COST AND MANAGEMENT ACCOUNTANCY

Written for Postgraduate, Honours & General Course students of Calcutta, North Bengal, Burdwan, Vidyasagar, and various other Indian universities. Also helpful to ICWA (Inter), CA (Inter), and CS (Inter) students.

COST AND MANAGEMENT ACCOUNTANCY

For BCom New Syllabus

Dr A K Chakrabarti MCom, PhD, FASM

Ex-Head of the Dept. of Commerce, Shyamaprasad College, Kolkata
Formerly, Lecturer of Bhowanipur Education Society College
St. Xavier's College and Netaji Nagar College, Kolkata

To be had of

New Central Book Agency (P) Ltd

LONDON

HYDERABAD ERNAKULAM BHUBANESWAR

DELHI KOLKATA PUNE GUWAHATI

NCBA
REGD OFFICE
8/1 Chintamoni Das Lane, Kolkata 700 009, India
email: ncbapvtltd@eth.net
OVERSEAS
NCBA (UK) Ltd, 149 Park Avenue North, Northampton, NN3 2HY, UK
email: ncbauk@yahoo.com
EXPORT
NCBA Exports Pvt. Ltd, 212 Shahpur Jat, New Delhi 110 049
email: ncbaexports@ncbaindia.com
BRANCHES

208B Peacock Lane, Shahpur Jat
New Delhi 110 049
email: ncbadel@ncbapvtltd.com

Shop Nos. 3 & 4, Vinayak Towers
681/B Budhwar Peth, Appa Balwant Chowk
Pune 411 002
email: ncbapune@ncbapvtltd.com

Shop No. 15, Bharati Towers, Ground Floor
Forest Park, **Bhubaneswar** 751 001
email: ncbabub@ncbapvtltd.com

House No. 3-1-315, 1st Floor
Nimboliadda, Kachiguda, **Hyderabad** 500 027
email: ncbahydb@ncbapvtltd.com

GSS Shopping Complex, 1st Floor
Opposite College Post Office, Convent Road
Ernakulam 682 035
email: ncbaernk@ncbapvtltd.com

Radhamayee Complex (Second Floor)
Opp. SBI, Panbazar, Jaswanta Road
Guwahati 781 001
email: ncbaguwahati@ncbapvtltd.com

COST AND MANAGEMENT ACCOUNTANCY • A K Chakrabarti

First Published: September 1991
Sixth Edition (New Syllabus): January 2004
Reprinted: July 2009, July 2012

PUBLISHER
Central Educational Enterprises (P) Ltd
54B Patuatola Lane, Kolkata 700 009

TYPESETTER
New Central Book Agency (P) Ltd
8/1 Chintamoni Das Lane, Kolkata 700 009

PRINTER
New Central Book Agency (P) Ltd
Web-Offset Division, Dhulagarh, Sankrail, Howrah

COVER DESIGNER
Ankit, Kolkata

COVER PRINTER
Biswanath Studio, Kolkata

PROOF CHECKING
Subas Maitra

PROJECT SUPERVISOR
Himangshu Acharya

ISBN 81 7381 449 X (10 digit)
978 81 7381 449 5 (13 digit)

Price ₹ 350.00

Dedication

In loving memory of my father
Late Jatindranath Chakrabarti,
who left me in my very early age.

Preface to the Sixth Edition

The book **'Cost and Management Accountancy'** has been revised in conformity with the syllabus framed **for B.Com. (Honours) and M.Com. courses** of various Indian Universities. Recently, the syllabus of Calcutta University has also been revised which will commence from the academic session 2003-2004.

To keep pace with the changes, the following topics have been included in the present edition of the book.

Marginal Costing

Standard Costing

Budgetary Control

Acounting Ratios

The present edition, the author feels, can be profitably be used by the students pursuing and preparing for the different professional examination like C.A. (Inter), C.S. (Inter), I.C.W.A. (Inter) etc.

The author acknowledges his debt to Mr. Amitabha Sen, M.B.A., Director of New Central Book Agency (P) Ltd. for his valuable advice and sincere co-operation.

Thanks are also due to the production team consisting of Mr. Prabhat Jas, Mr. Himangshu Acharya and Mr. Shankar Bhattacharya.

The author is also thankful to Mr. Ashoke Kr. Sarkar, Mr. Pratha Sinha Roy, Mr. Amit Kr. Ganguly and others of the sales and distribution department.

The author is equally thankful to the members of the staff of New Central Book Agency (P) Ltd. who help the author directly or indirectly in bringing out this edition.

Author's efforts will amply be rewarded if the book receives due recognition from his colleagues and students.

Shubha Mahalaya
25 September, 2003

A. K. Chakrabarti

Preface to the First Edition

In our diverse fields of activity we try to make the best use of available resources with the intention to obtain the highest output from a given input. Of late, the focus of accounting has been expanded to the measurement of efficiency in managing resources including human resources and decision making activities. Obviously, Costing as a branch of accounting has a pivotal role to play in this respect especially in an underdeveloped country like ours. In this context the study of Costing at undergraduate level has become very much essential for our future professionals.

Many books on Cost Accountancy written by many eminent writers are available to the students at present. But I strongly believe that none of them, except one or two, meets the demand of the students of various universities of India at the undergraduate level. This book aims at serving the academic interest of the students belonging to different Indian universities at the undergraduate and postgraduate levels. The salient feature of the book is that the basic concepts and principles of Costing have been explained with the help of illustrations. A large number of problems set in different University examinations have been worked out with relevant working notes at the end. In the exercises, variety of problems have been presented to enable the students to practise them for attaining perfection and self-confidence.

Many of my colleagues and students have been urging me to write a simple book on Costing. After giving serious thought to their wish ultimately I ventured upon writing this book.

I take this opportunity to convey my sincere thanks to Prof. Manab Mukherjee, Prof. Debkumar Roychoudhury, Prof. Sampat Mukherjee of St. Xavier's College and Dr. S. Kr. Paul of Prafulla Chandra College for their moral support without which I would not have dared this attempt.

I also express my sense of gratitude to Sri Ashoke Sarkar for his active co-operation.

I shall be failing in my duty if I do not acknowledge my debt to my publishers Sri Amitabha Sen and Sri Arunabha Sen of New Central Book Agency (P) Ltd. for their continuous encouragement in course of my writing the book.

My maiden attempt will amply be rewarded if this book satisfies the academic need of those for whom it has been written.

A. K. Chakrabarti

The 15th August, 1991
Shyamaprasad College
Calcutta 700 026

Features of this Edition

1. *Theory of each topic has been discussed lucidly and in simple language.*
2. *Questions set in B.Com. (Hons. & General) Examinations of the University of Calcutta, Burdwan and Vidyasagar Universities have been solved.*
3. *A good number of problems with gradation have been given for practice to attain perfection and confidence.*

CONTENTS

COST AND MANAGEMENT ACCOUNTANCY

INTRODUCTION 1

Learning Objectives :

1. *Classification of Accounting.*
2. *Financial Accounting – Definition.*
3. *Limitation of Financial Accounting.*
4. *Difference between Financial and Cost Accounting.*
5. *Financial Accounting and Management Accounting.*
6. *Cost Accounting and Management Accounting.*
7. *Cost Accounting and Management.*
8. *Cost Accounting – Definition.*
9. *Costing – Definition.*
10. *Cost Accountancy – Definition.*
11. *Need for Cost Accounting.*
12. *Limitations of Cost Accounting.*
13. *Methods of Costing – Job and Batch Costing, Contract Costing, Process Costing, Operation Costing, Opportunity Cost, Uniform Costing, Replacement Costs, Imputed Costs.*
14. *Chart showing the Applicability of Method of Costing to Industries – An example.*
15. *Cost Centres – Definition, Utilities, Types.*
16. *Cost Unit – Definition, Examples.*
17. *Difference between Cost Centre and Cost Unit.*
18. *Chart showing Costing System.*

INTRODUCTION 1

1.1 Classification of Accounting :

Accounting may be classified as follows :

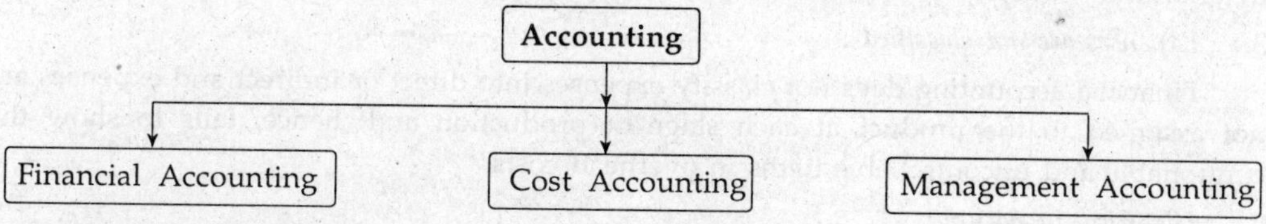

1.2 Financial Accounting :

According to American Accounting Association 'Accounting is a process of identifying, measuring and communicating economic information to permit informed judgements and decisions by the users of the information'.

But in recent years, the objectives of Accounting have undergone a sea change and accounting is moving rapidly towards social welfare objectives. In the language of AAA 1975 : "Accounting objectives are to provide information which is potentially useful for making economic decisions and which, if provided, will enhance social welfare". This social welfare aspect of accounting has been reflected in the recent development of social responsibility accounting. The social welfare theory of accounting calls for that the interest of employees, trade unions and consumers ought to be taken into account besides serving the interests of shareholders, investors, creditors and management.

1.3 Meaning and Limitations of Financial Accounting :

In any organisation the accounting system provides quantitative information for three main purposes :

(i) Accounting system of any organisation makes internal report to managers for using the information for planning and controlling routine operations.

(ii) It also makes report to the managers accounting information for use in making non-routine decisions and in formulation of major business plans and policies.

(iii) Accounting system provides accounting information to stockholders, government and other parties who are interested in the affairs of the company.

Financial accounting represents the historical, custodial and stewardship aspects of accounting. The field of financial accounting is concerned mainly with how accounting can serve external reporting. Its main purpose is to communicate all necessary accounting information to the outsiders like creditors, shareholders, financial institutions, banks, government, etc. Financial accounting seeks to reveal the financial result and financial position of the business on a particular day. It helps the management to portray a true and fair view of the state of affairs of the business. An analysis of the financial statement helps one to assess the overall performance, efficiency in the utilisation of available resources, financial solvency and weaknesses of a business unit.

In spite of new accounting devices, improved techniques, financial accounting fails to communicate adequate accounting information to the management. Financial accounting suffers from the following constraints :

1. *No classification is done in financial accounting* :

Financial accounting fails to classify the data regarding costs of different departments, processes products and units in the manufacturing division, by units of product lines and sales territories, by departments, services and functions in the administrative division.

2. *Materials and supplies are not properly controlled* :

Since financial accounting has no control over materials and supplies, misappropriation, deterioration, obsolescence and losses from scrap and defective parts result.

3. *Expenses are not classified* :

Financial accounting does not classify expenses into direct or indirect and expenses are not assigned to the product at each stage of production and, hence, fails to show the controllable and uncontrollable items in overhead costs.

4. *Historical in nature* :

In financial accounting data is summarised only at the end of the accounting period as a result of which day-to-day cost information cannot be obtained. It does not permit the computation of predetermined costs because of absence of budgetary elements.

5. *It fails to throw light on operating efficiency* :

Financial accounting fails to depict a clear picture of operating efficiency when prices go up or come down on account of inflation or trade depression.

6. *Price determination not possible* :

In financial accounting costs are not available and, as such, prices of products, services, production orders or lines of products cannot be determined.

7. *It fails to supply data to the management* :

It does not supply useful data to management for taking various financial decisions with regard to introduction of new products, replacement of labour by machines, price in normal or special circumstances, purchase of part of its product from outside or producing a part of its product in the factory.

8. *Analysis of losses* :

Analysis of losses due to idle plant and equipment, showing cost variations between active and inactive periods and seasonal conditions in the industry cannot be made.

9. *Comparison of cost data is not possible* :

It does not provide cost data as a result of which the cost data of the period under reference cannot be compared with those of previous period. For this reason, efficiency cannot be properly measured.

10. *Efficiency of labour is not rewarded* :

In financial accounting wages and labour are not recorded by jobs, processes, departments or services and are not interpreted in the light of cost factors and, as such, no company-wise system of incentives may be used to compensate labourers, salesmen and executives for their better performance.

11. *Fails to help in cost reduction* :

It is not possible to maximise profits since cost reduction is not possible under the financial accounting system, as it fails to analyse costs of different departments.

The above-mentioned deficiencies have facilitated the introduction of Cost Accounting in a business unit. A close study of the relationship of Cost Accounting with other branches of accountancy will lead us to understand clearly the scope, objects and functions of Cost Accounting.

1.4 Difference between Financial Accounting & Cost Accounting :

Points	*Financial Accounting*	*Cost Accounting*
1. Subject Matter	It deals with the whole of the business.	It is a part of financial accounting. It deals with the various costs of the products manufactured by the unit.
2. Objectives	It seeks to measure the financial performance of the business as a whole.	Its main objectives are : (i) Ascertainment of cost, (ii) Cost control and (iii) Cost analysis for decision making.
3. Applicability	It is applicable to all types of business.	It is applicable to Manufacturing Concern.
4. Accounting System	Double Entry System.	System useful to the management is applied.
5. Application of Accounting principles	It adheres to generally accepted accounting principles.	It adheres to costing concepts and principles.
6. Types of Data used	It makes use of historical, quantitative, monetary and objective data.	Cost Accounting uses descriptive, statistical, subjective data.
7. Transactions	Financial accounts are concerned with external transactions.	Cost Accounting is concerned with internal transactions.
8. Control	It does not lay emphasis on control.	It provides a detailed system of control for materials, labour, overheads.
9. Frequency of reporting	Generally reporting is done at the end of the financial year.	Cost control reports are submitted daily, weekly or fortnightly as required by the management.
10. Unit of measurement	Historical value i.e. Rupees.	Any monetary or physical unit such as labour hour rate, machine hour rate, etc.
11. Valuation of Stock	Stocks are valued at cost or market price whichever is less.	Stocks are always valued at cost.
12. Kind of Information	Financial accounts fail to provide information on relative efficiencies of Workers, Plants and Machineries.	It provides valuable information on the relative efficiencies of Labour & Plant and Machineries.

1.5 Financial Accounting and Cost Accounting :

Financial Accounting is concerned with historical cost. It consists of recording, classification (ledger) and analysis of the business transactions in a subjective manner. It presents income statements showing the financial result of the business for a particular financial year and a Balance Sheet on a specific date to exhibit the state of affairs of a business unit. It fails to throw light on the aspects of planning, control and decision making. For these purposes, we need Cost Accounting. To achieve the above objectives Cost Accounting records business expenditures in an objective manner, i.e. according to the purpose for which costs are incurred. It would be better for us if we take a simple example to make the position clear :

Illustration

Alfa Ltd. manufactures three products, namely, product X, Y and Z. Its financial accounts present the following data for the financial year ending on 31st March 1990 :

Materials Consumed	Rs. 4,00,000
Direct Wages paid	Rs. 3,00,000
Other Overheads	Rs. 3,60,000
	Rs. 10,60,000
Total Sales	Rs. 12,00,000

From the above financial data, we can calculate the Gross Profit earned by the company during the financial year 1989-90 :

	Rs.	Rs.
Sales		12,00,000
Less : Materials Consumed	4,00,000	
Wages	3,00,000	
Overheads	3,60,000	10,60,000
Gross Profit		1,40,000

Now, let us assume that Cost Accounting presents us with the following data :

	Product X Rs.	Product Y Rs.	Product Z Rs.
Materials	1,20,000	1,60,000	1,20,000
Wages	1,00,000	1,20,000	80,000
Overheads	1,10,000	1,40,000	1,10,000
Total Cost	3,30,000	4,20,000	3,10,000
Sales	4,20,000	4,00,000	3,80,000
	90,000	(–) 20,000	70,000

In the above problem, the financial accounting records give us the total Gross Profit without analysing the product-wise costs. But Cost Accounting records clearly show that product Y incurred a loss of Rs. 20,000. Another aspect it reveals in respect of Product X the company has earned a profit of 27.27%, while in respect of product Z the Company has earned a profit of 22.58% on cost. Now the Company can decide whether the production of Product Y should be stopped or the company should exercise more control on cost to make it viable economically, or to allocate more resources for production of product X. So, cost accounting helps the management in taking decisions.

As functions of management, Cost Accounting provides for the proper classification and subdivision of costs; control of materials; wages; overhead costs; reduction of wastes and measurement of efficiency. Moreover, Cost Accounting helps the management in determining business policies – whether to go for expansion or for contraction.

1.6 Financial and Management Accounting :

Financial accounting and management accounting can be better explained as external and internal accounting, respectively. Financial accounting prepares reports of an organisation for external users like creditors, banks and the investors and also for the government for the determination of income-tax and sales tax liabilities. Management accounting, on the other hand, emphasises the preparation of reports of an organisation for its internal users i.e. for company's management at different levels of management.

Distinctions between Financial and Management Accounting :

Points of difference	*Financial Accounting*	*Management Accounting*
1. Subject matter	Financial statements like income statements and balance sheet report on the overall performance of the business.	Management accounting deals with the internal details of an organisation.
2. Nature	Financial accounting is concerned with historical records.	Management accounting is concerned with the future plans and policies.
3. Primary Users	Managers of an organisation and outside parties use the accounting information communicated by financial accounting.	Top level, medium level and lower level managers are the users of accounting information communicated by management accounting.
4. Accounting system	Double entry system is followed.	Not restricted to double entry system. Ratio analysis, Fund Flow statement, marginal costing are used for having various managerial information.
5. Focal points of analysis	Business entity as a whole is considered for financial analysis.	Various segments of business entity are considered separately for various information for a particular segment.
6. Types of information	Monetary information is used only.	Both monetary and non-monetary information are used for various managerial analysis.
7. Reporting to authority and users	Income statements and balance sheet are prepared annually for communicating accounting information to internal and external users.	Reporting is made on regular basis to management for analysis and taking managerial decisions for efficient running of the business.
8. Degree of reliability	Financial accounting is relatively more precise and less approximations are used.	It is heavily subjective for planning purposes and objective data are needed when relevant. In this sense, it is dependent upon financial accounting.
9. Nature of dependence accounting.	Financial accounting is independent in nature.	Management accounting is dependent on both financial and cost

1.7 Cost Accounting and Management Accounting :

The American Accounting Associations' (AAA's) Committee on Management Accounting has defined Management Accounting "as the application of appropriate techniques and concepts in processing the historical and projected economic data of an entity to assist management in establishing plans for reasonable economic objectives and in the making of rational decisions with a view towards achieving these objectives. It includes the methods and concepts necessary for effective planning for choosing among alternative business actions and for control through the evaluation and interpretation of performance. Its study involves consideration of ways in which accounting information may be accumulated, synthesized, analyzed and presented in relation to specific problems, decisions and day to day tasks of business management".

Management Accounting embraces both Financial and Cost Accounting. Management Accounting emphasizes the preparation of reports of an organisation, for its internal users such as Board of Directors, Managing Director and for other top level management for the formulation of business policies. Thus, management accounting reports attempt to fill the information needs of managers with respect to a specific problem, situation, or decision.

Management Accounting is generally indistinguishable from Cost Accounting. They are closely linked as both of them use common basic data and reports. Cost Accounting largely uses data about production, sales, wages, overheads. Management Accounting uses the same data to prepare budgets, performance reports, control reports for making decisions in different areas.

Gray and Ricketts establish the relationship of Management Accounting with Cost Accounting in the following language :

"The historical data on labour cost might be used to estimate the labour cost for the coming year, to determine the size of work-force needed to meet anticipated production requirements and to estimate the cash requirements to meet weekly pay rolls. This represents the use of cost accounting data to develop managerial accounting data for planning decisions. The historical data on labour costs might be compared with the estimated labour costs to determine if labour is being used effectively and efficiently. This represents the use of cost accounting data to develop managerial accounting data for control decisions".

There is an intimate relationship between Cost Accounting and Management Accounting. Management Accounting communicates various information useful to the management for making decisions for the efficient running of the business. For this purpose, management accounting uses various techniques which include standard costing, marginal costing, uniform costing, budgetary control, break even and cost benefit analysis. In fact, management accounting is an extension of the managerial aspects of cost accounting; it utilizes the principles and practices of both cost accounting and financial accounting in the best interests of the business.

Financial Accounting determines the financial results for a period and the state of affairs on the last day of the period. From this point of view financial accounting may be treated as *Stewardship Accounting*.

Cost Accounting, on the other hand, generates information for controlling operations with a view to maximising efficiency and profit. So, it may be termed as *Control Accounting*.

Since Management Accounting communicates necessary information to the manage-ment for efficient running of the business, it is known as *Decision Accounting*.

1.8 Cost Accounting and Management :

Cost Accounting provides useful data to management for taking managerial decisions in the following areas :

i) Establishing business unit's profit goal;

ii) Determining departmental goals;

iii) Measuring and controlling business performance with the help of budgetary control;

iv) Making decisions about improvements and adjustments in the operation of the business for achieving predetermined business objectives ; and

v) To coordinate the entire organisational efforts and tasks. In doing so, cost accounting performs the following tasks :

1. Cost Accounting helps in determination and analysis of costs and income of a business unit. This facilitates comparison of costs of one period with those relating to a different period in order to evaluate the operating effficiency of each division or segment or product.

Control of Materials

2. It helps management in controlling cost. In every type of cost accounting, materials and supplies are accounted for—in terms of departments and processes. A rational and scientific system of receiving, handling and issuing materials is strictly observed. The perpetual inventory method is used to control properly the materials in stores. Control of raw materials and of parts follows production until goods are completed.

Control of Wages and Salaries

Labour cost is controlled through proper accounting for labour by jobs and by operations. In many manufacturing concerns, daily summary reports are prepared to show the number of hours and wage rate for each worker, per job or operation.

In cost accounting, costs are classified into direct and indirect items, indirect costs are generally termed as overheads. Overheads are further classified as controllable and uncontrollable items. This classification allows the cost accountant to concentrate his attention on those costs which can be reduced or eliminated.

3. *Cost Accounting as an aid in price determination*

Cost Accounting helps management in making revenue decisions like pricing new products or reducing or increasing the price of a product.

It also helps the management in taking short-term and long-term product mix decisions.

Cost data also helps the management in achieving the best combination of factors being used in the business enterprises. Cost data assists the management in making sound decisions like reducing price, increasing the volume of sales, increasing the price or improving turnover. In fact, the problem of properly regulating prices and output is largely dependent upon a knowledge of production, distribution and administrative costs per unit of product or of service.

4. *Curtailment of losses due to seasonal conditions*

In many industries higher costs and lower profits arise due to seasonal changes in activities. The cost accountant may make an attempt to alleviate the situation by presenting figures showing costs and losses that result from irregular employment of labour, plant and machinery. The cost reports can exhibit the idle time of workers and machinery, cost of storing raw materials and finished products, unabsorbed overhead costs and general decay in the morale of personnel that result from subnormal operations. The use of budgetary control combined with cost accounting may go a long way to bring about stability in industrial activity which will ultimately benefit the shareholders, employers and the society at large.

5. *Cost Accounting and expansion policy*

Every business unit has to face national and international changes that occur frequently due to changes in governments' political and economic policies. These changes have considerable effect on costs. Moreover, the management has to adopt policies to face the ever growing competition, to develop new markets for its products. The cost accountant is required to investigate and to prepare reports to keep the maangement abreast of the relative advantages and profitability of one policy as compared to others.

6. *Budgeting*

Participation of cost accounting in the formulation and execution of budgets and standards

Cost information for managerial decision making and planning is the most important justification of a sound cost accounting system. The following diagram shows the accounting cycle by which information reaches the decision makers :

Inputs

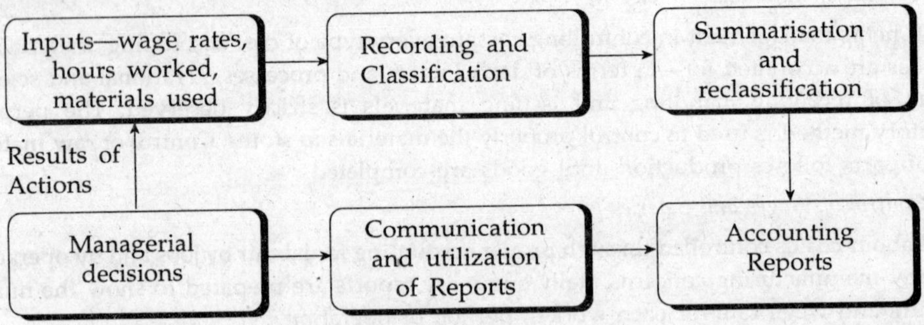

The use of budget helps the management to correct inefficiencies. It helps to identify the weak areas by making a comparative study of estimated figures with the actuals. Variances are studied carefully and corrective measures are taken in time to avoid wastage and losses.

We may now conclude that cost accounting is so closely linked with management that it becomes difficult to indicate where the work of the cost accountant ends and managerial control begins. In brief, it may be said that : "Cost accounting is to serve management in the execution of policies and in the comparison of actual and estimated results in order that the value of each policy may be appraised and changed to meet future conditions"—Blocker.

1.9 Cost Accounting Definition :

I.C.M.A., London, defines Cost Accounting as "an application of accounting and costing principles, methods and techniques in the ascertainment of costs and the analysis of savings and/or excesses as compared with previous experience or with standards".

In the language of **Wheldon** : "costing is the classifying, recording, and appropriate allocation of expenditure for the determination of costs of products or services; the relation of these costs to sales values; and the ascertainment of profitability".

"These costs may be ascertained :

i) Historically; i.e. after they have been incurred; or

ii) By predetermined standards combined with subsequent analysis of variances between these standards, and the actual cost incurred; and

iii) By the use of marginal methods of presentation for either (a) or (b), involving the differentiation between "fixed" and "variable" costs.

In the light of the above definitions we may define Cost Accounting as a process or mechanism by means of which costs of products and services are ascertained with a reasonable degree of accuracy. In a broader view, cost accounting is concerned with the field of responsibility for advising the management in both historical and future costs and, thereby, helping managerial planning, control and decision making. It provides the management with a variety of information to plan, control and make decisions. The following table gives us the examples of the information provided by a typical costing system and how it is used for different purposes by the management.

Information provided by the Management	*Possible uses by Management*
i) Cost per unit of production or for a process	Used as a factor in Pricing Decisions, Production Planning, and Cost Control.
ii) Cost of running a section, department or factory	Organisational planning, cost control.
iii) Wage costs for a unit of production or per period of production	Production planning, decision on alternative methods, wages, cost control.
iv) Rectification of costs	Material cost control, production planning.
v) Cost behaviour with varying levels of activity	Profit planning, make or buy decisions and cost control.

The examples provided by the table are not exhaustive. In practice, much more information is produced and used. The usefulness of costing information is enhanced when the actual results and costs are compared with some target or standard figure.

1.10 Costing :

The I.C.M.A, London, has defined costing as "the ascertainment of costs". So, it refers to the techniques and process of ascertaining cost. It also studies the principles concerning the determination of costs of products and services. Different types of costing are used in different industries, such as historical costing, absorption costing, marginal costing, standard costing. In other words, it is an aid to management for various management purposes.

1.11 Cost Accountancy :

The Institute of Cost and Works Accountants of the U.K. has defined Cost Accountancy as the "application of costing and cost accounting principles, methods and techniques to the science, art and practice of cost control and ascertainment of profitability as well as presentation of information for the purpose of managerial decision taking. So, the term Cost Accountancy is used in a broader sense. It embraces costing, cost accounting, cost control, cost audit and budgetary control".

1.12 Need for Cost Accounting :

Cost Accounting serves various purposes which justify its introduction in a business unit. The following are the purposes of Cost Accounting :

1. *Ascertainment of cost of product*

Product cost is ascertained through the mechanism of cost accounting. For this purpose, various costing methods are applied.

2. *Determination of selling price*

A business unit is required to determine the selling price at which its products are to be sold. In doing so, a unit should fix up the selling price for its products in such a way so that the costs of the product are recovered. Moreover, in fixing selling prices, regard must be had to the cost structure, conditions of the market, types of consumers and the demand and supply of the product.

3. *Analysis and classification of cost of production*

Cost Accounting helps to analyse and classify various items of cost incurred which lead to the revelation of various forms of waste, whether of materials, time or expense. Analysis of the causes of unsatisfactory results may suggest possible remedial measures to attain efficiency in the utilisation of resources.

4. *Submission of quotations and tenders*

To provide information with the supply of cost data upon which estimates and tenders are based. It provides the scope for price adjustment to meet market conditions, so as to ensure that no orders for supply of products are lost.

5. *Management tool for identifying and controlling efficiency*

It is used as a mangement tool to indicate to the management inefficiencies of various departments, plants and machinery. The management—through cost analysis—can identify the weak areas of operations and can take proper and prompt action and, thus, can lead the business unit to its desired goal.

6. *Preparation of budgets and standard costs*

It provides data to the management for the preparation of budgets and standard costs. An analysis of variances between budgeted figures and actuals or standard and actuals throw light on the weak areas of business operations and guides the management in taking corrective action to remove the unfavourable cost variances.

7. *Preparation of Financial Statements*

It is used to provide data for the preparation of periodical Profit and Loss Account and Balance Sheet at such intervals as may be desired.

It also provides a perpetual inventory of stores and other materials, so that interim financial statements can be prepared without stock taking.

So, an important objective of cost accounting is the creation of useful cost data and information for the purpose of planning and control. They influence and facilitate both short— and long-run decisions. Cost accounting provides for a basis for operating policies like, (a) determination of cost-volume-profit relationship, (b) whether it would be economical to buy certain articles or components from outside, (c) whether to replace the existing plant and machinery, or (d) whether to continue the business or to shut it down.

Thus, there is a direct relationship between information needs of management, cost accounting objectives, and techniques and tools used for the analysis.

1.13 Advantages of Cost Accounting :

Cost Accounting benefits the management in various ways as discussed earlier. It serves a business unit by rendering the following benefits to business enterprises :

i) The cost accounting system provides data about pofitable and unprofitable products or activities. By studying and interpreting cost data, the management can take corrective measures to improve the profitability of the concern.

ii) Production methods may be changed or improved so that costs can be controlled to increase profits.

iii) Cost data helps the management in minimising the loss and wastages.

iv) Cost data and information are provided to the management to determine the price of the product.

v) Cost data can be compared with the standard costs by the introduction of standard costing. Inter-firm comparisons will enable the management to study the causes of unfavourable developments and to institute procedures for their elimination.

vi) Inefficiencies in plant operation are very costly. The inefficiencies do occur due to wastage of materials, use of obsolete machinery and wrong man power planning. Proper use of cost accounting may remove these inefficiencies.

vii) Cost accounting helps the management in knowing the costs of different alternatives and selecting the most advantageous course of action. Decisions like produce or buy, continue or drop a product, operate or shut down, etc. and other short-term decisions can be made easily with the help of cost accounting data.

viii) More reliable and accurate financial accounts can be prepared with the help of perpetual inventory system of stock control.

ix) The introduction of effective costing system prevents manipulation and fraud.

x) An effective cost accounting system ensures maximum utilization of physical and human resources and helps the employees in achieving their basic goal of earning higher wages. It also helps the employer in maximising the profit of the concern.

1.15 Limitations of Cost Accountancy :

Cost Accountancy is an art which has developed in course of time through theories and practices. The theories are based on reasoning and practical experience of cost accountants. Many of the theories have been recognised and accepted in due course of time. So, the accepted theories have grown up through changes to be recognised as conventions. It is not a full proof system. Cost Accountancy is not regarded as an exact science in the sense that accepted principles of cost accounting still keep on changing with the passage of time. It suffers, like any other branch of accounting, from some limitations. Some of the limitations are :

1. *Lack of uniformity*

The greatest limitation of cost accounting is its failure to conform to any uniform procedure. No cost can be said to be exact as they involve a large number of conventions and flexible factors like, materials issue pricing based on FIFO, LIFO, Average or Standard costs; arbitrary allocation of overheads to cost centres; arbitrary allocation of joint costs; adoption of Marginal costs and Standard costs etc.

2. *Large number of conventions*

The existence of a large number of conventions and practices in regard to the valuation of stocks, materials issued to different cost centres, apportionment of joint costs stands in the way of finding out 'time cost' of a product. Cost—as ascertained by the application of costing principles—is not a true cost but an estimate.

3. *Applicability*

In small and medium sized industries, it becomes impractical to introduce costing since it becomes too expensive for the unit.

1.16 Installation of Costing System :

Every undertaking which wants to instal costing system has to design the system in such a manner so that it can satisfy the needs of the concern. But there are certain principles which are to be considered before the introduction of costing system. The principles are :

(a) The existing organisation of the unit should be disturbed as little as possible;

(b) It is better to introduce the system gradually with an eye to the needs of the organisation;

(c) Since the success of an efficient costing system depends on the cooperation of the staff, they should be taken into confidence and made to understand the utility of the system. So, confidence building is an essential factor for the installation of costing system;

(d) The system must be made simple for its easy operation.

Prerequisites or Steps

The introduction of costing system calls for a strong infrastructure to make it efficient and effective. The following steps are recommended as prerequisites for the installation of costing system :

1. *Determination of objectives*

The objectives for which the costing system is installed are to be determined. In fact, if the objectives are not predetermined and well defined, the costing system will fail to accomplish the desired goal.

2. *Size, layout and nature of the business*

A close study of the size, layout and nature of the business is very much essential to design the costing system. The choice of method of costing largely depends upon the nature of the business.

3. *Production stages*

Every costing system should follow the production stages because the cost at each stage of production is to be determined. The costing system should be designed in a way so that it can determine the cost at each significant stage.

4. *Organisational structure of the business*

The organisational set up of the business is to be closely studied. The methods of purchase, receipt of materials, issue and storage of materials should be examined and changes, if required, are to be made so that these departments can feed the costing department with the supply of accurate cost data. The maximum amount of required information should flow to the system.

5. *Easy, simple, economical and flexible*

The system to be introduced should be simple and easy to operate. For this, form and records of original entry should be designed in such a way as to minimise clerical work and expenditure. The cost of the system to be installed should be considered. It should be kept in mind that the installation and operation of the system should be economic.

6. *Coordination and cooperation*

Various departments that are involved in the system should be well coordinated so that they can function harmoniously and with a sense of cooperation to make the system effective. The benefits that accrue from the system should be explained to various persons concerned and the sense of awareness should be created.

7. *Cost Control*

The system should be so designed that cost control can effectively be exercised.

8. *Communication of information*

The costing system should incorporate a suitable procedure for communicating required information with promptness to the various levels of management for making appropriate decisions.

9. *Interlocking of financial and cost accounts*

The cost and financial accounts could be interlocked into a single integral accounting system. If, that is done, the results of separate sets of accounts could be reconciled by means of control accounts for accuracy.

Conclusion

To make the costing system efficient, meaningful and useful, the following factors are to be taken into consideration :

i) The system should be appropriate to the organisation and the manufacturing process.

ii) It should ensure that the reports, statements and analyses produced by the costing system contain the relevant information for the intended purpose.

iii) The reports and statements are produced at appropriate intervals and early enough to be effective.

iv) The reports and statements are properly addressed to the person responsible for planning, control and decision making.

v) The system has to ensure that the information is produced in a relevant form and to a sufficient degree of accuracy for the intended purpose.

1.15 Methods of Costing :

The term 'Costing' refers to the processes or techniques that are used for the determination of costs of a product manufactured or service rendered. To ascertain costs, different methods are applied—depending upon the nature of the product, production method and specific business conditions.

The following are the principal methods of costing :

i) *Classification of methods on the basis of manufacturing process*

(a) Job costing, (b) Process costing.

ii) *Classification on the basis of time* :

(a) Historical costs; (b) Predetermined costs like (i) Estimated costing and (ii) Standard costing.

iii) *Classification for making managerial decisions* :

(a) Marginal costing; (b) Uniform costing; (c) Opportunity costs; (d) Replacement costs; (e) Imputed costs.

Now we propose to discuss the different methods of costing one by one :

Job Costing

This is a method of costing by which the cost of a definite job, or of a specific order or a batch of finished products is determined. This method of costing is applied in those business concerns where production is carried out as per specific order.

Under this method, costs are collected and recorded under a specific production order. When an order is received, production control allots a number to it. In job costing all costs of direct materials, direct labour and other direct expenses are directly charged to the specific job or product.

Job cost sheets are used for the accumulation of job costs. The job cost sheets serve a control function.

This method is very much popular in enterprises engaged in house building, ship building, production of machinery and repairs.

Batch costing, contract costing and composite costing are the other variations of job costing.

Batch Costing

Batch costing refers to that method of costing which determines the cost of a group of identical products. This method is applied to general engineering factories which produce components in economical batches for subsequent assembly.

Batch costing can conveniently be applied to companies engaged in manufacturing radios, televisions, watches, cars, electronic goods, medicines, biscuits, confectionery, etc.

Contract Costing

This method of costing is based on the principle of job costing. A specific contract becomes the cost unit. A particular contract is treated as a whole job and the cost of the contract is ascertained. It is also known as Terminal Costing since the job cost is completed with the completion of the work. Contract costing is used in building and civil engineering works, ship building and aircraft manufacture.

Composite Costing or Multiple Costing

Under this method of costing, costs for each component or each group of components to be assembled into a final product are ascertained separately. Industries which manufacture radios, televisions, motor car, aircraft, etc. make use of this method of costing.

Process Costing

Process costing is a system which applies costs to like products that are mass produced in continuous fashion through a series of production steps known as processes. The finished goods of earlier processes become the raw materials of the latter processes. Costs are identified for each process and charged to that process. Cost of each process is ascertained separately. Chemical industries, oil refineries, gas and electricity generating concerns, textiles, paints, flour, food processing, paper, mining and cement industries etc. make use of this system of costing.

Other variations of process costing are : operating cost, operation cost and single or output cost.

Operation Cost

The cost unit is the 'operation' instead of the process. This system is used by the manufacturing concern where methods of production consist of a number of distinct operations. The per unit cost is arrived at the end of each accounting period by dividing the cost of an operation by the number of units completed in the operation centre.

Operating Cost

Operating cost is used for finding out the cost of the appropriate cost unit for a particular service. It is used by those organisations which render services such as transport, power house, schools, catering, hospitals, boiler houses etc.

Single or Output Cost

This method is employed where production is uniform and consists of a single product or two or three types of similar products. The per unit cost is obtained by dividing the total cost by the total number of units manufactured.

1.16 Techniques of Costing :

Historical Cost

These costs represent the cost of actual operational performance. It is a method of costing under which costs are determined after they have been incurred. Historical costs are 'postmortem' costs. Historical data are considered for predicting estimated costs of the alternative actions under consideration. By making comparisons, one of these alternative actions is selected and the decision is translated into action. So, in a decision-making process, historical costs play an important role.

(i) *Standard Costing*

It is a technique where standard costs are prepared in advance and used. Standard costs are fixed on the historical data. After the production, actuals are compared with the standard costs and variances are identified. Once the variances are determined, the management finds out the reasons for such variances for taking remedial measures. So, it is a tool in the hands of the management to control cost and ensures accountability, as also efficiency in the use of factors of production. It is an extension of budgetary control. This system of costing is useful in repetitive industries and jobbing industries.

I.C.M.A.'s definition of standard costing summarises its concept and purposes :

"A pre-determined calculation of how much costs should be under specified working conditions.

It is built up from an assessment of the value of cost elements and corelates technical specifications and the qualification of materials, labour and other costs to the prices and/or wage rates expected to apply during the period in which the standard cost is expected to be used.

Its main purposes are to provide bases for control through variance accounting, for the valuation of stocks and work-in-progress, and in some cases, for fixing selling prices".

(ii) *Marginal Costing*

In marginal costing, costs are classified into fixed and variable costs. The fundamental approach of marginal costing is to relate variable costs to cost units; while fixed costs are attributed to the business in general. Variable costs are charged to production; fixed costs will be written off in full in the period to which they are attributable.

Marginal costing assumes that the excess of sale price over variable cost contributes to a fund which will cover the fixed costs and provide the undertaking's profit. In other words, fixed overhead is not allocated to cost units.

(iii) *Uniform Costing*

Uniform costing is not a system of costing. This system refers to a system used by several undertakings. They use the same costing principles or practices to enable them to enjoy benefits of a uniform system. This method of costing is useful to make inter-firm comparisons.

Opportunity Costs

These costs refer to costs which result from the use of material, labour and other facilities, in a particular manner and which have been discarded in favour of an alternative use. In other words, the benefit from resources which has been foregone for not being used in the manner originally planned. So, opportunity cost is the foregone benefit which might have been drawn from the resources had they been used in an alternative manner. For example, a saving of Rs. 50,000 may earn an interest of Rs. 6,000 if deposited with a bank for two years or more. Now, this amount is invested in a business for earning profit. Here, the opportunity cost will be the amount of interest, i.e. Rs. 6,000 which has been foregone for its alternative use.

Replacement Costs

This cost refers to the cost of replacement of an asset at current market price. Suppose, the written down value of a particular machine is Rs. 30,000. If the machine is bought at current market price, it would cost, say, Rs. 35,000. So, the amount of Rs. 35,000 is the replacement cost of the machine. In replacement cost, the current market price of an asset or materials is considered but not its original cost or written down cost.

Imputed Costs

These are notional costs. They do not involve cash outlay. From this point of view, it is similar to opportunity cost. These costs are computed only for the purpose of decision making. They are also used for evaluating the performance of profit centres.

Chart showing the method of costing applicable to industry

Industries	*Method of Costing*
1. Chemical Industries Cement Soap Steel Oil Refinery Leather Sugar	Process Costing
2. Electric light and power undertakings Railways Hospitals, Road transport	Operating Costing
3. Furniture manufacturing Readymade garments Toy making Biscuit manufacturing	Batch Costing
4. Baby Food Paints and Decorating	Job Costing
5. Ship building Construction of Road, building	Contract Costing
6. Bicycle Locomotives Air Conditioners	Multiple Costing

Problem 1

Given below is a list of ten industries. Give the method of costing and the unit of cost against each industry.

(i) Nursing Home, (ii) Road Transport, (iii) Steel, (iv) Coal, (v) Bicycles, (vi) Bridge Construction, (vii) Interior Decoration, (viii) Advertising, (ix) Furniture, (x) Sugar company having its own sugarcane fields.

[C.A.(Inter) May 1988—Adapted]

Solution

	Industry	*Method of Costing*	*Unit of Cost*
1.	Nursing Home	Operating	Per Bed per day
2.	Road Transport	Operating	Per Tonne kilometer or Per Mile
3.	Steel and Oil Refinery	Process	Per Tonne
4.	Coal	Single	Per Tonne
5.	Bicycles	Multiple	Each Unit
6.	Bridge Construction	Contract	Each Contract
7.	Interior Decoration	Job	Each Job
8.	Furniture	Multiple	Each Unit
9.	Advertising	Job	Each Job
10.	Sugar Company having its own sugarcane fields	Process	Per Tonne

COST CENTRE

Definition

According to the Terminology of the Institute of the Cost and Management Accountants of England a cost centre, "is a location, person or item of equipment (or group of these) for which costs may be ascertained and used for the purposes of Cost Control". So, a cost centre may be an individual, a machine, or a 'shop' in the factory. It is very much necessary to divide the business into logical parts to which costs can conveniently be charged. Each part is known as cost centre. For example, the factory overheads may be allocated to several machines on the basis of some rational principles to ascertain the 'machine hour rate'. So, the machine is a cost centre.

The selection of a cost centre depends upon a number of factors, namely, organisational division of work, condition of incidence of cost, communication aids and availability of information and needs of costing and management policy regarding the choice of a course of action from various alternatives.

Utilities of Cost Centres

Cost centres have the following utilities :

i) Cost centres identify the spheres of responsibilities. The manager of a particular cost centre is assigned the responsibility for the control of costs in relation to that particular cost centre. He remains accountable to the higher authority for cost escalation or wastage.

ii) Cost centres are meant to assemble all costs at one area for which a common base of recovery can reasonably be used.

Types of Cost Centres

i) *Personal Cost Centre*

Personal cost centre consists of a person or group of persons.

ii) *Production Cost Centres*

These centres are engaged in production work. It is a centre where production is carried on. Machine shops and welding shops are examples of production cost centre. Cost of direct materials, direct labour, chargeable expenses and factory overheads are charged to this centre.

iii) *Service Cost Centre*

These centres render services to production centres. Only indirect costs are charged to this centre. Important service centres are :

(a) Material Service Centre – which deals with handling and upkeep of stores, internal transport ;

(b) Personnel service centres like personnel department.

(c) Plant maintenance centre.

(d) Administration centres like general office, accounts office, etc.

Cost Unit

Cost unit is a quantitative unit of product or service in relation to which costs are ascertained. The Institute of Cost and Management Accountants of England defines a unit of cost as "a unit of quantity of product, service or time in relation to which costs may be ascertained or expressed". Thus, cost units may be units of production, e.g. tonnes of cement, gallons/liters of gas, typewriters or units of service, like consulting hours, patent rights, kilowatt hours etc.

Distinction between Cost Centre and Cost Unit

The following are the points of difference between Cost Centre and Cost Unit :

i) Cost centre is the smallest organisational sub-unit. A cost unit is a devise for the purpose of breaking up or separating costs into smaller sub-divisions.

ii) Cost centre can be a location, person or item of equipment. Cost unit refers to a unit of quantity of output.

iii) In case of a cost centre the total cost is ascertained while in case of a cost unit, cost per unit is ascertained.

iv) Each cost centre consists of a department or a sub-department or item of equipment. In case of a cost unit the smaller subdivisions are attributed to products or services to determine product cost or cost of time spent for a particular job. We can determine the cost per tonne of steel, cost per machine hour. The forms of measurement used as cost units are usually the units of physical measurements like number, area, length, time etc.

v) Cost centre is helpful for cost control, cost unit is helpful for price determination and fixation of sale price.

vi) Cost centre is a unit of activity relating to a department while cost unit is a quantitative unit of product or service.

vii) The total costs of a cost centre is ascertained first, then the cost per unit is ascertained.

Examples of Cost Units

Examples of cost units are given in a tabular form for easy understanding :

Industry	*Cost Unit*	*Industry*	*Cost Unit*
Motor Car	Per Car	Building	Per Sq. ft.
Ship Building	Per Ship	Brewery	Per Barrel
Aircraft	Per Aircraft	Power	Kilowatt hour
Television	Per Set	Nuts and Bolts	Gross
Oil Refinery	Per Ton	Transport	Ton-kilometer
Coal, Iron ore	Per Ton		Passenger km
Steel	Per Ton	Cable	Meter
Fertilizers	Per Ton	Cement	Ton
Chemicals	Per Kg./Liter	Gas	Cubic meter
Electricity	Per Unit	Metal Plating	Square meter
Brick	Per thousand bricks		

CHART SHOWING COSTING SYSTEM

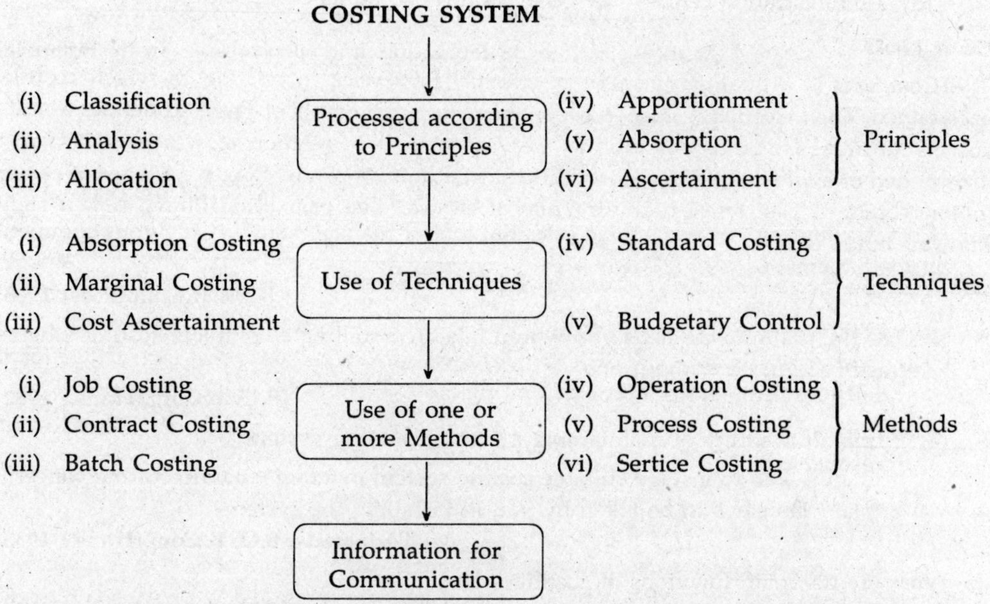

ASSIGNMENT

Theoretical Questions

1. What is meant by Cost Accounting ?

   How does Cost Accounting differ in technique and procedures from Financial Accounting?

2. What is Financial Accounting ? What are its limitations ?

3. What is Costing ? What are its objects and advantages ?

   [C.U. B.Com.(Pass) 1986]

4. "Cost Accounting has become an essential tool of management"—Give your comment on the Statement.

   [C.U. B.Com.(Pass) 1985]

5. Discuss the preliminary steps you would take in installing a complete costing scheme in a factory hitherto without one.

   [B.U. B.Com.(Hons.) 1982]

6. (a) Explain the utility of maintaining a cost accounting system.

   (b) You are asked to instal a suitable costing system in a large manufacturing concern. Explain the steps to be taken by you in installing the system.

   [Adapted—B.U. B.Com.(Hons.) 1983]

7. What are the main functions of costing system ?

   [C.U. B.Com.(Hons.) 1994]

8. (a) Define cost. Distinguish between costing and cost accounting.

   (b) Discuss the relationship between cost accounting and other branches of accounting.

   [B.U. B.Com.(Hons.) 1985]

9. (a) What is the importance of cost accounting to management in the discharge of their functions ?

   (b) What factors should a cost accountant consider in installing a sound system of costing in a manufacturing concern ?

   [B.U. B.Com.(Hons.) 1986]

10. Explain the following :

    (i) Job Costing ; (ii) Batch Costing ; (iii) Process Costing ; (iv) Operating Costing ; (v) Multiple Costing ; (vi) Operation Costing.

    [C.U. B.Com.(Hons.)]

11. Explain the following :

    (i) Historical Costing ; (ii) Marginal Costing ; (iii) Uniform Costing ; (iv) Standard Costing.

    [C.U. B.Com.(Hons.)]

12. Distinguish between Costing and Cost Accounting.

    What are the functions of Cost Accounting ? **[C.U. B.Com.(Hons.)]**

13. Discuss the advantages of Cost Accounting.

14. Explain the limitations of Cost Accounting.

15. What do you mean by Cost Centre and Cost Unit. How does Cost Centre differ from Cost Unit ? Discuss the main purposes of Cost Centre.

    [C.U. B.Com.(Hons.) 1992]

16. Can a modern manufacturing concern do without Cost Accounting ? State reasons. Enumerate the techniques of Costing.

    [C.U. B.Com.(Hons.) 1989]

17. (a) What do you mean by Costing and what are its objectives ?
    (b) What method of Costing would you recommend for the following industries ? Give reasons. Oil refinery, Toy making, Ship building, Printing and Radio.

[C.U. B.Com.(Hons.) 1991]

18. How do you distinguish between Financial and Cost Accounting ?

[C.U. B.Com.(Hons.) 1990]

19. What is 'Cost Accounting'? Explain the difference between Cost Accounting and Financial Accounting in technique and procedure.

[C.U. B.Com.(Hons.) 1993]

20. What are the main functions of a Costing System ?

[C.U. B.Com.(Hons.) 1994]

21. Distinguish between Cost Centre and Cost Unit.

[C.U. B.Com.(Hons.) 1997]

22. Discuss how does Cost Accounting contribute to the effective and efficient management of an industrial establishment.

[C.U. B.Com.(Hons.) 1996]

23. Why is Cost Accounting necessary ? Mention the steps which should be taken to instal Cost Accounting ?

[V.U. B.Com.(Hons.) 1995]

24. (a Define 'Cost', 'Costing' and 'Cost Accounting'
    (b) What are the differences between Cost Accounting and Financial Accounting ?

[V.U. B.Com.(Hons.) 1997]

ELEMENTS OF COST 2

Learning Objectives :

1. *Concept of Cost.*
2. *Classification.*
3. *Elements of Cost : (i) Direct Materials, (ii) Direct Wages, (iii) Direct Expenses, (iv) Indirect Materials, (v) Indirect Wages, (vi) Indirect Expenses, (vii) Overheads.*
4. *Cost Sheet : (i) Definition, (ii) Objectives, (iii) Preparation of Cost Sheet*
5. *Treatment of some Items : (i) Work-in-Progress, (ii) Defective Materials, (iii) Sale of Scrap, (iv) Defective Product, (v) Abnormal loss of Materials, (vi) Normal loss of Materials.*
6. *Treatment of Finished Goods.*
7. *Specimen of Cost Sheet.*
8. *Cost Unit : (i) Definition, (ii) Examples.*
9. *Worked out Problems.*
10. *Assignment.*

ELEMENTS OF COST 2

2.1 Concept of Cost

Cost is the amount of resources used up in exchange for some goods or services. The resources used up are expressed in terms of money or, if not in terms of money, they are expressed in monetary units. "Cost is a measurement, in monetary terms, of the amount of resources used for some purposes"—Anthony and Welsch.

Cost has been defined by the Committee on Terminology of the American Institute of Certified Public Accountants as : "Cost is the amount, measured in money, of cash expended or other property transferred, capital stock issued, services performed, or a liability incurred in consideration of goods and services received or to be received."

The term'Cost' has been defined in different ways, so as to encompass various types of costs. The term itself is not a significant one unless it is used with an adjective or phrase, when only it communicates the meaning for which it is intended. For example, when we say prime cost, direct cost, fixed cost, variable cost etc. we like to convey a definite meaning which is important in computing, measuring, analysing the cost which, in turn, will achieve three basic objectives of cost accounting – cost determination, cost analysis and cost control.

2.2 Cost objectives

"A Cost may be defined as a sacrifice or giving up of resources for a particular purpose'. Initially, costs are recorded in elementary form and then they are grouped in different ways to help managers in various ways.

Cost objective can be defined as any activity for which a separate measurement of costs is desired. The managers want to know the cost of something which helps them to take decisions in various areas of operation. The costs are accumulated and grouped in ways to help managers make decisions, such as evaluating the performance of subordinates and sub-units of the organisation, expanding or deleting products or territories, and replacing equipment etc.

2.3 Classification of Cost

Need for Classification

For decision making purpose, management is to be fed with necessary data. Cost data are useful to the management for the following reasons :–

(a) Planning profit by means of budgets ;

(b) Measuring annual or periodic profit ;

(c) Controlling Costs ;

(d) Fixing selling prices ;

(e) Framing price policy ;

(f) Making decisions.

So, to achieve the above objectives, it is necessary to analyse and classify costs. Classification is required to arrive at the detailed costs of various jobs, processes or departments

Classification is the arrangement of items in logical groups having regard to their nature. So, before any attempts are made to collect, analyse and control cost, it is imperative that all items should precisely be classified. The way items are classified must be related to the objectives of the systems using the classification. For example, the classification of materials must aid all the systems involved with materials. Thus, materials can be classified in a typical manufacturing company as raw materials ; components and assemblies ; work-in-progress ; consumable stores, maintenance materials ; office materials and tools.

The different bases of cost classification that are found in practice are based on cost characteristics. They are :

1. Natural characteristics (material, labour and overheads) ;
2. Changes in activity or volume (fixed and variable) ;
3. Relation to the product ;
4. Traceability to the product (direct and indirect cost) ;
5. Function ;
6. Cost analysis and decision making purposes.

2.4 Elements of Cost

This classification is based on the natural characteristics of cost, i.e. on the basis of the three elements of cost, namely, (i) **Materials cost,** (ii) **Labour cost,** and (iii) **Expenses.**

2.5 Direct Material

Definition

Materials are substances from which products are manufactured. Materials may be classified as direct and indirect.

Direct materials are those substances which can be directly identified with any cost centre, product or a group of products. Direct materials refer to those raw materials which become an integral part of the finished product. They can conveniently and economically be traced in specific units of output. For example, steel and aluminium are the direct materials that are used for making an automobile body, or raw cotton for making textiles, etc.

2.6 Examples

The following materials are treated as direct materials :

(i) All materials that are purchased for a particular job, process or product.

(ii) Materials acquired and subsequently requisitioned from the stores.

(iii) Components or parts or sub-assemblies bought for incorporation in the product.

(iv) Materials passing from one process to another. For example, finished product of a spinning mill becomes the raw material of a weaving mill.

(v) Primary packing materials, e.g. wrappings, cardboard boxes, etc.

Direct materials are also known as process material ; prime cost material ; production material, stores material etc.

In ascertaining the cost of materials used for production purpose, the following items of expense should be added to their invoiced price :

(a) Import duties ; (b) Dock charges ; (c) Carriage inward ; (d) Storing of materials ; (e) Cost of purchasing and receiving materials and (f) Cost of rectifying materials.

2.7 How is the Cost of Direct Materials Consumed ascertained ?

Cost of raw materials consumed			
	Opening stock of raw materials		×××
Add :	Purchase of raw materials	×××	
Add :			
	(a) Import duty	×××	
	(b) Dock charges	×××	
	(c) Carriage inward/transport cost for bringing the raw materials into stores	×××	
	(d) Primary packing materials	×××	×××
			×××
Less :	Abnormal loss of materials	×××	
Less :	Return of raw materials to stores	×××	
Less :	Closing stock of raw materials	×××	×××
Raw Materials consumed			×××

2.8 Direct Labour

Labour is defined as human effort by the application of which utility is created. Direct labour refers to direct wages paid to the workers (both skilled and unskilled) who are directly connected with production. Direct labour, like direct materials, can be identified with the manufacture of a single product or group of products. The term 'direct wages' refers to the remuneration paid to the workers who are directly connected with production. Direct wages may be defined as the measure of direct labour in terms of money—wages paid to the machine man, workers working in the productive department, workers of the assembly section, machine operators. Direct labour is also known as process labour, operating labour, productive labour.

2.9 Direct Expenses

Direct expense refers to any expense other than direct materials and direct labour which is incurred on a specific cost unit. This type of expense can be easily identified with cost units. direct expenses are also known as chargeable expenses and are charged directly to the product.

Examples : (a) Cost of special lay-out, design and drawings, (b) hire charges of tools and equipment for a particular production, (c) maintenance cost of such equipment, (d) royalty paid per unit for copyright design, (e) hire charges for plant for a particular job or batch.

2.10 Prime Cost

Prime cost is the primary cost of a product or group of products. Prime cost is the sum total or direct costs. Prime cost is the total of Direct Materials, Direct Labour and Direct Expenses. So, PRIME COST = Direct Materials + Direct Wages + Direct Expenses + Opening Stock of W.I.P. at prime cost – Closing Stock of W.I.P. at prime cost.

Problem 1

From the following particulars of a manufacturing concern, ascertain the Prime Cost :

	Rs.
Opening stock of raw materials	20,000
Closing stock of raw materials	30,000
Purchase of raw materials	1,05,000
Import duty paid on raw material purchased	15,000
Carriage Inward	5,000
Primary packing materials	3,000
Productive wages	95,000
Opening stock of work-in-progress at prime cost	17,000
Closing stock of work-in-progress at prime cost	10,000
Hire charge paid on plant	14,000
Other chargeable expenses	6,000

Solution

Statement showing the Prime Cost

		Rs.	Rs.
	Opening Stock of raw materials		20,000
Add :	Purchase of raw materials	1,05,000	
Add :	Import duty	15,000	
	Carriage Inward	5,000	
	Primary packing materials	3,000	1,28,000
			1,48,000
Less :	Closing Stock of raw materials		30,000
	Raw materials consumed		1,18,000
Add :	Direct wages		95,000
Add :	Direct Expenses		
	Hire charges on plant	14,000	
	Other chargeable expenses	6,000	20,000
			2,33,000
Add :	Opening Stock of W.O.P. at prime cost		17,000
			2,50,000
Less :	Closing Stock of W.I.P. at prime cost		10,000
	PRIME COST		2,40,000

2.11 Overhead

Definition

Overhead may be defined as total cost of indirect materials, wages and other expenses that are associated with manufacturing process. Overhead also includes cost of services. It comprises all expenses which cannot be traced or identified with the finished goods but are incurred for carrying on production process and in connection with the general organisation and operation of the business. Alternatively, overheads are all expenses that are not direct expenses.

2.12 Indirect Materials

There are certain materials which are used in the course of manufacture and do not themselves form a part of finished product or they do not enter into finished product.

Consumable stores, cotton waste, lubricant and stationeries are examples of indirect materials that are used in the factory.

2.13 Indirect Labour or Wages

Indirect wages may be defined as remuneration paid to the workers who are not directly engaged in production but they definitely contribute to such work and to the completion of the product and its movement up to the point of despatch. For example, the Works Manager's salary or wages paid to the workers who work in the factory for delivering goods to the production departments and carrying goods from the Assembly Section to the Stores, etc.

I.C.M.A. London defined indirect wages cost as "wages other than direct wages cost". In other words, wages paid to workers which cannot be allocated but can be apportioned to or absorbed by cost centres or cost units.

Examples of indirect wages :

Remuneration paid to :

Supervisors, Foremen and Chargehands ; Employees of inspection department ; Labourers for general handling of materials ; Storekeepers ; Work checkers and recorders ; Instructors ; Employees of Drawing Office, Tool room, Clerical staff, Gatemen ; Employees of Transport department ; Security officers and Security guards ; Office staff.

2.14 Indirect Expenses

Definition

Indirect expenses are those expenses which cannot be allocated directly to any cost centre job or cost unit. But indirect expenses can be apportioned to and absorbed by cost centre, cost unit or any particular job.

Examples of indirect expenses are :

Rent, rates and taxes of factory and office buildings, insurance, depreciation on fixed assets used in factory and office, power, electricity expenses, canteen subsidies, repairs and renewals, expenses for welfare of workers and any other expenses.

2.15 Classification of Overheads

Overheads can be classified as :

(i) Production overheads or Factory overheads ;

(ii) Office and Administration overheads ;

(iii) Selling overheads ; and

(iv) Distribution overheads

This classification is done with reference to the various activity divisions of a manufacturing concern.

2.16 Production Overhead

Production overhead is the sum total of costs of indirect materials, labour and other expenses including service expenses incurred in the factory or in carrying on manufacturing process.

Factory overhead covers all indirect expenses that are incurred from the receipt of the raw materials until the completion of products. It embraces all indirect expenses incurred within the four walls of the factory.

Production overhead is also known as 'Manufacturing overhead', 'Works overhead'. Factory overhead may be fixed and variable.

Examples

(a) Rent, rates and insurance chargeable against the factory.

(b) Depreciation of Factory buildings, plant and machinery and other equipments.

(c) Factory heating, lighting and air conditioning, fuel.

(d) Indirect labour such as salary of works manager, wages of foremen, salaries to factory staff.

(e) Insurance of plant and machinery ; maintenance cost of factory building, plant and machinery, tools etc.

(f) Stock keeping expenses, store keeping expenses.

(g) Cost of materials of little individual value used in production such as screws, bolts, paints.

(h) Normal wastage of materials, cost of rectification of defective works, idle time.

(i) Indirect materials such as oil, cotton waste, rags, lubricant, grease, small tools.

(j) Canteen subsidies, welfare expenses for the workers like recreation, first aid, news papers, magazines for the factory, T.V. and radio etc.

2.17 Administrative Overhead

Administration overhead consists of expenses that are incurred 'in the direction, control and administration of an undertaking'. It comprises the indirect materials cost, indirect wages and indirect expenses that are incurred in the direction, control and administration of an undertaking.

Examples

The following are some of the examples of administration overhead :

i) Indirect materials – Printing and Stationery which includes books of accounts, files, ink, paper, pin, james clip, broomstick, carbon paper, stencil paper etc.

ii) Indirect wages—Salaries to office staff, salaries paid to administrative directors, secretaries, accountants, cashier, internal auditors and other office supervisors and staffs of different departments like personnel, accounts, audit, credit approval, cash etc.

iii) Indirect expenses – Rent, rates and taxes of office buildings, depreciation on fixed assets used in the office, lighting, heating, cleaning of general offices, insurance for office buildings and equipment, repairs of office buildings and equipment, legal charges, travelling allowances to office staff, audit fees, postage, telephone etc.

So, **Administration Overhead = Indirect Materials + Indirect Wages + Indirect Expenses** of the offices of an undertaking.

2.18 Selling Overhead and Distribution Overhead

Selling overhead consists of indirect material cost, indirect wages and indirect expenses that are incurred from the time the products are in a saleable state until they are sold and delivered. This overhead comprises the expenses that are incurred by the producers for soliciting and securing orders for the articles dealt in, and for finding new customers and retaining the old. It includes all indirect material cost, indirect wages and indirect expenses that are incurred by the manufacturer for expansion of market for its products.

Distribution overhead consists of indirect material cost, indirect wages and indirect expenses for making the goods fit for despatch and make them available to customers. In other words, it comprises all expenses incurred from the time the product is completed in the factory until it reaches its destination.

Examples :

Selling Overhead :

i) *Indirect materials* : Printing and stationery, mailing literature, price lists, materials used for display etc.

ii) *Indirect wages* : Salaries and commission paid to Sales Manager, Sales Representatives, salaries of staff working in sales office.

iii) *Indirect expenses* : Rent, rates and taxes of showrooms and sales offices, lighting, advertisement expenses, bad debt, discount allowed to customers, collection charges, expenses for 'after sales service'.

Distribution Overhead :

i) Indirect materials : Printing and stationery, packing materials, oil, grease, spare parts for delivery vans, petrol, diesel for delivery vans.

ii) Indirect wages : Wages paid to staff and workers engaged in connection with delivery of goods, such as despatch clerks, workers for loading and unloading, packers, van drivers, mechanics, salaries to warehouse staff.

iii) Indirect expenses : Freight and carriage outwards, rent, rates and taxes for warehouses, insurance, repair and renewals of warehouse, repairs and depreciation and other running expenses of delivery vans, etc.

2.19 Behaviour-wise Classification

This classification is made on the basis of behavioural pattern of costs. There are certain costs which remain unaffected by changes in output, while some costs do change with the change in output. Many costs also tend to rise while volume increases but not in direct proportion. These costs are known as semi-variables.

The analysis of costs in this perspective is a matter of great importancee to the management for effective control and decision taking.

On the basis of behaviour, costs may be classified as :

i) Fixed costs ; ii) Variable costs ; and iii) Semi-variable costs.

1. Fixed Costs

Variable and Fixed costs are usually defined in terms of how a total cost changes in relation to changes in activity of a chosen cost objective which may be measured in units of product manufactured or sold.

A cost which remains unaffected up to certain level of production by fluctuations in volume of output or turnover. "If a total cost remains unchanged for a given time period despite wide fluctuations in activity, it is fixed" – Horngreen.

Hindusthan Motor Limited incurs, say, Rs. 3,00,000 for a financial year for payment of rent, rates and taxes for factory building, executive salaries and depreciation. These costs are fixed in the sense that they do not fluctuate with the increase in volume of production. The important characteristic of fixed costs is that during a given time span, it becomes progressively smaller on a per unit basis as volume of production increases. But it is to be noted that then costs remain fixed only in relation to a given range of activity called the "relevant range".

Examples

Depreciation of plant and machinery, depreciation of buildings, pay and allowances of executives, printing and stationery, legal charges, bank charges, salaries of works managers and supervisors, canteen expenses are the examples of fixed costs.

Fixed costs enable a business firm to do a business, but they are not incurred purely for manufacturing. Examples of fixed costs are rent, property taxes, supervising salaries, depreciation on office facilities, advertising, insurance, etc. These fixed costs originate because of contractual obligations and management decisions. They accrue or are incurred with the passage of time and not with the production of the product or the job.

Any fixed cost can be represented by the following graph :

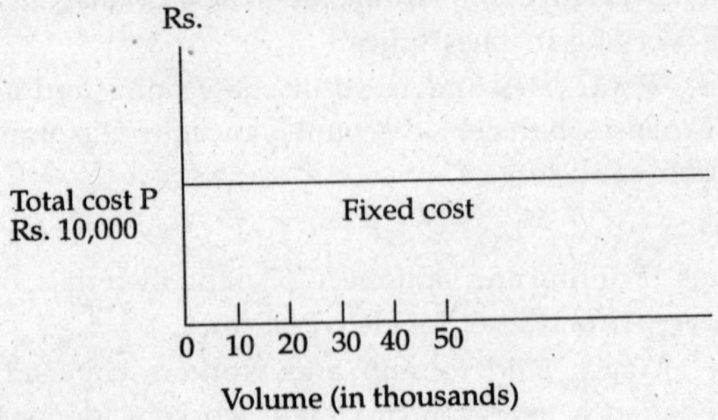

Fig. 2.1 : Fixed Cost

However, it should be improper to say that fixed costs never change in amount. Rents, insurance rates, taxes, salaries and other similar items may go up or down—depending on the circumstances. The basic concept is that the term "fixed" refers to fixity (non-variability) related to specific volume (or relevant range); the term does not imply that there will be no changes in fixed cost. The following are the fixed costs at different levels of production :

1. Rs. 50,000 fixed cost between 20,000 and 80,000 units of production.

2. Rs. 60,000 fixed cost in excess of 80,000 units. This assumes that increase in production after a certain level (80,000 units) requires increase in fixed expenses which have been fixed earlier, e.g., additional supervision, increase in quality control costs.

2. Variable Cost

Variable cost may be defined as a cost which varies in direct proportion to changes in the volume of output or turnover. "If a given cost changes in total, in direct proportion to changes in activity, it is variable"—Horngreen.

The cost of direct material is a variable cost as it changes in direct proportion to changes in output. For example, if one ton of iron ore is required to manufacture one ton of steel, surely two tons of iron ore will be required to manufacture two tons of steel.

Examples of Variable Costs

Indirect labour, indirect materials, power and fuel, repairs and maintenance, tools and spares, defective work, overtime pay, etc. are some of the examples of variable cost.

Difference between Fixed Cost and Variable Cost

The following are the points of difference between fixed cost and variable cost :

(i) Fixed costs do not vary directly with volume of output. On the other hand, variable costs vary directly and proportionately with the output.

(ii) Fixed costs arise due to contractual obligation and management decisions. For example rent, rates and taxes. Variable costs are related to production or operation. For example, cost of materials.

(iii) Fixed costs are generally apportioned to various departments while variable costs are directly allocated to cost centres.

(iv) Variable cost per unit is constant but the total cost changes corresponding to the level of output. Fixed cost per unit decreases with the increase in the volume of output.

(v) Fixed costs are always expressed in terms of time while variable costs are expressed in terms of units.

Graphical Presentation of Variable Cost

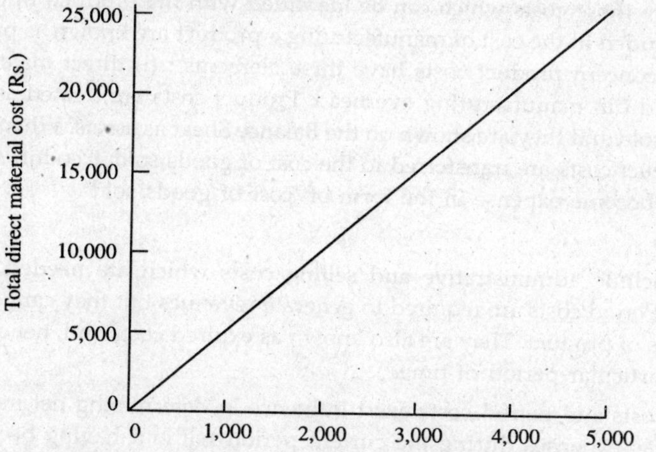

Fig. 2.2 : Behaviour of Variable Costs

3. Semi-variable Cost

A cost that contains both fixed and variable elements is known as semivariable cost. This type of cost is partly affected by fluctuations in the volume of output or turnover and is partly fixed up to a certain volume of production.

Examples

Examples of semi-variable costs are :

(a) Cost of supervision, inspection, maintenance and repairs of machinery and plant equipment.

(b) Cost of pay roll department services,

(c) Cost of personnel department services,

(d) Cost of factory office services,

(e) Cost of cost department services, etc.

The following graph depicts the nature of fixed, variable and semivariable costs.

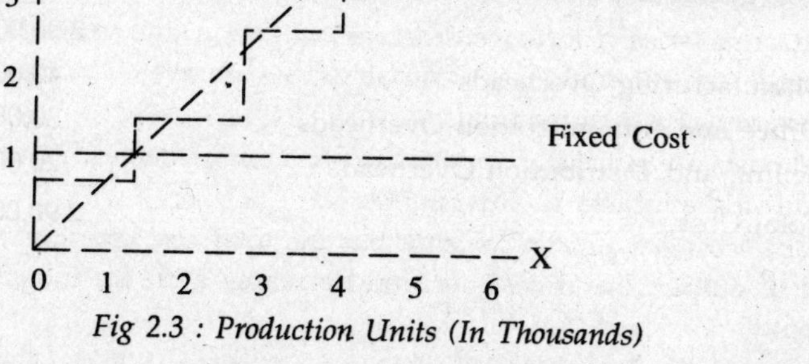

Fig 2.3 : Production Units (In Thousands)

2.21 Relation to the Product

Costs can be classified into product costs and period costs.

1. Product Costs

Product costs are those costs which can be identified with the product. In other words, the costs that are included in the cost of manufacturing a product are known as product costs. In a manufacturing concern product costs have three elements : (i) direct material cost, (ii) direct labour cost and (iii) manufacturing overhead. Product costs are treated as inventories so long they are not sold and they are shown on the Balance Sheet as assets. When the finished goods are sold, product costs are transferred to the cost of goods sold account. As the goods are sold, their costs become expense in the form of 'cost of goods sold'.

2. Period Costs

Period costs include administrative and selling costs which are needed to keep the business operating. Period costs are required to generate revenues but they cannot be directly associated with units of product. They are also known as expired costs and, hence, are treated as expenses for a particular period of time.

Both product costs and period costs exert influence in determining net income. Period costs are deducted as expenses during the current period without having been previously classified as product costs.

2.22 Traceability to the Product

Cost can also be divided into direct and indirect cost in terms of degree of traceability to the product.

1. Direct Cost

Costs which can be traced to or identified easily with a product are known as direct costs. In other words, direct costs represent costs and resources that can be traced to or identified with the finished product. The raw materials used and wages incurred in manufacturing one tonne of steel can easily be traced. If the cost of raw materials used for producing one tonne of steel is, say, Rs. 2,000 and direct wage paid to the workers is Rs. 2,500, the amount of direct cost is to be taken as Rs. 4,500.

2. Indirect Cost

Indirect costs are costs which are difficult or impossible to trace to a single product because they are common to several products. They cannot be identified with any single product. For example, the salary of a factory manager, rent, rates and taxes paid for the factory and office building cannot be traced to a single product.

The following cost sheet will explain clearly the nature of direct and indirect costs :

		Rs.	
	Cost Sheet		
	Cost of Raw Materials Consumed	1,00,000	Direct Costs
Add :	Direct wages	90,000	
Add :	Chargeable Expenses	10,000	
		2,00,000	
Add:	Manufacturing Overheads	40,000	Indirect Costs
Add :	Office and Administration Overheads	30,000	
Add :	Selling and Distribution Overheads	20,000	
	Total Cost	2,90,000	

2.23 Functional Classifications

Costs can be classified on the basis of the functions a business unit performs. In a manufacturing concern, costs are incurred for various functions. Under this approach, costs are classified under the headings of manufacturing, administrative and *selling costs.*

(i) Manufacturing costs consist of material cost, direct labour cost, direct expenses and factory overheads i.e. indirect materials cost, indirect labour cost and indirect expenses incurred in connection with factory. So, manufacturing costs are all production costs incurred to manufacture the products and to bring them to a saleable condition.

(ii) Administrative costs are cost of materials used in the office, salaries paid to office staff and all other expenses incurred in connection with office.

Examples :

Stationery used in office, rent, rates and taxes of office building, salaries paid to office staff, depreciation on office building and office equipment and furniture, electricity etc.

(iii) *Selling and distribution* costs are those which are incurred for performing selling and distribution function. These costs consist of cost of materials, wages and salaries and other expenses incurred for the selling department of an organisation.

Examples :

Cost of packing materials, stationery used, salaries to staff, depreciation on delivery van, sales representatives' commission, carriage outward, warehousing and storage, repairing and re-conditioning empty cartons, cases etc.

Functional classification is important because it provides an opportunity for the evaluation of the efficiency of different departments performing different functions in the organisation. It helps the management in **planning, control** and **decision making.**

2.24 Cost Analysis for Decision Making Purposes

Costs can conveniently be classified for effective cost analysis and also for decision making purposes. Here, some of the important costs have been discussed :

(i) *Opportunity Costs*

Opportunity cost is the cost of opportunity lost. Opportunity cost can be defined as the benefits lost by rejecting the best competing alternative to the one chosen. Opportunity cost of any asset is the amount that can be received if the asset is utilised in its next best alternative For example, assume that a manufacturer can sell his semi-finished product at Rs. 1,00,000. But he decides to finish it. Here, the opportunity cost of the semi-finished product is Rs. 1,00,000 because this is the amount of economic resources foregone by the manufacturer to finish the product.

Opportunity costs are very important in decision-making and evaluating alternatives. Decision-making in selecting the best alternative is facilitated with the help of opportunity cost.

(ii) *Sunk Cost*

This is the cost which has been incurred already or is yet to be incurred; but it will be the same no matter which alternative course of action is selected. Therefore, this cost is not relevant to decision making process. This is historical cost and sunk in the past.

For example, when the management decides to purchase new machinery to replace the old ones, the depreciated value of the old machinery becomes irrelevant in this decision- making process, as the amount is a sunk cost and will be written off at the time of replacement.

(iii) *Controllable and Non-controllable Costs*

The I.C.W.A. (U.K.) defines controllable cost as "a cost which can be influenced by the action of a specified member of an undertaking" and a non-controllable cost as "a cost which cannot be influenced by the action of a specified member of an undertaking". In other words, a manager has direct and complete decision authority over a controllable cost. Indirect labour, lubricants, cutting tools and power costs incurred in machining department are the examples of controllable cost.

According to **Ahmed Balkaoui**

(i) all *variable costs* are controllable and all *fixed costs* are non-controllable;

(ii) all direct costs are controllable, and *indirect costs* are non-controllable;

(iii) all *long-run costs* are controllable and all *short-run costs* are non-controllable.

The concept of controllable and non-controllable cost contributes effectively to the achievement of the objectives of cost control and responsibility accounting.

2.25 Cost Sheet

Definition

Cost sheet is a statement wherein detailed information about costs is depicted and a total cost of product manufactured during a particular period of time is ascertained. The cost sheet is prepared for a particular period, e.g. monthly, quarterly etc.

Advantages of Cost Sheet

The cost sheet is prepared with the following objectives :

i) It ascertains the total cost and cost per unit for a particular period.

ii) It enables the management to fix up sale price of products.

iii) It helps to present a comparative study of current costs with the costs of the corresponding period.

iv) The management can identify the causes of inefficiencies and wastages and can take corrective measures.

v) It provides management with suitable information for management control.

vi) It also helps the management considerably in formulating suitable and definite production policy.

vii) Cost sheet enables the businessman to submit quotation against tenders.

2.26 Preparation of Cost Sheet

The following steps are to be taken to prepare the cost sheet :

Step 1

Find out the Prime Cost

Definition of Prime Cost

Prime Cost is the sum total of direct materials consumed, direct or productive wages and direct or chargeable expenses and the difference of opening of work-in-progress and closing of work-in-progress at prime cost.

Thus, **Prime Cost = Direct Materials + Direct Wages + Direct Expenses + Opening Balance of W.I.P. at prime cost – Closing Balance of W.I.P. at prime cost.**

Problem 2

How to determine materials consumed?

From the following figures obtained from the costing records of product A ascertain the PRIME COST for the month of August 1997.

		Rs.
Opening stock of raw materials (1.8.97)	–	10,000
Raw materials purchased	–	80,000
Raw materials returned	–	5,000
Carriage Inward for raw materials purchased	–	4,000
Raw materials on 31.8.1997	–	6,000
Work-in-Progress at Prime Cost on 1.8.97	–	8,000
Work-in-Progress at Prime Cost on 31.8.97	–	4,000
Chargeable expenses	–	10,000
Productive Wages	–	40,000

Solution

Statement showing the Prime Cost for the month of August 1997

		Rs.	Rs.
	Opening Stock of raw materials		10,000
Add :	Purchase of raw materials	80,000	
Less :	Return	5,000	
		75,000	
Add :	Carriage Inward	4,000	79,000
			89,000
Less :	Stock of raw materials on 31.8.97		6,000
	Raw Materials Consumed		83,000
Add :	Productive Wages		40,000
Add :	Chargeable Expenses		10,000
			1,33,000
Add :	Opening Stock of W.I.P. at Prime Cost		8,000
			1,41,000
Less :	Closing Stock of W.I.P. at Prime Cost		4,000
	PRIME COST		1,37,000

Step 2

Find out the Works Cost

Works Cost = Prime Cost + Factory Overheads + Opening Stock of Work-in-Progress at Factory Cost – Closing Stock of Work-in-Progress at Factory Cost.

Problem 3

From the following information ascertain the Works Cost for the month of August 1997 :

		Rs.
Stock of raw materials on 1.8.1997	–	40,000
Work-in-Progress on 1.8.1997	–	25,000
Purchase of raw materials	–	1,00,000
Carriage Inwards	–	10,000
Direct Wages	–	60,000

Contd.

		Rs.
Cost of special drawing	–	15,000
Hire charge for machinery	–	12,000
Return of raw material	–	20,000
Carriage on return	–	3,000
Rent, rates and insurance of works	–	6,000
Cost of factory supervision	–	4,000
Sale of Scrap	–	500
Cost of rectification of defective works	–	1,500
Stock of raw materials on 31.8.1997	–	15,000
Stock of W.I.P. on 31.8.1997	–	12,000

Solution

Statement showing the Works Cost for the month of August 1997.

		Rs.	Rs.
	Opening Stock of raw materials	40,000	
Add :	Purchase	1,00,000	
		1,40,000	
Add :	Carriage Inwards	10,000	
		1,50,000	
Less :	Return of raw materials	20,000	
		1,30,000	
Less :	Closing stock of raw materials	15,000	
	Raw materials consumed		1,15,000
Add :	Direct wages		60,000
Add :	Chargeable Expenses :		
	Cost of Special drawings	15,000	
	Hire charge of machinery	12,000	27,000
	PRIME COST		2,02,000
Add :	Factory Overheads		
	Rent, rates and insurance of works	6,000	
	Cost of factory supervision	4,000	
	Cost of rectification of defective works	1,500	
	Carriage on return	3,000	
		14,500	
Add :	Opening Stock of W.I.P.	25,000	
		39,500	
Less :	Closing Stock of W.I.P.	12,000	
		27,500	
Less :	Sale of Scrap	500	
			27,000
	WORKS COST		2,29,000

Step 3

Ascertain Cost of Production and Cost of Goods Sold

(a)	**Cost of Production = Works Cost (Step 2) + Office and Administrative Overheads**	×××
(b)	**Cost of goods sold = Cost of Production (Step 3)**	×××
Add :	Opening Stock of Finished Goods	×××
Less :	Closing Stock of Finished Goods	×××
	COST OF GOODS SOLD	×××

Step 4

Ascertain Total Cost or Cost of Sales

	Cost of Goods sold	×××
Add :	Selling and Distribution Overheads	×××
	TOTAL COST	×××

Step 5

Find out the Sale Price and Profit

(a)	When sale price is given	
	Sale Price	×××
Less :	Total Cost	×××
	Profit	×××

Method for Calculation of percentage of profit

(i) When Percentage is calculated on Cost : $\frac{\text{Profit} \times 100}{\text{C.P.}}$

(ii) When percentage is calculated on Sales : $\frac{\text{Profit} \times 100}{\text{S.P.}}$

C.P. = Cost price

S.P. = Sale price

Calculation of profit as a percentage of cost price or sales

(v) When profit is to be calculated as a percentage on sales but S.P. is not given.

$$\frac{\text{'Actual' Cost} \times \text{\% of profit}}{100 - \text{\% of profit}}$$

Example : Assume that the cost of sales of a product A is Rs. 4,00,000. Now, the business wants to make profit at 20% on sales. We do not know the sale price.

The amount of profit is to be calculted as follows :

$$\frac{4,00,000 \times 20}{80(100-20)} = \text{Rs. } 1,00,000 \text{ i.e. S.P. } 5,00,000 \times \frac{20}{100} = 1,00,000$$

2.27 Expenses that are not treated in Cost Sheet

Items of expenses relating to capital assets, capital losses, payments by way of distribution of profits and matters of pure finance should not form a part of the costs.

Examples of such expenses are :

Income-tax, dividend, abnormal wastage of material, abnormal idle time, interest on capital, bad debt, provision for bad debt, cash discount received or allowed, discount on issue of shares and debentures, preliminary expenses, underwriting commissions and capital expenditure :

2.28 Treatment of some items in Cost Sheet

(a) Work-in-Progress :

Work-in-Progress means incomplete units at the end of the given period of time. Work-in-Progress may be valued at (i) prime cost and (ii) at factory cost.

W.I.P. at Prime Cost

When the Work-in-Progress is valued at prime cost the opening balance of W.I.P. is added to the total of direct materials, direct wages and direct expenses. Closing stock of W.I.P. is then deducted from the total Prime Cost. So, both opening and closing balances of Work-in-Progress are taken into consideration in the determination of Prime Cost e.g.,

		Rs.
	Direct materials consumed	×××
	Productive or direct wages	×××
	Other chargeable expenses	×××
Add :	Opening stock of Work-in-Progress at Prime Cost	×××
		×××
Less :	Closing Stock of Work-in-Progress at Prime Cost	×××
	PRIME COST	×××

At factory cost

If Work-in-Progress is valued on the basis of factory cost, both opening and closing balances of Work-in-Progress are considered while ascertaining the factory cost.

(b) **Treatment of Defective Materials**

If the defective materials are returned to the store or supplier, the value of defective materials is to be deducted from the value of raw materials consumed. When the defective materials are sold, the cost of materials consumed should be reduced by the amount received on account of sale of defective material.

(c) **Sale of Scrap**

In the course of manufacturing a product, some materials may be wasted or may be rendered useless. If these materials are sold as scrap at cost price, the amount realised from the sale of scrap should be deducted from the factory overheads.

(d) **Defective Product**

Sometimes, some of the products manufactured during a particular period of time may turn out to be defective. The cause of defects may be normal or abnormal. Defective products may be brought upto the standard of specification by incurring additional expenditure. Additional expenditure for rectifying the defects to bring the product up to the standard of specification will be treated as factory overhead and is to be added to the factory cost provided such defects have been caused due to normal reasons.

If the defects are caused due to abnormal reasons, additional cost for rectification will be transferred to Costing Profit and Loss A/c.

Problem 4

The following particulars have been collected from a manufacturing concern for the year ended 31.3.1998 :

	Rs.
Raw materials :	
Stock on 1.4.1997	70,000
Purchase during the year	5,00,000
Stock on 31. 3. 1998	50,000
Direct wages	1,00,000
Stores overhead on materials 10% on cost of materials.	
Factory overhead 50% of wages.	

10% of the casting was rejected and a sum of 6,000 was realised on sale as scrap.

10% of finished products was found to be defective and the defective products were rectified at an additional expenditure which is equivalent to 20% of proportionate direct wages.

The total output was 10,000 tonnes during the year.

Ascertain the manufacturing cost per tonne.

Solution

Statement of cost for the year ended 31st March 1998 – Output 9,000 tonnes

	Particulars		*Total Cost*	*Cost per Unit*
		Rs.	Rs.	Rs.
	Opening Stock of raw materials	70,000		
Add :	Purchase during the year	5,00,000		
		5,70,000		
Less :	Closing stock of raw materials	50,000		
	Cost of raw materials consumed		5,20,000	
	Direct Wages		1,00,000	
	PRIME COST		6,20,000	
Add :	Stores overhead @ 10% of cost of materials		52,000	
	Works overhead – 50% of direct wages		50,000	
			7,22,000	
Less :	Sale of Scrap		6,000	
			7,16,000	
Add :	Additional expenditure for rectification of defective products (NOTE 2)		1,800	
			7,17,800	79·756

Working Notes :

(1) Units rectified — 10,000 gross output

Less 10% rejected — 1,000

Finished product — 9,000

So, 10% of 9,000 were rectified, i.e. 900 tonnes.

(2) Additional expenditure = 20% of proportionate wages

$$\text{for 900 units} = \frac{20}{100} \times \frac{1,00,000}{10,000} \times 900 = \text{Rs. } 1,800$$

$$\text{(3) Cost per unit} = \frac{7,17,800}{9,000} = \text{Rs. } 79.756$$

2.29 Direct Cost

Direct Cost is the sum total of cost of direct materials consumed, direct wages and direct expenses incurred for a particular period of time.

Direct Cost = Cost of Materials Consumed + Direct Wages + Direct Expenses or Chargeable Expenses.

Treatment of Finished goods

If there is any balance of finished goods at the beginning of the month or year and unsold stock of finished goods at the end of the year, these balances are to be adjusted to ascertain the actual cost of goods sold. Moreover, if there is any missing figure like units produced or units sold, appropriate adjustments are to be made to determine the missing figure.

(i) **To find out the units sold :**

	Opening Stock of finished goods	×××
Add :	Units manufactured during the period	×××
		×××
Less :	Closing Stock of finished goods in units	×××
	Units Sold	×××

(ii) **To find out units manufactured**

	Units sold	×××
Add :	Units of unsold stock	×××
		×××
Less :	Units of stock at the beginning	×××
	Units manufactured	×××

POINTS TO NOTE

The students are to note that after making the above adjustments, Selling and Distribution Overheads should be added to ascertain the Cost of Sales or Total Cost. **Normal loss of materials will not be treated in the cost sheet.**

To make the above discussed matter easily understandable the following chart has been drawn.

ELEMENTS OF COST

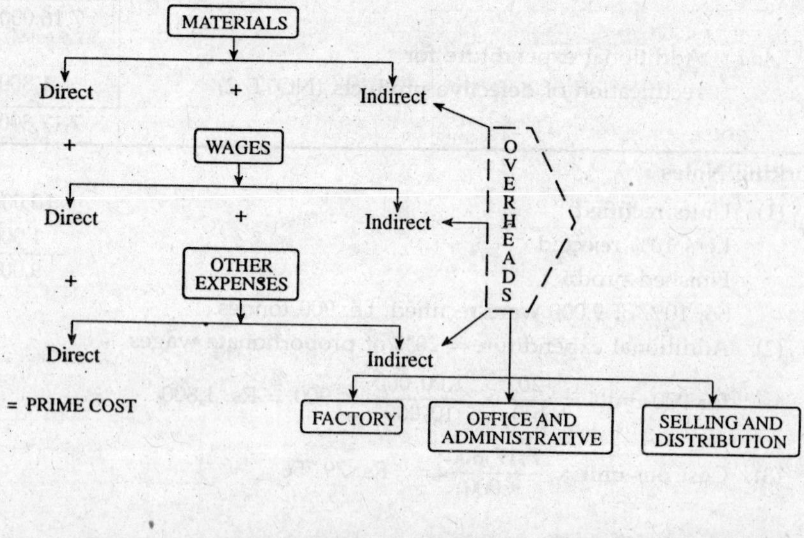

COST SHEET — How to prepare
[When goods are produced and sold]

Direct Materials + Direct Wages + Direct Expenses	⇨	PRIME COST
		+
Factory Indirect Materials + Factory Indirect Wages + Factory Indirect Expenses	⇨	FACTORY OVERHEADS
		=
		WORKS COST
		+
Indirect Materials used in office + Indirect Wages paid to office and Administrative staff. + Indirect Expenses for office and Administration.	⇨	OFFICE AND ADMINISTRATIVE OVERHEADS
		=
		COST OF PRODUCTION
		+
		OPENING STOCK OF FINISHED GOODS
		–
		CLOSING STOCK OF FINISHED GOODS
		=
		COST OF GOODS SOLD
Indirect Materials used in sales department. + Indirect Wages paid to staff of sales dept. + Indirect Expenses for sales dept.	⇨	SELLING & DISTIBUTION OVERHEADS
		=
		COST OF SALES
		+
		PROFIT
		=
		SALE PRICE

SPECIMEN OF COST SHEET

SEWIL & CO.

Cost Sheet for period ending – Product | Division/Department/Unit/Plant

Units Produced

Particulars	Total cost Standard	Total cost Actual
	Rs.	Rs.
Opening Stock of raw materials		
Purchases of raw materials		
Carriage Inwards,		
Less : Closing Stock		
Direct Materials consumed		
Direct Wages		
Direct Expenses		
Prime Cost		
Add : **Factory or Works overheads :**		
Works Consultancy		
Indirect Wages		
Power and Fuel		
Lighting, Heating, Cooling and Air-conditioning		
Factory Rents, Rates, Lease		
Depreciation, repairs and Maintenance of Factory Premises		
Depreciation of Factory Plant & Loose Tools		
Factory Employees' State Insurance		
Factory Employees' Welfare Services		
Factory Office (Personnel, Stationery, Machines, Communication, etc.)		
Cost of rectification of defective goods		
Insurance – Fixed Asset – Stocks		
Salaries of Works Manager, Supervisors and other similar personnel.		
Less : Sale of scrap		
Indirect Materials		
Works or Factory Cost		
Add : **Office and Administrative overheads**		
Office Consultancy salaries		
Rent, Lease, Rates and Taxes		
Lighting, Heating, Cooling and Air-conditioning		
Insurance		
Maintenance, Repairs,		
Upkeep of Office Building		

Contd.

Particulars	Total cost	
	Standard	Actual
	Rs.	Rs.
Printing and Stationery		
Postage, Telephone, Telex, etc.		
Depreciation of Office Building		
Legal Charges		
Bank Charges		
Audit Fees		
Misc. Expenses or General Office expenses		
Cost of Production		
Add : **Selling and Distribution overheads**		
Marketing Consultancy		
Sales Office (Personnel, Stationery, Machines, Communications, etc.)		
Lease, Rent, Rates and Taxes,		
Lighting, Heating, Cooling and Air-conditioning.		
Salaries of the Sales Staff, Commission,		
Travelling Expenses		
Advertising		
Bad Debts		
Carriage Outwards		
Depreciation and Running Expenses of Delivery Trucks, Vans, etc.		
Samples, Free gifts, etc.		
Misc. Expenses		
Cost of Sales		
Add : Net Profit or		
Deduct Net Loss		
Sales		

Problem 5

The following particulars have been obtained from the cost records for the year 1997 :

	Rs.
Materials used in manufacturing	1,10,000
Materials used in primary packing	20,000
Materials used in selling the product	3,000
Materials used in the factory	1,500
Productive Wages	30,000
Factory Supervision expenses	4,000
Materials used for office	2,500
Chargeable expenses	10,000
Indirect expenses – factory	2,000

Contd.

	Rs.
Administration expenses	3,000
Depreciation on Factory Building	3,500
Depreciation on Office Building	1,500
Freight on materials purchased	5,000
Depreciation on Delivery Van	1,000
Salary paid to the driver of Delivery Van	3,600
Advertisement	2,000
Bad Debt	1,500

Assume that all products manufactured during the year have been sold to earn a profit of 20% on selling price.

Solution

Statement of Cost and Profit
for the year 1997

		Rs.	Rs.
	Direct Materials		
	Direct Materials used	1,10,000	
	Materials used in primary packing	20,000	
	Freight on materials purchased	5,000	
			1,35,000
	Direct Labour		
	Productive wages		30,000
	Direct Expenses		
	Chargeable expenses		10,000
	PRIME COST		1,75,000
Add :	Factory Overheads		
	Materials used in factory	1,500	
	Factory supervision expenses	4,000	
	Factory indirect expenses	2,000	
	Depreciation on factory building	3,500	11,000
	WORKS COST		1,86,000
Add :	Office and Administrative Overheads		
	Materials used in office	2,500	
	Administration expenses	3,000	
	Depreciation on office building	1,500	7,000
	COST OF PRODUCTION		1,93,000
Add :	Selling Overheads		
	Materials used in selling the product	3,000	
	Advertisement	2,000	
	Bad Debt	1,500	6,500
			1,99,500
Add :	Distribution Overheads		
	Depreciation on Delivery van	1,000	
	Salary to driver of delivery van	3,600	4,600
	COST OF SALES/TOTAL COST		2,04,100
Add :	Profit @ 20% on sales i.e. 25% on cost		51,025
	SALE PRICE		2,55,125

Working Note : When sale price is 100, cost is Rs. 80 and Profit is Rs. 20

$$\text{So, Profit} = \frac{\text{Cost} \times 100}{100 - 20} = \frac{2,04,100 \times 20}{80} = \text{Rs. } 51,025.$$

$$\text{or, 25\% of Cost} = 2,04,100 \times \frac{1}{4} = 51,025$$

WORKED OUT PROBLEMS

Problem 6

From the following particulars prepare a Cost Sheet showing the Prime Cost, Factory Cost, Cost of Production and Cost of Sales :

Total Output : 50,000 units

	Rs.	Rs.
Raw materials consumed		2,00,000
Direct Wages		1,60,000
Direct Expenses (Factory)		40,000
Wages of foremen		40,000
Wages of indirect workers in the factory		10,000
Wages of storekeeper in the factory		20,000
Oil lubricants and wastes		6,000
Lighting and Power		
Factory	40,000	
Office	10,000	
Marketing Division	10,000	60,000
Rental and Leases		
Factory	40,000	
Office	50,000	
Marketing Division	30,000	1,20,000
Repairs and Renewals		
Factory Plant	20,000	
Office Machines	8,000	
Machines in Marketing Division	6,000	34,000
Depreciation		
Office Premises	12,000	
Plant and Machinery	28,000	
Office Machines	20,000	
Office Machines in the Marketing Division	12,000	
		72,000
Consumable Stores		80,000
Works Director's Salary		80,000
Office Manager's Salary		40,000
Marketing Director's Salary		60,000
Company Secretary's Salary		40,000
Office Printing and Stationery		20,000
Telephone, Postage, Telegram		36,000

Contd.

Salary		Rs.
Office	50,000	
Salesmen	70,000	1,20,000
Packing etc. (Sales Division)		52,000
Salesmen's Commission		12,000
Salesmen's travelling expenses		25,000
Advertising		32,000
Warehousing		4,000
Carriage outward		6,000
Entertainment		
Office	15,000	
Marketing Division	13,000	28,000
Fees of the Board		37,000

Solution

Notes : 1. The different heads of expenses should be segregated and classified into those relating to factory, office & marketing, etc. for the purpose of preparing the cost sheet.

2. Since the standard costs are not given, the columns relating to standard costs have not been used.

COST SHEET

Total Output 50,000 units

Particulars		*Total Cost*		*Cost per Unit*	
		Actual	*Standard*	*Actual*	*Standard*
		Rs.	Rs.	Rs.	Rs.
Direct materials :					
Raw materials consumed		2,00,000		4.00	
Direct Wages		1,60,000		3.20	
Direct Expenses		40,000		0.80	
Prime Cost		4,00,000		8.00	
Add : **Factory or Works Overheads**					
Indirect materials :	Rs.				
Consumable Stores	80,000				
Oil, Lubricants and Wages	6,000	86,000		1.72	
Indirect Labour :					
Wages of foreman	40,000				
Wages of indirect workers	10,000				
Wages of storekeeper	20,000				
Works Director's Salary	80,000	1,50,000		3.00	
Indirect Expenses :					
Lighting and Power	40,000				
Rent and Lease	40,000				
Repairs and Renewals	20,000				
Depreciation :					
Plant and Machinery	28,000	1,28,000		2.56	
Works or Factory Cost			7,64,000		15.28

Contd.

Particulars	*Total Cost*		*Cost per Unit*	
		Actual		*Actual*
	Rs.	Rs.	Rs.	Rs.
B.F.		7,64,000		15.28
Add : **Office or Administrative overheads**				
Indirect Material :				
Office printing and stationery		20,000		0.40
Indirect Labour :				
Office Manager's Salary	40,000			
Company Secretary's Salary	40,000			
Salary of Office Staff	50,000			
Fees of the Board	37,000	1,67,000		3.34
Indirect Expenses :				
Lighting and Power	10,000			
Rent and Leases	50,000			
Repairs and Renewals of office machines	8,000			
Depreciation of office machines	20,000			
Telephone, Postage and Telegrams	36,000			
Office entertainment	15,000			
Depreciation	12,000	1,51,000		3·02
Total Cost of Production		11,02,000		22·04
Add : **Selling and Distribution overheads**				
Indirect Material, Packing etc.		52,000		1.04
Indirect Labour :				
Marketing Director's Salary	60,000			
Salaries of Salesmen	70,000			
Salesmen's Commission	12,000	1,42,000		2.84
Indirect Expenses :				
Lighting and Power	10,000			
Rent and Leases	30,000			
Repairs and Renewals	6,000			
Depreciation of machines	12,000			
Salesmen's travelling expenses	25,000			
Advertising	32,000			
Warehousing	4,000			
Carriage outward	6,000			
Entertainment	13,000	1,38,000		2.76
Cost of Sales		14,34,000		28.68

Treatment of Abnormal and Normal Loss of Materials.

Abnormal Loss

Abnormal loss means the loss which could have been avoided had care been taken properly. This is not an inherent loss. For example, materials destroyed by fire, materials stolen etc. If materials are insured, a sum may be realised from insurance company.

The amount of abnormal loss should be subtracted from materials purchased or total cost of materials. The actual loss (abnormal loss – amount realised from insurance company) should be debited to Costing Profit and Loss Account.

Normal Loss

Normal loss is naturally, unavoidable i.e. it is inherent in production process. Sometimes normal loss of materials which are rendered useless for production may be sold as scrap. The sale price of such materials surely reduces the cost of materials consumed. Therefore, the sale price of scrap should be deducted from the cost of materials consumed.

The following example will clarify the concept.

	Rs.
Raw Materials purchased	2,00,000
Opening stock of raw materials	30,000
Carriage paid on materials purchased	5,000
Materials stolen	10,000
Amount received from Insurance Company against materials stolen	8,000
Normal loss of materials	6,000
Sale as Scrap	800
Closing Stock of Raw materials	20,000
Find out the amount of materials consumed	

Solution

	Raw Materials consumed	
	Opening stock of raw materials	30,000
Add :	Purchase of raw materials	2,00,000
Add :	Carriage on materials purchased	5,000
		2,35,000
Less :	Materials stolen	10,000
		2,25,000
Less :	Sale of Scrap	800
		2,24,200
Less :	Closing Stock of raw-materials	20,000
	Raw materials consumed	2,04,200

Problem 7

From the following particulars prepare a statement showing clearly all the elements of cost in the manner you consider best :

	Rs.
Direct wages	3,60,000
Stock of materials on 1.4.1989	5,00,000
Purchase of materials during 1989-90	14,00,000
Materials returned to suppliers	40,000
Stock of materials as on 31.3.1990	3,76,000
Wages paid to non-production workmen	40,000
Salaries paid to office staff	1,00,000
Carriage on materials purchased	10,000
Carriage on goods sold	30,000
Rent, rates and taxes on the works	50,000
Depreciation on Machinery	28,000
Maintenance and Repairs to Plant and Machinery	12,000
Office stationery and other expenses	30,000
Abnormal loss of materials	24,000
Chargeable expenses	16,000
Advertisement and sales promotion	24,000

[C.U. B.Com. (Pass) 1991]

Solution

COST SHEET
for the year 1989-90

		Rs.	Rs.
	Stock of materials on 1.4.1989	5,00,000	
Add :	Purchase of materials during 1989-90	14,00,000	
		19,00,000	
Less :	Materials returned to suppliers	40,000	
		18,60,000	
Less :	Abnormal loss of materials	24,000	
		18,36,000	
Less :	Closing stock of materials (31.3.1990)	3,76,000	
		14,60,000	
Add :	Carriage on materials purchased	10,000	
	Materials Consumed		14,70,000
Add :	Direct wages		3,60,000
	Chargeable expenses		16,000
	Prime Cost		18,46,000
Add :	*Factory overhead*		
	Wages paid to non-production workmen	40,000	
	Rent, Rates and Taxes on the works	50,000	
	Depreciation on Machinery	28,000	
	Maintenance and Repairs to Plant & Machinery	12,000	1,30,000
	Works Cost		19,76,000
Add :	*Office and Administrative overheads*		
	Salaries paid to office staff	1,00,000	
	Office stationery and other expenses	30,000	1,30,000
	Cost of Production		21,06,000
Add :	*Selling and Distribution overheads*		
	Carriage on goods sold	30,000	
	Advertisement and Sales promotion	24,000	54,000
	Total Cost		21,60,000

CLOSING STOCK IS TO BE VALUED

Problem 8

From the following information prepare a statement of Cost for the year 1996 showing therein (a) Prime Cost; (b) Works Cost; (c) Cost of Production; (d) Profit or Loss.

	Rs.
Raw Materials consumed	60,000
Direct Wages	40,000
Direct Expenses	8,000
Indirect Wages	10,000
Depreciation on Machinery	12,000
Office Overhead	20% of Works Cost
Selling Overhead	Rs. 3 per unit
Units Produced	15,000
Units Sold	12,000 @ Rs. 15 each

[C.U. B.Com. (Pass) 1997]

Solution

COST SHEET
for the year 1996

		Rs.	Rs.
	Raw Materials consumed		60,000
	Direct Wages		40,000
	Direct Expenses		8,000
(a)	**Prime Cost**		1,08,000
Add :	Factory Overhead		
	Indirect Wages	10,000	
	Depreciation on Machinery	12,000	22,000
(b)	**Works Cost**		1,30,000
Add :	Office Overhead – 20% of Works Cost	$\frac{20}{100} \times 1,30,000$	26,000
(c)	**Cost of Production**		1,56,000
Less :	Closing Stock (see note below)		31,200
	Cost of goods sold		1,24,800
Add :	Selling Overhead @ Rs. 2 per unit	12,000 × 3	36,000
	Cost of Sales or Total Cost		1,60,800
(d)	**Profit (Balancing figure)**		19,200
	Sale Price @ Rs. 15 per unit	12,000 × 15	1,80,000

Working notes :

(1) Closing Stock = Units produced – Units sold = 15,000 – 12,000 = 3,000 units.

Cost price of 3,000 units = Rs. $\frac{1,56,000}{15,000} \times 3,000$ = Rs. 31,200.

Problem 9

Calculate Prime Cost, Factory Cost, Cost of Production, Cost of Sales and Profit from the following particulars relating to the year 1997 :

	Rs.		Rs
Direct Materials	2,00,000	Consumable Stores	5,000
Productive Wages	60,000	Manager's Salary	5,000
Chargeable Expenses	10,000	Discount allowed	2,000
Lighting :		Director's fees	5,000
Factory	4,000	Office stationery	1,000
Office	2,000	Oil and Water	1,000
Depreciation :		Rent :	
Factory Plant	1,000	Factory	10,000
Office Premises	2,500	Office	6,000
Wages of foreman	5,000	Repairs and Renewals	
Electricity – factory	1,000	Factory Plant	7,000
Storekeeper's Wages	1,000	Office Premises	1,200
Carriage Outward	875	Telephone charges	400
Transfer to Reserve	6,000	Salesmans' salaries	4,000
Warehouse charges	1,600	Travelling expenses	1,500
Sales	4,00,000	Advertisement expenses	2,000
		Income-Tax	10,000
		Dividend	8,000

Solution

COST SHEET

		Rs.	Rs.
	Direct Materials		2,00,000
	Direct Wages		60,000
	Chargeable expenses		10,00
	Prime Cost		2,70,000
Add :	*Factory Overheads :*		
	Lighting	4,000	
	Depreciation – factory plant	1,000	
	Wages of foreman	5,000	
	Electricity	1,000	
	Storekeeper's wages	1,000	
	Consumable stores	5,000	
	Oil and Water	1,000	
	Rent – factory	10,000	
	Repairs and Renewals	7,000	
			35,000
	Works Cost		3,05,000
Add :	*Office and Administration Overheads*		
	Lighting	2,000	
	Depreciation – Office premises	2,500	
	Manager's salary	5,000	
	Director's fees	5,000	
	Office stationery	1,000	
	Rent – office	6,000	
	Repairs – Office premises	1,200	
	Telephone charges	400	
			23,100
	Cost of Production		3,28,100
Add :	*Selling and Distribution Overheads*		
	Carriage outward	875	
	Warehouse charges	1,600	
	Salesmen's salary	4,000	
	Travelling expenses	1,500	
	Advertisement expenses	2,000	
			9,975
	Total Cost/Cost of Sales		3,38,075
	Profit		61,925
	Sale Price		4,00,000

Problem 10

From the following information prepare a Statement of Cost for the year 1993 showing therein (a) Prime Cost, (b) Works Cost, (c) Cost of Production and (d) Total Cost :

		Rs.
Opening Stock of	Raw Materials	18,000
	Finished goods	5,000
Closing Stock of	Raw Materials	10,000
	Finished goods	6,000
Purchase of Raw Materials		90,000
Indirect Wages (Factory)		3,000
Factory Supervision		2,000
Direct Wages		18,000
Power and Fuel		5,000
Depreciation on Plant and Machinery		7,000
Carriage Outward		3,000
Office Salaries		8,000
Office Rent		6,000
Sundry Office expenses		9,000
Salesman's salaries		3,000

[C.U. B.Com. (Pass) 1994]

Solution

COST SHEET
for the year 1993

		Rs.	Rs.
	Opening Stock of Raw Materials	18,000	
Add :	Purchase of Raw Materials	90,000	
		1,08,000	
Less :	Closing Stock of Raw Materials	10,000	
	Raw Materials consumed		98,000
Add :	Direct Wages		18,000
(a)	**Prime Cost**		1,16,000
Add :	*Factory Overhead*		
	Indirect Wages	3,000	
	Factory supervision	2,000	
	Power and Fuel	5,000	
	Depreciation on Plant and Machinery	7,000	17,000
(b)	**Works Cost**		1,33,000
Add :	*Office and Administration Overheads*		
	Office Salaries	8,000	
	Office Rent	6,000	
	Sundry Office expenses	9,000	23,000
(c)	**Cost of Production**		1,56,000
Add :	Opening Stock of Finished goods		5,000
			1,61,000
Less :	Closing Stock of Finished goods		6,000
	Cost of Goods Sold		1,55,000
Add :	*Selling and Distribution Overheads*		
	Carriage Outward	3,000	
	Salesmen'ssalaries	3,000	6,000
(d)	**Total Cost**		1,61,000

Problem 11

On the basis of the information given below in respect of production of a certain product prepare a statement of Cost and find out its selling price.

	Rs.
Direct Materials	5,000
Direct Wages	3,000
Chargeable expenses	1,000

Works on cost at 30% of Direct Wages; Office on cost at 12% of Works Cost; Profit at 20% of selling price is required.

[C.U. B.Com. (Pass) 1996]

Solution

COST SHEET

for the year ....

		Rs.	Rs.
	Direct Materials		5,000
	Direct Wages		3,000
	Chargeable Expenses		1,000
	Prime Cost		9,000
Add :	Works on Cost @ 30% of Direct Wages	$\frac{30}{100} \times 3,000$	900
	Works Cost		9,900
Add :	Office on Cost @ 12% of Works Cost	$\frac{12}{100} \times 9,900$	1,188
	Cost of Production		11,088
Add :	Profit @ 20% on Selling price i.e., 25% on Cost		2,772
	Selling Price		13,860

Treatment of Abnormal and Normal Loss of Raw materials

Problem 12

The following data have been extracted from the books of Usha Engineering Co. for the year 1997. You are required to prepare a Cost Sheet for the period showing therein the Prime Cost, Works Cost, Cost of Production, Cost of Goods Sold and Cost of Sales.

	Rs.
Balance as on 1.1.1997	
Raw materials	20,000
Work-in-progress	30,000
Finished goods (5,000 units)	50,000
Purchase of raw materials	2,30,000
Raw materials returned to suppliers	5,000
Raw materials stolen	6,000
Cash received from Insurance Company against raw materials stolen	4,000
Carriage on raw materials purchased	5,000
Normal loss of raw materials	4,000
Cash received by sale of scrap in respect of normal loss of materials	2,500

Contd.

Productive wages	1,20,000
Indirect wages	10,000
Electricity	8,000
Motive power	5,000
Rent, rates and taxes	12,000
Salaries paid to staff (office)	30,000
Chargeable expenses	20,000
Materials used in the office	5,000
Packing materials for factory	10,000
Selling overheads @ Rs. 2 per unit sold	
Distribution overhead @ Re. 1 per unit	
Balance on 31.12.1997	
Raw materials	10,000
Work-in-progress	15,000
Finished goods (10,000 units)	?
Goods manufactured during the year	35,000 units

Rent, rates, taxes and electricity shall be apportioned between Factory and Office in 3 : 2.

COST SHEET
for the year 1997

		Rs.	Rs.
	Opening stock of raw materials	20,000	
Add :	Purchase of raw materials	2,30,000	
		2,50,000	
Less :	Return to suppliers	5,000	
		2,45,000	
Less :	Abnormal loss (materials stolen)	6,000	
		2,39,000	
Add :	Carriage on raw materials	5,000	
		2,44,000	
Less :	Cash received for sale of scrap	2,500	
		2,41,500	
Less :	Closing stock of raw materials	10,000	
	Materials Consumed		2,31,500
Add :	Productive Wages		1,20,000
	Chargeable Expenses		20,000
	Prime Cost		3,71,500
Add :	*Factory Overheads*		
	Indirect Wages	10,000	
	Electricity (3/5th of Rs. 8,000)	4,800	
	Motive power	5,000	
	Rent, rates and taxes (3/5th of Rs. 12,000)	7,200	
	Packing materials	10,000	37,000
			4,08,500
Add :	Opening work-in-progress		30,000
			4,38,500

Contd.

		Rs.	Rs.
	B.F.		4,38,500
Less :	Closing work-in-progress		15,000
	Works Cost		4,23,500
Add :	*Office and Administrative overheads*		
	Electricity $\left(\frac{2}{5} \times \text{Rs. } 8,000\right)$	3,200	
	Rent, Rates and Taxes $\left(\frac{2}{5} \times \text{Rs. } 12,000\right)$	4,800	
	Materials for office	5,000	13,000
	Cost of Production		4,36,500
Add :	Opening Stock of finished goods		50,000
			4,86,500
Less :	Closing Stock of finished goods (Note 1)		1,24,714
	Cost of Goods Sold		3,61,786
Add :	Selling overheads @ Rs. 2 per unit	30,000 × 2	60,000
Add :	Distribution overheads @ Re. 1 per unit	30,000 × 1	30,000
	Total Cost		4,51,786

Working Notes :

1. Cost of 35,000 units = Rs. 4,36,500

   Cost of 10,000 units = Rs. $\frac{4,36,500 \times 10,000}{35,000}$ = Rs. 1,24,714.

2. Units sold

	Opening stock of finished goods	5,000 units
Add :	Units manufactured	35,000 units
		40,000 units
Less :	Closing stock of finished goods	10,000 units
	Units sold	30,000 units

Problem 13

Prepare a cost sheet to show the cost of production and cost of production per unit of goods manufactured by a company for the month of July 1992 and also find the cost of sales :

	Rs.
Stock of raw materials on 1.7.1992	3,000
Purchase of raw materials	28,000
Stock of raw materials on 31.7.1992	4,500
Manufacturing wages	7,000
Depreciation on Plant	1,500
Loss on sale of a part of plant	300
Factory rent and rates	3,000
Office rent	500
General expenses	400
Discount on sales	300
Advertisement	600
Income-tax paid	2,000
Number of units produced during July 1992	3,000

The stock of finished goods was 200 and 400 units on 1.7.92 and 31.7.92, respectively. The total cost of the unit on hand on 1.7.92 was Rs. 2,800. All these units had been sold during the month.

[B.Com. Delhi]

Solution

COST SHEET

for the month of July 1992

			Cost per unit
	Rs.	Rs.	Rs.
Opening Stock of raw materials	3,000		
Add : Purchase of raw materials	28,000		
	31,000		
Less : Closing Stock of raw materials	4,500	26,500	
Add: Manufacturing wages		7,000	
Prime Cost		33,500	
Add : *Factory Overhead* :			
Depreciation on plant	1,500		
Factory rent and rates	3,000	4,500	
Work Cost		38,000	
Add : *Office Overhead*			
Office rent	500		
General Expenses	400	900	
Cost of Production		38,900	12.97
Add : Opening Stock of Finished goods		2,800	
		41,700	
Less: Cost of closing stock of finished goods $\frac{38,900}{3,000} \times 400$		5,187	
		36,513	
Add : Selling overhead—Cost of advertisement		600	
Cost of Sales		37,113	

Problem 14

The following figures are extracted from the Trial Balance of Gogetter Co. on 30th September 1997 :

	Rs.	Rs.
Inventories :		
Finished Stock	80,000	
Raw Materials	1,40,000	
Work-in-Process	2,00,000	
Office Appliances	17,400	
Plant and Machinery	4,60,500	
Buildings	2,00,000	
Sales		7,68,000
Sales Return and Rebates	14,000	
Materials Purchased	3,20,000	
Freight incurred on Materials	16,000	

	Rs.	Rs.
Purchase Returns		4,800
Direct Labour	1,60,000	
Indirect Labour	18,000	
Factory Supervision	10,000	
Repairs and Upkeep – Factory	14,000	
Heat, Light and Power	65,000	
Rates and Taxes	6,300	
Miscellaneous Factory Expenses	18,700	
Sales Commission	33,600	
Sales Travelling	11,000	
Sales Promotion	22,500	
Distribution Dept. :		
Salaries and Expenses	18,000	
Office Salaries and Expenses	8,600	
Interest on Borrowed Funds	2,000	

Further details are available as follows :

(i)	Closing Inventories:	
	Finished Goods	1,15,000
	Raw Materials	1,80,000
	Work-in-Process	1,92,000
(ii)	Accrued expenses on :	
	Direct Labour	8,000
	Indirect Labour	1,200
	Interest on Borrowed Funds	2,000
(iii)	Depreciation to be provided on :	
	Office Appliances	5%
	Plant and Machinery	10%
	Buildings	4%

Distribution of the following costs :

Heat, Light and Power to Factory, Office and Distribution in the ratio 8 : 1 : 1.

Rates and Taxes two-thirds to Factory and one-third to Office.

Depreciation on Buildings to Factory, Office and Selling in the ratio 8 : 1 : 1.

With the help of the above information, you are required to prepare :

(i) A statement of cost sharing various elements of cost

and

(ii) A statement of profit.

[C.A. Inter, Nov. 1986 – Modified]

Solution

COST SHEET

	Rs.	Rs.	Rs.
Opening Raw Material Inventory		1,40,000	
Add : Materials purchased		3,20,000	
Freight on Material		16,000	
		4,76,000	
Less : Purchases Returns	4,800		
Closing Raw Material Inventory	1,80,000	1,84,800	
Material Consumed			2,91,200
Add : Direct Labour (1,60,000 + 8,000)			1,68,000
Prime Cost			4,59,200
Add : Factory Overheads :			
Indirect Labour (18,000 + 1,200)		19,200	
Factory Supervision		10,000	
Repairs and upkeep—Factory		14,000	
Heat, Light and Power ($\frac{4}{5}$ of 65,000)		52,000	
Rates and Taxes ($\frac{2}{3}$ of 6,300)		4,200	
Misc. Factory Expenses		18,700	
Depreciation on Plant (10% of Rs. 4,60,500)		46,050	
Depreciation on Building $\left(\frac{4}{100} \times 2,00,000 \times \frac{4}{5}\right)$		6,400	1,70,550
Gross Works Cost			6,29,750
Add : Opening Work-in-Progress inventory			2,00,000
			8,29,750
Less : Closing Work-in-Progress inventory			1,92,000
Work Cost			6,37,750
Add : Administration Expenses			
Office Salaries and Expenses		8,600	
Depreciation on Office Appliances (5% of Rs. 17,400)		870	
Depreciation of Building		800	
Heat, Light and Power		6,500	
Rates and Taxes		2,100	18,870
Cost of Production			6,56,620
Add : Opening Finished Goods inventory			80,000
			7,36,620
Less : Closing Finished Goods inventory			1,15,000
Cost of Goods Sold			6,21,620
Add : Selling & Distribution Expenses :			
Sales Commission		33,600	
Sales Travelling		11,000	
Sales Promotion		22,500	
Distribution Department—Salaries and Expenses		18,000	
Heat, Light and Power		6,500	
Depreciation on Building		800	92,400
Cost of Sales			7,14,020

STATEMENT OF PROFIT

		Rs.	Rs.
	Sales	7,68,000	
Less :	Returns	14,000	7,54,000
Less:	Cost of Sales		7,14,020
	Net Operating Profit		39,980
Less :	Interest on Borrowed Funds		4,000
	Net Profit		35,980

[Where missing figures are to be ascertained]

Problem 15

The following information has been obtained from the cost records of Aditya Chemicals Ltd. for 1997 :

		Rs.
Finished goods on	1.1.1997	50,000
Raw Materials	1.1.1997	10,000
Work-in-Progress	1.1.1997	14,000
Direct Labour		1,60,000
Purchase of Raw Material		98,000
Indirect Labour		40,000
Heat, Light and Power		20,000
Factory Insurance and Taxes		5,000
Repairs to Plant		3,000
Factory supplies		5,000
Depreciation—Factory building		6,000
Depreciation—Plant		10,000
Other information made available is		
Factory cost of goods produced in 1997		2,80,000
Raw Material consumed in 1997		95,000
Cost of goods sold in 1997		1,60,000

No office and administration expenses were incurred during the year 1997. Prepare a Statement of Cost for the year ending 1997 giving maximum possible information and its break-up.

[B.Com. (Hons.) Delhi]

Solution

ADITYA CHEMICALS LTD.
COST SHEET
for the year ended 31st Dec. 1997

		Rs.	Rs.
	Stock of Raw Materials on 1-1-1997	10,000	
Add :	Purchases	98,000	
	Materials available for use	1,08,000	
Less :	Stock on 31st December 1997 (missing)	13,000	
	Cost of Materials Consumed		95,000
Add :	Direct Labour		1,60,000
	Prime Cost		2,55,000

Contd.

		Rs.	Rs.
	B.F.		2,55,000
	Factory overheads :		
	Indirect Labour	40,000	
	Heat, Light and Power	20,000	
	Insurance and Taxes	5,000	
	Repairs to Plant	3,000	
	Factory Supplies	5,000	
	Depreciation— Plant	10,000	
	Building	6,000	89,000
			3,44,000
Add :	Work-in-Progress on 1.1.1997		14,000
			3,58,000
Less :	Work-in-Progress on 31.12.1997 (missing)		78,000
	Factory Cost (given)		2,80,000
Add :	Finished goods stock on 1.1.1997		50,000
	Cost of goods available for sale 1997		3,30,000
Less :	Stock of Finished goods on 31.12.1997 (missing)		1,70,000
	Cost of Goods sold		1,60,000

Problem 16

The Modern Manufacturing Company submits the following information on 31st March 1997 :

	Rs.	Rs.
Sales for the year		2,75,000
Inventory at the beginning of the year :		
Finished goods	7,000	
Work-in-Progress	4,000	
Purchase of materials for the year		1,10,000
Materials inventory at the beginning		
of the year	3,000	
and at the end of the year	4,000	
Direct Labour		65,000
Factory overhead was 60% of the direct labour cost		
Inventories at the end of the year :		
Work-in-Progress		6,000
Finished goods		8,000
Other expenses for the year :		
Selling expenses 10% of sales		
Administrative expenses 5% of sales		

Prepare a statement of cost.

[C.A. Inter. May]

Statement of Cost of Modern Manufacturing Company
for the year ending 31st March 1997

			Total Cost
		Rs.	Rs.
	Materials consumed :		
	Inventory at the beginning of the year	3,000	
	Purchases during the year	1,10,000	
		1,13,000	
Less :	Inventory at the end of the year	4,000	1,09,000
	Direct Labour		65,000
	Prime Cost		1,74,000
	Factory overheads @ 60% of direct labour		39,000
	Gross Works Cost		2,13,000
Add :	Work-in-Progress at the beginning of the year		4,000
			2,17,000
Less :	Work-in-Progress at the end of the year		6,000
	Works Cost		2,11,000
Add:	Administrative Expenses 5% of Sales = $\frac{5}{100} \times 2{,}75{,}000$		13,750
	Cost of Production		2,24,750

Profit or Loss Statement
for the year ending 31st March 1997

		Rs.	Rs.
	Opening inventories of finished goods	7,000	
	Cost of goods produced during the year	2,24,750	
		2,31,750	
Less :	Closing inventories of finished goods	8,000	
	Cost of goods sold		2,23,750
Add:	Selling Expenses @ 10% of sales i.e. $\frac{10}{100} \times 2{,}75{,}000$		27,500
	Total cost of goods sold		2,51,250
	Profit of the balancing figure (Sales Rs. 2,75,000 – Cost Rs. 2,51,250)		23,750
	Sales		2,75,000

Problem 17

From the following particulars relating to production and sales for the year ended 31st Dec. 1995 prepare a statement of cost showing, inter alia, the Prime Cost, Factory Cost, Cost of Production, Cost of Goods Sold and Sale Price :

	As on 1.1.95	As on 31.12.95
	Rs.	Rs.
Raw Material	16,000	19,600
Work-in-Progress	12,600	4,600
Finished goods	16,400	?
(at cost)	(3,000 units)	(2,500 units)

Contd.

	Rs.
Other information for the year :	
Purchase of Raw Materials	1,11,600
Sale of finished goods (40,500 units)	2,83,500
Productive wages	67,200
Office and Administrative Expenses	20,800
Selling and Distribution Expenses :	50 paise per unit sold
Machine Hours worked :	8,000 hours
Machine Hour Rate :	Rs. 2.50

[Adapted—B.Com. (Hons). C.U.]

Solution

Statement of Cost Sheet
for the year ended 31.12.95

		Rs.	Rs.
	Opening Stock of Raw Materials	16,000	
Add :	Purchases of Raw Materials	1,11,600	
		1,27,600	
Less :	Closing Stock of R.M.	19,600	
	Materials consumed	1,08,000	
Add :	Productive Wages	67,200	
	Prime Cost		1,75,200
Add :	*Factory Overhead* :		
	Machine hours worked	8,000 × 2.50	20,000
Add :	Opening Work-in-Progress		12,600
			2,07,800
Less :	Closing Work-in-Progress		4,600
	Work Cost		2,03,200
Add :	*Office and Administrative Exp.*		20,800
	Cost of Production (40,000 units as per Note 1)		2,24,000
Add :	Opening finished goods		16,400
			2,40,400
Less :	Closing finished goods (Note 2)		14,000
			2,26,400
Add :	*Selling and Distribution Exp.*	(40,500 × 0.50)	20,250
	Total Cost		2,46,650
	Profit (Balancing figure)		36,850
	Sale Price		2,83,500

Working Note :

Ascertainment of goods (in units) manufactured during the year

1.	Units sold	40,500
	Add : Closing stock of finished goods	2,500
		43,000
	Less : Opening stock of finished goods	3,000
	Units manufactured	40,000

2. Value of closing stock of finished goods

Cost price of 40,000 units = Rs. 2,24,000

$$\text{Cost price of 2,500 units} = \frac{2,24,000 \times 2,500}{40,000} = \text{Rs. } 14,000$$

Problem 18

Total Production in 1990 (tonnes)	5,000
	Rs.
Cost of Raw Materials	20,00,000
Carriage inwards	2,00,000
Direct wages	20,00,000
Indirect wages (in factory)	1,00,000
Office expenses	10,00,000
Public relations expenses	50,000
Expenses on testing lab.	60,000
Selling overheads	10,00,000
Salary of managing director	50,000
Payment of income-tax	3,00,000

Note : (i) A profit margin of 50% on cost is provided (ii) The Government grants a special exports subsidy of Rs. 1,000 per tonne.

[B.Com. Pass, Delhi]

Prepare a Cost Sheet showing the price to the quoted.

Solution

COST SHEET

for the year 1990

(5,000 tonnes)

	Details		Total	Per tonne
			Rs.	Rs.
	Cost of Raw Materials		20,00,000	400
	Carriage inwards		2,00,000	40
	Direct wages		20,00,000	400
	Prime Cost		42,00,000	840
Add :	Indirect Factory wages	1,00,000		
	Expenses of testing lab	60,000	1,60,000	32
	Works Cost		43,60,000	872
Add :	*Office and Administrative expense*			
	Office expenses	10,00,000		
	Public relation expenses	50,000		
	Salary of managing director	50,000	11,00,000	220
	Cost of Production		54,60,000	1,092
Add :	Selling overheads		10,00,000	200
			64,60,000	1,292
Add :	50% Profit on cost		32,30,000	646
			96,90,000	1,938
Less :	Subsidy granted by the government			1,000
	Price to be quoted			938

Notes : 1. Payment of income-tax does not affect cost of production and will not be taken into account while computing cost.

2. Special export subsidy of Rs.1,000 per tonne will not be taken into consideration while computing cost, i.e. incentive and is kept in view while offering competitive price in the International market.

Problem 19

From the following particulars relating to the production and sales for the year ended 30, June 1997, prepare a cost statement showing therein : (i) Prime cost, (ii) Works cost, (iii) Cost of Production, (iv) Cost of sales, and (v) Profit.

	Rs.	Rs.
Raw Materials as on 1.7.96		12,500
Work-in-Progress as on 1.7.96		
At Prime Cost	15,000	
+ Manufacturing Expenses	3,000	18,000
Finished goods at cost as on 1.7.96 (8,000 units)		60,000
Raw Materials purchased		1,10,000
Freight on Raw Materials purchased		5,000
Loss of materials by fire		5,000
Factory expenses		70,000
Chargeable expenses		25,000
Direct labour		1,35,000
Administrative expenses		Rs. 2 per unit
Selling expenses		Re.1 per unit
Distribution expenses		15,000
Sale of finished goods (28,000 units)		4,00,000
Raw Materials as on 30.6.97		20,000
Work-in-progress as on 30.6.97		
At Prime Cost	10,000	
+ Manufacturing Exp.	8,000	18,000
Stock of finished goods on 30.6.97		10,000 units

Assume that sales are made on FIFO basis.

[Adapted—C.U. B.Com. (Hons.) '88]

Solution

COST SHEET

for the year ended 30th June 1997

Particulars	*Amount* Rs.	*Amount* Rs.	*Amount* Rs.
Raw Materials as on 1.7.96		12,500	
Raw Materials purchased	1,10,000		
Add : Freight on Raw materials	5,000	1,15,000	
		1,27,500	
Less : Materials lost by Fire	5,000		
Less : Closing Stock of R.M.	20,000	25,000	
Raw material consumed		1,02,500	
Add : Direct wages		1,35,000	
Add: Chargeable expenses		25,000	
		2,62,500	
Add : Opening W.I.P. at prime cost		15,000	
		2,77,500	
Less : Closing W.I.P. at prime cost		10,000	
Prime Cost			2,67,500

Contd.

	Rs.	Rs.	Rs.
B.F.			2,67,500
Add : *Factory overhead* :			
Factory expenses			70,000
			3,37,500
Add : Opening W.I.P. (Manufacturing exp.)			3,000
			3,40,500
Less : Closing W.I.P. (Manufacturing exp.)			8,000
Work Cost			3,32,500
Add : *Administrative expenses*	30,000 × 2		60,000
Cost of Production			3,92,500
Add : Opening finished goods			60,000
			4,52,500
Less: Closing finished goods $\frac{3,92,500}{30,000} \times 10,000$			1,30,833
			3,21,667
Add : *Selling and Distribution overhead* :			
Selling expenses	28,000 × 1	28,000	
Distribution expenses		15,000	43,000
Cost of Sale			3,64,667
Profit (Balancing figure)			35,333
Sale Price			4,00,000

Profit per unit = Rs. $\frac{35,333}{28,000}$ = Rs. 1.26.

Working Notes : 1. Units produced during the year

	Units sold	28,000 units
Add :	Closing stock of finished goods	10,000 units
		38,000 units
Less :	Opening stock of finished goods	8,000 units
		30,000 units

2. **Students are to note that under FIFO basis opening stock of goods have been sold out first. So, the closing stock is to be valued at current price.**

Problem 20

The following figures for the month of April 1992 were extracted from the records of a factory :

		Rs.
Opening Stock of Finished Goods (5,000)		45,000
Purchase of Raw Materials		2,57,100
Direct Wages		1,05,000
Factory Overhead	100% of Direct Wages	
Administration Overhead	Re. 1 per unit	
Selling and Distribution Overhead	10% of Sale	
Closing stock of Finished Goods (10,000 units)		
Sales (45,000 units)		6,60,000

Prepare a cost sheet for the month of April 1992, assuming that sales are made on the basis of first-in-first-out principle.

[C.U. B.Com. (Hons.)]

Solution

Cost Sheet
for the month of April 1992

		Rs.
	Purchase of Raw Materials	2,57,100
	Direct Wages	1,05,000
	Prime Cost	3,62,100
Add :	Factory Overhead 100% of direct wages	1,05,000
	Works Cost	4,67,100
Add :	Administrative Overhead @ Re 1 per unit = 50,000 × 1	50,000
	Cost of Production	5,17,100
Add :	Opening Stock of Finished Goods	45,000
		5,62,100
Less :	Closing Stock of Finished Goods (See Note 2)	1,03,420
	Cost of Goods Sold	4,58,680
Add :	Selling and Distribution Overhead @ 10% of sales	66,000
	Cost of Sales	5,24,680
	Profit (Balancing figure)	1,35,320
	Sales (given)	6,60,000

Working notes :

1. Calculation of units produced during the month :

Sales	45,000
Add : Closing Stock of Finished Goods	10,000
	55,000
Less: Opening Stock of Finished Goods	5,000
Units produced during the month	50,000

2. Cost of Closing Stock of Finished Goods : $\frac{5,17,100 \times 10,000}{50,000}$ = Rs. 1,03,420

Problem 21

The following data relate to the manufacture of a standard product during four weeks to 31st March 1987 :

		Rs.
Raw Materials consumed		2,000
Direct wages		1,200
Machines hours worked		950
Machine hour rate	20 paise	
Office Overhead	10% on work cost	
Selling Overhead	6 paise per unit	
Units prouced		20,000 units
Units sold	@30 paise	18,000 units

You are required to prepare a cost sheet in respect of the above showing :

(a) the cost per unit,

(b) the profit for the period.

[Adapted—Bombay, M.Com.]

Solution

Cost Sheet showing the Cost per unit and Profit

Output 20,000 units — Period 4 weeks ended 31st March 1987

		Total Cost	Cost per unit
		Rs.	Rs.
	Raw Materials consumed	2,000	0.10
	Direct Wages	1,200	0.06
	Prime Cost	3,200	0.16
	Factory Overhead		
	(Machine hours worked × machine hour rate) = 950 × 0.20	190	
	Works Cost	3,390	0.169
Add :	*Office overhead* @ 10% on Works Cost	339	0.017
	Cost of Production	3,729	0.186
Less :	Cost of closing stock (2,000 × 0.186)	372	
	Cost of goods sold	3,357	
Add :	*Selling overhead* @ 6 paise per unit (18,000 × 0.06)	1,080	0.060
	Cost of Sales	4,437	0.246
	Profit (Balancing figure)	963	0.054
	Sale Price (given) 18,000 × 0.30	5,400	0.300

Problem 22

The following is the Manufacturing and Profit and Loss Account of Swastik Ltd. for the year ended 30th June 1998 :

	Rs.	Rs.		Rs.	Rs.
Opening Stock :			Sales		5,00,000
Materials	2,000		Closing Stock :		
Finished goods	3,000	5,000	Materials	18,500	
Purchase of materials		1,50,000	Finished goods	3,000	21,500
Direct wages		1,20,000			
Power		15,500			
Carriage on material		2,000			
Royalty		24,000			
Cost of a special design		5,000			
Gross profit c/d		2,00,000			
		5,21,500			5,21,500
Rent and Rates					
Office	5,000				
Factory	7,000	12,000	By Gross Profit		2,00,000
Telephone		3,000	" Discount Received		6,250
		15,000			2,06,000

Contd.

	Rs.	Rs.		Rs.	Rs.
B.F.		15,000	B.F.		2,06,250
Advertisement		7,500	" Sale of Scrap		750
Electricity :					
Office	3,000				
Factory	4,500	7,500			
Provision for bad debts		10,000			
Depreciation :					
On plant and machinery	6,000				
On delivery vans	2,000	8,000			
Income-tax		12,000			
Salaries		25,000			
Donations		7,000			
Establishment Expenses		10,000			
Depreciation on furniture :					
Office	2,500				
Factory	2,000	4,500			
Rent of warehouse		6,500			
Net Profit		94,000			
		2,07,000			2,07,000

You are required to prepare a statement showing classification of costs under different components from the above information after due consideration to the following facts :

(1) 60% of telephone expenses relate to Office and 40% to Sales Department.

(2) 25% of the salaries relate to Factory, 50% to Office and 25% to Sales Dept. and

(3) 50% of the establishment expenses relate to Office and 50% to Sales Department.

Solution

Statement of Cost of Swastic Ltd.
for the year ending 30th June 1998

		Rs.	Rs.
	Opening stock of materials	2,000	
	Purchase of materials	1,50,000	
		1,52,000	
Less :	Closing Stock of materials	18,500	
		1,33,500	
Add :	Carriage on materials	2,000	
	Value of raw materials consumed	1,35,500	
Add :	Direct wages	1,20,000	
	Direct Expenses :		
Add :	Royalty	24,000	
	Cost of a special design	5,000	
	Prime Cost		2,84,500

Contd.

			Rs.	Rs.
	B.F.			2,84,500
Add :	*Factory overheads :*			
	Power		15,500	
	Factory, Rent and Rates		7,000	
	Electricity		4,500	
	Depreciation on Plant and Machinery		6,000	
	Salaries	25% of Rs. 25,000	6,250	
	Depreciation on factory furniture		2,000	41,250
				3,25,750
Less :	Sales of Scrap			750
				3,25,000
Add :	*Office and administrative overheads :*			
	Office rent and rates		5,000	
	Telephone expenses		1,800	
	Electricity		3,000	
	Salaries 50% of Rs. 25,000		12,500	
	Depreciation on office furniture		2,500	
	Establishment expenses	50% of Rs. 10,000	5,000	29,800
	Cost of Production			3,54,800
Add :	Opening Stock of finished goods			3,000
				3,57,800
Less :	Closing Stock of finished goods			3,000
	Cost of Goods Sold			3,54,800
Add :	Selling and distribution overheads :			
	Telephone expenses		1,200	
	Advertisement		7,500	
	Depreciation on delivery vans		2,000	
	Salaries	25% of Rs. 25,000	6,250	
	Establishment	50% of Rs. 10,000	5,000	
	Rent of warehouse		6,500	
				28,450
	Total Cost			3,83,250
	Profit (*balancing figure*)			1,16,750
	Sales			5,00,000

Note : Items relating to the financial accounts have been excluded from cost accounts, which are :

Provision for bad debts ; Income-tax ; Interest on loan ; Discount received ; Donations.

Problem 23

The following particulars relating to the year 1997 have been taken from the books of a Chemical Works, manufacturing and selling a chemical mixture :

	Kg.	Rs.		Kg.	Rs.
Stock on 1.1.1997			Salaries :		
Raw materials	2,000	2,000	Factory		72,220
Finished mixture	500	1,750	Office		37,220
Factory stores		7,250	Selling		41,500

Contd.

	Kg.	Rs.		Kg.	Rs.
Purchases :			Expenses :		
Raw materials	1,60,000	1,80,000	Direct		18,500
Factory stores		24,250	Office		18,200
Sales			Selling		18,000
Finished mixture	1,53,050	9,18,000	Stock on 31.12.1990		
Factory scrap		8,170	Raw materials	1,200	?
Factory wages		1,78,650	Finished mixture	450	?
Power		30,400	Factory stores		5,550
Depreciation of machinery		18,000			

The stock of finished mixture at the end of 1997 is to be valued at the factory cost of mixture for that year. The purchase price of raw materials remained unchanged throughout 1997.

Prepare statement giving the maximum possible information about cost and its break-up for the year 1997.

[Adapted—Delhi B.Com. (Hons.)]

STATEMENT OF COST
for the year 1997

	Kg	Rs.	Rs.
Materials consumed			
Opening Stock	2,000	2,000	
Purchases	1,60,000	1,80,000	
	1,62,000	1,82,000	
Less : Closing Stock $\left(\frac{1,200}{1,60,000} \times 1,80,000\right)$	1,200	1,350	
	1,60,800		1,80,650
Factory wages			1,78,650
Direct Expenses			18,500
PRIME COST			3,77,800
Add : Factory Overheads			
Power		30,400	
Depreciation on machinery		18,000	
Salary (factory)		72,220	
FACTORY STORES			
Opening Stock	7,250		
Purchase	24,250		
	31,500		
Less : Closing Stock (Note a)	5,550	25,950	
		1,46,570	
Less : Sale of scraps (Note b)	7,800	8,170	1,38,400
WORKS COST			5,16,200
Add : Office and Administration Overheads			
Salary (Office)		37,220	
Office Expenses		18,200	55,420
COST OF PRODUCTION			5,71,620

Contd.

		Kg	Rs.	Rs.
	B.F.			5,71,620
Add :	Opening Stock Finished Mixture			1,750
				5,73,370
Less :	Closing Stock Finished Mixture (See note below)			1,518
	COST OF GOODS SOLD			5,71,852
Add :	*Selling and Distribution Overheads*			
	Salary (selling)		41,500	
	Selling Expenses		18,000	59,500
	TOTAL COST			6,31,352
	Profit (balancing figure)			2,86,648
	SALE PRICE			9,18,000

Working Note :

(a) **Valuation of closing stock of finished mixture on the basis of works cost.**

	Quantity of mixture manufactured :	
	Sale of quantity –	1,53,050 kgs
Add :	Closing Stock of Finished Mixture	450 kgs
		1,53,500 kgs
Less :	Opening Stock of Finished Mixture	500 kgs
		1,53,000 kgs

Works cost of 1,53,000 kg = Rs. 5,16,200

Works cost of 450 kg = Rs. $\dfrac{5,16,200 \times 450}{1,53,000}$ = Rs. 1,518

(b) **Calculation of quantity of factory scrap sold**

	Quantity of finished mixture sold	1,53,050 kgs
Add :	Closing stock of finished mixture	450 kgs
		1,53,500 kgs
Less :	Opening stock of finished mixture	500 kgs
	Quantity produced	1,53,000 kgs
	Quantity of scrap sold (balancing figure)	7,800 kgs
	Materials consumed	1,60,800 kgs

Problem 24

The following extracts of costing information relate to commodity A for the year ended 31.3.93 :

		Rs.
Purchase of Raw Materials		48,000
Direct Wages		40,000
Stock on 1.4.1992		
Raw Materials		8,000
Finished Goods	1,600 quintals	6,400
Stock on 31.3.1993		
Raw Materials		8,800
Finished Goods	3,200 quintals	?
Works on Cost		16,800
Work-in-Progress :		
1st April 1992		1,920
31st March 1993		6,400
Office and Administrative Overheads		3,200
Sales (Finished Products)		1,20,000

Advertising, discount allowed and selling cost is Re 0.40 per quintal. During the year, 25,600 quintals of commodity were produced.

Calculate the cost of production and extend the Cost Sheet to include profit also so that it may also be called Production Statement.

[B.Com. Delhi.]

COST SHEET

for the year ended 31st March 1993

			Total Cost	Unit Cost
	Raw Material Used :	Rs.	Rs.	Rs.
	Opening Stock	8,000		
Add :	Purchases	48,000		
		56,000		
Add :	Closing Stock	8,800	47,200	
	Direct wages		40,000	
	Prime Cost		87,200	
	Factory Overheads		16,800	
			1,04,000	
Add :	Opening Work-in-Progress		1,920	
			1,05,920	
Less :	Closing Work-in-Progress		6,400	
	Works Cost		99,520	3.89
Add :	Office on Cost		3,200	0.12
	Cost of Production	25,600 qu.	1,02,720	4.01
Add :	Opening Stock of Finished Products	1,600 qu.	6,400	
		27,200 qu.	1,09,120	4.01
Less :	Closing Stock of Finished Products $\left(\text{Rs.}\frac{1,02,720}{25,600} \times 3,200\right)$	3,200 qu.	12,840	
	Cost of Goods Sold	24,000 qu.	96,280	4.01
Add :	Selling Cost @ Re 0.40 per unit sold		9,600	0.40
	Total Cost		1,05,880	4.41
	Profit		14,120	0.59
	Sales		1,20,000	5.00

Problem 25

From the following particulars relating to the production and sales for the year ended 31st March 1989, prepare a statement of cost showing therein (i) Prime Cost, (ii) Work Cost, (iii) Cost of Production, (iv) Cost of Sales and (v) Profit per unit :

		Rs.
Opening Inventory (1.4.88.)		
Raw Materials		6,000
Work-in-Progress		9,620
Finished Goods	1,000 units	13,680
Closing Inventory (31.3.89)		
Raw Materials		7,000
Work-in-Progress		8,020

Contd.

	Rs.
Finished Goods	?
Raw Materials Purchased	72,000
Productive Wages	18,000
Machine Hours worked (in hours)	21,600
Machine Hour Rate	1.50
Chargeable Expenses	16,400
Office and Administrative Overhead	1.00 per unit
Selling Overhead	0.90 per unit
Units Sold	8,000 units
Units Produced	8,200 units
Profit on Sale	10%

Assumed that sales are made on FIFO basis.

[C.U. B.Com. (Hons.) '90]

Cost Sheet

for the year ended 31.3.89

		Rs.	Units	Total	Per Unit
				Rs.	Rs.
	Opening Stock of Material			6,000	
Add :	Purchases			72,000	
				78,000	
Less :	Closing Stock of Material			7,000	
	Material Consumed		8,200	71,000	8.659
	Productive Wages			18,000	2.195
	Chargeable Exp.			16,400	2.000
	Prime Cost		8,200	1,05,400	12.854
	Works Overhead :				
	21,600 Machine Hrs. @ Rs. 1.50	32,400			
Add :	Opening W.I.P.	9,620			
		42,020			
Less :	Closing W.I.P.	8,020		34,000	4.146
	Works Cost			1,39,400	17.00
Add :	*Office and Adm. Overhead* @ Re. 1 per unit		8,200	8,200	1.00
	Cost of Production		8,200	1,47,600	18.00
Add :	Opening stock of Finished Goods		1,000	13,680	
			9,200	1,61,280	
Less :	Closing stock of Finished Goods		1,200	21,600	
	Cost of Goods Sold		8,000	1,39,680	17.46
	Selling Overhead @ Re. 0.90 per unit (8,000 × 0.90)			7,200	0.90
	Cost of Sales			1,46,880	18.36
	Profit $\left(\frac{1}{9} \times 1,46,880\right)$ which is 10% on sales			16,320	2.04
	Sales		8,000	1,63,200	20.40

FIXED AND VARIABLE COST

Problem 26

The New Pottery Works Ltd. prepares four types of articles A, B, C & D. The same raw materials are used for manufacture of all these articles. The manufactured articles that pass inspection and tests are called 'finished articles' and sold to the public. The articles which are found defective on inspection are called 'defective articles' and are sold only to the employees at concessional rate.

The ratio of defective articles is 10% of the finished articles. In other words, for every 100 finished articles there are 10 defective articles.

The following data are collected from the Manufacturing Account of the New Pottery Works Ltd. for the month of November 1993 :

Type	*Finished articles*	*Labour*	*Amount realised from sales of defective articles*
A	2,000	Re. 0.50 p each	Rs. 200
B	4,000	Re. 0.75 p each	Rs. 1,000
C	6,000	Re. 1.00 p each	Rs. 1,200
D	8,000	Rs. 1.50 p each	Rs. 2,000

One type of article requires one kg of raw materials at Rs. 4 per kg.

Factory Overhead : Fixed 200% / Variable 100% — on direct labour

Find out the Factory Cost of each article.

[Adapted—B.Com. Rajasthan]

Solution

Cost Sheet
for the Month of November 1993

Total	A	B	C	D
No. of total articles produced	2,200	4,400	6,600	8,800
No. of finished articles (less 10%)	2,000	4,000	6,000	8,000
	Rs.	Rs.	Rs.	Rs.
Materials @ Rs. 4 per article	8,800	17,600	26,400	35,200
Labour A @ 0.50 p. for A	1,100			
B @ 0.75 p.		3,300		
C @ 1.00			6,600	
D @ 1.50				13,200
Prime Cost of total output	9,900	20,900	33,000	48,400
Add : Factory Overhead :				
Fixed @ 200% of Labour	2,200	6,600	13,200	26,400
Variable @ 100% of Labour	1,100	3,300	6,600	13,200
	13,200	30,800	52,800	88,000
Less : Amount realised from Sale of defective articles	200	1,000	1,200	2,000
Factory Cost	13,000	29,800	51,600	86,000
Factory Cost per article	6.50	7.45	8.60	10.75

$$\text{Factory Cost per article} = \frac{\text{Factory Cost}}{\text{No. of finished articles}}$$

Problem 27

A Radio manufacturer produces three brands of Radio. The following particulars were collected from the books of accounts for the year ended 31st December 1997 :

Stock of finished goods (1. 1. 1997) :	
Janata Model	50 Nos. @ Rs. 225
Standard Model	40 Nos. @ Rs. 300
Luxury Model	30 Nos. @ Rs. 375

Additional information :

	Rs.
Opening work-in-progress	10,500
Cost of materials consumed	80,500
Cost of other stores	24,000
Productive wages	35,000
Works overhead	1,20,000
Closing work-in-progress	15,000

The production and sales during the year were :

	Production	Sales
Janata Model	400 Nos.	380 Nos.
Standard Model	300 Nos.	280 Nos.
Luxury Model	200 Nos.	210 Nos.

The average selling rates were Rs. 300, Rs. 400 and Rs. 500 for each for the respective models.

The cost of production is to be apportioned on the basis of sales value of production. Find out the gross trading profit in a tabular form.

[Adapted—V.U. B.Com. (Hons.)]

Solution

1. Cost of Production

		Rs.
	Materials consumed	80,500
	Production wages	35,000
	Prime Cost	1,15,500
Add :	Works overhead	1,20,000
	Cost of other stores	24,000
	Opening work-in-progress	10,500
		2,70,000
Less :	Closing work-in-progress	15,000
	Cost of Production	2,55,000

2. Sales value of Production

Janata—400 × 300 = 1,20,000
Standard—30 × 400 = 1,20,000
Luxury—200 × 500 = 1,00,000

Particulars	Janata Model	Standard Model	Luxury Model
	Rs.	Rs.	Rs.
Production cost in 6 : 6 : 5	90,000	90,000	75,000
Add : Opening stock	11,250	12,000	11,250
	(50 × Rs. 225)	(40 × Rs. 300)	(30 × Rs. 375)
	1,01,250	1,02,000	86,250
Less : Closing stock	15,750	18,000	7,500
(See working notes)			
Cost of Sales	85,500	84,000	78,750
Gross Profit	28,500	28,000	26,250
Sale Price	1,14,000	1,12,000	1,05,000
(No. of units sold × sale price per unit)			

Working Notes :

1.

	Janata in units	*Standard in units*	*Luxury in units*
Opening stock	50	40	30
Add : Production	400	300	200
	450	340	230
Less : Sales	380	280	210
Unsold stock	70	60	20

		Rs.	Rs.	Rs.
2.	Production cost per unit	90,000 ÷ 400 = 225	90,000 ÷ 300 = 300	75,000 ÷ 200 = 375
3.	Value of Closing stock	70 × Rs. 225 = Rs. 15,750	60 × Rs. 300 = Rs. 18,000	20 × Rs. 375 = Rs. 7,500

FIXED, VARIABLE AND SEMIVARIABLE OVERHEADS

Problem 27

The details of expenses incurred on the manufacture of two kinds of drums in the past are given below :

Expenses incurred on the manufacture of drums :

	Type 1	Type 2
	Rs.	Rs.
Direct materials	3.50	6.50
Direct wages	1.00	1.50
Plant and machine usage allocated on hourly basis	3.00	2.00
General overheads apportioned at 200% of direct wages	2.00	3.00
	9.50	13.00

Contd.

Cost records for the month of April 1994 show :

Direct materials used		26,500
Direct wages		5,850
Expenses of Plant and Machines		16,250
No. of drums manufactured :		
Type 1	2,000	
Type 2	3,000	

Prepare a consolidate cost sheet showing the total cost of production of each type according to different elements of cost showing also cost per drum.

[B.Com.—Andhra]

Solution

Consolidated Cost Sheet

Items of expenses	*Drums*				
		Type 1		*Type 2*	*Total*
		Cost per drum		Cost per drum	
No. of drums manufactured		2,000		3,000	
	Rs.	Rs.	Rs.	Rs.	Rs.
Direct Materials	7,000	3.50	19,500	6.50	26,500
Direct Wages (Note 1)	1,800	0.90	4,050	1.35	5,850
Prime Cost	8,800	4.40	23,550	7.85	32,350
Expenses on plant and machines	8,125	4.06	8,125	2.70	16,250
Work Cost	16,925	8.46	31,675	10.55	48,600
Add : General Overhead @ 200% of direct wages	3,600	1.80	8,100	2.70	11,700
Total Cost	20,525	10.26	39,775	13.25	60,300

Working Notes :

1. Apportionment of direct wages :

Type 1 = 2,000 × 1 = 2,000

Type 2 = 3,000 × 1.50 = 4,500

6,500, i.e. ratio is 2,000 : 4,500, i.e. 4 : 9.

$$\text{Type 1} = \frac{4}{13} \times 5{,}850 = \text{Rs. } 1{,}800$$

$$\text{Type 2} = \frac{9}{13} \times 5{,}850 = \text{Rs. } 4{,}050$$

2. Expenses on plant and machine :

Type 1 = 2,000 × 3 = 6,000

3,000 × 2 = 6,000

Ratio : – 6,000 : 6,000 i.e. 1 : 1

$$\text{Type 1} = \frac{1}{2} \text{ of } 16{,}250 = 8{,}125$$

$$\text{Type 2} = \frac{1}{2} \text{ of } 16{,}250 = 8{,}125$$

Fixed, variable and semi-variable overheads

Problem 29

A factory has undertaken a contract for the manufacture of 4,000 articles. The following information has been obtained for each article :

	Rs.
Materials cost	12
Direct wages	10
Selling price	35

The overhead charges consist of (a) fixed Rs. 6,000, (b) variable Rs. 3,600 and (c) semi-variable (of which 60% is fixed) Rs. 2,400.

Calculate the profit per article. What would be the profit per article if the number of articles manufactured was 5,000 and the nature of overhead expenditure remained the same.

[V.U. B.Com. (Hons.) 1997]

Solution

	Production 4,000 units		*Production 5,000 units*	
	Total cost	*Cost per Unit*	*Total cost*	*Cost per Unit*
	Rs.	Rs.	Rs.	Rs.
Material Cost	48,000	12.00	60,000	12.00
Direct wages @ 10 per unit	40,000	10.00	50,000	10.00
Prime Cost	88,000	22.00	1,10,000	22.000
Add : Fixed overhead Rs. 6,000	6,000	1.50	6,000	1.200
Variable overhead Rs. 3,600 ÷ 4,000	3,600,	0.90	4,500	0.900
Semivariable overheads				
Fixed (60% of Rs, 2,400)	1,440	0.36	1,440	0.288
Variable (40% of Rs. 2,400) ÷ 4,000	960	0.24	1,200	0.240
	1,00,000	25.00	1,23,140	24.628
Profit (balancing figure)	40,000	10.00	51,860	10.372*
Sale Price	1,40,000	35.00	1,75,000	35.00

* The average cost per unit comes down due to increased production and fixed cost is reduced per unit.

Problem 30

The Metal Products Company produces a sewing machine that sells for Rs. 300. An increase of 15% in cost of materials and of 10% in cost of labour is anticipated.
If the only figures available are given below, what must be the selling price to give the same percentage of gross profit as before ?

(a) Material costs have been 45% of cost of sales.

(b) Labour costs have been 40% of cost of sales.

(c) Overhead costs have been 15% of cost of sales.

The anticipated increased costs in relation to the present sale price would cause a 35% decrease in the amount of the present gross profit.

[C.U. B.Com. (Hons.), D.U. B.Com. (Hons.)]

Solution

Statement showing Cost of Sales

Assumed that the cost of sales = Rs. 100.

	Assumed present cost of sales	*Increase*	*Anticipated cost of sales*
	Rs.		Rs.
Material	45	15%	51.75
Labour	40	10%	44.00
Overhead	15	–	15.00
	100		110.75
Profit	x		.65 x
	100 + x		110.75 + .65 x

Or, 110.75 + .65x = 100 + x or, 100 + x = 110·75 + ·65x or ·35x = 10·75 or x = Rs. 30·714

In absolute figures

	Percentage	Product Cost Rs.	Increase in percentage	Anticipated cost Rs.
Materials	45%	103.28	15%	118.77
Labour	40%	91.80	10%	100.98
Overhead	15%	34.43	–	34.43
		229.51		254.18
Profit		70.49*		45.82
		300.00		300.00

* When SP.	Then Profit
130.714	30.714
300	?

$$\frac{30.714 \times 300}{130.714} = \text{Rs. } 70.49$$

ESTIMATED COST SHEET

Problem 31

The following data relate to the manufacture of a standard product during the four weeks to July 27, 1996 :

	Rs.
Raw Materials consumed	25,000
Manual and Machine Labour Wages (Directly Chargeable)	15,000
Chargeable Expenses	4,500
Machine Hours Worked	1,000 hours
Machine Hour Rate	2.5
Establishment and General Expenses	4,700
Selling and Distribution Overhead per Unit	8 Paise
Unit Produced	10,000
Unit Sold	8,000
Selling Price per Unit	6

(a) You are required to prepare a Cost Sheet in respect of the above showing therein the cost per unit under each element of cost and the profit for the period. Also show the percentage that the works overhead cost bears to the Manual and Machine Labour Wages and the percentage that the Establishment and General Expenses bears to the Works Cost.

(b) What price should the company quote to produce 1,000 units of another product which will require an expenditure of Rs. 8,000 for raw materials and Rs. 6,000 for direct wages, so that it will yield a profit of 25% on the Cost of Sales ?

[C.U. B.Com. (Hons.) 1997]

COST SHEET

for the period of 4 weeks to July 27, 1996

		Rs.	Rs.
	Raw Materials consumed	25,000	
	Mannual and Machine Labour Wages	15,000	
	Chargeable Expenses	4,500	
	Prime Cost		44,500
Add :	Factory Overhead		
	Machine hours worked × Machine hour rate	1,000 × 2.50	2,500
	Works Cost		47,000
Add :	Establishment and General Expenses		4,700
	Cost of Production		51,700
Less :	Closing Stock of Finished goods (10,000 – 8,000)	$\frac{51,700}{10,000} \times 2,000$	10,340
	Cost of Goods sold		41,360
Add :	Selling and Distribution Overhead		
	@ Re. 0.08 per unit sold	8,000 × 0.08	640
	Cost of Sales		42,000
	Profit		6,000
	Sale Price @ Rs. 6 per unit	8,000 × 6	48,000

Working Notes :

(a) Calculation of Factory overhead as a percentage of Direct Wages

$$\frac{\text{Factory overhead} \times 100}{\text{Direct wages}} = \frac{2,500 \times 100}{15,000} = 16.67\%$$

(b) Establishment & General Expenses as a percentage of Works Cost = $\frac{4,700 \times 100}{47,000} = 10\%$

EXTIMATED COST SHEET

Production 1,000 units

		Rs.	Rs.
	Raw Materials		8,000
	Direct Wages		6,000
			14,000
Add :	*Factory overhead* @ 16.67% of wages		1,000
	Works Cost		15,000
Add :	*Establishment and General Expenses* @ 10% of works cost		1,500
	Cost of Production		16,500
Add :	*Selling and Distribution* @ 0.08 per unit		80
	Cost of Sales		16,580
Add :	Profit @ 25% of Cost of Sales		4,145
	Price to be quoted		20,725

Problem 32

The following figures are available from the books of Best Manufacturing Company for the year ended 31.12.1990 :

Materials :	Rs.
Stock on 1.1.1990	1,000
Stock on 31.12.90	2,000
Purchased during 1990	10,000
Wages	7,500
Profit for the year	6,090
Selling Overhead	5,250
Factory Overhead	4,500
Administrative Overhead	4,200

(a) Prepare a Cost Sheet showing prime cost, works cost, cost of production, cost of sales and sales.

(b) In 1991, the factory receives an order for a job which will require materials Rs. 1,200 and wages Rs. 750. Ascertain the sale price of the job if the factory intends to earn a profit 10% higher than that in 1990. Assume that Factory Overhead has gone up by $16\frac{2}{3}$% and Selling Overhead has gone down by 20% in 1991. Further assume that Factory Overhead is recovered as a percentage of Direct Wages.

[Adapted—C.U. B.Com. (Hons.)]

Step I

Cost Sheet

for the year ended 31st Dec. 1990

Particulars	*Amount*	*Amount*
	Rs.	Rs.
Stock of Raw Materials on 1.1.90	1,000	
Add : Purchases during the year 1990	10,000	
	11,000	
Less : Stock 31.12.90	2,000	
Raw Materials consumed		9,000
Add : Direct wages		7,500
Prime Cost		16,500
Add : Factory overhead		4,500
Works Cost		21,000
Add : Administrative overhead		4,200
Cost of Production		25,200
Add : Selling overhead		5,250
Cost of Goods Sold		30,450
Add : Profit		6,090
Sales Price		36,540

Step II

Calculation of percentage of Overheads and Profit

1. When Direct Wages is 7,500, then Factory overhead is 4,500

   When Direct Wages is 100 then Factory overhead $\frac{4,500 \times 100}{7,500} = 60\%$

2. When works cost is 21,000 then Adm. overhead is 4,200

   When works cost is 100 then Adm. overhead $\frac{4,200 \times 100}{21,000} = 20\%$

3. When works cost is 21,000 then selling overhead is 5,250

   When works cost is 100 then selling overhead is $\frac{5,250 \times 100}{21,000} = 25\%$

4. When cost of sales is 30,450 then profit is 6,090

   When cost of sales is 100 then profit is $\frac{6,090 \times 100}{30,450} = 20\%$

Step III

Cost Sheet

for the year ended 31 Dec. 1991

	Particulars	*Amount*	*Amount*
		Rs.	Rs.
	Materials consumed		1,200
Add :	Wages		750
	Prime Cost		1,950
Add :	Factory overhead (60% of Direct wages. But now increased by $16\frac{2}{3}$% So, 70% of Direct wages. i.e. 60% + $16\frac{2}{3}$% of 60%)		525
	Work Cost		2,475
Add :	Administrative overhead (20% of works cost)		495
	Cost of Production		2,970
Add :	Selling overhead (25% of works cost. But, now decreased by 20%. So 20% of works cost, i.e. 25% – (20% of 25%)		495
	Cost of Good Sold		3,465
Add :	Profit (20% of cost of goods sold. But, now 10% higher. So, 30% of cost of good sold)		1,040
			4,505

Hint :

Method of solving problem

When the precentage of overheads increases or decreases and cost of materials and wages are given

Step One : Prepare the cost sheet for the past year on the usual basis.

Step Two : Calculate the precentage of overheads on the basis of principles given or recognised principles.

Step Three : Prepare the cost sheet for the present year.

Problem 33

In respect of a factory, the following figures have been obtained for the year 1987 :

	Rs.
Cost of materials	6,00,000
Direct wages	5,00,000
Factory overheads	3,00,000
Administrative overheads	3,36,000
Selling overheads	2,24,000
Distribution overheads	1,40,000
Profit	4,20,000

A work order has been executed in 1988 and the following expenses have been incurred : Materials Rs. 8,000 and Wages Rs. 5,000.

Assuming that, in 1988, the rate of factory overheads have increased by 20%, distribution overheads have gone down by 10% and selling and administration overheads have each gone up by $12\frac{1}{2}$%, at what price should the product be sold so as to earn the same rate of profit on the selling price as in 1987 ?

Factory overhead is based on direct wages while all other overheads are based on factory cost.

Solution

Statement of Cost for the year 1987

		Rs.
	Materials	6,00,000
	Direct wages	5,00,000
	Prime Cost	11,00,000
Add :	Factory overheads	3,00,000
	Works Cost	14,00,000
Add :	Administrative overheads	3,36,000
	Cost of Production	17,36,000
Add :	Selling overheads	2,24,000
	Distribution overheads	1,40,000
	Cost of Sales	21,00,000
Add :	Profit	4,20,000
	Sales	25,20,000

II. Calculation of percentage of various overheads on the basis given in the Problem :

(a) Percentage of Factory overheads on Direct Wages

$$= \frac{3,00,000}{5,00,000} \times 100 = 60\%$$

(b) Percentage of Administrative Overheads on Works Cost

$$= \frac{3,36,000}{14,00,000} \times 100 = 24\%$$

(c) Percentage of Selling Overheads on Works Cost

$$= \frac{2,24,000}{14,00,000} \times 100 = 16\%$$

(d) Percentage of Distribution Overheads on Works Cost

$= \frac{1,40,000}{14,00,000} \times 100 = 10\%$

(e) Percentage of Profit on Cost

$= \frac{4,20,000}{21,00,000} \times 100 = 20\%$

Calculation for 1988

(a) Percentage of Factory Overheads in 1988

60% of wages + 20% thereof = 72%

(b) Perentage of Administrative Overheads

24% of Works Cost + $12\frac{1}{2}$% thereof = 24 + 3 = 27%

(c) Percentage of Selling Overheads

16% + $12\frac{1}{2}$% thereof = 16 + 2 = 18%

(d) Percentage of Distribution Overheads

10% of Works Cost – 10% thereof = 10 – 1 = 9%

Estimate for Work Order for 1988

		Rs.
	Materials	8,000
	Wages	5,000
	Prime Cost	13,000
Add :	Factory Overheads @ 72% of wages	3,600
	Works Cost	16,600
Add :	Administrative Overheads @ 27% of works cost	4,482
	Cost of Production	21,082
Add :	Selling Overheads @ 18% of works cost	2,988
Add :	Distribution Overheads @ 9% of works cost	1,494
	Cost of Sales	25,564
Add :	Profit @ 20% on cost	5,113
	Selling Price	30,677

Problem 34

Following figures are extracted from the records of a company for the year 1989-90 :

	Rs.
Direct Materials	60,000
Direct Wages	50,000
Works Overhead	30,000
Administrative Overhead	33,600
Selling Overhead	22,400
Distribution Overhead	14,000
Profit	52,500

One material had been manufactured and supplied to Mr. X in 1990-91 for which following expenses were incurred :

	Rs.
Direct Materials	4,000
Direct Wages	2,000

In 1990-91 works overhead was increased by 20%, distribution overhead had been decreased by 10% and selling and administrative overhead each was increased by 12.5%.

At what price the above supply is to be billed to Mr. X so as to earn the same rate of profit on selling price as earned in 1989-90.

[C.U. B.Com. (Hons.) 1992]

Solution

COST SHEET

for the year 1989-90

		Rs.	Rs.
	Direct Materials		60,000
	Direct Wages		50,000
	Prime Cost		1,10,000
Add :	Works Overhead		30,000
	Works Cost		1,40,000
Add :	Administrative Overhead		33,600
	Cost of Production		1,73,600
Add :	Selling Overhead	22,400	
	Distribution Overhead	14,000	36,400
			2,10,000
	Profit (given)		52,500
	Sale Price		2,62,500

Calculation of percentages :

1. Percentage works overhead on wages = Rs. $\frac{30,000 \times 100}{50,000} = 60\%$

2. Administration overhead to works cost = Rs. $\frac{33,600 \times 100}{1,40,000} = 24\%$

3. Selling overhead on works cost = Rs. $\frac{22,400 \times 100}{1,40,000} = 16\%$

4. Distribution overhead on works cost = Rs. $\frac{14,000 \times 100}{1,40,000} = 10\%$

5. Profit percentage on sale price = Rs. $\frac{52,500 \times 100}{2,62,500} = 20\%$.

Estimated Cost Sheet

		Rs.	Rs.
	Direct Materials		4,000
Add :	Direct Wages		2,000
	Prime Cost		6,000
	Works overhead @ 60% of wages	1,200	
Add :	Increase 20% [or, 60% + (20% of 60%) = 72%]	240	1,440
	Works Cost		7,440
Add :	Administrative overhead 27% of works cost (24% + 12.5 × 24%)		2,008.8
	Cost of Production		9,448.8
Add :	Selling overhead @ 18% of works cost [16% + (12.5% of 16%)] = 16 + 2 = 18%		1,339.2
			10,788
Add :	Distribution overhead @ 9% of works cost [10% – (10% of 10%)]		669.6
	Cost of Sales		11,457.6
Add :	Profit @ 20% on selling price or 25% on cost		2,864.4
	Price to be quoted		14,322

Problem 35

A factory produce and sold 1,000 units of a product in July 1997 for which the following particulars are available :

	Rs.
Stock of Direct Materials on 1.7.97	6,000
Purchase of Direct Materials during July	1,44,000
Direct wages paid in cash in July 1997 (which includes Rs. 3,000 in respect of June 1997 and an advance of Rs. 2,000)	55,000
Works overhead charges for the month	60,000
Stock of Direct Materials on 31.7.97	10,000
Administrative and Selling overheads	25 per unit
Sales Price	300 per unit

From the above particulars you are required to (a) prepare a cost statement for July 1997,

(b) Estimate the sale price of a unit of the same product in August 1997 assuming :

i) 20% increase in direct material cost,

ii) 10% increase in direct wages,

iii) 5% increase in works overhead charges,

iv) 20% reduction in administration and selling overhead charges, and

v) same percentage of profit on sale price as in July 1997.

[Adapted—C.U. B.Com. (Hons.)]

Solution

Statement of Cost
for July 1997

	Total Amount		*Cost/unit*
	Rs.	Rs.	Rs.
Materials consumed :			
Stock as on 1-7-91	6,000		
Purchases during the month	1,44,000		
	1,50,000		
Less : Stock as on 31-7-91	10,000	1,40,000	140
Direct wages – paid in July	55,000		
Less : Payment for June	(3,000)		
	52,000		
Less : Advance payment	(2,000)	50,000	50
Prime Cost		1,90,000	190
Works overhead		60,000	60
Works Cost or Cost of Production		2,50,000	250
Administration and Selling overheads @ Rs. 25 per unit (1,000 × Rs. 25)		25,000	25
Cost of Sales		2,75,000	275
Profit (*balancing figure*)		25,000	25
Selling price @ Rs. 300		3,00,000	300

Estimate of Selling price per unit in August 1997

		Rs.
Direct Materials	$\frac{120}{100} \times 140$	168.00
Direct Wages	$\frac{110}{100} \times 50$	55.00
Prime Cost		223.00
Works Overhead	$\frac{105}{100} \times 60$	63.00
Works cost or Cost of production		286.00
Administration and Selling Overheads	$\frac{80}{100} \times 25$	20.00
Cost of Sales		306.00
Profit @ $8\frac{1}{3}$% on sale or $\frac{1}{12}$th of sales i.e., $\frac{1}{11}$th of cost[1]		27.82
Selling Price		333.82

Working Note :

[1]Ratio of profit to sales in July '91 = $\frac{25,000}{3,00,000} = \frac{1}{12}$th or $8\frac{1}{3}$%.

Problem 36

Bharat Electronics Ltd. furnishes the following information for 10,000 T.V. valves manufactured during the year 1997 :

	Rs.		Rs.
Materials	90,000	Clerical salaries and management expenses	33,500
Direct Wages	60,000	Selling expenses	5,500
Power and Consumable Stores	12,000	Sale proceeds of Scraps	2,000
Factory indirect wages	15,000	Plant repairs, maintenance and depreciation	11,500
Lighting of factory	5,500		
Defective work (cost of rectification)	3,000		

The net selling price was Rs. 31.60 per unit sold and all the units were sold.

As from 1st January 1998 the selling price was reduced to Rs. 31.00 per unit. It was estimated that production could be increased in 1998 by 50% utilising spare capacity. Rates of materials and direct wages will increase by 10%.

You are required to prepare :

(a) Cost sheet for the year 1997 showing various elements of cost per unit and

(b) Estimated cost and profit for 1998 assuming that 15,000 units will be produced and sold during the year. Factory overheads are recovered as a percentage of direct wages and office and selling expenses as a percentage of works cost.

[Adapted—C.A. (Inter)]

Solution

Cost Sheet

Output : 10,000 units — Period : year ended 31st Dec. '97

	Total Amount			Cost per unit
	Rs.	Rs.	Rs.	Rs.
Materials		90,000		9.00
Wages		60,000		6.00
Prime Cost		1,50,000		15.00
Factory overheads :				
Power and consumable stores	12,000		1.20	
Factory indirect wages	15,000		1.50	
Lighting of factory	5,500		0.55	
Defective work (cost of rectification)	3,000		0.30	
Plant repairs and maintenance and depreciation	11,500		1.15	
	47,000		4.70	
Less : Sale of scraps	2,000	45,000	0.20	4.50
Works Cost		1,95,000		19.50
Office and Selling expenses :				
Clerical salaries and management expenses	33,500		3.35	
Selling expenses	5,500	39,000	0.55	3.90
Cost of Sales		2,34,000		23.40
Profit (*balancing figure*)		82,000		8.20
Sales		3,16,000		31.60

Estimated Cost Sheet

Estimated output 15,000 units

		Total	Per Unit
		Rs.	Rs.
Materials :	15,000 × Rs. 9.90	1,48,500	9.90
Wages :	15,000 × Rs. 6.60	99,000	6.60
Prime Cost		2,47,500	16.50
Factory overheads @ 75% of wages1		74,250	4.95
Works Cost		3,21,750	21.45
Office and Selling expenses @ 20% of works cost2		64,350	4.29
Cost of Sales		3,86,100	25.74
Estimated profit (balancing figure)		78,900	5.26
Sales	(15,000 × Rs. 31)	4,65,000	31.00

Note : The cost of rectification of defective work has been included in factory overheads on the assumption that the defectives are normal.

Problem 37

The following extract of costing information relates to a commodity for the year ended 31st March 1984.

Stock on 1st April 1983

	Rs.
Raw Materials	5,000
Finished product (1,000 tonnes)	4,000
Stock on 31st March 1984 :	
Raw Materials	5,560
Finished Products (2,000 tonnes)	8,000
Raw Materials purchased	30,000
Direct Wages	25,000
Rent, Rates and Taxes of Works	10,000
Carriage Inwards	360
Work-in-Progress on 1st April 83	1,200
Work-in-Progress in 31st March 84	4,000
Cost of Factory Supervision	2,000
Sales of Finished goods	75,000

Advertisement and Selling expenses amount to 0.25 paise per tonne sold. 16,000 tonnes were produced during the year.

Prepare Statement showing (a) The value of raw materials used; (b) The cost of the output for the year; (c) The cost of the turnover for the year; (d) The net profit for the year; and (e) The net profit per tonne of the commodity.

[C.U. B.Com. (Hons.) 1984]

Solution

Cost Sheet
for the year ended 31.3.84

	Elements of Costs	Amount Rs.	Total Cost Rs.	Cost/unit Rs.
Add :	Raw Materials Consumed :			
	Opening Stock	5,000		
Add :	Purchases	30,000		
		35,000		
Less :	Closing Stock	5,560		
	(a) Value of raw materials used		29,440	
	Carriage Inwards		360	
	Direct Wages		25,000	
	Prime Cost		54,800	
	Factory Overheads :			
	Rents, Rates and Taxes	10,000		
	Cost of Factory Supervision	2,000	12,000	
	Work-in-Progress		66,800	
	Opening Stock	1,200		
Less :	Closing Stock	– 4,000	– 2,800	
	(b) **Works Cost/Cost of Production**		64,000	
	Office Overheads		Nil	
	Finished Goods			
	Opening Stock	4,000		
Less :	Closing Stock	– 8,000	– 4,000	
	(c) **Cost of Goods Sold**		60,000	
	Selling & Distribution Overheads			
	(@ 25 p. for 15,000 Tonnes) $15{,}000 \times \frac{25}{100}$		3,750	
			63,750	
Add :	(d) Profit (Balancing figure)		11,250	0.75 per tonne
	Sale Price		75,000	

Working Notes :

	Production	=	16,000	Tonnes
Add :	Opening Stock	=	1,000	"
			17,000	"
Less :	Closing Stock	=	2,000	Tonnes
	Total Goods Sold	=	15,000	Tonnes

Problem 38

Where purchase of materials is not given

The books and records of the Anand Manufacturing Company present the following data for the month of August 1988 :

Direct Labour Cost – Rs. 16,000 (160% of factory overhead)

Cost of goods sold – Rs. 56,000.

Inventory accounts showed these opening and closing balances :

	August 1	August 31
	Rs.	Rs.
Raw Materials	8,000	8,600
Work-in-Progress	8,000	12,000
Finished goods	14,000	18,000
Other data :		
Selling expenses		3,400
General and Administration expenses		2,600
Sales for the month		75,000

You are required to prepare a statement showing cost of goods manufactured and sold, and profit earned. **[C.A. Inter.]**

Solution

Anand Manufacturing Company Ltd.

Statement of cost of goods manufactured and sold and profit earned for the month of August 1988

		Rs.	Rs.
	Raw Materials Consumed :		
	Opening Stock	8,000	
Add :	Purchases (Note 2)	36,000	
		44,000	
Less :	Closing Stock	8,600	
	Materials Consumed (Note 1)		35,400
Add :	Direct Labour (being 160% of Factory overheads)		16,000
	Prime Cost		51,400
Add :	Factory Overhead $\frac{16,000 \times 100}{160}$		10,000
			61,400
Add :	Opening Work-in-Progress		8,000
			69,400
Less :	Closing Work-in-Progress		12,000
	Factory Cost		57,400
Add :	General and Administration expenses		2,600
	Cost of Production		60,000
Add :	Opening Stock of finished goods		14,000
			74,000
Less :	Closing Stock of finished goods		18,000
	Cost of Goods Sold (given)		56,000
Add :	Selling expenses		3,400
	Cost of Sales		59,400
	Profit (Sale Price – Cost of sales)		15,600
	Sales		75,000

Working Notes :

Note 1

In this problem the amount of raw materials purchased is not given, so, we are to make back calculation to ascertain the amount of raw materials consumed :

			Rs.
	Cost of goods sold		56,000
Add :	Closing Stock of finished goods		18,000
			74,000
Less :	Opening Stock of finished goods		14,000
	Cost of Production		60,000
Less :	General and Administration expenses		2,600
	Works Cost		57,400
Add :	Closing W.I.P.		12,000
			69,400
Less :	Opening W.I.P.		8,000
			61,400
Less :	Factory Overheads	10,000	
	Direct labour	16,000	26,000
	Raw Materials Consumed		35,400

Note 2

	Raw Materials purchased :	
	Raw Materials consumed	35,400
Add :	Closing Stock of Raw Materials	8,600
		44,000
Less :	Opening Stock of Raw materials	8,000
	Raw Materials Purchased	36,000

Problem 39

Cooling Limited manufactured and sold 1,000 refrigerators at the year ending 31st December 1988. The summarised Trading and Profit and Loss Account is set out below :

	Rs.	Rs.		Rs.	Rs.
To Cost of Material		80,000	By Sales		4,00,000
To Direct Wages		1,20,000			
To Other manufacturing cost		50,000			
To Gross Profit c/d		1,50,000			
		4,00,000			4,00,000
To Management and Staff Salary		60,000	By Gross Profit b/d		1,50,000
To Rent, Rates and Insurance		10,000			
To Selling expenses		30,000			
To General expenses		20,000			
To Net Profit		30,000			
		1,50,000			1,50,000

For the year ended 31st December 1989, it is estimated that :

(a) Output and Sales will be 1,200 refrigerators. Prices of materials will go up by 20% on the level of the previous year.

(b) Wages will rise by 5%.

(c) Manufacturing costs will rise in proportion to the combined cost of materials and wages.

(d) Selling cost per unit will remain unaffected.

(e) Other expenses will remain constant.

You are required to submit a statement to the Board of Directors showing the price at which the refrigerator should be marked so as to show profit at 10% on Selling Price.

[B.Com. Bombay]

Solution

Cost Sheet

for the year ending 31st December 1988

1988 – Output – 1,000 refrigerators	*Total Cost* Rs.	*Unit Cost* Rs.
Cost of Materials	80,000	80.00
Direct Wages	1,20,000	120.00
Prime Cost	2,00,000	200.00
Add : Manufacturing expenses	50,000	50.00
Works Cost	2,50,000	250.00
Add : Office and Administrative Overheads		
Management and Staff Salaries	60,000	60.00
	3,10,000	310.00
Add : Rent, Rates and Insurance	10,000	10.00
	3,20,000	320.00
Add : General Expenses	20,000	20.00
	3,40,000	340.00
Add : Selling and Distribution Overheads – Selling expenses	30,000	30.00
Total Cost	3,70,000	370.00
Profit	30,000	30.00
	4,00,000	400.00

Estimated Cost Sheet for 1,200 Refrigerators

	Rs.	Rs.
Materials Rs. 80 + 16 = 96 (20% increase)	96.00	1,15,200
Direct Wages Rs. 120 + 6 = 126 (5% increase)	126.00	1,51,200
Prime Cost	222.00	2,66,400
Manufacturing expenses (25% of Prime Cost)	55.50	66,600
Works Cost	277.50	3,33,000
Add : Administrative and Office Overheads :		
Management and Staff Salaries	50.00	60,000
Rent, Rates and Insurance	8.33	10,000
Other expenses	16.67	20,000
Cost of Production	352.50	4,23,000
Add : Selling Overheads :		
Selling Expenses	30.00	36,000
Total Cost	382.50	4,59,000
Add : Profit @ 10% on selling price, i.e. $\frac{1}{9}$th on cost	42.50	51,000
	425.00	5,10,000

Working Notes :

(1)	Cost of materials :		Rs.
	Previous Price =		80
Add :	Increase @ 20% =	$\frac{80 \times 20}{100}$ =	16
			96
(2)	Direct Wages :		
	Previous rate =		120
Add :	5% increase =	$\frac{120 \times 5}{100}$ =	6
			126

Manufacturing expenses :

When Prime Cost is 2,00,000 manufacturing expenses 50,000

When " " " 100 " " $\frac{50{,}000 \times 100}{2{,}00{,}000} = 25\%$.

Problem 40

One Company furnishes you with the following information about its 100 TV sets manufactured and all sold during the year :

	Rs.		Rs.
Materials	90,000	Office Administration Expenses	34,000
Direct Wages	50,000	Selling & Distribution Expenses	6,000
Power and Stores	12,000	Sale of Scrap	2,000
Factory Indirect Wages	15,000	Sale of 100 T.V. sets	3,10,000
Factory Lighting	6,000	Repairs and depreciation of	
Cost of rectifying defective work	3,000	machinery	10,000

Prepare the Cost Sheet for the above year, showing the elements of cost per unit. Prepare also the estimated Cost Sheet for the next year assuming that :

(i) Materials Cost and Direct Wages Cost will increase by 10% and 15% respectively.

(ii) Factory Overhead will be recovered as a percentage of Direct Wages, as last year.

(iii) Office Overhead and Selling Overhead will be recovered as percentage of Works Cost, as last year, and

(iv) 150 Sets will be produced and sold at Rs. 3,300 each in the next year.

[Adapted—Audit & Accounts Service Exam. 1989.]

Cost Sheet for 100 T.V. Sets

(Output 100 T.V. Sets)

			Cost/Unit
	Rs.	Rs.	Rs.
Material		90,000	900.00
Direct Wages		50,000	500.00
Prime Cost		1,40,000	1,400.00
Add : *Factory Overheads* :			
Factory indirect wages	15,000		
Factory Lighting	6,000		
Power and Stores	12,000		
Repairs and depreciation of machinery	10,000		
	43,000	1,40,000	1,400.00

Contd.

	Rs.	Rs.	Rs.
B.F.	43,000	1,40,000	1,400.00
Cost of rectifying defective works	3,000		
	46,000		
Less : Sale of Scrap	2,000	44,000	440.00
Works Cost		1,84,000	1,840.00
Add : Office Administration Expenses		34,000	340.00
Cost of Production		2,18,000	2,180.00
Add : Selling and Distribution Expenses		6,000	60.00
Total Cost		2,24,000	2,240.00
Add : Profit (Sale Price – Total Cost)		86,000	860.00
Sale Price		3,10,000	3,100.00

Estimated Cost

		Rs.
(i)	Materials cost per unit for the next year	
	Present cost per unit	900
Add :	10% increase	90
		990

So, Material cost for 150 units = 990 × 150 = 1,48,500

(ii) Direct Wages $500 + \left(500 \times \frac{15}{100}\right) = 575 \times 150 = 86{,}250$

(iii) Factory Overhead as a percentage of Direct wages.

Factory Overhead = 44,000

Direct Wages = 50,000

Percentage of Factory Overheads on Direct wages $= \frac{44{,}000 \times 100}{50{,}000} = 88\%$

(iv) Percentage of Office and Administration

Overheads on Works Cost $= \frac{34{,}000 \times 100}{1{,}84{,}000} = 18.47\%$

(v) Selling Overheads as a percentage on Works Cost $= \frac{6{,}000 \times 100}{1{,}84{,}000} = 3.26\%.$

Estimated Cost Sheet for 150 sets

(Output 150 T.V. Sets)

	Total Cost Rs.	*Cost/Unit* Rs.
Material (Note 1)	1,48,500	990.00
Direct Wages (Note 2)	86,250	575.00
Prime Cost	2,34,750	1,565.00
Add : *Factory overhead* (Note 3)		
88% of Direct Wages	75,900	506,00
Works Cost	3,10,650	2,071.00
Add : *Office and Administrative Overheads*		
@ 18.47% of works cost	57,377	382.51
Cost of Production	3,68,027	2,453.51
Add : *Selling & Distribution Overheads*		
@ 3.26% of works cost	10,127	67.51
Total Cost/Cost of goods sold	3,78,154	2,521.02
Add : **Profit** (Sale Price – Total Cost)	1,16,846	778.98
Sale Price (150 × Rs. 3,300)	4,95,000	3,300.00

REVISIONAL PROBLEMS

Problem 41

AB & Co. manufactures two types of pens P & Q. The cost data for the year ended 30th September 1990, is as follows :

	Rs.
Direct Materials	4,00,000
Direct Wages	2,24,000
Production Overhead	96,000
	7,20,000

It is further ascertained that :

(a) Direct materials in type P cost twice as much as direct materials in type Q.

(b) Direct wages for type Q were 60% of those for type P.

(c) Production overhead was of same rate for both types.

(d) Administration overhead for each was 200% of direct labour.

(e) Selling costs were 0.50 paise per pen for both types.

(f) Production during the year :

Type P 40,000

Type Q 1,20,000

(g) Sales during the year :

Type P 36,000

Type Q 1,00,000

(h) Selling prices were Rs. 14 per pen for type P and Rs. 10 per pen for type Q.

Prepare a statement showing per unit Cost of Production, Total Cost, Profit and also total sales value and profit separately for two types of pen P & Q.

[ICWA—Inter. - Dec. 1990]

Solution

Statement showing Per unit Cost,
Total Cost, Profit and Total Sales
for the year ended 30.9.1990

		Total	*Cost per unit*	*Total*	*Cost per unit*
		Rs.	Rs.	Rs.	Rs.
	Direct Material (Note 1)	1,60,000	4.00	2,40,000	2.00
Add :	Direct Wages (Note 2)	80,000	2.00	1,44,000	1.20
	Prime Cost	2,40,000	6.00	3,84,000	3.20
Add :	Production Overhead	24,000	0.60	72,000	0.60
	Works Cost	2,64,000	6.60	4,56,000	3.80
Add :	Administration Overhead @ 200% of Wages	1,60,000	4.00	2,88,000	2.40
	Cost of Production	4,24,000	10.60	7,44,000	6.20
Less :	Closing Stock	42,400	—	1,24,000	—
	Cost of goods sold	3,81,600	10.60	6,20,000	6.20
Add :	Selling expenses @ 0.50 per pen	18,000	0.50	50,000	0.50
	Cost of Sales	3,99,600	11.10	6,70,000	6.70
Add :	Profit	1,04,400	2.90	3,30,000	3.30
	Total Sales (S. P × No.)	5,04,000	14.00	10,00,000	10.00

Working Notes :

1. Suppose, the cost of Material for type Q = x

So the cost of Material of type P = 2x Or, 1,20,000 x + 80,000 x = 4,00,000

Or, 2,00,000 x = 4,00,000

Or, $x = \frac{4,00,000}{2,00,000}$ = Rs. 2 per unit

For type P = Rs. 2 × 2 = Rs. 4 per unit

2. Wages

Let us assume that the wages for P = x So, for Q it will be = $\frac{60}{100}$ x

$40,000\ x + 1,20,000 \times \frac{60}{100}\ x = 2,24,000$ Or, 40,000 x + 72,000 x = 2,24,000

Or, $x = \frac{2,24,000}{1,12,000}$ = Rs. 2.00 per unit

Cost of Wages for quality Q = $\frac{60}{100} \times 2 = \frac{120}{100}$ = Rs. 1.20 per unit

Problem 42

The following data are available from the Cost Ledger of Acme Industries for the year 1989 :

	Rs.
Plant Maintenance	25,000
Lighting	6,300
Depreciation on Plant	8,100
Rates and Taxes for the works	3,900
Staff Salaries	32,000
Management Salaries	22,000
Power (for this plant)	10,600
Rental for Leasehold Equipments	9,600
Indirect Wages	37,100
Rectification Cost of Defectives (Normal)	8,400
Consumable Stores	17,600
Selling expenses	30,000
General charges	15,600
Sale proceeds from Scrap	4,200

During the year 1989 total production was 1,20,000 units. The break-up of prime cost per unit was materials Rs. 2.20 and wages Rs. 1.80. The average selling price was Rs. 6.75 per unit and the entire quantity produced during the year was sold out.

With effect from January 1, 1990, the selling price was reduced to Rs. 6.40 per unit. It was envisaged that production could be enhanced during 1990 by $33\frac{1}{3}$% without incurring any overtime or extra-shift work or additional selling expenses.

You are required to prepare statements showing :

(i) Actual cost and profit for 1989.

(ii) Estimated cost and profit for 1990 assuming that the entire production will be sold during the year.

Assumption, if any, required to be made in the above exercise should be clearly stated.

[Adapted—I.C.W.A. (Inter) June, 1988]

ACME Industries
Units Cost Statement
for the year 1989

Output – 1,20,000

			Amount	*Cost/Unit*
		Rs.	Rs.	Rs.
	Direct Cost			
	Materials	(1,20,000 × 2.20)	2,64,000	
	Wages	(1,20,000 × 1.80)	2,16,000	
	Prime Cost		4,80,000	4.00
Add :	*Factory Overheads*			
	Variable Charges			
	Power	10,600		
	Consumable Stores	17,600		
	Rectification Cost of defective works	8,400		
		36,600		
Less :	Sale proceeds of Scrap	4,200	32,400	0.27
			5,12,400	4.27
Add :	Fixed Charges			
	Indirect wages	37,100		
	Plant maintenance	25,000		
	Lighting	6,300		
	Depreciation on Plant	8,100		
	Rates and Taxes for works	3,900		
	Rental for Leasehold Equipment	9,600	90,000	0.75
	Factory Cost		6,02,400	5.02
Add :	*Office Overheads*			
	Staff Salaries	32,000		
	Management Salaries	22,000		
	General Charges	15,600	69,600	0.58
	Cost of Production		6,72,000	5.60
Add :	*Selling Overhead*			
	Selling Expenses		30,000	0.25
	Total Cost		7,02,000	5.85
Add :	Profit (Sales – Total Cost)		1,08,000	0.90
	Sales (1,20,000 × Rs. 6.75)		8,10,000	6.75

Estimated Cost Statement for 1990

Estimated Output – 1,60,000 (1,20,000 + $\frac{1}{3}$ of 1,20,000)

	Particulars		Amount	Cost/Unit
			Rs.	Rs.
	Prime Cost @ Rs. 4.00 per unit		6,40,000	4.00
Add :	Variable charges			
Less :	Factory overheads @ Re. 0.27 per unit		43,200	0.27
			6,83,200	4.270
Add :	Fixed Charges			
	Works	90,000		
	Office	69,600		
	Selling	30,000	1,89,600	1.185
	Total Cost		8,72,800	5.455
Add :	Profit (Sale Price – Total Cost)		1,51,200	0.945
	Sale (1,60,000 × Rs. 6.40)		10,24,000	6.400

When goods are sold on LIFO basis

Problem 43

From the following particulars relating to the production and sales for the year ended 31st December 1992, prepare a cost statement showing therein (i) the Prime Cost, (ii) the Works Cost, (iii) the Cost of Production, (iv) the Cost of Sales, and (v) the Profit or Loss.

		Rs.	Rs.
	Stock as on 1.1.92		
	(a) Raw Materials		25,000
	(b) Work-in-Progress		
	At Prime Cost	30,000	
Add :	Manufacturing Expenses	6,000	36,000
	(c) Finished goods (at cost)		1,44,000
	Raw Materials Purchased		2,00,000
	Freight on raw materials		10,000
	Machine Hour Rate		3
	Machine Hours worked : 48,000 hours.		
	Chargeable Expenses		50,000
	Factory Wages for direct labour		2,70,000
	Administrative Expenses		1,00,000
	Selling Expenses		54,000
	Distribution Expenses		36,000
	Sale proceeds of finished goods (30,000 units)		9,00,000
	Stock as on 31st December 1992 :		
	(a) Raw Materials		45,000
	(b) Work-in-Progress		
	At Prime Cost	45,000	
Add :	Mfg. Expenses	9,000	54,000
	(c) Finished goods at cost (10,000 units)		?
	Finished goods produced 32,000 units		
	Apply LIFO principle in finished goods valuation.		

[C.U. B.Com. (Hons.) 1993]

Solution

COST SHEET

for the year ended 31st December 1992

		Rs.	Rs.
	Stock of Raw Materials	25,000	
Add :	Purchases of raw materials	2,00,000	
Add :	Freight on raw materials purchased	10,000	
		2,35,000	
Less :	Closing stock of raw materials	45,000	
	Raw Materials consumed		1,90,000
Add :	Direct wages		2,70,000
Add :	Chargeable Expenses		50,000
Add :	Work-in-progress at prime cost (opening)		30,000
			5,40,000
Less :	Work-in-progress at prime cost (closing)		45,000
	Prime Cost		4,95,000
Add :	*Factory Overhead*		
	Machine hours × Machine hour rate	48,000 × 3	1,44,000
			6,39,000
Add :	Work-in-progress at manufacturing expenses (opening)		6,000
			6,45,000
Less	Work-in-progress at manufacturing expenses (closing)		9,000
	Work Cost		6,36,000
Add :	*Administrative expenses*		1,00,000
	Cost of Production		7,36,000
Add :	Opening finished goods (8,000 units)		1,44,000
			8,80,000
Less :	Closing stock of Finished goods (10,000 units)		
	8,000 (units) Opening Stock	1,44,000	
	2,000 at current price (Note)	46,000	1,90,000
Add :	*Selling & Distribution Overheads*		6,90,000
	Distribution Expenses	36,000	
	Selling expenses	54,000	90,000
	Total Cost		7,80,000
Add :	Profit (balancing figure)		1,20,000
	Sale Price		9,00,000

Note for the students

Valuation of Closing Stock

Finished goods have been valued under LIFO Method.

Units sold during the year 30,000. These 30,000 units have been sold out of current stock of finished goods.

Closing Stock of finished goods :

From old Stock 8,000 units valued at Rs. 1,44,000 (given)

From current Stock 2,000 units valued at Rs. 46,000

$$\frac{\text{Cost of production} \times \text{closing stock (in units)}}{\text{No. of units produced}} = \left(\frac{7,36,000}{32,000} \times 2,000\right) = \text{Rs. } 46,000.$$

Problem 44

A certain type of factory produces a uniform type of article and has a capacity of producing 15,000 units per week of 48 hours. The following information shows the different elements of costs for three consecutive weeks of 48 hours each, when the output has changed from week to week.

Units produced	*Direct Materials*	*Direct Labour (Fixed and Variable)*	*Factory overheads*
4,000	8,000	16,000	38,000
5,000	10,000	20,000	40,000
8,000	16,000	32,000	46,000

You are required to find out the selling price per unit when the weekly output is 10,000 units and a profit of 8.33% on selling price will be made.

[B.U. B.Com. (Hons.) 1991]

Working notes :

Variable Costs

(i) Cost of materials per unit

Total Cost ÷ No. of units.

$= \text{Rs. } \frac{8,000}{4,000} = \text{Rs. } 2.00 \text{ per unit}$

(ii) Direct labour $= \frac{\text{Total Cost}}{\text{No. of units}} = \frac{16,000}{4,000} = \text{Rs. } 4.00 \text{ per unit}$

(iii) Variable factory overhead $= \frac{\text{Change in total cost}}{\text{Change in units}}$

$= \text{Rs. } \frac{2,000(\text{Rs. } 40,000 - 38,000)}{1,000(5,000 - 4,000)} = \text{Rs. } 2 \text{ per unit.}$

(iv) Fixed Factory Overhead = Total Cost of Factory Overhead – Variable Overhead

= Rs. 38,000 – Rs. 8,000 (4,000 × Rs. 2.00 per unit) = Rs. 30,000.

COST SHEET

Output 10,000 units

			Total Cost	*Cost per unit*
			Rs.	Rs.
	Materials	10,000 × Rs. 2	20,000	2.00
	Labour	10,000 × Rs. 4	40,000	4.00
	Prime Cost		60,000	6.00
Add :	*Factory Overhead :*			
	Fixed Factory Overhead		30,000	3.00
			90,000	9.00
	Variable Overhead	10,000 × Rs. 2	20,000	2.00
	Works Cost		1,10,000	11.00
Add :	Profit @ 8.33% on Selling price i.e. $\frac{1}{11}$th on cost		10,000	1.00
	Selling Price		1,20,000	12.00

Problem 45

A Co. makes two distinct types of vehicles A and B. The total expenses during a period is shown by the books for assembly of 600 of A and 800 of B, are as under :

	Rs.
Materials	1,98,000
Wages	12,000
Store Overhead	19,800
Running expenses of machine	4,400
Depreciation	2,200
Labour amenities	1,500
Works General Expenses	30,000
Administrative and Selling expenses	26,800

Other information :	A : B
Material cost ratio per unit	1 : 2
Wages	2 : 3
Machine utilisation	1 : 2

Calculate the cost of each vehicle giving reasons for the basis of apportionment adopted by you.

[Adapted—I.C.W.A.]

Working notes :

(i) Material cost has been apportioned in the ratio 3 : 8 which is calculated as follows:

Vehicle A = 600 × 1 = 600

Vehicle B = 800 × 2 = 1,600

The ratio = 600 : 1,600 = 3 : 8

(ii) Direct wages

Vehicle A = 600 × Rs. 2 = 1,200

Vehicle B = 800 × Rs. 3 = 2,400

The ratio = 1,200 : 2,400 = 1 : 2

(iii) Running expenses of machine and depreciation have been apportioned on the basis of machine utilisation which is as follows :

Vehicle A = 600 × 1 = 600

Vehicle B = 800 × 2 = 1,600

The ratio = 600 : 1,600 = 3 : 8

(iv) Stores Overhead as a percentage of material cost $= 19{,}800 \times \frac{100}{1{,}98{,}000} = 10\%$

(v) Works Overhead and labour amenities have been distributed as a percentage of wages :

Works Overhead $= 30{,}000 \times \frac{100}{12{,}000} = 250\%$

Labour Amenities $= 1{,}500 \times \frac{100}{12{,}000} = 12\frac{1}{2}\%$

(vi) Selling and Administration expenses have been distributed as a percentage of works cost :

Which is as follows : $\frac{26{,}800 \times 100}{2{,}67{,}900} = 10.03\%$

STATEMENT OF COST

	Vehicle A	*Vehicle B*	*Total*
	Rs.	Rs.	Rs.
Material (3 : 8)	54,000	1,44,000	1,98,000
Direct Wages (1 : 2)	4,000	8,000	12,000
Stores Overhead (10% of material cost)	5,400	14,400	19,800
Running expenses of machines (3 : 8)	1,200	3,200	4,400
Depreciation (3 : 8)	600	1,600	2,200
Labour Amenities ($12\frac{1}{2}$% of Wages)	500	1,000	1,500
Works General Expenses (250% of Wages)	10,000	20,000	30,000
Works Cost	75,700	1,92,200	2,67,900
Add : Administrative and Selling Expenses (10.03% of Work Cost)	7,583	19,217	26,800
Total Cost	83,283	2,11,417	2,94,700

Problem 46

A factory has undertaken a contract for the manufacture of 8,000 units and the following information has been obtained :

Material cost Rs. 25 for each article

Direct wages Rs. 20 for each article

Selling price Rs. 80 for each article

The overhead charges consist of (a) Fixed Rs. 20,000; (b) Variable Rs. 16,000; (c) Semi-variable (of which 60% is fixed) Rs. 9,600.

Calculate the profit per article. What would be the profit per article, if the number of articles manufactured were 10,000, the total fixed overhead charges remain unchanged ?

Solution

STATEMENT OF COST AND PROFIT

Particulars	8,000 units		10,000 units	
	Total Cost	*Cost/Unit*	*Total Cost*	*Cost/Unit*
	Rs.	Rs.	Rs.	Rs.
Material Cost	2,00,000	25.00	2,50,000	25.00
Direct wages	1,60,000	20.00	2,00,000	20.00
Prime Cost	3,60,000	45.00	4,50,000	45.00
Add : Variable Overhead	16,000	2.00	20,000	2.00
Fixed Overhead	20,000	2.50	20,000	2.00
	3,96,000	49.50	4,90,000	49.00
Add : Semi-variable Overhead				
60% Fixed Cost	5,760	0.72	5,760	0.58
Semi-variable 40% Variable	3,840	0.48	4,800	0.48
Total Cost	4,05,600	50.70	5,00,560	50.06
Add : Profit (*Balancing figure*)	2,34,400	29.30	2,99,440	29.94
Sales Price	6,40,000	80.00	8,00,000	80.00

Problem 47

The following particulars are obtained from the records of a factory :

	Rs.
Materials issued	64,000
Wages paid	56,000
Factory Overhead	60% of Wages

Out of materials issued, Rs. 800 worth of goods have been returned to stores and Rs.4,000 transferred to other jobs.

10% of the production has been scrapped as bad and a further 20% has been brought up to the specification by increasing the factory overhead to 80% of the wages. If the scrapped production fetches only Rs. 470, find the cost of production per unit of the finished goods, if the total product (including the quantity scrapped) be 100 units.

Solution

COST SHEET

	Amount Rs.	Total Cost Rs.	Cost/Unit Rs.
Materials cost	64,000		
Less : Returned to Stores	800		
	63,200		
Less : Transferred to other jobs	400		
Materials consumed		62,800	
Add : Direct wages		56,000	
Prime Cost		1,18,800	
Add : *Factory overhead @ 60% of Wages*	$\frac{60}{100} \times 56,000$	33,600	
		1,52,400	
Add : Cost of rectification by increasing the factory overhead to 80% of wages $\frac{80}{100} \times 56,000 = 44,800$			
Less : Wages already charged = 33,600		11,200	
		1,63,600	
Less : Value of Scrap realised		470	
Total Cost		1,63,130	
Cost per unit (100 units $- \frac{10}{100} \times 100 = 90$)	1,63,130 ÷ 90		1,812.56

Problem 48

A manufacturing company has an installed capacity of 60,000 units p.a. The cost structure of the products manufactured is as under :

(i) Variable cost (per unit)

Labour	Rs.	16.00
(subject to a minimum of Rs. 64,000 p.m.)		
Materials	Rs.	16.00
Overheads	Rs.	6.00
(ii) Fixed Overheads	Rs.	2,08,000 p.a.

(iii) Semi-variable Overheads Rs. 96,000 p.a. at 60% capacity, which increase by Rs. 12,000 p.a. for increase of every 10% of the capacity utilisation or any part thereof.

The capacity utilisation for the next year is estimated at 60% for 3 months, 75% for 5 months and 80% for the balance part of the year. If the company is planning to have a profit of 25% on the selling price, calculate the estimated selling price for each unit of production. Assume that there is no opening or closing stock.

Solution

Budgeted Production

		Production		(Units)
	Capacity at 100%	5,000 p.m.		
(a)	For 3 months @ 60%	3,000 × 3	=	9,000
	For 5 months @ 75%	3,750 × 5	=	18,750
	For 4 months @ 80%	4,000 × 4	=	16,000
				43,750

(b)	Calculation of Wages			
	First 3 months	@ Rs. 64,000 × 3	=	1,92,000
	For next 5 months	@ Rs. 64,000 × 5	=	3,20,000
	For next 4 months	4,000 × 16 × 4	=	2,56,000
				7,68,000

Note : To absorb the minimum wages of Rs. 64,000 the company is required to produce 64,000 ÷ 16 = 4,000 units.

(c) Calculation of Semi-variable Overheads

For 3 months @ 60% of capacity $= \text{Rs. } \dfrac{96,000}{12} \times 3 = \text{Rs. } 24,000$

For 5 months @ 75% capacity $= \text{Rs. } \dfrac{96,000 + 24,000}{12} \times 5 = \text{Rs. } 50,000$

For 4 months @ 80% of capacity $= \text{Rs. } \dfrac{96,000 + 24,000}{12} \times 4 = \text{Rs. } 40,000$

Total semivariable overheads = Rs. 24,000 + Rs. 50,000 + Rs. 40,000 = Rs. 1,14,000

Estimated Cost Sheet for 43,750 units

	Rs.	Rs.
Materials @ Rs. 16 per unit =	43,750 × 16	7,00,000
Wages as per Note (b)		7,68,000
Variable Overheads @ Rs. 6 per unit	43,750 × 6	2,62,500
Fixed Overheads		2,08,000
Semi Variable Overheads as per note (c)		1,14,000
Total Cost		20,52,500
Add : Profit @ 25% on sales i.e. $33\frac{1}{3}$% on Cost.		6,84,167
Sale Price		27,36,667

Selling Price per unit = Rs. 27,36,667 ÷ 43,750 = Rs. 62.55 per unit.

Problem 49

Following costs were incurred in producing 800 M.T. of MS Rods :

	Rs.
Materials	2,80,000
Labour	1,00,000
Processing charges	1,00,000
	4,80,000

Of the total output 10% was defective and had to be sold after a discount of 10% of the normal price. The scrap arising out of the production realised a sum of Rs. 8,700. The sale price is calculated to yield 15% profit on sales. You are required to find out the normal price as well as the discounted price of per M.T. of MS Rods.

[Adapted—I.C.W.A. June 1991]

Solution

Cost of Production of MS Rods

		Rs.
	Materials	2,80,000
	Labour	1,00,000
	Processing Charges	1,00,000
		4,80,000
Less :	Sale of Scrap	8,760
	Cost of Production	4,71,240
	Profit 15% of sales, i.e. 15/85 of cost	83,160
	Sales	5,54,400
Units Sold		
	Total production	800 M.T.
Less :	Defective 10%	80 M.T.
		720
Add :	Equivalent of Defective Production @ 90% of 80 M.T.	72 M.T.
	Price of goods produced $\frac{5,54,000}{792 \text{ M.T.}}$ = Rs. 700	792

Discounted price of defective production @ 10% discount = Rs. 700 – 70 = Rs. 630

Problem 50

Delta Engineering Limited produces a uniform type of product and has a manufacturing capacity of 3,000 units per week of 48 hours. From the cost records of the company, the following data are available relating to output and cost for three consecutive weeks :

Week No.	*Units Manufactured*	*Direct Materials*	*Direct Labour*	*Factory Overhead (variable & fixed)*
		Rs.	Rs.	Rs.
1	1,200	9,000	3,600	31,000
2	1,600	12,000	4,800	33,000
3	1,800	13,500	5,400	34,000

Assuming the company charges a profit of 20% on sales, find out the selling price per unit when the weekly output is 2,000 units.

[Adapted—I.C.W.A. (Inter) June 1990]

Solution

(i) **Calculation of Variable Cost**

Week	Units	Factory Overheads
		Rs.
2	1,600	33,000
1	1,200	31,000
Difference	400	2,000

Variable cost per unit = Rs. 2,000 ÷ 400 = Rs. 5.00 per unit

(ii) **Calculation of Fixed Overheads**

	Total overheads for 1,200 units	Rs. 31,000
Less :	Variable cost @ Rs. 5 per unit	Rs. 6,000
	Fixed Costs	Rs. 25,000

(iii) **Cost Sheet for 2,000 Units**

	Total Cost	***Cost/Unit***
	Rs.	Rs.
Direct Materials Rs. $\frac{9,000}{1,200} \times 2,000$	15,000	7.50
Direct Labour (Rs. 3,600 ÷ 1,200 × 2,000)	6,000	3.00
Variable Overheads @ Rs. 5.00	10,000	5.00
Fixed overheads	25,000	12.50
	56,000	28.00
Add : Profit @ 20% on Selling price i.e. $\frac{1}{4}$th on cost or 25% on cost	14,000	7.00
	70,000	35.00

Sale price per unit is Rs. 35.00

Problem 51

The books of Adarsh Manufacturing Company present the following data for the month of April 1992 :

Direct labour cost Rs. 17,500, being 175% of works overheads.

Cost of goods sold excluding administrative expenses Rs. 56,000.

Inventory accounts showed the following opening and closing balances :

	April 1	April 30
	Rs.	Rs.
Raw Materials	8,000	10,600
Works-in-process	10,500	14,500
Finished goods	17,600	19,000

Other data are :

	Rs.
Selling expenses	3,500
General and administrative expenses	2,500
Sales for the month	75,000

You are required to :

(i) Compute the value of materials purchased.

(ii) Prepare a cost statement showing the various elements of cost and also the profit earned.

[Adapted C.A. (Inter) May 1992]

Solution

(i) **COMPUTATION OF THE VALUE OF MATERIALS PURCHASED**

		Rs.
	Cost of goods sold (given)	56,000
Add :	Closing stock of Finished goods	19,000
		75,000
Less :	Opening Stock of Finished goods	17,600
		57,400
Add :	Closing Stock of work-in-progress	14,500
		71,900
Less :	Opening stock of work-in-progress	10,500
		61,400
Less :	Factory Overheads (17,500 × 100 ÷ 175)	10,000
	Works Cost	51,400
Less :	Direct labour (175% of works overhead)	17,500
	Raw Materials Consumed	33,900
Add :	Closing stock of raw materials	10,600
		44,500
Less :	Opening Stock of Raw Materials	8,000
	Raw Materials Purchased	36,500

(ii) **STATEMENT SHOWING ELEMENTS OF COSTS**

		Rs.	Rs.
	Raw Materials Consumed (as per note above)		33,900
Add :	Direct labour cost		17,500
	Prime Cost		51,400
	Factory Overheads		10,000
	Works Cost		61,400
Add :	Opening work-in-progress		10,500
			71,900
Less :	Closing work-in-progress		14,500
			57,400
Add :	Opening Stock of Finished goods		17,600
			75,000
Less :	Closing Stock of Finished goods		19,000
	Cost of goods sold		56,000
Add :	General and Administration expenses	2,500	
	Selling expenses	3,500	6,000
			62,000
Add :	Profit (Balancing figure)		13,000
	Sale Price (Given)		75,000

ASSIGNMENT

Theoretical Questions

1. What are the elements of Cost?
2. What is Prime Cost? How is it ascertained?
3. What is Cost Sheet? What are its objectives?
4. Explain the items (i) Direct expenditure and (ii) Indirect expenditure and state the elements of cost comprised in each.

[C.U. B.Com. (Hons.)]

5. You are required to state why is it important to distinguish between 'fixed' and 'variable' expenses in Cost Accounting and give two examples of each type of expense.

[C.U. B.Com. (Hons.)]

6. Explain the distinction between direct and indirect expenditure giving suitable illustrations. When the 'Works Costs' has been determined, what are the further elements to be added thereto to determine the 'Cost of Sales' ?.

[C.U. B.Com. (Hons.)]

7. Name and explain the elements of cost in detail.

[C.U. B.Com.(Hons.) 1994]

8. (a) Classify costs according to element and function and give three examples of each.
   (b) 'Direct Costs and controllable are not necessarily the same'—Discuss.

[C.U. B.Com.(Hons.) 1995]

9. (a) Distinguish between Direct Cost and Indirect Cost.
   (b) Fixed Cost and Variable Cost.

[C.U. B.Com.(Hons.) 1997]

Practical Problems

1. From the following particulars of a manufacturing firm prepare a statement showing :
   (a) Cost of materials used ;
   (b) Works cost ;
   (c) Cost of Production ;
   (d) Percentage of works overheads to works cost

	Rs.
Stock of materials on 1st January 1985	40,000
Purchase of raw materials in January 1985	11,00,000
Stock of finished goods on 1st January 1985	50,000
Productive wages	5,00,000
Finished goods sold	24,00,000
Works overhead charges	1,50,000
Office and general expenses	1,00,000
Stock of materials on 31st January 1985	1,40,000
Stock of finished goods on 31st January 1985	60,000

[B.Com. Punjab, 1976]

Ans : (a) Rs. 10,00,000, (b) Rs. 16,50,000, (c) Rs. 17,50,000, 0.09 per cent.

2. From the following particulars prepare a cost sheet for the month of January 1996 :

	Rs.
Stock on 1.1.96 :	
Raw Materials	1,200
Work-in-Progress	3,100
Finished goods	6,700
Stock on 31.1.96 :	
Raw Materials	1,500
Work-in-Progress	4,000
Finished goods	3,800
Raw Materials purchased	20,800
Carriage on purchase	600
Sale of finished goods	60,000
Direct wages	15,300
Non-productive wages	300
Chargeable expenses	700
Factory overheads	$33\frac{1}{3}$% of wages
Office overheads	2,700
Selling overheads	2,800

[Adapted—C.U. B.Com. Pass]

Ans : Total Cost: Rs.50,000, Profit: Rs.10,000, Prime Cost: Rs.37,100, W.C: Rs.41,600.

3. The following information has been obtained from the cost records of Bengal Steel Products of 1997 :

	Rs.
Stock as on 1.1.1997 :	
Finished goods	50,000
Raw Materials	10,000
Work-in-Progress	14,000
Direct Labour	1,60,000
Purchase of Raw Materials	98,000
Indirect labour	40,000
Heat, Light and Power	20,000
Factory Insurance and Taxes	5,000
Repairs to Plant	3,000
Factory supplies	3,000
Depreciation :	
Factory Building	6,000
Plant	10,000
Other information :	
Factory cost of goods produced in 1997	2,80,000
Raw Materials consumed in 1997	95,000
Cost of goods sold in 1997	1,60,000

[W.B.C.S. 1996]

Ans : Closing stock of Raw Materials Rs. 13,000; Closing stock of work-in-progress Rs. 76,000; Closing stock of finished goods Rs. 1,70,000.

4. Prepare a Cost Sheet to show the total cost of production and cost per unit of goods manufactured by a company for the month of December, 1998. Also find out the cost of sales.

	Rs.
Stock of raw materials on 1.12.98	3,000
Raw materials purchased	28,000
Stock of raw materials on 31.12.98	4,500
Manufacturing wages	7,000
Depreciation on plant	1,500
Loss on sale of part of plant	300
Factory rent and rates	3,000
Office rent	500
Discount on sales	300
Income tax paid	4,000
Provision for Bad Debt	400
General expenses	400
Discount on sale	300
Advertisement expenses	600
Transfer to Reserve	1,500

The number of units produced during December, 1998 was 3,000. The stock of finished goods was 200 and 400 units on 1.12.1998 and 31.12.98 respectively. The total cost of units in hand on 1.12.1998 was Rs. 2,800. All these have been sold during the month.

Ans. :

		Total cost
(i)	Prime cost	Rs. 33,500
(ii)	Cost of production	Rs. 38,900
(iii)	Cost of sales	Rs. 37,416

5. From the following particulars prepare a cost sheet for the month of January 1998 :

	Rs.
Stock of raw materials on 1.1.1998	3,000
Purchase of raw materials	28,000
Stock of raw materials on 31.1.98	4,500
Productive wages	6,300
Depreciation	2,000
Factory rent	1,800
Materials destroyed by fire	200
Office rent	4,800
General expenses	600
Selling overhead	1,500
Number of units produced during the month 4,000 units	
Stock of finished goods on 1.1.98 2,000 units valued at	3,000
Stock of finished goods on 31.1.98 – 500 units	
Apply FIFO method.	

[Adapted—C.U. B.Com. (Pass)]

Ans : Materials consumed Rs. 26,300; Prime cost Rs. 32,600; Works cost Rs. 36,400; Cost of production Rs. 41,800; Cost of goods sold Rs. 39,575; Cost of sales Rs. 41,075.

6. The particulars of a manufacturing company are given below :

	Rs.		Rs.
Opening Stock :			
Raw Materials	30,000	Wastage of raw materials	1,500
Finished goods	40,000	Salaries	20,000
Raw materials purchased	3,00,000	Stationery for office	1,000
Productive wages	1,80,000	Stationery for factory	500
Rent, rates and taxes of factory	10,000	Depreciation on Factory assets	10,000
Lubricants	5,000	Depreciation on office equipment	4,000
Packing materials (factory)	3,000	Commission to travelling agents	13,000
Power	20,000	Depreciation on Delivery van	2,500
Factory lighting	8,000	Carriage on raw materials	1,600
Chargeable expenses	12,000		

Salaries to be apportioned between factory and office in 3 : 2.

From the above information prepare a cost sheet showing therein : (i) Prime Cost, (ii) Works Cost, (iii) Cost of production and (iv) Cost of sales.

Ans. : (i) 5,22,100, (ii) 5,90,600, (iii) 6,03,600, (iv) 6,43,600, (v) 6,59,100.

7. From the following particulars prepare a cost sheet showing the profit or loss for the year ended 31st December 1997 :

	Jan. 1.1997 Rs.		Dec. 31.1997 Rs.
Stock of raw materials	12,550		10,910
Work-in-progress	6,600		7,200
Finished Stock	13,660		14,500
Other data for the year are :			
Purchase of raw materials	2,25,500	Factory overhead	87,600
Productive wages	1,12,000	Chargeable expenses	15,200
Selling overhead	40,000	Office and Administrative overhead	34,500
Sales	5,92,250		

[C.U. B.Com. (Pass)]

Ans : (i) Prime Cost Rs. 3,54,340; (ii) Works Cost Rs. 4,41,340; (iii) Cost of Sales Rs. 5,15,000; (iv) Profit Rs. 77,250.

8. From the following particulars prepare a statement in such form as you consider most suitable for showing clearly all elements of cost :

	Rs.		Rs.
Opening stock of raw materials	25,000	Carriage on goods sold	1,500
Purchase of raw materials	70,000	Rent and rates of workshop	2,500
Raw materials returned to suppliers	2,000	Fuel, gas, water etc.	1,000
Closing stock of raw materials	18,800	Repairs to plant	600
Wages paid to :		Depreciation on machinery	1,400
Productive workers	18,000	Office expenses	1,500
Non-productive workers	2,000	Direct chargeable expenses	800
Salaries paid to office staff	5,000	Advertising	1,200
Carriage on raw materials purchased	500	Abnormal loss of materials	1,200

[N.B.U. B.Com. (Hons.)—Adapted]

Ans : Materials consumed Rs. 73,500; Prime Cost Rs. 92,300; Works Cost Rs. 99,800; Cost of production Rs. 1,06,300; Cost of sales Rs. 1,09,000.

9. From the following particulars and sales for the year ended 31st December 1985, prepare a statement of cost showing, *inter alia*, the Prime Cost, Factory Cost, Cost of Production, Cost of goods sold and total and per unit cost of sales and profit.

	As on 1.1.85	As on 31.12.85
	Rs.	Rs.
Raw Materials	16,000	19,600
Work-in-progress	12,600	4,600
Finished goods (at cost)	16,400 (3,000 units)	? (2,500 units)

Other information for the year :	Rs.
Purchase of Raw Materials	1,11,600
Sales of finished goods (40,500 units)	2,83,500
Productive wages	67,200
Office and Administrative Expenses	20,800
Selling and Distribution Expenses	0.50 paise per unit sold
Machine hours worked	8,000 hours
Machine hour rate	Rs. 2.50 per hour

Assume that sales are made on the basis of 'First In First Out' principle.

[C.U. B.Com. (Hons.) 1986]

Ans : Prime Cost Rs. 1,75,200; Works Cost Rs. 2,03,200; Cost of Production Rs. 2,24,000; Cost of goods sold Rs. 2,26,400; Cost of sales Rs. 2,46,650; Cost of sales per unit Rs. 6.09; Profit per unit Re. 0.9019 or Re. 0.91.

10. The following figures were extracted from the books of a manufacturer at 31st December 1997 :

	Rs.
Stock at 1.1.97	
Raw materials	32,000
Work-in-progress	20,000
Finished goods	48,000
Purchase of raw materials	1,10,000
Carriage Inwards	2,400
Direct wages	56,000
Supervisory wages	15,200
Rent and rates	9,200
Heating and Lighting	14,000
Office salaries	12,800
Plant and Machinery at cost	1,36,000
Sales	2,81,200
Stock at 31.12.1997	
Raw materials	40,000
Work-in-progress	38,000
Finished goods	28,800

The following information is relevant :

i) Rent and rates are to be apportioned 75% to the factory and 25% to office.

ii) Heating and lighting expenses are to be allocated 80% to the factory and 20% to office.

iii) Plant and Machinery to be depreciated at 5% on the straight line method.

You are required to prepare a detailed cost statement showing :

(a) Prime cost, (b) Works cost, (c) Cost of production, (d) Cost of goods sold and the profit.

Ans : (a) Prime Cost Rs. 1,60,400; (b) Works Cost Rs. 1,82,500; (c) Cost of Production Rs. 2,00,400; (d) Cost of goods sold Rs. 2,19,600; (e) Profit Rs. 61,600.

11. From the following particulars you are required to prepare a statement showing (a) the cost of materials used; (b) the works cost; (c) the total cost; (d) the percentage of works on cost to direct wages, and (e) the percentage of office on cost to works cost :

	Rs.
Stock of finished goods on 1.1.1987	56,000
Stock of raw materials on 1.1.87	25,600
Purchase of raw materials	5,84,000
Direct wages	3,97,600
Sales of finished goods	11,84,000
Stock of finished goods on 31.12.87	60,000
Stock of raw materials on 31.12.87	27,200
Works overhead charges	87,472
Office and general expenses	71,048

[Adapted—B.Com. C.U.]

Ans : (a) Rs. 5,82,400, (b) Rs. 10,67,472, (c) Rs. 11,34,520, (d) 37.2% and (e) 6.67%.

12. A factory produces a standard product. The following information is given to you from which you are required to prepare Cost Sheet for January 1988 :

		Rs.
Raw Materials consumed		91,000
Direct wages		29,000
Other Direct expenses		11,000
Factory Overheads	80% of direct wages	
Office Overheads	10% works cost	

Selling and distribution expenses Rs. 2 per unit sold. Units produced and sold during the month 10,000. Also find out selling price per unit on the basis that profit mark up is uniformly made to yield a profit of 20% of the selling price. There was no stock or Work-in-Progress either at the beginning or at the end of the period.

[B.Com. Delhi – Pass]

Ans : Cost of Sales Rs. 1,89.620 and Profit Rs. 47,405.

13. From the following particulars prepare a cost sheet showing cost of sales and profit :

	Rs.
Opening Stock :	
Raw Materials	25,000
Finished goods	17,000
Work-in-Progress	8,000
Closing Stock :	
Raw Materials	26,000
Finished goods	16,000
Work-in-Progress	9,000
Purchase of raw materials	30,000

Direct wages	17,000
Works Expenses	8,800
Office Expenses	3,000
Selling and Distribution expenses	4,000
Sale of finished goods	77,000
Depreciation on Plant and Machinery	8,000
Sale of Scrap	3,000

[C.U. B. Com. (Pass) 1983]

Ans : Materials consumed Rs. 29,000; Prime Cost Rs. 46,000; Works Cost Rs. 58,800; Cost of Production Rs. 61,800; Cost of goods sold Rs. 62,800; Cost of Sales Rs. 66,800; Profit Rs. 10,200.

14. A manufacturing company submits the following information on 31st March 1992 :

	Rs.	Rs.
Sale for the Year		2,75,500
Inventories at the beginning of the year :		
Materials	3,000	
Finished goods	7,000	
Work-in-Progress	4,000	
Purchase of raw materials for the year		1,10,000
Direct labour		65,000
Inventories at the end :		
Materials	4,000	
Work-in-Progress	6,000	
Finished goods	8,000	
Other expenses for the year :		
Selling expenses @ 10% of sales		

Factory Overheads @ 60% of direct labour cost. Administrative expenses @ 5% of sales.
Prepare a Statement of Cost. **[C.U. B.Com. (Hons.)]**

Ans : Prime Cost Rs. 1,74,000; Works Cost Rs. 2,11,000; Cost of Production Rs. 2,24,775; Cost of goods sold Rs. 2,23,775; Profit Rs. 24,175.

15. A company manufacturing refrigerators and the following details are furnished in respect of its factory operations for the year ended 31st December 1993 :

	Rs.	Rs.
Work-in-Process on 1st January 1993		
At Prime cost	51,000	
Manufacturing expenses	15,000	66,000
Work-in-Process on 31st December 1993		
At Prime Cost	45,000	
Manufacturing expenses	9,000	54,000
Stock of raw materials on 1st Jan. 1993		2,25,000
Purchase of raw materials		4,77,000
Direct labour		1,71,000
Stock of raw materials on 31st Dec. 1993		2,04,000
Manufacturing expenses		84,000

On the basis of the above data prepare a statement showing the Cost of Production. Also indicate separately the amount of manufacturing expenses which enter into the Cost of Production.

[B.Com. Punjab, C.U. B.Com. (Hons.)]

Ans : Cost of production Rs. 7,65,000; Manufacturing expenses Rs. 90,000.

Hint :

	Manufacturing expenses	Rs.	84,000
Add :	Manufacturing expenses included in opening stock of work-in-process	Rs.	15,000
		Rs.	99,000
Less :	Manufacturing expenses in closing balance of work-in-process	Rs.	9,000
		Rs.	90,000

16. From the following particulars prepare a statement in such form as you consider most suitable for showing clearly all elements of cost :

	Rs.
Opening stock of raw materials	25,000
Purchase of raw materials	70,000
Raw materials returned to suppliers	2,000
Closing stock of raw materials	18,800
Wages paid to productive workers	18,000
Wages paid to non-productive workers	2,000
Salaries paid to office staff	5,000
Carriage on raw materials purchased	500
Carriage on goods sold	1,500
Rent and rates of workshop	2,500
Fuel, gas and water	1,000
Repairs to plant	600
Depreciation on machinery	1,400
Office expenses	1,500
Direct chargeable expenses	800
Advertisement	1,200
Abnormal loss of raw materials	1,200
Normal loss of materials	500

[N.B.U. B.Com. (Hons.)—Adapted]

Hints : 1. Abnormal loss of materials should be deducted.

2. Normal loss – no treatment should be made since it is a part of cost and to be absorbed in cost.

Ans : Materials consumed Rs. 73,500; Work Cost Rs. 99,800; Cost of Sales Rs. 1,09,000.

17. From the following particulars prepare a statement in a manner you consider ideal, for showing clearly all the elements of cost :

	Rs.
Stock of materials on 1.1.87	2,50,000
Purchase of materials during the year 1987	7,00,000
Materials returned to Suppliers	20,000
Stock of materials as at 31.12.1987	1,88,000
Wages paid to productive workmen	1,80,000
Wages paid to non-productive workmen	20,000
Salaries paid to office staff	50,000
Carriage paid on materials purchased	5,000
Carriage paid on goods sold	15,000

Rent, rates and taxes of the works	25,000
Depreciation on machinery	14,000
Repairs to Plant and Machinery	6,000
Office stationery and other expenses	15,000
Abnormal loss of materials	12,000
Chargeable expenses	8,000
Advertising and Sales publicity	12,000

[C.U. B.Com. (Pass) 1988]

Ans : Total Cost Rs. 10,80,000; Prime Cost Rs. 9,23,000; Works Cost Rs. 9,88,000; Cost of Production Rs. 10,53,000.

18. From the information given below prepare a Cost Sheet (in the usual form) :

	Rs.
Direct Materials	50,000
Direct Wages	30,000
Direct Expenses	?
Work-in-progress (Opening)	30,000
Work-in-progress (Closing)	20,000

Other relevant information :

(a) Units sold – 10,000 units @ Rs. 20 per unit

(b) Profit made – 25% on cost

(c) Administrative overheads incurred were equal to the Selling Overheads which amounted to Re 1.00 per unit sold.

(d) Works Cost was 140% of the prime cost.

[B.U. B.Com. (Hons.)1988]

Ans : Direct expenses Rs. 20,000; Works Cost Rs. 1,40,000; Total Cost Rs. 1,60,000; Profit Rs. 40,000.

19. From the following particulars prepare a statement, in a manner you consider ideal, for showing clearly all the elements of cost :

	Rs.
Stock of Materials on 1.7.1991	3,50,000
Purchase of Materials during the period from 1.7.1991 to 31.12.1991	8,00,000
Materials returned to suppliers	50,000
Stock of Materials on 31. 12. 1991	1,90,000
Wages paid to productive workmen	1,75,000
Wages paid to non-productive workmen	50,000
Salaries paid to office staff	60,000
Carriage on materials purchased	4,000
Carriage on goods sold	12,000
Customs duty and port charges paid on imported materials	4,000
Rent, rates and taxes of the works	25,000
Depreciation on Machinery	12,000
Repairs and maintenance of machinery	8,000

Office stationery and other expenses	15,000
Chargeable expenses	8,000
Advertising and sales promotion expenses	12,000
Bank charges on imported materials	250
Abnormal loss of materials	12,000
Electricity (including Rs. 2,000 for administrative office)	5,000

[C.U. B.Com. (Pass) 1993]

Ans : P.C. Rs. 10,89,250; W.C. Rs. 11,87,250; Cost of production Rs. 12,64,250; Cost of Sales Rs. 12,88,250.

20. Inventory accounts showed these opening and closing balances :

	August 1 Rs.	August 31 Rs.
Raw Materials	8,000	8,600
Work-in-Progress	8,000	12,000
Finished Goods	14,000	18,000
Selling Expenses		3,400
General and Administrative Expenses		2,600
Sales for the month		75,000

You are required to prepare a statement showing cost of goods manufactured and sold and profit earned.

[Adapted—C.A. Inter.]

Hint : Raw Materials Consumed Rs. 32,000
Raw Materials purchased Rs. 32,600

Ans : Cost of goods sold Rs.52,600; Cost of Sales Rs.56,000; Profit Rs.19,000; Sales Rs.75,000.

21. From the following particulars prepare a Cost Sheet showing (a) Cost per unit, (b) Profit for the period in April 1992.

	Rs.
Raw material consumed	15,000
Direct labour	9,000
Machine Hours worked	900 hours.
Machine Hour Rate	Rs. 5
Administrative overheads	20% on works cost
Selling Overheads	0.50 per unit
Units produced	17,100
Units sold 16,000 @ Rs. 4 per unit	

[Mysore B.Com. Part II 1990]

Ans : Prime Cost Rs. 24,000; Works Cost Rs. 28,500; Cost of Production (Rs. 2 per unit) Rs. 34,200; Cost of Sales (Rs. 2.50 per unit) Rs. 40,000; Profit Rs. 24,000;

22. From the following particulars prepare a cost sheet showing the profit or loss for the year ended 31.12.1984 :

	Jan 1, 1984 Rs.	December 31, 1984 Rs.
Stock of raw materials	12,550	10,910
Work-in-process	6,600	7,200
Finished stock	13,660	14,500

Other data for the year are :

Purchase of raw materials	2,25,500
Productive wages	1,12,000
Selling overheads	40,000
Sales	5,92,250
Factory overheads	87,600
Chargeable expenses	15,200
Office and administrative overheads	34,500

[C.U. B.Com. (Pass) 1985]

Ans : Prime Cost Rs. 3,54,340; Works Cost Rs. 4,41,340; Cost of Production Rs. 4,75,840; Cost of Sales Rs. 5,15,000; Profit Rs. 77,250.

23. From the following particulars prepare a Cost Sheet for the month of January, 1986 :

	Rs.
Stock of raw materials on 1.1.86	3,000
Purchase of raw materials	28,000
Stock of raw materials on 31.1.1986	4.500
Productive wages	6,300
Depreciation	2,000
Factory rent	1,800
Materials destroyed on fire	200
Office rent	4,800
General expenses	600
Selling Overhead	1,500

Number of units produced during the month 4,000.

Stock of finished goods on 1.1.86 2,000 units valued at Rs.3,000

Stock of finished goods on 31.1.1986 – 500 units

Apply FIFO method.

[C.U. B.Com. (Pass) 1986]

Ans : Materials Consumed Rs. 26,300; Prime Cost Rs. 32,600; Works Cost Rs. 36,400; Cost of Production Rs. 41,800; Cost of Sales Rs. 41,075.

24. From the following particulars of a manufacturing firm prepare a statement showing : (a) Cost of materials used, (b) Prime Cost, (c) Works Cost, (d) Cost of Production, (e) Percentage at works overheads to productive wages, (f) Percentage of general overheads to works cost.

	Rs.
Stock of materials on 1.1.1993	40,000
Purchase of raw materials	11,00,000
Stock of finished goods on 1.1.1992	50,000
Productive wages	5,00,000
Finished goods sold	24,00,000
Cost of goods sold	17,40,000
Works overhead charges	1,50,000
Stock of raw materials on 31.1.1993	1,40,000
Stock of finished goods on 31.1.1993	60,000

[Adapted—I.C.S.I.(Inter)]

Hint : Office and Administrative Overheads Rs. 1,00,000.

Ans : (a) Materials used Rs.10,00,000; (b) Prime Cost Rs.15,00,000; (c) Works Cost Rs.16,50,000; (d) Cost of Production Rs.17,50,000; (e) 30%; (f) 6.06%.

25. Work out in Cost Sheet the unit cost of production per ton of special paper, manufactured by a Paper Mill in December, 1991 from the following data :

Direct Materials :

Paper pulp – 500 tons @ Rs. 50 per ton

Other materials 100 tons @ Rs. 30 per ton

Direct Labour :

80 skilled men @ Rs. 3 per day for 25 days

40 unskilled men @ Rs. 2 per day for 25 days

Direct Expenses :

Special Equipment	Rs. 3,000
Special Dyes	Rs. 1,000

Works Overhead :

Variable @ 100% and

Fixed @ 60% on Direct Wages

Administration Overhead @ 10% and Selling and Distribution Overhead @ 15% on Work Cost.

400 tons of special paper was manufactured and Rs. 800 was realised by the sale of waste material during the course of manufacture. The Scrap Value of special equipment after utilisation is nil.

[Adapted—C.A. (Inter.)]

Ans : Total Cost – Rs. 65,000; Cost per unit i.e. per ton – Rs. 162.50.

26. A company manufactures two products A and B. During a month 500 units of product A and 400 units of product B have been manufactured. The total expenses incurred in the said month had been as follows :

	Rs.	
Materials	3,00,000	
Wages (Direct)	20,000	
Stores Overhead	30,000	
Machinery Maintenance	9,000	
Depreciation	4,500	
Workmen welfare expenses	2,300	
General works expenses	20,000	(to be charged as a % of direct wages)

Administration and selling expenses 20,500. (to be charged as a % of works cost).

Other data available are :

	A		B
Material cost ratio per unit	2	:	5
Direct labour cost ratio	2	:	3
Machine utilisation ratio	3	:	5

Calculate cost per unit of each product.

[C.U. B.Com. (Pass) 1992]

Ans : A Rs. 284.37 (Approx.); B Rs. 660.28 (Approx.).

27. A company makes two distinct types of electronic toys x and y. The total expenses during a period as shown by the books for assembly of 600 of x and 800 of y are as under :

	Rs.		Rs.
Materials	1,98,000	Depreciation	2,200
Direct wages	12,000	Labour amenities	1,500
Stores overhead	19,800	Works general	30,000
Running expenses of machines	4,400	Administration and Selling	26,800

Other data available to you are :	x		y
Material cost ratio per unit	1	:	2
Direct labour ratio per unit	2	:	3
Machine utilisation ratio per unit	1	:	2

Calculate the cost of each type of toy per unit giving reasons for the basis of apportionment of expenses adopted by you.

[C.U. B.Com. (Hons.) 1995]

Ans : Type x Rs. 138.805 per unit, Type y Rs. 264.271 per unit.

28. The following figures are extracted from the books of Fashions Ltd. for the year ended 30.9.1987. Prepare a cost sheet showing the cost per unit under various elements, and also profit or loss per unit.

		Rs.
Direct Materials		24,00,000
Direct labour		5,00,000
Depreciation of factory building		15,000
Branch offices expenses		40,000
Depreciation of office building		8,000
Depreciation of staff cars		12,000
Insurance of staff cars		1,500
Insurance for office building		1,200
Insurance for factory building		1,500
Delivery van maintenance and running expenses		10,000
Salaries including :		3,00,000
Sales Manager	Rs. 25,000	
Factory Chief Engineer	Rs. 25,000	
Finished goods warehoue expenses		20,000
Electricity (including Rs. 4,000 for administrative office)		40,000
Advertisement		20,000
Sundry factory expenses		3,40,000
Sales promotion		5,000
Office and administration expenses		50,000
Expenses for participating in industrial exhibition		10,000
Sales		42,00,000
Units produced	10,000	

[I.C.W.A. (Inter)]

Ans : Prime Cost Rs. 29,00,000; Factory Cost Rs. 33,17,500; Total Cost Rs. 37,74,200; Profit Rs. 4,25,800.

29. In a factory two, types of radio sets are manufactured, viz. King and Queen models. From the following particulars prepare a statement showing cost and profit per unit sold. There is no opening and closing stock :

	King	Queen
	Rs.	Rs.
Materials	27,300	1,08,680
Labour	15,600	62,920

Works overhead is charged at 70% on labour and office overhead is taken at 20% on Works Cost. The selling price of a King set is Rs. 1,000 while that of a Queen set is Rs. 500. 78King radio sets and 572 Queen radio sets were sold. Selling expenses were Rs. 5 per set.

[B.Com. Punjab]

Ans : Profit : King Rs. 13,026, Queen Rs. 24,367.20.

30. The following figures are extracted from the books of Fancy Ltd. for the year ended 30.9.1988. Prepare a cost sheet showing the cost under various elements.

	Rs.	Rs.
Direct materials		20,00,000
Direct labour		3,00,000
Depreciation of factory building		10,000
Branch office expenses		40,000
Depreciation of office building		6,000
Depreciation of staff cars		12,000
Insurance for office building		1,200
Insurance for factory building		1,500
Delivery van maintenance and running expenses		10,000
Salaries including		3,00,000
Sales Manager	20,000	
Factory Chief Engineer	25,000	
Finished goods warehouse expenses		15,000
Electricity (including Rs. 4,000 for administrative office)		40,000

Ans : Total Cost Rs. 27,35,700.

31. The following data relate to the manufacture of a standard product during the four weeks to July 31st, 1989 :

	Rs.
Raw materials consumed	2,000
Direct wages	1,200
Machine hours worked	950
Office overhead	10% on Works Cost
Selling overhead	0.06 P. per unit
Machine hour rate	Re. 0.20
Units produced	20,000
Units sold	18,000 @ 0.30 P. per unit

You are required to prepare a Cost Sheet in respect of the above showing (a) Cost per unit, (b) Profit for the period.

[C.U. B.Com. (Hons.) Old]

Ans : (a) 0.1865, (b) Rs. 963.90.

32. From the following cost data prepare a cost sheet of Maa Sarada Engineering Company for the year ended 31st March 1994 :

	Rs.
Opening Stock as on 1.4.1993 :	
Raw Materials	1,00,000
Finished goods	4,00,000
Work-in-process	40,000
Purchase of raw materials	8,00,000
Raw Materials returned to suppliers	50,000
Raw Materials stolen	10,000
Insurance claim recovered against raw materials stolen	4,000
Normal loss of raw materials	5,000
Direct wages	6,00,000
Indirect wages 20% of direct wages :	
Depreciation on plant and machinery	30,000
Office and Administration overhead 50% of works cost	
Selling and distribution overhead 20% of cost of production	

If all the units have been sold at a profit of 20% on sales, find out also the sale price.

Additional information :

	Rs.
Stock as on 31. 3. 1994 :	
Raw Materials	50,000
Work-in-progress	30,000
Finished goods	2,00,000

Hint : Materials consumed : Rs. 7,90,000. No treatment for normal loss of materials is to be made. The total amount of Rs. 10,000 for materials stolen should be deducted since it is an abnormal loss. The balance of Rs. 6,000 (Rs. 10,000 – 4,000) to be debited to costing P & L A/c.

Ans : Prime Cost Rs. 13,90,000; Works Cost Rs. 15,50,000; Cost of Production Rs. 23,25,000; Total Cost Rs. 29,90,000.

33. From the following information prepare a cost sheet showing (a) the value of materials consumed, (b) the cost of production, (c) the cost of sales.

	Rs.
Purchase of raw materials	2,64,000
Direct wages	2,20,000
Carriage Inwards	3,168
Work on cost	88,000
Stock on 1.1.89 :	
Raw Materials	44,000
Work-in-Progress	10,500
Finished goods (1,600 tons)	35,200
Stock on 31.12.89	
Raw Materials	48,928
Work-in-Progress	35,200
Finished goods (3,200)	70,400
Sales	6,60,000
Office on cost	17,600

Selling expenses amount to 0.75 paisa per ton, 25,600 tons were produced during the year.

[Audit & Accounts Serv. Exam. 1982.]

Ans : (a) Rs. 2,62,240, (b) Rs. 5,63,140, (c) Rs. 5,45,940.

34. From the following particulars prepare a cost statement showing the component of total cost and profit for the year ended 31st December 1998 :

	On 1st Jan.		On 31st Dec.
	Rs.		Rs.
Stock of finished goods	6,000		15,000
Stock of raw materials	40,000		50,000
Work-in-progress	15,000		10,000
Dividend	1,000	Income tax	500
Parchase of raw materials	4,75,000	Debenture Interest	5,000
Carriage Inward	12,500	Transfer to Sinking Fund for	
Wages	1,75,000	replacement of machinery	10,000
Work Manager's salary	30,000	Payment of sales tax	16,000
Factory Employees' salary	60,000	Goodwill written-off	10,000
Factory rent, taxes and insurance	7,250		
Power Expenses	9,500		
Other Production Expenses	43,000		
General Expenses	32,500		
Sales for the year	8,60,000		

[Andhra U. B.Com.]

Ans. : (i) Prime Cost Rs. 6,52,500; (ii) Works Cost Rs. 8,07,250; (iii) Cost of goods sold Rs. 8,30,750; (iv) Profit Rs. 29,250.

35. M/s M. T. Shoe Co. manufactures two types of shoes A and B. Production costs for the year ended 31st March 1991 were as follows :

	Rs.
Direct Materials	7,50,000
Direct wages	4,20,000
Production Overheads	1,80,000
	13,50,000

It is ascertained that :

(a) Direct material in type A shoes consists twice as much as that in type B shoes.

(b) The direct wages for B type shoes were 60% of those for type A shoes.

(c) Production overhead was the same per pair of A & B type.

(d) Administrative overhead for each type was 150% of wages.

(e) Selling cost was Rs. 1.50 per pair.

(f) Production during the year were as follows :
type A – 40,000 pairs and type B – 1,20,000.

(g) Units sold during the year :
type A – 36,000 and type B – 1,00,000 units.

(h) type A was sold at a profit of 25% on sales and type B was sold at a profit of 10% on cost.

Prepare a cost sheet showing :

(a) Total cost

(b) Total sale price.

Ans : (a) Type A Rs. 7,02,000, Type B Rs. 12,00,000; (b) Total Sales : A Rs. 9,36,000; B Rs. 13,20,000.

36. The Modern Manufacturing Company submits the following information on the 31st May 1989.

	Rs.	Rs.
Analysis and Classifiction of Cost :		
Sales for the year		2,75,000
Inventories at the beginning of the year :		
Finished goods	7,000	
Work-in-progress	4,000	
Purchase of materials for the year	1,10,000	
Material inventory at the beginning of the year– Rs. 3,000 and at the end of the year – Rs. 4,000.		
Direct Labour	65,000	
Factory Overhead was 60% of the direct labour cost.		
Inventories at the end of the year :		
Work-in-progress	6,000	
Finished goods	8,000	
Other expenses for the year :		
Selling expenses	10% of sales	
Administrative expenses	5% of sales	

Prepare a statement of cost.

[C.A. – Inter.]

Ans : Cost of production Rs. 2,24,750, Profit Rs. 43,750.

37. From the following figures you are required to prepare a cost sheet for the quarter ended 31st March 1996, assuming stock of finished goods at the end of the period to be valued at cost, showing :

Analysis and classification of cost :

(a) Value of material consumed, (b) Cost of production, (c) Cost of goods sold, (d) Net profit for the period.

	Rs.
Work-in-progress on 31.3.96	34,500
Raw Materials on 1.1.96	1,00,000
Raw materials on 31.3.96	1,23,500
Finished goods on 1.1.96	71,500
Finished goods on 31.3.96	42,000
Work-in-progress on 1.1.96	31,000
Purchase of Raw Materials	88,000
Wages – Direct	70,000
Wages – Indirect	2,500
Work charges	37,000
Administration expenses	13,000
Selling expenses	15,000
Sales	2,90,000

Ans : (a) Rs. 64,500, (b) 1,83,500, (c) Rs. 2,13,000, (d) Rs. 62,000.

38. From the understated particulars you are required to prepare a monthly cost sheet of Plastic Toy Manufacturers Ltd., showing cost and profit per 1,000 toys. Show also, in the form of a summary, the Cost of Sales, Net Profit, and Sales for the month. The company manufactures only one type of toy. The opening stock was valued at the same price per 1,000 toys as the production for the month concerned.

Materials :	
Basic Raw Materials	1,400 tonnes at Rs. 5 per ton.
Stores	Rs. 5,000
Labour :	
Direct	Rs. 16,000
Indirect	Rs. 3,000
On Cost :	
Works	25% of direct labour
Office	10% of work total cost.

Production for the month was 10 lakh toys. Sales for the month was 9 lakh toys @ Rs. 50 per 1,000.

Stock in the beginning was 2 lakh toys. Stock at the close was 3 lakh toys.

Ans : Cost of sales Rs. 34,650; Sales Rs. 45,000; Profit Rs. 10,350.

39. A manufacturing company submits the following information on 31st March 1995 :

	Rs.	Rs.
Sales for the year		2,75,000
Inventories at the beginning of the year :		
Materials	3,000	
Finished goods	7,000	
Work-in-progress	4,000	
Purchase of Raw Materials for the year	1,10,000	
Direct Labour	65,000	
Inventories at the end of the year :		
Materials	4,000	
Work-in-progress	6,000	
Finished goods	8,000	
Other expenses for the year:		
Selling Expenses @ 10% of Sales		
Factory Overhead @ 60% of Direct Labour cost		
Administrative Expenses @ 5% of Sales		

Prepare statement of cost.

[Calcutta, B.Com.]

Ans : Prime Cost Rs. 1,74,000, Cost of Production Rs. 2,24,750, Cost of Sales Rs. 2,51,250.

40. From the following particulars relating to production and sales for the year ended 31st December 1994, prepare Statements of Production Cost and Cost of Goods sold showing, inter alia, the Prime Cost and the cost per unit. Also prepare the Costing Profit and Loss Account.

	Rs.	
Raw Materials as on 1.1.94	25,000	
Work-in-progress as on 1.1.94	36,000	
Finished Goods as on 1.1.94 (8,000 units)	1,44,000	(at cost)
Raw Materials purchased	2,00,000	
Factory Wages	2,70,000	
Factory Expenses	90,000	
Administration Expenses	54,000	
Selling Expenses	36,000	
Distribution Expenses	36,000	
Sales proceeds of finished goods (30,000 units)	9,00,000	
Raw materials as on 31.12.94	45,000	
Work-in-progress as on 31.12.94	54,000	
Finished goods as on 31.12.94 (10,000 units)	at cost	

[Calcutta, B.Com.]

Ans : Prime Cost Rs. 4,50,000, Works Cost Rs. 5,22,000, Cost of Production Rs. 5,76,000, Cost of Sales Rs. 6,48,000, Profit Rs. 2,52,000.

41. From the following particulars prepare a cost sheet for the month of January 1994 :

	Rs.	
Stock on 1.1.84		
Raw Materials	1,200	
Work-in-Progress	3,100	
Finished Goods	6,700	
Stock on 31.12.84		
Raw Materials	1,500	
Work-in-Progress	4,000	
Finished Goods	3,800	
Raw Materials purchased	20,800	
Carriage on purchase	600	
Sale of finished goods	60,000	
Direct wages	15,300	
Non-productive Wages	300	
Chargeable expenses	700	
Factory Overhead	$33\frac{1}{3}\%$	of wages
Office Overhead	2,700	
Selling Overhead	2,800	

[Calcutta, B.Com.]

Ans : Prime Cost Rs. 37,100, Works Cost Rs. 41,600, Cost of Sales Rs. 50,000.

42. The following data have been extracted from the books of M/s Moonshine Industries Ltd. for the calendar year 1992 :

		Rs.
Opening Stock of Raw Materials		25,000
Purchase of Raw Materials		85,000
Closing Stock of Raw Materials		40,000
Carriage Inward		5,000
Wages – Direct		75,000
– Indirect		10,000
Other Direct Charges		15,000
Rent and Rates	– Factory	5,000
	– Office	500
Indirect consumption of materials		500
Depreciation	– Plant	1,500
	– Office furniture	100
Salary	– Office	2,500
	– Salesmen	2,000
Other Factory expenses		5,700
Other Office expenses		900
Managing Director's remuneration		12,000
Other selling expenses		1,000
Travelling expenses of salesmen		1,100
Carriage and freight outward		1,000
Sales		2,50,000
Advance Income-Tax paid		15,000
Advertisement		2,000

The Managing Director's remuneration is to be allocated Rs. 4,000 to factory, Rs. 2,000 to office and Rs. 6,000 to selling department.

From the above information prepare Cost Sheet showing : (a) Prime Cost, (b) Works Cost, (c) Cost of Production, (d) Cost of Sales (e) Net Profit.

[Delhi, B.Com. (Pass)]

Ans : (a) Rs.1,65,000, (b) Rs.1,91,700, (c) Rs.1,97,700, (d) Rs.2,10,800, (e) Rs.39,200.

43. The following is the Manufacturing and Profit and Loss Account of Swastik Ltd. for the year ended 30th June 1992 :

	Rs.	Rs.		Rs.	Rs.
To Opening Stock			By Sales		5,00,000
Materials	2,000		" Closing Stock		
Finished goods	3,000	5,000	Materials	18,500	
" Purchase of Materials		1,50,000	Finished good	3,000	21,500
" Direct Wages		1,20,000			
" Power		15,500			
" Carriage on Materials		2,000			
" Royalty		24,000			
" Cost of special design		5,000			
" Gross Profit		2,00,000			
		5,21,500			5,21,500

	Rs.	Rs.		Rs.	Rs.
To Rent and rates					
Office	5,000		By Gross Profit		2,00,000
Factory	7,000	12,000	" Interest on loan		4,550
To Telephone		3,000	" Sale of Scrap		750
" Avertisement		7,500	(at works cost)		
" Electricity Office	3,000		" Discount received		1,700
" Factory	4,500	7,500			
" Provision for Bad Debts		10,000			
" Depreciation on :					
Plant and Machinery	6,000				
" On Delivery Vans	2,000	8,000			
" Income-Tax		12,000			
" Salaries		25,000			
" Donations		7,000			
" Establishment Expenses		10,000			
" Depreciation of Furniture :					
Office	2,500				
Factory	2,000	4,500			
" Rent of warehouse		6,500			
" Net Profit		94,000			
		2,07,000			2,07,000

You are required to prepare a statement showing classification of costs under different components from the above information after giving due consideration to the following facts:

(1) 60% of telephone expenses relate to office and 40% to sales department.

(2) 25% of salaries relate to factory, 50% to office, 25% to sales departments and

(3) 50% of the establishment expenses relate to office and 50% to sales department.

[Raj University – B.Com.]

Hints : Donation, Discount Received, Income-Tax, Interest on Loan, Provision for Doubtful Debts will not be treated in Cost sheet as these are financial items.

Ans : Prime Cost Rs. 2,84,500; Works Cost Rs. 3,25,000; Cost of Production Rs. 3,51,800; Cost of goods sold Rs. 3,54,800; Profit Rs. 1,16,750.

44. A firm has purchased a plant to manufacture a new product, the cost data for which is given below :

Estimated Annual Sales	24,000	units
Estimated costs :	Rs.	
Materials	4.00	per unit
Direct labour	0.60	per unit
Overheads	24,000	Per year
Administrative Expenses	28,800	" "
Selling expenses	15% of sales.	

Calculate the selling price of profit per unit is Rs. 1.02.

[I.C.W.A. (Inter.) Dec. 1990]

Ans. : Sale price per unit Rs. 9.20

ESTIMATED COST SHEET

45. The following data are available for 1989 :

Production 50,000 units	Rs.
Materials consumed	75,000
Direct Wages	50,000
Variable production overhead	1,00,000
Variable selling overhead	2,00,000
Fixed Expenses	75,000
Selling price per unit	12

It is expected that in 1990 :

(i) Production will be 1,00,000 units

(ii) Prices of materials will go up by $33\frac{1}{3}\%$

(iii) Variable selling overhead and fixed expenses will rise by 25% and Rs. 25,000, respectively.

What would be the cost per unit and selling price in 1990, if it is desired to maintain the same rate of profit on sales as in 1989 ?

[Adapted—C.U. B.Com. – Pass, 1984]

Ans : Cost per unit in 1990 – Rs. 11.00, Selling price – Rs. 13.20 per unit.

46. Following are the particulars for the production of 2,000 sewing machines of Modern Engineering Co. Ltd. for the year 1992.

	Rs.
Cost of Materials	1,60,000
Wages	2,40,000
Manufacturing Expenses	1,00,000
Salaries	1,20,000
Rent, Rates and Insurance	20,000
Selling Expenses	60,000
General Expenses	40,000
Sales	8,00,000

The company plans to manufacture 3,000 sewing machines during 1993. You are required to submit a statement showing the price at which machines would be sold, so as to show a profit of 10% on selling price. The following additional information is supplied to you :

(a) Price of materials is expected to rise by 20%, (b) Wages rates are expected to show an increase of 5%, (c) Manufacturing expenses will rise in proportion to the combined cost of material and wages, (d) Selling expenses per unit will remain the same, (e) Other expenses will remain unaffected by the rise in output.

[Maharaja Manindra Chandra College – Test Exam. – 1987]

Ans : Profit Rs. 1,22,500.

47. An electric computer manufacturer desired to quote for a contract for the supply of 5,000 computers on 31st July 1990. From the following data prepare statement showing the price to be quoted to give the same percentage of net profit on turnover as was realised during the six months to 30th June 1990 :

	Rs.
Stock of Raw Materials on 1st January 1990	50,000
Stock of Raw Materials 30th June 1990	7,000
Purchase of Raw Materials (six months)	75,000
Factory Wages	1,50,000
Indirect Charges	25,000
Sales	2,70,000
Finished Stock on 1st January 1990	Nil
Finished Stock on 30th June 1990	50,000

The number of computers manufactured during six months was 2,000, including those sold and those in stock at the close of the period. The computers to be quoted for are of uniform size and quality and are similar to those manufactured during the six month period. As from 1st July 1990, the cost of factory labour increased by 10% and that of material by 15%.

[Adapted M.Com. – Agra]

Hint : Profit on Sale – 10%. Indirect charges have been taken as a percentage of Direct Wages.

Ans : The Tender price Rs. 1,44,756 (Approx.)

48. Bharat Electronics Ltd. furnishes the following information for 10,000 TV valves manufactured during the year 1992 :

	Rs.
Materials	90,000
Direct Wages	60,000
Power and Consumable Stores	12,000
Factory Indirect Wages	15,000
Lighting of Factory	5,500
Defective work (Cost of Rectification)	3,000
Clerical Salaries and Management Expenses	33,500
Selling Expenses	5,500
Sale Proceeds of Scraps	2,000
Plant Repairs and Maintenance and Depreciation	11,500

The net selling price was Rs. 31.60 per unit sold and all the units were sold.

As from 1st January 1993, the selling price was reduced to Rs. 31.00 per unit. It was estimated that production could be increased in 1993 by 50% due to spare capacity. Rates for Materials and Direct Wages will increase by 10%.

You are required to prepare :

(a) Cost Sheet for the year, 1992, showing various elements of cost unit, and,

(b) Estimated cost and profit for 1993 assuming that 15,000 units will be produced and sold during the year and factory overheads will be recovered as a percentage of Direct Wages and Office and Selling expenses as a percentage of Works Cost.

[C.A. – Inter]

Ans : (a) Prime Cost Rs. 15.00, Cost of Sales Rs. 23.40, (b) Cost of sales Rs. 3,86,100, Profit Rs. 78,900.]

49. The following figures relate to the costing of a manufacture of electric fans (of uniform size and quality) for a period of 3 months :

	Rs.
Complete Stock 1.10.89	Nil
Complete Stock on 31.12.89	20,250
Stock of Raw Materials on 1.10.89	5,000
Stock of Raw Materials on 31.12.89	3,500
Factory Wages	75,000
Indirect Wages	12,500
Materials purchased	32,500
Sales	1,12,500

The number of fans manufactured during the three months was 3,000.

Prepare a statement showing the cost per fan and the price to be quoted for 750 fans to realise the same percentage of profit as realised during the three months referred to above, assuming identical costs.

Ans : Cost of Sales Rs. 1,01,250, Price to be quoted Rs. 33,750.

50. The following particulars are available for the previous year's production of fans for M/s Eastern Engineering Co. :

		Rs.
(i)	Total production	1,000 units
(ii)	Total cost of raw materials Consumed	Rs. 12,000
(iii)	Total cost of direct labour	20,000
(iv)	Total works Overhead expenses	40,000
(v)	General Overhead expenses	36,000
(vi)	Total selling and distribution overhead expenses	16,000
(vii)	Total sale price for 800 units sold	1,12,640

On the basis of the undernoted instructions prepare a detailed price quotation per unit of fan for the current year :

(a) Cost of raw materials and direct labour are to be increased by 10% and 15% respectively over the previous year's level.

(b) Works Overheads general overhead as well as selling and distribution overheads are to be charged at the same respective percentage as in the previous year.

(c) Profit is to be estimated at the same percentage on total cost as earned in the previous year.

[C.U. B.Com. (Hons.)]

Ans. : Price to be quoted Rs. 160.71

51. The following figures are available from the books of Best Manufacturing Co. for the year ended 31.12.97 :

	Rs.
Materials :	
Stock 1.1.97	1,000
Stock on 31.12.97	2,000
Purchased during 1997	10,000
Wages	7,500
Profit for the year	6,090
Selling Overhead	5,250
Factory Overhead	4,500
Administration Overhead	4,200

(a) Prepare a Cost Sheet showing Prime cost, Cost of Production, Cost of Sales and Sales.

(b) In 1998 the factory receives an order for a job which will require materials Rs. 1,200 and wages Rs. 750. Ascertain the sale price of the job if the factory intends to earn a profit of 10% higher than the percentage of profit earned in 1989. Assume that Factory Overhead has gone up by $16\frac{2}{3}$% and Selling Overhead has gone down by 20% in 1998. Further assume that Factory Overhead is recovered as a % of the Wages and Administration and Selling Overhead as a % of Works Cost.

[Calcutta, B.Com.]

Ans : (a) Prime Cost Rs. 16,500, Works cost Rs. 21,000, Cost of Sales Rs. 30,450, and Sales Rs.36,540. (b) Rs. 4,504 (approx).

52. The accounts of the Steelways Engineering Co. Ltd. show for 1994 :

	Rs.
Materials used	1,80,000
Manual and Machine Labour wages directly chargeable	1,60,000
Works Overhead Expenditure	40,000
Establishment and General Expenses	19,000

(a) Show the works cost and total cost, the percentage that the works overhead cost bears to the Manual and Machine Labour Wages and the percentage that the Establishment and General expenses bear to the works cost.

(b) What price should the company quote to manufacture a machine which, it is estimated, will require an expenditure of Rs. 8,000, in material and Rs. 6,000 in wages, so that it will yield a profit of 25% on the total cost or 20% on selling price ?

[Calcutta, B.Com.]

Ans : (a) Rs. 3,80,000, 3,99,000, 25%; 5% and (b) Rs. 20,344.

53. The following particulars have been extracted from the accounts of Janata Motor Manufacturing Company for the year ended 31st December 1997 :

	Rs.
Opening Stock of Raw Materials	1,00,000
Purchase of Raw Materials	24,00,000
Carriage on Raw Materials	1,20,000
Wages of manual and machine labour for manufacturing motor cars	14,00,000
Works overhead expenses	3,92,000
Establishment and General Charges	2,98,340
Closing Stock of Raw Materials	1,50,000

Find out works cost and total cost of motor cars, the percentage of works overhead cost to wages and percentage of establishment and general charges to works cost.

Work out what price the company should quote for a motor car, which, it is estimated, will require an expenditure of Rs. 11,000 in raw materials and Rs. 8,000 in wages, so that it would yield profit at 25% on the total.

Ans : Works cost Rs. 42,62,000; Total Cost Rs. 45,60,340, percentage of works overhead cost to wages 28 per cent, percentage of general charges to works cost 7 per cent, price to be quoted Rs. 28,409 (Approx.).

54. The following figures have been obtained from the cost records of a Radio Manufacturing Company for the year 1991 :

	Rs		Rs.
Cost of Materials	2,40,000	Administration Expenses	1,34,400
Wages for Labour	2,00,000	Selling Expenses	89,600
Factory Overhead	1,20,000	Profit	1,68,000
Distribution Expenses	56,000		

A work order has been executed in 1992 and the expenses have been incurred – Cost of materials Rs. 32,000 and wages for labour Rs. 20,000.

Assuming that in 1992, the factory overhead went up by 20%, distribution charges went up by $12\frac{1}{2}$%. At what price should the product of the job be quoted so as to earn the same rate of profit on the selling price? Show the full working. Distribution, Administration and Selling charges are based on the Factory Cost.

[Andhra – B.Com.]

Ans : Price to be quoted Rs. 1,20,516.

55. The accounts of Steelways Engineering Co. Ltd. show for 1993 :

	Rs.
Materials used	1,80,000
Manual and machine labour wages directly chargeable	1,60,000
Work overhead expenditure	40,000
Establishment and general expenses	19,000

(a) Show that works cost and total cost, the percentage that the works overhead cost bears to the manual and machine labour wages and the percentage that the establishment and general expenses bear to the works costs.

(b) What price should the company quote to manufacture a machine which, it is estimated, will require an expenditure of Rs. 8,000 on materials and Rs. 6,000 on wages so that it will yield a profit at 25% on the total cost or 20% on selling price?

[C.U. B.Com. (Hons.)]

Hints : (a) Percentage of works overhead to manual and machine labour – 25%

(b) Percentage of establishment and general expenses to works cost – 5%.

Ans : Price to quote Rs. 20,344.

56. The Books of Accounts of the Peerless Engineering Co. show the following particulars for the year 1991 :

	Rs.
Direct Materials used	40,000
Direct Wages	60,000
Works Overhead Expenditure	50,000
Establishment and General Expenses	18,000

(a) Calculate, from the above particulars, the Works Cost and the Total Cost, the percentage that the works Overhead Expenditure bears to the direct wages and the percentage that the Establishment and General Expenses bear to the Works Cost.

(b) What price should the Company quote to manufacture a Machine ? It is estimated that Rs. 10,000 for Direct Materials and Rs. 8,000 for Direct Labour will be required. A profit of 20% on selling price is required.

[C.U. B.Com. (Pass) 1993.]

Ans : (a) Work Cost Rs. 1,50,000, Total Cost Rs. 1,68,000, 83.333%, 12% (b) Rs. 34,534 (Approx.)

57. A television manufacturing company finds that, in 1990, it cost Rs. 6,16,000 to manufacture 200 televisions which the company sold at Rs. 4,000 each. Cost was made up of :

	Rs.
Materials	2,00,000
Direct Wages	3,00,000
Factory Overhead Expenses	60,000
Office Overhead Expenses	56,000
	6,16,000

For 1991 season, the company estimates :

(a) that each television will require materials to the value of Rs. 1,000 and wages of Rs. 1,500.

(b) that the factory overhead expenses will bear the same relation to direct wages as in the previous year.

(c) the percentage of office overhead expenses on factory cost will be the same as in the previous year.

Prepare a statement showing the profit the company should make per unit if it enhances the price of the television by Rs. 80.

[Adapted—B.Com. Banaras]

Ans : Profit per unit Rs. 1,000.

58. The accounts of Eagle Engineering Co. show the following particulars for the year ended 31.12.1992 :

	Rs.
Materials Consumed	50,000
Direct Wages	70,000
Overhead Expenditure	60,000
Establishment and General Expenses	12,000

(a) Show from the above particulars the Works Cost and Total Cost, the percentage that the overhead expenditure bears to the Direct Wages, and the percentage that the Establishment and General expenses bear to the works cost.

(b) What price should the company quote to manufacture a machine ? It is estimated that Rs. 10,000 in materials and Rs. 8,000 in labour will be required on the machine. A profit of 20% on selling price is required.

[C.U. B.Com. (Pass) 1991]

Ans : (a) Works Cost — Rs. 1,80,000
Total Cost — Rs. 1,92,000
% of Work Overhead Expenditure — Rs. 85.714%
% of Establishment and General Exp. — 6.667%
(b) Rs. 26,514 to be quoted.

REVISIONAL PROBLEMS

59. From the following particulars prepare Cost Sheet showing, (a) Prime Cost; (b) Works Cost; (c) Cost of Production and (d) Cost of Sales :

	Rs.	Rs.
Raw Materials	20,000	25,000
Work-in-Progress	10,000	12,000
Finished Goods (3,000 units)	30,000	(2,000 units) ?

Other Information :

	Rs.	
Raw Materials purchased	1,00,000	
Freight on Materials purchased	10,000	
Chargeable Expenses	4,000	
Loss of Materials	2,000	
Wages (productive)	50,000	
Machine hours worked	3,000	hours
Machine hour rate	5	per hour
Selling Overhead	1	per unit
Units Sold	9,000	
Profit on sale	10%	
Office expenses	2	per unit

During the year a new order has been received for which Prime Cost was estimated at Rs. 13,000. Machine hours required 500 hours. All other expenses were in the same percentages but office expenses have gone up by 20%. Profit percentage was as before. Calculate the new cost of sales and the amount of profit.

Ans : Cost of sales Rs. 17,982, Profit Rs. 1,798.

60. The following particulars are obtained from the books of Mr. Somil for the year 1991.

Production and Sale	2,000 Units
	Rs.
Direct Materials	1,50,000
Direct Wages	80,000
Direct Expenses	20,000
Works Overheads	60,000
Office Overheads	30,000
Selling Overheads	40,000
Profit	38,000
	4,18,000

It is ascertained that 60% of the Works Overheads fluctuate directly with production and 80% of the Selling Overheads fluctuate with sales.

During 1992, it is anticipated that the production and sale will be 5,000 units. Direct wages per unit will be increased by 10%, fixed works overheads will increase by Rs. 6,000; office overheads and fixed selling overheads will increase by 20%, but otherwise no changes are anticipated.

Prepare a Cost Sheet for 1992 showing the price at which the unit will be sold so as to earn the same rate of profit on cost as in the year 1991.

[Gujrat University – B.Com.]

Ans : Total Cost in 1992 Rs.8,90,600; Profit Rs.89,060; Price per unit Rs.195.93.

61. A factory has undertaken a contract for the manufacture of 4,000 articles and the following information has been obtained :

For each article	Rs.
Material Cost	12
Direct Wages	10
Selling Price	35

The overhead charges consist of (a) Fixed Rs. 6,000; (b) Variable Rs. 3,600, and (c) Semi-variable (of which 60% is fixed) Rs. 2,400.

Calculate the profit per unit.

What would be the profit per article if the number of articles manufactured were 5,000 and the total fixed overhead charges remain unchanged ?

[Calcutta University, M.Com.]

Ans : Profit per article Rs. 10.372.

62. A factory can produce 60,000 units p.a. at its optimum (100%) capacity. Estimated cost of production is as under :

Materials	Rs. 3 per unit
Wages	Rs. 2 per unit
Overheads :	
Fixed	Rs. 1,50,000 p.a.
Variable	Rs. 5 per unit
Semi variable	Rs. 50,000 p.a. up to 50% capacity, Rs. 10,000 for every 25% increase in capacity or part thereof.

If the production programme is as follows and the factory wants to make a profit of Rs.1,00,000 for the year, determine the average sale price :

First 3 months –	50% capacity
Next 9 months –	80% capacity

[Adapted—Audit and Acct. Servs. Exam. and I.C.W.A. (Inter)]

Ans : Total Cost Rs. 6,50,000; Sale Price Rs. 7,50,000 (17.248).

63. A manufacturing company has an installed capacity of 1,20,000 units per annum. The cost structure of the products manufactured is as under :

(i) Variable Cost per unit

Materials	Rs. 8.00
Labour	Rs. 8.00
(subject to a minimum of Rs. 56,000 per month)	
Overheads	Rs. 3.00

(ii) Fixed Overheads Rs. 1,04,000 p.a.

(iii) Semi-variable Overheads Rs. 48.000 p.a. at 60% capacity which increase by Rs.6,000 p.a. for increase of every 10% of the capacity utilisation or any part thereof.

The capacity utilisation for the next year is estimated at 60% for 2 months, 75% for 6 months and 80% for remaining part of the year. If the Company is planning to have a profit of 25% on the Selling Price, calculate the estimated selling price for each unit of production. Assume that there is no Opening or Closing Stock.

[Adapted—I.C.W.A. (Inter.) June. 1990]

Hints :

(i) Production in units

60% of 10,000 × 2	=	12,000
75% of 10,000 × 6	=	45,000
80% of 10,000 × 4	=	32,000
		89,000

(ii) Estimated
Total Sales = Rs. 24,92,000.

Ans : Estimated Selling Price per unit = Rs. 28.00.

64. X & Co. manufactures two types of pens—X and Y. The cost data for the year ended 30.9.1990 is as follows :

	Rs.
Direct Materials	2,00,000
Direct Wages	1,12,000
Production Overhead	48,000
	3,60,000

It is further ascertained that :

(i) Direct materials in type X cost twice as much as direct materials in type Y.

(ii) Direct wages for type Y were 60% of those for type X.

(iii) Production Overhead was of the same rate for both types.

(iv) Administration Overhead for each was 100% of direct labour.

(v) Selling costs were 100 paise per pen for both types.

(vi) Production during the year

Type P 20,000 units

Type Q 60,000 units

(vii) Sale during the Year :

Type X 18,000

Type Y 50,000

(xi) Selling prices were Rs. 20 per pen for type X and Rs. 15 per pen for type Q.

Prepare a Statement showing per unit Cost of Production, Total Cost, Profit and also Total Sales Value separately for two types of pen X & Y.

Ans : Cost of production :	X	Rs.	8.70
	Y	Rs.	5.00
Total Cost :	X	Rs.	1,74,600
	Y	Rs.	3,00,000
Total Profit	X	Rs.	1,85,400
	Y	Rs.	4,50,000

65. A factory uses job costing system. The following cost data are available from the books for the year ended 31st March 1995 :

	Rs.
Direct Materials	9,00,000
Direct Wages	7,50,000
Profit	6,09,000
Selling and Distribution Overhead	5,25,000
Administrative Overhead	4,20,000
Factory Overhead	4,50,000

Required :

i) Prepare a Cost Sheet indicating the Prime Cost, Works Cost, Production Cost, Cost of Sales and Sales Value.

ii) In 1995-96, the factory has received an order for a number of jobs. It is estimated that the direct materials would be Rs, 12,00,000 and direct labour cost would be Rs. 7,50,000. What would be the price of these jobs if the factory intends to earn the same rate of profit on sales, assuming that the selling and distribution overhead has gone up by 15%? The factory recovers factory overhead as a percentage of direct wages and administrative and selling and distribution overheads as a percentage of works cost based on the cost rates prevalent in the previous year.

[Adapted—C.A. (Inter) Nov. 1989]

Ans : (i) (a) Prime Cost Rs.16,50,000, (b) Works Cost Rs. 21,00,000, (c) Production Cost Rs. 25,20,000, (d) Cost of sales Rs. 30,45,000, (e) Total Cost Rs. 36,54,000.

(ii) Sales value Rs. 42,84,000.

66. From the understated particulars you are required to prepare a monthly cost sheet of Plastic Toy manufacturing Ltd. showing cost and profit per 1,000 toys. Show also in the form of a summary, the cost of sales, net profit and sales for the month. The company manufacturers only one type of toy. The opening stock was valued at the same price per 1,000 toys as the production for the month concerned :

Materials :	
Basic raw materials	14,000 tonnes @ Rs. 5 per tonne
Stores	Rs. 5,000
Labour :	
Direct	Rs. 16,000
Indirect	Rs. 3,000
On cost :	
Works	25% of direct labour
Office	10% of works total cost
Production for the month (March 1999)	10,00,000 toys
Sales for the month	9,00,000 toys Rs. 50 per 1,000
Stock on 1st March, 1999	2,00,000
Stock on 31st March, 1999	3,00,000

[Adapted—C.U. M.Com]

Ans. :		Total	Per unit
	Cost of Sales	Rs. 34,650	Rs. 38.50
	Profit	Rs. 10,350	Rs. 11.50
	Sale price	Rs. 45,000	Rs. 50.00

67. Factory uses a job costing system. The following cost data are available from the books for the year ended 31st March 1989 :

	Rs.
Direct Materials	9,00,000
Direct wages	7,50,000
Profit	6,09,000
Selling and Distribution Overheads	5,25,000
Administrative Overheads	4,20,000
Factory Overhead	4,50,000

Required :

(a) Prepare a cost sheet indicating the prime cost, works cost, production cost, cost of sales and sales value.

(b) In 1989-90 the factory has received an order for a number of jobs. It is estiamted that the direct materials would be Rs. 12,00,000 and direct labour would cost Rs. 7,50,000. What would be the price for these jobs if the factory intends to earn the same rate of profit on sales, assuming that the selling and distribution overhead has gone up by 15%. The factory recovers factory overheads as a percentage of direct wages and administrative and selling and distribution overheads as a percentage of works cost, based on the cost rates prevalent in the previous year.

[C.A. Inter]

Ans. : Price for the jobs Rs. 42,84,000

68. Music India Ltd. has furnished the following information in relation to the production of 1,000 compact discs manufactured by it during the year 1998 :

		Rs.
(i)	Cost of material	1,00,000
(ii)	Direct wages paid	70,000
(iii)	Cost of power and consumable stories (20% fixed)	15,000
(iv)	Factory indirect wages paid (40% fixed)	20,000
(v)	Cost of lighting in the factory (fixed)	10,000
(vi)	Office expenses in worked (fixed)	30,000
(vii)	Selling expenses paid (70% variable)	50,000
(viii)	Depreciation of plant (under straight-line method)	10,000

The entire output were sold at Rs. 350 per unit.

For the year 1999, it is estimated that the production will be increased by 50% by utilising the spare capacity and the rates for materials and direct wages will increase by 10% and 20% respectively.

The expenses of the company are either fixed or variable and the company assumes that the nature of the expenses will not change in the coming days.

You are required to prepare :

(i) A cost sheet for the year 1998 showing the cost/unit.

(ii) A statement showing estimated cost and profit for the year 1999 assuming that all the goods produced would be sold at a price of Rs. 340/unit

[C.U. B.Com (Hons.) 1999]

[Ans. : (i) Cost/unit Rs. 305; profit Rs. 45,000; (iii) Cost/unit Rs. 307; profit Rs. 54,500]

MATERIALS 3

SECTION A

Learning Objectives

Introduction—Inventory defined—Materials defined—Material control—Purchasing of materials—Purchase routine—Purchase requisition—Bill of materials—Time of purchase—Purchase quantity—Purchase order—Purchasing proceedure.

Store Keeping

Importance of Store—Functions of a storekeeper—Organisation of Stores—Stores ledger layout—Centralised Stores—Economic Order Quantity (EOQ)—Determination of EOQ—Stock level—Minimum Level—Reorder Level—Maximum Stock Level—Materials Record—Bin Card—Stores Ledger—Difference between Stores ledger and Bin Card—Material Control procedures—Necessity of Bin card.

Inventory Systems

Perpetual Inventory Systems : Definition—Advantages—Continuous physical stock taking—Difference between perpetual inventory system and continuous stock taking—ABC analysis—Advantages of ABC Analysis—Limitations of ABC Analysis.

SECTION B

Materials—Pricing of issues and stocks

Introduction—Objectives of materials pricing—Features of pricing system—Determination of cost of incoming materials—Trade discount—Quantity discount—Cash discount—Freight and carriage—Value added tax—Containers; Methods of pricing of materials issues—First-in-first-Out—Advantages; Disadvantages; Applicability; Working out examples—Last-in-First-Out; (i) Advantages Disadvantages; (ii) Applicability—Comparison of FIFO and LIFO during inflation—Highest In-First-Out—Base Stock Price Method—Simple average method—Weighted average method—Advantages; Disadvantages—Treatment of some important items—Specimen of material transfer note—Selection of methods—Material control procedures—Worked out problems—Assignment.

MATERIALS 3

SECTION A

3.1 Introduction

In this chapter we propose to explain the essentials of materials control process. Material is an important constituent of production in a manufacturing concern. Material management is very important so far as cost of the product is concerned.

Efficient material control reduces cost as well as helps to produce better quality of goods. So, the objective of cost accounting can be better achieved through efficient and scientific inventory management.

3.2 Inventory defined

The International Accounting Standards Committee has defined inventories as "tangible property (a) held for sale in the ordinary course of business; (b) in the process of production for such sale or (c) to be consumed in the production of goods or services for sale".

A manufacturing organization holds the following types of inventory :

(i) Raw material inventory; (ii) Work-in-Progress inventory; and (iii) Finished goods inventory.

Inventory also includes components, spares, consumable stores and sundry supplies. Materials are a part of inventory.

3.3 Materials defined

Materials mean the commodities which are consumed in the process of production or of rendering service or for transformation into products.

We require iron ore, manganese, limestone, dolomite etc. for manufacturing steel. So, these items are treated as raw materials for steel. The costs of all such materials form part of the total cost of jobs, products or operations for which they are utilized.

3.4 Material Control

Definition

The American Production and Inventory Control (APIC) defines materials control as : "The function of maintaining a constantly available supply of raw materials, purchased parts and supplies that are required for the manufacture of products. Functional responsibilities include the requisitioning of materials for purchase in economic quantities at the proper time and their receipts, storage and protection, the issuing of materials to production upon authorised requests, and the maintenance and verification of inventory records."

The above definition clarifies that an efficient material control system should aim at efficient purchasing of materials, their efficient storing and efficient use and maintenance of proper records to provide material cost information for **decision making and financial reporting to the management of a business firm.**

3.5 Objectives of Material Control

A good system of material control should have the following objectives :

(i) Supply of the desired quality and quantity shall be ensured for efficient and uninterrupted production.

(ii) Materials should be purchased in economic quantities to enjoy the benefits of economic purchases.

(iii) Materials are to be properly stored to preserve quality and quantity and to avoid pilferage and obsolescence.

(iv) The investment in materials shall be maintained at lowest level to avoid unnecessary blockage of working capital.

(v) Purchase of materials must be made at the most favourable prices under the best possible terms.

(vi) Issues of materials should be properly authorised and accounted for.

(vii) Materials received should be properly inspected to test the quality of materials.

(viii) Payment should be made only when payment vouchers have been properly passed by authorised officer.

(ix) Payment should be made for those materials which have been received after proper inspection.

3.6 Its Importance

In an effective cost accounting system there must be a proper system for the control of material from the time an order is placed until the material is issued to production. Since materials represent an important asset and is the largest single item of cost in almost every manufacturing concern, the success or failure of a concern may depend largely upon efficient materials purchasing, storage, utilisation and proper accounting.

Where materials are not systematically controlled, excess stocks of some items are likely to occur as a result of which unnecessary tying up of capital and loss through obsolescence and deterioration take place. Further more, haphazard buying and lack of control of materials is bound to result in the purchase of material of too good or too poor a quality for the purpose for which it is intended. An efficient buyer makes a valuable contribution to the success of a business by ordering the right quality and quantity of material at the most favourable price and by ensuring the continuous flow of materials to the production departments.

Efficient material control cuts out losses and forms of wastes. So, incoming materials should be checked against orders to ensure that the correct quantity and quality have been received. Theft, breakage, deterioration, and the use of excessive floor space can be reduced to a minimum by proper controls. Finally, the most important thing to the cost accountant is that, it is impossible to produce reliable costing information system if the records of material issues are unsatisfactory. So, an efficient purchase officer should know **when to purchase, how much to purchase, where to purchase.**

Therefore, effective material control is very important in order to :

(i) provide better quality of goods to the customers at reasonable price by eliminating wastage and by reducing cost,

(ii) produce goods at the maximum efficiency,

(iii) manage inventories to control investment in inventories,

(iv) avoid abnormal wastage by exercising direct control,

(v) avoid over-stocking of materials by making proper planning of materials and fixation of levels well in advance. The stock should be maintained at such a level so that materials can be supplied to production departments as and when they require. It is also to be seen that working capital is not blocked unnecessarily in stock of materials.

3.7 Essentials of Materials Control

The essentials of materials control from the costing viewpoint can be summarised as follows :

(i) Materials of appropriate quality and specification should be purchased.

(ii) The suppliers of materials chosen should represent an appropriate balance between quality, price and delivery.

(iii) Materials should be properly inspected and received.

(iv) Appropriate storage facilities should be provided to preserve the quality of materials.

(v) There must exist co-ordination and co-operation between the various departments like Purchase, Inspection, Storage, Accounts and Cost.

(vi) Efficient purchase organisation.

(vii) The documentation, accounting systems and controls at each stage should be well designed and effective.

(viii) Planning of requirement of materials is to be done very carefully.

(ix) Well organised system of reporting to management regarding materials purchase, storage, utilization, returns, spoilage, defective goods, obsolete stocks and inventory balances should be introduced.

(x) Direct materials used in production should be charged to production on an appropriate and consistent pricing basis.

(xi) Stock taking must be well organised to ensure that sufficient quantities of stock on hand are available when required.

(xii) There must be efficient system of internal checks and internal audit.

Materials control consists of controls at two levels : (i) **quantity controls and** (ii) **financial controls.** The production department in a manufacturing organisation aims at quantity controls while the finance department aims at keeping the investment on materials at the lowest point. So, in materials control an equilibrium has to be maintained between the two opposite needs.

In the opinion of **A. Matz, O. J. Curry and George W. Frank**—"A basic objective of good materials control is to be able to place an order at right time from the right source to acquire the right quantity at the right price and quality".

Inefficient materials control results in loss through misuse, and waste of resources may be caused by many factors like buying the wrong articles, buying materials of inadequate quality, buying too much, buying too little. Financial loss results from materials stolen, piltered, spoilage and damage to materials before use, scrap and spoilage during use. All these lead to ineffective employment of working capital. An inadequate system of material control proves to be costly to the business firm and reduces competitiveness in the market because of high cost of the product.

3.8 Advantages of Material Control

The following are the advantages of material control :

(i) efficient material control eleminates wastages in course of purchases, storage handling and production;

(ii) it ensures continuous flow of materials for use in production;

(iii) it also facilitates preparation of accurate monthly, or periodical statement required for management information;

(iv) reduces to the minimum the working capital locked up in various inventories;

(v) reduces the risk of fraud and theft;

(vi) provides for accountability on the part of those who are involved in the process of material management.

3.9 Materials Planning

Materials planning is a scientific way of determining the requirements of raw materials, components, spares and other items. Materials budgets are prepared on the basis of Sales Budget to ascertain the total requirements of different types of materials for a particular period of time. In doing so, the following decisions are required to be taken :

(a) Whether to adopt centralised purchases and storage or to decentralise them;

(b) How materials should be codified and standardised;

(c) Fixation of different levels of stocks; like maximum, minimum and re-ordering levels of stock.

(d) Investment policies.

3.10 Organisation of Material Control

Various departments like Purchasing department, Receiving and Inspection department, Stores, Production departments of a manufacturing concern are invloved in material control. The co-operation of the above departments is imperative to make the material control effective. Each department discharges its own functions. Their functions are integrated to achieve some objectives like better accountability, better co-ordination, better performance and better environment for growth. In short, an integrated materials management aims at bringing together conflicting and yet interrelated-functions such as materials planning, purchasing, receiving, inspection, stores, inventory control, scrap and surplus disposal etc.

For better understanding a chart is given below :

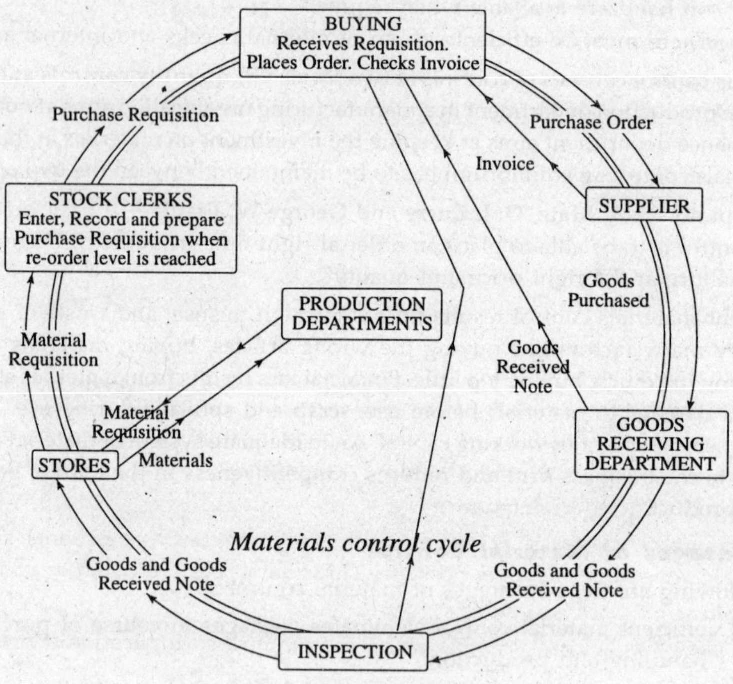

Fig. 3.1 : Materials control cycle

3.11 Purchasing of Materials

In a manufacturing concern there is a separate purchase department under the control of purchasing officer. The main functions of purchase department are to purchase required quantity of materials in time so that the store can feed the production departments with the continuous supply of materials, to purchase better quality of materials at reasonable price. The purchase officer has to play an important role since much money can be saved or lost by him. He requires a good technical knowledge of the industry and a large measure of administrative ability. He should also be aware of the policy of the management and the financial resources of the concern. He should also be aware of the market conditions and must have the knowledge of the sources of supply, reliable suppliers, price and purchasing formalities. He must keep himself abreast of the government policies regarding import and export restrictions and various duties and taxes on commodities. He must have a working knowledge of laws relating to contracts and sale of goods, so that he can negotiate and enter into contract on behalf of his employer.

3.12 Centralised and Decentralised Purchase

Centralised buying means purchase of materials by one specialised department. The purchase department is manned by personnel having specialised knowledge in respect of all aspects of materials. The purchase department has the authority to make purchases for the whole organisation. Under this system the requirements of the whole organisation are ascertained through the preparation of *Purchase Budget* and the purchase department makes the purchases following the accepted principles and distributes the materials to the respective poduction departments according to their requirements. In most of the cases the purchase department purchases material on the basis of *Requisition Slip* issued by the *Store.* The suppliers deliver the materials to the *Materials Receiving Section.* Where centralised purchase is followed, no individual department is allowed to purchase its own materials.

3.13 Advantages of Centralized Purchase

The following advantages can be derived from the Centralised buying :

(a) **Advantages of bulk purchase**

Since materials are purchased in bulk, materials can be bought at a much cheaper rate because of higher rate of trade discount, better credit facilities and increased bargaining power, quantity, discount.

(b) **Maintenance of quality**

Since all the purchases are made by the Purchase Department manned with persons having specialised knowledge in the quality of goods, quality of materials can be maintained which will ultimately lead to production of better quality of finished goods. Better quality of goods surely enhances the goodwill of the business which, in turn, results in increased turnover leading to a greater profit.

(c) **Reduction in transport cost**

Under this system materials are purchased in bulk as a result of which transportation cost is reduced substantially. This has a positive impact on the total cost or per unit cost of material. This will enable the organisation to be more competitive.

(d) **Advantage of specialisation**

As the Buying Department is manned with expert purchasing personnel, right purchases from the right type of suppliers is possible. This guarantees both quality and price.

(e) **Duplication can be avoided**

As one person is held responsible for all the purchases, duplication of purchasing work can be avoided.

(f) **Planned purchase**

Due to planned purchase holding of excess stores can be dispensed with, better space management becomes possible and **unnecessary blocking of working capital** can easily be avoided.

3.14 Limitations

The following are the limitations of Centralised Buying :

(a) **Expensive**

The administrative cost of the purchasing department is likely to be very expensive as a result of which the total cost is sure to increase and the very purpose of costing to reduce cost is defeated.

(b) **Acts as a hindrance to smooth functioning**

In case the materials which are required by one production department are not available, it has to wait till purchases are made by the purchasing department. This delay will lead to stoppage of production which will again lead to increased cost.

3.15 Decentralised Purchase

Decentralisation of purchases means each department is allowed to purchase materials according to its own needs. So, the authority to make purchases lies with the individual departments.

Advantages :

(a) **Benefits of local purchase**

If the production unit is situated far away from the main unit, it is beneficial to allow the unit to make local purchases. Benefits of basic low price, seasonal prices can be enjoyed which will cut out cost.

(b) **Reduction in Transportation Cost**

On account of local supply of materials, transport cost will be reduced substantially.

(c) **Quick settlement of issues**

Disputes arising out of rejections, shortages, returns can be settled easily and quickly.

3.16 Conclusion

If we carefully study the comparative advantages of Centralised and Decentralised Buying we will find that Centralised Buying is certainly advantageous and should always be adopted as a matter of policy. But if circumstances demand decentralised buying is also to be adopted especially where production units are located in different places of the country. Moreover, certain individual departments should be permitted to make their own purchases of small values to ensure smooth functioning of the factory. So, it is logical to adopt an integrated purchase policy.

3.17 Purchase Routine

Generally the following routine is followed for the purchase of materials :

(i) Request for purchase. The request is made by the Store Officer.

(ii) Inviting tenders and quotations for the supply of requisite quantity of materials.

(iii) Placing of order with suppliers after considering the tenders and quotations submitted by different suppliers.

(iv) Receiving of materials after proper inspection.

(v) Verifying and passing suppliers bill for payment.

3.18 Purchase Requisition

The decision for purchase of materials is taken by the purchase department after receiving requisition for such purchase from any authorised department. Requests for purchases are made by the authorised department to the purchase department on a prescribed form known as Purchase Requisition. A Purchase Requisition supplies three basic information which help the purchase officer to carry on the function of purchasing efficiently.

The information are :

(i) What materials are to be purchased (purchase of right quality).

(ii) When they are to be purchased (right time).

(iii) How much is to be purchased (right quantity).

Purchase Requisition

From .... Department — No. ....

To Purchase Department — Date ....

Please arrange to purchase the following materials which is required on .... for utilization against Production Order No. ..../for Stock.

Particulars of Materials	Code No.	Unit of Quantity	Quantity
			Signature

(To be filled in by the Purchase Department)

Purchase Order No. ....

Supplier ....

Fig. 3.2

Purchase requisition is received by the Purchase Officer from :

(i) the store-keeper for all standard materials;

(ii) the production control department for non-standard materials required for production.

(iii) the plant and maintenance engineer for special maintenance and capital expenditure.

(iv) head of the departments for special items, like office sundries.

The Purchase Requisition is prepared in triplicate—two copies are sent to the purchase department where one copy is retained as an evidence of authorisation and the other copy is returned to the indentor after quoting therein the details of the order placed which indicates the action taken by the purchase department. The third copy is retained by the Store for office record and for future reference.

3.19 Specification of Materials or Bill of Material

Purchase Requisition contains the particulars and specification of the materials to be purchased. Specification of materials is known as Bill of Material. It is initiated in the Production Control department or in the department of plant and maintenance engineer. Bill of Material is a complete schedule of materials or parts required by a particular job or work order prepared by the drawing office. Bill of Material is prepared for all production orders and a copy thereof is sent to the store-keeper.

Specimen of Bill of Materials

ABC CO. LTD.

BILL OF MATERIALS

Job Order No. .... — No. ....

Date ....

Item No.	Description	Code No.	Quantity or Weight	For Office Use	
				Rate Rs.	Amount Rs.

Drawing Office .... — Storekeeper .... — Accounts Officer ....

Fig. 3.3

3.20 Advantages of Bill of Materials

The following advantages can be obtained by various departments from Bill of Materials :

(i) On receipt of Bill of Materials the purchase department can place order with the selected supplier. So, Bill of Materials serves the purpose of Purchase Requisition.

(ii) A Bill of Materials authorises the Store to issue materials.

(iii) The foreman is not required to prepare detailed materials requisitions because the Bill of Materials contains the details of materials to be used by a job or work order. So it saves time and facilitates easy drawal of materials.

3.21 Time of Purchase

The Purchase Requisition indicates the date by which the materials are required for use. The Store-keeper places requisition to the purchase officer as soon as the materials reach the re-ordering level. The purchase officer on receipt of the Purchase Requisition places order to the supplier mentioning the date of delivery. The date of delivery is fixed keeping in view the rate of consumption of the material and the minimum level fixed for it.

Purchase is also made when the market condition is favourable in spite of the fact that there is no immediate requirement of material for production. In an inflationary economy, materials are purchased in bulk with the expectation that the price will rise further. In case of raw materials like jute, cotton, sugarcane, bulk purchases are made in the season to take advantage of quantity, quality and price. Sometimes long-term contracts are entered into with the suppliers for the purchase of materials for a specified period at a specified rate to safeguard against the possible rise in price in future. But, in doing so, the purchase officer should take into account the following factors :

(i) storage facilities to preserve quantity;

(ii) financial resources of the concern;

(iii) cost of transport, cost of capital and cost of storage etc.

3.22 Purchase Quantity

Before placing an order with the supplier the purchase officer is to ensure that only the right quantity of stores is purchased. The following factors are to be kept in view in deciding the quantity to be purchased :

(i) The stock level of materials is to be maintained in such a way that production department's requirement can be satisfied;

(ii) Production is not hampered for want of raw materials;

(iii) There should be no over-stocking to block working capital unnecessarily nor under-stocking of materials;

(iv) Availability of funds.

3.23 Purchase Order

Definition

Purchase order is an agreement between the buyer and supplier of materials. It is a request made by the purchaser to the supplier to supply a specific quantity and quality of goods in accordance with the terms and conditions laid down in the agreement. It also signifies the commitment on the part of the buyer to take delivery of the goods and make payment as per the terms and conditions stated in the purchase order.

After carefully fixing up the quantity to be purchased, the purchasing department must place orders with the chosen suppliers. Those suppliers are to be chosen who can provide the necessary goods at competitive prices and at the right time. Quotations are invited from the suppliers. Quotations received from different suppliers are compared and then the acceptable supplier is selected. After completing the above formalities the purchase order is issued to the supplier for the supply of requisite quantity of goods at specified time. The purchase order is issued in prescribed form and prepared in quadruplet (4 copies) and are sent to the following departments for reference and co-ordination :

(i) the first copy is sent to the supplier.
(ii) one copy is sent to the department originating the purchase requisition.
(iii) one copy is sent to the stores or goods inward department.
(iv) one copy is retained in the purchase department as a permanent record.
(v) a copy is sent to the Accounts department.

A specimen of Purchase Order is given below :

A.B.C. Co. Ltd.
PURCHASE ORDER

To ....
....

Serial No. ....
Date ....
Purchase Order No. ....
Purchase Requisition No. ....

Please supply, in accordance with the terms and conditions of purchased attached :

Quantity	*Description*	*Code*	*Delivery date*	*Price*	*Per*

Delivery at ....
Discount ....
Excise duty ....
Sales Tax ....
Freight ....
Terms of payment ....
Other particulars............

Special instructions ....

For ABC Co. Ltd.

Signature
Purchase Manager

(For Office use only)

Received on ....
Date of delivery ....
Challan No. ....Date .... Invoice No......... Date ....

Reminder ....

Fig. 3.4

3.24 Purchase Procedures

The Purchase Department has to follow certain procedures for efficient buying. The purchase procedures involve the following steps :

(1) Purchase requisition

Receiving the purchase requisition, which may be received from the stores, production control department, Departmental Managers. The volume of materials to be bought should be determined judiciously.

(2) Search for supplier

The Purchase Department has to search for prospective suppliers. Care should be taken in choosing the correct supplier. Once the suppliers are identified they should be asked to submit quotation or tender. The tenders are to be opened and supplier should be selected after considering the terms and conditions stated in the tenders.

(3) Placing order for purchase

Once the supplier is selected the purchase order should be given to the selected supplier. Copy of purchase order should be sent to the originating department, Accounts Department and one copy to Costing Department.

(4) Receipt of Materials

Materials received should be entered in the Goods Received Note and are to be sent to Inspection Department for inspection. After receiving inspection report, the materials are sent to the stores for despatch to the production departments.

For better understanding a chart in this respect is given below :

Purchasing Procedures

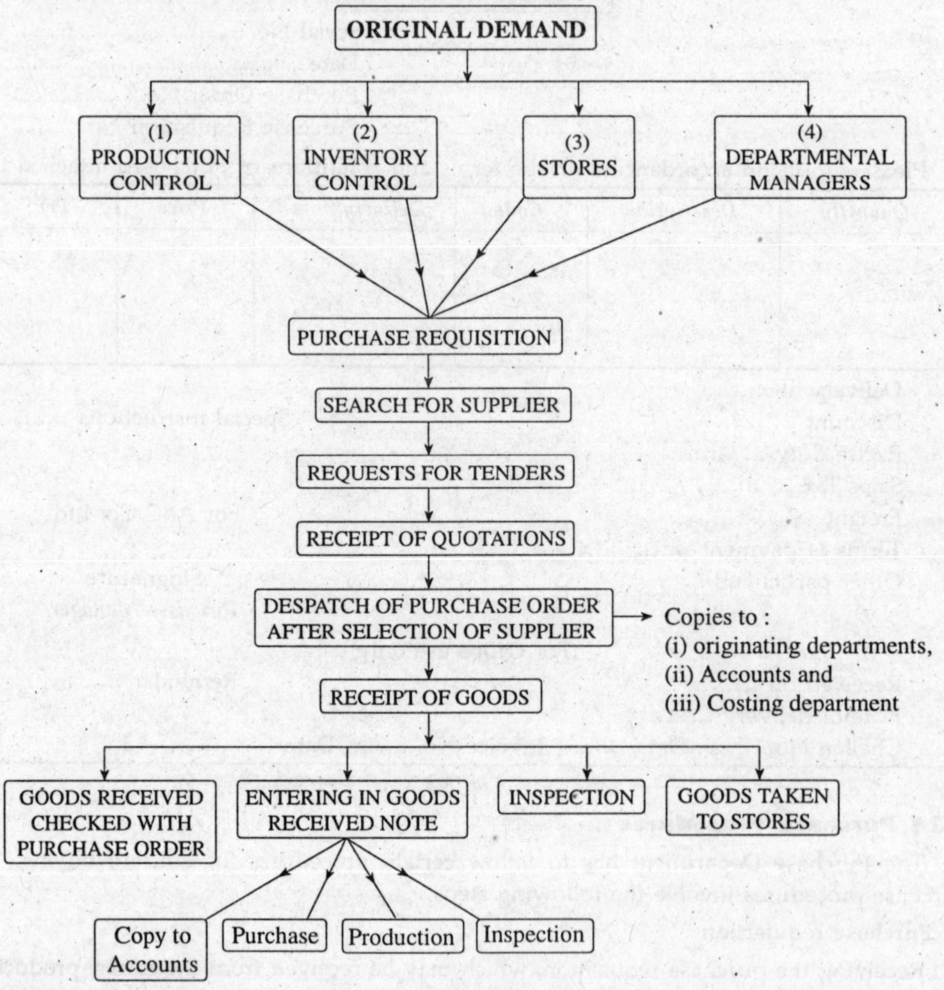

Fig. 3.5

RECEIPT OF GOODS

The following chart depicts the Reception and Inspection procedures of materials :

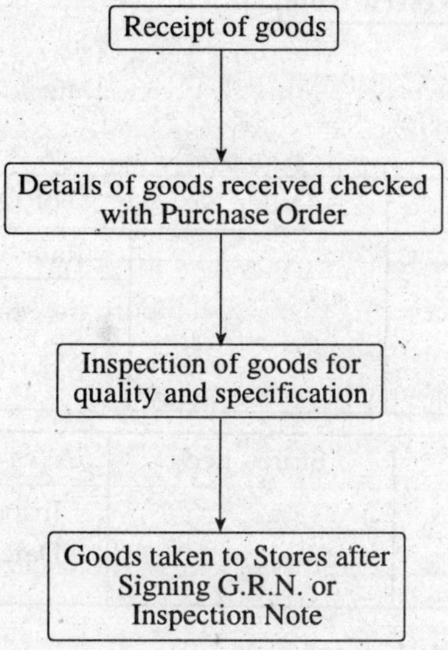

Documents used
↓
Goods Received Notes
↓
Copies to :

(i) Accounts Dept.
(ii) Purchase Dept.
(iii) Production Control
(iv) Inspection Dept.
(v) Stores
(vi) Retained

Inspection Note
Copies to :

(i) Accounts Dept.
(ii) Purchase Dept.
(iii) Production Control
(iv) Stores
(v) Retained for file

Fig. 3.6 : Reception and Inspection procedures

A goods receiving department is usually set up at the entrance to the factory. All carriers of goods are supposed to report to this department. After receiving delivery note or an advice of despatch from the supplier, the receiving department should make arrangements for unloading the goods. The receiving office should receive the goods after comparing the quantity, quality and other details incorporated in the Purchase Order which he should already possess.

On receipt of goods they should be checked either by weighing or by counting or by inspecting. If there is any damage or shortage, the fact should be noted on the carrier's copy or challan. After being satisfied in all respects the receiver of the goods should sign the carrier's copy of challan.

Particulars of goods should then be entered in a Goods Received Note (given below). Goods Received Note is an important document and is necessary so that the supplier's invoice can be verified and passed for payment. Goods Received Note is prepared with additional copies to be distributed as follows :

(i) to the purchase department to update purchase record;

(ii) to the department originating the purchase requisition;

(iii) to the accounting and stock control department;

(iv) to the store-keeper;

(v) retained in the receiving department for record and future reference.

3.25 GOODS RECEIVED NOTE (GRN)

A Specimen of Goods Received Note is given below :

ABC Co. Ltd.
Goods Received Note

From .... No. ....
Supplier .... Date ....
....

Goods	Quantity	Packages	Order No.	For Office use	
				Rate	Rs.

Carrier	Received by	Bill No.	Stores Ledg.	A/cs reference
				Inspector .... Date ....

Fig. 3.7 : Goods Received Note

It is a testimony to the goods received which are in accordance with the purchase order. Where this is not so the supplier is informed by a formal communication. If some adjustments are to be made on account of damaged or defective goods it is customary to send a debit note to the supplier for the value of the damaged or rejected items plus cost of carriage for returning them.

3.26 Checking of purchase invoices

Along with the goods the supplier sends an invoice which contains the details of the materials supplied and the price to be paid for it. On receipt of materials the purchase clerk checks the accuracy of the particulars with reference to the following documents :

(i) Purchase Order

(ii) Goods Received Note.

(iii) Inspection Report.

(iv) Debit Note, if any.

If the invoices are found correct they are signed by the responsible authority of the purchase department with a rubber stamp and passed to the accounts department for payment. The invoices are now checked by the authorised person of accounts department to ensure that the calculations are correct. The invoice is entered in the Purchase Day Book from which the supplier's account is credited. Periodically the total of the Purchase Journal is debited to Purchase Account in the General Ledger.

STORE KEEPING

3.27 Importance of Store

The cost of materials is one of the largest elements of cost. Proper storing of materials is very important to prevent losses from damage, pilferage and deterioration in quality of materials. The stores must, therefore, be properly organised and equipped for the handling of raw materials. Ideal stock levels must be maintained for every item of raw material so that the production departments get their required quantity of materials in time, and excessive working capital is not unnecessarily locked up in overstocking. Moreover, overstocking enhances the cost of production. However, the store department should be under the control of a technically qualified Store Officer.

3.28 Functions of a Store-keeper

The Store keeper is a responsible person and should be placed in a high position in the management hierarchy since he has to control the stores from every point of view. He is expected to help the cost department for its effective functioning. His duties and responsibilities are :

(i) To receive the materials from receiving department.

(ii) To maintain proper records of stores.

(iii) To make arrangement for proper storage of materials and finished goods.

(iv) To issue materials to production departments against proper and authorised requisition.

(v) To keep an eye on different stock levels and issue purchase requisition to the purchase department in time.

(vi) To report on waste, scrap and obsolete stock.

(vii) To prevent unauthorised persons from entering the stores.

(viii) Periodic comparison of physical stocks and book figures and to reconcile the discrepencies, if any.

(ix) To keep stores clean, tidy.

(x) To make suitable arrangement for maintenance and preservation of the materials during storage.

(xi) To take back surplus materials returned from departments or shops.

The above functions of the Store-keeper demonstrate that store-keeping is an important factor and can make a substantial contribution to the efficient operations of a business unit. Store-keeping includes the following activities :

(i) Efficient and speedy issue of materials and tools to production departments which is absolutely necessary for increased production.

(ii) Receipt of materials from goods reception and from production departments.

(iii) Organising storage in logical sequences so as to ensure that all items can be identified precisely and storage space is used economically and effectively.

(iv) Organising stock checks either on a continuous or a periodic basis so as to be able to provide accurate stock figures when required.

(v) Protecting materials from damage and deterioration.

(vi) Securing the stores from pilfering, theft and fire.

3.29 Organisation of Stores

In a large organisation the management is faced with the problem of adopting the type of organisation of store.

There are mainly three types of organisation namely :

(a) Central Store.

(b) Central Store with sub-stores.

(c) Independent stores situated in various departments.

Central store indicates centralised buying and handling of stores.

The **advantages** of centralised stores are :

(a) It is economical because there is economy in floor space, office overheads, stationery etc.

(b) It ensures better control and supervision because of availability of specialised knowledge and experience of stores staff.

(c) Better lay-out is possible.

(d) It facilitates inventory checks.

(e) The amount of capital invested in stock is minimised.

(f) Since all stores are located in one place, it becomes convenient to control the physical stock balances more effectively.

(g) Concise reports on scrap, obsolete stocks can be prepared regularly.

(h) Better security arrangement can be made.

But centralised stores have some **disadvantages**. The disadvantages are :

(a) It takes time to deliver materials to production departments if store is situated at some distance from many departments. So it causes inconvenience and delay.

(b) There is a greater risk of loss by fire because of concentration of all types of materials in one place.

(c) There is increased transportation cost.

(d) Breakdowns in transport in central store may cause production stoppage leading to increased cost.

(e) Administration becomes too complicated in a very large store.

3.30 Store Layout

As we have seen in our previous discussion that store plays an important role in the efficient and effective management of factory, the layout of store should be carefully and judiciously planned to ensure maximum efficiency. The stores department should conveniently be located so that it can receive materials from the suppliers and issue materials to production department without making much delay. It must have easy access to any part of the factory to minimise expense. So, it is desirable that store should be located centrally to discharge its responsibilities efficiently.

In large factories having many departments the store cannot be situated in a place from where materials can conveniently be delivered and at the same time its location shall be near the receiving department. So, it is necessary to set up substores situated conveniently to serve a particular part of the organisation.

The layout of the stores department requires thoughtful considerations. Racks, bins, shelves etc. must be arranged for easy access. There must be enough provision for open space for the passage of trucks. Special arrangement should be made for the storage of materials which are affected by atmospheric conditions. Heavy and bulky goods which cannot be kept in racks or bins are to be kept on floor. In that case, the area of the floor where these materials are to be kept should be marked with white lines indicating the area kept reserved for storing those materials.

3.31 Centralised Stores

A large factory may choose to have subsidiary stores within productive departments. This facilitates the spontaneous supply of materials required by the production department. It is very difficult to take a decision on whether a factory should have subsidiary stores or a centralised store. Before taking a decision the advantages of a centralised store must be taken into consideration.

3.32 Advantages of a Centralised Store

1. Purchase order can be placed for the total requirements of the firm and the larger order results in cost savings.
2. As there are many small stocks, the total buffer stock is much higher which leads to :
   (a) Less capital investment in Stocks ;
   (b) Less space taken up ;
   (c) Less danger of obsolescence and deterioration ; and
   (d) Less time taken for checking stock balances.
3. Better supervision is possible for using specialised skills and equipment.
4. Administration cost relating to stock recording is less.
5. Better layout of Stores is possible which results in efficiency in stock control.
6. Absence of any worker does not affect the work since staff become acquainted with different types of stores.
7. Better security arrangements can be made,

3.33 Possible disadvantages

The centralised storage of materials suffers from the following disadvantages :

1. It involves increased transportation costs.
2. It causes inconvenience and delay in supply of materials as the production departments have to obtain supply from the store situated at a distance.
3. More frequent movements of small quantities of materials may increase costs and cause production control problems.
4. Greater risks of loss by fire.

3.34 Control of Stock or Inventory Control

Inventory control can be defined as the system used in a manufacturing concern to control the firms investment in Stock. The system involves the recording and monitoring of various stock levels, forecasting future demands and deciding when and how much quantity or order. The overall objective of inventory control is to minimise the costs associated with stock. These costs can be classified into three groups :

1. Carrying Costs—**Carrying Costs include** :
   (a) Rent, rates, lighting, heating, refrigeration and air-conditioning costs of stores.
   (b) Material handling costs.
   (c) Insurance and security costs.
   (d) Stores staffing, equipment, maintenance and running costs.
   (e) Deterioration and obsolescence.
   (f) Pilferage, evaporation and damage.
   (g) Interest on Capital invested in stocks.
2. Costs of obtaining stock or **Ordering Costs include** :
   (a) Clerical and administrative costs of Purchasing, Accounting and Reception of Goods.
   (b) Transport Costs.
   (c) Set up and tooling costs where goods are manufactured internally and planning, production control costs associated with the internal order.

3. Costs of being without Stock or Stock-out Costs :
   (a) Cost of production stoppages caused by want of raw materials.
   (b) Extra costs associated with urgent and small quantity, replenishment orders.
   (c) Loss of future sales because customers may find out other sources.

Having considered the costs involved in stock we find that one of the major objectives of a stores control system is to ensure that 'Stock outs' do not occur and surplus stocks do not exist. Stocks out hampers production while surplus stocks lock up working capital. Both are equally harmful. Understock leads to loss of customers' goodwill and reduced profits. On the other hand, surplus stocks result in increased storage costs which also leads to reduced profits. So, it is very essential to maintain ideal stock levels to obviate the demerits of both overstocks and understocks. Every factory maintains different stock levels to achieve the objectives of efficient inventory control.

Some common inventory control items are defined and illustrated as follows :

3.35 Inventory Control Terminology

(i) **Lead time**—This is a period of time between ordering and replenishment.

(ii) **Economic Order Quantity [EOQ]**

This is a calculated recorder quantity which minimises the balance of cost between carrying costs and ordering costs.

(iii) **Buffer Stock or Minimum Stock or Safety Stock**

This is a stock allowance to cover the demand of materials during the lead time. This is the level below which stock is not allowed to fall.

(iv) **Maximum level**

This is a stock level calculated as the maximum desirable stock to be maintained and is an indicator to the management to show when stocks have risen too high.

(v) **Reorder level**

This is the level of stock at which a further replenishment order should be placed. This stock level is dependent on the lead time and the rate of consumption during the lead time.

(vi) **Reorder quantity** : The quantity of the replenishment order.

3.36 Economic Order Quantity [EOQ]

The main objectives of inventory decision are to minimise the total relevant costs of inventory and to avoid overstocking and understocking. In order to achieve these objectives two important decisions are to be taken— (i) how much to be bought and (ii) when should they be bought. So, any inventory planning model focuses on the twin problems of size and timing.

Definition

Economic Order Quantity may be defined as the most favourable quantity or the optimum quantity of materials which can ideally be purchased each time most economically. The EOQ is the size that will result in minimum total annual costs of the item of material in question.

Factors to be considered in deciding EOQ

The following factors are to be carefully considered while determining EOQ :

(a) The cost of materials.
(b) The inventory carrying charges.
(c) The ordering cost.

So, the total costs of an inventory policy consist of : Total acquisition cost + Total ordering cost + Total carrying cost.

Carrying Costs

Carrying costs usually consist of :

(i) Loss of interest on investments in inventory.
(ii) Cost of storage space.
(iii) Loss that may arise out of breakage, obsolescence, deterioration, pilferage etc.
(iv) Cost of insurance.
(v) Taxes on inventories.

Ordering Costs

Ordering costs consist of :

(i) Clerical costs of preparing a purchase order.
(ii) Postage, telegram charges and telephone bills for placing an order.
(iii) The costs of stationery and other consumables required by the purchasing department relating to the number of orders.
(iv) Processing and receiving costs relating to the number of orders processed.

Determination of EOQ

The EOQ can be determined by the application of the following formula :

$$\text{EOQ} = \sqrt{\frac{2AS}{C}} \text{ or } \sqrt{\frac{2C^3R}{C^1}}$$

where, A = Annual usage in units or R
S = Ordering cost or C^3
C = Annual carrying cost per unit or C^1

Example Units purchased = 6,000
Cost per unit = Rs. 2.50
Ordering cost per order = Rs. 15.00
Carrying cost is 20% of the average inventory value.
Calculate the EOQ.

Solution

$$\text{EOQ} = \sqrt{\frac{2AS}{C}} = \sqrt{\frac{(2 \times 6{,}000 \times 15)}{\frac{20}{100} \times 2.50}} = \sqrt{\frac{\text{Rs. } 1{,}80{,}000}{0.50}} = \sqrt{3{,}60{,}000} = 600 \text{ units.}$$

Problem 1

(a) A manufacturer uses 200 units of a component every month and he buys them entirely from outside supplier. The order placing and receiving cost is Rs. 100 and annual carrying cost is Rs. 12. From this set of data calculate the Economic Order Quantity.

(b) P. Ltd. uses three types of materials A, B & C for production of X, the final product. The relevant monthly data for the components are as given below :

	A	B	C
Normal usage	200 units	150 units	180 units
Minimum usage	100 "	100 "	90 "
Maximum usage	300 "	250 "	270 "
Reorder Quantity	750 "	900 "	720 "
Reorder period (in month)	2 to 3	3 to 4	2 to 3

Calculate for each component :

(a) Re-order level

(b) Minimum level

(c) Maximum level

(d) Average stock level

[Adapted, I.C.W.A. (Inter)]

Solution

(a) $EOQ = \sqrt{\frac{2C^3R}{C^1}}$

where C^3 = ordering cost, C^1 = Carrying cost, R = Annual requirements, i.e.

= 200 × 12 = 2,400

$\therefore \; EOQ = \sqrt{\frac{2 \times 100 \times 200 \times 12}{12}} = \sqrt{40,000} = 200 \text{ units}$

(b)

		A	B	C
(i)	**Re-order level**			
	Maximum reorder period × Maximum Consumption	3 × 300 = 900	4 × 250 = 1,000	3 × 270 = 810
(ii)	**Minimum level**			
	Reorder level – Normal	$900 - \left(200 \times 2\frac{1}{2}\right)$	$1,000 - \left(150 \times 3\frac{1}{2}\right)$	$810 - \left(180 \times 2\frac{1}{2}\right)$
	Usage × Average delivery	900 – 500	1,000 – 525	810 – 450
	time	= 400 units	= 475 units	= 360 units
(iii)	**Maximum level**	900 – 100 × 2 + 750	1,000 – 100 × 3 + 900	810 – 90 × 2 + 720
	Reorder level – Minimum consumption × Minimum reorder period	= 900 – 200 + 750	= 1,000 – 300 + 900	= 810 – 180 + 720
	+ Reorder quantity	= 1,450 units	= 1,600 units	= 1,350 units
(iv)	**Average Stock level**	$\frac{400 + 1,450}{2}$	$\frac{475 + 1,600}{2}$	$\frac{360 + 1,350}{2}$
	Minimum level + Maximum level ÷ 2	= 925 units	= 1,038 units	= 855 units

3.37 Stock levels (How much to purchase)

Maintenance of various stock levels is very important from costing point of view. For efficient control of both stocks and purchases certain stock levels are fixed up for every item of stores. Adequate stocks of raw materials, components and parts are needed for various reasons.

Advantages

(i) Ideal stock levels guarantee a constant flow of raw materials to production departments.

(ii) Adequate stocks ensure that production does not come to a standstill.

(iii) Overstocking leads to increased cost. Stock levels avoid overstock.

(iv) Maintenance of ideal stock levels guarantees that working capital is not unnecessarily locked up.

(v) Various stock levels serve as indices for initiating action on time.

(vi) Risk of loss due to depreciation in quantity, deterioration in quality and obsolescence of the materials during storage can be avoided if proper stock levels can be maintained.

3.38 Levels of Materials

The various levels fixed for effective stock control to achieve the above advantages are : (i) Maximum level; (ii) Re-ordering level; (iii) Minimum level and ; (iv) Danger level.

(i) Maximum Level

Maximum level is the level above which stocks are not allowed to rise. It is advisable to keep the level as low as possible.

In fixing the maximum level of stock the following factors are to be carefully considered :

(i) Maximum requirement of the store for production at any point of time.

(ii) The rate of consumption of the material.

(iii) The time necessary to obtain delivery of the materials.

(iv) Nature and features of the store.

(v) Storage facilities.

(vi) Cost of storage and insurance.

(vii) Availability of funds and the price of the store.

(viii) Economy in prices.

Maximum, Minimum and re-order levels are not static. They must be varied to suit changing circumstances. Thus, alterations will take place if the usage of certain materials is increased or decreased, if the re-order period changes, or if, in the light of a review of Capital available, it is decided that the overall inventory must be increased or decreased.

Determination of Maximum Level

Re-order level + Re-order quantity Minus (Minimum consumption × Minimum time required for delivery).

Illustration

From the following information calculate Maximum level :

Re-order quantity — 6,000 units

Time required—2 to 4 months

Re-order level—6,000 units

Minimum consumption—500 units

Maximum Level = Reorder level + Reorder quantity less (Minimum consumption × minimum time for delivery)

= 6,000 + 6,000 – (500 × 2) = 12,000 – 1,000 = 11,000 units.

(ii) Reorder Level

Reorder level is the point at which purchase requisition for fresh supplies is initiated by the store. This point is lower than the maximum level and fixed to avoid excess stock. It is higher than minimum stock level so as to cover emergencies like delay in supply or abnormal usage of the material.

How to determine ?

Reorder level is determined by the application of the following formula :

Maximum reorder period × maximum usage.

Illustration

From the following information find out reorder level :

Maximum consumption 2,000 units per month. Time required for delivery 2 – 4 months.

The Reorder level = Maximum usage × Maximum reorder period

= 2,000 × 4 = 8,000 units.

(iii) Minimum Stock Level

This is the level below which stocks are not allowed to fall. If stocks go below this level, store will fail to supply materials to production department which will lead to stoppage of production. This level of stock is a 'buffer stock' which is maintained to make the materials available in emergencies arising out of delay in supply. The following factors are to be taken into consideration in fixing the minimum level :

(i) Nature of the item of materials

For special items of materials which are purchased against customers' specific orders, no minimum level is required.

(ii) The maximum time required for delivery.

This is known as lead time. This indicates the time lag between the date of placing order with the supplier and receiving date of materials.

(iii) Rate of consumption of the material.

Here, the normal rate of consumption is to be considered.

How to find out Minimum Level?

Minimum level = Reorder level – (normal usage × average reorder period.)

Problem 2

From the following particulars find out (i) Re-order stock level, (ii) Minimum stock level, (iii) Maximum stock level and (iv) Average stock level.

Re-order quantity – 10,000 units

Time required for delivery 2 – 4 months

Maximum consumption 2,500 units p.m.

Normal consumption 2,000 units p.m.

Minimum consumption 1,500 units p.m.

[Adapted—M.Com. Mysore]

Solution

(a) *Reorder Stock level*

Maximum consumption × Maximum Reorder period = 2,500 × 4 = 10,000 units

(b) *Minimum Stock level*

Reorder level – (Normal consumption × Normal reorder period)

= 10,000 – (2,000 × 3) = 10,000 – 6,000 = 4,000 units

(Normal reorder period = $\frac{4+2}{2} = \frac{6}{2} = 3$ months.)

(c) *Maximum Stock level*

Reorder quantity + Reorder level – (Minimum consumption × Minimum reorder period)

$= 10,000 + 10,000 - (1,500 \times 2) = 20,000 - 3,000 = 17,000$ units

(d) *Average Stock level*

$$\text{Maximum level + Minimum level} = \frac{17,000 + 4,000}{2} = \frac{21,000}{2} = 10,500 \text{ units}$$

3.39 Materials Records

In a store the basic prerequisite of stock control is that the stock movements are to be recorded very accurately.

The most frequently used records of stocks are **(i) Bin Cards** and **(ii) Stock Record Cards.**

3.40 Necessity of Bin Card

It is often argued that the bin card is an unnecessary duplication of work. Undoubtedly it is a duplication of work, but it is advantageous to maintain both the sets of records for the following reasons :

(i) Since Bin Cards are not accounting records, it is essential that these be kept in stores.

(ii) In Store Ledger, posting is made periodically so it fails to show the uptodate balance of the stores materials.

(iii) Store Ledger constitutes a second check on the quantity recorded on the Bin Cards.

(iv) In case of discrepancy in regard to materials, store clerk may be held responsible for such discrepancy.

(v) Store Ledger is maintained centrally in the Cost Office from where consolidated information regarding stock position of the materials can be obtained.

(vi) An overall review of stores balances can frequently be made.

(vii) Maintenance of Bin Cards facilitates the continuous flow of stores of materials to production departments.

To conclude it can be said that the necessity of maintaining bin cards will depend on the proximity of the stores records office to the store and the accuracy and speed with which stock control records are updated.

3.41 Merits of a Bin Card

1. Effective control of stock

Bin Card records all receipts and issues of materials in detail. So a detailed record is made in the Bin Card regarding quantity of materials received and issued on different dates. Moreover, it assists the store keeper to control the Stock effectively. He can keep a constant vigil on the position of materials since the maximum reordering and minimum levels are stated on the Bin Card.

2. It facilitates ordering of further supply

When the quantity of materials reaches *Re-ordering level,* the storekeeper places order with the Purchase Department asking for fresh supply.

3. It feeds the production departments with regular supply of materials

This is possible because of strict observance of Maximum, Reordering and Minimum levels of each type of material with the help of Bin Card. As a result, production is soldom hampered.

4. It helps perpetual inventory system

It is a part of perpetual inventory system. So, it has a positive contribution to make the perpetual inventory system successful.

3.42 Treatment of discrepancies

A continuous record of materials is maintained in a perpetual inventory system in the form of bin cards and store ledger. Under this system any discrepancy in physical stock and accounting stock can be detected very quickly. The discrepancies may arise for any one of the following reasons :

(i) for wrong entry or omission of an entry;
(ii) for materials not being placed properly;-
(iii) inaccurate counting, weighing at the time of receipts or issues;
(iv) losses due to shrinkage, evaporation, spoilage, breakage etc.
(v) losses due to theft, manipulation, pilferage and misappropriation.

3.43 Adjustments

Discrepancies are required to be adjusted. But before making any adjustment, the reasons for such discrepancies must be studied carefully and should be reported to the proper authority. Approval from the appropriate authority should be obtained for adjustments.

Discrepancy arising out of normal circumstances like evaporation, shrinkage etc. should be adjusted by trnasfer to the Inventory Adjustment Account. But discrepancies due to abnormal circumstances like fire, theft etc. should be charged to costing Profit and Loss Account.

3.44 Bin Cards

In a store, materials are kept in appropriate bins, drawers or other receptacles; some are stacked while other racked. For each kind of material, separate record is kept on a bin card. Details of receipts and issues of materials are shown on the bin card. Bin card also assists the store keeper to control the stock. On the bin card the maximum level, re-ordering and minimum levels are maintained. Where the stock clerk is responsible for reordering material, he is reminded by the bin card when the stock reaches the minimum level to ensure that production departments do not starve from paucity of stock. To facilitate ordering of further supplies, the normal quantity to order is sometimes stated at the head of the card. Where bin cards are in use, they are attached to or adjacent to the actual materials and the entries are made at the time of issue, either by the storeman or a store clerk.

Specimen of a Bin Card

X Y Z Co. Ltd.
Bin Card

Description .... Bin No. ....
Stores Ledger No. .... Code No. ....
Minimum Level .... Unit ....
Reorder Level ....
Maximum Level ....

Date	*Received*		*Issued*		*Balance*	
	Ref.	*Quantity*	*Ref.*	*Quantity*	*Quantity*	*Check*

Fig. 3.8

3.45 Store Ledger Card

Stores Ledger Card is the key to stock control, as it is the basic record used to maintain optimum stock levels. Moreover, it provides the detail necessary to ascertain accurate stock values and to check physical stocks. To obtain a full picture of the stock position of an item it is necessary to know not only the physical stock balance but also the Free Stock Balance.

It is to be remembered that in all cases the pattern of demand is not easily determined, e.g. new materials, or where it is erratic. For such materials, as soon as an order is received from a customer, detailed material requirements are sent to the stores and stock of such materials are reserved against those orders so that materials are available for production. **Thus, the free stock is reduced by the quantity of reserved materials. When the free stock falls below the re-order level, then purchase requisition is sent to purchase department.** Free Stock Balance may be defined as Physical Stock + Outstanding replenishment order – Unfulfilled requirements. A typical Stock Record Card is shown below :

X Y Z Co. Ltd.
Stores Ledger Card

Description........... Unit..................... Location.................... Code...............................
Maximum............. Minimum............ Re-order level.......... Re-order Quantity..........

Receipt			*Issues*			*On Order*			*Free Balance*
Date	*Ref.*	*Quantity*	*Date*	*Ref.*	*Quantity*	*Physical Balance*	*Date*	*Ref.*	*Cumulative Quantity*

Fig. 3.9

3.46 Store Ledger

Store Ledger is maintained in the cost department. It is more or less identical with the bin cards with the exception that money values of materials are shown in Store ledger. Store ledger is used to record all receipts and issues of materials to different production departments. The ledger is usually of loose leaf or card type and contains an account for each class of material. This ledger is a subsidiary ledger to the main cost ledger. The specimen form of stores ledger is given below :

Specimen of Store Ledger

SWIL Limited
Store Ledger

Material.. Folio..
Code No. .... Maximum level...............................
Minimum level...............................
Re-ordering level............................

Date	*Received*				*Issued*				*Balance*			*Remarks*
	G.R.N. No.	*Qnt.*	*Rate*	*Amt.*	*Requisition No.*	*Qnt.*	*Rate*	*Amt.*	*Qnt.*	*Rate*	*Amt.*	

Fig. 3.10

3.47 Difference between Store Ledger and Bin Card

The following are the points of difference between store ledger and bin card :

Store Ledger	*Bin Card*
1. Store Ledger is maintained by the store-keeper.	Bin Card is maintained by the costing department.
2. Store Ledger is a record of both quantities and values.	Bin Card is a record of quantities only.
3. Posting of transactions is done after the transactions take place.	Posting is done before the transactions take place.
4. Transactions may be summarised and posted periodically.	Each transaction is posted individually.
5. It is a basic accounting record of materials.	It is not a basic accounting record.
6. Usually Bin Card is kept outside the stores.	It is kept inside the stores.
7. In case of any discrepancy in regard to materials, the person in charge of store ledger is not held responsible.	In case of any discrepancy, the person in charge of this document is held responsible.
8. Store Ledger helps in the preparation of Profit and Loss Statement as it supplies the inventory value.	It assists the store clerk to place purchase requisition to ensure the supply of materials to production departments. It facilitates ordering of further supplies.

3.48 Materials Control Procedures

In brief, the materials control procedures include :

(i) Purchasing, Receipt, Storage and issue, Inventory control and associated costing procedures.

(ii) The purchasing function is of paramount importance which aims at buying proper type of materials at competitive price. It aims for an appropriate balance of price, quality and delivery.

(iii) The purchase requisition giving precise details of quantity required, specification, delivery etc. initiates the main purchasing procedures.

(iv) The purchasing procedures consist of search for Supplier, Selection of Supplier, placing of order to the selected supplier and expediting the deliveries.

(v) Goods supplied must be properly received. Before taking delivery of goods they should be verified with reference to Purchase Order, inspected and to be entered in Goods Received Note (G R N).

(vi) The G. R. N. is an acknowledgement of goods received and is used for making payment to supplier.

(vii) Store keeping involves receipt and issue of materials, preservation of materials and storage space organisation.

(viii) Materials should be issued to production departments on the basis of Materials Requisition to be issued by a responsible authority of the production department concerned.

(ix) Ideal stock levels should be maintained by the stores so that replenishment of stock can take place at an appropriate time. It should see that the production departments do not suffer from dearth of mateials.

(x) Stock taking is carried out on a periodic or continuous basis. Continuous stock taking is essential for perpetual inventory systems.

3.49 INVENTORY SYSTEMS

1 Perpetual Inventory System

Definition

In the words of Wheldon : "Perpetual Inventory System may be defined as a method of recording store balances after every receipt and issue, to facilitate regular checking and to obviate closing down for stock-taking".

The Institute of Cost and Works Accountants (U.K.) has defined Perpetual Inventory System as : "a system of records maintained by the controlling department which reflects the physical movement of Stock and their current balance. A perpetual inventory is usually checked by a programme of continuous stock taking".

The perpetual inventory system gives information such as goods ordered, expected delivery date and unit costs. An essential feature of the perpetual inventory method is that items of stocks are checked periodically, normally at least once or twice in a year. This ensures that stock balances as per book records tally with the physical stocks which is vital for effective stock control. Perpetual inventory system comprises : (i) Bin Cards; (ii) Store Ledger and (iii) Continuous Stock-taking.

Advantages

The following advantages can be derived from Perpetual Inventory System :

(i) The long and costly work of a stock-taking count can be avoided.

(ii) It does not become necessary to stop production at the time of carrying out of physical stock taking.

(iii) Discrepancies and errors can be detected and localised promptly and remedial measures can be adopted to prevent their occurrence in future.

(iv) This system has a direct effect on the morale of the staff and acts as a deterrent to dishonesty.

(v) This system ensures that adequate stocks are maintained within the prescribed limits as the actual stocks with the authorised maxima and minima can be compared.

(vi) The stocks being kept within the prescribed limits, the working capital sunk in storing materials does not exceed the desired amount.

(vii) The disadvantages of excessive stocks can be avoided. The disadvantages of excessive stock arise because of :

  (a) loss of interest on capital locked up in stock;

  (b) loss through deterioration;

  (c) fall in market value;

  (d) obsolescence.

(viii) As the storekeeper remains responsible for maintaining different prescribed stock levels, the production departments do not suffer from shortage of raw materials. It helps to prevent delays and stoppage in production.

(ix) Profit and Loss Account and Balance Sheet at interim period, if required, can be prepared on the basis of prompt information about the stock of raw materials to be supplied by the Store Ledger.

(x) It acts as an internal check since a detailed and reliable check can be conducted by experienced men.

(xi) Perpetual inventory records provide details about cost of materials for individual products, jobs, processes, production orders etc. These information are helpful to management in exercising control over costs.

(xii) More effective control through greater opportunity for using specialised skills and equipment.

2 Continuous Physical Stock taking

The perpetual inventory system remains incomplete and ineffective without a systematic procedure for physical verification of stores. Physical check reveals the actual balances of materials on hand on a particular day. But it is to be noted that continuous stock taking is a part of perpetual inventory system.

3.50 Difference between perpetual inventory system and continuous stock-taking

(i) Perpetual inventory system signifies a complete process of inventory control while continuous stock-taking is a part of perpetual inventory system.

(ii) Perpetual inventory means the system of records, whereas continuous stock-taking means the physical checking of those records with actual stocks.

3 Periodic Stock Verification

Periodic Stock verification is another system of inventory control. Under this system the entire stock is verified all at a time at periodic intervals, usually once in a year. The verification of physical stock at the close of the financial year facilitates the valuation of stores for depicting in the final accounts. Periodic stock taking is to be completed as soon as possible since it necessitates the shut down of the factory resulting in stoppage of production and increased costs.

Periodic verification is necessary for stores that do not find a place in the perpetual inventory records, such as work-in-progress, consumable stores, capital assets, loose tools and spare parts lying in the shop.

3.51 Comparison

Wixon, Kell and **Bedford** compare both the methods in these words :

"Perpetual inventory assists management in planning future purchases, reduces possibilities of stock shortages and aids in the reduction of waste, spoilage etc., but more costly. The periodic inventory system is simple in concept and application. Yet it normally requires the shut down of operation while it is carried out; it is error-prone due to inexperience of inventory takers; it cannot pin-point shortages resulting from theft or waste".

Thus, we can **differentiate between Perpetual Inventory system and Periodic Inventory system** in the following way :

(i) Perpetual Inventory system is a management tool which helps the management in planning purchase and reduction of waste and spoilage. But this system is somewhat complex and more costly.

(ii) Periodic Inventory system is simple in concept and application but this is error-prone. Like Perpetual Inventory System it fails to identify shortages resulting from theft or waste.

3.52 ABC Analysis

In case of a big manufacturing unit which uses a large number of items for production purpose, it becomes difficult to comprehend such enormous number of items, the unit has to keep in stock. Sometime a modern industrial unit has to keep 30,000 to 50,000 units. So, many manufacturing units find it useful to divide materials, parts, supplies and finished goods into subclassifications for purposes of effective stock control. ABC method is a technique under which items of stocks are subclassified in "step-by-step" fashion by (i) itemizing total annual purchase cost of each time needed and (ii) grouping in decreasing order of annual consumptions cost". Under this system different materials are grouped into three classes :

(i) High priced materials (A)

(ii) Medium priced materials (B)

(iii) Low priced materials (C)

Materials to be handled under each category are converted into a percentage of the total value of the material.

The following figure will demonstrate the technique of ABC analysis of material inventory.

ABC Analysis of Material inventory

Step I

Item	*Average usage*	*Unit price*	*Total consumption cost*
		Rs.	Rs.
M10	2,000	10.00	20,000
M11	2,000	0.25	500
M12	20,000	0.50	10,000
M13	18,000	1.00	18,000
M14	1,20,000	0.10	12,000

Step II

Class	*Items*	*% of total*	*Total Cost*	*% of total*
			Rs.	
A	2,500	5%	14,00,000	70%
B	12,500	25%	4,00,000	20%
C	35,000	70%	2,00,000	10%
	50,000	100%	20,00,000	100%

Source—Horngren

The above chart demonstrates that "A" items consist of only 5% of total items handled but they represent 70% of the total value of stock-holding of the business. The second category "B" consists of 25% of total items representing 20% of the total value of stock, while the third category "C" consisting of 70% of total items represent only 10% of total cost of inventory.

At the time of classifying the items the following factors should be considered :

(i) Value of consumption.

(ii) Investment value.

(iii) Sales or profit potential.

3.53 Advantages of the ABC Analysis

(i) This method ensures availability of supplies at all times.

(ii) Clerical cost can be reduced and inventory is placed and maintained at the optimum level.

(iii) Close and strict control on costly items can be exercised.

(iv) Working capital management can be better planned.

(v) Frequency of placing order for different classes of items can reasonably be judged.

(vi) There exists the element of flexibility in material control management. Very strict control, moderate control and loose control can be exercised for A, B & C categories of items, respectively.

3.54 Limitations of ABC Analysis

1. In order to be fully effective, *ABC* analysis should be carried out with standardisation and codification.
2. As ABC analysis is based on gradation of different items, this gradation may include a lot of subjective elements.
3. The result of *ABC* analysis should be reviewed periodically and updated.

Despite these limitations, *ABC* analysis is a powerful tool in the direction of cost reduction, as it helps to control inventory items with a selective approach.

Graphical Presentation of ABC Analysis

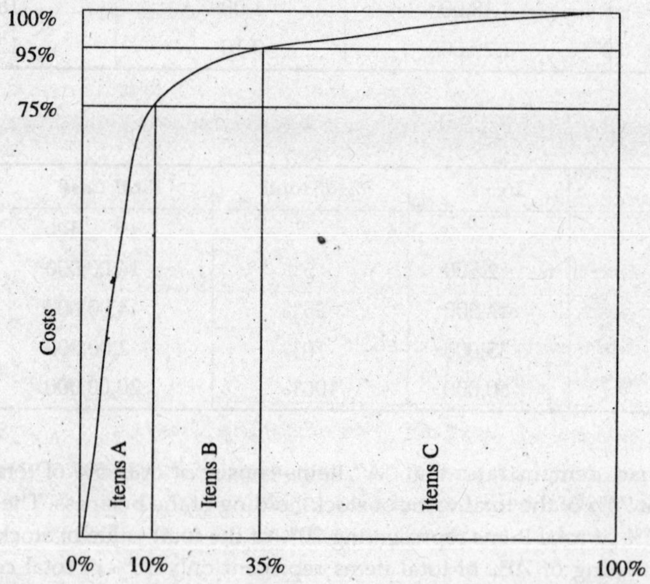

Fig. 3.11 : No. of items

SECTION B

PRICING OF MATERIALS

3.55 Introduction

In this section we shall discuss the costing problems relating to materials issued to a particular job and those of pricing issues. The various pricing methods have been discussed with their respective advantages and disadvantages. The effect of pricing system used on stock valuation is also discussed.

3.56 Objectives of Material Pricing

There are two main objectives of material pricing—

(a) To charge the cost of materials issued to production on a realistic and consistent basis.

(b) To provide a satisfactory basis of valuation of stock on hand on the closing day.

The above objectives can be achieved by adopting simplest effective pricing system which is realistic from administrative point of view.

Problems

The following factors are responsible for making the problem of pricing materials issues more complicated :

(i) The stock of any given material is usually made up of several deliveries at different prices.

(ii) Rapidly changing prices for materials and components.

(iii) Difficulties in identifying items with their delivery consignment.

(iv) The sensitivity of profit calculations to the pricing method adopted especially where materials form a substantial part of total cost.

It is to be noted carefully that no one method has all the advantages. So, it is necessary to use the most appropriate system to fulfil the requirements of a particular situation.

3.57 Features of Pricing System

When an issue is made from Stores, the Materials Requisition from the production department is passed to the Cost Department to be priced so that the appropriate ledger entries can be made.

The entries would be :

(i)	Work-in-Progress Control A/c (for direct materials issued)	Dr.
	Overhead Control A/c (for indirect materials issued)	Dr.
	To Stores ledger Control A/c	

3.58 Determination of Cost of Incoming Materials

Practically speaking, it is a problem to value materials properly. The question arises as to what elements of cost should be included in the valuation of materials. The following adjustments are to be made to the original purchase price of materials.

(a) Trade discount

Trade discount is an allowance or reduction in price given by a supplier to a retailer. It is allowed to cover the expenses and profit of the retailer. In arriving at the material cost price the amount of trade discount is deducted from the purchase price.

(b) Quantity discount

It refers to the allowance made by the supplier to all large users of the product. It is an inducement to the buyer to encourage him to place bulk orders. The buyer enjoys the economies of bulk purchase. The discount varies according to the size of the order. It is deducted from the purchase price in arriving at the material cost price.

(c) Cash discount

Cash discount is an allowance offered by the supplier to his customers for making payment within a stipulated time. Since it is a matter of financial nature, it is not considered as an element of cost in cost accounts.

(d) Freight and Carriage

Freight or other transport charges incurred on incoming materials are treated as part of cost and hence, should be included in material cost price. Freight and transport charges include sea, land and air freight, insurance, duties, dock charges, import duties etc. Where such costs are small and to be apportioned over a number of items included in the consignment, it is expedient to treat such charges as factory overhead.

(e) Value added tax

It is excluded from the cost of materials and debited to a separate account like VAT Account and later on set off against VAT collected from sales.

3.59 Containers

Treatment of cost of container varies as follows :

(a) If the buyer of materials does not pay for the container, no accounting entry is required. But if the containers are sold, the sale proceeds is to be credited to the overhead.

(b) Where the buyer has to pay for the containers and the containers are not returnable, cost price of such containers should be added to the cost of materials.

(c) When the containers are separately charged but they are returnable at a price less than the price charged, the difference is to be added to the cost of material. But if they are accepted by the supplier at charged out price, the cost of such containers is not to be added to the cost of the material.

3.60 Methods of pricing of Materials Issues

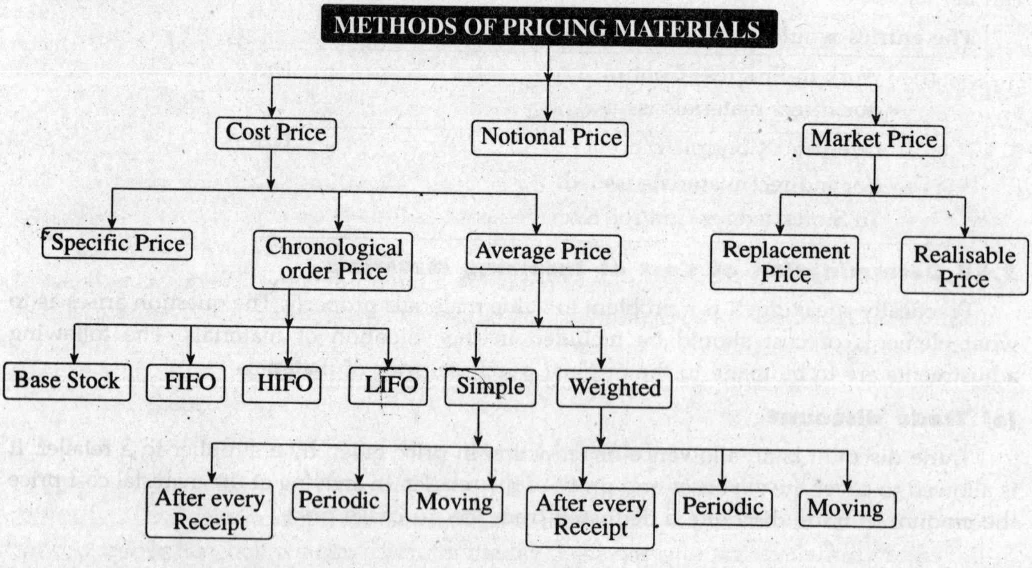

3.61 Methods of Pricing

The following are the different methods for pricing materials issued from stores to various jobs or orders. In practice, it is very difficult to choose an appropriate method. Once a particular method is chosen it is advisable to follow it consistently.

Methods—Various methods have been devised. They fall under the following 4 basic types :

(1)	Based on Cost price	(a)	Specific Price
		(b)	First in First out (FIFO)
		(c)	Last in First out (LIFO)
		(d)	Highest in First out (HIFO)
		(e)	Next in First out (NIFO)
		(f)	Base Stock.
(2)	Average Price Method	(a)	Simple Average
		(b)	Weighted Average
		(c)	Periodic Simple Average
		(d)	Periodic Weighted Average
		(e)	Moving Simple Average
		(f)	Moving Weighted Average
(3)	Market Price	(a)	Replacement Price
		(b)	Realisable Price
(4)	Notional Price	(a)	Standard Price
		(b)	Inflated Price.

3.62 BASED ON COST PRICE

(a) Specific Price Method

Under this method the specific price of materials issued to a particular job is charged to the job. This method is used where mateials are purchased specifically for a job work order.

(b) First-in-First-out (FIFO)

Under this method materials purchased first are to be issued first. Materials from the second lot will be issued only when the first lot is completely exhausted. Under this system of materials pricing the production or job is charged with earlier cost or cost of the earlier consignment. The idea behind this method is to sell the oldest units first and maintain a current inventory representing the most recent purchase.

3.63 Advantages

1. FIFO represents an approximation of the specific identification of unit costs, so, this method has an advantage that the management has little or no control over the selection of units in order to influence recorded profits.
2. This method has also the advantage of not being influenced by the arbitrary or whimsical choices of customers. As a result, valuation of inventory and cost of goods manufactured are consistent and realistic.
3. It also provides an appropriate base for comparisons among different firms in the same industry and among several years.
4. This method is very simple and easy to understand.
5. An objective of FIFO is the presentation of closing inventory at the most recent costs in the Balance Sheet which may be assumed to approximate replacement costs. When the inventory turns over rapidly, the stock valuation under this method will reflect current

prices unless prices change considerably after the recent purchases.

6. It is useful where transactions are not too many and prices of materials are fairly steady. This method may suitably be used for bulky materials with high unit prices.

3.64 Disadvantages

The following are the objections to this method of pricing inventory :

1. When consignments are received very frequently at varying prices, calculations become complicated and cumbersome.
2. For one requisition for supply of materials, more than one price may be adopted because two lots of different prices may be involved.
3. Though ending inventory closely represent the current cost, current production is matched with costs that date back in time. In case the prices rise rapidly the production cost is understated.
4. As the production cost does not match the current cost, revenue from sales will not produce enough income to cover the cost of raw materials used for production.
5. This method fails to achieve the objective of matching current costs with current revenues. It also fails to report separately the gains and losses from price changes.

3.65 Applicability

The FIFO method is suitable where (1) the size and cost of materials units are large ; (2) materials can be easily identified as belonging to a particular purchased lot ; (3) and not more than two or three different receipts of materials are on hand at one time.

Conclusion

FIFO is most suitable for use where the materials are of comparitively high value and not in frequent demand. It is also appropriate where there are relatively few changes of purchase price, or where the ratio of number of issues to the number of receipts is not large.

Problem 3

The following is the summary of the receipts and issue of materials in a factory during January 1991 :

Jan. 1	Opening balance 500 units @ Rs. 25 per unit.
3	Issue 70 units
4	Issue 100 units
8	Issue 80 units
13	Received from supplier 200 units @ Rs. 24.50 per unit
14	Returned to store 15 units @ Rs. 24 per unit
16	Issue 180 units
20	Received from supplier 240 units @ 24.75 per unit
24	Issue 304 units
25	Received from supplier 320 units @ Rs. 24.50 per unit
26	Issue 112 units
27	Returned to store 12 units @ Rs. 24.50 per unit
28	Received from supplier 100 units @ Rs. 25 per unit.

Work out on the basis of First-in-First-out.

There was a shortage of 5 units on 15th and another on 27th of 8 units.

[Adapted—C.A. Inter]

Solution

Store Ledger Account (FIFO)

Date	*Receipts*			*Issues*			*Balance*		
1991	*Qnt.*	*Rate*	*Amt.*	*Qnt.*	*Rate*	*Amt.*	*Qnt.*	*Rate*	*Amt.*
Jan. 1							500	25.00	12,500
" 3				70	25	1,750	430	25.00	10,750
" 4				100	25	2,500	330	25.00	8,250
" 8				80	25	2,000	250	25.00	6,250
" 13	200	24.50	4,900				250	25.00	6,250
							200	24.50	4,900
" 14	15	24.00	360				250	25.00	6,250
		(Return)					200	24.50	4,900
							15	24.00	360
" 15				5	25	125	245	25.00	6,125
					(Shortage)		200	24.50	4,900
							15	24.00	360
" 16				180	25	4,500	65	25.00	1,625
							200	24.50	4,900
							15	24.00	360
" 20	240	24.75	5,940				65,	25.00	1,625
							200	24.50	4,900
							15	24.00	360
							240	24.75	5,940
" 24				65	25.00	1,625			
				200	24.50	4,900			
				15	24.00	360			
				24	24.75	594	216	24.75	5,346
" 25	320	24.50	7,840				216	24.75	5,346
							320	24.50	7,840
" 26				112	24.75	2,772	104	24.75	2,574
							320	24.50	7,840
" 27	12	24.50	294				104	24.75	2,574
							320	24.50	7,840
							12	24.50	294
" 27				8	24.75	198	96	24.75	2,376
					(Shortage)		320	24.50	7,840
							12	24.50	294
" 28	100	25.00	2,500				96	24.75	2,376
							320	24.50	7,840
							12	24.50	294
							100	25.00	2,500

Closing Stock 528 valued at Rs. 13,010

(c) LIFO Method (Last in First out)

Under this method, materials that are purchased last are issued to the production first. The cost of the last lot of materials received is used to price requisitions until the lot is exhausted. This method of materials pricing ensures that materials are issued at current cost. Thus, the inventory is valued at oldest costs. **The very objective of this method is to match the current costs with current revenues.** This method has gained popularity because it eliminates the reporting of gains and losses from the holding of inventories as the inventories are valued at earlier costs which is a conservative valuation for the purpose of Balance Sheet.

3.66 Advantages

1. It is a method of pricing material issued to production which is systematic and realistic.
2. It provides a better matching of current costs with current revenues.
3. This method is simple to operate and is useful when the transactions are not too many.
4. In case of sharp price fluctuations this method minimises unrealised gains and losses from holding inventories.
5. Income is reported only when it is available for distribution as dividends.
6. Price changes over the business cycle do not result in the reporting of unrealised gains or losses arising from the holding of the initial and increasing amount of inventory.
7. In times of rising prices, this method of pricing materials issues helps in showing lower profit because the production or job is charged with increased price. The lower profit reduces tax burden. As long as the prices of materials do not decline, the tax benefit remains but if the tax rates go up, the tax saving facility will be eliminated with higher tax rates.

3.67 Disadvantages

The main arguments against the LIFO can be enumerated as follows :

1. **One of the principal objections to LIFO is that the value of the inventory shown in the balance sheet reflects prices of some past period which is meaningless in the context of current conditions.**
2. The computation of working capital ratio and other financial ratios become useless since the valuation of inventory is dependent on the level of prices in the year the LIFO method was adopted.
3. For pricing a single requisition, more than one price has frequently to be adopted.
4. This method adjusts income only for price changes of materials and only for price changes since the last purchase. From this point of view, as a method of solving price-level problem, LIFO is incomplete.
5. This method as a procedure for matching current costs and revenues is not perfect in the sense that unless both purchases and sales occur regularly in even quantities, the revenues will not be matched with the current costs at the time of sale particularly if prices and costs change rapidly.
6. During falling prices, issues are priced at lower rates and inventory is shown at higher rate which requires adjustments for showing the stock on the principles of valuation of stock at the 'lower of the cost and market price'.

3.68 Applicability

Hendriksen suggests that LIFO is considered to be appropriate when (1) the inventory consists of basic and homogeneous goods; (2) these goods form a substantial part of the cost of the final product sold; (3) the inventory is large in relationship to the total assets of the firm; (4) the inventory turnover is slow; and (5) changes in raw materials prices tend to be reflected quickly in the prices of the finished product.

3.69 Conclusions

The use of LIFO is advocated by those who follow the principle that cost should be related as closely as possible to current price levels. This method of pricing materials has considerable advantages in a period of rising prices as it puts sales and cost of sales on the same footing and automatically eliminates the windfall profit that would otherwise be shown. Advocates of this plan claim that the profits shown tend to be more stable and the resulting accounting information provides a better guide to the management.

3.70 Comparison of the FIFO and the LIFO during inflation

FIFO	FIFO
1. Pricing under FIFO method results in increasing in the valuation of closing stock as closing inventory is priced at current price. This leads to increase in profits.	Since closing inventory is valued at an earlier price, there is a decrease in profit.
2. The closing stock is valued at current costs, and, therefore, working capital is stated in more realistic figure.	On the contrary, as ending stock is valued at old figures, working capital is shown at lower values.
3. Under this system revenues are not properly matched with costs since the materials used in production are charged at lower prices.	It represents better matching of revenues and current cost of goods sold.
4. It cannot present realistic profits. So, decision-making becomes difficult.	It presents a more realistic profits than that presented by FIFO. So, it facilitates decision-making.
5. If prices continue to rise unabated, the total income depicted by income statement will be more.	Under this method the total income displayed by income statement will be less.
6. This method of pricing materials fails to pass the inflationary effect on prices on to the customers.	This method of pricing materials tends to pass on the inflationary impact on cost to the customers.

(d) Highest in First out (HIFO)

Under this method materials purchased at highest price are issued first. This will have the effect of pricing materials issued at the highest price and inventory valuation is made at the lowest possible prices. This method has not gained popularity. It is mainly used in case of monopoly products.

3.71 Average Price Method

(a) Simple Average Method

This method of pricing materials is based on the principle that materials are to be issued to production or job on an average price of two previous receipts regardless of their quantity. The average price is adopted for pricing issues till another consignment of materials is received. A new average rate is computed after every receipt.

Average price is calculated by dividing the total of the prices of the materials in the stock from which the material to be priced could be drawn by the number of prices used in the total. The issue price is determined as follows :

$$\text{Issue Price} = \frac{\text{Unit prices of materials in stock}}{\text{Number of prices}}$$

Advantages

(i) It is easy to calculate the price at which the issues are to be made.

(ii) Simplicity is another advantage of this method.

(iii) A particular purchase at higher or lower rate does not disturb the price to a great extent because the particular difference in the price is averaged out.

Disadvantages

This method suffers from the following disadvantages :

(i) Mateial cost does not represent the actual cost price

(ii) Since the identity of individual material price is lost, the closing stock figure cannot be verified.

(iii) This method does not consider the quantities of materials held in stock.

(iv) During the period of frequent rise in prices, the value of closing stock may show a credit which is not at all realistic.

This method can suitably be adopted where materials are received in uniform quantities. If the quantity varies widely, the simple average of prices will lead to erroneous costs.

Problem 4

From the following particulars find out the value of closing stock when materials are issued under simple average method :

1997			
Feb. 1	Balance	200 units	Rs. 1,000
3	Received	300 units	@ Rs. 6.00 per unit
4	Issues	350 units	
6	Issues	50 units	
10	Receipts	200 units	@ Rs. 6.50 per unit
15	Issues	150 units	

Store Ledger

(Simple Average Method)

Date	Receipts			Issues			Balance		
	Qnt.	*Rate*	*Cost*	*Qnt*	*Rate*	*Cost*	*Qnt.*	*Rate*	*Cost*
1997		Rs.	Rs.		Rs.	Rs.		Rs.	Rs.
Feb. 1							200	5	1,000
3	300	6	1,800				500	5.50	2,800
4				350	5.50	1,925	150	—	875
6				50	5.50	275	100	—	600
10	200	6.50	1,300				300		1,900
15				150	6.25	937.5	150		962.5

***Notes :** Issue rate on 4th and 6th Feb. (Rs. 5 + Rs. 6) ÷ 2 = Rs. 5.50
Issue rate on 25th Feb. (Rs. 6 + Rs. 6.50) ÷ 2 = Rs. 6.25

(b) Weighted Average Method

According to I.C.M.A. "A price which is calculated by dividing the total cost of materials in the stock from which the materials to be priced could be divided by the total quantity of materials in that stock".

Thus, the weighted average price takes into account both the price and quantity of the materials in store.

Advantages

1. The method is logical, rational and consistent as it absorbs the cost of materials while determining the average for pricing material issues. Weightage is given to both quantity and price to bring about consistency and uniformity.
2. This method recovers the cost of materials from production.
3. Under this method materials are issued at a price as near to the market price.
4. It is considered to be the best especially when prices fluctuate considerably.
5. Closing inventory represents the average cost price of materials in hand.

Disadvantages

1. When there is too much change in the prices of materials, simplicity and convenience are lost.
2. Since an average price is not based on actual price incurred, pricing of materials does not become realistic.

WEIGHTED AVERAGE METHOD

Problem 5

Show the Store Ledger entries as they would appear when using weighted average method of pricing issues in connection with the following transactions :

April 1990		Units	Value (Rs.)
1	Balance	300	600
2	Purchased	200	440
4	Issued	150	—
6	Purchased	200	460
11	Issued	150	—
19	Issued	200	—
22	Purchased	200	480
27	Issued	250	—

[Adapted—I.C.W.A. Inter)

Solution

Store Ledger Account

Code No. ....

Weighted Average Method
Minimum level
Reordering level
Maximum level

Date	Receipts			Issues			Balance		
1990	*Qnt.*	*Rate*	*Amt.*	*Qnt.*	*Rate*	*Amt.*	*Qnt.*	*Rate*	*Amt.*
April		Rs.	Rs.		Rs.	Rs.		Rs.	Rs.
1							300	2.00	600
2	200	2.20	440				500	2.08	1,040
4				150	2.08	312	350	2.08	728
6	200	2.30	460				550	2.16	1,188
11				150	2.16	324	400	2.16	864
19				200	2.16	432	200	2.16	432
22	200	2.40	480				400	2.28	912
27				250	2.28	570	150	2.28	342

Notes :

1. 4th April = 1,040 ÷ 500 = Rs. 2.08
2. 11th + 19th April = $\frac{1,188}{550}$ = Rs. 2.16
3. 27th = 912 ÷ 400 = Rs. 2.28

3.72 Base Stock Method

Under this method a certain minimum stock of a material is always carried and is priced at the original cost, generally at the lowest purchase price. The portion of stock above this level is issued and priced either under FIFO or LIFO method.

This method works well in tanning, and mining industries.

Advantages

This method of pricing materials has the following advantages :

1. The work of valuing inventory is simplified because base or normal stock values are fixed.
2. Unrealised profits are eliminated.
3. Inventories are consistently shown in balance sheet at conservative values.

Disadvantages

1. Balance Sheet shows misleading picture of working capital as inventories are under stated.
2. Profit and Loss Account shows a misleading profit since it fails to recognise gains and losses on inventories.
3. This method of pricing materials is not recognised by the Income-tax Authorities.

Problem 6

The following information is available for the month of January 1998 :

1998	Receipts Qnt. (Units)	Rate Rs.	Issues Units
Jan. 4	2,000	4.00	
" 12	3,000	4.80	
" 15			1,500
" 20	2,500	5.20	
" 30			1,000

Prepare Store ledger showing base stock method of inventory valuation with LIFO method of pricing material issues. The normal base stock quantity is 500 units.

Solution

STORE LEDGER

Base Stock with LIFO Method

Date	*Receipts*			*Issues*			*Balance*		
1998	*Qnt.*	*Rate*	*Amount*	*Qnt.*	*Rate*	*Amount*	*Qnt.*	*Rate*	*Amount*
		Rs.	Rs.		Rs.	Rs.		Rs.	Rs.
Jan. 4	2,000	4.00	8,000				2,000	4.00	8,000
" 12	3,000	4.80	14,400				2,000	4.00	8,000
							3,000	4.80	14,400
" 15				1,500	4.80	7,200	2,000	4.00	8,000
							1,500	4.80	7,200
" 20	2,500	5.20	13,000				2,000	4.00	8,000
							1,500	4.80	7,200
							2,500	5.20	13,000
" 30				1,000	5.20	5,200	2,000	4.00	8,000
							1,500	4.80	7,200
							1,500	5.20	7,800

The value of closing inventory comprises the following :

		Rs.
Base stock 500	units @ Rs. 4.00	2,000
1,500	@ Rs. 4.00	6,000
1,500	@ Rs. 5.20	7,800
1,500	@ Rs. 4.80	7,200
		23,000

3.73 Highest-in-first-out Method

Under this method it is assumed that highest priced materials are issued first. When the whole lot of highest priced materials are exhausted, the next lot of materials purchased at next higher price should be used for pricing the issue. Thus, the inventory value of materials is kept at the lowest possible price. This method has no practical use.

Disadvantages

This method suffers from the following **disadvantages** :

1. This method of pricing issues involves cumbersome calculations.
2. The cost of production is grossly overstated.
3. During a period of rising prices this method will be similar to LIFO method and during a period of falling prices it will be the same as the FIFO method.
4. Under this method comparison among similar jobs becomes a difficult exercise.
5. **Inventory is shown on the Balance Sheet at a lower value and as such Balance Sheet fails to exhibit true financial position.**

3.74 Periodic Simple Average Method

Under the method of Periodic Simple Average rate is calculated for a particular period and not whenever consignment is received. Thus, Periodic Simple Average is calculated by dividing the total of materials purchased during the accounting period during which the materials to be priced are used, by the number of prices used to calculate the average price.

Periodic Simple Average Price

$$= \frac{\text{Total of purchase prices of materials in a particular accounting period}}{\text{No. of prices used in the period}}$$

Advantages

The following advantages can be enjoyed :

(i) This method is very easy to operate.

(ii) It smoothenes out the price fluctuations of materials during a particular period.

(iii) This method can suitably be used in process industry.

Disadvantages

(i) The costing of the product gets delayed since pricing is done at the end of the period.

(ii) This method cannot be used suitably where each individual order must be priced at each stage up to completion.

(iii) It involves heavy clerical work.

(iv) A substantial profit or loss may arise only due to the use of this method.

3.75 Moving Simple Average Method

Under this method, periodic simple average prices are further averaged. The moving simple average price is the average of the periodic simple average prices for a given number of periods. **This price is computed by dividing the total of the periodic simple average prices of a given number of periods by the number of periods.** The period chosen should cover the period in which the material is issued.

Advantages

(i) This method is very useful where prices of materials are subject to constant price fluctuations.

(ii) High and low prices are removed from the computation and do not influence the average after six or seven months.

(iii) This method helps to stabilise the charges to work-in-process even during the period of frequent price fluctuations.

Disadvantages

(i) It involves substantial clerical work

(ii) The value of closing stock may be under-valued or over-valued. When prices rise, the issue price worked out is lower than the periodic average prices for the period concerned and vice versa.

3.76 Periodic Weighted Average Method

Under this method weighted average price is calculated by dividing the total cost of material purchased during the accounting period, in which the material to be priced is used by the total quantity of material purchased during that period.

Thus, Periodic Weighted Average Price

$$= \frac{\text{Total cost of purchase during the period}}{\text{Total quantity purchased during the period}}$$

Advantages

(i) It is easy to operate.

(ii) It can be used in process industry advantageously.

(iii) It eliminates the effect of price fluctuations.

Disadvantages

(i) Under this method costing of materials issues gets delayed upto the end of the period.

(ii) This method of pricing issues of materials cannot be used in job order industry.

(iii) It invloves lot of clerical work.

(iv) Under this method the value of closing stock will not correspond to the value of closing stock determined under conventional method of valuation of closing stock, i.e., market price or cost price, whichever is less.

3.77 Moving Weighted Average Method

Under this method, price is calculated by taking the average of periodic weighted average prices i.e. total of periodic weighted average prices of a given number of periods is divided by the number of periods.

The advantages and disadvantages of this method are more or less similar to those of Simple Average Method excepting that this method considers not only the prices but also the quantity used during the related period.

The use of this method of pricing issues of materials yields a very representative price for costing the material issues.

3.78 Standard Cost Method

The price of issues for each item is pre-determined for a particular period taking into account all the factors that affect price, e.g., market trends, transportation costs etc. Standard prices are determined for each material. All issues are made at standard price. The standards are revised from period to period. The actual price is compared with standard price.

Advantages

The following are the advantages of Standard Cost Method :

1. This method is easy to apply.
2. This helps to prepare material price variance account and material usage variance account.

3. The preparation of variance accounts help to determine the efficiency of material purchase department. The efficiency in the use of materials can also be measured.
4. Quick determination of selling prices is possible.
5. The use of this method results in reduction of clerical work.

Disadvantages

1. This method does not conform to accepted accounting practices.
2. This method does not reflect the market price.
3. The fixation of standard cost is a difficult exercise as it requires a lot of effort and experience.
4. This method can effectively be used when standard costing system is in use.

3.79 Choice of Method

In a period of *falling price,* it is conservative to value on the *FIFO* or *Average Method,* as the older or more expensive items are then absorbed into cost first and the less expensive items are left in stock. This brings the inventory reasonably into line with the value which will be used for financial accounting purposes.

In a period of rising prices, the pricing methods based on cost tend to show inflationary profits which appear to be highly satisfactory, but may nevertheless conceal factory losses and inefficient production. On the other hand, the pricing methods based on market value (LIFO) maintain a balance between material cost and selling price, but as the stock balances include goods at the earliest prices, the inventory is considerably undervalued.

The standard cost method can satisfactorily be operated in either a rising or a falling market as price fluctuations are automatically segregated into variance accounts. The variances may be written-off at the time of purchase or be held in suspense and charged to the Profit and Loss Account at the time if issue.

Other factors affecting the choice of method are :

(i) The nature of the business;
(ii) The relative number of issues compared with receipts;
(iii) The frequency with which prices change;
(iv) The proportion which raw materials bear to total cost;
(v) The necessity for maintaining uniformity within an industry;
(vi) Relative rate of stock turnover;
(vii) Customs and practices within the industry.

3.80 Treatment of some Important Items

If the stock verifier finds any shortage of stock on a particular day during physical verification, such shortage of materials should be treated as issues and to be entered in the issue column and to be valued as per the method adopted i.e. FIFO or LIFO.

1. Pricing of Materials Returned to Supplier

Materials purchased may be returned to the supplier. In cost accounting the following rules are generally applicable as to the valuation of such returns :

(i) When FIFO method is followed, the materials returned would be valued at the price of the *oldest goods in stock* on the date of such return.

(ii) In case of LIFO the returned materials would be valued at the price of *latest units in stock.*

(iii) In case the business firm follows average price method, purchase returns would be valued at *average price.*

The quantity and value of materials returned are shown generally in the *issue column*. They may also be shown in *Receipt column in red ink.*

2. Pricing of Materials Returned from Production Department

Problems arise when excess of defective materials are returned from the requisitioning departments to store. The following rules apply in regard to pricing of such materials in store ledger :

(i) In case the firm follows FIFO or LIFO method, the returned materials should be recorded in the Store Ledger at a price they were *originally issued.* Those units will be issued *at the old price* on the next requisition which is received. *Alternatively,* those units may be treated as a new purchase and may be issued according to the principles of method adopted.

(ii) If the firm follows *average price method,* the returned materials should be entered in the Receipt column at a price, the materials were originally issued. *A new average* cost is to be computed as if the goods returned were a new purchase.

The quantity and value of materials returned may be shown in issue column in red ink or alternatively, they may be shown in the Receipt column.

Materials Return Note

Excess materials on a particular job or in a department are returned to the storeroom with a note duly signed by the Foreman. These notes are coloured differently for easy identification. The materials returned are placed in the appropriate Bins and entered in the Bin Card. A specimen of Materials Return Note is given below :

ABC Co. Ltd.
Materials Return Note

Department .... No. ....
Credit Job No. .... Date ....

Code No.	*Quantity or or weight*	*Description*	*For office use*		*Remarks*
			Rate Rs.	*Amount* Rs.	

Authorised Bin No. ....
Price entered by Received by ....
Stores Ledger Folio Storekeeper ....

Fig. 3.12

3. Transfer of Materials from One Job to Another

Materials issued to one job may be transferred to another job. This is done when the need for one job is more urgent. To obviate unauthorised transfers, malpractices and manipulations in materials consumption, such transfers should take place on the basis of a document known as **Materials Transfer Note**. Valuation of such materials is done at the price at which they were originally issued. No entry is required to be made in the store ledger.

Specimen of Materials Transfer Note

SWIL LIMITED
Materials Transfer Note

Serial No. ....
Date ....

The following materials have been transferred—
From Job No................ to Job No................

Code	*Description*	*Quantity*	*Cost Office*		
			Rate	*Unit*	*Amount*

Authorised Delivered Received Priced

Fig. 3.13

4. Treatment of Material and Production Losses

Material and production losses may arise due to *Waste, Scrap, Spoilage* and *Defective work.*

The difference between the input of material and output in a process may be in the form of **waste, scrap, spoilage** or **defectives.**

In the production process waste represents discarded substances having no value, Waste comprises invisible loss or visible loss of material. Examples of waste are smoke, dust, gases, slag etc. Input loss of material may be either physical or economic. Physical loss may occur prior to production (evaporation) or during the production process. An economic loss signifies the loss of value although some residual may physically remain.

3.81 Accounting treatment

(i) *Normal waste* : This is unavoidable and uncontrollable and treated as a part of product cost. The cost of waste is borne by the good units. So, loss on normal wastage is usually charged to production thereby inflating the unit price of material used.

(ii) *Abnormal Waste* : Abnormal waste is the excess of material losses over the normal losses. The causes of abnormal waste are pilferage, careless handling of materials defective workmanship, obsolescence due to irrational issues etc.

Abnormal waste is transferred to costing Profit and Loss Account.

In most of the industrial units waste report is submitted periodically by the foreman or production incharge.

The specimen of waste report is given below :

Finolex Co. Ltd.
Waste Report

Department ....
Cost Centre .... No. ....
Job/Process No. .... Date ....

Particulars	*Normal waste%*	*Actual waste*			
		%	*Quantity*	*Value if any*	*Remarks*

Entered by Signature of Inspector
Action taken by

Fig. 3.14

5. Scrap

Scrap is a residue incidentally obtained from manufacturing processes having a small value which is recoverable without further processing.

Examples of scrap are :

Metal from stamping operation, clipping of wood, off-cuts of sheet metal. Scrap normally occurs in engineering industries where operations like boring, drilling, turning etc. are carried out. Scrap may arise in the form of Sawdust in Timber Industry, off-cuts and cut-pieces in leather industry.

Accounting treatment of scrap

(i) When the scrap is sold

(a) Treatment by neglect

If the value of Scrap is negligible, the sale of Scrap is treated as other income in profit and loss account. Under this method unit cost of production includes cost of scrap.

(b) Credited to Job or Work-in-Progress Account

If the value of scrap is significant and the quantity varies from job to job, the sale value of scrap is credited to the job account. The following journal entries will be passed :

(i) Scrap A/c Dr.
To Job A/c or Work-in-Progress A/c

(ii) For cash received
Cash A/c Dr.
To Scrap A/c

(c) Credited to Manufacturing Overhead

When the scrap cannot be identified with the individual jobs, the sale of scrap is credited to Manufacturing Overhead Account. As a result of this, the overhead rate is reduced.

Journal Entries

(i) Scrap A/c Dr.
To Manufacturing Overhead A/c

(ii) Cash A/c Dr.
To Scrap A/c

(ii) When Scrap is Reprocessed

Sometimes scrap can be reprocessed to convert it into useful raw materials for subsequent production of basic products. If the scrap is used for reprocessing, the most recent acquisition price is considered.

It may be necessary to process the scrap to make it worthy of reprocessing. In such a situation, the amount by which the cost of work-in-progress is to be reduced will depend upon the cost to be incurred for its further processing for re-use.

Control of Scrap

Management should take appropriate steps to keep scrap output within the acceptable limits. Managerial efforts should be made to produce maximum from a given quantity of raw materials.

Following points are relevant for effective Control of Scrap :

1. *Designing stage*

Scrap control begins form the product designing stage but not at the production stage. Therefore, attention must be given to avoid scrap at the stage of designing the product.

2. *Selection of right material and equipment*

The use of good quality of material and sophisticated equipment reduces the occurrence of scrap to a great extent.

3. *Selection of skilled personnel*

Right type of personnel with proper training and experience in material processing should be selected.

4. *Determination of acceptable limits*

For control of scrap, it is very much necessary to ascertain the acceptable limits of scrap output. Product design, material specification and labour force are to be considered primarily for this purpose. The determination of acceptable limits requires a lot of trial runs, experience and analytical study of required data available for the industry.

5. *Scrap reports*

Different scrap reports should be used for control of scrap. These reports may differ in contents in different organisations according to specific requirements. A common format for scrap report is given below :

SCRAP REPORT

Department No. ....
Cost Centre

Type of Scrap	*Basic Product*	*Process or Job*	*Good Production*	*Normal Scrap*			*Abnormal Scrap*			
				%	*Qnt.*	*Value*	*%*	*Qnt.*	*Value*	*Causes & action taken*

Entered by Signature of
Action taken by Inspector

Fig. 3.15

6 Spoilage

Sometimes in manufacturing operations materials are so damaged that they are taken out of process and disposed of since such materials cannot be repaired or reconditioned. Such materials are known as spoilage. Spoilage occurs due to some defect in operations or materials.

For the sake of control, spoilage can be classified as :

(i) Normal Spoilage and (ii) Abnormal Spoilage. If the spoilage is well within limits, it is treated as normal spoilage while spoilage exceeds the limits of normal spoilage, it is referred to as abnormal spoilage.

Accounting Treatment of Spoilage

Following accounting treatment may be adopted :

1. **Losses due to normal spoilage are charged to process or job since normal spoilage forms part of cost of good production.**
2. Cost of abnormal Spoilage represents avoidable losses, so, it does not for a part of cost of good production. For this reason loss on account of abnormal Spoilage should be charged to Profit and Loss Account.
3. If spoiled units are reused as raw material in the same manufacturing process, no separate accounting treatment is required. If spoilage is used for any other process or job, credit is given to relevant process or job account.

A systematic reporting goes a long way to exercise control over spoilage. Spoilage of each department should be communicated to departmental heads for taking appropriate measures for controlling spoilage.

A specimen format of spoilage report is given below for easy understanding :

Finolex Ltd.
Spoilage Report

Department — Number
Cost Centre — Week ending

Process Job No.	*Total units produced*	*Spoiled units*	*Actual Spoilage %*	*Standard Spoilage %*	*Cost of Spoilage*	*Cost of abnormal spoilage*	*Reasons*

Action taken — Signature of Inspector

Fig. 3.16

7. Defective Work/Rejects

Defectives are that portion of the process loss which can be converted into a finished product by incuuring further materials and expenses. Defective work may be the result of a number of factors like poor quality of materials, careless planning, poor workmanship, incompetent supervision. Defective units are subsequently reworked and rectified. There may also be defective finished goods, which have been in stock for too long a time and have become defective.

Accounting Treatment of Defective Work

1. **Treatment by neglect**
   When the defective work has a nominal value, the amount of loss is absorbed completely by good units.
2. **Charging to Overhead**
   The additional cost of rectification of defective is charged to factory overheads and apportioned to various goods as part of the factory overheads. If a particular department is responsible for the additional cost of rectification, it can be charged to that department.
3. **Charging to specific job**
   If the defective units can be traced to a specific job/order, the additional costs can be charged to the job or order.
4. **Charging to Costing Profit & Loss Account**
   If the defectives are abnormal and due to uncontrollable factors, the additional costs are charged to Costing Profit and Loss Account.

Defective Report

At each stage of production, defective and spoiled goods are separated. If reconditioning work has to be done, a report is prepared and attached to the production order representing the defective work. Reconditioning work should be approved by a senior official.

Specimen of Defective Work Report

Defective Work Report

Production Order No. .... No. ....

No. of units .... Date ....

Department responsible ....

Nature of Defects ....

Department (Job No.)	*Description of additional work*	*Rework Costs*			*Total Costs*	*Remarks*
		Material Cost	*Labour Cost*	*Applied overhead*		

Prepared by Checked by

Fig. 3.17

WORKED OUT PROBLEMS

Problem 7

A lorry load of materials of mixed goods was purchased for Rs. 9,000. These were sorted out into the following goods whose market rate is shown against each :

Grade A 5,000 units Selling Rate @ Rs. 1.20

B 3,000 units Selling Rate @ Re. 1.00

C 2,000 units Selling Rate @ Re. 0.50

Find out the purchase rate per unit of each grade of the material assuming that all grades yield same rate of profit.

[I.C.W.A. (Inter)]

Solution

	Total Sale Price			Profit = Rs. 10,000 – 9,000 = Rs. 1,000.
A	5,000 × Rs. 1.20	=	Rs. 6,000	
B	3,000 × Re. 1.00	=	Rs. 3,000	
C	2,000 × Re. 0.50	=	Rs. 1,000	
			10,000	

$$\text{Percentage of profit on sale price} = \frac{1,000 \times 100}{10,000} = 10\%$$

Therefore cost per unit :

			Profit		Sale Price – Profit = Cost Price
A =	$1.20 \times \frac{10}{100}$	=	0.12	=	1.20 – 0.12 = 1.08
B =	$1.00 \times \frac{10}{100}$	=	0.10	=	1.00 – 0,10 = 0,90
C =	$0.50 \times \frac{10}{100}$	=	0.05	=	0.50 – 0.05 = 0.45

Problem 8

The particulars relating to the import of Sealing Ring made by AB & Co. during December 1990 are given below :

(a) Sealing Ring – 1,000 pieces invoiced @ £ 2.00 C.I.F., Bombay Port.

(b) Customs duty was paid @ 100% on Invoice value (which was converted to Indian Currency by adopting an Exchange rate of Rs. 17.20 per £)

(c) Clearing charges – Rs. 1,800 for the entire consignment.

(d) Freight charges – Rs. 1,400 for transporting the consignment from Bombay Port to Factory premises.

It was found on inspection that 100 pieces of the above material were broken and, therefore, rejected. There is no scrap value for the rejected part. No refund for the broken material would be admissible as per the terms of contract. The management decided to treat 60 pieces as normal loss and the rest 40 pieces as abnormal loss. The entire quantity of 900 pieces was issued to production.

Calculate :

(a) Total cost of material and (b) Unit cost of material issued to production.

Also state briefly how the value of 100 pieces rejected in inspection will be treated in costs.

[I.C.W.A. (Inter)]

Solution

AB & Co.

Computation of total cost of Materials

	Invoice value – £ 2 × 1,000 = £ 2,000		Rs.
Add :	(£ 1 = Rs. 17.20) 2,000 × Rs. 17.20	=	34,400
	Customs Duty @ 100% of Invoice value	=	34,400
	Clearing charges	=	1,800
	Freight charges	=	1,400
	Total Cost	=	72,000

Chargeable units = 1,000 – 60 – 40 = 900 units

			Rs.
	Total material cost	=	72,000
Less :	Cost of abnormal loss of 40 pieces $\frac{72,000}{1,000} \times 40$	=	2,880
			69,120

Issue rate per unit = Rs. $\frac{69,120}{900}$ = Rs. 76.80

Note : Cost of abnormal loss should be written-off against costing Profit & Loss A/c while cost of normal loss should be absorbed.

Treatment of Abnormal Loss

The cost of abnormal loss of Rs. 2,880 should be charged to the costing Profit and Loss A/c for the period.

Problem 9

A manufacturing organisation has imported four types of materials. The invoice reveals the following data :

		Quantity Kgs	Rate U.S. $ per Kg.
Material	A	1,000	1.50
	B	2,000	1.25
	C	1,500	2.00
	D	3,000	1.00

Import duty – 23% of invoice value

Insurance – 2% of invoice value

Freight and clearing – Rs. 30,000

Exchange rate U.W. $ 1 = Rs. 16.00

50% of the materials imported are issued to production centres. While determining the value of closing stock 5% allowance is provided to cover up storage loss. Determine the value of closing stock of each type of materials.

[Adapted—I.C.W.A. (Inter) Dec. 1989]

Solution

Statement showing the Materials Cost

	Materials	A	B	C	D	Total
	Units (in Kgs)	1,000	2,000	1,500	3,000	7,500
	Rate U.S.$ per Kg.	1.50	1.25	2.00	1.00	
	Value in U.S.$	1,500	2,500	3,000	3,000	10,000
Add	Import duty @ 23%	345	575	690	690	2,300
	Insurance @ 2%	30	50	60	60	200
	Total Cost ($)	1,875	3,125	3,750	3,750	12,500
	Total cost converted into	Rs.	Rs.	Rs.	Rs.	Rs.
	Rupees @ $1 = Rs. 16	30,000	50,000	60,000	60,000	2,00,000
Add	Freight and clearing charges (in 2 : 4 : 3 : 6 = quantity ratio)	4,000	8,000	6,000	12,000	30,000
	Total Cost in rupees	34,000	58,000	66,000	72,000	2,30,000
	Issued to production departments @ 50%	17,000	29,000	33,000	36,000	1,15,000
	Balance of Stock	17,000	29,000	33,000	36,000	1,15,000
Less	Allowance @ 5% for storage loss	850	1,450	1,650	1,800	5,750
	Value of closing stock	16,150	27,550	31,350	34,200	1,09,250

Problem 10

The following details are available in respect of a consignment of 1,250 Kgs of material 'X' :

(a) Invoice price – Rs. 20 per kg

(b) Excise duty – 25% on Invoice price

(c) Sales Tax – 8% on Invoice price including Excise Duty

(d) Trade discount – 10% on Invoice price

(e) Insurance – 1% of aggregate net price

(f) Delivery charges – Rs. 250

(g) Cost of containers @ Rs. 60 per container for 50 kgs of material. Rebate is allowed @ Rs. 40 per container if returned within six weeks, which is a normal feature.

(h) One container load of material was rejected on inspection and not accepted.

(i) Cost of unloading and handling @ 0.25% or the cost of materials ultimately accepted.

On the basis of the above you are required to find out the landed cost of per kg of material 'X'.

[Adapted—I.C.W.A. (Inter) June 1991]

Solution

Computation of landed Cost of Material 'X'

		Total Cost	Cost per unit
		Rs.	Rs.
	Invoice price @ Rs. 20 per kg.	25,000.00	20.00
Less	Trade discount @ 10%	2,500.00	2.00
		22,500.00	18.00
Add	Excise Duty @ 25% on Invoice price	6,250.00	5.00
Add	Sales Tax @ 8% on Invoice price including	2,500.00	2.00
	Excise Duty	31,250.00	25.00
Add	Insurance @ 1% on the above net price	312.50	0.25
		31,562.50	25.25
Add	Delivery Charges @ Rs. 60	250.00	0.20
		31,812.50	25.45
Add	Cost of Container – $\frac{1,250}{50}$ × Rs. 60	1,500.00	1.20
		33,312.50	26.65
Less	Cost of material rejected (1 container of 50 kgs)	1,332.50	—
		31,980.00	26.65
Add	Cost of handling @ 0.25%	79.95	0.07
		32,059.95	26.72
Less	Credit for containers returnable	960.00	0.80
	(24 containers × Rs. 40 per container)		
	Total Landed Cost	31,099.95	25.92

Problem 11

From the following information given below determine the Economic Order Quantity :

Annual consumption – 400 units

Cost per unit – Re 1

Order Placing cost per order Rs. 5

Carrying cost on inventory 10%

[C.U. B.Com. (Pass) 1997]

Solution

Formula

$$EOQ = \sqrt{\frac{2AO}{C}}$$ where A = Annual Consumption

O = Cost for placing an order

C = Carrying cost.

$$\sqrt{\frac{2 \times 400 \times 5}{\frac{10}{100} \times 1}} = \sqrt{\frac{4,000}{0.10}} = 200 \text{ units}$$

Problem 12

From the information given below determine the EOQ :

Annual usage	8,000 units
Purchase price per unit	Rs. 10
Ordering cost per order	Rs. 80
Carrying cost	20% p.a. per unit cost.

[C.U. B.Com. (Pass) 1995]

Solution

$\sqrt{\dfrac{2AO}{C}}$ where A = Annual consumption

O = Ordering cost per order

C = Carrying cost

$\sqrt{\dfrac{2 \times 8,000 \times 80}{2}} = 800$ units

Problem 13

A Steel Rolling Mill uses a particular type of iron costing Rs. 500 per ton. Its annual consumption of that iron is 200 tons. The cost of placing an order is Rs. 100 and the rate of interest is 10% p.a. Work out the optimum quantity to be ordered by the Mill :

[V.U. B.Com. (Hons.) 1993]

Solution

$\text{EOQ} = \sqrt{\dfrac{2AO}{C}}$ Where, A = Annual consumption

O = Cost of placing an order

C = Carrying cost

$= \sqrt{\dfrac{2 \times 200 \times 100}{10\% \text{ of Rs.. } 500}} = \sqrt{\dfrac{40,000}{50}} = \sqrt{800} = 28.28$ units or Say, 29 units

Problem 14

From the following information calculate Re-order level, Maximum level and Minimum level of stock :

Reorder quantity – 6,000 units

Minimum stock level to allow for emergencies – 5 weeks.

Average lead time – 4 weeks.

Average consumption rate per week 500 units

Minimum consumption in 4 weeks 1,600 units.

[B.U. (Hons.) 1986]

Solution

(a) Reorder level

Minimum stock level + Average lead time × Average rate of consumption

= (5 × 500) + (4 × 500) = 2,500 + 2,000 = 4,500 units.

(b) Maximum Stock level

Reorder level + Reorder quantity – (Minimum consumption* × Lead time)

= 4,500 + 6,000 – (400 × 5) = 10,500 – 2,000 = 8,500 units

---

* Minimum consumption = $\dfrac{1,600}{4}$ = 400 units

(c) Minimum Stock level

Reorder level – (Average consumption × Average lead time)

= 4,500 – (500 × 4) = 4,500 – 2,000 = 2,500 units.

Problem 15

The following information is available in respect of a material of Y & Co. Ltd. :

Re-order quantity	12,000	units
Lead time	4 to 8	weeks
Maximum consumption	4,000	units per week
Normal consumption	3,000	units per week
Minimum consumption	1,550	units per week

Ascertain the following from the above information :

(a) Re-order level, (b) Minimum stock level, (c) Maximum stock level.

[B.U. B.Com. (Hons.) 1984]

Solution

(a) Reorder level = Maximum usage × Maximum reorder period = 4,000 × 8 = 32,000 units.

(b) Minimum Stock level = Reordering level –(Normal or average usage × Lead time)
= 32,000 – (3,000 × 6) = 32,000 – 18,000 = 14,000 units

(c) Maximum level = Reorder level – (Minimum consumption × Minimum reorder period) + Reorder quantity = 32,000 – (1,550 × 4) + 12,000 = 32,000 – 6,200 + 12,000 = 25,800 + 12,000 = 37,800.

Problem 16

The Ganges Company uses about 75,000 valves per year and the usage is fairly constant at 6,250 per month.

The valves cost Rs. 1.50 per unit when bought in quantities and the carrying cost is estimated to be 20% of average inventory investment on the annual basis. The cost to place an order and process the delivery is Rs. 18. It takes 45 days to receive from the date of an order and a safety stock of 3,250 valves is required.

You are required to determine :

(i) The most economic order quantity and frequency of orders, (ii) The order point and (iii) The most economic order quantity if the valves cost Rs. 4.50 each instead of Rs. 1.50 each.

[Adapted—M. Com. Delhi]

Solution

(i) $EOQ = \sqrt{\frac{2UO}{IC}}$ or $\sqrt{\frac{2\times 75{,}000 \times 18}{20\% \text{ of } 1.50}} = \sqrt{90{,}00{,}000}$

= 3,000 units or 25 orders per year.

(ii) Order point

Safety stock + (Average rate of consumption × Lead time)

= 3,250 + (6,250 units × 1.5 months) = 3,250 + 9,375 = 12,625 units.

(iii) $EOQ = \sqrt{\frac{2 \times 75{,}000 \times 18}{4.50 \times 20\%}} = \sqrt{30{,}00{,}000}$ = 1,733 units approximately per year.

Problem 17

Materials X and Y are used as follows :

Minimum usage – 50 units each per week, Maximum usage – 150 units each per week, Normal usage – 100 units each per week. Ordering quantities X = 600 units, Y = 1,000 units. Delivery period X = 4 to 6 weeks, Y = 2 to 4 weeks.

Calculate for each material :

(a) Minimum level; (b) Maximum level; (c) Order level.

[C.A. (Inter)]

Solution

For Material X

(c) Order level = Maximum usage × Maximum delivery period = 150 × 6 = 900 units

(a) Minimum level = Ordering level – (Normal usage × Normal delivery period) = 900 – (100 × 5) = 900 – 500 = 400 units

(b) Maximum level = (Reorder level + Ordering quantity) – (Minimum usage × Minimum delivery period) = 900 + 600 – (50 × 4) = 1,500 – 200 = 1,300 units.

For Material Y

Ordering level = 150 × 4 = 600 units

Minimum level = 600 – (100 × 3) = 600 – 300 = 300 units

Maximum level = 600 + 1,000 – (50 × 2) = 1,600 – 100 = 1,500 units

Working Notes

Calculation of normal period of delivery of Material X = $\frac{4 + 6}{2}$ = 5 weeks,

Material Y = $\frac{2 + 4}{2}$ = 3 weeks.

Problem 18

A Company uses annually 50,000 units of an item each costing Rs. 1.20. Each order costs Rs. 45 and carrying costs 15% of the annual average inventory value.

(i) Find the EOQ

(ii) If the Company operates 250 days a year, the procurement time is 10 days and safety stock is 500 units. Find reorder level, maximum, minimum and average inventory.

[Adapted—C.A. Final '87]

Solution

(i) $\text{EOQ} = \sqrt{\frac{2AO}{C}}$ C = 15% of Rs. 1.20 = Re. 0.18.

So, $\text{EOQ} = \sqrt{\frac{2 \times 50{,}000 \times 45}{0.18}} = \sqrt{\frac{45{,}00{,}000}{0.18}}$

$= \sqrt{2{,}50{,}00{,}000} = 5{,}000$ units

(ii) Consumption per day = $\frac{50,000}{250}$ days = 200 units

Re-order level = Safety stock + (Lead time × consumption per day).

= 500 + (10 × 200) = 500 + 2,000 = 2,500 units

Maximum level = Reorder level – (Minimum consumption during lead time) + EOQ. = 2,500 – (10 × 200) + 5,000 = 2,500 – 2,000 + 5,000 = 500 + 5,000 = 5,500.

Minimum Inventory = ROL – (Normal consumption during lead time)

= 2,500 – 10 × 200 = 2,500 – 2,000 = 500 units

Average Inventory = $\frac{\text{Maximum} + \text{Minimum}}{2} = \frac{5,500 + 500}{2}$

= $\frac{6,000}{2}$ = 3,000 units.

Problem 19

Kapil Motors purchase 9,000 motor spare parts for its annual requirements ordering one month's requirement at a time. Each spare part costs Rs. 20. The ordering cost per order is Rs. 15 and the carrying charges are 15% of the average inventory per year. You have been asked to suggest a more economical purchasing policy for the company.

[I.C.W.A. Final—June 87]

Solution

Cost as per present purchasing policy

Carrying cost	= $\frac{15}{100} \times 20$	=	Rs. 3.
Ordering one month usage	= $\frac{9,000}{12}$	=	750 units.
Cost of ordering	= 12 × 15	=	Rs. 180.00
Carrying cost	= $\frac{750}{2} \times 3$	=	Rs.1,125.00
			Rs.1,305.00

Economical Cost

EOQ = $\sqrt{\frac{2AO}{C}} = \sqrt{\frac{2 \times 9,000 \times 15}{3}}$ = 300 units

No. of orders in a year	= $\frac{9,000}{300}$	=	30
Ordering cost	= 30 orders × Rs. 15	=	Rs. 450
Carrying cost	= $\frac{300}{2} \times 3$	=	Rs. 450
			Rs. 900

Comment

If the Company follows the second alternative purchase policy, it will save Rs. 1,305 – Rs. 900 = Rs. 405 annually.

Problem 19

A manufacturer uses 200 units of a component every month and he buys them entirely from outside supplier. The order placing and receiving cost is Rs. 100 and annual carrying cost is Rs. 12. From this set of data calculate Economic Order Quantity.

[I.C.W.A.—Inter—June 1984]

Solution

$$\text{Economic Order Quantity} = \sqrt{\frac{2C_3R}{C_1}}$$

C_3 = ordering cost; C_1 = Carrying cost; R = requirements per unit of time.

Here C_3 = Rs. 100, C_1 = Rs. 12, R =200 units × 12 = 2,400 units.

$$EOQ = \sqrt{\frac{2 \times 100 \times 2,400}{12}} = \sqrt{\frac{4,80,000}{12}} = \sqrt{40,000} = 200 \text{ units.}$$

Problem 20

From the following particulars find out the Economic Order quantity :

Order Quantity :

(i)	Annual Demand	12,000 units
(ii)	Ordering Cost	Rs. 90 per order.
(iii)	Inventory carrying cost per annum—	Rs. 15.

[I.C.W.A.—Inter—Dec. 1990]

Solution

$$EOQ = \sqrt{\frac{2AP}{S}}$$

where E = Order size; A = Annual quantity used in units ;

P = cost per purchase order ; and

S = Annual cost of carrying one unit in stock for one year.

Substituting we get :

$$EOQ - \sqrt{\frac{2 \times 12,000 \times 90}{15}} = \sqrt{\frac{\text{Rs. } 21,60,000}{15}} = \sqrt{1,44,000} = 380 \text{ units.}$$

Problem 21

A manufacturer buys casting equipment from outside suppliers @ Rs. 30 per unit. Total annual needs are 800 units. The following further data are available : .

Annual return on investment 10%.

Rent, insurance and taxes per unit per year Re. 1

Cost of placing an order Rs. 100

Determine the economic order quanity.

[Adapted—C.U. M.Com.]

Solution

$$EOQ = \sqrt{\frac{2AB}{C}} = \sqrt{\frac{2 \times 800 \times 100}{4`}} = \sqrt{40,000} = 200 \text{ units}$$

Working notes

Calculation of carrying cost per unit

(a) Cost of interest = $\frac{800 \times \text{Rs. } 30 \times 10}{100}$ = Rs. 2,400

Interest cost per unit = Rs. 2,400 ÷ 800 = Rs. 3

So, total carrying cost per unit

Interest cost p.u. Rs. 3 + other carrying cost like rent, insurance and taxes Re. 1 per unit = Rs. 3 + Re. 1 = Rs. 4.

Problem 22

P Ltd. uses three types of materials A, B and C for production of 'X', the final product. The relevant monthly data for the components are as given below :

	A	B	C
Normal usage (in units)	200	150	180
Minimum usage (")	100	100	90
Maximum usage (")	300	250	270
Reorder Quantity (")	750	900	720
Reorder period (in month)	2 to 3	3 to 4	2 to 3

Calculate for each component :

(a) Reorder level; (b) Minimum level; (c) Maximum level; (d) Average Stock level.

[I.C.W.A.—Inter—June 1984]

Solution

	A (in units)	B	C
(a) **Reorder level** = Maximum Reorder period × Maximum usage	3 × 300 = 900	4 × 250 = 1,000	3 × 270 = 810
(b) **Minimum level** = Reorder level – (Normal usage × Average Delivery time) =	$900 - (200 \times 2\frac{1}{2})$ = 900 – 500 = 400 units	$1{,}000 - (150 \times 3\frac{1}{2})$ = 1,000 – 525 = 475 units	$810 - (180 \times 2\frac{1}{2})$ = 810 – 450 = 360 units
(c) **Maximum level** = Reorder level – (Minimum consumption × Minimum Reorder period) + Reorder quantity	900 – (100 × 2) + 750 = 900 – 200 + 750 = 1,450 units	1,000 – (100 × 3) + 900 = 1,000 – 300 + 900 = 1,600 units	810 – (90 × 2) + 720 = 810 – 180 + 720 = 1,350 units
(d) **Average Stock** = Minimum level + Maximum level ÷ 2	$\frac{400 + 1{,}450}{2}$ = 925 units	$\frac{1{,}600 + 475}{2}$ = 1,038 units	$\frac{1{,}350 + 360}{2}$ = 855 units

Problem 23

Sriram Enterprises manufactures a special product "ZED". The following particulars were collected for the year 1988 :

(a) Monthly demand of 1,000 units.
(b) Cost of placing an order Rs. 100.
(c) Annual carrying cost per unit Rs. 15.
(d) Normal usage 50 units per week.
(e) Minimum usage 25 units per week.
(f) Maximum usage 75 units per week.
(g) Re-order period 4 to 6 weeks.

Compute from the above

(1) Re-order Quantity
(2) Re-order level
(3) Minimum level
(4) Maximum level
(5) Average Stock level.

[Adapted—C.A. Inter, November 1987]

Solution

1. **Re-order Quantity of units used** $= \sqrt{\dfrac{2AS}{C}}$

where A = Annual demand of input units,
S = Cost of placing an order,
C = Annual carrying cost per unit

$$= \sqrt{\frac{2 \times 12{,}000 \times 100}{15}} = 400 \text{ units.}$$

2. **Re-order Level** = Maximum re-order period × maximum usage
= 6 weeks × 75 units = 450 units

3. **Minimum Level** = Re-order level – (normal usage × average re-order period)
= 450 units – 250 units = 200 units.

4. **Maximum Level** = Re-order level + Re-order quantity – (Minimum usage × Minimum order period) = 450 units + 400 units – (25 units × 4 weeks) = 750 units.

5. **Average Stock Level** $= \frac{1}{2}$(Minimum Stock level + Maximum Stock level)

$= \frac{1}{2}$ (200 units + 750 units) = 475 units.

Problem 24

From the following estimated consumption figures of a manufacturing company in respect of a particular kind of raw material for the year 1995, calculate :

(a) Maximum level, (b) Minimum level, (c) Re-ordering level and (d) Average Stock level.

Normal usage (in units)	5,000
Minimum usage (in units)	4,000
Maximum usage (in units)	6,000
Re-order quantity (in units)	16,000
Re-order period (in months)	2 to 4

[C.U. B.Com. (Pass) 1996]

Solution

Re-order Level	=	Maximum usage × Maximum reorder period
	=	6,000 × 4 = 24,000 units
Maximum Level	=	Re-order quantity + Re-order level
		– (Minimum usage × Minimum reorder period)
	=	16,000 + 24,000 – (4,000 × 2)
	=	40,000 – 8,000 = 32,000 units
Minimum Level	=	Reorder level – (Normal usage × Normal reorder period)
	=	24,000 – (5,000 × 3)
	=	24,000 – 15,000 = 9,000 units

Note 1. Normal reorder period $= \frac{\text{Maximum} + \text{Minimum}}{2}$

$$= \frac{4 + 2}{2} = \frac{6}{2} = 3 \text{ months}$$

2. In solving the problem we have to ascertain the Reorder Level first because on the basis of Reorder level, Maximum and Minimum levels are to be ascertained.

Average stock levels $= \frac{\text{Maximum} + \text{Minimum}}{2}$

$$= \frac{32,000 + 9,000}{2} = \frac{41,000}{2} = 20,500.$$

Problem 25

(a) Find the Economic Order Quantity from the following data.

Annual consumption – 18,000 units (p.a.)

Cost per unit – Rs. 1.50

Cost of plaining order and processing the delivery – Rs. 12 per order

Inventory carrying cost 20% of unit value.

(b) Calculate Maximum Level, Minimum Level and the Re-ordering Level from the following data :

Re-ordering Quantity	:	1,200 units
Reordering Period	:	4 to 6 weeks
Maximum consumption	:	300 units
Minimum consumption	:	200 units per week
Normal consumption	:	250 units per week

[C.U. B.Com. (Hons.) 1990]

Solution

(a) EOQ $= \sqrt{\frac{2AO}{C}}$. Where A = Annual consumption,

O = Ordering cost

C = Carrying cost

$$= \sqrt{\frac{2 \times 18,000 \times 12}{20\% \text{ of Rs. } 1.50}} = \sqrt{\frac{36,000 \times 12}{0.3}} = \sqrt{\frac{4,32,000}{0.3}}$$

$$= \sqrt{14,40,000} = 1,200 \text{ units}$$

(b) **Re-order Level** = Maximum consumption × Maximum re-order period

= 300 × 6 = 1,800 units

Maximum Level = Re-order quantity + Reorder level – (minimum consumption × minimum delivery period)

= 1,200 + 1,800 – (200 × 4)

= 3,000 – 800 = 2,200 units

Minimum Level = Re-order Level – (Normal consumption × Normal delivery period)

= 1,800 – (250 × 5)

= 1,800 – 1,250 = 550 units

Problem 26

From the following data work out the EOQ of a particular component.

Annual Demand	5,000 units
Ordering Cost	Rs. 60 per order
Price per unit	Rs. 100
Inventory carrying Cost	15% on average inventory

[I.C.W.A. Inter June 1986]

Solution

$$EOQ = \sqrt{\frac{2AB}{C}} \text{ or } \sqrt{\frac{2AO}{C}} = \sqrt{\frac{2 \times 5,000 \times 60}{15\% \text{ of } 100}} = \sqrt{\frac{6,00,000}{15}} = 200 \text{ units.}$$

Problem 27

Following information relating to a type of raw material is available :

Annual Demand	2,400 units
Unit price	Rs. 2.40
Ordering cost per order	Rs. 4.00
Storage Cost	2% p.a.
Interest rate	10% p.a.
Lead time	Half month.

Calculate Economic Order Quantity and total annual inventory cost in respect of the particular raw material.

[Adapted—I.C.W.A. (Inter) June 1988]

Solution

$$\text{Formula for EOQ} = \sqrt{\frac{2AB}{CS}}$$

where A = Annual consumption

B = Buying cost per order

C = Cost per unit

S = Storage and interest.

Therefore, $EOQ = \sqrt{\dfrac{2 \times 2,400 \times 4}{Rs.\ 2.40 \times \dfrac{(10 + 2)}{100}}} = \sqrt{\dfrac{4,800 \times 4}{2.40 \times \dfrac{12}{100}}} = \sqrt{\dfrac{19,200}{0.288}}$ = 258 units

Total Annual Inventory Cost :

	Rs.
Cost of 2,400 units @ Rs. 2.40	5,760.00
No. of order = $\dfrac{2,400}{258}$ = 9.3 or 10 orders	
So, Ordering Cost = 10 × 4	40.00
Carrying cost of average inventory $\dfrac{258}{2} \times 2.40 \times \dfrac{12}{100}$ =	37.15
	5,837.15

Problem 28

Pumkin Pump Company uses about 75,000 valves per year and the usage in fairly constant at 6,250 valves per month. The valves cost Rs. 1.50 per unit when bought in quantities and the carrying cost is estimated to be 20% of average inventory investment on the annual basis. The cost to place an order and process the delivery is Rs. 18. It takes 45 days to receive delivery from the date of an order and a safety stock of 3,200 valves is desired.

You are required to determine :

(i) the most economical order quantity and frequency of order :

(ii) the order point.

[Adapted—C.S. June 1991]

Solution

(i) $EOQ = \sqrt{\dfrac{2 \times R \times P}{C \times I}}$ where P = Ordering cost per unit

R = Annual Consumption

C = Cost of material per unit

I = Storage cost as percentage of Inventory (20%).

$$EOQ = \sqrt{\frac{2 \times 75,000 \times 18}{Rs.\ 1.50 \times 20\%}} = \sqrt{\frac{27,00,000}{Re.\ 0.30}}$$

$$= \sqrt{\frac{27,00,000 \times 100}{30}} = \sqrt{90,00,000} = 3,000 \text{ units.}$$

(ii) **Calculation of order point :** (Lead time × normal usage) + safety stock

= (1.5 months × 6,250 units per month) + 3,200 units = (9,375 + 3,200) units

= 12,575 units.

Problem 29

(a) A company uses 50,000 units of an item each costing Rs. 1.20. Each order costs Rs. 45 and inventory carrying cost is 15%. Find the E.O.Q.

(b) If the company operates 250 days a year, the procurement time is 10 days, a safety stock is 500 units. Find the Re-order level, Maximum and Minimum levels of the inventory.

[Adapted—Test Exam. Herambo Chandra College]

Solution

(a) $EOQ = \sqrt{\frac{2AO}{C}} = \sqrt{\frac{2 \times 50,000 \times 45}{1.20 \times \frac{15}{100}}}$

$= \sqrt{\frac{2 \times 50,000 \times 45 \times 100}{18}} = \sqrt{25,00,00,000} = 5,000$ units

(b) **Reorder point** = Safety stock + (Average rate of consumption × Lead time)

= 500 + (200 × 10) = 500 + 2,000 = 2,500 units

Minimum level = Reorder level – (Average consumption × Lead time)

= 2500 – (200 × 10) = 2,500 – 2,000 = 500 units

Maximum level = Reorder level – (Minimum consumption × Minimum reorder period) + Reorder quantity = 2,500 – (200 × 10) + 5,000

= 2,500 – 2,000 + 5,000 = 5,500 units.

Working Notes :

Calculation of Average rate of consumption $= \frac{\text{E.O.Q}}{\text{No. of orders}} = \frac{5,000}{25} = 200$

No. of orders $= \frac{\text{No. of days of operation}}{\text{Procurement time}} = \frac{250}{10} = 25$

Problem 30

Your factory buys and uses a component for production at Rs. 10 per piece. Annual requirement is 2,000 numbers. Carrying cost of inventory is 10% p.a. and ordering cost is Rs. 40 per order. The Purchase Manager agrees that as the ordering cost is very high, it is advantageous to place a single order for the entire annual requirement. He also says that if we order 2,000 at a time, we can get a 3% discount from the supplier. Evaluate this proposal and make your recommendation.

[Adapted—I.C.W.A (Final)]

Solution

Ordering quantity	*No. of order*	*Ordering Cost* Rs.	*Carrying Cost on average inventory* Rs.	*Total Cost* Rs.
200	10 (2,000 ÷ 200)	400 (10 × 40)	10% of 100 × 10 = 100	500
400	5 (2,000 ÷ 400)	200 (5 × 40)	10% of 200 × 10 = 200	400
500	4 (2,000 ÷ 500)	160 (4 × 40)	10% of 2,250 × 10 = 250	410
1,000	2 (2,000 ÷ 1000)	80 (2 × 40)	10% of 500 × 10 = 500	580
2,000	1 (2,000 ÷ 2,000)	40 (1 × 40)	10% of 1,000 × 10 = 1,000	1,040

Recommendation

Buying 400 units at a time is most economical.

Calculation of total cost when 2,000 units are purchased at a discount of 3% :

Amount of discount = 2,000 units × Rs. 10 cost per unit = Rs. 20,000

Less Discount @ 3% = $20{,}000 \times \frac{3}{100}$ = Rs. 600

Total Cost	Rs.
Cost of ordering = 1 × 40	40.00
Carrying Cost of average inventory = $1{,}000 \times 9.70 \times \frac{10}{100}$ =	970.00
	1,010.00
Less Discount as calculated above	600.00
Net total cost	410.00

The total cost comes to Rs. 410 when 2,000 units are bought, while the total cost comes to Rs. 400 when 400 units are ordered. Hence, it is commercially logical that Economic Order Quantity must be 400 units.

Problem 31

From the following particulars with respect to a particular item of materials of a manufacturing company, calculate the best quantity to order :

Ordering quantities (Tonnes)	**Price per Tonne** Rs.
Less than 250	6.00
250 and above but less than 800	5.90
800 and above but less than 2,000	5.80
2,000 and above but less than 4,000	5.70
4,000 and above	5.60

The annual demand for the material is 4,000 tonnes. Stock holding costs are 20% of material cost p.a.

The delivery cost per order is Rs. 6.00.

[Adapted—I.C.M.A.]

Solution

Statement showing the best quantity to order

Order size (tonnes)	200	250	800	2,000	4,000
No. of Order (Annual Demand ÷ order size)	20	16	5	2	1
Value per Order (Rs.) (Order size × Price per ton)	1,200	1,475	4,640	11,400	22,400
Average Inventory (Rs.) (Value per order ÷ 2)	600	738	2,320	5,700	11,200
Ordering Cost (Rs.) No. of order × ordering cost per order	120	96	30	12	6
Carrying Cost (20% of average Inventory)	120	148	464	1,140	2,240
	240	244	494	1,152	2,246
Annual Cost of Materials	24,000	23,600	23,200	23,800	22,400
Total Cost	24,240	23,844	23,694	24,952	24,646

The analysis of the above statement suggests that the best quantity to be ordered is 800 tonnes, the cost of which is Rs. 23,694 being the lowest.

Problem 32

From the following particulars calculate the best quantity to be ordered :

Ordering quantity (in k.g.)	Price per k.g. Rs.
Less than 500	10.00
500 and less than 1,600	9.60
1,600 and less than 4,000	9.40
4,000 and less than 8,000	9.20
8,000 and above	9.00

The annual requirement of the material is 8,000 kg. Stock holding cost is 20% of material cost p.a. Ordering cost per order is Rs. 10.

[C.U. B.Com. (Hons.) 1992]

Solution

Statement showing the Optimum Ordering Quantity of Materials

1. Order size (kg)	400	500	1,600	4,000	8,000
2. No. of orders (8,000 kg ÷ order size)	20	16	5	2	1
3. Value per order (Rs.)	4,000	4,800	15,040	36,800	72,000
4. Average Inventory (Rs.)	2,000	2,400	7,520	18,400	36,000
Ordering Cost. (Rs.)	200	160	50	20	10
Carrying Cost (Rs. 20% of average inventory	400	480	1,504	3,680	7,200
Cost of the Materials	80,000	76,800	75,200	73,600	72,000
	80,600	77,440	76,754	77,300	79,200

The above statement reveals that the best quantity to order is 1,600 units in which case the total cost is minimum.

Problem 33

A publishing house purchases 2,000 units of a particular item per year at a unit cost of Rs. 20, the ordering cost per order is Rs. 50 and the inventory carrying cost is 25%. Find the optional order quantity and minimum total cost including purchase cost.

If a 3% discount is offered by the supplier for purchases in lots of 1,000 or more, should the publishing house accept the proposal ?

[I.C.W.A Final (June) 1986]

Solution

1. **Without Discount**

$$\text{EOQ} = \sqrt{\frac{2AO}{C}} = \sqrt{\frac{2 \times 2{,}000 \times 50}{25\% \text{ of Rs. } 20}} = \sqrt{40{,}000} = 200 \text{ units.}$$

So, 10 orders are to be placed $\left(\frac{2{,}000}{200}\right)$

			Rs.
Total Cost = Cost price of 2,000 units @ Rs. 20			40,000
Ordering cost 10×50			500
Carrying Cost of average inventory $\frac{200}{2}$	$= 100 \times 5$		500
Minimum total cost			41,000

2. With Discount

			Rs.
Purchase price per unit = 20 – 0.60 = Rs. 19.40			
Carrying Cost = $\frac{25}{100} \times$ Rs. 19.40 = Rs. 4.85 P.			
Ordering Cost for 2 orders =	Rs. 50×2	=	100
Carrying Cost =	$\frac{1,000}{2} \times$ Rs. 4.85	=	2,425
Cost of raw materials =	$2,000 \times$ Rs. 19.40	=	38,800
			41,325

The former is cheaper. So, the second offer is to be rejected.

Problem 34

Following information relating to a type of raw material is available :

Annual Demand	2,400 Units
Unit price	Rs. 2.40
Ordering Cost per order	Rs. 4.00
Storage Cost	2% p.a.
Interest rate	10% p.a.
Lead time	Half month

Calculate Economic Order Quantity and total annual inventory cost in respect of particular raw material.

[Adapted I.C.W.A. (Inter), June 1988]

Solution

$$EOQ = \sqrt{\frac{2AO}{C}} \quad C = 10\% + 2\% \text{ of Rs. } 2.40 = 0.289$$

$$EOQ = \sqrt{\frac{2 \times 2,400 \times 4}{0.289}} = \sqrt{\frac{19,200}{0.289}} = 258 \text{ units}$$

Calculation of total Annual Inventory Cost

				Rs.
Cost of material	=	$2,400 \times$ Rs. 2.40	=	5,760
Ordering Cost	=	$\frac{2,400}{258} = 9.3 = 10$ orders		
Cost of per order	=	$10 \times$ Rs. 4	=	40
Carrying Cost	=	$\frac{258}{2} = 129 \times 0.289$	=	37
				5,837

Problem 35

The Purchase Department of your organisation has received an offer of quantity discounts on its orders of materials as under :

Price per tonne Rs.	Tonnes
1,400	Less than 500
1,380	500 and less than 1,000
1,360	1,000 and less than 2,000
1,340	2,000 and less than 3,000
1,320	3,000 and above.

The annual requirement of the material is 5,000 tonnes. The delivery cost per order is Rs. 1,200 and the annual stock holding cost is estimated at 20% of the average inventory.

The Purchase Department wants you to consider the following purchase options and advise which among them will be the most economical ordering quantity, presenting the relevant information in a tabular form.

The purchase quantity options to be considered are 400 tonnes, 500 tonnes, 1,000 tonnes, 2,000 tonnes and 3,000 tonnes.

[Adapted C.A. (Inter) May 1994]

Solution

Working notes

Annual requirement 5,000 tonnes

Order quantity (tonnes)	Stock holding cost (Rs.)
Less than 500	20% of 1,400 = 280
500 and less than 1,000	20% of 1,380 = 276
1,000 and less than 2,000	20% of 1,360 = 272
2,000 and less than 3,000	20% of 1,340 = 268
3,000 and above	20% of 1,320 = 264

Statement showing the EOQ under Trial and Error method

Ordering Qnty. (tonnes)	*Price per tonne (Rs.)*	*Purchase Cost of 5,000 tonnes (Rs.)*	*Ordering Cost (Rs.)*	*Carrying Cost (Rs.)*	*Total Cost (Rs.)*
400	1,400	70,00,000	15,600 (13 × 1,200)	56,000 $\left(\frac{400}{2} \times 280\right)$	70,71,600
500	1,380	69,00,000	12,000 (10 × 1,200)	69,000 $\left(\frac{500}{2} \times 276\right)$	69,81,000
1,000	1,360	68,00,000	6,000 (5 × 1,200)	1,36,000 $\left(\frac{1,000}{2} \times 272\right)$	69,42,000
2,000	1,340	67,00,000	3,600 (3 × 1,200)	2,68,000 $\left(\frac{2,000}{2} \times 268\right)$	69,71,600
3,000	1,320	66,00,000	2,400 (2 × 1,200)	3,96,000 $\left(\frac{3,000}{2} \times 264\right)$	69,98,400

Note : In case of varying prices we have to determine EOQ by means of Trial and Error method

Advice to Purchase Department

The most economical ordering quantity is 1,000 tonnes since it appears from the above statement that the total cost at this level is the least.

Problem 36

A Company's monthly requirement of an inventory item is 1,800 units. The cost of processing an order is Rs. 5 and the carrying cost per unit is 20 paise. The company's supplier agrees to offer quantity discount as under :

Lot size (in units)	up to 400	401 – 600	601 – 800	801 – 1,000	Above 1,000
Discounts (in Rupees)	Nil	6	10	15	20

Lead time is 2 days and the company wishes to keep a safety stock equal to 50% of the usage in the lead time.

(a) Find out the economic order quantity without considering the order of discount;

(b) Calculate the reorder point taking 30 working days in a month;

(c) Tabulate different types of cost as also effect of discount on different order sizes taking 1, 2, 3, ...7 orders a month and indicate the EOQ.

Solution

(a) EOQ $= \sqrt{\frac{2AO}{C}}$ A = Annual consumption = 1,800 × 12 = 21,600 units

$= \sqrt{\frac{2 \times 21{,}600 \times 5}{0.20}} = \sqrt{10{,}80{,}000} = 1{,}039$ units

(b) **Reorder point** = Safety stock + usage during lead time

Usage in a day $= \frac{1{,}800}{30} = 60$ units

Safety stock = 50% of usage in lead time in one day usage.

Reorder point = 1 day usage + 2 days usage

= 3 days usage

= 60 + 120 units = 180 units

(c) Table showing EOQ with discount :

1. No. of orders	1	2	3	4	5	6	7
2. Order size	1,800	900	600	450	360	300	257
3. Average Inventory	900	450	300	225	180	150	129
Ordering cost (in Rs.)	5	10	15	20	25	30	35
Carrying cost of average inventory at Re. 0.20 per unit	180	90	60	45	36	30	26
	185	100	75	65	61	60	61
Less : Discount	20	15	10	6	—	—	—
	165	85	65	59	61	60	61

Therefore, EOQ is 450 units at which the cost is minimum.

Where annual consumption is not given

Problem 37

T P Limited, manufacturers of a special product, follows the policy of EOQ (Economic Order Quantity) for one of its components. The components details are as follows :

	Rs.
Purchase price per component	200
Cost of an order	100
Annual cost of carrying one unit	10% of purchase price
Total cost of inventory and ordering per annum	4,000

The company has been offered a discount of 2% on the price of the component provided the lot size is 2,000 components at a time.

You are required to :

(a) Compute the EOQ.

(b) Advise whether the quantity discount offer can be accepted.
(Assume that the inventory carrying cost does not vary according to discount policy)

(c) Would your advice differ if the company is offered 5% discount on a single order?

[Adapted C.S. Nov. 1994]

Solution

In order to find out EOQ, we have to ascertain the Annual Consumption first since this figure is missing.

(a) $\sqrt{\frac{2AO}{C}}$ or $\sqrt{2AO}$ = C or $\sqrt{2A \times \text{Rs. } 100 \times 20}$ = Rs. 4,000

or $\sqrt{\text{Rs.} 4{,}000 \text{ A}}$ = Rs. 4,000 or $\left(\sqrt{4{,}000 \text{ A}}\right)^2 = (4{,}000)^2$ or A = 4,000 units.

So, Annual consumption = 4,000 units.

Now, EOQ = $\sqrt{\frac{2 \times 4{,}000 \times \text{Rs. } 100}{\text{Rs. } 20}}$ = 200 units

(b) **No of orders**

When order size is 2,000 units number of order is 2 (4,000 ÷ 2,000)

Total cost = Ordering cost + Carrying cost

= $(2 \times \text{Rs. } 100) + \left(\frac{1}{2} \times 2{,}000 \text{ units} \times \text{Rs. } 20\right)$.

= Rs. 200 + Rs. 20,000 = Rs. 20,200

∴ Extra cost = Rs. 20,200 – Rs. 4,000 = Rs. 16,200

Amount of discount received = 2% of 4,000 × Rs. 200

= $\frac{2}{100} \times 8{,}00{,}000$ = Rs. 16,000.

Therefore, the discount offer should not be accepted since there is an additional expenditure of Rs. 200 (Rs. 16,200 – Rs. 16,000).

(c) When order size is 4,000, Number of order is $\frac{4,000}{4,000} = 1$

Total cost = 1 × Rs. 100 + $\frac{1}{2}$ × 4,000 units × Rs. 20 = Rs. 40,100.

Extra cost = Rs. 40,100 – Rs. 4,000 = Rs. 36,100

Amount of discount = $\frac{5}{100}$ × 4,000 × Rs. 200 = Rs. 40,000.

This offer should be accepted since there is a reduction in total cost of carrying and ordering of inventory to the tune of Rs. 3,900 (Rs. 40,000 – Rs. 36,100).

Problem 38

Annual Inventory Cost and Savings due to EOQ

Anil company buys its annual requirement of 36,000 units in 6 instalments. Each unit costs Re. 1.00 and the ordering cost is Rs. 25. The inventory carrying cost is estimated at 20% of unit value. Find the total annual cost of the existing inventory policy. How much money can be saved by Economic Order Quantity?

[C.A. Final, May 1986]

Solution

		Rs.
	Ordering cost (6 orders @ Rs. 25)	150
	Carrying cost of average inventory	
	36,000 ÷ 6 = 6,000 units per order.	
	So, average inventory = 6,000 ÷ 2 = 3,000 units.	
	Carrying cost = 20% of Re. 1.00 = Re. 0.20. = 3,000 × 0.20	600
(A)	Total Cost	750

$$\text{EOQ} = \sqrt{\frac{2AC}{CS}} = \sqrt{\frac{2 \times 36{,}000 \times 25}{1.00 \times 20\%}} = 3{,}000 \text{ units}$$

Number of orders = 36,000 ÷ 3,000 = 12 orders.

		Rs.
	Ordering cost (12 × Rs. 25)	300
	Carrying cost of average inventory (3,000 × 0.20) ÷ 2 =	300
(B)	Total Cost	600

Savings due to EOQ = A – B = Rs. 750 – Rs. 600 = Rs. 150.

STORE LEDGER

Return from Job Order & Shortage of Stock

Problem 39

The following is the history of the receipts and issues of materials in a factory during February 1987 :

February			
1	Opening balance	500	quintals @ Rs. 25.00
3	Issue	70	"
4	Issue	100	"
8	Issue	80	"
13	Received from the suppliers	200	quintals @ Rs. 24.50
14	Return of surplus from a work order	15	" @ Rs. 24.00
16	Issue	180	"

20	Received from the suppliers	240	"	@ Rs. 24.375
24	Issue	304	"	
25	Received from the suppliers	320	"	@ Rs. 24.375
26	Issue	112	"	
27	Return of surplus from a work order	12	"	@ Rs. 24.50
28	Received from the suppliers	100	"	@ Rs. 25.00

Issues are to be priced on the principle of "First in First out" method. The stock verifier of the factory noticed that on 15th he had found a shortage of 5 quintals and on 27th another shortage of 8 quintals. Write out the Stores ledger account recording the above transactions.

[Adapted – Andhra]

Solution

STORE LEDGER ACCOUNT – FIFO METHOD

Date	*Receipts*				*Issues*				*Balance*			
1987	*GRN*	*Qnt.*	*Rate*	*Amt.*	*SR*	*Qnt.*	*Rate*	*Amt.*	*Qnt.*	*Rate*	*Amt.*	*Remark*
Feb.	No.		Rs.	Rs.	No.		Rs. .	Rs.		Rs.	Rs.	
1									500	25.00	12,500	
3.						70	25.00	1,750	430.	25.00	10.750	
4						100	25.00	2,500	330	25.00	8,250	
8						80	25.00	2,000	250	25.00	6,250	
13		200	24.50	4,900					250	25.00	6.250	
									200	24.50	4,900	
Feb. 14	Return	15	24.00	360					250	25.00	6,250	
									200	24.50	4,900	
									15	24.00	360	
15					Shortage	5	25.00	125	245	25.00	6,125	
									200	24.50	4,900	
16									15	24.00	360	
						180	25.00	4,500	65	25.00	1,625	
									200	24.50	4,900	
									15	24.00	360	
20		240	24.375	5,850					65	25.00	1,625	
									200	24.50	4,900	
									15	24.00	360	
									240	24.375	5,850	
24						65	25.00	1,625				
						200	24.50	4,900				
						15	24.00	360				
						24	24.375	585	216	24.375	5,265	
25		320	24.375	7,800					216	24.375	5,265	
									320	24.375	7,800	
26						112	24.375	2,730	424	24.375	10,335	
27	Return	12	24.50	294					424	24.375	10,335	
									12	24.50	294	
27					Shortage	8	24.375	195	416	24.375	10,140	
									12	24.50	294	
28		100	25.00	2,500					416	24.375	10,140	
									12	24.50	294	
									100	25.00	2,500	

Total value of stock on 28. 2. 1987 = Rs. 12,934.

Problem 40

From the following particulars write up Store Ledger using FIFO method

1993	January	1	Opening Stock	1,000	units	@ Rs. 10
	"	5	Received	500	"	@ Rs. 11
	"	10	Issued	1,200	"	
	"	12	Received	800	"	@ Rs. 11.50
	"	20	Returned	100	"	@ Rs. 10
	"	25	Issued	500	"	
	"	30	Issued	200	"	

[C.U. B.Com. (Pass) 1993]

Solution

STORE LEDGER—FIFO

Date	Particulars	Receipts			Issues			Bal		
		Qnt.	Rate	Amount	Qnt.	Rate	Amount	Qnt.	Rate	Amount
			Rs.	Rs.		Rs.	Rs.		Rs.	Rs.
1993										
Jan. 1	Opening stock							1,000	10	10,000
5	Received	500	11	5,500				1,000	10	10,000
								500	11	5,500
10	Issued				1,000	10	10,000			
					200	11	2,200	300	11	3,300
12	Received	800	11.50	9,200				300	11	3,300
								800	11.50	9,200
20	Returned	100	10	1,000				300	11	3,300
								800	11.50	9.200
								100	10	1,000
25	Issued				300	11	3,300	600	11.50	6,900
					200	11.50	2,300	100	10	1,000
30	Issued				200	11.50	2,300	400	11.50	4,600
								100	10	1,000

Value of closing stock – 400 units @ 11.50 = 4,600
100 units @ 10.00 = 1,000
Rs. 5,600

Problem 41

On 1st January the stock of a component in the stores was 554 units at Rs. 35 per hundred. During three months the receipts and issues were as follows :

1997	Purchased			Issued
January	434 units	@ Rs. 37.50	per hundred	400 units
February	500 "	@ Rs. 40.00	" "	610 "
March	750 "	@ Rs. 42.00	" "	950 "

When the stock was taken at 31st March, a discrepancy of 49 units was revealed Prepare a Store Ledger Card under the FIFO method and show how would you deal with the discrepancy.

[V.U. B.Com. (Hons.) 1994]

Solution

STORE LEDGER—FIFO

Date	*Receipts*			*Issues*			*Balance*			*Remarks*
	Qnt	*Rate*	*Amount*	*Qnt.*	*Rate*	*Amount*	*Qnt.*	*Rate*	*Amount*	
		Rs.	Rs.		Rs.	Rs.		Rs.	Rs.	
1997 Jan. 1							554	35 (per hundred	193.90	
Jan.	434	37.50 (per hundred)	162.75				554 434	35..00 37.50	193.90 162.75	
Jan.				400	35.00	140	154 434	35.00 37.50	53.90 162.75	
Feb.	500	40.00 (per hundred)	200.00	154 434 22	35.00 37.50 40.00	53.90 162.75 8.80	478	40.00	191.20	
March	750	42 (per hundred)	315.00	478 472	40.00 42.00	191.20 198.24	278	42.00	116.76	
March 31				49	42.00	20.58	229	42.00	96.18	Shortage

Value of closing stock on 31.3.1997, 229 units @ Rs. 42 per hundred = Rs. 96.18

Problem 42

The following is an extract of the record of receipts and issues of sulphur in a Chemical factory during November 1988 :

November	1	Opening balance 300 tonnes @ Rs. 300
	4	Issue 100 tonnes
	5	Issue 50 tonnes
	12	Received from supplier 200 tonnes @ Rs. 280
	16	Returned from department 20 tonnes
	20	Issue 200 tonnes
	22	Received from supplier 220 tonnes @ Rs. 310
	25	Issue 250 tonnes
	27	Returned from department 50 tonnes
	30	Received from supplier 150 tonnes @ Rs. 320

Issues are to be priced on the principle of 'First-in-First-out'. The stock verifier of the factory had found a shortage of 20 tonnes on 24th and left a note accordingly. Draw up Store Ledger showing the above transactions.

Solution on page No. 217

Problem 43

Following are the details of Raw Materials of Bird Ltd. for the month of January, 1993

Jan. 1	Opening stock	100	kg. @ Rs. 10
5	Issued	44	kg.
10	Received from vendor	60	kg. @ Rs. 12
15	Surplus returned from department	10	kg. @ Rs. 10
18	Shortage adjusted	8	kg.
20	Issued	34	kg.
25	Issued	30	kg.
30	Received from vendor	50	kg. @ Rs. 11
31	Issued	30	kg.

Show the Store Ledger Account under FIFO system assuming a Base Stock of 40 kg.

[C.U. B.Com. (Hons.) 1992]

Solution on Page No. 218

Solution

STORE LEDGER—FIFO

Date	Particulars	Receipts			Issues			Balance			Remarks
		Qnt.	Rate	Total	Qnt.	Rate	Total	Qnt.	Rate	Total	
1988		(tonnes)	Rs.	Rs.	(tonnes)	Rs.	Rs.	(tonnes)	Rs.	Rs.	
Nov. 1	Balance b/d	—	—	—	—	—	—	300	300	90,000	
4	Requistion Slip No.	—	—	—	100	300	30,000	200	300	60,000	
5.	Requisition Slip No.	—	—	—	50	300	15,000	150	300	45,000	
12	Goods Received Note No.	200	280	56,000	—	—	—	150	300	45,000	
								200	280	56,000	
16.	Material Returned Note No.	20	300	6,000	—	—	—	170	300	51,000	Return from
								200	280	56,000	department
20	Requisition Slip No.				170	300	51,000				
					30	280	8,400	170	280	47,600	
22	Materials Received Note	220	310	68,200				170	280	47,600	
								220	310	68,200	
24	Credit Note				20	280	5,600	150	280	42,000	
								220	310	68,200	Deficiency
25	Requisition Slip No.				150	280	42,000				
					100	310	31,000	120	310	37,200	
27	Materials Returned Note	50	310	15,500	—	—	—	50	310	15,500	Return from
								120	310	37,200	Department
30	Materials Received Note	150	320	48,000	—	—	—	50	310	15,500	
								120	310	37,200	
								150	320	48,000	

Note : Value of stock on 30.11.1988 = Rs. 1,00,700

Solution

STORE LEDGER ACCOUNT — Base Stock 40 kg. FIFO

Date	Particulars	Receipts			Issues			Balance			Remark
		Qnt	Rate	Amt.	Qnt.	Rate	Amt.	Qnt.	Rate	Amt.	
1993		Kg	Rs.	Rs.	Kg	Rs.	Rs.	Kg	Rs.	Rs.	
Jan. 1								100	10	1,000	
5					44	10	440	56	10	560	
10		60	12	720				56	10	560	
								60	12	720	
15		10	10	100				56	10	560	Returned
								60	12	720	from
								10	10	100	Department
18					*8	10	80	56	10	560	Storage
								60	12	720	
								2	10	20	
20					*2	10	20				
					16	10	160				
					16	12	192	40	10	400	
								44	12	528	
25					30	12	360	40	10	400	
								14	12	168	
30		50	11	550				40	10	400	
								14	12	168	
								50	11	550	
31					14	12	168				
					16	11	176	40	10	400	
								34	11	374	

Note : On 18 shortage of 8 kg has been priced @ Rs. 10 and shown in issue column out of materials returned by the department on 15th. The remaining 2 kgs have been issued first on 20th January, 1993.

Problem 44

	Date Receipts of meterials (in kg)	Rate per kg (Rs.)	Date	Issue of materials (in kg)
1997				
July 1	400	12	July 9	600
8	1,000	10	12	500
15	800	12	18	500
20	1,000	11	22	1,00
25	600	13		

Stock at the beginning of the month of July was 100 kg @ Rs. 10 per kg.

On July 26, 100 kg out of purchase made on July 20 has been returned to supplier.

On July 27 a shortage of 100 kg of materials was noted.

From the above transactions :

(i) draw up Store Ledger A/c under FIFO method;

(ii) find stock at the end of the month; and

(iii) determine the amount of material consumed during the month.

[Kalyani University B.Com. (Hons.) 1995]

STORE LEDGER ACCOUNT—FIFO

(i)

Date	Particulars	Receipts			Issues			Balance			
		Qnt	Rate	Amt.	Qnt.	Rate	Amt.	Qnt.	Rate	Amt.	
1997		kg	Rs.	Rs.	kg	Rs.	Rs.	kg	Rs.	Rs.	
July 1								100	10	1,000	
1		400	12	4,800				100	10	1,000	
								400	12	4,800	
8		1,000	10	10,000				100	10	1,000	
								400	12	4,800	
								1,000	10	10,000	
9					100	10	1,000				
					400	12	4,800				
					100	10	1,000	900	10	9,000	
12					500	10	5,000	400	10	4,000	
15		800	12	9,600				400	10	4,000	
								800	12	9,600	
18					400	10	4,000				
					100	12	1,200	700	12	8,400	
20		1,000	11	11,000				700	12	8,400	
								1,000	11	11,000	
22					700	12	8,400				
					300	11	3,300	700	11	7,700	
25		600	13	7,800				700	11	7,700	
								600	13	7,800	
26					100	11	1,100	600	11	7,700	Returned to
								600	13	7,800	supplier
27					100	11	1,100	500	11	5,500	Shortage
								600	13	7,800	

		Units Rate		Rs.
(ii) Stock at the end of the month	=	500 × 11	=	5,500
		600 × 13	=	7,800
				13,300

(iii) Materials consumed :	on 9.7.	Rs.	6,800
	12.7.	Rs.	5,000
	18.7.	Rs.	5,200
	22.7	Rs.	11,700
		Rs.	28,700

Problem 44

The particulars of receipts and issues of materials in a factory in January 1985 are as under :

January 1	Opening Balance	1,500	Kgs. @ Rs. 12 per Kg.
2	Issued	650	Kgs.
5	Purchased	400	Kgs. @ Rs. 12.50 per Kg.
9	Issued	300	Kgs.
10	Purchased	200	Kgs. @ Rs. 12.50 per Kg.
11	Issued	300	Kgs.
12	Returned from workshop issued on 2nd Jan.	20	Kgs.
13	Issued	450	Kgs.
16	Purchased	500	Kgs. @ Rs. 13.00 per Kg.
18	Issued	400	Kgs.
22	Purchased	300	Kgs. @ Rs. 12.00 per Kg.
30	Issued	200	kgs.

Pricing of issues is to be done on FIFO basis. A shortage of 10 Kg. was noticed on 17th January. Prepare the Store Ledger for the month of January 1985.

[Adapted—C.U. B.Com.(Hons.) 1985]

Solution

STORES LEDGER UNDER FIFO METHOD

Date	*Particulars*	*Receipts*			*Issues*			*Balance*			*Remarks*
1988		*Qty.*	*Rate*	*Amt.*	*Qty.*	*Rate*	*Amt.*	*Qty.*	*Rate*	*Amt.*	
Jan.		Kg	(Rs.)	(Rs.)	Kg	(Rs.)	(Rs.)	Kg	(Rs.)	(Rs.)	
1		—	—	—	—	—	—	1,500	12.00	18,000	
2	Req. Slip No.	—	—	—	650	12.00	7,800	850	12.00	10,200	
5	G.R.N.	400	12.50	5,000	—	—	—	850	12.00	10,200	
								400	12.50	5,000	
										15,200	
9	Req. Slip No.	—	—	—	300	12.00	3,600	550	12.00	6,600	
								400	12.50	5,000	
										11,600	
10	G.R.N.	200	12.50	2,500	—	—	—	550	12.00	6,600	
								600	12.50	7.500	
										14,100	
11	Req. Slip No.	—	—	—	300	12.00	3,600	250	12.00	3,000	
								600	12.50	7,500	
										10,500	
12	G.R.N.	20	12.00	240	—	—	—	270	12.00	3.240	Return
								600	12.50	7,500	from
										10,740	workshop
13	Req. Slip No.	—	—	—	270	12.00	3,240				
					180	12.50	2,250	420	12.50	5,250	
16	G.R.N.	500	13.00	6,500	—	—	—	420	12.50	5,250	
								500	13.00	6,500	
										11,750	
17		—	—	—	10	12.50	125	410	12.50	5,125	Shortage
								500	13.00	6,500	
										11,625	
18	Req. Slip No.	—	—	—	400	12.50	5,500	10	12.50	125	
								500	13.00	6,500	
										6,625	
22	G.R.N.	300	12.00	3,600	—	—	—	10	12.50	125	
								500	13.00	6,500	
								300	12.00	3,600	
										10,225	
30	Req. Slip No.	—	—	—	10	12.50	125	310	13.00	4,030	
					190	13.00	2,470	300	12.00	3,600	
										7,630	

Problem 46

The particulars of receipts and issues of a certain material during January, 1987 are given below :

Receipts				Issues	
Date		Units	Rate per unit	Date	Units
Jan. 6	Purchased	450	Rs. 25.00	Jan 3	600
" 12	Purchased	600	Rs. 24.50	" 8	500
" 15	Return from workshop (Issued on Jan. 3)			" 13	250
		50		" 24	300
" 22	Purchased	350	Rs. 26.00	" 27	500
" 28	Purchased	500	Rs. 27.00	" 31	300

Further information :

Opening balance on January 1, 1987 – 1,000 units @ Rs. 24.00 per unit.

A shortage of 15 units was noticed and recorded on January 9, 1987.

Prepare Store Ledger in respect of the materials for the month of January 1987 under the LIFO system. **[C.U. B.Com.(Hons.)]**

STORES LEDGER ACCOUNT UNDER THE LIFO METHOD

Date 1987	*Particulars*	*Receipts*			*Issues*			*Balance*			*Remarks*
		Qty	*Rate*	*Amt.*	*Qty*	*Rate*	*Amt.*	*Qty*	*Rate*	*Amt.*	
Jan.		Kg	(Rs.)	(Rs.)	Kg	(Rs.)	(Rs.)	Kg	(Rs.)	(Rs.)	
1		—		—	—	—	—	1,000	24	24,000	
3	Req. Slip No.	—	—	—	600	24	14,400	400	24	9,600	
6	G.R.N.	450	25	11,250	—	—	—	400	24	9,600	
								450	25	11,250	
8	Req. Slip No.	—	—	—	450	25	11,250				
					50	24	1,200	350	24	8,400	
9		—	—	—	15	24	360	335	24	8,040	
12	G.R.N.	600	24.50	14,700	—	—	—	335	24	8,040	
								600	24.50	14,700	
13	Req. Slip No.	—	—	—	250	24.50	6,125	335	24	8,040	
								350	24.50	8,575	
15	G.R.N.	50	24	1,200	—	—	—	385	24	9,240	}
								350	24.50	8,575	}
22	G.R.N.	350	26	9,100	—	—	—	385	24	9,240	}
								350	24.50	8,575	}
								350	26	9,100	}
24	Req. Slip No.	—	—	—	300	26	7,800	385	24	9,240	}
								350	24.50	8,575	}
								50	26	1,300	}
27	Req. Slip No.	—	—	—	50	26	1,300				
					350	24.50	8,575				
					100	24	2,400	285	24	6,840	
28	G.R.N.	500	27	13,500	—	—	—	285	24	6,840	
								500	27	13,500	
31	Req. Slip No.	—	—	—	300	27	8,100	285	24	6,840	
								200	27	5,400	
										12,240	

SIMPLE AVERAGE METHOD

Problem 45

From the following details write Stores Ledger under Simple Average Method :

1982		
November 1	Opening Balance	100 Kgs. @ Rs. 5.00
5	Received	50 Kgs. @ Rs. 5.20
8	Issued	120 Kgs.
10	Issued	10 Kgs.
15	Received	80 Kgs. @ Rs. 5.40
18	Issued	50 Kgs.
20	Received	100 Kgs. @ Rs. 5.60
25	Issued	40 Kgs.
29	Issued	60 Kgs.

The stock verifier found a shortage of 10 Kgs. on 16.11.82 and another shortage of 10 Kgs. on 26.11.82.

[Adapted—C.U. B.Com (Hons.) 1983]

Solution

STORES LEDGER UNDER AVERAGE METHOD

Date	*Particulars*	*Receipts*			*Issues*			*Balance*			*Remarks*
1982		*Qty.*	*Rate*	*Amt.*	*Qty.*	*Rate*	*Amt.*	*Qty.*	*Rate*	*Amt.*	
		Kg	(Rs.)	(Rs.)	Kg	(Rs.)	(Rs.)	Kg	(Rs.)	(Rs.)	
Dec. 1		—	—	—	—	—	—	100	5.00	500	
5	G.R.N.	50	5.20	260	—	—	—	150		760	
8	Req. Slip No.	—	—	—	120	5.10	612	30		148	
10	Req. Slip No.	—	—	—	10	5.10	51	20		97	
15	G.R.N.	80	5.40	432	—	—	—	100		529	
16		—	—	—	10	5.30	53	90		476	Shortage
18	Req. Slip No.	—	—	—	50	5.30	265	40		211	
20	G.R.N.	100	5.60	560	—	—	—	140		771	
25	Req. Slip No.	—	—	—	40	5.50	220	100		551	
26		—	—	—	10	5.50	55	90		496	
29	Req. Slip No.	—	—	—	60	5.50	330	30		166	

Value of closing stock on 30.11.1982—Rs. 158.00.

Working Note :

Calculation for simple average price :

For issue on 8th Dec. $\frac{(5.00 + 5.20)}{2} = 5.10$

For issue on 10th Dec. $= 5.10$

For Shortage on 16th Dec. $\frac{(5.20 + 5.40)}{2} = 5.30$

For issue on 18th Dec. $\frac{(5.20 + 5.40)}{2} = 5.30$

For issue on 25th Dec. $\frac{(5.40 + 5.60)}{2} = 5.50$

For shortage on 26th Dec. $= 5.60$

For issue on 29th Dec. $= 5.60$

Note to Ponder : Since there is only one lot while issuing on 10th, and 29th Dec. the question of averaging does not arise.

Problem 47

Show the year-end value of inventory under LIFO method for the following data :
Opening balance : 12000 units @ Rs. 2.00 per unit.

	Received (Units)	Issued (Units)
1st quarter	20,000 @ Rs. 2.20	16,000
2nd quarter	30,000 @ Rs. 2.40	26,000
3rd quarter	25,000 @ Rs. 2.30	32,000
4th quarter	10,000 @ Rs. 2.25	8,000

Assume that purchases were made on the first day of the quarter.

[B.Com—Andhra]

Solution

STORES LEDGER ACCOUNT LIFO METHOD

Date	*Receipts*				*Issues*				*Balance of Stock*		
1988	*G.R.N.*	*Qty.*	*Rate*	*Amt.*	*S.R.*	*Qty.*	*Rate*	*Amt.*	*Qty.*	*Rate*	*Amt.*
Jan.	No.	No.	Rs.	Rs.	No.	No.	Rs.	Rs.	No	Rs.	Rs.
Opening Balance									12,000	2.00	24,000
1st quarter		20,000	2.20	44,000					32,000		68,000
"						16,000	2.20	35,200	16,000		32,800
2nd quarter		30,000	2.40	72,000					46,000		104,800
"						26,000	2.40	62,400	20,000		42,400
3rd quarter		25,000	2.30	57,500					45,000		99,900
"						25,000	2.30	57,500			
						4,000	2.40	9,600			
						3,000	2.20	6,600			
						32,000		73,700	13,000		26,200
4th quarter		10,000	2.25	22,500					23,000		48,700
"						8,000	2.25	18,000	15,000		30,700

Problem 48

The following transactions took place in respect of a raw material during the month of January 1993 :

Date	Particulars	Kg.	Rate per Kg (Rs.)
January 1	Balance	1,000	9
2	Purchased	1,500	10
5	Issued	390	—
8	Shortage	10	—
15	Surplus returned by Production Department	200	12
20	Issued	1,000	—
25	Received from vendor	300	14
28	Issued	1,200	
31	Issued	100	

You are required to write up Store Ledger Account applying the Simple Average Method of pricing issues.

[C.U. B.Com.(Hons.) 1993]

Solution

STORE LEDGER

Simple Average Method

Date	*Receipts*			*Issues*			*Balance*			*Remarks*
1988	*Qty*	*Rate*	*Amt.*	*Qty*	*Rate*	*Amt.*	*Qty*	*Rate*	*Amt.*	
	kg	Rs.	Rs.	kg	Rs.	Rs.	kg	Rs.	Rs.	
January 1							1,000	9	9,000	
2	1,500	10	15,000				2,500		24,000	
5				390	9.50	3,705	2,110		20,295	
8				10	9.50	95	2,100		20,200	
15	200	12	2,400				2,300		22,600	
20				1,000	10.33	10,330	1,300		12,270	
25	300	14	4,200				1,600		16,470	
28				1,200	12	14,400	400		2,070	
31				100	12	1,200	300		870	

Notes :

(i) Issue on 20th involving 3 prices shall have to be considered since the balance on 1.1. has not been exhausted. So, average of 3 prices e.g. $\frac{\text{Rs. } 9 + \text{Rs. } 10 + \text{Rs. } 12}{3}$ = Rs. 10.33 per unit

(ii) Issue Price on 28th January also involves 3 prices since the second lot has not been exhausted.

So, Average Price = $\frac{\text{Rs. } 10 + \text{Rs. } 12 + \text{Rs. } 14}{3}$ = Rs. 12 per unit.

Problem 50

The stock of an item of materials as on 1st July 1998 was 500 units at Re. 1 per unit. Following purchases and issues of this item were made during July 1998 :

Date	*Purchases*		*Issues*	
1998	*Unit*	*Rate*	*Date*	*Units*
		Rs. p.		
July 6	100	1. 12	July 9	300
July 15	700	1. 22	July 16	700
July 20	400	1. 16	July 23	500
July 25	800	1. 21	July 31	600

Write up the Materials Account in the Stores Ledger pricing the issues under

(a) First-in-First-out Method

(b) Average Cost Method

Which of these two methods is more suitable for this example and why ?

[B.Com. Andhra]

Solution

Stores Ledger

(a)

First-In-First-Out Method

Date 1998	Receipts G.R.N. No.	Receipts Qnt.	Receipts Rate Rs.	Receipts Amt. Rs.	Issues R.S. No.	Issues Qnt.	Issues Rate Rs.	Issues Amt. Rs.	Balance of Stock Qnt.	Balance of Stock Rate Rs.	Balance of Stock Amt. Rs.
July 1									500	1.00	500.00
" 6		100	1.12	112.00					600		612.00
" 9						300	1.00	300.00	300		312.00
" 15		700	1.22	854.00					1000		1,166.00
" 16						200	1.00	200.00			
						100	1.12	112.00			
						400	1.22	488.00			
						700		800.00	300		366.00
" 20		400	1.16	464.00					700		830.00
" 23						300	1.22	366.00			
						200	1.16	232.00			
						500		598.00	200		232.00
" 25		800	1.21	968.00					1000		1,200.00
" 31						200	1.16	232.00			
						400	1.21	484.00			
						600		716.00	400	1.21	484.00

(b)

Stores Ledger—Material A/c
Average Cost Method

Date 1998	Receipts G.R.N. No.	Receipts Qnt. No.	Receipts Rate Rs.	Receipts Amt. Rs.	Issues R.S. No.	Issues Qnt. No.	Issues Rate Rs.	Issues Amt. Rs.	Balance of Stock Qnt. No	Balance of Stock Rate Rs.	Balance of Stock Amt. Rs.
July 1									500	1.00	500.00
" 6		100	1.12	112.00					600		612.00
" 9						300	1.06	318.00	300		294.00
" 15		700	1.22	854.00					1,000		1148.00
" 16						700	1.113	779.10	300		368.90
" 20		400	1.16	464.00					700		832.90
" 23						500	1.19	595.00	200		237.90
" 25		800	1.21	968.00					1,000		1205.90
" 31						600	1.185	711.00	400		494.90

Notes :

Rs.

Issue price on 9.7.98 $= \frac{1.00 + 1.12}{2} = \frac{2.12}{2} = 1.06$

" " on 16.7.98 $= \frac{1.00 + 1.12 + 1.22}{3} = \frac{3.34}{3} = 1.113$

" " on 23.7.98 $= \frac{1.22 + 1.16}{2} = \frac{2.38}{2} = 1.19$

" " on 31.7.98 $= \frac{1.16 + 1.21}{2} = \frac{2.37}{2} = 1.185$

Weighted Average Method

Problem 51

From the following details of stores receipts and issues of material 'EXE' in a manufacturing unit, prepare the Store Ledger using "Weighted Average" method of valuing the issues :

1990

November 1 Opening Stock 2,000 units @ Rs. 5.00 each
" 3 Issued 1,500 units to Production Department
" 4 Received 4,500 units @ Rs. 6.00 each
" 8 Issued 1,600 units to Production Department
" 9 Returned to Stores 100 units by Production Department (from the issue of Nov. 3)
" 16 Received 2,400 units @ 6.50 each
" 19 Returned to supplier 200 units out of quantity received on Nov. 4
" 20 Received 1,000 units @ Rs. 7.00 each
" 24 Issued to Production 2,100 units.
" 27 Received 1,200 units @ Rs. 7.50 each
" 29 Issued to Production 2,800 units (use rates up to two decimal places)

[Adapted—I.C.W.A. June '88]

Solution

STORE LEDGER FOR MATERIAL 'EXE'

(Weighted Average)

Date	*Particulars*	*Receipts*			*Issues*			*Balance*		
1990		*Qnt.*	*Rate*	*Amt.*	*Qnt.*	*Rate*	*Amt.*	*Qnt*	*Rate*	*Amt.*
Nov.		(Kg)	(Rs.)	(Rs.)	(Kg)	(Rs.)	(Rs.)	(Kg.)	(Rs.)	(Rs.)
1	Opening Balance							2,000	5.00	10,000
3	Issue to Production				1,500	5.00	7,500	500	5.00	2,500
4	Receipts	4,500	6.00	27,000				5,000		29,500
8	Issue to Production				1,600	5.90	9,440	3,400		20,060
9	Returned by Prod. Dept.	100	5.00	500				3,500		20,560
16	Receipts	2,400	6.50	15,600				5,900		36,160
19	Returned to Suppliers				200	6.13	1,226	5,700		34,934
20	Receipts	1,000	7.00	7,000				6,700		41,934
24	Issued to Production				2,100	6.26	13,146	4,600		28,788
27	Receipts	1,200	7.50	9,000				5,800		37,788
29	Issued				2,800	6.52	18,256	3,000		19,532

Value of Stock on 30.11.1990 – Rs. 19,558.

Problem 52

The following are the details supplied by J. K. Corporation in respect of its raw materials for the month of December 1988 :

	Receipts		Issues
Date	Units	Price per unit	Units
1. 12. 1988	2,000	Rs. 5.00	
7. 12. 1988	1,000	Rs. 6.00	
10. 12. 1988			2,500
15. 12. 1988	2,000	Rs. 6.50	
31. 12. 1988			2,200

On 31. 12. 1988 a shortage of 100 units was found. Find the values of issues and resulting stocks on different dates using (i) LIFO, (ii) FIFO and (iii) Simple Average methods.

[C.U. B.Com. (Hons.) 1989]

Solution

STORE LEDGER

FIFO

Date	*Receipts*			*Issues*			*Balance*		
1988	*Qty.* (Kg)	*Rate* (Rs.)	*Amt.* (Rs.)	*Qty.* (Kg)	*Rate* (Rs.)	*Amt.* (Rs.)	*Qty.* (Kg.)	*Rate* (Rs.)	*Amt.* (Rs.)
Dec. 1							2,000	5.00	10,000
7	1,000	6.00	6,000				2,000	5.00	10,000
							1,000	6.00	6,000
10				2,000	5.00	10,000			
				500	6.00	3,000	500	6.00	3,000
15	2,000	6.50	13,000				500	6.00	3,000
							2,000	6.50	13,000
31				500	6.00	3,000			
				1,700	6.50	11,050			
				100	6.50	650	200	6.50	1,300

LIFO

Date	*Receipts*			*Issues*			*Balance*		
1988	*Qty.* (Kg)	*Rate* (Rs.)	*Amt.* (Rs.)	*Qty.* (Kg)	*Rate* (Rs.)	*Amt.* (Rs.)	*Qty.* (Kg.)	*Rate* (Rs.)	*Amt.* (Rs.)
Dec. 1							2000	5.00	10,000
7	1,000	6.00	6,000				2000	5.00	10,000
							1000	6.00	6,000
10				1,000	6.00	6,000			
				1,500	5.00	7,500	500	5.00	2,500
15	2,000	6.50	13,000				500	5.00	2,500
							2000	6.50	13,000
31				2,000	6.50	13,000			
				200	5.00	1,000			
				100	5.00	500	200	5.00	1,000

SIMPLE AVERAGE

Dec. 1							2,000	5.00	10,000
7	1,000	6.00	6,000				3,000	—	16,000
10				2,500	5.50	13,750	500	—	2,250
15	2,000	6.50	13,000				2,500	—	15,250
31				2,200	6.25	13,750			
				100	6.50	650	200	6.50	1,300

Notes : 1. Value of Stock on 10.12.1988 = $\frac{6.00 + 5.00}{2}$ = 5.50

2. Value of Stock issued on 31.12.88 = $\frac{6.00 + 6.50}{2}$ = 6.25

3. Value of shortage – Since the whole lot of materials received on 15. 12. 1988 has been issued on 31.12.88, valuation of shortage has been done @ Rs. 6.50 i.e. at the cost of the latest arrival.

Problem 53

From the following information select the most suitable method of pricing material issues and write up a Store Ledger Card based on that method :

1996		
January 1	Opening balance	24,000 Kg. @ Rs. 7,500 per tonne
1	Purchased	44,000 Kg. @ Rs. 7,600 per tonne
3	Issued	10,000 Kg.
5	Issued	16,000 Kg.
12	Purchased	10,000 Kg. @ Rs. 7,800 per tonne
13	Issued	24,000 Kg.
18	Issued	25,000 Kg.
22	Purchased	50,000 Kg. @ Rs. 8,000 per tonne
28	Issued	20,000 Kg.
31	Issued	22,000 Kg.

On 24 Jan., 1996, a shortage of 200 Kg. noticed in stock taking.

[C.U. B.Com. (Hons.) 1996]

Solution

STORE LEDGER LIFO

Date	*Receipts*			*Issues*			*Balance*		
1996	*Qnt.*	*Rate*	*Amt.*	*Qnt.*	*Rate*	*Amt.*	*Qnt.*	*Rate*	*Amt.*
	(Kg)	(Rs.)	(Rs.)	(Kg)	(Rs.)	(Rs.)	(Kg.)	(Rs.)	(Rs.)
Jan. 1							24,000	7.5	1,80,000
1	44,000	7.6	3,34,400				24,000	7.5	1,80,000
							44,000	7.6	3,34,400
3				10,000	7.6	76,000	24,000	7.5	1,80,000
							34,000	7.6	2,58,400
5				16,000	7.6	1,21,600			
							24,000	7.5	1,80,000
							18,000	7.6	1,36,800
12	10,000	7.8	78,000				24,000	7.5	1,80,000
							18,000	7.6	1,36,800
							10,000	7.8	78,000
13				10,000	7.8	78,000	24,000	7.5	1,80,000
				14,000	7.6	1,06,400	4,000	7.6	30,400
18				4,000	7.6	30,400			
				21,000	7.5	1,57,500	3,000	7.5	22,500
22	50,000	8.0	4,00,000				3,000	7.5	22,500
							50,000	8.0	4,00,000
28				20,000	8.0	1,60,000	3,000	7.5	22,500
							30,000	8.0	2,40,000
31				22,000	8.00	1,76,000	3,000	7.5	22,500
							8,000	8.0	64,000

Note : 1,000 kg. = one tonne

Problem 54

The following are the details supplied by J. K. Corporation in respect of its raw materials for the month of December 1988 :

Date	Receipts Units	Receipts Amount (Rs.)	Issues Units
1. 11. 1990	1,000 (Opening)	6,000	
10. 11. 1990	500	3,500	
15. 11. 1990			1,200
20. 11. 1990	1,000	8,000	
30. 11. 1990			1,100

On 30th November 1990 a shortage of 50 units was found. Find the values of issues and resulting stocks on different dates using (a) LIFO, (b) Simple Average, and (c) Weighted Average.

[C.U. B.Com. (Hons) 1991]

Solution

(a)

STORE LEDGER

AB Limited

Material Code No. LIFO

Date 1990	Receipts Qnt. (Kg)	Receipts Rate (Rs.)	Receipts Amt. (Rs.)	Issues Qnt. (Kg)	Issues Rate (Rs.)	Issues Amt. (Rs.)	Balance Qnt. (Kg.)	Balance Rate (Rs.)	Balance Amt. (Rs.)
Nov. 1							1,000	6.00	6,000
10	500	7.00	3,500				1,000	6.00	6,000
							500	7.00	3,500
15				500	7.00	3,500			
				700	6.00	4,200	300	6.00	1,800
20	1,000	8.00	8,000				300	6.00	1,800
							1,000	8.00	8,000
30				1,000	8.00	8,000			
				150	6.00	900			
							150	6.00	900

Maximum level ....
Reordering level ....
Minimum level ....

(b)

Material Code No. SIMPLE AVERAGE

Date 1988	Receipts Qnt. (Kg)	Receipts Rate (Rs.)	Receipts Amt. (Rs.)	Issues Qnt. (Kg)	Issues Rate (Rs.)	Issues Amt. (Rs.)	Balance Qnt. (Kg.)	Balance Rate (Rs.)	Balance Amt. (Rs.)
Nov. 1							1,000	6.00	6,000
10	500	7.00	3,500				1,500	—	9,500
15				1,200	6.50	7,800	300	—	1,700
20	1,000	8.00	8,000				1,300	—	9,700
30				1,100	7.50	8,250	200	—	1,450
				50	7.50	375	150	—	1,075

(c) WEIGHTED AVERAGE

Date	Receipts			Issues			Balance		
	Qnt.	Rate	Amt.	Qnt.	Rate	Amt.	Qnt.	Rate	Amt.
1990	(Kg)	(Rs.)	(Rs.)	(Kg)	(Rs.)	(Rs.)	(Kg.)	(Rs.)	(Rs.)
Nov. 1							1,000		6,000
10	500	7	3,500				1,500	–	9,500
15				1,200	6.33	7,596	300		1,904
20	1,000	8	8,000				1,300		9,904
30				1,100	7.61	8,371	200		1,533
30				50	7.61	381	150		1,152

Notes I : Value of issue of materials on 15. 11. 1990 = 9,500 ÷ 1,500 = Rs. 6.33.

II : on 30.11.90 Rs. 9,904 ÷ 1,300 = Rs. 7.61.

Problem 55

Oil India is a bulk distributor of high octane petrol. A periodic inventory of petrol on hand is taken when the books are closed at the end of each month. The following summary of information is available for the month of June 1996 :

	Rs.
Sales	9,45,000
General Administration Cost	25,000
Opening Stock 1,00,000 litres @ 3 per litre	3,00,000
Purchases (including freight in)	
June 1—2,00,000 litres @ Rs. 2.85 per litre.	
June 30—1,00,000 litres @ Rs. 3.03 per litre.	
Closing Stock on June 30—1,30,000 litres	

Compute the following data by the first-in-first-out, weighted average method and last-in-last-out methods of inventory costing :

(a) Value of Inventory on June 30.

(b) Amount of the cost of goods sold for June.

(c) Profit or loss for June.

[Adapted—C.A. Inter]

Solution

Materials issued during June :

	Opening Stock	1,00,000	litres
Add	Purchases	3,00,000	litres
		4,00,000	litres
Less	Closing Stock on June 30	1,30,000	
		2,70,000	litres

(a) **Value of Closing Inventory under FIFO Method**

			Rs.
(i)	30,000 litres @ Rs. 2.85	=	85,500
	1,00,000 litres @ Rs. 3.03	=	3,03,000
			3,88,500
(ii)	**Under Weighted Average Method**		
	1,30,000 litres @ Rs. 3 per litre		3,90,000
	(Calculated as follows)		

Date	*Receipts*			*Issues*			*Balance*		
	Qty.	*Rate*	*Amt.*	*Qty.*	*Rate*	*Amt.*	*Qty.*	*Rate*	*Amt.*
1990	Kg	Rs.	Rs.	Kg	Rs.	Rs.	Kg.	Rs.	Rs.
June 1							1,00,000	3.00	3,00,000
June 1	2,00,000	2.85	5,70,000				3,00,000	—	8,70,000
1st Issue and 2nd Issue				2,70,000	2.90	7,83,000	30,000	—	87,000
June 30	1,00,000	3.03	3,03,000				1,30,000	—	3,90,000

Weighted Average Rate = Rs. 3,90,000 ÷ 1,30,000 = Rs. 3 per litre.

(iii) **LIFO Method**

		Rs.
30,000	litres @ Rs. 3 per litre	90,000
1,00,000	litres @ Rs. 3.03 per litre	3,03,000
		3,93,000

* First and Second issues were made before 30th June 1996. Under LIFO Method 1st and 2nd issues to the extent of 2,00,000 litres were made out of purchase made on June 1, 1996 and remaining 70,000 litres were issued out of opening stock leaving balance of 30,000 litres @ Rs. 3 per litre.

(b) **Cost of goods sold**

		FIFO	*Weighted Average*	*LIFO*
		Rs.	Rs.	Rs.
	Opening Stock	3,00,000	3,00,000	3,00,000
Add :	Purchases			
	June 1	5,70,000	5,70,000	5,70,000
	June 30	3,03,000	3,03,000	3,03,000
		11,73,000	11,73,000	11,73,000
Less :	Closing Stock	3,88,500	3,90,000	3,93,000
	Cost of goods sold	7,84,500	7,83,000	7,80,000

(c) **Profit**

		FIFO	Weighted Average	LIFO
		Rs.	Rs.	Rs.
	Sale Price	9,45,000	9,45,000	9,45,000
Less :	Cost of goods sold	7,84,500	7,83,000	7,80,000
		1,60,500	1,62,000	1,65,000
Less :	General Administration cost	25,000	25,000	25,000
	Profit	1,35,500	1,37,000	1,40,000

TREATMENT OF ABNORMAL LOSS

Problem 56

On 1st January the Stock of a component in the Stores was 545 units at Rs. 35 per hundred. During the three months the receipts and issues were as follows :

	Purchased	Issued
January	444 @ Rs. 37.50 per hundred	400 units
February	500 @ Rs. 40.00 per hundred	610 "
March	750 @ Rs. 42.00 per hundred	950 "

When stock was taken on 31st March, a discrepancy of 49 units was revealed. Prepare a Store Ledger Card under the FIFO method and show how would you deal with the discrepancy.

[Adapted—I.C.W.A. (Inter)]

Solution

STORE LEDGER ACCOUNT – FIFO

Code No. ....

Date	*Receipts*				*Issues*				*Balance*		
	G R	*Qnt.*	*Rate*	*Value*	*R.*	*Qnt.*	*Rate*	*Value*	*Qnt.*	*Rate*	*Value*
	No.	Rs.	Rs.	Rs.	No.	Rs.	Rs.	Rs.	Rs.	Rs.	Rs.
									545	35.00	190.75
Jan 1		444	37.50	166.50					545	35.00	190.75
									444	37.50	166.50
						400	35.00	140.00	145	35.00	50.75
									444	37.50	166.50
Feb 1		500	40.00	200.00					145	35.00	50.75
									444	37.50	166.50
									500	40.00	200.00
						145	35.00	50.75			
						444	37.50	166.50			
						21	40.00	8.40	479	40.00	191.60
Mar 1		750	42.00	315.00					479	40.00	191.60
									750	42.00	315.00
						479	40.00	191.60			
						471	42.00	197.82	279	42.00	117.18
Mar 31						49	42.00	20.58	230	42.00	96.60

Treatment of Normal and Abnormal Loss

Problem 57

From the following particulars prepare Store Ledger Account for the quarter Jan 90 to March, 90 of Martin Ltd. after taking into consideration the following information :

a) a provision for normal loss @ 1% on the Stores Account balance at the beginning of each month.

On 1st January 1990, the Stock was 1,000 @ 10 each. The following transactions took place during Jan. 1990 to March 1990 :

	Quantity	Purchase	Issues
January 1990	4,000	10	2990
February 1990	8,000	12	5980
March 1990	10,000	15	8960

On 31st March, 1990 stock taking revealed a shortage of 2,000 units.

Solution

STORES ACCOUNT

Date	Receipts			Issues			Balance		
1990	Qnt.	Rate	Amt.	Qnt.	Rate	Amt.	Qnt.	Rate	Amt.
		Rs.	Rs.		Rs.	Rs.		Rs.	Rs.
Jan 1							1000	10	10,000
" 1							10		
							990		10,000
Jan 1 to 31	4,000	10	40,000				4,000	10	40,000
Jan 31				990	10	10,000			
				2,000	10	20,000	2,000	10	20,000
				Shortage @ 1%					
Feb 1				20			1,980		20,000
Feb 1 to 28	8,000	12	96,000				8,000	12	96,000
				1,980		20,000			
				4,000	12	48,000	4,000	12	48,000
				Shortage @ 1%					
March 1				40			3,960		48,000
Mar. 1 to 31	10,000	15	1,50,000				3,960		48,000
Mar. 1 to 31							10,000	15	1,50,000
"				3,960		48,000			
				5,000	15	75,000	5,000	15	75,000
"				200	15	30,000	3,000	15	45,000
				Shortage @ 1%					
April 1				30	–		2,970		45,000

ASSIGNMENT

Theoretical Questions

1. Outline the procedure to be followed in a modern factory for purchase of raw materials. **[C.U. B.Com. (Pass)]**
2. What is Materials Requisition ? Draw up a specimen of a Materials Requisition. **[C.U. B.Com.(Hons.)]**
3. What is Goods Received Note ? What purpose does it serve ? Give a specimen form. **[C.U. B.Com. (Hons.)]**
4. What are the advantages and disadvantages of centralised store ?
5. What do you mean by the expression 'Maximum level', 'Minimum level' and 'Re-ordering level' ? What factors are to be taken into account in fixing those levels ? **[C.U. B.Com.(Hons) 1988]**
6. What is Perpetual Inventory System ? Describe its advantages. **[C.U. B.Com. (Hons.) 1989]**
7. Give a proforma of a Bin Card and enter therein two specimen items of receipt and two specimen items of issue of material. **[C.U. B.Com. (Hons.) 1988]**
8. What is ABC Analysis ? Describe its advantages.
9. What do you mean by Economic Order Quantity ? **[C.U. B.Com. (Hons.) 1987]**
10. Define Store Ledger. How does it differ from Bin Card ?
11. Write short notes in :
    (1) Stores Requisition, (ii) Bin Card (iii) Bill of Materials, (iv) Store Ledger. **[C.U. B.Com. (Pass)]**
12. What is the importance of material control? **[B.Com (Hons.) C.U.]**
13. Discuss broadly what records would you keep of the receipt of materials for a manufacturing concern. **[C.U. B.Com. (Hons.) 1994]**
14. Explain the difference between the store records kept in the stores and that in the Accounts Department. **[C.U. B. Com.(Hons.) 1995]**
15. What are the considerations necessary for selecting a particular method of pricing issues of materials? **[C.U. B.Com. (Hons.) 1996]**

PRACTICAL PROBLEMS

1. (a) A lorry load of material of mixed goods was purchased for Rs. 9,000. These were sorted in the following goods whose market rate is shown against each :

Order	A 5,000	units	selling	rate	@ Rs. 1.20
"	B 3,000	"	"	"	@ Re. 1.00
"	C 2,000	"	"	"	@ Rs. 1.50

Find the purchase rate per unit on each grade of the material assuming that all grades yield same rate of profit.

[New Alipore College – Test Exam. 1987]

Ans. : A–Re. 0.90, B–Re 0.75 and C–Rs. 1.125

2. Calculate the Economic Order Quantity from the following :

(a) Quantity	600 units
(b) Ordering Cost	Rs. 12 per order
(c) Carrying cost	20%
(d) Price per unit	Rs. 20.

Ans : EOQ = 60 units.

3. A manufacturer has to supply his customers 600 units of his product per year. Shortages are not allowed and the inventory carrying cost amount to Re. 0.60 per unit per year. The set up cost per run is Rs. 80. Find :
   i) The EOQ
   ii) The minimum average yearly cost.
   iii) The optimum number of orders per year.
   iv) The optimum period of supply for optimum order.

[I.C.W.A. 85]

Ans : i) EOQ 400 units, ii) Rs. 280, iii) $1\frac{1}{2}$ or 2 orders, iv) 8 months.

Hint : For 600 units – 12 months

For 400 units — ?

$$\frac{400 \times 12}{600} = 8 \text{ months}$$

4. The following data are available from the records of M/s Naveen Industries Ltd. using two types of materials A and B for the manufacture of their product :

	A	B
Normal Usage (units p.m.)	250	200
Minimum Usage	100	200
Maximum Usage	350	400
Reorder quantity	900	1,000
Reorder period (in months)	3	3 to 4

Compute for each type of material, the following levels :

(i) Reorder level ; (ii) Minimum level ; (iii) Maximum level ; (iv) Average Stock level.

[I.C.W.A. Inter]

	A	B
(i)	1,050	1,600
(ii)	300	900
(iii)	1,650	2,000
(iv)	975	1,450

5. Find out the Economic Order Quantity and order schedule for raw materials and packing materials with the following data given to you :

1. Cost of ordering	:	Raw materials Rs. 1,000 per order. Packing materials Rs. 5,000 per order
2. Cost of holding inventory	:	Raw materials Re. 0.1 per unit p.m. Packing materials Re. 0.5 per unit p.m.
3. Production rate	:	2,00,000 units p.m.

[C.S. Examination (N.S.)]

Ans. : (i) Raw materials 2,00,000 units and one order in a month
(ii) Packing materials 2,00,000 units and one order in a month.

6. A manufacturer uses 75,000 units of a particular material per year. The material cost is Rs. 1.50 per unit and the carrying cost is estimated to be 25% p.a. of average inventory cost. The cost of placing an order is Rs. 18.

You are required to determine the economic order quantity and frequency of order p.a.

[C.U. B.Com(Hons.) 1994]

Ans. : EOQ = Rs. 2,684 units
No. of order 28

7. From the information given below determine the EOQ. Annual usage-8,000 units; Purchase price per unit-Rs. 10 ; Ordering cost per order-Rs. 80; Carrying cost-20% p.a. per unit cost.

[C.U. B.Com(Hons.) 1995]

Ans. : EOQ = 800 units

8. Certain purchases part of which annual requirements are 8,000 units, involves ordering costs equal to Rs. 12.50 per order, cost per piece Re. 1 and the annual carrying cost is 20%. In addition, average daily usage is 32 units (based on 250 operating days per year), lead time is 10 days and the safety stock has been calculated to be 100 units.

Calculate the (a) Economic Order Quantity and (b) Reorder Point.

Ans. : EOQ = 1,000 units
Reorder Point = 420 units

Hint : Reorder Point = Safety Stock + (lead time × average daily usage)

9. The following information is obtained from a factory. The factory uses 5,126 units of a component in a year. The purchase price per unit of the component is Rs. 5 and the carrying cost including interest is estimated at 20% of the average inventory investment on annual basis. The cost of placing the order and processing the delivery is Rs. 10.

You are asked to ascertain the EOQ and the number of order to be placed for the component in a year.

Ans. 321 units; 16 orders.

10. From the following particulars find out the Economic Order Quantity :

Annual Demand	12,000 units
Ordering Cost	Rs. 90 per order
Inventory Carrying cost per annum	Rs. 15

11. From the following data for the twelve months, compute the average stock level for a component :

Maximum usage	300 Nos.
Minimum usage	200 Nos.
Average usage per month	225

Ans. : 380

Time lag in procurement of material :
Maximum 6 months, minimum 2 months.

Reorder quanity—	750 Nos

[Vidyasagar University, B.Com. (Hons.) 1991]

Ans. :			
	Reorder level	1,800	units
	Maximum level	2,150	"
	Minimum level	900	"
	Average stock level	1,525	"

12. If the price per unit of material is Rs. 15 and the annual consumption is 4,000 units, the interest and store-keeping charges are 20% of the value and the cost of placing an order and receiving the goods is Rs. 60, how much material should be ordered at one time?

[Adapted—A.I.M.A.]

Ans. : 400 Units.

13. A manufacturer buys certain equipment from outside suppliers at Rs. 30 per unit. Total annual needs are 800 units. The following further data are available :

Annual return on investment 10%, rent, insurance, taxes per unit per year Re. 1.00. Cost of placing an order Rs. 100. Determine the Economic Order Quantity.

[C.U. M.Com.—Adapted]

Ans. : EOQ 200 units.

Hint : Carrying cost per unit = Rs. 3.00 $\left(30 \times \frac{10}{100}\right)$ + Re. 1.00 = Rs. 4.

14. Find out the Economic Order Quantity for raw materials and packing materials with the following data given to you :

(i)	Cost of ordering :	
	Raw materials	Rs. 1,000 per order
	Packing materials	Rs. 5,000 per order
(ii)	Cost of holding inventory :	
	Raw materials	0.01 paisa per unit p.m.
	Packing materials	0.05 paisa per unit p.m.
(iii)	Production rate :	2,00,000 units p.m.

[Adapted—Company Secretaries]

Ans. : EOQ — 2,00,000 unit each.

15. From the following particulars in respect of a material, calculate the Economic Order Quantity :

Total Consumption per year—	20,000 units
Procurement cost per order—	Rs. 16
Cost per unit—	Rs. 10
Storage and carrying cost—	10%

[C.U. B.Com. (Pass)—1990]

Ans. : 800 units.

16. From the following data work out the EOQ of a particular component :

Annual demand – 5,000 units; Ordering Cost Rs. 60 per order, price per unit Rs. 100; Inventory carrying cost – 15% on average inventory.

[Adapted—ICWA (Inter) June—1986]

Ans. : EOQ – 200 units

17. From the following determine the EOQ :

Annual usage	8,000 units
Purchase price per unit	Rs. 10
Ordering cost per order	Rs. 80
Carrying cost 20% p.a.	

Ans. : EOQ 800 units

18. The following information is available in respect of a material of Y & Co. Ltd.

Re-order quantity	12,000 units
Lead time	4 to 8 weeks
Maximum consumption	4,000 units per week
Normal consumption	3,000 units per week
Minimum consumption	1,550 units per week

Ascertain the following from the above information :

(i) Reorder level
(ii) Minimum Stock level
(iii) Maximum stock level

Ans. : (i) 32,000 units, (ii) 14,000 units, (iii) 37,800 units

19. From the following particulars compute (i) Maximum stock level, (ii) Minimum stock level; (iii) Re-order stock level :

Normal consumption per month	1,000 litres
Maximum consumption p.m.	8,000 litres
Minimum consumption p.m.	400 litres
Lead time	2 – 4 months
Reorder quantity	10,000 litres.

[B.U. B.Com. (Hons.) 1982]

Ans. : (i) 41,200 litres, (ii) 29,000 litres, (iii) 32,000 litres.

20. From the following data prepare economic ordering quantity for the item :

Total annual consumption—	1,20,000 units
Purchase price (per unit)—	Rs. 1.50
Ordering cost	Rs. 80 per order
Cost of carrying inventory	20% per annum

[Adapted—C.S. June 1988]

Ans. : 8,000 units

21. A Company uses 10,000 units per year of an item costing Rs. 5 each. The cost of processing a purchase order is Rs. 100 and the stock holding cost amounts to 20% per year of the money value of inventory. How much should the company buy at a time (in a single order) in order to minimise the inventory cost?

[ICWA Final—Adapted]

Ans. : 1,414 units (Approx.)

22. Calculate Economic Order Quantity from the following information. Also state the number of orders to be placed in a year :

Consumption of materials p.a.	10,000 kg.
Order placing cost per order	Rs. 50
Cost per kg. for raw materials	Rs. 2
Storage costs	8% on average inventory

[Adapted—B.Com Madurai]

Ans. : (i) 2,500 kg.
(ii) No. of orders 4

23. (a) A manufacturer uses 200 units of a component every month and he buys them entirely from outside supplier. The order placing and receiving cost is Rs. 100 and annual carrying cost is Rs. 12. From this set of data calculate the Economic Order Quanity.

(b) XYZ Company uses three types of materials A, B and C for production of S, the final product. The relevant monthly data for the components are given below :

	A	B	C
Normal Usage (in units)	200	150	180
Minimum usage (in units)	100	100	90
Maximum usage (in units)	300	250	270
Reorder quantity (in units)	750	900	720
Reorder period (in months)	2 to 3	3 to 4	2 to 3

Calculate for each component :

(i) Reorder level, (ii) Minimum level, (iii) Maximum level, (iv) Average stock level.

[Test Examination – Sivnath Sashtri College]

Ans. : (a) 200 units

(b)

	A	B	C
Reorder level	900	1,000	810
Minimum level	400	475	360
Maximum level	1,450	1,600	1,350
Average Stock	925	1,038	855

24. From the given particulars of X & Co. Ltd. calculate :

(i) EOQ, (ii) How many orders should the Company place each year ? (iii) At what inventory level should an order be placed?

Particulars :

Order must be placed in multiples of 100 units
Requirements for the year 3,00,000 units
Purchase price is Rs. 3 per unit
Carrying Cost is 25% of the purchase price of goods
Cost per order placed is Rs. 20.
Desired safety stock is 10,000 units
Three days are required for delivery.

Ans. : (i) EOQ = 4,000 units
(ii) 75 orders; (iii) 13,000

Hint : Assuming that there are 300 working days in the factory in a year :

25. (A) From the following find out :

(i) Maximum level; (ii) Minimum level, (iii) Re-ordering level

Reorder Quantity	1,500 units
Reorder period	4 to 6 weeks
Maximum consumption	400 units per week
Minimum consumption	250 units per week
Normal consumption	300 units per week

(B) Calculate the EOQ of a material from the following information :

Annual usage	80,000 units
Buying cost per unit	Rs. 20
Inventory carrying cost	10% of Cost
Cost per unit	Rs. 50

Ans. : (A) (i) 2,900 units, (ii) 900 units, (iii) 2,400 units :
(B) 800 units

26. Two components A and B are used as follows :

Normal usage	50 per week each
Minimum usage	25 per week each
Reordering quantity	A—300 units; B—500 units
Reorder period	A—4 - 6 weeks; B—2 – 4 weeks

Calculate for each component :

(i) Re-ordering level; (ii) Minimum level ; (iii) Maximum level, (iv) Average stock level.

Ans. : Reorder level—	A—450,	B — 300
Minimum level—	A—200,	B—150
Maximum—	A—650,	B—750 units
Average stock level—	A—425 units,	B—450 units.

Hints : Maximum usage is to be claculated in the following manner :

Let Maximum usage = X

So, $\frac{\text{Minimum usage + X}}{2}$ = Normal usage (Average usage)

Or, $\frac{25+X}{2} = 50$

Or, $25 + X = 100$

Or, $X = 100 - 25 = 75$

Hint : Value of stock for theft Rs. 10,206 should be written-off against Costing Profit and Loss.

27. (i) A manufacturer uses 200 units of a component every month and he buys then entirely from an outside supplier. The order placing and receiving cost is Rs. 12. From this set of date, calculate the Economic Order Quantity.

(ii) P. Ltd. uses three types of materials A, B and C for production of X, the final product. The relevant monthly data for the components are as given below :

	A	B	C
Normal usage (in units)	200	150	180
Minimum usage (in units)	100	100	90
Maximum usage (in units)	300	250	270
Reorder Quantity (in units)	750	900	720
Reorder period (in months)	2 to 3	3 to 4	2 to 3

Calculate from each component :

(a) Re-order level, (b) Minimum level, (c) Maximum level, and (d) Average stock level.

[ICWA (Inter)—Adapted]

Ans. : (i) EOQ = 200 units (ii) (a) Reorder level

	A		B		C	
	900	(units)	1,000	(units)	810	(Units)
(b)	400	"	475	"	360	"
(c)	1,450	"	1,600	"	1,350	"
(d)	925	"	1,038	"	855	"

28. In a factory component A is used as follows :

Normal usage	50 kg. per week
Minimum usage	25 kg. per week
Maximum usage	75 kg. per week
Reorder quantity	300 kg.
Reorder period	4 to 6 weeks

Calculate for component A :

(i) Re-order level, (ii) Maximum level; (iii) Minimum level and (iv) Averge stock level.

[C.U. B.Com (Hons.) 1994]

Ans. : (i) 450 units; (ii) 650 units; (iii) 200 units, (iv) 425 units

29. Two components, A and B are used as follows :

Normal usage	3,000	units per week
Minimum usage	1,500	units " "
Maximum usage	4,500	units per week
Reorder quantity	A : 13,000	units ; B. 4,000 units
Reorder period	A. 4 to 6	weeks; B. 2 to 4 weeks

Calculate for each component :

(a) Reorder level, (b) Minimum level; (c) Maximum level, and (d) Average stock level.

[Adapted—Bangalore—M. Com.]

Ans. : (a) Reorder level—A—27,000 units
B—18,000 "
(b) Minimum level :
A : 12,000 units
B : 9,000 "
(c) A : 34,000 "
B : 29,000 "
(d) A : 18,500 units
B : 16,000 units

30. In a factory two components P and Q are used as follows :

Normal usage	900	units per week each
Maximum usage	1,350	" " " "
Minimum usage	450	" " " "
Reorder Quantity :		
P :	7,200	units
Q :	9,000	"
Reorder period :		
P :	2 – 4	weeks
Q :	4 – 6	weeks

Calculate for each component

(i) Re-order level, (ii) Minimum level; (iii) Maximum level and (iv) Average stock level.

[V.U. B.Com. (Hons.) 1995]

Ans. : P— (i) 5,400 units; (ii) 2,700 units
(iii) 11,700; (iv) 7,200 units
Q— (i) 8,100 units; (ii) 3,600 units;
(iii) 15,300 units; (iv) 9,450 units

31. Two components X & Y are used as follows :

Normal usage	50 units each per week
Minimum usage	25 units each per week
Maximum usage	75 units each per week
Re-order quantity	X : 400 units ; Y : 600 units
Re-order period	X : 4 to 6 weeks; Y : 2 to 4 weeks

Calculate for each component (1) the re-order level, (2) the minimum level (3) the maximum level and (4) the average stock level.

[M. Com.—Calicut]

Ans. : (a) Reorder level : X = 450 units, Y = 300 units
(b) Minimum level : X = 200 units, Y = 150 units
(c) Maximum level : X = 750 units, Y = 850 units
(d) Average stock : X = 475 units, Y = 500 units

32. Two Components, A and B, are used as follows :

Normal usage		50 units per week each
Minimum usage		25 units per week each
Maximum usage		75 units per week each
Reorder quantity	A :	300 units
	B :	500 units
Reorder Period	A :	4 to 6 weeks
	B :	2 to 4 weeks

Calculate for each component :

(a) Re-order level
(b) Minimum level
(c) Maximum level
(d) Average Stock level

[B. Com. Poona]

Ans. : Re-order level A – 450 units ; B – 300 units
Maximum level A – 650 units ; B – 750 units
Minimum level A – 200 units ; B – 150 units
Average Stock level A – 425 units ; B – 450 units

33. (a) EXE Limited has received an offer of quantity discounts on its order of materials as under :

Price per tonne (Rs.)	Tonnes Nos.
1,200	Less than 500
1,180	500 and above but less than 1,000
1,160	1,000 and above but less than 2,000
1,140	2,000 and above but less than 3,000
1,120	3,000 and above.

The annual requirement for the material is 5,000 tonnes. The ordering cost per order is Rs. 1,200 and the stock holding cost is estimated at 20% of material cost per annum.

You are required to compute the total economical purchase level.

(b) What will be your answer to the above question if there are no discounts offered and the price per tonne is Rs. 1,500?

[Adapted—C.A. (Inter) Nov. 1990]

Ans. : (a) 1,000 units at a total cost of Rs. 59,22,000 (b) 200 tonnes.

34. Sachin Ltd., furnishes the following information :

(i) Consumption 300 units per quarter; (ii) Cost per unit Rs. 40; (iii) Cost of processing on order Rs. 600; (iv) Obsolescence 15%; (v) Insurance on inventory 25%.

Compute : (a) Economic order quantity; (b) No. of orders per year; (c) time between two consecutive orders.

A supplier offers a discount of 2% on a purchase of 600 units should it be accepted?

[Adapted : Calcutta University B.Com. Hons.]

[Ans. : (b) (i) 300 units : (ii) 4; (iii) 3 months;
(iv) Cost taking 300 units (EOQ) as the order quantity Rs. 52,800;
(offer is not acceptable since the total cost is Rs. 52,800)]

35. A firm is able to obtain quantity discounts on its orders of material as follows :

Price per tonne Rs.	Tonnes
6.00	Less than 250
5.90	250 and less than 800
5.80	800 and less than 2,000
5.70	2,000 and less than 4,000
5.60	4,000 and over

The annual demand for the material is 4,000 tonnes. Stock holding costs are 20% of material cost per annum. The delivery cost per order is Rs. 6.00.

You are required to calculate the best quantity to order.

[Mangalore M. Com.]

Ans. : 800 tonnes.

36. Shrivam Enterprises manufactures a special product "ZED". The following particulars collected for the year 1993 are :

(a) Monthly demand of ZED – 1,000 units
(b) Cost of placing an order – Rs. 100
(c) Annual carrying cost per unit – Rs. 15
(d) Normal usage 50 units per week
(e) Minimum usage 25 units per week
(f) Maximum usage 75 units per week
(g) Reorder period 4 to 6 weeks

Compute from the above :

(1) Re-order Quantity.
(2) Re-order level.
(3) Minimum Level.
(4) Maximum Level.
(5) Average Stock Level.

[Adapted—C.A. (Inter) Nov. 1987]

Ans. : (1) 400 units, (2) 450 units, (3) 200 units, (4) 750 units, (5) 475 units.

37. (a) Discuss briefly what records would you keep of the receipt of materials for a manufacturing concern.

(b) In a factory, component A is used as follows :

Normal usage 50 kg per week
Minimum usage 25 kg per week
Maximum usage 75 kg per week
Re-order quantity 300 kg.
Re-order period 4 to 6 weeks

Calculate for component A

(i) Reorder level
(ii) Maximum level.
(iii) Minimum level.
(iv) Average stock level.

[C.U. B.Com. (Hons.) 1994]

Ans. : (i) 450 kgs.; (ii) 650 kgs.; (iii) 200 kgs.; (iv) 425 kgs.

38. (a) Calculate for each component Maximum Level, Minimum Level and Reorder Level from the following data :

Reordering Quantity—	A = 500 units
	B = 400 units
Reorder period—	A = 2 to 4 weeks
	B = 4 to 6 weeks

Normal consumption – 60 units per week each
Minimum consumption – 40 units per week each
Maximum consumption – 80 units per week each.

(b) A manufacturer uses 200 units of a component every month and he buys then entirely from outside suppliers. The order placing and receiving cost is Rs. 100 per order and annual carrying cost is Rs. 12.

On the basis of the above data calculate Economic Order Quantity.

Ans. 200 units.

39. The following information is provided by Sunrise Industries for the fortnight of December 1992 :

Materials Exe

Stock on 1.12.1992 – 100 units @ Rs. 5 per unit.

Purchases

5.12.1992	300 units at Rs. 6
8.12.1992	500 units at Rs. 7
12.12.1992	600 units at Rs. 8

Issues

6.12.1992	250 units
10.12.1992	400 units
14.12.1992	500 units

You are required to calculate using FIFO and LIFO methods of pricing issues :

(a) the value of materials consumed during the period,
(b) the value of stock of materials on 15.12.1992

[Adapted—C.A. (Inter) May 1989]

Ans. :	**(a)**	**(i)**	**FIFO—**	**Rs. 7,800**
		(ii)	**LIFO—**	**Rs. 8,300**
	(b)	**(i)**	**FIFO—**	**Rs. 2,800**
		(ii)	**LIFO—**	**Rs. 2,300**

40. From the following particulars write up the Store Ledger Account for the material 'M':

1.6.90	Opening Stock 1,600 units @ Rs. 9
7.6.90	Purchased 1,200 units @ Rs. 10
12.6.90	Issued 800
15.6.90	Purchased 500 units @ Rs. 11
20.6.90	Issued 700 units
21.6.90	Issued 300 units
22.6.90	Purchased 500 units @ Rs. 12
29.6.90	Purchased 600 units @ Rs. 12
30.6.90	Issued 800 units

The issues are valued on LIFO Method. On actual Stock Verification at the end of the month, the actual stock was found to be 1,750 units only. Out of the shortage, 16 units were normal and other units were due to theft.

[Audit & Acct. Exam. 1986]

Ans. : Value of stock Rs. 14,892

41. From the following particulars, write the Store Ledger of a matérial X for 3 months, after writing-off the normal wastage at the end of each month at 1% of opening stock for that month (calculating such wastage in approximate whole number of units) and, after valuing on FIFO— Method :

Jan. 1. 1989	Opening Stock	540 units @ Rs. 3.50
	Purchase	Issue
January 1989	440 units at Rs. 3.75	480 units
February 1989	500 units at Rs. 4.00	600 units
March 1989	640 units at Rs. 3.50	500 units

By physical verification on 31.3.1989, the actual stock in hand was found to be only 500 units. The Store Ledger balance was adjusted accordingly.

[Audit & Acct. Service Exam. 1986]

Ans. : 500 @ 3.5—Rs. 1,750

Hints : Abnormal loss of 28 units @ Rs. 3.50 should be shown as issue.

42. The following is the information regarding receipts and issues of pigments and the stores record of a paint manufacturing factory :

		Kg.
April 1	Opening stock of pigments (there were no issues or receipts during the last week of March)	25,000
2	Issue on Requisition No. 1	13,000
3	Received from a supplier by Challan No. 13 of 3 – 4 – 70 as per stipulated date of delivery	30,000
3	Issued on Requisition No. 3	10,000
4	Issued on Requisition No. 4	5,000
6	Received from supplier by Challan No. 48	10,000
7	Issued on Requisition No. 5	4,500

Examination by the store verifier on 6th morning recorded a shortage of 500 kg.

Maximum limit was	50,000 kg.
Minimum limit was	8,000 kg.
Ordering-level was	25,000 kg.

You are required to prepare Bin Card No. 36 for the item of pigment for which the symbol alloted is X = 40.

[C.A.—Inter]

Ans. : Balance : 32,000 kg.

43. The following are the transactions in respect of purchase and issues of components forming part of an assembly of a product manufactured by a firm which requires to update its costs of production very often for bidding tenders and finalising cost plus contracts :

Date	Quantity	Particulars
1986		
Jan. 5	1,000 units	Rs. 1.20 each
11	2,000 units	Issued
1986		
Feb. 1	1,500	Purchased @ Rs. 1.30 each
18	2,400	Issued
26	1,000	Issued
March 8	1,000	Purchased at Rs. 1.40 each
17	1,500	Purchased at Rs. 1.30 each
28	2,000	Issued

The stock on January 1, 1986 was 5,000 units at Rs. 1.10. State the method you would adopt in pricing the issue of components giving reasons.

[Adapted—ICWA (Inter) Dec. 1986]

Ans. : LIFO value of closing Stock =	**500 units @ 1.40**	**= Rs. 700**
	2,100 units @ Rs. 1.10	**= Rs. 2,310**
	2,600 units	**= Rs. 3,010**

44. Prepare a store ledger account from the following information applying Weighted Average Method.

A manufacturing company purchased and issued a certain material as follows :

Date	Particulars	Units	Units cost
1990			Rs.
Jan. 1	Purchases	600	4.00
4	Purchases	300	4.20
6	Issues	500	—
10	Purchases	700	4.40
15	Issues	800	—
20	Purchases	300	5.00
25	Issues	100	—

[C.U. B.Com. (Pass)]

Ans. : Balance of Stock valued Rs. 2,484.

45. From the following transactions prepare Store Ledger Account properly using the following pricing methods :

(a) FIFO, (b) Simple Average and (c) Weighted Average.

1995		
Oct. 2	Purchased	4,000 units @ Rs. 4 per unit
20	Purchased	500 units @ Rs. 5 per unit
Nov. 5	Issued	2,000 units
10	Purchased	6,000 units @ Rs. 6 per unit
12	Issued	4,000 units
Dec. 4	Issued	1,000 units
8	Issued	2,000 units
20	Purchased	4,500 units @ Rs. 5.50 per unit
31	Issued	2,500 units

[Adapted—B.Com. Osmania]

Ans. : FIFO Rs. 19,250
Simple Average Rs. 18,375
Weighted Average Rs. 19,204

46. Prepare a store ledger account from the following information applying Weighted Average Method :

A manufacturing company purchased and issued a certain material as follows :

Date	Purchase	Units	Unit Cost
1990			
Jan. 1	Purchases	600	4.00
4	Purchases	300	4.20
6	Issues	500	—
10	Purchases	700	4.40
15	Issues	800	—
20	Purchases	300	5.00
25	Issues	100	—

[C.U. B.Com. (Pass). 1991]

Ans. : 500 units @ Rs. 4.644 = Rs. 2,322

47. Prepare a Stores Ledger Account from the following details using LIFO method of pricing the issue of materials :

19...			
April 1	Opening balance	10,850 kg.	@ Rs. 130.00 per kg.
2	Purchased	20,000 kg.	@ Rs. 134.00 per kg.
3	Issued	6,750 kg.	to production
5	Issued	8,500 kg.	to production
6	Received back	550 kg.	from issue on 3rd April.
7	Purchased	17,550 kg.	@ Rs. 128.00 per kg.
8	Issued	11,250 kg.	to production
9	Physical stock verfication revealed loss of	250 kg.	
10	Issued	8,950 kg.	to production
12	Issued	6,300 kg.	to production
15	Purchased	10,000 kg.	@ Rs. 132.00 per kg.
16	Issued	7,750 kg.	to production

Ans. : 6,950 × 130 = Rs. 9,03,500
2,250 × 132 = Rs. 2,97,000
12,00,500

48. The particulars of receipts and issues of a material in a factory in August, 1995 are as under :

Aug. 1	Opening balance	1,500 kg.	@ 12.00 per kg.
2	Issued	100 kg.	
3	Issued	250 kg.	
4	Issued	300 kg.	
5	Received (purchase)	400 kg.	@ 12.500 per kg.
9	Issued	300 kg.	
10	Received (purchase)	200 kg.	@ 12.50 kg.
11	Issued	300 kg.	
12	Returned from workshop out of issues on 3rd August	20 kg.	
13	Issued	450 kg.	
16	Received (purchase)	500 kg.	@ 13.00 per kg.
18	Issued	400 kg.	
20	Returned from workship out of issues on 9th August	60 kg.	
22	Issued	300 kg.	
26	Received (purchase	400 kg.	@ 12.00 per kg.
29	Issued	200 kg.	

Pricing of issues is to be done on FIFO basis. A shortage of 10 kg. was noticed on 16th August. Prepare the Stores Ledger Account for the month of August, 1995 in respect of the material.

[C.U. B.Com. Hons.]

Ans. : 70 × Rs. 13 = Rs. 910
400 × Rs. 12 = Rs. 4,800
Rs. 5,710

49. From the following transactions prepare separately the Store Ledger Accounts using the following pricing methods :

(i) the FIFO, (ii) LIFO

1997		
Dec. 1	Opening balance 100 units of Rs. 5 each
5	Received 500 units @ Rs. 6 each
20	Issued 300 units
Jan. '98	
5	Issued 200 units
6	Received 600 units @ Rs. 5.00 each
Feb. '98	
10	Issued 300 units
12	Issued 250 units

Ans. : FIFO = 150 units @ Rs. 5 per unit = Rs. 750
LIFO = 100 units @ Rs. 5 per unit = Rs. 500
50 units @ Rs. 5 per unit = Rs. 250
Rs. 750

50. From the following transactions prepare Store Ledger Accounts using LIFO method of pricing :

Jan.	1	Opening balance 100 units @ Rs. 5.00 each
	5	Received 400 units @ Rs. 6.00 each
	20	Issued 200 units
Feb.	6	Issued 200 units
	10	Received 600 units @ Rs. 6 each
Mar.	8	Issued 400 units
	12	Issued 250 units

[Vidyasagar University, B.Com. (Hons.) 1988]

Ans. : Stock 50 units @ Rs. 5.00 each = Rs. 250.00.

51. From the following particulars prepare Store Ledger Account showing the pricing of materials issues, following First-in-First-out method :

1992			
Feb.	1	Opening stock	500 units at Rs. 2.00 each
	3	Purchase	400 units at Rs. 2.10 each
	5	Issued	600 units to Job K vide MR No. 15
	7	Purchased	800 units at Rs. 2.30 each
	9	Issued	600 units to Job P vide MR. No. 21
	12	Returned from Job K	150 units
	17	Purchased	350 units at Rs. 2.50 each
	19	Returned from Job P	100 units
	25	Issued	700 units to Job K vide MR No. 16

[Vidyasagar University B.Com. (Hons.) 1989]

Ans. : Value of Stock—Rs. 980.

Hints : (i) 100 × 2.30 = Rs. 230

300 × 2.50 = Rs. 750

52. From the following details of receipts and issues of ammonia in a chemical factory, draw up a priced Store Ledger for the material. Issues are to be priced on the principle of First-in-First-out.

Dec.	1	Balance 50,000 litres @ Rs. 2 per litre
	8	Issued 25,000 litres
	12	Received from Suppliers 20,000 litres @ Rs. 1.90 per litre
	15	Issued 18,000 litres
	21	Received from Suppliers 24,000 litres @ Rs. 1.80 per litre
	23	Issued 30,000 litres
	24	Received from Suppliers 32,000 litres @ Rs. 1.90
	27	Issued 20,000 litres
	29	Returned from production department out of issues made on 8.12 – 1,000 litres.

At the time of verification of physical stock on 31.12.1992 a shortage of 1,000 litres was noticed.

[C.U. B.Com. (Pass) 1988]

Ans. : Value of closing stock : 1,000 units @ 1.80 = Rs. 1,800

32,000 units @ 1.90 = Rs. 60,800

Rs. 62,600

53. From the following particulars write up the Stores Ledger using FIFO method :

1993			
Jan. 1	Opening Stock	1,000	units @ Rs. 10.00
5	Received	500	" @ Rs. 11.00
10	Issued	1,200	"
12	Received	800	" @ Rs. 11.50
20	Returned	100	" @ Rs. 10.00
25	Issued	500	"
30	Issued	200	"

[C.U. B.Com. (Pass) 1995]

Value of Stock

Ans. : 500 × Rs. 11.50 = Rs. 5,750

54. From the following particulars as stated below prepare the Stores Ledger Account for the month of March 1995, following the "First-in-First-out" basis :

1995	
March 1	Opening stock 250 units at Rs. 12 per unit
3	Issued 50 units to Dept. A
10	Issued 150 units to Dept. B
12	Purchased 300 units at Rs. 13 per unit
15	Issued 150 units to Dept. A.
20	Purchased 150 units @ Rs. 14 per unit
25	Issued 225 units to Dept. A
27	Returned to vendors 25 units out of the purchases on 20th March
30	Purchased 300 units at Rs. 15 per unit
30	Issued 50 units to Dept. B

[C.U. B.Com. (Pass) 1996

Ans. : Value of Stock	**50 × Rs. 14**	**= Rs. 700**
	300 × Rs. 15	**= Rs. 4,500**
		Rs. 5,200

55. The following are the particulars of receipts and issues of a material in a factory during January. 1990 :

Jan. 1	Opening Balance	1,000 kg. @ Rs. 20 per kg.
10	Issued to Jobs	500 kg.
12	Received from Supplier	400 kg. @ Rs. .30 per kg.
14	Returned of surplus from Job	30 kg. @ Rs. .25 per kg.
15	Issued to Jobs	305 kg.
20	Received from Supplier	600 kg @ Rs. 34 per kg.
25	Issued to Jobs	550 kg.
29	Received from Supplier	600 @ Rs. 35 per kg.
31	Issued to Jobs	350 kg.

You are required to prepare Store Ledger under the FIFO and LIFO methods.

[N.B.U. B.Com. (Hons.)]

Ans. : FIFO—Rs. 32,050

LIFO—Rs. 24,200.

56. Prepare Store Ledger Account from the following information applying Weighted Average method :

Date	Particulars	Units	Unit cost
1990			Rs.
Jan. 1	Purchases	600	4.00
4	Purchases	300	4.20
6	Issues	500	—
10	Purchases	700	4.40
15	Issues	800	—
20	Purchases	300	5.00
25	Issues	100	—

[C.U. B.Com. (Pass) 1991]

Ans. : Value of Stock Rs. 2,319.70]

57. From the following information, prepare the Stores Ledger Account under LIFO method:

1.2.95	Opening balance	100 units at Rs. 10 each
2.2.95	Received	200 units at Rs. 10.50 each
5.2.95	Received	300 units at Rs. 10.60 each
7.2.95	Issued	400 units
10.2.95	Issued	120 units
15.2.95	Received	400 units at Rs. 11 each
19.2.95	Issued	200 units
24.2.95	Received	300 units at Rs. 11.40 each
27.2.95	Issued	200 units
28.2.95	Issued	200 units

[Madras University—B.Com. 1997]

Closing stock of Materials :

80 × Rs. 10	**= Rs. 800**
100 × Rs. 11	**= Rs. 1,100**
	Rs. 1,900

58. At the beginning of July, Sunshine Box Co. had 10,000 Kg of Card-board in stock at 2.00 per kg. Following purchases of Card board are made during the month—

8th July	2,000 kgs @ Rs. 2.50 per kg.
11th July	5,000 kgs @ Rs. 3.00 per kg.
24th July	20,000 kgs @ Rs. 3.50 per kg.

Following issues were made to the Production Department :

15th July	16,000 kgs
30th July	20,000 kgs.

What would be the value of closing stock at the end of the month if the materials were issued according to (i) FIFO, (ii) LIFO and (iii) Weighted Average Method?

[W.B.A. & A. Service Exam. 1988]

Ans. :	**FIFO— 1,000 × Rs. 3.50**	**= Rs. 3,500**
	LIFO— 1,000 × Rs. 2.00	**= Rs. 2,000**
	Weighted Average— 1,000 × Rs. 3.398	**= Rs. 3,398**

59. With the help of the following information prepare the store ledger card based on the weighted average method of pricing issues :

Sept.	1	Opening balance 24,000 kgs @ Rs. 7,500 per ton.
	1	Purchased 44,000 kgs @ Rs. 7,600 per ton.
	1	Issued 10,000 kgs
	5	Issued 16,000 kgs
	12	Issued 24,000 kgs
	13	Purchased 10,000 kgs @ Rs. 7,800 per ton
	18	Issued 24,000 kgs
	22	Purchased 50,000 kgs @ Rs. 8,000 per ton
	28	Issued 30,000 kgs
	30	Issued 22,000 kgs.

[ICWA (Inter)]

Ans. : (a) Cost of materials issued = Rs. 9,76,448

(b) Value of closing stock = Rs. 15,952.

60. The following transactions occurred in purchases and issues of material in an organisation during December 1992 :

Date	Quantity	Rate	Per unit
4.12.1992	200 units	Rs. 24.00	per unit
10.12.1992	150 units	Rs. 23.00	per unit
18.12.1992	100 units	Rs. 24.00	per unit
22.12.1992	100 units	Rs. 23.50	per unit
Issued dated	Quantity		
5.12.1992	250 units		
12.12.1992	200 units		
25.12.1992	250 units		

The stock on 1.12.1992 was 200 units @ Rs. 25 per unit.

Prepare the Store Ledger Account first by adopting FIFO method of charging material issued and secondly by LIFO method.

[Delhi B.Com. (Pass)]

Ans. : Value of Stock FIFO—Rs. 1,175

LIFO—Rs. 1,250

61. Enter the following in the Store Ledger pricing the materials issued under Average Price method.

Purchases were :

Store Received Note No. 10 of 4th July 1992	20 @ Rs. 30 p.u.
Stores Received Note No. 53 of 17th July 1992	30 @ Rs. 28 p.u.
Stores Received Note No. 78 of 2nd August 1992	40 @ Rs. 29 p.u.
Stores Received Note No. 105 of 30th August 1992	30 @ Rs. 26 p.u.

The issues were :

25 on 20th July vide Requisition slip	No. 160
40 on 5th August vide Requisition slip	No. 32
45 on 31st August vide Requisition slip	No. 203

On 28th August, 1992 2 units issued on 20th July were received back.

On 29th August '92, one of them was found damaged and had to be discarded.

[B.U. B.Com. (Hons.) 1991]

Ans. : Value of Stock Rs. 277.50

62. The Store Ledger Account of material 'C' in the books of Chemical Processors Ltd. revealed the following Transactions for the month of November 1992 :

1992	
Nov. 1	Opening Stock 200 kg. @ 7.50 per kg.
5	Received from supplier S_1 400 kg. @ 7.75 per kg. (GRN No. 448)
8	Issued to production department 240 kg. (S.R. No. 897)
10	Issued to production department 160 kg. (S.R. No. 897)
12	Received from Supplier S_2 500 kg @ Rs. 7.90 per kg. (GRN No. 455)
15	Issued to production dept. 400 kg. (S.R. No. 912)
16	Received from Supplier S_3 250 kg. @ Rs. 8 per kg. (GRN. No. 461)
19	Received from Supplier S_4 600 kg. @ Rs. 8.25 per kg. (GRN No. 469)
21	Issued to production dept. 350 kg. (S.R. No. 946)
24	Issued to production dept. 260 kg. (S.R. No. 959)
27	Issued to production dept. 340 kg. (S.R. No. 974).

You are required to price the issues and draw out the closing balances in the Store Ledger Account under the pricing method suitable for any of the following two alternatives :

(a) The closing balance should be closely related to the current prices.

(b) The material costs charged to production should be closely related to current prices.

[Adapted—ICWA (Inter)]

Ans. : (a) 200 @ Rs. 8.25 = Rs. 1,650

(b) 200 @ Rs. 7.50 = Rs. 1,500

Hints : (a) FIFO method should be adopted

(b) LIFO method is to be adopted

63. On 1st January, 1988; the stock of a component in the store was 550 units of Rs. 35 per hundred. In January and February the receipts and issus were as below :

Date	Purchase	Rate	Issued
10.1.1968	440	Rs. 39 per hundred	
15.1.1988			450 units
10.2.1988	500 units	Rs. 45 per hundred	
15.2.1988			500 units

When the stock was taken on the last date of the month of February 1988 a shortage of 40 units was revealed.

Prepare Store Ledger under FIFO and Weighted Average method.

Show how would you deal with the shortage.

[B.U. B.Com.(Hons.)—1989]

Ans. : Balance under FIFO method 500 units @ .45 = Rs. 225.

Weighted Average Method – 500 @ .407 = Rs. 203.66.

64. The following transactions occur in the purchase & issue of a material :

Jan.	2	Purchased 4,000 units @ Rs. 4.00 per unit
Jan.	20	Purchased 500 units @ Rs. 5.00 per unit
Feb.	5	Issued 2,000 units
Feb.	10	Purchased 6,000 units @ Rs. 6.00 per unit
Feb.	12	Issued 4,000 units
March	2	Issued 1,000 units
March	5	Issued 2,000 units
March	15	Purchased 4,500 units @ Rs. 5.50 per unit
March	20	Issued 3,000 units

From the above, prepare the stores ledger account in two ways :

(a) first, by adopting FIFO method of charging materials issues and

(b) second, by adopting the LIFO Method.

What would be the value of stock in hand at the end of the period acording to each of the two methods?

[B.Com. (Hons.) Delhi]

Ans. : Closing stock under FIFO method : 3,000 units – Rs. 16,500;
Closing stock under LIFO method : 3,000 units – Rs. 14,250.

65. At the beginning of October 1995, the Bangalore Tin Co. had 10,000 Ibs of ten @ per Ib. Further purchases were made during the month as follows :

4th October	—	2,000 lbs @ Rs. 2.50 per Ib.
10th October	—	6,000 lbs @ Rs. 2.00 per Ib.
20th October	—	10,000 lbs @ Rs. 3.50 per Ib.

The issues to manufacture were as follows :

12th October	—	16,000 lbs
22nd October	—	10,000 lbs

Write the store ledger cards with the above transactions based on both the FIFO and the LIFO methods. What will be the value of the closing stock is each case?

[B.Com. Bangalore University]

Ans. : FIFO : Closing Stock 2,000 units—Rs. 7,000
LIFO : Closing Stock 2,000 units—Rs. 4,000

66. Show the year end value of inventory under (a) FIFO and (b) LIFO methods from the following data :

Opening balance—12,000 units @ Rs. 2.00 per unit.

Received (Units)	Issued (Units)
1st quarter 20,000 @ Rs. 2.20	16,000
2nd quarter 30,000 @ Rs. 2:40	26.000
3rd quarter 25,000 @ Rs. 2.30	32,000
4th quarter 10,000 @ Rs. 2.25	8,000

Assume that purchases were made on the first day of the quarter.

[Adapted—B.Com. Andhra]

Ans. :	(a) FIFO—	5,000 × Rs. 2.30	= Rs. 11,500
		10,000 × Rs. 2.25	= Rs. 22,500
			Rs. 34,000
	(b) LIFO—	12,000 × 2.00	= 24,000
		1,000 × 2.20	= 2,200
		2,000 × 2.25	= 4,500
			30,700

67. From the following particulars prepre Store Ledger Account showing the pricing of materials issued by adopting LIFO method for the month of December 1995 :

Dec. 1 Opening Stock 500 units @ Rs. 2 per unit.
3 Purchased 400 units @ Rs. 2.10 per unit
5 Issued 600 units to Job K
7 Purchased 800 units @ Rs. 2.40 per unit
9 Issued 500 units to Job P
12 Returned from Job K 200 units
17 Purchased 400 units @ Rs. 2.50 per unit
25 Issued 600 units to Job Y.

[Adapted—Karnataka, B.Com.]

Ans. : Stock balance—600 units—Rs. 1,320.

Hints : Materials returned from Job K will be issued on 25th on LIFO basis since they were issued on 5th December 1990.

68. At the beginning of October, 1990; the Bombay Tin Company had 10,000 lbs of tin at Rs. 2.00 per lb. Further purchases were made during the month as follows :

4th October	2,000 lbs @ Rs. 2.50 per lb.
10th "	5,000 lbs @ Rs. 3.00 per lb.
20th "	10,000 lbs @ Rs. 3.50 per lb.

The issues to manufacture were as follows :

12th October 16,000 lbs.
28th October 10,000 lbs.

What wuld be the value of Closing Stock at the end of the month if the materials were issued according to :

(a) First-in-First-out.
(b) Last-in-First-out method
(c) Weighted Average method?

[Adapted—ICWA]

Ans. : (a) FIFO— 1,000 lbs × 3.5 = Rs. 3,500
(b) LIFO— 1,000 × 2.00 = Rs. 2,000
(c) Weighted Average Method – 1,000 × Rs. 3.395 = Rs. 3,396 (approx.)

69. A manufacturing concern purchases from time to time large quantities of a commodity used in the manufacture of its products. The following are the details of purchase during the six months ended 31st December 1995 :

1995	Quantity	Cost price 100 units
August 2	10,000	Rs. 10.00
September 15	25,000	Rs. 10.50
October 20	20,000	Rs. 9.50
November 5	15,000	Rs. 9.00
December 1	12,000	Rs. 9.00
December 20	3,000	Rs. 8.50

There were 15,000 units in stock on July 1, 1995, which were valued at Rs. 9.50 per 100 units.

Quantities issued from Stores during the six months were :

1995	Quantity	1995	Quantity
July 25	10,000	October 30	20,000
Aug. 28	8,000	November 15	18,000
Sept. 29	25,000	December 29	5,000

Prepare a Store Ledger Account under LIFO and FIFO methods of pricing issues of materials.

[B.U. B.Com. (Hons.) 1983]

Ans. : Value of stock FIFO – Rs. 1,245, LIFO – Rs. 1,280.

70. The stock of materials of a company on 1.1.1998 was 10,000 units at Rs. 2 per unit. Further purchases were made during the month as follows :

4th Jan., 98	2,000	units @ Rs. 2.50 per unit
10th Jan., 98	5,000	units @ Rs. 3.00 " "
20th Jan., 98	10,000	units @ Rs. 3.50 " "

The issues during the period were as follows :

12th Jan., 1998	16,000	units
28th Jan., 1998	9,000	units

What would be the vlaue of the closing stock at the end of the month on the basis of materials being treated to have been issued according to :

(i) First-in-first-out method

(ii) Last-in-first-out method

(iii) Weighted average method.

[Adapted—C.U. B.Com. (Hons.)]

Ans. : (i) 2,000 units @ Rs. 3.50 per unit = Rs. 7,000

(ii) Rs. 5,500 (1,000 × Rs. 2) + (1,000 × Rs. 3.50)

(iii) 2,000 @ Rs. 3.396 = Rs. 6,788.

71. From the following particulars, prepare Store Ledger Account showing the pricing of materials issues, following FIFO Method :

1996

Feb. 1	Opening stock	500 units at Rs. 2.00 each
3	Purchased	400 units at Rs. 2.10 each
5	Issued	600 units to a job K (Vide MR No. 15)
7	Purchased	800 units at Rs. 2.30 each

9 Issued	600 units to Job P (Vide MR No. 22)
12 Returned from Job K	150 units
17 Purchased	350 units at Rs. 2.50 each
19 Returned from Job P	100 units
25 Issued	700 units to Job K (Vide MR No. 16)

[V.U. B.Com. (Hons.) 1996]

Ans. : Value of Stock Rs. 990

Note : It is assumed that materials issued to Production Department have been used on FIFO basis. So, materials returned by Job K have been valued as 150 @ Rs. 2.10 and at the time of issue materials returned by Production department have been issued first before issuing new arrivals.

72. The following information is extracted from the Store Ledger :

Material X

Opening Stock	Nil
Purchases :	
Jan. 1	100 units @ Re. 1.00 per unit
Jan. 20	100 units @ Rs. 2.00 " "
Issues :	
Jan. 22	60 units for Job W 16
Jan. 23	60 units for Job W 17

Complete the receipts and issues valuation by adopting the First-in-First-out, Last-in-First-out and Weighted Average Method. Tabulate the values allocated to Job W–16, W–17 and the closing stock under the aforesaid methods .

[Adapted—C.A. (Inter) 1985]

Ans. :

	FIFO	LIFO	Weighted Average
Material for Job W–16	**Rs. 60**	**Rs. 120**	**Rs. 90**
Material for Job W–17	**Rs. 80**	**Rs. 100**	**Rs. 90**
Closing stock	**Rs. 160**	**Rs. 80**	**Rs. 120**

73. The following transactions took place in respect of an item of material :

Date	*Receipts (quantity)*	*Rate Rs.*	*Issues (quantity)*
2.3.91	200	2.00	—
10.3.91	300	2.40	—
15.3.91	—	—	250
18.3.91	250	2.60	—
20.3.91	—	—	200

Prepare a priced ledger sheet pricing the issues at (i) simple average rate and (ii) weighted average rate.

[Adapted—ICWA (Inter)]

Ans. : Value of stock : (i) Rs. 720, (ii) Rs. 726

74. At the beginning of October 1992; Quantity Brush Company had in stock 10,000 brushes valued at Rs. 10 each. Further purchases were made during the month as follows :

7th October	4,000	brushes @ Rs. 12.50
14th October	6,000	brushes @ Rs. 15.00 each
24th October	8,000	brushes @ Rs. 16.50 each

Issues to shop floor were as follows :

16th October	16,000	brushes
28th October	10,000	brushes

(a) You are required : to prepare Stores Ledger card for the month of October on the assumption that materials were issued on the Frist-in-First-out principle and (b) to state the value of the closing stock at the end of October if issues are priced by the Weighted Average Method.

[C.A.—Inter]

Ans. : Value of closing stock : (a) Rs. 33,000; (b) Rs. 30,000.

75. Prepare Stores Ledger Account for the following transactions : Issues are to be priced on the basis of "Last-in-First-out" :

Opening balance	12,000 kgs @ Rs. 75 per M. Ton
Purchased	22,000 kgs @ Rs. 76 per M. Ton
Issued	5,000 kgs.
Issued	7,000 kgs.
Surplus returned from production department	2,000 kgs.
Issued	12,000 kgs.
Purchased 25,000 kgs. @ Rs. 74 per M. Ton	
Issued	7,000 kgs.
Issued	6,000 kgs.

Stock was verified and 500 kgs were found to be excess and adjusted accordingly.

[ICWA—Inter]

Ans. : Closing Stock 12 M. Tonnes @ Rs. 75 per M. Ton and 12.5 M. Tonnes @ Rs. 74 per M. Ton.

Hints. 1. One M. Ton = 1,000 kgs.

2. Excess of $\frac{1}{2}$ ton has been valued at Rs. 74 per M. Ton.

76. Adarsh Company purchased and issued the materials in the following order :

1998		Units	Unit Cost (Rs.)
Jan. 1	Purchases	300	3
4	Purchases	600	4
6	Issues	500	—
10	Purchases	700	4
15	Issues	800	—
20	Purchases	300	5
31	Issues	100	—

Ascertain the quantity of closing stock as on 31.1.98 and state its value under each of the following methods of pricing the issues. (a) Weighted Average (b) FIFO, (c) LIFO

Ans. : (a) Rs. 1,717, (b) Rs. 2,300, (c) Rs. 1,900

77. Discuss the effects of adopting LIFO and FIFO on profits, with the help of the following figures :

January 1 Opening balance 10 units @ Rs. 30
January 10 Purchases 10 units @ Rs. 33 units
January 12 Issued 10 units
January 31 Closing balance 10 units
January 12 Purchases 10 units @ Rs. 36 per unit

January 12 Issued 10 units
February Purchases 10 units @ Rs. 40 per unit
Sales during these two months amounted to Rs. 1,000.

[ICWA Inter]

Ans. : Materials Issues FIFO Rs. 630 Profit FIFO Rs. 370
" " LIFO Rs. 690 Profit LIFO Rs. 310

78. The following are the particulars of the receipt and issues of materials in a factory during January 1983 :

Jan. 2 Opening balance	1,000	kgs. @ Rs. 30 per kg.
Jan. 2 Issued	140	kgs.
Jan. 4 Issued	200	kgs.
Jan. 8 Issued	160	kgs.
Jan. 13 Received	400	kgs. @ Rs. 35 per kg.
Jan. 15 Return of surplus from a work	30	kgs. @ Rs. 28
Jan. 16 Issued	360	kgs.
Jan. 18 Received from vendor	600	kgs. @ Rs. 32
Jan. 20 Issued	550	kgs.
Jan. 22 Received	400	kgs. @ Rs. 34
Jan. 24 Issued off	250	kgs.
Jan. 29 Return of surplus from a work order	40	kgs. @ Rs. 32.00
Jan. 30 Received from vendor	200	kgs. @ Rs. 36 per kg.

Prepare a Store Ledger under LIFO and FIFO methods.

[C.U. B.Com. (Hons.)]

Ans. : Value of stock : LIFO Method – Rs. 32,630, FIFO Method – Rs. 33,920.

79. The particulars of receipts and issues of materials in a factory in August, 97 are as under :

August 1	Opening balance	1,500	kgs. @ Rs. 12.00 per kg.
2	Issued	100	kgs.
3	Issued	250	kgs.
4	Issued	300	kgs.
5	Received (Purchased)	400	kgs. @ Rs. 12.50 per kg.
9	Issued	300	kgs.
10	Received	200	kgs. @ Rs. 12.50 per kg.
11	Issued	300	kgs.
12	Returned from workshop issued on 3rd August	20	kgs.
13	Issued	450	kgs.
16	Purchased	500	kgs. @ Rs. 13.00 per kg.
18	Issued	400	kgs.
20	Returned from workshop issued on 9th August	60	kgs.
22	Issued	300	kgs.
25	Purchased	400	kgs. @ Rs. 12.00 per kg.
29	Issued	200	kgs.

Pricing of issues to be done on FIFO basis. A shortage of 10 kgs. was noticed on 16th August. Prepare the Stores Ledger Account for the month of August 1997 in respect of materials.

[B. Com. (Hons.) C.U.]

Ans. : Rs. 5,710.

80. Following information about material is available in respect of a manufaturing company :

(i)	March 1	1987	Purchased 3,000 kgs. @ Rs. 15 per kg.
(ii)	2	1987	Purchased 5,000 kgs. @ Rs. 16 per kg.
(iii)	3	1987	Issued 5,000 kgs.
(iv)	4	1987	Purchased 2,000 kg.s @ Rs. 18 per kg.

Determine the value of stock on 4.3.1987 (at closing hour) under :

(i) FIFO Method :
(ii) LIFO Method :
(iii) Simple average method and
(iv) Weighted average method.

[B.U. B.Com. (Hons.) 1887]

Ans. : FIFO Rs. 84,000, LIFO Rs. 81,000
Average Rs. 83,500; Weighted Average Rs. 82,850.

81. A manufacturing concern purchases from time to time large quantities of a commodity used in the manufacture of its products. The following are the details of purchases during the six months ended 31st December 1996 :

1996	Quantity	Cost per 100 units
August 2	10,000	Rs. 10.00
September 15	25,000	Rs. 10.50
October	20,000	Rs. 9.50
November 5	15,000	9.00
December 1	12,000	9.00
December 20	3,000	8.50

There were 15,000 units in stock on July 1st, 1996, which were valued at Rs. 9.50 per 100 units.

Quantities issued from Stores during the six months were :

1996	Quantity	1996	Quantity
July 25	10,000	October 30	20,000
August 28	8,000	November 15	18,000
September 29	25,000	December 29	5,000

Prepare a Store Ledger Account under LIFO and FIFO Methods of pricing issues of materials.

Ans. : LIFO = 4,000 @ 9.50 per hundred = Rs. 380
10,000 @ 9.00 per hundred = Rs. 900
Rs. 1,280

FIFO 11,000 @ Rs. 9.00 per 100 = 990
3,000 @ Rs. per 100 = 255
Rs. 1,245

82. The following is the history of the receipts and issues of materials in a factory during February 1989 :

February 1	Opening balance	500	quantals	@ Rs. 25.00
3	Issue	70	"	
4	Issue	100	"	
8	Issue	80	"	
13	Received from the suppliers	200	"	@ Rs. 24.50

14	Returned of surplus from a work order	15	"	@ Rs. 24.00
16	Issue	180	"	
20	Received from the suppliers	240	"	@ Rs. 24.375
24	Issue	304	"	
25	Received from the suppliers	320	"	@ Rs. 24.375
26	Issue	112	"	
27	Refund of surplus from a work order	12	"	@ Rs. 24.50
28	Received from the suppliers	100	"	@ Rs. 25.00

Issues are to be priced on the principle of " First-in-First-out" method. The sotck verifier of the factory noticed that on 15th he had found a shortage of 5 quintals and on 27th another shortage of 8 quintals.

Write out the Store Ledger Account, recording the above transactions.

[Andhra B.Com.]

Ans. : Rs. 12,934

83. The Fair Deal Grannery was not maintaining a perpetual inventory system for its stocks until recently. Only physical inventory was taken at the end of each month. The physical inventory at the end of December 1984 showed 200 bags of fine rice at Rs. 212.25 per bag. The following purchases were made in January 1985 :

3rd	400 bags at Rs. 218 per bag.
10th	900 bags at Rs. 223.50 per bag.
15th	400 bags at Rs. 220.00 per bag.
28th	700 bags at Rs. 213.00 per bag.
30th	300 bags at Rs. 224.00 per bag.

On 31st January 1985 the physical stock was 1,200 bags. You are required to calculate the value of the stock on 31st January 1985 according in First-in-First-out, Last-in-First-out Method.

[ICWA Inter]

Ans. : LIFO 1,200 – Rs. 263,750.

FIFO 1,200 – Rs. 2,60,300.

Hints :	FIFO	200 × 220	LIFO	200 × 212.25
		700 × 213		400 × 218
		300 × 224		600 × 223.50

84. A Ltd. furnishes the following store transactions for September 1, 1987 :

1.9.87	Opening balance	25 units value Rs. 162.50
4.9.87	Issues Req. No. 85	8 units
6.9.87	Receipts from B & Co. GRN No. 26	50 units @ Rs. 5.75 per unit
7.9.87	Issues Req. No. 97	12 units
10.9.87	Returns to B & Co.	10 units
12.9.87	Issues Req. No. 108	15 units
13.9.87	Issues Req. No. 110	20 units
15.9.87	Receipts from M. & Co. GRN No. 33	25 units @ Rs. 6.10
17.9.87	Issues Req. No. 121	10 units
19.9.87	Received replacement from B & Co. GRN No. 38	10 units
20.9.87	Returned from department, materials issued on 17th of B & Co. MRN No. 4	5 units

22.9.87	Transfer from Job 182 to Job 187 in the department MTN 6	5 units
26.9.87	Issues Req. No. 146	10 units
29.9.87	Transfer from Department A to Dept. B MTN No.	5 units
30.9.87	Shortage in stock taking	2 units

Write-up the priced stores ledger on the FIFO method and discuss how you would treat the shortage in stock taking.

[C.A. Inter, No

Ans. Value of closing stock Rs. 169.75

Hints : No record for transfer from one job to another.

85. Chandramouli & Company follows Simple Average cost method for the valuation of its issue of materials to jobs. The following are the transactions held in January. Prepare the store ledger in its specifical form :

Jan.	1	Purchased 1,000 lbs @ Rs. 4.50 per lb.
	5	Purchased 2,000 lbs @ Rs. 4.00 per lb.
	8	Issued 800 lbs
	15	Issued 1,200 lbs
	19	Purchased 1,500 Ibs @ Rs. 4.20 per Ib.
	22	Issued 1,000 Ibs.
	24	Purchased 800 Ibs at Rs. 4.50 per Ib
	27	Purchased 800 Ibs at Rs. 4.50 per Ib.
	28	Issued 800 Ibs
	30	Issued 400 Ibs
	31	Purchased 500 Ibs at Rs. 4.60 per Ib.

Ans. : Closing stock 2,400 Ibs valued at Rs. 10,420.

Hints : Issue price on 8th Jan. Rs. 4.25

Issue Price on 22nd Jan. Rs. 4.10

Issue Price on 28th Jan. Rs. 4.40 $\left(\frac{\text{Rs. } 4.20 + \text{Rs. } 4.50 + \text{Rs. } 4.50}{3}\right)$

86. The following is an extract of the record of receipts and issues of sulphur in a chemical factory during Feb. 1990 :

Feb.	1	Balance 500 tonnes @ Rs. 200
	3	Issue 70 tonnes
	4	Issue 100 tonnes
	8	Issue 80 tonnes
	13	Received from supplier 200 tonnes @ Rs. 210
	14	Returned from Department 15 tonnes (Issued on 8.2.1990)
	16	Issue 180 tonnes
	20	Received from supplier 240 tonnes @ Rs. 220
	24	Issue 300 tonnes
	25	Received from supplier 320 tonnes @ Rs. 225
	26	Issue 115 tonnes
	27	Returned from Department 35 tonnes (issued on 26.2.1990)
	28	Received from supplier 100 tonnes @ Rs. 230

Issues are to be priced on the principle of 'First-in-First-out'. The stock verifier of the factory had found a shortage of 10 tonnes on 22nd Feb. Draw up Store Ledger for the material, showing the above transactions.

Ans. : Value of stock Rs. 1,24,700.

87. The following transactions occurred in purchases and issues of material in an organisation during January 1993 :

Date	Receipts Qty.	Rste Rs.
4.1.1993	200 units	24.00 p.u.
10.1.1993	150 units	23.00 p.u.
18.1.1993	100 units	24.00 p.u.
22.1.1993	100 units	23.50 p.u.
Issues :		
5.1.1993	250 units	
12.1.1993	200 units	
24.1.1993	250 units	

The Stock on 1.1.1993 was 200 units @ Rs. 25.00 per unit. Prepare the Store Ledger Account under FIFO and LIFO methods.

[B.Com. (Pass) Delhi]

Ans. : FIFO 50 units @ Rs. 23.50 p.u. = Rs. 1,175
LIFO 50 units @ Rs. 25.00 p.u. = Rs. 1,250

88. The following are the receipts and isues of stores material Y in a manufacturing concern :

1992	
July 1	Opening stock 100 units at Rs. 10.00 p.u.
2	Issued 25 units to Department A
7	Reeived 425 units at Rs. 11.00 per unit
10	Issued 200 units to Department B
12	Returned to stores 10 units from Department A
15	Returned to vendor 20 units out of the quantity received on 7th
17	Received 110 units at Rs. 12.50 per unit
25	Received 100 units at Rs. 10.00 per unit
29	Issued 200 units to Dept. B
30	Received 100 units at Rs. 11.00 per unit

Enter the above transactions in the Store Ledger Account of material Y using the average (weighted) method. (Average Cost to be calculated correct to two decimal places of a rupee.)

[Adapted—ICWA (Inter)]

Ans. : Value of Store on 31.7.1992 – 400 units = Rs. 4,406.00.

Hints : (i) Return to vendor to be valued @ Rs. 11.00 per unit

(ii) Issues are valued as Rs. 10.00, Rs. 10.85, Rs. 11.00 and Rs. 11.02, respectively.

89. From the records of an oil distributing company, the following summarised information is available for the month of March 1986 :

Sale for the month – Rs. 19,25,000

Opening Stock as on 1.3.1986 – 1,25,000 litres @ Rs. 6.50 per litre.

Purchases (including freight and insurance) :

March 5 1,50,000 litres @ 7.10 per litre

27 1,00,000 litres @ Rs. 7.00 per litre

Closing stock as on 31.3.1986—1,30,000 litres

General Administrative Expenses for the month Rs. 45,000.

On the basis of the above information work out the following using FIFO and LIFO methods of inventory valuation, assuming pricing of issues is done at the end of the month after all receipts during the month :

(i) Value of closing stock as on 31.3.1986
(ii) Cost of goods sold during March 1986
(iii) Profit or loss for March 1986.

[Adapted—ICWA (Inter) June 1987]

Ans. :

	LIFO	**FIFO**
	Rs.	**Rs.**
Value of closing stock	**8,48,000**	**9,13,000**
Cost of goods sold	**17,29,500**	**16,64,500**
Profit	**1,50,500**	**2,15,500**

90. The stock-ledger account for material X in a manufacturing concern reveals the following data for the quarter ended September 30, 1989 :

Date	*??*	*Receipts*		*Issues*	
		Qnt. Units	*Price*	*Qnt.*	*Price Amount*
		Rs.			Rs.
July 1	Balance b/d	1,600	2.00	—	—
9		3,000	2.20	—	—
13				1,200	2,556
Aug. 5				900	1,917
17		3,600	2.40	—	—
24		—	—	1,800	4,122
Sept. 11		2,500	2.50	—	—
27		—	—	2,100	4,971
29				700	1,656

Physical verification on September 30, 1989 revealed an actual stock of 3,800 units.

You are required to :

(a) Indicate the method of pricing employed in the above.

(b) Complete the above account by making entries you would consider necessary including adjustments, if any, and giving explanation for such adjustments.

[Adapted—ICWA (Inter) June 1990]

Ans. : **(a) Weighted Average Method**

(b) Closing Stock 3,800 units @ Rs. 2.37 = Rs. 8,995.

Hints : The last issue was 200 units.

SECTION ONE

COST OF LABOUR

Learning Objectives

1. ***Introduction***
2. ***Controlling labour cost***
3. ***Time-booking and Time keeping,*** *Difference between Time-booking and Time-keeping.*
4. ***Specimen of Pay Roll***
5. ***Pay Roll Department****—Payment of Wages, Preparation of Pay Roll*
6. ***The Cost Accounting Department***
7. ***Direct and Indirect Labour****—Definition and Distinction*
8. ***Job Evaluation and Merit Rating****—Definition, Objects, Difference between Job Evaluation and Merit Rating.*
9. ***Treatment of Some Items****—Overtime, Holiday and Vacation Pay, Leave with Pay, Attendance Bonus, Apprentices' Wages, Shift Premium, Fringe Benefits, Idle Time, Treatment of Idle Time, Casual Workers, Out Workers.*
10. ***Labour Turnover****—Definition, Causes of Labour turnover, Effects, Measurement, Cost of Labour turnover, Treatment in Cost Accounts. Labour Turnover Report.*
11. ***Payment of Wages****—Preparation of Pay Rolls, Source documents for the preparation of Pay Rolls, Disbursement of Wages, Prevention of Fraud, Daily Time Sheet, Job Card, Pay Roll Accounting, Chart for Wage Procedures.*
12. ***Workedout Problems***

SECTION TWO

METHODS OF WAGE PAYMENT

Learning Objectives

1. ***Introduction***
2. ***Requisites of a good wage payment plan***
3. ***Methods of Remunerating Labour***
   (i) Time Rate Plan—Advantages and Disadvantages–Illustration. (ii) Piece Rate—Advantages and Disadvantages. Difference between Time and Piece Rate.
4. ***Incentive Wage Plan****—Principles, Features.*
5. ***Incentive Scheme****—Differential Piece Rate. (i) Taylor's Differential Piece Work System–Illustration. (ii) Merrick's Differential Piece Rate—Illustration.*
6. ***Premium Bonus Scheme****—(i) Definition, fundamentals of premium bonus plan. (ii) Halsey Plan–Illustration, Advantages and Disadvantages. (iii) Rowan Plan—Illustration, Advantages and Disadvantages. (iv) Difference between Halsey and Rowan plans Bedaux Point Plan—Illustration. (v) Emerson Efficiency Plan.*
7. ***Group Incentive Plans****—Advantages and Disadvantages–Illustration*
8. ***Bonus Scheme for Indirect Workers****—Illustrations*
9. ***Group Incentive Plans****—Advantages and Disadvantages–Illustration*
10. ***Bonus Scheme for Indirect Workers****—Illustrations*
11. ***Workedout Problems***
12. ***Assignment***

LABOUR 4

SECTION ONE

COST OF LABOUR

4.1 Introduction

One of the basic elements of cost is labour cost. Labour cost consists of the total amount of wages paid to the workers and other expenses relating thereto. Labour being the major factor of production it assumes the most important element of cost. In a labour intensive industry like Jute and Cotton, labour cost forms a major part of the total cost. So, the cost of a product is greatly influenced by labour cost. Efficient labour force contributes to a great extent to increased productivity and production. On the other hand, inefficient labour force contributes to increased cost. The total cost may increase or may be excessive due to inefficiency of labour force; high idle time, overtime payments, increase in spoilage, waste and defective goods do take place due to lack of efficient and effective supervision and inspection. The above reasons call for effective control of labour cost.

Labour costs involve various items of expenses incurred on workers. Labour costs include :

1. Monetary Benefits

Monetary benefits are regular in nature. They include :

(i) Basic wages; (ii) Dearness Allowance; (iii) House Rent Allowances (iv) Employer's contribution to provident fund; (v) Employer's contribution to Employee's State Insurance Scheme; (vi) Production Bonus; (vii) Profit Bonus; (viii) Leave Salary; (ix) Old age pension (x) Gratuity etc.

2. Fringe Benefits

Fringe Benefits include : (i) Subsidised food; (ii) Subsidised Housing; (iii) Subsidised education to the children; (iv) Medical facilities; (v) Holiday Pay, (vi) Recreational facilities etc.

4.2 Controlling labour cost

Effective labour cost control depends upon the cooperation and efficient functioning of some departments like :

i) Personnel Department
ii) Engineering Department
iii) Time-keeping Department
iv) Payroll Department
v) Cost Accounting Department

Let us see how the above departments function in controlling labour cost.

4.3 Personnel Department

Most firms of any size have a Personnel Department which has responsibility for numerous tasks involving labour. The tasks include :

(i) Advertising, recruiting and engaging labour.

(ii) Discharge, transfer and administration of and appraisal of schemes.

(iii) Industrial relations and negotiations with unions to settle industrial disputes.

(iv) Staff development, training and educational schemes including day release, apprenticeships and courses.

(v) Execute the policies regarding appointment, promotion, wage and incentive systems etc.

(vi) Communication of information to the management on such matters as absenteeism, lateness, labour turnover, normal and overtime worked.

(vii) Welfare, sports and social facilities, safety and medical facilities.

(viii) Manpower planning and forecasting.

In brief, the personnel department has the responsibility to provide an efficient labour-force which is cost effective and to keep labour turnover to a minimum.

4.4 Engineering Department

This department helps to maintain control over working conditions, production methods, job performance. It is also responsible for maintaining safety and efficient working conditions. It has to initiate and supervise research and development (R & D) and to make method study, motion study and time study. Making job evaluation, merit rating and job analysis are the important functions of the Engineering Department. This department should aim at improving labour efficiency or productivity, thereby cutting down the effective labour cost. The Engineering Department maintains control over working conditions and production methods for each job or process by performing the above functions.

4.5 Time-Keeping Department

The function of this department is to maintain the exact time for which each worker has worked. Proper time-keeping in labour costing and control is very important because of the following reasons :

(a) It accumulates the total number of hours worked by each worker so that his total periodical earnings can be computed.

(b) Absence of proper time-keeping arrangement is sure to create frustration among sincere and punctual employees. This situation will adversely affect the morale of employees resulting in low productivity and production and increased costs.

(c) Certain retirement benefits like pension, gratuity, leave with pay, provident fund and salary are linked with continuity of service of employees. Attendance records can be immensely helpful and useful in the determination of various retirement benefits and other fringe benefits.

(d) Time-keeping is of paramount importance in the task of apportionment of overhead costs on the basis of labour hours.

(e) Time-keeping records are also useful for analysis purposes.

4.6 Time Recording for Piece Worker

Time recording for workers who are paid on piece rate basis is essential for the following reasons :

(i) Time recording is necessary to ensure discipline in the factory.

(ii) When the workers are guaranteed minimum wages, time recording becomes necessary to ascertain the time spent by the workers irrespective of their individual output.

(iii) Time recording is important because it facilitates the preparation of pay roll as a whole and calculation of dearness allowance.

(iv) In fixing up differential wage rates, time recording becomes essential.

(v) Time recording also facilitates the apportionment of overheads on the basis of labour hours.

4.7 Objects of Time-keeping

The main objectives of time keeping function are :

(i) to maintain workers' activity records to meet statutory requirements;

(ii) to maintain basic data required for the preparation of payroll;

(iii) to generate statistical data to ascertain productivity of labour and to control labour cost;

(iv) to find out the labour cost and to control labour cost;

(iv) to find out the labour cost of a job or product or service;

(v) to maintain discipline in attendance; provide;

(vi) to nationalise basis of overhead distribution in various situations;

(vii) to calculate overhead cost of a job.

4.8 Time-booking

Time booking signifies the time spent by a worker on each job, process or operation. It is more important in case of direct workers as compared to indirect workers. Time booking aims at fulfilling the following purposes :

4.9 The objectives of Time-booking :

The objectives of time-booking are :

(i) to calculate the labour cost of jobs done;

(ii) to apportion overheads against jobs;

(iii) to evaluate performance of labour and to make comparison of actual labour time with budgeted time;

(iv) to ascertain idle time for the purpose of control;

(v) to determine overhead rates for absorbing overhead expenses under labour hour and machine hour methods;

(vi) to calculate bonus and wages provided the system of payment of wages depends on the time taken.

4.10 Methods of time-booking

There are two main methods of booking time—manual and mechanical.

The manual method can be classified as :

(i) Daily time Sheets, (ii) Weekly time Sheets; (iii) Job tickets and (iv) Job cards.

(i) **Daily time sheets**

It gives in detail the activities of the worker and the time spent in each job. One sheet is alloted to each worker and a daily record is made therein.

It is suitable for small organisation where the number of employee and job is small.

DAILY TIME SHEET

Worker's Name .... Date..........................

Worker's No. Department ....

Work order No.			*Time*		*Total Hours*		*Cost*	
Direct	*Indirect*	*Particulars*	*From*	*To*	*Ordinary*	*Overtime*	*Ordinary* **Rs.**	*Overtime* **Rs.**

....

Worker Foreman Costing Dept.

(ii) **Weekly Time Sheets**

Each worker is given a time sheet wherein jobs done in a week are recorded. It is quite similar to Daily Time Sheet. It reflects a consolidation of the total hours worked during a particular week. This method is useful where there are few jobs in a work.

4.11 Job Cards or Job Tickets

A separate job card for each job or operation is prepared. This card is alloted to each worker whenever a worker takes up a particular job. In this card the worker enters the time of commencement of a job as well as time of finishing the job.

The entries in the job card may be made with the help of machines like time-recording clock.

JOB CARD/JOB TICKET

Worker's Name .... Job No ....

Worker's No .... Date ....

Department .... Hourly rate of pay ....

Job Description	*Work*		
	Product	*Accepted*	*Rejected*

Time–From .... to ....

Total hours taken ....

Total cost ....

Signature

4.12 DISTINCTION BETWEEN TIME-KEEPING AND TIME-BOOKING

The following are the points of difference between Time-keeping and Time-booking :

Time-keeping	*Time-booking*
(i) Time-keeping is the process of recording each worker's attendance, that is his coming in and going out of the factory	It is the process of recording the time spent by a worker on different jobs carried out by him during his period of stay in the factory.
(ii) The time-keeper does the job of time-keeping	Workers themselves mark the time in the designated document counter signed by the supervisor.
(iii) Proper Time-keeping is required for payment of wages including overtime wages	Time-booking is used for computing direct labour cost for different jobs on which time is spent.
(iv) It includes time booked as well as time lost or idle time	It excludes time lost and idle time. It is related only to time spent on jobs.
(v) It aims at maintaining discipline in attendance.	It finds out the time during which a worker stays in the factory and it is properly utilised.

4.13 Payroll Department

The tasks of preparing pay rolls are complicated as some specified amounts like income tax, professional tax, cooperative loan, contribution to P.F., employees' contribution to E.S.I. etc. are withheld from the earnings of employees. There are three major problems that involve the preparation of payrolls : (a) allocating labour costs to products, departments ; (b) accurate computation of earnings and prompt payment to individual employees ; and (c)computing and remitting withholdings to proper authorities like government, local authority etc. From the view-point of employees, promptness of payments and pinpoint accuracy are the foremost criteria for judging the merits of any payroll system.

The functions of a payroll department is an intermediary function between the time-keeping and the cost accounting departments. The main functions of pay roll department are :

(i) to compute employees' wages accurately ;

(ii) to make prompt payment to employees ;

(iii) to compute the deductions to be made from employee's earnings under different heads and to remit them to the appropriate authority in time, for example, income tax, professional tax, E.S.I. etc. ;

(iv) to compile labour statistics for management to formulate labour policy ;

(v) to maintain a permanent pay roll record for each employee ;

(vi) to maintain a record of job classification, department and wage rate for each employee;

(vii) to verify and summarise the time of each worker as shown on the daily time cards.

4.14 Payment of Wages

Due care should be taken for payment of wages to employees to ensure proper payment i.e. right amount to the right persons. In order to maintain a control to safeguard the payroll against the inclusion of ghost workers or the names of those employees who have already left their jobs, the paymaster should require the identity of each employee at the time of payment of wages by one of the following :

(i) Personal identification by foreman or authority of the department ;

(ii) Identification card or badge ;

(iii) Signed receipt for comparison with a personal signature on file in the personnel department.

4.15 Preparation of Pay Roll

The preparation of pay roll is the responsibility of the pay roll accounting department. Wages for each worker is calculated in wage sheet or pay roll.

The following documents are used to prepare the pay roll of the workers :

(i) Time cards

(ii) Piece-work cards, and

(iii) Job cards.

Care should be taken at the time of preparing pay roll to avoid errors and frauds. It is to be seen that no wage bill has been drawn in the names of dummy workers.

4.16 Cost Accounting Department

This department is responsible for the accumulation and classification of all the cost data of which labour cost is one of the most important elements. There must be a proper coordination and close relationship between cost department and time keeping and pay roll departments. In the determination of labour cost time keeping and pay roll departments feed the costing department with necessary data in respect of time taken (labour hours) by each worker and his remuneration. Time-keeping is the first function in the labour accounting process. The pay roll department computes the earnings of each employee after making necessary deductions. The cost accounting department is responsible for the accumulation and classification of all cost information of which labour is one element.

DIRECT AND INDIRECT LABOUR

4.17 Direct Labour

The Institute of Cost and Management Accountants (U.K.) defines direct labour cost as "the cost which can be identified with, and allocated to, cost centre or cost units". In the words of Horngren—"All labour that is physically traceable to the finished goods in an economically feasible manner".

So, direct labour costs are identifiable with individual units of product or job orders as far as practicable.

Examples :

Wages paid to machine operators and assemblers are treated as direct labour costs.

4.18 Indirect Labour

According to the Institute of Cost and Management Accountants (U.K.) indirect labour costs mean "wage costs other than direct wage costs".

According to Horngren indirect labour refers to that activity of employees which is not possible and economically feasible to trace to any specific products via physical observation. Otherwise, the indirect labour cost is the cost which cannot be allocated to any specific job but can be apportioned or absorbed by cost centres or cost units.

Examples :

Factory Supervisors' salary, Storekeepers' salaries, Foremen's salaries etc. are examples of indirect labour costs.

4.19 Distinction Between Direct and Indirect labour cost

The distinction between direct labour cost and indirect labour cost is very important for the following reasons : :

(i) to provide a more accurate product cost ;

(ii) to provide a strict control over labour costs because direct labour efficiency can be measured by the number of units completed by direct labour ;

(iii) if this distinction is not made, proper allocation of overheads will be erroneous.

Direct labour cost is the cost for employees' efforts and skills used directly for a product or saleable service. The nature of the work of an employee is to be considered for making a distinction between direct labour and indirect labour. A machineman's work is treated as direct labour but while he spends time to repair a machine or to clean it up, his labour for doing so is to be treated as indirect labour because it is not directly connected with production process.

From this view-point, labour activities can be classified into the following categories to draw a line of distinction between direct and indirect labour :

(i) *Contribution Activities* : They refer to those activities which are directly connected with the production of goods or services which generate the firm's income. The costs of these activities are treated as direct labour cost.

(ii) *Service Activities* : These activities are those which support contribution activities but do not generate income. All such labour is treated as ***indirect labour.***

(iii) *Control Activities* : These are the activities which are necessary to control the employees. They relate to the control or supervision or managerial aspect of the whole show. These activities do not create income for the firm but help to generate income in a better way. All such labour is treated as indirect labour.

4.20 Need for distinguishing between direct and indirect labour

The distinction between direct and indirect labour is essential from costing point of view for the following reaons :

(a) The distinction between direct and indirec labour is important for calculating labour cost accurately which provides a basis for labour control;

(b) It facilitates the measurement of labour efficiency;

(c) Such distinction helps allocation of overheads.

(d) Introduction of incentive schemes for payment of wages becomes feasible and easy.

(e) It also helps to estimate total labour cost.

4.21 Job Evaluation and Merit-Rating

It is really a very difficult job in any wage system to decide on a fair rate to pay the employees. Generally, wage rate may be set at national level, particularly in an organised unit by collective bargaining or by the government in some cases. But the value of paying above agreed rates to efficient workers is recognised and this requires job evaluation of workers.

4.22 Definition

Job evaluation is the technique of analysis and assessment of jobs to determine their relative value within the firm so that a fair wage and salary structure can be established for various jobs. It is the process of close scrutiny and assessment of the relative value of jobs in an organisation to ascertain their relative labour worth. Job evaluation is the first step towards formulation of a proper wage structure.

4.23 Objects

Following are the objectives of Job Evaluation :

(i) It aims at developing a systematic and rational wage structure.

(ii) It aims at establishing consistency between the wage and salary structure adopted within the firm and that of the other firms.

(iii) Proper job evaluation helps to settle disputes relating to salaries between the employers and employees and thus helps promoting industrial peace and harmony.

(iv) It discloses characteristics and conditions relating to different jobs which are very helpful at the time of recruitment.

(v) Wage and salary structure established on the basis of job evaluation tends to be logical, rational and fair. In determining wage rate on the basis of job evaluation worker's competence, skill and education are properly reckoned with.

(vi) It also helps in eliminating discrepancies among employees of a group of organisation in any particular industry.

4.24 Steps for Job Evaluation

The following steps are suggested for Job Evaluation :

1. Identify and isolate component tasks in a job.
2. Identify the main duties involved.
3. Identify the main areas of responsibility.
4. Identify the personal demands which a job makes on an individual.
5. Examine how tasks are performed.
6. Examine why tasks are performed as they are.

4.25 Advantages of Job Evaluation

The following advantages can be derived from Job Evaluation :

1. It analyses human input brought to a job.
2. Comparative decisions can be made between two jobs since job evaluation seeks to assemble the information in a logical manner.
3. It facilitates cost control. Its use avoids anomalies, confusion and unrest.
4. It helps to develop an equitable wage structure.
5. It leads to simplification.

MERIT RATING OR PERFORMANCE APPRAISAL

4.26 Definition

Merit Rating is the comparative evaluation and analysis of the individual merits of the employees. It seeks to measure the individual performance efficiency of the workers who are working on similar jobs. In this sense it is more than job evaluation.

Merit rating has the following objectives :

(i) To evaluate the merit of individual worker for awarding different incentives like promotion, increment.

(ii) To analyse the merit of an employee and thereby help him in developing his skill and productivity.

(iii) To determine the suitability of an employee for his placement in the job for which he is best suited.

(iv) It helps the supervisor in planning the employee's further training.

(v) It infuses a spirit of competition among workers and this results in better performance.

4.27 Difference between Job Evaluation and Merit Rating

There are some points of difference between Job Evaluation and Merit Rating.

They are :

(i) Job evaluation aims at the assessment of the relative worth of jobs within the business while merit rating is the assessment of the relative worth of an employee with respect to a job.

(ii) Job evaluation helps to establish a rational wage or salary structure but merit rating helps in fixing fair rate of pay or fair wages for each worker after taking into consideration his skill and performance.

(iii) Job evaluation brings uniformity in wage structure but merit rating aims at providing fair wages to employees.

(iv) Job evaluation is concerned with the workers as a whole while merit rating is concerned with individual worker. So, the approach of the former is collective while that of the latter is individualistic.

Conclusion

Both job evaluation and merit rating can be useful to the employee in seeking to improve himself and to employer in selecting keen workers for promotion or special assignments provided they are applied fairly.

4.28 Time and Motion Study

Time study is defined as a work measurement technique for recording the times and rates of working for the elements of a specified job carried out under specified conditions and for analysing the data to determine the time necessary for carrying out the job at a defined level of performance.

Motion study implies dividing the work into fundamental elements or basic operations of a job or a process with the object of eliminating unnecessary or defective elements in a job. After investigating all movements in a job, process or operation it finds out the most scientific and systematic method of performing the operation or completing the job. Thus, time study fixes the standard time for a job or a process while motion study eliminates wasteful motions or the movement of a worker on the job. Both are complimentary to each other.

4.29 Objectives

Objectives of time and motion study are :

1. They eliminate unnecessary motions, fatigue, and seek to improve human efforts in doing a job.
2. They bring about improvement in method, procedure, techniques and processes relating to a job.
3. They make effective utilisation of materials, machines, human resources.
4. They also improve layout and design of plant and equipment and working environment.

4.30 Benefits

The following benefits are derived by the Management from time and motion study :

1. Optimum utilisation of materials, plant, labour and financial resources is possible.
2. Labour requirements can be properly assessed.
3. Determination of fair wage rates and effective wage incentive schemes can be determined.
4. Setting of labour cost standards and control of the labour cost are possible.
5. Labour budgets can be prepared.
6. Job can be standardised.
7. Improvement in work methods by making comparison between time taken to complete a job and time taken to complete the same type of job under different methods.
8. Effective cost control and proper planning can be made with the help of time and motion study.

4.13 TREATMENT OF SOME ITEMS

(i) Overtime

Overtime is the work put in by a worker beyond normal working hours. The wage rate for overtime is generally $1\frac{1}{2}$ times of usual rate. It is double or triple if the work is performed on any holiday or Sunday or on weekly holiday. In costing, the cost of overtime premium must be separated from regular earnings. Additional payment for overtime may be charged to the (i) job directly if overtime is worked at the customer's request with the object of completing the job within a specified period ; (ii) to the department which has been responsible for causing delay ; (iii) to the Costing Profit & Loss Account if overtime is necessary to make up the time lost due to breakdown of machinery, power failure etc. ; (iv) to the prime cost if the work is on a peak load due to seasonal rush in the factory.

Of late, it has been a regular feature to grant overtime work to the workers for the reasons beyond the control of the management, so it will be logical and rational to charge the extra payment for overtime direct to production.

(ii) Holiday and Vacation Pay

Workers enjoy some holidays like Independence Day, Republic Day, Mahatma Gandhiji's birthday and other Festival holidays with full pay. Production on these days remains suspended. Though payment for holidays is unproductive, the expense is treated as direct labour cost and charged to production.

(iii) Leave with Pay

According to the Factories Act. workers are entitled to annual leave with pay for some days as specified. This leave is known as earned leave. Moreover, they are entitled to casual leave, medical leave, special leave etc. with full pay. Practically speaking, the wages paid to workers for the period in which they do not contribute to production may be treated as unproductive wages. It is not generally treated as a direct charge to a product or to a job but is treated as factory overhead and recovered through departmental overhead rates. Alternatively, an inflated rate of direct wages cost can be applied to absorb both normal wages and an appropriate portion of leave with pay.

(iv) Attendance Bonus

Sometimes workers are paid extra wages for their regular and punctual attendance. This extra payment of wage is known as attendance bonus. It is generally treated as direct wages and charged to a product or job. But it can also be treated as factory overhead and may be recovered through departmental overhead rates.

(v) Apprentices' wages

In many factories it is the practice that new workers have to work as apprentice for some time before they are absorbed in regular work-force. As they are novice they are less efficient than the skilled and regular workers. During training period they are likely to cause more scrap and wastes. Moreover, they take more time than normal to complete a job assigned to them. For the reasons stated earlier they are paid a lower rate of wage per hour.

The wages paid to them are treated as production overhead and should be charged to the annual output by including it in the factory overheads. But, if learners' wages can be easily identified with a job, they should be treated as direct wages.

(vi) Shift Premium

When there is an unusual pressure of work, workers may be asked to work in the evening or night shifts. Generally, higher rate of wages or additional payment is made for night shift work. This additional payment can be treated in two ways :

1. Where workers are asked to work in night shift at the request of the customers to complete their job within a specified time, extra payments are charged directly to the job concerned.
2. When the workers are paid extra for working in night shifts in order to increase the output of a whole or to make up production backlog, the premium element should be separated from direct wages and is to be treated as a production overhead.

(vii) Fringe Benefits

An employee's pay roll generally consists of basic wages, dearness allowance, house rent allowance, city compensatory allowance etc. Besides these, a variety of benefits are provided to the workers. These benefits are known as fringe benefits. Fringe benefits are not directly related to the direct efforts of the employee.

Fringe benefits may comprise :

(i) Holiday pay ; (ii) Leave pay ; (iii) Sick pay ; (iv) Employer's contribution to provident fund ; (iv) State insurance and medical benefits ; (v) Gratuity : (vi) Good attendance bonus ; (vii) Cheap canteen supplies etc.

Treatment in Cost Accounts

The expenses in way of fringe benefits cannot be treated as direct labour cost and, as such, cannot be allocated to cost units as direct cost. They may be treated as items of departmental overhead and booked to standing order numbers alloted to each type of such expenditure. If the amounts are not uniform in each accounting period, an amount is estimated in advance for the whole year and a proportionate charge is made for each period.

In some companies, however, cost of fringe benefits related to direct labour are charged as an additional direct labour cost. Horngren suggests that the latter approach is conceptually preferable because these costs are a fundamental part of acquiring labour services.

(viii) Idle time

Idle time is the difference between the time for which workers are paid and the time for which the workers do work. So, idle time represents the time for which the employer makes payment but from which the employer does not gain anything in terms of production. Virtually, during idle time, the workers remain idle and contribute nothing to the production. Idle time includes some unavoidable losses like time taken in travelling between the factory gate and the department in which the worker concerned is engaged ; time lag between the completion of one job and the commencement of the next ; tea breaks, tiffin breaks ; personal needs and the time when production is stopped or interrupted for machine maintenance.

The wastage of time for the above reason or reasons cannot be avoided and the employer has to bear the financial loss arising out of such reasons. Idle time that results from unavoidable causes is treated as normal idle time.

Abnormal idle time is the result of causes which are avoidable. The following are the examples of abnormal idle time :

(i) time lost through the breakdown of machinery due to inefficiency or bad maintenance or for power failure which is frequent in our country ;

(ii) time lost through non-availability of materials ;

(iii) time lost due to stoppage of work on account of strikes, fire etc ;

(iv) bottlenecks in production ;

(v) time lost for waiting for instruction from the superior. These above causes are also known as administrative and productive causes. Idle time due to productive and administrative causes can be avoided if little care is taken in respect of maintenance of machineries ; proper store control, performance of purchase department and coordination between store and purchase department. All the above factors responsible for controllable and avoidable idle time can be regulated in favour of increased production if every aspect is planned well ahead.

Treatment of idle time

Cost of unavoidable and normal idle time should be charged as ovehreads. Idle time—which is abnormal and can be controlled—is to be charged to Costing Profit and Loss Account.

IDLE TIME CARD
VENUS Co. Ltd.

Clock No. .... Normal Code ....
Name .... Machine No. ....
Date ....

Particulars	*Reasons Code*	*Time*		*Hours*	*Rate*	*Cost*
		On	*Off*			*Rs.*

Reason Code :

A. No work D. No Machine
B. No Instruction E. No Tools
C. No Materials F. Machine break-down

Signed (worker)	Certified	Calculated by	Cost office reference

(ix) Casual workers

A worker who is employed on a temporary basis is known as casual worker. A casual worker is employed as a substitute of a worker who is on leave or may be employed to perform a specific job for a short period of time. When casual worker is employed on production job, job card should be issued in his name and work done by him should be certified by the authority i.e. by the foreman or by the supervisor. In the event casual workers are employed for miscellaneous indirect jobs, time sheets should be issued and a proper check on them should be kept. At the time of termination of service prior intimation to this effect should be sent to time keeping and wage departments so that no over-payment is made.

(x) Out workers

Out workers are sent to sites or customers' premises for performing work. A close control over the work performed and payment made to these workers is necessary. If the workers employed are few in number and for a short period of time, the record for their attendance may be kept by the foreman in charge. When the number of such workers is large and the duration of work for which they have been deputed is long, clock system for recording their attendance may be installed.

LABOUR TURNOVER

4.32 Definition

Labour turnover refers to the rate at which employees leave employment. Labour turnover can be evaluated by relating the number of employees leaving their employment during a period of time to the total or average numbers employed in that period. It may also be defined as engagements and losses in the working force as related to the total number of employees who were on the pay roll at the beginning of the period in question.

Example

Let us assume that in a factory there were 2,000 employees on an average during the year 1990 and 100 persons left the company during this period. So, the labour turnover will be $\frac{100 \times 100}{2,000} = 5\%$.

Generally, it is measured by the following formula :

$$\frac{\text{No. of employees leaving during the period}}{\text{Average number of employees employed durings such period}} \times 100$$

4.33 Causes of labour tunrover

Causes of labour turnover can be classified as (i) Avoidable and (ii) Unavoidable.

Avoidable causes are :

(i) Lower wages ; (ii) bad working conditions, (iii) unsympathetic attitude of the management ; (iv) lack of opportunities for promotion ; (v) lack of proper training ; (vi) improper manpower planning ; (vii) lack of proper incentives ; (viii) bitter relationship between management and workers ; (ix) lack of conveyance, accommodation, medical and educational facilities and recreational amenities etc.

Unavoidable causes :

Sometimes workers have to leave the organisation because of management requirements and administrative actions. They also leave their employment at their own will, that is, on personal reasons. In the latter case the management can do nothing but remains a helpless onlooker. So, unavoidable causes may be administrative or personal.

Administrative causes

(i) Termination of service due to indiscipline, insubordination, bad conduct etc.

(ii) Retrenchment or lay-off due to shortage of resources, low demand for recession.

Personal causes

(i) Change for better job ; (ii) death ; (iii) retirement due to old age ; (iv) change for better working conditions, better environment ; (v) change for secured job ; (vi) marriage, especially of women workers ; (vii) illness and accident rendering the worker permanently incapable of doing any work ; (viii) domestic need and responsibility etc.

4.34 Effects of labour turnover

Labour turnover is harmful and costly. It results in increased cost of production due to the following reasons :

(i) With frequent changes in labour force, production planning cannot be properly executed resulting in substantial loss in production

(ii) Since the new workers have no previous experience in production there is loss arising out of defective work, increased spoilage and wastage resulting in high cost of production.

(iii) Newly recruited workers are likely to mishandle tools and equipment which results in breakages.

(iv) The organisation has to incur extra cost for workers' training.

(v) Labour turnover causes increased replacement cost.

(vi) Labour cost increases because of lower productivity of newly recruited workers as they do not possess the same expertise as the old workers who have left the organisation.

4.35 Measurement of labour turnover

Labour turnover rate can be measured by the application of any one of the following three methods :

(i) Separation method :

$$\frac{\text{No. of separations during the period}}{\text{Average number of workers in the same period}} \times 100$$

(ii) Replacement method :

$$\frac{\text{No. of workers replaced during the period}}{\text{Average number of workers in same period}} \times 100$$

(iii) Flux method :

$$\frac{\text{No. of separations No. of replacements}}{\text{Average number of workers in the same period}} \times 100$$

Problem 1

From the following data given by the Personnel Department calculate the labour turnover rate by the application of above three methods :

No. of workers on the Pay Roll :

At the beginning of the month Jan, 91	900
At the end of the month	1,100

During the month 10 workers left, 40 persons were discharged and 150 workers were recruited. Of these, 25 workers were recruited in the vacancies of those leaving, while the rest were engaged for an expansion scheme.

[Adapted—A.I.C.W.A. (Inter) December 1988]

Solution

(a) Separation method $\frac{10 + 40}{1,000} \times 100 = 5\%$

(Note – Average number of workers during the month = $\frac{900 + 1,100}{2} = 1,000$)

(b) Replacement metod $\frac{25}{1,000} \times 100 = 2.5\%$

(c) Flux method $\frac{50 + 25}{1,000} \times 100 = \frac{75}{1,000} \times 100 = 7.5\%$

4.36 Cost of Labour Turnover

The cost of labour turnover is the monetary value of the loss of output and the cost of services involved in dealing with labour turnover and labour replacements.
The cost of labour turnover may be classified as :

(i) Preventive costs and

(ii) Replacement costs.

(i) Preventive Costs :

Preventive costs are incurred to keep the labour turnover minimum. These costs are the costs of benefits extended to the working force for keeping them satisfied so that they do not leave the organisation. These costs comprise the expenditure on the following :

(i) Safety measures ;

(ii) Welfare amenities to workers like medical, housing, recreational and educational facilities free of cost or at subsidised rates ;

(iii) Good retirement benefits;

(iv) Introduction of job evaluation and merit rating to introduce fair wage structure and for payment of incentives and suitable merit awards to skilled and competent workers;

(v) Selection and training on scientific basis.

(2) Replacement Costs :

Replacement costs arise from replacement of labour. These costs include :

(i) Cost of selection including cost of advertisement of the job, interviewing the candidates, training etc ;

(ii) Loss arising from inefficiency like higher spoilage of materials, outputs and time;

(iii) Loss due to machine breakdown due to mishandling of machineries ;

(iv) Increase in overhead costs due to wastage, spoilage, production of inferior goods etc ;

(v) Cost of additional supervision for training the new workers who have little or no experience in production function.

LABOUR TURNOVER REPORT

August 1994

		This Month	Last Month	Year to Date This year	Year to Date Last year
Average labour force		900	900	800	700
Number of separations		27	22	114	81
Labour turnover	%	3.0	2.4	14.2	11.6
REASON FOR LEAVING :					
(a) *Voluntary* :					
Higher wages		5	4	22	9
Better prospects		3	2	9	7
Unhappy at job		2	3	14	10
Conditions of work		2	1	7	8
Distance to travel		1	–	2	3
Retiral and death		1	–	5	4
Marriage		–	2	6	5
Other reasons		1	–	3	2
	Total	15	12	68	48
	%	1.7	1.3	8.5	6.9
(b) *Dismissals* :					
Insubordination		2	2	9	10
Incompetence		5	4	20	12
Health		1	–	4	2
Redundancy		2	1	6	2
Absenteeism		1	–	1	1
Timekeeping		1	2	4	4
Other reasons		–	1	2	2
	Total	12	10	46	33
	%	1.3	1.1	5.7	4.7

Note : High labour turnover mainly due to wage rates below average for this area. Best quality of labour cannot be obtained at present rates — hence large number of dismissals for incompetence.

4.37 LABOUR TURNOVER REPORT

The personnel department will normally maintain detailed records of overtime and shift work. As overtime is paid for at higher rates than normal daywork, most workers are only too anxious to take advantage of opportunities to undertake it, and the overtime develops among the workers.

To do away with this, all overtime working should be sanctioned by the proper authority. The departmental manager should prepare a list of overtime workers and pass it to the personnel department for approval. The personnel department has a duty to ensure that regulations laid down by the Factories Act have not been infringed. A weekly report showing the number of normal and overtime hours worked in each department should be submitted to the management to maintain a check on overtime, similar records will be kept of the number of times each worker is late or absent and the total amount of time lost. Regular reports should be sent to the departmental managers so that disciplinary action can be taken in the cases of persistent offenders.

4.38 Treatment in Cost Accounts

Preventive costs are allocated to different departments in proportion to the respective labour force. Replacement costs are, however, charged directly to the department where such replacement takes place. But, when the replacement does take place because of general management policy but not due to the fault of the department concerned, in such a case, it is desirable to treat such costs as overhead and should be apportioned and allocated to all the departments on the basis of number of workers on the pay roll.

If, however, labour turnover costs cannot be classified or identified as preventive or replacement costs, they are usually treated as overhead expenses and should not be charged direct to any job order.

4.39 Payment of Wages

The tasks of preparing pay rolls are complicated in the sense that specified amounts are withheld from the earnings of the employees to meet the government requirements for taxation and other statutory obligations. There are three major problems :

(i) allocating labour costs to functions, departments and products ;

(ii) accurate computation of earnings and prompt payment to workers ;

(iii) computation of deductions to be made from the employee's earnings and remitting them to the proper authorities. For example, the amount of Income Tax deducted from employees' earning should be deposited with the government in time, any failure to do so will attract penalty.

So, promptness of payment and pinpoint accuracy are the foremost criteria for judging the merits of any payroll system from the viewpoint of employees.

From the government's point of view, collection of taxes and their timely deposit are very much essential. There are other withholdings like repayment of loans, deduction for fines etc., contribution to group life insurance plans and other saving plans. These withholdings are funneled to the third parties through the employer.

Moreover, it is the responsibility of the wage department to prepare the pay rolls for the genuine workers. Utmost care should be taken that **dummy workers have not been included** in pay roll and wages have been paid to them.

4.40 Preparation of Pay Rolls

The Pay Roll is a record of (i) the gross wages earned by each worker for a specific wage period, (ii) the deductions in respect of provident fund contribution, professional tax, Income Tax, repayment of loans from P.F. or cooperative society made from gross wages and (iii) the net wages payable to him.

The essential information to be shown in the Pay Rolls are as :

1. Name of the Department
2. Wage period
3. Worker's clock number

4. Worker's production during the wage period
5. Hours of attendance
6. Overtime hours, if any
7. Worker's production during the wage period
8. Hourly rate of wage
9. Rate per unit of production
10. Basic wages
11. Dearness Allowance
12. Production Bonus
13. Overtime
14. Other Allowances
15. Deductions – P.F., P. Tax, I. Tax, Repayment of loans etc.
16. Net wage payble.

Proforma of Pay Roll see page no. 285

4.41 Source documents for the preparation of Pay Rolls

The basic data for the pay roll is the records of attendance or records of production which are collected from clock cards and piece-work tickets.

Where clock cards and piece-work tickets are not in use, the departmental attendance register or departmental record of production can be used as documents for the above information. The first step in the preparation of pay roll is to fill up the pay roll with the basic data. After filling up the required information the pay roll is sent to the cost department to reconcile and check the data entered into pay roll with those of production records and with the hours booked against jobs. After doing this, necessary deductions are made to arrive at net wages payable. Every calculation in the pay roll should be made by one clerk and checked by another. Once the pay roll is prepared, a wage ticket is made out for each worker and distributed to the worker concerned a day before the actual date of payment.

4.42 Disbursement of wages

The first step in the distribution of wages is to prepare pay packet containing exact cash that will be required for the payment of wages to each worker. In a big factory coin analysis of the exact cash to be required for payment of wages to each shift or department is prepared to ensure that no shortage or surplus in cash arises at the time of payment. Exact amount of cash to be paid to each worker is put in an envelope. All the envelopes are arranged in the same order as they appear in the attendance register of the department concerned. On the scheduled date, as fixed earlier, the payment is made in the department in presence of the departmental foreman.

4.43 Prevention of fraud

In order to minimise the risk of fraud, rigid control should be exercised over the calculation and payment of wages. In doing so the following points should be taken into consideration :

1. The wage office is to see that the wages for dummy workers' have not been included in the wage sheet or pay roll.
2. A number of persons should be associated with the preparation of wage sheet. One such person may be asked to insert the rate of wages payable on the payroll, and another should calculate the deductions to be made on various accounts and to ascertain the net wage payable to each worker.

SPECIMEN OF PAY ROLL

Department				Shift													Month/Week Ended ....
Serial No.	Worker's No.	Worker's Name	No. of Hrs. worked	Normal hours	Overtime	Bonus	Rate	Wages									
								Gross wage	Allowances	Total	P.F.	E.S.I.	I. Tax	P. Tax	Recovery of loans	Total	Net wages payable

Prepared by :

i)

ii)

3. The pay roll after its completion should be verified by a responsible person and, being satisfied with the entries and deductions made, he should put his signature on the pay roll. Each person responsible for the preparation of pay roll should put his initial on the pay roll.
4. Unpaid wage packets should be kept by the cashier and the reason for unclaimed pay packets should be established. If the pay packets remain undelivered for a few days, they should be opened and the contents should be deposited into a special bank account pending enquiry.
5. Time-cards should be compared at regular intervals with the pay roll by an official who is in no way connected with the wage office.
6. It is desirable that from time to time a senior officer should personally be present when the wages are being paid.
7. Wages should not be handed over to any person other than the worker concerned and that too on proper identification.

4.44 Specimen of the documents that are used in the wage office

1. Daily Time Sheet

EVERGREEN CO. LTD.

Daily Time Sheet

Name .... Date ....

Department ....

Clock Tocket No. ....

Work Order No.	*Description of work*	*Quantity*	*Time*		*Hour*	*Rate*	*Cost*
			Start	*Finish*			

Signature of the worker | Certified by Foreman | Cost Dept.

2. Job Card for each worker

EVERGREEN LTD.
Job Card for each worker

Name.................................... Clock No. ....
Dept...................................... Hourly Rate .... Week ending ....

Job No.		*Mon*	*Tues*	*Wed*	*Thurs*	*Fri*	*Sat*	*Total hours*	*Cost*
	Start Finish Start Finish Start Finish								

Total hours Normal overtime Idle Time

Checked and verified Foreman | Worker | Cost Office reference

3. JOb Card for each job

JOB CARD FOR EACH JOB

Job No.. Time Started......................................
Job description .... Time Finished ....
Drawing No.. Hours on Job ....
Operation No. .... Time allowance ....

Date	Operation	Department	Hourly Rate	Time Start	Time Hours	Hours	Cost

Total for the Job

Checked and verified Cost office reference

Foreman

Pay Roll Accounting

1) When payment of wages is made :

Wages Control A/c	Dr.	
To Cost Ledger Control A/c		

2)

Work-in-Progress Control A/c	Dr.	For Direct wages
Factory Overhead Control A/c	Dr.	For Indirect wages
Administrative Overhead Control or		For Indirect wages for Office and Administration
Selling and Distribution Overhead Control A/c	Dr.	For Indirect wages for Selling and Distribution
To Wage Control Account		

Posting in Financial Account

1)

Wages A/c (Gross Amount)	Dr.	
To Cash A/c		
To Income Tax A/c		Deductions
To Professional Tax A/c		
To Co-operative Society A/c		
To P.F. A/c		
To P.F. Loan A/c		
To E.S.I. A/c		

2) *For disbursement of withholdings to proper authorities* :

P.F. A/c	Dr.
E.S.I. A/c	Dr.
Professional Tax A/c	Dr.
Income Tax A/c	Dr.
To Cash/Bank	

4.45 IN BRIEF

CHART OF WAGE PROCEDURES

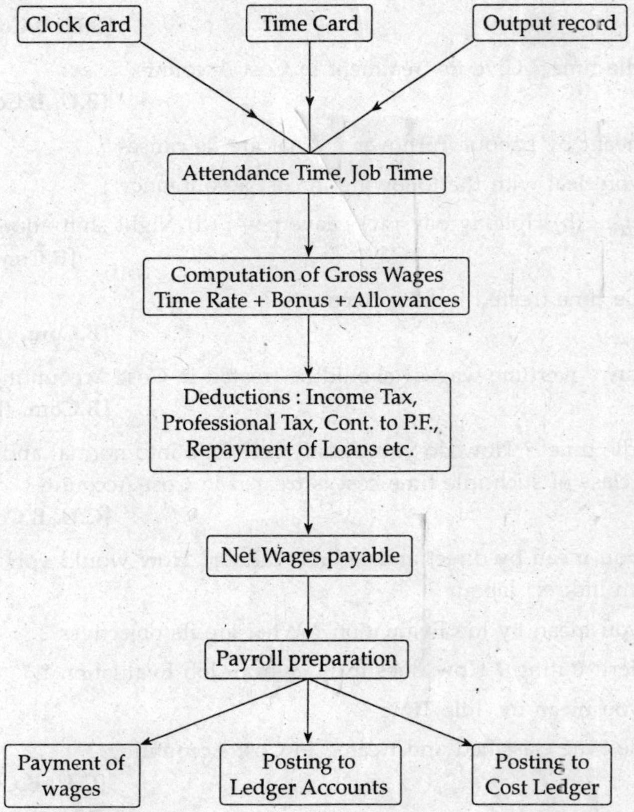

ASSIGNMENT

1. What is time keeping ? State the essential features of a good time keeping system. Explain the treatment of overtime premium in Cost Accounts.

[B.U. B.Com. (Hons.) 1985]

2. (a) Distinguish between time keeping and time booking.

   (b) Why is time keeping important even in case of piece-rate of wage system ?

[B.U. B.Com. (Hons.) 1986]

3. Write short notes on :

   (a) Time Booking ; (b) Overtime.

[B.U. B.Com. (Hons.) 1984]

4. What is idle time ? Give its treatment in Cost Accounts.

[B.U. B.Com. (Hons.) D.U.]

5. What is meant by Labour Turnover ? What are its causes ?
6. How do you deal with the following in cost accountancy :

   (a) Idle time ; (b) Holiday pay ; (c) Leave pay ; (d) Night shift allowance ?

[B.Com. Kerala Part III]

7. How is idle time treated in Cost Accounts ?

[B.Com. (Hons.) C.U. 1981]

8. Discuss how "overtime wages" should be treated in Cost Accounting.

[B.Com. (Hons.) C.U. 1984]

9. What is 'idle time' ? How do you classify idle time into normal and abnormal ? State how each class of such idle time cost is treated in Cost Accounts.

[C.U. B.Com. (Hons.) 1985]

10. What do you mean by direct and indirect labour? How would you distinguish direct labour from indirect labour ?
11. What do you mean by Job Evaluation ? What are its objectives ?
12. What is Merit Rating ? How does it differ from Job Evaluation ?
13. What do you mean by 'Idle Time' ?

    How is idle time classified and treated in Cost Accounting ?

[C.U. B.Com (Hons.) 1996]

[B.U. B.Com. (Hons.) 1995]

SECTION TWO

METHODS OF WAGE PAYMENT

4.46 Introduction

In this chapter we propose to discuss the various methods of wage payments. We have seen earlier that labour is an essential element of cost. Remuneration paid to the workers is known as wages. It is really a difficult job to fix up fair wages for the workers. In a modern industrial unit, workers' wages are based upon job evaluation, negotiation with trade unions and the government. In our country wages in some industries in the public sector like steel are determined by the government. Determination of wages is a sensitive and delicate issue since it concerns human psychology and behaviour. But both employer and employees are interested in the wage policy of a concern. The employer seeks to ensure that his personnel policy will result in maximum cost-effectiveness of labour while the employee may be seeking such facilities as (i) regular high wages; (ii) security of employment; (iii) good working conditions and (iv) some fringe benefits. To achieve increased production and productivity, the employer should adopt such a wage policy which will ensure good labour relationship.

Wage determination is a complex area where a good number of factors are involved. The factors vary in importance from one organisation to another and no simplistic, generalised statements can be made.

The following are the factors that are involved in wage determination :

(i) General economic climate of industry
(ii) Government policy
(iii) Profitability of the firm
(iv) Cost structure of the firm and industry
(v) Availability of skilled workers
(vi) Extent of hazardous or dangerous working conditions
(vii) Bargaining power of the union
(viii) Strategic importance of firm and industry.

4.47 Methods of Remunerating Labour

Methods of remuneration may be grouped under four headings :

(a) Time work – Time Rate
(b) Payment by results i.e. Piece Rate
(c) Group Bonus Schemes
(d) Profit-sharing and Co-partnership.

4.48 Requisites of a Good Wage Payment Plan

A good wage payment plan must have the following requisites :

(i) The wage payment system should be simple and easy to understand. There should not exist any ambiguity.
(ii) The wage policy should be flexible so that it can be adapted to the socio-economic changes.
(iii) It should guarantee a minimum living wage to the employees.
(iv) There should be uniformity. The wage rate in an industry should be comparable with the wages prevailing in same type of industry located in the region.
(v) The wage rate should take into account the skill and merits of the workers.

(vi) It should minimise labour turnover to avoid its inherited disadvantages.

(vii) It should satisfy both the employees and employer to create good industrial relationship for maintaining industrial harmony for increased production.

(viii) It should encourage and motivate the workers for increaed productivity and production.

(ix) Administration and operation cost should be minimised to increase competitiveness.

(x) The workers should be able to maximise output, but not at the cost of quality.

(xi) It should minimise absenteeism.

4.49 TIME RATE PLAN

The method which is related to the hours of work is known as Time Rate Plan. Under this method the worker is paid at an hourly, daily or weekly rate and his remuneration, thus, depends upon the time for which he is employed and not upon his contribution to production.

This method of wage payment is suitable where :

(1) The quality of the work is of paramount importance ;

(2) The output of the individual workers cannot be measured ;

(3) The speed of production cannot be influenced by the energy of the worker ;

(4) Where close supervision of work is possible ;

(5) Where increased production and productivity do not commensurate with the incentive paid.

4.50 Calculation of Earnings

Earnings = Clock hours worked ¥ Rate per hour.

OR

Earnings = Number of days worked ¥ Rate per day

Time work is most suitable for the two extreme grades of workers, viz. the highly skilled and the unskilled including learners and apprentices.

4.51 Advantages

Time-wage system offers the following advantages :

(i) *Stable wages and security*

It provides the worker with job security and stability of wages. The inefficient workers are assured of stable earnings.

(ii) *Better industrial relationship*

This wage system is readily acceptable to unions as it serves the workers on equity basis. This helps to promote better industrial relationship.

(iii) *Simplicity*

Wage calculation is simple.

(iv) *Economy*

The system is economical in the sense that it involves less clerical expenditure resulting in saving of overheads.

(v) *Quality Output*

Time wages result in better quality of output since workers are not in hurry to complete the jobs.

4.52 Disadvantages

The following are the disadvantages of time wage system :

(i) The efficient workers are economically penalised for their efficiency since they are not paid for it. In course of time they lose initiative and become inefficient.

(ii) With the decrease of productivity labour cost increases resulting in reduction in profit.

(iii) It contributes to creation of bottlenecks in production by upsetting production schedules and, thus, increases the cost per unit.

(iv) To make this system cost effective strict supervision is required. Thus, the additional cost of supervision will increase the labour cost per unit.

(v) Lack of strict supervision encourages the workers to idle away time since they know that they will be paid for the time, not for the work. This will increase cost of labour.

(vi) This system encourages the payment of overtime. The workers are reluctant to complete the assigned job within the working hours. The employer, however, is forced to pay overtime to get the work done in time. This becomes very costly.

(vii) It becomes very difficult to set the standards for labour under this system.

Under this system the employer bears all the loss arising from his employee's inefficiency, and all the gains arising from employees' extra efficiency. From the employees' point of view, inefficient workers gain while efficient workers stand to loose. The straight-time wage is still the most effective plan for workers such as clerks, stenographers, accountants, factory helpers, members of the supervisory staff and officers whose work cannot be standardised and measured satisfactorily. Here, the quality of work is more important than volume.

Problem 2

Calculate the normal and overtime wages payable to a workman from the following data :

Days	Hours worked		Rate
Monday	8 hours	Normal working hours	8 hours per day
Tuesday	10 "		
Wednesday	11 "	Normal Rate	Rs. 5.00 per hour
Thursday	12 "	Overtime Rate	Up to 9 hours in a day
Friday	8 "		at single rate and
Saturday	4 "		beyond 9 hours in a
	53 hours		day at double rate.

Solution

Day	Normal working hours	Total	At Normal rate	Overtime: Single rate	Overtime: Double rate
Monday	8	8	8	–	–
Tuesday	8	10	8	1	1
Wednesday	8	11	8	1	2
Thursday	8	12	8	1	3
Friday	8	8	8	–	–
Saturday	8	4	4	–	–
	48	53	44	3	6

Normal wage on time rate		=	44 hours × 5	=	Rs. 220.00
Overtime wages –	Single rate	=	3 hours × Rs. 5	=	Rs. 15.00
	Double rate	=	6 hours × Rs. 10	=	Rs. 60.00
	Total wages			=	Rs. 295.00

4.53 PIECE RATE

This system is also known as payment by result.

Under this system the payment of wages is based on performance. This system is the oldest and is widely applicable in many industries like garment manufacture, ancillaries of various kinds, plastic, footwear, printing etc. Payment of wages is based on the number of units of a product produced by a worker irrespective of the time taken. The earning of a worker is calculated as :

E = N × R; where E = Earning, N = Number of units produced, R = Rate of wages per unit.

If a worker completes 100 units of product 'X' in a month and the rate per unit is Rs. 2.75, then the worker's earning will be Rs. 275 per month (100 × Rs. 2.75).

The piece rate system can advantageously be applied to work of a standard or repetitive nature, where fixation of piece rate is easier. Under this system the employee, not the employer, stands to gain or lose as a result of his attained efficiency. In the words of Wheldon, the general principle underlying this system may be stated as **"produce more, earn more ; produce less —earn less"**.

4.54 Advantages

The following are the advantages of Piece Rate System of wage payment :

1. This system encourages the workers to produce more since their remuneration is proportionate to their efforts. Thus production is increased which leads to minimisation of cost per unit.
2. This system is more equitable since reward is related to effort.
3. There is an increase in productivity, more output is turned out in a shorter period of time. The overhead cost per unit of production is lowered.
4. Computation of labour cost in advance of production is possible since the fixed rate per unit has already been determined.
5. Calculation of wages is simple and easy.

4.55 Disadvantages

1. Production is encouraged at the expense of quality.
2. Having earned a desirable amount which the workers might have fixed in their minds and to avoid incidence of taxation, they may frequently absent themselves from work, thereby disturbing the production flow of the factory.
3. Under this system of wage payment only the worker's output is considered, his other qualities are ignored.
4. This system tends to develop the tendency of increasing imperfections, defectives and spoiled work and higher depreciation costs because of considerable wear and tear of plant and machinery.

4.56 Difference between Time Rate and Piece Rate Wages

Time Rate Wages	*Piece Rate Wages*
1. Wages payable to workers are calculated on the basis of time taken by a worker to do a job.	1. The worker is paid on the basis of output achieved by him.
2. This system of wage payment is better where the output cannot be measured.	2. This system is better where output can be measured.
3. This system can be applied for work over which the operator has no control.	3. It is applied where the operator has control over the quantity of output.
4. This system is better to adopt where quality is more important than quantity.	4. This system is better where the consideration for quality is less important.
5. Worker will concentrate on quality since he is paid on the basis of actual time taken by him to complete a job.	5. Under this method quality of work is sure to suffer.
6. It is easier to fix time rate wages.	6. Fixation of piece rate wages involves problems.
7. It is suitable where the methods and equipment are not standardised.	7. It is suitable where methods and equipment are standardised.
8. It is suitable where the work is not of repetitive nature.	8. It is suitable where the work is of repetitive nature.
9. The employer enjoys all gains arising from higher output.	9. The worker takes all the gains of higher output.

4.57 INCENTIVE WAGE PLANS

Premium Bonus Systems are variations of the piece rate systems and they mainly differ in showing of bonus. The mechanism of this system is that the results of efficiency are shared by the employer and employee on some agreed basis. The basic purpose of an incentive wage is to induce worker to produce more so that he can earn a higher wage. It aims at both increased productivity and production. The factory overhead cost per unit is reduced because of increased production i.e. greater number of units are produced.

4.58 Principles

The principles of good incentive scheme are :

1. There must be full consultation with the various employees' unions to ensure mutual agreement between the employer and employees. Any disagreement at a later stage may make the scheme futile.
2. Before reaching any agreement the objectives to be attained should be set out and clearly defined. There must not exist any ambiguity in the agreement.
3. No limits should be placed on additional earning under the scheme.
4. The scheme should be simple to administer.
5. The incentive system must be related closely to the efforts involved in the performance of the job.
6. The wage incentive system should be based upon standards of performance, time and motion studies, job evaluation and merit rating.

7. It is highly desirable that indirect personnel should be covered by the scheme, that is, they have a share in the scheme.
8. Performance above standard should be rewarded. For this reason there must be provision for higher wages for efficient workers whose efficiency goes beyond the standard.
9. The level of productivity required by the scheme must be attainable by the average employee. Performance levels should be in reach of the average worker.
10. Individual incentives should be used wherever possible.

4.59 Features

The following features are common to all types of premium bonus plans :

(i) Minimum wage is guaranteed to every worker.
(ii) Savings arising out of employee's higher efficiency are shared by both the employer and the employee
(iii) Labour cost decreases with the increase in production and productivity.
(iv) Employees are provided with modern facilities, equipment and latest techniques to increase productivity and production.

Incentive wage plans involve differential piece rates and bonus plans. The premium bonus plan may be individual or group.

4.60 INCENTIVE SCHEMES

Incentive schemes have been classified under the following categories :

1. Differential Piece Rate.
2. Premium Bonus Scheme.
3. Group Bonus Plan.
4. Bonus Schemes for indirect workers.

1. Differential Piece Rate

Under this system efficient workers are rewarded with higher wages for their increased output. This system aims at the maximisation of output which has a direct bearing on reduction of cost per unit.

This system can be suitably applied in the following circumstances :

(i) Where the nature of the work is repetitive and the methods of working, as also equipment can be standardised.
(ii) Where the output of each worker can be measured.
(iii) Where the standard time for each job can be set separately.
(iv) Where fixed overhead is high in comparison with direct wages.

Differential piece work systems are complicated and very expensive to operate. They are very difficult for the workers to understand. The labour cost per unit of production increases with the increase in production efficiency since it involves high rate of wages. A stage of production is reached where the advantages of increased production and reduced overhead cost may not neutralise the rising labour cost.

Some of the well-known systems of payment of wages by results are discussed below :

1. **Taylor's Differential Piece Work System**

Under this system two wage rates prevail—higher wage rate for above-standard performance and lower wage rate for output below standard. This system encourages the workers to increase their production to earn higher rate of wages. This system discourages the below average workers by providing no guaranteed hourly wage.

Problem 3

Standard output	–	120 units
Daily working hours	–	8
Anil's output	–	100 units
Sunil's output	–	140 units
Higher piece rate	–	0.20 paise per unit
Lower piece rate	–	0.15 paise per unit

Solution

	Output	Wages
Anil's remuneration	100 (below standard)	100 × 0.15 = Rs. 15.00
Sunil's remuneration	140 (above standard)	140 × 0.20 = Rs. 28.00

2. **Merrick's Differential Piece Rate**

This system is also known as Multiple Piece Rate System. This is an improvement over the Taylor system. Like Taylor's system this system does not guarantee time rate. It has a three-tier system having the following rates of remuneration :

Level of efficiency	Piece Rate
Up to 83%	Normal Piece Rate
From 83% to 100%	110% of normal Piece Rate
Above 100%	120% of normal Piece Rate

Problem 4

From the following particulars calculate the wages of 3 workers Amar, Akbar and Anthony under Merrick's Differential Piece Rate. Piece Rate is 40 paise per unit, standard output 30 units per day of 8 hours. Outputs : Amar – 24 units, Akbar – 27 units and Anthony – 36 units.

Solution

Efficiency of each worker as a percentage of standard :

Level of efficiency

Amar = $\frac{24}{30} \times 100 = 80\%$ = below 83%

Akbar = $\frac{27}{30} \times 100 = 90\%$ = above 83% but below 100%

Anthony = $\frac{36}{30} \times 100 = 120\%$ = above 100%

Calculation of Wages

1. Amar= 24 × 0.40 = Rs. 9.60
2. Akbar = 110% of normal wage rate

   i.e. $\frac{110}{100} \times$ Re. 0.40 × 27 units = Rs. 11.88
3. Anthony = 120% of normal piece rate = $\frac{120}{100} \times 0.40 \times 36$ = Rs. 17.28.

3. **Premium Bonus Scheme**

Premium Bonus Plan

Under time rate system of wage payment all the gains contributed by the efficient workers benefit the employer while, under piece rate system, it is the workers who gain or lose.

Under premium bonus system, the gains are shared by the employer and employees in agreed ratio. Apart from the minimum guaranteed wages, the efficient workers get bonus depending on the time saved. Under this system a standard time is fixed for performing a job. If a worker can perform the job within the time less than standard time, he is eligible to get bonus at his specific rate of wages for a percentage of time saved. Standard time in determined on the basis of time and motion study.

The object of a premium plan is to increase production by giving inducement in the form of bonus as a reward of a worker's efficiency.

The incentive wage payment plans are useful both for employees and employers. Employees are benefited by increased earnings while the employer gets the benefit of cost reduction.

The difference between premium bonus and efficiency bonus is that the former is a system of initial remuneration of a direct labour who completes the job in less than the alloted time while efficiency bonus is the additional remuneration which may be paid to both direct and indirect workers.

4.61 Fundamentals of Good Premium Bonus plan

1. Standard time should be fixed on the basis of careful time and motion study.
2. Standard time should be guranteed.
3. The plan should be simple and easily understandable to the workers.
4. It should appear reasonable both to the employer and employees.
5. The workers should be rewarded generously for increased output.
6. The incentive should be sufficiently high for the more efficient worker.
7. The standard one fixed should not be unnecessarily altered.
8. The employees' earnings should not be affected by the matters beyond his control. He should be compensated for break-downs and other hold-ups for which he is not responssible.
9. The scheme should be coupled with a sound routine of inspections to ensure that workers are paid only for good production.
10. The scheme should facilitate supervision and assist in production control. If possible, it should provide a basis for budgetary control and standard costing.
11. The main aim of the scheme should Influence the worker's morale. Every effort should be made to promote workers' understanding of the scheme and their support for it.
12. The scheme must take account of any relevant national or local trade agreement.
13. The scheme should provide for worthwhile and attainable objectives, with standards of performance not beyond the capabilities of the average worker.

4.62 Limitations of Premium Bonus Plan

The following are the limitations of incentive scheme :

1. It is the common belief among the workers that the scheme in operation is complicated

2. Generally the workers are of opinion that the standard time set for performing a job is unfair and standards are set by using fast workers underrating efforts.
3. A belief among workers exists that workers are treated as commodities. They feel that their opinions and feelings are not considered at the time of making time study.
4. The incentive wage system becomes successful only when the workers have confidence in Company's management.
5. Workers believe that incentive schemes are so formulated so as to confuse them and exploit their ignorance.

The following are some of the important Premium Bonus Schemes :

(i) Halsey Plan ; (ii) Halsey-Weir Plan ; (iii) Rowan Plan ; (iv) Bedaux Point Scheme
(v) Emerson's Efficiency Scheme.

1. **Halsey Plan**

This scheme was originated by F. A. Halsey in 1891. In this plan time rate is guaranteed. A standard time is fixed for the performance of a particular job. If a worker can complete the job before standard time, he is paid bonus for the time saved at a fixed percentage. The percentage varies from 30% to 70%. Generally, the worker is paid bonus @ 50% of standard time saved.

$$\text{Total wages} = \text{Time taken} \times \text{Rate} + \frac{50}{100} \text{ of Time saved} \times \text{Rate per hour.}$$

Under the Halsey Premium Plan, with time wages guaranteed up to standard, the employee receives time wages until he produces in less than standard time. For production above standard, the employee's remuneration is increased by the addition of a bonus, but as the savings are shared with the employer the rate of increase is lower than under straight piece-work.

Labour cost falls sharply as output increases up to standard, in the same way as it does with straight time rates. The cost per unit continues to fall when output exceeds standard, but it does not do so as rapidly as before.

4.63 Advantages of Halsey Plan

1. *Simplicity*

This scheme is simple to operate. It is also easily understandable to all workers. The worker knows the method of calculating the premium.

2. *Efficiency is rewarded*

Individual efficiency of workers is taken care of and rewarded.

3. *Benefit of time saved*

Benefit of time saved is equally shared by the employer and employee.

4. *Increased labour productivity*

Since worker is motivated in a better way, his earnings increase which leads to increased productivity.

5. *Feeling of security*

As the plan assures a minimum hourly rate or guaranteed wage, it helps to create a feeling of security among workers. Moreover, if a worker fails to perform his job well, he is not penalised.

6. *Reduction in fixed overhead*

Fixed overhead cost per unit comes down because of increased production.

4.64 Disadvantages

1. *Not scientific*

The plan is not scientific since it is difficult to fix standard time for a particular job.

2. *Quality deteriorates*

As the workers are attracted by higher income they complete the job in hurry as a result of which quality may suffer.

3. *More labour cost*

If the standard time cannot be properly fixed, the amount of bonus payable to workers may involve a large amount of money.

4. *More wastage, spoilage, defectives etc.*

As the worksers do the work hastily to earn more, there are possibilities of more wastage and defective goods resulting in high labour cost per unit.

2. **Halsey -Weir Plan**

The Halsey plan was modified by Weir. This is based on $33\frac{1}{3}\% : 66\frac{1}{3}\%$ sharing plan.

Worker's earning = Time taken × Rate per hour + ($33\frac{1}{3}\%$ of time saved × Rate per hour.)

Problem 5

Standard Time = 12 hours

Time taken = 8 hours

Time Rate = Rs. 5.00 per hour.

Compute the total earnings under Halsey and Halsey-Weir Plans.

Solution

Earnings under Halsey Plan

Total Earnings $= T \times R + 50\%$ of time saved $\times$ R. $= 8 \times 5 + \left(\frac{50}{100} \times 4 \times 5\right)$

= Rs. 40 + Rs. 10 = Rs. 50.

Under Halsey-Weir Plan

Earnings $= T \times R + \left(33\frac{1}{3}\% \text{ of time saved } \times R\right) = 8 \times 5 + \left(\frac{1}{3} \times 4 \times 5\right)$

= Rs. 40 + Rs. 6.67 = Rs. 46.67.

4.65 Rowan Plan

Games Rowan was the first to introduce the scheme in 1898. This scheme is similar to Halsey Plan. Under this scheme bonus is calculated as the proportion of time taken which the time saved bears to the time allowed. The bonus is paid at time rates. The Rowan Scheme protects the employer from loose rate-fixing by reducing the bonus at high production levels. For this reason this scheme of bonus is unpopular with the workers. The important features of this plan are (i) there is guaranteed day wage and (ii) the incentive is based on time worked compared with the standard time for completing the job.

Calculation of bonus

$$\text{Bonus} = \frac{\text{Time taken}}{\text{Time allowed}} \times \text{time saved} \times \text{time rate}$$

or

$$= \frac{\text{Time saved}}{\text{Standard Time}} \times \text{time taken} \times \text{rate per hour}$$

Problem 6

A worker takes 10 hours to complete a job on daily wages and 6 hours on a scheme of payment by results. His day rate is Rs. 5.00 an hour. The material cost of the product is Rs.10 and the overheads are recovered at 150% of the total direct wages. Calculate the factory cost of the product under Rowan Plan.

Solution

	Rs.
Wages for actual time taken 6 × Rs. 5.00 =	30.00
Bonus = $\frac{\text{Time taken}}{\text{Time allowed}} \times$ time sage × rates	
= $\frac{6}{10} \times 4 \times$ Rs. 5.00	12.00
	42.00

Computation of Factory Cost

Materials Cost	10.00
Add : Wages	42.00
Add : overhead @ 150% of wages $\frac{150}{100} \times 42$	63.00
	115.00

4.66 Advantages of Rowan Plan

1. Increased production is one of the important advantages of Rowan Plan.
2. The benefit arising out of increased production is shared also by the employer.
3. Up to 50% of the time saved the rate of bonus is higher than that under Halsey Plan. So, relatively slow workers enjoy good incentive.
4. It protects the employer against loose rate-setting.
5. As the premium increases at a decreasing rate above 50% of time saved, the employees do not complete the job quickly, so wastage and defective goods are less.
6. This scheme encourages the employer to better the working conditions.
7. The system is encouraging to beginners and learners.

4.67 Disadvantages

1. It is a complicated system which the workers do not understand easily.
2. At higher level of production, the incentive becomes lower. So, above a point of higher production, the efficient workers feel discouraged to produce more since there is a ceiling of bonus above a certain level of production.
3. If the standard of Plant and Machinery, Tools, Materials and Working condition cannot be maintained, the scheme will fail to serve any useful purpose.

GRAPH OF COMPARATIVE EARNINGS UNDER ALTERNATIVE BONUS SCHEMES.

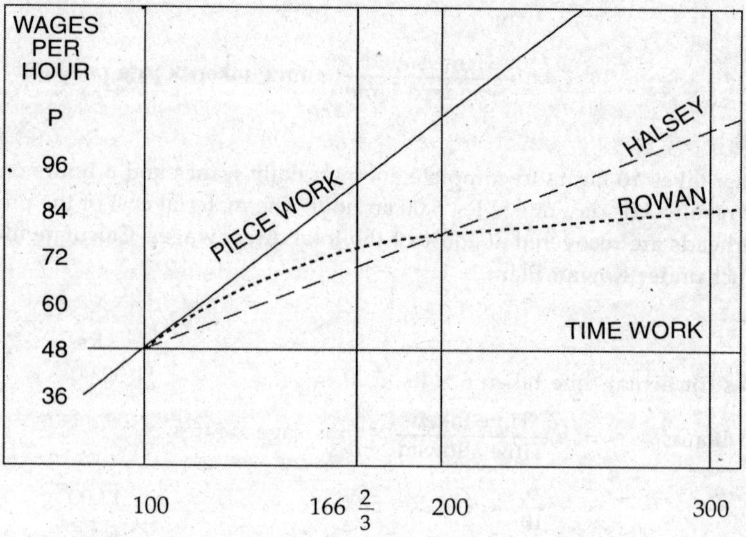

PRODUCTION–PIECES PER HOUR

(Time rate 48p pr hour. *Time allowed 1 hour per 100. + Production level for normal incentive earnings $166\frac{2}{3}$ per hour.)

It will be seen that the Rowan plan provides a better bonus than the Halsey 50-50 scheme until the job is performed in half standard time, when the bonus is the same under both schemes. When the job is completed in less than half the standard time the Rowan bonus is smaller than the Halsey one. It will also be seen that on the basis of the above figures 84p, or time plus 40 per cent is being paid under the Rowan scheme when the job is performed at normal incentive speed.

It has been shown that the bonus under the Rowan scheme rises faster than that under the Halsey until the job is performed in half the standard time. As the bonus is an increasing proportion of a reducing number of hours the increase in earnings beyond this point is relatively small and wages can never be doubled. The Rowan scheme is used extensively where it is difficult to set accurate standard times. It provides a good incentive while protecting the employer against a claim of unreasonably high wages.

4.68 Points of distinction between the Halsey Plan and the Rowan Plan

The following are the points of distinction between Halsey and Rawan Plan of Wage payment :

(i) Under the Halsey Plan the rate of bonus varies between $33\frac{1}{3}\%$ and $66\frac{2}{3}\%$ of the wages of time saved. But under Rowan Plan premium rate is fixed and is calculated as follows :

$$\frac{S - T}{S} \times T \times R$$

(ii) Under Halsey Plan the rate of premium is usually 50% which does not serve as a strong incentive for relatively more efficient worker. On the other hand, under the Rowan Plan, bonus is paid on the basis of ratio of time saved and standard time in relation to time taken. So, it provides a strong incentive to more efficient worker.

(iii) The effective labour rate per hour in the Rowan Plan is higher up to 50% of the time saved and fall thereafter. Under Halsey Plan, the effective labour rate per hour is lower up to 50% of the time saved and can be doubled thereafter. For this reason, workers who cannot save 50% of standard time prefer Rowan Scheme.

(iv) Under Halsey Plan, quality of work does suffer because to earn more bonus the workers go for quantity rather than for quality. But this does not happen in case of Rowan Plan because bonus increases at a diminishing rate at higher level of efficiency.

4.69 Bedaux Point Plan

Under this Plan an hourly guaranteed rate is paid until standard production is attained. Additional wage is paid for units in excess of standard.

The workers are paid the basic time wages and wages @ 75% of time saved, the remaining 25% of time saved is paid to personnel who help to attain the standard.

The formula for calculation of earnings is :

$$W = T \times R + \frac{75}{100} \times B's \times \frac{R}{60}, \text{ where}$$

W = Total wages ; T = time worked ; R = time rate, B's = Number of points (B's) saved. (Note : Number of points means time units. The time unit is one minute, which is known as B. Thus, where the standard time is one hour for a job, it consists of 60B's.).

Problem 7

Standard points (B's) for a job are 360 and actual number of points earned are 400. If the hourly rate is Rs. 6.00, calculate the wages under the Bedaux Plan.

Solution

$$W = T \times R + \frac{75}{100} \times B's \times \frac{R}{60}$$

$$= W = 6 \text{ hours} \times 6 + \left(\frac{75}{100} \times 40 \times \frac{6}{60}\right) = W = \text{Rs. } 36.00 + \text{Rs. } 3.00 = \text{Rs. } 39.00$$

4.70 Emerson Efficiency Plan

Under the Emerson Efficiency Plan minimum daily wage is guaranteed. A standard time for each job is determined. This plan is a combination of time and piece rates. The features of this plan are :

1. A standard output or time is fixed which serves as a yardstick of measuring efficiency of each worker.
2. Actual performance is compared with the standard to ascertain the amount of bonus.
3. Minimum basic time wage is guaranteed to all types of workers.

Calculation of bonus

Efficiency of each worker is determined by dividing actual hours into the standard time for the units produced. Emerson suggested that bonus should be paid if a worker attains $66\frac{2}{3}\%$ efficiency of the standard set and, thereafter, a graded scale of bonus has been suggested. He used 2 differentials so that each worker can enjoy the maximum benefit.

Group Incentive Plans

Group Bonus system is employed in cases where the ultimate production is dependent on the efficiency of a group of workers. In some cases a job is divided into different operations, each of which is performed by a different worker but the operations are very much interlinked in such a manner that the whole work is completed by the collective efforts of a group of persons. The important feature of this system is that a man's work depends on the work done by one or more of his colleagues. The workers forming a group is treated as a unit and the combined output of the unit is measured for the purpose of wage payment.

Advantages

Group system of payment enjoys the following advantages :

(i) It encourages the sense of cooperation and team-work among the workers. This leads to increased productivity and has positive impact on labour relations which is very much needed for increased production.

(ii) This system discourages absenteeism.

(iii) A less efficient worker can be identified by the efficient co-workers of the team. This reduces supervision cost.

(iv) It involves less clerical work and the use of stationery is reduced because the production of the individual worker is not recorded, the production of the group only is recorded. As a result, costing record becomes simple and less complicated.

(v) It helps to achieve maximum production at minimum cost by reducing spoilage, idle time etc.

Disadvantages

(i) Careful selection of workers who are to constitute the group is necessary. If the composition of the group is heterogeneous, with variations of skill, efficiency and seniority of individual workers, there may arise some discontent.

(ii) An efficient worker is economically penalised for his efficiency for he has to share the reward with other inefficient, if any, co-workers.

(iii) Rivalry among the members of the group may defeat the very object of the system.

(iv) Calculation of wages becomes complicated.

Area of Application

Group bonus scheme can generally be employed :

(i) Where individual output cannot be measured;

(ii) When the output of a product depends on the combined efforts of a group;

(iii) Where management wishes to encourage team spirit.

The following problem will clarify the method.

Problem 8

Following cost information is available for a week. Standard production – 100 units per work. No. of workers in a group – 10. Bonus – for every 10% increase in production a bonus of Rs. 200 will be shared prorata among the workers of the group.

Actual production 150 units.

Calculate bonus payable to each member of the group.

Solution

Actual production	—	150 units	
Standard production	—	100 units	
Increase in productionin percentage	—	50%	
Bonus–for each 10% @ Rs. 200		=	5×200 = Rs. 1,000
Therefore, Bonus for each worker		=	$\frac{1,000}{10}$ = Rs. 100

The important group bonus schemes are :

(i) Budgeted expense bonus, (ii) Cost defficiency bonus, (iii) Priestman System

Some Formula for Calculation of Bonus

Bonus Scheme	*Formula*
1. Halsey	50% of Time Saved × Rate per hour
2. Halsey – Wier	$33\frac{1}{3}$% of Time Saved × Time Rate
3. Rowan	$\frac{\text{Time save}}{\text{Time Allowed}}$ × Time Taken × Time Rate.
4. Gantt's Task and Bonus Plan	(i) Output below standard Time rate is guaranteed (ii) Output at Standard — Bonus is 20% of time rate. (iii) Output above standard High piece rate on the entire output.
5. Taylor's Differential Piece Rate	There are two or more fixed piece rates. One piece rate is used for production below standard and a higher rate when production is higher than standard.
6. Taylor's Differential Piece Rate	Up to $83\frac{1}{3}$% of efficiency – Normal piece rate. Above $83\frac{1}{3}$% but up to 100%–10% above normal rate. Above 100%—20% above normal rate

Contd.

Bonus Scheme	*Formula*
7. Emeson's Efficiency Differential Piece Rate	Standard time is set for each job or operation or a volume of output. (i) Below 66.7% efficiency—payment is at hourly rate. (ii) Above 66.7% but up to 100% efficiency = Hourly Rate × Time Taken plus increas in bonus according to degree of efficiency. (iii) Above 100% efficiency—additional bonus of 1% of the hourly rate for each 1% increase in efficiency.
8. Barth Timing Plan	$\sqrt{\text{Standard time} \times \text{Time Taken} \times \text{Rate per hour}}$

Problem 9

Ronalled Limited operates in one of its departments a group incentive scheme. A minimum hourly rate is guaranteed to each of the six employees in the group if actual output for the week is less than the standard output. If actual output is greater than the standard output, the hourly rate of each employee is increased by 4% for each additional 600 units of output produced. The standard output for the group is 12,000 units for a 40 hour week.

During the week ended December 31, 1989 each employee in the group worked 40 hours ; actual output and minimum hourly rates were as follows :

Employee	*Actual output (in units)*	*Minimum hourly rate*
Lal	2,500	0.60
Hari	2,700	1.00
Mohan	2,400	0.60
Shyam	2,500	0.80
Hanuman	2,460	0.60
Krishna	2,440	0.40

You are required to :

(i) Calculate the earnings of each employee.

(ii) Appraise the effectiveness to the company of this group incentive scheme.

[Adapted—C.A. Final]

Solution

Statement showing the earning of each employee in the group during the week ending 31st December, 1989.

Employee	*Minimum*	*Hourly premium*	*Total*		*Total wages for the week*
	Re.	Re.	Re.		Rs.
Lal	0.60	0.12	0.72 × 40	=	28.80
Hari	1.00	0.20	1.20 × 40	=	48.00
Mohan	0.60	0.12	0.72 × 40	=	28.80
Shyam	0.80	0.16	0.96 × 40	=	38.40
Hanuman	0.60	0.12	0.72 × 40	=	28.80
Krishna	0.40	0.08	0.48 × 40	=	19.20
					192.00

Working Notes :

1. Calculation of percentage increase in the hourly wage rate due to higher efficiency :

	Output (40 hrs. week)
Standard	12,000 units
Actual	15,000 units
Additional production	3,000 units

Increase in wage rate is 4%

for each additional 600 units.

Therefore, total increase $= \dfrac{3{,}000 \times 4}{600} = 20\%$

2. There is a saving of Rs. 8 (Standard Wages Rs. 200–Actual Wage Rs. 192). This saving has been shared both by the employer and employee.

3. Standard wages $= \dfrac{160 \times 15{,}000}{12{,}000} =$ Rs. 200.

Problem 10

Ten men work as a group. Where the weekly production of the group exceeds standard (200 pieces per hour) each man of the group is paid a bonus for the excess production in addition to his wages at hourly rates. The bonus is computed thus :

The percentage of production in excess of the standard amount is found and one half of this percentage is considered as the man's share. Each man in the group is paid as a bonus this percentage of wage rate of £ 0.665 per hour. There is no relationship between the individual workman's hourly rate and the bonus rate. The following is one week's record :

	Hours worked	Production
Monday	90	22,100
Tuesday	88	20,600
Wednesday	90	24,200
Thursday	84	20,100
Friday	88	20,400
Saturday	40	10,200
	480	1,17,600

(a) Compute the rate and amount of bonus for the week.

(b) Compute the total pay of Jones who worked 41.5 hours and was paid £ 0.475 per hour basic, and of Smith who worked 44.5 hours and was paid £ 0.525 per hour basic.

[Adapted—I.C.M.A.]

Solution

We shall have to find out the percentage of excess production in relation to standard.

Actual Production	1,17,600 units
Standard output 200 × 480 hours	96,000 units
Excess Production	21,600 units

Percentage of excess production over standard $\frac{21,600}{96,000} \times 100 = 22.5\%$

Men's share of bonus being the half $= \frac{22.5}{2} = 11.25\%$

Bonus Rate @ 11.25% of £ 0.665 = £ 0.0748 per hour (approx.)

Amount = 480 hours @ £ 0.0748 = £ 35.90.

Statement showing the total wages

Worker	*Hours worked*	*Rate per* *Basic*	*Bonus*	*Basic wages (Hrs × Rate)*	*Bonus (e)*	*Total wages*
	(a)	(b)	(c)	(d) = (a × b)	= (a × c)	(d + e)
Jones	41.5	£ 0.475	£ 0.0748	£ 19.712	£ 3.104	£ 22.816
Smith	44.5	£ 0.525	£ 0.0748	£ 23.362	£ 3.328	£ 26.690

4.74 Bonus Schemes for Indirect Workers

Introduction of Incentive schemes for indirect workers is essential for increasing efficiency of service they provide to direct labour or to induce the supervisory staff in the factory to increase the efficiency of the department concerned and thereby to reduce overhead costs. Since it is very difficult to measure the output of indirect workers it becomes necessary to group indirect workers with the group of direct workers with whom they are directly associated. This will facilitate the computation of bonus on the basis of the output of the direct workers.

In order to determine the suitable scheme for giving bonus to indirect workers, they may be grouped as follows :

(i) Those who are directly associated with the direct workers and,

(ii) Those who render some general services e.g., maintenance workers, ambulance men, canteen workers, sweepers etc.

4.75 Bonus to foremen and supervisors

Supervisors and foremen are paid bonus which is based upon :

(i) Output of the department ;

(ii) Quality of the product ;

(iii) Saving in time ;

(iv) Reduction of waste, spoilage, defective goods ;

(v) Reduction in labour turnover.

4.76 Bonus to the executives and the clerical staff

Bonus for executives and clerical staff is paid out of profit of the concern. Bonus is fixed on the basis of efficiency in performance of each department.

4.77 Bonus to repairs and maintenance staff

Group bonus system can be introduced on the basis of performance of the department i.e. reduction in the number of complaints or reduction in breakdown of machinery, vehicle etc.

WORKED OUT PROBLEMS

Problem 11

From the following data ascertain the total earnings of each worker separately under (i) Halsey Scheme (ii) Rowan Scheme. Also calculate the effective hourly rate of wages of the workers under both the schemes :

Name of workers	Amal	Bimal
Time Allowed (Hours)	5	5
Actual time taken (Hours)	4	6
Basic rate of wages per hour	Rs. 3.00	Rs. 3.00

[C.U. B.Com. (Hons.) 1990]

Solution

	Amal	Bimal
(a) Time allowed	5 hours	5 hours
(b) Time Taken	4 hours	6 hours
Time saved.(a – b)	1 hour	Nil

	Halsey Plan	Rowan Plan
Amal	$4 \times 3 + \left(\frac{50}{100} \times 1 \times 3\right)$	$4 \times 3 + \left(\frac{1}{5} \times 4 \times 3\right)$
	= Rs. 12 + 1.50 = Rs. 13.50	= Rs. 12 + 2.40 = Rs. 14.40
Bimal	Rs. 18.00	Rs. 18.00

Effective hourly rate

	Halsey Plan	Rowan Plan
Amal	Rs. 13.50 ÷ 4 = Rs. 3.375 p.h.	Rs. 14.40 ÷ 4 = Rs. 3.60 p.h.
Bimal	Rs. 3.00 p.h. (Rs. 18 ÷ 6)	Rs. 3.00 p.h. (Rs. 18 ÷ 6).

Problem 12

During a certain week in the month of September, 1987, a worker manufactured 240 articles. Working hours during a week are 48 hours, standard rate Rs. 5.00 per hour and standard time to manufacture an article is 15 minutes. Calculate his gross wages for the week according to :

(i) Piece work with guaranteed weekly wages

(ii) Rowan Premium Bonus Plan.

(iii) Halsey Premium Bonus Plan.

[C.U. B.Com. Hons. – 1988]

Solution

1. Standard time for producing 240 article is

$$\frac{240}{60} \times 15 = 60 \text{ hours}$$

2. Time taken = 48 hours

Time Saved 12 hours.

3. Wages for the week = 48 × Rs. 5 = Rs. 240

Standard production during the week $\frac{240 \times 48}{60}$ = **192 pieces**

Piece Rate Rs. 240 ÷ 192 = Rs. 1.25

(i) Wages according to piece rate = 240 × 1.25 = **Rs. 300.00**

(ii) Wages according to Rowan Plan

Wages =

$$\text{Time taken} \times \text{Rate per hour} + \left(\frac{\text{Time saved}}{\text{Time allowed}} \times \text{Time taken} \times \text{Rate}\right)$$

$$\text{Wages} = (48 \times 5) + \left(\frac{12}{60} \times 48 \times 5\right) = \text{Rs. } 240 + 48 = \textbf{Rs. 288}$$

(iii) Wages according to Halsey Plan

$$\text{Wages} = \text{Time taken} \times \text{Rate} + \left(\frac{50}{100} \times \text{Time saved} \times \text{Rate per hour}\right)$$

$$\text{So, Wages} = 48 \times \text{Rs. } 5 + \left(\frac{50}{100} \times 12 \times 5\right) = \text{Rs. } 240 + 30 = \textbf{Rs. 270.}$$

Problem 13

From the data given below, calculate the comparative Works Cost for a job in Factory A and Factory B :

	Factory A	**Factory B**
Method of payment of wages	Halsey Plan (50%)	Rowan Plan
Standard time for the job	250 hours	240 hours
Actual time taken	200 hours	210 hours
Hourly rate of wages	Rs. 2.50	Rs. 3.00
Material cost for the job	Rs. 1,000	Rs. 900
Factory Overhead	150% of wages	$133\frac{1}{3}$% of wages.

[C.U. B.Com. (Hons.)1986]

Solution

	Factory A	*Factory B*
1. Calculation of Bonus	50% of time saved × Rate	$\frac{\text{Time saved}}{\text{Time allowed}}$ × Time taken × Rate per hour
=	$\frac{50}{100}$ × (250–200) × 2.5	$\frac{240-210}{240}$ × 210 × 3
=	$\frac{50}{100}$ × 50 × 2.50 = Rs. 62.50	$\frac{18,900}{240}$ = Rs. 78.75
2. Total Wages= Time wages + Bonus		Time wages + Bonus
=	(200 × Rs. 2.50) + Rs. 62.50	= (210 × Rs. 3.000) + Rs. 78.75
=	Rs. 500 + 62.50 = Rs. 562.50	= Rs. 630 + 78.75 = Rs. 708.75

3. Computation of Factory Cost

	A	B
	Rs.	Rs.
Cost of Materials	1,000	900
Add : Wages	562.50	708.75
Add : Factory overheads @ 150% of wages	843.75	945.00
	2,406.25	2,553.75

Problem 14

The following piece rate system is followed in a small concern manufacturing a single product :

(i) Basic piece rate up to 85% efficiency.

(ii) 110% of basic piece rate between 85% and 100% efficiency.

(iii) 120% of basic piece rate above 100% efficiency.

Guaranteed day rate is equal to 70% efficiency. Assuming that 100% efficiency is 100 pieces per day of 8 hours and the piece rate is 50 paise per piece, calculate labour cost per piece at 5% intervals between 60% and 120% efficiency.

[Adapted—I.C.W.A. Inter]

Solution

1. Guaranted piece rate up to 60% efficiency = 70 × 0.50 = Rs. 35.00

   Piece rate = Rs. $\frac{35}{60}$ = Re. 0.583

2. Guaranted piece rate up to 65% efficiency = $\frac{70 \times 0.50}{65}$ = Re. 0.538

3. Guaranteed piece rate from 70% to 85% efficiency = $\frac{35}{70}$ = Re. 0.50

4. Piece rate from 90% to 100% efficiency = 110% of basic rate = $\frac{110}{100}$ × 0.50 = Re. 0.55 paise

5. Piece rate above 100% = 120% of basic piece rate = $\frac{120}{100}$ × 0.50 = Re. 0.60

Statement showing labour cost per piece different efficiency levels at 5% interval from 60% to 120%

Level of efficiency	60%	65%	70%	75%	80%	85%	90%	95%	100%	105%	110%	115%	120%
Labour Cost per piece (Re)	0.583	0.538	0.50	0.50	0.50	0.50	0.55	0.55	0.55	0.60	0.60	0.60	0.60

Problem 15

Calculate the normal and overtime wages payable to a workman on the basis of the following particulars :

Days	Hours worked
Monday	9
Tuesday	8
Wednesday	10
Thursday	11
Friday	9
Saturday	5

Normal working hours are 8 hours per day and the normal rate of wages is Rs. 1.25 per hour. Overtime pay is at the undernoted rates :

Up to 9 hours in a day at single rate and over 9 hours in a day at double rate. Or, up to 48 hours in a week at single rate and over 48 hours at double rate.

Whichever is more beneficial to the workman ?

[Adapted—C.U. B.Com. (Hons.)]

Solution

Calculation of total wages on Daily Basis

Day	*Hours worked*	*Hours at normal rate*	*Overtime hours*	
			at Single rate	*at Double rate*
Monday	9	8	1	–
Tuesday	8	8	–	–
Wednesday	10	8	1	1
Thursday	11	8	1	2
Friday	9	8	1	–
Saturday	5	5	–	–
Total	52	45	4	3

Total wages on hourly basis Rs.

		Rs.
(i)	Normal wages for 45 hours @ Rs. 1.25	56.25
(ii)	Overtime wages at single rate for 4 hrs @ Rs. 1.25 = 4 × 1.25	5.00
(iii)	Overtime wages at double rate for 3 hours @ Rs. 2.50 = 3 × 2.50	7.50
	Total wages (i + ii + iii)	68.75

Total Wages on weekly basis

Overtime on weekly basis = 52 – 48	4 hrs.
Normal wages at single rate for 48 hours @ Rs. 1.25 = 48 × 1.25	Rs. 60.00
Overtime at double rate for 4 hrs @ Rs. 2.50 (1.25 × 2) = 4 × 2.50	Rs. 10.00
Total wages	Rs. 70.00

From the above calculations it can be concluded that the total wages on weekly basis is more beneficial to the workman as he gets Rs. 1.25 (70 – 68.75) more than what he is supposed to receive on hourly basis.

Problem 16

From the following particulars given below, prepare the labour cost per man day of 8 hours :

(a)	Basic Pay	Rs. 10.00 per day
(b)	Dearness Allowance	Re. 1.00 for every point over 100 cost of living Index. Current cost of Living Index – 1,000 points
(c)	Leave Salary	20% of (a) and (b).
(d)	Employer's contribution to Provident Fund	10% of (a), (b) & (c)
(e)	Employer's contribution to State Insurance	2.5% of (a), (b) & (c)
(f)	Expenditure on amenities to labour	Rs. 20 per head per mensem (p.m.)
(g)	No. of working days in a month	26 days of 8 hours each.

Solution

Statement of labour cost per day

		Labour cost per day Rs.
(a) Basic pay		10.00
(b) Dearness Allowance for 900 points @ Re. 1.00 per point	$\frac{900 \times 1}{26} = \frac{900}{26} =$	34.61
		44.61
(c) Leave Salary @ 20% of Rs. 44.61		8.92
		53.53
(d) Employer's contributioin to Provident Fund @ 10% of (a), (b) & (c) =	$\frac{10}{100} \times 53.53$	5.35
(e) Employer's contribution to State Insurance @ 2.5%	$\frac{25}{100} \times 53.53$	1.33
(f) Expenditure on amenities =	$\frac{20}{26}$	0.77
		60.98

Problem 17

Ram Pujan Singh works in a factory where the following rates apply :

Normal rate per hour – Rs. 2.50

Normal piece rate – 20% more of time rate.

Expected output 25 units per hour. Ram Pujan Singh produces 150 units in a eight hour day. Calculate his wages for the day on (i) Time Basis and (ii) Piece Basis.

Solution

(i) **Wages on Time Basis**

No. of hours worked × Rate per hour = 8 × Rs. 2.50 per hour = Rs. 20.

(ii) **On Piece Basis**

Normal rate	Rs. 2.50	per hour
Add : 20% of normal rate –	0.50	
	Rs. 3.00	

$$\text{Piece rate} = \frac{3.00}{25} = 0.12 \text{ Paise per piece}$$

$$\text{Total wages} = \text{Piece} \times \text{rate per piece} = 150 \text{ units} \times 0.12 = 150 \times \frac{12}{100} = \text{Rs. } 18$$

Problem 18

Following are the particulars for April 1999 relating to four employees working in Department 'M' of a factory, exclusively for Job No. 120.

Name	Designation	Wages Rs.	P.m./p. day
A	Foreman	800	p.m.
B	Mechanic	15	p.d.
C	Machine Operator	12	p.d.
D	Workman	10	p.d.

The normal working hours per week of six days are 48, at 8 hours per day. Sundays are paid holidays. There was no other holiday during the month.

Provident fund contribution was 8% of monthly wages by the employee.

Provident Fund Contribution was 8% of monthly wages by the employer.

Employee State Insurance contribution was 3% of monthly wages by employee and 5% of monthly wages by employer.

From the foregoing data, calculate :

(a) Net wages payable by the employer for the month.

(b) The total amount of Provident Fund contribution to be deposited by the employer.

(c) Employee's State Insurance contribution to be deposited by the employer.

d) Total labour cost to the employer for the month of April chargeable to the job and

(e) The total cost of the job requiring materials valued at Rs. 6,000 and overheads at 50% of prime cost.

[Adapted—I.C.W.A. (Inter)]

Solution

(a) Net wages payable

		Rs.
Gross wages for April, 1999		
A Foreman @ Rs. 800 p.m.		800.00
B Mechanic @ Rs. 15 per day	= 15 × 30	450.00
C Machine operator @ Rs. 12	= 12 × 30	360.00
D Workman @ Rs. 10 per day	= 10 × 30	300.00
		1,910.00

			Rs.
B.F.			1,910
	Less : Deductions :		
(i)	Employees own contribution to Provident Fund		
	@ 8% of wages i.e. $\frac{8}{100} \times 1,910$ =	152.80	
(ii)	E.S.I. contribution @ 3% = $\frac{3}{100} \times 1,910$	57.30	210.10
			16,99.90
(b)	Total amount of Provident fund to be deposited :		
	Employees' own contribution		152.80
	Employer's contribution to P. F.		152.80
			305.60
(c)	Employee's State Insurance		
	Employees' share of E.S.I. (5% of Rs. 1910) =		95.50
	Employer's share of E.S.I. (3% of Rs. 1910) =		57.30
			152.80
(d)	Total Labour Cost		
	Gross wages (a)		1,910.00
	Employer's share of P.F.		152.80
	Employer's share of E.S.I.		95.50
			2,158.30
(e)	**Total cost of Job**		
	Materials		6,000.00
	Labour cost (as per d)		2,158.30
	PRIME COST		8,158.30
Add :	Overheads at 50% of Prime Cost		4,079.15
	Total Cost of the Job		12,237.45

Problem 19

A worker takes 48 hours to do a job for which the time allowed is 60 hours. His wage rate is Rs. 10 per hour.

Calculate the works cost of the job under the following methods of payment of wages :

(a) Halsey Plan, (b) Rowan Plan.

Additional information

Material cost Rs. 1,000

Overheads @ 150% of wages.

[C.U. B.Com (Pass) 1997]

Solution

Halsey Plan :

Time Saved = Time Allowed – Time Taken = 60 hrs – 48 hrs = 12 hours

Formula

Time Taken × Rate per hour + (50 % of Time Saved) × Rate per hour.

$$48 \times \text{Rs. } 10 + \left(\frac{50}{100} \times 12\right) \times \text{Rs. } 10$$

= Rs. 480 + (6 × 10) = Rs. 480 + Rs. 60 = Rs. 540

Rowan Plan

Formula

Earning = Hours taken × Rate per hour

$$+ \left(\frac{\text{Time Saved}}{\text{Time Allowed}} \times \text{Time Taken} \times \text{Rate per hour}\right)$$

$$= 48 \times 10 + \left(\frac{12}{60} \times 48 \times 10\right) = \text{Rs. } 480 + \text{Rs. } 96 = 576$$

Cost Sheet Showing Job Cost

	Halsey Plan	Rowan Plan
	Rs.	Rs.
Material Cost	1,000	1,000
Wages	540	576
Overheads @ 150% of wages	810	864
Work Cost	2,350	2,440

Problem 20

Calculate the wages and bonus of a worker from the following particulars :

(a) Rowan Premium Bonus Plan

(b) Halsey Weir Premium Bonus (50% of Time Saved)

Job commenced at 8 a.m. on 1st January. Job completed at 10 a.m. on 6th January. Quantity of work given 680 units. Work actually done 600 units. Time allowed 10 units per hour. Wages allowed for the work Rs. 5 per hour. Assume that a worker has worked 9 hours per day.

Solution

Time Allowed =	10 units per hour	
	So, for 600 units = $\frac{600}{10}$ = 60 hours.	
Hours Worked =	The worker worked for :	
	from 1st January to 5th January	
	@ 9 hours per day =	45 hours
Add :	2 hours on 6th January	
	i.e. from 8 am to 10 a.m	2 "
		47 hours
Time Saved =	Time Allowed – Time worked = 60 – 47 = 13 hours.	

(a) **Rowan Premium Bonus** = Hours worked × Rate per hour

$$+ \left(\frac{\text{Time Saved}}{\text{Time Allowed}} \times \text{Time Taken}\right) \times \text{Rate per hour}$$

$$47 \times \text{Rs. } 5 + \left(\frac{13}{60} \times 47\right) \times \text{Rs. } 5$$

Rs. 235 + Rs. 50.92 = Rs. 285.92

(b) **Halsey Weir Premium**

Formula

Earnings = (Hours worked × Rate per hour) + (50% of Time saved × Rate per hour.)

$$= 47 \times \text{Rs. } 5 + \left(\frac{50}{100} \times 13 \times \text{Rs. } 5\right) = \text{Rs. } 235 + \text{Rs. } 32.50 = \text{Rs. } 267.50$$

Problem 21

A worker takes 6 hours to complete a job under a scheme of payment by results. Standard time allowed for the job is 9 hours. His wage rate is Rs. 1.50 per hour. Material cost of the job is Rs. 16 and overheads are recovered at 150% of total direct wages. Calculate factory cost of the job under (a) Rowan and (b) Halsey. Schemes of incentive payments.

[Adapted—I.C.W.A. (Inter)]

Solution

Standard time 9 hours – time taken 6 hours , Time saved = 9 – 6 = 3 hours.

(i) Earning under Rowan Plan

$$E = T \times R + \left(\frac{TS}{TA} \times \text{Time taken} \times \text{Rate per hour}\right)$$

TS = Time Saved.

TA = Time Allowed

$$= 6 \times 1.50 + \left(\frac{3}{9} \times 6 \times 1.50\right) = 9 + 3 = \text{Rs. } 12$$

(ii) Earnings under Halsey Plan

$$E = T \times R + \left(\frac{50}{100} \times TS \times R\right)$$

$$E = 6 \times 1.50 + \left(\frac{1}{2} \times 3 \times 1.50\right) = \text{Rs. } 9 + 2.25 = \text{Rs. } 11.25$$

Factory Cost of the Job

	Under Rowan Plan	*Halsey Plan*
	Rs.	Rs.
Materials	16.00	16.00
Direct wages (i) & (ii)	12.00	11.25
Overhead @ 150% of wages	18.00	16.87
	46.00	44.12

Problem 22

An analysis of the time card of a worker on a machine shows that of the total 48 hours, he worked 45 hours (including 4 hours overtime) on production and that 3 hours was idle due to machine break down.

The rate of wages is Re. 1.00 per hour, but overtime is paid at 50 per cent extra.

You are required to allocate the total wages paid to the workers between 'direct' and 'indirect' labour indicating reasons thereof.

[C.A. Final]

Allocation of wages

	Total	Direct	Indirect
	Rs.	Rs.	Rs.
Normal wages – 41· × Re. 1.00	41.00	41.00	–
Overtime wages – @ Rs. 1.50 = 4 × 1.50	6.00	4.00	2.00
Idle time wages @ Re. 1.00 = 3 × 1.00	3.00		3.00
	50.00	45.00	5.00

Note : Normal wages for idle time is to be taken as indirect wage as this type of wage is unproductive. Excess wage paid for overtime is also to be treated as indirect wage since it does not contribute any additional production.

Problem 23

From the following particulars, find out the amount of cash required for wages in a factory for a particular month.

		Rs.
(i)	Wages for normal hours worked	20,500
(ii)	Wages for overtime	2,200
(iii)	Leave wages	2,700
(iv)	Deduction of employee's share of State Insurance	500
(v)	Employees contribution to P.F.	1,600
(vi)	House rent is to be recovered from 30 employees @ Rs. 10 p.m.	

[I.C.W.A. Inter]

Solution

Statement showing the payment of wages

		Rs.	Rs.
	Wages for normal hours		20,500
	Wages for overtime		2,200
	Leave wages		2,700
			25,400
	Less : Deductions		
i)	Employee's Contribution to State Insurance	500	
ii)	Employee's Contribution to P.F.	1,600	
iii)	House Rent @ Rs. 10 p.m. for 30 employees – 30 × Rs. 10	300	2,400
	Total cash requirement for wage payment		23,000

Problem 24

Calculate the effective hourly rate of labour wages in the following case where bonus is paid under the Rowan Premium Plan :

Basic rate of wages per hour	–	Rs. 4.50
Time allowed for the job	–	20 hours
Time actually taken	–	16 hours

[C.U. B.Com. Hons.]

Solution

Earning of a labour under Rowan Premium Plan :

Standard time	20 hours
Less : Time taken	16 hours
Time saved	4 hours

$$= \text{Time taken} \times \text{rate} + \left(\frac{\text{Time saved}}{\text{Time Allowed}} \times \text{Time Taken} \times \text{Rate}\right)$$

$$= 16 \times 4.50 + \left(\frac{4}{20} \times 16 \times 4.50\right)$$

$$= 72 + \left(\frac{16}{5} \times 4.50\right)$$

= 72 + 14.40 = Rs. 86.40 total wages.

Effective hourly rate = Rs. 86.40 ÷ 16 hours = Rs. 5.40

Problem 25

From the following data prepare statement showing the cost per day of 8 hours of engaging a particular type of labour :

(a)	Monthly salary (basic plus dearness allowance)	Rs. 200
(b)	Leave salary payable to the workman	5% of salary
(c)	Employer's contribution to Provident Fund	8% of Salary (Items a and b)
(d)	Employer's contribution to State Insurance	$2\frac{1}{2}$% of salary (Items a and b)
(e)	Pro rata expenditure on amenities to labour	Rs. 17.95 per head per month
(f)	No. of working hours in a month	200

Solution

Statement of Cost per day of 8 hours

	Rs.
Monthly salary	200.00
Leave salary – 5% of salary	10.00
Employer's contribution to Provident Fund	
8% of Rs. 210 = $\frac{8}{100}$ × Rs. 210 =	16.80
Employer's contribution to State Insurance	
$2\frac{1}{2}$% of Rs. 210 =	5.25
Pro rata expenditure on amenities to labour	17.95
Total	250.00

Cost per day of 8 hours = Rs. $\frac{250}{25}$ = Rs.10

200 ÷ 8 = 25 days

Problem 26

From the following particulars you are required to calculate under 'Average Wage Rate' the labour cost chargeable to Job No. 'A' which was completed in 1990.

Basic wage rate is Rs. 2 per hour and overtime rates are as follows :

Before or after working hours – 150% of basic wage rate.

Sundays and Holidays – 200% of basic wage rate.

During the year, 1990 the following hours were worked :

Normal time	2,00,000 hours
Overtime before or after working hours	30,000 hours
Overtime on Sundays and holidays	20,000 hours
Total	2,50,000 hours

For Job 'A', 3,500 hours were spent as follows :

Normal time	3,000 hours
Before and after working hours	300 hours
Sundays and Holidays	200 hours

[C.U. B.Com. (Hons) 1991]

Solution

Average wage rate during the previous year

Particulars	*Hours worked*	*Rate per hour* Rs.	*Wages paid* Rs.
Normal time	2,00,000	2	4,00,000
Overtime before or after Working hours	30,000	3	90,000
Overtime on Sunday and Other holidays	20,000	4	80,000
	2,50,000		5,70,000

Therefore, wage rate = Rs. $\dfrac{5,70,000}{2,50,000}$ = Rs. 2.28

Computation of labour cost chargeable to Job No. 'A' under "Average wage rate" :

Particulars	**Job No. 'A'**
Total hours spent	3,500 hrs.
Average wage rate	Rs. 2.28

Therefore, labour cost chargeable = 3,500 hrs. @ Rs. 2.28 per hour = Rs. 7,980.

Problem 27

Calculate the earnings of workers A and B from the following particulars for a month and allocate the earnings to each of the jobs X, Y and Z.

		A	B
(a)	Basic wages	Rs. 100.00	Rs. 100.00
(b)	Dearness Allowance	50%	55%
(c)	Provident Fund (on basic wages)	8%	8%
(d)	Employee's State Insurance (on basic wages)	2%	2%
(e)	Overtime	10 hours	
(f)	Idle time and leave		16 hours

The normal working hours for the month are 200 hours. Overtime is paid at double the normal wages including Dearness Allowance. Employer's contribution to State Insurance and Provident Fund are at equal rate with the employee's contribution. The month contains 25 working days and one paid holiday. Two workers were employed on jobs X, Y and Z in the following proportions :

Job	X	Y	Z
Worker A	40	30	30
Worker B	50	20	30

Overtime was done on job Y.

[Adapted—I.C.W.A. Inter]

Solution

Statement showing Net Earnings of Workers

		A	B
		Rs.	Rs.
	Basic wages	100.00	100.00
	Dearness Allowance @ 50%	50.00	55.00
	Overtime wages (Basic wages + D.A.) [1.50 × 10]	15.00	
		165.00	155.00
Less : (a)	P.F. contribution @ 8% of wages	8.00	8.00
		157.00	147.00
(b)	E.S.I. contribution @ 2% of wages	2.00	2.00
		155.00	145.00

Allocation of Wages to Jobs

Particulars	Total	X	Y	Z
		Jobs		
Worker A	Rs.	Rs.	Rs.	Rs.
Wages (4 : 3 : 3) (Note I)	160.00	64.00	48.00	48.00
Overtime Wages (Note II)	15.00		15.00	
Worker B				
Wages (5 : 2 : 3) (Note I)	165.00	83.00	33.00	49.00 (approx.)
	340.00	147.00	96.00	97.00

Working Notes :

		A	B
(1)	**Calculation of Gross wages**		
	Basic wages	100.00	100.00
Add :	Dearness Allowance @ 50% and 55%	50.00	55.00
Add :	Employer's contribution P.F. @ 8% of basic wages	8.00	8.00
Add :	Employer's contribution to State Insurance @ 2% of wages	2.00	2.00
		160.00	165.00

Note (2) **Calculation of Overtime**

Worker A

Wages and DA = Rs. 150 for 200 hours

So, hourly of rate = $\frac{150}{200}$ = 0.75p. per hour.

Rate of overtime = 0.75 × 2 = Rs. 1.50

(being double)

For 10 hours overtime wages — Rs. 1.50 × 10 = Rs. 15.00

Problem 28

From the following particulars calculate the earning of X, Y and Z under :

a) Time Rate
b) Straight Piece Rate
c) Straight Piece Rate based on std. hours
d) Differential Piece Rate
e) Halsey Scheme
f) Rowan Scheme.

Total hours worked in a week : 48 hrs.

	Hours actually worked	No. of units produced
X	45	400
Y	40	440
Z	36	380

Standard Production per hour	8 units.
Rate per hour	Rs. 2
Rate per piece	25 paise
Differential Piece Rate –	
Production below standard	80% of Normal Rate
100% efficiency	Normal Rate
100% – 110%	105% of Normal Rate
110% – 120%	110% of Normal Rate
Above 120%	115% of Normal Rate

Solution

a) **Earning under Time Rate**

X → 45 hrs	@ Rs. 2	= Rs. 90
Y → 40 "	@ Rs. 2	= Rs. 80
Z → 36 "	@ Rs. 2	= Rs. 72

(b) **Earning under Straight piece Rate**

X → 400 units	@ 25 P.	= Rs. 100
Y → 440 "	@ 25 P.	= Rs. 110
Z → 380 "	@ 25 P.	= Rs. 95

(c) Earning based on Straight Rate on standard hours.

$$\text{Output in terms of standard hours} = \frac{\text{Actual output}}{\text{Standard output per hour}}$$

$$\text{X's standard outut in terms of hrs} = \frac{400}{8} = 50 \text{ hrs.}$$

$$\text{Y's standard output in terms of hrs} = \frac{440}{8} = 55 \text{ hrs.}$$

$$\text{Z's standard output in terms of hrs} = \frac{330}{8} = 47.5 \text{ hrs.}$$

∴ Earning of :

X →	50 hrs	@ Rs. 2	= Rs. 100
Y →	55 hrs	@ Rs. 2	= Rs. 110
Z →	47.5 hrs	@ Rs. 2	= Rs. 95

(d) Earning under Differential piece Rate

$$\text{X's eefficiency} = \frac{400}{384} \times 100 = 104.16\%$$

$$\text{Y's efficiency} = \frac{440}{384} \times 100 = 114.58\%$$

$$\text{Z's efficiency} = \frac{380}{384} \times 100 = 98.95\%$$

[Standard output = 48 hrs × 8 units per hour = 384 units]

$$\therefore \quad \text{X will get @ 105\% of Normal rate} = 0.25 \times \frac{105}{100}$$

$$\text{Y will get @ 110\% of normal rate} = 0.25 \times \frac{110}{100}$$

$$\text{Z will get @ 80\% of normal rate} = 0.25 \times \frac{80}{100}$$

∴ Earning :

$$X = 400 \times 0.25 \times \frac{105}{100} = \text{Rs. } 105$$

$$Y = 440 \times 0.25 \times \frac{110}{100} = \text{Rs. } 121$$

$$Z = 380 \times 0.25 \times \frac{80}{100} = \text{Rs. } 76$$

(e) **Earning under Halsey Scheme** :

Earning = (H.W. × R.P.H.) + (50% × T.S. × R.P.H.)

$$X = 45 \times 2 + \left(\frac{50}{100} \times 5 \times 2\right) = 90 + 5 = \text{Rs. } 95$$

$$Y = 40 \times 2 + \left(\frac{50}{100} \times 15 \times 2\right) = 80 + 15 = \text{Rs. } 95$$

$$Z = 36 \times 2 + \left(\frac{50}{100} \times 5 \times 2\right) = 72 + 11.5 = \text{Rs. } 83.5$$

(f) Earning under Rowan plan

$$\text{Earning} = \text{H.W.} \times \text{R. P. H.} + \frac{\text{T.S}}{\text{T.A.}} \times \text{H.W.} \times \text{R.P.H.})$$

$$X = 45 \times 2 + \left(\frac{5}{50} \times 45 \times 2\right) = 90 + 9 = \text{Rs. } 99.00$$

$$X = 40 \times 2 + \left(\frac{15}{55} \times 40 \times 2\right) = 80 + 21.81 = \text{Rs. } 101.81$$

$$X = 45 \times 2 + \left(\frac{11.5}{47.5} \times 45 \times 2\right) = 90 + 9 = \text{Rs. } 89.43$$

Problem 29

Bharat Shawl Works has introduced the following sliding scale for its workers :

Within the first 10% of saving in Standard time, bonus is	40% of time saved
Within the next 20% of saving in Standard time, bonus is	50% of time saved
Within the next 30% of saving in Standard time, bonus is	60% of time saved
For the balance, bonus is	70% of time saved

Sm. Rekha Paul, a worker whose basic rate per hour is Rs. 2.00, completed a particular job in 120 hours (time allowed 200 hours).

[C.U. B.Com. (Hons.) 1989]

Solution

Standard Time	200 hours
Time Taken	120 hours
Time Saved	80 hours

$$\text{Time saved as a percentage of standard time} = \frac{80 \times 100}{200} = 40\%$$

Calculation of Bonus hours		Bonus Hours	
For the first 20 hours saved i.e. 10% of Standard time	=	40% of 20 hours	= 8 hours
For the next 20% standard time	=	50% of 40 hours	= 20 hours
$\frac{20}{100} \times 2{,}0000 = 40$ hours			
For the last 20 hours i.e. (80–60)	=	60% of 20 hours	= 12 hours
			40 hours

Rekha Paul is entitled to wages including wages for bonus hours

= (120 hours × Rs. 2.00) + (40 hours × Rs. 2.00) = Rs. 240 + Rs. 80 = Rs. 320.

Problem 30

A manufacturing concern has introduced a bonus system of wage payment at a slab rate based on cost reduction towards labour and overheads, the slab rate being :

Up to 10% of saving	—	5% of the earning
Up to 20% of saving	—	15% of the earning
Up to 40% " "	—	30% " " "
Up to 70% " "	—	40% " " "
Over 70% " "	—	50% " " "

The rates per hour for 3 workers X, Y and Z are Re 0.50, Re 0.60 and Re 0.55, respectively.

The overhead recovery rate is 500% on productive wages. The standard cost towards wages and overhead per unit is determined at Rs. 1.20 per unit.

If the time taken by X, Y & Z to finish 100 units is 26 hours, 30 hours and 20 hours respectively, what is the amount of bonus earned by each worker ?

[B.Com. – Madras]

Solution

Statement showing the amount of Bonus

	Particulars	X	Y	Z
	Time taken	26 hrs.	30 hrs.	20 hrs.
(a)	Standard Cost of Wages @ 0.20 per unit	Rs. 20.00	Rs. 20.00	Rs. 20.00
(b)	Actual wages	Rs. 13.00 (26 hrs × Re. 0.50)	Rs. 18.00 (30 hrs × Re. 0.60)	Rs. 11.00 (20 hrs × Re. 0.55)
(c)	Savings in wages (a – b)	Rs. 7.00	Rs. 2.00	Rs. 9.00
(d)	Standard cost of overheads for 100 units @ Re. 1.00 per unit	100.00	100.00	100.00
(e)	Actual overheads being 500% of wages	Rs. 65.00 (13 × 5)	Rs. 90.00 (18 × 5)	Rs. 55.00 (11 × 5)
(f)	Savings in Overheads (d – e)	Rs. 35.00	Rs. 10.00	Rs. 45.00
(g)	Total saving in wages and overheads (c + f)	Rs. 42.00	Rs. 12.00	Rs. 54.00
(h)	Percentage of savings in wages and overheads	35%[1]	10%[2]	45%[3]
(i)	Bonus earned	30% of Rs. 13.00 = Rs. 3.90	5% of Rs. 18.00 = Re. 0.90	40% of Rs. 11.00 = Rs. 4.40

Working Note

Calculation of percentage of savings in wages and overheads :

1. X = Total standard cost of overheads and wages = Rs. 120.00

Total savings = 7 + 35 = Rs. 42.00

So, percentage of savings $= \frac{42 \times 100}{120} = 35\%$

2. Y = Total standard cost = 100 + 20 = Rs. 120.00

Total saving = 10 + 2 = 12

Percentage of savings $= \frac{12 \times 100}{120} = 10\%$

3. Z = Total standard cost = 100 + 20 = Rs. 120

Total savings = 45 + 9 = Rs. 54.

Percentage of savings $= \frac{54 \times 100}{120} = 45\%$

Problem 31

An operator, engaged in machining certain components, receives an ordinary day rate of Rs. 1.60 per day of 8 hours. The standard output for machining the components has been fixed at 80 pieces per hour (time as fixed for premium bonus). On a certain day, the output of the worker on this machine is 800 pieces. Find the labour cost per 100 pieces and the wages that should have been actually earned by the workman under the following :

(a) If a bonus of Re. 0.23 is paid per 100 of the extra output.

(b) If paid for on straight piece work basis at the standard rate.

(c) If Halsey Premium system is being adopted.

[Adapted—I.C.W.A. (Inter)]

Solution

(a) Standard output = $= 8 \times 80 = 640$ units

So, wages for one day for 640 units = Rs. 1.60

Bonus for extra output (800 – 640) $= \left(160 \times \frac{23}{100}\right) =$ Re. 0.37

Total wages per day for 800 units = Rs. 1.97

Labour cost per 100 pieces $= \frac{1.97}{8} =$ Rs. 0.246

(b) Piece rate for 640 pieces = Rs. 1.60

Piece rate for 800 pieces $= \frac{\text{Rs. } 1{\cdot}60 \times 800}{640}$ Rs. 2.00

Labour cost per 100 pieces Rs. 0.25

(c) Wages per day for 640 pieces = Rs. 1.60

Bonus (for half of 160 pieces) $\frac{1.60}{640} \times \frac{50}{100} \times 160$ Rs. 0.20

= Rs. 1.80

Labour cost of 100 pieces = $\frac{1.80}{800} \times 100$ = Re. 0.225

Problem 32

A worker, whose day-work wages is Rs. 2.50 an hour, received production bonus under the Rawan Plan. He carried out the following work in a 48 hour week :

Job 1 — 1,500 items at 4 hours per 1,000

Job 2 — 1,800 items at 3 hours per 1,000

Job 3 — 9,000 items at 6 hours per 1,000

Job 4 — 1,500 items for which no standard time was fixed and it was arranged that the worker would be paid a bonus of 25%. Actual time on the job was 4 hours.

Job 5 —2,000 items at 8 hours each, item was estimated to be half-finished.

Job No 2 was carried out on a machine running at 90% efficiency and an extra allowance of 1/9th of actual time was given to compensate the worker.

4 hours were lost due to power cut. Calculate the earnings of the worker, clearly stating your assumptions for the treatment given by you for the hours lost due to power cut.

[I.C.W.A. (Inter) Dec. 1986]

Calculation of Standard time

		Hours
Job 1—1,500 items at 4 hours per 1,000 =		6.00
Job 2—1,800 items at 3 hours per 1,000 =	5.40	
and extra time $\frac{1}{9}$th	0.60	
		6.00
Job—39,000 items at 6 hours per 1,000 =		54.00
Job 4—1,500 items actual time 4 hours + bonus 25%		5.00
Job 5—1,000 items $\left(\frac{1}{2} \times 2{,}000\right)$ at 8 hours per thousand		8.00
		79 .00 hours

Time taken :

Total time	48 hours
Less : Time lost due to power cut	4 hours
	44 hours

Time saved :

Time allowed – time taken = 79 hours – 44 hours = 35 hours.

Total Earnings :

$$= T \times R + \left(\frac{S-T}{S} \times T \times R\right) = 48 \times 2.5 + \left(\frac{79-44}{79} \times 44 \times 2.50\right)$$

$$= \text{Rs. } 120 + \left(\frac{35}{79} \times 44 \times 2.5\right) = \text{Rs. } 120 + 48.73 = \text{Rs. } 168.73$$

The worker is not entitled to bonus for the lost time caused by power cut.

Problem 33

In a factory, bonus hours are credited to the employee in the proportion of time taken which time saved bears to time allowed. Jobs are carried forward from one week to another. No overtime is worked and payment is made in full for all units worked on, including those subsequently rejected. From the following, you are required to calculate for each employee :

(i) the bonus hours and the amount of bonus earned ;

(ii) the total cost ;

(iii) the wage cost of each good unit produced

Employee	A	B	C
Basic wage rate per hour	Rs. 5	Rs. 8	Rs. 7.50
Units issued for production	2,500	2,200	3,600
Time allowed for 100 units	2 hrs 36 mts	3 hrs.	1 hr. 30 mts.
Time taken	52 hrs	75 hrs	48 hrs
Rejects	100 units	40 units	400 units

[Adapted—I.C.W.A.]

Solution

Employee	A	B	C
Time allowed	2 hrs 36 mts × 25	3 hrs × 22	1 hr. 30 mts × 36
	= 65 hrs	= 66 hrs	= 54 hrs
Time taken	52 hrs	75 hrs	48 hrs
Time saved	13 hrs.	Nil	6 hrs.
Bonus $\left(\frac{TS}{TA} \times TT \times R\right)$	$13 \times \frac{52}{65} \times 5$	Nil	$6 \times \frac{48}{54} \times 7.50$
	= Rs. 52		= Rs. 40

Statement showing the earnings

Employee	A	B	C
Basic wages	Rs. 260.00	Rs. 600.00	Rs. 360.00
	(52 × 5)	(75 × 8)	(48 × 7.50)
Bonus (as calculated)	Rs. 52.00	–	Rs. 40.00
(a) Total wages	Rs. 312.00	Rs. 600.00	Rs. 400.00
(b) Good units	(2500 – 100)	(2200 – 40)	(3600 – 400)
	= 2,400	= 2,160	= 3,200
Cost of wages per unit (a ÷ b)	$\frac{312.00}{2,400}$	$\frac{600.00}{2,160}$	$\frac{400.00}{3,200}$
of good output	= Re. 0.13	= Re. 0.278	Re. 0.125

Problem 34

Determine on the basis of Halsey premium plan the total earnings of a worker in the following case :

Standard time for job	12 hours
Actual time taken	8 hours
Rate per hour	80 paisa

[C.U. B.Com. Hons.]

Solution

E = Time taken × Rate + (50% of time saved × Rate)

Standard time	12 hours
Time taken	8 hours
Time saved	4 hours

$$E = 8 \times 0.80 + \left(\frac{50}{100} \times 4 \times 0.80\right) = 6.40 + (2 \times 0.80) = 6.40 + 1.60 = \text{Rs. } 8.00.$$

Problem 35

From the following data ascertain the total earnings of each worker separately under Halsey and (ii) Rowan Scheme of incentive payment :

		A	B	C
(a)	Worker	A	B	C
(b)	Time Allowed (hours)	3	4	5
(c)	Actual time (hours) taken	5	3	3
(d)	Basic rate of wages per hour	2	2	2

[C.U. B.Com. Pass]

Solution

Total earnings of A :

a) Under Halsey Plan = Time taken × rate = 5 × 2 = Rs. 10

b) Under Rowan Plan = Time taken × rate = 5 × 2 = Rs. 10

Earnings of B

a) Under Halsey Plan

Time allowed	4 hours
Time taken	3 hours
Time saved	1 hour

Earning = 3 × 2 + [50% of (4 – 3) × 2] = Rs. 7.00

b) Under Rowan Plan $= 3 \times 2 + \left(\frac{1}{4} \times 3 \times 2\right)$

= Rs. 6 + Rs. 1.50 = Rs. 7.50

Earning of C

Time allowed	5 hours
Time taken	3 hours
Time saved	2 hours

a) Under Halsey Plan $= 3 \times 2 + \left(\frac{50}{100} \times 2 \times 2\right)$ = Rs. 6 + Rs. 2 = Rs. 8.00

b) Under Rowan Plan $= 3 \times 2 + \left(\frac{2}{5} \times 3 \times 2\right)$ = Rs. 6 + Rs. 2.40 = Rs. 8.40

Problem 36

Calculate total monthly remuneration of workers A, B, C and D on the basis of the following information for the month of December, 1997.

(i) Standard production for each worker – 1,000 units

(ii) Rate of wages – 10 paisa per unit

(iii) Bonus – Rs. 5 for each 1% increase over 90% of the standard.

(iv) Dearness Allowance per month – 100% of piece wage.

The units completed by the factory workers were as under :

A : 950 units B : 900 units
C : 960 units D : 850 units

[C.U. B.Com. Hons.]

Answer

	Standard production	% over standard	Increase in % of saving over 90%
A	1,000	$\frac{950 \times 100}{1,000} = 95\%$	5%
B	1,000	$\frac{900 \times 100}{1,000} = 90\%$	nil
C	1,000	$\frac{960 \times 100}{1,000} = 96\%$	6%
D	1000	$\frac{850 \times 100}{1,000} = 85\%$	nil

Statement showing the total remuneration

Items	A Rs.	B Rs.	C Rs.	D Rs.
Wage	(950 × 0.10) = 95	(900 × 0.10) = 90	(960 × 0.10) = 96	(850 × 0.10) = 85
Bonus	5 × 5 = 25	– –	6 × 5 = 30	– –
Dearness Allowance				
100% of piece wage =	95	90	96	85
Total remuneration	215	180	222	170

Problem 37

From the following data calculate total monthly remuneration of 3 workers X, Y & Z.

i) Standard production per month per worker is 1,000 units.

ii) Actual production during a month :
X — 800 units ; Y — 700 units ; Z — 900 units.

iii) Piece work rate per unit of actual production 15 paise.

iv) D.A. Rs. 40 per month (fixed).

v) House rent allowance – Rs. 20 p.m.

vi) Additional production bonus @ Rs. 5 for each percentage of actual production exceeding 75% actual production over standard.

[Adapted—I.C.W.A. – Inter]

Solution

Here, we are to find out the efficiency of each worker over standard since bonus is payable for each percentage exceeding 75% over standard production.

Standard production = 1,000 units

X's efficiency over standard = Actual production – 800 units

So, percentage of production over standard is $\frac{800}{1,000} \times 100 = 80\%$

Likewise, Y's efficiency = $\frac{700}{1,000} \times 100 = 70\%$

Z's efficiency = $\frac{900}{1,000} \times 100 = 90\%$

Now, we can draw a statement showing the total remuneration of 3 workers X, Y & Z.

Statement of monthly remuneration

		X Rs.	Y Rs.	Z Rs.
1.	Wages @ 0.15 per unit	120	105	135
2.	Dearness Allowance @ Rs. 40 p.m.	40	40	40
3.	House Rent Allowance @ 20 p.m.	20	20	20
4.	Bonus @ Rs. 5 for each percentage over 75%	25	–	75
		205	165	270

Note : Calculation of bonus :

X = 80% – 75% = 5% @ Rs. 5 = 25

Y = Nil, since his percentage is below 75%

Z = 90% – 75% = 15% × 5 = 75.

Problem 38

During first week of January 1991 Mr. Amitava, a workman, manufactured 150 articles. He receives wages for a guaranteed 48 hours week at the rate of Rs. 8 per hour. The estimated time to produce one article is 20 minutes and under incentive scheme the time allowed is increased by 20%. Calculate the gross wages according to :

(a) Piece work with a guaranteed weekly wage ;

(b) Rowan Premium Bonus and

(c) Halsey Premium Bonus @ 50% to workman.

Solution

Estimated time for producing one article = 20 minutes

Standard time to produce one article = 20 + (20% of 20 minutes) = 20 + 4 = 24 minutes.

Standard time for producing 150 articles = $150 \times \frac{24}{60}$ = 60 hours

Time taken = 48 hours

Time saved = 60 – 48 = 12 hours.

(a) If he is paid wages according to piece work :

Wages for 60 hours @ Rs. 8.00 = Rs. 480.

(b) When paid according to Rowan Plan :

$$\text{Earning} = T \times R + \left(\frac{S - T}{S} \times T \times R\right) \text{ Where, S = Standard time T = Time taken.}$$

$$E = 48 \times 8 + \left(\frac{24}{60} \times 48 \times 8\right)$$

= Rs. 384 + Rs. 76.80 = Rs. 460.80

Problem 39

From the following data calculate total monthly remuneration of three workers A, B and C :

(i) Standard production per month per worker is 1,000 units.

(ii) Actual production during a month :

A – 850 units, B – 720 units, C – 960 units.

(iii) Piece work rate per month of actual production – 20 paise

(iv) Dearness Allowance – Rs. 50 p.m. (fixed)

(v) House Rent Allowance Rs. 20 p.m. (fixed)

(vi) Tiffin Allowance Rs. 20 p.m. (fixed)

(vii) Additional production bonus @ Rs. 5 for each percentage of actual production exceeding 80% of the standard.

[C.U. B.Com.]

Solution

$$\text{A's output is 85\% of standard} = \frac{850 \times 100}{1{,}000} = 85\%$$

$$\text{B's output} = \frac{720 \times 100}{1{,}000} = 72\%$$

$$\text{C's output} = \frac{960 \times 100}{1{,}000} = 96\%$$

Statement showing the total monthly remuneration

	A Rs.	B Rs.	C Rs.
Wages @ 0.20 paise per unit	170.00	144.00	192.00
Dearness Allowance (fixed)	50.00	50.00	50.00
House Rent Allowance (fixed)	20.00	20.00	20.00
Time Allowance	20.00	20.00	20.00
Additional Production Bonus @ Rs. 5.00 for each percentage exceeding 80% of the standard (5 × 5)	25.00		(16 × 5) 80.00
	285.00	234.00	362.00

Problem 40

Jobs are issued to operater X to make 189 units and to operater Y to make 204 units for which a time allowance of 20 standard minutes and 15 standard minutes per unit respectively, is credited. For every hour saved a bonus is paid at 50% of the base rate, which is Rs. 6 per hour for both the employees. The basic working week is 42 hours. Hours in excess are paid at time rate plus one-third.

X completes his units in 45 hours and Y completes his units in 39 hours (but works a full week). Due to defective materials, six of X's units and four of Y's units are subsequently scrapped, although all units produced are paid for.

You are required to calculate for each of X and Y :

(i) the amount of bonus payable ;

(ii) the total gross wages payable ;

(iii) the wage cost per good unit made.

[I.C.W.A. U.K.—Adapted]

Solution

	X	Y
Time allowed	$189 \times \frac{20}{60} = 63$ hrs	$\frac{204 \times 15}{60} = 51$ hrs
Time taken	45 hrs	39 hrs
Time saved	18 hrs	12 hrs

Wages for the week

		X	Y
(a)	Bonus @ 50% of Rs. 6 for every hour saved	Rs. 3 × 18 = Rs. 54.00	3 × 12 = Rs. 36.00
	Wages for the week	42 × Rs. 6 = 252.00	39 × 6 = 234.00
	Overtime for 3 hours (45 – 42) @ Rs. 6 + $\left(\frac{1}{3} \times 6\right)$	3 × Rs. 8 = 24.00	–
		Rs. 330.00	Rs. 270.00
(b)	Good units produced		
	Units produced	189	204
	Less : Units scrapped	(–) 6	(–) 4
		183	200
	Labour cost per unit	Rs. 330 ÷ 183 = Rs. 1.80	Rs. 270 ÷ 200 = Rs. 1.35

(Where wage rate is to be ascertained)

Problem 41

Two workmen, Vishnu and Shiva, produce the same product using the same material. Their normal wage rate is also the same. Vishnu is paid bonus according to Rowan System while Shiva is paid bonus according to the Halsey System. The time allowed to make the product is 100 hours. Vishnu takes 60 hours while Shiva takes 80 hours to complete the product. The factory overhead rate is Rs. 10 per man hour actually worked. The factory cost for the product for Vishnu is Rs. 7,280 and for Shiva it is Rs. 7,600.

You are required :

(a) to find the normal rate of wages ;

(b) to find the cost of materials ;

(c) to prepare a statement comparing the factory cost of the product as made by the two workmen.

[C.A. Inter – May 1988]

Solution

Factory Overhead :

Vishnu = 60 × 10 = Rs. 600

Shiva = 80 × 10 = Rs. 800

Let us assume that :

Cost of Materials = M

Cost of Labour = Y

∴ Cost of Production = M + Y + 1,400 = 7,280 + 7,600

Labour Cost :

Vishnu (Rawan)

$$E = \text{Hours worked} \times \text{Rate per hour} + \left(\frac{\text{Time Saved}}{\text{Time Allowed}} \times \text{Rate per hour.}\right)$$

$$= 60Y + \left(\frac{40}{100} \times 60Y\right) = 60Y + 24Y = 84Y$$

Shiva (Halsey)

E = Hours worked × Rate per hour + (50% of Time saved) × Rate per hour

$$= 80 \times Y + \left(\frac{50}{100} \times 20Y\right) = 80Y + 10Y = 90Y$$

So, M + 84 Y + 600 = 7,280 (i)

M + 90 Y + 800 = 7,600 (ii)

Or, M + 84 Y = 7,280 – 600

M + 90 Y = 7,600 – 800

Or, M + 84 Y = 6,680 (i)

M + 90 Y = 6,800 (ii)

By subtracting (i) from (ii) we get—

Or, 6 Y = 120

$$\text{Or, } Y = \frac{120}{6} = \text{Rs. } 20$$

Material Cost = M + 84 × 20 = 6,680; or, M + 1,680 = 6,680; or, M = 6,680 – 1,680; or, M = Rs. 5,000

Vishnu

$$E = HW \times HR + \left(\frac{TS}{TA} \times HW \times HR\right)$$

$$E = 60 \times 20 + \left(\frac{40}{100} \times 60 \times 20\right) \text{ Or, } 1{,}200 + 480 = \text{Rs. } 1{,}680$$

Shiva

$E = HW \times HR + (50\% \text{ of T.S.} \times HR)$, Or, $80 \times 20 + \left(\frac{50}{100} \times 20 \times 20\right)$

Or, 1,600 + 200 = Rs. 1,800

Cost of products

	A	B
Cost of Materials	5,000	5,000
Labour Cost	1,680	1,800
Factory Overhead	600	800
	7,280	7,600

Problem 42

For a certain work order the standard time is 20 hours, wage Rs. 5 per hour, the actual time taken is 13 hours and factory overhead charges are 80% of direct wages for standard time.

Set out a comparative statement showing the effect of paying wages on :

(i) Halsey and (ii) Rowan Incentive Bonus System

[C.U. M.Com.]

Solution

Standard Time	20	hours
Less : Actual time taken	13	"
Time saved	7	hours

Normal time wages

for 13 hours @ Rs. 5 per our Rs. 65.00

Bonus under Halsey Plan

50% of time saved × rate

$\frac{1}{2} \times 7 \times \text{Rs. } 5 = \text{Rs. } 17.50$

Bonus under Rowan Plan

$\frac{\text{Time saved}}{\text{Time allowed}} \times \text{Time taken} \times \text{Rate}$

$\frac{7}{20} \times 13 \times 5 = \text{Rs. } 22.75$

Employer's savings under Halsey Plan

Standard wages 20 hours @ Rs. 5 per hour	= Rs.	100
Less : Actual wages Rs. 65 + Rs. 17.50	= Rs.	82.50
Saving in overheads		17.50
80% of standard wages	Rs.	80
Less : 80% of wages paid under Halsey Plan		
$\frac{80}{100} \times 82.50$	Rs.	66
	Rs.	14

Total savings :

In direct wages	Rs. 17.50
In over heads	Rs. 14.00
	Rs. 31.50

Employer's savings under the Rowan plan.

	Savings in direct wages. Rs. 100–Rs. 87.75	= Rs. 12.25
Add :	Savings in overhead :	
	80% of Rs. 12.25 (Rs. 100– Rs. 87.75)	= Rs. 9.80
		Rs. 22.05

Comparative Statement showing payment of wages under Halsey and Rowan plan

Incentive System	*Normal wages*	*Bonus*	*Total Earnings*	*Effective Rate*	*Employor's Saving.*
	Rs.	Rs.	Rs.	Rs.	Rs.
Halsey Plan	65.00	17.50	82.50	6.35	31.50
Rowan	65.00	22.75	87.75	6.75	22.05

Note : Effective rate = $\frac{\text{Total earning}}{\text{Actual time taken}}$

Halsey plan = $\frac{\text{Rs. } 82.50}{13}$ = Rs. 6.35

Rowan plan = $\frac{\text{Rs. } 87.75}{13}$ = Rs. 6.75

Problem 43

From the following particulars you are required to work out the earnings of a worker for a week under (a) Straight piece rate, (b) Differential Piece Rate, (c) Halsey Premium Scheme (50% sharing) and (d) Rowan Premium Scheme :

Weekly working hours	48
Hourly wage rate	Rs. 7.50
Piece rate per unit	Rs. 3.00
Normal output per week	120 pieces
Time taken per piece	20 minutes
Actual output for the week	150 pieces
Differential piece rate	80% piece rate when output is below normal and 120% of piece-rate when output above normal.

[Adapted—I.C.W.A. (Inter) Dec. 1989]

Solution

(a) **Straight Piece rate** = Actual output × piece rate = 150 × Rs. 3.00 = Rs. 450.00

(b) **Differential Piece rate** = Actual output × 120% of piece rate since output was above normal $= 150 \times \frac{120}{100} \times$ Rs. 3.00 = Rs. **540.00**

(c) **Halsey Premium Scheme**

Time taken × rate + (50% of time saved × rate per hour)

$= 48 \times \text{Rs. } 7.50 + \left(\frac{50}{100} \times 2 \times \text{Rs. } 7.50\right) = \text{Rs. } 360 + \text{Rs. } 7.50 = \text{Rs. } \mathbf{367.50}$

(d) **Rowan Premium Scheme**

$\text{Time taken} \times \text{rate} + \left(\frac{\text{Time Saved}}{\text{Time Allowed}} \times \text{Time taken} \times \text{Rate}\right)$

$= 48 \times \text{Rs. } 7.50 + \left(\frac{2}{50} \times 48 \times \text{Rs. } 7.50\right) = \text{Rs. } 360 + \text{Rs. } 14.40 = \text{Rs. } \mathbf{374.40}$

Working Note :

1. Time allowed :

   120 pieces in 2,400 minutes (120 × 20)

   (1 piece in 20 minutes).

   $150 \text{ piece} = \frac{2{,}400 \times 150}{120} = 3{,}000 \text{ minutes or } = \frac{3{,}000}{60} = 50 \text{ hours}$

2. Time taken = 48 hours

   So, time saved = 50 – 48 = 2 hours.

Problem 44

In an engineering concern, the employees are paid incentive bonus in addition to their normal wages at hourly rates. Incentive bonus is calculated in proportion of time taken to time allowed, of the time saved. The following details are made available in respect of employees X, Y and Z for a particular week :

	X	Y	Z
Normal wages (Rs. per hour)	4.00	5.00	6.00
Completed units of production	6,000	3,000	4,800
Time allowed (per 100 units)	0.8 hr.	1.5 hrs.	1 hr.
Time taken	42 hrs	40 hrs	48 hrs

You are required to work out for each employee :

(i) the amount of bonus earned ;

(ii) the total amount of wages received ;

(iii) the total wages cost per 100 units of output.

[Adapted—I.C.W.A. (Inter) – June, 1989]

Solution

	X	Y	Z
Time Allowed	$\left(\frac{6,000}{100} \times 0.8 \text{ hrs}\right)$	$\left(\frac{3,000}{100} \times 1.5 \text{ hrs}\right)$	$\left(\frac{4,800}{100} \times 1 \text{ hrs}\right)$
	= 48 hrs	= 45 hrs	= 48 hrs
Time taken	42 hrs	40 hrs	48 hrs
Time saved	6 hours	5 hours	Nil
Bonus =	$\left(\frac{6}{48} \times 42 \times 4\right)$	$\left(\frac{5}{45} \times 40 \times 5\right)$	—
	= Rs. 21.00	= Rs. 22.22	–
Normal wages earned	Rs. 168.00	Rs. 200.00	Rs. 288
Total wages	Rs. 189.00	Rs. 222.22	Rs. 288
Wages Cost per 100 units	$\left(\frac{\text{Rs. } 189}{60}\right)$	$\left(\frac{\text{Rs. } 222.22}{30}\right)$	$\left(\frac{\text{Rs. } 288}{48}\right)$
	= Rs. 3.15	= Rs. 7.41	= Rs. 6.00

Problem 45

Standard time 8 hours; Standard output 8 units; Wage rate per hour Rs. 5, units produced : 5, 6, 7, 8 and 10.

The premium table is as under :

Efficiency %	Premium %
67 – 70	5
71 – 80	7
81 – 90	10
91 – 99	15
100	20

Determine wage payment as per Emerson plan and wage cost per unit.

[B.U. B.Com. (Hom.) 1996]

Solution

$$\text{Level of performance} = \frac{\text{Actual output}}{\text{Standard Output}} \times 100$$

Level of performance	*Output* 5	*Output* 6	*Output* 7	*Output* 8	*Output* 10
Percentage of performance	$\frac{5}{8} \times 100$ = 62.5 %	$\frac{6}{8} \times 100$ 75%	$\frac{7}{8} \times 100$ 87.5%	$\frac{8}{8} \times 100$ 100%	$\frac{10}{8} \times 100$ 125%
Wages	8 hours × 5 = 40	(8 × 5) + (7% of wages) 40 + $\left(\frac{7}{100} \times 40\right)$ = Rs. 40 + Rs. 2.80 = Rs. 42.80	8 × 5 + (10% of 40) = Rs. 40 + Rs. 4 = 40 + 4 Rs. 44	8 × 5 + (20% of Rs. 40) = Rs. 40 + 8 = Rs. 48	8 × 5 + (20% of Rs. 40) = Rs. 40 + Rs. 8 = Rs. 48.

Problem 46

Calculate the earnings of a worker at Re. 1.00 per hour when he takes 140 hours to do a volume of work for which the standard time allowed is 200 hours. The plan of payment of bonus is on a sliding scale as under :

Within the first 10% of saving in standard time, bonus is	40% of time saved.
Within the second 10% of saving in standard time, bonus is	50% of time saved.
Within the third 10% of saving in standard time, bonus is	60% of time saved.
Within the fourth 10% of saving in standard time, bonus is	70% of time saved.
For the rest	75% of time saved.

Solution

Standard time	200 hours
Actual time taken	140 hours
Saving in time 200 – 140 =	60 hours
10% saving in standard time = $200 \times \frac{10}{100}$ =	20 hours.

Total percentage saving in standard time = 10% + 10% + 10% = 30%

$$\text{Or, } \frac{60}{200} \times 100 = 30\%$$

The earnings including bonus will be :

$$140 \times 1.00 + \left(20 \times \frac{40}{100} \times 1.00\right) + \left(20 \times \frac{50}{100} \times 1.00\right) + \left(20 + \frac{60}{100} \times 1.00\right)$$

$= 140 + 8.00 + 10.00 + 12.00 = 170.00.$

Problem 47

The standard hours of Job is 100 hours. The job has been completed by Amar in 60 hours, Akbar in 70 hours and Anthony in 95 hours.

The bonus system applicable to the job is as follows :

Percentage of time saved to time allowed	Bonus
Saving up to 10%	10% of time saved
From 11% to 20%	15% of time saved
From 21% to 40%	20% of time saved
From 41% to 100%	25% of time saved.

The rate of pay is Re. 1.00 per hour. Calculate the total earnings of each worker and also the rate of earnings per hour.

[Adapted—C.A. (Inter)] May 1990]

Solution

Statement showing the total earnings and rate of earning per hour

	Amar	Akbar	Anthony
Standard hours	100 hours	100 hours	100 hours
Time taken	60 hours	70 hours	95 hours
Time saved	40 hours	30 hours	5 hours
Percentage of time saved to time allowed	40%	30%	5%
Bonus eligible (On the basis of slab)	20%	20%	10%
Bonus hours	8 hours $\left(40\times\frac{20}{100}\right)$	6 hours $\left(30\times\frac{20}{100}\right)$	0.50 hour $\left(5\times\frac{10}{100}\right)$
Total hours to be paid	(60 + 8) 68 hrs	(70 + 6) 76 hrs	(95 + 0.5) 95.5 hrs
Total Earning @ Re. 1.00 per hour	Rs. 68.00	Rs. 76.00	Rs. 95.50 P.
Rate of Earning per hour	Rs. $\frac{68}{60}$ = Re. 1.133	Rs. $\frac{76}{70}$ = Re. 1.0857	Rs. $\frac{95.50}{95}$ = Re. 1.0005

Problem 48

In a manufacturing concern bonus to workers is paid on a slab rate based on cost saving towards labour and overheads. The following are the slab rates :

(i) Up to 10% saving 5% of the earning
(ii) Up to 15% saving 9% of the earning
(iii) Up to 20% saving 13% of the earning
(iv) Up to 30% saving 21% of the earning
(v) Up to 40% saving 28% of the earning
(vi) Above 40% saving 32% of the earning

The wage rates per hour of 4 workers – P, Q, R and S are respectively Re. 1.00, Rs. 1.10, Rs. 1.20 and Rs. 1.40. Overhead is recovered on direct wages @ 200%. Standard cost under wages and overhead per unit of production is fixed at Rs. 30. The workers have completed one unit each in 8, 7, $5\frac{1}{2}$ and 5 hours respectively. Calculate in respect of each worker –

(i) Amount of bonus earned
(ii) Total earnings
(iii) Total earnings per hour.

[Adapted—I.C.W.A. (Inter)]

Solution

		P	Q	R	S
	Time taken (in hours)	8	7	$5\frac{1}{2}$	5
	Rate per hour (Rupees)	1.00	1.10	1.20	1.40
(a)	Wages Payable (Rupees)	8.00	7.70	6.60	7.00
		(8 × 1)	(7 × 1.10)	$(5\frac{1}{2} \times 1.20)$	(5 × 1.40)
(b)	Overheads @ 200% of wages	16.00	15.40	13.20	14.00
(c)	Total Cost (a + b)	24.00	23.10	19.80	21.00
(d)	Standard Cost (Rupees)	30.00	30.00	30.00	30.00
(e)	Savings in Cost (d – c)	6.00	6.90	10.20	9.00
	Percentage of saving in cost	20%	23%	34%	30%
		$\left(6 \times \frac{100}{30}\right)$	$\left(6.90 \times \frac{100}{30}\right)$	$\left(10.20 \times \frac{100}{30}\right)$	$\left(9 \times \frac{100}{30}\right)$
	Bonus payable on slab rate as a percentage	13%	21%	28%	21%
(f)	Bonus earned (Rupees)	1.04	1.62	1.85	1.47
(g)	Total earnings (a + f)	9.04	9.32	8.45	8.47
(h)	Total earnings per hour	1.13	1.33	1.54	1.69
	(in Rupees)	$\left(\frac{\text{Rs. } 9.04}{8}\right)$	$\left(\frac{\text{Rs. } 9.32}{7}\right)$	$\left(\frac{\text{Rs. } 8.45}{5.5}\right)$	$\left(\frac{\text{Rs. } 8.47}{5}\right)$

Problem 49

Bharat Shawal works has introduced the following sliding scale for its workers :

Within the first 10% of saving in standard time, bonus is	40% of time saved
Within the next 30% of saving in standard time, bonus is	60% of time saved
For the balance bonus is	75% of time saved.

Sm. Rekha Pal, a worker whose basic rate per hour is Rs. 2, completed a particular job in 120 hours (time allowed 200 hours).

Compute her earning from the job.

[Adapted—B.Com. (Hons.) 1989]

Solution

	Time allowed	200 hours
Less :	Time taken	120 hours
	Time saved	80 hours

Percentage of time saved in standard time = $\frac{100 \times 80}{200}$ = 40%

Bonus hours

10% of standard time $= \frac{200}{100} \times 10 = 20$ hours

30% of standard time $= \frac{30}{100} \times 200 = 60$ hours

$$\text{Total earning} = 120 \text{ hrs} \times 2 + \left(\frac{40}{100} \times 20 \times 2\right) + \left(\frac{60}{100} \times 60 \times 2\right)$$

$$= 240 + (8 \times 2) + (36 \times 2) = \text{Rs. } 240 + \text{Rs. } 16 + \text{Rs. } 72 = \text{Rs. } 328$$

Problem 50

Payment of wage bonus is made in a concern on the following scale on the basis of the percentage of time saved on time allowed :

Time saved (% of standard)	Bonus (% of time saved)
Up to 25%	up to 10%
Above 25% and up to 35%	(i) Plus 20% of time saved above 25% and up to 35%
Above 35%	(ii) Plus 30% of time saved beyond 35%

Calculate the earnings of a worker (wage rate Rs. 1.20 per hour) who takes 50 hours to complete a job the standard time allowed for which is 100 hours.

[I.C.W.A. – Inter]

Solution

Standard time to complete a job =	100 hours
Less : Time taken	50 hours
Time saved	50 hours

Percentage of time saved = 50%. of standard time

Calculation of bonus hours :

The worker is entitled to get bonus for :

On 1st 25% of standard time 10% of time saved	2.5 hrs.
On above 25% and upto 35% i.e. 10% of standard time 20% $\left(10 \times \frac{20}{100}\right)$	2.0 hrs.
On the balance i.e. 50 – 35 = 15% of standard time 30% $\left(15 \times \frac{30}{100}\right)$	4.5 hrs.
	9.0 hrs.

Worker's earning =	Time wage = 50 × 1.20 =	Rs. 60.00
	Bonus = 9 × 1.20 =	Rs. 10.80
Total Earning		Rs. 70.80

Problem 51

A manufacturer has introduced a bonus system of wage payment at a slab rate based on cost reduction towards labour and overheads, the slab rate being :

Up to 10% saving	5% of the earning
Up to 20% "	30% of the earning
Up to 40% "	40% of the earning
Up to 70% "	50% of the earning

The rates per hour for 3 workers X, Y & Z are Re. 0.50, Re. 0.60 and Re. 0.55, respectively. The overhead recovery rate is 500% on productive wages. The standard cost towards wage and overhead per unit is determined at Rs. 1.20 per unit.

If the time taken by X, Y & Z to finish 100 units is 26 hours, 30 hours and 20 hours respectively, what is amount of bonus earned by each worker ?

[B.Com. Madras]

Solution

	No. of hours	*Wages*	*Overhead*	*Wages & overhead*	*Wages and overhead per unit*
X	26	13.00	65.00	78.00	0.78
Y	30	18.00	90.00	108.00	1.08
Z	20	11.00	55.00	66.00	0.66

Percentage of saving over Standard Cost

	Standard Cost	*Wages and overhead*	*Saving*	*% of saving*
X	1.20	0.78	0.42	35% (0.42 × 100 ÷ 1.20)
Y	1.20	1.08	0.12	10% (0.12 × 100 ÷ 1.20)
Z	1.20	0.66	0.54	45% (0.54 × 100 ÷ 1.20)

Bonus

X will get 30% of earning since % of saving is over 20% but up to 40%

i.e. $\frac{40}{100} \times 13$ = Rs. 5.20

Y will get 5% of earning since he has saved 10% of standard cost

i.e. $\frac{5}{100} \times 18$ = Re. 0.90

Z will get 50% of his earning as he has saved 45% which is above 40% but within 70% of saving

i.e. $\frac{50}{100} \times 11$ = Rs. 5.50

Problem 52

Payment of wage bonus is made in a concern on the following scale on the basis of the percentage of time saved on time allowed :

Time saved (% of standard) up to 25%	Bonus (% of time saved) 10%
Above 25% and up to 35%	(i) Plus 20% of time saved
Above 35%	(ii) Plus 30% of time saved

Calculate the earnings of a worker (Wage rate Rs. 1.20 per hour) who takes 50 hours to complete a job, the standard time allowed for which is 100 hours.

[I.C.W.A. Inter]

Solution

Standard time	100 hours
Less : Actual time taken	50 hours
Time saved	50 hours

Percentage of time saved to standard time = $\frac{50}{100} \times 100 = 50\%$.

Earnings of a worker

	Rs.
Wages for 50 hours @ Rs. 1.20 per hour (50 × 1.20)	60.00
Bonus (as per Note 1)	10.80
Total wages	70.80

Note I

1st slab

Bonus hours = up to 25% of standard time i.e. 10% of 25 hours = 2.50 hours

In the 2nd slab

10% of standard time i.e. 20% of 10 hours = 2.00 hours

3rd slab 15% of standard time i.e. 30% of 15 hours = 4.50 hours

9.00 hours

Bonus for 9 hours @ Rs. 1.20 per hour = 9 × 1.20 = Rs. 10.80

Problem 53

From the following particulars calculate the total earnings of a worker :

Wage bonus is being paid on the following scale on the basis of percentage of time saved on time allowed.

Time saved (% of standard)	Bonus (% of time saved)
up to 25%	10%
Above 25% and upto 35%	Plus 20% of time saved above 25% and un to 35%
Above 35%	Plus 30% of time saved above 35%

The worker whose wage rate is Rs. 2.40 per hour takes 50 hours to complete a job, the standard time allowed for which is 100 hours.

[C.U. B.Com (Hons.) 1992]

Solution

	Standard time to complete the job	100 hours
Less :	Time taken	50 hours
	Time saved	50 hours

Percentage of time saved 50%

The worker is entitled to get bonus for :

On 1st 25% of time saved, bonus is

10% of time saved $= \frac{25}{100} \times 100 \times \frac{10}{100}$ $= 2.5$ hours.

on next 10% of standard, bonus 30%

(35% – 25%) 10% of Standard time

$= \frac{10}{100} \times 100 = 10$ hours

So, Bonus hours $= \frac{20}{100} \times 10$ $= 2.0$ hours.

On 3rd slab – above 35% of Standard time

(50% – 35%) = 15% of Standard time

$= \frac{15}{100} \times 100 = 15$ hours

30% of 15 hours $= \frac{30}{100} \times 15$ Bonus hours $= 4.5$ hours

9 hours

So, the worker will get wages for 9 hours in addition to his normal wages.

	Rs.
Normal Wages = 50 hours × Rs. 2.40	120.00
Bonus for 9 hours @ Rs. 2.40 per hour = 9 × Rs. 2.40	21.60
Total Earnings.	141.60

Problem 75

In an assembly shop four workmen A, B, C, D work together as a team and are paid on group piece rate. They also work individually on hourly rate jobs. In a 44 hour week, the following hours have been spent by them on group piece work : A – 40 hours, B – 40 hours, C – 30 hours, D – 20 hours. The balance of the time in the week has been booked by each worker on day work job. Their hourly rates are as follows :

A – Rs. 3.00, B – Rs. 4.50, C – Rs. 6.00, D – Rs. 6.00

The group piece rate is Rs. 6.00 per unit and the team has produced 150 units. Calculate the gross weekly earning of each workman taking into consideration that each individual is entitled to dearness allowance of Rs. 50.00 per week.

[C.U. B.Com. (Hons.). 1993]

Calculation of share in group earning

Ratio of group earning :

A	40 hours × rate = 40 × 3	=	Rs. 120
B	40 hours × rate = 40 × 4.50	=	Rs. 180
C	30 hours × rate = 30 × 6.00	=	Rs. 180
D	20 hours × rate = 20 × 6.00	=	Rs. 120

Rate = A : B : C : D = 2 : 3 : 3 : 2

Total group wage = 150 units × Rs. 6 per unit = Rs. 900

A's share	=	$\frac{2}{10} \times 900$	=	Rs. 180
B's Share	=	$\frac{3}{10} \times 900$	=	Rs. 270
C's Share	=	$\frac{3}{10} \times 900$	=	Rs. 270
D's Share	=	$\frac{2}{10} \times 900$	=	Rs. 180
			=	Rs. 900

A's remuneration in work job =	44 – 40	=	4 × Rs. 3	=	Rs. 12.00
B's " " " "	44 – 40	=	4 × Rs. 4.50	=	Rs. 18.00
C's " " " "	44 – 30	=	14 × Rs. 6.00	=	Rs. 84.00
D's " " " "	44 – 20	=	24 × Rs. 6.00	=	Rs. 144.00

Calculation of total earning of each workman

	A	B	C	D
	Rs.	Rs.	Rs.	Rs.
Pay in group work	180.00	270.00	270.00	180.00
Pay in Job work	12.00	18.00	84.00	144.00
D. A.	50.00	50.00	50.00	50.00
	242.00	338.00	404.00	374.00

Problem 55

In a manufacturing concern 20 workmen work in a group. The concern follows a group incentive bonus system whereby workman belonging to the group is paid a bonus on the excess output over the hourly production standard of 250 pieces; in addition to his normal wages at hourly rate. The excess of production over the standard is expressed as a percentage and two-thirds of this percentage is considered to be the share of the workman and is applied on the notional hourly rate of Rs. 6.00 (considered only for the purpose of computation of bonus).The output data for a week are stated below :

Days	Man-hours worked	Output (In pieces)
Monday	160	48,000
Tuesday	172	53,000
Wednesday	164	40,000
Thursday	168	52,000
Friday	160	46,000
Saturday	160	42,000
	984	2,81,000

You are required to :

(i) Work out the amount of bonus for the week and the average rate at which each workman is to be paid the same.

(ii) Compute the total wages including bonus payable to Ram Jadav who worked for 48 hours at an hourly rate of Rs. 2.50 and to Francis Williams who worked for 52 hours at an hourly rate of Rs. 3.00.

[Adapted—A.I.C.W.A. – (Inter) December 1990]

Solution

(a) *Actual production during the year 2,81,000 units*

Standard production :

Standard output per hour × Actual hours = 984 × 250 units = 2,46,000 units

Excess production = 2,81,000 – 2,46,000 = 35,000 units

Percentage of excess production over standard = $\frac{35,000 \times 100}{2,46,000}$ = 14.22%

Bonus = $\frac{2}{3}$rd of 14.22 = 9.48%.

Rate of bonus = 9.49% of Rs. 6 = 0.57 (approx.) per hour.

Total bonus = 0.57 × 984 hours = Rs. 560.88

(b) *Statement of wages*

Worker	Hours worked	Rate per hour Basic	Rate per hour Bonus	Basic wages (Hrs. × R)	Bonus (Hrs. × R)	Total wages
Ram Jadav	48	2.50	0.57	120.00	27.36	147.36
Francis William	52	3.00	0.57	156.00	29.64	185.64

Problem 56

In a factory, two workers A & B produce the same product using the same material. Their normal wage rate is also the same. They are paid bonus according to Rowan System. The time allocated to the product is 40 hours. A takes 25 hours and B takes 30 hours to finish the product. The factory cost of the product for A is Rs. 193.75 and for B Rs. 205.00. The factory overhead rate is one rupee per man hour. Find out the normal rate of wages and the cost of materials used for the product.

[I.C.W.A. Inter]

Solution

Remuneration of A

Suppose the Rate of Wage is X and Cost of Material is M

Factory cost 25 hours × Re. 1.00 = Rs. 25.00

Time saved 40 – 25 = 15

So, Earnings of A = $25X + \left(\frac{15}{40} \times 25 \times X\right)$ ...... (i)

For B

Cost of wages = X ; Time saved = 40 – 30 = 10 hrs.

Factory overhead = 30 × 1.00 = Rs. 30

$$E = 30X + \left(\frac{10}{40} \times 30X\right)$$

Factory Cost = $M + 25X + \left(\frac{15}{40} \times 25 \times X\right) + 25 = 193.75$ ...... (i)

$M + 30X + \left(\frac{10}{40} \times 30 \times X\right) + 30 = 205$ ...... (ii)

Or, $M + 25X + \left(\frac{75}{8}\right) X = 193.75 - 25$

$M + 30X + \left(\frac{15}{2}\right) X = 205.00 - 30$

Or, $M + \frac{275}{8} X = 168.75$ ...... (iii)

$- M - \frac{75}{2} X = - 175.00$ ...... (iv)

By subtracting (iv) from (iii), we get

Or, $\frac{275 - 300}{8} X = - 6.25$, Or, $- \frac{25}{8} X = -6.25$

Or, $X = \left(\frac{6.25 \times 8}{25}\right)$ = Rs. 2 per hour.

Putting the value of X in equation no. (iii)

We get $M + \left(\frac{275}{8}\right) \times 2 = 168.75$, Or, $M = 168.75 - \frac{275}{4}$

Or, M = Rs. 168.75 – Rs. 68.75 Or, M = Rs. 100.

So, rate of wages is Rs. 2 per hour and cost of materials is Rs. 100.

Problem 57

In a factory bonus system, bonus hours are credited to the employee in the proportion of time taken which time saved bears to time allowed. Jobs are carried forward from one week to another. No overtime is worked and payment is made in full for all units worked, including those subsequently rejected.

From the following information you are required to calculate for each employee :

(i) The bonus hours and amount of bonus earned.

(ii) The total wages cost, and

(iii) The wages cost of each unit of product

	A	B	C
	Rs.	Rs.	Rs.
Basic wage rate per hour	0.25	0.40	0.30
Units produced	2,500	2,200	3,600
Time allowed per 100 units	2 hrs 36 min.	3 hrs.	1 hr. 30 min
Time taken	52 hrs	75 hrs	48 hrs
Rejects	100 units	40 units	400 units

[Adapted—I.C.W.A. (Inter)]

Solution

Particulars	A	B	C
Basic wage rate	0.25	0.40	0.30
Units produced	2,500	2,200	3,600
(a) Time allowed	65 hrs	66 hrs	54 hrs
$\left(\frac{2,500}{100} \times \text{hrs } 36\right)$	$\left(\frac{2,200}{100} \times 3\right)$	$\left(\frac{3,600}{100} \times 1\frac{1}{2}\right)$	
(b) Time taken	52	75	48
(c) Time Saved (a – b)	13 (65 – 52)	Nil	6 (54 – 48)
Ratio of time saved to time allowed	$\frac{13}{65} = \frac{1}{5}$th	Nil	$\frac{6}{54} = \frac{1}{9}$th
Bonus hours	$\frac{1}{5} \times 52 = 10\frac{2}{5}$hrs	Nil	$\frac{1}{9} \times 48 = 5\frac{1}{3}$hrs
(d) Bonus earned	$\frac{52}{5} \times \frac{25}{100}$ = Rs. 2.60	Nil	$\frac{16}{3} \times \frac{30}{100}$ = Rs. 1.60
(e) Wages	$52 \times \frac{25}{100}$ = Rs. 13.00	$75 \times \frac{9.40}{100}$ = Rs. 30.00	$54 \times \frac{30}{100}$ = Rs. 14.40
(f) Total wages (d + e)	Rs. 15.60	Rs. 30.00	Rs. 16.00
Units produced	2,500	2,200	3,600
Less Units rejected	100	40	400
(g) Good units produced	2,400	2,160	3,200
Wage cost of each good units	15.60 ÷ 2,400 = 0.0065	30.00 ÷ 2,160 = 0.0139	16.00 ÷ 3,200 = 0.0050
(i) Bonus hours	$10\frac{2}{5}$hrs	Nil	$5\frac{1}{3}$hrs
(ii) Total wage Cost	Rs. 15.60	Rs. 30.00	Rs. 16.00
(iii) Wage cost per unit	0.65 P	Rs. 1.39 P	Re. 0.50

Problem 58

The standard hours of job X is 100 hours. The job has been completed by Amar in 60 hours, Akbar in 70 hours and Antony in 95 hours.

The bonus system applicable to the job is as follows :

Percentage of time saved to time allowed	Bonus
Saving up to 10 %	10% of time saved
From 11% to 20%	15% of time saved
From 21% to 40%	20% of time saved.
From 41% to 100%	25% of time saved.

The rate of pay is Re. 1/- per hour. Calculate the total earnings of each worker and also the rate of earnings per hour.

[Adapted—C.A. (Inter) May 1990]

Solution

Statement showing the total earnings and rate of earning per hour of each worker

	Amar	Akbar	Anthony
Bonus hours (as per note I)	8	6	0.50
Hours worked	60	70	95
Total hours for which remuneration to be paid	68	76	95.5
Total Earnings @ Re. 1.00 per hour	68.00	76.00	95.50

Working notes

I. **Calculation of bonus hours :**

(a) Amar :

Standard time	100 hours
Time taken =	60 hours
Time saved	40 hours

So, bonus hours = $\frac{20}{100} \times 40$ hours = 8 hours.

(b) Akbar :

Standard time	100 hours
Time taken =	70 hours
Time saved =	30 hours

Percentage of time saved to time allowed = 30% (in 100 hours)

So, bonus hours = $\frac{20}{100} \times 30$ hours = 6 hours.

(c) Antony :

Standard time	100 hours
Time taken =	95 hours
Time saved =	5 hours

Percentage of time saved – 5%

Bonus hours = $\frac{10}{100} \times 5$ hours = 0.50 hour, or 1/2 hour.

II. Rate of Earning per hour :

$= \frac{\text{Total Earning}}{\text{Total time taken on the job}}$

Amar	=	Rs. 68 ÷ 60 hours	=	Re. 1.133
Akbar	=	Rs. 76 ÷ 70 hours	=	Re. 1.0857
Anthony	=	Rs. 95.50 ÷ 95 hours	=	Re. 1.0005

Problem 59

Calculate total monthly remuneration of workers A, B, C and D on the basis of the following information for the month of December, 1991.

(i) Standard production for each worker – 1,000 units
(ii) Rate of wages – 0.10 paise per unit.
(iii) Bonus – Rs. 5 for each 1% increase over 90% of the standard.
(iv) Dearness allowance per month – 100% of piece wages.

The units completed by the four workers nere as under :–

A – 950 units: B – 900 units: C – 960 units; D – 850 units.

[Adapted—C.U. (B. Com.)]

Solution

Percentage of Standard production

$$A = \frac{950 \times 100}{1,000} = 95\%$$

$$B = \frac{900 \times 100}{1,000} = 90\%$$

$$C = \frac{960 \times 100}{1,000} = 96\%$$

$$D = \frac{850 \times 100}{1,000} = 85\%$$

Statement of monthly remuneration of workers A, B, C & D

	A	B	C	D
Piece work wage @ 0.10 paise	95	90	96	85
Productive Bonus @ 1% increase over 90%	25	–	30	–
Dearness Allowance @ 100% of piece wage	95	90	96	85
	215	180	222	170

Problem 60

A worker takes 80 hours to do a job for which the time allowed is 100 hours. His daily rate is Rs. 6.00 per hour. Calculate the works cost of the job under the following methods of payment of wages :

(i) Time rate, (ii) Piece rate, (iii) Halsey Plan and (iv) Rowan Plan.

[C.U. B.Com. (Pass) 1991]

Solution

(i) *Time rate* = Hours worked × Rate = 80 × 6 = Rs.480

(ii) *Piece rate* = Rs. 80 × Rs. 6 = Rs. 480

(iii) *Halsey Plan* =

Time Saved =	Time allowed	x x x
Less	Time taken	x x x
	Time Saved	x x x

So, time saved – 100 hours – 80 hours = 20 hours.

Wages = Time taken × Rate of wages + 50% of time saved × Rate of wage

$$= 80 \times 6 + \frac{50}{100} \times 20 \times 6 = \text{Rs. } 480 + 10 \times 6 = \text{Rs. } 480 + 60 = \text{Rs. } 540$$

(iv) **Rowan Plan** = Time taken × Rate + $\frac{\text{Time Saved}}{\text{Time Allowed}}$ × Time taken × Rate

$= 80 \times 6 + \frac{80}{100} \times 80 \times 6 =$ Rs. 480 + Rs. 96 = Rs. 576.

Statement showing the work cost of the Job

Particulars	*Time Rate*	*Piece Rate*	*Halsey Plan*	*Rowan Plan*
	Rs.	Rs.	Rs.	Rs.
Material Cost	800	800	800	800
Wages (as per step I)	480	480	540	576
Prime Cost	1,280	1,280	1,340	1,376
Add Factory				
Overhead @ 125% of wages	600	600	675	720
Work Cost	1,880	1,880	2,015	2,096

Problem 61

Calculate the labour-hour rate of a worker P from the following data

Basic Pay	Rs. 200 p.m.
D. A	Rs. 150 p.m.
Fringe	Rs. 100 p.m.

Number of working days in a year 300. 30 days full pay and 20 days half-pay leave in a year is availed and allowed. Assume 8 hourly day.

What would be effect on hourly rate if only 30 days full pay leave is allowed ?

[C.S. (Inter) June 1990]

Solution

Calculation of effective working hours

	Total working days in a year	300 days
Less :	Non-productive days	
	(leave with full and half pay when no production is made) 30 + 20 =	50 days
		250 days

Total effective working hours = 250 × 8 = 2,000 hours.

	Total wages paid in a year	Rs.
	Basic pay @ Rs. 200 p.m.	2,400
	D.A @ Rs. 150 p.m.	1,800
	Fringe benefits Rs. 100 p.m.	1,200
		5,400
Less :	20 days half pay or 10 days full pay = $\frac{5,400}{300} \times 10 =$	180
		5,220

Hourly rate = Rs. $\frac{5,220}{2,000}$ hours = Rs. 2.61.

(b) Effective working hours in case of 30 days full pay leave :

	=	300 − 30 = 270 × 8	=	2,160 hours.
Total wages payable			=	Rs. 5,400
Hourly Rate	=	5,400 ÷ 2,160	=	Rs. 2.50
Effect on hourly rate	=	Rs. 2.61 − Rs. 2.50	=	Re. 0.11.

Problem 62

A, an employee of XYZ & Co., gets the following emoluments and benefits :

(a)	Salary	Rs. 250 per month
(b)	Dearness Allowance	
	On 1st Rs. 100 of Salary	Rs. 400
	On next Rs. 100 of Salary	Rs. 100
	On balance every Rs. 100	Rs. 50 or part thereof.
(c)	Employer's contribution to	
	Provident Fund	8% of salary and D.A.
	E.S.I.	4% of salary and D.A.
(d)	Bonus	20% of salary and D.A.
(e)	Other Allowances	Rs. 2,725 p.a.

A works for 2,400 hours per annum, out of which 400 hours are non-productive but treated as normal idle time. A worked for 18 effective hours in Job No. 13, where the cost of direct material equals A's earnings and the overhead applied is 100% of Prime Cost. The sale value of the job is quoted to earn a profit of 10% on such value.

You are requested to find out :

(a) Effective hourly cost of A and

(b) The expected sale value of Job No. 13.

[Adapted – I.C.W.A. (Inter) June 1991]

Solution

XYZ & Co.

		Rs.	Rs.
(A)	*Earnings of A per annum*		
	Salary & Rs. 250 p.m.	250 × 12	3,000
	Dearness allowance		
	On 1st Rs. 100 of salary	400	
	On next Rs. 100 of salary	100	
	On the balance of salary of Rs. 50	25	
		525 × 12	= 6,300
	Salary and Dearness Allowance		9,300
	Employer's contribution to P.F. @ 8%	$9{,}300 \times \frac{8}{100}$	744
	Employer's contribution to E.S.I. @ 4%	$9{,}300 \times \frac{4}{100}$	372
	Bonus @ 20% of Salary and D.A.	$\frac{20}{100} \times 9{,}300$	1,860
	Other Allowances (as given)		2,725
			15,001

Calculation of effective working hours

Gross working hours	2,400 hours
Less : Normal Idle time	400 hours
Effective working hours	2,000 hours

$$\text{Hourly cost of A} = \text{Rs. } \frac{15{,}001}{2{,}000} \text{ hours} = \text{Rs. } 7.50 \text{ per hour.}$$

COST SHEET OF JOB No. 13

		Rs.
Direct wages 18 hours =	18 × 7.50	135.00
Direct Materials @ 100% of Direct wages		135.00
Prime Cost		270.00
Add : Overhead @ 100% of Prime Cost		270.00
TOTAL COST		540.00
Add : Profit @ 10% on sales i.e. $\frac{1}{9}$ of cost		60.00
SALE VALUE		600.00

Problem 63

For a certain work order the standard time is 20 hours, wage is Rs. 5.00 per hour, the actual time taken is 13 hours and factory overhead charges are 80% of direct wages for standard time.

Set out a comparative statement showing the effect of paying wages under (i) the Halsey and (ii) the Rowan Incentive Bonus System.

[C.U. M.Com.]

Solution

	Standard time	20 hours
Less :	Actual time taken	13
	Time saved	7 hours

Normal time wages

for 13 hours @ Rs. 5 per hour — Rs. 65.00

Bonus under Halsey Plan

50% of time saved × rate = $\frac{1}{2} \times 7 \times$ Rs. 5 — Rs. 17.50

Bonus under Rowan Plan

$\frac{\text{Time Saved}}{\text{Time Allowed}} \times \text{Time taken} \times \text{Rate} = \frac{7}{20} \times 13 \times 5 =$ Rs. 22.75

Employer's savings under Halsey Plan

	Standard wages 20 hours @ Rs. 5 per hour	Rs. 100
Less :	Actual wages Rs. 65 + Rs. 17.50	82.50
	Saving in wages	17.50

Saving in overheads

		Rs.
	80% of standard wages	80
Less :	80% of wages paid under Halsey Plant = $\frac{80}{100} \times 82.50$	66
		14

Total savings :

	Rs.
In direct wages	17.50
In overheads	14.00
	31.50

Employer's savings under the Rowan Plan

Savings in direct wages.	(Rs. 100 – Rs. 87.75)	=	Rs. 12.25
Savings in overhead 80% of Rs. 12.25	(Rs. 100 – Rs. 87.75)	=	Rs. 9.80
			Rs. 22.05

Comparative Statement Showing payment of wages under Halsey and Rowan plan.

Incentive system	*Normal wages*	*Bonus*	*Total Earnings*	*Effective Rate*	*Employer's Saving*
	Rs.	Rs.	Rs.	Rs.	Rs.
Halsey Plan	65.00	17.50	82.50	6.35	31.50
Rowan	65.00	22.75	87.75	6.75	22.05

Note : Effective rate $= \dfrac{\text{Total Earing}}{\text{Actual time taken}}$

Halsey Plant $= \text{Rs. } \dfrac{82.50}{13} = \text{Rs. } 6.35$

Rowan Plant $= \text{Rs. } \dfrac{87.75}{13} = \text{Rs. } 6.75$

Problem 64

In an engineering factory, wages are paid on a weekly basis (48 hours per week) at a guaranteed hourly rate of Rs. 3.00. A study has revealed that the time required to manufacture a product is 12 minutes. However, a contingency allowance of 25% is to be added to this for normal idle time, setting up time etc. During the first week of June, 1992 Mr. X produced 224 pieces. Compute his wages under the following methods of wage payment.

(a) Time Rate ; (b) Piece rate with a Guaranteed Time Rate : (c) Rowan Premium Bonus Scheme, (d) Halsey Premium Bonus Scheme.

[Adapted—I.C.W.A (Inter)]

Solution

(a) **Time rate** – HW × RH = Rs. 48 × 3 = Rs. 144

(b) **Piece rate with guaranteed Time rate**

Time required =	12 minutes
Add : Contingency Allowance @ 25%=	3 minutes
	15 minutes

Hourly rate = Rs. 3.00

$\therefore$ Piece Rate $= \dfrac{3}{60} \times 15 = \text{Re. } 0.75$

Piece rate wage = 224 × 0.75 = Rs. 168

(c) **Rowan Plan**

Time saved = 56 – 48 = 8 hours.

$$E = H.W \times \text{Rate} + \left(\frac{TS}{TA} \times H.W \times RH\right)$$

$$= 48 \times 3 + \frac{8}{56} \times 48 \times 3 = \text{Rs. } 144 + \text{Rs. } 20.57 = \text{Rs. } 164.57.$$

(d) **Halsey**

$$E = H.W \times RH + \left(\frac{50}{100} \times T.S \times RH\right)$$

$$= 48 \times 3 + \left(\frac{50}{100} \times 8 \times 3\right)$$

= Rs. 144 + (4 × 3) = Rs. 144 + Rs. 12 = Rs. 156.

[Time taken to perform a job to be ascertained]

Problem 65

In an organisation, where Rowan Plan is in operation Anka Babu and Butchi Babu can earn Rs. 32.00 and Rs. 33.75, respectively, on a job, for which standard time is fixed at 12 hours. Rate is Rs. 3 per hour. Calculate what will be their earnings if Halsey Plan on 50 : 50 basis is adopted.

[Mysore B. Com. Part II 1992]

Solution

Let time taken by Anka Babu be x hrs. So, total earning = $T \times R + \left(\frac{S - T}{S} \times T \times R\right)$

where T = Time taken, R = Rate and S = Standard time

$$3x + \left(\frac{12 - x}{12}\right) \times 3x = 32,$$

Or, $3x + \left(\frac{12 - x}{4}\right)x = 32$, Or, $\frac{12x + 12x - x^2}{4} = 32$

Or, $24x - x^2 = 128$, Or, $x^2 - 24x + 128 = 0$

Or, $x^2 - 16x - 8x + 128 = 0$.

Or, $x(x - 16) - 8(x - 16) = 0$

Or, $(x - 16)(x - 8) = 0$,

∴ either $(x - 16) = 0$, i.e., $x = 16$, Or, $(x - 8) = 0$, i.e., $x = 8$.

Since maximum time for working is 12.

So, Anka Babu worked for 8 hrs.

Again, let time taken by Butchi Babu be y hrs.

$$3y + \frac{(12 - y)}{12} \times 3y = \frac{3,375}{100}$$

Or, $3y + \frac{(12 - y)}{4} \times y = \frac{135}{4}$ or $12y + 12y - y^2 = 135$

Or, $y^2 - 24y + 135 = 0$, Or $y^2 - 15y - 9y + 135 = 0$

Or $(y - 15)(y - 9) = 0$

Either $(y - 15) = 0$ ∴ $y = 15$

$(y - 9) = 0$ ∴ $y = 9$

Since maximum time = 12 hours. y = 15 is not possible ∴ y = 9

[Calculation of works Cost under different methods of incentive plans]

Problem 66

A worker takes 80 hours to do a job for which the time allowed is 100 hours. His daily rate is Rs. 6.00 per hour. Calculate the works cost of the job under the following methods of payment of wages :

(i) Time rate; (ii) Piece rate ; (iii) Halsey plan (iv) Rowan plan.

Additional information :

(a) Material Cost – Rs. 800

(b) Factory Overhead – 125% of Wages.

[C.U. B.Com. (Pass) 1991]

Solution

Calculation of wages :

(i) Time rate = Time taken × Rate = 80 hours × Rs. 6.00 = Rs. 480

(ii) Piece rate = Standard hours × Rate = 100 × Rs. 6.00 = Rs. 600

(iii) Halsey plan = $\text{Time taken} \times \text{Rate} + \left(\frac{50}{100} \text{ of time saved } \times \text{Rate per hour}\right)$

$= 80 \times 6 + \left(\frac{50}{100} \times 20 \times 6\right)$ = Rs. 480 + Rs. 60 = Rs. 540.

(iv) Rowan Plan = $\text{Time taken} \times \text{Rate} + \frac{\text{Time Saved}}{\text{Time Allowed}} \times \text{Time taken} \times \text{Rate}$ per hours.

$= 80 \times 6 + \left(\frac{20}{100} \times 80 \times 6\right)$ = Rs. 480 + Rs. 96 = Rs. 576.

Calculation of works cost

Elements of Cost	*Time Rate*	*Piece Rate*	*Halsey Plan*	*Rowan Plan*
	Rs.	Rs.	Rs.	Rs.
(a) Material Cost	800	800	800	800
(b) Direct wages	480	600	540	576
PRIME COST	1,280	1,400	1,340	1,376
Add :				
(c) FACTORY OVERHEAD				
@ 125% of Wages	600	750	675	720
WORKS COST	1,880	2,150	2,015	2,096

Problem 67

A worker takes 80 hours to do a job for which the time allowed is 100 hours. His daily rate is Rs. 2.50 per hour. Calculate the works cost of the job under the following methods of payment of wages :

(i) Time rate; (ii) Halsey Plan; (iii) Rowan Plan.

Additional information :

(a) Materials at Cost – Rs. 120

(b) Factory Overhead – 125% of Wages.

[C.U. B.Com.]

Solution

Calculation of Wages

(i) **Under Time Rate**

Wage = 80 × Rs. 2.50 per hour = Rs. 200

(ii) **Under Halsey Plan**

Time Saved = 100 hours – 80 hours = 20 hours.

$$\text{Earning} = \text{Time taken} \times \text{Rate} + \left(\frac{50}{100} \times \text{Time saved} \times \text{Rate per hour.}\right)$$

$$= 80 \times \text{Rs. } 2.50 + \left(\frac{50}{100} \times 20 \times \text{Rs. } 2.50\right) = \text{Rs. } 200 + (10 \times 2.50)$$

$$= \text{Rs. } 200 + 25 = \text{Rs. } 225$$

(iii) Under Rowan Plan

$$\text{Wages} = \text{Time taken} \times \text{Rate} + \frac{\text{Time Saved}}{\text{Time Allowed}} \times \text{Standard time} \times \text{Rate}$$

$$80 \times 2.50 + \left(\frac{20}{100} \times 80 \times \text{Rs. } 2.50\right) = \text{Rs. } 200 + (16 \times 2.50)$$

$$= \text{Rs. } 200 + 40 = \text{Rs. } 240.$$

Statement showing the works cost under different methods of payment of wages

Particulars	*Time Rate*	*Halsey Plan*	*Rowan Plan*
	Rs.	Rs.	Rs.
Cost of Materials	120.00	120.00	120.00
Wages	200.00	225.00	240.00
PRIME COST	320.00	345.00	360.00
Add Factory Overhead @ 125% of Wages	250.00	281.25	300.00
WORKS COST	570.00	626.25	660.00

Problem 68

During the first week of April 1991 the workman, Mr. Kalyan, manufactured 300 articles. He receives wages for a guaranteed 48 hours a week at the rate of Rs. 4 per hour. The estimated time to produce one article is 10 minutes and under incentive scheme the time allowed is increased by 20%. Calculate the gross wages according to :

(i) Piece-work with a guaranteed weekly wage

(ii) Rowan Premium Bonus.

(iii) Halsey Premium Bonus @ 50% to workman.

[Adapted—C.A. (Inter)]

Solution

(a) Piece work with a guaranteed weekly wage.

Estimated time – 10 minutes per article.

Add : 20% increase i.e., 2 minutes per article = 10 + 2 = 12 minutes.

Standard time for 300 articles

For 1 article = $\frac{12}{60}$ hour

for 300 articles = $\frac{12}{60} \times 300 = 60$ hours

∴ Wages for 60 hours @ Rs. 4 per hour = Rs. 240.00.

(b) **Rowan Plan**

Time saved = 60 – 48 = 12 hours.

$$\text{Wages} = \text{Time taken} \times \text{Rate} + \left(\frac{\text{Time Saved}}{\text{Time Allowed}} \times \text{Time taken} \times \text{Rate}\right)$$

$$= 48 \times 4 + \left(\frac{12}{60} \times 48 \times \text{Rs. } 4\right) = \text{Rs. } 192 + \text{Rs. } 38.40 = 230.40$$

(c) **Halsey Plan**

$$\text{Wages} = \text{Time taken} \times \text{Rate} + \left(\frac{50}{100} \times \text{Time Saved} \times \text{Rate}\right)$$

$$= 48 \times 4 + \left(\frac{50}{100} \times 12 \times 4\right) = \text{Rs. } 192 + 24 = 216.00.$$

Problem 69

Two fitters, a labourer and a boy, undertake a job on piece rate for Rs. 1,290. The time spent by each of them is 220 ordinary working hours. The rate of pay on time rate basis are Rs. 1.50 per hour for each of the two fitters, Re. 1 per hour for the labourer and Re. 0.50 per hour for the boy.

Calculate :

(a) The amount of piece-work premium and the share of each worker, when the piece-work premium is divided proportionately to the time wages paid.

(b) The selling price of the above job on the basis of the following additional data :

Cost of direct material Rs. 2,010, works overhead at 20% of Prime Cost, Selling overhead at 10% of Works Cost and Profit at 25% on Cost of Sales.

[Adapted—I.C.W.A. (Inter) June 1988]

Solution

(a) Calçulation of wages on time basis

	Rs.
Wages of 2 fitters @ Rs. 1.50 each for 220 hours (2 × Rs. 1.50 × 220)	660
Wages of 1 labourer @ Re. 1.00 for 220 hours (220 × Re. 1.00)	220
Wages of 1 boy @ Re. 0.50 for 220 hours (220 × 0.50)	110
Total wages	990

(b) Piece work Premium

	Agreed wages on Piece Rate	1,290
Less :	Wages on time basis	990
	Piece work Premium	300

Amount of Premium will be paid in the ratio of 660 : 220 : 110 i.e. 6 : 2 : 1

Two fitters	—	$\frac{6}{9} \times$ Rs. 300	=	200
One labourer	—	$\frac{2}{9} \times$ Rs. 300	=	66.67
One boy	—	$\frac{1}{9} \times$ Rs. 300	=	33.33
				300.00

Statement showing the Selling Price of the Job

		Rs.
	Direct Materials	2,010
	Direct Wages	1,290
	PRIME COST	3,300
Add :	Works overhead at 20% of Prime Cost	660
	WORKS COST	3,960
Add :	Selling overhead at 10% of Works Cost	396
	COST OF SALES	4,356
Add :	Profit at 25% on Cost of Sales	1,089
	SELLING PRICE	5,445

Problem 70

Calculate the earnings of A and B from the following particulars for a month and allocate the labour cost to each job X, Y and Z :

		A	B
(i)	Basic wages	Rs. 100	Rs. 160
(ii)	Dearness Allowance	50%	50%
(iii)	Contribution to Provident fund (on basic wages)	8%	8%
(iv)	Contribution to Employees State Insurance (on basic wages)	2%	2%
(v)	Overtime	Hours 10	

The normal working hours for the month are 200. Overtime is paid at double the total of normal wages and dearness allowance, Employer's contribution to State Insurance and Provident fund are at equal rates with employee's contributions. The two workers were employed on jobs X, Y and Z in the following proportions :

	Jobs		
	X	Y	Z
Worker A	40%	30%	30%
Worker B	50%	20%	30%

Overtime was done on job Y

[Adapted C.A. (Inter) May 1992

Solution

Statement showing Earnings of workers A & B

	A	B
	Rs.	Rs.
Basic wages	100	160
Dearness Allowance (50% of basic wages)	50	80
Overtime wages (as per note below)	15	nil
	165	240

Labour Cost per hour	A	B
	Rs.	Rs.
Gross wages (excluding overtime)	150	240
Employer's Contribution to Provident Fund @ 8% of basic wages	8	12.80
Employer's Contribution to E.S.I. @ 2% of basic wages	2	3.20
	160	256
Labour rate per hour	160 ÷ 200 = Rs. 0.80	256 ÷ 200 = Rs. 1.28

Statement showing allocation of wages to jobs

		Jobs		
	Total Wages	X	Y	Z
	Rs.	Rs.	Rs.	Rs.
Worker A				
Ordinary Wages (4 : 3 : 3)	160	64	48	48
Overtime	15	–	15	–
Worker B				
Ordinary Wages (5 : 2 : 3)	256	128	51.20	76.80
	431	192	114.20	124.80

Working notes :

Calculation of Overtime wages

$$2 \times \frac{(\text{Basic wages} + \text{D.A.})}{200} \times 10 \text{ hours}$$

$$2 \times \frac{(\text{Rs. } 150)}{200} \times 10 = \text{Rs. } 15 \times 10 = \text{Rs. } 15$$

Problem 71

Merrick Differential Piece Rate

On the basis of the following information, calculate the earnings of A, B, C and D under Merrick Differential Piece Rate :

Standard Production per hour			12 units
Normal rate per hour			Re. 0.60
In an 8 hour day :			
A	Produced	—	64 units
B	Produced	—	96 units
C	Produced	—	84 units
D	produced	—	100 units

Solution

STATEMENT SHOWING THE EARNINGS UNDER MERRICK DIFFERENTIAL PIECE RATE

Particulars	A	B	C	D
Standard production per hour (units)	12	12	12	12
Standard production per day (units)	96	96	96	96
Actual production	64	96	84	100
% of Efficiency	66.67%	100%	87.5%	104.17%
Piece rate applicable (in Rs.)	0.60	0.66	0.66	0.72
Total Earnings (in Rs.)	38.40	63.36	55.44	72.00

Note for consideration

According to Merrick Differential Piece Rate, the following rates are applicable according to efficiency :

Up to 83%	ordinary piece rate
84% to 100%	110% of ordinary piece rate
Over 100%	120% of ordinary piece rate.

Problem 72

From the following particulars you are required to calculate under 'Average Wage Rate' the labour cost chargeable to Job No. 'A' which was completed in 1990.

Basic wage rate is Rs. 2 per hour and overtime rates are as follows :

Before or after working hours—150% of basic wage rate. Sundays and Holidays—200% of basic wage rate. During the year 1990 the following hours were worked :

Normal time	2,00,000	hours
Overtime before or after working hours	30,000	"
Overtime on Sundays and Holidays	20,000	"
	2,50,000	"

For Job 'A' 3,500 hours were spent as follows :

Normal time	3,000	"
Before or after working hours	300	"
Sundays and Holidays	200	"
	3,500	"

[C.U. B.Com (Hons.) 1991]

Solution

Basic wage rate		Rs. 2	per hour.
Before or after working hours 150%			
of basic wage i.e.	2 × 150% =	Rs. 3	per hour.
Sundays and Holidays @ 200% =		Rs. 4	per hour

Annual wages for 1990

For Normal time	2,00,000	× Rs. 2		=	4,00,000
Before or after working hours	30,000	×	3	=	90,000
Sundays & Holidays	20,000	×	4	=	80,000
	2,50,000				5,70,000

Average labour cost per hour = 5,70,000 ÷ 2,50,000 = Rs. 2.28 per hour

The above average rate is to be applied to Job 'A' since overtime has been worked regularly for shortage of labour. Hence, overtime cost will be part of labour cost.

Labour cost for Job No 'A' = 3,500 hours × Rs. 2.28 per hour
= 3,500 × 2.28 = Rs. 7,980.

Problem 73

From the following particulars, work out the total amount payable to three workemen A, B. and C and the rate earned per hour by them under (a) Halsey and (b) Rowan premium bonus systems :

Standard time allowed	:	12 hours
Actual time taken	:	A 8 hours, B 6 hours and C 4 hours
Hourly wages rate	:	Rs. 150

[B.Com. Andhra]

Solution

(a) ***Halsey system*** :

Formula : Earning = Hours worked × Rate per hour + (50% of time saved × Rate per hour)

Particulars	A	B	C
(i) Standard time allowed	12 hours	12 hours	12 hours
(ii) Actual time taken	8 hours	6 hours	4 hours
(iii) Time saved	4 hours	6 hours	8 hours
(iv) Total amount payable i.e. earnings	8 × 1.50 + (50% × 4 × 1.50) = 12 + 3	6 × 1.50 + (50% × 6 × 1.50) = 9 + 4.50	4 × 1.50 + (50%× 8 × 1.50) = 6.00 + 6.00
(v) Rate earned	= Rs. 15.00	= Rs. 13.50	= Rs. 12.00
per hour	$\frac{15.00}{8}$ = Rs. 1.875	$\frac{13.50}{6}$ = Rs. 2.25	$\frac{12}{4}$ = Rs. 3.00

(b) ***Rowan Premium Bonus System :***

Particulars	A	B	C
Formula : Time taken × Rate + $\left(\frac{TS}{TA} \times TT \times Rate\right)$			
(i) Standard time	12 hours	12 hours	12 hours
(ii) Actual time taken	8 hours	6 hours	4 hours
(iii) Time saved	4 hours	6 hours	8hours
(iv) Wages Payable	8 × Rs. 1.50 + $\left(\frac{4}{12} \times 8 \times 1.50\right)$ = Rs. 12 + Rs. 4 = Rs. 16	6 × Rs. 1.50 + $\left(\frac{6}{12} \times 6 \times \text{Rs. } 1.50\right)$ = Rs. 9 + Rs. 4.50 = Rs. 13.50	4 × Rs. 1.50 + $\left(\frac{8}{12} \times 4 \times \text{Rs. } 1.50\right)$ = Rs. 6 + Rs. 4 = Rs. 10
(v) Rate per hour Total wages ÷ hours taken	Rs. 16 ÷ 8 = Rs. 2 per hour	Rs. 13.50 ÷ 6 = Rs. 2.25	Rs. 10 ÷ 4 = Rs. 2.50

Problem 74

From the following data, calculate Works Cost for jobs performed by Ajay and Saurav :

	Ajay	**Saurav**
Time allowed (per 100 units)	40 hours	42 hours
Rate per unit	Rs. 3	Rs. 4
Rate per hour	Rs. 8	Rs. 12
Actual time taken	48 hrs.	70 hrs
Actual units produced	150 units	200 units
Material cost for jobs	Rs. 668	Rs. 1,020
Bonus plan	Halsey	Rowan
Factory overhead	150% of wages	100% of wages.

[C.U. B.Com. (Hons.) 1998]

Solution

	Ajay	Saurav
Standard time for units produced	$\frac{*40 \times 150}{100} = 60$ hours	$\frac{**42 \times 200}{100} = 84$ hours
Time Allowed	60 hours	84 hours
Less : Time taken	48 hours	70 hours
	12 hours	14 hours

Wages earned by Ajay under Halsey Plan

Time taken × Rate + (50% of time saved × Rate)

$$48 \times 8 + \left(\frac{50}{100} \times 12 \times 8\right) = \text{Rs. } 384 + 48 = \text{Rs. } 432$$

Wages earned by Saurav under Rowan Plan

$$\text{Time Taken} \times \text{Rate} + \left(\frac{\text{Time Saved}}{\text{Time Allowed}} \times \text{Time Taken}\right) \times \text{Rate}$$

$$70 \times \text{Rs. } 12 + \left(\frac{14}{84} \times 70 \times 12\right) = \text{Rs. } 840 + \text{Rs. } 140 = \text{Rs. } 980.$$

* For 100 units time allowed 40 hours.

For 200 " " " $\frac{40 \times 150}{100} = 60$ hours.

* For 100 units time allowed 42 hours.

For 200 " " " $\frac{42 \times 200}{100} = 84$ hours.

COST SHEET

		Ajay	Saurav
		Rs.	Rs.
	Material cost	668	1,020
Add :	Wages	432	980
	Prime Cost	1,100	2,000
Add :	Factory Overhead		
	@ 150% of wages	648	980
	@ 100% of wages		
	Works Cost	1,748	2980

Problem 75

An Engineering firm determines the standard time for every job that it undertakes. In respect of Job No Y 0012, the standard time allowed is 20 hours. The normal wages rate of the firm is Re 0.75 per hour.

The material cost of the Job is Rs. 25 and the works overhead is Re 0.50 per labour hour. The firm follows a labour incentive scheme under which a worker receives wages for actual hours worked plus half of the hours saved.

Find out the labour cost and works cost of the job if it is completed in

(a) 16 hours

(b) 14 hours

[Andhra Univ. B.Com.]

Solution

Calculation of Labour Cost

In this case, incentive scheme followed is **Halsey Plan**

Formula :

Earnings = Hours worked × Rate per hour + (50% of time saved × Rate per hours)

	Condition (a)	Condition (b)
Time allowed	20 hours	20 hours
Hours worked	16 hours	14 hours
Time saved	4 hours	6 hours
Earnings	16 × 0.75 + (50% of 4 × 0.75)	14 × 0.75 + (50% of 6 × 0.75)
	Rs. 12 + Rs. 1.50 = Rs. 13.50	Rs. 10.50 + Rs. 2.25 = Rs. 12.75

Statement showing works cost of Job 0012

	Particulars	*When Job is completed*	
		16 hours	14 hours
		Rs.	Rs.
	Material cost	25.00	25.00
	Wages	13.50	12.75
	Prime Cost	38.50	37.75
Add :	Factory overhead		
	16 × 0.50	8.00	
	14 × 0.50		7.00
	Works Cost	46.50	44.75

Problem 76

From the following data ascertain the total earnings of each worker separately. Also calculate effective hourly rate of wages of the workers :

	Sajeeb	Sanjeeb
Time Allowed (Hours)	50	60
Actual Time taken (Hours)	38	48
Basic Rate of wages (Rs.)	8	8
Income Scheme	Halsey	Rowan

[C.U. B.Com. (Pass) 1993]

Solution

	Sajeeb	Sanjeeb
Time Allowed	50 hrs	60 hrs
Less : Time Taken	38 hrs	48 hrs
Time Saved	12 hours	12 hours

Total Earnings

Sajeeb (Halsey)

$$\text{Time taken} \times R + \left(\frac{50}{100} \times \text{T. S.}\right) \times R$$

$$= 38 \times \text{Rs. } 8 + \left(\frac{50}{100} \times 12\right) \times 8$$

$$= \text{Rs. } 304 + \text{Rs. } 48 = \text{Rs. } 352$$

Sanjeeb (Rowan)

$$\text{Time Taken} \times \text{Rate} + \left(\frac{\text{T.S.}}{\text{T.A.}} \times \text{T.T.}\right) \times R$$

$$= 48 \times \text{Rs. } 8 + \left(\frac{12}{60} \times 48\right) \times 8$$

$$= \text{Rs. } 384 + \text{Rs. } 76.80 = 460.80$$

Effective Hourly Rate of wages

	Sajeeb	Sanjeeb
(a) Total Earnings (Rs.)	352	460.80
(b) Hours worked (Hours)	38	48
(c) Effective hourly rate (a ÷ b)	9.26	9.60

Problem 77

The three workers Govind, Ram and Shyam produced 80,100 and 120 pieces of a product 'X' on a particular day in May 1997 in a factory. The time allowed for 10 units of product 'X' is one hour and their hourly rate is Rs. 4. Calculate for each of these workers the following :

(i) Earning for the day; and

(ii) Effective rate of earnings per hour under :

(a) Straight piece rate

(b) Halsey Premium Bonus (50% sharing) and

(c) Rowan Premium Bonus method of labour remuneration

(Adapted—I.C.W.A. (Inter)]

Solution

(a) **Straight Piece Rate**

$$\text{Piece Rate} = \frac{\text{Hourly rate}}{\text{Hourly units}} = \frac{\text{Rs. 4}}{\text{10 units}} = 0.40 \text{ Paisa}$$

Earning for the day	Govind	Ram	Shyam
	Rs.	Rs.	Rs.
Units produced × piece rate			
(80 × 0.40)	32		
(100 × 0.40)		40	
(120 × 0.40)			48
Effective rate of Earnings per hour			
= Earnings ÷ Hours	$\frac{32}{8}$ = Rs. 4	$\frac{40}{8}$ = Rs. 5	$\frac{48}{8}$ = Rs. 6

(b) **Halsey Premium Plan**

	Govind	Ram	Shyam
Time Allowed* (Note 1)	8 hrs.	10 hrs.	12 hrs.
Time taken	8 hrs.	8 hrs.	8 hrs
Time saved	nil	2 hrs.	4 hrs

Earnings:Time taken × Rate per hour + (50% of time saved × R)

Govind	Ram	Shyam
$8 \times 4 + \left(\frac{50}{100} \times \text{nil}\right) \times R$	$8 \times 4 + \left(\frac{50}{100} \times 2 \times 4\right)$	$8 \times 4 + \left(\frac{50}{100} \times 4 \times 4\right)$
= Rs. 32	= Rs. 32 + 4 = Rs. 36	= Rs. 32 + 8 = Rs. 40

Effective Rate of Earning

Govind	32 ÷ 8	=	Rs. 4
Ram	36 ÷ 8	=	Rs. 4.50
Shyam	40 ÷ 8	=	Rs. 5.00

(c) **Rowan plan**

$$\text{Time taken} \times \text{Rate per hour} + \left(\frac{TS}{TA} \times TT \times R\right)$$

When, TS = Time Saved

TA = Time Allowed

TT = Time Taken

Govind = 8×4 = Rs. 32

Ram = $8 \times 4 + \left(\frac{2}{10} \times 8 \times 4\right)$ = Rs. 32 + Rs. 6.40 = Rs. 38.40

Shyam = $8 \times 4 + \left(\frac{4}{12} \times 8 \times 4\right)$ = Rs. 32 + Rs. 10.67 = Rs. 42.67

Effective Rate :

Govind	Rs. 32 ÷ 8	= Rs. 4
Ram	Rs. 38.40 ÷ 8	= Rs. 4.80
Shyam	Rs. 42.67 ÷ 8	= Rs. 5.33

Working notes

(i) Time Allowed :

Govind 10 units for 1 hour

80 Units $1 \times \frac{80}{10}$ = 8 hours

Ram $\frac{100}{10}$ = 10 hours

Shyam $\frac{120}{10}$ = 12 hours

Problem 78

The normal working hours per week are fixed at 44 hours in a factory. An analysis of the time card of a worker shows that during a week he actually worked for 43 hours (including 4 hours overtime) on production and remained idle for the remaining 5 hours due to machine break-down.

Normal rate per hour is Rs. 5. Overtime rate is 150% of the normal rate and the rate of wages for idle time is 80% of the normal.

Calculate total wages payable to the worker and show how the total amount shall be treated in Cost Accounts.

[C.U. B. Com (Hons.) 1994]

Solution

			Rs.
(i)	Wages for normal time @ Rs. 5 per hour		
	for 39 hours	(43 – 4) = 39 × 5	195.00
(ii)	Wages for overtime @ Rs. 7.50 per hour (150% of Rs. 5)		
	for 4 hours =	4 × 7.50	30.00
(iii)	Wages for idle time @ 4.00 (80% of Rs. 5) for 5 hours		20.00
	Total wages.		245.00

Problem 79

In an Assembly shop of a Motor cycle Factory 4 workmen A, B, C & D work together as a team and are paid on group piece rate. They also work individually on day rate jobs. In a 44 hour week the following hours have been spent by A, B, C & D on group piece work, viz, A – 40 hours, B – 40 hours, C – 30 hours and D – 20 hours. The balance of the time has been booked by each worker on day work jobs. Their hourly rates are :

A	–	0.50 paise
B	–	0.75 paise
C	–	Re. 1.00
D	–	Re. 1.00

The group piece rate is Re. 1.00 per unit and the team has produced 150 units. Calculate the gross weekly earning of each workman taking into consideration that individual is entitled to Dearness Allowance of Rs. 20 per week.

[B.Com. Calcutta]

Solution

			Rs.
Group wages for 150 units @ Re. 1.00 per unit			150.00
Less : Individual Wages		Rs.	
	A	– 40 × 0.50	20
	B	– 40 × 0.75	30
	C	– 30 × 1.00	30
	D	– 20 × 1.00	20

So, the earning of the group will be distributed in the ratio 20 : 30 : 30 : 20.

Or 2 : 3 : 3 : 2

Thus, group earning of Rs. 150 (150 × Re 1) will be distributed as :

A $\frac{2}{10}$ × Rs. 150 = Rs. 30

B $\frac{3}{10}$ × Rs. 150 = Rs. 45

C $\frac{3}{10}$ × Rs. 150 = Rs. 45

D $\frac{2}{10}$ × Rs. 150 = Rs. 30

Rs. 150

Total earning will be

	Group earning	*Individual earning*	*Dearness Allowance*	*Total*
	Rs.	Rs.	Rs.	Rs.
A	30.00	2.00 (4 × 0.50p)	20.00	52.00
B	45.00	3.00 (4 × 0.75p)	20.00	68.00
C	45.00	14.00 (14 × 1.00)	20.00	79.00
D	30.00	24.00 (24 × 1.00)	20.00	74.00

Note

A has worked individually	=	44 hrs. – 40 hrs.	=	4 hrs.
B " "	=	44 hrs. – 40 hrs.	=	4 "
C " " "	=	44 hrs. – 30 hrs.	=	14 "
D " " "	=	44 hrs. – 20 hrs.	=	24 "

Problem 79

Wages negotiations are going on in a Company with the recognised Labour Union and the Management requests you as the Cost Accountant of the Company to formulate an incentive wage scheme with a view to increasing productivity.

The case of three representatives X, Y and Z who produce, respectively, 1,500 units, 1,200 units and 900 units in a normal week of 40 hours is taken up for study.

Assuming that day wages would be guaranteed at Rs. 5 per hour and the piece rate would be based on the standard hourly output of 25 units, calculate the earnings and labour cost per 100 pieces of each of the above three workers under :

(i) Piece work with a guaranteed weekly wage,

(ii) Halsey-Premium Plan, and

(iii) Rowan Premium Plan.

Also calculate the average wage cost for the Company to produce 100 pieces under each of the above methods.

[C.U. B.Com (Hons.) 1995]

Solution

(i) *Piece work*

Standard Production for 40 hours = 25 × 40 = 1,000 units

Rate per piece with guaranteed wages.

Guaranteed wages for 40 hours = 40 × Rs. 5 = Rs. 200

So, piece rate $= \frac{\text{Rs. } 200}{1{,}000 \text{ units}}$ = Re. 0.20

X will get for 1,500 units = 1,500 × 0.20 = Rs. 300

Y will get for 1,200 units = 1,200 × 0.20 = Rs. 240

Z will get for 900 units = 900 × 0.20 = Rs. 180

but he is entitled to get guaranteed weekly wages i.e. 40 × Rs. 5

Average wages for 100 pieces $= \frac{\text{Rs. } 740 \times 100}{3{,}600 \text{ units}}$ = Rs. 20.56 (approx.)

(Total units produced 1,500 + 1,200 + 900)

(ii) *Halsey Premium Plan*

Standard time for producing :

X	1,500 ÷ 25	=	60 hours
Y	1,200 ÷ 25	=	48 hours
Z	900 ÷ 25	=	36 hours.

Time saved :

X	60 hours – 40 hours	=	20 hours
Y	48 hours – 40 hours	=	8 hours
Z	36 hours – 40 hours	=	nil

Total Earnings :

X = Time taken × Rate per hour + (50% of time saved × Rate p.h.)

$= 40 \times \text{Rs. } 5 + \left(\frac{50}{100} \times 20\right) \times \text{Rs. } 5$

= Rs. 200 + (10 × Rs. 5) = Rs. 200 + Rs. 50 = Rs. 250

$Y = 40 \times \text{Rs. } 5 + \left(\frac{50}{100} \times 8\right) \times \text{Rs. } 5 = \text{Rs. } 200 + \text{Rs. } 20 = \text{Rs. } 220$

Z = 40 × Rs. 5 = Rs. 200

(Z will not get bonus since he has not saved any time)

Total wages = Rs. 250 + Rs. 220 + Rs. 200 = Rs. 670

$\text{Average wage cost per 100 pieces} = \text{Rs. } \frac{670 \times 100}{3,600} = \text{Rs. } 18.61$

(iii) **Rowan Premium Plan**

$\text{Earning} = \text{Time taken} \times \text{Rate} + \left(\frac{\text{Time Saved}}{\text{Time allowed}} \times \text{Time taken} \times \text{Rate}\right)$

X	$40 \times \text{Rs. } 5 + \left(\frac{20}{60} \times 40\right) \times \text{Rs. } 5 = \text{Rs. } 200 + \text{Rs. } 66.67$	=	Rs. 266.67
Y	$40 \times \text{Rs. } 5 + \left(\frac{8}{48} \times 40\right) \times \text{Rs. } 5 = \text{Rs. } 200 + \text{Rs. } 33.33$	=	Rs. 233.33
Z	40 × Rs. 5	=	Rs. 200.00
			Rs. 700.00

$\textbf{Average wage cost} = \text{Rs. } \frac{700 \times 100}{3,600} = \text{Rs } 19.44$

Problem 80

The following information relates to week ending 25th March 1996 for two workers X and Y :

	A	B
Work issued (in units)	1,800	3,168
Time allowed	30 mts. per dozen	3 hours per gross
Output rejected	444	756
Basic hourly wage rate	Rs. 4	Rs. 6
Hours worked	48	54

Bonus is paid @ $\frac{2}{3}$rd of the basic rate for all time saved and for all output without any deductions for rejected output. The basic working week is 42 hours, the first six hours of overtime being paid at the basic time rate plus one half.

Using the information given above, present in calculated summary form for each employee :

(a) number of bonus hours earned and amount of bonus earned;

(b) basic wages including overtime premium and gross wages; and

(c) direct wages cost per dozen if finished output (nearest paisa) when overtime is worked :

(i) regularly throughout the year as company policy due to labour shortage;

(ii) specifically at the customer's request to expedite delivery.

[Adapted—I.C.W.A. (Inter)]

Solution

In case of X

Time Allowed = @ 30 mts per dozen

$$12 \text{ units for } \frac{1}{2} \text{ an hour}$$

$$1{,}800 \text{ units} = \frac{1}{2} \times \frac{1{,}800}{12} = 75 \text{ hours.}$$

(a) Calculation of Bonus

Time Allowed	=	75 hours
Time Taken	=	48 hours
Time saved	=	27 hours

$$\text{Bonus for 27 hours} = 27 \text{ hours} \times \frac{2}{3} \times \text{Rs. } 4 = \text{Rs. } 72$$

(b) Basic wages

Hours worked	=	48
Working hours per week	=	42
Over time hours	=	6 hours
Wages for 42 hours @ Rs. 4	=	Rs. 168

$$\text{Wages for 6 hours} = 6 \times 4 + \left(\frac{1}{3} \times 4 \times 6\right) = 24 + 8 = 32$$

Gross Wage Rs. 168 + Rs. 32 + Rs. 72 = Rs. 272

Worker Y

(a) Calculation of Bonus

Time allowed	=	144 units for 3 hours	
	=	3168 " " $\frac{3 \times 3{,}168}{144}$ = 66 hours.	
∴ Time Allowed	=	66 hours	
Time taken	=	54 hours	
Bonus hours	=	12 hours	
Bonus	=	$\frac{2}{3} \times 12 \times \text{Rs. } 6$	= Rs. 48

Calculation of wages

Overtime	=	54 – 42 hours = 12 hours.	
Wages for 42 hours @ Rs. 6	=	42 × 6	= Rs. 252
First 6 hours @ $\frac{1}{3}$ of wage rate	=	$6 \times 6 + \left(\frac{1}{3} \times 6 \times 6\right)$	
	=	Rs. 36 + Rs. 12	= 48
For second 6 hours @ of wage rate	=	$6 \times \text{Rs. } 6 + \frac{1}{2} \times 6 \times 6$	
	=	Rs. 36 + Rs. 18 = 54	54
			402

Direct wage cost

Good units

A	=	(1,800 – rejected 444)	=	1,356
B	=	(3,168 – rejected 756)	=	2,412
				3,768 units

ie, 3,768 units = 3,768 ÷ 12 = 314 dozens

∴ **Direct wages cost per dozen**

(i) **When overtime is considered as overhead**

A	=	Rs. 168 + Rs. 24 + Rs. 72	=	Rs. 264*
B	=	Rs. 252 + Rs. 72 + Rs. 48	=	Rs. 372*
				Rs. 636
	=	Rs. 636 ÷ 314 dozens	=	Rs. 2.025

* Basic wages for normal hours + Wages for overtime + Bonus.

(ii) **When overtime is done at the request of the customer**

A	=	Rs. 272
B	=	Rs. 402
		Rs. 674

Direct wage cost per dozen = Rs. 674 ÷ 314 = Rs. 2.15

Problem 81

You are presented with the following information by one engineering company relating to the first week of December 1995 :

(a) **Materials**

The transactions in connection with the materials are as follows :

Receipts

Days	*Units*	*Rate per unit (Rs.)*	*Issues (units)*
1st	40	15.00	—
2nd	20	16.50	—
3rd	—	—	30
4th	50	17.10	—
5th	—	—	20
6th	—	—	40

Calculate the cost of materials issued under FIFO, LIFO and Weighted Average method of issue of materials and value of closing stock under the methods aforesaid.

(b) **Labour**

The firm employs five workers at an hourly rate of Rs. 2.00. During the week they worked for four days for a total period of 40 hours each and completed a job for which the standard time was 48 hours for each worker. Calculate per labour cost under the Halsey and Rowan Methods of incentive plan payments.

(c) Compute the prime cost of the job completed under different methods of valuing materials issues and calculation of labour costs.

[Adapted—C.S. (Inter)]

Solution

(a) Materials

Days	*Receipts*			*FIFO*			*LIFO*			*Weighted Average Method*		
		Rs.	Rs.		Rs.	Rs.		Rs.	Rs.		Rs.	Rs.
1st	40	15	600									
2nd	20	16.50	330									
				30	15	450	20	16.50	330	30	15.50	465
							10	15.00	150			
4th	50	17.10	855	10	15	150	20	17.10	342	20	16.50	330
5th				10	16.50	165						
6th				10	16.50	165	30	17.10	513	40	16.50	660
				30	17.10	513	10	15.00	150			
Total	110		1785	90		1443	90		1485	90		1455

(b) **Labour**

Hours worked	200 hours
Standard Hours	240 "
Time Saved	40 " (240 – 200)
Time Rate	Rs. 2 per hour.

Wages under Halsey Method

Time taken × Time Rate + (50% of Time Saved × Time Rate)

$$= 200 \times 2 + \left(\frac{50}{100} \times 40 \times 2\right) = \text{Rs. } 440$$

Wages under Rowan Plan

$$\text{Hours worked} \times \text{Time Rate} + \left(\frac{\text{Time Saved}}{\text{Time Allowed}} \times \text{Hours worked} \times \text{Rate}\right)$$

$$= 200 \text{ hours} \times \text{Rs. } 2 + \left(\frac{40 \text{ hours}}{240 \text{ hours}} \times 200 \text{ hours} \times \text{Rs. } 2\right) = \text{Rs. } 467$$

Statement Showing Prime Cost

	FIFO		*LIFO*		*Weighted Average*	
	Rs.	Rs.	Rs.	Rs.	Rs.	Rs.
Material Cost	1,443	1,443	1,485	1.485	1,455	1,455
Wages	440	467	440	467	440	467
	1,883	1,910	1,925	1,952	1,895	1,922

Problem 82

Standard time for a job is 60 hours. The hourly rate of guaranteed wages is Rs. 0.75. Because of the saving in time, a worker A gets an effective hourly rate of wages of Rs. 0.90 under Rowan Premium Bonus System. For the same saving in time, calculate the hourly rate of wages a worker B will get under Halsey-Weir Premium bonus System assuring 40% to worker.

[I.C.W.A (Inter)]

Solution

Let us assume that time taken is X hours. So, time saved = 60 – X.

Under Rowan Scheme :

$$0.90X = X \times 0.75 + \left(\frac{60 - X}{60} \times X \times 0.75\right) \text{ Or } 0{\cdot}90X = 0{\cdot}75X + \left(\frac{60 - X}{60} \times 0{\cdot}75X\right)$$

$$\text{Or, } 0.90X = 0.75X \left(1 + \frac{60 - X}{60}\right),$$

$$\text{or,, } 0.90X = 0.75X \left(\frac{120 - X}{60}\right), \text{ Or, } 6 = 5\left(\frac{120 - X}{60}\right), \text{ dividing both sides by 0.15.}$$

$$\text{or, } 6 = \left(\frac{120 - X}{12}\right) \quad \text{Or, } 72 = 120 - X, \text{ or, } X, = 120 - 72 \;\therefore\; X = 48 \text{ hours}$$

Hourly wages of B :

Standard time	=	60 hours
Time taken	=	48 hours
Time saved	=	12 hours

$$\text{Earnings} = \text{Time taken} \times \text{Rate} + \left(\frac{40}{100} \text{ of time saved} \times \text{Rate}\right)$$

$$= 48 \times 0.75 + \left(\frac{40}{100} \times 12 \times \text{Re. } 0.75\right) = \text{Rs. } 36 + 3.60 = \text{Rs. } 39.60.$$

Hourly rate of Wages :

Wages ÷ hours taken = Rs. 39.60 ÷ 48 = Re. 0.825.

ASSIGNMENT

Theoretical questions

1. Discuss the principal methods of remunerating workers.
2. Explain any two methods of paying bonus to factory workers and critically explain the advantages and disadvantages of one of them in a big manufacturing concern.
[C.U. B.Com. (Hons.)]
3. What do you mean by premium bonus scheme of remunerating labour ? Explain with illustration any one of the premium schemes that you are acquainted with.
[C.U. B.Com. (Hons.)]
4. What are the advantages of Piece Rate and Time Rate System of wage payment ?
5. What do you mean by Halsey Plan ? What are its advantages and disadvantages ?
6. What do you mean by Rowan Plan ? Explain its advantages and disadvantages.
7. What do you mean by Group Bonus Scheme? Discuss its advantages and disadvantages.
8. Discuss the advantages and disadvantages of the following premium bonus schemes :
(a) Halsey, (b) Halsey-Weir, (c) Rowan.
[B.Com. Madurai University]
9. (a) What are the objectives of incentive plans of wage payment ?
(b) How are payments to workers in respect of idle time and set-up time treated in cost accounting ?
[B.Com. (Hons.) Delhi]
10. What do you mean by 'Card Time Recording System' ?
[C.U. B.Com. (Hons.) 1993]
11. Discuss the various advantages and disadvatages of remunerating labour under time rate system or piece-work rate system.
[C.U. B.Com. (Hons.) 1994]
12. What are the objectives and characteristics of incentive wage scheme?
[C.U. B.Com. (Hons.) 1996]
13. What is a group bonus ? What are its advantages over individual bonus ?
[V.U. B.Com. (Hons.) 1997]

Practical Problems

1. Ramhari does a job in 70 hours as against 100 hours allowed. His hourly rate is Rs. 2.00. He is entitled to Dearness Allowance of Rs. 8.00 per day of 8 hours. Calculate the wages payable under (i) Halsey and (ii) Rowan Plan.
[C.U. B.Com. Pass 1982]
Ans. : (i) Rs. 240 ; (ii) Rs. 252.
2. From the following data ascertain the total earnings of each worker separately under (i) Halsey and (ii) Rowan Schemes of incentive payment :

(a)	Worker	A	B	C
(b)	Time allowed (hours)	3	4	5
(c)	Actual time taken (hours)	5	3	3
(d)	Basic rate of wages per hour (Rs.)	2	2	2

[C.U. B.Com. (Pass) 1984]
Ans. : (i) A – Rs. 10 ; B – Rs. 7 and C – Rs. 8.
(ii) A – Rs. 10; B – Rs. 7.50 and C – Rs. 8.40.

3. A workman is paid at the rate of Rs. 2.00 per hour under Halsey Premium Plan. He also gets dearness allowance of Rs. 40 per week plus a house rent allowance @ $12\frac{1}{2}$% of pay excluding incentive bonus but including dearness allowance. From the following details, calculate the workman's earning for the week :

Job No.	*Time Allowed*	*Time taken*
106	36 hours	24 hours
192	33 hours	22 hours
Waiting time		2 hours

[C.U. B.Com. (Pass) 1987]

Ans. : Rs. 176

4. Describe the Halsey Premium Plan and determine on this basis the total earnings of worker in the following case :

Standard time for the job	12 hours
Actual time taken	8 hours
Rate per hour	0.80 paise

[C.U. B.Com. (Hons.)]

Ans. : Rs. 8.00

5. Calculate the effective hourly rate of labour wages in the following case where bonus is paid under the Rowan Premium Plan :

Basic Rate of wages per hour	Rs. 4.50
Time allowed for the job	20 hours
Time actually taken	16 hours

[C.U. B.Com. (Hons.)]

Ans. : Total earning – Rs. 86.40

Hourly rate = Rs. 5.40.

6. A factory working on the Job Order System pays its workers under the Rowan Premium Bonus Scheme. Workers also get dearness allowance of Rs. 12 per week of 48 hours.

A worker's basic wage is Rs. 2.00 per day for 8 hours and his time sheet for a week is summarised below :

Job No.	*Time Allowed*	*Time taken*
1844	25 hours	20 hours
1226	30 hours	20 hours
Idle time (waiting)		8 hours
		48 hours

Calculate the Gross wage he has earned for the week.

[C.U. B.Com. (Hons.)]

Ans. : Rs. 26.67 P.

7. Production department of a Company pays its workers standard wages @ Rs. 2.00 per hour plus a bonus under the Rowan Premium Bonus Scheme and Dearness Allowance of Rs. 50 per week of 55 hours. At the end of a particular week the Time Sheet of a worker is summarised below :

Job No.	*Time Allowed*	*Time taken*
205	30 hours	25 hours
105	25 hours	20 hours
12	5 hours	3 hours
Idle time (waiting)		7 hours
		55 hours

Calculate the Gross wages (including bonus and D.A.) of the worker for the week.

[N.B.U. – B.Com. (Hons.)]

Ans. : Rs. 178.73 P.

8. A worker takes 80 hours to do a job for which the time allowed is 100 hours. His daily rate is Rs. 6.00 per hour. Calculate the works cost of the job under the following methods of payment of wages :

   (i) Time rate; (ii) Piece rate; (iii) Halsey Plan and (iv) Rowan Plan.

   Additional information

   (a) Material cost Rs. 800, (b) Factory Overhead 125% of wages.

   [C.U. B.Com. (Pass) 1990]

   Ans. : (i) Rs. 1,880, (ii) Rs. 2,150, (iii) Rs. 2,015, (iv) Rs. 2,096.

9. A worker takes 60 hours to do a job for which time allowed is 80 hours. His daily rate is Rs. 6 per hour.

   Calculate the works cost of the job under the following methods of payment of wages :

   (i) Time rate, (ii) Halsey Plan and (ii) Rowan Plan.

Additional information

Material costs Rs. 600, Factory Overheads @ 125% of wages.

[C.U. B.Com. (Pass) 1989]

Ans. : (i) Rs. 1,410, (ii) Rs. 1,545, (iii) Rs. 1,680.

10. From the following particulars calculate the total monthly remuneration of each of the three workers A, B and C :

    (a) Standard production per month per worker 1,000 units

    (b) Actual production during a month :
    A—850 units, B—720 units and C—960 units.

    (c) Piece work rate per unit of actual production Rs. 1.50

    (d) Dearness wages Rs. 200 p.m. (fixed)

    (e) Additional production bonus @ Rs. 5 for each percentage of actual production exceeding 80% of the standard.

    [C.U. B.Com. (Pass) 1994]

    Ans. : A Rs. 1,500
    B Rs. 1,280
    C Rs. 1,720

11. A worker takes 48 hours to do a job for which the time allowed is 60 hours. His wage rate is Rs. 10 per hour.

    Calculate the works cost of the job under the following methods of payment of wages :

    (a) Halsey Plan, (b) Rowan Plan.

    Materials cost Rs. 1,000, overheads 150% of wages.

    [C.U. B.Com. (Pass) 1997]

    Ans. : (a) Rs. 2,350, (b) Rs. 2,440.

12. From the data as given below determine the total remuneration of a worker both in terms of Halsey and Rowan Schemes :

Time Allowed	10 hours
Time Taken	7 hours
Time Rate	Rs. 5

[C.U. B.Com. (Pass) 1995]

Ans. : (1) Halsey Plan—Rs. 42.50
(2) Rowan Plan—Rs. 45.50

13. Calculate total monthly remuneration of four workers A, B, C and D on the basis of the following information for the month of March 1995 :

(i) Standard production per month per worker 1,000 units
(ii) Actual production during the month :
A—920 units, B—900 units, C—960 units and D—850 units
(iii) Piece-work rate per unit of actual production 10 paise
(iv) Dearness Allowance per month 80% piece wages
(v) House Rent Allowance Rs. 40 p.m. (fixed)
(vi) Additional production bonus @ Rs. 5 for each percentage of actual production exceeding 90% of the standard.

[V.U. B.Com. (Hons.) 1995]

Ans. : A Rs. 215.60, B—Rs.202,
C Rs. 242.80, D—Rs. 193.

14. A worker takes 9 hours to complete a job on daily wages and 6 hours on a scheme of payment by results. His day rate is 75 paise an hour, the material cost of the product is Rs. 4 and the overheads are recovered at 150% of the total direct wages.

Calculate the factory cost of the product under (a) Piece work Plan, (b) Rowan Plan and (c) Halsey Plan.

[B.Com. Poona]

Ans. : (a) Piece work Plan—Rs. 20.88
(b) Rowan Plan—Rs. 19.00
(c) Halsey Plan—Rs. 18.07

15. From the following data ascertain the total eanings of each worker separately under (i) Halsey Plan (50%), (ii) Rowan Scheme. Also calculate the effective hourly rate of wages of the workers under both the schemes :

Name of worker	Amal	Bimal
Time Allowed (hours)	5	5
Actual time taken (hours)	4	6
Basic rate of wages per hour (Rs.)	3.00	3.00

[C.U. B.Com. (Hons.) 1990]

Ans. : Halsey Plan
Amal Rs. 13.50, Rs. 3.375;
Bimal Rs. 18, Rs. 3.00
Rowan Plan : Rs. 14.40, Rs. 3.60;
Rs. 18, Rs. 3.00.

16. The standard output of a product has been fixed at 6 units per day of 8 hours. The normal wage per day is Rs. 12.

Determine the total wages payable under :

(i) Time Rate, (ii) Piece Rate, (iii) Halsey Plan and (iv) Rowan Plan. When the outputs are 5, 8, 12 and 15 units per day. Calculate also the labour cost per unit in each case

[Madras B.Com. 1988]

For production of 5 units

Ans. : (i) Rs. 12.00, Rs. 2.40, (ii) Rs. 10.00, Rs. 2.00,

(iii) Rs. 12.00, Rs. 2.40, (iv) Rs. 12, Rs. 2.40.

When production is 8 units

(i) Rs. 12.00, Rs. 1.50, (ii) Rs. 16.00, Rs. 2.00,

(iii) Rs. 14.00, Rs. 1.75, (iv) Rs. 16.00, Rs. 2.00.

When production is 12 units

(i) Rs. 12.00, Rs. 1.00, (ii) Rs. 24.00, Rs. 2.00,

(iii) Rs. 18.00, Rs. 1.50, (iv) Rs. 24.00, Rs. 2.00.

When productioin is 15 units

(i) Rs. 12.00, Re. 0.80, (ii) Rs. 30, Rs. 2.00,

(iii) Rs. 21.00, Rs. 1.40, (iv) Rs. 30, Rs. 2.00.

Hint :

$$\text{Bonus} = \frac{50}{100} \times 12 \times 2 + \frac{50}{100} \times 11 \times 2 = \text{Rs. } 23.$$

17. During first week of April 1990 the workman Mr. Kalyan manufactured 300 articles. He receives wages for a guaranteed 48 hours a week @ Rs. 4 per hour. The estimated time to produce one article is 10 minutes and under incentive scheme the time allowed is increased by 20%. Calculate his gross wages according to :

(a) Piece-work with a guaranteed weekly wage,

(b) Rowan premium bonus, and

(c) Halsey premium.

[C.A. (Inter) 1977]

Ans. : (a) Rs. 240.00; (b) Rs. 230.40; (c) Rs. 216.00.

18. Workmen of a particular grade working on 8 hour shift duty are guaranteed a wage of Rs. 32. An incentive scheme is in operation according to which production bonus is earned directly proportional to performance but only after 100% performance is reached. Four workmen A, B, C & D produce 48, 60, 75 and 90 units, respectively, in 6 hours spent in working on a job which has a standard time of 6 minutes per unit as measured work content. Remaining 2 hours of the shift are spent in doing unmeasured work for which no incentive bonus can be paid.

Find for each workman :

(i) the production performance level achieved ;

(ii) total earnings for the day.

[I.C.W.A. (Inter) 1984]

Ans. : (i) 80%, 100%, 125% & 150%

(ii) Rs. 32, Rs. 32, Rs. 38, Rs. 44.

Hints :

(a) Wage rate – 32 ÷ 8 = Rs. 4 per hour.

(b) Standard minutes :– 48 × 6, 60 × 6, 75 × 6 & 90 × 6. Time taken 360 minutes.

19. A worker takes 6 hours to complete a job under a scheme of payment by results. Standard time allowed for the job is 9 hours. His wage rate is Rs. 1.50 per hour. Material cost of the job is Rs. 16 and overheads are recovered at 150% of total direct wages. Calculate factory cost of the job under :

(a) Rowan and (b) Halsey Systems of incentive payments.

[Adapted—I.C.W.A. (Inter) 1985]

Ans. : (a) Rs. 46, (b) Rs. 44.12.

20. In an engineering works the standard time for a job is 16 hours and the basic wage is Rs. 2 per hour. A bonus scheme is instituted so that the worker is to receive his normal rate for hours actually worked and, in addition for half the hours saved. Materials cost for the job is Rs. 20 and factory overhead is charged on the basis of Rs. 2 per labour hour.

(a) Calculate wages and effective rate of earnings per hour if the job is completed (i) in 12 hours and (ii) in 14 hours. (b) Also ascertain the factory cost on the job on the same basis.

[SAS 83]

Ans. : (a) (i) 2.33 and (ii) 2.14
(b) Rs. 72 and Rs. 78.

21. From the following data, calculate the remuneration of each of the 3 workers X, Y & Z for the month :

(i) Standard production per month per worker is 1,000 units.
(ii) Actual production during the month were :
X – 800 units, Y – 700 and Z – 900
(iii) Piece rate per unit produced is Re. 0.25
(iv) D.A. Rs. 40 p.m. for each (fixed)
(v) House Rent Allowance Rs. 30 p.m. for each (fixed).
(vi) Additional production bonus at Re. 0.20 for each produced, which will be in excess of 75% over the standard production.
(vii) Calculate the effective Direct Labour Cost per unit under each of the 3 workers above.

[Adapted—Audit & Acct. Service Exam. 1986]

Ans. : Re. 0.35, Re. 0.35, Re. 0.36.

22.

Standard Time	–	60 hours
Time taken	–	40 hours
Hourly rate of wages	–	Rs. 2
Dearness Allowance	–	@ 0.50 paise per hour.

From the above information calculate the earnings of a worker :

(a) Time rate method ; (b) Halsey Plan and (c) Rowan Plan.

Ans : (a) Rs. 100.00 ; (b) Rs. 120.00 ; (c) Rs. 126.67.

23. In a light engineering concern, the standard time fixed for a job is 20 hours and basic wages Re. 1.00 per hour. A bonus scheme has been introduced so that the worker may get his normal rate for the hours actually worked and for half the hours saved. What will be the earnings of the worker and his effective earnings per hour if the job is completed in (a) 15 hours and (b) 18 hours. If the material of the job costs Rs. 50.00 and the factory overhead is to be charged at Rs. 2.00 per hour, calculate the factory cost of the job in both the above cases.

[B.Com.—Bangalore]

Ans. : (a) Rs. 17.50 and Rs. 19.00 ;
(b) Earning per hour : – Rs. 1.66 and Rs. 1.05 ;
(c) Factory Cost = (i) Rs. 97.50, (ii) Rs. 105.00.

24. An operator engaged in machining certain components receives an ordinary rate of Rs.1.60 per day of 8 hours. The standard output for machining components has been fixed at 80 pieces per hour (time as fixed for premium bonus). On a certain day the output of the worker on this machine is 800 pieces. Find the labour cost per 100 pieces and the wages that would have been earned by the workman under the following :
   (a) If a bonus of Rs. 0.23 is paid per 100 of the extra output.
   (b) If paid for on a straight piece-work basis at the standard rate.
   (c) If Halsey premium bonus system is adopted.

[I.C.W.A. Inter]

Ans. : (a) Rs. 1.97 ; (b) Rs. 2.00 ; (c) Rs. 1.80.

25. An employee working under a bonus scheme saves 4 hours in a job for which the standard time is 32 hours. Calculate the rate per hour worked and wages payable for the time taken under the following alternative scheme (award rate is Re. 1 per hour) :
   (i) Employee receives an increase in the hourly rate based on percentage.
   (ii) A bonus of 10 percent on award rate is payable when standard time (namely, 100% efficiency) is achieved plus a further bonus of 1 percent award rate for each 1 percent in excess of 100 percent efficiency.

[I.C.W.A. Inter]

Ans. : (i) Wages Rs. 31. 50 ; (ii) Rate per hour Rs. 1.24.

26. From the following information, prepare the earnings of a worker under Halsey Plan and Rowan plan :

Time Allowed	60	hours
Time Taken	50	hours
Rate per hour	Rs. 2.	

[Madras Univ. B.Com. 1997]

Ans. : (i) Under Halsey Plan Rs. 110
(ii) Under Rowan Plan Rs. 103.33

Calculate the earnings of a worker under Halsey and Rowan Plan :

Standard Time — 36 hours, Actual Time – 30 hours

Rate per hour — Rs. 10

[M.U. B.Com. 1997]

Ans. : Halsey Plan — Rs. 330
Rowan Plan — Rs. 350

27. From the following data calculate total monthly remuneration of 3 workers X, Y & Z :
   (i) Standard production per month per worker is 1,000 units.
   (ii) Actual production during a month :
   X – 800 units ; Y – 700 units ; Z – 900 units.
   (iii) Piece-work rate per unit of actual production 15 paise.
   (iv) D.A. Rs. 40 p.m. (fixed)
   (v) House Rent Allowance Rs. 20 p.m. (fixed)
   (vi) Additional production Bonus @ Rs. 5 for each percentage of actual production exceeding 75% of actual production over standard.

[I.C.W.A. Inter]

Ans. : X – Rs. 205 ; Y – Rs. 165 and Z – Rs. 270.

28. From the following particulars, find out the amount of cash required for payment of wages in a factory in a particular month :

		Rs.
(i)	Wages for normal hours worked	20,600
(ii)	Wages for overtime	2,200
(iii)	Leave wages	1,700
(iv)	Deduction of employees' share to State Insurance Corporation	500
(v)	Employee's Contribution to Provident Fund	1,600
(vi)	House Rent is to be recovered from 30 employees @ Rs. 10 p.m.	

[I.C.W.A. Inter]

Ans. : Rs. 22,100

29. A worker under the Halsey method of remuneration has a day rate of Rs. 12 per week of 48 hours plus a cost of living bonus of 10 p per hour worked. He is given an 8 hour task to perform, which he accomplishes in 6 hours. He is allowed 30% of the time saved as premium bonus. What would be his total hourly rate of earnings and what difference would it make if he was paid under the Rowan method ?

[B.Com.—Rajasthan]

Ans. : Halsey rate of earning = Re. 0.375
Rowan – Re. 0.225

30. On the basis of the following information, calculate the earnings of A and B under straight piece-rate system and Taylor's Differential piece rate system :

Standard Production 8 units per hour
Normal time rate Re. 0.40 per hour
Differential to be applied :
80% of piece rate below standard.
120% of piece rate at or above standard.
In a nine hour day, A produces 54 units and B produces 75 units.

[Adapted—Kerala—B.Com.]

Ans. : A – Rs. 2.16, B – Rs. 4.50

Hints :

Standard production per day = 9 × 8 = 72 units

Normal Piece rate = Re. $\frac{0.40}{8}$ = 0.5 paise.

Low piece rate below standard = $0.5 \times \frac{80}{100}$ = 0.4 paise

High piece rate = $0.5 \times \frac{120}{100}$ = 0.6 paise.

31. A worker produced 200 units in a week's time. The guaranteed weekly wage payment for 45 hours is Rs. 81. The expected time to produce one unit is 15 minutes which is raised further by 20% under the incentive scheme. What will be the earnings per hour of that worker under Halsey (50% sharing) and Rowan Bonus Schemes ?

[Adapted—C.S. (Inter) May 1995]

Ans. : Earnings per hour HalseyRs. 2.10; Rowan 2.25

32. During first week of April 1999 the workman Mr. Kalyan manufactured 300 articles. He receives wages for a guaranteed 48 hours a week @ Rs. 4 per hour. The estimated time to produce one article is 10 minutes and under incentive scheme the time allowed is increased by 20%. Calculate his gross wages according to :

(a) Piece-work with a guaranteed weekly wage.

(b) Rowan premium bonus, and

(c) Halsey premium bonus @ 50% to workman.

[C.A. (Inter)]

Ans. : (a) Rs. 240.00, (b) Rs. 230.40, (c) Rs. 216.00.

33. There are two piece-workers, Rakhal and Upendra, who are paid Rs. 5 for each piece work executed which costs Rs. 15 per piece in materials.

In a working day of 8 hours, Rakhal can complete 4 pieces and Upendra only 3. If the work head charges be Rs. 1.50 per hour show which of the two piece workers is more useful to the factory.

[I.C.W.A. Inter]

Ans. : Cost of production :
Rakhal – Rs. 23 per unit,
Upendra – Rs. 24 per unit.

34. The standard time taken to complete production is 12 hours at 25 p. per hour. Time wages are allowed to workers taking more than the time allowed. But workers who complete the job in standard time or less receive a straight piece work-rate plus 10% bonus, i.e. 12 hours at Re. 0.275.

Calculate the wage earned by A, B, C and D who complete the job in 15, 12, 10 and 8 hours, respectively. What will be their effective hourly rate ?

If the overhead rate chargeable to production is Re. 0.50 per hour, what will be the cost of conversion (labour and overhead) per piece produced by each worker ?

[C.A. Inter]

Ans. : Effective hourly rate
Re. 0.25, 0.275, 0.33, 0.4125.
Cost of conversion Rs. 11.25, 9.30, 8.30, 7.30.

35. Using the following data find the earnings of a worker under (a) Rowan and (b) Halsey Premium Bonus systems

Time allowed	48 hours
Time taken	40 hours
Rate per hour	Re. 1.00

[B.Com.—Andhra]

Ans. : (a) Rs. 46.67 ; (b) Rs. 44.00.

36. From the following particulars, calculate the remuneration of one worker for the month, under each of the basis separately—

(i) Halsey Scheme, (ii) Rowan Scheme, (iii) Piece Rate, (iv) Time Rate.

(a) Hourly Rate	Rs. 2.00
(b) Normal time for producing one piece	2 hours
(c) No. of working days in the month	25 days
(d) No. of working hours per day	8 hours
(e) Actual production during the month by the worker	125 pieces

[A and A S Exam.—W.B. 1987]

Ans. : (i) Rs. 450; (ii) Rs. 480; (iii) Rs. 500; (iv) Rs. 400.

37. Calculate total monthly remuneration of 3 workers A, B and C from the following data :

(a) Standard production per worker – 1,000 units
Actual production during a month : A – 850 units, B – 750 units and C – 950 units.

(b) Piece work rate 0.10 P. per unit.

(c) Additional Production bonus is Rs. 10 for each percentage of actual production exceeding 80% of standard production.

(d) Dearness Pay (fixed) – Rs. 50 per month.

[Adapted—I.C.W.A.]

Ans. : A – Rs. 185, B – Rs. 125, C – Rs. 295.

38. A workman whose basic rate of pay is Rs. 2.00 per hour is working under the "Rowan System" of premium bonus. In addition, he receives a cost of living bonus of Rs. 33 per week of 44 hours. During the week he does the following jobs : (i) Job A, for which 30 hours are allowed, in 20 hours ; (ii) Job 'B', for which 36 hours allowed, in 20 hours. During the week his waiting time amounts to 4 hours.

Calculate the worker's earnings and the amounts to be charged to each job and to overhead.

[I.C.W.A., U.K.]

Ans. : Job A Rs. 68.33; Job B Rs. 75.77; Overhead Rs. 8.00; Total Earnings Rs. 152.10.

39. From the information given below calculate the earnings of each employee under any two of the following methods of wage payments :

(i) Halsey-Weir Premium Bonus Scheme.

(ii) Halsey Premium Bonus Scheme.

(iii) Rowan Premium Bonus Scheme.

Employee	A	B	C
Time allowed – hours per 100 units	35	40	42
Wages per unit	Rs. 2	3	4
Hourly rate	Rs. 7	8	10
Actual time taken in hours	50	48	46
Actual units produced	200	150	125

[Adapted—I.C.W.A.]

Ans. :	*Condition* (i)	*Condition* (ii)	*Condition* (iii)
A	396.67	420.00	450.00
B	416.00	432.00	460.80
C	481.67	492.50	516.95

40. An employee working under a bonus scheme saves 12 hours in a job for which the standard time is 60 hours. Calculate the rate per hour worked and wages payable to a worker if incentive bonus of 10% on the hourly rate is payable when standard time (namely 100% efficiency) is achieved, and a further incentive bonus of 1% on hourly rate for each 1% in excess of that 100% efficiency is payable.

Assume that the normal rate of payment is Rs. 5.00 per hour.

[C.A. (Inter)—Adapted]

Ans. : Wage payable – Rs. 324.

41. A Company's basic wage rate is Rs. 3.00 per hour and its overtime rates are :

Evenings	Time and one-third
Weekends	Double time

During the previous year the following hours were worked :

	Hours
Normal time	2,20,000 hours
Time plus one-third	20,000 hours
Double time	10,000 hours

The following times have been worked on these jobs :

	Job A Clock hours	Job B Clock hours	Job C Clock hours
Normal time	3,000	5,000	4,000
Evening Overtime	300	600	1,050
Weekend Overtime	100	50	300
	3,400	5,650	5,350

From the following particulars you are required to calculate under 'Average Wage Rate' the labour cost chargeable to Job A, Job B and Job C.

[Adapted—Andhra Univ. B.Com.]

Ans. : Job A — Rs. 10,880; Job B — Rs. 18,080; Job C — Rs. 17,120.

42. Calculate total monthly remuneration of workers A, B, C & D on the basis of the following information for the month of December 1980 :
   (i) Standard production for each worker – 1,000 units.
   (ii) Rate of wages – 0.10 paise per unit.
   (iii) Bonus – Rs. 5 for each 1% increase over 90% of the standard.
   (iv) Dearness Allowance per month – 100% of piece wage.

The units completed by the four workers were as under :

A : 950 units B : 900 units

C : 960 units D : 850 units

[C.U. B.Com. (Hons.) 1981]

Ans. : A – Rs. 215 ; B – Rs. 180 ; C – Rs. 222 ; D – Rs. 170.

43. From the following particulars given below, prepare the labour cost per man day of 8 hours :

(a)	Basic Salary	Rs. 2 per day.
(b)	Dearness Allowance	0.25 paise per every point over 100 cost of Living Index for working class – current cost of living index – 700 points.
(c)	Leave Salary	10% of (a) & (b)
(d)	Employer's contribution to Provident Fund	8% of (a), (b) & (c).
(e)	Employer's contribution to State Insurance	2.5% of (a), (b) and (c).
(f)	Expenditure on amenities to labour	Rs. 20 per head per mensem.
(g)	Number of working days in a month	25 days of 8 hours each

[I.C.W.A. Inter]

Ans. : Rs. 10.52

44. Calculate total monthly remuneration of 3 workers A, B & C from the following data :
   (a) Standard production per month per worker 1,000 units
   (b) Actual production during the month : A 850 units; B 750 units; C 950 units
   (c) Piece work rate 10 Paise per unit
   (d) Additional production bonus is Rs. 10 for each percentage of actual production exceeding 80% over standard.
   (e) Dearness pay fixed : Rs. 50 p.m.

[I.C.W.A. Inter]

Ans. : A – Rs. 185, B – Rs. 125, C – Rs. 295.

45. What will be the earning of a worker at 0.55 Paise per hour when he takes 140 hours to do a volume of work for which the standard time allowed is 200 hours.

The plan payment of bonus on sliding scale is as under :

(a) Within the first 10% saving in standard time, the bonus is 40% of the time saved.

(b) Within the second 10% saving in standard time, the bonus is 50% of the time saved.

(c) Within the third 10% saving in standard time, the bonus is 60% of the time saved.

(d) Within the fourth 10% saving in standard time, the bonus is 70% of the time saved.

(e) For the rest the bonus is 75% of the time saved.

[I.C.W.A. Inter]

Ans. : Bonus – Rs. 16.50, Total wages – Rs. 93.50.

Hint : Bonus hours :

On 1st slab	8 hours
On 2nd slab	10 hours
On 3rd slab	12 hours
	30 × 0.55 = Rs. 16.50.

46. The following particulars for the first week of September 1999 relate to A and B, two workers employed in a Factory :

	A	B
(1) Job Completed (Units)	3,600	4,200
(2) Out of above, output rejected which became unsaleable	540	450
(3) Time allowed	12 minutes per dozen	3 hours per 200 units
(4) Basic wage rate per hour	Rs. 5.00	Rs. 6.00
(5) Hours worked	45	50

The normal working hours per week are fixed at 42 hours. Bonus is paid @ $\frac{2}{3}$rd of basic wage rate of gross time worked and gross output produced without deduction for the rejected output. The rate of overtime for the first four hours is paid at time plus $\frac{1}{3}$rd and for the next 4 hours is paid at time plus $\frac{1}{2}$.

From the above data calculate for each employee :

(a) Number of bonus hours earned and the amount of bonus earned.

(b) Total wages earned including basic wages, overtime premium and bonus.

(c) Direct wages cost per 100 Saleable units.

[Adapted—I.C.W.A. Inter]

Ans. : (a) A – 15 hrs ; Rs. 50 ; B – 13 hrs ; Rs. 52.

(b) A – Rs. 280 ; B – Rs. 372.

(c) When O.T. is regular then A – Rs. 8.99 and B – Rs. 9.31.

When O.T. is at the request of the customers – A – Rs. 9.15, B – Rs. 9.84.

47. A worker takes 18 hours to complete a job on daily wages and 12 hours on a scheme of payment by results. His day rate is 75 paise per hour, the material cost of the product is Rs. 6 and the overheads are recovered at 150% of the total direct wages. Calculate the factory cost of the product under :

(i) Piece work plan ; (ii) Halsey Plan and (iii) Rowan Plan.

[Bangalore B.Com.]

Ans. : Rs. 9.00 ; Rs. 11.25 and Rs. 12.00

Factory Cost : Rs. 28.50 ; Rs. 34.13 and Rs. 36.00.

48. Jobs are issued to operative X to make 189 units and to operative Y to make 204 units, for which a time allowance 20 standard minutes and 15 standard minutes per unit respectively, is credited. For every hour saved a bonus is paid at 50% of basic rate, which is Rs. 6 per hour for both employees. The basic working week is 42 hours. Hours in excess are paid at time plus one-third.

X completes his units in 45 hours and Y completes his units in 39 hours (but works a full week) due to defective material. Six of X's unit and four of Y's units are subsequently scrapped, although all units produced are paid for.

You are required to calculate for each of X and Y :

(a) The amount of bonus payable

(b) The total gross wages payable

(c) The wages cost per good unit made.

[I.C.W.A., U.K. (Adapted)]

Ans. : (a) Bonus : X – Rs. 54 ; Y – Rs. 36.

(b) Wages : X – Rs. 330 ; Y – Rs. 270.

(c) Labour cost per unit :

X – Rs. 1.80; Y – Rs. 1.35.

Hint :

X : 189 – 6 = 183 units

330 ÷ 183,

Y : 204 –4 = 200, Rs. 270 ÷ 200

49. During the first week of May 1995 the workman X manufactured 300 articles. He receives wage for a guaranteed 48 hour-week at the rate of Rs. 5 per hour. The estimated time to produce one article is 10 minutes and under incentive scheme the time allowed is increased by 20%. Calculate his gross wage according to :

(i) Piece-work with guaranteed weekly wage,

(ii) Rowan Premium Bonus Plan

(iii) Halsey Premium Bonus Plan (50 : 50 sharing scheme)

[K.U. B.Com. (Hons.) 1996]

Ans. : Piece Rate – Rs. 300 and Rs. 6.25 rate per hour

Rowan Plan – Rs. 288 and Rs. 6.00 per hour

Halsey Plan – Rs. 270 and Rs. 5.625 per hour.

50. From the following particulars calculate the total monthly remuneration of each of the three workers A, B and C :

(a) Standard production per month per worker : 1,000 units; (b) Actual production during a month : A — 850 units, B — 720 units and C — 960 units; (c) Additional Production

Bonus @ Rs. 5 for each percentage of actual production exceeding 80% of the standard; (d) Piece Work Rate per unit of actual production Rs. 1.50; (d) Dearness wages @ Rs. 200 p.m. (fixed).

[C.U. B.Com. (Pass) 1994]

Total monthly remunerations

Ans. : A—Rs. 1,500; B—Rs. 1,280; C—Rs. 1.720.

51. From the following data ascertain the total earnings of each worker separately. Also calculate effective hourly rate of wage of the workers :

	Rajeeb	Sanjeeb
Time allowed (Hrs.)	50	60
Actual time taken (Hrs.)	38	48
Basic rate of wage per hour	Rs. 8.00	Rs. 8.00
Incentive Scheme	Halsey	Rowan

[C.U. B.Com. (Pass) 1993]

Ans. : Rajeeb – Rs. 352.00, Rs. 9.26
Sanjeeb – Rs. 460.80, Rs. 9.60

52. In a factory 2 men X and Y produce the same product using the same materials. Their normal wage rate is the same. They are paid bonus according to Rowan system. The time alloted to the product is 40 hours. A takes 25 hours and B takes 30 hours to finish the product. The factory cost of the product for A is Rs. 193.75 and for B Rs. 205. The factory overhead rate is Re 1.00 per man hour. Find out normal rate of wages and the cost of the materials used for the product.

Ans. : (i) Cost of materials used Rs. 100
(ii) Wages of X—Rs. 68.75
Y—Rs. 75.00

53. In a factory of two workmen A and B produce the same product using the same material. They are paid bonus according to Rowan system. The time alloted to the product is 40 hours. A takes 25 hours and B takes 30 hours to finish the product. The factory cost of the product for A is Rs. 193.75 and for B Rs. 205. The factory overhead rate is one rupee per man-hour. Find the normal rate of wages and the cost of materials used for the product.

[I.C.W.A. Inter]

Ans. : Cost of materials Rs. 100
Rate of wages – Rs. 2.00 per hour (approx.).

54. The rate per hour for three workers X, Y and Z are Re. 0.50, Rs. 0.60 and Re 0.55, respectively. The overhead recovery rate is 500% on production wages. The standard cost towards wages and overheads per unit is determined at Rs. 1.20 per unit.

If the time taken by X, Y and Z to finish 100 units is 26 hours, 30 hours, 20 hours, respectively, What is the amount of bonus earned by each worker ?

[B.Com. Madras]

Ans. : X – Rs. 3.90, Y – Re. 0.90, Z – Rs. 4.40.

Hints.

(i) Cost of Savings (S–A) = 42,12,54

$$\% \text{ of Savings} = \frac{\text{Cost of Savings}}{\text{Standard}} \times 100$$

= X–35%, Y–10%, Z–45%.

55. A, B and C in a particular day had produced 200, 250 and 300 pieces of a product 'P'. The time allowed for production of 25 units of 'P' is one hour and the hourly rate of wage payment is Rs. 8. Calculate for each of these three workers the following under Halsey Premium Bonus (50% sharing) and Rowan Premium Bonus Methods of Labour Remuneration :

(i) Earning for the day (8 hours per day) and

(ii) Effective Rate of Earnings per hour.

[Adapted I.C.W.A. (Inter)]

Ans. : (a) Rs. 64; Rs. 72; Rs. 80
(b) Rs. 64, Rs. 76.80; Rs. 85.33
(c) Halsey : Rs. 8; Rs. 9; Rs. 10
Rowan Rs. 8; Rs. 9.60; Rs. 10.

56. The standard output of a product has been fixed at 6 units per day of 8 hours. The normal wage per day is Rs. 12.

Determine the total wages payable under (i) Time rate; (ii) Piece rate; (iii) Halsey Plan and (iv) Rowan Plan when the outputs are 5, 8, 12 and 15 units per day. Calculate the labour cost per unit in each case.

[M.U. B.Com. 1988]

Ans. : When production :	5 units		8 units	12 units	15 units
	Rs.		Rs.	Rs.	Rs.
(i)	12.00	2.40	12.00	12.00	12.00
(ii)	10.00	2.00	16.00	24.00	30.00
(iii)	12.00	2.40	14.00	18.00	21.00
(iv)	12.00	2.40	16.00	24.00	30.00

57. Alpha Company pays its workers a guaranteed wage of Rs. 2 per hour. In addition, a bonus is paid for effective production and time saved @ Rs. 2 per hour. Calculate the amount of wages and bonus earned by each of the following workers :

Worker	Hours worked	Standard output	Actual output
A	40	80 units	3,360 units
B	38	80 units	3,648 units
C	40	80 units	3,000 units

[Karnataka B.Com. 1986]

Ans. : A – Rs. 84, B – Rs. 91.20, C – Rs. 80.

58. In an engineering concern, the employees are paid incentive bonus in addition to their normal wages at hourly rates. Incentive bonus is calculated in proportion of time taken to time allowed of the time saved. The following details are made in respect of employees X, Y and Z for a particular week.

	X	Y	Z
Normal wages (Rs. per hour)	4.00	5.00	6.00
Completed units of production	6,000	3,000	4,800
Time allowed (per 100 units)	0.8 hour	1.5 hours	1 hour
Actual time taken (Hours)	42	40	48

You are required to work out for each employee :

(i) the amount of bonus earned;

(ii) the total amount of wages earned;

(iii) the total wage cost per 100 units of output.

[Adapted—I.C.W.A (Inter) June 1989]

Ans. : (i) Rs. 21.00, Rs. 22.22p, Nil.; (ii) Rs. 189, Rs. 222.22, Rs. 288; (iii) Rs. 3.15, Rs. 7.41, Rs. 6.00.

59. From the following data ascertain the total earning of each worker separately under (i) Halsey and (ii) Rowan scheme of incentive payment :

Worker	A	B	C
Time allowed (hours)	3	4	5
Time taken (hours)	5	3	3
Basic Rate of wages per hour (Rs.)	2	2	2

[Vidyasagar University B.Com. (Hons.) 1990]

Ans. :

	A	B	C
	Rs.	Rs.	Rs.
Halsey Plan	10.00	7.00	8.00
Rowan Plan	10.00	7.50	8.40

60. Calculate the total monthly remuneration of workers A, B, C & D on the basis of the following information for the month of December 1989 :

(i) Standard production per worker – 1,000 units

(ii) Rate of Wage – 10 paise per unit

(iii) Bonus – Rs. 5 for each 1% increase over 90% of the standard.

(iv) Dearness Allowance per month – 100% of piece wage

The units completed by the workers were as under :

A – 950 units, B – 960 units, C – 900 units and D – 850 units.

[Vidyasagar University B.Com. (Hons.) 1989]

Ans. : A – Rs. 215.00, C – Rs. 180.00, B – Rs. 222.00, D – Rs. 170.00.

Hint : C and D will not get any bonus.

61. From the following particulars you are required to work out the earnings of a worker for a week under (a) Straight piece rate, (b) Differential piece rate; (c) Halsey premium scheme (50% sharing) and (d) Rowan premium scheme :

Weekly working hours	48
Hourly wage rate	Rs. 7.50
Piece rate per unit	Rs. 3.00
Normal time taken per piece	20 minutes
Normal output per week	120 pieces
Actual output for the week	150 pieces
Differential piece rate	80% of piece rate when output below normal and 120% of piece rate when output above normal.

[I.C.W.A. (Inter) Dec. 1989]

Ans. : (i) Rs. 450, (ii) Rs. 540; (iii) Rs. 367.50; (iv) Rs. 374.40.

62. From the following particulars calculate Group Bonus payable and the amounts that will be paid to each member of the group :

Standard production in a week is 120 units.

It is agreed that for every 10% increase in production, bonus of 5% of the total wages payable for the week will be paid and the same will be shared by the group consisting of 4 members in proportion to their total wage of the week.

Total production for the week is 145 units and wages earned by the four members of the group (A, B, C & D) are Rs. 80, Rs. 78, Rs. 72 and Rs. 68.

[Adapted—I.C.W.A. Inter]

Ans. : Total wages payable
A = Rs. 88.33, B = Rs. 86.13
C = Rs. 79.50 and D = Rs. 75.08

Hints :

Excess production $\frac{25}{120} \times 100 = 20.833\%$

Production Bonus $\frac{50}{100} \times 20.83 \times$ Rs. 298

Group Bonus = Rs. 31.04

A $\frac{80}{298} \times 31.04 =$ Rs. 8.33.

63. A manufacturing enterprise has introduced a bonus system of wage payment on a slab rate based on cost reduction towards labour and overheads, the slab rate being :

Up to	10% of Saving	5% of the earning
"	20% of Saving	15% " "
"	40% "	30% " "
"	70% "	40% " "
Above	70% "	50% " "

The rate per hour for 3 workers A, B and C are Re. 1.00, Rs. 1.20, Rs. 1.10, respectively. The overhead recovery rate is 500% on productive wages. The standard cost towards wages and overhead per unit is determined at Rs. 2.40 per unit.

If time taken by A, B and C to finish 100 units is 26 hours, 30 hours and 20 hours respectively, what is the amount of bonus earned by each worker ?

Ans. : Bonus : A – Rs. 7.80 ; B – Rs. 1.80 ; C – Rs. 8.80.

64. Jobs are issued to operator X to make 189 units and to operator Y to make 204 units, for which a time allowance of 20 standard minutes and 15 standard minutes per unit, respectively, is credited. For every hour saved, bonus is paid 50% of the basic rate which is Rs. 4 per hour for both the employees. The basic working week is 42 hours. Hours in excess are paid at time rate plus one-third.

X completes his units in 45 hours and Y completes his units in 39 hours (but works a full week). Due to defective materials six of X's units and four of Y's units are subsequently scrapped, although all units produced are paid for.

You are required to calculate for each of X and Y :

(i) the amount of bonus payable;
(ii) the total gross wage payable;
(iii) the wage cost per good unit made.

[Adapted—I.C.W.A. Eng.]

Ans. : (i) Rs. 36.00; Rs. 24.00
(ii) Rs. 220.00; Rs. 192.00
(iii) Rs. 1.202; Re – 0.96.

Hints : Basic Pay for the week for Y – 42 hours × Rs. 4 = Rs. 168.

65. The standard time for a job is 60 hours. The hourly rate of guaranteed wages is Re. 0.75. Because of the saving in time, worker A gets an hourly wage of Re 0.90 under Rowan premium bonus system for the same saving in time. Calculate the hourly rate of wages that worker B will get under Halsey-Weir premium bonus system (assuming 40% to worker).

[Adapted—I.C.W.A. (Inter)]

Ans. : Re. 0.825.

66. Calculate the earnings of workers A and B from the following particulars for a month and allocate of each to jobs X, Y and Z.

	A	B
(a) Basic wages (Rs.)	1,000	1,000
(b) Dearness Allowance	150%	155%
(c) Provident Fund (on basic wages)	8%	8%
(d) Employees' State Insurance (on basic wages)	2%	2%
(e) Overtime	10 hours	
(f) Idle time and leave		16 hours.

The normal working hours for the month are 200 hours. Overtime is paid for at double the normal rate plus D.A. Employer's contribution of State Insurance and Provident Fund are at equal rate with the employee's contributions. The month has 25 working days and one paid holiday.

The two workers were employed on jobs X, Y and Z in the following proportions :

	Jobs X	Y	Z
A	40	30	30
B	50	20	30

It is to be noted that overtime was done on job Y.

Ans. : Earnings : A Rs. 2,850
B Rs. 2,650
Job Cost X—Rs. 1,182.50
Y—Rs. 775.00
Z—Rs. 787.50

67. In a manufacturing company the daily wage rate guaranteed for a worker is Rs. 1.87 and the standard output fixed for the month is 1,000 articles, representing 100% efficiency. The daily wage rate is paid without bonus to those workers who show upto 662–3 % of the efficiency standard. Beyond this, there is a bonus payable in a graded scale in a fixed ratio to be increased output as under :

Efficiency	Bonus payable
90%	10%
100%	20%

Further increase of 1% is given for every 1% further rise in efficiency.

Find out the total earnings of A, B, C & D who have worked for 26 days in a month.

The workers' outputs are :

A—500 articles, B – 900 articles, C—1,000 articles and D—3,100 articles.

[B.Com. Punjab]

Ans. : A – Rs. 48.62 ; B – Rs. 53.48 ;
C – Rs. 58.34 and D – Rs. 63.20.

68. In a workshop 10 workers form a group. Standard production of the group is 10 units per minute. The group is paid a bonus equal to 80% of the time saved.

During the week ended 31.12.1992 the production was as follows :

Date	Hours worked	Production in unit
25.12.1992	90	78,000
26.12.1992	80	72,000
27.12.1992	85	66,000
28.12.1992	70	42,000
29.12.1992	80	62,000
30.12.1992	75	52,000
	480	3,72,000

A worked for 48 hours during the week and B 46 hours. Their hourly rates of pay are Re.1.00 and Rs. 1.25, respectively. They are also entitled to Dearness Allowance @ 150% of pay. Calculate their earnings, including share of Group Bonus for the week ended 31.12.1992.

[Adapted—B.Com. (Pass) C.U. 1988]

Ans. : A = Rs. 56.00 + D.A. 84.00 = Rs. 140.00
B = Rs. 167.71.

69. Calculate the earnings of A and B from the following particulars for a month and allocate the labour cost to each job X, Y and Z .

		A	B
(i)	Basic wages	Rs. 100	Rs. 160
(ii)	Dearness Allowance	50%	50%
(iii)	Contribution of Provident Fund (on basic wages)	8%	8%
(iv)	Contribution to Employee's State Insurance (on basic wages)	2%	2%
(v)	Overtime	10 hours	

The normal working hours for the month are 200 hours. Overtime is paid at double the total of normal wages and dearness allowance. Employer's contribution to State Insurance and Provident Fund are at equal rates with employee's contributions. The two workers were employed on jobs X, Y and Z in the following proportions :

	Jobs		
	X	Y	Z
Worker A	40%	30%	30%
Worker B	50%	20%	30%

[C.A. (Inter) May 1992]

Overtime was done on job Y

Ans. : Net wages—A Rs. 155; B—Rs. 224.
Allocation of wages
X—Rs. 192; Y—Rs. 114.20; Z—Rs. 124.80.

70. From the following particulars you are required to calculate according to 'Average Wage Rate' the labour cost chargeable to job no. P-301 which was cmpleted in 1998.

Basice wage rate is Rs. 15 per hour, and overtime rate are as follows :

Before or after working hours 150% of basic wage rate.

Sundays and other holidays 200% of basic wage rate.

During the year 1998 the following labour hours were worked.

Normal time	4,00,000 hours
Overtime working after or before hour	50,000 hours.
Overtime on Sundays and holidays	40,000 hours
	4,90,000 hours

For jon no. P-301, 4,000 hours were spent as follows :

Normal time	3,000 hours
Before or after working hours	700 hours
Sundays and holidays	300 hours

[C.U. B.Com.(Hons.) 1999]

Ans. : Average wage rate Rs. 17;

Labour cost chargeable to job no. P-301`—Rs. 69,750.

OVERHEADS

5

Learning Objectives :

1. *Introduction*
2. *Definition*
3. *Indirect Materials, Indirect Wages and Indirect Expenses*
4. *Absorption of Overheads*
5. *Bases of Absorption and Selection of base*
   – Advantages and disadvantages of different bases
6. *Source documents*
7. *Classification of Overheads :*
   (i) Function-wise; (ii) Element-wise; (iii) Behaviour-wise; (iv) Control-wise
8. *Accounting for Overhead Costs*
9. *Cost Apportionment and Cost Allocation*
10. *Chart showing Apportionment and Allocation*
11. *Difference between Cost Apportionment and Cost Allocation*
12. *Bases of Apportionment of Factory Overheads*
13. *Pre-determined Overheads :*
    (i) Definition, (ii) Objects.
14. *Over–absorption and Under–absorption of Overheads*
15. *Treatment of Over–absorption and Under–absorption*
16. *Machine Hour Rate :*
    (i) Definition; (ii) Advantages; (iii) Method of Computation; (iv) Basis of Apportionment
17. *Comprehensive Machine Hour Rate*
18. *Setting Time and Idle Time —Treatment in Cost Accounts*
19. *Worked out Problems*
20. *Assignment.*

OVERHEADS 5

5.1 Introduction

In this chapter we propose to explain in detail the process of overhead absorption and the various bases used. The effect of under or over-absorption is also explained.

5.2 Definition

In the words of **Harold J. Wheldon : "Overhead may be defined as the cost of indirect materials, indirect labour and such other expenses including services as cannot conveniently be charged to a specific unit. Alternatively, overheads are all expenses other than direct expenses".**

According to **W. W. Bigg : "In cost accounting language, all indirect costs are termed as overheads".**

In the **Terminology of Cost Accountancy, Overhead is defined as "the aggregate of indirect material cost, indirect wages and indirect expenses".**

Overhead expenses refer to those expenses which are not identifiable with any particular peoduct, process, operation, job. So, they are to be apportioned or allocated to such cost centre on some equitable and fair basis.

Therefore, **Overheads = Cost of Indirect Materials + Indirect wages + Indirect expenses** pertaining to factory, office and administration, selling and distribution of products.

Let us now acquaint ourselves with the words 'Indirect materials', 'Indirect wages' and 'Indirect expenses'.

5.3 Indirect Materials

Indirect materials are those which do not enter in final product but are used in the process of manufacture of a product. The cost of such materials cannot be directly allocated to a cost centre. But they do form a part of total cost and, hence, they are to be apportioned to or absorbed by cost centres or cost units.

Moreover, there are some materials which are used in such small quantities that it is often considered logical to regard them as an indirect expense. For example, in the construction of a building, nails are used but the cost of such nails is so insignificant compared to the total cost of the building that cost of nails is treated as indirect material cost.

On the other hand, there are some materials which do not seem as direct but are treated as direct. In brick-making, large amount of coal or coke are used in firing the kilns. Though the fuel does not enter into the final product yet this may be treated as direct cost in the sense that the fuel is used to make hard-baked brick and the cost of fuel can be directly charged to the cost of brick.

In the words of **Wheldon : "It may be generally accepted that indirect materials are those which are used asancillary to manufacture and cannot be traced into the finished product".**

Examples

Screws, nails, bolts, nuts, paint, oil, rags, stationeries, cotton waste, lubricant etc. are the examples of indirect materials.

5.4 Indirect wages

I.C.M.A., London, defined indirect wages cost as **"wages other than direct wages cost"**.

In a factory there are workers who are not directly connected with production activities but indirectly help the direct workers in carrying out their activities. The employees who work in the office, sales and purchase departments are also known as indirect workers. In other words, wages paid to all workers who do not help directly in 'changing the shape or composition' of the raw materials from which a product is made.

Examples

Wages paid to foremen, storekeepers, employees of purchase department; salaries of office executives, commission payable to sales representatives; salaries paid to office staff etc.

5.5 Indirect Expenses

Indirect expenses refer to those expenses which are not direct or chargeable to any cost centre or unit. These expenses can be apportioned to or absorbed by cost centres or cost units. Most of the expenses of an organisation are indirect expenses since they are incurred for the business as a whole.

Examples

Rent, rates and taxes of factory premises ; lighting, power, depreciation, canteen subsidies ; fire insurance premium, advertising, repairs and renewals etc.

5.6 Classification

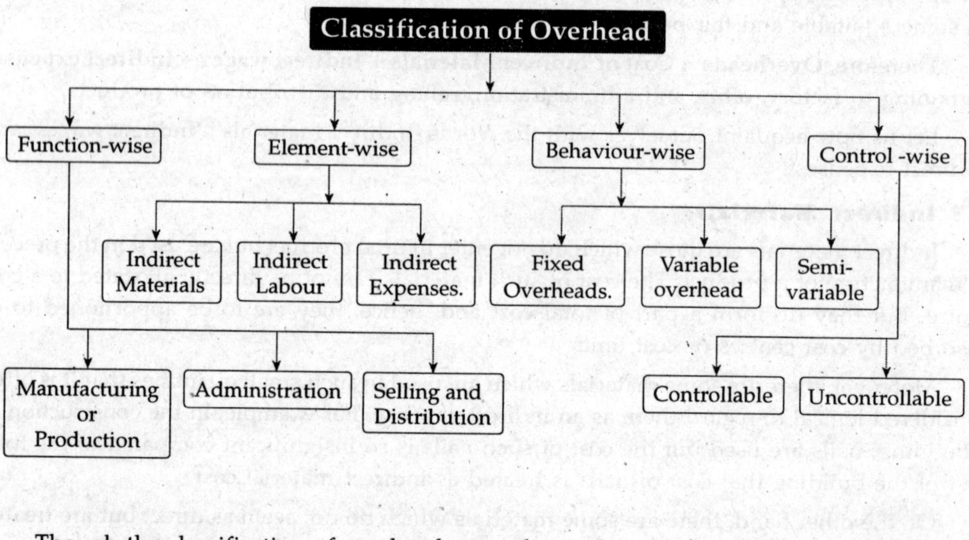

Though the classification of overhead expenditure depends upon the type and size of a manufacturing concern and the nature of the product it manufactures, or the nature of the service it renders, the following are the principal methods :

(i) Function-wise classification,

(ii) Element-wise classification,

(iii) Behaviour-wise classification, and

(iv) Control-wise classification.

5.7 Function-wise classification

Classification of overhead expenses on a functional basis is done with reference to the various activities of a concern. The main groups consist of :

(a) Manufacturing overhead costs,

(b) Office and Administration overhead costs,

(c) Selling overhead costs, and

(d) Distribution overhead costs.

Manufacturing Overhead Costs = Indirect Materials used in factory + Indirect or unproductive wages paid for the factory + Indirect expenses incurred in the factory.

In the words of **W. M. Harper** : "Overheads incurred in production i.e. overhead incurred within the four walls of the factory proper" are known as Production Overheads.

Students are to note that production overhead is also known as factory overhead or works overhead or production overhead.

Production overhead includes the following indirect expenses :

Factory rent, rates and taxes ;

Lighting, heating, power and fuel ; depreciation, repairs and insurance for factory assets ;

State Insurance, retirement pension premiums, wages of indirect workers ; salaries and related costs of production management ;

Indirect materials and materials of little individual value used in production – screws, nails, bolts, nuts etc. ;

Carriage inwards on materials purchased ;

Normal wastage of materials ;

Canteen and Welfare expenses ;

Tool room expenses, production control and progress department expenses ;

Oil, rags and other factory supplies.

5.8 Office and Administration Overhead Costs

Cost of Indirect materials used, indirect remuneration paid to the office and administrative staff and indirect expenses incurred in office management are the constituent factors of office and administration overhead costs. It is the sum total of those costs of general management, and of secretarial, accounting and administrative services, which cannot be directly related to the production, marketing, research and development functions of the enterprise.

Office and administration overhead costs include the following :

Office rent, rates and taxes and insurance.

Office lighting, heating and cleaning.

Repairs to office buildings, furniture and fittings and equipment.

Salaries, overtime, bonus of office staff, printing and stationery used in the office.

Salaries of administrative directors and other managerial personnel.

Audit fees, legal charges and bank charges.

5.9 Marketing, Selling and Distribution Overhead Costs

Marketing Cost has been defined by the **I.C.M.A., London**, as "the Cost incurred in publicizing and presenting to customers the products of the undertaking in suitably attractive forms and at acceptable prices, together with the costs of all relevant research work, the securing of orders and, usually, delivery of the goods to customers. In certain cases, after-sales service and/or order processing may also be included".

Sometimes it becomes useful in most businesses to subdivide the marketing cost into selling, publicity and distribution costs.

Marketing overhead costs include the following indirect materials, labour costs and indirect expenses incurred in connection with marketing the products :

Selling

Salaries, commissions and travelling expenses of technical representatives and sales engineers and salesmen.

Bad debts written-off.

Maintenance and administration costs of Sales Offices.

Publicity

Cost of advertisement,

Cost of printing catalogues, price lists,

Cost of maintenance of showrooms,

Salaries of showroom personnel,

Stationery used in showrooms,

Cost of participation in industrial exhibitions.

Distribution

Carriage outwards,

Cost of packing materials,

Packing charges,

Costs of running and maintaining of delivery vehicles,

Costs of maintenance of warehouse.

Research and Development Costs

They include the following expenses :

Salaries of Laboratory technicians, Work-study engineers, Research Associates etc.

Cost of raw materials used in research.

Depreciation of Laboratory Equipment.

Cost of technical journals.

Patent fees.

Subscriptions for Research Association etc.

5.10 Element-wise classification

Under this method total indirect expenses are classified as (i) Indirect materials ; (ii)Indirect labour and (iii) Indirect expenses. These have bee discuss and earlier.

5.11 Behaviour-wise classification

Overhead costs can be classified into (i) Fixed ; (ii) Variable ; and (iii) Semi-variable costs.

(i) **Fixed Costs**

Definition : Fixed Costs are those which remain fixed and do not vary with the increase or decrease in volume of output for a given period of time.

Examples : Rent of building, Property taxes, Management salaries, Building depreciation, Salaries of Works Managers, Supervisors, Accountants, Stationery, Printing etc.

(ii) **Variable Costs**

Definition : Variable Costs refer to those costs which do vary with the change in the level of production. This type of cost tends to vary in direct proportion to changes in the volume of output.

Examples : Indirect labour ; Indirect material ; Power and Fuel ; Lighting ; Power ; Repairs and Maintenance ; Tools and Spares ; Overtime pay etc.

(iii) **Semi-variable Costs**

Definition : Costs that contain both fixed and variable elements, which are, therefore, partly affected by fluctuations in the volume of output or turnover are known as semi-variable costs. These costs remain fixed in total amount over a relatively short range of variation in output and then are abruptly changed to a new level of production.

Examples : Normal maintenance of buildings, salaries and wages of administration, stationery and postage, wages of service department, wages of supervisors etc.

5.12 Control-wise classification

Costs may also be classified as (i) Controllable and (ii) Uncontrollable costs.

Controllable costs refer to those costs which can be controlled effectively if proper managerial control is exercised.

Uncotrollable costs are those which are beyond the control of the management. They are bound to occur.

5.13 Absorption of Overhead

Definition

Overhead absorption is a process by which overheads are included in the total cost of a product.

According to **Terminology of Cost Accountancy overhead absorption is defined as "the charging overheads to cost units by means of rates separately calculated for each cost centre. In most cases the rates are pre-determined".**

When dissimilar products are made which require different production processes or for jobs using identical facilities, overhead absorption becomes very much essential.

The overhead to be absorbed by a cost unit is computed with reference to two factors :

(i) the overheads attributable to a given cost centre ; and (ii) the number of units of the absorption base i.e. labour hours, machine hours etc.

So, Overhead Absorption Rate

$$= \frac{\text{Total overheads}}{\text{No. of units of absorption base applicable to cost centre}}$$

5.14 Bases of absorption

The objective of overhead absorption process is to include in the total cost of a product an appropriate share of a firm's total overheads. Various bases to absorb overheads have been developed. These bases are :

(i) Direct labour hour overheads absorption rate (OAR) .
Total overheads ÷ Direct labour hours.

(ii) Direct wages OAR = **Total overheads ÷ Direct wages × 100.**

(iii) Direct Materials OAR = **Total overheads ÷ Direct Materials used.**

(iv) Prime Cost OAR = **Total overheads ÷ Prime Cost × 100.**

(v) Machine hour OAR = **Total overheads ÷ Total Machine Hours.**

5.15 Selection of base

Certain factors are considered for choosing a particular and appropriate base for absorption of overheads, but final choice is a matter of judgement and common sense. Let us discuss them one by one.

1. **Direct labour hour basis**

This method of absorbing overhead is most appropriate in a labour intensive cost centre. Moreover, it is easy to use. Nowadays, most production methods involve substantial use of machinery and so the labour hour method may become increasingly inappropriate.

2. **Machine hour rate**

This method is most appropriate in a mechanised cost centre, i.e. where production is mainly carried on mechanically. In such a cost centre, many of the overheads are related to the machinery, this method of absorption of overheads reflects more accurately the incidence of overheads in the total cost. So, where a large part of the overhead is incurred by the use of machinery, the use of machine hour rates can be suggested.

3. **Direct Material**

This method of overhead absorption is not commendable since its use leads to some absurd anomalies. Though this method is simple and easy to understand and apply, it suffers from the following disadvantages :

(i) There is no logical relationship between direct materials cost of a product and factory overhead.

(ii) Nowadays, in every economy, material prices fluctuate substantially. This change in price leads to high or low overhead costs, even though overhead costs remain unchanged.

(iii) Most of the overhead expenses vary with time, they accrue on time basis and not on materials consumed. The use of direct materials cost as the basis of absorption totally ignores the time factor which is considered as an important factor in allocation of overhead.

(iv) This method is not rational when part of the materials passes through all processes and part through only some processes.

4. **Direct Wages**

This method is frequently used in practice. This is computed in the following way :

$$\frac{\text{Factory Overhead}}{\text{Direct Labour cost}} \times 100$$

This method is simple to operate and understand. It considers the time factor and so it is a rational method for the absorption of factory overheads. Under this method, labour cost is computed by multiplying number of hours spent on work by an hourly labour rate. This signifies that the more hours worked, the higher the labour cost and greater the charge for factory overheads.

This method is beneficial where production is uniform.

The following are the **demerits** of this method :

(i) It does not consider the share of other factors of production other than direct labour. In many concerns, machinery is considered the major factor of production but not the labour. In such case, machine hour is recommended as the base of absorption.

(ii) It does not take into account the variations in the rates of wages for different personnel. Where wage rates vary and different incentive schemes are in existence, corelation between wages paid and time elapsed does not exist. If there is only one rate of wage per hour paid throughout a cost centre and no form of incentive scheme exists then the Direct Wages system would be more appropriate to use. But such a situation is a distant possibility.

5. **Prime Cost**

This method combines the total of direct materials cost and direct labour cost.

The formula is : $\dfrac{\text{Total Factory Overhead}}{\text{Prime Cost}} \times 100$

Advantages

This method is simple to operate as the prime cost data is easily available.

Disadvantages

(i) It ignores time factor in absorbing factory overhead.

(ii) Since the method is a combination of direct materials and direct wages, it suffers from the shortcomings of both the methods.

(iii) Where the cost of materials forms a larger part of prime cost, the time factor will be ignored.

(iv) Additional costs which arise due to the use of costlier machines are ignored and thus, this method is likely to result in an inequitable allotment of overheads.

Pre-determined Overhead Rates

5.16 Definition

We know from our earlier discussion that in most cases the overhead absorption rates are pre-determined. This means that the overhead absorption rates are calculated or computed prior to the accounting period, using estimated or budgeted figures for overheads and units of the absorption base chosen. Once we again repeat the formula of computing O.A.R.

The formula is $\dfrac{\text{Budgeted total overheads for cost centre}}{\text{Budgeted total number of units of absorption base}}$

5.17 Objects

The main object of using predetermined overhead rates is that the actual overheads and actual number of base units are not available in total until the end of the period. Hence, overhead absorption rate (OAR) cannot be calculated until the end of the financial period. This would obviously mean the costs of products could not be calculated and would cause unacceptable delays in estimating costs for submission of quotations and tenders.

Pre-determined overhead rates can advantageously be used in both job and process cost accounting. Its basic approach is to develop an overhead absorption rate that closely approximates the amount of actuals.' Predetermined rates also can be effectively applied to standard costing and budgetary programmes as they use estimated costs.

Problem 1

The following are the figures relating to Cost Centre 10

	Rs.
Total Overhead for the period	24,000
Total Direct Labour hours	3,200
Total Direct Wages	6,400
Total Direct Materials used	12,000
Total Machine hours	4,800
Total Units produced	180

Using the above data the following absorption rates could be calculated using the above formula :

Direct Labour hour OAR $= \text{Rs. } \dfrac{24{,}000}{3{,}200} = \text{Rs. } 7.5$

Direct Wages' OAR $= \text{Rs. } \dfrac{24{,}000}{6{,}400} \times 100 = 375\%$ of wages

Direct Materials Overhead

Absorption rate $= \text{Rs. } \dfrac{24{,}000}{12{,}000} \times 100 = 200\%$ of materials

Prime Cost OAR $= \text{Rs. } \dfrac{24{,}000}{18{,}400} \times 100 = 130\%$ of Prime Cost

Machine Hour OAR $= \text{Rs. } \dfrac{24{,}000}{4{,}800} = \text{Rs. } 5.00$ per machine hour

Cost Unit OAR $= \text{Rs. } \dfrac{24{,}000}{180 \text{ units}} = \text{Rs. } 133.33$ overhead per unit produced.

5.18 Method of Absorption of Overheads—Choice of Method

It is really a difficult task to choose the proper method of absorption of overhead. Out of the methods discussed previously the direct labour hour method is usually the best method because most of the factory overheads are period costs as they relate to time and not to the production. If all the workers in a department or in a Cost Centre are paid wages at the same rate, direct labour hour method is to be followed. If the workers are paid at different rates, direct wages percentage rate is to be adopted. The circumstances under which each method is followed are :

Circumstances	*Method to be followed*
1. If the cost centre is labour intensive and the workers are paid at the same rate of wages	Direct labour method
2. If the cost centre is labour intensive and the workers are paid at different rates of wages	Direct wages percentage rate
3. If the cost centre is machine intensive	Machine hour rate
4. If the cost of materials is predominant	Direct materials cost percentage
5. If the prime cost is predominant	Prime cost percentage rate.

5.19 Source Documents

The following are some of the primary documents from which overhead expenses can be collected :

1. Store requisitions – Indirect materials
2. Job cards or tickets – Indirect labour
3. Purchase vouchers – Indirect materials
4. Salary or Pay Bills – Indirect labour
5. Subsidiary records – Indirect expenses
   Cash vouchers, Cash Book
6. Plant Register – Depreciation
7. Lease Deed – Rent
8. Local government assessment – Rates.

5.20 Items not included in Cost Accounts

Certain items of expense, though dealt with in Financial Accounts of a business unit, are not considered as elements of cost and are excluded from Cost Accounts. These items fall into three main categories :

1. Appropriations and other deductions

These items consist of :

(a) Income tax and Corporation tax.
(b) Transfers to reserves.
(c) Provisions.
(d) Charity and donations to any institution wherefrom the employees do not derive any benefit.
(e) Dividends.
(f) Amount of goodwill, preliminary expense, discount on issue of shares and debentures, expenses of capital nature and issue written-off.
(g) Directors' fees (not remuneration to directors).
(h) Appropriations to sinking funds created for the redemption of liability.

2. Financial Overheads

Items of this nature include :

(a) Interest, dividends received on investments.
(b) Capital losses or profits.
(c) Interest received on bank deposits.

3. Adjustments

Some items are there for which adjustments are made. Certain items of expense are charged in financial accounts whereas they are not considered in cost accounts. Depreciation on plant under construction is not considered in cost accounts while it is prudent to provide for it in financial account. So, the differences arising out of adopting different methods of treatment must be computed carefully and should be brought into reconciliation statement prepared for reconciling the profit shown by cost accounting and financial accounting.

5.21 ACCOUNTING FOR OVERHEAD COSTS

The following steps are involved in accounting for overheads :

Step I The overhead expenses incurred by various departments are collected and accumulated under appropriate standing order numbers.

Step II The next step is to allocate the overhead expenses to production and service departments.

Step III Apportionment of such overheads which cannot be allocated directly between the production and service departments is done on the basis of accepted and logical principles.

Step IV The total cost of service department or departments is distributed proportionately to different production departments on the basis of service rendered by them to production departments. Here, the total cost means **direct materials, and direct labour costs plus total apportioned overhead costs.**

Step V An overhead rate is computed for each department.

Step VI The overhead rate computed as per Step V is charged to the cost of products manufactured by different departments at a predetermined rate.

5.22 Cost apportionment and Cost allocation

The indirect costs are required to be divided between various cost centres to determine the total cost of the product. The procedure for allotting indirect costs to cost units involves apportionment, allocation and absorption.

(i) **Cost apportionment**

I.C.M.A., London, has defined cost apportionment as the division of costs among two or more cost centres in proportion to the estimated benefit received. If an overhead cannot be allocated directly to cost centre, it is apportioned on the basis of accepted and logical principles.

Expenses like light and rent are to be apportioned to all departments using such items. Generally these expenses are apportioned on the basis of floor area occupied by each department. In cost accounting, the function of apportionment is known as *primary distribution of overhead.*

(ii) **Cost Allocation**

I.C.M.A., London, has defined cost allocation as "the allotment of whole items of cost to cost centres or cost units". It is the charging of discrete identifiable items of cost to cost centres or cost units. Some overhead costs like repair and maintenance expenses incurred in specific departments, indirect materials can be directly identified with a particular department or cost centres as having been incurred for that cost centre. Though these items cannot be traced to product or job, they can definitely be allocated to departments or jobs.

5.23 Difference between apportionment of costs and allocation of costs

The distinctions between cost apportionment and cost allocation are:

1. Cost allocation deals with the whole items, while apportionment deals with only a proportion of items of cost.
2. Cost allocation means direct allocation of costs to cost centre, while apportion means distribution of total cost among different cost centres. Distribution is made on some rational and equitable bases.

3. Allocation is a much wider term than apportionment.
4. Allocation refers to distribution of overhead expenses on a departmental basis, while apportionment of the departmental overhead expenses means the method of distribution of the cost of one department to the other departments. For example, cost of service department is apportioned between different production departments proportionately. This apportionment is known as **secondary distribution.**

The following chart demonstrates the method of apportionment of overheads.

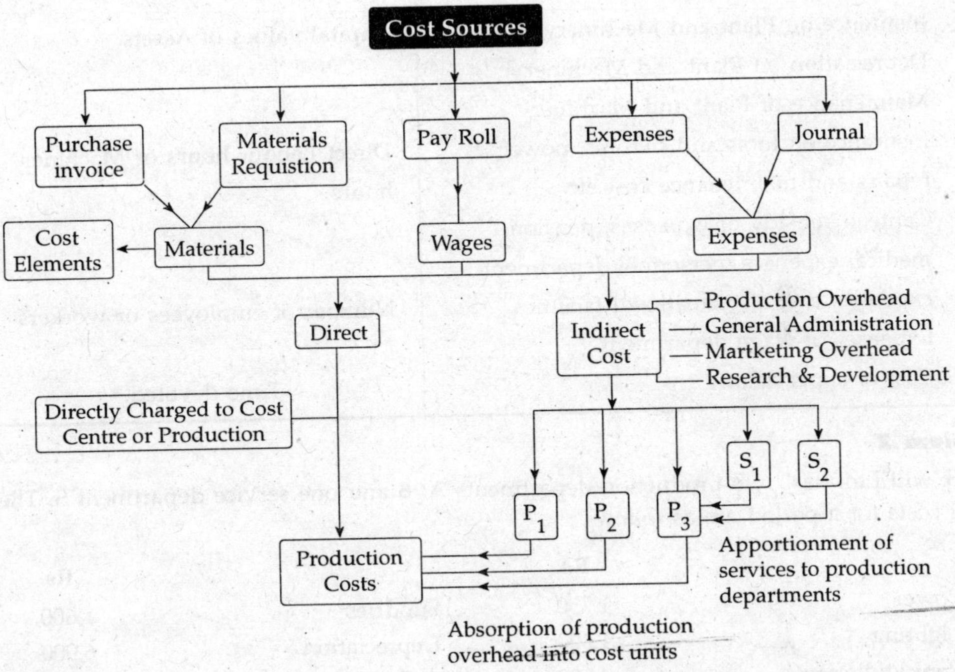

Fig. 5.1

The above chart demonstrates how the overheads are apportioned and ultimately absorbed into cost centre or job.

5.24 Primary Distribution of Overhead

Primary distribution involves apportionment or allocation of overhead to all departments in a factory on logical and rational basis. This process of apportionment is also known as departmentalisation of overhead. It is to be carefully noted that at the time of making primary distribution, the distinction between production and service departments is ignored.

Following points should be considered for primary distribution of items of overheads:

(i) basis for distribution should be equitable and practicable;

(ii) method adopted for distribution should not be time–consuming;

(iii) overhead expenses should be distributed among different departments on the basis of benefits received by departments;

For the purpose of primary distribution, a departmental distribution summary is prepared in the following way :

Basis of Apportionment of Factory Overhead

Expenses	*Base*
1. Lighting, heating, rent, rates and taxes, depreciation on building, repair cost of building, caretaking etc.	Floor area occupied by each department. Light points for lighting.
2. Insurance on Plant and Machinery, Building; Depreciation on Plant and Machinery; Maintenance of Plant and Machinery.	Capital values of Assets.
3. Insurance on tools and fixtures, power, repairs and maintenance cost etc.	Direct Labour hours or Machiner hours.
4. Canteen subsidy or expenses, pension, medical expenses, personnel department expenses, cost of recreational facilities. Expenses of wage department	Number of employees or workers
5. Cost of supervision	Time devoted.

Problem 2

S. will Ltd. has two production departments A, B and one service department S. The actual costs for a period are as follows :

	Rs.		Rs.
Power	1,750	Sundries	1,600
Lighting	1,600	Depreciation on Machinery	6,000
Rent and Rates	6,000		
Indirect wages	4,000		

The other particulars are :

	Production Departments A	B	Service Department S
Working Hours	4,000	3,000	2,000
Direct wages (Rs.)	3,000	2,000	3,000
Cost of Machinery	75,000	50,000	25,000
H.P. of Machinery	60	30	10
Light points	18	12	10
Floor Area (sq. ft.)	1,000	1,200	800

Apportions the costs of the various departments on most equitable basis.

Solution

Primary Distribution Summary

Items	*Basis of Apportionment*	*Total Rs.*	*A Rs.*	*B Rs.*	*S Rs.*
Power	Horse Power × hours 24 : 9 : 2	1,750	1,200	450	100
Lighting	Light points 9 : 6 : 5	1,600	720	480	400
Rent and Rates	Area occupied 5 : 6 : 4	6,000	2,000	2,400	1,600
Indirect Wages	Direct wages 3 : 2 : 3	4,000	1,500	1,000	1,500
Sundries	Direct wages 3 : 2 : 3	1,600	600	400	600
Depreciation	Cost of Machinery 3 : 2 : 1	6,000	3,000	2,000	1,000
		20,950	9,020	6,730	5,200

5.25 Secondary Distribution

In a factory a product does not pass through Service department (S), but service department renders service to production departments for carrying on production function. It is, therefore, logical that the product cost should bear the equitable share of cost of service department. Under this backdrop, the second step is to distribute the total cost of service departments among the production departments. The process of redistributing *the cost of service* departments among production departments is known as **secondary distribution**. Here, the cost of service department means the apportioned overheads **plus** direct materials **plus** direct labour and direct expenses of concerned service department.

Bases for Secondary Distribution

Service Department Costs	*Basis of Redistribution*
(i) Employment department	(i) Rate of labour-turnover or number of employees.
(ii) Maintenance department	(ii) Hours worked for each department.
(iii) Purchase department	(iii) No. of purchase orders or value of materials purchased.
(iv) Store keeping	(iv) No. of requisitions.
(v) Canteen, welfare and recreation	(v) No. of employees of each department.

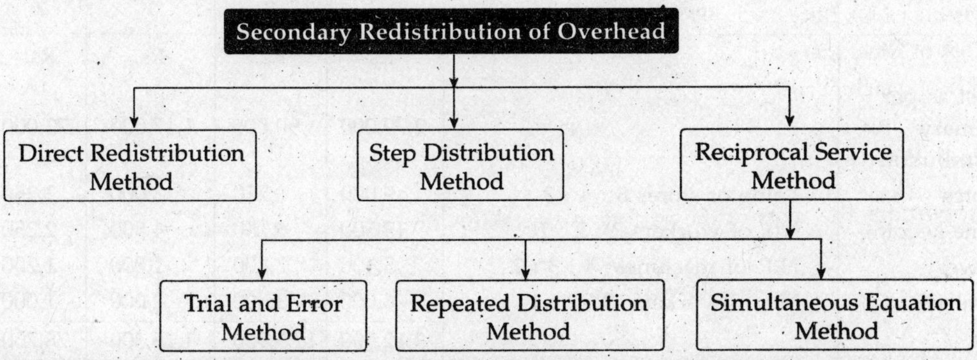

(i) **Direct Redistribution Method**

Under this method, service department's costs are apportioned to production departments only ignoring service rendered by one service department to another. When this method is followed, the number of secondary distribution will be equal to number of secondary department.

Problem 3

Finolex Co. Ltd. has three production departments and four service departments. The expenses of these departments as per primary distribution summary were as follows :

Production Departments		
	Rs.	Rs.
X	90,000	
Y	1,17,000	
Z	72,000	
		2,79,000
Service Departments		
Stores	9,000	
Time-keeping and accounts	13,500	
Power	(5,400) 5,400	
Canteen	6,000	33,900
		3,12,900

The following information is also available in respect of production departments :

	X	Y	Z
H.P. of machines	1,200	900	600
No. of workers	120	80	40
Value of store requisitioned (Rs.)	7,500	6,000	4,500

Apportion the cost of various service departments to the production departments.

Solution

Secondary Distribution Summary

Item	*Basis of apportionment*	*Total*	*Production departments*		
			X	*Y*	*Z*
		Rs.	Rs.	Rs.	Rs.
Cost as per primary distribution	—	2,79,000	90,000	1,17,000	72,000
Stores	Value of stores 5 : 4 : 3	9,000	3,750	3,000	2,250
Time-keeping	No. of workers 3 : 2 : 1	13,500	6,750	4,500	2,250
Power	H.P. of machines 4 : 3 : 2	5,400	2,400	1,800	1,200
Canteen	No. of workers 3 : 2 : 1	6,000	3,000	2,000	1,000
		3,12,900	1,05,900	1,28,300	78,700

2. **Step Method**

This method of redistribution gives cognizance to the service rendered by one service department to another service department.

The cost of service department which renders service to the largest number of other departments is distributed first. After this is done, the cost of service department serving the next largest number of department is apportioned. This process continues till the cost of last service department is apportioned. The cost of last service department is apportioned among production departments only.

Problem 4

A manufacturing company has two production departments X and Y, and three service departments, Stores, Time-keeping and Maintenance. The departmental distribution summary showed the following expenses for March 1998 :

	Rs	Rs.
Production Departments		
X	1,20,000	
Y	1,00,000	
		2,20,000
Service Departments		
Stores	20,000	
Time-keeping	12,000	
Maintenance	9,000	
		41,000
		2,61,000

Additional information

	Production Departments		Service Departments		
	X	*Y*	*Stores*	*Time-keeping*	*Maintenance*
No of employees	40	30	20		10
No. of stores requisitioned	25	20	—	—	5
Machine Hours	2,400	1,600			

Apportion the cost of Service Departments to Production Departments :

Solution

Departments	*As per primary distributions*				
Service Departments	Rs.	Rs.	Rs.	Rs.	Rs.
Time-keeping (4 : 3 : 2 : 1)	12,000	–12,000			
Stores (5 : 4 : 1)	20,000	2,400	–22,400		
Maintenance (3 : 2)	9,000	1,200	2,240	–12,440	
Production Departments					
X	1,20,000	4,800	11,200	7,464	1,43,464
Y	1,00,000	3,600	8,960	4,976	1,17,536
	2,61,000	—	—	—	—

3. **Reciprocal Distribution Method**

There may be two or more service departments in a factory and they may render service to each other. In that situation it is logical to give weight to inter-departmental services while distributing the expenses of service departments.

There are *three methods* for dealing with the distribution of inter-departmental services :

A) Trial and Error Method

B) Repeated Distribution Method

C) Simultaneous Equation Method.

A. Trial and Error Method

Under this method, the cost of one service department is apportioned to another service department and the cost of another service department *plus* the share received from first service department is again apportioned to first service department and this process is continued till the balancing figure is negligible.

Problem 5

Suppose the cost of service department X is Rs. 4,000 and that of Y is 4,800; an analysis reveals that X department renders 20% of its service to Y and Y renders 30% of its service to X.

Under Trial and Error Method distribution will be made in the following way .

	X Rs.	Y Rs.	
	4,000.00	4,800.00	
		800.00	20% of Rs. 4,000
		5,600.00	
30% of Rs. 5,600 =	1,680.00		
		336·00 =	20% of Rs. 1,680
30% of Rs. 336 =	100.80		
		20·16 =	20% of Rs. 100·8
30% of Rs. 20·16 =	6.05		
		1·20 =	20% of Rs. 6·05
30% of Rs. 1·20 =	0.36		
	5787.21	5,957·36	

B. Repeated Distribution System

Under this method, costs of one service department are apportioned to other service departments and production departments on agreed percentages and this process is repeated till the figures of service departments are too small to be reckoned for further apportionment. The following steps are involved in this method :

(i) Apply the given percentages to distribute the primary total of first service department. After proper distribution the account of first service department will be closed.

(ii) Apply the given percentages to the second service department whose total is made up of primary charges *plus* amount apportioned from Service Department 1. This will close the amount of second service department.

(iii) Repeat this process.

(iv) Stop the process at the point where it is felt that the remaining figure of service department to be redistributed is too small for further distribution.

Problem 6

Swill Co. Ltd. has three production departments and two service departments. From the following information show the distribution of service departments cost under the ***repeated distribution method.***

Production Departments

	Rs.	Rs.
P_1	4,800	
P_2	4,200	
P_3	3,000	12,000

Service Departments

	Rs.
X	1,000
Y	1,200

The expenses of service departments' are charged on a percentage basis which is as follows :

	Production Departments			*Service Departments*	
	P_1	P_2	P_3	X	Y
X	20%	40%	30%		10%
Y	40%	20%	20%	20%	

Solution

Primary Distribution Summary

Items	*Production Dept.*			*Service Dept.*	
	P_1	P_2	P_3	X	Y
	Rs.	Rs.	Rs.	Rs.	Rs.
As per primary distribution	4,800	4,200	3,000	1,000	1,200
Service Dept X—20%, 40%, 30% & 10%	200	400	300	(1,000)	100
Service Dept Y—40%, 20%, 20%, 20%	520	260	260	260	(1,300)
Service Dept. X	52	104	78	(260)	26
Service Dept. Y	10.40	5.20	5.20	5.20	(26)
Service Dept X	1.04	2.08	1.56	(5.2)	:52
Service Dept Y	0.26	0.13	0.13		(.52)
	5583.70	4,971.41	3644.89	—	—

C. Simultaneous Equation Method

Under this method, the true costs of service department are ascertained first with the help of simultaneous equations. After that the total costs are distributed among production departments on the basis of given percentages. The following problem will exemplify the method.

Problem 7

A manufacturing company has three production departments and two service departments. The primary distribution summary of March 1999 gives the following information :

	Rs.	Rs.
Production Departments		
X	32,000	
Y	24,000	
Z	12,000	
		68,000
Service Departments		
S_1	4,500	
S_2	8,000	
		12,500
		80,500

The service departments' expenses are charged on a percentage basis which is as follows :

	Production Departments			*Service Departments*	
	X	Y	Z	S_1	S_2
S_1	20%	25%	35%		20%
S_2	25%	25%	40%	10%	

Solution

Let	A	=	total overhead of department S_1	
	B	=	total overhead of department S_2	
or,	A	=	Rs. 4,500 + 10% of B	.... (i)
and	B	=	Rs. 8,000 + 20% of A	.... (ii)
or	A	=	Rs. 4,500 + .1B	.... (iii)
and	B	=	Rs. 8,000 + .2A.	.... (iv)

By eliminating the decimal and rearranging

$$10A = 45,000 + B \quad \text{......... (v)}$$

$$10B = 80,000 + 2A \quad \text{......... (vi)}$$

Or. $10A - B = 45,000$

$10B - 2A = 80,000$

By multiplying equation (vi) by 5 we get

$$10A - B = 45,000 \quad \text{......... (vii)}$$

$$-10A + 50B = 4,00,000 \quad \text{......... (viii)}$$

By adding (vii) and (viii), we get $49B = 4,45,000$

or $B = \dfrac{4,45,000}{49}$ = Rs. 9,082 (Aprox.)

Substituting the value of B in equation (v) we get

$10A - 9,082 = 45,000$ or, $10A = 45,000 + 9,082$

or, $A = \dfrac{54,082}{10}$ = Rs. 5,408

Statement showing the secondary distribution

Item	*Total*	*Production Departments*		
		X	Y	Z
	Rs.	Rs.	Rs.	Rs.
As per primary distribution	68,000	32,000	24,000	12,000
Department S_1 (80% of Rs. 5,408) distributed in the ratio 4 : 5 : 7	4,326	1,082	1,352	1,892
Department S_2 (90% of Rs. 9,082) in 5 : 5 : 8	8,174	2,271	2,271	3,632
	80,500	35,353	27,623	17,524

Problem 8

The following particulars related to the production department of a factory for the month of June, 1998 :

	Rs.	
Material used	80,000	
Direct wages	72,000	
Direct labour hours worked		20,000
Hours of machine operation		25,000
Overhead charges allocated to the department	90,000	

Cost data of a particular work order carried out in the above department during June, 1998 are given below :

Material used	8,000	
Direct wages	6,250	
Labour hours booked		3,300
Machine hours booked		2,400

What would be the factory cost of the work order under the following methods of charging overheads :

(i) Direct labour cost rate

(ii) Machine hour rate and

(iii) Direct Labour hour rate.

[I.C.W.A. (Inter)]

Solution

$$\text{Overheads charging rate} = \frac{\text{Overheads}}{\text{Basis}}$$

(i) Direct Labour Cost rate = $\frac{90,000}{72,000} \times 100 = 125\%$

(ii) Machine Hour rate = $\frac{90,000}{25,000}$ = Rs. 3.60 per machine hour.

(iii) Direct Labour Hour rate = $\frac{90,000}{20,000}$ = Rs. 4.50 per direct labour hour

Problem 9

A manufacturing company has two producing departments, Department A and Department B, and three service departments—Stores, Power house and Repair shop.

From the following information prepare a manufacturing expense budget and calculate overhead recovery rates for the two production departments as percentages of direct labour :

Direct Labour :	Rs.
Deptt. A	15,000
Deptt. B	30,000
Store	650
Power house	896
Repair shop	624
Indirect labour :	
Deptt. A	8,190
Deptt. B	11,500
Fuel (Power House)	1,780
Factory supplies :	
Power house	219
Repair shop	151
Deptt. A	2,400
Deptt. B	3,510

Contd.

Depreciation calculated as a % of original cost :

Building	2,500
Store equipment	100
Power house machinery	280
Repair shop machinery	400
Deptt. A	3,000
Deptt. B	2,800

Floor space occupied (sq. ft.) :

Store 1,000, Power house 500, Repair shop 500.
Deptt. A 4,000, Deptt. B 4,000.

Distribution of :

Power house	:	20% of repair shop, 20% to Deptt. A and 60% to Deptt. B.
Store	:	10% to Power house, 20% to Repair shop.
	:	30% to Deptt. A and 40% to Deptt. B
Repair shop	:	20% to Power house, 30% to Deptt. A and 50% to Deptt. B

[I.C.W.A. (Inter)]

Solution

Statement of Manufacturing expense distribution and recovery rates

Particulars	*Basis of apportion-ment*	*Total*	*Production Deptt.*			*Service Deptts.*	
			A	*B*	*Store*	*power House*	*Repair shop*
		Rs.	Rs.	Rs.	Rs.	Rs.	Rs.
Indirect Labour	Actuals	19,690	8,190	11,500	—	—	—
Fuel	"	1,780	—	—	—	1,780	—
Factory Supplies	"	6,280	2,400	3,510	—	219	151
Depreciation on Building	Floor space	2,500	1,000	1,000	250	125	125
Depreciation	Actuals	6,580	3,000	2,800	100	280	400
Total		36,830	14,590	18,810	350	2,404	676
Store	3 : 4 : 1 : 2		105	140	(–) 350	35	70
Power House	6 : 2 : 2		488	1,463	—	(–) 2,439	488
Repair Shop	3 : 5 : 2		370	617	—	247	(–) 1,234
Power House			49	148	—	(–) 247	50
Repair Shop			15	25	—	10	(–) 50
Power House			2	6	—	(–) 10	2
Repair Shop			1	1	—	—	(–) 2
Total Overhead		36,830	15,620	21,210	—	—	—

Overhead recovery Rate (ORR) as % of Direct Labour =

A: $\frac{15,620}{15,000} \times 100 = 104.13\%$

B: $\frac{21,210}{30,000} \times 100 = 70.7\%$

Problem 10

You are supplied with the following information and required to work out the production hour rate of recovery of overhead for departments A, B and C :

Particulars	*Total*	*Production Departments*			*Service Departments*	
		A	*B*	*C*	*P*	*Q*
	Rs.	Rs.	Rs.	Rs.	Rs.	Rs.
Rent	12,000	2,400	4,800	2,000	2,000	800
Electricity	4,000	800	2,000	500	400	300
Indirect labour	6,000	1,200	2,000	1,000	800	1,000
Depreciation	5,000	2,500	1,600	200	500	200
Sundries	4,500	910	2,143	847	300	300
Estimated working hours		1,000	2,500	1,400		

Expenses of service Departments P & Q are apportioned as under :

A	B	C	P	Q	
P	30%	40%	20%	—	10%
Q	10%	20%	50%	20%	

[Adapted—C.A. (Inter)]

Solution

Overhead Distribution Summary

Particulars	Total	A	B	C	P	Q
	Rs.	Rs.	Rs.	Rs.	Rs.	Rs.
Rent	12,000	2,400	4,800	2,000	2,000	800
Electricity	4,000	800	2,000	500	400	300
Indirect labour	6,000	1,200	2,000	1,000	800	1,000
Depreciation	5,000	2,500	1,600	200	500	200
Sundries	4,500	910	2,143	847	300	300
Total	31,500	7,810	12,543	4,547	4,000	2,600

(1) **Continued Distribution Method (secondary distribution)**

	A	B	C	P	Q
	Rs.	Rs.	Rs.	Rs.	Rs.
As per Primary Distribution	7,810	12,543	4,547	4,000	2,600
Cycle I					
Expenses of P being distributed in 3 : 4 : 2 : 1	1,200	1,600	800	(–) 4,000	400
	9,010	14,143	5,347	—	3,000
Cycle II					
Expenses of Q being distributed in 1 : 2 : 5 : 2	300	600	1,500	600	(–) 3,000
Total	9,310	14,743	6,847	600	—
Cycle III					
Expenses of P Deptt. being redistributed in 3 : 4 : 2 : 1	180	240	120	(–) 600	60
	9,490	14,983	6,967	—	60

Contd.

	A	B	C	P	Q
	Rs.	Rs.	Rs.	Rs.	Rs.
B.F.	9,490	14,983	6,967	—	60
Cycle IV					
Expenses of Q Deptt. being					
redistributed in 1 : 2 : 5 : 2	6	12	30	12	(–) 60
	9,496	14,995	6,997	(–) 12	—
Cycle V					
Expenses of P Deptt.					
in 3 : 4 : 2	4	5	3	(–) 12	—
	9,500	15,000	7,000		
Working hours	1,000	2,500	1,400		
Rate per hour	$\frac{9,500}{1,000}$ = Rs. 9.50	$\frac{15,000}{2,500}$ = Rs. 6.00	$\frac{7,000}{1,400}$ = Rs. 5.00		

(2) **Simultaneous Equation Method**

Let X be the expense of Deptt. p and Y be the expense of Deptt. Q.

Then, $X = 4{,}000 + \frac{1}{5}$th of Y (20% of Y); $Y = 2{,}600 + \frac{1}{10}$th of X (10% of X).

putting the value of X we get :

$Y = 2{,}600 + \frac{1}{10}$ of $(4{,}000 + \frac{1}{5}$ or Y,) or $Y = 2{,}600 + 400 + \frac{1}{50}$ Y.

or, $Y = 3{,}000 + \frac{1}{50}$ Y, or, 50 Y = 1,50,000 + Y, ... multiplying by 50

or, 50Y – Y = 1,50,000; or, 49 Y = 1,50,000; or, $Y = \frac{1,50,000}{49}$ = Rs. 3,061.

Putting the value of Y we get $X = 4{,}000 + \frac{1}{5}$ or 3,061, or, X = 4,000 + 612 = Rs. 4,612.

Overhead Distribution Summary

Particulars	A	B	C	P	Q
	Rs.	Rs.	Rs.	Rs.	Rs.
Total as per Primary distribution	7,810	12,543	4,547	4,000	2,600
Expense of Deptt. P being					
redistributed in 3 : 4 : 2 : 1	1,384	1,845	922	(–) 4,612	461
Expenses of dept. Q Rs. 3,061 being					
redistributed in 1 : 2 : 5 : 2	306	612	1,531	612	(–) 3,061
(a) Total allocated overhead	9,500	15,000	7,000		
(b) No. of hours	1,000	2,500	1,400		
Rate per hour (a ÷ b)	= 9.50	= 6.00	= 5.00		

5.26 Over-absorption or under-absorption of overheads

Definition

Usually overheads are absorbed on the basis of predetermined rates. Since predetermined overhead rates are based on budgeted overheads and budgeted production, invariably the overheads absorbed by this process do not agree with the actual overheads incurred for the period.

If the absorbed overheads at predetermined rates are greater than actual overheads, this is known as OVER-ABSORPTION. Conversely, if absorbed overheads ae less than the actual overheads, this is known as UNDER-ABSORPTION.

Problem 11

Cost Centre—100 Data for 1990

	Budgeted	Actual
Overheads	Rs. 12,000	Rs. 13,000
Direct labour hours	1,600	1,575
Direct wages	Rs. 3,200	Rs. 3,410
Direct materials	Rs. 6,000	Rs. 5,900
Machine hours	2,400	2,345
Unit produced	90	92

The predetermined overhead absorption rate for direct labour hours was Rs. 7.5 per hour.

Solution

Total overheads absorbed by actual activity of 1,575 labour hours

= 1,575 × 7.50 = Rs. 11,812.50 absorbed into production but actual overheads were Rs. 13,000.

Under-absorbed Overheads = Rs. 13,000 – 11,812.50 = Rs. 1,1857.50

It is to be noted that under or over-absorption may arise from either actual overheads differing from budget or a difference between the actual and budgeted amount of the absorption base or a combination of these two factors.

5.27 Treatment of over-absorption or under-absorption

There are many factors that are responsible for the difference between absorbed overheads and actual overheads. But it is actual overhead that is to be absorbed to ascertain the actual cost which finally determines the profit. The total of actual costs must appear in the final income statement and not merely those calculatd product costs which include actual prime cost plus overheads based on predetermined overhead rates.

Accordingly, the amount of under-absorbed overheads should be added to total costs before the profit is calculated and, conversely, the amount of over-absorbed overheads should be subtracted from the total cost.

The following illustration will make the concept clear :

Actual Direct material	*Actual Direct labour*	*Prime Cost*	*Absorbed Overheads*	*Calculatd Production Cost*	*Under absorption*	*Total Cost of production*	*To be debited to P & L A/c*
Rs.	Rs.	Rs.	Rs.	Rs.	Rs.	Rs.	
4,000	2,000	6,000	3,000	9,000	400	9,400	

This treatment can be made when under or over-absorption of overheads is caused by abnormal factors.

In a seasonal business firm, the balance (being the difference between predetermined absorbed overheads and actuals) may be carried forward to a subsequent period expected to be counter balanced at the end of the accounting period.

A supplementary rate can be used to adjust the amount of under or over-absorption. The supplementary rate is determined as follows :

$$\frac{\text{Amount of Under or Over absorption}}{\text{Actual absorption base}}$$

Under-absorption is adjusted by using a plus supplementary rate while a minus supplementary rate is used to correct over absorption.

Problem 12

In a manufacturing company overhead was recovered at a predetermined rate of Rs. 25 per manday. The total factory overhead expenses incurred and the mandays actually worked were Rs. 41.50 lakhs and Rs. 1.50 lakhs days, respectively.

Out of the 40,000 units produced during a period, 30,000 were sold.

On analysing the reasons, it was found that 60% of the unabsorbed overheads were due to defective planning and the rest were attributable to increase in overhead costs.

How would under-absorbed overheads be treated in cost accounts?

[B.Com. (Hons.) Delhi]

Solution

Recovered Overheads

Actual mandays × Rate = 1.50 lakhs × Rs. 25 = Rs. 37.50 lakhs

Actual Overheads = Rs. 41.50 lakhs

Under Recovery = Rs. 4.00 lakhs

Reasons for under-absorption

(i) Due to defective planning $= \frac{60}{100} \times 4{,}00{,}000 =$ Rs. 2,40,000

(ii) Increase in Overhead Cost $= \frac{40}{100} \times 4{,}00{,}000 =$ Rs. 1,60,000

4,00,000

5.28 Treatment in Cost accounts

(i) Rs. 2,40,000 should be transferred to Costing Profit & Loss Account as under-absorption has been caused by abnormal factors.

(ii) Rs. 1,60,000 should be charged to units produced.

So, the distribution should be as follows :

Cost of Sales A/c $= \frac{1{,}60{,}000 \times 30{,}000}{40{,}000} =$ Rs. 1,20,000

Finished Goods Stock A/c $= \frac{1{,}60{,}000 \times 10{,}000}{40{,}000} =$ Rs. 40,000

(Ratio 3 : 1 i.e. 40,000 – 30,000 = 10,000 finished goods stock).

Problem 13

The factory overhead costs of four production departments of a company engaged in executing job orders, for a accounting year, are as follows :

	Rs.
A	19,300
B	4,200
C	4,000
D	2,000

Overhead has been applied as under :

Dept.	A	R. 1.50 per machine hour for 14,000 hours
"	B	Rs. 1.30 per Direct Labour hour for 3,000 hours
"	C	80% of Direct Labour cost of Rs. 6,000
"	D	Rs. 2 per piece, for 950 pieces.

Find out the amount of department-wise under or over-absorbed factory overheads.

What are the methods that could be considered for disposal of the resultant Under or over-absorbed factory overheads?

[I.C.W.A (Inter)]

Solution

Amount of Under- or Over absorbed Factory Overheads

Department		*Factory Overhead absorbed*	*Factory Overhead incurred*	*Over-absorbed (+) Under-absorbed (–)*
		Rs.	Rs.	Rs.
A	14,000 × 1.50	21,000	19,300	(+) 1,700
B	3,000 × 1.30	3,900	4,200	(–) 300
C	80% of 6,000	4,800	4,000	(+) 800
D	950 × 2	1,900	2,000	(–) 100
	Total	31,600	29,500	(+) 2,100

Methods for disposal of under- or over-absorption of factory overheads :

1. Apportionment through supplementary rates.
2. Transfer to Costing Profit and Loss Account
3. Carry over to next year's Accounts.

5.29 Machine Hour Rate

Definition : Machine hour rate is a rational method for absorption of factory overhead. The factory overhead costs are allocated to a machine or a group of machines doing the same type of job and the cost per hour of the machine is ascertained dividing the total allocated overhead costs to the machine by number of hours the machine worked during the same period of time for which the costs have been considered. In this method of overhead absorption each machine is considered as cost centre. The formula used to derive the machine-hour rate is given below :

$$\text{Machine hour rate} = \frac{\text{Estimated factory overhead costs for the period}}{\text{Estimated machine hours for the period}}$$

The machine-hour method is based on the principle that, in plants where production processes are primarily mechanical, machines constitute a more important and costly element than labour. Factory overhead costs are equitably apportioned to production on the basis of some rational and accepted principles. This method of overhead absorption can satisfactorily be used when all production overheads are departmentalised and the overheads of the service departments are apportioned to the production departments.

5.30 Treatment of machine setting time and idle time

It is the usual practice to find out the total potential hours for the computation of machine hours. The cost of idle time may be calculated separately.

Alternatively, only effective machine hours may be ascertained by making allowance for idle time or setting time. By doing this, the machine hour rate is inflated by absorbing the machine hour cost for idle time.

For example :

The total indirect cost allocated to a particular machine is Rs. 20,000. Machine hours are 2,200 out of which 200 hours are for idle time. The machine hour rate will be :

$$\frac{20,000}{2,000} = \text{Rs. } 10$$

Effective machine hours = 2,200 hours – 200 hours (idle time) = 2,000 hours.

5.31 Classification of Expenses

Machine Expenses

Fixed Expenses or Standing Charges	Variable or Machine Expenses
(i) Rent	(i) Depreciation
(ii) Supervision	(ii) Power
(iii) Insurance on building	(iii) Lubricating oil
(iv) Consumable stores	(iv) Insurance on machinery
(v) Indirect wages	(v) Repairs and maintenance

5.32 Advantages of Machine Hour Rate

The following are the advantages of Machine Hour Rate :

(i) It is perhaps the most realistic and accurate method of allocating expenses to each job from cost accounting point of view.

(ii) This is the best and logical method of charging overheads where one operator attends to several machines or several operators are engaged on one machine.

(iii) It is a scientific method of absorbing overheads since it takes into consideration the time factor completely.

(iv) From the management point of view, it is the best method of absorption of overheads since it is a scientific and logical method and it can be used easily.

(v) Under-absorption will reveal the extent to which the machines remained idle.

5.33 Disadvantages of Machine Hour Rate

The following are the disadvantages of Machine Hour Rate :

(i) This method involves increased costing work.

(ii) This method of absorption can be applied to job which is performed by machines only.

5.34 Method of computation

The following steps have to be taken for the computation of machine-hour rate :

Expenses are apportioned on the basis of accepted principles.

Step I All standing or fixed expenses for a particular period of time say for a year or for a month, are added up. The total standing expenses thus arrived at, is divided by number of hours the machine worked i.e. machine hours for that period of time. It is essential that standing charges for the machine or group of machines which has been considered as cost centre should be considered. The resultant figure will give us the fixed expenses per hour. Fixed expenses are rent, rates and taxes for the factory, insurance, lighting, supervision expenses, canteen and other welfare expenses.

Step II Variable expenses pertaining to the cost centre, i.e. machine or group of machines are considered. Variable expenses comprise depreciation, power, fuel, repairs and renewals. An hourly rate is calculated by dividing each item of variable expenses by normal working hours of the machine.

Step III Hourly rate of standing charges and hourly rates of each item of variable expenses are added up to derive the total machine hour rate.

Basis of apportionment of standing and variable expenses pertaining to the machine :

Expenses	*Basis*
Standing Charges	
1. Rent, rates and taxes	Floor area occupied by each machine
2. Lighting and heating	Number of light points or floor are occupied
3. Lubricating oil and consumable stores	Past experience or Machine hours
4. Insurance	Actual or cost of machines
5. Supervision	Time devoted
6. Canteen subsidies	No. of workers
7. National Insurance Scheme	No. of workers
8. Manager's salary	Time devoted
Variable expenses	
9. Repairs and renewals	Actual
10. Steam, water and power	Machine hours worked or actual consumption or Horse power
11. Insurance	Cost of machine
12. Lubricants, rags and cotton waste	Cost of machine
13. Depreciation	Actual*

* **Calculation of depreciation**

Cost of the Machine :	Price paid plus expenses incurred up to the point of installation i.e. import duty, clearing charges, carriage inward and installation charges.
Less : Scrap Value	If any.
Divide by :	Span in terms of effective working hours.

$$\frac{\text{Cost machine} - \text{Scrap value}}{\text{Estimated working hours} - \text{Idle time}}$$

5.35 Comprehensive of composite Machine Hour Rate

Generally, in the computation of Machine hour Rate only indirect expenses in connection with the factory are apportioned or allocated. Machine operator's wages are treated as *direct wages* and charged to the job directly. But, **machine operator's wages are included,** in certain cases, in the machine hour rate itself. The machine hour rate so arrived at is known **as a comprehensive or composite machine hour rate.** This rate is useful where not only the operator but a distinct group of workers can be identified directly with the machine or group of machines. It is to be noted that this method converts the elements of prime cost (direct labour) into factory overhead. It is, therefore, of advisable to compute comprehensive machine hour rate.

5.36 Setting Times and Idle Time

In a factory, machines do not work for the full working hours. Certain hours become unproductive because machines remain idle for some hours because of certain factors like setting of tools, waiting for raw materials. In estimating the total machine hours for the computation of the machine hour rate it is the general practice to consider the total potential hours including the possible idle hours. The positive aspect of this method is that the cost of idle time can be separately worked out which will help the management in controlling the idle expenses from period to period.

Conversely, in computing machine hour rate, only the net effective or productive hours are considered. The object of this treatment is to absorb the idle time cost into cost of production.

Similarly, certain machine hours are lost in tool setting. Logically, the tool setting time should form a part of the actual machine hours against the job and the setting hours are also charged to the jobs at the same machine hour rate.

In practice, many Cost Accountants favour the method of finding out machine hour rate for effective productive hours which is calculated as follows :

Effective hours = Machine Hours – Idle time – Setting time

5.37 Base of Apportionment

The following table amplifies what has already been stated with regard to the bases of apportionment commonly used in connection with overhead other than that concerned solely with selling and distribution :

Bases of Apportionment

(Commencing with the most common or most appropriate basis where several bases are stated)

Canteen	Number of employees. Total wages.	Unless the extent to which the canteen is used varies greatly between departments.
Caretaking	Area of floor space. Value of buildings.	
Charitable subscriptions and donations	Number of employees. Total wages.	
Cleaning—		
Buildings.	Area of floor space.	
Windows.	Area of windows.	
Depreciation—		
Buildings	Area of floor space. Cubic capacity.	
Plant and Machinery	Value Cost or written down value.	Details of actual cost obtainable from an analysis of Plant register.
Vehicles	Cost or written down value.	Details of actual cost obtainable from an analysis of Vehicle Register.
Design	Chargeable man-hours.	
Drawing Office	Number of drawings made. Chargeable man-hours.	
Electro Lighting	Area of floor space. Estimates of consumption based on wages of lamps. Number of lamps.	
Electric Power	Horse-power hours of plant.	Unless separate meters are provided.
Fire Prevention	Area of buildings. Cubic capacity of buildings. Value of buildings, stock, etc. Estimated usage.	Unless separate meters are provided.
Goods Transport	Ton-miles operated. Miles run. 100 cu. ft. of materials transported. Gallons of liquid transported. Value of goods transported.	
Heating	Area of floor space.	
Holiday Pay	Total wages.	Unless accumulated on the payroll itself on a cost centre basis.

Contd.

Idle Time		Should always be accumulated by cost centres; otherwise the information is useless for cost control.
Insurance— Accident	Total wages. Number of employees.	Unless the probability of accident is greater in some departments than in others, when weighing must be resorted to.
Buildings	Area of floor space. Cubic feet capacity. Value of building.	
Employer's Liability	Total wages. Number of employees.	
Plant and Machinery	Value.	
Vehicles	Number. Value.	Unless separately recorded.
Jigs, Tools, and Fixtures	Machine operating hours. Chargeable man-hours required to produce particular tools, etc.	
Lighting	Area of floor space. Number of lamps. Wattage of lamps.	
Maintenance— Buildings	Area of floor space. Value of building (amongst a group).	Maintenance costs are usually recorded separately, building by building, and apportionment amongst buildings is not usually required.
Plant and Machinery	Value of machinery.	Normally recorded separately, machine by machine.
Vehicles	Value of vehicles.	Normally recorded separately vehicle by vehicle.
Material handling	Number of requisitions handled. 100 cu. ft. of materials handled. Number of employees served. Value of materials handled.	
Materials storage	100 cu. ft. of materials handled. Value of materials stored. Number of requisitions handles.	
Medical, Dental, and First-aid	Number of employees. Total wages.	Unless medical examination is confined to certain trades or grades.
National Insurance	Number of Employees Total wages.	Usually allocated specifically to cost centres.

Contd.

Oil and Grease	Estimated usage.	Machine hours operated or transport-miles run may assist in the making of the estimate. Generally, there is a direct charge to the centres using the materials.
Passenger transport	Number of passenger miles.	
Pensions	Total wages. Number of employees.	Unless allocated direct to cost centres.
Personnel Department	Number of employees. Total wages.	
Planning and Progress	Machine operating hours. Direct labour hours.	
Power	Horse-power hours of plant. Machine operating hours.	Frequently separately metered.
Production Control	Machine operating hours. Direct labour hours.	
Profit-sharing payments	Number of employees. Total wages.	Unless treated as a "non--costing" item.
Purchasing	Value of materials. Number of orders.placed.	
Rates	Area of floor space. Cubic feet capacity of building. Value of particular buildings or floors therein.	
Recreation	Number of employees. Total wages.	
Rent or Equivalent	Area of floor space.	
Rent Charge	Cubic feet capacity of building. Value of particular buildings or floors therein.	
Storage	Number of requisitions handled.100 cu. ft. of material stored. Gallons of liquid stored. Value of material stored.	
Superannuation	Total wages. Number of employees.	Usually allocated direct to cost centres.
Supervision	Number of employees. Total wages.	Unless some centres require for more supervision than is apparent from a consideration of the ersonnel employed or their total remuneration.
Telephone— Calls	Number of calls made.	Unless records of the actual cost of each call are maintained and used as the basis of direct charges.

Contd.

Provision of Instruments	Number of stations.	
Time Office	Number of employees. Total wages.	
Training	Number of trainees.	Unless the cost of training is suficiently high to justify the separate recordig of the cost of training individuals or groups.
Transport	Number of vhicle-operating hours.	
Ventilation	Area of floor space. Cubic feet capacity.	Unless made necessary by some particular process.
Wages department	Number of employees. Total wages.	Unless the partial application of bonus schemes, etc., make the cost of paying certain personnel for greater than that of paying others.
Washrooms, etc.	Number of employees. Total wages.	
Watching and Patrolling	Area of floor space. Value of buildings stocks, etc. Area of windows.	
Window Cleaning and Maintenance.	Number of studies made.	
Work Study	Number of employees served. Number of chargeable man-hours occupied by the studies.	

5.38 Treatment of some items of Expenses

Generally, cost which can definitely be identified to a product or department or job or process should be charged directly. Otherwise, the expenses (indirect) should be apportioned on some rational basis. In doing so, it should be noted that *Normal Losses* are borne by the good output while *Abnormal Losses* are charged directly to Costing Profit and Loss Account.

The following items are discussed :

1. **Design and Drawing office costs :**

Where design and drawing office renders specific service to a job, the costs thereof shall be charged to job concerned directly. But where drawing office provides general service to the undertaking as a whole, its costs are treated as production overheads and apportioned on the basis of number of drawings made, chargeable manhours etc.

2. **Materials Carriage, handling and storage expenses :**

When the cost of carriage inward is incurred for a particular material then it is treated as a part of material cost. But where carriage inwards cover a large number of materials then it is treated as an item of production overhead. Materials handling and storage expenses may be apportioned on the basis of value, weight and value of materials or number of material requisitions handled.

3. **Transport Charges :**

Internal transport costs incurred for movement of materials viz., from stores to production departments, interdepartmental movement of stores, components are distributed to different products or departments on the basis of distance traversed, volume, value or weight of stores carried etc. Cost of external transport, i.e. delivery of goods to customers is treated as distribution overhead and is apportioned on the basis of truck hours, truck kilometres, weight of the products carried etc.

4. Royalties and Patent Fees :

When Royalty is paid on the basis of a fixed percentage of output, the expenditure is charged to the cost of product. When the royalty is paid on the basis of sales it is treated as *selling overheads*.

The expenditure incurred for registering and renewal of patents is treated as *Administration Overheads*.

5. Light, Heat and Air-conditioning :

The expenditure is apportioned to works administration and Selling and Distribution overheads on the basis of light points if voltage is equal, otherwise on the basis of area occupied by each department. Expenses for air-conditioning and heating may be apportioned on the basis of *area occupied* or on the basis of cubic capacity of the department concerned.

6. Repairs renewals and Maintenance :

If the expense incurred is on account of normal maintenance and minor repairs, it is treated as overhead costs. The expense incurred for plant and machinery and factory building is charged to factory or works overhead costs. Expenses in connection with capital assets used in the general office, selling and distribution departments will be charged to administration, selling and distribution overheads, respectively.

7. Material losses and wastages :

Material losses or wastages may arise in (i) transit, (ii) storage and (iii) manufacturing.

(i) Loss in transit

Incoverable losses are treated as overhead. In case of heavy loss, such loss should be charged to the Costing Profit and Loss Account.

(ii) Loss during storage

Some materials are lost in handling. Loss may arise due to pilferage, evaporation, and shrinkage. This type of loss is sure to occur and unavoidable. Such a loss is a normal loss and is treated as a factory overhead. Losses that arise due to theft, fire, and mismanagement are known as *abnormal losses* and should be excluded from the cost accounts and should be charged to Costing Profit and Loss Account.

(iii) Loss during manufacturing

The materials which are wasted during manufacturing process should be charged to the job. But if the wastage is abnormal in nature it should be transferred to Profit and Loss Account.

8. Inspection Charges :

If expenses incurred in connection with inspection of goods can be identified to a specific product, process or department, it should be charged directly to the product, process or department. Otherwise it is treated as an item of factory overhead. Inspection charges relating to raw materials and packing materials are merged with materials handling and storage expenses. Inspection cost of finished product is treated as distribution overhead.

9. Insurance Costs :

Insurance charges paid at the time of purchase of raw materials are charged direct to cost of materials or assets purchased. Premium paid for stock of raw materials is treated as manufacturing overhead. Insurance premium paid for warehouse stock is treated as distribution overhead while premium paid against loss of profit or burglary is treated as an item of administration overhead. Insurance premium paid to cover the risks of general loss and fire in respect of plant and machinery, factory building and equipment is treated as production overhead and apportioned to the different departments on the basis of value insured.

10. **Canteen Expenses :**

Canteen expenses are apportioned to different Cost Centres on the basis of direct wages, number of employee, number of meals served etc.

11. **Training Costs :**

Training costs pertaining to workers are apportioned to different Cost Centres on the basis of number of trainees, direct wages. If the trainees perform productive work, a part of estimated cost is charged to the production order concerned.

12. **Cost of container and packing cases :**

Cost of primary containers which are exhausted by one use becomes a part of production cost. Cost of secondary containers which are returnable by the customers forms a part of selling and distribution overhead.

13. **Cost of small tools :**

Generally, cost of small tools is charged to all departments on the basis of actual issues. There is a alternative treatment which is not popular. Small tools are treated as assets and depreciation thereon is charged as overhead.

14. **Cost office expenses :**

It is treated as overhead and apportioned to factory administration and selling divisions on the basis of estimated benefit obtained by each division.

15. **Directors' fees and salaries :**

These expenses form a part of administration overhead. Sometimes directors' remuneration may be apportioned to production, administration and selling and distribution functions on the basis of time devoted by the directors. Where there are separate directors for different functions like purchase, sales, finance etc., separate allocation can be made to different functions.

16. **Subscription and donations :**

Subscriptions and donations to welfare schemes or institutions from which workers can obtain benefit are treated as an item of factory overhead. Subscriptions to mercantile agencies for obtaining different information as to the financial status of a prospective buyer should be treated as selling overhead. Subscription and charitable donations from which no benefit is derived by the workers or the business unit are kept outside the ambit of cost accounts.

17. **Market Research and Development (R & D) :**

"Research and Development costs have been defined by **ICMA, London,** as follows :

"Research cost is the Cost of seeking new or improved products, applications of materials or methods. Development cost is the cost of the process which begins with the implementation of the decision to produce a new or improved product or to employ a new or improved method, and ends with the commencement of formal production of that product or by that method."

Research may be of two types, namely, fundamental research and applied research. Fundamental research aims at increasing the knowledge of the technicians. Applied research aims at a achieving the following objectives :

(i) to improve the quality of the existing product:
(ii) to improve the existing method of production;
(iii) to search for new product;
(iv) to search for new method of production;
(v) to search for new application of materials.

Treatment in Cost Accounting

(i) **Fundamental research**

Expenses incurred on fundamental research are treated as manufacturing overhead.

(ii) **Applied research**

When expenses on applied research are incurred for bringing about improvement on the existing methods of production and products, such expenses incurred for a particular period should be treated as manufacturing overhead of that period. But if such expenses are ear-marked for any specific product, all expenses will be charged directly to the product.

When expenses are incurred for searching new products or new methods of production, each research project should be given a specific project number and cost should be allocated accordingly. If the research project becomes a failure the cost should be debited to Costing Profit and Loss Account. But if it becomes a success it should be debited to development cost. If the project results are relating to a particular product, it would be a direct charge to that product, but if a production method is related to any project, it should be treated as an item of manufacturing overhead:

18. **Dismantling of Plant :**

Where it becomes essential to dismantle the existing plant and machinery and re-erect the plant at a different place, the expenditure involved is charged to works overhead. When an asset is prematurely dismantled on being obsolete, the costs of dismantling should be charged to the account of dismantled asset, and set off against any salvage or compensation moneys or sale proceeds received. The final gain or loss on realisation should be transferred direct to Profit and Loss Account, unless some element of any gain is considered to be a Capital Profit which ought to be properly transferred to Capital Reserve.

19. **Installation of new Plant and Machinery :**

The cost incurred for installation of a new machine is generally capitalised and such cost is written-off as depreciation along with the asset.

20. **Moving and refixing existing plant :**

The cost may be treated as production overhead as it does not add to the value of the asset.

21. **Set up Cost :**

Cost of setting up for a particular job order or production order is a direct charge to that job order. But when setting cost is not meant for a particular job and is high, it is treated as production overhead and is apportioned to all the jobs accordingly.

22. **Depreciation :**

Generally, depreciation is charged on the capitalised value of a fixed asset.

Depreciation on fixed assets used in the factory is treated as an item of Factory Overhead. Depreciation on fixed assets used in the office and sales departments is treated as an item of Office and Administration and Selling and Distribution Overhead, respectively.

It is suggested that when prices are rising, the amount of depreciation should be calculated on 'Replacement Cost' rather than on original cost. Providing of depreciation on replacement cost is a controversial issue. Arguments for and against it are discussed below :

Points in favour of providing depreciation :

1. After the expiry of the life of the asset, sufficient funds are made available to replace the old asset. Moreover, unless the firm provides depreciation on a replacement cost basis, it will have insufficient funds to keep its capital intact.
2. True profits are not closed under the original cost basis as depreciation is either undercharged or overcharged depending upon inflation or deflation.
3. The depreciation charge on the replacement cost in the cost accounts represents the true cost in as much as the cost so arrived at is comparable with the current selling price.
4. In case the value of the asset has gone up and depreciation is provided at the usual old rates, true price cannot be revealed.
5. Overstatement of profits in the original cost method results in higher taxation.
6. The inflated profits may be paid away in the form of dividend which may affect the financial position of the concern.

Points against

The following are arguments against providing depreciation on replacement cost of an asset :

1. Depreciation is a charge for diminution in the book value of an asset and has nothing to do with the appreciation in its value or its replacement cost.
2. The actual cost of an asset should be taken into account for costing purposes. Providing depreciation on replacement cost is misleading and is a departure from costing principles.
3. 'Replacement Reserve' can be created to provide sufficient funds for replacement of an asset.
4. This method is not approved by the Revenue Department. In India, the Income tax Act approves the charging of depreciation on the original cost of the asset.
5. In an inflationary economy it becomes very difficult to ascertain the true replacement cost of an asset. So, the practical application of this method also has certain difficulties.

23. **Cost office expenses :**

Expenses incurred in connection with Cost Office are treated as an item of administration overhead. Sometimes they are apportioned to factory, administration and selling divisions on the basis of estimated benefit obtained by each.

24. **Profit sharing bonus :**

In a profit sharing bonus scheme the bonus is paid out of profit and so this should be excluded in cost accounts. Since bonus is a part of wages, some accountants prefer to treat bonus as an overhead and is apportioned to different departments on the basis of wages of each department. When payment of bonus becomes obligatory it is to be apportioned to these functions.

25. **After-Sales Service Costs :**

After-sales service costs include salaries paid to staff engaged in after-sales service, rectification expenses during the warranty period. These costs are treated as product costs. In some cases, after-sales service costs are treated as part of selling overhead and pro-rated to different products on the basis of sales achieved.

26. **Interest on Capital :**

Whether interest on capital is to be treated as an element of cost is a controversial issue. The arguments for and against the inclusion of interest are discussed below :

Arguments for

(i) It is argued that interest on Capital is a reward of the capital invested in the business and should be treated as an element of cost like wages.

(ii) If interest is excluded comparison of different operations and processes would be different which may lead to erroneous conclusions.

(iii) Inclusion of interest would take into consideration the time element, for it is one of the most important factors in production. Where a considerable amount of capital is locked up for quite a long period the interest factor is of utmost importance in the calculation of total cost.

(iv) Carrying cost of inventory cannot be ascertained without taking into consideration the effect of interest on capital involved.

(v) Where old plant and machineries are replaced by modern machinery the result of such replacement cannot be accurately ascertained or decided without studying the interests on capital borrowed for the purpose. Advantages that can be derived from such replacement should be compared with the amount of interest which is likely to be lost on the capital locked up.

(vi) If interest is paid it should be included in cost accounts for expenditure incurred is taken into account at the times of cost ascertainment.

Arguments against

(i) It is argued that payment of interest is a matter of finance and hence is not in any way connected with the cost of production. Payment of interest does not affect the manufacturing cost but affects the quantum of profit.

(ii) The reward for capital is covered by profits. Interest paid on borrowed capital should be included in cost but not the interest payable on owned capital as a reward.

(iii) Actual expense is considered for the determination of total cost. Therefore, interest not payable should not be included in Cost.

(iv) If interest is included in cost accounts, the value of closing stock and work-in-progress is likely to be inflated.

(v) Cost accounts will unnecessarily become complicated if interest is included because for the purpose of computation of interest it is difficult to determine the exact capital employed as well as the fair rate of interest.

Conclusion

Cost Accountants generally agree that the amount of interest paid should be included in cost accounts, but they differ on the point whether or not interest not paid should be included in the cost. Some cost accountants are strictly against such inclusion.

Considering the arguments for and against the inclusion of interest in cost accounts, it is advisable that debenture interest and interest on loans may be treated in cost accounts but not interest on capital.

According to **W. W. Bigg**, it is desirable to include an amount of interest specially in those cases where the job takes a long time to complete and where a choice between alternative projects is involved.

5.39 Items excluded from cost accounts

The following items are excluded from cost accounts :

1. Charity and donations from which company's employees derive no direct benefit.
2. Transfer to Reserves.
3. Income Tax and Corporation tax.
4. Dividends.
5. Directors' fees (as distinct from emoluments as executives).
6. Amounts written-off to fictitious assets like preliminary expenses, underwriting commission, Discount on issue of Debentures, expenses of Capital issues.
7. Amounts written-off to fixed intangible assets like goodwill, patent rights etc.
8. Appropriations to sinking funds created for the redemption of loans.
9. Interest received on bank deposits.
10. Interest, dividend received on investments.
11. Profits or losses on sales of assets.

WORKED OUT PROBLEM

Problem 14

The budgeted working conditions for a cost centre are as follows :

Normal working per week	42 hours
No. of machines	14 "
Normal weekly loss on maintenance etc.	5 hours per machine
No. of weeks worked per year	48
Estimated annual overheads	Rs. 1,24,320
Estimated direct wage rate	Rs. 4 per hour
Actual results in respect of a week period are :	
Wages incurred	Rs. 9,000
Overheads incurred	Rs. 10,200
Machine hours	2,000

You are required to calculate :

(a) The overhead rate per machine hour ; and

(b) The amount of under or over-absorption of overheads.

[Adapted – I.C.W.A. (Inter)]

Solution

			Rs.
(a)	**Calculation of overhead rate per machine hour**		
	Estimated annual overhead		1,24,320
	Normal working hours	42 × 48 × 14 =	28,224 hours
Less :	Loss of hours on maintenance	5 × 48 × 14 =	3,360 "
	Net working hours =		24,864 "

$$\text{Overhead rate per machine} = \text{Rs. } \frac{1,24,320}{24,864} = 5.00$$

(b)	Overheads incurred		10,200
	" absorbed	2,000 hours × 5	10,000
	Under-absorption of overheads		200

Problem 15

The following is the budget of Superb Engineering works for the year 1988 :

	Rs.
Factory Overheads	62,000
Direct labour cost	98,000
Direct labour hours	1,55,000
Machine hours	50,000

(a) From the above figures prepare the overhead application rates using the following methods :

(i) Direct Labour Hour

(ii) Direct Labour Cost

(iii) Machine Hour.

(b) Prepare a comparative statement of cost, showing the result of application of each of the above rates to Job No. 555 from the under mentioned data :

	Rs.
Direct Material Cost	45
Direct Labour – Wages	50
Direct Labour Hours	40
Machine Hours	30

[Adapted—I.C.W.A. (Inter)]

Solution

(a) **Overhead application rates :**

(i) Direct Labour Hour Method = $\frac{62,000}{1,55,000}$ = 0.40 p.

(ii) Direct Labour Cost Method = $\frac{62,000}{98,000} \times 100 = 63.27\%$

(iii) Machine Hour Rate = $\frac{62,000}{50,000}$ = Rs. 1.24 per machine hour.

(b) **Statement showing Comparative Cost**

	Direct Labour Hour Method	*Direct Labour Cost Method*	*Machine Hour Method*
	Rs.	Rs.	Rs.
Direct Materials	45.00	45.00	45.00
Direct labour	50.00	50.00	50.00
Overhead	16.00 (40 × 0.4)	31.63 (50 × 63.27)	37.20 (30 × Rs. 1.24)
	111.00	126.63	132.20

Problem 16

The following are the maintenance costs incurred in a Machine shop per six months with corresponding machine hours :

Month	*Machine Hours*	*Maintenance Costs*
		Rs.
January	2,000	300
February	2,200	320
March	1,700	270
April	2,400	340
May	1,800	280
June	1,900	290
	12,000	1,800

Analyse the Maintenance Cost which is semi-variable into fixed and variable element.

[I.C.W.A. (Inter) 1985]

Solution

February machine hours	2,200	Rs. 320
January machine hours	2,000	Rs. 300
	200	Rs. 20

∴ Variable Cost = Rs. 20 ÷ 200 = 0.10 paise per machine hour.

Analytical Statement

Month	*Machine Hours*	*Maintenance Cost*	*Fixed Cost*	*Variable Cost*
		Rs.	Rs.	Rs.
January	2,000	300	100	200
February	2,200	320	100	220
March	1,700	270	100	170
April	2,400	340	100	240
May	1,800	280	100	180
June	1,900	290	100	190

Problem 17

The following is the budget of a manufacturing concern for the year 1989 :

Factory Overheads	Rs. 1,24,000
Direct Labour Cost	Rs. 1,96,000
Direct Labour hours	3,10,000
Machine hours	10,000

(a) From the above figures prepare the overhead application rates using methods : (i) Direct labour hours; (ii) Direct labour cost and (iii) Machine hour.

(b) Prepare a comparative statement of cost showing the result of application of each of the above rates to Job No. 551 from the undermentioned data :

	Rs.
Direct materials cost	90.00
Direct labour cost	180.00
Direct labour hours	150.00
Machine hours	60.00

[Adapted—B.U. B.Com. (Hons.) 1986]

Solution

(i) Direct labour overhead absorption rate

$$= \text{Rs. } \frac{1,24,000}{1,96,000} \times 100 = 63.26\% \text{ of Wages}$$

(ii) Direct labour hour overhead absorption rate

$$= \text{Rs. } \frac{1,24,000}{3,10,000} = \text{Re. } 0.4 \text{ per labour hour}$$

(iii) Machine hour OAR

$$= \text{Rs. } \frac{1,24,000}{10,000} = \text{Rs. } 12.40 \text{ per machine hour.}$$

Comparative Statement showing the cost for Job 551

	Direct Labour Cost OAR	*Direct Labour Hour OAR*	*Machine Hour OAR*
	Rs.	Rs.	Rs.
(i) Direct Material Cost	90.00	90.00	90.00
(ii) Direct Wages	180.00	180.00	180.00
PRIME COST	270.00	270.00	270.00
Add : Factory overhead (absorbed @ predetermined overhead rates)	113.87 (@ 63.26% of wages)	60.00 (150 × 0.40)	744.00 (60 × 12.40)
WORKS COST	383.87	330.00	1,014.00

Problem 18

The ABC Company produces its own power which is used by other departments – production and service.

Basic data for the month of March 1999 are as follows :

SCHEDULE OF HORSE POWER HOURS

	Production Departments		*Service Departments*	
	A	B	X	Y
Needed at capacity operations	10,000	20,000	12,000	8,000
Used during the month of March 1999	8,000	13,000	7,000	6,000

During the month of March, the expenses of operating the power service department amounted to Rs. 93,000, of which Rs. 25,000 was considered to be fixed cost and the remainder variable cost.

It is required to –

(i) Calculate the rupee amounts of power service department expense to be allocated to each production and service department.

(ii) Enumerate the reasons for allocating the cost of one service department to other service department and production departments.

[B.Com., Hons., Delhi]

Solution

Statement showing Apportionment of Cost of The Power Service Department

	Total	Production Departments		Service Departments	
		A	B	X	Y
Horse Power Hours					
Needed at Capacity production	50,000	10,000	20,000	12,000	8,000
Use during the month	34,000	8,000	13,000	7,000	6,000
Apportionment of cost	Rs.	Rs.	Rs.	Rs.	Rs.
1. **Variable Cost :**					
Rs. 2 per hour $\frac{\text{Rs. } 68,000}{34,000}$	68,000	16,000	26,000	14,000	12,000
2. **Fixed Cost :**					
Re. 0.50 paise $\frac{\text{Rs. } 25,000}{50,000}$					
Per hour of capacity needed	25,000	5,000	10,000	6,000	4,000
Total (1 + 2)	93,000	21,000	36,000	20,000	16,000

LABOUR HOUR RATE

Problem 19

Calculate Direct Labour Hour Rate from the following :

Total no. of workers	100
Working days in a year	300
No. of hours per day worked	8
Short and Idle time 5%	
Factory overheads	Rs. 11,400
Gift to workers	Rs. 1,000

[B.Com. Pass, Delhi]

Solution

CALCULATION OF LABOUR HOUR RATE

(A) Factory overheads — Rs. 11,400

(B) No. of Labour hours worked

No. of workers × Working days in a year × No. of hours per day worked less short and Idle time

= (100 × 300 × 8) less 5% = 2,40,000 − 12,000 = 2,28,000 hours

$$\text{Labour Hour Rate} = \frac{\text{Factory overheads (A)}}{\text{No. of labour hours worked (B)}}$$

$$= \text{Rs. } \frac{11,400}{2,28,000} = 0.05 \text{ paise per hour}$$

Note : Gifts to workers will be included in Administration Overhead and not in Factory Overheads.

Problem 20

The following particulars related to the production departments of a factory for the month of June,1997 :

Materials used	Rs. 80,000
Direct Wages	Rs. 72,000
Direct labour hours worked	20,000
Hours of machine operation	25,000
Overhead charges allocated to the department	Rs. 90,000

Cost data of a particular work order carried out in the above department during June 1997 are given below :

Materials used	Rs. 8,000
Direct wages	Rs. 6,250
Labour hours booked	3,300
Machine hours booked	2,400

What would be the factory cost of the work order under the following methods of charging overheads :

(i) Direct Labour cost rate ;

(ii) Machine Hour Rate; and

(iii) Direct Labour Hour Rate?

[Adapted—I.C.W.A (Inter)]

Solution

(i) Direct Labour Cost Rate $= \frac{\text{Rs. } 90,000}{72,000} \times 100 = 125\%$

(ii) Machine Hour Rate $= \text{Rs. } \frac{90,000}{25,000} = \text{Rs. } 3.60$

(iii) Direct Labour Hour Rate $= \text{Rs. } \frac{90,000}{20,000} = \text{Rs. } 4.50$

Factory Cost of Work Order

	Direct Labour Cost rate	*Machine Hour rate*	*Direct Labour Hour rate*
	Rs.	Rs.	Rs.
Materials used	8,000	8,000	8,000
Direct wages	6,250	6,250	6,250
Overheads @ 125% of wages	* 7,812.50	**8,640	***14,850
Factory cost of work order	22,062.50	22,890	29,100

Note : * Overhead = 125% of wages = Rs. $6,250 \times \frac{125}{100}$ = Rs. 7,812.50

** Overhead = 2,400 hours × Rs. 3.60 per machine hour = Rs. 8,640

*** Overhead = 3,300 labour hour × Rs. 4.50 per direct labour hour = Rs. 14,850.

Problem 21

Naidra Enterprises has two departments A and B. Work is done manually in department A and through machines in department B. You are required to compute :

(i) Direct labour cost percentage

(ii) Machine hour rate method of absorption of overheads from the data (annual) given below :

	Rs.
Direct wages	1,00,000
Factory Overheads allocated to department A	60,000
Factory Overheads allocated to department B	90,000

Factory overheads not traceable directly to both departments amount to Rs. 20,000 and are to be shared equally between the two departments.

There are 5 machines of similar size. Each machine works 40 hours in a week. Each machine remains idle on account of repairing and holidays, etc, for 80 hours annually :

[D.U. B. Com (Pass) 1987]

Solution

Department A

Total overhead = Rs. 60,000 + Rs. 10,000 = Rs. 70,000

Direct labour cost percentage = Rs. $\frac{70,000 \times 100}{1,00,000}$ = 70%

Department B

Total overhead = Rs. 90,000 + Rs. 10,000 = Rs. 1,00,000

For each machine = Rs. 1,00,000 ÷ 5 = Rs. 20,000

Machine Hour Rate = Rs. $\frac{20,000}{2,000}$ = Rs. 10 per hour

[(40 × 52) = 2,080 – 80 = 2,000 hours]

Problem 22

In a factory there are three production departments and one service department. The actual expenses in 1992 were as follows :

Power Rs. 900; Light Rs. 500; Repair to plant Rs. 4,500; Rent Rs. 5000; Depreciation Rs. 2,700, Supervision Rs. 7,500 and Canteen Expenses Rs. 3,000.

With above noted expenses and the following further particulars determine the total overhead cost of production Departments. Cost of the Service Department is apportioned to Production Departments in 2 : 2 : 1 ratio.

	Production Departments			*Service Department*
	A	B	C	S
Area (Sq. mt.)	1,250	550	450	250
Cost of Plant (Rs.)	1,20,000	90,000	90,000	—
No. of Employees	24	18	12	6
Wages (Rs.)	30,000	20,000	15,000	10,000
Light Points	8	7	6	4
H.P. of Machines	6	4	5	—

[C.U. B. Com. (Pass) 1993]

Solution

Overhead Distribution Chart

Expenses	*Basis of Apportionment*	*Total*	*Production Dept.* A	B	C	*Service Dept.* S
		Rs.	Rs.	Rs.	Rs.	Rs.
Power	H.P. of Machines 6 : 4 : 5	900	360	240	300	
Light	Light Points 8 : 7 : 6 : 4	500	160	140	120	80
Repairs to Plant	Cost of Assets 12 : 9 : 9	4,500	1,800	1,350	1,350	
Rent	Floor Area 25 : 11 : 9 : 5	5,000	2,500	1,100	900	500
Depreciation	Cost of Assets 12 : 9 : 9	2,700	1,080	810	810	
Supervision	No. of Employees 4 : 3 : 2 : 1	7,500	3,000	2,250	1500	750
Canteen Expenses	No. of Employees 4 : 3 : 2 : 1	3,000	1,200	900	600	300
Total allocated overheads		24,100	10,100	6,790	5,580	1,630
Add : wages		10,000				10,000
Total Expenses						11,630
Expenses of S apportional to Production department in 2 : 2 : 1			4,652	4,652	2,326	(–) 11630
		34,100	14,752	11,442	7,906	Nil.

Problem 23

From the following particulars, calculate the overheads allocable to Production Departments : P and Q.

There are also two service departments S_1 and S_2. S_1 renders service worth Rs. 6,000 to S_2 and the balance to P and Q as 3 : 2. S_2 renders service to P and Q as 9 : 1.

	P	Q	S_1	S_2
Floor area (Sq. ft)	2,500	2,000	500	500
Assets (Rs. in lakh)	5	2.5	1.5	0.5
H.P. of machines	500	250	200	50
No. of workers	100	50	50	25
Light and Fan points	50	30	20	20

Expenses and charges	Rs.		Rs.
Depreciation	95,000	Rent, Rates and Taxes	18,000
Insurance	7,600	Power	10,000
Canteen Expenses	5,400	Electricity	2,400

[C.U. B. Com (Hons.) 1998]

Solution

Primary Distribution Statement

Item	*Basic*	*Total*	*P*	*Q*	S_1	S_2
Depreciation	Value of assets 5 : 2.5 : 1.5 : 0.5 or 10 : 5 : 3 : 1	95,000	50,000	25,000	15,000	5,000
Insurance	Value of Assets 10 : 5 : 3 : 1	7,600	4,000	2,000	1,200	400
Canteen Expenses	No. of workers 4 : 2 : 2 : 1	5,400	2,400	1,200	1,200	600
Rent, Rates and Taxes	Floor Area 5 : 4 : 1 : 1	18,000	8,182	6,545	1,636	1,637
Power	H.P. of Machines 10 : 5 : 4 : 1	10,000	5,000	2,500	2,000	500
Electricity	Light & Fan points 5 : 3 : 2 : 2	2,400	1,000	600	400	400
		1,38,400	70,582	37,845	21,436	8,537
Rs. 6,000 of S_1 allocated to S_2 and the balance allocated to P & Q in 3 : 2 i.e. 21,436 – 6,000 = 15,436			9,262	6,174	(–) 21436	6,000
Expenses of S_2 allocated to P & Q in 9 : 1			13,083	1,454		14,537 –14537
		1,38,400	92,927	45,473	—	—

Determination of Departmental Overhead Rate

Problem 24

The following information is available for 3 months ending on 31.3.1998 of a large manufacturing concern. You are required to calculate the departmental overhead rates for each Production Department, assuming that the overheads are recovered as a percentage of direct wages.

The expenses for 3 months :

Rent and Rates—Rs. 5,000; Repairs and maintenance Rs. 6,000; Depreciation—Rs. 30,000; Electricity charges—Rs. 2,000; Power—Rs. 12,000; Supervision Expenses—Rs. 3,000; General Expenses—Rs. 1,500.

	Production Departments			*Service Departments*	
	A	B	C	D	E
Direct Wages (Rs.)	12,000	8,000	5,000	3,000	2,000
Floor Space (Sq. ft.)	8,000	6,000	4,000	4,000	3,000
Value of Machines (Rs.)	1,00,000	80,000	60,000	40,000	20,000
H P. of Machines	50	30	20	20	—
No. of light points	80	40	40	30	10

Total expenses of Service Department E are to be distributed equally and those of Service Department D are to be distributed in the ratio of 2 : 2 : 1 over the Production Departments A, B and C.

[Adapted C.U. B. Com. (Hons.)]

Solution

Distribution of overheads.

Expenes	Basis of apportionment	Total Rs.	A Rs.	B Rs.	C Rs.	D Rs.	E Rs.
			Production Depts.			Service Depts	
Rent and Rates	Area accupied 8 : 6 : 4 : 4 : 3	5,000	1,600	1,200	800	800	600
Repairs and Maintenance	Value of asset 5 : 4 : 3 : 2 : 1	6,000	2,000	1,600	1,200	800	400
Depreciation	Value of asset 5 : 4 : 3 : 2 : 1	30,000	10,000	8,000	6,000	4,000	2,000
Electricity charges	Light points 8 : 4 : 4 : 3 : 1	2,000	800	400	400	300	100
Power	H.P. of machines 5 : 3 : 2 : 2	12,000	5,000	3,000	2,000	2,000	—
Supervision Expenses	Direct wages 12 : 8 : 5 : 3 : 2	3,000	1,200	800	500	300	200
General Expenses	Direct wages 12 : 8 : 5 : 3 : 2	1,500	600	400	250	150	100
Direct wages		5,000				3,000	2,000
		64,500	21,200	15,400	11,150	11,350	5,400
Expenses of Dept. D allocated to A B & C	2 : 2 : 1.		4,540	4,540	2,270	(–) 11350	(–) 5400
Expenses of E allocated to A, B and C	1 : 1 : 1		1,800	1,800	1,800	—	(–) 5,400
		64,500	27,540	21,740	15,220	—	—

Calculation of departmental overhead rate

$$\text{Departmental overhead rate} = \frac{\text{Allocated overhead}}{\text{Direct wages}} \times 100$$

A	B	C
$\frac{27,540 \times 100}{12,000}$	$\frac{21,740 \times 100}{8,000}$	$\frac{15,220 \times 100}{5,000}$
= 229.5%	= 271.75%	= 304.40%

Problem 25

Merrut Manufacturing Company makers several product lines which are processed through three production departments—X, Y and Z.

The information concerning the relevant data for a year is as follows :

	Factory Overhead (including share of service department)	*Direct Labour hours*	*Direct Labour Cost.*
	Rs.	Rs.	Rs.
Department X	1,24,000	80,000	1,60,000
Department Y	2,30,000	1,15,000	2,41,500
Department Z	5,46,000	1,05,000	1,99,500

Production records at the end of the year indicated the following for the product line 'Krish' :

Unit produced 20,000 units

	Dept. X	Dept. Y	Dept. Z
	Rs.	Rs.	Rs.
Prime Cost	45,000	10,500	59,500
Direct Labour Hours	10,000	5,000	30,000

You are required to :

(a) Calculate the departmental and plant-wise overhead rate based on direct labour hours;

(b) Compute the cost . 'Krish' line for the year by using (i) plant-wise rate and (ii) departmental rates.

[D.U. B. Com. (Hons.) 1994

Solution

(a) **Departmental Overhead Rates**

Department X = Rs. $\frac{1,24,000}{80,000}$ = Rs. 1.55

" Y = Rs. $\frac{2,30,000}{1,15,000}$ = Rs. 2.00

" Z = Rs. $\frac{5,46,000}{1,05,000}$ = Rs. 5.20

Plant-wise Overhead Rate

Factory overheads ÷ Total Direct Labour Hours

or (Rs. 1,24,000 + Rs. 2,30,000 + Rs. 5,46,000) ÷ (Rs. 80,000 + Rs. 1,15,000 + Rs. 105,000)

or, Rs. 9,00,000 ÷ 3,00,000 = Rs. 3.00

(b) **Computation of Cost of 'Krish' line using Department Rates :**

	X	Y	Z
	Rs.	Rs.	Rs.
Prime Cost	45,000	10,500	59,500
Factory overheads (as per note below)	15,500	10,000	1,56,000
	60,500	20,500	2,15,500

Calculation of Factory overhead

X	=	10,000 (labour hours) × 1.55 (hourly rate)	=	Rs. 15,500
Y	=	5,000 (labour hours) × 2.00 (hourly rate)	=	Rs. 10,000
Z	=	30,000 (labour hours) × 5.20 (hourly rate)	=	Rs. 1,56,000

Calculation of cost of 'Krish' line using plant-wise rate

	Prime Cost = Rs. 45,000 + Rs. 10,500 + 59,500	=	Rs. 1,15,000
Add :	Factory Overheads 45,000 × Rs. 3	=	Rs. 1,35,000
	Work Cost		Rs. 2,50,000

Notes : Prime Cost includes direct labour cost.

Repeated Distribution Method

Problem 26

Using Repeated Distribution Method, solve the problem given below :

(a) Service Department A—Expenses are to he allocated in the ratio 30 : 30 : 20 : 20 to Production Departments X, Y, & Z and Service Department B.

(b) Service Department B—Expenses are to be allocated in the ratio of 50 : 20 : 20 : 10. to the Production Departments X, Y and Z and Service Department A.

(c) Expenses of production Departments :

X	Rs. 50,000
Y	Rs. 20,000
Z	Rs. 25,000

(d) Expenses of production Departments :

A	Rs. 5,000
B	Rs. 8,000

[Calicut—B.Com]

STATEMENT SHOWING APPORTIONMENT OF OVERHEADS

Items	*Basis of apportionment*	*Total Rs.*	Production Depts *X Rs.*	*Y Rs.*	*Z Rs.*	Service Departments *A Rs.*	*B Rs.*
	Allocated Overhead	1,08,000	50,000	20,000	25,000	5,000	8,000
Expenses of Dept							
A	30 : 30 : 20 : 20		1,500	1,500	1,000	(–) 5000	1,000
B	50 : 20 : 20 : 10		4,500	1,800	1,800	900	(–) 9,000
A	30 : 30 : 20 : 20		270	270	180	(–) 900	180
B	50 : 20 : 20 : 10		90	36	36	18	(–) 180
A	30 : 30 : 20 : 10		5	5	4	(–) 18	4
B	50 : 20 : 20 : 10		2	1	1		(–) 4
		1,08,000	56,367	23,612	28,021		

Under and over absorption

Problem 27

During the year ended 31st March 1993 the factory overhead costs of three production departments of an organisation are as under :

	Rs.
X	48,950
Y	89,200
Z	64,500

The basis of apportionment of overheads is given below :

Department X— Rs. 5 per machine hour for 10,000 hours.

Y— 75% of Direct Labour Cost of Rs. 1,20,000

Z— Rs. 4 per piece for 15,000 pieces.

Calculate department-wise under or over-absorption of overheads and present the data in a tabular form.

[Adapted—I.C.W.A. (Inter) June 1993]

Solution

Statement of under-or over-absorption of overheads

Department	*Basis of apportion*	*Overheads Absorbed*	*Overheads Incurred*	*Under absorption*	*Over absorption*
		Rs.	Rs.	Rs.	Rs.
X	Machine hours 10,000 × 5	50,000	48,950		1,050
Y	Direct Labour Cost 75% of Rs. 1,20,000	90,000	89,200		800
Z	Piece Rate 15,000 × 4	60,000	64,500	4,500	
		2,00,000	2,02,650	4,500	1,850

Net Under-absorption = Rs. 4,500 – Rs. 1,850 = Rs. 2,650.

Problem 28

The following information relating to the productions of Nalanda Fabricators for 1983 at standard capacity has been collected :

Direct Labour Cost :

Machining	Rs. 1,00,000
Assembling	Rs. 50,000

Floor Space Occupied :

Machining Department	60 per cent
Assembling Department	30 per cent
Factory Office	10 per cent

Factory Overhead tracable to Departments :

Machining Department	Rs. 92,000
Assembling Department	Rs. 53,000
Factory Office	Rs. 41,000

Factory Overheads not tracable to Departments :

Factory Rent, Taxes and Insurance	Rs. 10,000

It has been decided that the costs of Factory Office, which is a service department, can be equitably apportioned to other departments on a direct labour cost basis.

The Machining Department operates on a 40 hour week. There are five machines in the Department and every machine has remained idle for 280 hours in 1983 for vacations, holidays, repairs, etc.

Calculate overhead absorption rate based on machine hours for Machining Department and overhead absorption rate based on direct labour cost for Assembling Department.

[B.Com. Hons., Delhi 1984]

Solution

Overhead Analysis Sheet

		Production Dept.		Service Dept.
		Machining	*Assembling*	*Factory Office*
		Rs.	Rs.	Rs.
Director Labour Cost :				
Factory Overheads		92,000	53,000	41,000
Factory Rent, Taxes & Insurance [6 : 3 : 1]	10,000	6,000	3,000	1,000
Total		98,000	56,000	42,000
Factory Office apportioned among production departments [2 : 1]		28,000	14,000	(– 42,000)
		1,26,000	70,000	
Machine Hour [40 × 5 × 52] =	10,400			
Less : Holidays 280 × 5	1,400			
	9,000			
Machine Hour Rate 1,26,000 ÷ 9,000 =		Rs. 14 p.m.h.		
Direct Labour Cost			50,000	
Direct Labour cost percentage			$\frac{70,000}{50,000} \times 100$ = 140%	

Problem 29

A fire occurred in a factory and records containing information about the allocation of overhead charges were destroyed. It is, however, known that Work Overhead is a certain percentage of Wages and Office Overhead is also a fixed percentage of Factory Cost.

The following further information regarding two previous jobs is also available :

Job No.	*Materials*	*Wages*	*Direct total cost)*	*Profit % on total cost*	*Selling Price*
	Rs.	Rs.	Rs.		Rs.
381	20,000	16,000	4,000	10%	80,080
552	32,000	24,000	2,000	15%	1,22,360

Find out the percentage for Works Overhead and Office Overhead.

[B.Com., Madras]

Solution

The cost of production of Job No. 381 = Rs. 72,800 being $\frac{10}{11}$ of Rs. 80,080 ; and the cost of production of Job. No. 552 = Rs. 1,06,400 being $\frac{100}{115}$ of Rs. 1,22,360.

The cost of production = Material + Wages + Direct Expenses + Works overheads + Office overheads.

Let work overheads be x% of wages and the office overheads be y% on works cost.

Then we have

$$72{,}800 = 20{,}000 + 16{,}000 + 4{,}000 + \left(16{,}000 \times \frac{x}{100}\right) + \left[\frac{y}{100} \times (40{,}000 + 160x)\right]$$

$$\text{or} \quad 72{,}800 = 40{,}000 + 160x + 400y + 1.60xy \text{ ; or, } 32{,}800 = 160x + 400y + 1.60xy \quad \ldots \text{(i)}$$

$$1{,}06{,}400 = 32{,}000 + 24{,}000 + 2{,}000 + \left(24{,}000 \times \frac{x}{100}\right) + \left[\frac{y}{100} \times (58{,}000 + 240x)\right]$$

$$48{,}400 = 240x + 580y + 2.4xy \quad \ldots \text{(ii)}$$

Multiplying equation (i) by 3, we get $98{,}400 = 480x + 1.200y + 4.80\,xy$

Multiplying equation (ii) by 2, we get $\frac{96{,}800}{1{,}600} = 480x + \frac{1{,}160y}{40y} + 4.80\,xy$

or y = 40% by subtracting equation (ii) from (i), we get

Substituting the value of y in equation (i), we get

$32{,}800 = 160x + 16{,}000 + 64x$

or, $224x = 16{,}800$; or, $x = 16{,}800 \div 224 = 75\%$.

Problem 30

In a factory the average annual charge for direct wages bill amounts to Rs. 2,40,000.

The following are some of the expenses (average figure for a year) incurred inside the factory :

(i) Works Manager's salary and other emoluments : Rs. 25,000.

(ii) Factory rent and rates : Rs. 18,000. The total area of the factory is 45,000 sq metre, of which the shops occupy 40,000 sq. metre.

(iii) Wages of caretaker, peons, sweepers, etc. amount to Rs. 3,500.

(iv) Other Factory overhead charges amount to Rs. 26,500.

In a shop occupying 3,000 sq. metre, a work order is executed requiring Rs. 5,000 in wages. If the total wages for all the work orders executed in this shop amount to Rs. 80,000, calculate the total amount of factory overhead charges to be debited to the account of the work order in question.

Solution

Total area of the factory = 45,000 sq. metres
Area occupied by the shop = 40,000 sq. metres
Factory rent and rate = Rs. 18,000

Rent and rates attributed to the shop $= \text{Rs. } \frac{18{,}000 \times 40{,}000}{45{,}000} = \text{Rs. } 16{,}000.$

(in proportion of floor space occupied)

The balance of Rs. 2,000 is attributed to the rest of the factory.

The work order is executed in a shop occupying 3,000 sq. metres and the rent and rates for the shop shall be $= \text{Rs. } 16{,}000 \times \frac{3{,}000}{40{,}000} = \text{Rs. } 1{,}200$

The wages paid for the shop work order are Rs. 5,000.

The wages paid for all work orders are Rs. 80,000.

Hence, (i) proportionate amount applicable to the order on the basis of wages in respect of rent and rates shall be $1{,}200 \times \frac{5{,}000}{80{,}000} = \text{Rs. } 75.$

Other Factory Overheads

	Rs.
Works Manager's Salary etc.	25,000
Factory rent and rates	2,000
Sundry wages	3,500
Other charges	26,500
	57,000

The proportionate amount of it on the basis of wages for the work order shall be :

(ii) $\text{Rs. } \frac{57{,}000}{2{,}40{,}000} \times 5{,}000 = \text{Rs. } 1{,}187.50$

Therefore, Total Factory Overheads chargeable for the work order shall be ;

	Rs.
(i) Rent and Rates of shop	75.00
(ii) Other Factory Overheads	1,187.50
	1,262.50

Problem 31

Following data is available relating to a company for a certain month :

	Territory I	Territory II	Territory III
	Rs.	Rs.	Rs.
Selling expenses	7,600	4,200	6,240
Distribution Costs	4,000	1,800	2,000
No. of unit sold	16,000	6,000	10,000
Sales	76,000	28,000	52,000

The Company adopts sales basis and quantity basis for application of selling and distribution costs, respectively. Compute (a) The territory-wise overhead recovery rates sepa- rately for Selling and Distribution Costs and (b) The amounts of selling and distribution costs chargeable to a consignment of 2,000 units of a product sold in each territory at Rs. 4.50 per unit.

[Adapted—I.C.W.A. (Inter) Dec. 1986]

Solution

(a) Calculation of Overhead recovery rates

1. Selling Cost recovery rate $= \frac{\text{Selling Expenses}}{\text{Sales}} \times 100$

2. Distribution Cost recovery rate $= \frac{\text{Distribution Costs}}{\text{No. of units sold}}$

Territory	*Selling Cost recovery rate*	*Distribution Costs recovery rate*
I	$\frac{7,600}{76,00} \times 100 = 10\%$	4,000 ÷ 16,000 = 0.25 paise per unit
II	$\frac{4,200}{28,000} \times 100 = 15\%$	1,800 ÷ 6,000 = 0.30 paise per unit
III	$\frac{6,240}{52,000} \times 100 = 12\%$	2,000 ÷ 10,000 = 0.20 paise per unit

(b) Calculations of amounts of selling and distribution costs chargeable to the consignment.

		I	II	III
		Rs.	Rs.	Rs.
(a)	No. of units sold	2,000	2,000	2,000
(b)	Sales @ Rs. 4.50 per unit	9,000	9,000	9,000
(c)	Selling cost chargeable @ 10%, 15% and 12% respectively	900	1,350	1,080
(d)	Distribution cost chargeable @ 0.25 paise, 0.30 and 0.20 paise respectively per unit	500	600	400
	Total (c) + (d) Selling + Distribution Overhead chargeable	1,400	1,950	1,480

Problem 32

In a certain factory, there are two production departments X and Y, two service departments A and B. Total expenses of the service department A are apportioned between X, Y and B in the ratio 3 : 2 : 1, and the expenses of the service department B are allocated between X & Y equally. From the following particulars calculate the overheads to be calculated to Production Departments X and Y :

	X	Y	A	B
Floor space (sq. ft)	5,000	4,000	1,000	2,000
Assets (Rs. in lakhs)	10	5	3	1
H. P. of Machine	100	50	40	10
No. of workers	100	50	50	25
Light points	25	15	10	10
Direct wages (Rs.)	10,000	8,000	5,000	3,000
Direct Materials (Rs.)	15,000	10,000	4,000	—

Total expenses and charges are :

	Rs.
Depreciation	38,000
Rent, rates and taxes	18,000
Power	12,500
Insurance on Assets	9,500
Canteen expenses	5,400
Electricity	3,600

[C.U. B. Com. (Hons.) 1988]

Solution

Statement Showing overhead Distribution

Expenses	*Basis for Apportionment*	*Total*	*X*	*Y*	*A*	*B*
			Rs.	Rs.	Rs.	Rs.
Direct Material	Actual	4,000			4,000	
Direct Wages	Actual	8,000			5,000	3,000
Rent, rates and taxes	Floor Area 5 : 4 : 1 : 2	18,000	7,500	6,000	1,500	3,000
Depreciation	Cost of Asset 10 : 5 : 3 : 1	38,000	20,000	10,000	6,000	2,000
Power	H.P. of Machine 10 : 5 : 4 : 1	12,500	6,250	3,125	2,500	625
Insurance on assets	Cost price of assets 10 : 5 : 3 : 1	9,500	5,000	2,500	1,500	500
Canteen Expenses	No. of workers 4 : 2 : 2 : 1	5,400	2,400	1,200	1,200	600
Electricity	Light points 5 : 3 : 2 : 2	3,600	1,500	900	600	600
Total		99,000	42,650	23,725	22,300	10,325
(i) Expenses of A allocated apportioned to X, Y and B in 3 : 2 : 1			11,150	7,433	(–) 22,300	3,717
			53,800	31,158	Nil	14,042
(ii) Expenses of Service Dept. B allocated to X and Y in 1 : 1			7,021	7,021		(–) 14,042
		99,000	60,821	38,179		Nil

Labour Hour Rate

Problem 33

Calcutta Engineering Co. has three Production Departments X, Y and Z and one Service Department S.

From the following particulars calculate Labour Hour Rate of each of the departments X, Y and Z :

Expenses	Rs.
Rent	34,000
Power	18,400
Depreciation on Machinery	22,000
Indirect Wages	5,300
Canteen Expenses	5,700
Electricity	4,600

Further information :

	X	Y	Z	S
Floor area (sq. m.)	2,000	3,000	2,500	1,000
Light points	18	12	10	6
Cost of machines (Rs.)	80,000	50,000	60,000	10,000
Horse power ratio	3	2	4	1
No. of workers	7	5	5	2
Direct Wages (Rs.)	15,000	16,000	18,000	4,000

There were 125 working days of 8 hours each. Services rendered by the Service Department are to be apportioned to the Production Departments X 50%, Y 25% and Z 25%.

[C.U. B.Com. (Hons.) 1982]

Solution

Statement showing apportionment of overhead

Expenses	*Basis of Apportionment*	*Total*	*Production Department Dept.*			*Service Dept.*
			X	Y	Z	S
		Rs.	Rs.	Rs.	Rs.	Rs.
Direct Wages		4,000				4,000
Rent	Floor space (sq. m) 4 : 6 : 5 : 2	34,000	8,000	12,000	10,000	4,000
Power	H. P. Ratio 3 : 2 : 4 : 1	18,400	5,520	3,680	7,360	1,840
Depreciation on machinery	Cost of machine (Rs.) 8 : 5 : 6 : 1	22,000	8,800	5,500	6,600	1,100
Indirect Wages	Direct Wages (Rs.) 15 : 16 : 18 : 4	5,300	1,500	1,600	1,800	400
		83,700	23,820	22,780	25,760	11,340

Contd.

Expenses	Basis of Apportionment	Total	Production Department			Service
			X	Y	Z	S
		Rs.	Rs.	Rs.	Rs.	Rs.
B.F.		83,700	23,820	22,780	25,760	11,340
Canteen expenses	No. of workers 7 : 5 : 5 : 2	5,700	2,100	1,500	1,500	600
Electricity	No. of light points 9 : 6 : 5 : 3	4,600	1,800	1,200	1,000	600
		94,000	27,720	25,480	28,260	12,540
Apportionment of service department expenses	Ratio of service rendered 50% : 25% : 25%		6,270	3,135	3,135	– 12,540
(a) Total allocated Expenses			33,990	28,615	31,395	—
Labour hours worked[1]			7,000	5,000	5,000	—
Labour hour rates[2] (a ÷ b)			4.86	5.72	6.28	

Working Notes :

1) Labour Hours Worked :

X : $125 \times 8 \times 7 = 7{,}000$

Y : $125 \times 8 \times 5 = 5{,}000$

Z : $125 \times 8 \times 5 = 5{,}000$

2) Labour Hour Rates :

X : Rs. $\frac{33{,}990}{7{,}000} = 4{\cdot}855$ or $4{\cdot}86$

Y : Rs. $\frac{28{,}615}{5{,}000} = 5{\cdot}72$

Z : Rs. $\frac{31{,}395}{5{,}000} = 6{\cdot}279$ or $6{\cdot}28$

2) Calculation of Labour Hours = Hours × No. of workers.

	X	Y	Z
125 × 8 = 1,000 × No. of workers =	1,000 × 7 = 7,000	1,000 × 5 = 5,000	1,000 × 5 = 5,000 hrs.

Problem 34

Moonlight Engineering Company has three production departments. A, B and C and Service department S. Following are the particulars of a month of 25 working days of 8 hours each. Calculate the labour hour rate for each of the production departments :

		Rs.	Rs.
Indirect Material			
Dept. A	–	1,735	
Dept. B	–	930	
Dept. C	–	935	
Dept. S	–	300	
			3,900
Indirect Wages	–		9,000
Rent	–		8,800
Canteen Expenses	–		1,800
Lighting	–		2,200
Depreciation @ 12% p.a.			

Other Information :

	Dept. A	Dept. B	Dept. C	Dept. S
No. of workers	20	25	30	15
Area (sq. metre)	100	100	150	50
Direct Wages (Rs)	8,000	10,000	12,000	6,000
No. of Electric points	40	30	20	20
Value of Assets (Rs)	5,000	6,000	6,000	3,000

Service rendered by the service departments to production departments. A, B and C is in the ratio of 2 : 2 : 1, respectively.

[Adapted C.U. B. Com.(Hons.) 1986]

Solution

Statement showing apportionment of overhead

Items of Expenses	*Basis of Apportionment*	*Total*	*Production Departments*			*Service Dept.*
			A	B	C	S
		Rs.	Rs.	Rs.	Rs.	Rs.
Direct Wages		6,000				6,000
Indirect Material	Actual	3,900	1,735	930	935	300
Indirect Wages	Direct Wages 4 : 5 : 6 : 3	9,000	2,000	2,500	3,000	1,500
Rent	Area (sq. m) 2 : 2 : 3 : 1	8,800	2,200	2,200	3,300	1,100
Canteen expenses	No. of workers 4 : 5 : 6 : 3	1,800	400	500	600	300
Lighting	No. of el. pts. 4 : 3 : 2 : 2	2,200	800	600	400	400
Depreciation' @ 12%	Value of assets 5 : 6 : 6 : 3	2,400	600	720	720	360
		34,100	7,735	7,450	8,955	9,960
Apportionment of service dept. expenses	Ratio of service rendered 2 : 2 : 1		3,984	3,984	1992	– 9,960
Total Allocated Exp.	(a)	34,100	11,719	11,434	10,947	–
Labour Hours worked[2]	(b)		4,000	5,000	6,000	–
Labour Hour Rate[3]	(a ÷ b)		2.93	2.29	1.83	–

Working Note :

1) Total value of assets : 5,000 + 6,000 + 6,000 + 3,000 = 20,000

Depreciation @ 12% = $20,000 \times \frac{12}{100} = 2,400$

2) Labour Hours Worked

A : 25 × 8 × 20 = 4,000

B : 25 × 8 × 25 = 5,000

C : 25 × 8 × 30 = 6,000

3) Labour Hour Rate

A : 11,719 ÷ 4,000 = 2·93

B : 11,434 ÷ 5,000 = 2·29

C : 10,947 ÷ 6,000 = 1·83

Problem 35

K.S.D. Ltd. has three manufacturing departments A, B, C and one service department S.

The following particulars are available for one month of 25 working days of 8 hours each day. All departments work all days with full attendance.

Expenses	*Total*	*Production Department*			*Service Dept.*
		A	B	C	S
Power and lighting	1,100	240	200	300	360
Supervisor's Salary	2,000				
Rent	500				
Welfare	600				
Others	1,200	200	200	400	400
Supervisor's Salary		20%	30%	30%	20%
Number of workers		10	30	40	20
Floor area in sq. ft.		500	600	800	600
Service rendered by Service department to production departments		50%	30%	20%	

Calculate the labour hour rate of each of the departments A, B and C.

[Karnataka M.Com.]

Solution

Computation of Labour Hour Rate

Particulars	*Basis*	*Production Dept.*			*Service Dept.*
		A	B	C	S
		Rs.	Rs.	Rs.	Rs.
Power & Lighting	Actual	240	200	300	360
Supervisor's salary	Given 2 : 3 : 3 : 2	400	600	600	400
Rent	Floor area 5 : 6 : 8 : 6	100	120	160	120
Welfare	No. of employees	60	180	240	120
Others	Actual	200	200	400	400
		1,000	1,300	1,700	1,400
Share of S dept.	Given	700 (50%)	420 (30%)	280 20%)	(–) 1,400
Total Overheads (a)		1,700	1,720	1,980	
Labour hours (b)		2,000	6,000	8,000	
Hourly rate	$\frac{\text{Total Overheads}}{\text{Labour Hours}}$ =	0·85	0·29	0·25	

Working Notes :

Total Labour Hours

A	=	25 × 8 × 10	=	2,000
B	=	25 × 8 × 30	=	6,000
C	=	25 × 8 × 40	=	8,000

Problem 36

Deccan Manufacturing Ltd. have three departments which are regarded as production departments. Service departments' costs are distributed to these production departments using the 'Step Ladder Method' of distribution. Estimates of factory overhead costs to be incurred by each department in the forthcoming year are as follows. Data required for distribution is also shown against each department.

Department	*Factory Overhead*	*Direct Labour Hours*	*No. of employees*	*Area in sq. m.*
Production				
X	1,93,000	4,000	100	3,000
Y	64,000	3,000	125	1,500
Z	83,000	4,000	85	1,500
Service				
P	45,000	1,000		500
Q	75,000	5,000	50	1,500
R	1,05,000	6,000	40	1,000
S	30,000	3,000	50	1,000

The Overhead costs of the four service departments are distributed in the same order, viz., P, Q, R and S, respectively, on the following basis :

Department	Basis
P	No. of Employees
Q	Direct Labour Hour
R	Area in sq. metres
S	Direct Labour Hours.

You are required to :

i) Prepare a schedule showing the distribution of Overhead Costs of the four Service departments to the three production departments, and

ii) Calculate the overhead recovery rate per direct labour hour for each of the three production departments.

[Adapted—C.A. (Inter) 1988]

Solution

DECCAN MANUFACTURING LIMITED

Statement showing the distribution of Overhead Costs to Production Departments

	Service Departments				*Production Departments*		
	P	*Q*	*R*	*S*	*X*	*Y*	*Z*
	Rs.	Rs.	Rs.	Rs.	Rs.	Rs.	Rs.
Overhead Costs (Actual)	45,000	75,000	1,05,000	30,000	1,93,000	64,000	83,000
Distribution of Cost of Dept. P in 50 : 40: 50 : 100 : 125 : 85	– 45,000	5,000	4,000	5,000	10,000	12,500	8,500
Cost of Dept. Q (Direct labour hour) Note I		– 80,000	24,000	12,000	16,000	12,000	16,000
Cost of Dept. R (6 : 3 : 3 : 2)			– 1,33,000	19,000	57,000	28,500	28,500
Cost of Depts (Note II)				– 66,000	24,000	18,000	24,000
					3,00,000	1,35,000	1,60,000

(b) Direct Labour Hours

	X	Y	Z
	$\frac{3,00,0000}{4,000}$	$\frac{1,35,000}{3,000}$	$\frac{1,60,000}{4,000}$
	= Rs. 75.00	= Rs. 45.00	= Rs. 40.00

Problem 37

A Limited Company has three Manufacturing Departments A, B and C and one Service Department 'S'. The following figures are available for one month of 25 working days of 8 hours each day. All these departments work for all the days and with full attendance.

Expenditure	*Amount Total*	*Production Departments*			*Service Dept.*
		A	*B*	*C*	*S*
	Rs.	Rs.	Rs.	Rs.	Rs.
Power and lighting	1,100	200	300	360	240
Supervisor's salary	2,000				
Rent	500				
Welfare	600				
Others	1,200	200	200	400	400
	5,400				
Supervisor's salary		20%	30%	30%	20%
Number of workers		10	30	40	20
Floor area in sq. ft.		500	600	800	600
Service rendered by service department		50%	30%	20%	

Calculate labour hour rate for each of the departments A, B and C.

[Adapted—C.A. Inter]

Solution

OVERHEAD DISTRIBUTION SUMMARY

Expenses	*Basis*	*Total*	*Departments*			
			S	***A***	***B***	***C***
			Rs.	Rs.	Rs.	Rs.
Power and lighting	Actual	1,100	240	200	300	360
Supervisor's salary	2 : 3 : 3 : 2	2,000	400	600	600	400
Rent	Floor Area i.e. 6 : 5 : 6 : 8	500	120	100	120	160
Welfare	No. of workers i.e. 2 : 1 : 3 : 4	600	120	60	180	240
Others	Given	1,200	200	200	400	400
		5,400	1,080	1,160	1,600	1,560
Allocation of expenses of Service Department to other departments in 5 : 3 : 2 ratio.		—	– 1,080	540	324	216
		5,400	—	1,700	1,924	1,776

Calculation of Labour Hour Rate

	A	B	C
Number of Hours in a month 25 × 8 =	200	200	200
Labour hours in a month	200 × 10 = 2,000	200 × 30 = 6,000	200 × 40 = 8,000
Labour hour rate	Rs.1,700 ÷ 2,000 = Re. 0.85	Rs.1,924 ÷ 6,000 = Re. 0.32	Rs.1,776 ÷ 8,000 = Re. 0.222

Problem 38

In a certain factory, three products are made from different materials by similar processes. For a typical period, production costs are as under :

	Product A	Product B	Product C
	Rs.	Rs.	Rs.
Materials used	1,600	2,000	800
Direct Labour Cost	1,200	1,000	400
Overhead (actual)	800	650	350

Overhead is charged to cost of each product @ 25% on Prime Cost.

Do you see something wrong in principle in this method of charging overheads ? If so, suggest a preferable method.

[Adapted—I.C.W.A. – Inter, June 1984]

Solution

	A	B	C
	Rs.	Rs.	Rs.
Overhead incurred (actual)	800	650	350
Overhead absorbed @ 25% on Prime Cost	700	750	300
	(25% of 2,800)	(25% of 3,000)	(25% of 1,200)
Over-under-absorption	(100)	100	(50)

In the problem it is revealed that the relationship between material and direct labour cost is not uniform. So, it is not logical to recover overhead @ 25% on Prime Cost. Product consuming higher proportion of materials will be burdened with higher share of overhead.

The following analysis will justify to charge overhead as a percentage of direct labour cost :

Product A — $\frac{800}{1,200} \times 100 = 66.67\%$

Product B — $\frac{650}{1,000} \times 100 = 65\%$

Product C — $\frac{350}{400} \times 100 = 87.5\%$

Problem 39

Bharat Engineering Works has three production departments A, B & C and one service department S. From the undermentioned particulars calculate labour hour rate for each of production departments.

Expenses for the period of 12 months :

	Rs.
Rent	36,000
Power	8,250
Indirect wages	5,200
Depreciation on Machinery	22,000
Electricity	5,600
Canteen Expenses	6,500

Additional information :

	A	B	C	S
Light points (Nos.)	7	7	9	5
Floor Space (sq. m.)	300	250	450	200
Horse Power of Machine (H.P.)	65	30	30	40
No. of workers (Nos.)	2	3	6	2
Direct wages (Rs.)	12,000	14,000	18,000	8,000
Cost of Machine (Rs.)	50,000	60,000	80,000	10,000

Working days : 200 days of 8 hours each.

Service rendered by Service department S to Production departments A, B, C is 30%, 20% and 50%, respectively.

[C.U. B.Com.(Hons.) 1990]

Solution

Statement showing the apportionment of overhead expenses amongst three Depts. A, B & C and one Service Dept. S together with Overhead Recovery Rate per labour hour

Particulars	*Basis of Apportionment*	*Total*	*Production Department* A	B	C	*Service Dept.* S
		Rs.	Rs.	Rs.	Rs.	Rs.
Rent	Floor Space 6 : 5 : 9 : 4	36,000	9,000	7,500	13,500	6,000
Power	H. P. of Machines 13 : 6 : 6 : 8	8,250	3,250	1,500	1,500	2,000
Indirect Wages	Direct wages 6 : 7 : 9 : 4	5,200	1,200	1,400	1,800	800
Depreciation	Cost of machine 5 : 6 : 8 : 1	22,000	5,500	6,600	8,800	1,100
Electricity	Light points 7 : 7 : 9 : 5	5,600	1,400	1,400	1,800	1,000
Canteen Exp.	No. of workers 2 : 3 : 6 : 2	6,500	1,000	1,500	3,000	1,000
Direct Wages	Allocated	8,000	–	–	–	8,000
Primary Dist. Cost		91,550	21,350	19,900	30,400	19,900
Apportionment of Cost of Service Dept.	3 : 2 : 5		5,970	3,980	9,950	– 19,900
Total Cost	(a)	91,550	27,320	23,880	40,350	–
Total Labour Hours	(b) 200 × 8 × No. of workers		27,320 3,200	23,880 4,800	40,350 9,600	
Labour Hour Rate	(a) ÷ (b)		= 8.54	= 4.98	= 4.20	

Simultaneous Equation Method

Problem 40

Swanirvar Co. Ltd. has three Production Departments A, B and C and two Service Departments D and E. From the following information available from the records of the Company, calculate the overhead rates per labour hour for the Production Departments.

	Rs.
Indirect materials	15,000
Indirect wages	10,000
Depreciation on machinery	25,000
Depreciation on buildings	5,000
Rent, rates and taxes	10,000
Electric power for machinery	15,000
Electric power for lighting	500
General Expenses	15,000
	95,500

Items	Total	A	B	C	D	E
	Rs.	Rs.	Rs.	Rs.	Rs.	Rs.
Direct materials (Rs.)	60,000	20,000	10,000	19,000	6,000	5,000
Direct wages (Rs.)	40,000	15,000	15,000	4,000	2,000	4,000
Value of machinery	2,50,000	60,000	1,00,000	40,000	25,000	25,000
Floor area (sq. ft.)	50,000	15,000	10,000	10,000	5,000	10,000
Horse power of machines	150	50	60	30	5	5
No. of light oints	50	15	10	10	5	10
Labour hours	15,000	5000	5,000	2,000	1,000	2,000

The expenses of Service Departments D and E are to be apportioned as follows:

Expenses of	A	B	C	D	E
D	20%	40%	30%	—	10%
E	40%	20%	20%	20%	—

[V.U. B. Com (Hons.) 1994]

Solution

Primary Distribution Sheet

Items	Basis of apportionment	Total	Department A	B	C	D	E
		Rs.	Rs.	Rs.	Rs.	Rs.	Rs.
Indirect materials	Direct materials 20 : 10 : 19 : 6 : 5	60,000	20,000	10,000	19,000	6,000	5,000
Indirect wages	Direct wages 15 : 15 : 4 : 2 : 4	40,000	15,000	15,000	4,000	2,000	4,000
Depreciation on Machinery	Value of machinery 60 : 100 : 40 : 25 : 25	25,000	6,000	10,000	4,000	2,500	2,500
Depreciation on Building	Floor Area 15 : 10 : 10 : 5 : 10	5,000	1,500	1,000	1,000	500	1,000
Rent, rates and taxes	Floor Area 15 : 10 : 10 : 5 : 10	10,000	3,000	2,000	2,000	1,000	2,000
Electric power machinery	Horse power 10 : 12 : 6 : 1 : 1	15,000	5,000	6,000	3,000	500	500
Electric power for lighting	Light points 3 : 2 : 2 : 1 : 2	500	150	100	100	50	100
General expenses	Direct wages 15 : 15 : 4 : 2 : 4	15,000	5,625	5,625	1,500	750	1,500
		1,70,500	56,275	49,725	34,600	13,300	16,600

Secondary Distribution Sheet

	Dept. A	Dept. B	Dept. C	Service D	Service E
	Rs.	Rs.	Rs.	Rs.	Rs.
Balance as per Primary Distribution Sheet	56,275	49,725	34,600	13,300	16,600
Department D	3,392	6,784	5,088	(–)16960	1,696
Department E	7,318	3,659	3,659	3,660	(–) 18296
	66,985	60,168	43,347	Nil	Nil
Labour Hour Rate = $\frac{\text{Expenses}}{\text{Labour hours}}$	$\frac{66,985}{5,000}$	$\frac{60,168}{5,000}$	$\frac{43,347}{2,000}$		
	Rs. 13.40	Rs. 12.03	Rs. 21.67		

Working Notes

Let X be the total cost of department D

and Y be the total cost of department E

Then,

$$X = 13,300 + \frac{20}{100} Y \text{ or } 13,300 + \frac{1}{5} Y \text{ .... (i)}$$

$$Y = 16,600 + \frac{10}{100} X \text{ or } 16,600 + \frac{1}{10} X \text{ .... (ii)}$$

$$\text{Or } Y = 16,600 + \frac{1}{10} (13,300 + \frac{1}{5} Y)$$

[Substituting the value of x in equation (ii)]

$$\text{Or } Y = 16,600 + 1,330 + \frac{1}{50} Y$$

$$\text{Or } 50Y = 8,30,000 + 66,500 + Y \text{ [Multiplying both by 50]}$$

$$\text{Or } 50Y - Y = 8,96,500$$

$$\text{Or } 49Y = \text{Rs. } 8,96,500 \text{ or } Y - \text{Rs. } 18,296$$

$$X = 13,300 + \frac{1}{5} Y$$

$$\text{Or } X = 13,300 + \frac{1}{5} \times 18,296$$

$$\text{Or } X = 13,300 + 3,650$$

$$\text{Or } X = \text{Rs. } 16,960$$

Problem 41

A factory comprises two Production Departments and three Service Departments. For the month of March 1991. The direct departmental expenses were as follows :

Production Departments	*Service Departments*	
A—Rs. 85,000	Power house	Rs. 47,350
B—Rs. 70,000	Store	Rs. 15,000
	Repair Shop	Rs. 60,500

The expenses of Service Departments are distributed on a percentage basis as under :

Power House : 25% to Repair shop; 25% to Department A and 50% to Department B.

Store : 10% to Power House; 20% to Repair Shop; 30% to Department A and 40% to Department B.

Repair Shop : 20% to Power House; 30% to Department A and 50% to Department B.

Prepare a statement showing the distribution of Service Departments' expenses to Production Departments using the simultaneous equation method.

[V.U. B.Com. (Hons.) 1991]

Solution

Secondary Distribution Summary

Item	*Basis*	*Product Departments*		*Service Departments*		
		A	*B*	*Power House*	*Store*	*Repair Shop.*
		Rs.	Rs.	Rs.	Rs.	Rs.
As per primary distribution		85,000	70,000	47,350	15,000	60,500
Expenses of Store	3 : 4 : 1 : 2	4,500	6,000	1,500	(15,000)	3,000
		89,500	76,000	48,850	—	63,500
Expenses of Power House	1 : 2 : 1	16,197	32,395	(64,790)	—	16,198
Expenses of Repair Shop	3 : 5 : 2	23,909	39,849	15,940		(79,698)
		1,29,606	1,48,244	nil	nil	nil

Working notes

Suppose total expenses of Power House = m

" " " " Repair shop = n

We get, $m = \text{Rs. } 48{,}850 + 20\% \text{ of } n = \text{Rs. } 48{,}850 + \frac{1}{5} \text{ of } n$ ...... (i)

$n = \text{Rs. } 63{,}500 + 25\% \text{ of } m = \text{Rs. } 63{,}500 + \frac{1}{4} \text{ of } m$ .... (ii)

Or $n = \text{Rs. } 63{,}500 + \frac{1}{4}\left(48{,}850 + \frac{1}{5} n\right)$

[Substituting the value of m in (ii)]

Or $\quad n = 63{,}500 + 12{,}213 + \frac{1}{20}n$

Or $\quad 20n = 12{,}70{,}000 + 2{,}44{,}260 + n$ (multiplying both sides by 20)

Or $\quad 19n = 15{,}14{,}260$

Or $\quad n = \frac{15{,}14{,}260}{19}$ = Rs. 79,698

Putting the value of n in equation (i) we get,

Rs. 48,850 + ($\frac{1}{5}$ × Rs. 79,698)

Or Rs. 48,850 + Rs. 15,940 = Rs. 64,790.

Problem 42

Maneka Company has three production centres and two service centres. The overhead analysis sheet gives the following overhead costs :

Production Centres	Rs.	*Service Centres*	Rs.
A	27,600	D	12,600
B	43,800	E	10,200
C	25,800		

The machine hours in different departments are :

A—3,284; B—2,606, C—1,752

The expenses of service centres are apportioned as follows:

	A	B	C	D	E
D	30%	40%	20%		10%
E	10%	20%	50%	20%	

You are required to calculate :

(a) The machine hour rate for each department,

(b) The cost of production of a product requiring Rs. 400 for materials and Rs. 600 for labour. The product has to pass through departments A, B and C for 5, 4 and 5 hours, respectively.

[B.U. B. Com. (Hons) 1997]

Solution

Secondary Distribution Summary

	Production Centres			*Service Centres*	
	A	*B*	*C*	*D*	*E*
	Rs.	Rs.	Rs.	Rs.	Rs.
As per primary distribution	27,600	43,800	25,800	12,600	10,200
Service Dept. D	3,780	5,040	2,520	(12,600)	1,260
Service Dept. E	1,146	2,292	5,730	2,292	(11460)
Service Dept. D	688	917	458	(2292)	229
Service Dept. E	23	46	115	45	(229)
Service Dept. D	13.50	18	9	(45)	4.5
Service Dept. E in 1 : 2 : 5 : 2	0.45	0.90	2.25	0.90	(4.50)
Service Dept. D in 3 : 4 : 3	0.30	0.40	0.20	–0.90	
	33,251.25	52,114.30	34634.45	nil	nil

(a) **Machine hour rate for**

each department $= \dfrac{\text{Total overhead}}{\text{Machine Hours}}$

$A = \text{Rs. } \dfrac{33{,}251.25}{3{,}284}$ $B = \text{Rs. } \dfrac{52{,}114.30}{2{,}606}$ $C = \text{Rs. } \dfrac{34{,}634.45}{1{,}752}$

= Rs. 10.13p. = Rs. 20 = Rs. 19.77

(B) **Cost Sheet**

	Rs.
Material cost	400.00
Wages	600.00
Overhead (5 × 10.13) + (4 × 20) + (5 × 19.77)	229.50
	1,229.50

Problem 43

In a manufacturing concern there are four departments viz A, B, C & D. A & B are Production Departments and C & D are Service Departments. C renders service worth Rs.12,000 to D and balance to A & B in the ratio of 3 : 2. D renders service to A & B in the ratio of 9 : 1.

The Overhead expenses incurred in a year are as follows :

	Rs.
Depreciation	95,000
Rent, Rates and Taxes	18,000
Insurance	7,600
Power	10,000
Canteen Expenses	5,400
Electricity	2,400

Following further information are given regarding the departments :

	A	B	C	D
Direct Materials (Rs.)	6,000	5,000	3,000	2,000
Direct Labour (Rs.)	20,000	10,000	10,000	5,000
Floor Space occupied (Sq. ft.)	5,000	4,000	1,000	2,000
Value of Assets (in lakhs)	10	5	3	1
H. P. of Machines	1,000	500	400	100
No. of workers	100	50	50	25
Light and Fan points	50	30	20	20

From the above particulars prepare a statement showing overhead expenses of Production Departments A & B after redistribution of Service Departments' expenses.

[Adapted—C.U. B.Com. (Hons.) 1992]

Solution

STATEMENT SHOWING THE DISTRIBUTION OF OVERHEADS

Expenses	*Basis of Apportionment*	*Total*	*Production Departments*		*Service Departments*	
			A	B	C	D
			Rs.	Rs.	Rs.	Rs.
Depreciation	Value of Assets 10 : 5 : 3 : 1	95,000	50,000	25,000	15,000	5,000
Rent, Rates and Taxes	Floor space 5 : 4 : 1 : 2	18,000	7,500	6,000	1,500	3,000
Insurance	Value of Assets 10 : 5 : 3 : 1	7,600	4,000	2,000	1,200	400
Power	H.P. of machines 10 : 5 : 4 : 1	10,000	5,000	2,500	2,000	500
Canteen Expenses	No. of workers 4 : 2 : 2 : 1	5,400	2,400	1,200	1,200	600
Electricity	Light and Fan points 5 : 3 : 2 : 2	2,400	1,000	600	400	400
Direct Materials	Actual	5,000			3,000	2,000
Direct Labour	Actual	15,000			10,000	5,000
		1,58,400	69,900	37,300	34,300	16,900
1. Expenses of Rs. 12,000 of Dept. C allocated to Dept. D					– 12,000	+ 12,000
Balance of Rs, 22,300 allocated to A and B Department in 3 : 2			+ 13,380	+ 8,920	– 22,300	
		1,58,400	83,280	46,220	—	28,900
2. Expenses of Dept. D allocated to Depts. A and B in 9 : 1			26,010	2,890	—	– 28,900
		1,58,400	1,09,290	49,110	—	—

SIMULTANEOUS EQUATION METHOD

Problem 44

A Company has three Production Departments and two Service Departments. The Overhead distribution sheet showed the following totals :

		Rs.
Production Department	A	25,000
	B	31,000
	C	28,000
Service Department		
	S	8,000
	T	13,900

Using the following bases of apportionment, distribute the cost of service departments under Simultaneous Equation Method.

		A	B	C	S	T
Department	S	30%	20%	40%		10%
Department	T	40%	15%	25%	20%	

[Kalyani University B.Com. (Hons.) 1992]

Solution

Let x be the expense of Department S

and y be the expense of Department T

Then x = Rs. 8,000 + $\frac{1}{5}$th of y (20% of y)

y = Rs. 13,900 + $\frac{10}{100}$ of x

Putting the value of x, we get :

y = Rs. 13,900 + $\frac{1}{10}$ of (8,000 + $\frac{1}{5}$th of y)

Or, y = Rs. 13,900 + Rs. 800 + $\frac{1}{50}$ y

Or, y = Rs. 14,700 + $\frac{1}{50}$ y, or, 50 y = 7,35,000 + y

Or, 50y − y = Rs. 7,35,000, or, 49y = Rs. $\frac{7,35,000}{49}$ = Rs. 15,000

Putting the value of y we get

x = Rs. 8,000 + $\frac{1}{5}$th of y, or, x = Rs. 8,000 + $\frac{1}{5}$ of Rs. 15,000

Or, x = Rs. 8,000 + Rs. 3,000, or, x = Rs. 11,000.

Total expense of dept. S Rs. 11,000

Total expense of dept. T Rs. 15,000

Overhead Distribution Summary **Departments**

Particulars	A	B	C	S	T
	Rs.	Rs.	Rs.	Rs.	Rs.
Total as per Primary Distribution	25,000	31,000	28,000	8,000	13,900
Distribution of expenses of Dept. S in the ratio 3 : 2 : 4 : 1	3,300	2,200	4,400	– 11,000	1,100
Distribution of expenses of Dept. T in the ratio 8 : 3 : 5 : 4	6,000	2,250	3,750	3,000	–15,000
	34,300	35,450	36,150	—	—

Problem 45

Ascertain the composite machine hour rates in respect of the following production departments A, B and C from the data furnished below. There are two more service departments S_1 and S_2 in the factory.

The total of budgeted expenses for the year as well as the basis of distribution are given below :

Expenses	*Total Expenses*	*Basis of distribution*
	Rs.	
Indirect Labour	3,78,000	Rs.49,000 to dept A: Rs. 35,000 to S_2. The balance to the remaining departments on the basis of direct labour hours.
Management Salaries	8,85,000	On the basis of direct labour hours.
Maintenance	12,50,000	On the basis of cost of machinery—the amount includes materials for construction Rs. 1,50,000 and raw materials Rs. 1,00,000
Factory rent	1,25,000	Floor space
Fuel consumed in Service Dept. S_2 only	83,300	—
General Factory Expenses	5,60,000	On the basis of direct wages
Depreciation		Figures not available in the budget

The following further information is available from the factory records :

Items	*Total*	*Production Departments*			*Service Departments*	
		A	B	C	S_1	S_2
Floor Space (sq. ft.)	50,000	17,000	12,000	10,000	5,000	6,000
Direct labour hours	8,85,000	2,55,000	3,78,000	1,44,000	66,000	42,000
Machine hours	4,16,500	1,80,000	1,20,000	67,500	15,000	34,000
Cost of machinery (Rs.) in lakhs	200	70	60	40	10	20
Direct wages (Rs.) in lakhs	14	4	6	2	1	1
Depreciation %		10	8	9	10	12.5

Expenses apportioned to department S_1 are to be distributed to production and service departments on the basis of machine hours. Expenses apportioned to S_2 are to be distributed to production departments on the basis of direct labour hour.

[Adapted—I.C.W.A. (Inter)]

Solution

Statement showing apportionment and allocation of overheads

Items	*Basis of apportionment*	*Total*	*Production Depts.* A	B	C	*Service Depts.* S_1	S_2
		Rs.	Rs.	Rs.	Rs.	Rs.	Rs.
Indirect labour	Direct labour hours (378 : 144 : 66) to B, C and S_1	3,78,000	49,000	1,89,000	72,000	33,000	35,000
Management salaries	Direct labour hours (255 : 378 : 144 : 66 : 42)	8,85,000	2,55,000	3,78,000	1,44,000	66,000	42,000
Maintenance	Cost of machinery (70 : 60 : 40 : 10 : 20)	10,00,000	3,50,000	3,00,000	2,00,000	50,000	1,00,000
Factory Rent	Floor Space (17 : 12 : 10 : 5 : 6)	1,25,000	42,500	30,000	25,000	12,500	15,000
Fuel	Actual	83,300					83,300
General Factory Exp.	Direct wages (4 : 6 : 2 : 1 : 1)	5,60,000	1,60,000	2,40,000	80,000	40,000	40,000
Depreciation	As given	18,90,000	7,00,000	4,80,000	3,60,000	1,00,000	2,50,000
Direct wages	Allocated	14,00,000	4,00,000	6,00,000	2,00,000	1,00,000	1,00,000
		63,21,300	19,56,500	22,17,000	10,81,000	4,01,500	6,65,300
Overheads of S_1 allocated on the basis of M.H.R. (180 : 120 : 67.5 : 34)			1,80,000	1,20,000	67,500	–4,01,500	34,000
Overheads of S_2 allocated in (255 : 378 : 144) D.L.H			2,29,500	3,40,200	1,29,600		–6,99,300
		63,21,300	23,66,000	26,77,200	12,78,100	Nil	Nil

Calculation of Machine Hour Rate

Machine hours of Production Departments

A	B	C
1,80,000 hours	1,20,000 hours	67,500 hours

Machine Hour Rate = Overheads ÷ Machine hours

A = Rs. $\frac{23,66,000}{1,80,000}$ = Rs. 13.14	B = Rs. $\frac{26,77,200}{1,20,000}$ = Rs. 22.31	C = Rs. $\frac{12,78,100}{67,500}$ = Rs. 18.93

[Ascertainment of total Cost through working hours]

Problem 46

The New Enterprises Ltd. has three Production Departments, A, B & C and two Service Departments D & E. The following figures are extracted from the records of the Company :

	Rs.
Rent and rates	5,000
General lighting	600
Indirect wages	1,500
Power	1,500
Depreciation on machinery	10,000
Sundries	10,000

The following further details are available :

Particulars	*Total*	*A*	*B*	*C*	*D*	*E*
Floor Space (sq. ft)	10,000	2,000	2,500	3,000	2,000	500
Light points	60	10	15	20	10	5
Direct wages (Rs.)	10,000	3,000	2,000	3,000	1,500	500
H.P. of machines	150	60	30	50	10	
Value of machinery (Rs.)	2,50,000	60,000	80,000	1,00,000	5,000	5,000
Working hours		6,226	4,028	4,066		

The expenses of Departments D & E are allocated as follows :

	A	B	C	D	E
D	20%	30%	40%		10%
E	40%	20%	30%	10%	

What is the total cost of an article, if its raw materials cost is Rs. 50, labour cost Rs. 30 and it passes through departments A, B & C for 4, 5 and 3 hours, respectively ?

[Adapted—C.A. (Inter)]

Solution

Step I.

Apportionment of Overhead expenses between different departments

Statement Showing Overheads Apportionment (Primary Distribution)

Expenses	*Basis of apportionment*	*Total amount*	*Production Depts.*			*Service Depts.*	
			A	B	C	D	E
		Rs.	Rs.	Rs.	Rs.	Rs.	Rs.
Rent and Rates	Floor space (4 : 5 : 6 : 4 : 1)	5,000	1,000	1,250	1,500	1,000	250
General Lighting	Light points (2 : 3 : 4 . 2 . 1)	600	100	150	200	100	50
Indirect wages	Direct wages (6 : 4 : 6 : 3 : 1)	1,500	450	300	450	225	75
Power	H.P. of machine (6 : 3 : 5 : 1 : 0)	1,500	600	300	500	100	
Depreciation	Value of machine (12 : 16 : 20 : 1 : 1)	10,000	2,400	3,200	4,000	200	200
Sundries	Direct wages (6 : 4 : 6 : 3 : 1)	10,000	3,000	2,000	3,000	1,500	500
Direct wages	Actual	2,000				1,500	500
		30,600	7,550	7,200	9,650	4,625	1,575

Step II.

Allocation of overheads of Service departments D & E according to the simultaneous methods

$x = 4{,}625 + 10\%$ of y Or, $10x = 46{,}250 + y$

$y = 1{,}575 + 10\%$ of x $10y = 15{,}750 + x$

where x = Total overheads of dept. D and y = Total overheads of Dept. E.

Or, $10x - y = 46{,}250$ (i)

$-x + 10y = 15{,}750$ (ii).

$10x - y = 46{,}250$ By multiplying the equation (ii) by 10 we get

$-10x + 100y = 1{,}57{,}500$

$99y = 2{,}03{,}750$

Or, $y = \frac{2{,}03{,}750}{99}$ = Rs. 2,058 (approx.)

Substituting this value of y on equation we get

$10x - 2{,}058 = 46{,}250$, Or, $10x = 46{,}250 + 2{,}058$, Or, $10x = 48{,}308$

Or, $x = 48{,}308 \div 10$ = Rs. 4,831 (approx).

Step III.

Allocation of over-heads of Service Departments to Production Departments A, B & C

	A	B	C
	Rs.	Rs.	Rs.
Amount as per Primary Distribution	7,550	7,200	9,650
Allocation of expenses of dept. D			
Rs. 4,831 – Rs. 483 = Rs. 4,348 in the ratio 2 : 3 : 4	966	1,449	1,933
Department E (Rs. 2,058 – 206 = Rs. 1,852 in 4 : 3 : 2)	823	617	412
	9,339	9,266	11,995

Step IV.

Determination of Overheads per hour

$$\text{Overhead Per hour} = \frac{\text{Total Overheads as allocated}}{\text{Working Hours}}$$

	A	B	C
	Rs.	Rs.	Rs.
Total Overhead	9,339	9,266	11,995
Working Hours	6,226	4,028	4,066
Overheads per hour	$\frac{9{,}339}{6{,}226}$	$\frac{9{,}266}{4{,}028}$	$\frac{11{,}995}{4{,}066}$
	= Rs. 1.50	= Rs. 2.30	= Rs. 2.95

Step V

Determination of Total Cost

Statement Showing Total Cost of an Article

				Rs.	Rs.
Cost of Raw materials					50.00
Cost of labour					30.00
Prime Cost					80.00
Add Overheads :	A	=	4 × 1.50 =	6.00	
	B	=	5 × 2.30 =	11.50	
	C	=	3 × 2.95 =	8.85	
					26.35
					106.35

Problem 47

The company is having three production departments A, B and C and two service departments boiler-house and pump-room. The boiler-house has to depend upon the pump-room for supply of water and pump-room in its turn is dependent on the boiler-house for the supply of steam power for driving the pump. The expenses incurred by the production departmenrs are :

A : Rs. 4,00,000; B : Rs. 3,50,000; and C : Rs. 2,50,000

The expenses for boiler-house is Rs. 1,17,000 and the pump-room is Rs. 1,50,000.

The expenses of the boiler-house and pump-room are apportioned to the production departments on the following basis :

	A	*B*	*C*	*Boiler House*	*Pump Room*
Expenses of boiler-house	20%	40%	30%	—	10%
Expenses of pump-room	40%	20%	20%	20%	—

Show clearly as to how the expenses of boiler-house and pump-room would be apportioned to A, B and C departments?

[ACS Inter June, 88]

Solution

In view of inter-dependence of departments. Repealed distribution method is to be followed :

Apportionment of overheads—repeated distribution method : Basis of apportionment is the percentages given in the questions.

Particulars	*Production Deptt.*			*Service Deptt.*	
	A	*B*	*C*	*Boiler House*	*Pump room*
	Rs.	Rs.	Rs.	Rs.	Rs.
Expenses incurred	4,00,000	3,50,000	2,50,000	1,17,000	1,50,000
Boiler house	23,400	46,800	35,100	(–)1,17,000	11,700
Pump room	64,680	32,340	32,340	32,340	(–)1,61,700
Boiler house	6,468	12,936	9,702	(–)32,340	3,234
Pump room	1,293	647	647	647	(–)3,234
Boiler house	129	259	194	(–)647	65
Pump room	26	13	13	13	–65
Boiler house	4	5	4	(–)13	
	4,96,000	4,43,000	3,28,000		

Problem 48

You are supplied with the following information and required to work out the production hour rate of recovery of overhead in departments A, B and C :

Particulars	*Total*	*Production Depts.*			*Service Depts.*	
		A	B	C	P	Q
	Rs.	Rs.	Rs.	Rs.	Rs.	Rs.
Rent	12,000	2,400	4,800	2,000	2,000	800
Electricity	4,000	800	2,000	500	400	300
Indirect labour	6,000	1,200	2,000	1,000	800	1,000
Depreciation	5,000	2,500	1,600	200	500	200
Sundries	4,500	910	2,143	847	300	300
Estimated working hours		1,000	2,500	1,400		

Expenses of Service Departments P and Q are apportioned as under :

	A	B	C	P	Q
P	30%	40%	20%	–	10%
Q	10%	20%	50%	20%	–

[Adapted—C.A. Inter]

Solution

OVERHEAD DISTRIBUTION SUMMARY

Particulars	*Total*	*A*	*B*	*C*	*P*	*Q*
	Rs.	Rs.	Rs.	Rs.	Rs.	Rs.
Rent	12,000	2,400	4,800	2,000	2,000	800
Electricity	4,000	800	2,000	500	400	300
Indirect Labour	6,000	1,200	2,000	1,000	800	1,000
Depreciation	5,000	2,500	1,600	200	500	200
Sundries	4,500	910	2,143	847	300	300
	31,500	7,810	12,543	4,547	4,000	2,600

Allocation of expenses of Service departments P and Q under Continued Distribution Method.

Particulars	*Total*	*A*	*B*	*C*	*P*	*Q*
	Rs.	Rs.	Rs.	Rs.	Rs.	Rs.
As per primary Distribution		7,810	12,543	4,547	4,000	2,600
Allocation of Expenses						
Expenses of Dept. P. (3 : 4 : 2 : 1)		1,200	1,600	800	– 4,000	400
Total		9,010	14,143	5,337	–	3,000
Expenses of Dept. Q. (1 : 2 : 5 : 2)		300	600	1,500	600	– 3,000
Total		9,310	14,743	6,847	600	–
Cycle II						
Expenses of Dept. P. (3 : 4 : 2 : 1)		180	240	120	– 600	60
Total		9,490	14,983	6,967	–	60
Expenses of Dept. Q. (1 : 2 : 5 : 2)		6	12	30	12	– 60
		9,496	14,995	6,997	12	–

Contd.

Particulars	*Total*	*A*	*B*	*C*	*P*	*Q*
	Rs.	Rs.	Rs.	Rs.	Rs.	Rs.
B.F.		9,496	14,995	6,997	12	
Cycle III						
Expenses of P		4	5	3	– 12	–
(a) Total allocated overhead		9,500	15,000	7,000	–	–
(b) Working hours		1,000	2,500	1,400		
Rate per hour (a ÷ b)		Rs. 9.5	Rs. 6	Rs. 5		

Problem 49

A manufacturing company has two departments X and Y and all products pass through both the departments. Their production cost for March 1991 is :

	Dept. X	Dept. Y
	Rs.	Rs.
Direct labour hours	6,000	4,000
Machine hours	4,500	2,000
Direct Materials	1,00,000	50,000
Direct Wages	6,000	8,000
Overheads	45,000	10,000
Job Card for Job No. I shows :		
Raw Materials	3,000	1,000
Direct Wages	250	380
Direct Labour Hours	225	200
Machine Hours	200	600

Compute the cost of Job No. 1 under the method recommended by you and one other method of overhead absorption.

[B.U. B.Com. (Hons.) 1987]

Solution

Absorption of Overheads

	X	Y
(i) Direct Wages Method	$\left(\frac{45,000}{6,000}\right) \times 100 = 750\%$	$\left(\frac{10,000}{8,000}\right) \times 100 = 125\%$
(ii) Labour Hour Method	$\left(\frac{45,000}{6,000}\right)$ = Rs. 7.5	$\left(\frac{10,000}{4,000}\right)$ = Rs. 2.5
(iii) Machine Hour Method	$\left(\frac{45,000}{4,500}\right)$ Rs. 10	$\left(\frac{10,000}{2,000}\right)$ = Rs. 5

Statement showing the Cost of Job No. I using the Machine Hour Method

	X	Y	Total
Machine Hour Method	Rs.	Rs.	Rs.
Direct Materials	3,000	1,000	4,000
Direct Wages	250	380	630
Prime Cost	3,250	1,380	4,630
Add : Factory Overhead	(200 × 10) 2,000	(600 × 5) 3,000	5,000
	5,250	4,380	9,630

Contd.

	X	Y	Total
Direct Labour Hour Method			
Direct Materials	3,000	1,000	4,000
Direct Wages	250	380	630
PRIME COST	3,250	1,380	4,630
Add Factory Overhead	1,687.50	500	2187.50
	(225 × 7.50)	(200 × 2.5)	
	4,937.50	1,880	6,817.50

Problem 50

A company reapportions the costs incurred by two service cost centres, materials handling and inspection, to the three production cost centres of machining, finishing and assembly.

The following are the overhead costs which have been allocated and apportioned to the five cost centers :

	Rs. '000
Machining	400
Finishing	200
Assembly	100
Materials handling	100
Inspection	50

Estimates of the benefits received by each cost center are as follows :

	Machining	*Finishing*	*Assembly*	*Materials handlig*	*Inspection*
	%	%	%	%	%
Materials handling	30	25	35	—	10
Inspection	20	30	45	5	—

You are required to :

(a) Calculate the charge for overhead to each of the three production cost centers, including the amounts reapportioned from the two service centers, using :

(i) the continuous allotment (or repeated distribution) method, and

(ii) an algebraic method.

[CIMA London, November 1989]

Solution

(i) **Repeated Distribution Method.**

	Machining	*Finishing*	*Assembly*	*Materials handling*	*Inspections*
	Rs.	Rs.	Rs.	Rs.	Rs.
Initial cost	4,00,000	2,00,000	1,00,000	1,00,000	50,000
Reapportioned :					
Materials handling in 6 : 5 : 7 : 2	30,000	25,000	35,000	(1,00,000)	10,000
	4,30,000	2,25,000	1,35,000	—	60,000
Inspection in 4 : 6 : 9 : 1	12,000	18,000	27,000	3,000	(60,000)
	4,42,000	2,43,000	1,62,000	3,000	—

Contd.

	Machining	Finishing	Assembly	Materials handling	Inspections
	Rs.	Rs.	Rs.	Rs.	Rs.
B. F.	4,42,000	2,43,000	1,62,000	3,000	—
Materials handling in 6 : 5 : 7 : 2	900	750	1,050	(3,000)	300
	4,42,900	2,43,750	1,63,050	—	300
Inspection in 4 : 6 : 9 : 1	60	90	135	15	(300)
	4,42,960	2,43,840	1,63,185	15	—
Materials handling in 6 : 5 : 7	5	4	6	(15)	—
	4,42,965	2,43,844	1,63,191		

(ii) Algebraic Method

Let materials handling = x ; Let inspection = y

x = 1,00,000 + 0.05y .... (1)

y = 50,000 + 0.1x .... (2)

y = 20,00,000 – 20x .... (3) (By multiplying (1) by 20)

o = 20,50,000 – 19.9x .... (4) (By adding) = (2) + (3)

x = 20,50,000 ÷ 19.9 or x = Rs. 1,03,015

y = 50,000 + 0.1 (1,03,015) .... (2)

y = 50,000 + 10,301 or y = Rs. 60,301

		Machining	Finishing	Assembly
	Initial cost	Rs. 4,00,000	Rs. 2,00,000	Rs.1,00,000
(x)	Materials handling	(30) 30,905	(25) 25,754	(35) 36,055
(y)	Inspection	(20) 12,060	(30) 18,090	(45) 27,136
		4,42,965	2,43,844	1,63,191

Problem 51

Superclass Co. Ltd. has three production departments *X*, *Y* and *Z* and two service departments *A* and *B*.

The following estimated figures for a certain period have been made available :

	Rs.
Rent and Rates	10,000
Lighting and electricity	1,200
Indirect Wages	3,000
Power	3,000
Depreciation of Machinery	20,000
Other Expenses and Sundries	20,000

Following are further details which are also available :

	Total	X	Y	Z	A	B
Floor Space (Sq. mts.)	10,000	2,000	2,500	3,000	2,000	500
Light Points (Nos.)	120	20	30	40	20	10
Direct wages Rs.	20,000	6,000	4,000	6,000	3,000	1,000
Horsepower of machines	300	120	60	100	20	—
Cost of Machinery (Rs.)	1,00,000	24,000	32,000	40,000	2,000	2,000
Working hours		4,670	3,020	3,050	—	—

The expenses of the service departments A and B are to be allocated as follows :

	X	Y	Z	A	B
A	20%	30%	40%	—	10%
B	40%	20%	30%	10%	—

You are required to calculate the overhead absorption rate per hour in respect of the three production departments.

What will be the total cost of an article with material cost of Rs. 80 and direct labour cost of Rs. 40 which passes through *X*, *Y* and *Z* for 2, 3, and 4 hours, respectively ?

(I.C.W.A. Inter, June 1985)

Solution

Departmental Primary Distribution Summary

Items	*Basis of Apportioment*	*Total*	*Production Dept.*			*Service Dept.*	
			X	*Y*	*Z*	*A*	*B*
		Rs.	Rs.	Rs.	Rs.	Rs.	Rs.
1. Rent, Rates and Taxes	Floor Area	10,000	2,000	2,500	3,000	2,000	500
2. Lighting and Electricity	Light Points	1,200	200	300	400	200	100
3. Indirect Wages	Direct Wages	3,000	900	600	900	450	150
4. Power	Horse power	3,000	1,200	600	1,000	200	—
5. Dpreciation of Machinery	Cost of Machine	20,000	4,800	6,400	8,000	400	400
6. Other expenses and sundries	Direct wages	20,000	6,000	4,000	6,000	3,000	1,000
7. Direct wages	Only Service Dept.	4,000	—	—	—	3,000	1,000
		61,200	15,100	14,400	19,300	9,250	3,150

Secondary Distribution Summary

	X	Y	Z	A	B
	Rs.	Rs.	Rs.	Rs.	Rs.
As per primary distribution	15,100	14,400	19,300	9,250	3,150
Over heads of A in 2 : 3 : 4 : 1	1,850	2,775	3,700	(9,250)	925
Over head of B in 4 : 2 : 3 : 1	1,630	815	1,222	408	(4,075)
Over head of A in 2 : 3 : 4 : 1	82	122	163	(408)	41
Over head of B in 4 : 2 : 3 : 3 : 1	16	8	13	4	(41)
Overhead of A in 2 : 3 : 4	2	—	2	(4)	—
(a) Grand total	18,680	18,120	24,400		
(b) Working hours	4,670	3,020	3,050		
Rate per hour (Rs.) (a ÷ b)	4	6	8		

Statement of cost per unit

			Rs.	Rs.
Material cost			80	Rs.
Labour			40	
Prime cost				120
Overhead				
X	2×4.	=	8	
Y	3×6	=	18	
Z	4×8	=	32	58
Total production cost				178

Problem 52

Modern Manufacturers Ltd. have three Production Departments P_1 P_2, P_3 and two Service Departments S_1 and S_2, the details pertaining to which are as under :

	P_1	P_2	P_3	S_1	S_2
Direct Wages (Rs.)	3,000	2,000	3,000	1,500	195
Working Hours	3,070	4,475	2,419	—	—
Value of Machines (Rs.)	60,000	80,000	1,00,000	5,000	5,000
H.P. of Machines	60	30	50	10	—
Light Points	10	15	20	10	5
Floor Space (sq. ft.)	2,000	2,500	3,000	2,000	500

The following figures extracted from the accounting records are relevant :

	Rs.
Rent and Rates	5,000
General Lighting	600
Indirect Wages	1,939
Power	1,500
Depreciation on Machines	10,000
Sundries	9,695

The expenses of the Service Departments are allocated as under :

	P_1	P_2	P_3	S_1	S_2
S_1	20%	30%	40%	—	10%
S_2	40%	20%	30%	10%	—

Find out the total cost of product X which is processed for manufacture in Department P_1 P_2 and P_3 for 4, 5 and 3 hours respectively, given that its Direct Materials Cost is Rs. 50 and Direct Llabour cost Rs. 30.

[C.A Inter.]

Solution

Statement showing distribution of overheads of Modern Manufactures Ltd.

Particulars	*Basis*	*Total*	*Production Department*			*Service Department*	
			P_1	P_2	P_3	S_1	S_2
		Rs.	Rs.	Rs.	Rs.	Rs.	Rs.
Rent	Area 4 : 5 : 6 : 4 : 1	5,000	1,000	1,250	1,500	1,000	250
General Lighting	Light points	600	100	150	200	100	50
Indirect Wages	Direct Wages 600 : 400 : 600 : 300 : 39	1,939	600	400	600	300	39
Power	H.P.	1,500	600	300	500	100	—
Depreciation	Value of mach.	10,000	2,400	3,200	4,000	200	200
Sundries	Direct Wages	9,695	3,000	2,000	3,000	1,500	195
Direct wages		1,695				1,500	195
		30,429	7,700	7,300	9,800	4,700	929

Redistribution of Service Departments expenses over production department.

	P_1	P_2	P_3	S_1	S_2
Total Overhead	7,700.00	7,300.00	9,800.00	4,700	929.00
Overheads of Dept. S_1 (20 : 30 : 40 : 10)	940.00	1,410.00	1,880.00	(–)4,700	470.00
Overhead of Dept. S_2 (40 : 20 : 30 : 10)	559.60	279.80	419.70	319.90	(–) 1,399
Overhead of Dept. S_1 (20 : 30 : 40 : 10)	27.98	41.97	55.96	(–) 139.90	13.99
Overhead of Dept. S_2 (40 : 20 : 30 : 10)	5.60	2.80	4.20	1.39	(–) 13.99
Overhead of Dept. S_1 (20 : 30 : 40 : 10)	0.28	0.42	0.56	(–) 1.39	0.13
Overhead of Dept. S_2 (40 : 20 : 30)	0.06	0.03	0.04	—	(–) 0.13
Total	9,233.52	9,035.02	12,160.46	—	—
Working hours	3,070.00	4,475.00	2,419.00	—	—
Working rate per hour (Total cost ÷ working hrs.)	3.00	2.02	5.03		

Statement showing cost of Product *X*

	Rs.	Rs.
Direct material		50.00
Direct labour		30.00
Production overhead :		
Dept. P_1 (4 hrs. × Rs. 3.00)	12.00	
Dept. P_2 (5 hrs. × Rs. 2.02)	10.10	
Dept. P_3 (3 hrs. × Rs. 5.03)	15.09	37.19
Total Cost		117.19

STEP - LADDER METHOD

Problem 53

Deccan Manufacturing Ltd. have three departments which are regarded as production departments. Service departments, costs are distributed to these production departments using the 'Step-Ladder Method' of distribution. Estimates of factory overhead costs to be incurred by each department in the forthcoming year are as follows. Data required for distribution is also shown against each department :

Departments		*Factory Overhead*	*Direct Labour Hours*	*No. of Employees*	*Area in sq. mt.*
		Rs.	Rs.	Rs.	Rs.
Production :	X	1,93,000	4,000	100	3,000
	Y	64,000	3,000	125	1,500
	Z	83,000	4,000	85	1,500
Service :	P	45,000	1,000	10	500
	Q	75,000	5,000	50	1,500
	R	1,05,000	6,000	40	1,000
	S	30,000	3,000	50	1,000

The overhead costs of the four service departments are distributed in the same order, viz, *P, Q, R* and *S*, respectively on the following basis :

Department		*Basis*
P	—	Number of Employees
Q	—	Direct Labour Hours
R	—	Area in square metres
S	—	Direct Labour Hours

You are required to :

(a) prepare a schedule showing the distribution of overhead costs of the four service departments to the three production departments; and

(b) calculate the overhead recovery rate per direct labour hour for each of the three production departments.

[C.A. Inter, May 1988]

Solution

(a) Deccan Manufacturing Ltd.

Schedule showing the distribution of overhead costs of the four service departments.

	Service				*Production*		
	P	Q	R	S	X	Y	Z
	Rs.	Rs.	Rs.	Rs.	Rs.	Rs.	Rs.
Overhead	45,000	75,000	1,05,000	30,000	1,93,000	64,000	83,000
Distribution of Overhead of :							
Deptt. P.	(45,000)	5,000	4,000	5,000	10,000	12,500	8,500
Deptt. Q		(80,000)	24,000	12,000	16,000	12,000	16,000
Deptt. R			(1,33,000)	19,000	57,000	28,500	28,500
Deptt. S				(66,000)	24,000	18,000	24,000
Total *(i)*					3,00,000	1,35,000	1,60,000
Direct Labour Hours *(ii)*					4,000	3,000	4,000
(b) Overhead recovery rate *(i)* ÷ *(ii)*					Rs. 75	Rs. 45	Rs. 40

Problem 54

(Apportionment of Overheads to Production and Service Departments).

Self-help Ltd. has genset and produces its own power. Data for power costs are as follows :

Horse Power Hours	*Production Depts.*		*Service Depts.*	
	A	*B*	*X*	*Y*
Needed capacity production	10,000	20,000	12,000	8,000
Used during the month of May	8,000	13,000	7,000	6,000

During the month of May costs for generating power amounted to Rs. 9,300, of this Rs. 2,500 was considered to be fixed cost. Service Deptts. *X* renders service to *A*, *B* and *Y* in the ratio of 13 : 6 : 1 while *Y* renders Service to *A* and *B* in the ratio of 31 : 3. Given that direct labour hours in Deptts. *A* and *B* are , 1650 hours and 2,175 hours, respectively, find the power cost per labour hour in each of these two Departments.

[C.A. Inter.
B. Com. (Hons.) Delhi]

Solution

Statement showing the overhead distribution

Particulars	*Basis*	*Total*	*Production Departments*		*Services Departments*	
			A	*B*	*X*	*Y*
		Rs.	Rs.	Rs.	Rs.	Rs.
Fixed Cost	H.P. Hrs. at needed capacity (5 : 10 : 6 : 4)	2,500	500	1,000	600	400
Variable Cost	H.P. Hrs. used (8 : 13 : 7 : 6)	6,800	1,600	2,600	1,400	1,200
Total Cost		9,300	2,100	3,600	2,000	1,600

Redistribution of Service Depts. expenses to Production Departments

Particulars	*Total*	*Production Dept.*		*Services Dept.*	
		A	*B*	*X*	*Y*
	Rs.	Rs.	Rs.	Rs.	Rs.
Total Overheads	9,300	2,100	3,600	2,000	1,600
Dept. *X* overheads apportioned to Deptts. *A*, *B*, and *Y* in the ratio of 13 : 6 : 1		1,300	600	(2,000)	100
Dept. *Y* overhead apportional to Deptts. (*A* and *B* 31 : 3)		1,550	150		(1,700)
Total (i)		4,950	4,350		
Total Direct Labour Hrs. (ii)		1,650	2,175		
Power cost per labour hour (i) ÷ (ii)		3.00	2.00		

Problem 55

The Space Production Company manufactures components for radio and television satellites using two service departments and two production departments. The inter-departmental relationships and estimated overhead costs are given below :

Percentage of Services Provided to :

		Maintenance	*Scheduling*	*Moulding*	*Assembly*
From :	Maintenance	—	10%	40%	50%
"	Scheduling	20%	—	50%	30%
Total overhead costs		Rs. 7,50,000	4,00,000	3,78,000	2,76,000

Required :

(i) Using the direct method, show the amount of Scheduling Department costs to be allocated to Assembly Department.

(ii) Repeat *(i)* using the step method and allocating maintenance first.

(iii) Repeat *(i)* using the Reciprocal Method (method of Simultaneous Equations may be used.)

[I.C.W.A. Inter.]

Solution

(i) **Direct Method** : Scheduling department costs to be allocated to Assembly Department @ 30% of Rs. 4,00,000 = Rs. 1,20,000.

(ii) **Step method** : (Allocating maintenance cost first)

Particulars	*Service Departments*		*Production Departments*	
	Maintenance	*Scheduling*	*Moulding*	*Assembly*
	Rs.	Rs.	Rs.	Rs.
Total overhead costs	7,50,000	4,00,000	3,78,000	2,76,000
Maintenance in 10 : 40 : 50	(–) 7,50,000	75,000	3,00,000	3,75,000
Scheduling in 2 : 5 : 3	95,000	(–) 4,75,000	2,37,500	1,42,500
Maintenance in 10 : 40 : 50	(–) 95,000	9,500	38,000	47,500
Scheduling in 2 : 5 : 3	1,900	(–) 9,500	4,750	2,850
Maintenance in 10 : 40 : 50	(–) 1,900	190	760	950
Scheduling in 2 : 5 : 3	38	(–) 190	95	57
Maintenance in 10 : 40 : 50	(–) 38	4	15	19
Scheduling in 2 : 5 : 3		(4)	2	2
Total overheads	—	—	9,59,122	8,44,878

(iii) Allocation of Overheads using Reciprocal Method

Porticulars	*Production Departments*		*Service Departments*	
	Moulding	*Assembly*	*Maintenance*	*Scheduling*
	Rs.	Rs.	Rs.	Rs.
Total Overhead Costs	3,78,000	2,76,000	7,50,000	4,00,000
Maintenance	3,38,775	4,23,470	(8,46,939)	84,694
Scheduling	2,42,347	1,45,408	96,939	(4,84,694)
	9,59,122	8,44,878	Nil	Nil

(iv) **Simultenous Equation Method :**

Let m be the overheads of maintenance. Let s be the overheads of scheduling.

m = 7,50,000 + 0.2 s ...... (i) s = 4,00,000 + 0.1m .... (ii)

Rearranging *(i)* and *(ii)*

m – 0.2s = 7,50,000 (iii)

–0.1 m + s = 4,00,000 (iv)

Multiply *(iv)* by 10 (v)

– m + 10 s = 40,00,000

Adding equatiion *(iii)* and *(v)*,

we get 9.8 s = 47,50,000 or s = 4,84,694

Putting the value of s in *(i)*

m = 7,50,000 + 0.2 × 4,84,694 or m = 8,46,939

Allocation of overheads using Simultaneous Equation Method

	Particulars	*Production Moulding*	*Departments Assembly*
	Overheads allocated	3,78,000	2,76,000
(i)	Overheads of Maintenance allocated to Moulding and Assembly in 4 : 5 [Rs. 8,46,939 – (10% of Rs. 8,46,939)] Rs. 84,694 = Rs. 7,62,245	3,38,776	4,23,469
(ii)	Overheads of Scheduling allocated to Production departments in 5 : 3 [Rs. 4,84,694 – (20% of Rs. 4,48,694)] Rs. 96,939 = Rs. 3,87,755	2,42,346	1,45,409
		9,59,122	8,44,878

MACHINE HOUR RATE

Problem 56

Where Working Hours Are to be Determined

The following annual charges are incurred in respect of a machine in a shop where manual labour is almost nil and where work is done by means of five machines of exactly similar type and specification :

		Rs.
(i)	Rent and Rates (proportional to the floor space occupied) for the shop	4,800
(ii)	Depreciation on each machine	500
(iii)	Repairs and maintenance for the five machines	1,000
(iv)	Power consumed @ 05 paise per unit for the shop	3,000
(v)	Electric charges for lights in the shop	540
(vi)	Attendants : There are two attendants for the five machines and they are each paid Rs. 60 per month	
(vii)	Supervision : For the five machines in the shop there is one supervisor whose emoluments are Rs. 250 p.m.	

Contd.

		Rs.
(viii)	Sundry suppliers such as lubricants, jute and cotton waste, etc. for the shop	450
(ix)	Hire-purchase instalment payable for the machine (including Rs. 300 as interest)	1,200

The machine uses 10 units of power per hour.

Calculate the machine hour rate for the machine for the year.

Solution

Computation of Machine Hour Rate for the Year

Particulars	*Basis*	Rs.	Rs.
Standing Charges			
Rent and Rates	$\frac{1}{5}$th of Rs. 4,800	960.00	
Lighting Charges	$\frac{1}{5}$th of Rs. 540	108.00	
Attendant's salary	$\frac{1}{5}$th of Rs. 1,440 (60 × 2 × 12)	288.00	
Supervision per machine	$\frac{1}{5}$th of Rs. 3,000	600.00	
Sundry supplies per machine	$\frac{1}{5}$th of Rs. 450	90.00	
		2,046.00	
Hourly rate of standing charges		$\frac{2,046}{1,200}$	1.71
Variable Expenses			
Depreciation	$\frac{500}{1,200}$		0.42
Repairs and Maintenance	Rs. $\frac{200}{1,200}\left(\frac{1,000}{5 \times 1,200}\right)$		0.17
Power	10 units @ .05 per unit		0.50
Machine Hour Rate			2.80

Working Notes :

Total working hours :

Total cost of power consumed = Rs. 3,000

Cost of power consumed per hour = 0.05 × 10 = 0.50 paise

Total working hours $= 3,000 \times \frac{100}{50} =$ 6,000 hrs

Working hours per machine $= \frac{6,000}{5} =$ 1,200 hrs per year

Problem 57

From the following particulars calculate machine hour rate :

	Rs.
Cost of machine (including installation charges)	1,05,000
Rent of shop p.m.	1,000
Lighting of shop p.a.	1,500
Repairs p.a.	1,700
Supervisor's salary p.m.	1,200
Insurance premium of the machine per quarter	375

The life of the machine is 10 years with a scrap value of Rs. 5,000. It occupies $\frac{1}{5}$th of the shop area and consumes 3 units of power per hour @ $33\frac{1}{3}$ p. per unit. Supervisor devotes $\frac{1}{3}$rd his time to the machine. The machine has the capacity of working 5,000 hours p.a. but it actually worked 90% of the capacity.

[B.Com.(Hons.)C.U.]

Solution

Statement showing the computation of Machine Hour Rate

Deptt/Shop	Date of installation	Life 10 years
Machine No.	Cost Rs. 1,05,000	Scrap value Rs. 5,000
Effective working hours 4,500		

		Per year Rs.	Per hour Rs.
Fixed expenses :			
Rent of shop	$1,000 \times 12 \times \frac{1}{5}$	2,400	
Lighting of shop	$1,500 \times \frac{1}{5}$	300	
Supervisor's salary	$1,200 \times 12 \times \frac{1}{3}$	4,800	
Insurance premium of the machine	375 × 4	1,500	
Fixed expenses for 4,500 hours		9,000	
Variable expenses :		9,000 ÷ 4,500	2.00
Repairs	1,700 ÷ 4,500		0.38
Depreciation	(1,05,000 – 5,000) ÷ (4,500 × 10)		2.22
Power	$33\frac{1}{3} \times 3$		1.00
Machine Hour Rate			5.60

Problem 58

From the particulars furnished below compute the machine hour rate :

	Rs.	
Cost of machine	90,000	
Cost of installation	10,000	
Scrap value at the end of 10 years	5,000	
Indirect wages and materials for the machine	500	per year
Supervision cost for four similar machines	16,000	per year
Insurance premium for the machine	200	per quarter
Rent of the machine shop	400	p.m.
Electricity cost for the machine shop	100	p.m.

Power consumption of the machine is 20 units per actual working hour.

Power cost is 50 paise per unit.

The total area of the machine shop is 600 sq. metres of which this machine occupies only 150 sq. metres. There are 200 light points in the machine shop of equal wattage of which the machine utilises only 40 points.

It is estimated that the machine will normally work for 2,700 hours in a year, but it is apprehended that the machine will remain idle for 200 hours.

[C.U. B.Com.(Hons.) 1985]

Solution

Statement showing the computation of machine hour rate

Deptt/Shop	Date of installation	Life 10 years
Machine No.	Cost Rs. 90,000	Scrap value Rs. 5,000
	Installation expenses Rs. 10,000	

Effective working hours/year 2,500

	Basis	Per year	Per hour
		Rs.	Rs.
Fixed expenses :			
Rent of machine shop (Note 1)	$100 \times 12 \times \frac{1}{4}$	1,200	
Electricity	$\frac{1,200}{200} \times 40$	240	
Insurance Premium	200×4	800	
Supervision cost for similar machines	$16,000 \div 4$	4,000	
Fixed expenses for (2,700 – 200) or		6,240	
2,500 hours	$\frac{\text{Rs. } 6,240}{2,500}$		2.50
Variable Expenses :			
Depreciation	$(90,000 + 10,000 - 5,000) \div (2,500 \times 10)$		3.80
Power	$20 \times \frac{50}{100}$		10.00
Indirect wages and materials	$500 \div 2,500$		0.20
Machine Hour Rate			16.50

Working Note :

1. The machine's occupied area = 600 ÷ 150 = $\frac{1}{4}$

Problem 59

From the following particulars calculate the machine hour rate :

	Rs.
Cost of the machine	2,00,000
Installation charges	20,000
Rent of the shop per month	3,000
Insurance premium for the machine per annum 1% of capital cost	
Electricity charges for the shop per month	300
Repair and maintanance @ 0.5% of capital cost	
Supervisor's salary per month	1,800
Rate of power charges for 100 units	55

[The machine consumes 16 units of power per hour]

The machine occupies $\frac{1}{3}$rd of the shop area. Its life is 10 years and anticipated scrap value is Rs. 10,000. The supervisor devotes $\frac{1}{4}$th of his time to the machine.

Estimated Idle time : 50 hours in a year. Normal working days during a year : 250 days of 8 hours and 50 days of 5 hours. **[C.U. B.Com.(Hons.) 1987]**

Solution

Statement showing the computation of Machine Hour Rate

Deptt/Shop ...... Date of installation ...... Life 10 years

Machine No. .... Cost Rs. 2,00,000 Scrap value Rs. 10,000

Installation expenses Rs. 20,000

Effective working hours in a year 2,200 (See working note)

		Per year Rs.	*Per hour* Rs.
Fixed expenses :			
Rent	(Area occupied) $3{,}000 \times 12 \times \frac{1}{3}$	12,000	
Electricity	(Area occupied) $300 \times 12 \times \frac{1}{3}$	1,200	
Supervisor's salary	(Time devoted) $1{,}800 \times 12 \times \frac{1}{4}$	5,400	
Insurance Premium for the machine p.a.	(Actual) (2,00,000 + 20,000)		
1% of capital cost	$2{,}20{,}000 \times \frac{1}{100}$	2,200	
Fixed expenses for 2,200 hours (Note 1)	20,800 ÷ 2,200	20,800	9.45
Repair and maintenance	(2,00,000 + 20,000)		
p.m. 0.5% of capital cost	$[2{,}20{,}000 \times \left(\frac{5}{1{,}000}\right)] \div 2{,}200$		0.50
Variable expenses :			
Depreciation	(2,20,000 − 10,000) ÷ (2,200 × 10)		9.55
Power	$\frac{55}{100} \times 16$		8.80
Machine Hour Rate			28.30

Working Note :

1. Normal working days during a year :

250 × 8	=	2,000 hrs
50 × 5	=	250 hrs
		2,250 hrs
Less : Idle time		50 hrs
		2,200 hrs

Problem 60

Machine costing Rs. 28,700 excluding installation costs of Rs. 300 has an anticipated life of 10 years with residual value of Rs. 500.

The straight line method of depreciation is followed.

From the following details, compute machine hour rate on the basis of anticipated working hours :

(1) Rent and rates for the factory is Rs. 4,000 per annum and 5% of the effective area is occupied by this machine.

(2) Insurance for this machine is Rs. 150 per annum.

(3) Repairs and maintenance for the factory for the year is Rs. 1,000, $12\frac{1}{2}$% of this amount relates to this machine.

(4) Consumable stores etc. attributed to this machine is Rs. 275.

(5) Total of production services is Rs. 4,000. 10% of this amount is applicable to this machine.

(6) Power cost is 0.50 p. per working hour.

The year contains 250 working days of 8 hours each but it is anticipated that the machine will remain idle 20% of this time.

[B.Com. Madras]

Solution

COMPUTATION OF MACHINE HOUR RATE

Expenses	*Basis*	*Total*	*Hourly rate*
		Rs.	Rs.
Standing Charges :			
Rent and Rates	Area occupied 5% of Rs. 4,000	200	
Insurance	Actual	150	
Consumable stores	Actual	275	
Production Service	10% of Rs. 4,000	400	
Total		1,025	
Standing charges per hour	Rs. 1.025 ÷ 1,600[1] hrs.		0.64
Variable expenses			
Depreciation[2]	Rs. 28,500 ÷ 16,000		1.78
Repairs and Maintenance	Rs. 125 ÷ 1,600[1] hrs given		0.08
Cost of power	Actual		0.50
Machine Hour Rate			3.00

Notes :

		Rs.
1.	Total effective hours 250 × 8 =	2,000
	Less : 20% Idle time	400
		1,600
2.	Depreciation per hour = Rs. 28,700 + Rs. 300	29,000
	Less : Residual values	500
		28,500

Hourly Rate ÷ 28,500 + 16,000 (1,600 × 10) = Rs. 1.78.

Problem 61

The expenses of a machine cost centre for a particular month are as under :

(i) Power Rs. 50,000; (ii) Maintenance and repairs – Rs. 10,000; (iii) Machine operator's wages – Rs. 2,000; (iv) Supervision – Rs. 6,000; and (v) Depreciation Rs. 40,000.

Other particulars are given below :

Products	*Rate of production*	*Production Units.*
A	30 units per hour	1,800
B	10 units per hour	500
C	6 units per hour	300
D	4 units per hour	260

The entire production was to be offered to the government on cost plus 20% basis.

Material costs per unit are :

A – Rs. 40, B – Rs. 60, C – Rs. 100 and D – Rs. 300.

Prepare a statement showing product-wise 'Cost' and 'Offer price'.

[Adapted—I.C.W.A. (Inter), December 1988]

Solution

Statement showing the Machine Hour Rate

		Rs.
Power		50,000
Maintenance and Repairs		10,000
Wages		2,000
Supervision		6,000
Depreciation		40,000
Total expenses for machine Centre –		1,08,000
Machine Hour Rate	Rs. $\frac{1,08,000}{225}$	Rs. 480

Note :

Effective machine hours

A	=	1,800 ÷ 30	=	60 hours
B	=	500 ÷ 10	=	50 hours
C	=	300 ÷ 6	=	50 hours
D	=	260 ÷ 4	=	65 hours
				225 hours

(ii) **Statement showing the cost price product-wise**

Product	*Output*	*Machine hour rate*	*Machine hour*	*Total allocation*	*Cost per unit*	*Material cost per unit*	*Total cost per unit*
	(a)	(b)	(c)	(d)	(e)	(f)	(g)
A	1,800	480	60	28,800*	16	40	56
B	500	480	50	24,000*	48	60	108
C	300	480	50	24,000*	80	100	180
D	260	480	65	31,200*	120	300	420
			225	1,08,000			

Note :

*Total Allocation

A $= \frac{1,08,000 \times 60}{225} = 28,800$

B $= \frac{1,08,000 \times 50}{225} = 24,000$

C $= \frac{1,08,000 \times 50}{225} = 24,000$

D $= \frac{1,08,000 \times 65}{225} = 31,200$

Statement showing the offer price

Product	*Total Cost per unit*	*Profit @ 20% on Cost*	*Offer price per unit*
	Rs.	Rs.	Rs.
A	56	11.20	67.20
B	108	21.60	129.60
C	180	36.00	216.00
D	420	84.00	504.00

Problem 62

The normal expenses attributable to Machine III and the normal hours for which the machine is expected to be utilized in 1992 are indicated below :

	Rs.	Rs.
Expenses		
Fixed		2,000
Variable :		
Power	1,500	
Repairs	900	
Lubricants	600	3,000
		5,000

Predetermined normal hours of working :

To make ready	200 hrs
Running on jobs	800 hrs
	1,000 hrs

From the data furnished below compute the cost of Job No. 8237 :

	Rs.
Materials consumed :	
10 units at Rs. 5 per unit	50.00
Machine labour :	
To make ready : 2 hours at Re. 1.00	2.00
Running on Job 8 hours at Re. 1.00	8.00
	60.00

[Adapted—I.C.W.A. (Inter)]

Solution

Machine Hour Rate

		Rs.	Rs.
Fixed Expenses		2,000	
Total number of hours (800 + 200)	1,000		
Fixed expenses per hour –		Rs. 2,000 ÷ 1,000	2.00
ii) *Variable expenses per hour*			
Power	1,500		
Repairs	900		
Lubricants	600	3,000	
Variable expenses per hour = Rs. 3,000 ÷ 800 hrs =			3.75
			5.75

Cost of Job No. 8237

	Rs.	Rs.
Cost of materials 10 units @ Rs. 5		50.00
Wages 2 hours @ Re. 1.00	2.00	
To make ready		
8 hours @ Re. 1.00	8.00	10.00
PRIME COST		60.00
Add : Factory overhead in terms of machine hour rate :		
Fixed expense per hour to make the machine ready @ Rs. 2 per hour	2 × 2 = 4.00	
Machine hour rate for running the machine (fixed + variable)	5.75 × 8 = 46.00	50.00
TOTAL COST		110.00

Note : 200 hours to make ready has been treated as abnormal loss of time.

Problem 63

From the following particualrs compute a.comprehensive Machine Hour Rate :

(i) Cost of the machine : Rs. 1,00,000. Estimated life : 15 years. Residual value : Rs.10,000.

(ii) Machine Running Hours : 2040 hours per machine per annum including idle time of 40 hours due to routine repairs and maintenance and 20 hours due to break-down of machine.

(iii) Power consumption of the machine per hour : 20 units ; rate of power per 100 units Rs.80.

(iv) There are two operators in the shop and wages, workmen's compensation insurance etc. of an operator who is in charge of two machines Rs. 12,000 p.a.

(v) Rent, rates and taxes of the shop : Rs. 4,800 p.a.

(vi) Insurance premium for the machine : Rs. 400 per quarter.

(vii) General lighting of the shop per month : Rs. 600.

(viii) Repairs and maintenance expenses per month : Rs. 400 per machine.

(ix) Shop supervisor's salary per month : Rs. 1,500.

(x) Other factory overhead allocated to the shop : Rs. 6,000 p.a.

There are four indentical machines in the Machine Shop. The supervisor devotes one-fifth of his time for supervising the machine.

[C.U. B.Com.(Hons.) 1991]

Solution

MACHINE HOUR RATE

Department Shop — Machine No. ....

Effective life : 15 years

Working hours : 2,040 – 40 = 2,000 hours

		Fixed Cost per annum	*Variable Cost per hour*	*Total Cost per hour*
		Rs.	Rs.	Rs.
Fixed Expenses				
Rent and rates	$\left(\frac{4,800}{4}\right)$	1,200		
Insurance premium	(400 × 4)	1,600		
General lighting	$\left(600 \times \frac{12}{4}\right)$	1,800		
Supervisor's salary	$\left(1,500 \times \frac{12}{5}\right)$	3,600		
Factory overhead	$\left(\frac{6,000}{4}\right)$	1,500		
Total fixed cost p.a.			9,700	
Total fixed cost p. hr.			$\left(\frac{9,700}{2,000}\right)$	4.85
Variable Expenses				
Depreciation	$\frac{1,00,000 - 10,000}{15 \times 2,000}$		3.00	
			3.00	4.85

Contd.

		Rs.	Rs.
B. F.		3.00	4.85
Power	$\left[\frac{(20 \times 80)}{100}\right]$	16.00	
Repairs & maintenance	$\frac{(400 \times 12)}{2,000}$	2.40	
Total variable cost per hour		21.40	21.40
Machine Hour Rate			26.25
Wages of operator per hour	$\frac{12,000}{(2 \times 2000)}$		3.00
Comprehensive Machine Hour Rate			29.25

Problem 64

From the following particulars compute a comprehensive Machine Hour Rate :

(i)	Original purchase price of the machine (subject to depreciation at 10% per annum on original cost)	Rs.	21,600
(ii)	Normal working hours for the month (the machine works only 75% of capacity)		200 hours
(iii)	Wages of Machine-man	Rs.	4 per day (of 8 hrs)
(iv)	Wages of a helper (machine attendant)	Rs.	2 per day (of 8 hrs)
(v)	Power consumption (H.P.) estimated at Rs. 150 per mensem for the time worked		
(vi)	Supervision charges apportioned for the machine centre	Rs.	300 p.m.
(vii)	Electricity and lighting	Rs.	75 p.m.
(viii)	Repairs and maintenance (machine) including consumable stores per mensem	Rs.	150
(ix)	Insurance of Plant and Building (apportioned) per annum	Rs.	1,000
(x)	Other general expenses (overhead) per annum	Rs.	2,160

(xi) Production bonus payable to workers $33\frac{1}{3}$% in terms of an award of basic wages and dearness allowance

(xii) Workers are also paid a fixed dearness allowance of Rs. 75 p.m.

(xiii) Add 10% of the basic wages and dearness allowance against leave wages and holidays with pay to arrive at a comprehensive labour cost for debit to production.

[B.Com. Calcutta]

Solution

COMPUTATION OF COMPREHENSIVE MACHINE HOUR RATE

		Per month	*Rate per hour*
Standing Charges :	Rs.	Rs.	Rs.
Supervisor charges	Actual	300	
Supervision and Lighting	Actual	75	
Insurance	1,000 ÷ 12	83.33	
General Expenses	2,160 ÷ 12	180	
Total		638.33	
Standing charges per hour		$\frac{638.33}{150}$	4.26
Machine Expenses :			
Depreciation		$\frac{2,160}{12 \times 150}$	1.20
Wages of machine-man (See note)		$\frac{279.50}{150}$	1.86
Wages of Helper (See note)		$\frac{193.50}{150}$	1.29
Power		$\frac{150}{150}$	1.00
Repairs and Maintenance		$\frac{150}{150}$	1.00
Machine Hour Rate			10.61

Working Note :

Calculation of Wages

	Machine-man	Helper
	Rs.	Rs.
Wages 25 days @ Rs. 4 and Rs. 2, respectively	120	60
Dearness allowance	75	75
	195	135
Production bonus 1/3 wages and DA	65	45
	260	180
Allowance against leave wages and holiday with pay 10% of wages and DA	19.50	13.50
	279.50	193.50

Problem 65

A machine was purchased on January 1, 1990 for five lakhs. The total cost of all machinery inclusive of the new machine was Rs. 75 lakhs. The following further particulars are available :

Expected life of the machine is 10 years. Scrap value at the end of ten years Rs. 5,000. Repairs and maintenance for the machine during the year Rs. 2,000. Expected number of working hours of the machine per year 4,000 hours. Insurance premium annually for all machines Rs. 4,500.

Electricity consumption for the machine per hour (@ 0.75 paise per unit) 25 units.

Area occupied by the machine 100 sq. ft., area occupied by other machines 1,500 sq. ft. Rent per month of the department Rs. 800.

Lighting charges for 20 points for the whole department, out of which three points are for the machine, Rs. 120 per month.

Compute the machine hour rate for the new machine on the basis of the data given above.

[Adapted—C.A. (Inter), May 1990]

Solution

Computation of Machine Hour Rate

	Basis of Apportionment	*Total Expenses*	*Per hour*
		Rs.	Rs.
Standing Charges			
Depreciation	Actual (Note 1)	49,500	
Insurance Premium	Cost of machines $\frac{4,500 \times 5,00,00}{75,00,000}$	300	
Repairs and Maintenance	Actual	2,000	
Rent	Area occupied $\frac{9,600 \times 100}{1,600}$	600	
Lighting	No. of points $\frac{120 \times 12 \times 3}{20}$	216	
		52,616	
Hourly rate for standing charges		$\frac{\text{Rs. } 52,616}{4,000 \text{ hrs.}}$	13.154
Variable Expenses			
Electricity	25 units p.h. @ 0.75 P. per unit		18.750
Machine hour rate			31.904

Note :

Calculation of depreciation

	Cost of new machine	5,00,000
Less :	Scrap value	5,000
		4,95,000

Life of machine = 10 years

Depreciation per year = $\frac{4,95,000}{10}$ = Rs. 49,500

Problem 66

From the following information calculate Machine Hour Rate for a factory :

Normal working week per year	48
Normal working hours per week	40 hours
Normal weakly loss of hours on maintenance	4 hours
No. of machines	15
Estimated Annual Overheads	Rs. 1,55,520

At your calculated rate, what would be the amount of overheads to be charged to a job which took one month for completion in the factory ?

[B.U. B.Com. (Hons.) 1988]

Solution

			Total Expenses	*Houly Rate*
(a)	Machine Hour Rate			
	Total Overheads		Rs. 1,55,520	
	Total effective working hours of 15 machines =	48 × 40 × 15	28,800	
Less :	Normal weekly loss for maintenance @ 4 hours =	48 × 4 × 15	2,880	
			25,920	
	Machine Hour Rate =		Rs. $\frac{1,55,520}{25,920}$	6.00
(b)	Amount of Overhead to be charged to a job for one month =		$\frac{25,920}{12}$ × Rs. 6.00	12,960

Problem 67

A machine shop has 8 identical drilling machines manned by 6 operators. The machines cannot be worked without an operator wholly engaged on it. The original cost of all these 8 machines works out to Rs. 8 lakhs. These particulars are furnished for a 6-month period :

Normal available hours per month	208
Leave (with pay) – hours	20
Absenteeism (without pay) hours	18
Normal idle time (unavoidable) – hours	10
Average rate of wages per day of 8 hours	Rs. 20
Production bonus estimated	15% on wages.
Value of power consumed	Rs. 8,050
Supervision and Indirect Labour	Rs. 3,300
Lighting and Electricity	Rs. 1,200
These particulars are for a year :	
Repairs and maintenance including consumables 3% on value of machines.	
Insurance	Rs. 40,000
Depreciation 10% on original cost	
Other sundry works expenses	Rs. 12,000
General Management expenses allocated	Rs. 54,530

You are required to work out a comprehensive machine hour rate for the Machine shop.

[C.A. (Inter) 1986]

Solution

Computation of Comprehensive Machine Hour Rate

Expenses	*Basis of apportionment*	Rs.	Rs.
Wages for 6 operators	Actual 190 × 6 × 6 × Rs. 2.50	17,100	
Production Bonus	15% of Wages	2,565	
Power	Actual	8,050	
Supervision and Indirect Labour	Actual	3,300	
Lighting + Electricity	Actual	1,200	
Repairs and Maintenance	3% on 8 lakhs for 6 months	12,000	
Insurance	40,000 ÷ 2	20,000	
Depreciation	10% of 8 lakhs for 6 months	40,000	
Other Sundry works expenses	12,000 ÷ 2	6,000	
General Management expenses	54,530 ÷ 2	27,265	
		1,37,480	
Machine Hour Rate =	1,37,480 ÷ 5,760 =		Rs. 23.87

Working Notes :

(i) Effective Working Hours = 208 – 48 = 160 × 6 × 6 = 5,760 hours.

(ii) In computing comprehensive machine hour rate, the direct wages are to be considered.

Treatment of normal and abnormal loss of time

Problem 68

From the following data for the month of January 1992 compute the machine hour rate to be charged in respect of job carried out during the month on a printing machine in a job printing press :

Cost of printing machine	Rs.	77,000
Estimated life	10	years
Anticipated Scrap Value	Rs.	5,000
Normal working hours p.m.		600
Hours run on trial runs and job setting		20
Hours lost due to repairs (normal)		50
Hours lost due to power failure (abnormal)		80
Cost of maintenance	Rs.	3,300
Supervisor's Salary	Rs.	800
Cost of printing ink	Rs.	2,400
Electricity Charges	Rs.	720
Other fixed charges	Rs.	3,000
Overtime hours worked to complete job on time	100	hours
Rate of wages per hour (normal)		8
Rate of wages per hour (overtime)		12
Rate of wages per hour (during power failure)		4

[Adapted—I.C.W.A. (Inter)]

Solution

Computation of Machine-Hour Rate

Particulars	*Basis*	*Total Expenses*	*Machine hour rate*
		Rs.	Rs.
Standing charges			
Supervisor's salary	Actual	800	
Other fixed charges	Actual	3,000	
		3,800	
Machine hour rate (See Note 1)	$\frac{\text{Expenses}}{\text{Machine hours}}$	$\frac{3,800}{650}$	5.85
Variable expenses			
Depreciation (as per note 2)			0.92
Printing ink		2,400 ÷ 650	3.69
Electricity charges		720 ÷ 650	1.11
Cost of maintenance		3,300 ÷ 650	5.08
Machine-Hour-Rate			16.65

Note 1 :

	Calculation of effective hours for standing expenses :	Rs.
	Normal working hours	600
Less :	Hours lost for repairs (normal)	50
		550
Add :	Overtime	100
		650 hours.

Note 2 :

	Calculation of depreciation		
	Cost of machine		77,000
Less :	Scrap value		5,000
			Rs. 72,000
	Machine hour rate	= Rs. $\frac{72,000}{10 \times 12}$ =	Rs. 600 monthly
	Depreciation per hour	Rs. 600 ÷ 650 =	0.92

Note 3 :

	Machine hour rate during power failure	
	Machine-hour-rate as per statement	16.65
Add :	Wages per hour during power failure as given	4.00
		20.65

Note 4 :

	Comprehensive Machine-Hour Rate		
	Machine hours –		650 hours
Less :	Hours lost due to power failure		80 hours
			570 hours
	Normal Wages – 600 hours – 80 hours – (treated separately)		
		= 520 × Rs. 8 =	4,160
	For Overtime	100 hours × 12 =	1,200
			5,360
	Hourly rate =	Rs. 5,360 ÷ 570 =	9.40

Problem 69

Following particulars have been extracted from the books of Reliable Company.

	Rs.	Rs.
Indirect Materials		
Shop No. 1	12,000	
Shop No. 2	18,000	
Shop No. 3	6,000	
Tool Room	3,600	
Stores	4,800	
Factory Office	1,800	46,200
Indirect Wages		
Shop No. 1	12,600	
Shop No. 2	17,600	
Shop No. 3	16,000	
Tool Room	11,100	
Stores	4,500	
Factory Office	6,600	68,400
Factory Rent		30,000
Insurance		6,000
Depreciation 10%		30,000
Power		27,000
Light and heat		12,000
Total		2,19,600

Further information regarding the operations are given below :

Depreciation	*Area (Sq. meter)*	*Book value of Machinery*	*Effective H.P.*	*Direct labour Hours*	*Direct labour Cost*	*Machinery Hours*
		Rs.			Rs.	
Production						
Shop No. 1	1,000	75,000	90	3,00,000	90,000	1,60,000
Shop No. 2	750	1,35,000	90	3,00,000	60,000	2,40,000
Shop No. 3	1,500	30,000	—	2,00,000	50,000	—
Service						
Tool Room	500	45,000	20	—	50,000	—
Stores	750	7,500	—	—	—	—
Factory Office	500	7,500	—	—	—	—
	5,000	3,00,000	200	8,00,000	2,50,000	4,00,000

You are required to prepare an "Overhead Analysis Sheet" for departments of Reliable Co. for the year showing the basis of apportionment.

[ICWA (Inter) Dec. 1994]

Solution

Overhead Analysis Sheet

Overheads	*Basis of apportionment*	*Total*	*Production shop No.* 1	2	3	*Service* *Tool Room*	*Stores*	*Factory Office*
Indirect Materials	As given	46,200	12,000	18,000	6,000	3,600	4,800	1,800
Indirect wages	As given	68,400	12,600	17,600	16,000	11,100	4,500	6,600
Factory Rent	Area	30,000	6,000	4,500	9,000	3,000	4,500	3,000
Insurance	Book value of Machinery	6,000	1,500	2,700	600	900	150	150
Depreciation @ 10%	Book value of Machinery	30,000	7,500	13,500	3,000	4,500	750	750
Power	Notes 1 & 2	27,000	10,800	16,200	—	—	—	—
Light & Heat Heat	Area	12,000	2,400	1,800	3,600	1,200	1,800	1,200
Total Overheads		2,19,600	52,800	74,300	38,200	24,300	16,500	13,500

Notes: 1.

Shop No.	Effective H.P. × Machine kHours	Total
1	90 × 1,60,000	1,44,00,000
2	90 × 2,40,000	2,16,00,000

Ratio = 144 : 216 or 2 : 3

Shop No. 1. $27{,}000 \times \frac{2}{5}$ = Rs. 10,800

Shop No. 2 $27{,}000 \times \frac{3}{5}$ = Rs. 16,200

2. In the Tool Room, effective H.P. is 20 but Machine hours is nil. The machine has not worked. Hence, power charges have not been apportioned to Tool Room.

Computation of Machine Hour Rate when interest is included

Problem 70

An Engineering company has installed a machine (Horizontal Borer). Calculate the machine hour rate on the basis of the following particulars :

		Rs.
(i)	F.O.B. cost of the machine	24,00,000
(ii)	Customs duty, Insurance and Freight	11,00,000
(iii)	Installation expenses	3,00,000
(iv)	Cost of tools adequate for 2 years only	4,00,000
(v)	Cost of Machine Room	3,00,000
(vi)	Cost of air-conditioning for the machine room	2,00,000

Contd.

(vii)	Rate of interest on term loan to finance the above Capital Expenditure	12% p.a.
(viii)	Salaries for operators and supervisory Staff	2,00,000
(ix)	Cost of electricity	Rs. 11 per hour
(x)	Consumption of the stores	5,000 p.m.
(xi)	Other expenses	5,00,000 p.a.
(xii)	Rate of depreciation @ 10% p.a.	
(xiii)	Total working hours	200 hours p.m.
(xiv)	Loading and unloading time is 10% of machining time	

[Adapted—I.C.W.A. (Inter)]

Solution

Statement Showing Computation of Machine-Hour-Rate

Particulars	*Basis of apportionment*	*Amount p.a.*	*Rate per hour*
Variable Expenses		Rs.	Rs.
Depreciation	10% of Rs. 43,00,000	$\frac{4,30,000}{2,160}$	199.07
Electricity	Actual		11.00
Fixed Expenses			
Cost of tools	Actual $\left(\frac{4,00,000}{2}\right)$	2,00,000	
Interest on loan	Actual $\left(\text{Rs. } \frac{47,00,000 \times 12}{100}\right)$	5,64,000	
Stores consumption	Actual (5,000 × 12)	60,000	
Salaries for operators and Supervisory Staff	Actual	2,00,000	
Other Expenses		5,00,000	
Machine House Rate		15,24,000	
	$\frac{15,24,000}{2,160}$		705.56
			915.63

Notes :

(i) Capital Cost of the Machine :

	Rs.
Cost of Machine (FOB)	24,00,000
Custom duty, Insurance and Freight etc.	11,00,000
Installation Expenses	3,00,000
Machine Room Cost	3,00,000
Air Conditioning Cost	2,00,000
	43,00,000

(ii) Bank Loan

Capital cost as above	43,00,000
Cost of tools	4,00,000
	47,00,000

(iii) Effective working hours

Annual working hours 200 × 12 =	2,400
Less : Loading and unloading time when no production was carried out	240
Effective working hours –	2,160

Problem 71

A. T. Ltd., an Engineering Company having 25 different automatic machines, furnishes the following data for 1997-98 in respect of Machine 'B' :

	Rs.
Cost of the Machine	50,000 p.a.
Life 10 years	
Scrap value	Nil
Overhead Expenses	
Factory Rent	50,000 p.a.
Heating and Lighting	40,000 p.a.
Supervision	1,50,000 p.a.
Reserve Equipment for the machine	5,000 p.a.
Area of the Factory	80,000 sq. ft.
Area occupied by Machine B	3,000 sq. ft.

Power cost 0.50 paise per hour while in operation.

Wages of operator is Rs. 24 per day of 8 hours including all fringe benefits. He attends to one machine when it is under set up and two machines while under operation.

Estimated production hours	3,600 p.a.
Estimated set up time	400 hours p.a.

Prepare a schedule of comprehensive machine hour rate and find the cost of the following jobs :

	Job 1102	Job 1308
Set up time (hours)	80	40
Operation time (hours)	130	160

[Adapted—C.A. (Inter)]

Solution

Statement Showing Machine Hour Rate for Machine 'B'

Particulars	*Basis of Apportionment*	*Expenses p.a.*	*Machine hour rate*
		Rs.	Rs.
Fixed Expenses			
Depreciation	50,000 ÷ 10	5,000	
Rent	Area occupied $\frac{50,000}{80,000} \times 3,000$	1,875	
Heating and Lighting	Area occupied $\frac{40,000}{80,000} \times 3,000$	1,500	
Supervision	No. of machines $\frac{1,50,000}{25}$	6,000	
Reserve Equipment	Actual	5,000	
		19,375	
Machine Hour Rate	$\frac{\text{Total Expenses}}{\text{Machine Hours}}$	$\frac{19,375}{4,000}$	4.84
Operator's Wages	Actutal	$\frac{24}{8 \times 2}$	1.50
Variable Expense			
Power	Actual		0.50
(a) Machine hour rate while in operation			6.84
(b) Machine hour rate while under set up			
Fixed expenses (as calculated above)			4.84
Operator's Wages	Actual	24 ÷ 16	1.50
			6.34

Statement Showing the Cost of Jobs

	Job 1102			Job 1308		
	Hours	*Rate*	*Amount*	*Hours*	*Rate*	*Amount*
		Rs.	Rs.		Rs.	Rs.
Set up	80	6.34	507.20	40	6.34	253.60
In operation	130	6.84	889.20	160	6.84	1,094.40
			1,396.40			1,348.00

Point to highlight

During setting up time there was no production. Hence, only fixed expenses are to be considered for the computation of machine-hour-rate for setting up time.

Problem 72

In a manufacturing concern ABC Ltd., the machine shop has 8 identical machines manned by 6 operators. The machine cannot be worked without an operator wholly engaged on them. The total cost of the machines are Rs. 8,00,000.

Following information relates to a six monthly period ended 30.6.1998 :

Normal available hours per month	208
Absenteeism (without pay) hours p.m.	18
Leave (with pay) hours per month	20
Normal idle time (unavoidable) hours per month	10
Average rate of wages per day of 8 hours	Rs. 20
Production Bonus	15% of wages
Power and Fuel consumption	Rs. 9,000
Supervision and Indirect labour	Rs. 3,300
Electricity	Rs. 1,200
The following particulars are on a yearly basis :	
Repairs and renewals	3% of the value of machines
Insurance	Rs. 42,000
Depreciation	10% of original cost
Other factory expenses	Rs. 12,000
Allocated General Management Expenses	Rs. 63,670

You are required to work out a comprehensive machine-hour rate for the machine shop.

[I.C.W.A. (Inter)]

Solution

A B C Ltd.

Computation of Comprehensive Machine Hour Rate

for 6 months ended June 30th 1998

Expenses	*Basic*	*Total*	*Hourly Rate*
		Rs.	Rs.
Worker's wages (as per note)		17,100	
Production Bonus	@ 15% of wages	2,565	
Power & Fuel consumed	Actual	9,000	
Supervision and Indirect wages	Actual	3,300	
Electricity	Actual	1,200	
Repairs and Maintenance	Actual 3% of Rs. 8,00,000 for 6 months	12,000	
Insurance	Actual - $\frac{1}{2}$ of Rs. 42,000	21,000	
Other Factory Expenses	Actual $\frac{1}{2}$ of Rs. 12,000	6,000	
Allocated General Management Expenses	$\frac{1}{2}$ of Rs. 63,670	31,835	
Depreciation	$\frac{10}{100} \times$ Rs. 8,00,000 $\times \frac{1}{2}$	40,000	
		1,44,000	
Machine-Hour-Rate			
Total Expenses ÷ Hours worked		$\frac{1,44,000}{5,760}$	
			25.00

Notes :

1. Calculation of working hours

	Normal available hours		208 hours p.m.
Less :	Unutilised hours		
	Absenteeism (without pay)	18 hours	
	Leave (with pay)	20 hours	
	Normal idle time	10 hours	48 p.m.
			160 hours.

Since there are 6 operators for the shop, the total working hours for 6 months = 160 × 6 × 6 = 5,760 hours

2. Total wages

	Normal available hours	208 hours
Less :	Hours without pay	18 hours
	Hours with pay	190 hours

$$\text{Total wages} = \frac{190}{8} \times 20 \times 6 \times 6 = \text{Rs. } 17{,}100$$

Problem 73

Gemini Enterprises undertakes three different jobs A, B and C. All of them require the use of a special machine and also the use of a computer. The computer is hired and the hire charges work out to Rs. 4,20,000 p.a. The expenses regarding the machine are estimated as follows :

	Rs.
Rent per quarter	17,500
Depreciation per annum	2,00,000
Indirect charges per annum	1,50,000

During the first month of operation the following details were taken from the job register :

	A	B	C
Number of hours the machine was used :			
(a) Without the use of the computer	600	900	–
(b) With the use of the computer	400	600	1,000

You are required to compute the machine hour rate :

(a) For the firm as a whole for the month when the computer was used and when the computer was not used,

(b) For the individual job A, B and C.

[C.A. Inter]

Solution

(a) Machine Hour Rate for the firm as a whole for a month

When the computer was used Rs. $\frac{55,000}{2,000}$ hrs. = Rs. 27.50 per hour.

When the computer was not used Rs. $\frac{15,000}{1,500}$ hrs = Rs. 10.00 per hour.

(b) Machine Hour Rate for the individual job

Overheads	*Rate per hour*	*A*		*B*		*C*	
	Rs.	Hrs.	Rs.	Hrs.	Rs.	Hrs.	Rs.
Without Computer	10	600	6,000	900	9,000	–	–
With Computer	27.50	400	11,000	600	16,500	1,000	27,500
		1,000	17,000	1,500	25,500	1,000	27,500
			1,000		1,500		1,000
Machine hour rate			= 17		= 17		= 27.50

Working Notes :

i) Total machine hours used (600 + 900 + 400 + 600 + 1,000) 3,500.00

ii) Total machine hours without the use of computers (600 + 900) 1,500.00

iii) Total machine hours with the use of computers (400 + 600 + 1,000) 2,000.00

iv) Total overheads of the machine per month :

Rent	Rs. $\frac{17,500}{3}$ =	5,833.33
Depreciation	Rs. $\frac{2,00,000}{12}$ =	16,666.67
Indirect Charges	Rs. $\frac{1,50,000}{12}$ =	12,500.00
Total		35,000.00

v) Computer hire charge per month Rs. $\frac{4,20,000}{12}$ = Rs. 35,000

vi) Overheads for using machines without computer

= Rs. $\frac{35,000}{3,500}$ × 1,500 hrs = Rs. 15,000

vii) Overheads for using machine with computer

= Rs. $\frac{35,000}{3,500}$ × 2,000 hrs + Rs. 35,000 hire charge = Rs. 55,000.

Problem 74

The following data pertains to the machine shop of an engineering company relating to the year 1994. The machine shop has three cost centres A, B and C each having distinct set of machines.

	A	B	C	Total
No. of workers	400	400	800	1,600
No. of machine hours	50,000	50,000	60,000	1,60,000
Percentage of H.P.	45	25	35	100
Value of Assets (Rs. in lakhs)	20	35	30	85
Direct wages (Rs. in lakhs)	16	20	24	60
Indirect wages (Rs. in lakhs)				18
Supervisory Salaries (Rs. in lakhs)				7
Depreciation (Rs. in lakhs)				8.50
Insurance (Rs. in lakhs)				4.25
Electricity charges (Rs. in lakhs)				12.00
Welfare expenses (Rs. in lakhs)				9.00
Office and other expenses (Rs. in lakhs)				16.00

Work out a composite machine-hour rate for each of the cost centres, showing the basis of apportionment of expenses amongst the cost centres.

[ICWA (Inter) June, 1995]

Solution

Statement of Composite Machine Hour Rate

Particulars	*Basis of Apportionment*	*Total*	*Cost Centre* A	B (Rs. in lakhs)	C
Indirect wages	30% of Direct Wages	18.00	4.80	6.00	7.20
Supervisory salaries	Direct wages	7.00	1.87	2.33	2.80
Depreciation	Value of assets at 10%	8.50	2.00	3.50	3.00
Insurance	Value of assets at 5%	4.25	1.00	1.75	1.50
Electricity	Note 1	12.00	4.49	2.80	4.71
Selfare expenses	No. of workers	9.00	2.25	2.25	4.50
Office & Other Exp.	Direct wages	16.00	4.27	5.33	6.40
	Total	74.75	20.68	23.96	30.11
No. of Machine Hours Rate			50,000	50,000	60,000
Composite Machine Hour Rate (Rs.)			$\frac{20.68}{50,000}$	$\frac{23.96}{50,000}$	$\frac{30.11}{60,000}$
			41.36	47.92	50.18

Note : 1. Electricity charges are to be apportioned in proportion to the composite ratio of machine hours multiplied by Horse Power as follows :

A	50,000 × 40%	=	20,000
B	50,000 × 25%	=	12,500
C	60,000 × 35%	=	21,000
			53,500

A	$12.00 \times \dfrac{20,000}{53,500}$	$= \dot{4}.49$
B	$12.00 \times \dfrac{20,000}{53,500}$	$= 2.80$
C	$12.00 \times \dfrac{21,000}{53,500}$	$= 4.71$

2. If the amount of Direct wages is considered, the composite machine hour rate will be as follows :

Particulars	*Basis of Apportionment*	*Total*	*Cost Centre*		
			A	B	C
			(Rs. in lakhs)		
Total	As worked out in the above Stt.	74.75	20.68	23.96	30.11
Direct wages	As given	60	16	20	24
A Grand Total		134.75	36.68	43.96	54.11
B No. of Machine hours			50,000	50,000	60,000
Composite Machine Hour Rate	$\dfrac{\text{Total Expenses (allocated)}}{\text{No. of Machine hours}}$		$\dfrac{36,68,000}{50,000}$	$\dfrac{43,96,000}{50,000}$	$\dfrac{54,10,000}{60,000}$
			Rs. 73.36	Rs. 87.92	Rs. 90.17

Apportionment of Factory Overhead

Problem 75

X Ltd. is the manufacturer of four brands of toy – A, B, C & D. If the Company limits the manufacture to just one brand the monthly production will be :

A – 50,000 units
B – 1,00,000 units
C – 1,50,000 units
D – 3,00,000 units

You are given the following set of information from which you are requested to find out the profit or loss made on each brand showing clearly the following elements :

(a) Direct Cost or Prime Cost
(b) Works Cost
(c) Total Cost

	Brands			
	A	B	C	D
Actual Production (units)	6,750	18,000	40,500	94,500
Direct Wages (Rs.)	15,000	27,500	37,500	1,05,000
Direct Material Cost (Rs.)	50,000	92,500	1,27,500	3,80,000
Selling Price per unit (Rs.)	20	15	10	8

Factory Overhead expenditure for the month was Rs. 1,62,000. Selling and distribution cost should be assumed @ 20% of Works Cost. Factory Overhead expenses should be allocated to each brand on the basis of units which could have been produced in a month when single brand production was in operation.

[Adapted—I.C.W.A. (Inter)]

Solution

Note for students

In this problem the students are to allocate the total overhead expenditure to the departments proportionately. Hence, the ratio with proper weightage should be ascertained.

Department D can manufacture 3,00,000 units while A can manufacture 50,000 units.

So, D is taken as the basis for calculation

1 unit of A = 6 units of D

1 unit of B = 3 units of D

1 unit of C = 2 units of D

1 unit of D = 1 unit of D

So, the ratio = 6 : 3 : 2 : 1

Brand of Toys	Units		Weightage
A	6,750 × 6	=	40,500
B	18,000 × 3	=	54,000
C	40,500 × 2	=	81,000
D	94,500 × 1	=	94,500
			2,70,000

So, factory overhead per toy = Rs. $\frac{1,62,000}{2,70,000}$ = 0.60 paise

Apportionment of Factory Overhead :

				Rs.
A	=	0.60 × 6 × 6,750	=	24,300
B	=	0.60 × 3 × 18,000	=	32,400
C	=	0.60 × 2 × 40,500	=	48,600
D	=	0.60 × 1 × 94,500	=	56,700
				1,62,000

COST SHEET

Particulars	A	B	C	D	Total
	Rs.	Rs.	Rs.	Rs.	Rs.
Direct Materials (Given)	50,000	92,500	1,27,500	3,80,000	6,50,000
Direct Wages (Given)	15,000	27,500	37,500	1,05,000	1,85,000
PRIME COST	65,000	1,20,000	1,65,000	4,85,000	8,35,000
Add : Factory Overhead (See note above)	24,300	32,400	48,600	56,700	1,62,000
WORKS COST	89,300	1,52,400	2,13,600	5,41,700	9,97,000
Add : Selling and Distribution @ 20% of works Cost	17,860	30,480	42,720	1,08,340	1,99,400
TOTAL COST	1,07,160	1,82,880	2,56,320	6,50,040	11,96,400
PROFIT (Balancing figure)	27,840	87,120	1,48,680	1,05,960	3,69,600
	1,35,000	2,70,000	4,05,000	7,56,000	15,66,000

Problem 76

The Machine Shop of an auto engineering factory has five distinct groups of machines for which the recovery of expenses is at a rate per machine hour.

A budget for the machine shop for the year ended 31.12.98 is framed as under :

Groups :	1	2	3	4	5
	Rs.	Rs.	Rs.	Rs.	Rs.
Consumable Stores	210	420	700	850	1,260
Maintenance	630	840	1,500	2,000	1,800
Horse power hours ratio	5	15	20	25	35
Space occupied sq. ft.	200	400	600	300	500
Book value of machinery	30,000	90,000	25,000	60,000	45,000
Estimated utilisation hours	5,000	10,000	3,000	7,500	12,500

Common Expenses are :

	Rs.
Power	9,000
Rent, rates and taxes	25,000
Heat and Light	5,500
Insurance on building	2,400
Insurance on machinery	7,500
Depreciation	37,500
Shop Supervision	30,400
Other general expenses	60,800
Total	1,78,100

Calculate a machine hour rate for each group indicating the basis of allocation of expenses.

Solution

Computation of Machine Hour Rate for the year ended 31.12.98

Items	*Basis of apportionment*	*Total*	*Machine Groups*				
			1	2	3	4	5
		Rs.	Rs.	Rs.	Rs.	Rs.	Rs.
Consumable stores	Direct	3,440	210	420	700	850	1,260
Maintenance	Direct	6,770	630	840	1,500	2,000	1,800
Power	Horse power hour ratio (5 : 15 : 20 : 25 : 35)	9,000	450	1,350	1,800	2,250	3,150
Rent, rates and taxes	Space occupied (2 : 4 : 6 : 3 : 5)	25,000	2,500	5,000	7,500	3,750	6,250
Heat and light	As above	5,500	550	1,100	1,650	825	1,375
Insurance on building	As above	2,400	240	480	720	360	600
Insurance on machinery	Value of machinery (30 : 90 : 25 : 60 : 45)	7,500	900	2,700	750	1,800	1,350
Depreciation	Value of machinery (30 : 90 : 25 : 60 : 45)	37,500	4,500	13,500	3,750	9,000	6,750
Shop supervision	Estimated utiln. hrs. (50 : 100 : 30 : 75 : 125)	30,400	4,000	8,000	2,400	6,000	10,000
Other general expenses	As above	60,800	8,000	16,000	4,800	12,000	20,000
(a)	Total overheads Rs.	1,88,310	21,980	49,390	25,570	38,835	52,535
(b)	Estimated machine hours	—	5,000	10,000	3,000	7,500	12,500
Machine hour rate (a ÷ b) (Rs.)		—	4.40	4.94	8.52	5.18	4.20

Under/Over Absorption of Overhead

Problem 77

The budgeted working conditions for a cost centre are as follows :

Normal working hours in a week	42 hours
Number of machines	14
Normal weekly loss of hours on maintenance	5 hours per machine
Estimated annual overheads	Rs. 1,61,616
Estimated direct wages rate	Rs. 3 per hour
Number of weeks worked per year	48
Actual result in respect of a week period are :	
Overhead incurred	Rs. 13,270
Wages incurred	Rs. 7,620
Machine hours produced	2,100

You are required to calculate (a) the overhead rate per machine hour and (b) the amount of under-or over-absorption of both wages and overhead.

[I.C.W.A., Inter—Adapted]

Solution

(a) Normal working hours per year = 14 × 42 hrs week × 48 weeks = 28,224 hours

Normal loss of hours per year = 14 × 5 × 48 = 3,360 hours

Effective hours per year = 28,224 – 3,360 = 24,864

Machine hour rate = Rs. $\frac{1,61,616}{24,864}$ = Rs. 6.5

Overhead absorbed = 2,100 hours @ Rs. 6.5	=	Rs. 13,650
Overhead incurred	=	Rs. 13,270
Overhead over-absorbed	=	Rs. 380
Wages absorbed = 14 × 42 × 4 hours @ Rs. 3 per hour	=	Rs. 7,056
Wages incurred	=	Rs. 7,620
(b) **Wages under–absorbed**		Rs. 564

Problem 78

A production department of a manufacturing concern has three distinct machines—A, B and C. It is estimated that each machine will normally work for 50 weeks a year, 45 hours per week. But it is anticipated that the machines will remain idle 20% of this time due to normal repairs and maintenance.

The budgeted figures of the production departments for the year ended 31st March 1996 are as follows :

	Rs.
Rent and Rates	4,800
Lighting	900
Depreciation	10,500
Indirect wages	4,500
Canteen Expenses	2,500
Repairs and Maintenance	6,300
Sundries	3,000
Power	12,000

Other information

	Machine A	Machine B	Machine C
Space occupied (sq. ft.)	100	150	150
Light points	5	5	8
Cost of Machines (Rs.)	25,000	30,000	50,000
H.P. of Machines	2	2.5	3
No. of workers	3	3	4
Direct wages (Rs.)	6,000	4,000	5,000

During the 4 weeks of February 1996 the Machines worked at 80% capacity utilisation.

Actual overheads incurred were :

Machine A—Rs. 1,200, Machine B–Rs. 900 and Machine C—Rs. 2,000

You are required to calculate for each machine :

(a) pre-determined overhead rate based on effective working hours;

(b) the amount of under/over absorption of overhead;

(c) the revised overhead application rate.

[C.U. B.Com. (Hons.) 1996]

Solution

Items	*Basis of apportionment*	*Total*	*Machine A*	*Machine B*	*Machine C*
		Rs.	Rs.	Rs.	Rs.
Rent & Rates	Space occupied 2 : 3 : 3	4,800	1,200	1,800	1,800
Lighting	Light points 5 : 5 : 8	900	250	250	400
Depreciation	Cost of Machines 5 : 6 : 10	10,500	2,500	3,000	5,000
Indirect wages	Direct wages 6 : 4 : 5	4,500	1,800	1,200	1,500
Canteen Expenses	No. of workers 3 : 3 : 4	2,500	750	750	1,000
Repairs & Maintenance	Cost of Machines 5 : 6 : 10	6,300	1,500	1,800	3,000
Sundries	Direct wages 6 : 4 : 5	3,000	1,200	800	1,000
Power	H.P. of Machines 2 : 2.5 : 3	12,000	3,200	4,000	4,800
		44,500	12,400	13,600	18,500

	Machine A	Machine B	Machine C
(a) ***Predetermined Allocated overhead***			
Overhead rate	Rs.	Rs.	Rs.
Effective hours = 50 weeks × 45 hours	6.89	7.56	10.28
= 2,250 hours 80% of 2,250 = 1,800 hours	$\left(\text{Rs. } \frac{12,400}{1,800}\right)$	$\left(\text{Rs. } \frac{13,600}{1,800}\right)$	$\left(\text{Rs. } \frac{18,500}{1,800}\right)$

(b) ***Amount of over/under absorption of overhead***

	Machine A	*Machine* B	*Machine* C
	Rs.	Rs.	Rs.
Predetermine overhead	(–) 992	1,088	(–) 1,480
	(144 × R. 6.89)	(144 × 7.56)	(144 × 10.28)
Actual overhead	1,200	(–) 900	2,000
	208	188	520
	(Under absorbed)	(Over absorbed)	(Under absorbed)

(c) ***The revised overhead application rate***

	A	B	C
Actual overhead ÷ Machine hours	Rs.	Rs.	Rs.
	8.33	6.25	13.89
	(1,200 ÷ 144)	(900 ÷ 144)	(2,000 ÷ 144)

Effect of Overhead on Profit

Problem 79

A factory has a capacity of 20,000 units per annum. With a 50% production and selling each unit at Rs. 20, the total cost is Rs. 1,80,000 represented by direct charges Rs. 1,30,000 and indirect charges Rs. 50,000.

The management is considering two proposals, one to acccept an additional order for 5,000 units at Rs. 17.50 per unit and the other to spend Rs. 60,000 in advertising which is calculated to increase the output and sales to full capacity at Rs. 20 per unit.

Assuming that the direct and indirect charges increase in proportion to output, prepare a statement to show which proposal would be better.

[Punjab B.Com.]

Solution

Statement of Profit under first proposal

	10,000 Units	*5,000 Units*	*15,000 Total*
Direct Charges (Rs.)	1,30,000	65,000	1,95,000
Indirect Charges (Rs.)	50,000	25,000	75,000
Total Cost	1,80,000	90,000	2,70,000
	20,000	Loss(–)2.500	17,500
Sale Price	2,00,000	87,500	2,87,500

Statement of Profit under Second Proposal

		10,000 units	20,000 units
	Direct Charges (Rs.)	1,30,000	2,60,000
	Indirect Charges	50,000	1,00,000
		1,80,000	3,60,000
Add :	Selling Overhead		60,000
			4,20,000
Less :	Loss		20,000
	Sales @ Rs. 20 per unit		4,00,000

From the above statements it is clear that the first alternative is preferable since the amount of loss is less.

Preparation of Cost Sheet by using Overhead Application Rates

Problem 80

The following figures have been extracted from the books of Punjab Industrial Works. All jobs pass through two departments.

	Processing Department	*Finishing Department*
	Rs.	Rs.
Materials used	12,000	1,000
Direct labour	6,000	3,000
Facotry Overhead	3,600	2,400
Labour hours	24,000	10,000
Machine hours	20,000	4,000

The following information relates to Job No. 007 :

	Processing	*Finishing*
	Rs.	Rs.
Materials used	240	20
Direct labour cost	130	50
Direct labour hours	530	140
Machine hours	510	50

(a) Prepare normal overhead application rates using :

(i) Direct Labour-Hour Method

(ii) Direct Labour-Cost Method

(iii) Machine-Hour Rate Method

(b) Prepare a statement showing the different cost results for Job No. 007 under each of the three methods.

[Adapted—Andhra B.Com. and Delhi B. Com.]

Solution

(a) **Calculation of Overhead Rates**

	Processing	Finishing
	Re.	Re.
(i) *Direct Labour-Hour method*		
Overhead ÷ Labour hours	Rs. $\frac{3,600}{24,000}$ = 0.15	Rs. $\frac{2,400}{10,000}$ = 0.24
(ii) *Direct labour cost method*		
Overhead ÷ Direct labour cost	Rs. $\frac{3,600}{6,000}$ = 0.60	Rs. $\frac{2,400}{3,000}$ = 0.80
(iii) *Machine hour rate method*		
Overhead Cost ÷ Machine hours	Rs. $\frac{3,600}{20,000}$ = 0.18	Rs. $\frac{2,400}{4,000}$ = 0.60

(b) **Cost Sheet of Job 007 under three methods**

Particulars	*Direct labour hour*	*Direct labour cost*	*Machine hour rate*
	Rs.	Rs.	Rs.
Materials used	240 + 20 = 260.00	260.00	260.00
Direct labour	130 + 50 = 180.00	180.00	180.00
	440.00	440.00	440.00
Add : *Factory Overheads*			
Processing Department			
530 × 0.24	79.50		
130 × 0.60		78.00	
510 × 0.18			91.80
Finishing Department			
140 × 0.15	33.60		
50 × 0.80		40.00	
50 × 0.60			30.00
Works Cost	553.10	558.00	561.80

Problem 81

In a light Engineering Factory, the machine shop consists of three cost centres (A, B and C) each having their distinct set of machines. The following are the details of estimates for 1992 :

(Amounts are in lakhs of Rupees)

		Total	A	B	C
(i)	No. of workers	800	200	200	400
(ii)	No. of Machine Hours	1,00,000	30,000	30,000	40,000
(iii)	% of Horse Power	100	40	25	55
(iv)	Value of Assets	40	10	16	14
(v)	Direct wages	30	8	10	12
(vi)	Depreciation	4.00			
(vii)	Indirect labour	9.00			
(viii)	Insurance Charges	2.00			
(ix)	Electricity	3.00			
(x)	Supervisory Salary	1.60			
(xi)	Staff welfare expenses	3.00			
(xii)	Other expenses	6.00			

Work out composite machine hour rate for each of the three cost centres indicating clearly the basis of apportionment of expenses between the centres.

[I.C.W.A. Inter—Adapted]

Solution

Computation of Composite Machine Hour Rate

Items	*Basis of Apportionment*	*Total*	*Rupees in lakhs*		
			A	*B*	*C*
		Rs.	Rs.	Rs.	Rs.
Direct wages	Actual	30.00	8.00	10.00	12.00
Depreciation	Asset value	4.00	1.00	1.60	1.40
Indirect labour	Direct wages	9.00	2.40	3.00	3.60
Electricity	Horse Power	3.00	1.20	0.75	1.05
Insurance charges	Assets value	2.00	0.50	0.80	0.70
Supervision	No. of workers	1.60	0.40	0.40	0.80
Welfare expenses	No. of workers	3.00	0.75	0.75	1.50
Other expenses	Machine Hours	6.00	1.80	1.80	2.40
Total allocated expenses (in lakhs) (i)		58.60	16.05	19.10	23.45
(in lakhs) No. of Machine Hours (ii)			0.30	0.30	0.40
Composite Machine Hour Rate			53.50	63.67	58.63
Expenses ÷ Machine Hour. (i) ÷ (ii)					

Note : In the computation of composite machine hour rate, direct wages are to be considered.

Problem 82

From the following data of a textile factory machine-room, compute an hourly machine rate, assuming that the machine room will work at 90% capacity throughout the year and that a breakdown of 10% is reasonable.

There are 3 days holiday at Deepawali, 2 days at Holi and two days at Christmas, exclusive of Sundays. The factory works 8 hours a day and 4 hours on Saturday.

Number of machines (each of same type) 40.

Expenses p. a.	Rs.
Power	3,120
Light	640
Salaries to foreman	1,200
Lubricating oil	66
Repairs to machines	1,446
Depreciation	785.60
	7,257.60

[Adapted—C.A. Final (O.S.)]

Solution

Computation of Machine-Hour-Rate

		Rs.	Rs.
Standing Charges			
Salaries to Foreman		1,200	
Light		640	
		1,840	
Per hour =	$\frac{1,840}{72,576}$		0.025
Variable Expenses			
Power		3,120	
Lubricating oil		66	
Repairs		1,446	
Depreciation		785.60	
		5,417.60	
Per hour =	Rs. $\frac{5,417.60}{72,576}$		0.075
Machine Hour Rate			0.10
Calculation of Hours worked			
No. of days in a year			365
Less : Saturdays		52	
Sundays		52	
Holidays (3 + 2 + 2)		7	111
Full working days			254 days
No. of hours on full working days @ 8 hours per day		254 × 8	2,032
No. of hours on Saturdays		52 × 4	208
			2,240
Effective hours per machine at 90%		90% of 2,240	2,016
Total number of hours for 40 machines =		2,016 × 40	80,640
Less : 10% allowance for breakdown			8,064
Total hours worked			72,576

Problem 83

A machine shop of a factory has 3 cost centres having distinct sets of machines. The following estimates are available for the year 1994 :

	Total for the factory	*Centre I*	*Centre II*	*Centre III*
	Rs.	Rs.	Rs.	Rs.
Direct wages	1,60,000	50,000	50,000	60,000
Share of Service Expenses	5,000	1,000	1,500	2,500
Power	10,000			
Repairs and Maintenance	13,000			
Insurance	3,900			
Rent	3,000			
Lighting	1,800			

Contd.

	Total for the factory	*Centre I*	*Centre II*	*Centre III*
	Rs.	Rs.	Rs.	Rs.
Indirect wages	14,400			
Labour Welfare Expenses	20,000			
Value of Machines	3,25,000	1,00,000	75,000	1,50,000
Floor Area (Sq. Feet)		120	240	360
Power of Motor (H.P.)		10	10	20
Machine Hours		5,000	6,000	10,000
No. of Workers		12	10	18

Machines are depreciated of 10% p.a.

(a) Compute a suitable machine-hour-rate of overhead absorption for each of the machine centres.

(b) Job No. 201 passes through all the above three Cost Centres is :

Centre I – 4 hours, Centre II – 3 hours, Centre III – 8 hours.

What price should the Company quote for Job No. 201 to yield a profit of 20% on cost if its direct materials and direct labour costs are estimated at Rs. 500 and Rs. 300, respectively, and other expenses are 20% on works cost.

[C.U. B. Com. (Hons.) 1994]

Solution

Computation of Machine-Hour-Rate

Particulars	*Basis*	*Centre I*	*Centre II*	*CentreIII*
		Rs.	Rs.	Rs.
Share of Service expenses	Actual	1,000	1,500	2,500
Power	H.P. 1 : 1 : 2	2,500	2,500	5,000
Repairs and Maintenance	Cost of Machine	4,000	3,000	6,000
Insurance	4 : 3 : 6	1,200	900	1,800
Rent	Floor area 1 : 2 : 3	500	1,000	1,500
Lighting	1 : 2 : 3 (floor area)	300	600	900
Indirect Wages	Direct Wages 5 : 5 : 6	4,500	4,500	5,400
Labour Welfare Expenses	No. of Workers	6,000	5,000	9,000
Depreciation @ 10%	Asset values	10,000	7,500	15,000
		30,000	26,500	47,100
Machine Hour Rate	$\frac{\text{Overheads}}{\text{Hours}}$	$\frac{30,000}{5,000}$ = Rs. 6.00	$\frac{26,500}{6,000}$ = Rs. 4.42	$\frac{47,100}{10,000}$ = Rs. 4.71

Statement showing the Cost of Job No. 201

	Rs.	Rs.
Material Cost		500
Wages		300
Prime Cost		800
Factory Overhead		
Centre I = 4 × Rs. 6.00 =	24.00	
Centre II = 3 × Rs. 4.42 =	13.26	
Centre III = 8 × Rs. 4.71 =	37.68	
		74.94
Works Cost		874.94
Other Expenses 20% on works Cost		174.99
		1,049.93
Add : Profit @ 20% on Cost		209.99
PRICE TO BE QUOTED		1,259.92

Problem 84

The particulars relating to four machines are :

Machine Numbers	I	II	III	IV
Cost (Rs.)	50,000	40,000	30,000	20,000
Area occupied (sq. ft.)	500	450	300	250
Light points	10	8	6	4
No. of Workers	20	15	8	7
Direct Wages (Rs.)	1,500	1,200	1,000	500
Horse-Power of Machines	25	20	16	14
Consumable Stores (Rs.)	100	80	75	50

The Expenses incurred were :

	Rs.
Rent and Taxes	600
Lighting	140
Depreciation	2,800
Repairs & Maintenance	700
Power	375
Indirect Wages	840
Consumable Stores	305
Canteen Expenses	100
General Expenses	420

(a) Compute the machine hour rate for a month of 25 working days with 8 working hours on an average.

(b) Calculate the cost of production of one unit of product A, if the material cost is Rs. 10, Labour cost Rs. 20 and if processed for 1 hour in machine I, 2 hours in machine II, 3 hours in machine III, and 4 hours in machine IV.

[C.U. B. Com. (Hons.) 1997]

Solution

Computation of Machine Hour Rate

Items	*Basis of apportionment*	*Total*	*Machine I*	*Machine II*	*Machine III*	*Machine IV*
		Rs.	Rs.	Rs.	Rs.	Rs.
Rent and Taxes	Area occupied 10 : 9 : 6 : 5	600	200	180	120	100
Lighting	Light points 5 : 4 : 3 : 2	140	50	40	30	20
Depreciation	Cost of Machines 5 : 4 : 3 : 2	2,800	1,000	800	600	400
Repairs and Maintenance	Cost of Machines 5 : 4 : 3 : 2	700	250	200	150	100
Power	H.P. of Machines 25 : 20 : 16 : 14	375	125	100	80	70
Indirect Wages	Direct wages 15 : 12 : 10 : 5	840	300	240	200	100
Consumable stores	Actual	305	100	80	75	50
Canteen Expenses	No. of workers 20 : 15 : 8 : 7	100	40	30	16	14
General expenses	Direct wages 15 : 12 : 10 : 5	420	150	120	100	50
		6,280	2,215	1,790	1,371	904

Working hours = 25 × 8 = 200 hours.

	Machine I	*Machine II*	*Machine III*	*Machine IV*
	Rs.	Rs.	Rs.	Rs.
(a) Allocated Overheads	2,215	1,790	1,371	904
(b) Working Hours	200	200	200	200
Machine Hour Rate a ÷ b	= Rs. 11.08	= Rs.8.95	= Rs. 6.855	= Rs. 4.52

COST SHEET OF PRODUCT A

					Rs.
Material Cost					10
Labour Cost					20
Prime Cost					30.00
Add Factory Overhead				Rs.	
Machine I	=	1 × Rs. 11.08	=	11.08	
Machine II	=	2 × Rs. 8.95	=	17.90	
Machine III	=	3 × Rs. 6.855	=	20.56	
Machine IV	=	4 × Rs. 4.520	=	18.08	67.62
Cost per unit					97.62

Problem 85

From the following data work out the predetermined Machine Hour Rates for departments A and B of a factory :

	Total	Preliminary estimates of expenses	
		Dept. A	Dept. B
	Rs.	Rs.	Rs.
Power	15,000	—	—
Spare parts	8,000	3,000	5,000
Consumable Stores	5,000	2,000	3,000
Insurance on machinery	3,000	—	—
Depreciation on Machinery	30,000	10,000	20,000
Indirect Labour	40,000	—	—
Building Maintenance	7,000	—	—

The final estimates are to be prepared on the basis of the above figures after taking into consideration the following factors :

(a) An increase of 10% in the price of spare parts.

(b) An increase of 20% in the consumption of spare parts.

(c) Increase in the straight line method of depreciation from 10% on the original value of machinery to 12%

(d) 15% general increase in wage rates :

The following information is available :

	Dept. A	Dept. B
Estimated direct labour hours	80,000	1.20,000
Ratio of KW rating	3	2
Estimated machine hours	25,000	30,000
Floor space (sq. ft)	15,000	20,000

[I.C.W.A—Inter—Adapted]

Solution

Item	Basis of apportionment	Total	Dept A	Dept B
		Rs.	Rs.	Rs.
Power	K.W. rating 3 : 2	15,000	9,000	6,000
Spare parts	Direct on final estimate 1 : 2	9,900[1]	3,300	6,600
Consumable stores	Direct	5,000	2,000	3,000
Depreciation	Direct on final estimate 1 : 2	36,000[2]	12,000	24,000
Insurance on machinery	Depreciation ratio 1 : 2	3,000	1,000	2,000
Indirect Labour	Estimated Direct Labour Hour 2 : 3	46,000[3]	18,400	27,600
Building Maintenance	Floor Area 3 : 4	7,000	3,000	4,000
		1,21,900	48,700	73,200

Machine Hour Rate = $\frac{\text{Total Expenses}}{\text{Machine Hours}}$; Dept A: $\frac{48,700}{25,000}$ = Rs. 1.948 ; Dept B: $\frac{73,200}{30,000}$ = Rs. 2.440

Working notes

		Total	Dept. A	Dept. B
(1)	***Spare parts***	Rs.	Rs.	Rs.
	Preliminary estimates	8,000	3,000	5,000
Add :	Price increase 10%	800	300	500
		8,800	3,300	5,500
Add :	Increase in consumption @ 20%	1,100	—	1,100
		9,900		6,600
(2)	***Calculation of depreciation***			
	Depreciation	30,000	10,000	20,000
	20% increase in the rate	6,000	2,000	4,000
	(2% on 10% = 20% on 100%)	36,000	12,000	24,000
(3)	***Indirect labour***			
	Indirect wages	40,000		
Add	Increase @ 15%	6,000		
	Final estimates	46,000		

Problem 86

A Machine Shop cost centre contains machines of equivalent capacities. Three operators are employed on each machine, one at Rs.10 an hour and two at Rs. 5 per hour each. The factory works a forty-hour week which includes four hours for set-up time. The work is jointly done by the operators. The operators are paid fully for the forty hours. In addition they are paid a bonus of 10% on productive time. Costs are reported for this company on the basis of thirteen four-weekly periods.

The company for the purposes of computing machine hour rate includes the direct wages of the operators and also recoups the factory overheads allocated to the machines. The following details of factory overheads applicable to the cost centre are available :

(1) Set-up time as described above.

(2) Depreciation 10% per annum on original cost on each machine.
Original cost of each machine is Rs. 13,000.

(3) Maintenance and repairs per week per machine is Rs. 25.

(4) Consumable stores per week per machine Rs. 36.

(5) Power—20 units per hour per machine at 40 paise per unit.

(6) Apportionment to the cost centre

Rent per annum	Rs. 3,000
Heat and light per annum	Rs. 5,400
Foreman's salary per annum	Rs. 7,200

You are required to :

(*a*) Compute the cost of running one machine for a four-week period and

(*b*) The machine hour rate.

[C.A. Inter, December 1990]

Solution

Computation of Cost of running one machine for four-week period

		Per Annum	Rs.
	Standing Charges	Rs.	
	Rent	3,000	
	Heat and light	5,400	
	Foreman's salary	7,200	
	Total expenses for 6 machines	15,600	
	Total expenses for one machine for four-week period	$\frac{15,600}{6} \times \frac{4}{13}$	800
Wages	Hours per week = 40		
	Hours for 4 weeks = 40 × 4 = 160		
	160 hrs. (1 × Rs. 10 + 2 × Rs. 5)	3,200	
Bonus	10% of productive time i.e., for 144 hrs.		
	[144 hrs (1 × Rs. 10 + 2 × Rs. 5] × 10%	288	3,488
(i)	***Total standing charges***		4,288
	Machine Expenses		
	Depreciation Rs. $\frac{13,000 \times 4}{13} \times 10\%$		400
	Repairs and maintenance	(Rs. 25 × 4)	100
	Consumable stores	(Rs. 36 × 4)	144
	Powers–no power is consumed during set-up time (144 hrs. × 20 units × 40 paise)		1,152
(ii)	Total machine expenses	4,288 + 1,796	1,796
	Total Cost *(i)* + *(ii)*		6,084

Machine Hour Rate =

Total Cost ÷ Total productive time = Rs. 6,084 ÷ 144 hrs. Rs. 42.25 per hour.

Problem 87

A machine was purchased on January 1, 1990, for Rs. 5 lakhs. The total cost of all machinery inclusive of the new machine was Rs. 75 lakhs. The following further particulars are available :

Expected life of the machine 10 years.

Scrap value at the end of ten years Rs. 5,000.

Repairs and maintenance for the machine during the year Rs. 2,000. Expected number of working hours of the machine per year, 4,000 hours. Insurance premium annually for all the machines Rs. 4,500.

Electricity consumption for the machine per hour (@ 75 paise per unit) 25 units.

Area occupied by the machine 100 sq. ft.

Area occupied by other machines 1,500 sq. ft.

Rent per month of the department Rs. 800.

Lighting charges for 20 points for the whole department, out of which three points are for the machine Rs. 120 per month.

Compute the machine hour rate for the new machine on the basis of the data given above.

[C.A. Inter. May 1990]

Solution

Computation of Machine-Hour Rate

	Total	Per Hour
Expected number of machine hours	4,000 hours	
Standing charges :		
Depreciation (Rs. 5,00,000–5,000) ÷ 10 yrs.	49,500	
Repairs and maintenance	2,000	
Insurance premium (4,500 × Rs. 5 lakhs) ÷ Rs. 75 lakhs	300	
Rent (Rs. 800 × 12 months × 100 sq. ft.) ÷ 1600 sq. ft.	600	
Lighting charges Rs. (120 × 12 × 3 points) ÷ 20 points	216	
Total standing charges	52,616	
Per hour	(Rs. 52,616 ÷ 4,000)	Rs. 13.154
Electricity consumption	(25 units × Rs. 0.75)	18.750
Machine Hour Rate		31.904

Problem 88

The following particulars relate to a new machine purchased :

Purchase price of the machine	Rs. 4,00,000	
Installation expenses	1,00,000	
Rent per quarter	15,000	
General lighting for the total area	1,000	per month
Foreman's salary	30,000	per annum
Insurance premium for the machine	3,000	per annum
Estimated repair for the machine	5,000	per annum
Estimated consumable stores	4,000	per annum

Power–2 units per hour at Rs. 50 per 100 units.

The estimated life of the machine is 10 years and the estimated value at the end of the 10th year is Rs. 1 lakh. The machine is expected to run 20,000 hours in its life time. The machine occupies 25% of the total area. The foreman devotes 1/6th of his time for the machine. Calculate the machine hour rate for the machine.

[C.S. Inter, June 1989]

Solution

		Rs.	Rs.	Rs.
Standing charges :				
Rent for the year	($\frac{1}{4}$th share for this machine)		15,000	
Lighting	(Rs. 12,000 ÷ 4) for one year		3,000	
Foreman's salary	(Rs. 30,000 ÷ 6)		5,000	
Insurance Premium			3,000	
Depreciation :				
Cost of machine		4,00,000		
Add : Installation charges,		1,00,000		
		5,00,000		
Less : Residual value after 10 years		1,00,000		
		4,00,000		
For one year	(4,00,000 ÷ 10)		40,000	
			66,000	

Contd.

		Rs.	Rs.	Rs.
B.F.			66,000	
No. of hours worked during the year		2,000		
Hourly rate of standing charges (Rs. 66,000 ÷ 2,000 hrs.)			66,000 / 2,000	33.00
Operating charges :				
Consumable stores per hour	(Rs. 4000 ÷ 2000)			2.00
Repair per hour	(Rs. 5,000 ÷ 2000)			2.50
Power per hour	(2 units × Re. 0.50)			1.00
Machine Hour Rate				38.50

Problem 89

XYZ Ltd. a manufacturing company, having an extensive marketing network throught the country, sells its products through four zonal sales office viz. A, B, C & D. The budgeted expenditure for the year are given below :

			Rs.
Sales manager's salary			1,20,000
Expenses relating to sales manager's office			80,000
Travelling salesmen's salaries			3,20,000
Travelling expenses			36,000
Advertisements			30,000
Godown rent :			
Aone	A	15,000	
	B	25,200	
	C	9,800	
	D	18,000	68,000
Insurance on inventories			20,000
Commission on Sales @ 5% on sales			6,00,000

The following further particulars are also available :

Zone	*Sales in Rs. Lakhs*	*No. of Salesmen*	*Total Mileage*	*Allocation of Advertisement*	*Average Stock in Rs. Laksh*
A	36	5	6,000	30%	6
B	48	6	14,000	30%	8
C	16	2	4,500	20%	4
D	20	3	5,500	20%	2

Based on the above details, compute zonewise selling overheads, as a percentage to sales

[ICWA. Inter Dec. 1987]

Solution

Statement of Zonewise Selling Overheads

Selling overheads	*Basis of apportionment*	*Zone* A	B	C	D
Sales Manager's salary	Sales	36,000	48,000	16,000	20,000
Sales Manager's Office expenses	"	24,000	32,000	10,667	13,333
Travelling salesmen's salaries.	No. of Salesmen	1,00,000	1,20,000	40,000	60,000
Travelling expenses	Total mileage covered	7,200	16,800	5,400	6,600
Advertisement	% as given in the question	9,000	9,000	6,000	6,000
Godown Rent	As given	15,000	25,200	9,800	18,000
Insurance on Inventories	1% on Average Stock	6,000	8,000	4,000	2,000
Commission on sales	5% on sales	1,80,000	2,40,000	80,000	1,00,000
Total selling overheads	12,74,000	3,77,200	4,99,000	1,71,867	2,25,933
% on sales	$\frac{\text{Overheads} \times 100}{\text{Sales}}$	10.48	10.4	10.74	11.3

ASSIGNMENT

Theoretical Questions

1 What are the consequential problems arising out of the use of predetermined rate of absorption of factory overhead ? How do you deal with these problems ?

[B.U. B.Com. (Hons.) – 1986]

2 What are the source documents for collection of factory overheads ?

[B.U. B.Com. (Hons.) – 1986]

3 What is pre-determined overhead rate ? Why is it used ?

[B.U. B.Com. (Hons.) – 1985]

4 (a) Define overhead and state the different methods of classification of overhead, giving examples.

(b) What factors would you consider for determining overhead absorption rate ?

[B.U. B.Com. (Hons.) – 1985]

5 What do you understand by over-absorption and under-absorption of overheads ? What are the causes of such under-or over-absorption ? How are they treated in Cost Accounts ?

[B.U. B.Com. (Hons.) – 1984]

6 Discuss the treatment of Administrative Overhead in the books of accounts.

[B.U. B.Com. (Hons.) – 1984]

7 What are the different methods of absorption of factory overhead? Discuss at least four methods, illustrating your answer with imaginary figures.

[B.U. B.Com. (Hons.) – 1983]

8 Explain the meanings of the term 'Allocation', 'Apportionment' and 'Absorption'. What is predetermined rate of overhead ?

[B.U. B.Com. (Hons.) – 1995]

9 What is a pre-determined overhead rate ?

[B.U. B.Com. (Hons.) – 1985]

10 What do you mean by 'Primary Distribution' and 'Secondary Distribution' of overhead ? Briefly describe different methods of secondary distribution of overhead.

[B.U. B.Com. (Hons.) – 1994]

11. (a) What is Labour Hour Rate ?

(b) Under what circumstances labour hour rate would be suitable for absorption of overhead ?

[B.U. B.Com. (Hons.) – 1995]

12. Why are predetermined rates for overhead absorption used ? How do you solve the consequential problem arising out of the use of predetermined overhead rates ?

[B.U. B.Com. (Hons.) – 1997]

13 What are the methods of distribution of Service department overhead to Production departments ?

[V.U. B.Com. (Hons.) – 1991]

Practical Problems [Determination of overhead Rates]

1. The following is the budget of a manufacturing concern for the year 1989 :

	Rs.
Factory Overhead	1,24,000
Direct Labour Costs	1,96,000
Direct Labour Hours	3,10,000
Machine Hours	10,000

(1) From the above figures prepare the overhead application rates using the methods : (i) Direct Labour Hours, (ii) Direct Labour Cost, (iii) Machine Hour.

(2) Prepare a comparative statement of cost showing the result of application of each of the above rates to Job No. 551 from the undermentioned data :

Direct Materials	90.00
Direct Labour Cost	180
Direct Labour Hours	150
Machine Hours	60

(3) In this case which method do you think to be appropriate

[B.U. B.Com. (Hons.) 1986]

Ans. : (1) (i) Re. 0.400 (i) Rs. 0.632%, (iii) Rs. 12.40
(2) (i) Rs. 330.00, (ii) 383.76, (iii) 1014.00

2. The following information relates to the activities of a production department of a factory for a certain period :

Materials used	Rs. 36,000
Direct wages	Rs. 30,000
Labour hours worked	12,000 hours
Hours of machine operation	20,000 hours
Overhead chargeable to the department	Rs. 25,000

One order carried out in the department during the period, the relevant data were :

Materials used	Rs. 6,000
Direct wages	Rs. 4,950
Labour hours worked	1,650 hours
Machine hours	1,200 hours

Calculate the overheads chargeable to the job by three commonly used methods.

Ans. : Direct wage method Rs. 4,125.00
Labour hour method Rs. 3,437.50
Machine hour method Rs. 1,500.00

3. The following information relates to the activities of a production department of a factory for a certain period :

	Rs.	
Material used	36,000	
Direct wages	30,000	
Labour Hours worked		24,000 (hours)
Hours of machine operation		20,000 (hours)
Overhead Chargeable to the Department	25,000	

On the order carried out in the department during the period, the relevant data was :

	Rs.
Materials used	2,000
Direct wages	1,650
Labour hours	1,650
Machine hours	1,200

Calculate by three different methods the overhead chargeable to the job.

Ans : Overhead chargeable to the Job
(i) Rs. 1,716 – labour hour
(ii) Rs. 1,375 – labour wages
(iii) Rs. 1,500 – machine hour

4. From the budgeted figures of a factory :
   (a) Prepare normal overhead application rate using :
   (i) Direct Labour Hour Method
   (ii) Direct Labour Cost Method
   (iii) Machine-Hour Rate Method

Budgeted figures :

	Rs.
Estimated factory overhead for the year	5,80,000
Estimated direct labour hours for the year	13,46,000
Estimated direct labour cost for the year	9,78,000
Estimated Machine hours	5,05,000

(b) Prepare comparative statement of cost showing the result of application of each of the above rates to Job No. 101 from the data given below :

	Rs.
Cost of direct materials consumed	420
Direct labour wages	450
Direct labour hours	300
Machine hours	200.

(c) Indicate what method of overhead recovery would be preferable, giving reasons.

[B.U. B.Com. (Hons.) 1991]

Ans. : (a) (i) 43.09%; (ii) Re. 0.59 per labour hour; (iii) Rs. 1.148 per machine hour.
(b) (i) Rs. 1,063.90; (ii) Rs.1,047; (iii) Rs. 1,167.

Hint : For solution see worked out problem No. 5.

5. XYZ Company uses a historical cost system and applies overheads on the basis of 'predetermined rates'. The following data are available from the records of the Company for the year ended 31.3.1990 :

	Rs.
Manufacturing Overheads	8,50,000
Manufacturing Overheads applied	7,50,000
Work-in-Progress	2,40,000
Finished goods stock	4,80,000
Cost of goods sold	16,80,000

Apply two methods for disposal of under–absorbed Overheads showing the implications of each method on the profits of the company.

[Adapted I.C.W.A. (Inter) June 1990]

Ans. : Under–absorbed overheads = Rs.1,00,000.

Hints : (i) Can be treated as part of cost of sales

(ii) Can be apportioned as follows – W.I.P.—Rs. 10,000 ; F. Goods—Rs. 20,000 ; Cost of goods sold – Rs. 70,000 ; i.e. :- 1 : 2 : 7.

6. The following figures have been extracted from the books of Punjab Industrial Works. All jobs pass through two departments :

	Processing Department	*Furnishing Department*
Materials used (Rs.)	12,000	1,000
Direct labour (Rs.)	6,000	3,000
Factory Overhead (Rs.)	3,600	2,400
Direct Labour Hours	24,000	10,000
Machine Hours	20,000	4,000

The following information relates to Job No. 007.

	Processing	Firshing
Materials used	Rs. 240	Rs. 20
Direct labour	Rs. 130	Rs. 50
Direct labour hours	530	140
Machine hours	510	50

(a) Prepare normal overhead application rates using

(i) Direct Labour Hour Method

(ii) Direct Labour Cost Method

(iii) Machine Hour Rate Method

(b) Prepare a statement showing the different cost results for Job No. 007 under each of the three methods.

[Adapted Delhi Univ. B. Com]

Ans : (i) Direct labour hour method = Rs. 553.10

(ii) Direct labour Cost method = Rs. 558.00

(iii) Machine hour rate method = Rs. 561.80

7. In a light engineering factory, the following particulars have been collected for the three monthly period ended 31st December 1988. You are required to prepare production overhead distribution summary showing clearly the basis of apportionment where necessary.

Particulars	*Production Depts.*			*Service Dept.*	
	A	*B*	*C*	*D*	*E*
Direct Wages (Rs.)	2,000	3,000	4,000	1,000	2,000
Direct Materials (Rs.)	1,000	2,000	2,000	1,500	1,500
Staff (Nos.)	100	150	150	50	50
Electricity (Kwh.)	4,000	3,000	2,000	1,000	1,000
Light points (Nos.)	10	16	4	6	4
Asset Value (Rs.)	60,000	40,000	30,000	10,000	10,000
Area occupied	150	250	50	50	50

The expenses for the period were :

	Rs.
Motive power	550
Lighting power	100
Stores Overheads	400
Amenities to Staff	1,500
Depreciation	15,000
Repairs and Maintenance	3,000
General Overheads	6,000
Rent and Taxes	275

Apportion the expenses of Service department E proportionate to direct wages and those of Service department D in the ratio of 5 : 2 : 2 : 1 to departments A, B, C and E, respectively.

[Madras University, B.Com. 1989]

Ans : A— Rs. 12,543, B— Rs. 10,222, C— Rs. 10,060

8. A wool wear manufacturing company processes production through two departments : (i) Machine Department and (ii) Finishing Department. Overhead rates are predetermined on the basis of 'machine hours' in the Machine Department and 'direct wages' in the Finishing Department.

Figures for 1990-1991 based on which the overhead and direct labour rates were arrived at are furnished below :

		Machine Dept.	*Finishing Dept.*
		Rs.	Rs.
2.	Factory Overhead	16,00,000	15,00,000
3.	Direct Labour Hours	1,20,000	2,00,000
4.	Machine Hours	2,00,000	50,000

The cost sheet for part no. P 340 on Job order No. 1478 indicates as below :

		Machine Dept.	Finishing Dept.
		Rs.	Rs.
(a)	Materials Consumed	50.00	10.00
(b)	Direct Labour Hours	8	12
(c)	Machine Hours	7	2

Assuming that the above details relate to the manufacture of 10 units, prepare a cost sheet showing also the unit cost of the part.

[Adapted I.C.W.A. (Inter)]

Ans : Rs. 257.00 and Rs. 176.

9. A factory has 3 production departments A, B and C and 2 Service departments, D & E. The following figures are found :

	Rs.
Rent and rates	5,000
General lighting	600
Indirect wages	1,500
Power	1,500
Depreciation on Machinery	10,000
Sundry Expenses	10,000

Further details are :

	Total	A	B	C	D	E
Floor area (sq. ft.)	10,000	2,000	2,500	3,000	2,000	500
Light points (Nos.)	60	10	15	20	10	5
Direct wages	10,000	3,000	2,000	3,000	1,500	500
H. P. of machinery	150	60	30	50	10	–
Value of machinery (Rs.)	2,50,000	60,000	80,000	1,00,000	5,000	5,000

The expenses of D and E are allocated to A, B and C as under :

	A	B	C
D	30%	30%	40%
E	40%	30%	30%

Show necessary charts for allocating the indirect expenses among the 5 departments and for allocating the Service Dept. expenses to the Production Departments.

[Audit & Accounts Service Exam. – W.B. 1986]

Ans : A – Rs. 9,567; B – Rs. 9,060; C – Rs. 11,973.

10. A manufacturing company has three production and two service departments. Overhead allocated for a year to these departments is as follows :

	Production Dept.	Service Dept.
A	Rs. 5,000	1. Rs. 2,000
B	Rs. 3,000	2. Rs. 3,000
C	Rs. 2,500	

The following percentages are applicable for the apportionment of the costs of the service departments :

Dept.	A	B	C	1	2
1	40%	30%	10%	–	20%
2	20%	40%	30%	10%	

Find out the total costs of production departments after apportionment of the costs of the service departments taking into consideration inter-departmental services.

[B.U. B.Com. (Hons.) – 1985]

Ans : A – Rs. 6,631; B – Rs. 5,092; C – Rs. 3,777.

11. A manufacturing company has three production departments and two service departments. Overhead allocated for a period to these departments is as follows :

Production departments	P	Rs. 6,000
	Q	Rs. 5,000
	R	Rs. 8,000
Service departments	1	Rs. 3,000
	2	Rs. 4,000

A technical estimate for the apportionment of the costs of the service departments shows the following position :

Department	A	B	C	1	2
1	30%	40%	20%	–	10%
2	20%	30%	30%	20%	

You are required to show total overhead chargeable to the three production departments after apportionment of costs of the service departments using simultaneous equation method.

[B.U. B.Com. (Hons.) – 1983]

Ans : A—Rs. 8,041; B—Rs. 9068; C—Rs. 10,091

12. Calculate the overheads allocable to Production Departments X and Y. There are also two Service Departments A and B.

A renders service worth Rs. 15,000 to B and the balance to X and Y as 3 : 2. B renders Service to X and Y as 9 : 1.

	X	Y	A	B
Floor Space (sq. ft.)	5,000	4,000	1,000	2,000
Assets (Rs. in lakh)	10	5	3	1
H. P. of machines	1,000	500	400	100
Nos. of workers	100	50	50	25
Light and Fan Points	50	30	20	20

Expenses and Charges are :	Rs.
Depreciation	1,90,000
Rent, Rates and Taxes	36,000
Insurance	15,200
Power	20,000
Canteen Expenses	10,800
Electricity	4,800

[M.Com. C.U.]

Ans : X—Rs. 1,87,680; Y—Rs. 89,120

13. In a factory, there are two service departments P & Q and three production departments A, B and C. In April 1995, the departmental expenses were

Departments	Rs.
A	6,50,000
B	6,00,000
C	5,00,000
P	1,20,000
Q	1,00,000

The service department expenses are allotted on a percentage basis as follows :

Particulars	*Production Depts.*			*Service Depts.*	
	A	B	C	P	Q
P	30	40	15	–	15
Q	40	30	25	5	–

Prepare a statement showing the distribution of the two service department expenses to the three departments. Method of calculation should be shown clearly.

[I.C.W.A. – Final]

Ans : [Overheads after distribution

A—Rs. 7,35,340; B—Rs. 6,86,045; C—Rs. 548,615]

14. The following information are collected from the books of Roy & Co. for the month of. January 1994 :

Indirect materials :		Rs.
Production Departments	A	95
	B	120
	C	20
Maintenance Departments	X	150
Store Department	Y	40
Indirect wages :		
Department	A	90
	B	110
	C	30
	X	100
	Y	65
Power and Light		600
Rent and Taxes		280
Insurance of Machinery		100
Canteen Expenses		300
Depreciation		6% p.a. on Asset value.

Additional information are given below

Item	*Production Departments*			*Service Departments*	
	A	B	C	X	Y
Floor Area (sq. ft.)	4,000	4,000	3,000	2,000	1,000
Asset value (Rs.)	1,00,000	1,20,000	80,000	60,000	40,000
KWH	4,000	4,400	1,600	1,500	500
No. of workers	90	120	30	40	20

On the basis of the above information prepare the Departmental distribution summary of Ray & Co.

[B.U. B. Com. (Hons.) 1994]

Ans : A—Rs. 6,580; B—Rs. 7,880; C—Rs. 5040
X—Rs. 4,020 and Y— Rs. 2,580

15. Superfine Ltd. has furnished the following particulars for the half year ended of March 31, 1998. Compute the departmental overhead rates for each of the production departments, assuming that the overheads are recovered as percentage of direct wages.

Particulars	*Production Depts.*			*Service Dept.*	
Direct wages (Rs.)	4,000	6,000	8,000	2,000	4,000
Direct materials	2,000	4,000	4,000	3,000	3,000
Number of employees	100	150	150	50	50
Electricity (Kwh.)	8,000	6,000	4,000	2,000	2,000
Light points (No.)	10	16	4	6	4
Asset value (Rs.)	1,20,000	80,000	60,000	20,000	20,000
Area occupied in sq. m.	150	250	100	50	50

The overhead expenses of the period were :

	Rs.
Motive power	3,300
Lighting	400
Stores expenses	800
Staff welfare expenses	4,800
Depreciation	30,000
Repairs	15,000
Rent, Rates and Taxes	1,200
General expenses	12,000

Apportion the expenses of service department X in proportion to the direct wages and that of service department Y in the ratio of 5 : 3 : 2 to production departments A, B and C.

[Adapted—I.C.W.A., Inter, New.]

Ans : Overhead recovery rate :
Department A Rs. 671.8%;
Department B Rs. 369.7% and
Department C Rs. 269. 7%.

16. In a factory there are two Production departments A and B, two Service departments S_1 and S_2. Total expenses of department S_1 are apportioned between A and B and S_2 in the ratio of 3 : 2 : 1 and the expenses of department S_2 are allocated between A and B equally. From the following particulars calculate the overheads to be allocated to Production Departments A and B :

	A	B	S_1	S_2
Floor Area (Sq. ft)	5,000	4,000	1,000	2,000
Assets (in lakhs)	10	5	3	1
H.P. of Machine	50	50	30	20
No. of workers	80	80	30	20
Light points	30	20	10	10
Direct wages (Rs.)	10,000	10,000	5,000	5,000
Direct Materials (Rs.)	15,000	15,000		5,000

Total expenses and charges are :

	Rs.
Depreciation	57,000
Canteen Expenses	4,200
Rent, Rates and Taxes	12,000
Electricity	2,100
Insurance of assets	3,800
Power	2,100

[V.U. B.Com. (Hons.) 1992]

Ans : A–Rs. 58,160; B – Rs. 38,040

17. A manufacturing company has two production departments P_1 and P_2 and three service departments – Time keeping, Stores and Maintenance. The departmental summary shows the following expenses incurred in the month of January 1989 :

	Rs.	Rs.
Production Department		
P_1	16,000	
P_2	10,000	26,000
Service Department		
Time Keeping	4,000	
Stores	5,000	
Maintenance	3,000	12,000
		38,000

Other relevant information are as follows :

	Production Departments		*Service Departments*		
	P_1	P_2	*Time Keeping Keeping*	*Stores*	*Maintenance*
No. of employees	40	30		16	14
No. of store requisitors	24	20	–	–	6
Machine hours	1,400	1,600			

You are required to make departmental allocation of overhead and redistribution of service departments overheads to the production departments.

[V.U. B.Com. (Hons.) 1989]

Ans. : P_1 – Rs. 22,284.37; P_2 – Rs. 15,715.63

18. In a factory there are three Production departments and one Service department. The actual cost in 1992 were as follows :

Power Rs. 900 ; Light Rs. 500; Repair to Plant Rs. 4,500; Rent Rs. 5,000; Depreciation Rs.2,700; Supervision Rs. 7,500 and Canteen expenses Rs. 3,000.

With above noted expenses and the following further particulars determine the total overhead cost of Production departments. Cost of Service department is apportioned to production departments in 2 : 2 : 1 ratio.

	Production Department			*Service Dept.*
	A	B	C	S
Area (sq. metres)	1,250	550	450	250
Cost of Plant (Rs.)	1,20,000	90,000	90,000	–
No. of employees	24	18	12	6
Wages (Rs.)	30,000	20,000	15,000	10,000
Light points	8	7	6	4
H.P of machines	6	4	5	–

[C.U. B.Com. (Pass) 1993]

Ans : A – Rs. 14,752; B – Rs. 11,442; C – Rs. 7,906.

19. The following data were obtained from the books of Light Engineering Company for the half-year ended 30th September 1998. Calculate the departmental overhead rates for each of the production departments assuming that the overheads are recovered as a percentage of direct wages.

	Production Department			***Service Department***	
	A	B	C	X	Y
Direct wages (Rs.)	7,000	6,000	5,000	1,000	1,000
Direct materials (Rs.)	3,000	2,500	2,000	1,500	1,000
Employees (Nos.)	200	150	150	50	50
Electricity (Kwh.)	8,000	6,000	6,000	2,000	3,000
Light points (Nos.)	10	15	15	5	5
Assets values (Rs.)	50,000	30,000	20,000	10,000	10,000
Area occupied (Sq.Yds.)	800	600	600	200	200

The expenses for 6 months were :

	Rs.		Rs.
Stores Overhead	400	Depreciation	6,000
Mature Power	1,500	Repairs and Maintenance	1,000
Electric Lighting	200	General Overheads	10,000
Labour Welfare	3,000	Rent and Taxes	600

Apportion the expenses of Department X in the rates of 4 : 3 : 3 and that of department Y in proportion to direct wages, to department A, B and C, respectively.

[Mysore B.Com.]

Ans. : (a) A – Rs. 11,396 : B – Rs. 8,663 : C – Rs. 7,341

(b) A – 162.8% ; B – 144.4% ; C – 146.8%.

Hints : General Overhead have been apportioned on the basis of Direct wages and Stores Overhead on the basis of materials consumed.

20. There are three Production departments and one Service department in a factory. The cost for the year 1994 were as given below :

Rent–Rs. 5,200; Light–Rs. 480, Power–Rs. 1,800; Depreciation on plant — Rs. 3000, Canteen Expenses–Rs. 6,300, Supervision charges–Rs. 3150.

With the above–noted expenses and particulars as given below find out the total overhead expenses of each of the production departments. Cost of the service department is apportioned to production departments in the ratio of 2 : 2 : 1.

	Production Departments			***Service Department***
	A	B	C	S
No. of Employees	30	18	9	6
Cost of Plant (Rs.)	1,50,000	1,00,000	50,000	
Light Points	9	6	5	4
H.P. of Machines	10	5	3	
Wages paid (Rs.)	40,000	30,000	20,000	10,000
Area (Sq. mt.)	1,500	750	500	500

[C.U. B.Com. (Pass) 1995]

Ans : A—Rs. 14,292; B—Rs. 10,232; C—Rs.5406

21. A, B, C and D are four departments of an engineering concern. Services rendered by D to the production departments A,B,C are 30%, 20% and 50%, respectively. From the undermentioned particulars calculate labour hour rate for each of the production departments :

Expenses for the period of 12 months

	Rs.		Rs.
Rent	36,000	Depreciation on machinery	11,000
Power	8,250	Electricity	5,600
Indirect wages	5,200	Canteen Expenses	6,500

Additional information :

	A	B	C	D
Light points (Nos.)	7	8	8	5
Floor space (sq. m.)	300	250	450	200
H.P. of Machines (H.P.)	130	60	60	80
No. of workers (Nos.)	2	3	6	2
Direct wages (Rs.)	12,000	14,000	18,000	8,000
Cost of machine (Rs.)	25,000	30,000	40,000	5,000

Working days : 200 days of 8 hours each.

[V.U. B. Com (Hons.) 1996]

Ans : A—Rs. 6.876; B—Rs. 3.972; C—Rs. 3.278

22. Find out the labour hour rate of each Production Department and find out the total cost of product processed for production in Department P_1 P_2 and P_3 for 5,4 and 3 hours from the following information.

Material cost Rs. 150, Direct wages Rs. 70. The expenses for Production Departments and Service Departments for the year 1996-97 and other particulars of Production Departments and Service Departments are given below :

	Rs.		Rs.
Rent, Rates and Taxes	550	Repairs and Maintenance	6,000
Lighting expenses	200	Stores overhead	800
General Overhead	12,000	Depreciation	30,000
Motive power	1,100	Amenities to staff	3,000

	Production Departments			*Service Departments*	
	P_1	P_2	P_3	S_1	S_2
Direct wages (Rs.)	4,000	6,000	8,000	2,000	4,000
Number of staff	100	100	100	50	50
Direct Materials (Rs.)	2,000	4,000	4,000	3,000	3,000
Light points (Nos)	10	16	4	6	4
Electricity (KWH)	8,000	6,000	4,000	2,000	2,000
Assets Value (Rs.)	1,20,000	80,000	60,000	20,000	20,000
Area Occupied (SQM)	300	500	100	100	100

Expenses of the Service Department S_1 to be apportioned to production Departments in the ratio of 5 : 3 : 2 and that of S_2 to Production Departments on the basis of Direct Wages.

There were 125 working days of 8 hours each.

[W.B.C.S. 1997]

Ans : (a) Labour Hour Rate
P_1—Rs. 25.09
P_2—Rs. 20.94
P_3—Rs. 19.60
(b) Total Cost—Rs. 488

Hint : (a) General overhead has been apportioned on the basis of Direct wages.

23. B Banerjee has three production departments X, Y and Z and two service departments A and B. The departmental distribution summary gives the following figures :

		Rs.	Rs.
Production Departments :			
	X	1,600	
	Y	1,400	
	Z	1,000	4,000
Service Departments	A	468	
	B	600	1,068

Expenses of Service Departments are to be distributed as follows :

	X	Y	Z	A	B
Service Department A	20%	40%	30%	—	10%
Service Department B	40%	20%	20%	20%	

Prepare a statement showing re-distribution of overheads of service departments, A and B among production departments, X, Y and Z using the Simultaneous Equation Method.

[B.U. B. Com (Hons.) 1993]

Ans. : X— Rs. 1,984; Y—Rs. 1,772; Z— Rs. 1,312

24. From the following particulars calculate Labour Hour Rate of each of the departments X, Y, and Z :

(i) Expenses :

Rent Rs. 34,000; Electric power Rs. 18,400; Depreciation on machinery Rs. 22,000; Indirect wages Rs. 5,300, Canteen Expenses Rs. 5,700, Light charges Rs. 4,600

(ii) Further information

Particulars	*Production Departments*			*Service Department*	
	X	*Y*	*Z*	*S*	*Total*
Floor space (sq. m)	2,000	3,000	2,500	1,000	8,500
Light points	18	12	10	6	46
Cost of machines (Rs.)	80,000	50,000	60,000	10,000	2,00,000
H.P. of Machines	30	20	40	10	100
No. of workers	7	5	5	2	19
Direct wages (Rs.)	15,000	16,000	18,000	4,000	53,000

There were 125 working days of 8 hours each. Services rendered by the service department to the Production Departments are X—50%, Y— 25% and Z— 25%.

[B.U. B.Com. (Hons.) 1995]

Ans : X— Rs. 4.856; Y— Rs. 5.723; Z— Rs. 6.279.

25. You are supplied with the following information and required to work out the production hour rate of recovery of overheads for A, B & C under the repeated distribution method :

	Production Department			*Service Department*	
	A	B	C	X	Y
Primary Overhead (Rs.)	7,810	12,543	4,547	4,000	2,600

Expenses of Service Departments P and Q are apportioned as follows :

	A	B	C	X	Y
P	30%	40%	20%		10%
Q	10%	20%	50%	20%	

Estimated working hours of production are as under :

Dept. A – 1,000 hours ; B – 2,500 hours ; C – 1,400 hours.

[Bangalore B.Com.]

Ans : A – Rs. 9.50 ; B – Rs. 6.00 ; C – Rs. 5.0

26. From the particulars given below show a chart of allocation of overheads to the two Production Departments, P_1 and P_2. There are also two Service Departments, S_1 and S_2. S_1 renders service to S_2 to the extent of Rs. 15,000 and the balance to P_1 and P_2 in the ratio 3 : 2. S_2 renders service to P_1 and P_2 in the ratio 10 : 1.

	P_1	P_2	S_1	S_2
Floor Space (Sq. ft.)	5,000	4,000	1,000	2,000
Assets Value (in lacs of rupees)	10	5	3	1
H.P of machines	1,000	500	400	100
No. of workers	100	50	50	50
No. of light points	50	30	20	20

The expenses and charges are (for all four departments together)

	Rs.
Depreciation	1,90,000
Rent, Rates and Taxes	36,000
Insurance	20,900
Power	30,000
Canteen Expenses	12,500
Electricity	6,000

[A & A Service Examination 1987]

Ans : P_1— Rs. 2,00,707; P_2— Rs. 94,693

27. P. H. Ltd. is a manufacturing company having three production departments 'A', 'B' and 'C' and service departments 'X' and 'Y'. The following is the budget for December 1992 :

	Total	A	B	C	X	Y
	Rs.	Rs.	Rs.	Rs.	Rs.	Rs.
Direct Materials		1,000	2,000	4,000	2,000	1,000
Direct Wages		5,000	2,000	8,000	1,000	2,000
Factory Rent	4,000					
Power	2,500					
Depreciation	1,000					
Other Overhead	9,000					
Additional information :						
Area (Sq. ft.)		500	250	500	250	500
Machine hours		1,000	2,000	4,000	1,000	1,000
Capital value of Assets						
(Rs. in lakh)		20	40	20	10	10
Horse power of machines		50	40	20	15	25

A technical assessment for the apportionment of expenses of service departments is as under :

	A	B	C	X	Y
Service Dept X	45%	15%	30%		10%
Service Dept Y	60%	35%	5%		

(i) A statement showing distribution of overheads to various departments.

(ii) A statement showing redistribution of service departments expenses to production departments.

(iii) Machine hour rates of the production departments A, B and C

[Adapted—C.A (Inter)]

Ans : A – Rs. 9.57, B – 2.69, C – Rs. 1.87

28. Chandra Bhanu & Co. has 3 Production and 2 Service departments. Distribution of overheads is done as follows :

Production Departments		*Service Departments*	
	Rs.		Rs.
A	3,000	X	234
B	2,000	Y	300
C	1,000		

Expenses of Service departments are to be allocated on percentage basis as follows :

Departments	A	B	C	X	Y
X	20%	40%	30%	–	10%
Y	40%	20%	20%	20%	

Find out the amount to be distributed among Production departments under Simultaneous Equation.

[Adapted—Mysore University, Part II B.Com. 1990]

Ans : A—3192.24,; B—2185.78; C—1155.89

29. A manufacturing company produces various articles. The amount of overhead expenses incurred by the different departments are stated below :

	Expenses Rs.	*Direct labour*	*No. of hours worked*	*Floor space Sq.ft.*	*Power consumed K.W.*
Service Departments					
Maintenance	9,600	–			
Building Service	12,000	–	1,000	–	–
Power	4,000	–	400	2,000	–
Production Departments					
Cutting	16,000	14,660	1,600	4,000	3,60,000
Assembly	8,000	13,520	1,800	8,000	40,000

The service department costs are distributed to other service departments and to the production departments in the order shown above. The basis of distribution of costs is as follows :

Overhead expenses of	***Basis of distribution***
Maintenance Department	Hours worked in other departments
Building Service department	Floor space
Power Department	Power consumption.

[Adapted—C.U. B.Com. (Hons.)]

Ans. : (a) Cutting – Rs. 29,320 ;
Assembly – Rs. 20,280
(b) Percentage of overhead on Direct Labour –
Cutting Dept – 200%
Assembly Dept – 150%

Hints : Calculation of %

(a) Cutting Dept. – Rs. $\frac{29,320}{14,660} \times 100$; (b) Assembly Dept. – Rs. $\frac{20,280}{13,520} \times 100$.

30. In a light engineering factory, the following particulars have been collected for the three monthly periods ended 31st December 1991. Compute the departmental overhead rates for each of the production departments assuming that overheads are recovered as a percentage of direct wages.

Particulars	*Production Dept.*			*Service Dept.*	
	A	B	C	D	E
Direct Wages (Rs.)	2,000	3,000	4,000	1,000	2,000
Direct Materials (Rs.)	1,000	2,000	2,000	1,500	1,500
Staff (Nos.)	100	150	150	50	50
Electricity (Kws.)	4,000	3,000	2,000	1,000	1,000
Light Point (Nos.)	10	16	4	6	4
Assets Value Rs.	60,000	40,000	30,000	10,000	10,000
Area occuppied sq. yds.	150	250	50	50	50

The expenses for the period were :

	Rs.
Motive Power	550
Lighting Power	100
Stores Overhead	400
Amenities to staff	1,500
Depreciation	15,000
Repairs and maintenance	3,000
General Overhead	6,000
Rent and Taxes	275

Apportion the expenses of service department E proportionate to Direct wages and that of service department D in the ratio 5 : 3 : 2 to Departments A, B and C, respectively.

[I.C.W.A.]

Ans. : A – Rs. 12,444 ; B – Rs. 10,522 ; C – Rs. 9,859.

	A	B	C
Service Dept. D	Rs. 2,257	Rs. 1,355	Rs. 903
Service Dept. E	Rs. 1,336	Rs. 2,003	Rs. 2,671

31. Self-help Ltd. has gensets and produces its own power. Data for Power costs are as under :

Horse Power Hours	*Production Depts*		*Service Depts*	
	A	*B*	*X*	*Y*
Needed at capacity production	10,000	20,000	12,000	8,000
Used during the month of May	8,000	13,000	7,000	6,000

During the month of May costs for generating power amounted to Rs. 9,300; of this Rs. 2,500 was considered to be fixed cost. Service department X renders service to A, B and Y in the ratio 13 : 6 : 1, while Y renders service to A and B in the ratio 31 : 3. Given the direct labour hours in departments A and B are 1,650 hours and 2,175 hours respectively, find the Power Cost per labour hour in each of these two departments.

[Adapted—C.A. (Inter) Nov. 1985]

Ans. : Dept. A – Rs. 3.00; Dept. B – Rs. 2.00.

Hints : (a) Fixed cost of Rs. 2,500 to be apportioned on the basis of H.P. needed at capacity production.

(b) Variable cost of Rs. 6,800 to be apportioned on the basis of Horse Power hours used during May.

32. You are supplied with the following information and required to work out the production hour rate of recovery of overhead in Departments A, B and C :

Particulars	*Total*	*Production Depts.*			*Service Dept.*	
		A	*B*	*C*	*P*	*Q*
	Rs.	Rs.	Rs.	Rs.	Rs.	Rs.
Rent	12,000	2,400	4,800	2,000	2,000	800
Electricity	4,000	800	2,000	500	400	300
Indirect Labour	6,000	1,200	2,000	1,000	800	1,000
Depreciation of Machinery	5,000	2,500	1,600	200	500	200
Sundries	4,500	910	2,143	847	300	300
Estimated working hours	–	1,000	2,500	1,400		

Expenses of service departments P and Q are apportioned as under :

	A	B	C	P	Q
P	30%	40%	20%	–	10%
Q	10%	20%	50%	20%	–

Ans : Dept. A – Rs. 9.50, B – Rs. 6, C – Rs. 5.

33. The following figures have been extracted from the books of a manufacturing company. All jobs pass through the company's departments :

	Working Dept. Rs.	Finishing Dept. Rs.
Material used	6,000	500
Direct labour	3,000	1,500
Factory Overheads	1,800	1,200
Direct Labour Hours	12,000	5,000
Machine Hours	10,000	2,000

The following information relates to Job No. 17 :

	Working Dept. Rs.	Finishing Dept. Rs.
Material	120	10
Direct Labour	65	25
Direct Labour Hours	265	70
Machine Hours	255	25

You are required :

(a) To enumerate four methods of absorbing factory overheads by jobs, showing the rates for each department – under the method quoted ; and

(b) To prepare a statement showing the different cost results for Job No. 17 under each of four methods referred to.

[B.Com. Delhi]

Hints :

	Working Dept	Finishing Dept.
(a) Material Cost percentage	30%	240%
Direct Labour Rate	60%	80%
	Rs.	Rs.
Direct Labour Hour Rate	Rs. 0.15 per hour	Rs. 0.24 per hour
Machine Hour Rate	Rs. 0.18 per hour	Rs. 0.60 per hour

Comparative Statement of Job No. 17 for Working Dept. :

(b) Total Cost	Total Cost of Job 17 (Rs.)
Material Cost Percentage	221.00
Direct Labour Rate	224.00
Direct Labour Hour Rate	224.75
Machine Hour Rate	230.90

Comparative Statement of Job No. 17 for Finishing Dept. :

	Rs.
Material Cost Percentage	280.00
Direct Labour Rate	279.00
Direct Labour Hour Rate	276.55
Machine Hour Rate	280.90

34. Strongman Ltd. has three production departments A, B and C and two service departments X and Y.

The following particulars are available for the month of March 1991 concerning the organisation :

	Rs.
Rent	15,000
Municipal Taxes	5,000
Electricity	2,400
Indirect Wages	6,000
Power	6,000
Depreciation on Machinery	40,000
Canteen Expenses	30,000
Other labour related costs	10,000

Following further details are also available :

	Total	A	B	C	X	Y
Floor Space (Sq. mts.)	5,000	1,000	1,250	1,500	1,000	250
Light Point (Nos.)	240	40	60	80	40	20
Direct Wages (Rs.)	40,000	12,000	8,000	12,000	6,000	2,000
H. P. of machines (Nos.)	150	60	30	50	10	–
Cost of machines (Rs.)	2,00,000	48,000	64,000	80,000	4,000	4,000
Working hours		2,335	1,510	1,525		

The expenses of service departments are to be allocated in the following manner :

	A	B	C	X	Y
X	20%	30%	40%		10%
Y	40%	20%	30%	10%	

You are requested to calculate the overhead absorption rate per hour in respect of the three production departments.

[Adapted—I.C.W.A. (Inter), June 1991]

Ans. : A – Rs. 16.00 ; B – Rs. 24.00 ; C – Rs. 32.00

35. A factory comprises of two Production Departments and three Service Departments. For the month of July, the direct departmental expenses were as follows :

Production Department	***Service Department***
A – Rs. 85,000	Power House – Rs. 47,350
B – Rs. 70,000	Store – Rs. 15,000
	Repair Shop – Rs. 60,500

The expenses of service departments are distributed on a percentage basis as under :

Power House	:	25% to Repair Shop, 25% to Dept. A and 50% to Dept. B.
Store	:	10% to Power House, 20% to Repair shop, 30% to Dept. A and 40% to Dept. B.
Repair Shop	:	20% to Power House, 30% to Dept. A and 50% to Dept. B.

Prepare a statement showing the distribution of service department expenses to production departments using simultaneous equations method.

[C.U. M.Com.]

Ans. : A – Rs. 1,29,606 ; B – Rs. 1,48,244

Hint : Store expenses should be distributed first.

36. The following figures relate to a department having three machines A, B and C. Compute the machine hour rate of machine A from the data given below; the machine A is expected to work 200 hours.

	Rs.
Power	1,500
Lighting	200
Depreciation of machinery	3,000
Insurance on machinery	200
Indirect wages	1,500
First-aid cost	50
Civil maintenance	720
Repairs to machinery	1,000
Miscellaneous expenditure	1,000
	9,710

	A	B	C
Space occupied	100 sq. m.	200 sq. m.	200 sq. m.
Light points (Nos.)	2	6	12
Cost of machine	Rs. 75,000	Rs. 30,000	Rs. 45,000
No. of workers	1	2	2
Power units recorded	7,500	2,500	5,000
Direct wages	Rs. 300	Rs. 600	Rs. 600.

[Adapted—I.C.W.A. (Inter)]

Ans. : Rs. 17.62

Hints : (i) Civil maintenance has been allocated on the basis of space occupied and Miscllaneous on the basis of direct wages.

37. Aruna Perfumaries Ltd. has two production departments and one service department. The following figures are available for one month of 25 working days of 8 hours per day (per worker).

Particulars	*Total*	*Production Depts.*		*Service Dept.*
	Rs.	X	Y	Z
Lighting	1,200	–	–	–
Rent	590	–	–	–
Staff Amenities	510	–	–	–
Depreciation (Plant)	800	–	–	–
Supervisor's salary	500	–	–	–

Contd.

Particulars	*Total*	*Production Depts.*		*Service Dept.*
	Rs.	X	Y	Z
Motive Power	300	–	–	–
General Charges	180	–	–	–
Time devoted by the Supervisor	–	50%	30%	20%
No. of workers	–	10	5	2
No. of Light points	–	6	4	2
Electricity (Kwh.)	–	15	10	5
Floor space (Sq. Yd.)	–	3,000	2,000	900
Value of Plant (Rs.)	–	50,000	20,000	10,000
Direct wages (Rs.)	–	10,000	6,000	3,000
Service rendered by Dept. Z to Production Departments	–	60%	40%	–
Working Hours utilised	–	100%	100%	100%

You are required to calculate Labour Hour Rate of each of the Production Departments.

[N.B.U. B.Com. (Hons.)]

Ans. : X – Rs. 2.18, Y – Rs. 2.71

38. Particulars regarding three shops in a factory are as follows :

	Shop A	Shop B	Shop C
Floor area	3,000 sq. ft.	2,000 sq. ft.	1,000 sq. ft.
Number of workers	20	30	40
Capital Value of Plants	Rs. 5,00,000	Rs. 3,00,000	Rs. 2,00,000
Direct Machine Hours	4,000 p.a.	2,000 p.a.	1,000 p.a.
Number of lights	100	60	40
Wages paid	Rs. 10,000 p.a.	Rs. 15,000 p.a.	Rs. 10,000 p.a.

Different items of expenses incurred in respect of the factory are as follows :

Rent and Rates of Factory	Rs. 1,200 p.a,
Expenses of wage office in the factory	Rs. 1,800 p.a.
Repairs and maintenance of plants	Rs. 1,400 p.a.
Electricity Charges (factory)	Rs. 2,000 p.a.
Depreciation of Plants :	Rs. 20,000 p.a.
Canteen Expenses	Rs. 900 p.a.
Workmen's State Insurance	Rs. 2,100 p.a.

You are required to allocate the above expenses to the three shops in the factory.

[N.B.U. B.Com. (Hons.)]

Ans. : Shop A – Rs. 13,714; Shop B – Rs. 9,372; Shop C – Rs. 6,314

39. Calculate from the following data the machine hour rate for Machine A :

	Rs.
Cost of Machine	1,050
Estimate Scrap Value	50
Effective Working Life	20,000 hrs.
Running time 4 weekly Period	150 hrs.

Weekly Amount payable under a Maintenance Agreement covering all repairs.	Rs. 7.50
Standing Charges allocated to Machine per 4 weekly	Rs. 5.00
Period power used by Machine	5 units per hour at 6 paise per unit

[B.Com. Delhi]

Ans. : Rs. 0.58 per hour

40. Work out the machine hour rate for the following machine whose scrap value is nil :

1.	Cost of machine	Rs. 90,000
2.	Freight and installation	Rs. 10,000
3.	Working life	10 years
4.	Working hours	2,000 per year
5.	Repair Charges	50% of depreciation
6.	Power 10 units per hour @ 10 paise per unit.	
7.	Lubricating oil @ Rs. 2 per day of 8 hours.	
8.	Consumable stores @ Rs. 10 per day of 8 hours.	
9.	Wages of operator @ Rs. 4 per day.	

[Adapted B.Com. (Hons.) Delhi]

Ans. : Rs. 10.00

Hint : Excluding wages

41. Calculate the machine hour rate from the following :

Cost of machine	Rs. 8,000
Cost of installation	Rs. 2,000
Scrap value after 10 years	Rs. 2,000
Rates and rent for a quarter for the shop	Rs. 300
General lighting	Rs. 20 p.m.
Shop supervisor's salary	Rs. 600 per quarter
Insurance premium for a machine	Rs. 60 p.a.
Estimated repair	Rs. 100 p.a.
Power 2 units per hour, @ Rs. 5 per 100 units	
Estimated working hours p.a. 2,000.	

The machine occupies $\frac{1}{4}$th of the total area of the shop. The Supervisor is expected to devote $\frac{1}{6}$th of his time for supervising the machine. General lighting expenses are to be apportioned on the basis of floor area.

Ans. : Re. 0.96.

42. A machine costing Rs. 20,000 is expected to run for ten years at the end of which its scrap value is estimated to be Rs. 2,000. Installation charges are Rs. 200. Repairs during the entire ten years' life of the machine are estimated to be Rs. 1,800 and the machine is expected to run for 2,190 hours in a year.

Its power consumption would be 15 units per hour at Rs. 5 per 100 units. The machine occupies $\frac{1}{4}$ of the area of the Department and has two points out of a total of ten for lighting.

The foreman has to devote about $\frac{1}{3}$ of his time to this machine.

The rent for the Department is 300 per month and charges for lighting Rs. 80 per month. The foreman is paid a salary of Rs. 960 per month.

Find out the hourly rate assuming that insurance is @ 1% per annum of the capital cost of the machine and the expenses on oil etc are Rs. 9 per month.

[B.Com. (Hons.) Delhi]

Ans. : Rs. 4.05.

43. From the following details compute a comprehensive machine hour rate for a particular machine A, installed in a workshop consisting of 6 identical machines :

Normal working hours possible for Machine A in a year	2,500
Normal idle time for the machine	20%
Rent and taxes for the workshop per year	Rs. 72,000
Lighting for the entire workshop p.m.	Rs. 4,000
Repairs and maintenance expenses for Machine A p.a.	Rs. 6,000
Cost of power per 100 units	Rs. 25
Machine consumes 10 units per hour	
Indirect labour cost applicable to Machine A	Rs. 4 per hour
Shop supervisor's salary	Rs. 1,500 p.m.

The supervisor is to supervise the working of all the machines.

Machine A costs Rs. 2,60,000 and is expected to have a working life of 10 years, at the end of which a scrap value of Rs. 20,000 is expected to be realised from the machine.

[C.U. B.Com. (Pass) 1988]

Ans : Rs. 33.00.

44. Calculate Machine-Hour Rate from the following :
    1. Cost of Machine Rs. 19,200.
    2. Estimated scrap value Rs. 1,200.
    3. Average Repairs and Maintenance charges per month Rs. 150.
    4. Standing charges allocated to machine per month Rs. 50.
    5. Effective working life of machine 10,000 hours.
    6. Running time per month 166 hours.
    7. Power used by machine : 5 units per hour @ 19 paise per unit.

[B.Com. Punjab]

Ans : Rs. 3.95.

45. Calculate Machine Hour Rate of A Machine :

	Rs.	
Consumable Stores	600	for A Machine
Consumable Stores	1,000	for B Machine
Repairs	800	for A Machine
Repairs	1,200	for B Machine
Heat and Light	360	
Rent	1,200	
Insurance of Building	4,800	
Insurance of Machine	800	
Depreciation Machines	700	
Room Service	60	
General Charges	90	

Additional information :

	Working Hours (sq. meter)	Area (Rs.)	Book Value
A Machine	10,000	100	12,000
B Machine	25,000	500	20,000

[B.Com. Pass, Delhi]

Ans : A – Rs. 0.141, B – Re. 0.298.

46. Work out, in the appropriate form, the comprehensive machine hour rate of a Saw Mill with reference to the following items as information extracted from the account books of a Wood Working Shop :

		Rs.
(i)	Purchase price of the Saw Mill	40,000
(ii)	Railway freight, other incidental charges and installation charge incurred for the equipment	10,000
(iii)	Life of the Saw Mill is 10 years @ 2,000 working hours per year.	
(iv)	Repair charges – 40 per cent of depreciation.	
(v)	Consumption of electric power – 20 units per hour @ 10 P. per unit.	
(vi)	Lubricating oil @ Rs. 2 per day of 8 hours.	
(vii)	Consumable Stores @ Rs. 10 per day of 8 hours.	
(viii)	Wages of machine operator @ Rs. 4 per day of 8 hours.	

Note : The Residual Scrap value of the Saw Mill is nil.

[B.Com. Punjab]

Ans : Rs. 7.50

47. From the following details compute the hourly rate of a machine installed in a shop :

	Rs.
Cost of the machine	2,00,000
Installation charges	20,000
Estimated scrap value after the expiry of its life (15 years)	10,000
Rent and rates of the shop	7,200
General lighting of the shop p.m.	800
Insurance premium for the machine per quarter	720
Estimated repairs and maintenance cost of the machine p.a.	3,000
Power consumption of the machine – 20 units per hour	
Rate of power per 100 units	Rs. 20
Estimated working hours of the machine per year 2,300 hours	
Shop supervisor's salary – p.m.	1,800

The machine occupies $\frac{1}{4}$th of the total floor area of the shop. The supervisor is expected to devote $\frac{1}{5}$th of his time for supervising the machine. Normal idle time is estimated to be 300 hours p.a.

[Adapted—B.U. B.Com. (Hons.) 1984]

Ans. : Rs. 18.20

48. Ashok owns a machine shop. From the following details compute the hourly rate of machine newly installed for Rs. 24,000 in the shop.

Rent of the shop	Rs. 2,400	per year
Rate & Water	Rs. 1,200	per year
General Lighting & Heating	Rs. 1,800	per year
Power Consumption of the machine	Rs. 4,800	
Supervisor's Salary	Rs. 600	per month
Estimated working hours of the machine	1,500	per year
Insurance premium of the machine	Rs. 410	per year

The machine occupies $\frac{1}{4}$th of the total floor area of the shop. The Supervisor is expected to devote $\frac{1}{5}$th of his time for supervising the machine. General light and heating expenses are to be apportioned on the basis of the floor area. The life of the machine is 10 years without any scrap value.

[C.A. Inter]

Ans. : Rs. 6.93

49. Compute the machine hour rate from the following data :

Cost of machine	Rs. 1,00,000
Installation charges	Rs. 10,000
Estimated scrap value after the expiry of its life (15 years)	Rs. 5,000
Rent and Rates for the shop per month	Rs. 200
General Lighting for the shop per month	Rs. 300
Insurance Premium for the machine per annum	Rs. 960
Repairs and Maintenance expenses per annum	Rs. 1,000
Power consumption – 10 units per hour	–
Rate of power per 100 units.	Rs. 20
Estimated working hours per annum – 2,200	
– This includes setting up time of 200 hours	
Shop supervisor's salary per month	Rs. 600

The machine occupies $\frac{1}{4}$th of the total area of the shop. The supervisor is expected to devote $\frac{1}{5}$th of his time for supervising the machine.

[B.Com. (Hons.) Delhi]

Ans : Rs. 7.95.

50. Compute comprehensive machine hour rate from the following data :

(i) Total machine cost of one machine to be depreciated Rs. 2,30,000 ; Life 10 years ; Depreciation on Straight Line.

(ii) Departmental overheads (annual) :

Rent	Rs. 50,000
Heat and Light	Rs. 20,000
Supervision	Rs. 1,30,000

(iii)

Departmental area	70,000 square feet
Machine area	2,500 square feet

(iv)	26 machines are in the department	
(v)	Annual cost of reserve equipment for the machines	Rs. 1,500
(vi)	Hours run on production	1,800
(vii)	Hours for setting and adjusting	200
(viii)	Power cost Rs. 0.50 per hour of running time.	
(ix)	Labour (a) When setting and adjusting, full time attention (b) When machine is producing, one man can look after 3 machines.	
(x)	Labour rate Rs. 6 per hour	

[I.C.W.A.I. Inter]

Ans : Rs. 20.14

Hint : Labour Rs. 4,800 $(200 \times 6 + 1{,}800 \times \frac{6}{3})$.

51. Calculate Machine Hour Rate for recovery of overheads for a group of 4 machines from the following data :

Original cost of the 4 machines Rs. 76,800

Depreciation at 10% per annum ; Straight line method.

Maintenance cost average Rs. 8/- per day of 8 hours for the group of machines.

Power 25 paise per running hour (Per machine).

Supervision for the machine group Rs. 640 per month.

Allocation of building depreciation for the 4 machines on a floor area basis, Rs. 80 per month.

Share of manufacturing overheads, Rs. 240 per month, for the group.

Normal working days in the year, 300.

Normal Idle time, 20%

Normal running 1 shift of 8 hours.

[C.U. M.Com.]

Ans : Rs. 12.00.

52. A machine costs Rs. 90,000 and deemed to have a scrap value of 5% at the end of its effective life of 19 years. Normally the machine is expected to run for 2,400 hours p.a. but it is estimated that 150 hours will be the cost for normal repairs and maintenance and further 750 hours will be lost on account of load shedding, other details in respect of the machine shop are :

		Rs.	
(i)	Wages of two operators, each operator is in charge of two machines	6,000	p.a.
(ii)	Rent of the shop	3,000	p.a.
(iii)	General lighting of the shop	250	p.m.
(iv)	Insurance premium for the machines	200	per qu.
(v)	Cost of repairs per machine	250	p.m.
(vi)	Shop supervisor's salary	500	p.m.
(vii)	Power per machine per hour	20	units
(viii)	Rate of power per 100 units	10	
(ix)	Other factory overhead	4,000	p.a.

There are four identical machines in the shop. The supervisor devotes $\frac{1}{5}$th of his time for the machine.

Compute a comprehensive machine hour rate.

[Audit + Accounts Service Exam – 1982]

Ans : Rs. 8.70

Hints : Time lost on account of loadshedding has been considered as abnormal idletime

53. Prepare a machine hour rate computation for the month of December 1995 to cover the overhead expenses indicated below; relating to a particular machine :

Per annum	Rs.
Rent of the department (space occupied by the machine $\frac{1}{5}$th of the Department)	780
Lighting of department	240
Insurance etc.	36
Cotton waste, oil etc.	60
Salary of Foreman ($\frac{1}{4}$th of Foreman's time is occupied by this machine and the remainder equally upon two other machines)	6,000

The cost of the machine is Rs. 9,200 and it has an estimated scrap value of Rs. 200.

It is assumed from past experience :

(a) that the machine will work for 1,800 hours p.a.;
(b) that it will incur an expense of Rs. 1,000 for repairs and maintenance,
(c) that it consumes 5 units of power per hour at a cost of 10 paise per unit; and
(d) that the working life of the machine will be 10 years.

Ans. : Machine Hour Rate Rs. 2.06

54. Particulars of three machines used in a factory are as under (six-week period : 160 hours working) :

	Machine No. 1	Machine No. 2	Machine No. 3
Cost of Machine	Rs. 10,000	Rs. 15,000	Rs. 20,000
No. of workers	2	5	10
Direct wages	Rs. 300	Rs. 800	Rs. 1,200
Power	Rs. 45	Rs. 80	Rs. 150
Light	2	4	6
Area occupied	100 sq. ft.	250 sq. ft.	400 sq. ft.

The expenses incurred during the period were as follows :

	Rs.
Power	275
Lighting	48
Rent and Rates	450
Depreciation	1,350
Repairs	1,800
Indirect Wages	460
Canteen Expenses	51
Sundries	300

Compute the Machine Hour Rate for each machine.

[C.U. B.Com. (Hons.)]

Ans. : (i) Rs. 5.90 ; (ii) Rs. 9.82 ; (iii) Rs. 13.65.

Hint : Sundries have been apportioned on the basis of cost of machines.

55. A machine costing Rs. 12,000 is expected to run for 10 years and, at the end of its life, its scrap value is expected to be Rs. 2,000. Repairs and maintenance charges during the whole life of the machine are likely to be Rs. 2,960. The machine is expected to run 4,320 hours per year on an average. Electricity consumed by the machine is 20 units per hour and the rate per unit of electricity is Re. 0.10. The machine occupies $\frac{1}{3}$rd of the area of the department and the monthly rent of the department is Rs. 600. There are 5 light points over the machine out of 20 light points in the department and the lighting charges amount Rs. 200 per month. The foreman has to devote about 1–5th of his time to the machine and he is paid Rs. 850 per month. Wages paid to direct workers engaged on the machine amount to Rs. 1,000 per month. Expenses on oil, grease etc. are Rs. 1,200 per year and insurance charges are Rs. 600 per quarter. Find out the Machine Hour Rate.

[N.B.U. B.Com. (Hons.)]

Ans : Rs. 4.92

56. From the following particular compute machine-hour rate of machine no. 102 :

Cost of the machine	10,00,000
Import duty	10,000
Installation cost	30,000
Scrap value	5,000
Depreciation	10% p.a.
Other expenses per annum :	
Insurance for the machine	Rs. 250 per quarter
Rent for the shop	Rs. 1,000 per quarter
The machine occupies $\frac{1}{4}$ area of the shop.	
Electricity for shop	Rs. 500 p.m.
The machine consumes 40 units per hour.	
Cost of electricity is Rs. 2.50 per 10 units.	

The machine works for 250 days of 8 hours per day in a year.

Ans : Machine Hour Rate Rs. 18.50

57. Compute the Machine Hour Rate from the following data :

	Rs.
Cost of Machine	1,00,000
Installation charges	10,000
Estimated scrap value after the expiry of its life (15 years).	5,000
Rent and Rates for the shop per month	200
	Rs.
General lighting for the shop per month	300
Insurance Premium for the machine per annum	960
Repairs and Maintenance expenses per annum	1,000
Power Consumption 10 units per hour –	
Rate of power per 100 units	20
Estimated working hours per annum	2,200
(This includes setting up time of 200 hrs.)	
Shop Supervisor's salary per month	600

The machine occupies $\frac{1}{4}$th of the total area of the shop. The Supervisor is expected to devote $\frac{1}{5}$th of his time for supervising the machine.

[B.Com.(Hons.)]

Ans. : Machine hour rate Rs. 7.95.

58. The following particulars refer to a process in the treatment of material subsequently incorporated in a component forming part of an electrical appliance.

 (a) The original cost of the machine used (Purchased on June 1995) was Rs. 10,000. Its estimated life is 10 years, the estimated scrap value at the end of its life is Rs.1,000, and the estimated working life per year (50 weeks of 44 hours) is 2,200 hours of which machining maintenance etc. is estimated to take up 200 hours.

 No other loss of working time is expected; setting up time, estimated at 5% of total productive time, is regarded as productive time. (Bank holidays are to be ignored).

 (b) Electricity used by the machine during production is 16 units per hour at a cost of 0.09P. per unit. No current is taken during maintenance or setting up.

 (c) The machine requires a chemical solution which is replaced at the end of each week at a cost of Rs. 20 each time.

 (d) The estimated cost of maintenance per year is Rs. 1,200.

 (e) Two attendants control the operation of the machine together with five other identical machines. Their combined weekly wages insurance and the employer's contribution to holiday pay amount to Rs. 120.

 (f) Departmental and general works overheads allocated to this machine for the year 1995-96 amount to Rs. 2,000.

You are required to calculate the machine hour rate necessary to provide for recoupment of the costs of operating the machine.

[C.A. Final, M.Com. Agra]

Ans : Rs. 4.61 per hour

59. A machine shop contains four newly purchased machines, each occupying practically equal amount of space and costing, respectively : A – Rs. 20,000, B – Rs. 25,000, C – Rs. 30,000 and D–Rs. 40,000.

The following are the expenses per annum of the machine shop :

		Rs.
Rent		10,000
Rates and Water		4,250
Light and Heat		3,150
Overhead II		
Power :		Rs.
	A	5,100
	B	5,000
	C	12,000
	D	14,500
Administration		9,500
Running expenses and repairs		20,000

Prepare a machine hour rate for each machine assuming 45-hour week, 50 weeks per year, 80 per cent utilisation and the life of machines being 10 years without any scrap value.

Ans. : Standing charges per machine Rs. 3.74
Machine expenses of Machine A – Rs. 5.87,
B – Rs. 6.58, C – Rs. 11.23, D – Rs. 14.14.

Hint : Running expenses have been apportioned on the basis of capital values.

60. From the following data for the month of March 1990 compute the machine hour rate to be charged in respect of jobs carried out during the month on a Printing Machine in a Job Printing Press.

Cost of the Printing Machine	Rs. 77,000
Estimated life of the machine	10 years
Anticipated Scrap Value	Rs. 5,000
Normal working hours per month	600
Hours spent on trial run and job setting	20
Hours lost due to repairs (normal)	50
Hours lost due to power failures (abnormal)	80
Cost of maintenance materials and wages	3,300
Supervisor's salary	800
Cost of painting ink etc.	2,400
Electricity charges	720
Other fixed charges	3,000
Overhead hours worked to complete job in time	100
Rate of wages per hour (normal)	8
Rate of wages per hour (overtime)	12
Rate of wages per hour (during power failure)	4

[Adapted—I.C.W.A. (Inter)]

Ans. : Machine hour rate – Rs. 16.65
Composite machine hour rate – Rs. 26.05

61. A machine was purchased on January 1, 1990 for Rs. 5 lakhs. The total cost of all machinery inclusive of the new machine was Rs. 75 lakhs.

The following further particulars are available :

Expected life of the machine 10 years.

Scrap value at the end of 10 years Rs. 5,000. Repairs and maintenance for the machine during the year Rs. 2,000. Expected number of the working hours of the machine per year 4,000 hours. Insurance premium annually for all machines Rs. 4,500.

Electricity consumption for the machine per hour (@ 0.75 paise per unit) 25 units.

Area occupied by the machine – 100 sq. ft.

Area occupied by other machines 1,500 sq. ft.

Rent per month of the department Rs. 800.

Lighting charges for 20 points for the whole department, out of which three points are for the machine Rs. 120 per month.

Compute the machine hour rate for the new machine on the basis of the data given above.

[C.A. (Inter) May 1990]

Ans. : Machine hour rate Rs. 31.904

62. From the following details compute comprehensive machine hour rate :
 (i) Cost of the machine Rs. 44,200; Estimated life 10 years; Estimated scrap value Rs. 1,000.
 (ii) Normal working hours for the month 200 hours (the machine works only at 75% capacity).
 (iii) Wages to machineman Rs. 4 per day of 8 hours .
 (iv) Wages for a helper Rs. 2 per day of 8 hours
 (v) Power consumption Rs. 150 per month.
 (vi) Supervision charges apportioned for the machine Rs. 300 per month.
 (vii) Electricity and lighting Rs. 75 per month.
 (viii) Repairs and maintenance (including consumable stores Rs. 50 p.m.) Rs. 150 p.m.
 (ix) Insurance of plant and building (apportioned) per annum Rs. 1,000.
 (x) Other general expenses (overheads) Rs. 2,160 p.a.
 (xi) Workers are paid a fixed D.A. of Rs. 75 p.m.
 (xii) Workers are also paid leave wages @ 10% on their wages and D.A.

[V.U. B.Com. (Hons.) 1993]

Ans. : Rs. 10.98

63. A machine was purchased in January 1992 for 5 lakhs. The total cost of all other machinery in the machine shop was 70 lakhs.

Other particulars are as follows :

Expected life of the machine	10 years
Scrap value at the end of ten years	Rs. 5,000
Repairs and maintenance of the machine during the period of 10 yrs.	Rs. 20,000
Expected number of working hours of the machine per year	4,000 hours
Insurance premium annually for all machinery	Rs. 4,500
Electricity consumption for the machine per hour (@ 75 paise per unit)	25 units
Area ocupied by the machine	100 Sq. metres
Area occupied by other machines	1,500 Sq. metres
Rent per month for the department	Rs. 800
Lighting charges for 20 points for the whole department of which 3 relate to the machine	Rs. 120 p.m.

Compute the machine hour-rate for the new machine on the basis of the above noted data.

[C.U. B.Com. (Pass) 1993]

64. The normal expenses attributable to Machine No. III and the normal hours for which the machine is expected to be utilized in the year 1992 are indicated below :

	Rs.	Rs.
Expenses :		
Fixed		2,000
Variable		
Power	1,500	
Repairs	900	
Lubricants	600	3,000
Total		5,000

Predetermined normal hours of working :

To make ready	200 hours
Running on Jobs	800 hours
Total	1,000 hours

From the date furnished below compute the cost of Job No. 1,200 :

Materials consumed :		
10 units at Rs. 5 p.u.	=	Rs. 50
Machine labour :		
To make ready – 2 hours at Rs. 10.00	=	Rs. 20
Running on Job – 8 hours at Rs. 10.00	=	Rs. 80
		Rs. 150

Ans. : Machine Hour Rate :
Fixed Expenses – Rs. 2.00
Variable Expenses – Rs. 3.75
Total Cost of Job No. 1,200 = Rs. 200.

65. A department is having three machines. The figures indicate the departmental expenses. Calculate the machine hour rate in respect of these machines from the information given below :

	Rs.
Depreciation of machinery	12,000
Depreciation of building	2,880
Repairs to machinery	4,000
Insurance of machinery	800
Indirect wages	6,000
Power	6,000
Lighting	800
Miscellaneous expenditure	4,200
	36,680

	Machine I	Machine II	Machine III
Direct wages	Rs. 1,200	Rs. 2,400	Rs. 2,400
Power units	30,000	10,000	20,000
Number of workers	4	8	8
Light points	8	24	48
Space	400 (Sq. ft)	800 (Sq. ft)	800 (Sq. ft)
Cost of machines	Rs. 3,00,000	Rs.1,20,000	Rs. 1,80,000
Hours worked	200	300	300

[Adapted—I.C.W.A. (Inter)]

Ans. : Machine hour rate –

M_1	M_2	M_3
Rs. 70.48	Rs. 32.77	Rs. 42.71

Comprehensive machine hour rate :

M_1	M_2	M_3
Rs. 76.48	Rs. 40.77	Rs. 50.51

Hints : (i) Misc. Expenses have been apportioned on the basis of Direct wages and indirect wages on the basis of No. of workers.

(ii) Comprehensive machine hour rate includes direct wages of Rs. 1,200 and Rs.2,400 and Rs. 2,400, respectively.

66. The following annual charges are incurred in respect of a machine shop where manual labour is almost nil and where work is done by means of five machines of an exactly similar type and specification :

		Rs.
1.	Rent, Rate (Proportion to the floor space)	4,803
2.	Depreciation on machine	500
3.	Repairs and maintenance for the five machines	1,000
4.	Cost of power consumed @ $6\frac{1}{4}$ paise per unit for the shop	3,750
5.	Electric charges for light in the shop	540
6.	**Attendants** – there are two attendants for the five machines and they are each paid Rs. 60 p.m.	
7.	**Supervision** : There is one supervisor in the shop for the five machines and he is paid Rs. 250 p.m.	
8.	Sundry supplies such as lubricant, jute, cotton waste etc. for the shop.	494
9.	Hire-purchase instalments paid on the machines (including Rs. 300 as interest)	1,200
10.	The machine uses 10 units of power per hour	

Compute the machine hour rate for the year.

[Adapted C.A. (Final)]

Ans : Rs. 2.78 per hour

Hints : Calculation of machine hours

Power consumption for the machine $\frac{1}{5}$th of Rs. 3,750 = 750

Per hour cost $10 \times 6\frac{1}{4}$ p = Rs. 0.625

Machine hours = Rs. 750 ÷ 0.625 = 1,200 hours.

67. Compute machine hour rate of a machine in a shop consisting of three machines occupying equal floor space. Following details are supplied for the machine of which estimated working hours per year are fixed at 2,500 hours in which normal idle time is estimated at 20% of the standard time.

	Rs.
Rent and taxes of the shop p.a.	3,600
General electricity for the shop p.m.	200
Repairs and maintenance expenses for the machine per annum	600
Rate of power charges for 100 units (the machine consumes 10 units per hour)	3
Foreman's salary for supervising all the machines per month	750
Indirect labour cost Rs. 2 per hour for the machine	

The machine costs Rs. 1,30,000 and scrap value is estimated Rs. 10,000 and estimated life 10 years.

The foreman devotes equal time to each machine

[C.U. B.Com. (Hons.)]

Ans. : Machine-Hour Rate Rs. 11.10.

68. A machine shop of a factory has three cost centres having distinct sets of machines. The following estimates are available for the year 1992 :

	Total for the Factory	*Centre I*	*Centre II*	*Centre III*
Value of Machine (in Rs.)	6,50,000	2,00,000	1,50,000	3,00,000
Direct wages (in Rs.)	1,60,000	50,000	50,000	60,000
Power	20,000			
Repairs (Rs.)	65,000			
Insurance (Rs.)	1,300			
Rent (Rs.)	6,000			
Lighting (Rs.)	3,600			
Labour welfare expenses (Rs.)	40,000			
Power of motor (in h.p.)		25	25	25
Floor area (in square metres)		100	200	300
Machine hours		11,150	13,000	31,080
Share of Service expenses	10,000	2,000	3,000	5,000

Machines are depreciated at 10% p.a.

Compute machine hour rate of overhead absorption for each of the centres.

Job X passes through all the three cost centres as stated above and the time required in each centre is Centre I–4 hours, Centre II—3 hours and Centre III—8 hours.

Compute the cost of the job if its direct materials and direct labour cost are estimated at Rs. 500 and Rs. 300, respectively.

[B.U. B.Com. (Hons.)1983]

Ans : (a) I – Rs. 5.51, II – Rs. 4.15 and III – Rs. 3.07

(b) Rs. 859.05

69. During the year ended 31st March 1998 the factory overhead costs of three production departments of an organisation are as under :

Department	Rs.
X	48,950
Y	89,200
Z	64,500

The basis for apportionment of overheads is given below :

Department X Rs. 5 per machine hour for 10,000 hours.

Y 75% of Direct Labour Cost of Rs. 1,20,000

Z Rs. 4 per piece for 15,000 pieces.

Calculate the department wise under-or over-absorption of overheads and present the data in a tabular form.

[I.C.W.A. (Inter) June 93]

Ans. : Over-absorption—X— Rs. 1,050; Y— Rs. 800

Under-absorption—Z—Rs. 4,500

70. In a manufacturing unit, factory overhead was recovered at a predetermined rate of Rs. 25 per man-day. The total factory overhead expenses incurred and the man-days actually worked were Rs. 41,50,000 and 1,50,000 man-days respectively.

Out of the 40,000 units produced during a period, 30,000 units were sold.

On analysing the reasons, it was found that 60% of the unabsorbed overheads were due to defective planning and the rest were attributable to increase in overhead costs. How would unabsorbed overheads be treated in cost accounts ?

[Adapted—C.A (Inter)]

Ans. : Unabsorbed overhead of Rs. 4,00,000. (60% of Rs. 4,00,000, i.e Rs. 2,40,000, to be transferred to Costing Profit and Loss Account 40% of unabsorbed overhead; i.e. Rs. 1,60,000 to be recovered by a supplementary rate of Rs. 4 per unit and to be adjusted against Finished Goods Stock.

71. The expenses of a machine cost centre for a particular month are as under :

		Rs.
(i)	Power	50,000
(ii)	Maintenance and repairs	10,000
(iii)	Machine operator's wages	2,000
(iv)	Supervision	6,000
(v)	Depreciation	40,000

Other particulars are given below :

Products	Rate of production	Production units
A	30 units per hour	1,800
B	10 units per hour	500
C	6 units per hour	300
D	4 units per hour	260

The entire production is to be offered to the Government on 'Cost plus 20%' basis. Materials costs per unit are :

A Rs. 40, B Rs. 60, C Rs. 100, D Rs. 300

Prepare a statement showing product wise 'cost' and 'offer price'.

[Adapted—I.C.W.A.(Inter)]

Ans. : Productwise cost : A Rs. 56, B Rs. 108, C Rs. 180, D Rs. 420.
Offer price A Rs. 67.20, B Rs. 129.60, C Rs. 216, and D Rs. 504.

72. A manufacturing unit has added a new machine to its fleet of five existing machines. The total cost of purchase and installation of the machine is Rs. 7,50,000. The machine has an estimated life of 15 years and is expected to realise Rs. 30,000 as scrap at the end of its working life.

Other relevant data are as follows :

(i) Budgeted working hours is 2,400 based on 8 hours per day for 300 days. This includes 400 hours for plant maintenance.

(ii) Electricity used by the machine is 15 units per hour at a cost of Rs. 200 per unit. No current is drawn during maintenance.

(iii) The machine requires special oil for heating which is replaced once the every month at a cost of Rs. 2,500 on each occasion.

(iv) Estimated cost of maintenance of the machine is Rs. 500 per week of 6 working days.

(v) 3 operators control the operations of the entire battery of six machines and the average wages per person amounts to Rs. 450 per week plus 40% fringe benefits.

(vi) Departmental and general works overheads allocated to the operation during the last year was Rs. 60,000. During the current year it is estimated that there will be an increase of 12.5% of this amount. No incremental overhead is envisaged for the installation of the new machine.

You are required to compute the machine-hour rate for recovery of the running cost of the machine.

[Adapted—I.C.W.A. (Inter) June 1993]

Ans. : Rs. 95

Hints :

(a) Effective Machine Running hours 2,000 hours.

73. A machine shop has 6 identical machines manned by 5 operators. The machine cannot be worked without any operator wholly engaged on it. The original cost of all these 6 machines works out at Rs. 6 lakhs.

The following estimates are available for the year 1999 :

(a)	Normal working hours per month	220 hours
(b)	Absenteeism (without pay) per month	20 hours
(c)	Leave with pay per month	20 hours
(d)	Normal idle time (unavoidable)	20 hours
(e)	Average rate of wages per day of 8 hours	Rs. 40
(f)	Production Bonus	15% of wages
(g)	Cost of power for the period	Rs. 20,700
(h)	Supervision and indirect labour cost for the year	Rs. 8,100
(i)	Light and electricity per annum	Rs. 3,070
(j)	Repairs and maintenance of machines	2% of the value of the machines p.a.
(k)	Insurance charges	Rs. 30,000 p.a.
(l)	General management expenses as allocated for the year	Rs. 84,000
(m)	Depreciation under straight line method	15% on the original cost of machine

You are required to workout a comprehensive Machine Hour Rate for the machine shop.

[Adapted C.U. B.Com.(HOns.) 1999]

Ans. : Comprehensive Machine Hour Rate Rs. 33.

Hint : Effective working hour 9,600 hours.

JOB, BATCH AND CONTRACT COSTING 6

Learning Objectives

SECTION I

1. Job Costing

(i) Definition, (ii) Features, (iii) Applicability, (iv) Pre-requisites, (v) Advantages, (vi) Disadvantages, (vii) Source Documents, (viii) Specimen of Job Cost Sheet, (ix) Procedures, (x) Chart for procedures, (xi) Chart showing an outline of Job Costing, (xii) Accounting entries, (xiii) Worked out problems

SECTION II

2. Batch Costing

(i) Introduction, (ii) Application, (iii) Elements of Cost, (iv) How to find out Economic Batch Quantity (EBQ), (v) Worked out problems, (vi) Assignment.

SECTION III

3. Contract Costing

(i) Introduction, (ii) Definition, (iii) Features, (iv) Accounting Entries, (v) Method of valuation of work certified, (vi) Balance Sheet, (vii) Specimen of Contract Account, (viii) Method of calculation of profit to be taken to Profit & Loss A/c on incompleted contract.

JOB, BATCH AND CONTRACT COSTING 6

SECTION I

JOB COSTING

Introduction

In this chapter we propose to describe job costing and show how the cost of job is built up. The necessary procedures to support job costing have been described and the main records have been illustrated.

Definition

The formal definition is given below :

"That form of specific order costing which applies where work is undertaken to customers' special requirements and each order is comparatively for short duration. The work is carried out within a factory or workshop and moves through processes and operations as a continuously identifiable unit. The term may also be applied to work such as property repairs and the method may be used in the costing of internal capital expenditure jobs" – Terminology.

I.C.M.A., London, defines Job Costing as "that category of basic costing method which is applicable where the work consists of separate contract, jobs or batches each of which is authorised by specific order or contract".

Features of Job Costing

The following are the features of Job Costing :

(i) the production is always against customers' order and not for stock;

(ii) each job has its own characteristics and, therefore, needs special treatment;

(iii) there is no uniformity in the flow of production from department to department;

(iv) the department through which job has to be processed depends purely on the nature of each job;

(v) the work-in-progress differs from period to period according to the number of jobs on hand;

(vi) job cost system is essential, if costs tend to vary markedly from order to order and specific cost date is required for each order;

(vii) under job costing each job or order is given a number.

A system of job costing when applied to certain industries is often referred to by different names :

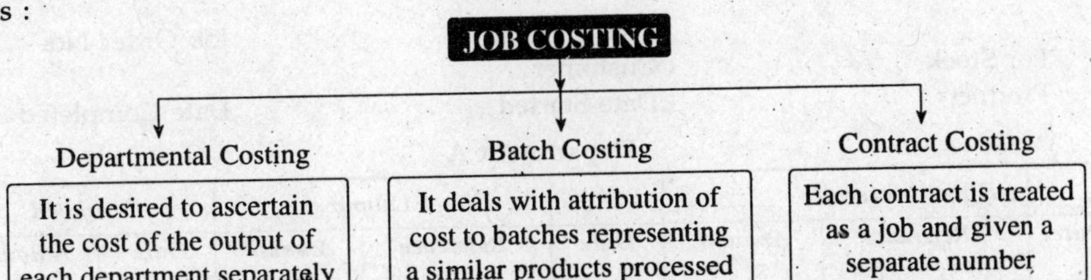

Applicability

Job costing is used by organisations whose products or services can readily be identified by individual units or batches. Each receives varying inputs of direct materials, direct labour and factory overhead. Industries that use job order methods include **construction, printing, aircraft, furniture** and **machinery.**

Non-manufacturing organisations that use job costing include **auto repair, auditing, consulting engagements, hospital cases, social welfare cases** and **research projects.**

Prerequisites for Job Costing

The presence of following factors is necessary to ensure job costing an *effective and workable* system :

1. There must exist a sound system of production control.
2. Comprehensive work documentations which include works order, bill of materials, materials requisition, tool requisitions etc.
3. An appropriate time booking system using either time sheets or piece work tickets.
4. A well organised basis to the costing system with clearly defined cost centres, good labour analysis, appropriate overhead absorption rates and relevant materials issue pricing system.

Advantages

The following are the recognised advantages :

1. Since all costs are compiled, more accurate costing is possible.
2. It is simple as the recording of direct materials and labour hours is done by job.
3. Job cost sheets can be used to attain efficiency and estimate future work.
4. It provides a basis for making comparison of cost of one job with that of the other.
5. Since spoilage and defectives from each job can be known separately, they can be easily controlled.
6. Profitability of each job can be ascertained easily.

Disadvantages

The following are the disadvantages :

1. It requires detailed and separate record keeping for each job.
2. The detailed and separate record keeping for different jobs may prove complicated.
3. Since it involves much clerical work to maintain detailed records it becomes costly.

Source Documents

The following are the relevant documents from which information flow :

(1) *Job Order or Job Cost Sheet :* This is the basic document used by a job order system to accumulate product costs. The job cost sheets for the uncompleted jobs make up the subsidiary ledger for Work-in-Process Control.

Specimen of Job Cost Sheet :

For Stock | X & Company | Job Order No.
Product | Customer |
 | Date Started | Date Completed

Department A

	Direct Material			Direct Labour		Overhead	
Date	Reference	Amount	Date	Reference	Amount	Date	Amount

Fig. 6.1

Department B

Direct Material			*Direct Labour*			*Overhead*	
Date	*Reference*	*Amount*	*Date*	*Reference*	*Amount*	*Date*	*Amount*

Fig. 6.2

Summary of Cost

	Dept. A	Dept. B	Total
Direct Material	X X X	X X X	X X X
Direct Labour	X X X	X X X	X X X
Factory Overhead	X X X	X X X	X X X

(2) *Store requisitions* : Store requisitions are used to charge job cost sheets for direct materials used.

(3) *Work tickets* : Work tickets are used to charge job cost sheets for direct labour used for a job.

(4) *Clock Card* : Clock Card is used for determining individual worker's earning. Each worker is required to punch cards for getting his time of attendance recorded. Many auto-machines must account for the worker's time. From punch cards a worker's hours of work can be ascertained and his wage bill prepared.

Procedures in a jobbing concern

It is necessary to consider the flow of administrative procedures which ensure a job is manufactured correctly, delivered on time and charged for. An outline showing the administrative procedures to complete a job is given below.

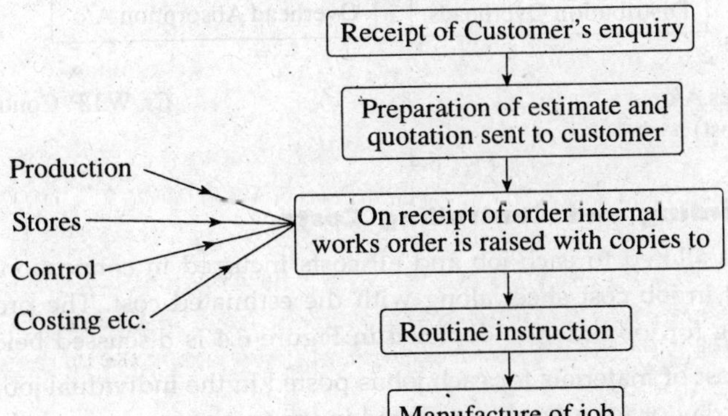

Fig. 6.3

Costing procedures

The main objective is to charge all costs incurred in connection with a particular job. The usual means by which this is done is by creating a job cost card which comprises the firm's work-in-progress and the detailed entries to the job cards would be debited in total to work-in-progress account.

Job Procedures :

An Outline of Job Costing

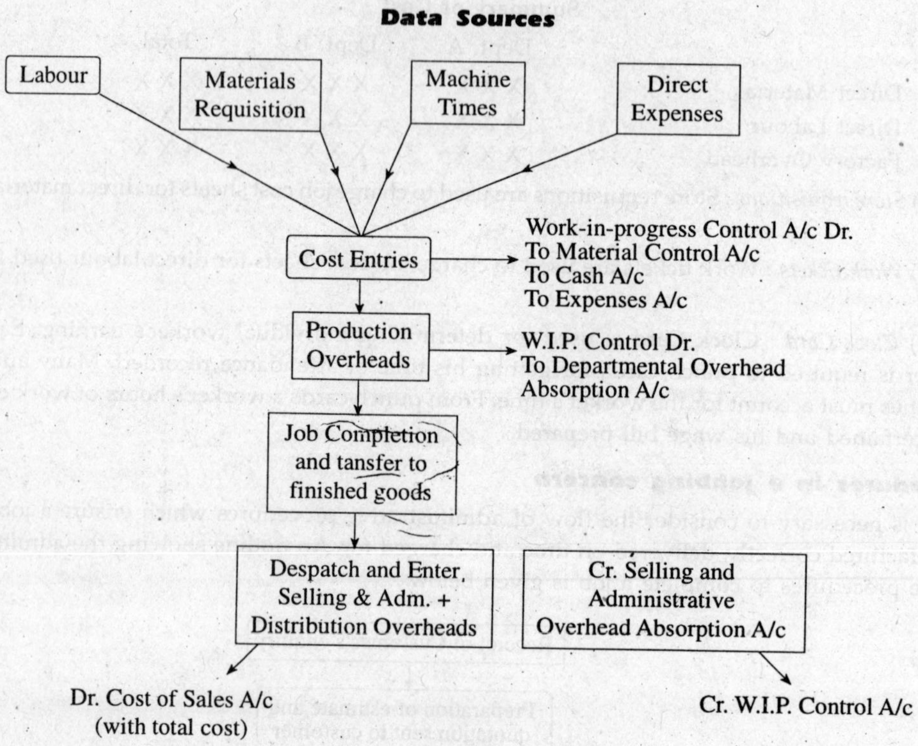

Fig. 6.4

Procedures for Recording and Controlling Costs

A specific number is alloted to each job and all costs incurred in connection with that specific job are recorded in job cost sheet along with the estimated cost. The procedure of recording and accounting for job order as depicted in Figure 6.4 is discussed below :

(1) **Materials :** The cost of materials for each job is posted in the individual job cost sheet and the total issues for a day or for a week are posted in the work-in-progress ledger control account.

Entry : Work-in-Progress Ledger Control A/c Dr.
To Store Ledger Control A/c.

Excess materials, if any, are returned to stores through the document **"Materials Return Note"**. If materials are returned to other job they are recorded in **'Materials Transfer Note'**

(2) **Wages or Labour Costs :** Direct labour costs are recorded through the document 'Job Time Tickets'. Job Time Tickets provide the necessary information to determine the total labour costs since they record the time spent by workers for the completion of the job. Earnings are computed using the workers' hourly rates.

Overtime Payment

A distinction is desired to be made between overtime, that is the time worked over and above the normal working hours, and over time premium, which is the additional remuneration paid over normal rate for worker's efficiency.

When the overtime is worked on a special job or when it is due to the insistence of a customer for completing the job within the specified time, the extra payment for overtime premium is logically charged to the job as direct labour. But, if the overtime is for the purpose of increased output, the cost of such overtime is treated as overhead and charged to a standing order number.

The total labour cost of each job is entered in the job cost accounts and the following entries are passed in cost accounts :

For direct wages : Work-in-Progress Ledger Control A/c Dr.
To Wages Control A/c.

For indirect wages : Factory Overhead Control A/c Dr.
To Wages Control A/c.

(3) **Direct Expenses :** Expenses directly chargeable to jobs are analysed and posted in job cost sheet.

Accounting entry

Work-in-Progress Ledger Control A/c Dr.
To General Ledger Adjustment A/c.

(4) **Overhead :** Overhead consists of cost of indirect materials, indirect wages and indirect expenses. Overhead expenses are apportioned to production and service departments on some appropriate and logical bases. The expenses of service departments are transferred to production departments. The total overhead of production departments (after apportionment) is allocated to products on some realistic bases, such as, machine or labour hour rate, as a percentage on direct wages or direct materials. The specific job is debited with the production overhead.

Accounting entries

(1) For any indirect expense paid : Factory Overhead Control A/c Dr.
To Cost Ledger Control A/c

(2) For charging overhead to job : Work-in-Progress Control A/c Dr.
To Factory Overhead Control A/c

(5) **Completed Job :** When the job is completed, its total cost is determined by totalling prime cost and absorbed overhead cost. The cost sheet is then marked 'completed' and removed from job ledger.

Accounting entires

(i) *For the total cost of completed Job :* Cost of Sales A/c Dr.
To Work-in-Progress Ledger Control A/c

(ii) *The balance of cost of Sales A/c is transferred to Costing Profit & Loss A/c :* Costing P & L A/c Dr.
To Cost of Sales A/c

(iii) For the sale value of job completed : Cost Ledger Control A/c Dr.
To Costing P & L A/c

WORKED OUT PROBLEMS

Problem 1

The account of Fair Deal Ltd. shows for 1998 :	Rs.
Materials used	18,000
Manual and Machine Labour Wages directly chargeable	16,000
Works overhead Expenditure	4,000
Establishment and General Expenses	1,900

(a) Show the works cost and total cost, the percentages that the works overhead cost bears to the Manual and Machine Labour Wages and the percentage that the Establishment and General Expenses bear to the works cost.

(b) What price should the Company quote to manufacture a machine which, it is estimated, will require an expenditure of Rs. 8,000 in material and Rs. 6,000 in wages, so that it will yield a profit of 25% on the total cost or 20% on the selling price.

[Calcutta, B.Com. – Adapted]

Solution

(a) **Job Cost Sheet :**

			Amount
			Rs.
(a) Materials used			18,000
(b) Direct wages			16,000
Prime Cost			34,000
(c) Works Overhead Expenditure – bears to the (b)	$\frac{4,000}{16,000} \times 100$	25%	4,000
Works Cost			38,000
(d) Establishment & General Expenditure			
–bears to Works Cost	$\frac{1,900}{38,000} \times 100$	5%	1,900
Total Cost			39,900

Quotation Price

Details	Amount
	Rs.
(a) Direct Materials	8,000
(b) Direct Wages	6,000
Prime Cost	14,000
(c) Works Overhead – 25% on (b)	1,500
Works Cost	15,500
(d) Establishment & General Expenses—5% on Works Cost	775
Total Cost	16,275
(e) Profit—25% on Total Cost i.e. 20% on selling price	4,069
Selling Price	20,344

Problem 2

The following direct costs were incurred on Job. No. 415 of Standard Radio Company.

			Rs.
Materials			4,010
Wages :	Deptt.	A – 60 hrs. – Rs. 3 per hr.	
	"	B – 40 hrs. – Rs. 2 per hr.	
	"	C – 20 hrs. – Rs. 5 per hr.	

Overhead expenses for these three departments were estimated as follows :

Variable Overheads :

Deptt. A – Rs. 5,000 for 5,000 labour hours
B – Rs. 3,000 for 1,500 labour hours
C – Rs. 2,000 for 500 labour hours

Fixed Overheads : Estimated at Rs. 20,000 for 10,000 normal working hours.

You are required to calculate the cost of Job 415 and calculate the price to give profit of 25% on selling price.

[Madurai, B.Com.]

Solution

STANDARD RADIO COMPANY

Job Cost Sheet

Customer : .... Job No. 415 ....

Job Details : .... Completion Date ....

Date	*MATERIAL COST*		*LABOUR COST*			
	Mat. Req. No.	*Amount*	*Dept.*	*Hours*	*Rate*	*Amount*
		Rs.			Rs.	Rs.
...	......	4,010	A	60	3	180
			B	40	2	80
			C	20	5	100
	Total	4,010		Total		360

OVERHEAD COST | COST SUMMARY

Nature	*Dept.*	*Hours*	*Rate*	*Amount*		*Amount*
				Rs.		Rs.
Variable	A	60	Rs. $\frac{5,000}{5,000}$ = Re. 1	60	Direct Material	4,010
	B	40	Rs. $\frac{3,000}{1,500}$ = Rs. 2	80	Direct Labour	360
					Overhead Costs	460
	C	20	Rs. $\frac{2,000}{500}$ = Rs. 4	80	Total Cost	4,830
				220	Profit – 25% on Selling Price	1,610
Fixed		120	Rs. $\frac{20,000}{10,000}$ = Rs. 2	240	i.e. $33\frac{1}{3}$% on cos	
	Total			460	Selling Price	6,440

Problem 3

By February, 1992 100 units of product X were produced on a Job Order No. 009 which commenced on 26 February, 1992.

The following are the particulars of expenses from which you are to prepare a Job Cost Sheet for the Job Order No. 009.

Materials used		*Wages incurred*	
Date	Rs.	Date	Rs.
26.2.92	60.00	26.2.92 (for 10 hours)	5.00
27.2.92	30.00	27.2.92 (for 50 hours)	25.00
28.2.92	20.00	28.2.92 (for 60 hours)	30.00
29.2.92	25.00	29.2.92 (for 60 hours)	30.00

Overhead expenses are 100% of wages.

[V.U. B.Com.(Hons.) 1992]

Solution

Cost Sheet for Job No. 009

	Rs.	Rs.
Material Cunsumed :		
26.2.92	60.00	
27.2.92	30.00	
28.2.92	20.00	
29.2.29	25.00	135.00
Add : Direct Wages		
26.2.92	5.00	
27.2.92	25.00	
28.2.92	30.00	
29.2.92	30.00	90.00
Prime Cost		225.00
Add : Overheads @ 100% of Wages		90.00
Total Cost		315.00

Problem 4

Budgeted figures :

Estimated factory overhead for the year	Rs. 1,16,000
Estimated direct labour hours for the year	2,32,000
Estimated direct labour cost for the year	Rs. 2,00,000
Estimated machine hours	1,00,000

Prepare a comparative statement of cost showing the result of application of each of the above rates to Job No. 200 from the data given below :

Cost of direct materials consumed	Rs. 1,000
Direct wages	Rs. 1,200
Direct labour hours	500
Machine hours	300

Solution

Overhead application rates

Formula $\frac{\text{Overhead incurred}}{\text{Basis of application}}$

(a) Direct labour hour rate $= \text{Rs.} \frac{1,16,000}{2,32,000} = 0.5$ per direct labour hour

(b) Direct labour cost $= \text{Rs.} \frac{1,16,000}{2,00,000} \times 100 = 58\%$

(c) Machine hours $= \text{Rs.} \frac{1,16,000}{1,00,000} = \text{Rs. } 1.16$ per machine hour

Comparative Statement of Cost of Job No. 200

		Direct labour hour as basis	*Direct Labour cost as basis*	*Machine hour as basis*
		Rs.	Rs.	Rs.
	Direct materials	1,000	1,000	1,000
	Direct wages	1,200	1,200	1,200
	Prime Cost	2,200	2,200	2,200
Add :	Factory Overheads			
	500 × Rs. 0.50	250		
	58% of Rs. 1,200		696	
	300 × Rs. 1.16			348
	Factory Cost	2,450	2,896	2,548

Problem 5

The following is the budget of Joy Engineering works for the year 1993 :

Factory Overhead	Rs. 1,24,000
Direct Labur cost	Rs. 1,96,000
Direct Labur hours	3,10,000 hours
Machine Hours	1,00,000 hours

(i) From the above figures prepare the overhead application rates, using the following mathods :

(a) Direct Labour Hours

(b) Direct Labour Cost

(c) Machine Hours

(ii) Prepare a comparative statement of cost showing the result of application of each of the above rates to Job order No. 501 from the undermentioned data :

Direct Material Cost	Rs. 90
Direct Wages	Rs. 100
Direct Labour Hours	80 hours
Machine Hours	60 hours

[Kalyani University B.Com. (Hons.)1995]

Solution

Calculation overhead application rates

(i) Direct Labour Hours Rates

$$= \frac{\text{Factory Overheads}}{\text{Labour Hours}} = \text{Rs. } \frac{1,24,000}{3,10,000} = \text{Re. 0.40 per hours}$$

(ii) Direct Labour Cost

$$= \frac{\text{Factory Overhead} \times 100}{\text{Direct Labour Cost}} = \text{Rs. } \frac{1,24,000 \times 100}{1,96,000} = 63.265\%$$

(iii) Machine Hours Rate

$$= \frac{\text{Factory Overhead}}{\text{Machine Hours}} = \text{Rs. } \frac{1,24,000}{1,00,000} = \text{Rs. 1.24 per hours}$$

(iv) **Comparative Statement of cost of Job Order No. 501**

	Direct Labour Hours	*Direct Labour Cost*	*Machine Hours*
	Rs.	Rs.	Rs.
Direct Material Cost	90.00	90.00	90.00
Direct Wages	100.00	100.00	100.00
Prime Cost	190.00	190.00	190.00
Add : Factory Overhead	32.00 (80 × 0.40)	63.27	74.40
	222.00	253.27	264.40

Problem 6

The following data relate to manufacture of a statdard product during the four weeks to July 28, 1996 :

Raw Matrials consumed	Rs. 25,000
Manual and Machine Labour Wages (Directly chargeable)	Rs. 15,000
Chargeable expenses	Rs. 4,500
Machine Hours worked	1,000
Machine Hour Rate	Rs. 2.5
Establishment and general expenses	Rs. 4,600
Selling and Distribution overhead per unit	0.08 paise
Units produced	10,000
Units sold	8,000
Selling price per unit	Rs. 6

(a) You are required to prepare a cost sheet in respect of the above showing therein the cost per unit, each element of cost and the profit for the period. Also show the percentage that the works overhead cost bears to the Manual and Machine Labour Wages and the percentage that the establishment and general expenses bear to the works cost.

(b) What price should the company quote to produce 1,000 units of another product which will require an expenditure of Rs. 8,000 for raw materials and Rs. 6,000 for direct wages, so that it will yield a profit of 25% on the cost of sales.

[C.U. B.Com. (Hons.) 1997]

Solution

(a)

Cost Sheet

for the four weeks to July, 1996

		Total Cost	Cost per unit
		Rs.	Rs.
Raw Materials consumed		25,000	2.50
Manual and Machine Labour Wages		15,000	1.50
		40,000	4.00
Chargeable Expenses		4,500	0.45
Prime Cost		44,500	4.45
Add : Factory Overhead Machine Hours Worked × Machine Hour Rate	1,000 × 2.5	2,500	0.25
Works Cost		47,000	4.70
Add : Office & Administration Overhead Establishment and general Expenses		4,700	0.47
Cost of Production		51,700	5.170
Less : Closing Stock of finished goods		10,340	1.034
Cost of goods Sold		41,360	4.136
Add : Selling & Distribution Overhead	8,000 × 0.08	640	0.064
Cost of sales/total cost		42,000	4.200
Add : Profit		6,000	0.600
Sales Price	8,000 × 6	48,000	4.800

(a) Percentage of works overhead to wages = Rs. $\frac{2,500 \times 100}{15,000}$ = 16.67%

(b) Percentage of general and Establishment = $\frac{4,700 \times 100}{47,000}$ = 10%

Notes : Value of closing stock of finished goods :

Cost of 2,000 units @ Rs. 5.17 = Rs. 10,340.

(b)

Estimated Cost Sheet for 1,000 Units

		Rs.	Rs.
	Rawmaterials		8,000
	Direct Wages		6,000
	Prime Cost		14,000
Add :	Work overhead @ 16.67% of direct wages	$6,000 \times \frac{16.67}{100}$	1,000
	Works Cost		15,000
Add :	Office and Administrative Overhead		
	@ 10% of works cost	$\frac{10}{100} \times 15,000$	1,500
	Cost of Production		16,500
Add :	Selling Overhead @ 0.08 p. per unit	1,000 × 0.08	80
	Cost of Sales		16,580
Add :	Profit @ 25% on cost	25% of Rs. 16,580	4,145
	Price tobe quoted		20,725

So, Price to be quoted = Rs. 20,725.

Problem 7

The following direct costs were incurred on Job No. 100 of an engineering works :

		Rs.
Materials		3,415
Wages :	Dept. 1 : 80 hours – Rs. 2.50 per hour	
	Dept. 2 : 60 hours – Rs. 4.00 per hour	

The overhead expenses were estimated as follows :

Variable : Dept. 1 : Rs. 5,000 for 4,000 direct labour hours.

Dept. 2 : Rs. 6,000 for 3,000 direct labour hours.

Fixed : Rs. 7,500 for 10,000 hours being the normal working hours of the factory.

Calculate the cost of Job No. 100 and estimate the percentage of profit earned if the price quoted at Rs. 4,750.

[Madras, B.Com.]

Solution

JOB COST SHEET (JOB NO. 100)

Details		Rs.	Rs.
Direct Materials			3,415
Direct Wages – (Dept. 1 : 80 × Rs. 2.50) +	(Dept. 2 : 60 × Rs. 4.00)		440
Overhead Expenses : (a) Variable :	Dept. 1 – 80 × Rs. 5,000 ÷ 4,000	100	
	Dept. 2 – 60 × Rs. 6,000 ÷ 3,000	120	
			220
(b) Fixed : (80+60) = 140 hrs. × Rs. 7,500 ÷10,000			105
Total Cost			4,180
Profit (13.6% on cost) – balancing figure			570
Sales Price			4,750

Problem 8

A factory is engaged in making standard products which pass through three departments. The Cost figures of the factory for the month of November, 1994 are furnished below :

Name of Expense	*Total*	*Dept. 'A'*	*Dept. 'B'*	*Dept. 'C'*
	Rs.	Rs.	Rs.	Rs.
Direct Material used	18,600	7,500	6,400	4,700
Labour Cost	15,000	6,000	5,000	4,000
Total Overhead expenses	7,500	3,000	2,500	2,000
	41,100	16,500	13,900	10,700

Prepare a simple cost sheet for products X and Y on the basis of the data furnished below :

		Dept. 'A'	Dept. 'B'	Dept. 'C'
		Rs.	Rs.	Rs.
Product X –	Materials	100	200	300
	Labour	50	60	70
Product Y –	Materials	50	90	140
	Labour	70	60	20

[Bangalore M.Com. – Adapted]

Solution

JOB COST SHEET

Customer ....

Products : X & Y

Job Details ....

MATERIALS | LABOUR COST

Dept.	*Product X*	*Product Y*	*Dept.*	*Product X*	*Product Y*
	Rs.	Rs.		Rs.	Rs.
A	100	50	A	50	70
B	200	90	B	60	60
C	300	140	C	70	80
Total	600	280	Total	180	210

OVERHEADS | COST SUMMARY

Dept.	*Product X*	*Product Y*	*Elements*	*Product X*	*Product Y*
	Rs.	Rs.		Rs.	Rs.
A	25	35	Materials	600	280
B	30	30	Labour Cost	180	210
C	35	40	Overheads	90	105
Total	90	105	Total Cost	870	595

Problem 9

A factory uses job costing. The following data are obtained from its books for the year ended 31st, December, 1989.

	Rs.		Rs.
Direct Materials	90,000	Selling & Distribution Overheads	52,500
Direct Wages	75,000	Administrative Overheads	42,000
Profit	60,900	Factory Overheads	45,000

(a) Prepare a Job Cost Sheet indicating the Prime Cost, Works Cost, Production Cost, Cost of Sales and Sales Value.

(b) In 1990, the factory receives an order for a number of jobs. It is estimated that direct materials required will be Rs. 1,20,000 and direct labour will cost Rs. 75,000. What should be the price for these jobs if factory intends to earn the same rate of profit on sales assuming that the selling and distribution overheads have gone up by 15% ? The factory recovers factory overheads as a percentage of direct wages and administration and selling and distribution overheads as a percentage of works cost, based on cost rates prevailing in the previous year.

[C.A. Inter – Adapted]

Solution

JOB COST SHEET

(a)

Details	%	Amount
		Rs.
(1) Direct Materials		90,000
(2) Direct Wages		75,000
Prime Cost		1,65,000
(3) Factory Overheads		
Related to Direct wages as $\left(\frac{45,000}{75,000} \times 100\right)$	60	45,000
Factory Cost		2,10,000
(4) Administrative Overheads		
Related to Factory Cost $\left(\frac{42,000}{2,10,000} \times 100\right)$	20	42,000
Cost of Production		2,52,000
(5) Selling & Distribution Overheads $\left(\frac{\text{Rs. } 52,500}{2,10,000} \times 100\right)$	25	52,500
Cost of Sales (a + b + c + d + c)		3,04,500
(6) Profit – Related to Sales $\left(\frac{60,900}{3,65,400} \times 100\right)$	16.67	60,900
(7) Sales		3,65,400

(b)

Estimated Cost Sheet for 1990

		Amount
		Rs.
(1)	Direct Materials	1,20,000
(2)	Direct Wages	75,000
	Prime Cost	1,95,000
(3)	Factory Overheads – 60% of Direct Wages	45,000
	Factory Cost	2,40,000
(4)	Administrative Overhead – 20% of Factory Cost	48,000
	Cost of Production	2,88,000
(5)	Selling and Distribution Overheads 25% of Rs. 2,40,000 + 15% of Rs. 60,000	69,000
	Cost of Sales	3,57,000
(6)	Profit – 16.67% on Sales i.e. $\frac{1}{5}$th on cost	71,400
	Sales Price	4,28,400

Problem 10

The budgeted costs of a manufacturing company for a normal year are as follows :

	Rs.	Rs.
Direct Materials		68,273
Direct Wages :		
Machine Shop (10,000 hours)	27,382	
Assembly Shop (8,000 hours)	22,780	50,162
Works Overhead		
Machine Shop	33,490	
Assembly	16,237	49,727
Administration Overhead		12,268
Selling Overhead		15,481
Distribution Overhead		13,290

The absorption method of costing is in operation. You are required to :

(1) prepare a schedule of overhead rates for this business from figures available ;

(2) prepare cost estimate for the following job based on the overhead rates so computed :

Direct Material : 20 kg ... Rs. 12 per kg.
15 kg ... Rs. 2 per kg.

Direct Labour : Machine Shop 15 hrs. at Rs. 6 per hour.
Assembly 25 hours at Rs. 7 per hour.

[I.C.W.A. Inter.]

Solution

1. **Schedule of Overhead Rates :**

(a) *Works Overhead :*		
(i) Machine Shop :	It has to work for 10,000 hrs. at a cost of Rs. 33,490, hence the rate is Rs. 33,490 ÷ 10,000 hrs.	Rs. 3.349 per hr.
(ii) Assembly Shop :	It has to work for 8,000 hrs. at a cost of Rs. 16,237, hence, the rate is Rs. 16,237 ÷ 8,000 hrs.	Rs. 2.03 per hr.
(b) *Percentage of Administration Overhead on Works Cost :* Works Cost = Direct Materials + Direct Wages + Works Overhead = 68,273 + 50,162 + 49,727 = Rs. 1,68,162. The percentage of Admn. Overhead on Works Cost = (12,268 × 100) ÷ Rs. 1,68,162		7.295%
(c) *Percentage of Selling & Distribution Overhead on Cost of Production :*		
Cost of Production	= Works Cost + Administration Overhead = Rs. 1,68,162 + 12,268 = Rs. 1,80,430	
∴ The Percentage	= [(15,481 + 13,290) × 100] × 1,80,430	15.946%

2. **Estimate of Cost for the Job :**

Detail		Rs. P.	Rs. P.
(a) Direct Materials :	20 kg ...... Rs. 12 per kg.	240.00	
	15 kg ...... Rs. 2 per kg.	30.00	270.00
(b) Direct Labour :	(i) Machine Shop 15 hrs. ... Rs. 6 per hr.	90.00	
	(ii) Assembly Shop 25 hrs. ... Rs. 7	175.00	265.00
(c) Works Overhead	(i) Machine Shop – 15 hrs. ... Rs. 3.349	50.24	
	(ii) Assembly Shop – 25 hrs. ... Rs. 2.03	50.75	100.99
(d) Works Cost (a + b + c)			635.99
(e) Administration Overhead = 7.295% on (d)			46.40
(f) Cost of Production			682.39
(g) Selling and Distribution Overhead = 15.946% on (f)			108.81
Total Estimated Cost			791.20

Problem 11

M/s. Perfect Printers Limited, is operating a printing press. During November 1989, the plant was operating at full capacity. The material and labour costs of Job 101, and all other jobs worked on, in November, are shown below :

	Job 101	All other jobs	Total Rs.
Material	10,000	70,000	80,000
Direct labour	12,000	28,000	40,000
Overtime premium	4,000		4,000

In addition to the foregoing costs, factory overhead incurred in November amounted to Rs. 40,000. Overhead is allocated to production on the basis of direct labour costs.

You are required to :

(i) Show what the factory profit or loss on Job 101 would be, using two different methods of accounting for overtime premium. Assume that the contract price for this job is Rs. 40,000

(ii) Indicate under what circumstances each method should be used.

(iii) State whether the profit or loss of the company during November would be affected by the choice of one method or another.

[I.C.W.A. – Inter. Adapted]

Solution

(i) (a) If overtime premium is fully charged to Job 101 :

JOB COST SHEET	JOB NO. 101	
		Rs.
	Materials	10,000
	Direct labour including overtime (12,000 + 4,000)	16,000
	Factory Overhead (recovered @ 100% of Direct Labour)	16,000
	Total Cost	42,000
Less :	Contract price	40,000
	Loss	2,000

(b) If overtime premium is charged pro rata to all the jobs :

	Rs.
Materials	10,000
Direct labour including overtime $\left[\text{Rs. } 12{,}000 + \left(4{,}000 \times \frac{12}{40}\right)\right]$	13,200
Factory Overhead (100% of Direct Labour)	13,200
Total Cost	36,400
Less : Contract price	40,000
Profit	3,600

Problem 12

An article undergoes three successive operations from raw materials to finished product stage. The following information is available from the production records of a particular period :

Operation No.	*No. of pieces put in*	*No. of pieces rejected*	*No. of pieces Output*
1.	36,000	12,000	24,000
2.	39,600	3,600	36,000
3.	28,800	4,800	24,000

Find what should be the input in the first operation and number of pieces to obtain a finished product of 100 pieces after the last product. Calculate cost of raw material required to produce one piece of finished product from the following particulars.

Weight of finished piece	100 gm. per piece.
Price of Raw Material	Rs. 10 per kg.

[I.C.W.A.—Adapted]

Solution

JOB COST SHEET

Operation No.	No. pieces put in	No. of Rejects	No. of output	Rejects (in %)	Ratio of in put to output of 100	Raw Material for 100 gm. of finished product
1	36,000	12,000	24,000	50%	198	198 gm.
2	39,600	3,600	36,000	10%	132	132 gm.
3	28,800	4,800	24,000	20%	120	120 gm.

Note : From the above Job Cost Sheet it is found that 198 number of pieces are to be put in the first operation to get 100 pieces of finished product. Raw material, cost of finished pieces of 100 gm. will be $\left[198 \times \left(\frac{10}{1,000}\right)\right]$ = Rs. 1.98.

Problem 13

The estimated material cost of a job is Rs. 5,000 and direct labour cost is likely to be Rs. 1,000. In machine shop it will require machining by Machine No. 8 for 20 hours, and by Machine No. 11 for 6 hours. Machine hour rates for Machine No. 8 and Machine No. 11 are respectively Rs. 10 and 15. Considering only machine shop cost, the direct wages in all other shops last year amounted to Rs. 80,000 as against Rs. 48,000 factory overhead. Last year factory cost of all jobs amounted to Rs. 2,50,000 as against Rs. 37,500 office expenses.

Prepare a quotation which guarantees 20% profit on selling price.

[Madras, M.Com.]

Solution

QUOTATION

	Rs.	Rs.
(a) Materials Cost of the job		5,000
(b) Direct Wages		1,000
Prime Cost (a + b)		6,000
(c) Factory Overheads : For Machine No. 8 – 20 hours – Rs. 10	200	
For Machine No. 11 – 6 hours – Rs. 15	90	
Factory on cost in the last year was $\left(\frac{48,000}{80,000} \times 100\right)$ = 60% of wages	290	
∴ For the subject job $\left(\text{Rs. } 1,000 \times \frac{60}{100}\right)$	600	890
Factory Cost (a + b + c)		6,890
(d) Administrative Overhead		
Last year it was $\left(\frac{37,500}{2,50,000} \times 100\right)$ = 15% of Factory cost		
For the job – 15% of Rs. 6,890		1,034
Cost of Production		7,924
(e) Profit (20% on Sales) i.e. 25% on cost $\frac{25}{100}$ × Rs. 7,924		1,981
Selling Price		9,905

Problem 14

You are required to prepare a Cost Sheet of an engineering works showing the actual and estimated costs of a batch of 100 units from the following information :

The batch passes through 3 departments, A, B and C. Materials used for the batch :

Dept. A : 600 units at Rs. 10 per unit.

Dept. C : 50 units at Rs. 20 per unit.

Factory Labour :

Dept. A : 100 hours at Rs. 2 per hour.

Dept. B : 20 hours at Rs. 2.50 per hour.

Dept. C : 100 hours at Rs. 1.50 per hour.

Factory Overhead :

Dept. A : 150 per cent on direct wages.

Dept. B : at Rs. 10 per labour hour.

Dept. C : $66\frac{2}{3}\%$ on the direct wages.

After the batch is complete, 100 units of raw materials issued to Dept. A are found to be surplus and returned to Stores.

A comparison of the actual costs with the estimated costs of the direct material and the factory overhead has shown that the actual costs exceed the respective estimated costs by 20%, whereas the estimated labour cost is 25% higher than actual costs.

You are required to show in the Cost Sheet, the costs of the batch and the difference between the estimated costs and the actual costs. Show detailed working separately.

[Bangalore, M.Com.]

Solution

Job COST SHEET

Customer .... Job No. ....

Job Details .... Batch Size : 100 Units

MATERIALS				LABOUR			
Dept.	*Actual*	*Estimated*	*Variance*	*Dept.*	*Actual*	*Estimated*	*Variance*
Rs.	Rs.	Rs.		Rs.	Rs.	Rs.	
A	5,000 (Rs. 6,000 – 1,000).	4,167 (5/6th of Rs. 5,000)	833(A)	A	200	250 (5/4th of Rs. 200).	50 (F)
B	...	...	...	B	50	63 (5/4th of Rs. 50).	13 (F)
C	1,000	833 (5/6th of Rs. 1,000)	167 (A)	C	150	188 (5/4th of Rs. 150)	38 (F)
Total	6,000	5,000	1,000(A)	Total	400	501	101(F)

OVERHEADS				COST SUMMARY			
Dept.	*Actual*	*Estimated*	*Variance*	*Elements*	*Actual*	*Estimated*	*Variance*
	Rs.	Rs.	Rs.		Rs.	Rs.	Rs.
A	300 (150% of Rs. 200)	250 (5/6th of Rs. 300)	50(A)	Materials	6,000	5,000	1,000(A)
B	200 (20 × 10)	167 (5/6th of Rs. 200)	33(A)	Labour	400	501	101(F)
C	100 ($66\frac{2}{3}$% of Rs 150)	83 (5/6th of Rs. 100)	17(A)	Overheads	600	500	100(A)
Total	600	500	100(A)	Total	7,000	6,001	999(A)

Problem 15

As a newly appointed Cost Accountant you find that the selling price of Job No. 1,000 has been calculated on the following basis :

	Rs.
Materials	12.08
Direct Wages – 22 hours as 0.25 per hour	5.50
(Department A – 10 hours	
B – 4 hours	
C – 8 hours)	
Prime Cost	17.58
Plus $33\frac{1}{3}$% on Prime Cost	5.86
Total	23.44

An analysis of the previous years P. & L. A/c. showed the following :

	Rs.	Rs.		Rs.
Material used		77,500	Sales	1,35,000
Direct Wages :				
Dept. A	5,000			
Dept. B	6,000			
Dept. C	4,000	15,000		
Factory Overhead :				
Dept. A	2,500			
Dept. B	4,000			
Dept. C	1,000	7,500		
Gross Profit c/d		35,000		
		1,35,000		1,35,000
Selling Costs		30,000	By Gross Profit b/d	35,000
Net Profit		5,000		
		35,000		35,000

You are required to : (a) Draw up a Job Cost Sheet.

(b) Calculate and enter the revised costs using the previous year's figure as a basis.

(c) Add to the total job cost 10% for profit and give the final selling price.

Solution

Calculation Factory Overhead rates

		Rs.
Dept. A :		
Factory Overhead		2,500
Direct Labour Hours :		
$\frac{\text{Total wages}}{\text{Hourly rate}}$	= Rs. $\frac{5,000}{0.25}$	20,000
Rate per hour (Rs. 2,500 ÷ 20,000)		0.125
Dept. B :		
Factory Overhead		4,000
Direct Labour Hours (Rs. 6,000 ÷ 0.25)		24,000
Rate per Hour		0.167
Dept. C :		
Factory Overhead		1,000
Direct Labour Hours (Rs. 4,000 ÷ 0.25)		16,000
Rate per Hour		0.063

Selling Cost : Rs. 30,000

Work Cost = Rs. 1,00,000 (i.e. Rs. 77,500 + 15,000 + 7,500)

% of Selling Cost on Works Cost = Rs. $\frac{30,000}{1,00,000} \times 100 = 30\%$.

JOB COST SHEET	JOB NO. 1234	
	Rs.	Rs.
Materials :		12.08
Direct Wages :		
Dept. A	2.50	
Dept. B	1.00	
Dept. C	2.00	5.50
Prime Cost		17.58
Factory Overhead		
Dept. A (10 hrs. @ Re. 0.125)	1.25	
Dept. B (4 hrs. @ Re. 0.167)	0.67	
Dept. C (8 hrs. @ Re. 0.063)	0.50	2.42
Works Cost		20.00
Selling Cost (30% of Works Cost)		6.00
Cost of Sales		26.00
Profit (10% on Cost)		2.60
Selling Price		28.60

Problem 16

In a factory following the Job Costing Method, an abstract from the Work-in-Process as at 30th September, 1990 was prepared as under :

Job No.	*Materials*	*Direct Labour*		*Factory Overheads*
	Rs.		Rs.	Rs.
115	1,325	400 hrs.	800	640
118	810	250 hrs.	500	400
120	765	300 hrs.	475	380
Total	2,900		1,775	1,420

Materials used in October, 1990 were as follows :

Materials Requisition	*Job No.*	*Cost*
		Rs.
54	118	300
55	118	425
56	118	515
57	120	665
58	121	910
59	124	720
		3,535

A summary of Labour Hours deployed during October, 1990 is as under :

Job No.	Number of hours.	
	Shop A	Shop B
115	25	25
118	90	30
120	75	10
121	65	–
124	20	10
	275	75
Indirect Labour		
Waiting for material	20	10
Machine breakdown	10	5
Idle time	5	6
Overtime premium	6	5

A shop credit slip was issued in October, that materials issued under requisition No. 54 was returned back to stores as being not suitable. A material transfer note issued in October indicated that the material issued under Requisition No. 55 for Job 118 was directed to Job 124.

The hourly rate in shop A per labour is Rs. 3 per hour while at shop B it is Rs. 2 per hour. The Factory Overhead is applied at the same rate as in September. Jobs 115, 118 and 120 were completed in October, 1990.

You are asked to compute the factory cost of the completed jobs. It is the practice of the management to put a 10% on the factory cost to cover administration and selling overheads and invoice the job to the customer on a total cost plus 20% basis. What would be the invoice price of these three jobs ?

[C.A. (Inter) Nov. 1985]

Solution

Statement showing the Cost and Invoice price of 3 Jobs.

Particulars	Job 115 Rs.	Job 118 Rs.	Job 120 Rs.
September, 1990			
Materials	1,325	810	765
Direct wages	800	500	475
Factory Overhead	640	400	380
(a)	2,765	1,710	1,620
October, 1990			
Materials used (Note 1)		515	665
Direct labour Shop A	75	270	225
Shop B	50	60	20
(as per Note 2)	125	845	910
Factory Overheads @ 80% of Direct Labour	100	264	196
(b)	225	1,109	1,106
Total Works Cost (a + b)	2,990.00	2,819.00	2,726.00
Administrative and Selling overheads at 10% on works cost	299.00	281.90	272.60
Total Cost	3,289.00	3,100.90	2,998.60
Profit at 20% on total cost	657.80	620.18	599.72
Invoice Price	3,946.80	3,721.08	3,598.32

Note 1 :

Cost of Materials consumed in October		Job 115 Rs.	Job 118 Rs.	Job 120 Rs.
As per Requisitions No. 54 to 56			1240	
Less: Materials transferred to Job 124	Rs. 425			
Less: Materials returned	Rs. 300		725	
			515	
As per Requisition No. 57				665

Note 2 :

Labour Cost	Job 115	Job 118	Job 120
Shop A (Labour hour × R)	25 × 3 = 75	90 × 3 = 270	75 × 3 = 225
Shop B (Labour hour × R)	25 × 2 = 50	30 × 2 = 60	10 × 2 = 20

Note 3 :

Factory Overhead as a percentage of direct wages :

$$\text{Job 115} = \frac{640 \times 100}{800} = 80\%$$

$$\text{Job 118} = \frac{400 \times 100}{500} = 80\%$$

$$\text{Job 120} = \frac{380 \times 100}{475} = 80\%$$

Problem 17

You are presented with the following information by Om Engineering Company relating to the first week of December, 1986 :

(a) **Matrials :** The transactions in connection with the materials are as follows :

Days	*Receipts* Units Rs.	Rate per unit	*Issues* (Units)
1st	400	15.00	—
2nd	20	16.50	—
3rd	—	—	30
4th	50	17.10	—
5th	—	—	20
6th	—	—	40

Calculate the cost of materials issued under FIFO method, LIFO method and weighted average method of issue of materials and value of closing stock under the methods aforesaid and discuss from different points of view which methods you would prefer.

(b) **Labour :** The firm employs five workers at an hourly rate of Rs. 200. During the week they worked for four days for a total period of 40 hours each and completed a job for which the standard time was 48 hours for each worker.

Calculate the labour cost under the Halsey method and Rowan method of incentive plan payments.

(c) Compute the prime cost of the job completed under different methods of valuing material issues and calculation of labour costs.

[A.C.S. Inter Dec. 1986]

Solution

(a) Statement of Cost of materials Issued and Value of closing stock

Day	*Receipts*			*Issues*					
				FIFO Method			*LIFO Method*		
	Units	*Rate*	*Amount*	*Units*	*Rate*	*Amount*	*Units*	*Rate*	*Amount*
1st	40	15.00	600						
2nd	20	16.50	330						
3rd				30	15.00	450	20	16.50	330
4th	50	17.10	855				10	15.0	150
5th				10	15.00	150	20	17.10	342
				10	16.50	165			
6th				10	17.50	165	30	17.10	513
				30	17.10	513	10	15.00	150
Total :	110		1,785	90		1,443	90		1,485
				20		342	20		300
				110		1,785	110		1,785

Sotres Ledger —Weighted Average Method

Day	Receipts			Issues			Balance of Stock		
	Units	Rate	Amount	Units	Rate	Amount	Units	Rate	Amount
1st	40	15.00	600				40	15.00	600
2nd	20	16.50	330				60	$\frac{930}{60}$ = 15.50	930
3rd				30	15.50	465	30		465
4th	50	17.10	855				80	$\frac{930}{60}$ = 16.50	1,320
5th				20	16.50	330	60		990
6th				40	16.50	660	20		330
Total :	110		1,785	90		1,455			

				Hours	
(b) Standard time	=	5 × 48	=	240	(i.e., Time Allowed).
Hours worked	=	5 × 40	=	200	
Time saved				40	

Halsey Method : $E = HW \times RH + (50\% \times TS \times RH)$

$= 200 \times 2 + (50\% \times 40 \times 2) = 400 + 40 =$ Rs. 440

Rowan Method : $E = HW \times RH + \left(\frac{TS}{TA} \times HW \times RH\right)$

$= 200 \times 2 + \left(\frac{40}{240} \times 200 \times 2\right)$

$= 400 + 67 =$ Rs. 467.

(c)

Statement of Prime Cost of the Job

Cost Element	FIFO Halsey	FIFO Rawan	LIFO Halsey	LIFO Rowan	Weighted Average Halsey	Weighted Average Rowan
Material Cost	1,443	1,443	1,485	1,485	1,455	1,455
Labour Cost	440	467	440	467	440	467
Prime Cost of the Job	1,883	1,910	1,925	1,952	1,895	1,922

Problem 18

A company has two manufacturing shops. The shopfloor supervisor presented the following cost for *Job No. A* to determine the selling price :

	Rs. (Per Unit)
Material	70
Direct wages 14 hrs. @ Rs. 2:50 per hour (Deptt. X-8 hrs. ; and Deptt. Y-6 hrs).	35
Chargeable expenses (stores)	5
	110
Add : 33 for expenses (overheads)	37
	147

Analysis of the profit and Loss account shows the following :

		Rs.		Rs.
Material used		1,50,000	Sales less returns	2,50,000
Direct wages :				
Deptt. X	10,000			
Deptt. Y	12,000			
		22,000		
Store expenses		4,000		
Overheads :				
Deptt. X	5,000			
Deptt. Y	9,000			
		14,000		
		1,90,000		
Gross profit c/d		60,000		
		2,50,000		2,50,000

It is noted that average hourly rates for the two department, X and Y are similar.

You are reuired to :

(i) Draw up a job cost sheet.

(ii) Calculate the revised cost using overheads figures shown in the profit and loss account as the basis for charging overheads to Deptt. X and Y.

(iii) Add 20% of total cost to determine price

[C.S. (Inter) June 91]

Solution

Working notes :

Overheads absorption on the basis of direct wages :

$$\text{Dept. X} = \frac{\text{Overheads}}{\text{Direct wages}} \times 100$$

$$= \frac{5{,}000}{10{,}000} \times 100 = 50\% \text{ of Direct Wages}$$

$$\text{Dept. Y} = \frac{9{,}000}{12{,}000} \times 100 = 75\% \text{ of Direct Wages}$$

Job Cost Sheet

Job No. A — Date started

Description — Date completed

Particulars	*Rate (hours)*	*Qty. (Rs.)*	*Amount*
Materials			70.00
Direct Wages :			
Deptt. X	2.50	8 × Rs. 2.50 = 20	
Deptt. Y	2.50	6 × Rs. 2.50 = 15	
			35.00
Chargeable expenses (store)			5.00
Prime Cost			110.00
Overhead :			
Deptt. X	50% of	20 = 10.00	
(50% of direct wages)			
Deptt. Y	75% of	15 = 11.25	
(75% of direct wages)			21.25
Total Cost			131.25
Add : 20% of total cost			26.25
Selling Price			157.50

Problem 19

You are presented with the following information by Sphinx Engineering Co. relating to the first week of September, 1992 :

A. Materials – The transactions in connection with the materials are as follows :

Days	*Receipts*		*Issues*
	Units	*Rate*	*Units*
		Rs.	
1st	40	15	
2nd	20	16.50	
3rd			30
4th	50	14.30	
5th			20
6th			40

Calculate cost of materials issued under FIFO and Weighted Average Method of issue of materials.

B. Labour – The firm employs 5 workers at an hourly rate of Rs. 2.00. During the week they worked for 4 days for a total period of 40 hours each and completed a job for which the standard time was 48 hours for each worker.

Calculate the labour cost under Halsey and Rowan method of incentive plan payments.

C. Compute the prime cost of a Job completed under the different methods of valuing materials issues and calculation of labour costs.

[Adapted – I.C.W.A. (Inter)]

Solution

Step I

Preparation of Store Ledger for pricing materials issued to the Job under FIFO and weighted average method –

STORE LEDGER FIFO

Date 1992	*Receipts*			*Isssues*			*Balance*		
	Unit	*Rate (Rs.)*	*Value (Rs.)*	*Unit*	*Rate (Rs.)*	*Value (Rs.)*	*Unit*	*Rate (Rs.)*	*Value (Rs.)*
Sept. 1st	40	15.00	600.00				40	15	600
2nd	20	16.50	330.00				40	15	600
							20	16.50	330
3rd				30	15	450	10	15	150
							20	16.50	330
4th	50	14.30	715				10	15	150
							20	16.50	330
							50	14.30	715
5th				10	15	150	10	16.50	165
				10	16.50	165	50	14.30	715
6th				10	16.50	165			
				30	14.30	429	20	14.30	286
						1,359			

So, materials issued to the job valued Rs. 1,359 (Total of Issue Column).

Step II

STORE LEDGER

2. (*Weighted Average Method*)

Date 1992	*Receipts*			*Isssues*					
	Unit (Rs.)	*Rate (Rs.)*	*Value*	*Unit (Rs.)*	*Rate (Rs.)*	*Value*	*Unit (Rs.)*	*Rate (Rs.)*	*Value*
Sept. 1st	40	15	600				40	15	600
2nd	20	16.50	330				60	15.50	930
3rd				30	15.50	465	30	15.50	465
4th	50	14.30	715				80	14.30	1,180
5th				20	14.75	295	60	14.75	885
6th				40	14.75	590	20	14.75	295
						1,350			

Step III

Calculation of Direct wages

	Halsey Plan (Rs.)	Rowan Plan (Rs.)
Normal wage	400.00 (40 × 5 × Rs.2)	400.00 (40 × 5 × Rs. 2)
Bonus	40.00	67.00
	440.00	467.00

Halsey Plan

Working notes : Time saved = 5 × 8 hours = 40 hours.

$$\text{Bonus} = \frac{1}{2} \times 40 \times 2 = \text{Rs. } 40$$

Rowan Plan

$$\text{Bonus} = \frac{\text{Time saved}}{\text{Standard time}} \times \text{Time taken} \times \text{Rate}$$

$$= \frac{40}{48 \times 5} \times 5 \times 40 \times 2 = \text{Rs. } 67.00$$

Calculation of Prime Cost

	FIFO/ Halsey	*FIFO/ Rowan*	*Wt. Average/ Halsey*	*Wt. Average/ Rowan*
	Rs.	Rs.	Rs.	Rs.
Material	1,359	1,359	1,350	1,350
Labour/Wages	440	467	440	467
PRIME COST	1,799	1,826	1,790	1,817

Problem 20

In a factory following the Job Costing Method, an abstract from the work in process as at 30th September was prepared as under.

Job No.	*Materials*	*Direct Labour*		*Factory Overheads*
	Rs.			Rs.
115	1,325	400 hours	Rs. 800	640
118	810	250 hours	Rs. 500	400
120	765	300 hours	Rs. 475	380
	2,900		Rs. 1,775	1,420

Materials used in October were as follows :

Materials Requisition No	Job No	Cost Rs.
54	118	300
55	118	425
56	118	515
57	120	665
58	121	910
59	124	720
		3,535

A summary of Labour Hours deployed during October is as under :

Job No.	*Number of hours*	
	Shop A	*Shop B*
115	25	25
118	90	30
120	75	10
121	65	–
124	20	10
	275	75
Indirect Labour		
Waiting for Materials	20	10
Machine Breakdown	10	5
Idle time	5	6
Overtime Premium	6	5
	316	101

A shop credit slip was issued in October, that material issued under Requisition No. 54 was returned to stores as being not suitable. A material transfer note issued in indicated that material issued under Requisition No. 55 for Job 118 was directed to Job 124.

The hourly rate in Shop A per labour hour is Rs. 3 per hour while at Shop B, it is Rs. 2 per hour. The Factory Overhead is applied at the same rate as in September to Jobs 115, 118 and 120 which were completed in October.

You are asked to compute the factory cost of the completed jobs. It is the practice of the management to put a 10% on the factory cost to cover administration and selling overheads and invoice the job to the customer on a total cost plus 20% basis. What would be the invoice price of these three jobs ?

[Adapted—C.A. (Inter)]

Solution

1. ***Materials consumed***

	Job 115	Job 118	Job 120
	Rs.	Rs.	Rs.
September	1,325	810	765
October	nil	515	665
	1,325	1,325	1,430

2. ***Direct Labour***

	Job 115	Job 118	Job 120
September	800	500	475
October	125	330	245
	925	830	720

3. Percentage of factory overhead on Direct Wages in September

Job 115 – $\frac{640 \times 100}{800} = 80\%$

Job 118 – $\frac{400 \times 100}{500} = 80\%$

Job 120 – $\frac{380 \times 100}{475} = 80\%$

STATEMENT SHOWING FACTORY COST AND INVOICE PRICE OF COMPLETED JOBS

		Job 115	Job 118	Job 120
		Rs.	Rs.	Rs.
	Materials (1)	1,325	1,325	1,430
	Direct Labour (2)	925	830	720
	Factory Overhead @ 80% of Direct Wages (3)	740	664	576
	FACTORY COST	2,990	2,819	2,726
Add :	Administration Cost @ 10% of Factory Cost	299	281.90	272.60
		3,289	3,100.90	2,998.60
Add :	Profit @ 20%on Cost	657.80	620.18	599.72
	INVOICE PRICE	3,946.80	3,721.08	3,598.32

Missing figures are to be ascertained

Problem 21

A firm has purchased a plant to manufacture a new product, the cost data for which is given below :

Estimated Annual Sales	24,000	units
Estimated costs	Rs.	
Material	4.00	per unit
Direct labour	0.60	per unit
Overheads	24,000	p.a
Administrative Expenses	28,800	p.a.
Selling Expenses	15%	of sales

Calculate the selling price if profit per unit is Rs. 1.02.

[Adapted I.C.W.A. (Inter) Dec. 1990]

Solution

COST SHEET

		Cost per unit
		Rs.
Material cost		4.00
Direct labour		0.60
Overheads	Rs. 24,000 ÷ 24,000 units	1.00
Administrative Expenses	Rs. 28,800 ÷ 24,000 units	1.20
Cost of Production		6.80

Selling expenses	=	15% of sales
Total Cost	=	Rs. 6.80 + 15% of Sales.
Selling price	=	Total Cost + Profit
Or, Selling Price	=	Rs. 6.80 + 0.15S + 1.02 where S = Selling Price
		Or, S – 0.15S = Rs. 6.80 + 1.02
		Or, .85S = 7.82
		Or, S = 7.82 ÷ .85 = Rs. 9.20
∴ Selling price	=	Rs. 9.20 per unit
Selling expenses	=	$\frac{15}{100}$ × Rs. 9.20 = Rs. 1.38.

Note : Reconciliations

		Rs.
	Cost of production per unit	6.80
	Selling expenses per unit	1.38
	Total Cost	8.18
Add	Profit	1.02
	Selling Price	9.20

SECTION II

BATCH COSTING

Definition

I.C.M.A. London has defined Batch Costing as that form of specific order costing which applies where similar articles are manufactured in batches either for sale or use within the Company. In most of the cases the costing is similar to job costing.

This is used when production consists of limited repetition work and a definite number of articles are manufactured in one batch.

In shoe industry, bakeries, toys, Batch Costing is used. In batch costing the unit is a batch. I.C.M.A., London, has defined a batch as a "Cost unit which consists of a group of similar articles which maintains its identity throughout one or more stages of production. Each batch is given a production order number".

The cost of each batch is determined separately by charging with its own costs.

Accounting Procedures

Materials issued are allocated directly to the batch. Wages are also charged to the batch. For the calculation of wages, **Time tickets** are used which show the amount of time devoted on each batch order number by direct workers. Overheads are absorbed according to the suitable basis of absorption. Per unit cost is determined by dividing the total cost of the batch by the total batch quantity.

Method of determination of Economic Batch Quantity (EBQ)

In order to determine the optimum quantity to constitute an economical batch the following factors are to be reckoned with :

i) the cost and time taken for setting up the tools ;
ii) the cost and time taken for manufacturing the parts ;
iii) the rate of interest on capital invested ;
iv) the cost of storage ;
v) the rate at which the parts are demanded.

We can now use the following formula for determining the EBQ (Economic Batch Quantity) :

(a) When the rate of interest and cost per unit is not given :

$$EBQ = \sqrt{\frac{2RS}{C}}$$

(b) When the rate of interest on capital and cost of production per unit is given –

$$EBQ = \sqrt{\frac{2RS}{C}}$$

R – stands for annual requirements,
S – stands for setting up costs,
C – stands for carrying cost,
I – stands for the rate of interest on capital.

Problem 22

Find out the Economic Batch Quantity from the particulars given below :

Annual demand	Rs. 9,600
Setting up Cost	Rs. 200
Cost of production per unit	Rs. 50
Rate of interest	10% p.a.

Solution

$$EBQ = \sqrt{\frac{2RS}{C}} = \sqrt{\frac{2 \times 9,600 \times 200}{0.1 \times 25}} = 1,239 \text{ (approx.)}$$

Problem 23

A Contractor has to supply 10,000 paper cones per day to a Textile unit. He finds that when he starts a production run he can produce 25,000 paper cones per day. The cost of holding a paper cone in stock for one year is 2 paise and the set up cost of a production run is Rs. 18. How frequently the production run be made.

[Adapted – I.C.W.A. – Final]

Solution

(i) Based on 300 days in the year.

Annual Sales = 10,000 × 300 = 30,00,000 Paper Cones.

Set up Cost = Rs. 18

Carrying Cost = Re. 0.02 per unit p.a.

$$EBQ = \sqrt{\frac{2RS}{C}} = \sqrt{\frac{2 \times 30,00,000 \times 18}{0.02}} = 73,500 \text{ units.}$$

73,500 ÷ 10,000 = 7.35

So, Production run should be made in 7 or 8 working days.

Problem 24

B K Bearing Ltd. is committed to supply 24,000 bearings per annum to Century Fans Ltd. on a steady daily basis. It is estimated that it costs 10 paise as inventory holding cost per bearing per month and that the set-up cost per run of bearing manufacture is Rs. 324.

(i) What should be the optimum run size for bearing manufacture?

(ii) What should be the interval between two consecutive optimum runs?

(iii) Assuming that the company has a policy of manufacturing 6,000 bearings per run, how much extra costs the company would be incurring as compared to the optimum run suggested in (i) above?

(iv) Find ut the minimum inventory holding cost.

[C.A. Inter. Nov. 1992—Adopted]

Solution

(i) Optimum run size

$$= \sqrt{\frac{2US}{C_c}} = \sqrt{\frac{2 \times 24{,}000 \times 324}{1.20}} = 3{,}600 \text{ units}$$

where U = units to be produced in a year

S = set-up cost

C_c = carrying cost per unit for one year (12 × 0.10 = Rs. 1.20)

$$\text{No. of runs} = \frac{24{,}000}{3{,}600} = \frac{20}{3}$$

(ii) Interval between two consecutive optimum runs :

$$\frac{365}{\text{No. of set-up per annum}} = \frac{365}{\frac{20}{3}} = 54.75 \text{ or } 55 \text{ calendar days.}$$

SECTION III

CONTRACT COSTING

Introduction

Now, we propose to define contract costing, and describe its characteristics. We shall also discuss the procedures for payments and the calculation of profit on uncompleted contract and the costing procedures. Book keeping entries are also shown and exemplified.

Definition :

Contract costing is known as terminal costing. Contract costing has many similarities to job costing and is usually applied to work which is :

(a) undertaken on customer's special requirements ;

(b) relatively long duration ;

(c) site based ;

(d) frequently of a construction nature.

Contract costing is generally applied to business engaged in building or other construction work. The basic principles of contract costing are similar to those that are applied in job costing system.

Difference between Job and Contract Costing

However, contract costing does differ from job costing in respect of the following :

i) A number of jobs in hand may be large while number of contracts that may be undertaken at a time may be few.

ii) Most of the expenses are directly charged to contract account but direct allocation of expenses to such extent is not possible in job costing.

iii) Since a contract may run for a longer period, the question of assessment of profit on incomplete contract at the end of the accounting period naturally arises while such a question does not arise in case of job costing.

iv) The analysis, apportionment, allocation and control of cost is simple in contract costing.

Features

The following features are common to most contract costing system :

(a) *Higher proportion of direct costs* :

Because of the self contained nature of most site operations, many items of indirect expenses can be identified specifically with a contract and, thus, can be charged directly. For example, telephones installed on site, site power usage, site vehicles, transportation design and planning salaries are charged directly to contract account.

(b) *Low indirect costs* :

For most contracts, the only item of indirect cost would be a charge for Head Office expenses. This forms a very small portion of the total cost of contract and is absorbed on some overall basis, such as a percentage of total contract cost.

(c) *Surplus Materials* :

All materials bought for a contract would be charged directly to the contract. At the end of the contract, the contract account would be **credited with the cost of materials not used**. If the materials are transferred to any other contract the new contract account is to be debited.

(d) *Difficulties of Cost Control* :

There exists frequently major problems of cost control concerning materials usage and losses, pilferage, labour supervision and utilisation, damage to and loss of plant and tools etc. because of the scale of some contracts and the size of the site.

(e) *Materials* :

Materials purchased or supplied from the stores **shall be debited to contract account**. Materials returned to stores and amount received from sale of materials will appear on the credit side. The accruing profit or loss being the difference between cost and sale price is transferred to Profit & Loss Account.

When the materials are transferred from one contract to another or from one site to another to avoid transportation, expenses in returning them to central stores and issuing them again, contract receiving the materials is debited with the cost of such materials and contract transferring the materials is credited.

Normal wastage of materials and store should be charged to the contract at a price at which they are priced out.

(f) *Wages* :

All workers employed at the contract site shall be treated as direct labour and, as such, wages paid to them should be debited to Contract Account.

(g) Contract Plant :

Plant includes cranes, trucks, excavators, mixers and lorries. The usual ways in which cost of plant is dealt with are as follows :

(1) *When plant is purchased* : The following two methods are in common use :

(i) Charge new plant at cost to the contract. When the plant is no longer required and is transferred to another contract, the original contract is credited with the depreciated value of the plant. In this way the contract bears the charge of depreciation.

(ii) Where plant is moved frequently from contract to contract, each contract is charged a daily or weekly rental.

(2) *When Plant is leased* : The leasing charges are charged directly to the contract.

Note : Whatever method is followed, the ordinary running costs like fuel, repairs and insurance, would be charged direct to the Contract Account.

Sub-Contract

Where a part work of the contract is done by a sub-contractor, the costs of sub-contract will be charged directly to the contract as direct expense.

Accounting Entries

1. *Materials issued to Contract*

   Contract A/c Dr.
   To Materials

2. *Materials at Site*

   Contract A/c Dr.
   Materials A/c

3. *Materials returned to Stores*

   Materials Returned A/c Dr.
   To Contract A/c

4. *Materials transferred to another Contract*

   Contract A/c (say A) Dr.
   To Contract A/c (say B)

5. *Materials sold at Site at a Profit*

   Bank Dr.
   To Contract A/c
   To P & L A/c

6. *For Materials lost*

   Profit & Loss A/c Dr.
   To Contract A/c

7. *Materials Stolen or lost and money realised from Insurance Co. in part*

   Bank Dr.
   Profit & Loss A/c Dr.
   To Contract A/c

8. *Special Plant Supplied*

   Contract A/c Dr.
   To Plant A/c

9. *Plant sold at a Profit*

   Bank Dr.
   To Contract A/c
   To Profit & Loss A/c

10. *Plant sold as Scrap*

    Bank Dr.
    Profit & Loss A/c Dr. (loss)
    To Plant A/c

11. *Plant at site at the end*

    Plant A/c Dr.
    To Contract A/c

12. *For Work-certified*

    Work-in-Progress A/c Dr.
    To Contract A/c

13. *Work uncertified* Work-in-Progress A/c Dr. To Contract A/c	15. *For Sale of Scrap* Bank Dr. To Contract A/c
14. *For all expenses like wages, paid or outstanding* Contract A/c Dr. To Wages A/c To Outstanding Expenses A/c	16. *Profit* Contract A/c Dr. To Profit & Loss A/c 17. *For Profit to be reserved* Contract A/c Dr. To Work-in-Progress

Work Certified and Retention Money

In the case of contracts which run for a long period of time, the contract normally provides for the contractee to make progress payments either at specific stage of the work e.g. when foundations are completed. The basis of interim payments is an architect's certificate. The architect's certificate shows the value of work done at selling prices. Normally, such payments are not received to the full extent of work certified but a small percentage, say, 10% or 15% or 20% of work certified is retained as retention money. The retention money acts as safeguard against non-fulfilment of one or more of the conditions laid down in the contract.

The book-keeping entries are :

1st Method

Contract Dr.
Retention Money A/c Dr.
To Contract Account

or'

(i) For amount due
Contractee Dr.
To Contract Account

(ii) On receipt of Cash
Cash Account Dr.
To Contractee

The retention money is released when the contract is fully completed.

2nd Method

The amount of work certified will be debited to the work-in-progress account and credited to the Contract Account. The Work-in-Progress Account is shown as an asset in the Balance Sheet after deducting the amount received from the contractee.

Journal entries :

(i)	Work-in-Progress A/c	Dr.
	To Contract A/c	
	(Being amount of work certified)	
(ii)	Bank	Dr.
	To Contractee's A/c	
	(Being amount received)	

Work not Certified

The work done but not certified by the Surveyor or Architect is termed as **'work uncertified'**. It is valued at cost and credited to contract account and debited to 'work-in-progress' account.

Work-in-Progress Account

In Contract Account the value of work-in-progress consists of :

(a) the cost of work completed ;

(b) the value of work uncertified ;

(c) the amount of profit taken as credit.

The amount of work-in-progress will appear in the Balance Sheet as an asset.

Method of Valuation of work-in-progress

Work-in-progress includes the amount of work certified and the cost of work uncertified.

Work-in-Progress — how to determine ?

	Value of work certified	X X X
Add :	Value of work not certified	X X X
		X X X
Less :	Reserve for unrealised profit	X X X
	ALTERNATIVELY	
(i)	Cost of Contract	X X X
Add :	Profit credited to P & L A/c	X X X
		X X X
Less :	Cash received	X X X
	Value of Work Certified	X X X

How to show in Balance Sheet

Balance Sheet as on ......

Asset Side

	Work-in-Progress :		
	Cost of work certified		X X X
	Cost of work uncertified		X X X
Less :	Cash received from contractee	X X X	
Less :	Profit Provision	X X X	
			X X X
	Work-in-Progress		X X X

Profit on Incomplete Contracts

A contract may take more than one financial year for its completion. In such a case problem arises as to how much profit shall be credited to P & L A/c. It becomes necessary to compute profit on partly completed contract and take credit for a part of it in the accounts at the year end.

The amount of profit that is to be credited to Profit & Loss A/c depends upon the fact that how far the contract has advanced i.e. the stage of completion it has reached.

The computation of profit is done in the following ways :

1. Profit should be considered in respect of work certified only. **Work uncertified should always be valued at cost.**
2. For contract which has been taken just in hand or which has not advanced far or **1/4th has been completed, no profit should be taken to the credit of Profit and Loss A/c.** This is because it would be too early to forecast or estimate profit with a reasonable degree of accuracy.
3. In case of a contract which is covered by Architect's certificate, profit is computed by deducting the cost of contract from work certified. A portion of this notional profit is taken to new Profit & Loss Account and the balance of notional profit is carried forward as profit in suspense. Conventionally, $\frac{1}{3}$ or $\frac{2}{3}$rds of profit is credited to Profit and Loss Account. If less than 50% but more than 25% of contract is completed then the portion of profit to be taken to the credit of profit and loss account is computed as follows :

   $$\frac{1}{3} \times \textbf{Notional profit} \times \textbf{(Cash received} \div \textbf{Work certified)}$$

   But, where more than 50% but less than 75% of contract is completed then Profit is computed for taking to Profit and Loss Account :

   $$\frac{2}{3} \times \textbf{Notional Profit} \times \textbf{(Cash received} \div \textbf{Work certified).}$$

4. Where the contract is almost complete, an estimated total profit is ascertained by deducting the total cost and additional expenditure to be incurred to complete the contract from the contract price. The Profit and Loss Account should be credited with that proportion of total estimated profit on a cash basis, which the work certified bears to the total contract price. The formula is as follows :

   Estimated total profit × (Value of work certified ÷ Contract price)

5. If there is any loss, the total loss should be transferred to Profit and Loss Account by crediting the Contract Account.

   Profit & Loss Account Dr.

   To Contract Account

The Costing entries

A separate account will be maintained for each contract with the object of finding out the overall Profit or Loss of the contract. To do this, a proforma of a contract account is shown on the next page :

CONTRACT ACCOUNT

for the year ended ......

Dr.			Cr.
	Debit entries		*Credit entries*
To	Cost of Materials, cost of labour	By	Materials returned to stores
"	Direct expenses (Plant hire,	"	Materials stolen
"	Subcontract Cost, Architect's fees etc.)	"	Closing balance of Plant
"	Cost of Plant bought	"	Materials sold from site
"	Materials, Plant transferred from contract	"	Sale of Scrap
"	Profit on materials sold	"	Materials transferred
"	Head office charges	"	Value of work certified
"	Accrued expenses	"	Value of work not certified
"	Notional Profit		
To	Profit & Loss A/c	By	Notional Profit b/d
"	Work-in-progress (Profit in suspense)		

WORKED OUT PROBLEMS

Problem 25

From the following particulars relating to a contract, prepare (a) the Contract Account, (b) Contractee's Account and (c) relevant entries in the Balance Sheet.

	Rs.
Materials sent to site	85,349
Labour engaged on site	74,375
Plant installed at cost	15,000
Direct expenditure	4,126
Establishment charges	3,167
Materials returned to stores	549
Work certified	1,95,000
Cost of work not certified	4,500
Materials on hand, Dec. 31	1,883
Wages accrued on December, 31	2,400
Direct expenditure accrued on Dec. 31	240
Value of plant, Dec. 31	11,000

The contract price has been agreed at Rs. 2,50,000. Cash has been received from the contractee amounting to Rs. 1,80,000.

[B.Com. Delhi]

Solution

Contract Account

Dr.			Rs.				Cr. Rs.
To	Materials sent to site		85,349	By	Materials returned to store		549
"	Wages	74,375		"	Materials on hand		1,883
	Add Accrued	2,400	76,775	"	Plant		11,000
"	Plant		15,000				13,432
"	Direct Exp	4,126		"	Work-in-Progress :		
	Add Accrued	240	4,366		Work certified	1,95,000	
"	Establishment charges		3,167		Cost of work		
"	Profit c/d		28,275		not certified	4,500	1,99,500
			2,12,932				2,12,932
"	Profit & Loss a/c		17,400	By	Profit b/d		28,275
"	Work-in-Progress		10,875				
			28,275				28,275

Contractee's Account

		Rs.			Rs.
To	Contract A/c	1,95,000	By	Bank	1,80,000
			"	Balanced c/d	15,000
		1,95,000			1,95,000

Balance Sheet

as on Dec. 31

	Rs.			Rs.
Outstanding wages	2,400	Work-in-Progress :		
Outstanding expenditure	240	Value of work certified	1,95,000	
		Cost of work uncertified	4,500	
			1,99,500	
		Less : Profit in suspense	10,875	
			1,88,625	
		Less : Cash received	1,80,000	
				8,625
		Materials on hand		1,883
		Plant at site		11,000

Note : Calculation of Profit taken to the credit of Profit and Loss Account :

$$\frac{2}{3} \times 28,275 \times (1,80,000 \div 1,95,000) = \text{Rs. } 17,400$$

Problem 26

The following information relate to contract 100 as at 31st Dec. 1998 :

	Rs.
Wages	42,000
Materials direct to site	54,000
Materials transferred to River-view site	1,500
Plant purchased at cost	12,500
Plant transferred from River-view site	5,300
Sub-contractors charges	19,500
Site expenses (power etc.)	5,000
Materials on site (31.12.98)	18,300
Plant on site (31.12.98)	14,750
Prepayments at 31.12.98	500
Accrued wages at 31.12.98	920
Cost of work done but not certified at 31.12.98	7,250
Head office charges are 10% of wages	
Materials from Stores	650

The contract value is Rs. 5,50,000. From the above information prepare the Contract Account for the year ended 31st December, 1998 clearly showing the profit for the year. Value of work certified by the architect was Rs. 1,37,500 and the contractor had made progress payments of this amount less 15% agreed retention percentage.

Solution

CONTRACT ACCOUNT No. 100

Dr.	Rs.	Rs.		Rs.	Cr. Rs.
To Wages	42,000				
Add Accrued	920	42,920	By Materials		
" Materials purchased	54,000		on site c/d		18,300
Materials from store	650	54,650	" Plant on site c/d		14,750
" Plant purchased	12,500		" Prepayment c/d		500
" Plant transferred	5,300	17,800	" Materials		
" Sub-contractors charges		19,500	transferred		1,500
" Site expenses		5,000	" Cost of contract		1,09,112
" Head office charges					
10% of wages		4,292			
		1,44,162			1,44,162
To Cost of contract b/d		1,09,112	By Value of		
" Profit & Loss A/c		10,097	Work certified		1,37,500
" Profit in Suspense A/c		25,541	Work not certified		7,250
		1,44,750			1,44,750
1st Jan, 1989			1st Jan. 1989		
To Prepayment b/d		500	By Profit in Suspense		25,541
" Materials b/d		18,300			
" Plant b/d		14,750			
" Work-in-Progress b/d		7,250			

Notes : Calculation of Profit to be taken to the credit of Profit and Loss A/c :

Notional Profit = Rs. 1,44,750 – 1,09,112 = Rs. 35,638

$\frac{1}{3}$ of 35,638 × $\frac{85}{100}$ = 10,097.

Problem 27

Calculate profit on work certified, cost of work in progress at the year end from the following :

(a) Materials sent to site Rs. 86,000 ; (b) Labour on site Rs. 70,000 ; (c) Plant at site Rs.80,000 ; (d) Direct Expenses Rs. 3,000 ; (e) Office expenses Rs. 4,000 ; (f) Materials returned to stores Rs. 600 ; (g) Work certified Rs. 1,90,000 ; (h) Work not certified Rs. 7,700 ; (i) Materials in stock at end Rs. 2,000 ; (j) Outstanding wages Rs. 300 ; (k) Cash received against bill Rs. 1,61,500 ; (l) Depreciation on plant Rs. 7,000.

[B.Com. Punjab]

Solution

Contract Account

Dr. *Cr.*

	Rs.	Rs.		Rs.	Rs.
To Materials		86,000	By Materials returned to store		600
" Wages	70,000		" Stock of materials		2,000
Add Outstanding	300	70,300	" Plant		73,000
To Direct Expenses		3,000	" Cost of contract (Balancing figure)		1,67,700
" Plant		80,000			
" Office Expenses		4,000			
		2,43,300			2,43,300
To Cost of contract b/d		1,67,700	By Contractee's A/c Value of work certified		1,90,000
" Profit & Loss a/c		8,500	Cost of work not certified		7,700
" Profit in suspense		21,500			
		1,97,700			1,97,700

Working Notes :

1. Assuming that 50% of contract has been completed and hence $\frac{1}{3}$ of notional profit has been considered.

2. $\frac{1}{3}$ × 30,000 × 1,61,500 + 1,90,000 = Rs. 8,500 credited to Profit and Loss A/c.

3. Value of Work-in-Progress :

		Rs.
	Cost of work not certified –	7,700
Add	Contractee's balance 1,90,000 – 1,61,500 =	28,500
		36,200
Less	Profit in Suspense	21,500
	Cost of Work-in-progress	14,700

Problem 28

X & Y Construction Company undertook the construction of a bridge. The value of the contract was Rs. 25,00,000 subject to a retention money of 20% until one year after the certified completion of the contract and final approval of the contractee's engineer. The following are the details as shown in the Books on 30. 6. 1987 :

	Rs.
Labour on site	8,10,000
Materials direct to site	6,40,000
Materials from Store	1,62,400
Hire and use of plant upkeep account	24,200
Direct Expenses	46,000
General Overhead	74,200
Materials on hand, June 30, 1987	12,600
Wages accrued on June 30, 1987	15,600
Direct expenses accrued on June 30, 87	3,200
Works not certified	33,000
Amount certified by the engineer	22,00,000
Cash received on account	17,60,000

Prepare (a) Contract Account, (b) Contractee's A/c; (c) Determine the cost of Work-in-progress :

[Andhra – B.Com.]

Contract Account

Dr. *Cr.*

	Rs.	Rs.		Rs.	Rs.
To Materials		6,40,000			
" Materials from Stores		1,62,400	By Materials on hand		12,600
" Wages	8,10,000		" Cost of contract		
Add Accrued	15,600	8,25,600	(balancing figure)		17,63,000
" Direct Expenses	46,000				
Add Accrued	3,200	49,200			
" Hire charge of Plant		24,200			
" General Overhead		74,200			
		17,75,600			17,75,600
To Cost of Contract b/d		17,63,000	By Contractee's A/c		22,00,000
" Profit & Loss A/c		2,50,667	work certified		
" Profit in Suspense		2,19,333	" Cost of work not		
			certified		33,000
		22,33,000			22,33,000
" Materials in hand		12,600	By Wage b/d		15,600
			" Direct Exp. b/d		3,200

Contractee's Account

Dr.	Rs.	Rs.		Rs.	*Cr.* Rs.
To Contract A/c		22,00,000	By Bank		17,60,000
(Value of work certified)			By Balance c/d		4,40,000
		22,00,000			22,00,000

Working Notes :

1. **Profit taken to the credit of P & L A/c :**

Notional Profit = Rs. 22,00,000 + 33,000 − 17,63,000 = Rs. 4,70,000

Since more than 75% of contract had been completed, profit to be taken to the credit of Profit & Loss A/c as follows :

$\frac{2}{3} \times 4{,}70{,}000 \times 17{,}60{,}000 \div 22{,}00{,}000$ = Rs. 2,50,667.

2. **Value of work-in-progress :**

	Rs.
Cost of work not certified –	33,000
Balance of Contractee's A/c	4,40,000
	4,73,000
Less Profit in Reserve –	2,19,333
Value of Work-in-progress :	2,53,667

Problem 29

Calcutta Construction Ltd. undertook a contract for construction of a bridge on 1st July, 1991. The contract price was Rs. 5,00,000. The Company incurred the following expenses up to December, 1991 :

	Rs.
Materials consumed	1,10,000
Wages	40,000
Direct expenses	20,000
Plant purchased on 1. 1. 1991	1,00,000
Materials in hand	5,000

Depreciation 10% p.a. on plant

Charge other works expenses @ 20% of wages and office expenses @ 10% of works cost.

The amount certified by the engineer was Rs. 3,00,000, retention money being 20% of the certified value.

Prepare the Contract Account showing therein the amount of profit that the company can reasonably take to its Profit and Loss Account.

[C.U. B.Com.(Hons.) 1985]

Solution

In the Books of

CALCUTTA CONSTRUCTION LTD.

Contract Account

for the half-year ended 31st Dec. 1984

Dr. *Cr.*

	Rs.		Rs.
To Materials purchased	1,15,000	By Materials in hand	5,000
" Wages	40,000	" Cost of Contract	2,01,800
" Direct Expenses	20,000		
" Works Expenses 20% of wages	8,000		
" Depreciation on Plant (for 6 months @ 10%)	5,000		
Works Cost	1,88,000		
" Office Expenses @ 10% of works cost	18,800		
	2,06,800		2,06,800
" Cost of Contract	2,01,800	By Work-in-Progress :	
" Profit & Loss A/c	52,373	Work certified	3,00,000
" Profit in Reserve	45,827		
	3,00,000		3,00,000
" Materials b/d	5,000	By Profit in Reserve	45,827
" Plant	95,000		

Note :

1. Depreciation has been charged for 6 months as the same has been used from 1st July, 1991 to 31st Dec. 1991.

2. In the problem the amount of materials consumed is given, so, no adjustment is required for closing stock of materials. Alternatively, materials sent to site can be determined as :

Materials consumed	1,10,000
Add : Materials in hand	5,000
	1,15,000

In this case, materials in hand will appear on the credit side of Contract Account.

3. Profit transferred to P & L A/c

$$\frac{2}{3} \times 98,200 \times \frac{80}{100} = \text{Rs. } 52,373$$

or, $\frac{2}{3}$ of Notional Profit × (Cash received ÷ work certified)

$$\frac{2}{3} \times 98,200 \times (2,40,000 \div 3,00,000) = \text{Rs. } 52,373.$$

Where value of work certified is to be determined

Problem 30

From the following particulars in respect of a particular contract for the year ended 31st December, 1986. Prepare Contract Account.

	Rs.
Materials sent to site	1,90,000
Wages paid	1,20,000
Wages outstanding	5,500
Direct Expenses	60,000
Establishment charges	52,000
Special Plant installed at cost	2,00,000
Cost of work not certified	25,000
Value of special Plant on 31. 12. 86	1,70,000
Materials at site on 31. 12. 86	21,000
Total Contract Price	12,00,000
Cash received	5,94,000
Retention – 10% of work certified	–
Sale of Scrap	2,000

General Plant costing to Rs. 1,20,000 was used for 3 months, depreciation on that is to be provided at 15% p.a.

[C.U. B.Com. (Hons.) 1987]

Contract Account

for the year ended 31st Dec. 1986

Dr.	Rs.		*Cr.* Rs.
To Materials sent to site	1,90,000	By Plant	1,70,000
" Wages	1,20,000	" Materials	21,000
" Outstanding wages	5,500	" Bank – Sale of Scrap	2,000
" Direct Expenses	60,000	" Cost of Contract	4,39,000
" Special Plant	2,00,000		
" Establishment Charges	52,000		
" Depreciation on general plant for 3 months @ 15% p.a.	4,500		
	6,32,000		6,32,000
" Cost of Contract	4,39,000	" Work-in-Progress	
" Profit and Loss A/c (2)	1,47,600	work certified (Note 1)	6,60,000
" Profit Provision		" Cost of work not	
(balancing figure)	98,400	certified	25,000
	6,85,000		6,85,000
" Materials b/d	21,000	" Wages b/d	5,500
" Plant b/d	1,70,000		
" W. I. P.	25,000	" Profit Provision	98,400

Notes :

i) Value of work certified :

Cash received = Rs. 5,94,000 being 10% of work certified.

So, when cash received 90 then value of w.c 100

... ... 5,94,000 ... ... ?

$$\therefore \frac{100 \times 5,94,000}{90} = \text{Rs. } 6,60,000$$

ii) Profit transferred to P & L A/c = $\frac{2}{3}$ of Rs. 2,46,000 (N.P.) × $\frac{90}{100}$ = Rs. 1,47,600.

Since more than 50% of Contract has been completed $\frac{2}{3}$ of notional profit has been transferred to P & L A/c.

Or, $\frac{2}{3} \times 2,46,000 \times (5,94,000 \div 6,60,000) = \text{Rs. } 1,47,600$

Problem 31

Mirik Construction Limited entered into a contract to construct a building. The contract value is Rs. 6,50,000 to be realised in instalments on the basis of the value of work certified by the architect subject to a retention of 10%. The work commenced on 1. 4. 88 but it remained incomplete on 31. 12. 1988 when the final accounts are to be prepared.

The facts and figures of the contract are :

	Rs.
Plant charged to Contract at the commencement	32,000
Materials charged to contract	1,80,000
Wages paid	87,000
Expenses incurred on the contract	38,750

Total establishment expenses amounted to Rs. 41,000 out of which 25% is attributable to this contract. Out of the materials issued to the contract, material costing Rs. 4,000 were sold for Rs. 5,000. A part of the plant (costing Rs. 2,000) was damaged on 1. 10. 1988 and the scrap realised Rs. 300 only. Plant costing Rs. 3,000 was transferred to another contract site on 31.12.1988.

Plant is to be depreciated @ 10% p.a. ;

Materials in hand on 31. 12. 88 Rs. 17,500

Cash received from Contractee Rs. 3,06,000

Cost of work yet to be certified Rs. 30,000

Prepare Contract Account showing therein the amount of Profit or Loss to be transferred to Profit & Loss Account.

[C.U. B.Com. (Hons.) 1989]

Solution

In the Books of

MIRIK CONSTRUCTION LTD.

Contract Account

for 9 months ending on 31st Dec. 1988

Dr.		Rs.			*Cr.* Rs.
To	Materials charged	1,80,000	By	Bank – materials sold	5,000
"	Wages	87,000	"	Bank – sale price of damaged plant as scrap	300
"	Expenses	38,750	By	Plant – transferred to another contract (Note 2)	2,775
"	Establishment Expenses – (25% of Rs. 41,000)	10,250	By	Materials in hand	17,500
"	Profit & Loss A/c (Profit on materials sold)	1,000	"	P & L A/c (loss on plant sold)	1,600
"	Plant charged to contract	32,000	"	Plant (Note 1)	24,975
			"	Cost of Contract	2,96,850
		3,49,000			3,49,000
"	Cost of Contract b/d	2,96,850	By	Work-in-Progress : Work Certified (4)	3,40,000
"	Profit & Loss A/c (3)	43,890	"	Cost of work not certified	30,000
"	Profit Provision	29,260			
		3,70,000			3,70,000
To	Plant b/d	24,975	By	Profit Provision	29,260
"	Materials b/d	17,500			
"	W. I. P.	30,000			

Note 1 : Calculation of Depreciation on Plant

		Rs.
	Total cost of Plant charged to contract	32,000
Less	Plant sold as scrap (cost price)	2,000
		30,000
Less	Plant transferred to another contract at cost (treated separately)	3,000
		27,000
Less	Depreciation for 9 months	2,025
	Depreciated value of Plant in hand	24,975

Note 2 : Depreciated value of Plant transferred

	Cost price of plant transferred	3,000
Less	Depreciation for 9 months @ 10% p.a.	225
	Depreciated value	2,775

Note 3 : Profit transferred to P & L A/c :

$\frac{2}{3}$ of Notional Profit × (Cash received ÷ Work certified)

$= \frac{2}{3} \times 73,150 \times (3,06,000 \div 3,40,000) = \text{Rs. } 42,930$

Since more than 50% of contract has been completed, $\frac{2}{3}$ of notional profit has been considered for transfer to P & L A/c.

Note 4 : Value of work certified

Cash received being 90% of work certified is Rs. 3,06,000

So, Work certified = $3,06,000 \times \frac{100}{90}$ = Rs. 3,40,000

Problem 32

United Construction Company got a contract in January, 1990 for construction of a bridge. The contract price was Rs. 5,00,000. The company incurred the following expenses upto 31.12.1990 :

	Rs.
Materials issued	1,10,000
Wages	40,000
Direct Expenses	20,000
Plant Purchased on 30. 6. 90	1,00,000
Materials in hand	5,000
Cost of uncertified work	2,000

Depreciation to be charged on plant @ 10% per annum. Other Works Expenses to be charged @ 20% of Wages and Office Expenses @ 10% of Works Cost.

The amount certified by the Engineer up to 31. 12. 90 was Rs. 3,00,000, retention money being 20% of the certified value.

Prepare a Contract Account showing therein the amount of profit or loss to be transferred to Profit & Loss Account. **[C.U. B.Com. (Hons.) 1991]**

Solution

In the Books of
UNITED CONSTRUCTION COMPANY
CONTRACT ACCOUNT
for the year ended 31st Dec. 1990

Dr. Cr.

Date	Particulars	Amount Rs.	Amount Rs.	Date	Particulars	Amount Rs.
1.1.90	To Material issued	1,10,000		31.12.1990	By Total Cost	1,95,800
	Less : Material in hand	5,000			(Balance c/d)	
	" Material consumed		1,05,000			
	" Wages		40,000			
	" Direct Expenses		20,000			
	Prime Cost :		1,65,000			
	" Works Overhead :					
	" Dep. on Plant	5,000				
	" Other works expenses	8,000				
	(20% of 40,000)		13,000			
	Works Cost		1,78,000			
	" Office Expenses		17,800			
	(10% of Works Cost)					
			1,95,800			1,95,800

Contd.

Date	Particulars	Amount Rs.	Amount Rs.	Date	Particulars	Amount Rs.
31.12.90	To Balance b/d. (Total Cost)		1,95,800	31.12.90	By Cost of Work uncertified	2,000
	" Notional Profit		1,06,200	31.12.90	" Value of Work certified	3,00,000
			3,02,000			3,02,000
31.12.90	To Profit & Loss A/c (Profit transferred)		56,640	31.12.90	By Notional Profit	1,06,200
	" Profit & Loss Reserve		49,560			
			1,06,200			1,06,200
1.1.91	To Material in hand b/d		5,000		By Profit provision b/d	49,560
	" Plant at site b/d		95,000			
	" W. I. P.		2,000			

Note : $\frac{2}{3} \times$ Rs. $1,06,200 \times \frac{80}{100}$ = Rs. 56,640

Problem 33

Following are the details for two contracts undertaken by M/s. Builders Association during the year ending on 31st December, 1998 :

	Contract A	*Contract B*
Date of commencement	1.1.1998	30.6.1998
	Rs.	Rs.
Total Contract Price	3,00,000	1,00,000
Value of plant installed	20,000	10,000
Materials issued	50,000	30,000
Wages paid	60,000	20,000
General expenses paid	20,000	12,000
Accrued wages on 31. 12. 98	3,000	2,000
Accrued General Expn. on 31. 12. 98	2,000	1,000
Material in hand on 31. 12. 98	1,200	500
Work certified till 31. 12. 98	1,75,000	60,000
Work uncertified on 31. 12. 98	15,000	5,000
Cash received from the Contractors	1,40,000	48,000

Plants at site are to be depreciated at 20% per annum.

You are required to (a) prepare Contract Accounts in columnar form showing the results to be reasonably transferred to the Profit and Loss Account for the year end, (b) show how the respective balances in relation to both the contracts are to appear in the Balance Sheet of M/s. Builders Association as on 31. 12. 1998.

[C.U. B.Com. (Hons.)]

Solution

In the Books of
Builders Association
CONTRACT ACCOUNTS A & B.

Dr.	A Rs.	B Rs.	Cr.	A Rs.	B Rs.
To Materials	50,000	30,000	By Materials		
To Wages paid	60,000	20,000	in hand	1,200	500
" Wages accrued	3,000	2,000	" Cost of		
" General exp.	20,000	12,000	Contract c/d	1,37,800	65,500
" General exp. accrued	2,000	1,000			
" Depreciation on plant	4,000	1,000			
	1,39,000	66,000		1,39,000	66,000
" Cost of Contract b/d	1,37,800	65,500	By Contractee A/c	1,75,000	60,000
" P & L A/c	27,840		Value of work certified		
Profit taken			By Cost of work uncertified	15,000	5,000
To Profit in Reserve	24,360	–	" P & L A/c. Loss	–	500
	1,90,000	65,500		1,90,000	65,500

Notes :

1. **Notional Profit**

	A Rs.	B Rs.
Value of work certified	1,75,000	60,000
Add : Value of work not certified	15,000	5,000
	1,90,000	65,000
Less : Cost of contract	1,37,800	65,500
	52,200 (Profit)	500 (Loss)

2. Contract A has been completed to the extent of more than 50%. Hence, profit taken to Profit & Loss A/c. is

$\frac{2}{3} \times$ Notional Profit $\times$ (Cash received $\div$ Value of work certified)

$\frac{2}{3} \times 52{,}200 \times (1{,}40{,}000 \div 1{,}75{,}000) =$ Rs. 27,840

3. In case of B, the whole of Loss is to be transferred to P & L A/c.

4. **Value of Work-in-Progress**

			A Rs.		B Rs.
	Cost of work not certified		15,000		5,000
Add	Contractee's balance				
	value of work certified	1,75,000		60,000	
Less	Cash received	1,40,000	35,000	48,000	12,000
	Total		50,000		17,000
Less	Profit in Reserve		24,360		Nil
	Value of Work-in-Progress				
			25,640		17,000

BALANCE SHEET
M/s. Builders Association
as on 31.12.98 (Extract)

Liabilities		Rs.	Assets		Rs.
P & L A/c.			Materials in hand		
Profit A	27,840		A	1,200	
Loss B (–)	500	27,340	B	1,500	2,700
Accrued wages			Plant		
A	3,000		A	20,000	
B	2,000	5,000	*Less* : Dep.	4,000	16,000
			B	10,000	
			Less : Dep.	1,000	9,000
Accrued General Exp.					
A	2,000				
B	1,000	3,000	Work-in-Progress		
			A	25,640	
			B	17,000	42,640

Problem 34

A firm of building contractors began to trade on April 1, 1998. The following was the expenditure on contract for Rs. 3,00,000.

	Rs.
Materials issued to Contract	51,000
Plant used for Contract	15,000
Wages incurred	81,000
Other expenses incurred	5,000

Cash received on account to 31st March, 1999 amounted to Rs. 1,28,000 being 80% of the work certified. Of the plant and materials charged to the contract, plant which cost Rs.3,000 and materials which cost Rs. 2,500 were lost. On March 31, 1999, plant, which cost Rs. 2,000 were returned to stores, the cost of work done but uncertified was Rs. 1,000 and materials costing Rs. 2,300 were in hand on site.

Charge 15 percent depreciation on plant, reserve $\frac{1}{2}$ of profit received and prepare a Contract Account from the above particulars.

[Meerut – B.Com.]

Solution

CONTRACT ACCOUNT
for the year ended 31.3.99

Dr. *Cr.*

	Rs.		Rs.
To Materials	51,000	By P & L A/c—Materials Lost	2,500
To Wages	81,000	" Materials at site	2,300
" Depreciation on plant 15%		" Cost of contract c/d	1,34,000
(15,000 – 3,000)	1,800		
" Other exp.	5,000		
	1,38,800		1,38,800

Contd.

	Rs.		Rs.
To Cost Contract c/d	1,34,000	By Contractee's A/c Value of work certified	
" P & L A/c (Profit transferred)	13,500	$1,28,000 \times \frac{100}{80}$	1,60,000
" Profit in Reserve (50% as given in question)	13,500	By Cost of work done but uncertified	1,000
	1,61,000		1,61,000

Note :

Plant Account

To Bank-purchase	15,000	By P & L A/c plant lost	3,000
		" Contract A/c - Dep.	1,800
		" Stores A/c	2,000
		" Balance c/d	8,200
	15,000		15,000

Problem 35

Deluxe Limited undertook a contract for Rs. 5,00,000 on 1st January 1997. The company furnishes the following details for the year ended 31st December, 1997 :

	Rs.
Materials consumed	1,65,000
Direct Expenses	5,000
Wages	30,000
Materials returned to stores	5,000
Materials stolen from site	10,000
Insurance claim admitted	6,000
Other works expenses @ 20% on wages	
Office expenses @ 10% on works cost	
Materials in hand on 31.12.1997	15,000
Cash received to the extent of 90% of works certified	2,70,000
Cost of work uncertified	11,000

Plant sent to site costing Rs. 60,000 with a scrap value of Rs. 10,000 and its useful life is 5 years. The plant was used in the contract for 146 days.

Prepare Contract Account showing therein the cost of materials issued to site and the amount of profit or loss to be transferred to the Profit & Loss Account. Show the value of work-in-Progress separately.

[C.U. B.Com. (Hons.) 1998]

Solution

Calculation of cost of materials issued at site

		Rs.
	Materials consumed	1,65,000
Add :	Materials stolen	10,000
	Materials returned to stores	5,000
	Materials in hand (31.12.1997)	15,000
		1,95,000

Contract Account

for the year ended 31st Dec. 1997

Dr.		Rs.			*Cr.* Rs.
To	Materials sent to	1,95,000	By	Matrials returned to store	5,000
"	Direct Expenses	5,000	"	Insurance claim	6,000
"	Wages	30,000	"	Profit & Loss A/c	4,000
"	Works Expenses 10% of wages	6,000	"	Materials in hand	15,000
"	Office Expenses— 10% of Works Cost (Note 1)	21,000	"	Cost of Contract	2,31,000
"	Depreciation on Plant	4,000			
		2,61,000			2,61,000
To	Cost of Contract b/d	2,31,000	By	Work in Progress :	
"	Notional Profit	80,000		Work certified	3,00,000
				Work uncertified	11,000
		3,11,000			3,11,000
To	Profit & Loss A/c (Note 2)	48,000	By	Notional Profit	80,000
"	Profit Provision	32,000			
		80,000			80,000

Working Notes :

1. **Calculation of works cost**

		Rs.
	Materials consumed	1,65,000
Add :	Direct Wages	30,000
	Direct Expenses	5,000
	Prime Cost	2,00,000
Add :	Works expenses	6,000
	Depreciation	4,000
		2,10,000

10% of Rs. 2,10,000 – Rs. 21,000.

2. **Profit to be credited to Profit & Loss A/c**

$$\frac{2}{3} \times \text{Notional Profit} \times \frac{\text{Cash received}}{\text{Work certified}}$$

$$= \frac{2}{3} \times 80{,}000 \times \frac{2{,}70{,}000}{3{,}00{,}000} = \text{Rs. } 48{,}000.$$

Value of Work-in-Progress

		Rs.
	Work certified	3,00,000
Add :	Work not certified	11,000
		3,11,000
Less :	Cash received from contracee	2,70,000
		41,000
Less :	Profit in Reserve	32,000
		9,000

Problem 36

A contractor makes up his accounts on 31st December in each year. Contract No. 21 commenced on 1st April, 1997. The costing records yield the following information as at 31st December, 1997 :

	Rs.
Materials charged out to site	21,500
Labour	50,110
Foremen's wages	6,310

A machine costing Rs. 15,000 has been on the site for 73 days. Its working life is estimated at five years and its final scrap value is Rs. 1,000.

A supervisor, who is paid Rs. 1,000 per month has spent approximately one half of his time on this contract.

All other expenses amount to Rs. 12,610.

Materials in store at site on 31st December, 1997 cost Rs. 2480.

The contract price is Rs. 2,00,000. On 31st December 1997, two-thirds of the contract was completed ; architect's certificates had been issued covering Rs. 1,00,000 ; Rs. 80,000 has so far been paid on account.

Prepare a contract account and state how much profit or loss should be included in the financial accounts to 31st December, 1997.

[B.Com.—Madras]

Solution

CONTRACT NO. 21 ACCOUNT
for 9 months ended 31st Dec. 1997

Dr.	Rs.		*Cr.* Rs.
To Materials	21,500	By Materials at site	2,480
" Labour	50,110	By Cost of contract c/d	89,110
" Foreman's wages	6,310		
" Depreciation on Machine $\frac{15,000 - 1,000}{5} \times \frac{37}{365}$	560		
" Supervisor's salary $\frac{1}{2}$ of 1,000	500		
" Admn. & other exp.	12,610		
	91,590		91,590
To Cost of contract b/d	89,110.00	By Contractee's A/c value of work certified	1,00,000
" P & L A/c—profit transferred (see note below)	17,689.33	" Cost of work not certified (see note below)	22,277.50
" Profit in Suspense c/d	15,478.17		
	1,22,277.50		1,22,277.50

Notes :

1. $\frac{2}{3}$ of contract was completed and $\frac{1}{2}$ of contract price was certified by the Architect.

Hence, the balance cost represents the cost of work not certified. i.e. $\left(\frac{2}{3} - \frac{1}{2}\right) = \frac{1}{6}$th of contract.

Cost of $\frac{2}{3}$ of contract = Rs. 89,110

Cost of $\frac{1}{6}$ of contract – ? = $\frac{1}{6} \times \frac{3}{2} \times 89{,}110$ = 22,277.50

2. Notional Profit

	Rs.	Rs.
Value of work certified		1,00,000.00
Cost of contract	89,110.00	
Less : Cost of work not certified	22,277.50	66,832.50
Notional Profit		33,167.50

3. Profit taken to P & L A/c :

As the amount of work certified is 50% of the contract price, the following formula is applied to find out the profit to be taken into P & L A/c.

$\frac{2}{3} \times$ Notional Profit $\times$ (Cash received $\div$ Value of Work certified)

$\frac{2}{3} \times 33{,}167.50 \times (80{,}000 \div 1{,}00{,}000)$ = Rs. 17,689.33

Problem 37

Sterling Construction obtained a contract for the building of an office for Rs. 3,00,000. Construction work commenced on 1st April, 1997 and at the end of the financial year they received payment of Rs. 1,20,000 representing 80% of the amount of work certified. The following information is available from the books of the contractors :

	Rs.
Materials issued	60,000
Materials on hand on 31. 3. 1998	2,500
Wages paid	80,000
Plant installed at site	60,000
Direct Expenses	11,000
Overheads allocated to this contract	5,500
Work finished but not yet certified at cost	5,000
Plant to be depreciated at 10%	

Prepare the contract account for the year ended 31.3.98 and show your calculation of the amount adjusted to the credit of Profit & Loss Account.

[B.Com. – Madras]

Solution

CONTRACT ACCOUNT

for the year ended 31.3.98

Dr.	Rs.		Cr. Rs.
To Materials	60,000	By Materials on hand	2,500
" Wages	80,000	" Plant	54,000
" Direct Expenses	11,000	" Cost of contract c/d	1,60,000
" Plant	60,000		
" Overheads	5,500		
	2,16,500		2,16,500
To Cost of contract b/d	1,60,000	By Contractee's A/c	
		Value of work certified	1,50,000
		" Cost of work not certified	5,000
		" Profit & Loss A/c	5,000
		(Loss transferred)	
	1,60,000		1,60,000

Note : The amount of loss is to be written off against P & L A/c.

Problem 38

The followin is the summary of the entries in a contract ledger as on 31.3.1998 in respect of contract No. 10. Prepare a contract Account.

	Rs.
Materials bought directly	1,20,000
Materials from stores	10,000
Wages	48,000
Chargeable expenses	12,000
Establishment charges	8,000
Plant	45,200
Scrap sold	2,500
Cost of sub-contract	17,500

You are further supplied with the following information :

(i) Accruals on 31.3.1998 are wages Rs. 1,900 and direct expenses Rs. 1,200.

(ii) Included in the above summary of entries are wages Rs. 1,000 and other expenses Rs. 1,500 since certification. The value of materials used since certification is Rs. 4,200.

(iii) Depreciation till 31.3.1998 on plant Rs. 4,520.

(iv) Materials on hand on 31.3.98 Rs. 10,000.

(v) The total contrct price is Rs. 2,00,000.

(vi) Rs. 1,25,000 had been certified upto 31.3.1998, when $\frac{5}{8}$th contract has been completed.

Solution

CONTRACT ACCOUNT

Dr.	Rs.	Rs.		Rs.	*Cr.* Rs.
31.3.1998			31.3.1998		
To Materials purchased	1,20,000		By Sale of scrap		2,500
Add : Materials from stores	10,000	1,30,000	" Plant		40,680
To Wages	48,000		" Materials		10,000
Add : Outstanding	1,900	49,900	" Work-in-progres :		
To Chargeable expenses	12,000		Work certified		1,25,000
Add : Outstanding	1,200	13,200	Works not certified :		
To Extablishment charges		8,000	Materials	4,200	
" Plant		45,200	Wages	1,000	
" Cost of sub-contract		17,500	Other Expenses	1,500	
					6,700
			" Profit and loss A/c		78,920
			(Loss transferred)		
		2,63,800			2,63,800
1.4.1998			1.4.1998		
To Balance b/d			By Balance b/d		
Materials		10,000	Outstanding wages		1,900
Plant		40,680	Outstnading Direct		
Work not certified		6,700	Expnses		1,200

CONTRACT WITH ESCALATION CLAUSE

Problem 39

Deluxe Limited undertook a contract for Rs. 5,00,000 on 1st July, 1988. On 30th June, 1989 when the accounts were closed, the following details about the contract were gathered :

	Rs.
Materials purchased	1,00,000
Wages paid	45,000
General expenses	10,000
Plant purchased	50,000
Materials on hand (30. 6. 89)	25,000
Wages accrued	5,000
Work certified	2,00,000
Cash received	1,50,000
Work uncertified	15,000
Depreciation of Plant	5,000

The above contract contained an escalation clause which reads as follows :

"In the event of prices of materials and rates of wages increase by more than 5%, the contract price would be increased accordingly by 25% of the rise in the cost of materials and wages beyond 5% in each case".

It was found that since the date of signing the agreement, the prices of materials and wage rates increased by 25%. The value of the work certified does not take into account the effect of the above clause.

Prepare the Contract Account. Workings should form the part of the answer.

[Adapted—C. A. (Inter) Nov. 1987]

Solution

CONTRACT ACCOUNT

for the year ending 30th June, 1989

Dr.	Rs.		Cr. Rs.
To Materials	1,00,000	By Materials on hand	25,000
" Wages	45,000		
" General Expenses	10,000		
" Plant	50,000		
" Wages Accrued	5,000		
		" Plant	45,000
		" Cost of Contract	1,40,000
	2,10,000		2,10,000
To Balance b/d	1,40,000	By Work in Progress	
" Profit and Loss A/c	20,000	Work certified	2,00,000
(Note 2)		Work uncertified	15,000
" Profit provision	60,000	Escalation of Contract	5,000
		(Note 1)	
	2,20,000		2,20,000
To Balance b/d		By Balance b/d	
Stock in hand	25,000	Accrued wages	5,000
Plant	45,000	Profit Provision	60,000

Working Notes :

1. Calculation of price escalation Increase

		Total	Upto 5%	Beyond 5%
Materials	$\left[\text{Rs. } 75{,}000 \times \frac{25}{125}\right]$	15,000	3,000	12,000
Wages	$\left[\text{Rs. } 50{,}000 \times \frac{25}{125}\right]$	10,000	2,000	8,000
		25,000	5,000	20,000

So, increase in Contract Price $= \frac{25}{100} \times 20{,}000 =$ Rs. 5,000.

2. Calculation of Profit to be credited to P & L A/c.

Since the contract has been completed between 25% and 50%, one-third of the Notional Profit shall be considered.

Profit $= \frac{1}{3} \times 80{,}000 \times \frac{1{,}50{,}000}{2{,}00{,}000} =$ Rs. 20,000.

PREPARATION OF BALANCE SHEET WHEN TRIAL BALANCE IS GIVEN

Problem 40

The following is the Trial Balance of Premier Construction Company engaged on the execution of Contract No. 747 for the year ended 31. 12. 1998.

	Rs.	Rs.
Contractee's Account :		
Amount received		3,00,000
Buildings	1,60,000	
Creditors		72,000
Bank balance	35,000	
Capital account		5,00,000
Materials	2,00,000	
Wages	1,80,000	
Expenses	47,000	
Plant	2,50,000	
	8,72,000	8,72,000

The work on Contract No. 747 commenced on 1st January 1998. Materials costing Rs.1,70,000 were sent to the site of the contract but those costing Rs. 6,000 were destroyed in an accident. Wages amounting to Rs. 1,80,000 were paid during the year. Plant costing Rs.50,000 was used on the contract all through the year. Plant with a cost of Rs. 2 lakhs was used from 1st January to 30th September and was then returned to the stores. Materials of the cost of Rs. 4,000 were at site on 31st December 1998.

The contract was for Rs. 6,00,000 and the contractee pays 75% of the work certified. Work certified was 80% of the total contract work at the end of 1998. Uncertified work was estimated at Rs. 15,000 on 31st December 1998.

Expenses are charged to contract at 25% of wages. Plant is to be depreciated at 10% for the entire year.

Prepare Contract No. 747 account for the year 1998 and make out the balance sheet as on 31st December 1998 in the books of Premier Construction Co.

[B. Com. (Hons.), Delhi]

Solution

CONTRACT NO. 747 ACCOUNT

for the year ending 31st Dec. 1998

Dr.	Rs.		*Cr.* Rs.
To Materials	1,70,000	By Profit and Loss A/c (abnormal loss)	6,000
" Wages	1,80,000	" Plant returned to store (Rs. 2,00,000 – 15,000)	1,85,000
" Expenses (25% on wages)	45,000	" Plant at site (Rs. 50,000 – 5,000)	45,000
" Plant	2,50,000	" Materials at site	4,000
" Profit and Loss (see Note 1)	45,000	" Work-in-progress :	
" W. I. P. (being reserve)	45,000	Work certified	4,80,000
		Work uncertified	15,000
	7,35,000		7,35,000

Balance Sheet

as on 31st Dec. 1998

Liabilities	Rs.	Rs.	Rs.	Assets	Rs.	Rs.
Capital			5,00,000	Buildings		1,60,000
Profit from contract		45,000		Plant :		
Less : Abnormal loss	6,000			In store		1,80,000
Depreciation on plant	5,000			At contract site		45,000
Unabsorbed expenses	2,000	13,000		Materials :		
			32,000	In store		30,000
Creditors			72,000	At contract site		4,000
				Work-in-Progress :		
				Work certified	4,80,000	
				Work uncertified	15,000	
					4,95,000	
				Less : Reserve	45,000	
					4,50,000	
				Less : Cash received from contractee	3,00,000	1,50,000
				Bank balance		35,000
			6,04,000			6,04,000

Working Notes :

1. The profit taken to the profit and loss account $90,000 \times \frac{2}{3} \times \frac{3}{4}$ = Rs. 45,000.

SUB-CONTRACT

Problem 41

From the following data relating to a contractor, prepare the Contract Account and show what profit or loss should be taken to the Profit & Loss A/c for the year ended December 31st, 1989 :

	Rs.
Materials (direct)	30,000
Materials (from stores)	6,500
Wages	17,210
Direct expenses	6,710
Establishment charges	8,000
Plant	34,200
Sale of scrap	1,820
Sub-contracts	7,210

The other information available are as follows :

1. Accruals on December 31, 1989 are wages Rs. 880 ; direct expenses Rs. 1,120.
2. Depreciation on plant up to December 31 is Rs. 8,850.
3. Included in above summary of entries are wages Rs. 1,000 and other expenses Rs.1,500 since certification. The value of materials since certification is Rs. 2,080.

4. Materials on site on December 31, 1989, costing Rs. 10,000.
5. Rs. 62,500 have been certified up to December 20, 1989, when $\frac{3}{8}$th of the contract remained uncompleted.
6. The contract price is Rs. 1,00,000.

[Adapted – M.Com. M.K.U.]

Solution

CONTRACT ACCOUNT

Dr. *Cr.*

	Rs.	Rs.		Rs.
To Materials		30,000	By Bank – Sale of scrap	1,820
" Materials (from Stores)		6,500	" Materials at site	10,000
" Wages	17,210			
Add Outstanding	880	18,090	" Work in Progress :	
To Direct Expenses	6,710		Work certified	62,500
Add Outstanding	1,120	7,830	Work uncertified (Note 1)	4,580
To Establishment Charges		8,000	" P & L A/c	7,580
" Depreciation on Plant		8,850	—Loss transferred	
" Sub-contracts		7,210		
		86,480		86,480

Working Note :

		Rs.
1. Work Uncertified :	Expenses since certification	
	Wages –	1,000
	Materials –	2,080
	Other expenses –	1,500
		4,580

Problem 42

M/s Excellent Erectors Ltd. took up a contract for the construction of a building at a contract price of Rs. 15,00,000. During the first year the following amounts were spent as against which a sum of Rs. 5,62,500, which represented 90% of the work certified received by the contractor.

	Rs.
Materials	2,62,500
Wages	1,50,000
Overhead expenses	37,500

During the second year, the firm spent the following amounts –

	Rs.
Material	3,75,000
Labour Cost	3,00,000
Overhead expenses	75,000

In the second year the contract was completed and a sum of Rs. 8,75,000 was received by the contractor.

You are required to prepare the Contract Accounts and Contractee's Account for both the years and calculate the profit.

Note : Consider only $\frac{2}{5}$th or 40% of the notional profit to be taken to the credit of P & L A/c in the first year as the work done is less than 50%.

[Adapted I.C.W.A. (Inter)]

Solution

EXCELLENT ERECTORS LTD.
CONTRACT ACCOUNT – FIRST YEAR

Dr.	Rs.		Cr. Rs.
To Materials	2,62,500	By Cost of Contract (balancing figure)	4,50,000
" Wages	1,50,000		
" Overheads	37,500		
	4,50,000		4,50,000
To Cost of Contract	4,50,000	By Value of work certified (Note 1)	6,25,000
" Profit and Loss A/c (Note 2)	70,000		
" Profit Provision c/d	1,05,000		
	6,25,000		6,25,000

CONTRACT ACCOUNT – SECOND YEAR

Dr.	Rs.		Cr. Rs.
To Materals	3,75,000	By Cost of Contract	7,50,000
" Wages	3,00,000		
" Overheads	75,000		
	7,50,000		7,50,000
To Cost of Contract	7,50,000	By Profit Provision A/c	1,05,000
" Profit & Loss A/c	2,30,000	" Value of work Certified (Note 3)	8,75,000
	9,80,000		9,80,000

Working Notes :

1. Value of work certified in first year = $5{,}62{,}500 \times \frac{100}{90}$ = Rs. 6,25,000.
2. Profit to be credited – $\frac{40}{100} \times 1{,}75{,}000$ = Rs. 70,000.
3. Value of work certified in 2nd year = Rs. 15,00,000 – Rs. 6,25,000 = Rs. 8,75,000.

Where the value of uncertified work is to be determined

[Value of Work not certified]

Problem 43

M/s Manholes and Sewers Ltd., undertook a contract for erection, sewerage treatment plant for a municipality for a total value of Rs. 24 lakhs.

It was expected that the contract would be completed by 31st January, 1996. You are required to prepare a contract account for the year ended 31st January, 1995 from the following particulars :

		Rs.
1.	Wages	6,00,000
2.	Special Plant	2,00,000
3.	Materials	3,00,000
4.	Overheads	1,20,000

5. Depreciation @ 10% to be provided on plant
6. Materials lying at the site on 31.1.1995 Rs. 40,000
7. Work certified was to the extent of Rs. 16,00,000 and 80% of the same was received in cash.
8. 5% of the value of material issued and 6% of wages may be taken to have been incurred for the portion of work completed but not yet certified.
9. Overheads are charged as a percentage of direct wages.
10. Ignore depreciation on plant for use on uncertified portion of the work.
11. Ascertain the amount to be transferred to Profit and Loss account on the basis of realised profit.

[I.C.W.A. – Inter]

Solution

CONTRACT ACCOUNT

Dr.	Rs.		*Cr.*	Rs.
To Wages	6,00,000	By	Materials at site	40,000
" Special Plant	2,00,000	"	Plant at site (cost less depreciation @ 10%)	1,80,000
" Materials	3,00,000			
" Overheads	1,20,000		Work certified	16,00,000
" Balance c/d	6,58,200		Work not certified	58,200
	18,78,200			18,78,200
" Profit and Loss Account	3,51,040	By	Balance b/d (Notional Profit)	6,58,200
" Work in Progress Account (Reserve)	3,07,160			
	6,58,200			6,58,200

Working Notes :

Calculation of Work uncertified :		Rs.
1.	Materials (5% of Rs. 3,00,000)	15,000
2.	Wages (6% of Rs. 6,00,000)	36,000
3.	Overheads (20% of Rs. 36,000)	7,200
		58,200

Contract for Consecutive 3 Years

Problem 44

Mr. Bhagwandas undertook a contract for Rs. 15,00,000 on an arrangement that 80% of the value of the work done as certified by the architect of the contractee, should be paid immediately and that the remaining 20% be retained until the contract was completed.

In 1995 the amounts expended were : Materials Rs. 1,80,000 ; Wages Rs. 1,70,000 ; Carriage Rs. 6,000; Cartage Rs. 1,000 ; Sundry Expenses Rs. 3,000. The work was certified for Rs. 3,75,000 and 80% of this was paid as agreed.

In 1996 the amounts expended were : Materials Rs. 2,20,000 ; Wages Rs. 2,30,000 ; Carriage Rs. 23,000 ; Cartage Rs. 2,000 ; Sundry expenses Rs. 4,000. Three-fourths of the contract was certified as done by 31st December and 80% of this was received accordingly. The value of unused stock and work-in-progress uncertified was ascertained at Rs. 20,000.

In 1997 the amounts expended were : Materials Rs. 1,26,000 ; Wages Rs. 1,70,000 ; Cartage Rs. 6,000 ; Sundry expenses Rs. 3,000 and on 30th June the whole contract was completed.

Show how the contract account and also contractee's account would appear in each of these years in the books of the contractor assuming that the balance due to him was paid on completion of the contract.

[M.Com. Raj Univ.]

Solution

CONTRACT ACCOUNT

Dr.	Rs.		Cr. Rs.
1995		**1995**	
To Materials	1,80,000	By Work-in-Progress :	
" Wages	1,70,000	Work certified	3,75,000
" Carriage	6,000		
" Cartage	1,000		
" Sundry Expenses	3,000		
" Profit c/d	15,000		
	3,75,000		3,75,000
To Profit and Loss A/c	4,000	By Profit b/d	15,000
" Work-in-Progess (Profit Provision)	11,000		
	15,000		15,000
1996		**1996**	
To Work-in-Progress (3,75,000–11,000)	3,64,000	By Work-in-Progress :	
" Materials	2,20,000	Work uncertified	20,000
" Wages	2,30,000	Work certified	11,25,000
" Carriage	23,000		
" Cartage	2,000		
" Sundry Expenses	4,000		
" Profit c/d	3,02,000		
	11,45,000		11,45,000
To Profit & Loss A/c	1,61,067	By Profit b/d	3,02,000
" Work-in-Progress	1,40,933		
	3,02,000		3,02,000
1997		**1997**	
To Work-in-Progress	10,04,067	By Contractee's A/c	15,00,000
" Materials	1,26,000		
" Wages	1,70,000		
" Cartage	6,000		
" Sundry Expenses	3,000		
" Profit and Loss A/c	1,90,933		
	15,00,000		15,00,000

CONTRACTEE'S ACCOUNT

Dr.			*Cr.*
1995		1995	
To Balance b/d	3,00,000	By Bank	3,00,000
1996		1996	
To Balance c/d	9,00,000	By Balance b/d	3,00,000
		" Bank	6,00,000
	9,00,000		9,00,000
1997		1997	
To Contract A/c	15,00,000	By Balance c/d	9,00,000
		Bank	6,00,000
	15,00,000		15,00,000

Working Notes :

1995 Profit to be credited to Profit and Loss A/c $\frac{1}{3} \times 15,000 \times \frac{80}{100}$ = Rs. 4,000

1996 Profit to be taken – $\frac{2}{3} \times 3,02,000 \times \frac{80}{100}$ = Rs. 1,61,067

1997 The whole amount to be credited to P & L A/c.

Problem 45

Crystal Construction Limited engaged in contract work has the following Trial Balance on 31st December, 1995 :

	Dr.	*Cr.*
Share Capital – Shares of Rs. 10 each		35,180
Profit and Loss A/c on 1st Jan. 95		2,500
Provision for Depreciation on Plant and Tools		6,300
Contractee's A/c Contract No. 707		1,28,000
Creditors		8,120
Land and Buildings (at cost)	7,400	
Plant and Tools (at cost)	5,200	
Bank Balance	4,500	
Contract No. 707 :		
Materials issued	60,000	
Direct Labour	83,000	
Expenses	4,000	
Plant and Tools at site (at cost)	16,000	
	1,80,100	1,80,100

Contract No. 707, having a contract price of Rs. 2,40,000 began on 1st Jan. 1995 and contractee pays 80% of the work completed and certified. The cost of work done since certification is estimated to be Rs. 1,600.

After the above Trial Balance was extracted on 31st December, 1995, plant costing Rs.3,200 was returned to the stores and materials at site on that date were valued at Rs.3,000.

Provision is to be made for sub-standard costs amounting to Rs. 600 incurred on Contract No. 707 and for depreciation of all Plant and Tools @ $12\frac{1}{2}$% on cost.

Prepare Contract No. 707 account showing the computation of profit, if any, for which credit may properly be taken in 1995 and prepare the Balance Sheet of the construction company on 31st December, 1995.

[Delhi, B.Com. (Hons.)]

Solution

CONTRACT NO. 707 ACCOUNT

Dr.			*Cr.*
1995	Rs.	1995	Rs.
To Materials	60,000	By Materials at site	3,000
" Direct Labour	83,000	" Cost of Contract c/d	1,46,600
" Expenses	4,000		
" Depreciation on Plant & Tools 12.5% of 16,000	2,000		
" Provision for sub-standard costs	600		
	1,49,600		1,49,600
To Cost of Contract b/d	1,46,600	By Contractee's account value of work certified $1,28,000 \times \frac{100}{80}$	1,60,000
" P & L A/c Profit taken (See Note 1 below)	8,000		
" Profit in suspense/reserve	7,000	" Cost of work done but not certified	1,600
	1,61,600		1,61,600

Balance Sheet

as on 31.12.1995

Liabilities	Rs.	Rs.	Assets	Rs.	Rs.
Share Capital		35,180	Land & Buildings		7,400
P & L Account	2,500		Plant & Tools		
Add : Profit on Contract 707	8,000		16,000 + 5,200 =	21,200	
	10,500		*Less* : Returned	3,200	
			to stores		18,000
Less : Depreciation on			Plant at Stores		3,200
Plant & Tools			Materials at site		3,000
12.5% on 5,200	650		Work-in-Progress		26,600
		9,850	(see Note 2 below)		
Provision for deprecation on			Bank		4,500
Plant & Tools		8,950			
(6,300 + 2,000 + 650)					
Provision for Sub-std. costs		600			
Creditors		8,120			
		62,700			62,700

Note :

1. Work has been completed to the extent of $66\frac{2}{3}\%$ i.e. $66\frac{2}{3}\% \times 2,40,000$ = Rs. 1,60,000.

			Rs.
	Value of work certified		1,60,000
	Cost of contract	1,46,600	
Less :	Cost of work done but not certified	1,600	1,45,000
	Notional profit :		15,000

$\frac{2}{3} \times 15,000 \times \frac{1,28,000}{1,60,000}$ = Rs. 8,000 profit to be transferred to P & L Account.

2.	Cost of work done but not certified	1,600
Add :	Contractee's balance 1,60,000 – 1,28,000 =	32,000
		33,600
Less :	Profit in suspense /reserve	7,000
	Value of work-in-progress	26,600

Problem 46

Mr. Sudhir undertook a contract for the construction of building on 1st January, 1997, the contract price being Rs. 7,50,000. The following details are available for the year 1997 :

	Rs.
Materials purchased	1,20,000
Materials issued from stores	1,50,000
Labour employed on site	45,000
Plant installed on site	60,000
Direct expenses	30,000
Proportionate establishment charges	7,500
Cash received (80% of work certified)	3,00,000
Work un-certified	75,000
Materials returned to stores	7,500
Materials in hand at the end	3,000
Plant in hand at the end	45,000
Wages outstanding	9,000
Direct expenses accrued	12,000

Prepare the Contract Account and show the amount that would appear in the Balance Sheet.

[B.Com. – Andhra]

Solution

CONTRACT ACCOUNT

Dr.	Rs.		Cr. Rs.
To Materials purchased	1,20,000	By Materials retuned to stores	7,500
" Materials issued from stores	1,50,000	" Materials in hand at the end	3,000
" Labour	45,000	" Cost of contract c/d	3,78,000
" Wages outstanding	9,000		
" Direct expenses	30,000		
" Direct expenses accrued	12,000		
" Depreciation on plant 60,000 – 45,000	15,000		
" Establishment charges	7,500		
Total	3,88,500		3,88,500
To Cost of contract b/d	3,78,000	By Contractee's account value of work certified (see note below)	3,75,000
" P & L Account (see note below)	38,400	" Cost of work uncertified	75,000
" Profit in Reserve	33,600		
	4,50,000		4,50,000

Balance Sheet

as on 31.12.97 (Extract)

Liabilities	Rs.	Assets	Rs.	Rs.
Wages outstanding	9,000	Materials in hand		3,000
Direct expenses accrued	12,000	Plant	60,000	
		Less : Dep.	15,000	45,000
Profit & Loss A/c	38,400	Work-in-Progress (see note below)		1,16,400

Notes :

1. **Value of work certified :**

If cash received is Rs. 80 the work certified is Rs. 100

If cash received is Rs. 3,00,000 ...... ? $3,00,000 \times \frac{100}{80}$ = Rs. 3,75,000.

2. **Profit taken to P & L Account :**

Value of work certified		3,75,000
Cost of contract	3,78,000	
Less : Cost of work uncertified	75,000	3,03,000
Notional Profit		72,000

$\frac{2}{3}$ × Notional Profit × (Cash received/Value of work certified)

$\frac{2}{3} \times 72,000 \times \frac{3,00,000}{3,75,000}$ = Rs. 38,400.

3. **Work-in-Progress :**

		Rs.
Cost of work un-certified		75,000
Contractee's Balance = 3,75,000 – 3,00,000		75,000
		1,50,000
Less : Profit in Reserve		33,600
	Total :	1,16,400
Alternatively,		
Cost of Contract		3,78,000
Profit taken to P & L Account		38,400
		4,16,400
Less : Cash received from contractee		3,00,000
	Total :	1,16,400

Problem 47

A firm of building contractors carrying out large contracts, kept in a contract ledger, separate accounts for each contract. On 30th June, 1995, the following was shown as being the expenditure in connection with a contract.

	Rs.
Materials purchased	58,063
Materials from stores	9,785
Plant which had been used on other contracts	12,523
Additional plant purchased	3,610
Wages	73,634
Direct expenses	2,026
Proportion of establishment charges	8,720

The contract which had commenced on 1st Feburary, 1995, was for Rs. 3,00,000 and the amount certified by the architect, after deduction of 20 per cent retention money was Rs.1,20,800, the work being certified to 30th June, 1995.

The materials on the site at that date were valued at Rs. 9,858.

A contract plant ledger was also kept in which depreciation was dealt with monthly, the amount debited in respect of plant on the contract to 30th June, 1995 was Rs. 1,130.

You are required to prepare an account showing the profit on the contract to 30th June, 1995.

[B.Com. – Andhra]

Solution

CONTRACT ACCOUNT

for the period from 1.2.95 to 30.6.95

Dr.		Rs.			Cr. Rs.
		Rs.			Rs.
To	Materials purchased	58,063	By	Materials on site	9,858
"	Materials from stores	9,785	"	Cost of contract c/d	1,43,500
"	Wages	73,634			
"	Direct expenses	2,026			
"	Depreciation on Plant	1,130			
"	Establishment charges	8,720			
		1,53,358			1,53,358
"	Cost of contract b/d	1,43,500	By	Value of work certified (see note below)	1,51,000
"	P & L A/c. Profit taken (see note below)	4,000			
"	Profit in Reserve	3,500			
		1,51,000			1,51,000

Notes :

			Rs.
1.	**Value of work certified**	Rs. $1,20,800 \times \frac{100}{80}$ =	1,51,000
Less :	Retention money 20%		30,200
	Cash received 80%		1,20,800

2. **Profit taken to P & L A/c :**

Notional Profit is Rs. 1,51,000 – 1,43,500 = Rs. 7,500

$\frac{2}{3} \times$ Notional Profit $\times$ (Cash received $\div$ Value of work certified)

$\frac{2}{3} \times 7,500 \times \frac{1,20,800}{1,51,000} \times$ Rs. 4,000 or $\frac{2}{3} \times 7,500 \times 80\%$ = Rs. 4,000.

Problem 48

M/s J. Das, contractors, undertook a contract for Rs. 4 lakhs on 1st January, 1997. The following expenses were incurred up to 31st December, 1997 :

	Rs.
Materials issued from stores	35,000
Materials charged direct	5,000
Direct charges	2,000
Wages	20,000

The amount of work certified was Rs. 80,000 of which contractors received 75% in cash. The transactions for 1998 are as under :

Material issued from stores	90,000
Wages	40,000
Direct Charges	4,000

The cost of plant issued on 1st January, 1998 was Rs. 80,000. Further, work certified amounted to Rs. 2,20,000, 75% of which was received; work done and not certified valued at Rs. 15,000. Plant is to be depreciated @ 25% per annum on the original cost. Materials on site valued at Rs. 10,000. The contract was completed on 31st January, 1999 up to which date the following expenses were incurred :

	Rs.
Material issued	40,000
Material charged direct	7,000
Wages	15,000
Direct charges	1,350

The General Reserve on cost each year to be taken at 5% of the amount of material consumed and wages paid during the year. The plant on 31st January, 1998 was valued at Rs.50,000. The materials at site were sold at Rs. 7,000 and those returned to store, amounted to Rs. 13,000.

Prepare contract account and contractee's account showing the result of the transactions assuming that the balance due from the contractee was duly received.

Solution

CONTRACT ACCOUNT

for the year ending 31.12.1997

Dr.	Rs.	Cr.	Rs.
To Materials issued from stores	35,000	By Cost of contract c/d	65,000
" Materials charged direct	5,000		
" Wages	20,000		
" Direct wages	2,000		
" General reserve on cost (5% of Material and wages)	3,000		
	65,000		65,000
To Cost of contract b/d	65,000	By Contractee's A/c value of work certified	80,000
" P & L A/c Profit taken	Nil		
" Profit in suspense c/d	15,000		
Total	80,000	Total	80,000

Note : As the amount of work certified is less than $\frac{1}{4}$th of value of contract for Rs. 4 lakhs, the profit taken to the credit of Profit and Loss Account is Nil.

CONTRACT ACCOUNT

for the year ending 31.12.1998

Dr.		Rs.		Cr. Rs.
To Materials		90,000	By Profit in suspense b/d	15,000
" Wages		40,000	" Materials on site	10,000
" Direct charges		4,000	" Cost of Contract c/d	1,35,000
" Depreciation on Plant 25% of 80,000		20,000		
" General Reserve on cost—5% of Materials i.e. 5% of 90,000	4,500			
Wages i.e. 5% of (40,000–10,000)	1,500	6,000		
		1,60,000		1,60,000
To Cost of Contract b/d		1,35,000	By Contractee's account of work certified	2,20,000
" P & L A/c —Profit taken		50,000	" Cost of work not certified	15,000
" Profit in Suspense		50,000		
		2,35,000		2,35,000

Notes : (a) The cumulative work has been completed to the extent of Rs. 3,00,000 (2,20,000 + 80,000) i.e., 75% of the amount of contract for Rs. 4 lakhs. Hence, the profit taken to the credit of P & L A/c.

$$\frac{2}{3} \times \text{Notional Profit} \times (\text{Cash received} \div \text{Value of work certified}).$$

(b) Notional Profit :

Value of work certified		2,20,000
Cost of contract	1,35,000	
Less : Cost of work not certified	15,000	1,20,000
Notional Profit		1,00,000

$$\frac{2}{3} \times 1,00,000 \times \frac{2,25,000}{3,00,000}$$

$$\text{Or, } \frac{2}{3} \times 1,00,000 \times \frac{75}{100}$$

= Rs. 50,000 to be taken to the credit of P & L A/c.

CONTRACT ACCOUNT

for the month ending on 31.1.1999

Dr.		Rs.			Rs. *Cr.*
To	Cost of work not certified	15,000	By	Profit in suspense b/d	50,000
"	Materials on site b/d	10,000	"	Cash account – (Materials at site sold)	7,000
"	Materials issued	40,000			
"	Materials charged direct	7,000	"	Materials returned to stores	13,000
"	Wages	15,000			
"	Direct charges	1,350	"	Cost of contract c/d	30,950
"	Depreciation on plant 60,000 – 50,000 =	10,000			
"	General reserve on cost 5% of Materials and Wages = Rs. 10,000 + 40,000 + 7,000 + 15,000 – 7,000 – 13,000 = 52,000	2,600			
		1,00,950			1,00,950
To	Cost of contract b/d	30,950	By	Contractee's account value of work certified (4,00,000 – 3,00,000) =	1,00,000
"	P & L A/c – Profit taken	69,050			
		1,00,000			1,00,000

Note : As the work has been completed by 31.1.1999, the profit has been fully taken to the credit of Profit and Loss Account.

CONTRACTEE'S ACCOUNT

			Rs.				Rs.
31.12.97	To	Contract A/c	80,000	31.12.97	By	Bank A/c	60,000
				"	"	Balance b/d	20,000
			80,000				80,000
1.1.98	"	Balance b/d	20,000	31.12.98	By	Bank A/c	1,65,000
31.12.98	"	Contract A/c	2,20,000	31.12.98	"	Balance c/d	75,000
			2,40,000				2,40,000
1.1.99	To	Balance b/d	75,000	31.1.99	By	Bank A/c	1,75,000
31.1.99	"	Contract A/c	1,00,000				
			1,75,000				1,75,000

Problem 49

The following balances have been extracted from the books of a building contractor on 31st March, 1997.

	Rs.
Materials issued at site	65,700
Wages paid	72,500
Wages accrued (due on 31.3.97)	650
Plant issued at site on 1.7.96	16,000
Direct charges paid	2,500
Direct charges accrued on 31.3.97	250
Establishment charges	6,400
Stock of materials at site on 31.3.97	7,200
Value of work certified as at 31.3.97	1,60,000
Cost of work not certified	5,600
Cash received on account of certified work	1,44,000

The work was commenced on 1.4.96. Prepare the Contract Account for the year, providing depreciation at 20% p.a. Calculate the profit or loss on the contract to date making such provisions as are considered desirable.

[Adapted – I.C.W.A. Final]

Solution

CONTRACT ACCOUNT

Dr.					*Cr.*
1996		Rs.	Rs.	Mar. 31 1997	Rs.
July 1	To Plant		16,000	By Balance c/d	
1997				Materials	7,200
Mar. 31					
	To Materials		65,700	" Plant	13,600
	" Wages paid	72,500			
	Add : Accrued	650	73,150	" Cost of Contract	1,43,200
	To Direct charges paid	2,500			
	Add : Accrued	250	2,750		
	To Establishment charges		6,400		
			1,64,000		1,64,000
	To Cost of contract		1,43,200	By Work certified	1,60,000
	" Profit & Loss A/c		13,440	" Work not certified	5,600
	" Reserve A/c		8,960		
			1,65,600		1,65,600
	To Balance b/d			By Wages Accrued	650
	Materials		7,200	" Direct charges accrued	250
	Plant		13,600		
	Work-in-Progress		1,56,640	" Reserve	8,960

WORK NOT CERTIFIED TO BE ASCERTAINED

Problem 50

The following figures have been extracted from the books of Ayan Dasgupta, a contractor, for the year ending 31st March, 1991 :

		Rs.	Rs.
	Work-in-Progress on 31st March, 1990	8,00,000	
Less :	Advance from Contractees	5,00,000	
			3,00,000
	Materials issued to Contract from stores		1,20,000
	Materials supplied to Contract directly		80,000
	Wages		1,05,000
	Other Expenses		30,000
	Materials returned to stores		5,000
	Work certified		3,50,000
	Contracts completed		4,67,000
	Administrative expenses (of which Rs. 4,000 chargeable to Profit & Loss A/c)		12,000
	Plant issued		25,000
	Materials returned direct to suppliers		6,000
	Profit taken upon contract		1,10,000
	Advances from contractees		4,50,000

Prepare Contract Account and Contractee's Account

Solution

CONTRACT ACCOUNT
for the year ending 31.3.1991

Dr.	Rs.		Cr. Rs.
To Work-in-Progress (1. 4. 90)	8,00,000	By Materials returned to stores	5,000
" Materials from stores	1,20,000	" Materials returned to suppliers	6,000
" Materials	80,000	" Contractee's A/c (Contract completed)	4,67,000
" Wages	1,05,000	" Work certified	3,50,000
" Other Expenses	30,000	" Work not certified (balancing figure)	4,50,000
" Administrative Expenses	8,000		
" Plant	25,000		
" Profit & Loss A/c	1,10,000		
	12,78,000		12,78,000

Note : Since profit on contract is given the balancing figure of contract account is to be considered as work not certified.

CONTRACTEE'S ACCOUNT

Dr.	Rs.		Cr. Rs.
To Contract A/c Contract completed	4,67,000	By Balance b/d	5,00,000
" Balance c/d	4,83,000	" Bank	4,50,000
	9,50,000		9,50,000

WHEN PROFIT IS CALCULATED IN RELATION TO ESTIMATED COST

Problem 51

Dastur Engineering Ltd. secured a contract to supply and erect machinery for a sum of Rs.6,50,000.

The Company commenced work on 1st April, 1990 and incurred the following expenses for the financial year 1990–1991 :

	Rs.
Plant and Tools	1,50,000
Machinery and Stores	1,00,000
Establishment Expenses	40,000
Wages	1,20,000

A part of machinery costing Rs. 30,000 was unsuitable to the contract and immediately sold at a profit of Rs. 3,000.

The value of Plant and Tools on 31.3.1991 was Rs. 20,000 and the value of machinery was Rs.10,000.

By 30th April a sum of Rs. 4,50,000 being 90% of the certified value of work done upto 31.3.1991 was received.

The Company estimated that the following further expenditure would be incurred in completing the contract. The Co. credited to Profit and Loss Account that proportion of the estimated net profit to be realised on contract which the certified value of the work done bore to the contract price.

The Company estimated :

i) that the contract would be completed in a further period of three months ;

ii) that the plant and tools would have a residual value of Rs. 5,000 upon the completion of the contract ;

iii) that the wages and establishment expenses up to 30th June, 1991 would be Rs.50,000 and Rs. 5,500 respectively ;

iv) that 3% of the total cost of the contract should be provided for contingencies.

v) cost of machinery and stores Rs. 40,000 including those in stock.

Prepare Contract Account for the year ended 31st March, 1991.

Solution

DASTUR ENGINEERING
CONTRACT ACCOUNT
for the year ended 31st March 1991

Dr.	Rs.		Cr. Rs.
To Plant and Tools	1,50,000	By Bank	33,000
" Machinery and Stores	1,00,000		
" Establishment Exp.	40,000	" Plant in hand	20,000
" Wages	1,20,000	" Machinery in hand	10,000
" Profit & Loss A/c (Profit on Sale of machinery)	3,000	" Cost of Contract c/d	3,50,000
	4,13,000		4,13,000

Contd.

	Rs.		Rs.
To Cost of Contract b/d	3,50,000	By Work-in-Progress	
" Profit and Loss A/c	1,35,142	Work certified	5,00,000
(Profit transferred)		$\left(\text{Rs. } 4,50,000 \times \frac{100}{90}\right)$	
" Work-in-Progress (Profit provision)	14,858		
	5,00,000		5,00,000

Note 1 : Calculation of Profit to be credited to Profit & Loss A/c :

		Rs.
Cost of the contract up to 31. 3. 1991		3,50,000
Add : Further estimated expenses : Machinery and Stores	40,000	
Wages	50,000	
Establishment Charges	5,500	
Plant and Tools (20,000 – 5,000)	15,000	
		1,10,500
Total estimated Cost of the Contract		4,60,500
Add : Provision for contingencies @ 3% = $\frac{3}{100} \times 4,60,500$ =		13,815
		4,74,315
Add : Estimated Profit (balancing figure)		1,75,685
Contract Price (given)		6,50,000

Profit to be credited –

$$\text{Estimated Profit} \times \frac{\text{Work certified}}{\text{Total Contract Price}} = 1,75,685 \times \frac{5,00,000}{6,50,000} = 1,35,142.$$

Problem 52

A contractor, who prepares his account on 31st December each year, commenced a contract on 1st April, 1998. The costing records concerning the said contract reveal the following information on 31st December, 1998 :

	Rs.
Materials charged to site	2,58,100
Labour cngagcd	5,60,500
Foremen's salary	79,300

Plant costing Rs. 2,60,000 had been on site for 146 days. Working life of the plant is estimated at 7 years and its final scrap value at Rs. 15,000. A supervisor, who is paid Rs. 4,000 per month, has devoted approximately three-fourths of his time to this contract. The administrative and other expenses amount to Rs. 1,40,000. Materials in hand at site on 31st December, 1998 cost Rs. 25,400. Some of the materials costing Rs. 4,500 was found unsuitable and was sold for Rs. 4,000 and a part of the plant (whose written down value on 31.12.98 was Rs. 5,500) was sold at a profit of Rs. 1,000 as it was unsuited to the contract.

The contract price was Rs. 22,00,000 but it was accepted by the contractor for Rs. 20,00,000. On 31st December 1995, two-third of the contract was completed. Architect's certificate has been issued covering 50% of the contract price and Rs. 7,50,000 has so far been paid on account.

Prepare Contract Account and state how much profit or loss should be included in the financial accounts to 31st December, 1998. Depreciation is charged on time basis. Also prepare the Contractee Account and show how these accounts would appear in the Balance Sheet as on 31st December 1998.

[C.A. Inter—Adapted]

Solution

CONTRACT ACCOUNT

Dr.		Rs.		Cr. Rs.
31.12.98			31.12.98	
To Materials		2,58,100	By Cash—sale of materials	4,000
" Labour		5,60,500	" Profit & Loss A/c	
" Foremen's salary		79,300	—Loss on sale of materials	500
" Supervisor's salary		27,000	" Materials at site c/d	25,400
" Depreciation of plant		14,000	" Balance c/d	
" Administrative and other		1,40,000	—cost to date	10,49,000
expenses		10,78,900		10,78,900
To Balance b/d		10,49,000	By Work-in-progress c/d	
			—cost of work not yet certified	2,62,250
			" Balance c/d	7,86,750
		10,49,000		10,49,000
To Balance b/d		7,86,750	By Work-in-progress	
" Profit & Loss A/c—propotion			—value of work certified	10,00,000
of profit transferred		1,06,625		
" Work-in-progress c/d				
—provision		1,06,625		
		10,00,000		10,00,000
1.1.1999				
To Materials at site b/d		25,400		
" Work-in-Progress b/d				
—cost of work not				
yet certified	2,62,250			
—value of work				
certified	10,00,000			
	12,62,250			
Less : Provision	1,06,625	11,55,625		

CONTRACTEE

Dr.	Rs.		Cr. Rs.
31.12.98		31.12.98	
To Balance c/d	7,50,000	By Bank	7,50,000

(Extract from)Balance Sheet
as at 31st December 1998

Liabilities		Rs.	Assets	Rs.	Rs.
Profit & Loss A/c (will include)			Plant at site		2,40,500
Profit on Contract No. ...	1,06,625		Materials at site		25,400
Profit on sale of plant	1,000		Work-in-progress	11,55,625	
	1,07,625		Less : Cash received on account	7,50,000	
Less : Loss on site of materials	500				
		1,07,125			4,05,625

Problem 53

GS Construction Ltd. undertook a contract for Rs. 8,00,000 from 1st January, 1995. The particulars in regard to the contract for the year ended 31st December, 1995, were as follows :

	Rs.
Materials purchased	1,25,000
Wages paid	90,000
Direct expenditure	10,000
General overhead	15,000
Depreciation of plant	12,000
Materials in hand on 31.12.95	29,000
Wages accrued on 31.12.95	10,000
Cash received from contractee (being 80% of work certified)	2,40,000
Uncertified work at cost	10,000

The contract deed contained an escalation clause as stated below :

"In the event of prices of materials and rates of wages increase by more than 5% the contract price would be increased accordingly by 25% of the rise in the cost of materials and wages beyond 5% in each case".

It was found that, from the date of signing the deed the prices of materials and wage rate increased by 20% and 25% respectively. The value of the work certified does not take into account the effect of the above clause.

Prepare the Contract Account showing the profit or loss on the contract to be transferred to Profit & Loss Account for the year ended 31.12.95.

[C.A. Inter—Adapted]

Solution

GS Construction Ltd.
CONTRACT ACCOUNT

Dr. *Cr.*

31.12.95		Rs.	31.12.95	Rs.
To Materials		1,25,000	By Materials on hand c/d	29,000
" Wages	90,000		By Balance c/d	2,33,000
Add : Accrued c/d	10,000	1,00,000		
" Direct expenditure		10,000		
" General overhead		15,000		
" Depreciation of plant		12,000		
		2,62,000		2,62,000

Contd.

	Rs.	Rs.		Rs.
To Balance b/d		2,33,000	By Work-in-progress c/d	
			—cost of uncertified work	10,000
			" Balance c/d	
			—cost of certified work	2,23,000
		2,33,000		2,33,000
To Balance b/d		2,23,000	By Work-in-Progress c/d	
" Profit & Loss A/c			—Value of certified work	
transferred		21,889	$\left(\frac{100}{80} \times 2,40,000\right)$	3,00,000
" Work-in-Progress c/d			—Excalation (Note 1)	7,000
—provision		62,111		
		3,07,000		3,07,000
1.1.96			1.1.96	
To Materials on hand b/d		29,000	By Accrued wages b/d	10,000
" Work-in-Progress b/d :				
Cost of uncertified work	10,000			
Value of certified work	3,00,000			
Escalation	7,000			
	3,17,000			
Less : Provision	62,111			
		2,54,889		

Working Notes

Escalation of contract price :

	Rs.	Rs.
Materials		
Increase in cost due to 20% increase in price :		
$\frac{20}{120} \times (1,25,000 - 29,000)$	16,000	
Less : 5% increase beyound which escalation clause		
applies $\frac{5}{20} \times 16,000$	4,000	12,000
Labour—		
Increase in cost due to 25% increase in wage rate :		
$\frac{25}{125} \times 1,00,000$	20,000	
Less : 5% increase beyond which escalation clause		
applies $\frac{5}{25} \times 20,000$	4,000	16,000
Total increase beyond 5%		28,000

Problem 54

Compute a conservative estimate of profit on a contract (which has been 80% complete) from the following particulars.

Total expenditure to date	85,000
Estimated further expenditure to complete the contract (including contingencies)	17,000
Contract Price	1,53,000
Works certified	1,00,000
Works not certified	8,500
Cash received	81,600

[Adapted I.C.W.A., Dec. 1984]

Solution

			Rs.
	Value of work certified		1,00,000
	Work not certified		8,500
	Total work done		1,08,500
Loss :	Total expenses		85,000
	Notional Profit		23,500
	Contract Price		1,53,000
Less :	Up-to-date expenses	Rs. 85,000	
Add :	Further estimated expenses for completion	Rs. 17,000	1,02,000
	Estimated total profit		51,000

Problem 55

M/s Tom and Dick obtained a contract to build quarters, the price being Rs. 1,00,000. Work was started on 1st April, 1990 and the following expenditure was incurred :

	Rs.
Plant	5,000
Stores	18,000
Wages	16,250
Sundry Expenses	1,325
Establishment Charges	2,925

A part of the material was unsuitable and was sold for Rs. 3,625 (cost being Rs. 3,000). A portion of the plant was scrapped and disposed of for Rs. 575.

The value of plant on 31. 3. 1991 was Rs. 1,550 and of stores Rs. 850. Cash received on account was Rs. 35,000, representing 80% of the work certified. The work uncertified was valued at Rs. 5,475 and this was certified later for Rs. 6,250.

M/s Tom and Dick decided to estimate the amount of further expenditure that would be required to complete the contract, to compute from this estimate and the expenditure that would be required to complete the contract, to compute from this estimate and the expenditure already incurred, the total profit that would be made on this contract and to take to credit of P & L A/c for the year 1990-91, that provision of the total which corresponded to the work certified on 31. 3. 1991.

Their estimate reveals that contract would be completed after 9 months, till then wages likely to be incurred Rs. 17,875. The cost of stores etc. required in addition to those in stock on 31.3.1991would be Rs. 17,875, and that further contract expenses would amount to Rs. 1,500. A further investment of Rs. 6,250 would be required on plant which would be valued on 31.12.1990 at Rs. 750. The establishment charges would be same on monthly basis, as in the preceding year.

Lastly, $2\frac{1}{2}$% of the total cost of contract should be kept in as reserve for contingencies.

Prepare Contract, Stores and Plant Accounts for the year ended 31st March, 1991 and also show your calculation of the amount credited to Profit & Loss A/c for the year.

[Adapted—C.A. Final England]

Solution

CONTRACT ACCOUNT

For the year ended 31. 3. 1991

Dr.	Rs.		Cr. Rs.
To Materials from Stores	14,150	By Cost of Contract c/d	37,525
" Plant	2,875		
" Wages	16,250		
" Sundry Expenses	1,325		
" Est. Expenses	2,925		
	37,525		37,525
		By Work-in-Progress :	
To Cost of Contract b/d	37,525	Work Certified	43,750
" Profit & Loss A/c (a)	5,993	Work not Certified	5,475
" Reserve A/c (balancing figure)	5,707		
	49,225		49,225

STORES ACCOUNT

Dr.	Rs.		Cr. Rs.
To Bank A/c	18,000	By Bank-materials sold	3,625
" Profit and Loss A/c (Profit on sale)	625	" Contract A/c (Balancing figure)	14,150
		" Balance c/d (given)	850
	18,625		18,625

PLANT ACCOUNT

Dr.	Rs.		Cr. Rs.
To Bank A/c	5,000	By Bank (sale)	575
		" Contract A/c	2,875
		" Balance c/d	1,550
	5,000		5,000

MEMORANDUM CONTRACT ACCOUNT

Up to 31. 12. 1991

Dr.	Rs.	Rs.		Rs.	Cr. Rs.
To Materials as per Contract A/c	14,150		By Closing Stock of Plant		750.00
Add : Closing balance	850		" Estimated total cost		86,301.25
Add : Additional Stores required given	17,150				
		32,150.00			
To Plant					
As per Contract A/c	2,875				
Add : Closing balance	1,550				
Add : Additional	6,250				
		10,675.00			
To Wages as per Contract A/c	16,250				
Add : Additional wages	17,875	34,125.00			
To Sundry Expenses	1,325				
Add : Additional	1,500				
		2,825.00			
To Establishment Charges	2,925.00				
Add : Additional for 9 months	2,193.75				
		5,118.75			
To Reserve 2.5% on total cost (b)		2,157.50			
		87,051.25			87,051.25

Computation of Net Profit

		Rs.
	Total Contract Price	1,00,000.00
Less :	Total Cost as per Memorandum Contract A/c	86,301.25
		13,698.75

Working Notes :

(a) Calculation of profit to be credited to P & L A/c on completed contract :

Net profit as per Memorandum Contract Account

= Estimating profit × Work Certified ÷ Contract Price

$$= \text{Rs. } 13{,}698.75 \times \frac{43{,}750}{1{,}00{,}000} = \text{Rs. } 5{,}993.20$$

(b) Total Cost without Reseve – Rs. 84,143.75

$$\text{Reserve @ 2.5\% on total cost} = \frac{84{,}143.75}{97.5} \times 2.5 = \text{Rs. } 2{,}157.50.$$

Problem 56

The following information relates to a Building contract for Rs. 10,00,000 :

	1991 Rs.	1992 Rs.
Materials Issued	3,00,000	84,000
Direct wages	2,30,000	1,05,000
Direct Expenses	22,000	10,000
Indirect Expenses	6,000	1,400
Work Certified	7,50,000	10,00,000
Work Uncertified	8,000	–
Materials on Site	5,000	7,000
Plant issued	14,000	2,000
Cash received	6,00,000	10,00,000

The value of plant at the end of 1991 and 1992 was Rs. 7,000 and Rs. 5,000 respectively.

Prepare Contract Account and Contractee's Account for the years 1991 and 1992.

[D.U. B.Com. (Hons)]

Solution

CONTRACT ACCOUNT

For the year ended 31st December, 1991

Dr.	Rs.	Cr.	Rs.
To Materials	3,00,000	By Materials on Site	5,000
" Direct wages	2,30,000	" Plant	7,000
" Direct Expenses	22,000	" Work Certifical	7,50,000
" Indirect Expenses	6,000	" Work not Certified	8,000
" Plant	14,000		
" Notional Profit (balancing figure)	1,98,000		
	7,70,000		7,70,000
To Profit & Loss A/c	1,05,600	By National Profit b/d	1,98,000
" Profit in Suspense	92,400		
	1,98,000		1,98,000

CONTRACT ACCOUNT

For the year ended 31st December, 1992

Dr.	Rs.	Cr.	Rs.
To Materials b/d	5,,000	By Materials on Site c/d	7,000
" Plant b/d	7,000	" Plant c/d	5,000
" Work Certified (Note below)	6,65,600	" Work Certified or contractee	10,00,000
" Materials issued	84,000		
" Direct wages	1,05,000		
" Direct Expenses	10,000		
" Indirect Expenses	1,400		
" Plant issued	2,000		
" Profit & Loss A/c	1,32,000		
	10,12,000		10,12,000

Note :

	Rs.
Value of work in Progress	
Value of work certified	7,50,000
Value of work not certified	8,000
	7,58,000
Less : Profit in Suspense or Reserve	92,400
	6,65,600

CONTRACTEE ACCOUNT

Dr.		Rs.			Cr. Rs.
1991	To Work Certified	7,50,000	1991	By Bank	6,00,000
				" Balance c/d	1,50,000
		7,50,000			7,50,000
1992	To Balance b/d	1,50,000		By Bank	4,00,000
	" Work certified	2,50,000			
		4,00,000			4,00,000

Alternatively

CONTRACTEE ACCOUNT

Dr.		Rs.			Cr. Rs.
1991	To Balance	6,00,000	1991	By Bank	6,00,000
		600,000			6,00,000
1992	To Contract A/c	10,00,000	1992	By Balance b/d	6,00,000
				" Bank (Amount received in full settlement)	4,00,000
		10,00,000			10,00,000

Note : Under the alterrnative method the amount paid in 1991 to the contractee is treated as advance. The Contractee's account is settled with the final payment.

Problem 57

AB contractors obtained a contract to build houses, the contract price being Rs. 4,00,000. Work commenced on 1st January, 1992 and the expenditure incurred during the year was plant and tools Rs. 20,000; stores and materials Rs. 72,000, wages 65,000 sundry expenses Rs. 5,300 and establishment expenses Rs. 11,700.

Certain materials costing Rs. 12,000 were unsuited to the contract and were sold for Rs. 14,500. A portion of the plant was scrapped and sold for Rs. 2,300.

The value of the plant and tools on the sites on 31st December 1992 was Rs. 6,200 and the value of materials and stores on hand Rs. 3,400. Cash received on account was Rs. 1,40,000 representing 80% of the work certified. The cost of the work done but not certified was Rs. 21,900 and this was certified for Rs. 25,000

AB decided (i) to estimate what further expenditure would be incurred in completing the contract, (ii) to compute from this estimate and expenditure already incurred, the total profit that would be made on the contract, and (iii) to take to the credit of the Profit and Loss Account for the year 1992 that proportion of the total which correspond to the work certified by 31st December. The estimate was as follows –

(a) That the contract would be completed by 30th September, 1993

(b) That the wages on the contract in 1993 would amount to Rs. 71,500.

(c) That the cost of stores and materials required in addition to those in stock on 31.12.1992 would be Rs. 68,600 and that the further expenses relating to the contract would amount to Rs. 6,000.

(d) That a further Rs. 25,000 would have to be laid out on plant and tools and that residual value of the plant and tools on 30th September, 1993 would be Rs. 3,000.

(e) That the establishment charges would cost the same per month as in 1992.

(f) That $2\frac{1}{2}$% of the total cost of the contract would be due to defects, temporary maintenance and contingencies.

Prepare Contract Account for the year ended 31st December, 1992 and show your calculations of the amount to be credited to the profit and loss account for the year.

[Adapted—Company Secretaries of India – Inter – June 1992]

Solution

CONTRACT ACCOUNT

Dr.			*Cr.*
	Rs.		Rs.
To Plant and Tools	20,000	By Cash – (materials sold)	14,500
" Stores and Materials	72,000	" Cash (Plant sold)	2,300
" Wages	65,000	" Plant and Tools in hand	6,200
" Sundry Expenses	5,300	" Stores and Materials	3,400
" Establishment Charges	11,700	" Cost of Contract	1,50,100
" P & L A/c profit on sale of materials	2,500		
	1,76,500		1,76,500
To Cost of Contract b/d	1,50,100	By Work-in-Progress : Work Certified $1{,}40{,}000 \times \frac{100}{80}$	1,75,000
" Notional Profit	46,800	" Work not Certified	21,900
	1,96,900		1,96,900
To Profit and Loss A/c (working note)	24,067	By Notional Profit b/d	46,800
" Work-in-Progress	22,733		
	46,800		46,800
1.1.93		1.1.93	
To Plant and Tools	6,200	By Work-in-Progress	22,733
" Stores and Materials	3,400		
" Work-in-Progress			
Work certified	1,75,000		
Work uncertified	21,900		

Calculation of total expenditure

		Rs.	Rs.
	Cost of Contract for the year 1992		1,50,100
Add :	Further estimated expenses –		
	Wages		71,500
	Further contract expenses		6,000
	Further materials	68,600	
Add :	Materials in hand	3,400	
			72,000
	Further Plant	25,000	
Add :	Plant in hand	6,200	
		31,200	
Less :	Residual Value	3,000	28,200
	Establishment charges for 9 months		
	@ last year i.e. $\frac{3}{4}$th of Rs. 11,700		8,775
			3,36,575
Add :	Provision for temporary maintenance and		
	contingencies @ $2\frac{1}{2}$% of total cost of Rs. 3,36,575		8,414
	Total Estimated Cost		3,44,989
Total Estimated Profit			
	Contract Price		4,00,000
Less :	Total Estimated Cost		3,44,989
			55,011

Profit to be transferred to Profit & Loss Account

$$\text{Total Estimated Profit} \times \frac{\text{Work certified}}{\text{Contract price}} = \text{Rs. } 55{,}011 \times \frac{1{,}75{,}000}{4{,}00{,}000} = \text{Rs. } 24{,}067$$

ASSIGNMENT

Theoretical Questions

1. What do you understand by Job Costing ? What are its special features ?
2. What is Batch Costing ? In what industries this can suitably be applied ?
3. What do you mean by Economic Batch Quantity ? How can it be determined ?
4. Describe the special features of contract costing. Give five examples of jobs where contract costing would be appropriate.

   [C.U. B.Com. (Hons.)]
5. State briefly how the profit on uncompleted contracts should be determined.

   [C.U. B.Com. (Hons.)]
6. What do you mean by Work-in-Progress in Contract Account ? State the basis of valuation of Work-in-Progress for the purpose of Balance Sheet.

Practical Questions

1. The following information for the year ended 31st December 1998 is obtained from the books and records of a factory :

Particulars	*Completed jobs*	*Work-in-Progress*
	Rs.	Rs.
Raw materials supplied	90,000	30,000
Wages	1,00,000	40,000
Chargeable expenses	10,000	4,000
Materials transferred to work-in-progress	2,000	2,000
Materials returned to stores	1,000	

Factory overhead is 80% of wages and office overhead 25% of factory cost.

The value of executed contracts during 1998 was Rs. 4,10,000. Prepare (i) Consolidated completed job account. (ii) Consolidated work-in-progress account.

[Adapted—C.A.]

Ans. : Profit – Rs. 53,750

2. The information given below has been taken from the costing records of an Engineering Works in respect of Job No. 1,303.

Materials –		Rs. 6,000
Wages – Dept.	A	60 hours @ Rs. 3 per hour
	B	40 hours @ Rs. 2 per hour
	C	20 hours @ Rs. 5 per hour

Overhead expenses for these 3 departments were estimated as follows :

Variable overheads :	Dept.	A	Rs. 5,000 for 5,000 labour hours
	"	B	Rs. 3,000 for 1,500 labour hours
	"	C	Rs. 2,000 for 1,000 labour hours

Fixed overheads – estimated at Rs. 20,000 for 5,000 normal working hours.

You are required to calculate the cost of the job 1,303 and calculate the price to give profit of 25% on selling price.

Ans. : S. P. – Rs. 8,000
Profit – Rs. 2,000.

3. Builders Ltd. was awarded a contract to build an office block in Calcutta and work commenced at the site on 1st May, 1995. During the period to 28th February, 1996, the expenditure on the contract was as follows :

	Rs.
Materials issued from stores	9,411
Materials purchased	28,070
Direct expenses	6,149
Wages	18,493
Charge made by the company of administration expenses	2,146
Plant and Machinery purchased on 1st May, 1995 for use at site	12,180

On 28th February, 1996, the stock of materials at the site amounted to Rs. 2,164 and there were amounts outstanding for wages Rs. 366 and direct expenses Rs. 49.

Builders Ltd. has received on account the sum of Rs. 64,170 which represents the amount of Certificate No. 1 issued by the architects in respect of work completed to 28th February, 1996 after deducting 10% retention money.

The following relevant information is also available :

(a) The plant and machinery has an effective life of 5 years, with no residual value, and

(b) The company only takes credit for two-thirds of the profit on work certified.

You are required :

(i) To prepare a contract account for the period to 28th February, 1996 and

(ii) To show your calculation of the profit to be taken to the credit of the company's profit and loss account in respect of the work covered by Certificate No. 1.

[C.U. B.Com. (Hons.)]

Ans. : Profit transferred to P & L A/c – Rs. 4,050

4. From the following particulars relating to a contract, prepare (a) the Contract Account : (b) Contractee's account, and also show the relevant entries in the balance sheet :

	Rs.
Materials sent to site	85,349
Labour engaged on site	74,375
Plant installed at cost	15,000
Direct expenditure	4,126
Establishment charges	3,167
Material returned to store	549
Work certified	1,95,000
Cost of work not certified	4,500
Materials on hand, December 31	1,883
Wages accrued due on December 31	2,400
Direct expenditure accrued due on December 31	240
Value of plant, December 31	11,000

The contract price has been agreed at Rs. 2,50,000. Cash has been received from the contractee amounting to Rs. 1,80,000.

[B.Com. Delhi]

Ans : P & L A/c – Rs. 17,400

5. The total value of the Contract is Rs. 10,00,000. The work on the contract was started on 1. 4. 89 and on 31st March, 1990, the position was as follows :

Materials sent to the contract – Rs. 2,00,000, wages paid Rs. 1,00,000. Overhead expenses incurred – Rs. 30,000, Plant issued to contract – Rs. 1,50,000.

Depreciation on Plant @ 10% p.a. is to be considered. 80% of the work certified being Rs.6,00,000 according to agreement has been received in cash.

As at 31. 3. 90 materials lying at site amounted to Rs. 38,000 and cost of uncertified work on that date was Rs. 15,000.

Prepare Contract Account.

[C.U. B.Com. (Pass) 1991]

Ans. : Rs. 3,07,000 – Cost of Contract. Profit transferred – Rs. 1,64,267.

6. A building contractor undertaking construction work at contract price of Rs. 5,00,000 began execution of work on 1st Jan. 1990. The following are the particulars of contract up to 31st December 1990 :

	Rs.
Machinery installed at site	30,000
Materials sent to site	1,70,698
Labour at site	1,48,750
Direct expenses	6,334
Overhead charges allocated	8,252
Materials returned from site	1,098
Works certified by architect	3,90,000
Cash received	3,60,000
Cost of work not yet certified	9,000
Materials on hand 31. 12. 1990	3,766
Wages accrued due on 31. 12. 1990	5,380
Value of machinery as at 31. 12. 1990	22,000

It was decided that profit made on the contract in the year should be arrived at by deducting the cost of works certified from the total value of the architect's.certificate and that a third of the profit so arrived should be regarded as provision against contingencies and that such provision should be increased by taking to the credit of Profit and Loss Account only such proportion of two-thirds profit as the cash received bore to work certified.

Prepare the Contract A/c for the year and show the amount taken to the credit of Profit & Loss A/c.

[Adapted—C.A.]

Ans : Profit – Rs. 34,738

7. The following particulars relate to a contract undertaken by a firm of engineers –

	Rs.
Materials issued	85,000
Labour	74,000
Plant as cost	15,000
Direct expenses	3,000
Establishment charges	4,000
Materials returned to stores	500
Works certified	2,00,000
Cost of work uncertified	4,500
Materials in hand (31st Dec.)	1,800
Wages outstanding	2,500
Value of plant (31st Dec.)	10,000

The contract price was agreed at Rs. 2,60,000. Cash received from the contractee was Rs.1,95,000.

Prepare Contract Account and Contractee's Account. Also show how the entries would appear in the Balance Sheet of the Contractors.

[M.Com. Sagar Univ.]

Ans. : Profit transferred to P & L A/c – Rs. 21,645

Profit in Reserve – Rs. 11,655.

8. The Bharat Construction Company's Site Accounts for the year 1990 showed the following expenses in respect of their project work at Namrup.

	Rs.
Materials issued to site	2,00,000
Wages	4,00,000
Overhead 20% on wages	
Special plant	1,60,000
Value of materials at site as on 31. 12. 90	19,000
Value of work done and not yet certified	50,000

The total value of the contract was Rs. 16,00,000. It was estimated that the project work at Namrup would be completed by 31. 12. 91. The value of work certified was Rs. 8,40,000 and Rs. 7,56,000 was received in cash. Provide depreciation on plant at 25% per annum.

Prepare Namrup Construction Project Account and determine what profit would be taken for the year 1990.

[B.Com. Andhra, Part II]

Ans : Transfer to P & L A/c – Rs. 1,13,400

9. Batliboi Construction Co. Ltd. has undertaken a contract to build Sewage Treatment Plant for New Bombay's Metropolitan Corporation for Rs. 15 lacs. As per the terms of the contract, the contractors are entitled to a retention of 20% of the amount due for a period of one year after the Engineer of the Corporation has certified the same. This money is to be refunded to the contractor after the final certificate is obtained from the Chief Executive Engineer of the Corporation.

The following are the details as shown in the books of the Company as on 31.12.94 :

		Rs.
1.	Labour on site	4,05,000
2.	Materials direct to site less returns	3,20,000
3.	Materials from stores	81,200
4.	Hire and use of plant	12,100
5.	General overheads allocated to the Contract	37,100
6.	Materials in hand on 31.12.94	6,300
7.	Wages accrued on 31.12.94	7,800
8.	Direct expenses accured on 31.12.94	1,600
9.	Work not yet certified (at cost)	16,500
10.	Amount certified by the Corporations' Engineer	12,00,000
11.	Cash received on account (Tax deducted at source at 2%)	9,40,800

You are required to prepare –

(a) Contract Account and (b) Contractee's Account.

[Bombay, M.Com.]

Ans. : Profit transferred to P & L A/c – Rs. 1,90,933.33

Reserve in Profit – Rs. 1,67,066.67

10. From the following particulars prepare (a) Contract Account (b) Contractee's Account, (c) Show calculation of profit which is to be credited to Profit and Loss Acount and (d) Value of work-in-progress with break up :

	Rs.		Rs.
Materials sent to site	85,349	Labour engaged to site	74,375
Plant installed at site at cost	15,000	Direct expenditure	3,167
Establishment charges	4,126	Materials returned to stores	1,549
Work certified	1,95,000	Cost of work not certified	4,500
Materials in hand at 31st Dec.	1,883	Wages accrued at 31st Dec.	2,400
Direct expenditure accrued at 31st. Dec.	240	Value of plant at 31st Dec.	11,000

The contract price has been agreed at Rs. 2,50,000 and cash has been received from the contractee amounting to Rs. 1,80,000.

[C.U. B.Com.]

Ans. : Profit to be credited Rs. 18,015.

11. The following are the particulars relating to a contract which has begun on 1st January 1990 :

	Rs.		Rs.
Contract Price	5,00,000	Overheads	8,240
Machinery	30,000	Materials returned	1,600
Material	1,70,600	Materials on hand, 31.12.90	3,700
Wages	1,48,750	Machinery on 31.12.90	22,000
Direct expenses	6,330	Value of work certified	3,90,000
Outstanding wages	5,380	Cash received	3,51,000
Uncertified work	9,000		

Prepare the Contract Account for the year 1990 showing the amount of profit that may be taken to the credit of the Profit and Loss Account of the year. Also show the amount of the work-in-progress as it would appear in the Balance Sheet of the year.

[Madurai, B.Com.]

Ans. : Profit – Rs. 34,200

12. The Gama Limited was engaged on a contract during 1998. The contract price was Rs.2,50,000. Of the plant and material charged to the contract, the plant which cost Rs.2,500 and materials which cost Rs. 2,000 were lost in an accident.

On 31st December, 1998, the plant which cost Rs. 2,500 was returned to the stores. The cost of work done but uncertified was Rs. 1,000. Materials costing Rs. 2,000 were in hand on site.

Charge depreciation on the plant at 10%. Transfer such profit to the Profit and Loss Account which you think reasonable after preparing a Contract Account :

Other details of the contract are given below :

Charged to contract :

	Rs.		Rs.
Materials	45,000	Wages	70,000
Plant	12,500	Expenses	3,500

Cash received on contract (80% of work certified) Rs. 1,00,000.

[Venkateshwara, B.Com. – Adapted]

Ans. : National Profit – Rs. 10,500. Transferred to P & L A/c Rs. 5,600.

13. Contractors Ltd. obtained a contract for the construction of a barrage. The particulars in regard to the contract for the year ended 31st March, 1996, were as follows :

	Rs.
Agreed value of the contract	2,00,00,000
Materials issued to the contract	30,00,000
Materials returned to stores	75,000
Materials in hand	1,80,000
Wages	60,00,000
Plant at cost (to be depreciated @ 20% p.a.)	50,00,000
Direct expenditure	90,000
General overhead (allocated to the contract)	75,000
Cost of completed work yet to be certified	6,00,000
Work was taken up on 1.4.95	

Up to the close of the period a total sum of Rs. 86,40,000 being 90% of the certified amount was received.

Prepare the Contract Account.

[Calcutta, B.Com.]

Ans. : Profit to be credited to Profit and Loss Account Rs. 1,74,000

Hint : $\frac{2}{3}$ of Notional Profit has been transferred to P & L A/c.

14. A construction company has undertaken to construct a bridge. The following particulars relate to the construction for the year ended 31.3.96.

	Rs.
Materials :	
Direct purchase	50,000
Issued from stores	10,000
Wages for labour	45,000
General plant in use	
(depreciation to be charged @ 10%)	1,00,000
Direct expenses	3,500
Share of general overhead	2,000
Materials in hand at 31.3.96	1,000
Materials lost by fire	500
Salvage value thereof	150
Wages accrued at 31.3.96	5,000
Direct expenses accrued at 31.3.96.	500
Value of work certified	1,59,000
Cost of uncertified work	4,500

The value of the contract is Rs. 2,15,000 and it is the practice of the contractee as per terms of the contract, to retain 10% of work certified.

From the above particulars, prepare the Contract account for the year ended 31.3.96.

[Calcutta, B.Com]

Ans. : Profit transferred – Rs. 23,400

15. A Contract Account in the books of Construction Ltd. appears as follows :

1996		Rs.
June 30.	Materials issued to site	5,000
	Plant	12,500
	Indirect labour	4,600
	Overhead expenses	1,950

You are informed that it is the practice of the firm to take credit for $\frac{2}{3}$rd of the profits earned on contracts in progress after taking into account the value of work certified for payment by architects. You are required to

(a) Complete the Contract A/c to June 30.

(b) Show the amount to be transferred to P & L A/c.

(c) Show relevant entries in the Balance Sheet as on 30.6.1996.

For this purpose you are given the following further information as at that date :

	Rs.
Value of work certified for payment	10,000
Cost of work carried, but uncertified	3,800
Stock unused	950
Value of plant at site 30.6.1996.	11,875

[Delhi, B.Com.]

Ans. : Profit to be taken to P & L A/c – Rs. 1,717.

16. The following is the summary of the entries in a Contract Ledger as on the 31st December, 1989 in respect of Contract No. 51 :

	Rs.		Rs.
Materials bought directly	35,000	Establishment charges	8,000
Materials from stores	7,000	Plant	34,200
Wages	18,000	Scrap sold	1,820
Direct expenses	7,000		

The further information is as follows :

1. Accruals on 31st December, 1989 were : Wages Rs. 900 and direct expenses Rs. 1,200.
2. The cost of the work uncertified included materials Rs. 2,600, wages Rs. 1,000 and expenses Rs. 1,500.
3. Rs. 2,000 worth of plant and Rs. 2,000 worth of materials were destroyed by fire.
4. Rs. 5,000 worth of plant sold for Rs. 3,000 and materials costing Rs. 5,000 sold for Rs. 6,000.
5. Depreciation till 31st December, 1989 on plant Rs. 10,000.
6. Materials at site Rs. 5,000.
7. Cash received from the contractee Rs. 60,000 being 80% of the work certified.
8. Contract price Rs. 1,00,000.

Show the Contract Account and Work-in-Progress Account. Show the same in the Balance Sheet.

[Mysore, B.Com.]

Ans. : Profit – Rs. 7,820

17. ABC Contractor & Co. undertook to construct a big building for EFGH Housing Co. on 1.4.1996 fora contract price of Rs. 12,00,000.

	Rs.
Materials issued from stores	3,00,000
Materials purchased for the contract	80,000
Normal loss of materials	2,000
Plant stalled at the site	1,40,000
Wages paid to the workers	4,80,000
Direct expenses paid for the contract	44,000
Extablishment Expenses paid	20,000
Direct expenses accrued on 31.3.1997	6,000

Of the plant and materials charged to the contract, plant which cost Rs. 10,000 and materials costing Rs. 8,000 were lost. Some materials costing Rs. 5,000 were sold for Rs. 6,000. On 31.3.1997 plant costing Rs. 4,000 was returned to stores and plant which cost Rs. 6,000 was transferred to other contract site.

The work certified Rs. 9,60,000 and 80% of the same was received in cash. Work completed but not certified upto 31.3.1997 was Rs. 6,000. Charge depreciation on plant @ 10% p.a.

Prepare Contract Account and Contractee's Account for the year 1996-97.

Ans. : Profit transferred to P & L A/c Rs. 19,200;
Profit provision Rs. 16,800.

Hint : Normal loss will not be considered

18. Fabrication Company Limited undertook the construction of a large reservoir and started its work on January 1, 1996. The value of the contract is Rs. 20 lakhs and for the year to December 31, 1996, the expenses and other details were as under :

	Rs.
Materials purchased	3,00,000
Materials from stores	80,000
Materials in hand on 31st December	40,000
Labour on site	2,75,000
Direct expenses	25,000
General overhead chargeable to the contract	10,000
Plant and machinery purchased on January 1, 1996, for use at site (effective life 5 years with no residual value)	2,00,000
Wages accrued on 31st December	15,000
Direct expenses accrued	3,000
Work certified	8,40,000
Cash received on account (80% of the value of work certified)	6,72,000

Assuming that the company takes credit for two-thirds of the profit on the work certified, prepare a Contract Account from the abovenoted data and work out the profit in respect of the work done up to date that the company should take to its Profit and Loss Account.

[Calcutta, B.Com.]

Ans. : Profit to be taken to P & L A/c – Rs. 70,400

19. The following particulars relate to a contract undertaken by a firm of engineers :

	Rs.
Materials issued	85,000
Labour	74,000
Plant at Cost	15,000
Establishment Charges	4,000
Direct Expanses	3,000
Materials returned to stores	500
Work Certified	2,00,000
Cost of work uncertified	4,500
Materials on hand (31.12)	1,800
Wages outstanding	2,500
Value of Plant (31.12)	10,000

The contract price was agreed at Rs. 2,60,000. Cash received from the contractee Rs.1,95,000.

[V. U. B.Com. (Hons.) 1988]

Ans : Profit Rs. 33,300

Profit transferred – Rs. 21,645

20. M/s Sunirman Ltd., undertook a contract for Rs. 2,50,000 for constructing a college building. The following is the information concerning the contract during the year 1990 :

	Rs.
Materials sent	85,349
Labour engaged	74,375
Plant installed (at Cost)	15,000
Direct Expenditure	3,167
Establishment charges	4,126
Materials returned to stores	549
Work certified	1,95,000
Cost of work not certified	4,500
Materials in hand on 31.12.90	1,883
Wages accrued 31.12.1990	2,400
Direct Expenditure accrued 31.12.90	240
Value of plant on 31.12.90	11,000
Cash received from contractee	1,80,000

Prepare Contract Account, Contractees Account and show the value of work-in-progress as on 31.12.1990.

(V. U. B. Com. (Hons.) 1991]

Ans. : Profit – Rs. 28,275

Profit transferred to P & L A/c – Rs. 17,400

Work-in-Progress Rs. 10,800

21. From the following particulars in respect of Contract No. 123 for the year ended 31.12.1987, prepare Contract Account :

	Rs.
Contract Price	6,00,000
Date of Commencement 1.1.1987	
Materials sent to site on 1.1.87	1,50,000
Plant sent to site on 1.1.87	2,00,000
Wages Paid	1,80,000
Wages due but not paid	3,000
Materials returned to store	5,000
Materials pilfered from the site	10,000
Other expenses on the contract	26,000
Cash received on account	3,60,000
Insurance claim admitted for materials pilfered	8,500
As at 31st December, 1987 there had been at site materials awaiting use	8,000
Work yet to be approved by the contractee at cost	11,000
The Plant is subjected to depreciation @ 7.5% p.a.	
Cash received on acccount has been, as per the contract, 90% of the value of work certified	

It is the practice to take credit in the Profit & Loss Account for two thirds of the realised profit on partly completed contract.

[Adapted—C.U. B.Com. (Pass)

Ans. : Profit – Rs. 60,000

Profit transferred to P & L A/c – Rs. 36,000

22. From the following particulars in respect of Contract No. 136 for the year ended 31.3.1993 prepare Contract Account :

	Rs.
Contract Price	12,00,000
Date of Commencement of Work	1.4.1992
Materials sent to site	3,00,000
Plant sent to site on 1.4.92	3,50,000
Wages paid	3,60,000
Wages due but not paid	6,000
Materials returned from the site to stores	10,000
Materials stolen from the site	20,000
Overhead Expenses	52,000
Cash received on account	7,20,000
Insurance claim admitted for materials stolen	17,000
Unused materials at site on 31.3.1993	16,000
Work yet to be approved by the contractee at cost	22,000
Depreciation on plant to be provided	10% p.a.

Cash received on account has been, as per contract, 90% of the work certified.

It is the practice to take credit in the Profit and Loss Account $\frac{2}{3}$rd of the profit realised in cash on partly completed contract.

(C.U. B.Com. (Pass) 1993]

Ans. : Profit transferred to P & L A/c Rs. 69,000

23. The total value of the Contract is Rs. 10,00,000. The work on the contract was started on 1.4.1989 and on 31st March, 1990 the position was as follows: Materials sent to the contract – Rs. 2,00,000, Wages paid – Rs. 1,00,000, Overhead expenses incurred Rs.30,000, Plant issued to the Contract Rs. 1,50,000.

Depreciation on Plant @ 10% p.a. is to be considered. 80% of the work certified being Rs.6,00,000 according to agreement has been received in cash.

As at 31.3.1990 materials lying at site amounted to Rs. 38,000 and cost of uncertified work on that date was Rs. 15,000.

Prepare Contract Account.

[C.U. B.Com. (Pass) 1991]

Ans. : Cost of Contract – Rs 3,07,000; Profit & Loss A/c – Rs. 2,44,267 (appr.)

24. Given below is a summary of entries in a Contract Ledger as at 31. 12. 89 in respect of Contract No. 532 :

	Rs.		Rs.
Materials	36,500	Establishment charges	8,000
Wages	24,420	Plant	34,000
Direct expenses	6,710	Sales of scrap	1,820

You are required to prepare an account for Contract No. 523 after taking into account the following information and to indicate what profit or loss should be taken to the Profit and Loss Account for the year ended 31.12.89 :

(a) Accruals at 31.12.89 are : Wages Rs. 800, other expenses Rs. 1,120.

(b) Depreciation of plant up to to 31.12.89 was Rs. 8,550.

(c) Included in the summary entries are : Wages Rs. 1,000, other expenses Rs. 1,500, materials used Rs. 2,080 since certification of work done.

(d) Materials on site at 31.12.89 : Cost Rs. 10,000.

(e) Rs. 62,500 had been the total work certified up to 20.12.89 when $\frac{3}{8}$thsof the contract remained uncompleted.

(f) The total contract price was Rs. 1,00,000.

[Bangalore, B.Com.]

Ans. : Loss Rs. 7,200 ;
Work uncertified Rs. 4,580

25. A building contractor undertook to construct a building for which the following details are supplied :

(i) Construction started on January 1, 1990 ; (ii) Total contract price Rs. 5,00,000 ; (iii)Raw Materials supplied Rs. 1,00,000 ; (iv) Direct Labour cost Rs. 60,000 ; (v) Other expenses Rs. 5,000 ; (vi) Plant installed at site Rs. 80,000 ; (vii) Materials in hand (on closing day) Rs. 2,000 ; (viii) Proportionate overhead expenses Rs. 20,000 ; (ix) Expenses accrued but not paid Rs. 1,000 ; (x) Value of work certfied Rs. 2,50,000 ; (xi) Cost of work not certified Rs.10,000 ; (xii) Cash received from contractee Rs. 2,00,000.

Prepare the Contract Account for the year ending 31st December, 1990 by transferring reasonable profit to Profit and Loss Account aftr adjusting depreciation on plant at 20% p.a.

[C.U. B.Com. (Hons.) 1989]

Ans. : Profit transferred to P & L A/c Rs. 32,000.

26. ABC Ltd. entered into a contract of road construction for a total contract price of Rs.10,00,000. For the year ending 31. 12. 1989 the following information is collected on account of the contract –

(i) Raw Materials Rs. 1,30,000 ; (ii) Wages Rs. 1,20,000 ; (iii) Plant installed at site (at cost) Rs. 2,00,000 ; (iv) Supervision expenses Rs. 60,000 ; (v) Proportionate share of office overhead Rs. 10,000 ; (vi) Materials in hand (on the closing day) Rs. 15,000 ; (vii) Materials returned to stores Rs. 3,000 ; (viii) Wages accrued Rs. 3,000 ; (ix) Depreciation on Plant at 10% p.a. (x) Contractee paid Rs. 2,80,000 (being 80% of work certified) ; (xi) Cost of work uncertified Rs. 35,000.

Show Contract Account.

[C.U. B.Com. (Hons.)]

Ans : Profit transferred to P & L A/c Rs. 16,000.

Hint : Since less than 50% of contract has been completed, $\frac{1}{3}$ of profit has been transferred to P & L A/c.

27. The Contract Ledger of a Company showed the following expenditure on account of Contract No. 1470 at 31st December 1990 :

	Rs.		Rs.
Materials	94,000	Wages	1,03,000
Plant	12,000	Establishment Charges	6,700

The Contract had commenced in January, 1990 and the contract price was Rs. 4,00,000. Cash received on account to date was Rs. 1,72,000 representing 80% of the work certified, the remaining 20% being retained until completion. The value of materials on hand was Rs.4,500 and the work finished but not certified was Rs. 4,000.

Prepare an account in respect of the contract showing profit to date, assuming depreciation on plant at 10% per annum and state the proportion of profit the company would be justified in taking to the credit of the Profit and Loss Account.

[Calicut, B.Com.]

Ans : Profit taken – Rs. 9,920

28. The following was the expenditure on a contract for Rs. 6,00,000 commenced in February 1990 –

	Rs.
Materials	1,20,000
Wages	1,64,000
Plant	20,000
Business charges	8,600

Cash received on account to 31st December 1990 amounted to Rs. 2,40,000 being 80 per cent of work certified ; the value of materials on hand at 31. 12. 1990 was Rs. 10,000.

Prepare the Contract Account for 1990 showing the profit to be credited to the year's Profit and Loss Account. Plant is to be depreciated at 10%.

Ans. : Profit transferred to P & L A/c – Rs. 8213.

Hint : Since 50% of contract has been completed $\frac{2}{3}$ of Notional Profit has been considered.

Profit transferred $\frac{2}{3}$rd of Notional profit × (Cash received ÷ Work certified)

29. Work out the Contract Account from the following information. The terms of the contract are Rs. 20 per sq. ft. of the covered floor area built and certified as correct by the engineer of the contractee.

Building materials at start of the work, Rs. 10,000. Purchase of materials during the contract work :

(a) Cement 9,000 bags at Rs. 10 per bag.
(b) Bricks 1,00,000 at Rs. 100 per 1,000 bricks.
(c) Sand 10,000 cft. at Rs. 20 per cft.
(d) Wood work 900 cft. at Rs. 20 per cft.

The value of materials on hand on completion of work, Rs. 20,000.

100 masons at Rs. 7 each per day for 40 days.

500 coolies at Rs. 2 each per day for 40 days.

Tools and Plant :

Two new concrete mixers were purchased at the commencement of the work costing Rs.10,000 each. The residual value of each of these after completion would be Rs. 3,500 each.

Supervision :

50% of the 4 engineers' pay at Rs. 500 per month each for two months.

50% of the 10 overseers' pay at Rs. 250 per month each for four months.

Administration overheads :

20% of the head office expenses for the period of the contract.

The head office expenses were Rs. 5,000.

Quantity of work done :

15,000 sq. ft. of the covered floor area certified as correct by the contractee.

[Mysore, B.Com.]

Ans. : Profit transferred to P & L A/c – Rs. 55,333.

30. Builders Ltd. was awarded a contract to build an office block in Calcutta and work commenced at the site on 1st May, 1989.

During the period to 28th February, 1990, the expenditure on the contract was as follows :

	Rs.
Materials	9,411
Materials purchased	28,070
Direct expenses	6,149
Wages	18,493

Charge made by the company for administration expenses Rs, 2,146

Plant and machinery purchased on 1st May, 1989 for use at site Rs. 12,180

On the 28th February, 1990, the stock of materials at the site amounted to Rs. 1,164 and there were outstanding wages Rs. 366 and direct expenses Rs. 49.

Builders Ltd. has received on account the sum of Rs. 64,170 which represents the amount of Certificate No. 1 issued by the architects in respect of work completed to 28th February, 1990, after deducting 10% retention money.

The following relevant information is also available :

(a) The plant and machinery has an effective life of 5 years with no residual value, and

(b) The company only takes credit for two-thirds of the profit on work certified.

You are required :

(i) to prepare Contract Account for the period to 28th February 1990, and

(ii) to show your calculation of the profit to be taken to the credit of the company's Profit and Loss Account in respect of the work covered by Certificate No. 1.

[Calcutta, B.Com.]

Ans. : Profit to be credited to Profit & Loss Account – Rs. 3,833

31. Raj Contractors obtained a contract for building an office for Rs. 3,00,000. Construction started on 1st April 1995. At the end of the financial year, i.e. 31st March, 1996, they received a sun of Rs. 1,20,000 being 80% of the amount of the Surveyor's certificate. Prepare the contract account showing the profit on contract as on 31.3.1996 from the following information.

	Rs.
Stores issued to contract	60,000
Stock on hand (31.3.1996)	2,500
Wages paid	60,000
Plant purchased for the contract	60,000
Direct Expenses	11,000
Overhead allocated to this contract	5,500
Plant to be depreciated @ 10% p.a.	

[Madras Univ. B.Com. 1997]

Ans. : Transferred to Profit & Loss Account Rs. 2,667

32. Hindusthan Construction Ltd. was engaged for the construction of a bridge in the year 1996. The following particulars are obtained as at 31.12.1996.

Date of commencement of the contract 1st January, 1996.

	Rs.
Contrct price	10,00,000
Materials delivered at the site	2,00,000
Materials issued from stores	80,000
Materials returned to stores	7,000
Architect's fees	10,000
Direct wages paid	2,10,000
Direct Expenses	90,000
Establishment charges	37,000
Plant installed of the value	1,20,000
Materials on site on December 31st	35,000
Expenses outstanding on December 31	9,000
Cost of contract not yet certified	36,000
Value of contract certified	6,80,000
Cash received from contractee	5,80,000
Value of plant on December 31st.	15,000

You are required to prepare :

(i) A contract Account and (ii) The contractee's Account.

[V.U. B.Com.(Hons.) 1996]

Ans. : Profit transferred Rs. 9,667

33. (a) The following information relates to two contracts of "X Ltd." in 1988 :

Particulars	*Contract A* Rs.	*Contract B* Rs.
Materials sent to sites	1,70,698	1,46,534
Labour	1,48,750	1,37,046
Plant	30,000	25,000
Direct expenses	6,334	5,718
Establishment charges	8,252	7,704
Materials returned to store	1,098	1,264
Work certified	3,90,000	2,90,000
Work uncertified	9,000	6,000
Materials at site (31. 12. 88)	3,766	3,472
Wages accrued (31. 12. 88)	4,800	4,200
Direct expenses accrued (31. 12. 88)	480	360
Value of plant (31. 12. 88)	22,000	19,000

The Contract price was Rs. 5,00,000 for A and Rs. 4,00,000 for B. The cash received from contractee was 80% of the value of work certified.

Prepare :

(i) The Contract Accounts,

(ii) The Contractee's Accounts.

[Madras Univ. B.Com. – 1989]

Ans. : Cont. A – P & L A/c – Rs. 30,160
Profit in Reserve – Rs. 26,390
Contract B – Loss – Rs. 6,826

34. The following information relates to a building contract for Rs. 10,00,000.

	1996 Rs.	1997 Rs.
Materials issued	3,00,000	84,000
Direct wages	2,30,000	1,05,000
Direct expenses	22,000	10,000
Indirect expenses	6,000	1,400
Work certified	7,50,000	10,00,000
Work uncertified	8,000	—
Materials at site	5,000	7,000
Plant issued	14,000	2,000
Cash recd. from contractor	6,00,000	10,00,000

The value of plant at the end of 1996 and 1997 was Rs. 7,000 and Rs. 5,000, respectively. Prepare (i) the contract account, and (ii) contractee account for two years 1996 and 1997 taking into consideration such profit for transfer to the profit and loss account as you think proper.

[B.Com. (Hons.), Delhi]

Ans. : 1996 P & L A/c – Rs. 105,600
1997 P & L A/c – Rs. 1,32,000

35. The following information relates to a contract for Rs. 7,50,000 (the contractee paying 90% of the value of work done as certified by the Architect and rest on completion of the contract) :

	1988	1989	1990
	Rs.	Rs.	Rs.
Materials	90,000	1,10,000	63,000
Wages	85,000	1,15,000	85,000
Direct Expenses	3,500	12,500	4,500
Indirect Expenses		1,500	2,000
Work certified	1,75,000	5,65,000	7,50,000
Work-in-Progress uncertified	—	10,000	—
Plant	10,000	—	—

The value of the Plant at the end of the 1988, 1989 and 1990 was Rs. 8,000, Rs. 5,000, Rs.2,000 respectively.

Prepare Contract Accounts.

[Adapted—Lucknow, B.Com. Final]

Ans. : 1988 – Loss – Rs. 7,000
1989 – Profit transferred to P & L A/c – Rs. 94,800
1990 – Profit transferred – Rs. 82,500

Hints -:

1989 – W.I.P. Opening Balance to be brought down – 1,75,000.

	Rs.
1990 – W.I.P. brought down – W. C.	5,65,000
Add : Work not certified –	10,000
	5,75,000
Less : W. I. O. (Reserve)	53,000
	5,22,000

36. A building contractor took a contract for the construction of a certain building on 1st January, 1996. The contract price was agreed at Rs. 4,00,000. The contractor had made the following expenditure during the year :

	Rs.		Rs.
Direct materials purchased	20,000	Plant	40,000
Direct materials issued from stores	5,000	Indirect expenses	10,000
Direct labour	15,000		

From the following further particulars, prepare a Contract Account for the year. Also show the amount of work-in-progress which will be shown in the Balance Sheet of the contractor :

	Rs.
Value of plant on 31st December, 1996	30,000
Stock of materials at the place of work on 31st December, 1996	5,000
Materials returned to stores	1,000
Work certified by the architect	75,000
Cash received	70,000
Cost of work not yet certified	4,000

[Kerala, B.Com.]

Ans. : Work-in-Progress – Rs. 54,000

37. Kurian Construction Company undertook the construction of a bridge. The value of contract was Rs. 75,000 subject to retention of 20% until one year after the certified completion of the contract and the final approval of contractee's engineer. The following are the details as shown in the books on 30th September, 1990 :

	Rs.
Labour on site	24,30,000
Materials direct to site	19,20,000
Materials from store	4,97,200
•Hire and use of plant – plant upkeep	72,600
Direct expenses	1,38,000
Overheads charged to contract	2,22,600
Materials on hand (30. 9. 90)	37,800
Wages accrued (30. 9. 90)	9,600
Work not yet certified –cost	99,000
Work certified	66,00,000
Cash received on account	52,80,000
Materials lost in fire accident	10,000

Prepare (a) Contract Account, (b) Contractee's Account. Show how the items relating to contract appear in the Balance Sheet.

[Osmania, B.Com.]

Ans. : Profit taken – Rs. 7,76,960

38. The following figures are available in respect of Contract No. 101 of the Construction Corporation Ltd., Calcutta.

	Rs.
Materials purchased and delivered to work site	45,000
Materials issued from site stores	4,500
Materials returned to store	500
Site Wages	15,000
Site office expenses	2,000
Plant issued and transferred to site	5,000
Plant returned from site	1,500
Consulting and design fees paid	1,300
Sub-contact work	5,200

Central Office overhead is @ 10% of site wages at the year end.

		Rs.
(a)	Plant at site	1,800
	Material at site	1,000
	Pre-payments	200
	Accruals	300
	Cost of work done but not yet certified	3,500
(b)	Value of work certified by architect	86,310

On account payment received by C. C. Ltd. less 10% retention money. You are required to prepare : (a) Contract Account; (b) Customer's Account.

[M.Com. – S.V. – April]

Ans. : Transferred to P & L A/c Rs. 20,760

39. The following is the summary of the expenditure on Job No. 50 to 31st December, 1995 :

	Rs.
Direct Wages	6,900
Direct Materials	34,000
Stores issued	3,800
Stores returned	550
Sub Contract costs	6,300
Plant	12,000

You obtain the following information :

1. The job began in 1995 and the total contract price was Rs. 60,000.
2. The architects had certified that $\frac{4}{5}$th of the contract had been completed on 15th December, 1995.
3. Depreciation on plant to 15th December, 1995 is Rs. 4,800.
4. The summary set out above includes items relating to the period since 15th December 1995 as follows : Wages Rs. 700, Materials used Rs. 1,520.
5. Materials on site on 31st December, '95 had cost Rs. 5,000 and stores on site had cost Rs.400.
6. Establishment charges are 40% on direct wages.
7. A fine of Rs. 1,000 is likely to be imposed for late completion.

You are required to prepare a job cost Ledger Account, to show what profit or loss has arisen on the work certified and to suggest what figures should be taken to Profit and Loss Account for the year to 31st December, 1995.

Hint : Provision for fine should be credited to provision A/c and to be debited to contract A/c.

[B.Com. – Madras]

Ans. : Loss Rs. 2,110

40. The following is the summary of the entries in a Contract ledger as on 31st March, 1999 in respect of Contract No. 51.

	Rs.
Materials bought directly	35,000
Materials from stores	7,000
Wages	18,000
Direct Expenses	7,000
Establishment charges	8,000
Plant	34,200
Scrap sold	1,820

Further information is as follows :

(i) Accruals on 31.3.1999 – Wages Rs. 900 ; Direct expenses – Rs. 1,200.

(ii) The Cost of uncertified work included materials Rs. 2,600, Wages – Rs. 1,000 and expenses Rs. 1,500.

iii) Rs. 2,000 worth of plant and Rs. 3,000 worth of materials were destroyed by fire.

iv) Rs. 5,000 worth of plant sold for Rs. 3,000 and materials costing Rs. 5,000 were sold for Rs. 6,000.

v) Depreciation till 31.3.1999 on plant Rs. 10,000.

vi) Materials at site Rs. 5,000.

vii) Cash received Rs. 60,000 being 80% of work certified.

viii) Contract price Rs. 1,00,000.

Show Contract Account and the Work-in-Progress.

[Adapted—Mysore, B.Com.]

Ans. : Profit – Rs. 7,820, Work-in-Progress – Rs. 16,450.

41. Pioneer Construction Company Ltd. obtained a contract for the erection of a multistoried building. Building operations started in July 1997. The contract price was Rs. 9,00,000. On 30th June 1998, the end of the financial year, the cash received on account was Rs.3,60,000, being 80% of the amount on the surveyor's certificate.

The following additional information is given below :

	Rs.
Materials issued to contract	1,80,000
Materials on hand at site as on 30th June 1998	7,500
Wages	2,46,000
Plant purchased specially for contract and to be depreciated at 10% per annum	30,000
Direct expenses incurred	12,900
General overhead allocated to contract	7,600
Work finished but not yet certified : cost	15,000

You are required to prepare the contract account and statement showing the profit on the contract to 30th June 1998, indicating what proportion of the profit the company would be justified in taking to the credit of the profit and loss account, and to show what entries in respect of the contract would appear in the balance sheet.

[C.A. Final, Nov. – Adapted]

Ans. : Cost of contract – Rs. 4,42,000

42. From the following particulars prepare a Contract Account for the year ended 31.12.1994 :

	Rs.
Machinery installed	50,000
Materials issued	1,60,000
Labour	1,30,000
Direct expenses	6,000
Overhead charges	5,000
Materials returned	2,000
Cash received	4,50,000
Retention money	20,100
Cost of work not certified	20,000
Materials on hand	4,000
Wages accrued	3,000
Value of machinery (depreciated)	38,000

General plant costing Rs. 1,00,000 was used for 3 months. Depreciation @ 20% p.a. is to be provided. Materials costing Rs. 2,000 were sold for Rs. 3,000. In addition scraps were sold for Rs. 1,000. Materials costing Rs. 8,000 were lost and Rs. 5,000 had been recovered from Insurance Company.

[Adapted—Audit & Account. Service Exam. – W.B.]

Ans. : Profit transferred to Profit & Loss A/c – Rs. 1,25,144 (Approx.)

43. The following figures are supplied to you by the contractor for the year ending 31st December, 1990 :

		Rs.	Rs.
	Work-in-Progress on 31. 12. 1989	85,000	
Less :	Cash received from the Contractee	55,000	
			30,000
During the year 1990 :			
	Wages paid		8,500
	Materials bought		6,000
	Materials issued from Stores		10,500
	Working expenses		1,500
	Administrative expenses		1,250
	(Rs. 250 chargeable to P & L A/c)		
	Plant		2,500
	Materials returned to supplier		450
	Materials returned to stores		550
	Work certified		15,000
	Contract finished		22,500
	Profit taken upon Contract		11,500
	Advances from the Contractee		40,000

Prepare Contract Ledger Account and the Contractee's A/c and show the Work-in-Progress as it would appear in the Balance Sheet.

[Adapted—B.Com. – Bombay]

Ans. : (a) Work uncertified – Rs. 88,000

(b) Contractee's A/c – Rs. 95,000

(c) Work-in-Progress – Rs. 63,000

44. A building contractor took a contract for the construction of a certain building on January 1, 1997. The contract price was agreed at Rs. 8,00,000. The contractor incurred the following expenditure during the year :

	Rs.
Direct material purchased	20,000
Material issued from stores	30,000
Direct labour	30,000
Plant	80,000
Direct expenses	20,000
	1,80,000

From the following further information prepare a contract account for the year. Also show the amount of Work-in-Progress which will be shown in the Balance Sheet of the contractor :

	Rs.
Value of plant on 31.12.1997	60,000
Stock of material at site on 31.12.97	10,000
Materials returned to store	2,000
Work certified by architect	1,50,000
Cash received from contractee	1,40,000
Cost of work not yet certified	8,000

[M.Com.—Agra]

[**Ans.** : The work certified being less than a quarter of the value of contract, no portion of profit would be taken to Profit and Loss A/c, Work-in-Progress Rs. 1,08,000.]

45. On 31st December 1998, the books of accounts of a contractor show the following particulars :

	Rs.	Rs.
Work-in-progress 31. 12. 1998	2,50,000	
Advance taken	1,50,000	1,00,000
Materials taken directly to contracts		20,000
Materials from stores		45,000
Wages		35,000
Expenses		5,000
Administration expenses		1,950
Plant given to contract		11,000
Materials returned to supplies.		2,500
Materials returned to stores		3,500
Completed contracts		1,10,000
Work certified		80,000
Profit determined on contracts		65,000
Advance taken in the year		2,50,000

Prepare Contract Account and Contractee's Account. Explain how you would show the Work-in-Progress as on 31.12.1998 in the Balance Sheet.

[Nagarjuna, B.Com.]

Ans. : Work uncertified – Rs. 2,36,950

46. Two contracts commenced on 1st January and 1st July 1996 respectively, were undertaken by a contractor and their accounts on 31st December 1996 showed the following position :

	Contract 1 Rs.	*Contract 2* Rs.
Contract price	4,00,000	2,70,000
Expenditure :		
Materials	72,000	58,000
Wages paid	1,10,000	1,12,400
General charges	4,000	2,800
Plant installed	20,000	16,000
Materials on hand	4,000	4,000
Wages accrued	4,000	4,000
Work certified	2,00,000	1,60,000
Cash received in respect thereof	1,50,000	1,20,000
Work done but not certified (at cost)	6,000	8,000

The plant was installed on the date of commencement of each contract ; depreciation thereon is to be taken at 10% per annum.

Prepare the Contract Account in the tabular form and ascertain the profit or loss to be taken to Profit and Loss Account.

[Kerala – B.Com.]

Ans. : Contract 1. Profit to be taken to P & L A/c Rs. 9,000. Profit in Reserve Rs. 9,000. Contract 2. Loss Rs. 6,000.

47. A contractor undertook five contracts during the year 1998. Contract No. I and II commenced on 1st Jan., Contract No. III on 1st April, Contract IV on 1st July and No. V on 1st October. A Plant was purchased for each contract at the date of commencement. Provide depreciation on plant @ 10% per annum. The particulars of the contracts are :

	I	II	III	IV	V
	Rs.	Rs.	Rs.	Rs.	Rs.
Contract price	35,000	1,12,000	75,600	84,000	56,000
Work certified	35,000	70,000	44,800	9,800	8,400
Cash received	35,000	52,500	42,000	8,400	5,600
Materials	21,000	20,160	23,240	5,600	4,200
Wages	9,800	32,480	40,250	4,410	4,900
General expenses	1,400	1,330	910	350	700
Plant installed	—	5,600	4,480	3,360	2,100
Materials in hand	—	1,120	1,120	560	140
Work uncertified	—	7,000	3,500	1,400	700

Prepare Contract Account in tabular form in the books of the Contractor and also show the Balance Sheet.

Ans. :

			Rs. P.
Contract	I	Profit	2,800.00
"	II	Profit	11,795.00
"	III	Loss	15,316.00
"	IV	No Profit transferred to Profit and Loss A/c.	
"	V	Loss	612.50

48. In 1990, British Contractor undertook three contracts, on 1st January, 1st July and 1st October respectively. On 31st December, when the accounts were made the position was :

	I	II	III
	Rs.	Rs.	Rs.
Contract price	3,00,000	2,02,500	2,25,000
Expenditure :			
Materials	54,000	43,500	15,000
Wages	82,500	84,300	10,500
General	3,000	2,100	750
Plant installed	15,000	12,000	9,000
Materials on hand	3,000	3,000	1,500
Wages accured	2,550	2,700	1,200
General expense accrued	450	300	150
Work certified	1,50,000	1,20,000	27,000
Cash received in respect thereof	1,12,500	90,000	20,250
Work finished but uncertified	4,500	6,000	1,575

The plant was installed on the dates of the contracts and depreciation is taken at 10% per annum. Prepare respective accounts in the Contract ledger and give suitable entries in the Company's Balance Sheet. Columnar form may be used and dates may be omitted.

[Adapted—Chartered Accountants (Final) – England]

Ans. : Profit to be credited to P & L A/c :
(i) Rs. 6,750 (Loss) to be debited to P & L A/c.
(ii) Rs. 4,500, (iii) Nil (Reserve 1,250).

49. The following particulars relate to two houses which a firm of builders had in course of construction under contract :

	House A Rs.	House B Rs.
Work-in-progress on 1st Jan. 1997 (excluding Rs. 800 estimated Profit which was taken to Profit and Loss Account in 1996)	14,000	—
Materials purchased	23,000	16,600
Wages	20,000	14,000
Electrical services and fittings	1,400	300
Road making charges	8,000	—
Contract price (including road making)	60,000	40,000
Cash received to work certified	60,000	24,000
Percentage of cash received to work certified	100	$66\frac{2}{3}$
Value of materials on hand on 31st Dec. 1997	400	540
Completed work not certified	—	2,500
Value of plant used on sites	12,000	6,000
Period of plant remained on sites during the year	10 months	8 months

The total establishment expenses incurred during the year 1997 amounted Rs. 12,240. These are to be charged to the two contracts in proportion to wages. Depreciation of plant is to be taken into account at the rate of 10 per cent per annum.

Prepare the two Contract Accounts (in columnar form) showing the profit or loss on each house for the year 1987 and the sums which you consider appropriately transferable to the Profit and Loss Account.

[B.Com. Agra]

Ans. : A – Rs. 15,000 Loss ;
B – Rs. 1,200 Profit transferred to P & L A/c.

50. Following is the trial balance of Bharat Construction Ltd., engaged in the construction of contract No. 999 for the year ended 31. 12. 1998 :

	Dr. Rs.	Cr. Rs.
Contractee A/c (cash received)		3,00,000
Buildings	1,60,000	
Creditors		72,000
Bank Balance	35,000	
Capital A/c		5,00,000
Materials	2,00,000	
Wages	1,80,000	
Expenses	47,000	
Plant	2,50,000	
	8,72,000	8,72,000

The Contract No. 999 was commenced on 1. 1. 1998. Materials costing Rs. 1,70,000 were sent to the site but those worth Rs. 6,000 were destroyed in a fire accident. Plant costing Rs.50,000 was used in the contract throughout the year. Another plant costing Rs. 2,00,000 was used in the contract only for 9 months and then returned to the stores. Materials of the value of Rs. 4,000 were at site on 31. 12. 1998. The contract was for Rs. 6,00,000 and the contractee pays 75% of the work certified. At the end of the year 80% of the work was certified and Rs.15,000 was uncertified work. Expenses are charged to the contract at 25% of wages. Depreciate plant at 10% per annum. Prepare the Contract A/c and also the B/S of the company as on December 1998.

[Madras University – M.Com., B.Com. Delhi – (Hons.)]

Ans. : Profit transferred – Rs. 45,000

Profit in Reserve – Rs. 45,000

51. Rex Limited commenced a contract on 1.7.1997. The total contract price was Rs. 5,00,000 but Rex Limited accepted the same for Rs. 4,50,000. It was decided to estimate the total profit and to take to the credit of Profit and Loss Account that proportion of estimated profit on cash basis which the work completed bore to the total contract. Actual expenditure till 31.12.1997 and estimated expenditure in 1998 are given below :

	Actuals till 31.12.1997	Estimate for 1998
	Rs.	Rs.
Materials	75,000	1,30,000
Labour	55,000	60,000
Plant purchased (Cost)	40,000	—
Misc. Expenses	20,000	35,500
Plant returned to Stores on 31. 12. 1997 at original cost	10,000	25,000 (as at 30.9.98)
Materials at site	5,000	Nil
Work Certified	2,00,000	Full
Work uncertified	7,500	Nil
Cash Received	1,80,000	Full

The Plant is subject to annual depreciation @ 20% of original cost. The contract is likely to be completed on 30.9.1998.

You are required to prepare the Contract Account for the year ended 31.12.1997.

[Adapted—C.A. (Inter)]

Ans. : Profit transferred to P & L A/c – Rs. 26,400.

Hints : (i) Estimated Profit Rs. 66,000 from 1.1.1998 to 30.9.1998.

(ii) Profit to be transferred =

$$\text{Estimated Profit} \times \frac{\text{Cash received}}{\text{Work certified}} \times \frac{\text{Work certified}}{\text{Total Contract Price}}$$

$$= 66{,}000 \times \frac{1{,}80{,}000}{2{,}00{,}000} \times \frac{2{,}00{,}000}{4{,}50{,}000} = \text{Rs. } 26{,}400.$$

(iii)	Plant at site on 30. 9. 1998 :		
	Original Cost	Rs.	5,000
Less	Depreciation	Rs.	1,250
	$5{,}000 \times \frac{20}{120} \times \frac{15}{12}$		3,750
(iv)	Plant returned to Stores		
	Original Cost	Rs.	10,000
Less	Depreciation for 6 months @ 20%	Rs.	1,000
		Rs.	9,000

52. On 1.1.1992 A undertook a contract for Rs. 5,00,000. He incurred the following expenses during the year :

	Rs.
Materials issued from Stores	50,000
Materials purchased for the contract	45,000
Plant installed at cost	35,000
Wages paid	1,00,000
Wages accrued due on 31.12.92	40,000
Direct Expanses paid	10,000
Direct Expenses accrued on 31.12.92	2,500
Establishment expenses	6,500

Of the plant and materials charged to the contract, the plant which cost Rs. 2,000 and materials costing Rs. 1,500 were lost. Some of the materials costing Rs. 2,000 were sold for Rs.2,500. On 31.12.1992 the plant which cost Rs. 500 was returned to the stores and a part of the plant which cost Rs. 200 was so damaged as to render itself useless.

The work certified was Rs. 2,40,000 and 80% of the same was recieved in cash. The cost of work done but uncertified was Rs. 1,000. Charge 10% p.a. on depreciation. Prepare Contract Account for the year ended 31.12.1992 by transferring to the Profit & Loss A/c the portion of the profit, if any, which you think reasonable. Show also the Balance Sheet.

[Bangalore University B.Com]

Ans. : Loss of Contract Rs. 12,780; B/S – Plant Rs. 29,070
W.I.P – Rs. 49,000; P & L A/c (Dr) – Rs. 15,980

53. Modern Constructions Ltd. has taken two contracts on 1st October, 1995. The position of contracts on 30th September, 1996 is as follows :

	Contract I	Contract II
	Rs.	Rs.
Contract price	27,00,000	60,00,000
Materials	5,80,000	10,80,000
Wages paid	11,24,000	16,50,000
Other expenses	28,000	60,000
Plant at site	1,60,000	3,00,000
Unused materials at site	40,000	60,000
Wages payable	36,000	54,000
Other expenses due	4,000	9,000
Work certified	16,00,000	30,00,000
Cash received	12,00,000	22,50,000
Work not certified	80,000	90,000

The plant at site is to be depreciated at 10%. Prepare the Contract Accounts in respect of each work showing the notional profit and also the profit to be transferred to Profit and Loss Account.

[A.C.S. (Inter)]

Ans. : Contract I – Loss Rs. 68,000.

Contract II – Transferred to Profit & Loss A/c – Rs. 1,33,500

Profit in Suspense – Rs. 1,33,500

52. The following information relates to a building contract for Rs. 10,00,000 and for which 80% of the value of work-in-progress as certified by the architect is being paid by the contractee :

	1st year	2nd year	3rd year
	Rs.	Rs.	Rs.
Materials issued	1,20,000	1,45,000	84,000
Direct wages	1,10,000	1,55,000	1,10,000
Direct expenses	5,000	17,000	6,000
Indirect expenses	2,000	2,600	500
Work certified	2,35,000	7,50,000	10,00,000
Uncertified work	3,000	8,000	–
Plant issued	14,000	–	–
Materials on site	2,000	5,000	8,000

The value of the plant at the end of 1st, 2nd and 3rd years were Rs. 11,200, Rs. 7,000 and Rs. 3,000, respectively. Prepare Contract Account for these three years taking into account such profit as you think proper on incomplete contract.

[Delhi B.Com.]

Ans. : 2nd year – Profit Rs. 1,06,347; 3rd year – Profit Rs. 1,33,553

Hint. : In first year no proift is to be transferred since less than $\frac{1}{4}$th of contract is completed.

53. Three contracts were commenced on the following months :

1st January, 1st July and 1st October. They were undertaken by a contractor and their accounts on 31.12.1992 showed the following position :

	Contract 1	Contract 2	Contract 3
	Rs.	Rs.	Rs.
Contract Price	4.00.000	2.70.000	3,00,000
Expenditure			
Materials	72,000	58,000	20,000
Wages paid	1,10,000	1,12,400	14,000
General Charges	4,000	2,800	1,000
Plant	20,000	16,000	12,000
Materials on hand	4,000	4,000	2,000
Wages accrued	4,000	4,000	1,800
Works certified	2,00,000	1,60,000	36,000
Cash received	1,50,000	1,20,000	27,000
Works not certified	6,000	8,000	2,100

Prepare the Contract Accounts. Depreciate Plant @ 10% p.a.

[Mysore B. Com. 1991]

Ans. : Profit tranferred Contract I Rs. 9,000;

Contract II Loss Rs. 6,000; Contract III profit Rs. 3,000

Hint : Since less than $\frac{1}{4}$th of the contract has been completed no profit is to be transferred.

54. Draw columnar contract accounts for Bayes Construction Ltd. who at present have two contracts in progress.

The following details were extracted at the 31st December, 1992 :

Contract No.	Y 282	Z 650
Commencement date	1st January	1st July
	Rs.	Rs.
Contract price	2,75,000	3,50,000
Expenditure		
Materials	12,680	19,280
Wages	48,643	37,218
Site expenses	6,500	8,620
Plant purchases	1,50,000	65,000
Materials on site on 31st December	2,100	6,400
Accrued wages	4,217	2,242
Work certified	1,10,000	85,000
Cash received on work certified	93,500	63,750
Work completed but not certified	3,500	2,200

Head office charges of Rs. 22,500 are charged to contracts in proportion to their prime costs. The plant was installed at the commencement of the contracts and depreciation is calculated at 20% p.a. Both contracts have been estimated to give an overall profit on completion.

[Adapted—Mysore – M.Com. Nov. 1991]

56. Nilcom Construction Company commenced a contract on 1.7.1991. The Contract price is Rs. 9,00,000. Actual Expenditure till 31.12.1991 and estimated expenditure in 1992 are given below :

	Actual till 31.12.1991	Estimated for 1992
	Rs.	Rs.
Purchase of Materials	1,50,000	2,60,000
Labour	1,10,000	1,20,000
Purchase of Plant (Original Cost)	80,000	–
Miscellaneous expenses	40,000	71,000
Return of Plant to stores on 31.12.1991 (Original Cost)	20,000	50,000
Materials at site	10,000	Nil
Work Certified	4,00,000	Full
Work uncertified	15,000	Nil
Cash received	3,60,000	Full

Depreciation is charged on plant @ 20% p.a. on original cost (calculation to be made on time basis). The contract is likely to be completed by 30.9.1992.

You are required to prepare Contract Account for the year ended 31.12.1991. It has been decided to estimate the total profit on the contract and to take to the credit of Profit & Loss Account that proportion of estimated profit on realised basis which the work actually certified bears to the total contract.

[C. A. (Inter)]

Ans. : Estimated Total Profit Rs. 1,32,000

Hint : Profit to be credited :

$$\frac{\text{Work certified}}{\text{Contract price}} \times \frac{\text{Cash received}}{\text{Work certified}} \times \text{Estimated Profit to be taken to P \& L A/c.}$$

Total Profit Rs. 52,800.

57. A Jobbing factory has undertaken to supply 200 pieces of a component per month for the ensuing 6 months. Every month a batch order is opened against which materials and labour hours are booked at actuals. Overheads are levied at a rate per labour hour. The selling price contracted for Rs. 8 per piece. From the follwing data present the cost and profit per piece of each batch order and overall position of the order for 1,200 pieces.

Month	*Batch output*	*Material Cost* (Rs.)	*Direct Wages* (Rs.)	*Direct labour* hours
January	210	650	120	240
February	200	640	140	280
March	220	680	150	280
April	180	630	140	270
May	200	700	150	300
June	220	720	160	320

The other details are :

Month	*Chargeable expenses* (Rs.)	*Direct labour hours*
January	12,000	4,800
February	10,560	4,400
March	12,000	5,000
April	10,580	4,600
May	13,000	5,000
June	12,000	4,800

[Adapted—I.C.W.A. (Inter)]

Ans. : Total Cost per unit – Rs. 7.34
Selling Price per unit – Rs. 8.00
Profit per unit – Re. 0.66

Hints : Chargeable expenses for January – Rs. $\frac{12,000}{4,800} = 2.50$

Chargeable expenses for the component – 240 × Rs. 2.50 = Rs. 600.

PROCESS COSTING 7

Learning Objectives

1. *Introduction*
2. *Definition*
3. *Applicability*
4. *Features*
5. *Distinction between Job Order Costing and Process Costing*
6. *Advantages of Process Costing*
7. *Elements of Process Costing*
8. *Treatment of Process Loss, Scrap and Wastages*
9. *Normal Loss, Abnormal Loss and Abnormal Gain*
10. *Worked-out Problems*
11. *Assignment.*

PROCESS COSTING 7

7.1 Introduction

This chapter is devoted to the study of Process Costing. Attempt has been made to explain the basis of all process costing systems and the ways in whch normal and abnormal process losses are dealt with in cost accounts.

7.2 Definition

Process Costing is a form of operation costing used where production follows a series of sequential process. According to I.C.M.A., London, "it is that form of operation costing where standardised goods are produced". "It is a system for applying costs to like products that are mass produced in continuous fashion through a series of production steps called processes" — Horgren.

7.3 Applicability

Process costing is used in a variety of industries which include oil refining, food processing, paper, chemical and drug manufacture, paint and varnish manufacture, soap making, biscuit works, textiles, canning factories, box making, milk dairy etc.

7.4 Features

The following are the common features that exist in most process costing systems :

(i) Process cost centres are clearly defined and all costs are accumulated by the cost centres. Both direct and indirect costs are accumulated in cost accounts.

(ii) The maintenance of accurate records of units and part units produced and the cost incurred by each process.

(iii) The averaging of the total costs of each process over the total production of that process.

(iv) The charging of the total cost of earlier process as the raw material input cost of the following process.

(v) Procedures for separating costs where the process produces two or more products (joint products) or where by-products arise during production are clearly defined.

(vi) If units are lost or spoiled in a process or department such loss is borne by the units completed and remaining within the department and thus average cost is increased.

7.5 Basis of Process Costing

The following figure depicts the basis of all process costing system :

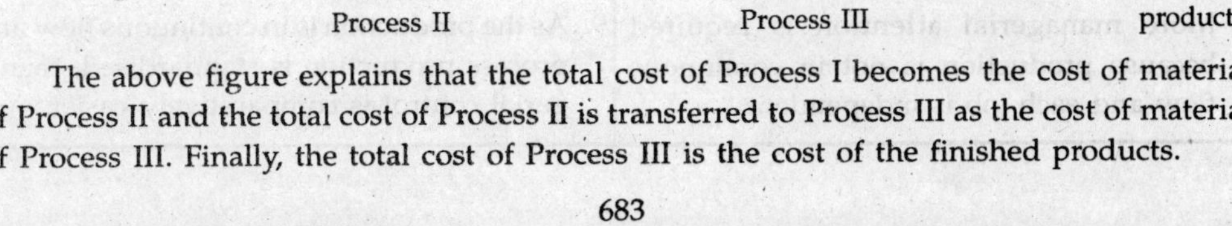

The above figure explains that the total cost of Process I becomes the cost of materials of Process II and the total cost of Process II is transferred to Process III as the cost of materials of Process III. Finally, the total cost of Process III is the cost of the finished products.

7.6 Distinction between Job Order Costing and Process Costing

Job Order Costing and Process Costing 'are the two polar extremes of product costing'. The main points of distinction between the two systems are

Job Costing	*Process Costing*
1. *Production of goods* Goods are produced against specific orders.	1. Uniform production is carried on in continuous flow.
2. *Cost Collection* Costs are accumulated for specific cost centre i.e. a specific job.	2. Costs are accumulated for the entire departments or processes.
3. *Applicability* Job costing is applicable where the objective is to identify the cost with specific job.	3. Process Costing is applied in case of mass production of similar units which continuously pass through different processes. Under process costing, individual products lose their identity.
4. *Time Period* In Job Costing the production period may be more than one accounting period. Here, time factor is ignored, only costs are accumulated. Job Costs are computed when the jobs are complete for a specific product.	4. In Process Costing costs are accumulated for processes for a given time period. Process costs are calculated at the end of the cost period.
5. *Transfer of Cost* Cost of product is not transferred from one job to another.	5. Costs of one process are transferred to another process. The finished product of one process becomes the raw materials of the next process until the goods are completely manufactured.
6. *Computation of Unit Cost* In Job Costing unit cost is obtained by dividing the cost of the job order by units produced in the job order.	6. Under Process Costing the unit cost is computed by dividing the process costs by the units produced by the process.
7. *Work-in-Progress* In Job Costing one work-in-progress account is maintained. Different jobs may or may not have opening or closing work-in-progress.	7. As the production is in continuous flow there is always an opening and closing balance of work-in-progress.
8. *Purpose* In Job Costing production is dependent on customers' orders and specifications.	8. Production is carried on for building stock and for future sale.
9. *Managerial Control* More managerial attention is required because production is not in continuous flow and each job is independent.	9. As the production is in continuous flow and process production is standardised, managerial control is comparatively easier.

7.7 Advantages

The following are some of the advantages of process costing :

(i) Method of finding cost is less expensive and simpler than the job costing.

(ii) More accurate cost for each process can be ascertained. Expenses can conveniently be allocated to each process of production.

(iii) Process Costs can be determined at short intervals especially where predetermined overhead rates are used.

(iv) As cost can be ascertained shortly, quotations may be submitted without difficulty.

(v) Evaluation of performance of each process can be made easily and as a result, exercise of managerial control becomes easier.

7.8 The Elements of Process Cost

The elements of Cost of a Process consist of :

(i) Material Cost ; (ii) Cost of Labour ; (iii) Direct Expenses and (iv) Production Overhead.

An account is maintained for each process to which all costs of material, labour, direct expenses and overhead are debited.

(i) **Materials**

Materials required for production are issued to the first process. The finished goods of first process are passed to the next process, each process merely performs some operation on the material passed from the earlier process. The finished goods of Process I become the raw materials of Process II and so on.

There are some systems where extra or new materials may be needed and added to the finished goods passed from earlier process and this may continue until completion. The method to be followed depends upon the nature of the product.

Whatever method is followed, sufficient supply of raw materials should be assured to meet production needs. It is to be seen that production does not come to a halt due to paucity of raw materials.

(ii) **Labour**

Both direct and indirect wages paid to direct workers and indirect workers like supervisory staff are debited to the Process Account. However, where workers are engaged in more than one process, the gross wages are distributed to each process on the basis of time spent on each process. Generally, the cost of direct labour forms a very small part of the cost of production in industries that adopt process costing.

(iii) **Direct Expenses**

Direct expenses which can easily be directly allocated to a particular process are known as direct expenses. Examples of such expenses are cost of design, cost of electricity, depreciation and hire charges of equipment. These expenses are debited to Process Account.

(iv) **Production Overhead**

In process costing the overhead element forms a major part of total cost. So, great care should be taken to ensure that each process is charged with a reasonable share of overhead. Overheads are to be apportioned where they cannot be directly allotted and actual overhead in respect of a particular process should be charged or debited to the Process concerned. Overhead may be recovered at a predetermined rates and charged to the Process.

Having discussed the elements of cost we now proceed towards the preparation of Process Account where there is no process loss.

7.9 Costing Procedure

Under process costing method a separate account is maintained for each process in respect of which the costs are to be ascertained. A proforma of a process account is given below

Process Account

Particulars	*Quantity units*	*Amount Rs.*	*Particulars*	*Quantity units*	*Amount Rs.*

The following steps are involved in costing procedure :

1. Debit the cost of basic raw materials to the first process account showing both quantity and amount.
2. Debit costs of other materials, direct labour and direct expences pertaining to each process.
3. Debit each process account with production overheads as given or on some equitable basis.
4. Credit the process account with realisable value of scrap.
5. Ascertain the total cost of the process and calculate average cost per unit.
6. If the whole output of a process has been transferred to the next process, the total cost may be shown on the credit side as transfer to next process and the same shall be shown on the debit side of the next process account.
7. If a portion of the output has been earmarked for sale or has been sold show its cost as transfer to stores and the balance as transfer to the next process. It should be noted that when a portion of output has been sold, the process account should credited only with its cost and not the sale value.
8. The cost of containers used for packaging the finished goods should be debited to the last process account.
9. The total cost of the last process shall be transferred to Finished Stock Account.

Problem - 1.

Prepare Process Cost Accounts from the following data

Items	*Total*	*Process I*	*Process II*	*Process III*
Direct Materials	8,800	7,200	1,200	400
Direct Wages	1,600	400	800	400
Direct Expenses	2,000	1,200	—	800

Production overhead incurred is Rs. 3,200 and is recovered @ 200% of direct wages. Production during the period was 200 units. Assume that there was no opening and closing work-in-process.

Solution

Process I Account

Dr.	Cost per unit	Amount		Cost per unit	Amount Cr.
	Rs.	Rs.		Rs.	Rs.
To Materials	36.00	7,200			
" Direct Wages	2.00	400	By Process II Account	48.00	9,600
" Direct Expenses	6.00	1,200			
" Production Overhead @ 200% of direct wages	4.00	800			
	48.00	9,600		48.00	9,600

Process II Account

Dr.	Cost per unit	Amount		Cost per unit	Amount Cr.
	Rs.	Rs.		Rs.	Rs.
To Output – Process I	48.00	9,600	By Output transferred to Process III	66.00	13,200
" Materials	6.00	1,200			
" Direct wages	4.00	800			
" Overhead @ 200% of wages	8.00	1,600			
	66.00	13,200		66.00	13,200

Process III Account

Dr.	Cost per unit	Amount Rs.		Cost per unit	Amount Cr.
	Rs.	Rs.		Rs.	Rs.
To Output from Process II	66.00	13,200	By Output transferred to Finished Stock	78.00	15,600
" Materials	2.00	400			
" Direct Wages	2.00	400			
" Direct Expenses	4.00	800			
" Production overhead @ 200% of wages	4.00	800			
	78.00	15,600		78.00	15,600

Problem 2

A Product passes through three processes as – A, B and C. The details of expenses incurred on the three processes during the year 1992 were as follows :

Process	A	B	C
Units issued	10,000		
Cost per unit Rs. 100	Rs.	Rs.	Rs.
Sundry Materials	10,000	15,000	5,000
Labour	30,000	80,000	65,000
Direct Expenses	6,000	18,150	27,200
Selling price per unit of output	120	165	250

Management expenses during the year were Rs. 80,000 and selling expenses were Rs.50,000, these are not allocable to the processes.

Actual output of the three processes was :

A – 9,300 units, B – 5,400 units and C – 2,100 units. Two-thirds of the output of process A and one-half of the output of process B was passed on to the next process and the balance was sold. The entire output of process C was sold.

The normal loss of the three processes, calculated on the input of every process was; Process A – 5%; B – 15% and C – 20%.

The loss of process A was sold at Rs. 2 per unit, that of B at Rs. 5 per unit and of Process C at Rs. 10 per unit.

Prepare the three Processes Accounts and the Profit & Loss Account.

[Adapted—C.A. (Inter) May, 1993]

Solution

Process A Account

Dr. *Cr.*

Particulars	*Units*	*Amounts*	*Particulars*	*Units*	*Amounts*
		Rs.			Rs.
To Input	10,000	10,00,000	By Normal Loss	500	1,000
(10,000 × Rs. 100)			$(10,000 \times \frac{5}{100})$		
" Sundry Materials		10,000	" Abnormal Loss	200	22,000
			(Note 1)		
" Labour		30,000	" Process B (6,200 × 110)	6,200	6,82,000
" Direct Expenses		6,000	" Profit & Loss A/c	3,100	3,41,000
			(3,100 × 110)		
	10,000	10,46,000		10,000	10,46,000

Process B Account

Dr. *Cr.*

Particulars	*Units*	*Amounts*	*Particulars*	*Units*	*Amounts*
		Rs.			Rs.
To Process A	6,200	6,82,000	By Normal Loss	930	4,650
Materials		15,000	$(6,200 \times \frac{15}{100})$ units		
Labour		80,000	" Process C A/c		
Direct Expenses		18,150	2,700 × 150	2,700	4,05,000
Abnormal Gain	130	19,500	" Profit & Loss A/c		
(Note 2)			(Cost of goods sold)	2,700	4,05,000
			(2,700 × Rs. 150)		
	6,330	8,14,650		6,330	8,14,650

Process C Account

Dr. Particulars	Units	Amounts	Cr. Particulars	Units	Amounts
		Rs.			Rs.
To Process B	2,700	4,05,000	By Normal Loss (20% of 2,700)	540	5,400
" Materials		5,000			
" Labour		65,000	" Abnormal Loss	60	13,800
" Direct Expenses		27,200	" Profit & Loss A/c (2,100 × Rs. 230)	2,100	4,83,000
	2,700	5,02,200		2,700	5,02,200

Profit and Loss Account

Dr. Particulars	Units	Amounts	Cr. Particulars	Units	Amounts
		Rs.			Rs.
To Process A	3,100	3,41,000	By Bank – Sale (Process A) @ Rs. 120 p.u.	3,100	3,72,000
" Process B	2,700	4,05,000			
" Process C	2,100	4,83,000	" Bank – Sale (Process B) @ Rs. 165 p.u.	2,700	4,45,500
" Management Expenses		80,000	" Bank – Sale	2,100	5,25,000
" Selling Expenses		50,000	(Process C) @ Rs. 250 p.u.		
" Abnormal Loss		34,800	" Abnormal Gain A/c		18,850
			" Net Loss		32,450
	7,900	13,93,800		7,900	13,93,800

Working notes :

1. (a) Per unit cost of normal production of Process A

$$\frac{\text{Rs. } 10,46,000 - \text{Rs. } 1,000}{9,500 \text{ units}} = \text{Rs. } 110 \text{ p.u.}$$

(b) Value of abnormal loss = 9,500 units – 9,300 units × Rs. 110 p.u. = Rs. 22,000

2. Per unit cost of normal production of Process B

(i) $$\frac{\text{Rs. } 7,95,150 - \text{Rs. } 4,650}{5,270 \text{ units}} = \text{Rs. } 150 \text{ p.u.}$$

(ii) Value of Abnormal loss 930 units – 800 units = 130 units × Rs. 150 = Rs. 19,500

3. (i) Per unit cost of normal production of Process C

$$\frac{\text{Rs. } 5,02,200 - \text{Rs. } 5,400}{2,160 \text{ units}} = \frac{\text{Rs. } 4,96,800}{2,160 \text{ units}} = \text{Rs. } 230$$

(ii) Value of abnormal loss = 2,160 units – 2,100 units = 60 units × Rs. 230 = Rs. 13,800.

Abnormal Loss Account

Dr. *Cr.*

Particulars	*Units*	*Rate*	*Amount*	*Particulars*	*Units*	*Rate*	*Amount*
		Rs.	Rs.			Rs.	Rs.
To Process A	200	100	22,000	By Bank	200	2	400
Process C	60	230	13,800	Bank	60	10	600
				P & L A/c			34,800
	260		35,800		260		35,800

Abnormal gain Account

Dr. *Cr.*

Particulars	*Units*	*Rate*	*Amount*	*Particulars*	*Units*	*Rate*	*Amount*
		Rs.	Rs.			Rs.	Rs.
To Normal Loss	130	5	650	By Process B	130	150	19,500
" P & L A/c			18,850				
	130		19,500		130		19,500

Note : Normal loss for 130 units in Process B has been written off against Abnormal Gain of Process B @ Rs. 5 p.u. and the balance has been transferred to costing Profit & Loss Account.

7.10 Treatment of Process Losses, Scrap and Wastage

In the course of production through different processes, some losses are bound to occur. The quantity and weight of the process output will be less than the quantity, weight or volume of the materials input. This may happen due to various reasons :

(i) Evaporation, residuals,

(ii) Unavoidable handling, breakage and spoilage losses.

So, it is imperative that accurate records are to be maintained to have control over materials. The cost department must be kept informed of the losses through the medium of scrap tickets, materials credit notes and loss reports. This information is essential for ascertainment of actual cost of the final product. Materials which have been processed and later on are found to be defective and scrapped have surely incurred their share of labour cost and overhead cost up to the point of rejection. More defective and scrapped materials mean financial loss to the concern.

Classification of Process Loss

Process losses may be classified as :

(i) Normal Process Loss and (ii) Abnormal Process Loss.

(i) *Normal Process Loss*

This type of loss is caused by the factors like evaporation, pilferage and which is inherent in large scale production. This loss cannot be avoided but sure to occur. This loss may not be a total loss but may often include scrap and waste. The amount of normal process loss is reduced by selling the scrap and waste.

(ii) *Abnormal Process Loss*

Abnormal Process Loss is caused by unexpected or abnormal conditions. The causes are substandard materials, accidents, carelessness. Moreover, it may happen sometimes that the percentage of wastage or loss may exceed the predetermined percentage of normal wastage or loss. So, any wastage exceeding the normal wastage is termed abnormal wastage or loss. All abnormal losses must be thoroughly investigated, and, where necessary, all possible steps should be taken to prevent its occurrence in future.

Treatment of Normal and Abnormal Loss in Costing :

(i) *Normal Process Losses*

Normal Loss is normally expressed as a percentage of the quantity of output. Loss arising out of normal wastage is absorbed in the cost of good units i.e. it becomes the part of total cost and surely, increases the total cost of output. If any value can be recouped from the sale of imperfect articles or materials then the amount so realised shall be credited to relevant Process Account which will reduce the cost of output of that process.

The following example will make the concept clear.

Problem 3

A food manufacturing process has a normal wastage of 5% which can be sold as animal feed stuff at Rs. 10 per tonne. The following data for a given period were collected :

Input materials 200 tonnes at Rs. 25 per tonne. Labour and Overheads Rs. 3,000. Losses were at the normal level. Compute the cost per tonne.

Solution

			Tonnes	Rs.	
Input	Materials	200	200 × 25	5,000	
	Labour and Overheads			3,000	
				8,000	
Less :	Normal Loss @ 5%	10	10 × 10	100	(cr)
		190		7,900	

So, Cost per ton = $\frac{7,900}{190}$ = Rs. 41.58

Process Account

Dr.	Cost per unit	Amount		Cost per unit	Amount *Cr.*
	Rs.	Rs.		Rs.	Rs.
To Materials	200	5,000	By Normal Wastage	10	100
" Labour & Overheads		3,000	" Next Process A/c	190	7,900
		8,000			8,000

Abnormal Process Losses

Abnormal loss or wastage is not treated as a part of production cost or total cost. Its value is credited to the concerned Process A/c and debited to Costing Profit & Loss Account. The value of abnormal loss is calculated with the help of the following formula :

$$\frac{\text{Normal Cost of Normal Production}}{\text{Units of Normal Production}} \times \text{Units of abnormal wastage}$$

A separate account is opened for abnormal losses to which is debited the cost of materials, labour and proportionate overhead incurred by the wastage. Since the value of abnormal loss is not treated as a part of cost of production it is written off to the Costing Profit and Loss Account.

WORKED OUT PROBLEMS

Problem 4

The following data have been collected from Ledger Accounts –

Input	Materials	1,000 tonnes	Rs. 50 per tonne
	Wages		Rs. 20,000
	Overheads		Rs. 10,000

Normal wastage @ 5% which can be sold at Rs. 5.00 per tonne. Actual production is 900 tonnes.

Compute the value of abnormal loss and show the relevant accounts.

Solution

Abnormal Loss = Actual Loss – Normal Loss = 100 – 50 = 50 tonnes.

Process Account

Dr. *Cr.*

	Qnt.	Rs.		Qnt.	Rs.
To Materials	1,000	50,000	By Normal Loss	50	250
" Wages		20,000	" Abnormal Loss	50	4,197
" Overhead		10,000	" Good Production transferred to Next process	900	75,553
	1,000	80,000		1,000	80,000

Calculation of value of abnormal loss.

	Total Cost =	Rs. 80,000
Less :	Amount realised from normal loss =	250
	Value of normal units of 950	79,750

So, value of abnormal loss = $\frac{\text{Rs. } 79,750 \times 50}{950}$ = Rs. 4,197

Abnormal Loss Account

Dr. *Cr.*

	Rs.		Rs.
To Process A/c	4,197	By Scrap Sales A/c (50 × 5)	250
		" Profit and Loss A/c	3,947
	4,197		4,197

Scrap Sales Account

Dr. *Cr.*

	Rs.		Rs.
To Process A/c	250		
" Abnormal Loss A/c	250		

7.11 Abnormal Gain

Abnormal Gain arises when the actual loss is smaller than estimated loss. ***According to Wheldon,*** "sometimes the actual loss in a process is smaller than was expected, in which case an abnormal gain results".

The value of abnormal gain is calculated at the rate at which the effective output would have been valued if normal wastage had taken place according to expectation. Relevant Process Account is debited with the value of Abnormal Gain and Abnormal gain A/c is credited by Process A/c. The Abnormal Gain A/c is debited with the Scrap Sales A/c and the balance is written off to Profit and Loss A/c.

Abnormal Gain = Normal Loss – Actual Loss

Value of Abnormal Gain

$$= \frac{\text{Normal Cost of Normal Production}}{\text{Normal Units}} \times \text{Units of abnormal effectives}$$

Problem 5

A product passes through Process I and II. The normal wastage is 5% and 10% respectively. The wastage of Process I is sold at Re. 1.00 per unit and that of Process II at Rs. 2.00 per unit. 10,000 of crude materials were introduced in Process I @ Rs. 2 per unit. The other expenses were :

	Process I	Process II
	Rs.	Rs.
Materials Consumed	2,000	4,000
Wages	6,000	8,000
Overheads	3,000	4,000

The output of each process had been as follows :

Process I – 8,500 and Process II – 7,800. Prepare Process Account and Abnormal Loss Account and Abnormal Gain A/c.

Process I Account

Dr.	Qnt.	Rs.		Qnt.	Rs. Cr.
To Raw Materials (units introduced)	10,000	10,000	By Normal Loss A/c	500	500
" Materials Consumed		2,000	" Abnormal Loss A/c	1,000	3,210
" Wages		6,000	" Process II A/c	8,500	27,290
" Overheads		3,000			
	10,000	31,000		10,000	31,000

Process II Account

Dr.	Qnt.	Rs.		Qnt.	Rs. Cr.
To Process I A/c	8,500	27,290	By Normal Loss	850	1,700
" Materials Consumed		4,000	" Finished Stock A/c	7,800	42,405
" Wages		8,000			
" Overheads		4,000			
" Abnormal Gain	150	815			
	8,650	44,105		8,650	44,105

Abnormal Loss Account

Dr.	Rs.	Cr.	Rs.
To Process I A/c	3,210	By Bank – Sale of Scrap @ Re. 1.00 per unit	1,000
		" Costing Profit & Loss A/c	2,210
	3,210		3,210

Abnormal Gain Account

Dr.	Rs.	Cr.	Rs.
To Normal Wastage (Short fall of 150 units @ Rs. 2 per unit	300	By Process II	815
" Costing Profit & Loss A/c	515		
	815		815

Working Notes :

Process I Value of Abnormal Loss $= \text{Rs. } \frac{30,500}{9,500} \times 1,000 = \text{Rs. } 3,210$

Process II Value of Abnormal Gain $= \text{Rs. } \frac{41,590}{7,650} \times 150 = \text{Rs. } 815$

Problem 6

Banerjee Enterprises produces an article through three successive processes. The following data relate to 31st March, 1991. Prepare Process Accounts showing Unit Cost at each process.

The output produced in March, 1991 is 200 units.

	Process I	Process II	Process III
	Rs.	Rs.	Rs.
Materials Consumed	20,000	8,000	3,000
Wages booked	16,000	28,000	18,000
Direct charges	4,000	10,000	5,000

Overhead amounts to Rs. 15,500 for the period. Overhead is recovered on the basis of direct wages.

[B.Com. (Pass) C.U. 1991]

Process I Account

Dr.	*Units*	*Unit Cost*	*Total*	Cr.	*Units*	*Unit Cost*	*Total*
		Rs.	Rs.			Rs.	Rs.
To Materials	200	100	20,000	By Process II A/c	200	220	44,000
" Wages		80	16,000				
" Direct Charges		20	4,000				
" Overheads*		20	4,000				
	200	220	44,000		200	220	44,000

* Overhead $= \text{Rs. } \frac{15,500}{31} \times 8$

Process II Account

Dr.	Units	Unit Cost	Total		Units	Unit Cost	Total *Cr.*
		Rs.	Rs.			Rs.	Rs.
To Process I A/c	200	220	44,000	By Process III	200	485	97,000
"Materials		40	8,000				
"Wages A/c		140	28,000				
"Direct Charges		50	10,000				
"Overhead*		35	7,000				
	200	485	97,000		200	485	97,000

*Overhead = Rs. $\frac{15,500}{31} \times 14$

Process III Account

Dr.	Units	Unit Cost	Total		Units	Unit Cost	Total *Cr.*
		Rs.	Rs.			Rs.	Rs.
To Process II A/c	200	485.00	97,000	By Finished Stock A/c	200	637.50	1,27,500
"Materials		15.00	3,000				
"Wages		90.00	18,000				
"Direct Charges		25.00	5,000				
"Overhead		22.50	4,500				
	200	637.50	1,27,500		200	637.50	1,27,500

*Overhead = Rs. $\frac{15,500}{31} \times 9$

Treatment of Normal Loss

Problem 7

The Bharat Manufacturing Company's product passes through two distinct processes, X and Y, and then to the finished stock. It is known from the past experience that wastage occurs in the process as under :

In Process X, 5% of the units entering the process.

In Process Y, 10% of the units entering the process.

The scrap value of the wastages in process X is Rs. 8 per 100 units and in process Y is Rs.10 per 100 units.

	Process X	Process Y
	Rs.	Rs.
Materials Consumed	6,000	3,000
Wages	7,000	4,000
Manufacturing expenses	2,000	2,000

10,000 units were brought into Process X, costing Rs. 5,000. The outputs were :

Process X	9,500 units
Process Y	8,500 units

Prepare Process Cost Accounts showing the cost of the output.

[Madras—B.Com.]

Solution

Process X Account

Dr.	Qnt.	Rate Rs.	Amount Rs.	Cr.	Qnt. Rs.	Rate Rs.	Amount
To Units introduced	10,000	0.50	5,000	By Normal Loss Scrap - 5% of 10,000	500	0.08	40
" Materials			6,000	" Process Y A/c (output transferred)	9,500	2.10	19,960
" Wages			7,000				
" Manufacturing Expenses			2,000				
	10,000		20,000		10,000		20,000

Process Y Account

Dr.	Qnt.	Rate Rs.	Amount Rs.	Cr.	Qnt. Rs.	Rate Rs.	Amount
To Process X A/c	9,500	2.10	19,960	By Normal Loss Scrap 10% of 9,500	950	0.10	95
" Materials			3,000	" Abnormal Loss	50	3.376	169
" Wages			4,000	" Output transferred to Finished Stock A/c	8,500	3.376	28,696
" Manufacturing Expenses			2,000				
	9,500		28,960		9,500		28,960

Working Notes :

Process X Cost per unit = $\frac{\text{Total Cost} - \text{Value of Scrap}}{\text{Normal Production}} = \frac{20,000-40}{9,500}$ = Rs. 2,101 approx.

Process Y Cost per unit = $\frac{28,960-95}{9,500-950} = \frac{28,865}{8,550}$ = Rs. 3.376

Problem 8

ABC Ltd. is producing the product "P" required to be processed in three continuous processes. They have laid down the standards to produce 75 litres of finished product as under :

	Process Number (1)	(2)	(3)
Raw Materials (litres)	100	—	—
Materials cost per litre (Rs.)	2	—	—
Waste percentage on input (%)	10	11.11	6.25
Direct labour hours	6	10	8
Labour rate per hour (Rs.)	7.50	10.00	12.50
Overhead rate per labour hour (Rs.)	3.5	3	8
Sale price per litre of finished goods (Rs.)	—	—	9

You are required to prepare the statement of standard cost and standard profit rate per 75 litres of finished product.

[Adapted—A.C.S. – Final, Dec. 1986]

Solution

Process I Account

Dr.	*Qnt.*	*Amount* Rs.	*Cr.*	*Qnt.*	*Amount* Rs.
To Raw Materials	100	200	By Normal Loss A/c @ 10%	10	—
" Direct Wages		45	" Process II A/c Output transferred	90	266
" Overheads 6 × 3.350		21			
	100	266		100	266

Process II Account

Dr.	*Qnt.*	*Amount* Rs.	*Cr.*	*Qnt.*	*Amount* Rs.
To Process I	90	266	By Normal Loss A/c @ 11.11%	10	—
" Direct Wages		100	" Output transferred to Process III	80	396
" Overhead 10 × 3		30			
	90	396		90	396

Process III Account

Dr.	*Qnt.*	*Amount* Rs.	*Cr.*	*Qnt.*	*Amount* Rs.
To Process II A/c output transferred	80	396	By Normal Loss A/c @ 6.25%	5	—
" Direct Wages		100			
" Overheads 8 × 8		64	" Finished Stock A/c	75	560
	80	560		80	560

Finished Stock Account

Dr.	*Qnt.*	*Amount* Rs.	*Cr.*	*Qnt.*	*Amount* Rs.
To Process III output transferred from Process III	75	560	By Sales 75 × 9	75	675
" Profit		115			
	75	675		75	675

Standard Cost of 75 litres = Rs. 560.00

Standard Profit = Rs. 115.00

Treatment of Normal and Abnormal Loss

Problem 9

The product of a manufacturing concern passes through two processes A and B and then to finished stock. It is ascertained that in each process normally 5% of the total weight is lost and 10% is scrap which from processes A and B realizes Rs. 80 per ton and Rs. 200 per ton, respectively.

The following are the figures relating to both the processes :

	Process A	Process B
Materials in tons	1,000	70
Cost of materials in rupees per ton	125	200
Wages in rupees	28,000	10,000
Manufacturing expenses	8,000	5,250
Output in tons	830	780

Prepare Process Accounts showing cost per ton of each process. There was no stock or work-in-progress in any process.

[Delhi – B.Com. (Hons.), 1977]

Solution

Process A Account

Dr. *Cr.*

	Qnt.	*Rate*	*Amount*		*Qnt.*	*Rate*	*Amount*
		Rs.	Rs.			Rs.	Rs.
To Materials	1,000	125	1,25,000	By Normal Loss 5%	50		
" Wages			28,000	" Scrap 10%	100	80	8,000
" Manufacturing Expenses			8,000	" Abnormal Loss	20	180	3,600
				" Process B	830	180	1,49,400
	1,000		1,61,000		1,000		1,61,000

Cost per unit = Rs. $\dfrac{1,61,000 - 8,000}{31850}$ = Rs. 180

Process B Account

Dr. *Cr.*

	Qnt.	*Rate*	*Amount*		*Qnt.*	*Rate*	*Amount*
		Rs.	Rs.			Rs.	Rs.
To Process A A/c	830	180	1,49,400	By Normal Loss 5% of 900	45	—	—
" Materials	70	200	14,000	" Normal scrap 10%	90	200	18,000
" Wages			10,000	" Finished goods	780	210	1,63,800
" Manufacturing Expenses			5,250				
" Abnormal gains	15	210	3,150				
	915		1,81,800		915		1,81,800

Working Note :

1. Cost per ton = $\dfrac{\text{Total Cost} - \text{Value of Scrap}}{\text{Output}} = \dfrac{1,78,650 - 18,000}{900 - 135}$ = Rs. 210 per ton

Problem 10

A product passes through 3 distinct processes to completion. During January, 1998, 500 units were produced. The cost books show the following information :

Particulars	A	B	C
	Rs.	Rs.	Rs.
Materials	3,000	1,500	1,000
Labour	2,500	2,000	1,500
Direct Expenses	500	2,160	905

The indirect expenses for the period were Rs. 1,400. The by-products of process B were sold for Rs. 145. Residue of process C was sold for Rs. 166. Prepare the accounts in respect of the processes showing its cost and cost of production of finished product per unit.

[Adapted—B.Com., Andhra]

Solution

Process A Account

Dr.			*Cr.*
	Rs.		Rs.
To Materials	3,000	By Process B A/c	6,000
" Labour	2,500		
" Direct Expenses	500		
	6,000		6,000

Process B Account

Dr.			*Cr.*
	Rs.		Rs.
To Process A Account	6,000	By Sale of by-product	145
" Materials	1,500	" Process 'C' Account	11,515
" Labour	2,000		
" Direct Expenses	2,160		
	11,660		11,660

Process C Account

Dr.			*Cr.*
	Rs.		Rs.
To Process B Account	11,515	By Sale of Residue	166
" Materials	1,000	" Finished Stock A/c (balancing figure)	14,754
" Labour	1,500		
" Direct Expenses	905		
	14,920		14,920

Process Stock Account

Dr.	Qnt.	Rate	Amount		Qnt.	Rate	Amount Cr.
		Rs.	Rs.			Rs.	Rs.
To Process C A/c	500	29.508	14,754	By Balance c/d	500	32.308	16,154
" Indirect Expenses		2.800	1,400				
	500	32.308	16,154		500	32.308	16,154

Note : Cost of Production of Finished product per unit = 16,154 ÷ 500 = Rs. 32.308.

Problem 11

The manufacture of product "Fanta" requires three distinct processes. On completion of the product is passed from Process 3 to finished stock. During the month of December 1992, the following information was obtained :

Elements of Costs	Total	Process I	Process II	Process III
	Rs.	Rs.	Rs.	Rs.
Direct materials	26,000	15,000	11,000	–
Direct labour	26,500	12,500	6,000	8,000
Direct expenses	8,000	3,000	–	5,000
Production Overhead	79,500			

Production Overhead is absorbed by processes at a percentage of direct wages. Production during the period was 1,000 kgs. There was no stock of raw materials or work-in-progress at the beginning or at the end of the month.

[C.U. B. Com. (Hons.) 1993]

Solution

Process I Account

Dr.	Rs.		Cr. Rs.
To Materials	15,000	By Process II	68,000
" Direct labour	12,500		
" Direct expenses	3,000		
" Production Overhead	37,500		
	68,000		68,000

Process II Account

Dr.	Rs.		Cr. Rs.
To Process I A/c	68,000	By Process III A/c	1,03,000
" Materials	11,000		
" Direct labour	6,000		
" Production Overhead	18,000		
	1,03,000		1,03,000

Process III Account

Dr.	Rs.		*Cr.* Rs.
To Process II A/c	1,03,000	By Finished Stock A/c	1,40,000
" Direct labour	8,000	1,000 kg	
" Direct Expenses	5,000		
" Production Overhead	24,000		
	1,40,000		1,40,000

Working notes :

Calculation of Production overhead as a percentage of direct wages.

When Direct wages	then P.O.
26,500	79,500
100	$\frac{79,500 \times 100}{26,500} = 300\%$

Problem 12

A product is produced through two distinct processes—Process I and Process II. On completion it is transferred to Finished Stock. From the following particulars during the month of December 1994, prepare Process Accounts and Finished Stock Account.

	Process I	Process II
Units introudced	10,000	9,000
Transfer to next process finished goods	9,000	8,250
Normal loss on inputs	10%	5%
Realisable value of normal loss (per unit)	Rs. 2	Rs. 4
Cost incurred	Rs.	Rs.
Direct Materials	40,000	
" Labour	20,000	20,000
" Expenses	12,000	10,050

Production overhead 100% of direct labour

Assume the there was no opening or closing stock of raw materials and work-in-progress.

[C.U. B.Com. (Hons.) 1995]

Solution

Process I Account

Dr.	*Qnt.*	*Rate*	*Amount*		*Qnt.*	*Rate*	*Amount* *Cr.*
		Rs.	Rs.			Rs.	Rs.
To Direct Materials	10,000		40,000	By Normal Loss	1,000	2	2,000
" Direct Labour			20,000	Process II A/c	9,000	10	90,000
" Direct Expenses			12,000				
" Overhead 100% of Direct Labour			20,000				
			92,000				92,000

Process II Account

Dr. *Cr.*

	Qnt.	Rate	Amount		Qnt.	Rate	Amount
		Rs.	Rs.			Rs.	Rs.
To Process I A/c	9,000	10	90,000	By Normal Loss A/c			
" Labour			20,000	5% of inputs	450	4	1,800
" Direct Expenses			10,050	" Abnormal Loss	300	16.170	4,851
" Overhead @ 100%			20,000	" Finished			
of Direct Labour				Goods A/c	8,250	16.170	1,33,399
	9,000		1,40,050		9,000		1,40,050

Process II Value of finished goods :

Total cost	Rs. 1,40,050
Less : Normal Loss	Rs. 1,800
	Rs. 1,38,250 ÷ 8,550 = Rs. 16.169 or Rs. 16.170.

Problem 13

A product passes through three processes viz. Process I, Process II and Process III.

The percentage of normal loss in each case computed on the basis of number of units entering the process concerned.

The loss in process I is sold @ Rs. 2.50 per unit and that Process II is sold at Rs. 5.00 per unit and that of Process III @ Rs. 10 per unit. 15,000 units of crude material were introduced in Process I @ Rs. 10 per unit. The other expenses, normal loss and output are :

	Process I	Process II	Process III
Materials consumed (Rs.)	15,000	22,500	7,500
Direct Labour (Rs.)	75,000	1,20,000	97,500
Direct Manufacturing Expenses (Rs.)	5,750	4,250	6,150
Normal loss (5%)	3	6	10
Output (units)	14,250	13,650	12,012
Overhead Expenses (50% of Direct wages)			

Prepare Process Accounts, Abnormal Loss and Abnormal gain Accounts.

[B.U. B.Com.(Hons.) 1997]

Process I Account

Dr. *Cr.*

	Qnt.	Rate	Amount		Qnt.	Rate	Amount
		Rs.	Rs.			Rs.	Rs.
To Inputs	15,000	10	1,50,000	By Normal Loss	450	2.50	1,125
" Materials			15,000	5% of 15,000			
" Direct Labour			75,000				
" Direct Manu-				" Abnormal Loss	300	19.39	5,817
facturing Exp.			5,750				
" Overheads			37,500	" Process II	14,250	19.39	2,76,308
50% of Rs. 75,000							
	15,000		2,83,250		15,000		2,83,250

Process II Account

Dr.	*Qnt.*	*Rate*	*Amount*		*Qnt.*	*Rate*	*Amount* *Cr.*
		Rs.	Rs.			Rs.	Rs.
To Process I	14,250	19.39	2,76,308	By Normal Loss 6% of 14,250	855	5	4,275
" Materials			22,500				
" Direct Labour			1,20,000				
" Direct Manufacturing Exp.			4,250				
" Overhead 50% of Rs. 1,20,000			60,000	By Process III	13,650	35.743	4,87,898
" Abnormal gain	255	35.743	9,115				
	14,505		4,92,173		14,505		4,92,173

$$\text{Rs. } \frac{4,83,050 - 4,275}{14,250 - 455} = \text{Rs. } 35.743$$

Process III Account

Dr.	*Qnt.*	*Rate*	*Amount*		*Qnt.*	*Rate*	*Amount* *Cr.*
		Rs.	Rs.			Rs.	Rs.
To Process II	13,650	35.743	4,87,898	By Normal Loss	1,365	10	13,650
" Materials			7,500				
" Direct Labour			97,500	" Abnormal Loss	273	51.620	14,092
" Direct Manufacturing Exp.			6,150	" Finished goods A/c	12,012	51.620	6,20,056
" Overheads 50% of Rs. 97,500			48,750				
	13,650		6,47,798		13,650		6,47,798

Abnormal Loss Account

	Units	Rs.		Units	Rs.
To Process I A/c	300	5,817	By Bank 300 × 2.50		750
" Process III A/c	273	14,092	" Bank 273 × 10		2,730
			" Profit & Loss A/c		16,429
		19,909			19,909

Abnormal Gain Account

	Units	Rs.		Units	Rs.
To Bank	255	1,275	By Process Ii A/c	255	9,115
" Profit & Loss A/c		7,840			
		9,115			9,115

Problem 14

A product passes through three processes for completion. In January, 1994, the cost of production was given below :

Processes

	I	II	III
	Rs.	Rs.	Rs.
Material	4,000	6,040	6,716
Wages	7,000	8,452	10,000
Production Overheads	3,000	3,556	5,000

1,000 units were issued to process I @ Rs. 5 per unit :

Normal loss in Process I	10%
Normal loss in Process II	5%
Normal loss in Process III	10%

Wastage realised at the rate of Rs. 10 per unit, Rs. 5 p.u. and Rs. 6 per unit in Process I, II and III respectively.

Actual Production

Process I	940 units
Process II	890 "
Process III	804 "

Prepare the Process Accounts

[B.U. B.Com.(Hons.) 1995]

Solution

Process I Account

Dr. *Cr.*

	Qnt.	*Rate*	*Amount*		*Qnt.*	*Rate*	*Amount*
		Rs.	Rs.			Rs.	Rs.
To Inputs	1,000	5.00	5,000	By Normal Loss A/c	100	100	1,000
" Materials			4,000	@ 10%			
" Wages			7,000				
" Production Overheads			3,000				
" Abnormal gain	40	20	800	By Process II	940	20	18,800
	1,040		19,800		1,040		19,800

Rate per unit = Rs. $\frac{18,000}{900}$ = Rs. 20.

Process II Account

Dr. *Cr.*

	Qnt.	*Rate*	*Amount*		*Qnt.*	*Rate*	*Amount*
		Rs.	Rs.			Rs.	Rs.
To Process I A/c	940	20	18,800	By Normal Loss A/c	47	5	235
" Materials			6,040	5% of 940			
" Wages			8,452	" Abnormal Loss	3	41	123
" Production Overheads			3,556	" Process III	890	41	36,490
			36,848				36,848

Cost per unit = Rs. $\frac{36,848 - 235}{900940 - 47}$ = Rs. 41.00.

Process III Account

Dr.	*Qnt.*	*Rate*	*Amount*	*Cr.*	*Qnt.*	*Rate*	*Amount*
		Rs.	Rs.			Rs.	Rs.
To Process II A/c	890		36,490	By Normal Loss @ 10% of 890	89	6	534
" Materials			6,716				
" Wages			10,000				
" Production Overheads			5,000				
" Abnormal gain	3	72	216	By Finished goods A/c	804	72	57,888
	893		58,422		893		58,422

$$\text{Rs. } \frac{58,206 - 534}{890 - 89} = \text{Rs. } 72.00.$$

Problem 15

The following are the details in respect of Process X and Process Y of a processing factory :

	Process X	Process Y
	Rs.	Rs.
Materials	10,000	—
Labour	10,000	14,000
Overheads	4,000	10,000

The output of Process X is transferred to Process Y at a price calculated to give a profit of 20% on the transfer price and the output of Process Y is charged to Finished Stock at a profit of 25% on the transfer price. The Finished department realised Rs. 1,00,000 for the finished goods received from Process 'Y'. You are asked to show Process Accounts and total profits assuming that there was no opening and no closing work-in-progress.

[C.A. (Inter.)]

Solution

Process X Account

Dr.	Rs.	*Cr.*	Rs.
To Materials	10,000	By Transfer to Process Y	30,000
" Labour	10,000		
" Overheads	4,000		
" Profit 20% of Transfer Price	6,000		
	30,000		30,000

Process Y Account

Dr.	Rs.	*Cr.*	Rs.
To Transfer from Process X	30,000	By Transfer to Finished Stock	72,000
" Labour	14,000		
" Overheads	10,000		
" Profit (25%) of the transfer price	18,000		
	72,000		72,000

Profit and Loss Account

Dr.	Rs.		Cr. Rs.
To Cost of Sale	72,000	By Sale	1,00,000
" Profit c/d	28,000		
	1,00,000		1,00,000
To Costing Profit & Loss A/c	52,000	" Profit on Process X	6,000
		" Profit on Process Y	18,000
		" Profit on Sales	28,000
	52,000		52,000

Problem 16

A product passes through three processes to completion. In January, 1998 the costs of production were as given below :

	Process I	Process II	Process III
Direct Materials	4,000	6,040	6,924
Wages	7,000	8,452	10,000
Production Overheads	3,000	4,000	5,000
2,000 units were issued to Process I @ Rs. 5 each			
Normal Loss	10%	5%	10%
Wastages realises	Rs. 3 per unit	Rs. 5 per unit	Rs. 6 per unit
Actual production (in units)	1,840	1,740	1,600

Prepare the necessary accounts.

Solution

Process I Account

Dr.	Units	Amount Rs.	Cr.	Units	Amount Rs.
To Input	2,000	10,000	By Normal Loss	200	600
" Material		4,000	" Process II	1,840	23,920
" Wages		7,000			
" Overheads		3,000			
" Abnormal gain	40	520			
	2,040	24,520		2,040	24,520

Process II Account

Dr.	Units	Amount Rs.	Cr.	Units	Amount Rs.
To Process I	1,840	23,920	By Normal Loss	92	460
" Material		6,040			
" Wages		8,452	" Abnormal Loss	8	192
" Overheads		4,000	" Process III	1,740	41,760
	1,840	42,412		1,840	42,412

Process III Account

Dr.	Units	Amount		Units	Amount Cr.
		Rs.			Rs.
To Process II	1,740	41,760	By Normal Loss	174	1,044
" Material		6,924	" Finished Stock	1,600	64,000
" Wages		10,000			
" Overheads		5,000			
" Abnormal gain	34	1,360			
	1,774	65,044		1,774	65,044

Normal Loss Account

Dr.	Units	Amount		Units	Amount Cr.
		Rs.			Rs.
To Process I	200	600	By Abnormal gain		
" Process II	92	460	" Process I	40	120
" Process III	174	1,044	" Process II	34	204
			" Bank	392	1,780
	466	2,104		466	2,104

Abnormal Loss Account

Dr.	Units	Amount		Units	Amount Cr.
		Rs.			Rs.
To Process II	8	192	By Cash	8	40
			" Costing P & L A/c		152
	8	192		8	192

Problem 17

Product Z is obtained after it passes three distinct process. The following information is obtained from the accounts for the month ending March 31st, 1991.

Items	Total	Process I	Process II	Process III
	Rs.	Rs.	Rs.	Rs.
Direct Materials	7,542	2,600	1,980	2,962
Direct Wages	9,000	2,000	3,000	4,000
Production Overhead	9,000			

1,000 units at Rs. 3.00 each were introduced to Process I. There was no stock of materials or work-in-progress at the beginning or at the end of the period. The output of each process passes direct to the next process and finally to finished stores. Production overhead is recovered @ 100% of direct wages. The following additional data are obtained :

Process	*Output during the month*	*Percentage of normal loss to input*	*Value of Scrap per unit*
I	950	5%	2
II	840	10%	4
III	750	15%	5

Prepare process cost accounts and abnormal gain or loss accounts.

[Adapted – B.Com.(Hons.)–Delhi and B.Com. – Andhra]

Solution

Process I Account

Dr.	*Units*	*Amount*	*Cr.*	*Units*	*Amount*
		Rs.			Rs.
To Inputs	1,000	3,000	By Normal Loss	50	100
" Materials		2,600	" Loss @ 5%		
" Wages		2,000	" Process II	950	9,500
" Overheads 100% of wages		2,000			
	1,000	9,600		1,000	9,600

Process II Account

Dr.	*Units*	*Amount*	*Cr.*	*Units*	*Amount*
		Rs.			Rs.
To Process I	950	9,500	By Normal Loss A/c 10%	95	380
" Materials		1,980	" Abnormal Loss	15	300
" Wages		3,000	" Process III	840	16,800
" Overheads 100% of wages		3,000			
	950	17,480		950	17,480

Process III Account

Dr.	*Units*	*Amount*	*Cr.*	*Units*	*Amount*
		Rs.			Rs.
To Process II A/c	840	16,800	By Normal Loss @ 15%	126	630
" Materials		2,962	" Finished Stock A/c	750	28,500
" Wages		4,000			
" Overheads		4,000			
" Abnormal gain	36	1,368			
	876	29,130		876	29,130

Abnormal Loss Account

Dr.	Units	Amount		Units	Amount Cr.
		Rs.			Rs.
To Process II	15	300	By Bank	15	60
			" Costing P & L A/c		240
	15	300		15	300

Abnormal Gain Account

Dr.	Units	Amount		Units	Amount Cr.
		Rs.			Rs.
To Normal Loss A/c	36	180	By Process III	36	1,368
" Costing P & L A/c		1,188			
	36	1,368		36	1,368

Normal Loss Account

Dr.	Units	Amount		Units	Amount Cr.
		Rs.			Rs.
To Process I	50	100	By Bank	235	930
" Process II	95	380	" Abnormal Gain A/c	36	180
" Process III	126	630			
	271	1,110		271	1,110

Problem 18

The following information is extracted from the cost accounts of a factory purchasing a commodity in the manufacture of which three processes are involved. Prepare process cost accounts showing the cost of the output and the cost per unit at each stage of manufacture.

You may presume that :

(i) the operations in each separate process are completed daily and

(ii) the value of which units are to be charged to process two and three is the cost per unit of processes one and one plus two, respectively :

Particulars	Process I	Process II	Process III
	Rs.	Rs.	Rs.
Direct wages	2,500	5,000	6,500
Machine expenses	1,400	1,200	1,200
Raw materials consumed	8,000	–	–
Factory on cost	1,100	1,550	900
	Units	Units	Units
Production (Gross)	2,750	–	–
Wastage	150	210	200
Stock at beginning	–	250	500
Stock at end	–	440	100

[Madras University – B.Com. 1988]

Solution

Process I Account

Dr.	Units	Amount Rs.	Cr.	Units	Amount Rs.
To			By Bank		
" Raw Materials	2,750	8,000	" Normal Wastage	150	–
" Direct Wages		2,500			
" Machine Expenses		1,400	" Process II	2,600	13,000
" Factory on Cost		1,100			
	2,750	13,000		2,750	13,000

Process II Account

Dr.	Units	Amount Rs.	Cr.	Units	Amount Rs.
To Opening Stock @ Rs. 5 per unit	250	1,250	By Normal Wastage	210	–
			" Closing Stock A/c @ Rs. 5	440	2,200
" Process I A/c	2,600	13,000			
" Direct Wages		5,000	" Process III @ Rs. 9.00 per unit	2,200	19,800
" Machine Exp.		1,200			
" Factory on Cost		1,550			
	2,850	22,000		2,850	22,000

Process III Account

Dr.	Units	Amount Rs.	Cr.	Units	Amount Rs.
To Opening Stock @ Rs. 9.00	500	4,500	By Normal Wastage	200	–
			" Closing Stock @ Rs. 9.00 per unit	100	900
" Process II	2,200	19,800			
" Direct Wages		6,500			
" Machine Exp.		1,200	" Finished Stock – @ Rs. 13.33 per unit	2,400	32,000
" Factory on Cost		900			
	2,700	32,900		2,700	32,900

Problem 19

A product passes through two Processes I and II and the normal loss is estimated at 2% for Process I and 5% for Process II of the respective inputs. The loss in each process is sold as scrap as under :

Process I	Rs. 10 per 100 units
Process II	Rs. 20 per 100 units

40,000 units of crude materials were introduced in Process I at a cost of Rs. 16,000. From the information supplied prepare the process accounts :

	Process I	Process II
	Rs.	Rs.
Materials consumed	8,000	2,800
Labour	12,200	14,000
Expenses	3,080	1,000
	Units	Units
Finished output	39,000	38,500
Stock on 1st January	4,000	6,000
Stock on 31st December	3,000	8,000
Stock valuation on 1st January	90 paise per unit	Rs. 1.47 per unit

Stock on 31st December is to be valued at the costs shown by the year's Process A/c.

[Madras University, M.Com. – 1988]

Solution

Process I Account

Dr. *Cr.*

		Units	*Amount*			*Units*	*Amount*
			Rs.				Rs.
"	Units introduced	40,000	16,000	"	Normal Loss @ 2%	800	80
"	Materials consumed		8,000	"	Abnormal Loss A/c	200	200
"	Labour		12,200	"	Process I Stock A/c	39,000	39,000
"	Expenses		3,080		@ Re. 1.00		
		40,000	39,280			40,000	39,280

Process I Stock Account

Dr. *Cr.*

		Units	*Amount*			*Units*	*Amount*
			Rs.				Rs.
To	Balance b/d	4,000	3,600	By	Process II	40,000	39,600
	@ 0.90 paise				(Balancing figure)		
"	Process I A/c	39,000	39,000	"	Balance	3,000	3,000
					@ Re. 1.00 per unit		
		43,000	42,600			43,000	42,600

Process II Account

Dr. *Cr.*

		Units	*Amount*			*Units*	*Amount*
			Rs.				Rs.
To	Input from Process I	40,000	39,600	By	Normal Loss @ 5%	2,000	400
"	Material Consumed		2,800				
"	Labour		14,000	"	Process II Stock A/c	38,500	57,740
"	Expenses		1,000		@ 1.499		
"	Abnormal Gain A/c	500	740				
		40,500	58,140			40,500	58,140

Process II Stock Account

Dr.	Units	Amount	Cr.	Units	Amount
		Rs.			Rs.
To Balance @ 1.47	6,000	8,820	By Finished Stock A/c	36,500	54,568
" Process II A/c	38,500	57,740	" Balance @ Rs. 1.499	8,000	11,992
	44,500	66,560		44,500	66,560

Abnormal Loss Account

Dr.	Units	Amount	Cr.	Units	Amount
		Rs.			Rs.
To Process I A/c	200	200	By Bank	200	20
			" Costing P & L A/c		180
	200	200		200	200

Normal Loss Account

Dr.	Units	Amount	Cr.	Units	Amount
		Rs.			Rs.
To Process I A/c	800	80	By Abnormal Gain A/c	500	100
" Process II A/c	2,000	400	" Bank (Balancing figure)	2,300	380
	2,800	480		2,800	480

Abnormal Gain Account

Dr.	Units	Amount	Cr.	Units	Amount
		Rs.			Rs.
To Normal Loss A/c	500	100	By Process II A/c	500	740
" Costing P & L A/c		640			
	500	740		500	740

Problem 20

A product is finally obtained after it passes through three distinct processes. The following information is available from the cost records :

Particulars	Process I	Process II	Process III	Total
	Rs.	Rs.	Rs.	Rs.
Materials	2,600	2,000	1,025	5,625
Direct wages	2,250	3,680	1,400	7,330
Production Overheads				7,330

500 units @ Rs. 4 per unit were introduced in Process I. Production overheads are absorbed as a percentage of direct wages.

The actual output and normal loss of the respective processes are given below :

	Output (units)	*Normal loss as a percentage of input*	*Value of scrap (per unit)* Rs.
Process I	450	10%	2.00
Process II	320	20%	4.00
Process III	270	25%	5.00

Prepare the process accounts and the abnormal gain/loss accounts.

[I.C.W.A. – (Inter) – June – 1991]

Solution

Process I Account

Dr.	*Units*	*Amount* Rs.	*Cr.*	*Units*	*Amount* Rs.
To Input	500	2,000			
" Materials		2,600	By Normal Loss A/c	50	100
" Direct wages		2,250			
" Production Overheads		2,250	" Process II A/c	450	9,000
	500	9,100		500	9,100

Process II Account

Dr.	*Units*	*Amount* Rs.	*Cr.*	*Units*	*Amount* Rs.
To Process I A/c	450	9,000	By Normal Loss	90	360
" Materials		2,000			
" Direct Wages		3,680	" Abnormal Loss	40	2,000
" Production Overheads		3,680	" Process III A/c	320	16,000
	450	18,360		450	18,360

Process III Account

Dr.	*Units*	*Amount* Rs.	*Cr.*	*Units*	*Amount* Rs.
To Process II A/c	320	16,000	By Normal Loss	80	400
" Materials		1,025			
" Direct wages		1,400			
" Production Overheads		1,400	" Finished Stock A/c	270	21,853
" Abnormal Gain A/c	30	2,428			
	350	22,253		350	22,253

Hints : Process I – Total cost 9,100 – Scrap realised Rs. 100 = Rs. 9,000.
Cost per unit Rs. 9,000 ÷ 450 = Rs. 20.

Problem 21

In a factory the output passes through three processes. The output of one process is transferred to the next process.

	A	B	C
	Rs.	Rs.	Rs.
Direct Wages	10,000	20,000	30,000
Machinery Expenses	5,000	13,000	20,000
On Cost	2,000	1,000	4,730
Materials consumed	23,000	–	–
	Units	Units	Units
Output (Gross)	21,000	–	–
Wastage	1,000	1,500	2,500
Opening Stock	–	2,000	3,500
Closing Stock	–	500	1,000

Prepare process accounts showing the cost per unit in each process and also the total cost in each process.

[Adapted—Andhra B. Com.]

Solution

Process A Account

Dr. *Cr.*

	Unit No.	*Rate* Rs.	*Amount* Rs.		*Unit* No.	*Rate* Rs.	*Amount* Rs.
To Materials			23,000	By Wastage A/c	1,000	–	–
" DirectWages			10,000	" Process B A/c	20,000	2.00	40,000
" Machinery							
" Expenses			5,000				
" On Cost			2,000				
			40,000				40,000

Process B Account

Dr. *Cr.*

	Unit No.	*Rate* Rs.	*Amount* Rs.		*Unit* No.	*Rate* Rs.	*Amount* Rs.
To Opening Stock*	2,000	4.00	8,000	By Wastage A/c	1,500	–	–
" Process A A/c	20,000	2.00	40,000	" Process C A/c	20,000	4.00	80,000
" Direct Wages			20,000	(transfer)			
" Machinery							
Expenses			13,000				
" On Cost			1,000	" Closing Stock	500	4.00	2,000
	22,000		82,000		22,000		82,000

Process C Account

Dr. *Cr.*

	Units	*Rate* Rs.	*Amount* Rs.		*Units*	*Rate* Rs.	*Amount* Rs.
To Opening Stock**	3,000	7.70	23,100	By Wastage	2,500	–	–
" Process B A/c	20,000	4.00	80,000				
" Machinery Expenses A/c			20,000	" Finished Stock A/c	19,500	7.70	1,50,150
" Direct Wages			30,000				
" On Cost			4,750	" Closing Stock	1,000	7.70	7,700
	23,000		1,57,850		23,000		1,57,850

Working notes :

* (a) Current cost of Process B = Rs. 40,000 + Rs. 20,000 + Rs. 13,000 + Rs. 1,000 = Rs. 74,000

(b) Current Production = 20,000 – 1,500 (wastage) = 18,500 units.

∴ Current cost of Process B Rs. 74,000 ÷ 18,500 = Rs. 4 per unit

This rate has been applied to both opening stock and closing stock.

** Current Cost of Process 'C' = Rs. 80,000 + Rs. 20,000 + Rs. 30,000 + Rs. 4,750 = Rs. 1,34,750

Current production = 20,000 units – wastage 2,500 units = 17,500 units (good)

∴ Current Cost of Process C = Rs. 134,750 ÷ 17,500 = Rs. 7.70 per unit

The above rate has been applied in the valuation of opening stock and closing stock of Process 'C'.

Problem 22

X Ltd. produces product 'Z' through two distinct processes—Process A and Process B. On completion, it is transferred to finished stock.

From the following information relating to the year 1997-98, prepare Process Account and Finished Stock Account.

	Particulars	Process A	Process B
(i)	Raw materials used	1,000 units	
(ii)	Cost per unit	Rs. 200	
(iii)	Transfer to next process/ Finished stock	940 kunits	870 units
(iv)	Normal loss (on inputs)	5%	10%
(v)	Direct wages	Rs. 15,600	Rs. 13,200
(vi)	Direct expenses	75% of direct wages	75% of direct wages
(vii)	Sundry expenses	—	Rs. 2,954
(viii)	Realisabble value of scrap per unit	Rs. 4.50	Rs. 5.75

800 units of finished goods were sold at a profit of 20% on Cost. Assume that there was no opening or closing stock of work-in-progress.

[C.U. B.Com. (Hons.) 1999]

Solution

Process A Account

Dr.	Units	Rs.	Cr.	Units	Rs.
To Raw materials	1,000	20,000	By Normal Loss A/c	50	225
" Direct wages		15,600	(5% of inputs)		
" Direct expenses		11,700	" Abnormal Loss A/c	10	496
(75% of wages)			Process B A/c	940	46,579
			—goods transferred		
	1,000	47,300		1,000	47,300

$$\text{Rate per unit} = \frac{\text{Rs. } 47,300 - \text{Rs. } 225}{1,000 - 50} = \text{Rs. } 49{\cdot}552$$

Process B Account

Dr.	Units	Rs.	Cr.	Units	Rs.
To Process A A/c	940	46,579	By Normal Loss A/c	94	541
" Direct wages		13,200	(10% of 940)		
" Direct expenses		9,900	" Finished goods A/c	870	74,137
(75% of wages)					
" Sundry expenses		2,954			
" Abnormal gain A/c	24	2,045			
	964	74,678		964	74,678

$$\text{Cost per unit} = \text{Rs. } \frac{72,633 - 541}{940 - 541} = \text{Rs. } \frac{72,092}{846} = \text{Rs. } 85.215$$

Problem 23

Product X is obtained after it passes through 3 distinct processes. You are required to prepare Process Accounts from the following information :

	Total Rs	Process I Rs.	Process II Rs.	Process III Rs.
Materials	15,084	5,200	3,960	5,924
Direct Wages	18,000	4,000	6,000	8,000
Production Overhead	18,000			

1,000 units @ Rs. 6 per unit were introduced in Process I. Production Overhead are to be distributed at 100% on direct wages.

	Actual output	Normal loss	Value of Scrap per unit
Process I	950	5%	Rs. 4.00
Process II	840	10%	Rs. 8.00
Process III	750	15%	Rs. 10.00

[Adapted—Andhra, B. Com.]

Solution

Process I Account

Dr. *Cr.*

	Units	Rate	Amount		Units	Rate	Amount
		Rs.	Rs.			Rs.	Rs.
To Input	1,000	6	6,000	By Normal Loss	50	4	200
" Materials			5,200	(5% of 1,000)			
" Direct wages			4,000	" Process II			
" Production				Account	950	20	19,000
Overhead			4,000				
(100% of wages)							
	1,000		19,200		1,000		19,200

Note : Cost per unit of output = Rs. $\frac{19{,}200 - 200}{1{,}000 - 50}$ = Rs. 20.

Process II Account

Dr. *Cr.*

	Units	Rate	Amount		Units	Rate	Amount
		Rs.	Rs.			Rs.	Rs.
To Process I A/c	950	20	19,000	By Normal Loss A/c	95	8	760
" Materials			3,960	(10% of 950)			
" Direct Wages			6,000	" Abnormal			
" Production				Loss A/c	15	40	600
Overhead			6,000	" Process III A/c	840	40	33,600
(100% of Wages)							
	950		34,960		950		34,960

Note : Cost per unit = Rs. $\frac{34{,}940 - 760}{950 - 95}$ = Rs. $\frac{34{,}200}{855}$ = Rs. 40 per unit

Process III Account

Dr. *Cr.*

	Units	Rate	Amount		Units	Rate	Amount
		Rs.	Rs.			Rs.	Rs.
To Process II A/c	840	40	33,600	By Normal			
" Materials			5,924	Loss A/c	126	10	1,260
" Direct Wages			8,000	(15% of 840)			
" Production Overhead			8,000	" Finished			
(100% of Wages)				Stock A/c	750	76	57,000
" Abnormal Gain A/c	36	76	2,736				
	876		58,260		876		58,260

Note : Cost per unit = Cost per unit = Rs. $\frac{55{,}524 - 1{,}260}{840 - 126}$ = Rs. $\frac{54{,}264}{714}$ = Rs. 76.00

Problem 24

In a factory the product passes through two processes A and B. A loss of 5% is allowed in Process A and 2% in Process B, nothing being realised by disposal of wastage. During April 1992, 10,000 units of materials costing Rs. 6 per unit were introduced in Process A. The other costs are as follows :

	Process A	Process B
	Rs.	Rs.
Materials	–	6,140
Labour	10,000	6,000
Overheads	6,000	4,600

The output was 9,300 units from Process A. 9,200 units were produced by Process B, which were transferred to the warehouse.

8,000 units of the finished product was sold @ Rs. 15 per unit, the selling and distribution expenses were Rs. 2 per unit.

Prepare (i) Process Accounts; and (ii) a statement of profit or loss of the firm for April, 1992, assuming there were no Opening Stock of any type.

[Adapted—D.U. B.Com. (Hons.)]

Solution

Process A Account

Dr. *Cr.*

	Units	*Amount*		*Units*	*Amount*
		Rs.			Rs.
To Materials	10,000	60,000	By Normal Loss	500	–
" Labour		10,000	" Abnormal Loss*	200	1,600
" Overheads		6,000	" Process B A/c	9,300	74,400
	10,000	76,000		10,000	76,000

Process B Account

Dr. *Cr.*

	Units	*Amount*		*Units*	*Amount*
		Rs.			Rs.
To Process A A/c	9,300	74,400	By Normal Loss	186	–
" Materials		6,140	" Finished Goods A/c	9,200	92,000
" Labour		6,000			
" Overhead		4,600			
" Abnormal Gain**	86	860			
	9,386	92,000		9,386	92,000

Profit and Loss Account

Dr.	Rs.		*Cr.* Rs.
To Cost of finished goods	92,000	By Sales (8,000 × 15)	1,20,000
" Selling and Distribution costs	16,000	" Closing Stock at cost	12,000
" Profit	24,000	(1,200 × 10)	
	1,32,000		1,32,000

STATEMENT OF PROFIT

	Rs.
Profit as per Profit & Loss A/c	24,000
Add : Abnormal Gain in Process B	860
	24,860
Less : Abnormal Loss in Process A	1,600
	23,260

Note : * Calculation of cost of Abnormal Loss in Process A

Cost of 9,500 units (10,000 – Normal loss 500) = Rs. 76,000

$$\text{Cost of 200 units} = \text{Rs. } \frac{76,000}{9,500} \times 200 = \text{Rs. } 1,600$$

** Calculation of value of Abnormal Gain

Cost of 9,114 units (9,300 – 186) = Rs. 91,140

$$\text{Cost of 86 units} = \text{Rs. } \frac{91,140}{9,114} \times 86 = \text{Rs. } 860$$

Problem 25

Product X is obtained after it is processed through three distinct processes. The following cost information is available for the operation :

	Total	*Proces I*	*Process II*	*Process III*
	Rs.	Rs.	Rs.	Rs.
Materials	5,625	2,600	2,000	1,025
Direct wages	7,330	2,250	3,680	1,400
Production Overheads	7,336	—	—	—

500 Units @ Rs. 4 per unit were introduced in process I. Production Overhead to be distributed as 100% on Direct Wages.

The Actual Output and Normal Loss of the respective process are :

	Output Unit	Normal Loss on Input	Value of Scrap per unit
			Rs.
Process I	450	10%	2
Process II	340	20%	4
Process III	270	25%	5

There is no stock or work-in-progress in any process.

Show

(a) The three Process Accounts

(b) The Normal Loss Account

(c) The Abnormal Loss and Abnormal Gain Accounts

[Adapted—I.C.W.A.]

Solution

Process I Account

Particulars	*Units*	*Cost per Unit*	*Amount*	*Particulars*	*Units*	*Cost per Unit*	*Amount*
		Rs.	Rs.			Rs.	Rs.
Units introduced	500	4.00	2,000	Normal Loss	50	2.00	100
Materials			2,600	Tfr. to Process II	450	20.00	9,000
Direct wages			2,250				
Production overhead			2,250				
	500		9,100		500		9,100

Process II Account

Particulars	*Units*	*Cost per Unit*	*Amount*	*Particulars*	*Units*	*Cost per Unit*	*Amount*
		Rs.	Rs.			Rs.	Rs.
Tfr. from Process I	450	20.00	9,000	Normal Los	90	4.00	360
Matrials			2,000	Abnormal Loss	20	50.00	1,000
Direct wages			3,680	Trnas. to Pr. II	340	50.00	17,000
Production overhead			3,680				
	450		18,360		450		18,360

Process III Account

Particulars	*Units*	*Cost per Unit*	*Amount*	*Particulars*	*Units*	*Cost per Unit*	*Amount*
		Rs.	Rs.			Rs.	Rs.
Transfer from Pr. II	340	50.00	17,000	Normal Loss	85	5.00	425
Materials			1,025	Transfer to Finished Stores	270	80.00	21,600
Direct Wages			1,400				
Production overhead			1,400				
Abnormal gain	15	80.00	1,200				
	355		22,025		355		22,025

Normal Loss Account

Particulars	*Units*	*Cost per Unit*	*Amount*	*Particulars*	*Units*	*Cost per Unit*	*Amount*
		Rs.	Rs.			Rs.	Rs.
Process I	50	2.00	100	Cash-sale of scrap			
Process II	90	4.00	360	Process I	50	2.00	100
Process III	85	5.00	425	Process II	90	4.00	360
				Process III	70	5.00	350
				Abnormal gain			
				Process I	15	5.00	75
	225		885		225		885

Abnormal Loss Account

Particulars	*Units*	*Cost per Unit*	*Amount*	*Particulars*	*Units*	*Cost per Unit*	*Amount*
		Rs.	Rs.			Rs.	Rs.
Process II	20		1,000	Cash-sale of scrap			
				Process II	20	4.00	80
				Costing P & L A/c			920
	20		1,000		20		1,000

Abnormal Gain Account

Particulars	*Units*	*Cost per Unit*	*Amount*	*Particulars*	*Units*	*Cost per Unit*	*Amount*
		Rs.	Rs.			Rs.	Rs.
Normal Loss A/c	15	5.00	75	Process III	15	80.00	1,200
Costing P & L A/c			1,125				
	15		1,200		15		1,200

Problem 26

A product passes through three processes A,B and C. The details of expenses incurred on the three processes during the year 1992 were as under :

Process	A	B	C
Unit issued/introduced	10,000		
Cost per unit Rs. 100	Rs.	Rs.	Rs.
Sundry Materials	10,000	15,000	5,000
Labour	30,000	80,000	65,000
Direct Expenses	6,000	18,150	27,200
Selling price per unit of output	120	165	250

Management expenses during the year were Rs. 80,000 and selling expenses were Rs. 50,000. These are not allocable to the processes.

Actual output of the three processes was :

A—9,300 units, B—5,400 units and C—2,100 units. Two-thirds of the output of Process A and one-half of the output of Process B was passed on to the next process and the balance was sold. The entire output of Process C was sold.

The normal loss of the three processes, calculated on the input of every process was : Process A—5% ; B—15% and C—20%.

The loss of Process A was sold at Rs. 2 per unit, that of B at Rs. 5 per unit and of Process C at Rs. 10 per unit.

Prepare the Three Process Accounts and the Profit and Loss Account.

C.A. (Inter.) May 1993

Solution

Process A Account

Particulars	*Units*	*Rate*	*Amount*	*Particulars*	*Units*	*Rate*	*Amount*
			Rs.				Rs.
To Units introduced	10,000	100	10,00,000	By Normal loss	500	2	1,000
" Sundry Materials			10,000	(5% of 10,000 units)			
" Labour			30,000	" Abnormal Loss	200	110	22,000
" Direct expenses			6,000	" Output transferred			
				to process B A/c	6,200	110	6,82,000
				" P & L A/c	3,100	110	3,41,000
	10,000		10,46,000		10,000		10,46,000

$$\text{Cost per unit} = \frac{\text{Total cost} - \text{Value of normal loss}}{\text{Input quantity} - \text{Normal loss quantity}} = \frac{10,46,000 - 1,000}{10,000 - 500} = \text{Rs. } 110$$

This rate is to be applied toabnormal loss and output.

Process B Account

Particulars	*Units*	*Rate*	*Amount*	*Particulars*	*Units*	*Rate*	*Amount*
			Rs.				Rs.
To Output from A' A/c	6,200	110	6,82,000	By Normal loss	930	5	4,650
" Sundry Materials			15,000	(15% of 6,200 units)			
" Labour			80,000	" Output transferred			
" Direct Expenses			18,150	to Process C A/c	2,700	150	4,05,000
	6,200		7,95,150	" P & L A/c	2,700	150	4,05,000
To Abnormal gain	130	150	19,500				
	6,330		8,14,650		6,330		8,14,650

$$\text{Cost per unit} = \frac{7,95,150 - 4,650}{6,200 - 930} = \text{Rs. } 150$$

This rate is to be applied to abnormal gain and output.

Process C Account

Particulars	Units	Rate	Amount	Particulars	Units	Rate	Amount
			Rs.				Rs.
To Output from B	2,700	150	4,05,000	By Normal Loss			
" Sundry Materials			5,000	20% of 2,700	540	10	5,400
" Labour			65,000	" Abnormal loss	60	230	13,800
" Direct Expenses			27,200	" P & L A/c	2,100	230	4,83,000
	2,700		5,02,200		27,000		5,02,200

$$\text{Cost per unit} = \frac{5,02,200 - 5,400}{2,700 - 540} = \frac{4,96,800}{2,160} = \text{Rs. } 230.$$

Profit and Loss Account

Particulars	Units	Rate	Amount	Particulars	Units	Rate	Amount
			Rs.				Rs.
To Process A	3,100	110	3,41,000	By Sales			
" Process B	2,700	150	4,05,000	Process A	3,100	120	3,72,000
" Process C	2,100	230	4,83,000	Process B	2,700	165	4,45,500
" Management Exp.			80,000	Process C	2,100	250	5,25,000
" Selling Expenses			50,000	" Abnormal			
" Abnormal loss A/c			34,800	gain (Note 2)			18,850
(Note : 1)				" Net loss			32,450
	7,900		13,93,800		7,900		13,93,800

Abnormal Loss Account

Particulars	Units	Rate	Amount	Particulars	Units	Rate	Amount
			Rs.				Rs.
To Process A	200	110	22,000	By Sales	200	2	400
" Process C	60	230	13,800	" Sales	60	10	600
				" P & L A/c			34,800
	260		35,800		260		35,800

Abnormal Gain Account

Particulars	Units	Rate	Amount	Particulars	Units	Rate	Amount
			Rs.				Rs.
To Normal Loss	130	5	650	By Process B	130	150	19,500
" P & L A/c			18,850				
	130		19,500		130		19,500

Problem 27

The finished product of a manufacturing company passes through three processes, viz., I, II and III. The normal wastage in each process is 5%, 7% and 10% for the processes I, II and III respectively (calculated with reference to the number of units fed into each process). The scrap generated out of wastage has a sale value of 70 paise per unit 80 paise per unit and Rupee 1 per unit in the processes I, II and III respectively. The output of each process is transferred to the next process and the finished output emerges from the process III is transferred to stock. There was no stock of work-in-progress in any process in a particular month. The details of cost data for the month are given below :

	Processes I	Processes II	Processes III
Materials used (Rs.)	1,20,000	40,000	40,000
Direct labour cost (Rs.)	80,000	60,000	60,000
Production expenses (Rs.)	40,000	40,000	28,000
Output in units (actuals)	38,000	34,000	32,000

Process I was fed with 40,000 units of raw input at a cost of Rs. 3,20,000.

Prepare the process accounts.

[I.C.W.A. (Inter.) June, 1996]

Solution

Process I Account

	Units	Amount (Rs.		Units	Amount Rs.
To Raw input	40,000	3,20,000	By Normal scrap 5% of 40,000 = 2,000 units at 70 paise	2,000	1,400
" Materials		1,20,000	" Output transferred to II	38,000	5,58,600
" Direct labour		80,000			
" Production Expenses		40,000			
	40,000	5,60,000		40,000	5,60,000

$$\text{Cost per unit} = \frac{\text{Total Cost} - \text{Value of normal scrap}}{\text{Input Qty} - \text{Normal loss Qty.}}$$

$$= \frac{5,60,000 - 1,400}{40,000 - 2,000} = \frac{5,58,600}{38,000} = \text{Rs. } 14.70 \text{ per unit}$$

This rate is applied to output 38,000 × 14.70 = Rs. 5,58,600

Process II Account

	Units	Amount (Rs.		Units	Amount Rs.
To Output from I	38,000	5,58,600	By Normal scrap 7% of 38,000 = 2,660 units at .80 paise	2,660	2,128
" Materials		40,000	" Abnormal loss	740	14,584
" Direct labour		60,000	" Output transferred to III	34,600	6,81,888
" Production Expenses		40,000			
	38,000	6,98,600		38,000	6,98,600

$$\text{Cost per unit} = \frac{6,98,600 - 2,128}{38,000 - 2,660} = \text{Rs. } 19.707753$$

This rate is applied to output & abnormal loss.

Abnormal loss	=	740 × 19.707753	=	Rs. 14,584
Output	=	34,600 × 19.707753	=	Rs. 6,81,888

Process III Account

	Units	Amount		Units	Amount
		(Rs.			Rs.
To Output from II	34,600	6,81,888	By Normal scrap 10% of 34,600 = 3,460 units at Rs. 1.00	3,460	3,460
" Materials		40,000			
" Direct labour		60,000			
" Production Expenses		28,000	" Output transferred to finished stock	32,000	8,28,699
	34,600	8,09,888			
" Abnormal gain	860	22,271			
	35,460	8,32,159		35,460	8,32,159

$$\text{Cost per unit} = \frac{7,09,888 - 3,460}{34,600 - 3,460} = \text{Rs. } 25.896852 \text{ per unit}$$

This rate is applied to output & abnormal gain.

Output	=	32,000 × 25.896852	=	8,28,699
Abnormal gain	=	860 × 25.896852	=	Rs. 22,271

Problem 28

A product passes through three processes : A, B and C. 10,000 units at a cost of Rs. 1.10 were issued to process A. The other direct expenses were as follows :

	Process A	Process B	Process C
	Rs.	Rs.	Rs.
Sundry materials	1,500	1,500	1,500
Direct Labour	4,500	8,000	6,500
Direct Expenses	1,000	1,000	1,503

The scrap of process 'A' was 5% and in process 'B' 4% on input. The scrap of process 'A' was sold at Re. 0.25 per unit and that of 'B' at Re. 0.50 per unit and that of C at Re. 1.00 per unit.

The overhead charges were 160% of direct labour. The final product was sold at Rs. 10 per unit fetching a profit of 20% on sales. Prepare 3 Process accounts and find out the number of units of scrap in process C.

[C.S. (Inter) Dec. 1994]

Solution

Process A Account

Dr. *Cr.*

Particulars	*Units*	*Rate*	*Amount*	*Particulars*	*Units*	*Rate*	*Amount*
			Rs.				Rs.
To Units issued	10,000	1.10	11,000	By Scrap 5% of 10,000	500	0.25	125
" Sundry Materials			1,500	" Output transferred to B	9,500	2.639	25,075
" Direct Labour			4,500				
" Direct Expenses			1,000				
" Overheads 160% of labour			7,200				
	10,000		25,200		10,000		25,200

$$\text{Cost of output} = \frac{\text{Total cost} - \text{Value of normal scrap / wastage}}{\text{Input} - \text{Normal scrap}}$$

$$= \frac{25,200 - 125}{10,000 - 500} = \frac{25,075}{9,500} = \text{Rs. } 2.639$$

Process B Account

Dr. *Cr.*

Particulars	*Units*	*Rate*	*Amount*	*Particulars*	*Units*	*Rate*	*Amount*
			Rs.				Rs.
To Output from A	9,500	2.639	25,075	By Scrap 4% of 9,500	380	0.50	190
" Sundry Materials			1,500	" Output transferred to C	9,120	5.283	48,185
" Direct Labour			8,000				
" Direct Expenses			1,000				
" Overheads at 160% of labour			12,800				
	9,500		48,375		9,500		48,375

Process C Account

Dr. *Cr.*

Particulars	*Units*	*Rate*	*Amount*	*Particulars*	*Units*	*Rate*	*Amount*
			Rs.				Rs.
To Output from B	9,120	5.283	48,185	By Scrap (See note benlow)	696	1.00	696
" Sundry Materials			1,500	" Output transferred to finished stock	8,424	8.00	67,392
" Direct Labour			6,500				
" Direct Expenses			1,503				
" Overheads at 160% of labour			10,400				
	9.120		68.088		9,120		68,088

Notes :

	Rs. per unit
Selling price of final product	10.00
Less : Profit at 20% on sales	2.00
Cost	8.00

Let the scrap in process C be 'S' units which can be sold at Re. 1.00 per unit. Cost per unit

$$\text{Cost per unit} = \frac{\text{Total cost} - \text{Value of Normal Scrap}}{\text{Input Quantity} - \text{Normal Scrap Quantity}}$$

$$8.00 = \frac{68{,}088 - (S \times 1.00)}{9{,}120 - S}$$

By Cross Multiplying

$8(9{,}210 - S) = 68{,}088 - S$

$72{,}960 - 8S = 68{,}088 - S$

$72{,}960 - 68{,}088 = 8S - S$

$4{,}872 = 7S$

$S = 4{,}872/7 = 696$ units of scrap in Process C.

Problem 29

The following details are extracted from the costing records of an oil mill for the year ended 31st March, 1999 :

Purchase of 500 tonnes copra, Rs. 2,00,000.

	Crushing	Refining	Finishing
	Rs.	Rs.	Rs.
Cost of Labour	2,500	1,000	1,500
Electric power	600	360	240
Sundry materials	100	2,000	—
Steam	600	450	450
Repairs of machinery	280	330	140
Factory expenses	1,320	660	220
Cost of casks			7,500

300 tonnes of crude oil were produced. 250 tonnes of oil were produced by the refining process. 248 tonnes of refined oil were finished for delivery. Copra sacks sold for Rs. 400. 175 tonnes of copra residue sold for Rs. 11,000. Loss in weight in crushing 25 tonnes. 45 tonnes of byproducts obtained from refining process valued at Rs. 6,750.

You are required to show the accounts in respect of each of the following stages of manufacture for the purpose of arriving at the cost per tonne of each process and the total cost per tonne of the finished oil : (a) Copra crushing process. (b) Refining process. (c) Finishing process including casking.

[B.Com., Karnataka : B.Com., Mysore]

Solution

Copra Crushing Process Account

	Tonnes	*Amount*		*Tonnes*	*Amount*
		Rs.			Rs.
To Copra used	500	2,00,000	By Sale of copra residue	175	11,000
" Labour		2,500	" Loss	25	.
" Electric power		600	Sale of copra sacks		400
" Sundry material		100	" Cost of crude oil	300	1,94,000
" Repairs to machinery		280	Rs. 646.67 per tonne		
" Steam		600			
" Factory expenses		1,320			
	500	2,05,400		500	2,05,400

Refining Process Account

	Tonnes	Amount		Tonnes	Amount
		Rs.			Rs.
To Crude oil	300	1,94,000	By Sale of byproducts	45	6,750
" Labour		1,000	" Loss	5	—
" Electric power		360	" Cost of refining		
" Sundry material		2,000	oil Rs. 768.2 per tonne	250	1,92,050
" Repairs to machinery		330			
" Steam		450			
" Factory expenses		660			
	330	1,98,800		300	1,98,800

Finishing Proces Account

	Tonnes	Amount		Tonnes	Amount
		Rs.			Rs.
To Refining process	250	1,92,050	By Loss	2	—
" Labour		1,500	" Cost of finished		
" Electric power		240	oil @ Rs. 784.68		
" Repairs to machinery		140	per tonne	248	1,94,600
" Steam		450			
" Factory expenses		220			
	250	1,94,600		250	1,94,600

Finished Stock Account

	Tonnes	Amount		Tonnes	Amount
		Rs.			Rs.
To Finishing process	240	1,94,600	By Balance at Rs. 814.02		2,02,100
" Cost of casks		7,500			
		2,02,100			2,02,100

Problem 30

Hydrabad Chemicals Ltd. manufactures a particular brand of phenyle. The phenyle passes through three important process. During the month of January, 1996, 600 gross of bottles were produced. The cost books show the following information :

	Process A	ProcessB	Process C
Materials (Rs.)	8,000	4,000	3,000
Labour (Rs.)	6,00	5,000	5,000
Direct Expenses (Rs.)	1,200	400	1,000
Cost of bottles (Rs.)	—	4,060	—
Cost of corks (Rs.)	—	—	650

The indirect expenses for this period were Rs. 3,200. The by-products of Process B were sold for Rs. 480 and the residue of Process C was sold for Rs. 250.

Prepare the Process Accounts, find out the cost of production in each process and the cost of finished product per gross of bottles.

[Andhra U. B.Com.]

Solution

Process A

Output 600 gross of bottles

	Rs.		Rs.
To Materials	8,000	By Process B	16,400
" Labour	6,000		
" Direct Expenses	1,200		
" Indirect Expenses (20% of labour)	1,200		
	16,400		16,400

Process B

	Rs.		Rs.
To Process A	16,400	By Bank—sale of by-product	480
To Materials	4,000	By Process C	30,380
" Labour	5,000		
" Direct Expenses	400		
" Indirect Expenses (20% of Direct labour)	1,000		
" Cost of bottles	4,060		
	30,860		30,860

Process C

	Rs.		Rs.
To Process B	30,380	By Bank—sale of residue	250
" Materials	3,000	" Finished Goods	40,780
" Labour	5,000		
" Direct Expenses	1,000		
" Indirect Expenses (20% of labour)	1,000		
" Cost of corks	650		
	41,030		41,030

Note : Indirect expenses have been apportioned as a percentage of Direct Labour "

$$\text{Rs. } \frac{3,200 \times 100}{16,000} = 20\%.$$

7.12 Concept of Equivalent Production

Equivalent Production represents the production of a process in terms of completed units. At the end of any given period there are likely to be partly completed units (work-in-process). It is evident that some of the costs pertaining to this period are attributable to the units which have not been completed. Just to spread the total costs equitably over part finished and fully complete units the concept of equivalent units is required. The number of equivalent units is the number of equivalent fully complete units which the partly completed units represent.

The following example will make the concept clear.

Let us assume that in a given period production was 3,000 complete units and 800 partly complete units. The partly complete units were deemed to be 75% complete.

Total equivalent production = Complete units + Equivalent units in Work-in-progress

$= 3{,}000 + \frac{3}{4}$ of $800 = 3{,}000 + 600 = 3{,}600.$

The total cost will be spread over the total equivalent production.

So, cost per unit = Total costs ÷ Total equivalent production (units).

Equivalent Units and Cost elements

In calculating equivalent units, each cost element must be treated separately and then the cost per unit of each element is added to ascertain the cost of a complete unit.

Problem 31

For the month of January, 1991, production and cost data were as follows :

Total Costs :	Materials	Rs. 3,000
	Wages	Rs. 4,500
	Overheads	Rs. 2,500
		Rs. 10,000

Production was 1,500 fully complete units and 200 partly complete. The degree of completion of the 200 units work-in-progress was as follows :

Materials	75%
Labour	60%
Overheads	50%

Calculate the total equivalent production, the cost per complete unit and the value of work-in-progress.

Solution

Cost element	*Equivalent units in WIP*	+ *Fully complete units*	*Total effective production*	*Total cost*	*Cost per unit*
				Rs.	Rs.
Materials	200 × 75% = 150	+ 3,000	3,150	3,000	0.952
Labour	200 × 60% = 120	+ 3,000	3,120	4,500	1.442
Overheads	200 × 50% = 100	+ 3,000	3,100	2,500	0.806
				10,000	3.200

Value of completed production = 3,000 × Rs. 3.20 = Rs. 9,600

Value of work-in-Progress :

Total Cost – Value of completed production = Rs. 10,000 – 9,600 = Rs. 400

7.13 Valuation of Opening work-in-progress

The partly completed units at the end of the one period will be the opening work-in-progress at the beginning of the next period. The value of opening work-in-process brought forward from the previous period, sometimes sub-divided into various elements of materials, labour and overheads each with a given degree of completion and value. In most practical situations there is both opening and closing work-in-progress and in such cases the problem arises of how to value the closing work-in-progress and the completed units transferred out.

There are two approaches to this problem, the FIFO method and the Average Cost method.

FIFO METHOD OF VALUATION

Under this method of valuation it is assumed that units are dealt with on a first-in– first-out basis which signifies that the first work done in a period is the completion of the opening work-in-process.

AVERAGE COST METHOD OF VALUATION

Under this method of valuation, an average unit cost is calculated using the total of the opening work-in-process plus the current period costs. The effect of this method is that both closing work-in-process and completed units are valued using the same average unit cost.

Problem 32

Process II receives units from Process I and after carrying out work on the units Process II transfers them to Process III. For one accounting period the relevant data were as follows :

Opening work-in-progress 200 units (25% completed) valued Rs. 2,500.

800 units received from Process I valued at Rs. 4,300. 840 units were transferred to Process III. Closing work-in-process 160 units (50% complete). The costs for the period were Rs.16,580 and no units were scrapped.

You are required to prepare the Process Accounts for Process II using :

(i) the FIFO method of valuation,

(ii) the average cost method of valuation.

Solution

On FIFO basis

Calculation of effective units of production :

	Completed units transferred	840	units
Add :	work contained in closing W.I.P. (160 × 50%)	80	units
		920	units
Less :	work contained in opening W.I.P (200 × 25%)	50	units
		870	units

$$\text{Period Cost per unit} = \frac{\text{Total cost for the period}}{\text{Effective units}} = \text{Rs. } \frac{16,580 + 4,300}{870} = \text{Rs. } 24$$

$$\text{Value of closing W.I.P.} = 160 \times \frac{50}{100} \times \text{Rs. } 24 = 80 \times 24 = \text{Rs. } 1,920.$$

Process II Account

	Units	Rs.		Units	Rs.
To Opening W.I.P.	200	2,500	By Process III	840	21,460
" Process I	800	4,300	" Closing W.I.P.	160	1,920
" Process Costs		16,580			
	1,000	23,380		1,000	23,380

On Average Cost Method

The effective units 840 + 80 = 920 units The total costs involved = Opening W.I.P. + Total Cost of units transferred + Closing W.I.P.

Problem 33

RP Limited furnishes you the following information relating to Process B for the month of October, 1998 :

(i) Opening work-in-progress – Nil

(ii) Units introduced 10,000 units @ Rs. 3 per unit

(iii) Expenses debited to the Process

	Rs.
Direct Materials	14,650
Labour	21,148
Overheads	12,000

(iv) Normal loss in process = 1% of input.

(v) Closing work-in-process – 350 units

Degree of completion – Materials	100%
Labour and Overheads	50%

(vi) Finished output – 9,500 units

(vii) Degree of completion of abnormal loss :

Materials	10%
Labour & Overheads	80%

(viii) Units scrapped as normal loss were sold at Re 1.00 per unit.

(ix) All the units of abnormal loss were sold at Rs. 2.50 per unit

Prepare :

1. Statement of Equivalent production;
2. Statement showing the cost of Finished goods, abnormal loss and closing work-in-progress.
3. Process B Account.

[Adapted—I.C.W.A.- (Inter)]

Solution

Statement of Equivalent Production [EQP]

Particulars	*Output*	*E Q P Materials Units*	*%*	*Labour Units*	*%*	*Overheads Units*	*%*
Finished output	9,500	9,500	100%	9,500	100%	9,500	100%
Normal Loss 1% of Rs. 10,000	100	–	–	–	–	–	–
Abnormal loss (10,000 – 9,500 —350 – 100 = 50)	50	50	100%	40	80%	40	80%
Closing W.I.P.	350	350	100%	175	50%	175	50%
	10,000	9,900		9,715		9,715	

Units introduced 10,000 × Rs. 3	Rs. 30,000			
Add : Direct Materials	Rs. 14,650			
	Rs. 44,650			
Less : Value of Normal loss	100			
	Rs. 44,550	44,550	21,148	42,000

Cost per unit of EQP $= \frac{\text{Cost}}{\text{Units}} = \frac{44,550}{9,900} \quad \frac{21,148}{9,715} \quad \frac{42,000}{9,715}$

= Rs.4.50 = 2.1768 = 4.3232

Statement of Cost

				Rs.
Finished goods (Rs. 1,07,798 – 100 – 485 – 2,713)			9,500 × Rs. 11	1,04,500
Abnormal loss				
Materials	50 units × Rs. 4.50	=	225	
Labour	40 × Rs. 2.1768	=	87	
Overheads	40 × Rs. 4.3232	=	173	485
Closing W.I.P.				
Materials	350 × Rs. 4.50	=	1,575	
Labour	175 × Rs. 2.1768	=	381	
Overheads	175 × Rs. 4.3232	=	757	2,713

Process B Account

Dr. *Cr.*

	Units	Rs.		Units	Rs.
To Opening W.I.P.		Nil	By Normal Loss	100	100
" Units introduced	10,000	30,000	" Abnormal loss	50	485
" Direct Materials		14,650	" Finished Goods	9,500	1,04,500
" Wages		21,148	" Closing W.I.P.	350	2,713
" Overheads		42,000			
	10,000	1,07,798		10,000	1,07,798

Abnormal Loss Account

Dr.	Units	Rs.		Units	Rs. Cr.
To Process B A/c	50	485	By Cash (sold @ Rs. 2.50)	50	125
			" Costing P & L A/c		360
	50	485		50	485

Problem 34

The following data are available in respect of Process I for February, 1990 :

(i) Opening Stock of work-in-process 800 units at a total cost of Rs. 4,000.

(ii) Degree of completion of opening work-in-process :

Materials	100%
Labour	60%
Overheads	60%

(iii) Input of materials at a total cost of Rs. 36,800 for 9,200 units

(iv) Direct wages incurred Rs. 16,740

(v) Production overhead Rs. 8,370

(vi) Units scrapped 1,200 units. The stage of completion of these units was :

Materials	100%
Labour	80%
Overheads	80%

(vii) Closing Work-in-process 900 units.

The stage of completion of these units was :

Materials	100%
Labour	70%
Overheads	70%

(viii) 7,900 units were completed and transferred to the next process.

(ix) Normal loss is 8% of the total input (Opening Stock plus units put in)

(x) Scrap value in Rs. 4 per unit.

You are required to :

(a) Compute equivalent production.

(b) Calculate the cost per equivalent unit of each element.

(c) Calculate the cost of abnormal loss (or gain), closing stock in process and the units transferred to the next process using the FIFO method.

(d) Show the Process Account for February, 1990.

[Adapted—C.A. (Inter) May, 1990]

Solution

STATEMENT OF EQUIVALENT PRODUCTION (FIFO METHOD)

Input (units)		*Units*	*Materials % of completion*	*Units*	*Labour*		*Overheads*	
					%	*units*	*%*	*units*
800	W.I.P.	800			40%	320	40%	320
9,200	Finished	7,100	100%	7,100	100%	7,100	100%	7,100
	Closing W.I.P.	900	100%	900	70%	630	70%	630
	Normal Loss (8%)	800	–	–	–	–	–	–
	Abnormal Loss	400	100%	400	80%	320	80%	320
10,000				8,400		8,370		8,370

(b) **Statement showing cost per equivalent units**

	Elements	Cost Rs.	Equivalent Production	Cost per equivalent unit
	Cost of Materials	36,800		
Less :	Sale of scrap 800 × 4	3,200		
		33,600	8,400	4.00
	Labour cost	16,740	8,370	2.00
	Overhead cost	8,370	8,370	1.00
				7.00

(c) **Cost of Abnormal loss** – (400 units)

			Rs.
Material Cost of 400 Equivalent units	@ Rs. 4 p.u.	=	1,600
Labour Cost of 320 Equivalent units	@ Rs. 2 p.u.	=	640
Overhead Cost of 320 Equivalent units	@ Re. 1 p.u.	=	320
			2,560

(d) **Cost of Closing W.I.P.** – 900 units

Material Cost of 900 equivalent units	@ Rs. 4.00 p.u.	=	3,600
Labour Cost of 630 Equivalent units	@ Rs. 2.00 p.u.	=	1,260
Overhead Cost of 630 equivalent units	@ Re 1.00 p.u.	=	630
			5,490

(e) **Cost of 7,900 units transferred to next process**

			Rs.
(i)	Cost of opening W.I.P.		4,000
(ii)	*Add* : cost incurred :		
	Material Cost		–
	Labour Cost of 320 equivalent units	@ Rs. 2.00 p.u.	640
	Overhead Cost of 320 equivalent units	@ Re 1.00 p.u.	320
			4,960
(iii)	Cost of 7,100 completed units	@ Rs. 7.00 p.u.	49,700
			54,660

Process Account

For February, 1990

Dr.	Units	Rs.	Cr.	Units	Rs.
To Opening W.I.P.	800	4,000	By Abnormal Loss	400	2,560
" Materials	9,200	36,800	" Normal Loss	800	3,200
" Labour		16,740	" Finished Goods	7,900	54,660
" Overhead		8,370	" Work-in-process	900	5,490
	10,000	65,910		10,000	65,910

Problem 35

A product passes through three Processes – A, B, C. 10,000 units at a cost of Rs. 1.10 per unit were issued to Process A. The other direct expenses were as follows :

	Process A	Process B	Process C
	Rs.	Rs.	Rs.
Sundry materials	1,500	1,500	1,500
Direct labour	4,500	8,000	6,500
Direct expenses	1,000	1,000	1,503

The wastage in Process A was 5% and in Process B 4%. The wastage of Process A was sold at Re. 0.25 per unit and that of B at Re. 0.50 per unit and that C at Re. 1.00 per unit.

The overhead charges were 160% of direct labour. The final product was sold at Rs. 10 per unit fetching a profit of 20% on sales. Find out the percentage of wastage in Process C.

[I.C.W.A. (Inter)]

Solution

Process A Account

Dr. Particulars	*Quantity (units)*	*Rate (Rs.)*	*Amount (Rs.)*	Cr.	*Quantity (units)*	*Rate (Rs.)*	*Amount (Rs.)*
To Input	10,000	1.10	11,000	By Wastage (5% of 10,000 units)	500	0.25	125
" Materials			1,500				
" Direct Labour			4,500				
" Direct expenses			1,000	" Process B A/c (output transferred)	9,500	2.6395	25,075
" Overheads (@ 160% of direct labour)			7,200				
	10,000		25,200		10,000		25,200

$$\text{Cost per unit} = \frac{25,200 - 125}{10,000 - 500} = \frac{25,075}{9,500} = \text{Rs. } 2.6395$$

Process B Account

Dr. *Cr.*

Particulars	*Quantity (units)*	*Rate (Rs.)*	*Amount (Rs.)*		*Quantity (units)*	*Rate (Rs.)*	*Amount (Rs.)*
To Process A A/c	9,500	2.6395	25,075	By Wastage (4% of 9,500 units)	380	0.50	190
" Materials			1,500				
" Direct labour			8,000				
" Direct expenses			1,000	" Process C A/c (transferred)	9,120	5.2834	48,185
" Overheads (160% of direct labour)			12,800				
	9,500		48,375		9,500		48,375

$$\text{Cost per unit} = \frac{48,375 - 190}{9,500 - 380} = \frac{48,185}{9,120} = \text{Rs. } 5.28$$

Process C Account

Dr. *Cr.*

Particulars	*Quantity (units)*	*Rate (Rs.)*	*Amount (Rs.)*		*Quantity (units)*	*Rate (Rs.)*	*Amount (Rs.)*
To Process B A/c	9,120	5.2834	48,185	By Wastage (7.63% of 9,120 units)	696	1.00	696
" Materials			1,500				
" Labour			6,500				
" Direct expenses			1,503	" Finished Stock A/c	8,424	8.00	67,392
" Overheads (160% of direct labout)			10,400				
	9,120		68,088		9,120		68,088

Working Note :

The Wastage of Process C

		Rs.
	Selling price per unit	10
Less :	Profit 20% on sales	2
	Cost of sales per unit	8

If 'x' be the quantity of wastage in Process C, output transferred to finished stock = (9,120 – x) units. Cost of output transferred to finished stock is also = 68,088 – (x × 1)

Hence, (9,120 – x) × Rs. 8 = Rs. 68,088 – (x × Re. 1)

Or, $72,960 - 8x = 68,088 - x$

Or $-7x = -4,872$

Or $x = \frac{4,872}{7} = 696$ units

Solving the equation, we get, X = 696 units.

$$\text{Percentage of Waste} = \frac{696}{9,120} \times 100 = 7.63\%.$$

Problem 36

From the following data find out the equivalent units of production to determine the per unit processing cost which was incurred evenly during the month of March, 1997.

Opening work-in-progress	5,000 units (80% completed)
Fresh units started	16,000 units
Finished goods	12,000 "
Closing work-in-progress	8,000 " (60% completed)

No loss was permissible in the process. Entire stock of opening work-in-progress was completed during the month of March, 1997 without any loss or rejection.

[Adapted D.U. B.Com.(Hons.)]

Solution

Equivalent Units of Production

Particulars	*Work done*		*Equivalent units*
Opening stock	5,000	80%	4,000
current year's production (12,000 – 5,000)	7,000	100%	7,000
Closing work-in-progress	8,000	60%	4,800
Unprocessed units	1,000	Nil	Nil
			15,800

Unprocessed units

	Fresh units started	16,000
Less :	Closing work-in-progress	8,000
		8,000
Less :	Units completed	7,000
	Unprocessed units	1,000

ASSIGNMENT

Theoretical Questions

1. What is Process Costing ? What are its characteristics ? Name three industries where Process Costing is used.

[C.U. B.Com. Pass]

2. State the points of difference between Process Costing and Job Costing.
3. Define Normal Loss and state how is it treated in Cost Accounting.
4. What is Abnormal Loss? How is it computed? How is it treated in Cost Accounting?
5. Explain normal and abnormal process losses and state how are they treated in Cost Accounts.
6. Define Process Costing. What are its advantages?
7. Discuss briefly what do you understand by 'Process Costing'.

[B.Com., C.U. 1973]

8. Describe the method known as Process Costing stating four types of manufacture which would be suitable for its purpose.

[C.A. Inter, England]

9. Describe the general features of Process Costing. Name three industries where process costing can be applied.

[B.Com., Andhra, July, 1973]

10. Describe briefly the procedure involved in the accumulation of costs under the process costing accounting system. How does the procedure differ from that under the Job Order System?

[B.Com., Kerala, December, 1975]

11. Explain normal loss, abnormal loss and abnormal effectives and elucidate how they will be treated in process cost accounts.
12. What do you understand by (a) normal and (b) abnormal loss in the process of manufacture? State briefly how each should be treated in Process Cost Accounts.

[B.Com., Andhra, Sept. 1977]

13. Explain how you would ascertain and deal with the following under process cost accounting method : (i) Normal loss, (ii) Abnormal loss, and (iii) Abnormal gain.

[B.Com., Kerala, 1974]

14. A steel factory has a grey iron foundry which supplies slag pots to blast furnaces and steel melting shops and pigmoulds to pig casting. In addition the foundry makes casting required by central maintenance and repair shops of the factory. Outline the costing system to be adopted in the foundry and elucidate how the process scrap i.e., such items as runners, feeder-heads, over-metal and melting losses will be treated in the costs.

[I.C.W.A. Final]

15. Components found defective in the course of manufacture can be rectified, salvaged for alternative use, or scrapped. Outline the steps to recover costs incurred on these rejects from persons responsible for the same. How will the cost involved be collected and controlled ?

Practical Problems

1. A product passes through three processes of production ; the output of the preceeding process is transferred to the next process. The output for November 1990 was 480 units. Prepare, process accounts from the figures given below :

	Process A	Process B	Process C
	Rs.	Rs.	Rs.
Direct materials	18,000	6,000	2,400
Direct labour	9,600	24,000	7,200
Other direct expenses	3,120	8,640	3,000

Manufacturing expenses during the month amounted to Rs. 10,200. No work-in-progress or process stocks existed at the beginning or the end of the month.

Ans. : Process A Rs. 33,120. Total cost per unit Rs. 69
Process B Rs. 77,760. Total cost per unit Rs. 162
Process C Rs. 92,160. Total cost per unit Rs. 192

2. The information given below is extracted from the cost accounts of a factory producing a commodity in manufacture of which three processes are involved. Prepare process cost accounts showing the cost of the output and cost per unit at each stage of manufacture.

(a) The operations in each separate process are completed daily.

(b) The value at which units are to be charged to process A, and B plus C, respectively.

	Process A	Process B	Process C
	Rs.	Rs.	Rs.
Direct wages	640	1,200	2,925
Machinery expenses	360	300	360
Factory on cost	200	225	240
Raw material consumed	2,400	–	–
	Units	Units	Units
Production (Gross)	37,000	–	–
Wastage	1,000	1,500	500
Opening cost	–	4,000	16,500
Closing stock	–	1,000	5,500

Ans. : Total cost for Process A, B and C is 3,600, Rs. 5,625 and Rs. 10,800 respectively while per unit is 0.10, 0.15 and 0.225 paise respectively.

[B.Com. – Agra]

3. The finished goods of a factory pass through three processes known as A, B and C, the production of each process being passed on to the next process. From the following figures, show the cost of each process.

	Process A	Process B	Process C
	Rs.	Rs.	Rs.
Wages and Materials	19,200	36,000	87,750
Works on cost	16,800	15,750	18,000
General on cost	9,000	10,000	12,000
	Units	Units	Units
Production for July, 1984	36,000	37,500	48,000
Stock on 1st July, 1984	–	4,000	16,500
Stock on 31st July, 1984	–	1,000	5,500

[B.Com. Kanpur, and B.Com., Guru Nanak Uni.]

Ans. : Cost of Production : Process A Rs.45,000; B Rs. 1,10,500 and C Rs. 2,60,663.

4. The products of Maharashtra Chemicals Ltd. passed through three processes of manufacture. The output of each process is transferred to the next process at cost. The stocks were to be valued at cost per unit of the previous process. Prepare Process Cost Accounts showing the per unit cost and total output cost at the end of each process. The available data is given below :

	P1	P2	P3
	Rs.	Rs.	Rs.
Direct wages	64,000	1,20,000	2,92,500
Other direct expenses	36,000	30,000	36,000
Manufacturing overheads	20,000	22,500	24,000
Materials consumed	2,40,000	–	–
	Units	Units	Units
Production (Gross)	18,500	–	–
Scrap	500	750	250
Stock on 1-4-1984	–	2,000	8,250
Stock on 30-4-1985	–	500	2,750

[M.Com., Poona Uni.]

Ans. : Cost per unit P1 – Rs.20, P2 – Rs.30, P3 – Rs.45
P1–Rs. 3,60,000, P2–Rs. 5,62,500, P3 Rs. 10,80,000

5. An article passes through three processes of manufacture. From the following details, show the cost of each of the three processes and the cost per article produced during the month of January, 1999

	Process I	Process II	Process III
	Rs.	Rs.	Rs.
Materials used	75,000	27,000	9,000
Labour	45,000	90,000	30,000
Direct Expenses	12,000	36,000	12,600

The indirect expenses amounted to Rs. 42,900 and may be apportioned on the basis of wages. No account need be taken of stocks in hand and work-in-process at the beginning and at the end of the month. The number of articles produced during the month was 1,200.

[C.U. B.Com. (Pass)]

Ans. : (i) Value of goods of Process I Rs. 1,43,700, Process II Rs. 3,20,100 and Process III Rs.3,79,500.
(ii) Cost per unit – Process I Rs. 119.75, Process II Rs. 266.67, Process III Rs. 316.25.

Hints : Indirect expenses are to be apportioned in the ratio 3 : 6 : 2.

6. Make out the necessary accounts from the following details :

	Process A	Process B
	Rs.	Rs.
Materials	30,000	3,000
Labour	10,000	12,000
Overheads	7,000	8,600
Input	20,000	17,500
Normal Loss	10%	4%
Sales value of wastage per unit	1.00	2.00

There was no opening or closing stock or work-in-process. Final output from Process B was 17,000 units.

[Adapted—C.U. M.Com.]

Ans. : Abnormal loss – Process A Rs. 1,250; Abnormal Gain – Process B Rs. 785; Value of finished goods Rs. 66,735

7. The information given below is extracted from the Cost Accounts of a Factory producing a commodity in the manufacture of which these processes are involved. Prepare Process Cost Accounts showing the cost of the output and the cost per unit at each stage of manufacture :

The operations in each separate process are completed daily :

	Process A	Process B	Process C
	Rs.	Rs.	Rs.
Direct wages	640	1,200	2,925
Machine expenses	360	300	360
Factory on Cost	200	225	240
Raw materials	2,400	–	–
	Units	Units	Units
Production Gross	37,000		
Wastage	1,000	1,500	500
Stock July 1, 1990		4,000	16,500
Stock July 31, 1990		1,000	5,500

[Adapted—M.Com. C.U.]

Ans. : Unit Cost : Process I – 0.100, Process II – 0.150, Process III – 0.225.

Hint : Wastages have been treated as normal loss.

8. Product X is obtained after it is processed through three distinct processes. The following cost information is available for the operation.

	Total	Process I	Process II	Process III
	Rs.	Rs.	Rs.	Rs.
Materials	5,625	2,600	2,000	1,025
Direct wages	7,330	2,250	3,680	1,400
Production Overheads	7,330			

500 units @ Rs. 4.00 per unit were introduced in Processes I. Production overheads to be distributed as 100% on Direct wages.

The Actual Output and Normal Loss of the respective processes are :

	Output in Units	Normal Loss on Input	Value of scrap per unit
Process I	450	10%	Rs. 2
Process II	340	20%	Rs.4
Process III	270	25%	Rs. 5

There is no stock or work-in-progress in any process.
Show :

(a) The three Process Accounts

(b) The Normal Loss Account

(c) The Abnormal Loss and Abnormal Gain Account.

[Adapted—I.C.W.A. (Inter)]

Ans. : Process I – Rs 9,000; Process II – Rs.17,000; Process III – Rs. 21,600.
Normal Loss I – Rs. 100; Normal Loss II – Rs. 360; Normal Loss III – 425.

Hints. Abnormal Gain transferred to P & L A/c– Rs. 1,200.

9 . The product of a manufacturing concern passes through two processes A and B and then to finished stock. It is ascertained that, in each process, normally, 5% of the total weight is lost and 10% scrap which realises Rs. 80 per ton and Rs. 200 per ton from processes A and B, respectively.

The following are the figures relating to both the processes :

	Process A	Process B
Materials	1,000 tons	70 tons
Cost of Materials per ton	Rs. 125	Rs. 200
Wages	Rs. 28,000	Rs. 10,000
Manufacturing expenses	Rs. 8,000	Rs. 5,250
Output	830 tons	780 tons

Prepare Process Accounts showing cost per ton of each process. There was no stock of work-in-progress in any process.

[C.U. B.Com. (Pass), 1983]

Ans. : Abnormal Loss – Process A – Rs. 3,600
Abnormal Gain – Process B – Rs. 3,150
Value of finished goods Rs. 1,63,800.

10. The products of a Company pass through three separate processes for completion, A, B and C processes. From past experience, it is estimated that wastage is incurred in such process, as 2%, 5% and 10% in Process A, B and C, respectively. In each case, the percentage of wastage is computed on the number of units entering the processes concerned.

The scrap values of the process A, B and C are Rs. 5, Rs. 20 and Rs. 10 per 100 units, respectively.

The output of each process is transferred immediately to the next process and the finished units are transferred from Process C to stock.

Other particulars are given below :

	Process A	Process B	Process C
	Rs.	Rs.	Rs.
Materials consumed	6,000	2,000	2,000
Direct Labour	4,000	3,000	3,000
Manufacturing expenses	1,000	2,000	1,000

20,000 units have been put into process A at a cost of Rs. 8,000. The output of the each process is as under :

Process A 19,600 units, Process B 18,400 units and Process C 16,700 units.

There is no stock or work-in-progress in any process.

Show how the Process Accounts will appear in the books.

[Adapted—C.U. M.Com.]

Ans. : (i) Value of Finished goods Rs. 31,560
(ii) Abnormal Loss – Tr. to P & L A/c Rs. 304
(iii) Abnormal Gain – Tr. to P & L A/c Rs. 265.

11. Prepare necessary accounts from the following details :

	Process A	Process B
	Rs.	Rs.
(1) Materials	30,000	3,000
(2) Labour	10,000	12,000
(3) Overheads	7,000	8,600
(4) Input	20,000	17,500
(5) Normal Loss	10%	4%
(6) Sales value of waste per unit	Re. 1	Rs. 2

There was no opening stock or closing stock or work-in-progress. Final output from Process B was 17,000 units.

[M.Com. Bombay.]

Ans. :

	Process A	Process B
Cost of production	43,750	66,735
Abnormal Loss	1,250	785

12. A product passes through two distinct processes A and B and then to finished stock. The output of A passes direct to B and that of B passes to finished stock. From the following information prepare the necessary accounts :

	Process A	Process B
	Rs.	Rs.
Materials added	10,000	6,610
Wages	10,000	12,000
Overhead – 200% of wages :		
Output (Units)	9,500	9,250
Normal wastage (percentage of input)	10%	2%
Value of normal wastage per unit	5.50	9.00

There was no opening or closing work-in-progress. 10,000 units were introduced in process A at Rs. 6 per unit.

[M.Com. Calcutta University]

Ans. : Normal Loss A – Rs. 1,000, B – Rs. 1,710

	Process A	Process B
	Rs.	Rs.
Cost of production	99,750	1,39,743.55

13. Triplex Industries produces a forged product Sunbeam after it passes through three distinct processes. The following information has been obtained from the cost accounts for the month ending 31st December, 1998 :

Item	Total Amount	Process I	Process II	Process III
	Rs.	Rs.	Rs.	Rs.
Direct materials	7,542	2,600	1,980	2,962
Direct wages	9,000	2,000	3,000	4,000
Production overheads	9,000			

1,000 units at Rs. 3 each were introduced in Process I. There was no stock of materials, work-in-progress and finished goods at the beginning or at the end of the period. The output of each process passed direct to the next process and finally to finished stock. Production overheads are recovered at 100 per cent of direct wages.

The following additional data are obtained :

Process	Output during the month	Percentage of normal loss to input	Value of scrap per unit Rs.
Process I	950	5%	2
Process II	840	10%	4
Process III	750	15%	5

Prepare process cost accounts.

[B.Com. (Hons.), Delhi Univ.]

Ans. :

	Cost of Production Total	Per Unit	Abnormal loss/gain Units	Rs.
	Rs.	Rs.		
Process I	9,500	10		
Process II	16,800	20	15 (loss)	300
Process III	28,500	38	36 (gain)	7,368

14. A product of a chemical enterprise passes through two processes A and B, and then to finished stock. The normal wastage of each process is as follows :

Process A	:	3 per cent
Process B	:	5 per cent.

Wastage of process A was sold @ Rs. 2.50 per unit and that of process B @ Rs. 5.00 per unit. 10,000 units were issued to process A in the beginning of April, 1999 at a cost of Rs. 10 per unit.

The other expenses were as under :

	Process A	Process B
	Rs.	Rs.
Sundry materials	10,000	15,000
Wages	50,000	80,000
Manufacturing expenses	10,500	11,800

Actual output of process A was 9,500 units and that of process B was 9,100 units. There were no opening or closing stocks.

Prepare the process accounts and determine the cost per unit of finished product. Briefly explain the treatment of wastage in process accounts.

[M.Com., Nagarjuna Univ.]

Ans. : Process A – Rs. 17.58; Process B – Rs. 30.39.

15. A product passes through two processes A and B thereafter it is transferred to finished stock. The output of A passes to B and that of B to finished stock. From the following information you are required to prepare process accounts :

	Process A	Process B
	Rs.	Rs.
Material consumed	24,000	14,000
Direct labour	28,000	18,000
Manufacturing expenses	23,100	26,468
Input in Process A – units	20,000	
Input in process A – value	20,000	
Output – units	18,800	16,600
Normal wastage-percentage of input	5%	10%
Value of normal wastage	10 per 100 units	10 per 100 units

[B.Com. Madras.]

Ans. : Process A – Cost per unit Rs. 5.00 and Process B – Cost per unit Rs. 9.

16. A product passed through three processes X, Y and Z. The normal wastage of each process is as follows :

Process X	3%
Process Y	5%
Process Z	8%

Wastage of process X was sold at Rs. 2.50 per unit and that of Y at Rs. 5.00 per unit and that of Z at Rs. 8.00 per unit.

10,000 units were issued to process X in the beginning of July, 1990 at a cost of Rs. 100 per unit.

	Process X	ProcessY	Process Z
Sundry materials	10,000	15,000	5,000
Labour	50,000	80,000	65,000
Direct expenses	10,450	15,995	20,090

Actual output was :

Process X	9,500
Process Y	9,700
Process Z	8,100

Prepare process accounts assuming that there was no opening or closing stocks. Also give abnormal wastage and abnormal gain accounts, if any.

[B.Com. Madurai Univ.]

17. The product of a soap factory has to pass through three stages before the article comes out in a finished form. These processes are known as A, B and C. The wastage in each of these processes is as follows :

Process A 2%, Process B 5%; and Process C 10%.

In each case, the percentage of wastage in computed on the number of units entering the process concerned. The wastage of each process possesses a scrap value. The wastage of Process A and B is sold at Rs. 4 per 100 units and that of Process C at Rs. 20 per 100 units. The output of each process passed immediately to the next process and the finished units are passed from Process C into stock.

The following further information is obtained :

	Process A	Process B	Process C
	Rs.	Rs.	Rs.
Materials consumed	8,000	4,000	2,000
Direct labour	12,000	8,000	6,000
Manufacturing expenses	2,000	2,000	3,000

40,000 units have been issued to Process A at a cost of Rs. 16,000. The output of each process has been as under :

Process A 39,000, Process B 37,600 and Process C 37,000. There is no stock or work-in-progress in any process. Prepare the process accounts and show the treatment of wastage in the process.

[B.Com., Part II Exam. Allahabad Univ.]

Ans. :	Process A	Process B	Process C
	Rs.	Rs.	Rs.
Cost of production (App.)	37,774	52,463	68,557
Abnormal loss transferred to Costing P & L (App.)	194	......	1,386
Abnormal gain transferred to Costing P & L A/c. (App.)	......	767	......

18. The product of a soap factory passes through three stages before the article comes out in finished form. The processes are known as A, B and C. The wastage in each process is as follows :

Process A 2%, Process B 5% and Process C 10%.

In each case, the percentage of wastage is computed on the number of units entering the process concerned. The wastage of each process is sold at Rs. 5 per 100 units in case of processes A and B and at Rs. 20 per 100 units in case of Process C. The output of each process passes immediately to the next process and the finished units are passed from Process C into stock.

The following additional information is available :

	Process A	Process B	Process C
	Rs.	Rs.	Rs.
Materials consumed	8,000	4,000	2,000
Direct labour	12,000	8,000	6,000
Manufacturing expenses	2,000	2,000	3,000

40,000 units have been issued to Process A at a cost of Rs. 16,000. The output of each process has been as under :

Process A 39,000; Process B 37,600 and Process C 32,000.

There is no stock or work-in-progress in any process.

Prepare process cost accounts showing per unit cost of product at each stage and the total cost per unit.

[B.Com., Bhopal]

Ans. : Process A Abnormal wastage 200 units, Cost Rs. 194, Output 32,000 units, Cost Rs. 37,766

Process B Abnormal effective 550 units, Cost Rs Output 37,600 units; Cost Rs. 52,435

Process C Abnormal wastage 1,840 units, Cost Rs. 3,408; Output 32,000 units; Cost Rs. 59,275

19. An article passes through three processes. From the following figures show the cost of each of the three processes during the month of January 1989 :

	Process I	Process II	Process III
	Rs.	Rs.	Rs.
Material used	15,000	5,000	2,000
Labour	8,000	20,000	6,000
Direct Expenses	2,600	7,200	2,500

The indirect expenses amounting to Rs. 8,500 may be apportioned on the basis of wages, the number of articles produced during the month 240.

[Adapted—Mysore University B. Com.]

20. The actual output and normal loss of the respective processes are :

	Output unit	Normal loss on Input	Value of Scrap per unit
			Rs.
Process I	450	10%	2
Process II	340	20%	4
Process III	270	25%	5

There is no stock or work-in-process.

Show :

(a) Three Process Accounts.

(b) The Normal Loss Account.

(c) The Abnormal Loss and Abnormal Gain Accounts.

	I	II	III
Normal Loss :	Rs. 100	Rs. 360	Rs. 425
Abnormal Loss :	–	Rs. 1,000	–

Transfer to 270 units @ Rs. 80.

Finished goods = Rs. 21,600.

21. The manufacture of product 'Fanta' requires 3 distinct processes. On completion the product is passed from Process 3 to Finished Stock. During the month of December 1992, the following information was obtained :

Elements of Costs	Total	Process I	Process II	Process III
	Rs.	Rs.	Rs.	Rs.
Direct Materials	26,000	15,000	11,000	—
Direct Labour	26,500	12,500	6,000	8,000
Direct Expenses	8,000	3,000	—	5,000
Production overhead	79,500	—	—	—

Production Overhead is absorbed by processes at a percentage of direct wages. Production during the period was 1,000 kg. There was no stock of raw materials or work-in-progress at the beginning or at the end of the month.

Show the Process Accounts and Finished Stock Account.

[C.U. B.Com. (Hons.) 1993]

22. Product 'X' is obtained after it is processed through three distinct processes. The following cost information is available for the operation :

	Total	Process I	Process II	Process III
	Rs.	Rs.	Rs.	Rs.
Materials	5,625	2,600	2,000	1,025
Direct Wages	7,330	2,250	3,680	1,400
Production Overheads	7,330	–	–	–

500 units @ Rs. 4.00 per unit were introduced in Process I. Production Overheads are absorbed as a percentage of Direct wages.

The actual output and normal loss of the respective processes are :

	Output in units	Normal loss in Input	Value of Scrap per unit
			Rs.
Process I	450	10%	2.00
Process II	340	20%	4.00
Process III	270	25%	5.00

There is no stock or work-in-progress in any process.

Show :

(i) the three processes accounts

(ii) the abnormal loss and abnormal gain accounts.

[Adapted—I.C.W.A. (Inter.) 1986]

Ans. : Transfer to Process II 450 units Rs. 9,000

" " " III 340 units Rs. 17,000

" " Finished goods – 270 units

Valued Rs. 21,600

Hints : Abnormal Loss for Process II – Rs. 1,000 ; and Abnormal Gain for Process III – Rs. 1,200 (15 units).

23. The product of a company passes through three distinct processes for completion. From past experience, it is ascertained that normal wastage in each process is as under :

Process	Wastage	Sale value of wastage
A	2%	Re. 0.25 per unit
B	4%	Re. 0.50 per unit
C	2.5%	Re. 0.60 per unit

The expenses were as follows :

	Process A	Process B	Process C
	Rs.	Rs.	Rs.
Materials	12,000	10,000	9,000
Direct labour	16,000	5,000	4,900
Manufacturing expenses	2,000	3,400	3,590
Other factory expenses	3,500	2,005	2,004

4,000 units were initially introduced in Process A at a cost of Rs. 13,560.

The output of each process was as under :

A	3,850 units
B	3,600 units
C	3,500 units

Prepare process accounts and also work out the sale price per unit of finished goods so as to realise 20% of profit on selling price.

[Adapted—C.A. (Inter.) O.S.]

Hints : Abnormal wastage : A – Rs. 840 (70 units), B – Rs. 1,728 (96 units), C – Rs. 240 (10 units).

Ans. : Transfer to : Process B – Rs. 46,200; Process C – Rs, 64,800 ; Finished Stock Rs. 84,000.

24. Y Ltd. produces a standard product through Process I and Process II. Finished product from Process I is used as raw material for Process II. From the following data prepare necessary accounts :

	Process I	Process II
Input (in units)	15,000	13,000
Materials (in Rs.)	30,000	4,000
Labour (in Rs.)	18,000	15,275
Overheads (in Rs.)	9,000	10,950
Normal loss	10%	5%
Scrap value (in Rs.)	2	3

There was no opening and closing work-in-progress. The final output from Process II was 12,500 units.

[V. U. B.Com. (Hons.) 1991]

Ans. : Process I – Abnormal Loss 500 units valued @ Rs. 4 = Rs. 2,000

Process II – Abnormal Gain 150 units @ Rs. 6.50 = Rs. 975

Value of Finished goods 12500 units @ Rs. 6.50 = Rs. 81,250.

25. From the following data relating to the product 'Bista' for the half year ended 31st December, 1992, prepare the cost sheet of each process :

Input to Process I – 20,000 units @ Rs. 4.00 per unit.

Output of Process	In units	% of normal loss acceptable
I	18,400	10%
II	17,400	5%
III	16,000	10%

The wastes, in each process realise Rs. 3, Rs. 5 and Rs. 5 per unit, respectively.

There has been no opening or closing stock of materials or work-in-progress in any of the processes. The output of each process is transferred to the next process, for further processing and the output of process III is the finished production available for sale. Manufacturing overheads are charged @ 50% of direct wages for that process. Other details are given below :

Process	I	II	III
	Rs.	Rs.	Rs.
Other Materials used	40,000	61,000	71,700
Direct Wages	60,000	40,000	50,000
Other Direct Expenses	36,000	41,000	44,700

[Adapted—C.U. B.Com. (Pass) 1988]

Ans. : Process I Abnormal Gain : 400 – Rs. 5,332
Process II Abnormal Loss : 80 – Rs. 1,838
Process III Abnormal Gain : 340 – Rs. 12,648.

26. A product is finally obtained after it passes through three distinct processes. The following information is available from the cost records.

	Process I	Process II	Process III	Total
	Rs.	Rs.	Rs.	Rs.
Materials	2,600	2,000	1,025	5,625
Direct wages	2,250	3,680	1,400	7,330
Production Overheads				7,330

500 units @ Rs. 4 per unit were introduced in Process I. Production overheads are absorbed as a percentage of direct wages.

The actual output and normal loss of the respective processes are given below :

	Output (units)	Normal loss as a percentage of input	Value of Scrap (per unit)
Process I	450	10%	Rs. 2.00
Process II	340	20%	Rs. 4.00
Process III	270	25%	Rs. 5.00

Prepare the Process Accounts and the Abnormal Gain or Loss Accounts.

[Adapted—I.C.W.A. (Inter.) June, 1991]

Ans : Abnormal Loss : Process I – Nil, Process II – 20 units Rs. 1,000,
Process III – Abnormal Gain 15 units Rs. 1,200.

27. The product of a company passes through three distinct processes A, B and C. It is ascertained that wastage in these processes is 2%, 5% and 10%, respectively. In each case, the percentage of wastage is computed on the number of units entering the process concerned. The wastage of each process possesses a scrap value. The wastage of processes A and B is sold at Rs. 5 per 100 units and that of process C at Rs. 20 per 100 units. The following information is obtained :

	PROCESS		
	A	B	C
Materials Consumed (Rs.)	4,000	2,000	1,000
Direct labour (Rs.)	6,000	4,000	3,000
Manufacturing Expenses (Rs.)	1,000	1,000	1,500

20,000 units have been issued to Process A at a cost of Rs. 8,000. The output of Process A, B and C is 19,500 ; 18,800 and 16,000, respectively. There is no stock or work-in-process in any process. Show the Process Accounts.

[C. S. (Inter.) June 1992]

Ans : Normal Wastage : A – 400 units Rs. 20, B – 975 units Rs. 49, C – 1,800 units Rs. 376
Value of Finished Stock – 16,000 units – Rs. 29,638.

28. The product of a manufacturing concern passes through two processes A and B and then to finished stock. It is ascertained that in each process normally 5% of the total weight is lost and 10% is scrap which from processes A and B realises Rs. 80 and Rs. 200, respectively.

The following are the figures relating to both the processes

	Process A	Process B
Material in tons	1,000	70
Cost of material in rupees (per ton)	125	200
Wages in rupees	28,000	10,000
Manufacturing expenses (in rupees)	8,000	5,250
Output in tons	830	780

Prepare process accounts showing cost per ton of each process. There was no stock or work-in-progress in any process.

[B.Com., Hons., Delhi]

Ans. : Process A – Rs. 180; Process B – Rs, 210.

29. A product passes through three processes for completion. During a month 1,000 units of raw material valued at Rs. 20,000 were put into the first process. Other information regarding the manufacture is as under :

	Process I	Process II	Process III
	Rs.	Rs.	Rs.
Sundry material	2,000	1,600	1,200
Direct labour	10,000	8,000	10,000
Cost of boxes	400	400	800
Cost of packing	–	8,216	–
Normal wastage	5%	10%	5%
Actual output – units	900	800	670
Sale of wastage (per unit)	4	8	10

Prepare process accounts and ascertain the cost of the product at the end of each process.

[B.Com., Mysore]

Ans. Abnormal Loss – P1 – 50 – Rs. 1,695; P2 – 10 – Rs. 593; P3 – 90 – Rs. 6,988.

30. A product passes through two distinct processes A and B and thereafter it is transferred to finished stock. From the following information you are required to prepare process accounts :

	Process A	Process B
	Rs.	Rs.
Material consumed	12,000	6,000
Direct labour	14,000	8,000
Manufacturing expenses	4,000	4,000
Input in Process A (Units)	10,000	
Input in Process A (Value)	10,000	
Output (Units)	9,400	8,300
Normal wastage percentage of input	5%	10%
Value of normal wastage (Per 100 units)	8	10

[I.C.W.A.]

Ans. :

	Abnormal Loss		Output transferred	
	Unit	Cost	Units	Cost
	Rs.	Rs.		Rs.
Process A	100	421	9,400	39,539
Process B	160	1,086	8,300	56,359

31. The output of different processes is partially sold and partially transferred to the next process. Robust Ltd., manufactures a patent material. The material is produced in three consecutive grades – soft medium and hard.

	Process I	Process II	Process III
Raw material used	1,000 tonnes		
Cost per tonne	Rs. 200		
Manufacturing wages and expenses	Rs. 87,500	Rs. 34,500	Rs. 10,710
Weight lost (% of the input of the process)	5%	10%	20%
Scrap (sale price Rs. 50 per tonne)	50 tonnes	30 tonnes	51 tonnes
Sale price of output per tonne	Rs. 350	Rs. 500	Rs. 800

Management expenses were Rs. 17,500 and selling expenses Rs. 10,000.

Two-thirds of the output of Process I and one-half of the output of Process II are passed on the next process and the balances are sold. The entire output of Process III is sold. Prepare the three Process Accounts and a Statement of Profit. Make approximations where necessary.

[B.Com. Andhra, 1977]

Ans. :

	Process I	Process II	Process III
Cost of production	Rs. 2,85,000	Rs. 2,23,000	Rs. 1,19,660
Total net profit	Rs. 1,260	–	–

32. In process X 6,000 units of raw materials were introduced during the month of April 90. The cost of the raw materials issued was Rs. 28,500. Other expenses incurred were as follows :

Material	Rs. 5,475
Labour	Rs. 10,500
Overhead	Rs. 7,912.50

The normal loss was estimated at 5% of the input. At the end of the month 900 units were incomplete. These units were complete 100% as regards raw materials, 75% as regards other matterial and 50% as regards labour and overhead and production of finished stock was 4,500 units.

Prepare Process X A/c.

Ans.: Abnormal loss 300 units Rs. 2,852.34. Work-in-progress 900 units Rs. 6,750 and Finished stock 4,500 units. Rs. 42,785.16.

33. G. H. and Co. manufactures a product in one process. The process costing is followed and work-in-progress stocks at the end of each month are valued on FIFO basis.

At the beginning of the month of June, 1990, the inventory of work-in-progress showed 400 units, 40% complete valued as follows :

	Rs.
Material	3,600
Labour	3,400
Overheads	1,000
	8,000

In June materials were purchased for Rs. 75,000 and wages and overheads in the month amounted to Rs. 79,800 and Rs. 21,280 respectively. Actual issue of materials to production was Rs. 68,500. Finished stock taken into stock in the month was 2,500 units. There was no loss in process.

At the end of the month the work-in-progress inventory was 500 units, 60% complete as to labour and overheads and 80% complete as to materials.

Prepare journal entries for recording the month's transactions and prepare a process cost sheet showing total and unit cost.

[Adapted—I.C.W.A.]

Ans. : Closing work-in-progress Rs. 21,485.

34. A company manufactures a product which involves two processes viz., pressing and polishing. For 1998 the following information is available:

	Pressing	Polishing
Opening stock	–	–
Input of units in process	1,200	1,000
Units completed	1,000	500
Units under process	200	500
Cost of materials	Rs. 9,600	Rs. 8,800
Conversion costs	Rs. 2,28,000	Rs. 52,000

For incomplete units in process charge material cost at 100% and conversion costs at 60% in the pressing process and at 50% in the polishing process. Prepare a statement of cost and calculate the selling price per unit which will result in 25% profit on sale price.

[C.A. Inter.]

Ans. : Cost per unit Rs. 415.38, selling price Rs. 553.71.

35. A particular brand of Phenyle passed through three important processes. During the week ended 31st January, 1991, 600 gross bottles are produced. The cost books show the following information :

	Process A	Process B	Process C
Materials	Rs. 4,000	2,000	1,500
Labour	Rs. 3,000	2,500	2,300
Direct expenses	Rs. 600	200	500
Cost of bottles	Nil	2,030	Nil
Cost of corks	Nil	Nil	325

The indirect expenses for the period were Rs. 1,600. The by-products of process B were sold for Rs. 240. The residue of process C was sold for Rs. 125.50.

Prepare the account in respect of each of the process showing its cost and cost of production of the finished product per gross bottle.

[Adapted—B.Com. (Hons.), Delhi]

Ans. :

	Cost per gross bottle
Process A	Rs. 13.69
Process B	Rs. 25.36
Process C	Rs. 33.65

36. In an oil refinery the product comes through three different processes. The following information is available for January 1991.

	Crushing Rs.	Refining Rs.	Finishing Rs.
Raw materials (500 tons of copra)	2,25,000	–	–
Wages	8,000	5,000	5,875
Power	1,200	1,000	4,500
Sundry material	500	1,900	–
Factory expenses	600	1,000	950

Cost of string drums for storing finished oil was Rs. 21,025 and 200 tons of cake were sold for Rs. 15,000 and 275 tons of crude oil were obtained, sundry by-products of the crushing process Rs. 900 (20 tons) and 250 tons of refined oil were obtained. 240 tons of finished oil were stored in drums and 10 tons were sold for Rs. 1,200.

Establishment expenses for the period amounted to Rs. 3,500 which are to be charged in three processes in proportion of 3 : 2 : 2. Prepare the Process Accounts.

[Adapted B.Com. Bihar]

Ans.	Cost per tone Crushing process	803.27
	Cost per ton Refining process	923.20
	Cost per ton Finishing process	995.52
	Cost per ton Finished store (storing)	1083.13

37. A product passes through three processes, namely 1, 2 and 3. From the following information prepare the Process Accounts :

	Process 1	Process 2	Process 3
	Rs.	Rs.	Rs.
Raw Materials used (tonnes)	1,000		
Cost per tonne (Rs.)	200		
Manufacturing Wages (Rs.)	72,500	40,800	10,710
Weight loss	5%	10%	20%
Scrap (sold at Rs. 50 per tonne)	50	30	51

Two-thirds of the Process 1 and $\frac{1}{2}$ of Process 2 are passed to the next process and the balances are sent to the warehouse for sale.

[Mysore University—B.Com. 1991]

38. X Ltd. produces product 'Z' through two distinct proces—Process A and Process B. On completion, it is transferred to finished stock.

From the following information relating to the year 1997-98 prepare proces accounts and finished stock account :

	Particulars	*Process A*	*Process B*
(i)	Raw materials used	1,000 units	
(ii)	Cost per unit	Rs. 200	
(iii)	Transfer to next process/finished goods	940 units	870 units
(iv)	Normal loss (on inputs)	5%	10%
(v)	Direct wages	Rs. 15,600	Rs. 13,200
(vi)	Direct expenses	75% of direct wages	direct wages
(vii)	Sundry expenses		Rs. 2,954
(viii)	Realisable value of scrap per unit	Rs. 4.500	Rs. 5.75

800 units of finished goods were sole at a profit of 20% on cost.

Assume that there was no opening or closiing stock of work-in-progress.

[C.U. B.Com.(Hons.) 1999]

Ans. : Cost per unit

Proces A—Rs. 239.03

ProcessB—Rs. 295.74

Balance of finished goods Rs. 20,702.

OPERATING COSTING 8

Learning Objectives :

After reading this chapter we shall learn :

1. *Definition of operating costing*
2. *Application of operating costing*
3. *Meaning of composite cost*
4. *Preperation at cost sheet under this system*
5. *Classification of costs.*
6. *Worked-out Problems*
7. *Assignment.*

OPERATING COSTING 8

Definition

Operating costing may be defined as the cost of the undertakings which provide and operate services. It is also known as **service costing**. Operating costing is a method of costing applied to determine the cost of rendering services by such undertakings as Airways, Railways, Road Transport, Hospitals, Electricity companies etc. The unit of cost in these industries is not the job, product or process but the services rendered. So, it is a method of costing applied to undertaking which provides services. These services may be internally used e.g., Canteen, delivery van, boiler house etc. Some undertakings render services to the public like transport corporations, electricity generating companies, hospitals etc. These services are known as external services. Therefore, operating or service costing is a method of determining the cost of services.

Generally, operating costs are period costs. Expenses accumulated for a period, say, quarterly, monthly are related to the quantum of services rendered during the period.

Applicability :

The important features of industries where operating costing is applied are :

(i) a uniform service is rendered to the consumers;

(ii) many processes and stages are involved in converting the basic materials and facilities to the ultimate services rendered;

(iii) the distinction between fixed cost and variable cost is very important as the economics and scale of operations considerably affect the unit cost of services.

The method of operating costing can be applied to the following operations :

(i) Transport—Airways, Railways, Roadways etc. (ii) Hospital; (iii) Canteen, (iv) Boiler House; (v) Goods transport, (vi) Electricity Boards, (vii) Hotel; (vii) Water supply service, (viii) Road Maintenance Department etc.

The following two points are to be considered for introducing operating costing :

(i) Cost unit and (ii) Collection of costing data.

(ii) Cost Unit

In operating costing the main problem is to determine the suitable cost unit to be used for ascertainment of cost. A proper unit of cost must be selected in order to ascertain the cost per unit of services provided; this is a very difficult job.

The following are some examples of cost units used in different organisations :

	Enterprise	*Cost per unit*
1.	Railways	Per passenger–kilo meter
2.	Road Transport–Bus	—do—
3.	Goods Transport–Lorry, Rail	Per Ton kilo-meter.
4.	Canteen	Meals served per person.
5.	Water Supply service	Per 1,000 gallons.
6.	Boiler House	Thousand kg of steam.
7.	Bricks	1,000
8.	Hotel	Per room/day

(i) **Collection of Costing Data**

After determining the unit of cost to which the total expenditure is to be allocated, the cost relating to the service rendered is collected. The cost thus collected is presented under the heads suitable for the purposes of control, ie, fixed expenditure and variable expenditure. Thus, under operating costing method all costs are collected and classified as fixed and variable expenses. This distinction between fixed and variable costs helps cost control by drawing the attention of the management to the fixed costs.

Some undertakings where operating costing is usually employed is explained below.

Motor Transport costing

In motor transport undertaking most of the data required for computation of cost and cost control purpose are obtained from Daily Log Book. The Log Book should be filled up by the driver of the vehicle furnishing necessary details of trips made by vehicle during a specified period of time—usually on daily basis. A specimen of Log Book is given below :

LOG SHEET

Vehicle No .... Date ....

License No .... Driver ....

Registration No .... Time of start ....

.... Time of Returning ....

Trip No.	*From*	*To*	*Goods out*	*Passenger collected en route*	*Kilometers*	*Time*		*Remarks*
						out	*in*	
Total								

Supplies	*Time spent*	*Loss of Time*
Petrol	Driver	Traffic delays
Oil	Conductor	Loading delay
Grease	Cleaner	Accident

The above log sheet helps the management to avoid unnecessary or duplicate trips, to avoid under-utilization of capacity by low burdening or over-utilization of extra loading and to avoid waste or idle running capacity.

Classification of Cost

For preparing a cost sheet the costs are classified into the following three broad heads :

1. Fished or standing charges
2. Maintenance charges
3. Operating and running charges.

1. ***Fixed and standing charges***

Fixed and standing charges include :

(i) Insurance Premium;

(ii) Salary of operating manager, supervisor etc.;

(iii) License Fees;

(iv) Road Tax;

(v) Garage Rent;

(vi) Interest on capital;

(vii) General supervision.

2. *Maintenance charges*

These include semi-variable charges, e.g.,

(i) Repairs and maintenance of vehicles.

(ii) Cost of Tyres and Tubes.

(iii) Cost of spares, accessories, paints, retreading etc.

(iv) Overhauling of vehicles.

3. *Operating and Running charges*

These are variable costs. They include :

(i) Cost of Fuel (petrol, diesel, mobil etc.)

(ii) Wages of drivers conductor and cleaner.

(iii) Commission of taking, if any.

Depreciation on vehicle may be treated as fixed or semi-variable cost depending upon the method of charging depreciation

Selection of unit

In transport costing, a composite cost unit such as passenger kilo-meter or ton kilo-metre is usually adopted. The main advantage of selecting of a composite unit cost is that it takes into account both the number of passengers or weight of goods carried and distance covered.

A proforma of cost sheet of a Transport Company is given below for easy understanding.

Arun Transport Company Ltd.
Cost Sheet
for the month of.........199

Expenses	*Vehicle No.*	*001*	*003*	*004*	*Total*
	Capacity (Tonne)	*5*	*8*	*10*	
		Rs.	Rs.	Rs.	Rs.
1. **Operating Costs :**					
Petrol					
Engine oil					
Lubricating oil					
Wages of Drivers					
Wages of cleaners					
Depreciation					
Total					

Contd.

Expenses	Vehicle No.	001	003	004	Total
	Capacity (Tonne)	5	8	10	
		Rs.	Rs.	Rs.	Rs.
2. **Maintenance Costs**					
Tyres and tubes					
Repairs					
Painting					
Overhauls					
Total					
3. **Fixed Costs**					
Motor vehicle Tax					
License Fee					
General supervision					
Insurance					
Garage rent					
Interest on capital					
Total					
Grand Total					
1 + 2 + 3					
Mileage run					
load carried (Tonne)					
Days on Road					
Capacity utilization(%)					
Tonne mile run					
Cost per tonne-mile					
Operating					
Maintenance					
Fixed					
Total					

CANTEEN COSTING

Proforma of Canteen Cost Sheet

Month.................... No. of meals..............

Particulars	*Total cost*	*Cost per meal*
1. **Wages and Salaries** Canteen Manager Supervisor Cooks Counter Helpers etc.		
2. **Provisions** Tea Coffee Cold drinks Bread and Cakes Biscuits Milk Egg etc.		
3. **Consumable stores** Table linen Cutlery Washing up clothes Cleaning materials.		
4. **Fuel and Power** Steam Gas Electricity and Lighting Coal		
5. **Miscellaneous** Rent and Rates Depreciation Insurance Maintenance etc.		
Total cost (1 + 2 + 3 + 4 + 5)		

Receipts from : Company subsidy
Sale

Total Profit or Loss.

At present many organisations provide facilities for canteen to workers. The workers are provided with food at subsidised prices. It may be considered a service by the company.

The following are the main items of costs relating to canteen costing :

(a) ***Provisions***

Provisions will include items like meat, fish poultry egg, tea, coffee, milk, flour, rice, soft drinks etc.

(b) ***Labour***

Labour will include :

Wages and salaries of canteen staff such as cooks, waiters, kitchen assistants, supervisors etc.

(c) ***Services***

It will include steam, gas, electricity, power, light and water.

(d) ***Consumable stores***

They will include items like linen, cutlery, crockery, glass wares, mops, washing up clothes, dustpans, cleaning materials and brushes

(e) ***Overheads***

Overhead charges will include rent, rates, insurance, depreciation

Receipts

The receipts will consist of :

(i) Subsidy received from company,

(ii) Sale of coupons.

BOILER HOUSE
COST SHEET

Steam produced in 1,000 1bs ....
Less Boiler House use. ....
Line losses ....
Total Consumption ....

Item	*Total cost*		*Cost per 1000 1bs steam*		*Remarks*
	This month	*year to date*	*This month*	*year to date*	
1. **Fuel and labour**					
Cost or Fuel oil					
Electric power					
Fuel handling					
Ash removal					
Stokers and coal wheelers					
2. **Water**					
Purchased					
Softening					

Contd.

Item	*Total cost*		*Cost per 1000 1bs steam*		*Remarks*
	This month	*year to date*	*This month*	*year to date*	
3. **Misc . Expenses** Supervision, Sweepers cleaners, Labour, Boiler cleaning					
4. **Maintenance** Fixed plants, Meters, Boilers Softening plant, Economisers Coal Bunkers Furnace, Machanical stokers Steam Service Pipe weighing Machine					
5. **Fixed Overheads** Rent, rates, Depreciation of plant, Building Interest on capital Steam mains Allocated factory overheads					
Total					

Remarks.

Prepared by ....

Checked by ....

WORKED OUT PROBLEMS

Problem 1

Union Transport Company supplies the following details in respect of a truck of 5-tonne capacity :

Cost of truck	Rs. 90,000
Estimated life	10 years
Diesel, oil, grease	Rs. 15 per trip each way
Repairs and maintenance	Rs. 500 per month
Driver's wage	Rs. 500 per month
Cleaner's wage	Rs. 250 per month
Insurance	Rs. 4,800 per year
Tax	Rs. 2,400 per year
General supervision charges	Rs. 4,800 per year

The truck carries goods to and from city covering a distance of 50 miles each way.

While going to the city, freight is available to the extent of full capacity.

Assuming that the truck runs on an average 25 days a month, work out :

(i) Operating cost per tonne-mile, and

(ii) Rate per ton per trip that the company should charge if profit of 50% on freightage is to be earned.

[B. Com., (Hons.) Delhi]

Solution

(i) **Operating Cost Statement**

		Rs.	Per month Rs.	Per tonne-mile Rs.
1.	**Fixed Costs :**			
	Driver's wage	500		
	Cleaner's wage	250		
	Insurance	400		
	Taxes	200		
	General supervision	400	1,750	0.233
2.	**Running Costs :**			
	Diesel oil, etc.	750		
	Repairs & maintenance	500		
	Depreciation	750	2,000	0.267
			3,750	
			7,500	0.500

(ii) **Calculation of Freight Rate**

Cost per ton-mile	Re. 0.50
Profit per ton-mile	Re. 0.50
Freight rate per ton-mile.	Re. 1.00

Freight rate per trip both ways = 300 × Re. 1.00 = Rs. 300

Tonne-miles are computed as under :

(50 × 5) + (50 × 1) × 25 = 7,500 tonne-mile.

Problem 2

The Kangaroo Transport operates a fleet of lorries. The records for lorry L-14 reveal the following information for September, 1990 :

Days maintained	30	
Days operated	25	
Days idle	5	
Total hours operated	300	
Total kms covered	2,500	
Total tonnes carried	200	(4 tonne-load per trip, journey empty)

The following information is made available :

A. ***Operating costs for the month***

Petrol Rs. 400, oil Rs. 170, grease Rs. 90, wages to driver Rs. 550, wages to khalasi Rs. 350.

B. ***Maintenance costs for the month.***

Repairs Rs. 170, overhead Rs. 60, Tyres Rs. 150, Garage charges Rs. 100.

C. ***Fixed costs for the month*** based on the estimates for the year :
Insurance Rs. 50, Licence, Tax etc. Rs. 80,
Interest Rs. 40, other overheads Rs. 190.

D. ***Capital costs***

Cost of acquisition Rs. 54,000

Residual value at the end of 5 years life is Rs. 36,000.

Prepare a Cost Sheet and performance statement showing :

(a) Cost per day maintained;

(b) Cost per day operated ;

(c) Cost per kilometer;

(d) Cost per hour;

(e) Cost per commercial tonne

[Adapted—I.C.W.A. Dec., 1990]

Solution

Cost Sheet for September 1990 (Lorry L–14)

	Rs.	Rs.
A. Operating Costs		
Petrol	400	
Oil	170	
Grease	90	
Wages to Driver	550	
Wages of khalasi	350	1,560
B. Maintenance Costs		
Repairs	170	
Overhand	60	
Tyres	150	
Garage charges	100	480
C. Fixed costs		
Insurance	50	
Licence, Tax etc.	80	
Interest	40	
Other overheads	190	360
D. Depreciation		
$\frac{\text{Rs. } 54{,}000 - \text{Rs. } 36{,}000}{5 \text{ years.}} = \text{Rs. } \frac{18{,}000}{5} = \text{Rs. } 3{,}600$		
$= \text{Rs. } 3{,}600 \div 12$		300
Total Cost for the month.		2,700

Performance Statement :

(a) Cost per day maintained Rs. $\frac{2,700}{30}$ = Rs. 90

(b) Cost per day operated Rs. $\frac{2,700}{25 \text{ days}}$ = Rs. 108

(c) Cost per kilo-meter Rs. $\frac{2,700}{2,500}$ = Rs. 1.08

(d) Cost per hour Rs. $\frac{2,700}{300 \text{ hours}}$ = Rs. 9.00

(e) Commercial tonne-kms

Outward – 4tonnes × 25 dyas × 50 kms =	5,000
Return = 0 × 25 × 50	nil
Total	5,000

Cost per commercial tonne-km Rs. $\frac{2,700}{5,000}$ = Re. 0.54

Problem 3

Mr. Sohan Singh has started transport business with a fleet of 10 taxis. The various expenses incurred by him are given below :

(a) Cost of each Taxi Rs. 75,000.

(b) Salary of Office staff Rs. 1,500. p.m.

(c) Salary of garage staff Rs. 2,000. p.m.

(d) Rent of garage Rs. 1,000. p.m.

(e) Drivers salary (per taxi) Rs. 400. p.m.

(f) Road Tax and Repairs per taxi Rs. 2,160. p.a.

(g) Insurance premium @ 4% of cost p.a.

The life of a taxi is Rs. 3,00,000 km. and at the end of which it is estimated to be sold at Rs. 15,000. A taxi runs on an average 4,000 km. per litre of petrol costing Rs. 6.30 per litre. Oil and other sundry expenses amount to Rs. 10 per 100 km.

Calculate the effective cost of running a taxi per kilometre. If the hire charge is Rs. 1.80 per kilometre, find out the profit Mr. Sohan Singh may expect to make in the first year of operation.

(ICWA–Inter Dec. '83)

Solution

Hire charges earned in the 1st year of operation :

A taxi runs on an average 4,000 km. per month of which 20% it runs empty

i.e., effective running will be 3,000 km. per month.

(i.e., 4,000 – 20% of 4,000)

Hence, total hire charges earned in the 1st year on 10 Taxis = 3,200 × 12 months × 10 Taxis. = 3,84,000 km. at Rs. 1.80 = Rs. 6,91,200.

Statement of Operating of a Taxi per km.

Particulars	*Basis of apportionment*		*Amount per month*	*per km.*
			Rs.	Rs.
A. **Fixed Costs**				
Salary of office staff	$\frac{1,500}{10}$	=	150.00	
Salary of garage staff	$\frac{2,000}{10}$	=	200.00	
Rent of garage	$\frac{1,000}{10}$	=	100.00	
Driver's Salary	per taxi	=	400.00	
Road Tax & Repairs	$\frac{2,160}{12}$	=	180.00	
Insurance 4% of 75,000 =	3,000 ÷ 12	=	250.00	
			1,280.00	
Total (A) :	1,280 ÷ 4,000	=		0.32
B. **Variable Costs :**				
Depreciation	$\frac{75,000-15,000}{3,00,000 \text{ km.}}$	=		0.20
Petrol	$\frac{6.30}{9}$	=		0.70
Oil & Other Sundry Exp.	$\frac{10}{100}$	=		0.10
Total (B) :	...	=		1.00
Operating Cost per km. (A + B) :	0.32 + 1.00	=		1.32
Effective cost of running a taxi per km.	$1.32 \times \frac{4,000}{3,200}$	=		1.65
Operating cost per month per taxi =	4,000 × 1.32	=		5,280
Operating cost per annum per taxi =	5,280 × 12	=		63,360
Operating cost per annum for 10 Taxis =	63,360 × 10	=		6,33,600
Hire charges earned in 1st Year =		=		6,91,200
Profit in the first year of opeation :				57,600

Or

Operation cost per km.			
effective running =	$1.32 \times \frac{4,000}{3,200}$	=	1.65
Hire charges per km.		=	1.80
Profit per km. (effective running)		=	0.15
Profit in 1st year = 3,84,000 effective km. at Rs. 0.15		=	57,600

Problem 4

Shanker has been promised a contract to run a tourist car on a 20 km. long route for the chief executive of a multinational firm. He buys a car costing Rs. 1,50,000. The annual cost of insurance and taxes are Rs. 4,500 and Rs. 900 respectively. He has to pay Rs. 500 per month for a garage where he keeps the car when it is not in use. The annual repair costs are estimated at Rs. 4,000. The car is estimated to have a life of 10 years, at the end of which the scrap value is likely to be Rs. 50,000.

He hires a driver who is to be paid Rs. 300 per month plus 10% of the takings as commission. Other incidental expenses are estimated at Rs. 200 per month.

Petrol and oil will cost Rs. 100 per 100 kms. The car will make 4 round trips each day. Assuming a profit of 15% on takings is desired and that the car will be on the road for 25 days on an average per month what should he charge per round-trip ?

[C.A. (Inter.) May, 1989]

Solution

Working Notes :

1. Total km. in a month :

   One Round Trip = 20 km. outward + 20 km. Inward = 40 km.

   Total km. = 40 km. × 4 × 25 days = **4,000 km.**

2. No. of round trips in a month = 25 × 4 = 100.
3. Petrol & Oil will cost Rs. 100 per 100 km. i.e., Re. 1 per one km.

Solution

Statement of Operating Cost

Particulars	*Basis of apportionment*	*Amount per month*	*per km.*
		Rs.	Rs.
A. **Standing Charges :**			
Depreciation	$\frac{1,50,000 - 50,000}{10}$	10,000	
Insurance		4,500	
Taxes		900	
Garage rent	500 × 12	6,000	
Annual repairs		4,000	
Driver's Salary	300 × 12	3,600	
Incidental exp.	200 × 12	2,400	
		31,400 ÷ 12	2,617
B. Variable Exp.			
Petrol & Oil.	4,000 km. × 1.00 per km.		4,000
Total Cost (excluding Commission) A + B =			6,617
Total Takings = T			
Driver's Commission = 10% of T i.e., 0.10 T.			
Profit = 15% of T i.e., 0.15 T			

Driver's Commission + Profit = 0.10 T + 0.15 T = 0.25 T.

Total Takings per month = Total Cost + Driver's Commission + Profit.

$T = 6{,}617 + 0.10\ T + 0.15\ T.$

$T = 6{,}617 + 0.25\ T$

$T - 0.25\ T = 6{,}617$

$0.75\ T = 6{,}617 \quad \text{or} \quad T = \text{Rs. } 6{,}617 \times \frac{100}{75}$

T = Rs. 8,822.67 per month.

$\text{Charge per round trip} = \text{Rs. } \frac{8{,}822.67}{100} = \text{Rs. } 88.23 \text{ say Rs. } 89.$

Problem 5

Mr. X owns a bus which runs according to the following schedule :

(i) Delhi to Chandigarh and back, the same day.
Distance covered : 150 kms. one way.
Number of days run each month : 8
Seating capacity occupied 90%.

(ii) Delhi to Agra and back, the same day.
Distance covered : 120 kms. one way.
Number of days run each month : 10
Seating capacity occupied 85%,

(iii) Delhi to Jaipur and back, the same day.
Distance covered : 270 kms. one way.
Number of days run each month : 6
Seating capacity occupied 100%

(iv) Following are the other details :

	Rs.	
Cost of the bus	6,00,000	
Salary of the driver	2,800	p.m.
Salary of the Conductor	2,200	p.m.
Salary of the part-time Accountant	200	p.m.
Insurance of the bus	4,800	p.m.
Diesel consumption 4 kms. per litre at	6	per litre
Road tax	1,500	p.a.
Lubricant oil	10	per 100 kms.
Permit fee	1,000	p.m.
Repairs and maintenance	315	p.m.
Depreciation of the bus		@ 20 % p.a.
Seating capacity of the bus		50 persons.

Passenger tax is 20% of the total takings. Calculate the bus fare to be charged from each passanger to earn a profit of 30% on total taking. The fares are to be indicated per passenger for the journeys :

(i) Delhi to Chndigarh (ii) Delhi to Agra
(iii) Delhi to Jaipur

C.A. (Inter) May, 1994

Solution

Working Notes

1. *Total Running Kms. per month*

Place	*Distance (km.)*	*Trips per day*	*Days per month*	*Km. per month*
Delhi to Chandigarh	150	2	8	2,400
Delhi to Agra	120	2	10	2,400
Delhi to Jaipur	270	2	6	3,240
				8,040

2. *Passenger Km. per month*

Delhi to Chandigarh & back	=	50 seats × 90% × 2,400	=	1,08,000
Delhi to Agra & back	=	50 seats × 85% × 2,400	=	1,02,000
Delhi to Jaipur & back	=	50 seats × 100% × 3,240	=	1,62,000
				3,72,000

Solution

Operating Cost Statement (per month)

Particulars	*Basis of apportionment*	*Amount* Rs.	*Total* Rs.
A. *Fixed Costs* :			
Salary of driver		2,800	
Salary of conductor		2,200	
Salary of Part-time Accountant		200	
Insurance	$\frac{4,800}{12}$ months	400	
Road Tax	$\frac{1,500}{12}$	125	
Permit Fee		315	
Repairs & Maintenance		1,000	
Depreciation	$\frac{6,00,000 \times 20}{100} \times \frac{1}{12}$	10,000	
Total A			17,040
B. *Variable Costs* :			
Diesel	$\frac{8,040 \times 6}{4}$	12,060	
Lubricant Oil	$\frac{8,040 \times 10}{100}$	804	
Total B			12,864
Total cost per month	A + B		29,904
Add : Passenger tax	20% of total takings		
Profit	30% of total takings		
	50% of total takings		
	i.e. 100% of total cost (Note 1)	29,904	29,904
Total takings			59,808

$$\text{Rate per passenger km} = \frac{\text{Rs. } 59,808}{3,72,000 \text{ passenger km.}} = 0.1607741.$$

i.e. Re. 0.161

Fare to be charged per passeenger :

				Rs.
(i) Delhi to Chandigarh	=	150 × 0.161	=	24.15
(ii) Delhi to Agra	=	120 × 0.161	=	19.32
(iii) Delhi to Jaipur	=	270 × 0.161	=	43.47

Note : 1

			Rs.
	Total takings		59,808
Less :	Passenger tax = 20% of total takings	= 11,961.60	
	Profit = 30% of total takings	= 17,942.40	29,904
	Total Cost		29,904

Problem 6

From the following data relating to two different vehicles A and B, compute the cost per running mile :

	Vehicle A	Vehicle B
Mileage run (annual)	15,000	6,000
	Rs.	Rs.
Cost of vehicle	25,000	15,000
Road licence (annual)	750	750
Insurance (annual)	700	400
Garage rent (annual)	600	500
Supervision and salaries	1,200	1,200
Driver's wages per hour	3	3
Cost of fuel per gallon	3	3
Miles run per gallon	20 miles	15 miles
Repairs and maintenance per mile	1.65	2.00
Tyre allocation per mile	0.80	0.60
Estimated life of vehicle	1,00,000 miles	75,000 miles

Charge interest at 5% per annum on cost of vehicles. The vehicles run 20 miles per hour on an average

(B. Com., Madras,)

Solution

Operating Cost Statement

		Vehicle A	Vehicle B
		Rs.	Rs.
A.	Fixed Cost per annum :		
	Road licence	750	750
	Insurance	700	400
	Garage rent	600	500
	Supervisory salaries	1,200	1,200
	Interest 5%	1,250	750
		4,500	3,600
	Mileage run per annum	15,000	6,000
	Fixed cost per mile	0.30	0.60
B	**Running Cost per mile :**		
	Drivers' wages (Rs. 3 per hour for 20 miles)	0.15	0.15
	Fule cost per mile	0.15	0.20
	Repairs and maintenance	1.65	2.00
	Tyre allocation	0.80	0.60
	Depreciation (cost ÷ estimated life)	0.25	0.20
	∴ Running cost per mile.	3.00	3.15
	Total Cost per Running Mile (A + B)	3.30	3.75

Problem 7

Agarwal Automobiles distribute its goods to a regional dealer using a single lorry. The dealer's premises are 40 kilometres away by road. The Lorry has a capacity of 10 tonnes and makes the journey twice a day fully loaded on the onward journeys and empty on return journeys.

The following information is available for a four weekly period during the year 1997 :

Petrol consumption	5 kilometres per litre
Petrol cost	Rs. 22 per litre
Oil	Rs. 150 per week
Driver's wages	Rs. 800 " "
Repairs	Rs. 100 " "
Garrage Rent	Rs. 300 " "
Cost of Lorry	Rs. 6,00,000
Life of Lorry	1,00,000 km.
Insurance	5% of cost of lorry
Cost of Tyres	Rs. 10,000
Estimated value of Lorry at the end of its life	Rs. 40,000.
Cost of Licence	Rs. 150 per week
Other overhead costs	Rs. 39,000 p.a.
Life of tyres	25,000 km.

The Lorry operates on a five day week.

You are required :

(i) to prepare a statement to show total cost of operating the vehicle for the four weekly period analysed into running and fixed costs;

(ii) to calculate the vehicle cost per kilo metre and per ton kilometre.

Solution

(i) **Statement of Total Cost of operating the vehicle for the four weekly period.**

Particulars	*Basis of apportionment*	*Amount* Rs.
A. **Fixed Costs**		
Garrage Rent	Rs. 300 × 4	1,200
Insurance	5% of Rs. 6,00,000	30,000
Licence Fees	Rs. 150 × 4	600
Other Over head	Rs. 39,000 × $\frac{4}{52}$	3,000
		34,800
B **Running Costs :**		
Petrol	40 × 2 = 80 km × 2 trips = 160 × 20 days = 32,000 km. $\frac{3,200}{5}$ = 640 litres @ Rs. 22	14,080
Oil	Rs. 150 × 4	600
Driver's wages	Rs. 800 × 4	3,200
Repairs	Rs. 100 × 4	400
Depreciation	$\frac{\text{Rs. } 6,00,000 - \text{Rs. } 40,000}{1,00,000}$ = Rs. 5.60 per. km. Rs. 5.60 × 3,200 km.	17,920
Cost of tyre	$\frac{\text{Rs. } 10,000 \times 3,200 \text{ km.}}{25,000}$	1,280
		37,480
Total cost A + B =	Rs. 34,800 + Rs. 37,480 =	72,280

Tonne kilometre

Outward 40 km. × 2 trips × 20 days × tonnes = 16,000 tonnes

Return 40 km × 2 trip × 20 days × 0 ton = Nil

16,000

$$\textbf{Cost per ton km} = \frac{\text{Total cost}}{\text{km}} = \frac{\text{Rs. } 72,280}{16,000} = \text{Rs. } 4.52 \text{ (Approx)}$$

Problem 8

The Union Transport Company has been given a twenty kilometer long route to ply a bus. The bus costs the company Rs. 5,00,000. It has been insured at 3% per annum. The annual Road Tax amounts to Rs. 10,000; Garage rent is Rs. 2,000 p.a. Annual Repair is estimated to cost Rs. 11,800. and the span of life of the bus is estimated for five years.

The salary of the driver and the conductor is Rs. 3,000 and Rs. 1,000 p.m. respectively in addition to 10% of takings as commission to be shared equally by them. The manager's salary is Rs. 3,500 p.m. and stationery will cost Rs. 500 p.m. Petrol and oil will cost Rs. 250

per 100 kilometers. The bus will make three round trips per day carrying on an average 50 passangers in each trip. Assuming 15% profit on takings and the bus will ply on an average 25 days in a month, prepare operating cost statement on a full year basis and also calculate the bus fare to be charged from each passenger per kilometer.

Solution

(i) **Statement of Operating Cost per year.**

Particulars	*Basis*	*Amount*
		Rs.
A. *Fixed charges*		
Manager's salary	Rs. 3,500 × 12	42,000
Driver's Salary	Rs. 3,000 × 12	36,000
Conductor's Salary	Rs. 1,000 × 12	12,000
Road Tax		10,000
Garrage Rent		2,000
Insurance	3% of Rs. 5,00,000	15,000
Stationery	Rs. 500 × 12	6,000
Depreciation	Rs. 5,00,000 ÷ 5 years	1,00,000
		2,23,000
B. *Maintenance and Repairs*		11,800
C. *Running charges*		
Petrol and oil	$\frac{\text{Rs. } 250}{100} \times 36{,}000$	90,000
		3,24,800

(ii) **Calculation of bus fare to be charged per passanger**

Passanger – KM

Onward Journey.

20 km × 3 trips × 50 passangers × 25 days × 12 months

	9,00,000	km
Return Journey	9,00,000	km
Total Passager km.	18,00,000	km

Total Cost

			Rs.
	Total operating cost		3,24,800
Add :	Commission to driver and Conductor	10% of takings	
Add :	Profit	15% of takings.	
		25% i.e., $\frac{1}{3}$rd of cost.	
		i.e., $\frac{1}{3}$rd of Rs. 3,24,800 =	1,08,267
Takings			4,33,067

Fare to be charged per passanger $= \dfrac{\text{Takings}}{\text{Total pasenger km.}}$

$= \dfrac{\text{Rs. } 4{,}33{,}067}{18{,}00{,}000} = 0.24$ paisa.

Working notes

1. **Distance to be covered in a year**	**Kilometer**
Onward 20 km. × 3 trips × 25 × 12	18,000
Return	18,000
	36,000

Problem 9

A manufacturing firm facing shortage of electric power supply from the state Electricity Board has set up its own power generation plant for efficient running of its production units in the factory. The following information has been taken from the records in connection with the generation of power for a month.

1) Number of units generated was 10,00,000 for the month of which 10% was utilised by the generator department.
2) Consumption data of materials, etc; for the month :
   a) Coal consumed = 300 MTS @ Rs. 3,600 per metric tonne.
   b) Oil consumed = 4.5 MTS @ Rs. 40,000 per MT.
   c) Cost of water extraction and treatment for 6 lakhs lts @ 1.25 per litre.
3) Steams boiler costs Rs. 20,00,000 with a residual value of Rs. 2,00,000 after a life of 10 years.
4) Salaries and wages per month :
   a) For staff of generating plant
      i) 100 skilled workers @ Rs. 3,000 per month.
      ii) 150 helpers @ Rs. 1,500 per month.
   b) For staff of boiler house :
      (i) 60 category A workers @ Rs. 1,500 per month.
      (ii) 100 category B workers @ Rs. 1,000 per month.
5) Cost of generating plant : Rs. 36 lakhs with no residual value. Depreciation @ 10% on straight line basis is to be charged.
6) Repairs and maintainenace of generating plant and boiler Rs. 50,000 per month.
7) Share of administrative charges Rs. 40,000 per month.
8) Sale value of ash disposed off Rs. 15,000 per month.

Calculate the per unit cost of electricity generated using a cost sheet format.

[ICWA (Inter) June, 1996]

Solution

Power House Cost Sheet

Elements of cost		*Total cost of the month*	*Cost per unit or KWH*
		Rs.	Rs.
1. ***Consumption of materials*** :			
a) Coal consumed	300 × 3,600 =	10,80,000	
b) Oil consumed	4.5 × 40,000 =	1,80,000	
c) Cost of water etc.	6,00,000 × 1.25 =	7,50,00	
		20,10,000	
		10,00,000	2.01

Contd.

		Rs.	Rs.
2. ***Salaries & Wages***			
a) For staff of generating plant			
	100 × 3,000 =	3,00,000	
	150 × 1,500 =	2,25,000	
b) For staff of boiler house :			
	60 × 1500 =	90,000	
	100 × 1000 =	1,00,000	
		7,15,000	0.715
3. Depreciation :			
a) Steam boiler	$\frac{20-2}{10} = \frac{1.80}{12}$	15,000	
b) Generating plant 10% of 36	$= \frac{3.60}{12}$	30,000	
		45,000	0.045
4. Repairs & Maintenance		50,000	0.050
Total 1 + 2 + 3 + 4		28,20,000	2.820
Less : Sale value of ash disposed		15,000	0.015
Worko cost		28,05,000	2.805
Add : Share of administrative charges		40,000	0.04
Cost of Electricity generated		28,45,000	2.845

Note : 1. Per unit cost of electricity generated is Rs. 2.845

Note : 2. Cost of units utilised by generator deportment 10% i.e. 10% i.e. 1,00,000 units utilised at Rs. 2.845 per unit = Rs. 2,84,500. This amount should be debited to generator department.

Problem 10

PQ Ltd. plans to start a lodging house at a tourist centre with a capacity of 32 single occupancy rooms. Costs per day per room have been estimated as under :

		Costs per day per room (Rs.)
(A) *When occupied*		
(a)	Electricity and utilities	4
(b)	Linen, laundry and sanitary supplies	9
(c)	Dusting, sweeping and cleaning	2
		15
(B) *When unoccupied*		2

Over and above these costs, the following expenses represent the estimate of fixed charges per annum (i.e., 365 days) :

	Rs.
Staff expenses	3,20,000
Other office expenses	64,000
Rates, taxes, insurance, maintenance and depreciation	42,320
	4,26,320

PQ Ltd. defines 100% occupancy to mean all the 32 rooms to fetch revenue for all the 365 days.

You are required to answer the following, using a planning period of the year :

(i) What should be the tariff per day per room in order to reach break-even at an occupancy level of 50%?

(ii) What would be the profits, if the occupancy level reaches : (a) 60%, (b) 70% and (c) 80% respectively?

(iii) What would be the profits, if the tariff per day is reduced by 10% from the answer in (i) above and the occupancy level is 100%?

[I.C.W.A. (Inter.) Dec. 1994]

Solution

(i)	Variable cost per day per room = Rs. 15 when occupied,		
	Variable cost at 50% occupancy level :		Rs.
	32 rooms × 50% = 16 rooms × 365 days × Rs. 15 =		87,600
Add :	Variable cost when unoccupied		
	32 rooms × 50% = 16 rooms × 365 days × Rs. 2		11,680
	Total Variable cost in a year		99,280
Add :	Fixed charges per annum		4,26,320
	Total Cost in a year		5,25,600

Note : Total Cost is equal to BEP

$$\text{Tariff per day per room} = \frac{\text{Rs. } 5,25,600}{16 \text{ rooms} \times 365 \text{ days}} = \text{Rs. } 90$$

	Total income = 16 rooms × 365 days × Rs. 90 =		5,25,600
Less :	Variable Cost		99,280
	Contribution		4,26,320
Less :	Fixed charges		4,26,320
	Profit		Nil
	(ii) **at 60% occupancy level** :		Rs.
	Income 32 rooms × 60% × 365 × Rs. 90		6,30,720
Less :	Variable cost when occupied 32 × 60% × 365 × 15 =	1,05,120	
	Variable cost when unoccupied 32 × 40% × 365 × 2 =	9,344	1,14,464
	Contribution		5,16,256
Less :	Fixed Charges		4,26,320
	Profit		89,936
(b)	**At 70% occupancy level** :		
	Income : 32 rooms × 70% × 365 days × 90 =		7,35,840
Less :	Variable cost when occupied 32 × 70% × 365 × 15 =	1,22,640	
	Variable cost when unoccupied 32 × 30% × 365 × 2 =	7,008	1,29,648
	Contribution		6,06,192
Less :	Fixed Charges		4,26,320
	Profit		1,79,872

			Rs.
(c)	80% occupancy level :		
	Income : 32 rooms × 80% × 365 days × Rs. 90 =		8,40,960
Less :	Variable cost when occupied 32 × 80% × 365 × 15 =	1,40,160	
	Variable cost when unoccupied 32 × 20% × 365 × 2 =	4,672	1,44,832
	Contribution		6,96,128
Less :	Fixed Charges		4,26,320
	Profit		2,69,808
(iii)	If tariff per day is reduced by 10%, it will be 90-10% = Rs. 81 per day per room at 100% occupancy level :		
			Rs.
	Income : 32 rooms × 100% × 365 days × Rs. 81 =		9,46,080
Less :	Variable cost when occupied 32 × 100% × 365 × 15 =		1,75,200
	Contribution		7,70,880
Less :	Fixed Charges		4,26,320
	Profit		3,44,560

Problem 11

A lodging home is being run in a small hill station with 50 single rooms. The home offers concessional rates during six off-season months in a year. During this period, half of the full-room rent is charged. The management's profit margin is targeted at 20% of the room rent. The following are the cost estimates and other details for the year ending 31st March, 1996, (assume a month to be of 30 days);

(a) occupancy during the season is 80%, while in the off-season is 40% only :

(b) expenses :

		Rs.
(i)	staff salary (excluding room attendants)	2,75,000
(ii)	repairs to buildings	1,30,500
(iii)	laundry & linen	40,000
(iv)	interior and tapestry	87,500
(v)	sundry expenses	95,400

(c) annual depreciation is to be provided, for buildings at 5% and on furniture and equipments at 15%, on straight line basis.

(d) room attendants are paid Rs. 5 per room-day on the basis of occupancy of rooms in a month.

(e) monthly lighting charges are Rs. 120 per room except in four months of winter when it is Rs. 30 per room and this cost is on the basis of full occupancy for the month.

(f) and total investments in the home is Rs. 100 lakhs of which Rs. 80 lakhs relate to building and balance for furniture and equipemnt.

You are required to work out the room rent chargeable per day both during the season and the off-season months, on the basis of the foregoing information.

[I.C.W.A. (Inter.) Dec. 1995]

Solution

Occupancy during Season :			Room days
	50 rooms × (80% × 6 months) × 30 days =		7,200
Off-season :	50 rooms × (40% × 6 months) × 30 days =		3,600
Total			10,800
Room Rent			
Full Room rent =		7,200 × 1	7,200
Half of full room rent =		3,600 × 0.5	1,800
			9,000
Expenses			Rs.
Staf salaries			2,75,000
Repairs to Buildings			1,30,500
Laundry & Linen			40,000
Interior & tapestry			87,500
Sundry expenses			95,400
Depreciation			
Buildings 5% of 80 lakhs			4,00,000
Furniture 15% of 20 lakhs			3,00,000
Payment to room attendants : 10,800 × 5			54,000
Lighting charges for 12 months :			
	120 × 6 months × 50 rooms × 80%	28,800	
	120 × 2 months × 50 rooms × 40%	4,800	
	30 × 4 months × 50 rooms × 40%	2,400	36,000
Total Cost			14,18,400
Add : Profit margin at 20% of room rent i.e. 25% of total cost			3,54,600
Room Rent			17,73,000

Room rent = $\frac{17,73,000}{9,000}$ = Rs. 197 per day during the season and Rs. 98.50 per day during the off season.

Reconciliation of Room-rent

During season : 7,200 × 197	14,18,400
Off season : 3,600 × 98.50	3,54,600
Total room rent	17,73,000

Problem 12

Prakash Automobiles distributes its goods to a regional dealer using a single Lorry. The dealers premises are 40 kilometres away by road. The Lorry has a capacity of 10 tonnes and makes the journey twice a day fully loaded on the outward journeys and empty on return journeys. The following information is available for a *Four-Weekly Period* during the year 1990 :

Petrol consumption	8 kilometres per litre
Petrol cost	Rs. 13 per litre
Oil	Rs. 100 per week
Drivers wages	Rs. 400 per week
Repairs	Rs. 100 per week
Garage rent	Rs. 150 per week

Cost of Lorry (Excluding Tyres)	Rs. 4,50,000
Life of Lorry	Rs. 80,000 Kilometres
Insurance	Rs. 6,500 kilometres
Cost of Tyres	Rs. 6,250
Life of Tyres	25,000 kilometres
Extimated sale value of Lorry at end of its life	Rs. 50,000
Vehicle Licence cost	Rs. 1,300 per annum
Other overhead cost	Rs. 41,600 per annum

The Lorry operates on a five-day-week.

Required :

(a) A statement to show the total cost of operating the vehicle for the *four-weekly period* analysed into running costs and fixed costs.

(b) Calculate the vehicle cost per kilometre and per tonne kilometre.

[C.A. Inter, May 1991]

Solution

(a) Before computing the total cost, it is necessary to find out the basic data as under :

1. Distance travelled in 4 week period : 40 km one way × 2 (return) × 2 trips × 5 days × 4 week = 3,200 km.
2. For Tonne km. working = Empty on return and as such for tonne km.
   = 3,200 ÷ 2 = 1,600 km.
3. Total consumption in 4 weeks = 3,200 km. ÷ 8 km/lt = 400 Ltr.
4. Tyre Cost = (Rs. 6,250 ÷ 25,000 km) × 3,200 km = Rs. 800.
5. Depreciation of Lorry in 4 weeks $\frac{(\text{Rs. } 4{,}50{,}000 - \text{Rs. } 50{,}000)}{80{,}000}$ km × 3,200

   = Rs. 16,000.

Operating cost Statement of Lorry of M/s Prakash Automobile

(for the 4 weeks period)

	Rs.
Running Costs	
Cost of petrol (400 litres × Rs. 13)	5,200
Oil (Rs. 100 per week × 4)	400
Drivers wages (Rs. 400 per week × 4)	1,600
Repairs (Rs. 100 × 4)	400
Cost of tyres (as at 4 above)	800
Depreciation (as at 5 above)	16,000
Total running cost ... (i)	24,400
Fixed Costs	
Garage rent (Rs. 150 × 4)	600
Insurance (Rs. 6,500 ÷ 52) × 4	500
Licence cost (Rs. 1,300 ÷ 52) × 4	100
Other overheads (Rs. 41,600 ÷ 52) × 4	3,200
Total fixed cost ...(ii)	4,400
Total cost ...(i) + (ii)	28,800

(b) Cost per km = Rs. 28,800 ÷ (1,600 × 10 tonne) = 1.80

Problem 13

SMS is a public school having five buses each plying in different direction for the transport of its school students. In view of a large number of students availing of the bus service, the buses work two shifts daily both in the morning and in the afternoon. The buses are garaged in the school. The work load of the students has been so arranged that in the morning the first trip picks up senior students and the second trip plying an bour later picks up the junior students. Similarly in the afternoon the first trip drops the junior students and an hour later the second trip takes the senior students home.

The distance travelled by each bus one way is 8 kms. The school works 25 days in a month and remains closed for vacation in May, June and December. Bus fee, however, is payable by the students for all the 12 months in a year.

The details of expenses for a year are as under :

Driver's salary	Rs. 450 per month per driver
Clearner's salary	350 per month per clearner
(Salary payable for all 12 months—one cleaner employed for all the five buses)	
Licence fee, taxes, etc.	860 per bus per annum
Insurance	1,000 per bus per annum
Repairs and maintenance	3,500 per bus per annum
Purchase price of the bus	1,50,000 each
Life	12 years
Scrap value	Rs. 30,000
Diesel cost	2.00 per litre

Each bus gives an average mileage of 4 km. per litre of diesel.

The seating capacity is fully occupied during the whole year.

Sealing capacity of each bus—50 students.

Students picked up and dropped within a range up to 4 km. of distance from the school are charged balf fare and fifty per cent of the students travelling in each tripare in this category. Ignore interest. Since the charges are to be based on average cost, you are required to :

(i) Prepare a statement showing the expenses of operating a single bus and the fleet of five buses for a year;

(ii) Work out the average cost per sutdent per month in respect of :

(a) Students coming from a distance of up to 4 km. from the school and

(b) Students coming for a distance beyond 4 km. from the school.

[C.A. Inter.]

Solution

SMS Public School

Statement showing the Operating Cost of the Fleet

	Particulars	*Per bus per annum*	*Fleed of 5 buses per annum*
		Rs.	Rs.
	Driver's salary @ Rs. 450 p.m. per driver	5,400	27,000
	Cleaner's salary @ Rs. 35 p.m. for one cleaner (one cleaner for 5 buses)	840	4,200
	Licence fee, taxes, etc. @ Rs. 860 per bus p.a.	860	4,300
	Insurance Rs. 1,000 per bus p.a.	1,000	5,000
	Repairs and maintenance Rs. 3,500 per bus p.a.	3,500	17,500
	Depreciation $\left(\text{Rs. } \frac{1,50,000}{30,000}\right) \times 12$	10,000	50,000
	Diesel cost (See note1)	7,200	36,000
	Total operating cost	28,800	1,44,000
(a)	Operating cost per month	2,400	12,000
(b)	Number of half fare students	150	750
(c)	Operating cost per half fare student (a) ÷ (b)	16.00	16.00
(d)	Operating cost per full fare student (c) × 2	32.00	32.00

Working Notes :

1. Calculation of diesel cost per bus

Number of trips of 8 kms. each day =	8 trips
Distance travelled per day by a bus : 8 × 8 km./trip =	64 kms.
Distance travelled during a month : 64 × 25 =	1,600 kms.
Distance travelled p.a. : 1,600 × 9 months =	14,400 kms.
(May, June and December being vacations)	
Mileage 4 kms. per litre	
Diesel required : 14,400 ÷ 4 =	3,600 litres
Cost of diesel @ Rs. 2 per litre =	Rs. 7,200 p.a. per bus.

2. Calculations of number of students per bus

Bus capacity	50 students
Half fare	50% i.e. 25 students
Full rate	50% i.e., 25 students
Full fare students as equivalent to half fare students, i.e.,	50 students
Total No. of half-fare students per trip	75 students
Total No. of half-fare students in 2 trips	150 students
On full-fare basis No. of students in 2 trips	75 students

Problem 14

Mr. Harry is a Travelling Inspector for the Environmental Protection Agency. He uses his own car and the agency reimburses him at Rs. 1.80 per kilometre. Mr. Harry claims he needs Rs. 2.20 per kilometre just to break-even. A scrutiny of his expenses by the agency reveals the following :

	Rs.
Oil change every 4,800 kms.	120
Maintenance (other than oil) every 9,600 kms.	1,800
Yearly insurance (comprehensive with accident benefits)	4,000
Cost of car, with an average residual value of Rs. 60,000 and with a useful life of 3 years	1,08,000

Petrol is Rs. 5 a litre and Harry gets 8 kms. per litre in his car. When Harry is on the road, he averages 192 kilometres a day. He works 5 days a week has 10 days vacation in a year besides 6 holidays and spends 15 working days a month in the office.

You are required to determine.

(a) An equitable rate of reimbursement on the basis of the schedule he presently follows; and

(b) The number of kilometres a year he would have to travel, to break-even at the current rate of reimbursement.

[I.C.W.A. Inter]

Solution

(a) Total kilometres covered by Mr. Harry in one year

Total number of days in one year			365
Less :	Vacation	10	
	Holidays	6	
	Week-ends (52 weeks × 2)	104	
	Days spent in office (12 Months × 15 days)	180	300
			65

Actual days of travelling in a year

Average kilometres in one day = 192

Total kilometres in 65 days = 192 × 65

Total distance covered = 12,489 kms.

Cost Incurred for Travelling 12,480 kms.	Rs.
Oil change (120 ÷ 4,800) × 12,480	312
Maintenance (1,800 ÷ 9,600) × 12,480	2,340
Yearly insurance	4,000
Depreciation $\dfrac{1,08,000 - 60,000}{3}$	16,000
Cost of petrol (12,480 ÷ 8) Rs. 5	7,800
Total cost to break-even	30,452
Cost per km. to break-even (30,452 ÷ 12,480)	2.44 per km.

(b) Number of kms. required to be travelled in a year to Break-even at Rs. 1.80 per km.

Fixed cost :

	Rs.
Yearly insurance	4,000
Depreciation	16,000
Total fixed cost	20,000

Variable Cost for Covering 9,600 kms.

Maintenance	1,800
Oil change (120 ÷ 4,800) × 9,600	240
Cost of petrol (9,600 ÷ 8) × Rs. 5	6,000

Variable cost per km. = 8,040 ÷ 9,600 or Re. 0.8375

Contribution per km. = Rs. 1.80 – 0.8375 = Re. 0.9625.

No. of kms. required to break-even = Rs. $\frac{20,000}{0.9625}$ = 20,779 km.

In order to get a contribution of Rs. 20,000, Harry has to travel 20,779 kilometres.

Problem 15

Ranjeet Hotel has three types of suites for its customers, viz., single room, double room and three rooms respectively. State the rent to the charged for each type of suite on the basis of following information.

(i) The number of suites of each type are :

(a)	Single room suites	100
(b)	Double room suites	30
(c)	Three room suites	20

(ii) The rent of double room suite is to be fixed as $1\frac{1}{2}$ times the single-room suite and that of three room as twice the single room suite.

(iii) The occupancy of each type of suite is as follows :

		Summer	Winter
(a)	Single room suites	90%	50%
(b)	Double room sutes	80%	20%
(c)	Three room suites	60%	20%

(iv) The annual expenses are as follows :

(a) Staff salaries Rs. 2,20,000

(b) Room attendent's wages when occupied :

	Summer	Winter
	Rs.	Rs.
Single room suites	2	3.00
Double room suites	3	4.50
Three room suites	4	6.00

(c) Lighting heating and power for full month, when occupied

	Lighting	Power
	Rs.	Rs.
Single room suites	40	20
Double room suites	60	30
Three room suites	80	40

(d)	Repairs and renovation	42,000
	Line etc.	45,000
	Interior decoration	50,000
	Sundries	31,550
(c)	Depreciation	
	Building @ 5% on Rs. 14,00,000	
	Furniture & Fixtures @ 10% on Rs. 1,00,000	
	Air-conditioner @ 10% on Rs. 2,00,000	

(v) Summer may be assumed for 7 months and winter for 5 months in a year. A month may be taken as of 30 days.

(vi) Profit including interest on investment @ 25% on cost.

Solution

Operating Cost Statement

(A)			Total cost per annum Rs.
	Staff salaries		2,20,000
	Attendant's wages (Working note 2)		93,150
	Repairs and renovation		42,000
	Lighting (Working note 3)		55,400
	Power (Working note 4)		27,700
	Linen		45,000
	Interior decoration		50,000
	Sundries		31,550
	Depreciation :		
	Building	70,000	
	Furniture & Fixture	10,000	
	Air-conditioner	20,000	1,00,000
	Total cost for the year		6,64,800
(B)	Profit 25% on cost		1,66,200
(C)	Total rent to be charged		8,31,000
(D)	Total single room days (Working note I)		41,550 days
(E)	Rent for one day		20
(F)	Rent for single room suite		20
(G)	Rent for double room suite $20 \times \frac{3}{2}$		30
(H)	Rent for three room suite (20×2)		40

Working Notes

1. Room days :

(a) Single room suite :

Summer : 100 rooms × 90% × 30 days × months =	18,900
Winter : 10 rooms × 50% × 30 days × 5 months	7,500
Total single room days	26,400

(b) Double room suite :

Summer : 30 rooms × 80% × 30 days × 7 months 5,040.

Winter : 30 rooms × 20% × 30 days × 5 months ; 900

Total double room days 5,940

(c) Three room suite :

Summer : 20 rooms × 60% × 30 days × 7 months = 2,520

Winter : 20 rooms × 20% × 30 days × 5 months ; 600

Total three rooms days 3,120

Total single room days

The rent of a double rom suite is to be 1* times and that of a three room suite as twice the single room suite.

	Single room days
Single room suite =	26,400
Double room suite $\left(5,940 \text{ days} \times \frac{3}{2}\right)$ =	8,910
Three rom suite (3,120 days ¥ 2) =	6,240
	41,550

2. Room attendant's wages

Summer	
Single room suite (18,900 days × Rs. 2) =	37,800
Double room suite (5,040 days × Rs. 3) =	15,120
Three room suite (2,520 days × 4) =	10,080
Winger	
Single room suite (7,500 days × Rs. 3) =	22,500
Double room suite (900 days × Rs. 4.5) =	4,050
Three room suite (600 days × Rs. 6) =	3,600
Total rom attendants wages	93,150

3. Lighting for full year

Single room suite $= \dfrac{26,400 \text{ days} \times \text{Rs. } 40}{30 \text{ days}} = 35,200$

Double room suite $= \dfrac{5,940 \text{ days} \times \text{Rs. } 60}{30 \text{ days}} = 11,880$

Three room suite $= \dfrac{3,120 \text{ days} \times \text{Rs. } 80}{30 \text{ days}} = 8,320$

55,400

4. Power for full year

Single room suite $= \dfrac{26,400 \text{ days} \times \text{Rs. } 20}{30 \text{ days}} = 17,600$

Double room suite $= \dfrac{5,940 \text{ days} \times \text{Rs. } 30}{30 \text{ days}} = 5,940$

Three room suite $= \dfrac{3,120 \text{ days} \times \text{Rs. } 40}{30 \text{ days}} = 4,160$

27,770

Problem 16

From the following data pertaining to the year 1996-97 prepare a cost sheet showing the cost of electricity generated per unit of kwh. by Chambal Thermal Power Station :

Total units generated	20,00,000 kwh.
Operating labour	Rs. 50,000
Repairs and maintenance	Rs. 50,000
Lubricants, spares and stores	Rs. 40,000
Plant supervision	Rs. 30,000
Administrative overheads	Rs. 20,000

Coal consumed per kwh. for the year is 2.5 kg.
@ Rs. 0.02 per kg
Depreciation charge @ 5% on capital cost of Rs. 2,00,000.

[B.Com., S.V. Univ.]

Solution

Power House Cost Sheet

Power House Station : Chambal Thermal; Year 96-97
Electricity generated : 20,00,000 kwh.

	Items			*Cost per kwh.*
			Rs.	Rs.
(A)	*Fixed costs* :			
	Depreciation @ 5% on Rs. 2,00,000			10,000
	Plant supervision			30,000
	Administration overheads			20,000
	Total fixed costs for the year $\left(\frac{60,000}{20,00,000}\right)$		60,000	0.030
(B)	*Variable cost* :			
	Coal :	2.5 kg × Re. 0.02	1,00,000	0.050
	Operating labour	50,000 ÷ 20,00,000	50,000	0.025
	Repairs and maintenance	50,000 ÷ 20,00,000	50,000	0.025
	Lubricants, spares and stores	40,000 ÷ 20,00,000	40,000	0.020
	Total variable costs		2,40,000	0.120
(C)	*Total Cost (A + B)*	Rs. 2,40,000 + Rs. 60,000	3,00,000	0.150
(D)	*Cost per kwh. of electricity generated*			0.150

Problem 17

A chemical factory runs its boiler on furnace oil obtained from Indian oil and Bharat Petroleum whose depots are situated at a distance of 12 kms. and 8 kms. from the factory site. Transportation of furnace oil is made by the company's own lorries of 5 tonne capacity each. Outward trips are made only on full load and the lorries return empty. The filling-in time takes an average 40 minutes for Indian Oil and 30 minutes. for Bharat Petroleum. But the emptying time in the factory is only 40 mins for all. From the records available it is seen that the average speed of the company's lorries works out to 24 km per hour. The varying operating charges average 60 p per km. covered and fixed charges given incidence of Rs. 7.50 per hour operation. Calculate the cost per tonne mile from each source.

[C.A. Inter]

Solution

Working Notes :

Particulars	Indian Oil	Bharat Petroleum
1. ***Variable cost of operating*** :		
Distance of Oil Depots from chemical factory	12 kms.	8 kms.
Distance covered per trip	12 × 2 = 24 kms	8 × 2 = 16 kms.
Variable cost @ 60 per km	24 × 0.60 = Rs. 14.40	16 × 0.60 = Rs. 9.60
2. ***Fixed Cost*** :		
Running time @ 24 km	60 mins.	40 mins.
Filling time	40 mins.	30 mins.
Emptying time	40 mins.	40 mins.
Total time per Trip	140 mins.	110 mins.
Fixed charges @ Rs. 7.50 per hour	Rs. $\frac{7.50}{60} \times 140$ = Rs. 17.50	Rs. $\frac{7.50}{60} \times 110$ = Rs. 13.50
3. Tonne-kilometres :		
Outward trip	5 × 12 = 60	5 × 8 = 40
Return trip	0 × 12 = 0	0 × 8 = 0
Total tonne-kilometres	60	40

While measuring service in terms of tonne-kilometres, distance travelled with load (and not total distance covered) should be considered.

Operating Cost Statement

Particulars	*Indian Oil*	*Bharat Petroleum*
	Rs.	Rs.
Variable Cost (Note-1)	14.40	9.60
Fixed Cost (Note-2)	17.50	13.75
Total Cost (A)	31.90	23.35
Tonne-kilometers (B) (Note 3)	60	40
Cost per tonne-kilometres [(A) ÷ (B)]	0.53	0.58

ASSIGNMENT

Theoretical Questions

1. What is 'Operating Cost'? To what industries is this method of costing applicable?
2. Draw up a pro-forma Cost Sheet for such a company showing distinctly the operational and maintenance cost.

[I.C.W.A. (Inter)]

3. How costs are classified in transport costing?
4. What are the features of operating costing?

Practical Problems

1. A truck starts with a load of 10 tonnes of goods from station P. It unloads 4 tonnes at station Q and rest of the goods at station R. It reaches back directly to station P after getting reloaded with 8 tonnes of goods at station R. The distance between P to Q, Q to R and then from R to P are 40 kms., 60 kms, and 80 kms respectively.

[C.A. (Inter.) May, 1990]

Ans. : 1,440 tonne km.

2. Calculate the cost per km of a vehicle from the following data :

	Rs.
Value of vehicle	15,000
Road licence fee per year	500
Insurance charges per year	100
Garage rent per year	600
Driver's wages per month	200
Cost of petrol per litre	Re 0.80
Kilometres per litre	8
Proportionate charge for tyre and maintenance per km.	Re 0.20
Estimated life	1,50,000 kms.
Estimated annual kilometreage	6,000
Ignore interest on capital	

Ans. : Cost per km. Re. 1.00

3. A transport company maintains a flet of buses as follows :

No. of Busses	*Carrying Capacity*
10	60 passengers each
5	40 passengers each

Each bus makes 4 trips (both upward and downward) in a day, covering a distance of 5 kilometres in each trip. On an average 75% of the seats are occupied in each trip. Assuming that the company operates its fleet 25 days in a month, ascertain operating cost per passenger kilometre, taking into account the following further information :

Wages of 5 drivers Rs. 250 each p.m., petrol oil and grease Rs. 3,000 p.m.; Repairs Rs. 1,500 p.m.; tyre-tube etc. Rs. 375 p.m.; Depreciation Rs. 90,000 p.a.; Garage rent Rs. 9,000 p.a.; Interest on capital Rs. 12,000 p.a.; General supervision charges Rs. 3,000 p.a.

[Adapted—C.U. M.Com.]

Ans. : Re. 0.030208

4. Work out in the in the appropriate Cost Sheet form, the unit cost per passenger-mile for the year 1997-98 for fleet of passenger buses run by a transport company. The following figures are extracted from the books of the company.

   Five passenger buses cost Rs. 50,000; Rs. 1,20,000; Rs. 45,000; Rs. 55,000 and Rs. 80,000 respectively. Yearly depreciation of vehicles 20% of cost. Annual repair, maintenance and spare parts 80% of depreciation; wages of 10 drivers @ Rs. 100 each p.m.; wages of 20 cleaners @ Rs. 50 each p.m.; Yearly rate of interest 4% of capital; Rent of six garages Rs. 50 each p.m. Director's Fees @ Rs. 400 p.m.; Office establishment expenses Rs. 1,000 p.m.; Licence and taxes Rs. 1,000 every six months; Realisation from sales proceeds of old tyres and tubes @ Rs. 3,200 for every six months; 900 passengers were carried over 1,600 miles during the year.

[Adapted—I.C.W.A.]

Ans. : Re. 0.1249

5. From the following data, calculate cost per kilometre of a vehicle :

	Rs.
Value of vehicle	15,000
Road licence fee per year	500
Insurance charges per year	100
Garage rent per year	600
Driver's wages per month	200
Cost of petrol per litre	3.60

   Kilometre per litre 8

   Proportionate charge for tyre and maintenance per km. Re. 0.20.

   Extimated life 1,50,000 kms.

   Extimated annual kilometreage 6,000.

   Ignore interest on capital.

[B.Com. Mysore]

Ans. : Cost per km. Rs. 1:35]

6. The Road Transport Co., which keeps a fleet of lorries, shows the following information :

Kilometres run for April, 1994	30,000
Wages for April	Rs. 2,000
Petrol, oil ect. for April	Rs. 4,000
Original cost of vehicles	Rs. 1,00,000

   Depreciation to be allowed @ 25% per annum on original cost.

Repairs for the month of April	6,000
Garage rent etc. for April	1,000
Licence, Insurance etc. for the year	6,000

   Prepare a statement for April, 1994 showing the cost per running km.

[M.Com. Madras Adapted]

Ans. : Cost per km. Re. 0.52

7. The following cost data pertaining to the year 1994-95 are collected from the books of ABC Power Co. Ltd.

Prepare a cost sheet showing the cost of generation of power per unit of Kwh.

Total units generated	15,00,000
	Rs.
Operating labour	16,500
Plant supervision	5,250
Lubricants and supplies	10,500
Repairs and maintenance	21,000
Administration overheads	9,000
Capital cost	1,50,000

Coal consumed per Kwh, for the year is 1.5 lb. and the cost of coal delivered to the power station is Rs. 33.06 per tonne. Depreciation rate chargeable is 4% per annum and interest on capital is to be taken at 7%.

[C.A. Inter]

Ans. : Cost per Kwh. = Paise 7.5

[Hint. : There are 2,205 lbs. in one tonne. Cost of coal is computed as follows :

*Cost of one tonne (2,205 lb.) = Rs. 33.06

Cost of 1.5 lb. (per Kwh.) = $\frac{33.06}{22.05} \times 1.5 =$ Paise 2.25

Total for 15,00,000 Kwh. = 15,00,000 × Paise 2.2 = Rs. 33,750]

INTEGRATION OF ACCOUNTS 9

Learning Objectives :

1. *Integrated Account—definition*
2. *Features of Integrated Accounting*
3. *Advantages of integrated Accounting*
4. *Important Journal Entries*
5. *Worked-out problems*
6. *Need for Reconciliation between Costing Proift and Financial proift*
7. *Reasons for disagreement*
8. *Method of preparation of Reconciliation Statement*
9. *Worked-out problems*
10. *Assignment.*

INTEGRATION OF ACCOUNTS 9

In cost accounting the cost books are basically maintained under the following two systems :

1. Integral or integrated cost accounting
2. Non-integrated cost accounting

Integral Accounts

A single book-keeping system which contains both financial and cost accounts is termed an integral accounting system. This system contains two types of account – (i) Simple accounts and (ii) Control accounts. The former represent assets, liabilities etc. ; while each of the latter forms a connecting link with a subsidiary ledger in which the detailed composition of the control account balance is recorded. In fact, this system tends to merge cost and financial accounting to form one inseperable accounting function and precisely, integrated accounting is a system of recording both financial and costing transactions in one integrated set of books.

Features of integrated acounting system

The essential features of integrated system are as follows –

(i) The integrated system records financial items not required for cost accounting. For examples – Accounts for capital expenditure, Sundry Debtors and Creditors, share capital, cash and bank balances, prepaid expenses and accruals are opened.

(ii) Store transactions are recorded in the Stores Control Account. For store purchased Store Control Account is debited and credited to Cash/Bank/Creditors Account.

(iii) Payment of wages is debited to Wage Control Account. Similarly, for overhead expenses incurred Overhead Control Account is debited and Sundry Creditors/ Cash/Bank Account is credited.

(iv) At the end of the accounting period, the total of Wages Control A/c, Stores Control A/c and Overhead Control A/c is transferred to Work-in-Progress Account. The entry is :

Work-in-Progress Control A/c Dr.
To Stores Control A/c
To Wages Control A/c
To Overhead Control A/c

(v) All accruals are debited and advance payments are credited. While capital expenditure is separated in the process of Cost analysis and debited to Capital Assets Account.

Advantages

The following are the advantages of integral accounting system –

1. Duplication in accounting and analysis can easily be avoided.
2. Since the need for maintaining of separate sets of financial and Cost accounts ledgers is absent, preparation of reconciliation statemet is not required.
3. There is an automatic check on the correctness of the cost data, which creates confidence in the management.
4. Centralisation of accounting function leads to economy.
5. As Cost accounts are posted immediately from the original entries, there is no delay in obtaining cost data.

Important jounral entries for posting into Control Account

Transactions	*Integrated Entry*	
1. Materials purchased		
(a) For Stock	Store Ledger Control A/c	Dr.
	To Financial Ledger Control A/c	
(b) For special jobs	Work-in-Progress Control A/c	Dr.
	To Financial Ledger Control A/c	
2. Materials Issued		
(a) Direct materials	Work-in-Progress Control A/c	Dr.
	To Stores Ledger Control A/c	
(b) Indirect materials	Overhead Control A/c	Dr.
	To Store Ledger Control A/c	
(c) Return to Supplier	Financial Ledger Control A/c	Dr.
	To Store Ledger Control A/c	
3. Materials returned from Shop floor	Stores Ledger Control A/c	Dr.
	To Work-in-Progress control A/c	
4. Labour		
(a) Wages and Salaries paid	Wage Control A/c	Dr.
	To Financial Ledger Control A/c	
(b) Allocation for direct labour	Work-in-Progress Control A/c	Dr.
	To Wage Control A/c	
(c) For indirect labour	Overhead Control A/c	Dr.
	To Wage Control A/c	
5. Direct Expenses	Work-in-Progress Control A/c	Dr.
	To Financial Ledger Control A/c	
6. Overheads		
(a) Incurred and Accrued	Overhead Control A/c	Dr.
	To Financial Ledger Control A/c	
(b) Recovered	Work-in-Progress Control A/c	Dr.
	(for works and administration)	
	Cost of Sales A;c	Dr.
	To Overhead Control A/c	
(c) Work-in-Progress	Work-in-Progress A/c	Dr.
	To Respective Overheads Suspense A/c	
7. Finished Stock		
(a) Produced	Stock Ledger Control A/c	Dr.
	To Work-in-Progress A/c	
(b) Stock Sold	(i) Cost to Sales A/c	Dr.
	To Stock Ledger Control A/c	
	(ii) Financial Ledger Control A/c	Dr.
	To Cost of Sales A/c	
8. Under-absorption of Overheads	Costing Profit & Loss A/c	Dr.
	To Respective Overhead Control A/c	
9. Over-absorption of Overheads	Respective Overhead Cofntrol A/c	Dr.
	To Costing Profit & Loss A/c	
10. Transfer of Net Profit	Costing Profit & Loss A/c	Dr.
	To Financial Ledger Control A/c	

SCHEME OF ENTRIES

For the sake of easy understanding entries to be passed under Integral and Non-integral accounting systems are given below :

Items	Financial Books	Cost Books	Integrated Books
(a) Purchase of Materials	Purchase Account Dr. To Bought Ledger Control (creditors) A/c	Stores Ledger Control A/c Dr. To General Ledger Adj. A/c (creditors) A/c	Stores Ledger Control A/c Dr. To Bought Ledger Control or (creditors) A/c
(b) Issue of Materials for Production	No Entry	Work-in-progress Ledger Control A/c Dr. To Stores Ledger Control A/c	Work-in-progress Ledger Control A/c Dr. To Stores Ledger Control A/c
(c) Payment of Wages	Wages A/c Dr. To Cash To Insurance To Tax	Wages A/c or (Wages Control A/c) Dr. To General Ledger Adjst. A/c	Wages A/c or (Wages Control A/c) Dr. To Cash
(d) Analysis and Distribution of Wages	No Entry	Work-in-progress A/c Dr. (for direct labour) Factory Overhead Control A/c Dr. (for indirect labour A/c) Adm. Overhead Control A/c Dr. (for office indirect labour) Selling & Distribution Overhead Control A/c Dr. (for selling and distribution indirect labour) To Wages Control A/c	Work-in-progress Control A/c Dr. Factory Overhead Control A/c Dr. Administration Control A/c Dr. Selling and Distribution Overhead Control A/c Dr. To Wages Control A/c

Items	Financial Books	Cost Books	Integrated Books
(e) Payment for Indirect expenses e.g., Power and repairs etc.	Expenses A/c Dr. To Cash To Creditors	Factory/Adm./Selling and Dis. Control A/c Dr. To General Ledger Adj. A/c	Factory/Office/Selling and Distribution Overheads Control A/c To Cash To Creditors
(f) Factory Overheads at pre-determined rates	No Entry	Work-in-progress Control A/c Dr. To Factory Overhead Control A/c	Work-in-progress Control A/c Dr. To Factory Overhead Control A/c
(g) Factory Overheads Over-absorbed	No Entry	Factory Overhead Control A/c Dr. To Costing Profit & Loss A/c (or the balance may be carried)	Factory Overhead Control A/c Dr. To Profit & Loss A/c
(h) Job completed	No Entry	Stock Ledger Control A/c To Work-in-progress Ledger Control A/c	Stock Ledger Control A/c To Work-in-progress Ledger Control A/c
(i) Sales	Cash A/c or Sales Ledger Control (or debtors) A/c Dr. To Sales A/c	General Ledger Adj. Dr. To Sales	Sales Ledger Control (Debtors A/c) Dr. To Sales A/c
(j) Rent of Own Premises	No Entry	Works or (Office) Expenses A/c Dr. To Cost Ledger Control A/c	Works or (Office) Expenses A/c Dr. To Rent (Notional) A/c
(k) Interest Paid	Interest A/c Dr. To Cash	No Entry	Interest A/c Dr. To Cash
(l) Abnormal idle time	No Entry	Costing Profit and Loss A/c Dr. To Wages A/c	Costing Profit and Loss A/c Dr. To Wages A/c

WORKED OUT PROBLEMS

Problem 1

The following figures have been extracted from the costing records and financial books of a factory. You are required to pass the necessary entries in the cost journal.

	Rs.
Purchases	3,90,000
Carriage Inward	5,850
Stores issued	3,58,800
Productive wages	3,46,320
Unproductive wages	1,21,680
Work on cost	3,48,400
Materials-used in repairs	3,120
Cost of completed jobs	12,80,630

[Adapted—C.A – Final]

Solution

Cost Journal

	Particulars		*Debit*	*Credit*
			Rs.	Rs.
1.	Stores Ledger Control A/c	Dr.	3,90,000	
	To Cost Ledger Control A/c			3,90,000
	(For purchase of materials)			
2.	Stores Ledger Control A/c	Dr.	5,850	
	To Cost Ledger Control A/c			5,850
	(Being Carriage Inward treated as part of material cost)			
3.	Work-in-Progress Ledger Control A/c	Dr.	3,58,800	
	To Stores Ledger Control A/c			3,58,800
	(Stores issued to production)			
4.	Wages Control A/c	Dr.	3,46,320	
	To Cost Ledger Control A/c			3,46,320
	(Being direct wages paid)			
5.	Factory Overhead Control A/c	Dr.	1,21,680	
	To Cost Ledger Control A/c			1,21,680
	(Being indirect wages incurred)			
6.	Factory Overhead Control A/c	Dr.	3,48,680	
	To Cost Ledger Control A/c			3,48,,680
	(Being works overhead incurred)			
7.	Factory Overhead Control A/c	Dr.	3,120	
	To Store Ledger Control A/c			3,120
	(Being materials used in repairs)			
8.	Finished Stock Ledger Control A/c	Dr.	12,80,630	
	To Work-in-progress Ledger Control A/c			12,80,630

Problem 2

A manufacturing company has approximately 600 weekly paid direct and indirect production workers. It incurred the following costs and deductions relating to the payroll for the week ended May 2.

	Rs.	Rs.
Gross wages		1,80,460
Deductions :		
Employees' national insurance	14,120	
Employees' pension fund contributions	7,200	
Income Tax	27,800	
Court order retentions	1,840	
Trade union subscriptions	1,200	
Private health care contributions	6,000	
Total deductions		58,160
Net wages paid		1,22,300

The employer's national insurance contribution for the week was Rs. 18,770.

From the wages analysis the following information was extracted :

	Direct workers	*Indirect workers*
	Rs.	Rs.
Paid for ordinary time	77,460	38,400
Overtime wages at normal hourly rates	16,800	10,200
Overtime permium (treat as overhead)	5,600	3,400
Shift premiums/allowances	8,500	4,500
Capital work-in-progress expenditure	—	2,300*
Statutory sick pay	5,700	3,300
Paid for idle time	4,300	—
	1,18,360	62,100

*Work done by building maintenance workers concerning floor area for a warehouse extension.

You are required to show journal entries to indicate clearly how each item should be posted into the accounts

(i) from the payroll, and

(ii) from the Wages Control Account to other accounts, based on the wages analysis.

[C.I.M.A. London, May 1992]

Note : Narrations for the journal entries are not required.

Solution

		Rs.	Rs.
(i) Wages Control A/c	Dr.	1,22,300	
To Bank A/c			1,22,300
Wages Control A/c	Dr.	58,160	
To Employees National Insurance			14,120
To Employees Pension Fund Contributions		7,200	
To Income Tax			27,800
To Court Order Retentions			1,840
To Trade Union Subscription			1,200
To Private Health			6,000
		1,80,460	1,80,460
Production Overhead Control A/c	Dr.	18,770	
To Employer's National Insurance			18,770
(ii) Work-in-progress Control Dr. (Wages)		77,460	
(Overtime Wages – Direct)		16,800	
Production Overhead Control—(O. T. Premium)9,000			
—(Shift Premium)13,000			
—(Indirect Wages)38,400			
O. T. Wages (indirect)			10,200
Assets in course of construction			2,300
Statutory Sick Pay			9,000
Idle time			4,300
To Wages Control A/c			1,80,460
		1,80,460	1,80,460

COST ACCOUNTS

Problem 3

Dutta Enterprises operates an integral system of accounting. You are required to pass the Journal Entries for the following transactions that took place for the year ended 30. 6. 1990.

(Narrations are not required)	Rs.
Raw Materials Purchased (50% on credit)	6,00,000
Materials Issued to production	4,00,000
Wages Paid (50% Direct)	2,00,000
Wages charged to production	1,00,000
Factory Overheads Incurred	80,000
Factory Overheads charged to production	1,00,000
Selling and Distribution Overheads incurred	40,000
Finished Goods at Cost	5,00,000
Sales (50% credit)	7,50,000
Closing Stock	Nil
Receipts from Debtors	2,00,000
Payments to Creditors	2,00,000

[C.A. Inter November, 1990]

Solution

Journal Entries-Integral System of Accounting

Stores Ledger Control A/c	Dr.	6,00,000	
To Sundry Creditors A/c			3,00,000
To Cash or Bank A/c			3,00,000
Work-in-progress Control A/c		4,00,000	
To Stores Ledger Control A/c			4,00,000
Wages Control A/c	Dr.	2,00,000	
To Cash			2,00,000
Work-in-Progress Control A/c	Dr.	1,00,000	
Factory Overhead Control A/c	Dr.	1,00,000	
To Wages Control A/c			2,00,000
Factory Overhead Control A/c	Dr.	80,000	
To Cash or Bank A/c			80,000
Work-in-Progress Control A/c	Dr.	1,00,000	
To Factory Overhead Control A/c			1,00,000
Selling and Distribution Overhead Control A/c	Dr.	40,000	
To Cash or Bank A/c			40,000
Finished Goods Ledger Control A/c	Dr.	5,00,000	
To Work-in-Progress Control A/c			5,00,000
Cost of Sales A/c	Dr.	5,40,000	
To Finished Goods Ledger Control A/c			5,00,000
To S & D Overhead Control A/c			40,000
Sundry Debtors A/c	Dr.	3,75,000	
Cash or Bank A/c	Dr.	3,75,000	
To Sales A/c			7,50,000
Cash or Bank A/c	Dr.	2,00,000	
To Sundry Debtors A/c			2,00,000
Sundry Creditors A/c	Dr.	2,00,000	
To Cash or Bank A/c			2,00,000

Problem 4

In the absence of the Chief Accountant, you have been asked to prepare a month's cost accounts for a company which operates a batch costing system fully integrated with the financial accounts. The following relevant information is provided to you:

	Rs.
Balance at the beginning of the month :	
Stores Ledger Control Account	25,000
Work in Progress Control Account	20,000
Finished Goods Control Account	35,000
Prepaid Production Overheads brought forward from previous month	3,000
Transactions during the month :	
Materials Purchased	75,000

	Rs.	Rs.
Materials Issued :		
To Production	30,000	
To Factory Maintenance	4,000	34,000
Materials transferred between batches		5,000
Total wages paid :		
To Direct workers	25,500	
To Indirect workers	~~5,000~~	30,000
Direct wages charged to batches		20,000
Recorded non-productive time of direct workers		5,000
Selling and Distribution Overheads Incurred		6,000
Other Production Overheads Incurred		12,000
Sales		1,00,000
Cost of Finished Goods Sold		80,000
Cost of Goods completed and transferred into finished goods during the month		65,000
Physical value of work in progress at the end of the month		40,000

The production overhead absorption rate is 150% of direct wages charged to work-in-progress.

Required :

Prepare the following accounts for the month :

(a) Stores Ledger Control Account.

(b) Work in Progress Control Account.

(c) Finished Goods Control Account.

(d) Production Overhead Control Account.

(e) Profit and Loss Account.

[Adapted—C.A. (Inter) May 1988]

Solution

(a) **Stores Ledger Control Account**

		Rs.			Rs.
To	Balance b/d	25,000	By	Work in progress Control A/c	30,000
"	Creditors (or bank)	75,000	"	Production Overhead Control A/c	4,000
			"	Balance c/d	66,000
		1,00,000			1,00,000

(b) **Work-in-Progress Control Account**

		Rs.			Rs.
To	Balance b/d	20,000	By	Finished Goods Control A/c	65,000
"	Store Ledger Control A/c	30,000	"	Balance c/d (Physical value)	40,000
"	Wages Control A/c	20,000			
"	Production Overhead Control A/c (150% of direct wages)	30,000			
"	Profit & Loss A/c (Stock Gains)	5,000			
		1,05,000			1,05,000

(c) **Finished Goods Control Account**

		Rs.			Rs.
To	Balance b/d	35,000	By	Cost of Goods A/c Or, Profit & Loss A/c	80,000
"	Work in progress Control A/c	65,000	"	Balance c/d	20,000
		1,00,000			1,00,000

(d) **Production Overhead Control Account**

			Rs.			Rs.
To	Balance b/d (Prepaid amount)		3,000	By	Work in progress Control A/c (150% of direct wages)	30,000
"	Stores Ledger Control A/c		4,000			
"	Wages Control A/c					
	Direct Workers	5,000				
	Indirect Workers	5,000	10,000			
"	Bank		12,000			
"	Profit & Loss A/c* (Over absorption- Balancing figure)		1,000			
			30,000			30,000

* Alternatively the over-absorbed overhead may be carried forward.

(e) **Profit & Loss Account**

		Rs.			Rs.
To	Finished goods Control A'c Or Cost of goods sold A/c	80,000	By	Sales A/c	1,00,000
"	Selling & Distribution Overheads A/c	6,000	"	Production Overhead Control A/c	1,000
"	Balance c/d	20,000	"	Work-in-progress Control A/c (Stock gain)	5,000
		1,06,000			1,06,000

Notes : 1. Materials transferred between batches will not affect the Control Accounts.
2. Non-production time of direct workers is a production overhead and therefore will not be charged to work in progress control A/c
3. Production overheads absorbed in work in progress Control A/c will be equal to Rs. 30,000 (150% of Rs. 20,000)
4. In the work in progress control A/c the excess physical value of stock is taken resulting in stock gain. Stock gain is transferred to Profit & Loss A/c.

INTEGRATED ACCOUNTS

Problem 5

Messrs. Essbee Ltd. maintain Integrated Account of Cost and Financial Accounts. From the following details write control accounts in the general ledger of the factory and prepare a trial balance :

	Rs.
Share Capital	3,00,000
Reserve	2,00,000
Sundry Creditors	5,00,000
Plant and Machinery	5,75,000
Sundry Debtors	2,00,000
Closing Stock	1,50,000
Bank and Cash balance	75,000
Transactions during the year were as follows :	
Stores purchased	10,00,000
Stores issued to production	10,50,000
Stores in hand	95,000
Direct wages incurred	6,50,000
Direct wages charged to production	6,00,000
Manufacturing expenses incurred	3,00,000
Manufacturing expenses charged to production	2,75,000
Selling and distribution expenses	1,00,000
Finished Stock production (at cost)	18,00,000
Sales at selling price	22,00,000
Closing Stock	95,000
Payment to Creditors	11,00,000
Receipt from Debtors	21,00,000

[I.C.W.A. Inter, June 1985]

Solution

Share Capital Account

	Rs.		Rs.
		By Balance b/d	3,00,000

Reserve Account

	Rs.		Rs.
To Balance b/d	5,15,000	By Balance b/d	2,00,000
		" Costing P & L A/c	3,15,000
	5,15,000		5,15,000
		Balance b/d	5,15,000

Sundry Creditors Account

	Rs.		Rs.
To Bank A/c	11,00,000	By Balance b/d	5,00,000
To Balance c/d	4,00,000	" Stock Control A/c	10,00,000
	15,00,000		15,00,000
		" Balance b/d	4,00,000

Plant & Machinery Account

	Rs.		Rs.
To Balance b/d	5,75,000		

Sundry Debtors Account

	Rs.		Rs.
To Balance b/d	2,00,000	By Bank A/c	21,00,000
" Sales	22,00,000	" Balance c/d	3,00,000
	24,00,000		24,00,000
To Balance b/d	3,00,000		

Stock Control Account

	Rs.		Rs.
To Balance b/f	1,50,000	By W.I.P. A/c	10,50,000
" Sundry Creditors	10,00,000	" Mfg. O. H. Control A/c	5,000
		" Balance c/d	95,000
	11,50,000		11,50,000
To Balance b/d	95,000		

* It is presumed that difference was issued for indirect materials.

Bank Account

	Rs.		Rs.
To Balance b/f	75,000	By Wages Control A/c	6,50,000
" Sundry Debtors	21,00,000	" Production O.H. Control A/c	3,00,000
		" Selling Expenses	1,00,000
		" Sundry Creditors	11,00,000
		" Balance c/f	25,000
	21,75,000		21,75,000
To Balance b/d	25,000		

W.I.P. Account

		Rs.			Rs.
To	Stores Control A/c	10,50,000	By	Finished Stock A/c	18,00,000
"	Wages Control A/c	6,00,000	"	Balance c/d	1,95,000
"	P.O.H. Control A/c	2,75,000			
		19,25,000			19,25,000
To	Balance b/f	1,25,000			

Wages Control Account

		Rs.			Rs.
To	Bank A/c	6,50,000	By	W.I.P. A/c	6,00,000
			"	P.O.H. A/c	50,000
		6,50,000			6,50,000

Production Overhead Control Account

		Rs.			Rs.
To	Stores Control A/c	5,000	By	W.I.P. A/c	2,75,000
"	Bank A/c	3,00,000	"	P & L A/c	80,000
"	Wages Control A/c	50,000		(under-absorption)	
		3,55,000			3,55,000

Selling & Distribution Overhead Control Account

		Rs.			Rs.
To	Bank A/c	1,00,000	By	Cost of Sales	1,00,000
	Cost of Sales A/c				
"	Finished Stock Control A/c	17,05,000	"	Costing P & L A/c	18,05,000
"	S & D Ovh. Control A/c	1,00,000			
		18,05,000			18,05,000

Finished Stock Control Account

		Rs.			Rs.
To	W.I.P. A/c	18,00,000	By	Cost of Sales A/c	17,05,000
			"	Balance c/d	95,000
		18,00,000			18,00,000

Sales Account

		Rs.			Rs.
To	Costing P & L A/c	22,00,000	By	S Debtors	22,00,000

Costing P & L Account

		Rs.		Rs.
To	Cost of Sales A/c	18,05,000	By Sales A/c	22,00,000
To	Prod. Ohd. Control A/c (under-absorption)	80,000		
To	Net Profit (transferred to Reserve)	3,15,000		
		22,00,000		22,00,000

Trial Balance

	Debit	Credit
	Rs.	Rs.
Share Capital		3,00,000
Reserve		5,15,000
Sundry Creditors		4,00,000
Plant and Machinery	5,75,000	
Sundry Debtors	3,00,000	
Stock-in-hand	95,000	
Stock of Finished Goods	95,000	
Bank	25,000	
Work-in-Progress A/c	1,25,000	
	12,15,000	12,15,000

RECONCILIATION OF COST AND FINANCIAL ACCOUNTS

Introduction

Cost accounts are maintained independent of financial accounts. The two accounts have a different order of recording revenue and expenses. In cost accounting expanses are analysed and recorded in objective form while in financial accounting expenses are recorded in the books of accounts in subjective form. As a result, there occurs a diference between profit shown by Cost accounting and that of financial accounting. Therefore, it becomes imperative to reconcile two accounts which enables to test the reliability of cost accounts.

Need for Reconciliation

In a manufacturing concern both financial and cost accounting are maintained. Naturally, two sets of accounts disclose profit which will not agree with each other. Profit disclosed by the financial accounting does not agree with the profit disclosed by the cost accounting But this does not happen when a manufacturing company uses an integrated accounting system i.e. no separate cost and financial accounts are maintained. So, when cost and financial accounts are maintained separately and independently of each other, profit disclosed by one system tends to differ from that of the other accounting systems. This difference in profit creates problems and the need of reconciling the accounting systems arises to arrive at one profit figure.

Reasons for Disagreement

Disagreement between Cost and Financial accounts generally arises due to the following factors :

1. Items that are included only in financial accounts

The following items of purely financial nature are included in financial accounts but not in cost accounts :

(i) Interest received on bank deposits
(ii) Profit on sale of assets
(iii) Rents receivable
(iv) Interest and dividend on investments
(v) Loss on sale of Assets
(vi) Loss on sale of investment
(vii) Interest paid on Bank Loan, Debentures
(viii) Damages payable
(ix) Payment of income-tax
(x) Payment of dividend
(xi) Transfer to Reserves
(xii) Creation of provisions
(xiii) Donations
(xiv) Writing off fictitious Assets like Preliminary expenes, Discount on issue of shares, debentures
(xiv) Writing of intangible fixed assets like Goodwill, Patent Rights etc.

2. Under or over-absorption of overhead expenses

In cost accounts overheads are absorbed at predetermined rates which are based on past data. On the other hand, in financial accounts the actual amount of expense incurred is only considered. Hence difference arises.

3. Adoption of different bases for stock valuation

In financial accounts stocks are valued either at cost or at market value whichever is less. But in cost accounts stock of materials are issued to production departments at cost by using FIFO, LIFO, Simple Average, Weighted Average method. This leads to a difference.

4. Bases of Depreciation

The methods of charging depreciation and the rates may be different which surely leads to difference.

Method of preparation of Reconciliation Statement

Step I	Start with the profits as per Cost Accounts	x x x
Step II	*Add* :	
	(i) Items of income included in financial accounts but not in cost accounts (profit increased in financial accounts)	x x x
	(ii) Item of expenditure included in cost accounts but not in financial accounts (Profit in financial accounts increased).	xx x
	(iii) Over absorption of overheads in cost accounts (Profit increases)	
	(iv) Amounts by which items of income have been shown in excess in financial accounts as compared to corresponding entries in cost accounts.	x x x
	(v) Amounts by which items of expenditure have been shown in excess in cost accounts as compared to the corresponding entries in financial accounts	x x x
	(vi) Over valuation of closing stock in financial accounts	x x x
	(vii) Under valuation of closing stock in financial accounts	x x x
		x x x

Step III	*Deduct*		
(i)	Items of income included in cost accounts but not included in financial accounts	x x x	
(ii)	Items of expenditure included in financial accounts but not in cost accounts	x x x	
(iii)	Under-absorption of overheads in cost accounts	x x x	
(iv)	The amount by which the closing stock of inventory is under valued in financial accounts	x x x	
(v)	The amount by which the items of expenditure have been shown in excess in financial accounts over the corresponding items of expenditure in cost accounts	x x x	
(vi)	The amount by which the opening stock of inventory is under valued in cost accounts	x x x	
(vii)	Amount by which the items of expenditure have been shown in excess in financial accounts over the corresponding items in financial accounts	x x x	
			x x x
	Profit as per Financial Accounts		x x x

WORKED OUT PROBLEMS

Problem 6

From the following figures prepare a Reconciliation Statement

	Rs.
Net profit as per financial records	1,28,755
Net profit as per costing records	1,72,400
Works Overheads under recovered in cost	3,120
Administration overhead recovered in excess	1,700
Depreciation charged in financial records	11,200
Depreciation recovered in costing	12,500
Interest received but not included in costing	8,000
Obsolescence loss charged in financial records	5,700
Income-tax provided in financial books	40,300
Bank interest credited in financial books	750
Store adjustments (credit in financial books)	475
Depreciation of stock charged in financial books	6,750

[Adapted—B.Com. Madras and Andhra]

Soluiton

Reconciliation Statement

		Rs.	Rs.
	Net Profit as per Cost records		1,72,400
Add :	Excess Depreciation charged (Rs. 12,500 – Rs. 11,200)	1,300	
	Excess Administration Overhead	1,700	
	Interest received not included in cost	8,000	
	Bank interest received not included in cost	750	
	Store adjustmnt (credit in financial records)	475	12,225
			1,84,625

Contd.

Less :	Works Overhead under recovered	3,120	
	Obsolescence loss not charged to cost accounts	5,700	
	Income-tax not provided in cost accounts	40,300	
	Depreciation in stock value	6,750	55,870
	Net profit as per financial records		1,28,755

Problem 7

From the following figures prepare a statement reconciling the profits as per the cost accounts and the profits as per the financial accounts.

	Rs.
Net profit as per the financial accounts	1,28,755
Net profit as per the cost accounts	1,72,400
Works overheads underrecovered	3,120
Administrative Overheads Over-recovered	1,700
Depreciation charged in the financial accounts	11,200
Depreciation charged in the cost accounts	12,500
Interest received but not included in the cost accounts	8,000
Loss due to obsolesence charged in the financial accounts	5,700
Income Tax provided in financial accounts	40,300
Stores adjustments credited in the financial accounts	475
Depreciation of Stock charged in the financial accounts	6,750
Bank interest credited in financial accounts	750

[Adapted—I.C.W.A (Inter) June, 1991]

Solution

Reconciliation Statement

			Rs.	Rs.
Net profit as per the cost Accounts				1,72,400
Add :	(i)	Administrative Overheads over-recovered	1,700	
	(ii)	Excess depreciation charged in cost accounts	1,300	
	(iii)	Interest received but not included in the cost accounts	8,000	
	(iv)	Stores adjustment credited in the financial accounts	475	
	(v)	Bank interest credited in the financial accounts	750	
				12,225
				1,84,625
Less :	(vi)	Works overheads under-recovered	3,120	
	(vii)	Loss due to obsolescence charged in financial accounts	5,700	
	(viii)	Income Tax provided in financial accounts	40,300	
	(ix)	Depreciation of stock charged in financial accounts	6,750	
				55,870
		Net profit as per financial Accounts		1,28,755

Problem 8

The Trading and Profit and Loss Account of M/s XYZ Co. Ltd. was as follows as at 31.3.1992

	Rs.		Rs.
To Purchase	21,000	By Sales	69,000
" Direct wages	10,000	" Stock of Materials	1,000
" Menufacturing Expenses	12,000	" Profit on Sale of Assets	2,500
" Selling Expenses	6,000		
" Distribution Expenses	2,000		
" Administration Expenses	5,000		
" Depreciation	1,000		
" Net Profit	15,500		
	72,500		72,500

Additional information – Profit as per Cost Accounts was Rs. 16,900

The following information was available in the Cost Accounts.

(i) Closing inventory of materials – Rs. 2,000

(ii) Manufacturing overhead was applied @ 15% on direct wages

(iii) Selling distribution and administrative expenses were applied @ 10% on sales

(iv) Depreciation charged Rs. 1,200

You are required to reconcile the financial accounts profit with that of Cost Accounts.

[Adapted—Punjab B.Com.]

Solution

Reconciliation Statement

			Rs.	Rs.
Profit as per Financial Accounts				15,500
Add :	(i) Difference in the value of Closing Stock (2,000 – 1,000)	1,000		
	(ii) Under absorption of Selling, distribution and administrative expenses			
	Amount charged	Rs. 13,000		
Less :	10% of Rs. 69,000	6,900	6,100	7,100
				22,600
Less :	(iii) Overabsorption of manufacturing expenses in Cost Accounts			
	Amount charged 150% of 10,000 =	Rs. 15,000		
Less :	Amount charged in financial accounts	Rs. 12,000	3,000	
	(iv) Depreciation overcharged in Cost Accounts		200	
	(v) Profit on sale of assets not considered in Cost Accounts		2,500	5,700
	Profit as per Cost Accounts			16,900

Problem 9

The following figures are available from the financial records of Nutan Manufacturing Co. Ltd. for the year ended 31. 3. 1992

		Rs.
Sales (20,000 units)		25,00,000
Materials		10,00,000
Wages		5,00,000
Factory Overheads		4,50,000
Office and Administrative Overheads		2,60,000
Selling and distribution Overheads		1,80,000
Finished goods (1,230 units)		1,50,000
Work-in-Progress :		
Materials	Rs. 30,000	
Labour	Rs. 20,000	
Factory Overheads	Rs. 20,000	70,000
Goodwill written off		2,00,000
Interest on Capital		20,000

In the costing records factory overhead is charged at 100% of wages; administrative overhead at 10% of factory cost and selling and distribution overhead @ Rs. 10 per unit sold.

Prepare a statement reconciling the profit as per cost records with the profit as per financial records.

[Bombay University M.Com.]

Solution

Step I. Prepare the Profit & Loss Account in Financial Accounts to find out the profit –

Profit & Loss Account
for the year ended 31.3.1992

Dr. *Cr.*

	Rs.		Rs.
To Materials	10,00,000	By Sales (20,000 units)	25,00,000
" Wages	5,00,000	" Stock :	
" Factory Overhead	4,50,000	Finished goods	
" Office & Administrative		(1.230 units)	1,50,000
Overhead	2,60,000	Work-in-Progress	70,000
" Selling & Distribution			
Overhead	1,80,000		
" Goodwill – written off	2,00,000		
" Interest on Capital	20,000		
" Net Profit			
(Balancing figure)	1.10,000		
	27,20,000		27,20,000

Step II. Prepare Cost Sheet to ascertain the profit as per Cost Accounts

COST SHEET

for the year ended 31st March 1992

		Rs.	Rs.
	Materials		10,00,000
	Wages		5,00,000
	PRIME COST		15,00,000
Add :	Factory Overhead @ 100% of Wages	100% of 5,00,000	5,00,000
			20,00,000
Less :	Closing work-in-progress		70,000
	FACTORY COST		19,30,000
Add :	Office and Administrative overheads (@ 10% of Factory Cost i.e. 10% of Rs. 19,30,000)		1,93,000
	COST OF PRODUCTION (of 21,230 units)		21,23,000
Less :	Closing Stock of finished goods (1,230 units) = $\frac{21,23,000}{21,230} \times 1,230$		1,23,000
	COST OF GOODS SOLD		20,00,000
Add :	Selling and Distribution overhead @ Rs. 10 per unit sold	20,000 × 10	2,00,000
	COST OF SALE		22,00,000
	PROFIT		3,00,000
	SALES (20,000 @ Rs. 125 per unit)		25,00,000

Step III. Prepare Reconciliation Statement

Reconciliation Statement

			Rs.	Rs.
		Profit as per Cost Accounts		3,00,000
Add :	(i)	Factory Overhead over-absorbed in Cost Accounts (Rs. 5,00,000 – Rs. 4,50,000)	50,000	
	(ii)	Selling and Distribution Overheads in Cost Accounts (Rs. 2,00,000 – Rs. 1,80,000)	20,000	
	(iii)	Difference in valuation of closing stock of Finished Goods (Rs. 1,50,000 – Rs. 1,23,000)	27,000	97,000
				3,97,000
Less :	(iv)	Office and Administrative Overheads under-absorbed in Cost Accounts (Rs. 2,60,000 – Rs. 1,93,000)	67,000	
	(v)	Goodwill written off in Financial Accounts but not in Cost Accounts	2,00,000	
	(vi)	Interest on Capital charged to Financial Accounts	20,000	2,87,000
		Profit as per Financial Accounts		1,10,000

Problem 10

A Company's Trading and Profit & Loss Account was as follows :

Dr. *Cr.*

		Rs.			Rs.
To	Purchases	25,210	By	Sales 50,000 units	
"	Wages	10,500	"	@ Rs. 1.50 each	75,000
"	Works Expenses	12,130	"	Discount Received	260
"	Selling Expenses	7,100	"	Profit on sale of land	2,340
"	Administration Expenses	5,340	"	Closing Stock	4,080
"	Depreciation	1,100			
"	Net Profit	20,300			
		81,680			81,680

The Profit as per cost accounts was only Rs. 19,770. Reconcile the finanial and cost profits using the following information –

(i) Cost accounts value of closing stock was Rs. 4,280.

(ii) The work expenses in the accounts were taken as 100% of direct wages.

(iii) Selling and administration expenses were charged in the cost accounts at 10% of sales and Re. 0.10 per unit respectively.

(iv) Depreciation in the cost accounts was Rs. 800.

[Adapted—C.A. (Inter)]

Solution

Reconciliation Statement

			Rs.	Rs.
Profit as per Cost Accounts				19,770
Add :	(i)	Profit on sale of land credited to Profit & Loss A/c but not in Cost Accounts (Profit increased)	2,340	
	(ii)	Over absorption of Selling Expenses in Cost Accounts (Profit increased in Financial Accounts) – (Rs. 7,500 – Rs. 7,100)	400	
	(iii)	Discount received credited to Profit & Loss A/c of Financial Accounts but not in Cost Accounts	260	3,000
				22,770
Less :	(iv)	Over-valuation of closing stock in Cost Accounts (Rs. 4,280 – Rs. 4,080)	200	
	(v)	Under-absorption of works Expenses (Rs. 12,130 – Rs. 10,500)	1,630	
	(vii)	Depreciation charged less in Cost Accounts (Rs. 1,100 – Rs. 800)	300	2,470
		Profit as per Financial Accounts		20,300

Problem 11

The following figures have been extracted from the Financial Accounts of a Manufacturing Firm for the first year of its operation :

	Rs.
Direct Materials consumption	50,00,000
Direct wages	30,00,000
Factory Overheads	16,00,000
Administrative Overheads	7,00,000
Selling and Distribution Overheads	9,60,000
Bad Debts	80,000
Preliminary Expenses written off	40,000
Legal Charges	10,000
Dividend received	1,00,000
Interest received on deposits	20,000
Sales (1,20,000 units)	1,20,00,000
Closing Stocks (4,000 units)	3,20,000
Work-in-Progress	2,40,000

The Cost Accounts for the same period reveal that the direct material consumption was Rs. 56,00,000. Factory Overhead is recovered at 20% on Prime Cost. Administration overhead is recovered at Rs. 6 per unit of production. Selling and distribution overheads are recovered at Rs. 8 per unit sold.

Prepare the Profit and Loss Accounts both as per Financial records and as per cost records. Reconcile the profits as per the two records.

[Adapted—C. A. (Inter) May, 1990]

Solution

Profit & Loss Account
(as per financial records)

Dr.	Rs.		Rs. Cr.
To Direct Materials	50,00,000	By Sales (1,20,000 units)	1,20,00,000
" Direct Wages	30,00,000	" Closing Stock	
" Factory Overheads	16,00,000	Work-in-Progress	2,40,000
" Gross Profit	29,60,000	Finished Goods (4,000 units)	3,20,000
	1,25,60,000		1,25,60,000
To Administration Overheads	7,00,000	By Gross Profit	29,60,000
" Selling and Distribution Overheads	9,60,000	" Dividend	1,00,000
" Bad Debts	80,000	" Interest	20,000
" Preliminary Expenses	40,000		
" Legal Charges	10,000		
" Net Profit	12,90,000		
	30,80,000		30,80,000

Statement of Cost & Profit

(As per Cost records)

		Rs.
	Direct Materials consumed	56,00,000
	Direct Wages	30,00,000
	PRIME COST	86,00,000
Add :	Factory Overhead @ 20% of Prime Cost	17,20,000
		1,03,20,000
Less :	Work-in-Progress (closing)	2,40,000
	WORKS COST (1,24,000 units)	1,00,80,000
Add :	Administration Overhead @ Rs. 6.00 per unit	7,44,000
	COST OF PRODUCTION	1,08,24,000
Less :	Finished Goods (4,000 units) @ Rs. 87.29 (Note I)	3,49,160
	COST OF GOODS SOLD	1,04,74,840
Add :	Selling and Distribution Overheads (1,20,000 × Rs. 8)	9,60,000
	COST OF SALES	1,14,34,840
	Net Profit (Balancing figure)	5,65,160
	SALES	1,20,00,000

Reconciliation Statement

			Rs.	Rs.
		Profit as per Cost Records		5,65,160
Add	(i)	Excess Materials consumed in Cost Accounts (Profit increased in financial records)	6,00,000	
	(ii)	Excess Factory Overhead in Cost Accounts	1,20,000	
	(iii)	Excess Administration Overhead	44,000	
	(iv)	Dividend credited to Profit & Loss A/c as per financial records (Profit increased)	1,00,000	
	(v)	Interest credited to financial Profit & Loss A/c	20,000	8,84,000
				14,49,160
Less	(vi)	Bad Debts in financial account but not in Cost Accounts	80,000	
	(vii)	Legal Charges debited to Financial Profit and Loss Accounts (Profit decreased)	10,000	
	(viii)	Preliminary expenses written off in Financial Accounts	40,000	
	(ix)	Overvaluation of Closing Stock in Cost Accounts (Rs. 3,49,160 – Rs. 3,20,000)	29,160	1,59,160
		Profit as per Financial Accounts		12,90,000

Note for the students :

Calculation of value of Closing Finished Goods

Cost of Production of 1,24,000 units is Rs. 1,08,24,000

$$\text{Cost of Production 1 unit} = \frac{1,08,24,000}{1,24,000} = \text{Rs. } 87.29$$

ASSIGNMENT

1 Calculate the amount of profit as per Profit and Loss account on the basis of the following information –

(i) The Profit as per Cost Accounts was Rs. 1,50,300

(ii) Works overhead were under recorded in cost accounts by Rs. 4,000

(iii) Administration expenses were under recorded in Financial Accounts by Rs.1,500

(iv) Depreciation charges were over-recorded in Cost Accounts by Rs. 950

(v) Interest recorded on investments during the year amounting to Rs. 459

(vi) Transfer fees amounting to Rs. 120 were received during the year in connection with registration of transfer of shares.

(vii) Provision for income-tax made in Financial Accounts was Rs. 48,500

[Adapted—Andhra B.Com.}

Ans. : Profit as per Financial Accounts – Rs. 1,00,829.

2 The profit as per Cost Accounts is Rs. 86,250. The following points are found out on comparison between cost accounts and Financial Accounts.

	Cost Account	*Financial Account*
	Rs.	Rs.
Opening Stock – Materials	10,300	10,500
Work-in-Progress	8,000	8,500
Closing Stock – Materials	15,000	14,200
Work-in-Progress	6,000	5,600

Dividend and interest received – Rs. 600

Loss on sale of investments – Rs. 1,000

Rs. 1,500 interest charged but not considered in Financial Accounts.

Goodwill Rs. 2,500 and preliminary expenses Rs. 3,000 have been written off during the year.

Overheads incurred Rs. 40,600 but overheads recovered amounted to Rs. 38,500.

Find out the profit as per Financial Accounts by drawing up Reconciliation Statement.

[Adapted—Punjab Univesity B.Com.]

Ans. : Profit as per Financial Accounts – Rs. 77,850.

3 Prepare the following statements from the particulars given below :

(a) A statement of profit as per Cost Accounts.

(b) Profit as per Financial Accounts.

(c) A Reconciliation Statement.

	Rs.
Raw Materials :	
Opening Stock	4,000
Purchases	24,000
Closing Stock	6,000

Finished goods	
Opening Stock	8,000
Closing Stock	2,000
Wages	10,000
Sales	65,000
Office Expenses	6,100
Works Expenses	7,750
Selling price Cost + 25%	

As per Cost Accounts factory overhead at 25% of Prime Cost and Office Overheads at 75% of Factory overheads.

[Adapted—Mysore Univ. B.Com. 1991]

4 The following figures are available from financial accounts for the year ended 31.3.1992 :

	Rs.
Materials consumed	2,50,000
Direct wages	1,00,000
Factory Overheads	3,80,000
Administration overhead	2,50,000
Selling and distribution overheads	4,80,000
Bad Debt	20,000
Prelimiary expenses written off	10,000
Legal charges	5,000
Dividend received	50,000
Interest on Deposit received	10,000
Sales 1,20,000 units	7,00,000
Closing Stock –	
Finished Stock– 40,000 units	1,20,000
Work-in-progress	80,000

The Cost Accounts reveal –

Direct materials consumption – Rs. 2,80,000

Factory Overhead recovered – at 20% on prime cost.

Administration Overhead at Rs. 3 per unit of production

Selling and distribution overhead at Rs. 4 per unit sold.

Prepare –

(i) Costing profit and loss account

(ii) Financial profit and loss account

(iii) Reconciliation statement

[Adapted—C.A. (Inter)]

Hint : Bad Debt, Preliminary expenses, Legal charges Dividend received and Interest on deposit will not be considered in costing P & L A/c.

Ans. : Loss as per Costing P & L Account Rs. 4,22,000

Loss as per Financial P & L Account Rs. 5,35,000

5. **The net profit of a Manufacturing Co. Ltd. appeared at Rs. 64,377 as per financial records for the year ended 31st December, 1992. The cost books, however, showed a net profit of Rs.86,200 for the same period. A scrutiny of the figures from both the sets of accounts revealed the folowing facts.**

	Rs.
Works Overheads under recovered in Cost	1,560
Administration overheads over recovered in Cost	850
Depreciation charged in financial accounts	5,600
Interest on investments not included in Cost	4,000
Loss due to obsolescence charged in financial accounts	2,850
Income tax provided in financial accounts	20,150
Bank interest in financial books	375
Store adjustments (credit in financial books)	237
Loss due to depreciation in stock values (charged in financial accounts)	3.375

Prepare a statement showing the reconciliation between the figures of net profit as per cost accounts and the figure of the net profit shown in the financial books.

[Andhra B.Com.]

6. A factory is producing two products, Anusha and Bhanusha. Their particulars are as follows :

	Anusha	Bhanusha
	Rs.	Rs.
Materials (per unit)	12.50	7.50
Wages (per unit)	10.00	6.00

Factory expenses are to be calculated at 100% of wages and office expenses at 25% of works Cost. Product Anusha was produced 200 units and Bhanusha 500 units. Price of product Anusha was Rs. 50 per unit and Bhanusha at Rs. 30. Actually factory expenses were Rs. 4,800 and office expenses Rs. 4,200. Reconcile both the profits.

[Mysore University B.Com. Part II 1990]

Anusha :	Financial Statement –	Profit Rs. 1,900
	Costing Profit –	Profit Rs. 1,875
Bhanusha :	Profit as per Financial Statement –	Profit Rs. 2,850.00
	Costing Profit –	Profit Rs. 2,811.50

Trading and Profit and Loss A/c

for the year ended 31.12.1992

Dr. *Cr.*

	Rs.		Rs.
To Opening Stock	1,200	By Sales	52,000
" Purchases	17,200	" Closing Stock	2,100
" Factory Overhead	7,500	" Dividend	600
" Office Overhead	6,000		
" Selling Overhead	200		
" Loss on sale of machinery	300		
" Preliminary expenses	500		
" Net Profit	13,800		
	54,700		54,700

Prepare a Reconciliation Statement after taking into consideration the following information available from cost books.

(a) Opening stock Rs. 1,900; Closing Stock Rs. 1,500.
(b) Factory Overhead charged at 90% of direct wages.
(c) Office Overhead charged Rs. 7,200
(d) Selling Overhead was ignored.
(e) Pofit Rs. 12,000

[C.U. B.Com. (Pass)]

7. The summarised Trading and Profit and Loss Account for the year ended 31.3.1992 :

Trading and Profit and Loss Account

Dr. *Cr.*

		Rs.			Rs.
To	Opening Stock	2,400	By	Sales	
"	Purchases	61,800		(1,300 units @ Rs.100 each)	1,30,000
"	Productive wages	19,000	"	Closing Stock	4,200
"	Factory Overhead	10,100	"	Bank Interest	950
"	Office and Administrative overhead	11,250			
"	Debenture Interest	600			
"	Preliminary expenses	300			
"	Selling Overhead	1,400			
"	Net Profit	28,300			
		1,35,150			1,35,150

Information received from Cost Books.

(i) Opening Stock Rs. 2,700; closing stock – Rs. 4,000.
(ii) Office and Administrative Overheads charged Rs. 11,500
(iii) Factory Overhead recovered at 50% of productive wages
(iv) Selling Overheads recovered @ Re 1.00 per unit sold
(v) Profit s. 28,200.

Prepare a Reconciliation Statement.

[Adapted—C.U. B.Com. (Pass)]

8. From the following summary of Trading and Profit & Loss Account of a company for the year ended 31st December, 1992, prepare Costing Profit & Loss Account and reconcile the profit disclosed with that shown in Financial Accounts.

Profit and Loss Account

Dr. *Cr.*

		Rs.				Rs.
To	Materials consumed	27,40,000	By	Sales (1,20,000 units)		60,00,000
"	Wages	15,10,000	"	Finished Stock (4,000 units)		1,60,000
"	Factory Expenses	8,30,000	"	Work-in-Progress		
"	Admn. Expenses	3,81,400		Materials	64,000	
"	Goodwill	40,000		Wages	36,000	
"	Selling and Distribution Exp.	4,50,000		Factory Exp.	20,000	1,20,000
"	Preliminary Exp. written-off	20,000	By	Dividend		18,000
"	Net Profit	3,26,600				
		62,98,000				62,98,000

In the Cost Accounts –

(i) Factory expenses have been allocated to the production at 20% on Prime Cost.

(ii) Administration expenses @ Rs. 3.00 per unit on units produced.

(iii) Selling and Distribution expenses at Rs. 4.00 per unit on units sold.

[B.Com. Andhra—adapted]

Ans. : Profit as per Cost Accounts – Rs. 3,40,645.

9. During the year ended 31st December, 1992 the pofit of a company as per Financial Profit and Loss Account was Rs. 33,248 as given below. Prepare a reconciliation satement and arrive at the profit as per Cost Accounts using the additional information given –

Profit and Loss Account

for the year ended 31.12.1992

Dr.			Rs.			*Cr.* Rs.
To	Opening Stock	4,94,358		By	Sales	6,93,000
"	Purchase	1,64,308		"	Sundry Income	632
		6,58,666				6,93,632
Less :	Closing Stock	1,50,242	5,08,424			
To	Direct wages		46,266			
"	Administration Expenses		19,690			
"	Selling Expenses		44,352			
"	Net Profit		33,248			
			6,93,632			6,93,632

The Costing records show :	Rs.
(i) Closing Stock	1,56,394
(ii) Direct wages absorbed	49,734
(iii) Factory Overheads absorbed	32,428
(iv) Administration Overhead calculated at 3% of sales	
(v) Selling expenses absorbed @ 5% of Sales.	

[Adapted I.C.W.A. (Inter)]

Ans. : Profit as per Cost Accounts – Rs. 46,126.

10 The following is the summary of the Trading and Profit & Loss Account of a manufacturing company for the year ended 31st March, 1990

		(Rs. '000)				(Rs. '000)
To	Material Consumed	2,740	By	Sales (1,20,000 units)		6,000
"	Wages	1,510	"	Finished Stock		160
"	Factory expenses	830		(4,000 units)		
"	Administration Expenses	382	"	Work-in-progress :		
"	Selling and Distribution			Materials	64	
	Expenses	450		Wages	36	
"	Preliminary Expenses	40		Factory Expenses	20	120
"	Goodwill (Written off)	20	"	Dividend		18
"	Net profit	326				
		6,298				6,298

In the Cost Accounts the following allocations have been made –

(a) Factory expenses at 20% on Prime Cost.

(b) Administration Expenses at Rs.3 per unit of production

(c) Selling and Distribution expenses at Rs. 4 per unit of sales.

You are required to prepare a costing Profit and Loss Account of the Company and to prepare Reconciliation Statement

[Adapted—C.S. (Inter) 1990]

Ans. : Net Profit as per Costing Profit & Loss Account Rs. 3,40,000

MARGINAL COSTING 10

Learning Objectives :

1. *Definition :*
   (i) Marginal Cost, (ii) Marginal Costing, (iii) Characteristics
2. *Absorption Costing :*
   (i) Definition,
   (ii) Difference between Marginal Costing and Absorption Costing
3. *Advantages and Disadvantages of Marginal Costing*
4. *Break-even Analysis*
5. *Break-even Charts—Assumptions, Limitations*
6. *Profit Volume Chart*
7. *Angle of Incidence*
8. *Concept of Contribution*
9. *Cost Volume Profit Analysis*

MARGINAL COSTING 10

Definitions

It is very difficult to give a precise definition of 'Marginal Costing'. Probably it is the most controversial subject in the field of Management Accounting. 'Marginal Costing' is used in U.K. and Europe while 'Direct Costing' or 'Variable Costing' is preferred in the USA.

Marginal Cost

The Institute of Cost and Management Accountant's publication **'A Report on Marginal Costing'** gives the following definition of marginal cost—***"The amount at any given volume of output by which aggregate costs are changed if the volume of output is increased or decreased by one unit."***

If we analyse the above definition we shall find that with the increase in one unit of output the total cost is increased and this increase in total cost due to change in the volume of output is known as **marginal cost.**

An example will clarify the matter. Suppose, a company produces 1,000 units of product A, Total Fixed Cost is Rs. 50,000 p.a., variable cost per unit is Rs. 200. So, total cost of 1,000 units comes to Rs. 50,000 + Rs. 2,00,000 (1,000 × Rs. 200) = Rs. 2,50,000.

If output is increased by one unit, the total cost of 1,001 units will be :

		Rs.
Variable Cost 1,001 × 200	=	2,00,200
Fixed Cost	=	50,000
		2,50,200
Therefore, Marginal Cost per unit	=	Rs. 2,50,200 – Rs. 2,50,000
	=	Rs. 200 per unit

It means **marginal cost is the variable cost**

Marginal cost is also known as **'direct cost', 'volume cost'** or **'activity cost'.**

We may conclude that marginal cost is a constant ratio which may be expressed in terms of an amount per unit of output.

Marginal Costing

The Institute of Cost and Management Accountants' publication **'A Report on Marginal Costing'** defines Marginal Costing : ***"The ascertainment, by differentiating between the fixed costs and variable cost, of marginal costs and of the effect on profit of changes in volume or type of output."***

In marginal costing procedure, total costs are separated into fixed and variable costs.

Marginal costing is not a system of costing, but a technique which presents management with required information enabling it to measure the profitability of an undertaking by considering the behaviour of costs. It is not a distinct method of ascertainment of costs such as process or job costing. On the other hand, it is a technique that applies the existing methods in a particular way to bring out the relationship between profit and volume of output.

Characteristics of Marginal Costing

The following are the features of marginal costing :

(i) Costs are separated into fixed and variable elements. All elements of cost—works, office and administration, selling and distribution—are classified into fixed and variable components. Even semi-variable costs are also analysed into fixed and variable elements. The usefulness of marginal costing depends upon a correct appreciation of the behaviour of the costs with changes in output.

(ii) The marginal costs or variable costs are treated as cost of the product. The values of stock of finished goods and work-in-progress also comprise only the variable costs.

(iii) Fixed costs are written-off and charged to Profit and Loss Account of the period during which they are incurred. So, fixed costs do not find place in product cost or in the inventories.

(iv) Prices of a product are based on marginal costs and marginal **'contribution'**. Contribution is the excess of sale price over variable costs of sales. For example, if the sale price is Rs. 30 per unit and variable cost is Rs. 15, then contribution is equal to Rs. 30 – Rs. 15 = Rs. 15.

(v) The relative profitability of products or departments can be determined after a study of the contribution made available by each product or department.

(vi) Marginal costing involves the techniques of both cost recording and cost reporting.

(vii) Break-even techniques and calculations which show the effect of increasing or reducing the volume of output or of changing the mixture or types of products are an integral part of the technique.

(viii) Profit in marginal costing is calculated in a difficult way. Marginal costs (variable costs) are deducted from sales revenue to arrive at the **'contribution'**. The excess of contribution over fixed cost is taken as **profit**.

(ix) A special form of Profit and Loss Account or Statement is prepared styled as Marginal Profit and Loss Account.

ABSORPTION COSTING

Definition

Absorption costing is an approach to product costing in which all manufacturing costs, variable costs and fixed costs are charged to the cost of goods manufactured and inventories. In absorption costing all manufacturing costs—variable and fixed—are charged to products; materials and labour costs by direct measurement while indirect manufacturing costs are charged by some method of apportionment. Under absorption costing some part of every cost is carried forward from period to period as inventories of work-in-process and finished goods. Absorption costing is a process of determining average total cost by charging all operating costs to the goods manufactured or sold.

Absorption Cost Equation

For the sake of convenience, the elements of costs in absorption costing can be explained with the help of an equation

P = S (R – T) where;

P = Total profit,
S = Sales volume,
R = Selling price per unit,
T = Total cost per unit.

Difference between Marginal Costing and Absorption Costing

The following are the points of difference between Absorption and Marginal Costing :

1. **Treatment of fixed cost and variable cost :**

Absorption costing is a total cost technique since the total cost is considered for the determination of profit. Both **fixed and variable costs** are charged to operations, processes or job.

In marginal costing only **variable costs** are charged to products, process or operations. Fixed costs are written-off against Profit and Loss Account.

2. **Valuation of W.I.P. and Finished Goods :**

In Absorption Costing work-in-process and stocks are valued at total cost which includes both variable and fixed costs.

In Marginal Costing work-in-process and stocks are valued at marginal cost only. This results in higher valuation of stock in absorption costing than in marginal costing.

3. **Apportionment of fixed cost :**

In Absorption Costing apportionment of fixed costs is done arbitrarily which may result in over-absorption or under-absorption of costs.

Arbitrary apportionment of fixed costs does not arise since fixed costs are written-off.

4. **Determination of profit :**

In absorption costing managerial decisions are taken on the basis of profit which is excess of sale price over total cost. But Marginal Costing focuses its attention on 'contribution' which is the excess of sales value over variable cost.

Contribution = Sales – Variable Costs.

The following illustration will show how profit is determined under Marginal Costing and Absorption Costing :

Problem 1

From the following cost, production and sales data of XY Co. prepare comparative income statement for three years under :

(i) the absorption costing method and

(ii) the direct costing method.

Indicate the unit cost for each year under each method. Also evaluate the closing stock. The company produces a single article for sale.

Production and Sales	1986	1987	1988
Opening Stock	—	—	10,000
Units produced	50,000	70,000	60,000
Units sold	50,000	60,000	66,000
Closing Stock	—	10,000	4,000
Costs incurred	Rs.	Rs.	Rs.
Direct Materials	1,00,000	1,44,000	1,27,200
Direct Labour	1,50,000	2,16,000	1,74,000
Direct Labour Hours	1,00,000	1,44,000	1,16,000
Direct Expenses	48,000	72,000	56,000
Factory and Administration Overhead	72,000	72,000	70,000
Variable Selling Costs	2,50,000	3,00,000	3,40,000
Fixed Selling Costs	50,000	50,000	50,000

Selling Price Rs. 20 per unit.

Fixed costs are to be recovered on actual activity. **[Adapted—I.C.W.A. (Inter)]**

Solution

OPERATING STATEMENT (MARGINAL COST METHOD)

		1986	1987	1988
		Rs.	Rs.	Rs.
(A)	Sales	10,00,000	12,00,000	13,20,000
		(50,000 × Rs. 20)	(60,000 × Rs. 20)	(66,000 × Rs. 20)
(B)	*Less* : **Marginal Cost of goods sold**			
	Direct Materials	1,00,000	1,44,000	1,27,200
	Direct Labour	1,50,000	2,16,000	1,74,000
	Direct Expenses	48,000	72,000	56,000
	Selling Expenses	2,50,000	3,00,000	3,40,000
		5,48,000	7,32,000	6,97,200
Marginal Contribution (A – B)		4,52,000	4,68,000	6,22,800
Less :	Fixed Cost	50,000	50,000	50,000
	Profit	4,02,000	4,18,000	5,72,800

OPERATING STATEMENT
(Absorption Costing System)

		1986	1987	1988
		Rs.	Rs.	Rs.
(A)	Sale	10,00,000	12,00,000	13,20,000
(B)	Direct Materials	1,00,000	1,44,000	1,27,200
	Direct Labour	1,50,000	2,16,000	1,74,000
	Direct Expenses	48,000	72,000	56,000
	Selling Expenses	2,50,000	3,00,000	3,40,000
	Fixed Cost	50,000	50,000	50,000
	Total Cost	5,98,000	7,82,000	7,47,200
	Net Profit (A – B)	4,02,000	4,18,000	5,72,800

ADVANTAGES OF MARGINAL COSTING

The technique of Marginal Costing is of immense importance for managerial decisions. It is also a significant tool for both cost control and profit planning.

The following benefits can be derived from the technique of Marginal Costing :

1. The Technique is less complicated

Since fixed overheads are not included in the cost of production there is no need for complicated and expensive method of finding out overheads recovery rate, its modification from time to time and allocating overheads. Thus, this technique is free from complications and confusion.

2. A Vehicle for Cost Control

Marginal Costing is essentially a managerial tool for cost control, cost analysis and cost presentation. It presents the data in a manner which helps the various levels of management for controlling costs. It is also an important tool for cost reduction. Since this technique recognises only variable costs, which are always controllable, it becomes easier to fix the responsibility for these costs and to effect control over them. On the other hand, fixed costs can be controlled effectively because they are treated as a whole in the determination of profit.

3. Meaningful Managerial Reporting

The technique of Marginal Costing serves as a good basis for managerial reporting. Reports prepared on the basis of this technique provide information based on sales rather than on production. Thus, it coveys real state of efficiency. The technique of marginal costing precisely and clearly reflects the effect of fixed costs on profit.

4. Profit Planning

Marginal Costing helps the management in the area of profit planning. Break-even Analysis and Margin of Safety are the tools for profit planning. It also facilitates the analysis of cost profit-volume relationship. The contribution ratio of marginal ratio—which is the ratio of marginal contribution to sales—indicates the relative profitability of the different sectors of business organisation whenever there is a change in variable costs, fixed costs, sale price or product mix.

5. Easy Understanding of Income Statement

Management can easily understand the income statement prepared by allocating fixed expenses and variable expenses separately. Moreover, stock valuation becomes easier since it is valued at marginal cost which remains constant.

6. Appraisal of Profitability

The technique of Marginal Costing serves as a tool of profitability appraisals. The different departments have different revenue earning potentialities. The performance of each department or segment can be measured or evaluated by means of marginal cost analysis.

7. Decision Making

The main utility of marginal costing lies in the fact that this technique helps the management in taking various important managerial decisions—particularly in dealing with problems that require short-term decisions.

8. Price Policy and Price Determination

This technique contributes significantly to the area of price policy and price determination. If the organisation faces the problem of fixing optimum price, minimum price, dumping price or price under recession, correct and sound decision may be taken on the basis of information revealed by the technique of marginal costing.

DISADVANTAGES OF MARGINAL COSTING

Though the Marginal Costing as a technique enjoys the above-mentioned advantages, several arguments are put forward to indicate its demerits.

The disadvantages from which this technique suffers are :

1. Emphasis on Sales

It lays too much emphasis on selling function of an organisation, thus, production function has been considered to be less significant. But it is to be kept in mind that both the functions are equally important from the point of view of business efficiency.

2. Valuation of Stock

It is not logical to value the stock at marginal cost because it may result in undervaluation from the financial point of view.

3. Long-term Price Policy

This technique fails to provide any long-term price policy.

4. External Reporting

This technique is not suitable for external reporting viz. for tax authorities where marginal income is not considered as taxable profit.

5. Time Factor

The technique of marginal costing does not take into consideration the importance of time factor.

IMPORTANT DECISION MAKING AREAS OF MARGINAL COSTING

Marginal Costing is a useful technique used by the management of most of the manufacturing concerns for taking various and important managerial decisions. Some of the important decision making areas where marginal costing technique is used are :

(i) **Fixation of Selling Price**

(a) Under normal circumstances,

(b) For special market (export) or for a special customer,

(c) During recession,

(d) At marginal cost or below marginal cost.

(ii) **Decision relating to the most Profitable Product Mix**

(a) Selection of Optimal Product Mix

(b) Substitution of one product for another

(c) Discontinuation or dropping of a product line

(iii) **Decision relating to make or buy**

The management has to take decision as to whether it will be profitable to manufacture the product or parts or to buy them from outside.

(iv) **Retaining or replacing a machine**

(v) **Selling the product in the home or in the export market**

(vi) **Expanding or contracting**

The management has to take decision whether to expand or contract the business under different economic conditions.

(vii) **Shut down or continue**

In certain economic conditions, the management has to take crucial decision whether to shut down the factory or to continue or to determine the level of output especially in period of recession.

(viii) **Decision making relating to Price-Mix.**

BREAK-EVEN ANALYSIS

The study of cost-volume-profit relationship is often referred to as **'break-even analysis'**. The term 'break-even analysis' is interpreted in narrow as well as broad sense. In its narrow sense, it is concerned with finding out the break-even point. **Break-even point is the point at which total revenue is equal to total cost,** it is **the point of no profit no loss.**

In its broad sense, break-even analysis refers to a system of analysis that can be used **to determine the probable** profit at any level of production. It may be shown both graphically as well as algebrically.

Break-even point can be calculated in the following ways :

1. Break-even point in units = $\dfrac{\text{Fixed Cost}}{\text{Contribution per unit}}$

2. Break-even point in sales value = $\dfrac{\text{Fixed Cost} \times \text{Selling Price per unit}}{\text{Contribution per unit}}$

Or

$$\frac{\text{Fixed Cost} \times \text{Sale Value (total)}}{\text{Contribution}} \text{ Or } \frac{\text{Fixed Cost}}{\text{P / V Ratio}}$$

3. $\text{BEP} = \dfrac{\text{Total Fixed Cost}}{1 - \dfrac{\text{Variable cost per unit}}{\text{Selling price per unit}}}$

Or $\text{BEP} = \text{Total Fixed cost} \times \dfrac{1}{\text{P / V Ratio}}$

Margin of Safety

Definition

The margin of safety is the difference between actual sales or output and the break-even sales or production. It may also be expressed in percentage. A greater margin of safety reflect the soundness of the business. If the margin of safety is small, any fall in sales value may even result in loss.

The margin of safety can be rectified by the management, by lowering fixed or variable costs, by increasing selling price or volume of sales, by substituting unprofitable product by profitable ones. It may be expressed as :

Margin of Safety = **Actual Sales or output – Break-even sales or productions**

or, $\text{M/S} = \dfrac{\text{Profit}}{\text{P / V ratio}}$

BREAK-EVEN CHART

The break-even chart is the graphic presentation that shows the varying costs along with varying sales revenue. It depicts the point of production at which neither profit nor loss can result (i.e., the break-even point) and also shows the estimated profit or loss at different levels of production.

Construction of Break-Even Chart : There are three methods of drawing a break-even chart. These have been explained as follows :

First Method : On the X-axis (i.e., on the horizontal line) of the graph is plotted the volume of production; and on the Y-axis (i.e., on the vertical line) the cost and sales revenue are shown. Plot the fixed cost on the vertical axis and draw fixed cost line passing through this point parallel to horizontal axis. This is so because fixed cost remains the same with any volume of production.

The variable cost line is shown above the fixed cost line. This line can be considered as a total cost line because it begins from the point where certain fixed cost has been incurred and variable cost at that point is zero. The sales revenue line is drawn from the point where there are no sales (Zero intersection of horizontal and vertical sales) and it goes upward, thereby depicting the increasing sales revenue due to increasing sale. The total costs and total sales line intersect each other at a point which is known as break-even point. **To the left of this point there is a loss and to the right of it there is profit.**

This chart shows clearly the Fixed Costs, Variable Costs, Profit and Margin of Safety, etc.

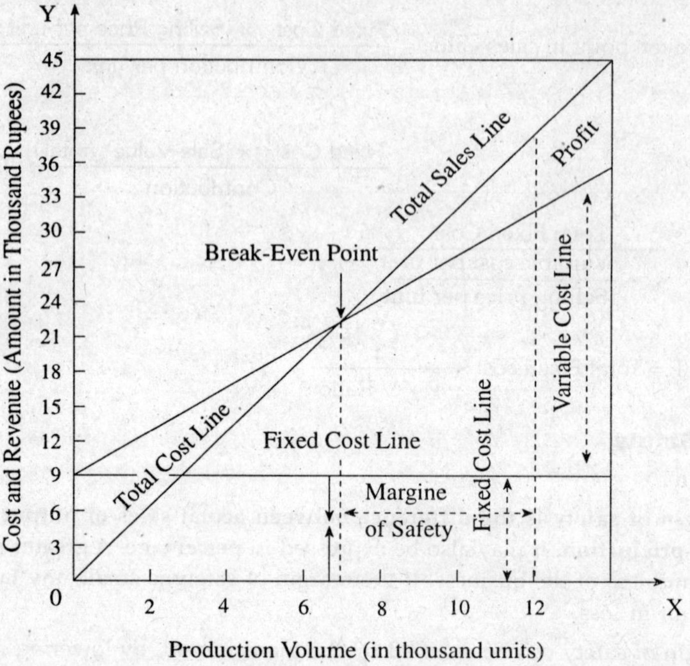

Second Method : Under this method, the fixed costs line is shown above the variable cost. This method has the advantage because of the fact that it reveals more clearly the recovery of fixed costs at various levels of production before profits are realized. This chart depicts the

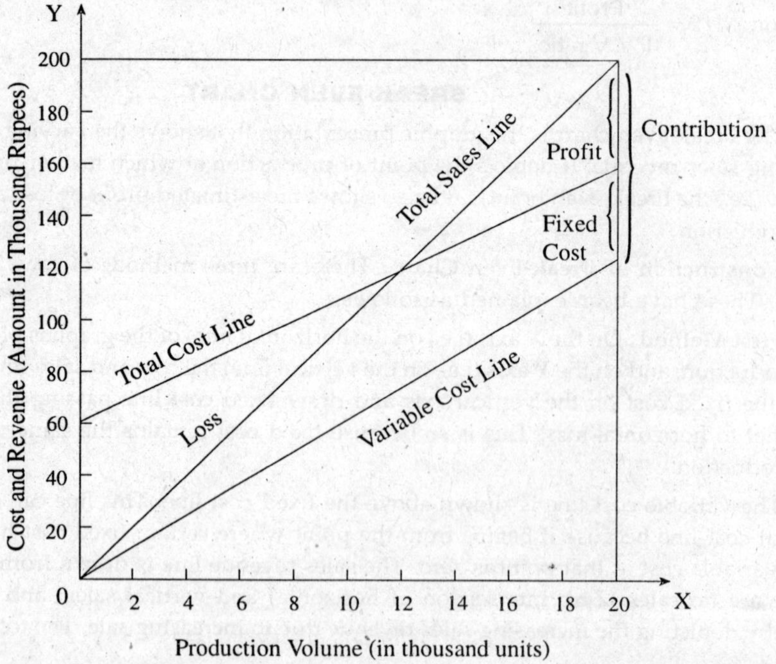

contribution at different levels of production more clearly than the previous one. The graph is drawn in a similar way, except that variable cost line is drawn first, then fixed cost and sales lines are drawn.

Third Method : This method is known as *Analysis (Detailed), Break-even chart*. It is prepared showing various details of variable costs under various elements of costs, such as direct material cost, direct labour cost. Variable factory overhead, variable administration, selling and distribution overheads etc. Similarly, appropriation of profit to taxes, dividends, reserves etc., is also depicted.

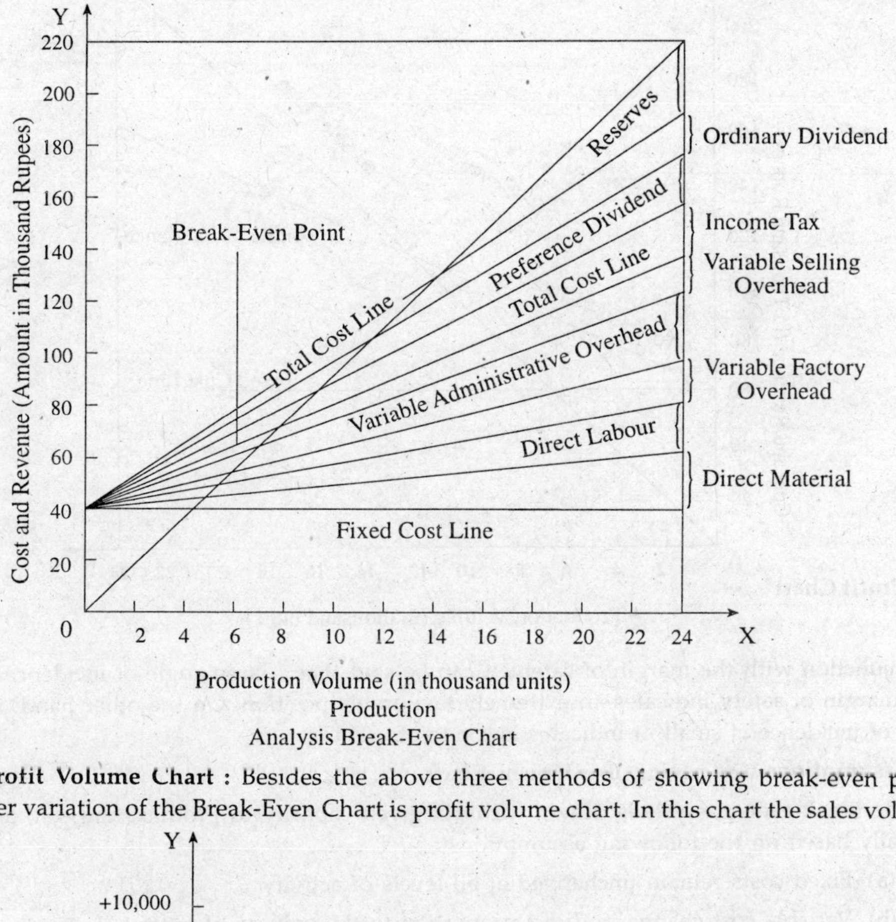

Production
Analysis Break-Even Chart

Profit Volume Chart : Besides the above three methods of showing break-even point another variation of the Break-Even Chart is profit volume chart. In this chart the sales volume

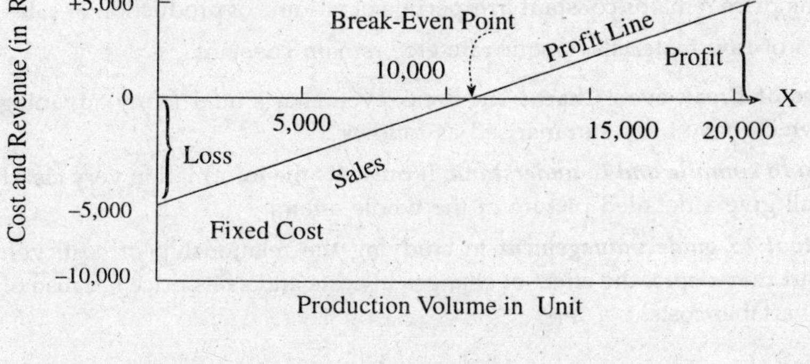

is depicted on the horizontal line and profit or loss on the vertical line. The profit line is plotted by determining the Profit or Loss (i.e., difference between sales revenue and total cost) at each volume. **The point where the profit line intersects the horizontal line is the Break-Event Point.**

Angle of Incidence : This is an angle at which sales line intersects the total cost line. If the angle of incidence is large it is an indication that profits are being earned at high rate. Taken

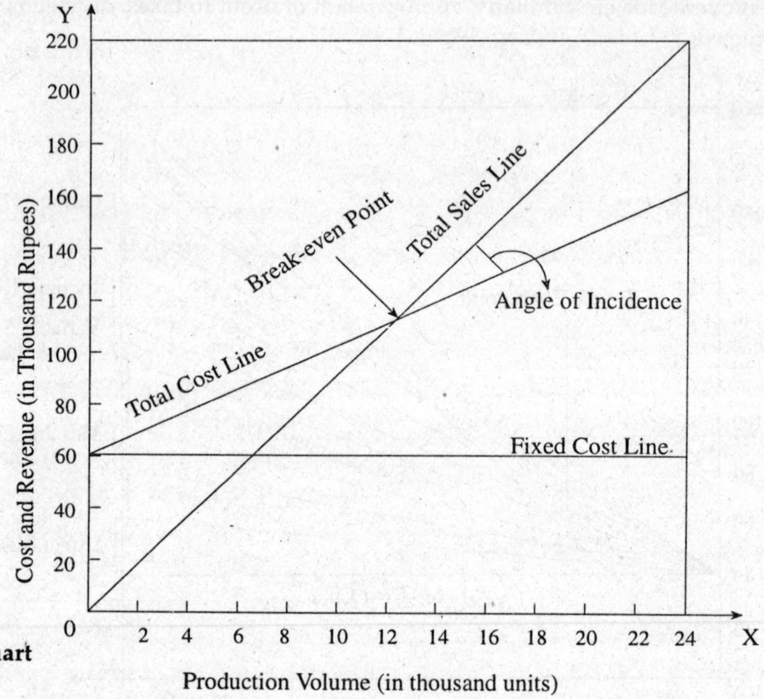

Profit Chart

in conjunction with the margin of safety, it can be said that a large angle of incidence with high margin of safety indicates an extremely favourable position. On the other hand, if the angle of incidence is small, it indicates low rate of earning.

Assumptions underlying Break-even Chart :

The break-even analysis is drawn within a given capacity to produce and sell, and is generally based on the following assumptions :

(a) Fixed costs remain unchanged at all levels of activity.

(b) Variable cost change in direct proportion to the volume of output.

(c) All indirect costs can be classified into fixed and variable elements.

(d) Selling price remains constant irrespective of volume of production or sales changes.

(e) Prices of raw materials, labour rate etc., remain constant.

Advantages of Break-even Chart : The break-even charts offer many advantages, more important of which have been summarised as follows :

1. ***It is easy to compile and to understand.*** It presents the information very clearly. A look or a glance shall give a detailed picture of the whole affairs.

2. ***Useful tool to guide management*** in studying the relationship of cost, volume and profits. The chart may depict the effect of changes in costs and sales price because of changes in fixed costs, variable costs.

3. ***Ascertainment of strength of the business and the profit earning capacity.***

By the study of Margin of Safety and angle of incidence together, many important policy decisions can be taken. Policy decisions like :

(a) to increase the selling price;

(b) to reduce the costs;

(c) to increase the level of production;

(d) to substitute the less profitable products by more profitable products may be taken on the basis of Margin of Safety and Angle of Incidence in the Break-even Chart.

4. ***It helps identifying product and sale-mix.***

It helps in selecting the most profitable product mix or sales-mix in making maximum profits.

Limitations of Break-Even Chart

1. The assumptions on the basis of which Break-even chart is drawn are unrealistic for the following reasons :

(a) It is not possible to separate or segregate all indirect costs into fixed costs and variable component accurately.

(b) Fixed costs are constant only in the short period; in the long period they are subject to change.

(c) Certain items of variable costs may not change in direct proportion to volume but may reduce on account of economies of bulk buying etc.

(d) The selling price does not also remain constant. Any increase or decrease in output is likely to have an influence on the selling price.

2. When a number of products are manufactured, separate break-even charts will have to be drawn up. This surely poses problem of apportionment of fixed expenses to each product.

3. Break-even chart does not take into account the amount of capital employed—which is one of the vital factors in the determination of profitability.

Problem 2

Two businesses A.B. Ltd. and C.D. Ltd. sell the same type of product in the same type of market. Their budgeted profit and loss accounts for the year ending 2001 are as follows :

			A.B. Ltd.		***C.D. Ltd.***
			Rs.		Rs.
	Sales		1,50,000		1,50,000
Less :	Variable costs	1,20,000		1,00,000	
	Fixed costs	15,000		35,000	
			1,35,000		1,35,000
	Net budgeted profit		15,000		15,000

You are required to :

(a) Calculate the break-even points of each business and

(b) State which business is likely to earn greater profits in conditions of

(i) heavy demand for the product

(ii) low demand for the product **[I.C.W.A.I. (Inter)]**

Solution

		A.B. Ltd.	C.D. Ltd.
		Rs.	Rs.
	Sales	1,50,000	1,50,000
Less :	Variable Costs	1,20,000	1,00,000
	Contribution	30,000	50,000
	P/V ratio = $\left(\frac{C}{S} \times 100\right)$	20%	$33\frac{1}{3}\%$
		15,000	35,000
	B. E. Sales = $\left(\frac{\text{Fixed Cost}}{\text{P / V ratio}}\right)$	20%	$33\frac{1}{3}\%$
		= 75,000	= 1,05,000
	Margin of safety = (Present Sales – B. E. Sales or P/V ratio)	75,000	45,000

Although total costs of both firms are the same, the fixed costs of A.B. Ltd. are lower than those of C.D. Ltd. As a result, the break-even point in first case is reached sooner (i.e., at a lower ratio of activity) as will be evident from the following graph.

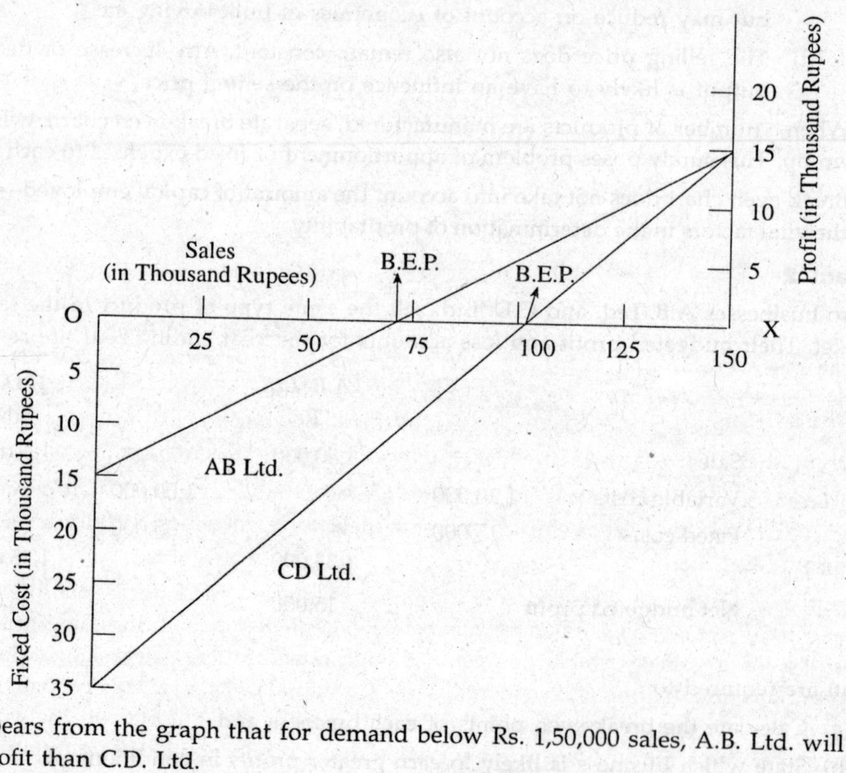

It appears from the graph that for demand below Rs. 1,50,000 sales, A.B. Ltd. will earn greater profit than C.D. Ltd.

At value of Rs. 1,50,000 both will earn same profit. Since the rate of profit earning in case of C.D. Ltd. is greater than that of A.B. Ltd. (vide angle incidence), for volume above Rs. 1,50,000 C.D. Ltd. will earn more profit than A.B. Ltd. Thus, in case of heavy demand, C.D.

Ltd. will earn greater profits; while A.B. Ltd. will earn greater profits in condition of low demand for the product.

Concept of Contribution

Contribution is the difference between selling price and variable cost. If selling price is Rs. 20 and its variable cost is Rs. 10, then contribution is Rs. 20 – Rs. 10 = Rs. 10. Otherwise we can say that contribution = **Fixed Cost + Profit.**

Thus, Contribution = **Selling Price – Variable Cost = Fixed Cost + Profit.**

Profit = Contribution margin – Fixed Cost.

= Selling price – Variable Cost – Fixed Cost.

Benefits

The knowledge of contribution margin is of great importance to the management as it acts as an aid to management in making various decisions. A few benefits are discussed below :

1. While considering the question of acceptance or rejection of any new order, contribution margin is of considerable help to the management in taking correct decision.
2. While choosing from among alternative methods of production, the method which yields the greatest contribution is to be adopted.
3. Contribution margin helps a lot in the selection of a product mix keeping in view that the products which give the minimum contribution margin are to be retained.

Contribution	=	S – V, or, Sales – Variable Cost
		or,
		Fixed Cost + Profit
Fixed Cost	=	S – V – Profit
Profit	=	S – V – FC

COST VOLUME PROFIT ANALYSIS

Definition

Profit of an undertaking depends upon a large number of factors, the most important of which are cost of manufacture, volume of sales and selling prices of products sold. The three factors of cost volume and profit are interlinked and Interdependent. As wc know, profit depends upon sales; selling price; to a great extent; depends upon cost; volume of sales depends upon volume of production which, in turn, is related to cost. In cost-volume-profit analysis an attempt is made to measure variation in cost with variation in volume.

Cost-Volume-Profit analysis is the analysis of three variables, viz., cost, volume and profit, that seek to explore the relationship existing amongst costs, revenues, activity levels and the resulting profit.

Profit, as a variable, is a reflection of a number of internal and external conditions which exert their influence on sales, revenue and costs. Revenue depends upon selling prices, costs, volume of sales, demand, competition etc. Although none of these can be singled out as the most important, the volume is considered to be a dominant factor. This is probably because changes in volume are more frequent, take place rapidly and are outside the purview of management control. Further, Costs rarely vary in direct proportion to the volume and hence, a small change in the volume may have a more than proportionate effect on profits than the other factors. It is thus, the volume which is perhaps the largest single factor that influences cost. Therefore, there exists an intimate relationship amongest costs, volume and profit.

The cost-volume-profit analysis is an extension of marginal costing and makes use of the principles of marginal costing. It is important tool of short-term planning and is more relevant where the proposed changes in the level of activity are relatively small. Therefore, it is very much useful in making short-run decisions.

Importance of Cost – Volume – Profit Analysis

The relationship between cost, volume and profit makes up the profit structure of an undertaking. This analysis may be useful for **profit planning, cost control** and **decision making.** The main objectives of cost-volume-profit analysis are discussed below :

1. Profit Planning

In Profit planning it becomes essential to know the relationship between cost, volume and profit. The most important feature of cost-volume-profit analysis is the manner in which it relates cost, selling price and volume and enables calculation to be made to show the effect of change in these on profit. Accordingly, the management can plan profit with reference to cost – volume – profit analysis.

2. Preparation of Flexible Budget

Cost – volume – profit analysis is of special help in the preparation of flexible budget that indicates cost and profit at various levels of activity.

3. Decision Making

Cost – volume – profit analysis is very much useful in making decisions like **make or buy, pricing, selection of a product mix, selection of the best channel of distribution, and selection of best method of production.**

4. Cost Control

In the area of cost control, **cost – volume – profit analysis** is of great assistance to the management. The effect on cost of changes in volume can be evaluated for the purpose of reviewing profits achieved and cost incurred.

Calculation of P/V Ratio

1. **P/V Ratio** $= \frac{S - V}{X} \times 100$ or $\frac{\text{Contribution}}{\text{Sales}} \times 100$

   Margin of Safety $= \frac{\text{Profit}}{\text{P / V Ratio}}$

2. **If the per unit information is available, then the ratio will be :** $\frac{\text{Contribution per unit}}{\text{Sales}} \times 100$

3. **P/V Ratio** $= \frac{\text{Change in Profit (Rs.)}}{\text{Change in Sales}} \times 100$

4. **P/V Ratio** $= \frac{\text{Profit}}{\text{Margin of Safety}} \times 100$

5. **P/V Ratio** $= \frac{\text{Fixed Cost}}{\text{BEP in Rupees}} \times 100$

6. **P/V Ratio** $= 100 - \left(\frac{\text{Variable Cost} \times 100}{\text{Sales}}\right)$

7. **Composite P/V Ratio** $= \frac{\text{Total Contribution} \times 100}{\text{Total Sales}}$

Problem 3

From the following data, calculate P/V ratio :

Sales 20,000 units @ Rs. 20 per unit = Rs. 4,00,000

Variable costs @ Rs. 15 per unit = Rs. 3,00,000

Fixed Costs Rs. 80,000.

Solution

(i) P/V Ratio $= \dfrac{S - VC}{S} \times 100 = \dfrac{\text{Rs. } 4{,}00{,}000 - \text{Rs. } 3{,}00{,}000}{\text{Rs. } 4{,}00{,}000} \times 100$

$= \dfrac{\text{Rs. } 1{,}00{,}000}{\text{Rs. } 4{,}00{,}000} \times 100 = 25\%$

(ii) P/V Ratio $= \dfrac{C}{S} \times 100 = \dfrac{\text{Rs. } 1{,}00{,}000}{\text{Rs. } 4{,}00{,}000} \times 100 = 25\%$

(iii) P/V Ratio $= 1 - \dfrac{VC}{S}$

$= 1 - \dfrac{\text{Rs. } 3{,}00{,}000}{\text{Rs. } 4{,}00{,}000} = \dfrac{\text{Rs. } 1{,}00{,}000}{\text{Rs. } 4{,}00{,}000} = 25\%$

(iv) P/V Ratio $= \dfrac{S - V}{S} \times 100$

$= \dfrac{\text{Rs. } 20 - \text{Rs. } 15}{\text{Rs. } 20} \times 100 = \dfrac{\text{Rs. } 5}{\text{Rs. } 20} \times 100 = 25\%$

Problem 4

The following is the standard cost data per unit of product "Flex" manufactured by Gama Limited :

			Rs.
Selling price			40
Costs :	Rs.		
Direct Material	8		
Direct Labour	5		
Variable Production Overhead	2		
Fixed Production Overhead	5	(Based on a budgeted normal output of 36,000 units p.a.)	
Variable Selling Overhead	6		

Further, the fixed selling expenses were Rs. 1,20,000 p.a. During a particular month, the company produced 2,000 units of the product and sold 1,500 units of the same. There was no opening stock.

You are required to :

(a) Prepare profit statements under :

(i) Marginal Costing and (ii) Absorption Costing Method.

[Adapted—C.S. (Inter)]

Solution

Statement showing profit under Marginal Costing Method

		Rs.	Rs.
	Sales (1,500 @ Rs. 40 per unit)		60,000
Less :	Variable production costs :		
	Material 2,000 × Rs. 8 =	16,000	
	Labour 2,000 × Rs. 5 =	10,000	
	Production Overheads 2,000 × Rs. 2 =	4,000	
		30,000	
Less :	Closing stock 500 × Rs. 15 =	7,500	
	Variable Production cost of goods sold	22,500	
Add :	Variable selling overheads 1,500 × 6 =	9,000	31,500
	Contribution		28,500
Less :	Fixed costs for the period		
	Production (36,000 × Rs. 5) ÷ 12 =	15,000	
	Selling Expenses (Rs. 1,20,000 ÷ 12) =	10,000	25,000
	Actual Profit		3,500

Calculation of Profit under Absorption Costing

		Rs.	Rs.
	Sale price (1,500 × Rs. 40) =		60,000
Less :	Cost of sales		
	Production Cost :		
	Material 2,000 × Rs. 8 =	16,000	
	Labour 2,000 × Rs. 5 =	10,000	
	Production Overhead 2,000 × Rs. 2 =	4,000	
		30,000	
Add :	Fixed Overhead 2,000 × 5 =	10,000	
	Total Production costs	40,000	
Less :	Closing Stock 500 units		
	= 500 × (Rs. 8 + Rs. 5 + Rs. 2 + Rs. 5) =	10,000	
	Production Cost of Saleable Units =	30,000	
Add :	Selling Expenses :		
	Variable (1,500 × Rs. 6) =	9,000	
	Fixed (Rs. 1,20,000 ÷ 12) =	10,000	49,000
			11,000
Less :	Adjustment for under absorbed overhead as per note		5,000
	Actual Profit		6,000
Note :	Fixed production overhead for the period (36,000 × Rs. 5) ÷ 12 =	15,000	
Less :	Fixed production overhead absorbed by the production = 2,000 × Rs. 5 =	10,000	
		5,000	

Problem 5

From the following data calculate :

(i) Break-even point expressed in amount of sales in rupees.

(ii) How many units must be sold to earn a net income of 10% of sales ?

Selling price	Rs. 20 per unit
Variable cost	Rs. 12 per unit
Fixed cost	Rs. 2,40,000

[D.U. B.Com.]

Solution

(i) $$\text{Break-even Point} = \frac{\text{Fixed Cost}}{\text{Contribution}} \times \text{Selling Price}$$

$$= \frac{\text{Rs. } 2,40,000}{8} \times 20 = \text{Rs. } 6,00,000$$

(ii) Suppose No. of units = x

Selling Price = Rs. 20 per unit

Total Sales = Rs. 20x

$$\text{Profit} = 10\% \text{ of Sales} = \frac{10}{100} \times 20x = 2x$$

$\therefore$ 20x = Rs. 2,40,000 + 12x + 2x

or, 20x – 12x – 2x = Rs. 2,40,000

$$\text{or } 6x = \text{Rs. } 2,40,000 \text{ or, } x = \frac{\text{Rs. } 2,40,000}{6} = 40,000$$

Therefore, total sales in units to earn a net income of 10% on sales = 40,000 units.

Problem 6

A company has fixed expenses of Rs. 90,000 with sales at Rs. 3,00,000 and a profit of Rs. 60,000. Calculate the profit/volume ratio. If in the next period the company suffered a loss of Rs. 30,000, calculate the sales volume.

[D.U. B.Com. (Hons.)]

Solution

Contribution = Fixed Cost + Profit = Rs. 90,000 + 60,000 = Rs. 1,50,000.

$$\textbf{P/V Ratio} = \frac{\text{Contribution}}{\text{Sales}} \times 100 = \frac{\text{Rs. } 1,50,000}{\text{Rs. } 3,00,000} \times 100 = 50\%$$

$$\text{Sales volume} = \frac{\text{Fixed Cost} - \text{Loss}}{\text{P / V Ratio}}$$

$$\frac{\text{Rs. } 90,000 - \text{Rs. } 30,000}{50\%} = \text{Rs. } 60,000 \times \frac{100}{50} = \text{Rs. } 1,20,000$$

Problem 7

From the following data calculate :

(i) P/V Ratio

(ii) Profit when sales are Rs. 20,000 and

(iii) New Break-even point if selling price is reduced by 20%

	Rs.
Fixed Expenses	4,000
Break-even point	10,000

[Adapted Delhi Univ. B.Com. (Hons.)]

Solution

Variable Cost = B.E.P. – Fixed Expenses (since there is no profit)

= Rs. 10,000 – Rs. 4,000 = Rs. 6,000

Here, Contribution = Fixed cost only

(i) P/V Ratio $= \frac{\text{Contribution}}{\text{Sales}} \times 100 = \frac{\text{Rs. } 4{,}000}{\text{Rs. } 10{,}000} \times 100 = 40\%$

(ii) When sales are Rs. 20,000

Contribution $= \text{Rs. } 20{,}000 \times \frac{40}{100} = \text{Rs. } 8{,}000$

Profit = Contribution – Fixed Cost

= Rs. 8,000 – Rs. 4,000 = Rs. 4,000

(iii) **Computation of new BEP**

New sale price = Rs. 20,000 – (20% of Rs. 20,000)

= Rs. 20,000 – Rs. 4,000 = Rs. 16,000

Variable Cost = Sales – Fixed Cost

= Rs. 16,000 – Rs. 4,000 = Rs. 12,000

Contribution = Rs. 16,000 – Rs. 12,000 (Sales – V.C.) = Rs. 4,000

P/V Ratio $= \frac{\text{Contribution}}{\text{Sales}} \times 100 = \frac{\text{Rs. } 4{,}000}{\text{Rs. } 16{,}000} \times 100 = 25\%$

$\therefore$ New B.E.P. $= \frac{\text{Fixed Cost}}{\text{P/V Ratio}} = \frac{\text{Rs. } 4{,}000}{25\%} = \text{Rs. } 16{,}000$

CALCULATION OF BEP

Problem 8

From the following information calculate the break-even point :

	Rs.
Fixed Cost	1,50,000
Sales	6,00,000
Direct Materials	2,00,000
Direct Labour	1,20,000
Direct Expenses	80,000

Solution

First Step

We shall find out the contribution :

Contribution = Sales – Variable cost

		Rs.	Rs.
	Sales		6,00,000
Less :	Variable Cost		
	Direct Materials	2,00,000	
	Direct Labour	1,20,000	
	Direct Expenses	80,000	4,00,000
	Contribution		2,00,000

Second Step

Find out the P/V Ratio

$$\text{P/V Ratio} = \frac{\text{Contribution}}{\text{Sales}} \times 100$$

$$= \frac{\text{Rs. } 2,00,000}{\text{Rs. } 6,00,000} \times 100 = 33.33\%$$

Third Step

Find out the **BEP in terms of value**

$$\text{BEP} = \frac{\text{Fixed Cost}}{\text{P / V Ratio}} = \frac{\text{Rs. } 1,50,000}{33.33\%}$$

$$= \frac{\text{Rs. } 1,50,000 \times 100}{33.33} = \text{Rs. } 4,50,000$$

Problem 9

From the following particulars find out the number of units to break-even. The firm produced 10,000 units.

	Rs.
Raw Materials	30
Direct Expenses	10
Variable Overheads	5
Fixed Overheads	5
Total cost per unit	50
Selling price	60
Profit	10

Solution

		Rs.	Rs.
	Selling Price		60
Less :	**Variable Costs**		
	Raw Materials	30	
	Direct Expenses	10	
	Variable Overheads	5	45
	Contribution		15
Less :	Fixed Cost		5
	Profit		10

$$\text{BEP} = \frac{\text{Fixed Cost}}{\text{Contribution}} = \frac{10,000 \times 5}{15} = \frac{50,000}{15} = \textbf{3,333 units}$$

DETERMINATION OF SALES AT BREAK-EVEN POINT IN TERMS OF QUANTITY AND VALUE

Problem 10

ABC Pvt. Limited manufactures and sells a standard product at fixed selling price. The budgeted figures for 2001-2002 are as under :

Production and sales	1,00,000 units
Variable Cost	Rs. 40 per unit
Fixed Cost	Rs. 26 lacs
Profit margin	$33\frac{1}{3}\%$ on selling price

You are required to determine the sale at break-even, both in terms of quantity and value for the budget year 2001-2002 at the above selling price.

Solution

		Per unit
		Rs.
Variable Cost		40
Fixed Cost =	$\frac{\text{Rs. } 26,00,000}{1,00,000}$	26
Total Cost		66
Profit @ $33\frac{1}{3}\%$		22
Selling Price		88

Contribution = Sale Price – Variable Cost = Rs. 88 – Rs. 40 = Rs. 48

P/V Ratio $= \frac{C}{S} \times 100 = \frac{48}{88} \times 100 = 54.55\%$

BEP in units $= \frac{\text{Fixed Cost}}{\text{Contribution per unit}} = \frac{\text{Rs. } 26,00,000}{48} = \text{Rs. } 54,167$

BEP (in value) $= \frac{\text{Fixed Cost}}{\text{P / V Ratio}} = \frac{\text{Rs. } 26,00,000}{54.55\%} = 4,76,626.94 \text{ or Rs. } 4,76,627$

Problem 11

From the following data calculate (i) P/V Ratio; (ii) Profit when sales are Rs. 20,000 and (iii) new Break-even point, if selling price is reduced by 20% :

	Rs.
Fixed Expenses	4,000
BEP	10,000

[Delhi B.Com. (Hons.)]

Solution

Break-even Point = Fixed Expenses + Variable Expenses

Rs. 10,000 = Rs. 4,000 + Variable Expenses

Or, Variable Expenses = Rs. 10,000 – Rs. 4,000 = Rs. 6,000

Contribution at BEP = Rs. 4,000 (Fixed Expenses)

(i) **P/V Ratio** $= \frac{\text{Contribution}}{\text{Sales (at BEP)}} = \frac{\text{Rs. } 4,000}{\text{Rs. } 10,000} \times 100 = 40\%$

(ii) **Profit** = (S × P/V Ratio) – Fixed Expenses

$= \left(\text{Rs. } 20,000 \times \frac{40}{100}\right) = \text{Rs. } 4,000$

= Rs. 8,000 – Rs. 4,000 = Rs. 4,000

(iii) **New Sales** $= \text{Rs. } 20,000 - \left(\frac{20}{100} \times 20,000\right)$

= Rs. 20,000 – Rs. 4,000 = Rs. 16,000

$$\text{Less : Variable Cost} = \frac{60}{100} \times 20{,}000 = \text{Rs. } 12{,}000$$

$$\textbf{Contribution} = \text{Rs. } 16{,}000 - \text{Rs. } 12{,}000 = \text{Rs. } 4{,}000$$

$$\textbf{New P/V Ratio} = \frac{\text{Contribution}}{\text{Sales}} \times 100 = \frac{\text{Rs. } 4{,}000}{\text{Rs. } 16{,}000} \times 100 = 25\%$$

$$\text{New BEP} = \frac{\text{Fixed Expenses}}{\text{P / V Ratio}} = \frac{\text{Rs. } 4{,}000}{25\%} = \text{Rs. } 4{,}000 \times \frac{100}{25} = \textbf{Rs. 16,000}$$

SALES WHEN THERE IS LOSS AND MARGIN OF SAFETY

Problem 12

(a) A company has fixed expenses of Rs. 90,000 with sales at Rs. 3,00,000 and a profit of Rs. 60,000. Calculate the P/V ratio. If in the next period the company suffered a loss of Rs. 30,000; calculate the sales volume.

(b) What is the margin of safety for a profit of Rs. 60,000 in (a) above?

[I.C.W.A. (Inter)]

Solution

(a) $$\text{P/V Ratio} = \frac{\text{Contribution}}{\text{Sales}} \times 100$$

Contribution = Fixed Expenses + Profit

So, Contribution = Rs. 90,000 + Rs. 60,000 = Rs. 1,50,000.

$$\text{P/V Ratio} = \frac{\text{Contribution}}{\text{Sales}} \times 100 = \frac{\text{Rs. } 1{,}50{,}000}{\text{Rs. } 3{,}00{,}000} \times 100 = 50\%$$

In the next period there is a loss of Rs. 30,000

So, Contribution = Fixed Expenses – Loss = Rs. 90,000 – Rs. 30,000 = Rs. 60,000

$$\textbf{Sales} = \frac{\text{Contribution}}{\text{P / V Ratio}} = \frac{\text{Rs. } 60{,}000}{50\%} = \text{Rs. } 1{,}20{,}000.$$

(b) $$\textbf{Break-even Sales} = \frac{\text{Fixed Cost}}{\text{P / V Ratio}} = \frac{\text{Rs. } 90{,}000}{50\%} = \text{Rs. } 1{,}80{,}000$$

Margin of Safety = Sales – BES = Rs. 3,00,000 – Rs. 1,80,000 = Rs. 1,20,000.

Problem 13

From the following data ascertain how much the value of sales must be increased to break-even :

	Rs.
Sales	2,00,000
Fixed Cost	90,000
Variable Cost	1,25,000

Solution

(i) **Find out the amount of contribution**

Contribution = Sales – Variable Cost = Rs. 2,00,000 – Rs. 1,25,000 = Rs. 75,000.

(ii) **Find out BEP**

$$\text{BEP} = \frac{\text{Fixed Cost}}{\text{Contribution}} \times \text{Sales} = \frac{\text{Rs. } 90{,}000}{\text{Rs. } 75{,}000} \times \text{Rs. } 2{,}00{,}000 = \text{Rs. } 2{,}40{,}000$$

So, sales will be increased by Rs. 40,000 (Rs. 2,40,000 – Rs. 2,00,000).

Alternatively

Find out the P/V Ratio

$$\text{P/V Ratio} = \frac{C}{S} \times 100 = \frac{\text{Rs. } 75{,}000}{\text{Rs. } 2{,}00{,}000} \times 100 = 37.5\%.$$

Now, Find out BEP

$$\text{BEP} = \frac{\text{Fixed Cost}}{\text{P/V Ratio}} = \frac{\text{Rs. } 90{,}000}{37.5\%} = \frac{\text{Rs. } 90{,}000}{37.5\%} = \text{Rs. } 2{,}40{,}000$$

Increased Sales = Rs. 2,40,000 – Rs. 2,00,000 = Rs. 40,000.

Problem 14

The projected output of a plant, when sold, would earn Rs. 70,000 in sales income to Mixers Ltd. The variable cost of this production volume would be Rs. 30,000. The fixed cost is Rs. 20,000. Determine the following :

(i) The break-even point of the company.

(ii) The profit or loss to the company on sales of Rs. 49,000 and Rs. 28,000.

(iii) The amount of sales that will enable the company to earn a net profit of Rs. 28,000.

[D.U. B.Com. (Hons.)]

Solution

(a) **At 100% capacity**

	Rs.
Sales	70,000
Variable Cost	30,000
Fixed Cost	20,000

$$\text{So, P/V Ratio} = \frac{S - V}{S} \times 100 = \frac{\text{Rs. } 70{,}000 - 30{,}000}{70{,}000} \times 100$$

$$= \frac{\text{Rs. } 40{,}000}{\text{Rs. } 70{,}000} \times 100 = 57.14\%$$

(i) $$\textbf{Break-even Point} = \frac{\text{Fixed Costs}}{\text{P/V Ratio}} = \frac{\text{Rs. } 20{,}000}{57.14\%} = \text{Rs. } 35{,}000$$

(ii) Sales Rs. 49,000 and Rs. 28,000

= When Sales Rs. 70,000, capacity 100%

" " Rs. 49,000 " $\frac{100 \times 49{,}000}{70{,}000} = 70\%$

When Sales Rs. 70,000, than capacity 100%

" Rs. 28,000 " $\frac{100 \times 28{,}000}{70{,}000} = 40\%.$

Statement

		Rs. 49,000	= 70% capacity	Rs. 28,000	= 40% Capacity
		Rs.		Rs.	
	Variable Cost	21,000	$\left(\frac{70 \times 30,000}{100}\right)$	12,000	$\left(\frac{40 \times 30,000}{100}\right)$
Add :	Fixed Cost	20,000		20,000	
	Total Cost	41,000		32,000	
		(+) 8,000	(Profit)	(–) 4,000	(Loss)
	Sale Price	49,000		28,000	

(iii) **Sales to earn a profit of Rs. 28,000**

$$\text{Sales} = \frac{\text{Fixed Cost + Desired Profit}}{\text{P / V Ratio}} = \frac{\text{Rs. } 20,000 + \text{Rs. } 28,000}{57.14\%}$$

$$\text{Or, Rs. } 48,000 \times \frac{100}{57.14} = \text{Rs. } 83,624 \text{ (approx.)}$$

Problem 15

When sale price is reduced

You are given the following information :

	Rs.
Fixed Cost	4,000
Break-even sales	20,000
Profit	1,000
Selling price per unit	20

Calculate :

(i) Sales and Marginal Cost of sales.

(ii) New BEP if selling price is reduced by 10%.

[B.Com. (Pass) Delhi]

Solution

In this problem contribution is equal to Fixed Cost since there is no profit in case of break-even sales. So, we can ascertain the P/V Ratio.

$$\text{P/V Ratio} = \frac{C}{S} \times 100 = \frac{\text{Rs. } 4,000}{\text{Rs. } 20,000} \times 100 = 20\%$$

Sales when there is profit of Rs. 1,000

$$\frac{\text{Fixed Cost + Profit}}{\text{P / V Ratio}} = \frac{\text{Rs. } 4,000 + \text{Rs. } 1,000}{20\%} = \frac{\text{Rs. } 5,000 \times 100}{20} = \text{Rs. } 25,000$$

(i) Marginal Cost (or Variable Cost) = Sales – Contribution

= Rs. 25,000 – Rs. 4,000 (FC) – Rs. 1,000 (Profit)

= Rs. 20,000

Alternatively, P/V Ratio = 20%.

∴ Marginal cost = 80% of sales

= 80% of Rs. 25,000 = Rs. 20,000

(ii) New Sale Price = Rs. 20 – (10% of Rs. 20) = Rs. 18

New Sale Price = Rs. 25,000 – (10% of Rs. 25,000)

= Rs. 25,000 – Rs. 2,500 = Rs. 22,500

New Contribution = S – VC = Rs. 22,500 – Rs. 20,000 = Rs. 2,500

New P/V Ratio $= \frac{C}{S} \times 100 = \frac{\text{Rs. } 2,500}{\text{Rs. } 22,500} \times 100 = 11.11\%$

∴ **New BEP** $= \frac{\text{Fixed Cost}}{\text{P / V Ratio}} = \frac{\text{Rs. } 4,000 \times 100}{11.11}$

= Rs. 36,003.6 or Rs. 36,000

Problem 16

A. Sen manufactures a single product with a sale price of Rs 16 per unit and a variable cost of Rs. 10 per unit. Fixed costs are Rs. 48,000 p.a.

Calculate :

(i) P/V Ratio; (ii) number of units to be sold to break-even; (iii) number of units to be sold to achieve a profit of Rs 30,000.

[C.U. B.Com. (Hons.) 1994]

Solution

(i) **P/V Ratio**

P/V Ratio $= \frac{C}{S} \times 100$

Contribution per unit = S – V.C. = Rs. 16 – Rs. 10 = Rs. 6.

∴ P/V Ratio $= \frac{6}{16} \times 100 = 37.5\%$.

(ii) **BEP** $= \frac{\text{Fixed Expenses}}{\text{Contribution per unit}}$

$= \frac{\text{Rs. } 48,000}{\text{Rs. } 6} = 8,000$ units

(iii) **Number of units to be sold to earn a profit of Rs. 30,000.**

$$\frac{\text{Fixed Expenses + Profit (desired)}}{\text{Contribution per unit}} = \frac{\text{Rs. } 48,000 + \text{Rs. } 30,000}{\text{Rs. } 6}$$

$$= \frac{\text{Rs. } 78,000}{\text{Rs. } 6} = 13,000 \text{ units}$$

Problem 17

Profit/volume ratio of a company is 50%, while its margin of safety is 40%. If sales volume of the company is Rs. 50,00,000, find out its break-even point and net profit.

[D.U. B.Com. (Hons.) 1999]

Solution

Profit = P/V ratio × M/S ratio × sales.

= 50% × 40% × 50 lakhs.

= Rs. 10,00,000

Calculation of Break-even Point

Break-even point = Sales – M/S Ratio

= Rs. 50 lakhs – 40% of Rs. 50 lakhs

$= \text{Rs. } 50{,}00{,}000 - \left(\frac{40}{100} \times 50{,}00{,}000\right)$

= Rs. 50,00,000 – Rs. 20,00,000

= Rs. 30,00,000

Problem 18

The sales turnover and profit during two years were as follows :

Year	Sales	Profit
	Rs.	Rs.
1998	1,50,000	20,000
1999	1,70,000	25,000

Calculate :

(a) P/V Ratio; (b) Break-even point; (c) Fixed Expenses, and (d) Profit, when sales are Rs. 2,50,000.

[Madras University, B.Com.]

Solution

Year	Sales	Profit
	Rs.	Rs.
1998	1,50,000	20,000
1999	1,70,000	25,000
Difference	20,000	5,000

(a) $\text{P/V Ratio} = \frac{\text{Change in Profit}}{\text{Change in Sales}} \times 100 = \frac{\text{Rs. } 5{,}000}{\text{Rs. } 20{,}000} \times 100 = 25\%.$

(b) $\text{Sales at Break-even Point} = \frac{\text{Fixed Cost}}{\text{P / V Ratio}} = \text{Rs. } 17{,}500 \times 25\% = \text{Rs. } 4{,}375.$

(c) Variable Cost = 100% – 25% = 75% of Sales

∴ Sales for 1998	Rs. 1,50,000
Less : Variable Cost – 75% of Rs. 1,50,000 =	Rs. 1,12,500
Contribution	Rs. 37,500
Less : Profit	Rs. 20,000
Fixed Cost	Rs. 17,500

Alternatively = Sales × P/V Ration = Contribution

∴ Rs. 1,50,000 × 25% = Rs. 37,500

Fixed Cost = Contribution – Profit

= Rs. 37,500 – 20,000 = Rs. 17,500.

(d) Profit when sales are Rs. 2,50,000

Profit = (S × P/V Ratio) – Fixed Cost = (Rs. 2,50,000 × 25%) – Rs. 17,500

= Rs. 62,500 – Rs. 17,500 = Rs. 45,000.

Problem 19

Present production and sales 8,000 units

Selling price per unit Rs. 20

Variable cost per unit :

Direct Materials Rs. 5.00

Direct Labour Rs. 2.50

Variable Overhead 100% of Direct Labour Cost

Fixed Cost, Rs. 40,000

Find out : (a) P/V Ratio; (b) Sales required to break-even; (c) Margin of safety.

Solution

		Rs.	Rs.
	Selling price		20
Less :	Variable expenses :		
	Direct materials	5.00	
	Direct labour	2.50	
	Variable Overhead		
	(100% of direct labour)	2.50	10
	Contribution per unit		10

(a) **P/V Ratio** $= \frac{S - V}{S} \times 100 = \frac{20 - 10}{20} \times 100 = 50\%$.

(b) **BEP** $= \frac{\text{Fixed Expenses}}{\text{P/V Ratio}} = \frac{\text{Rs. } 40,000}{50\%} = \text{Rs. } 80,000$.

(c) **Margin of Safety**

Actual sales – BEP sales

= Rs. 1,60,000 – Rs. 80,000 = Rs. 80,000

Problem 20

From the following data calculate—(i) P/V Ratio, (ii) Profit when sales are Rs. 20,000, and (iii) New Break-even point, if selling price is reduced by 20%.

	Rs.
Fixed Expenses	4,000
Break-even point	10,000

[Delhi B.Com. (Hons.)]

Solution

(i) **P/V Ratio**

BEP = Variable Cost + Fixed Expenses

Rs. 10,000 = Variable Cost + Rs. 4,000

Or, Variable Cost = Rs. 10,000 – Rs. 4,000 = Rs. 6,000.

Here, Fixed Cost = Contribution since there is no profit at break-even point

Therefore, P/V Ratio $= \frac{\text{Contribution}}{\text{Sales}} \times 100 = \frac{\text{Rs. } 4,000}{10,000} \times 100 = 40\%$.

Note : Variable cost is the complement of P/V ratio i.e. 100% – 40% = 60% of sales.

(ii) **Profit** = (P/V Ratio × Sales) – Fixed Cost

= (40% of Rs. 20,000) – Rs. 4,000

= Rs. 8,000 – Rs. 4,000 = Rs. 4,000.

(iii) **New sales**

	Rs.
Present Sales	20,000
Less : 20%	4,000
	16,000
Less : Variable Cost = 60% of Rs. 20,000	12,000
Contribution	4,000

$$\text{New P/V Ratio} = \frac{\text{Contribution}}{\text{Sales}} \times 100 = \frac{\text{Rs. } 4,000}{\text{Rs. } 16,000} \times 100 = 25\%.$$

Problem 21

If margin of safety is Rs. 2,40,000 (40% of sales) and P/V ratio is 30% of AB Ltd., calculate its (i) Break-even sales, and (ii) amount of profit on sales of Rs. 9,00,000.

[Adapted—C.A. (Inter)]

Solution

Margin of safety = Rs. 2,40,000 (40% of sales)

$$\therefore \quad \text{Sales} = \frac{\text{Rs. } 2,40,000}{40} \times 100 = \text{Rs. } 6,00,000$$

Margin of Safety × P/V ratio = Profit

$$\text{Or,} \quad \text{Rs. } 2,40,000 \times \frac{30}{100} = \text{Profit}$$

Or, Profit = Rs. 72,000.

Contribution = Sales × P/V ratio

$$= \text{Rs. } 6,00,000 \times \frac{30}{100} = \text{Rs. } 1,80,000.$$

Fixed Cost = Contribution – Profit = Rs. 1,80,000 – Rs. 72,000 = Rs. 1,08,000.

(i) Break-even Sales × P/V ratio = Fixed cost

$$\therefore \quad \text{BES} = \text{Rs. } 1,08,000 \times \frac{100}{30} = \text{Rs. } 3,60,000.$$

(ii) Amount of profit on sales of Rs. 9,00,000

S × P/V Ratio = Fixed Cost + Profit

Or, Rs. 9,00,000 × 30% = Rs. 1,08,000 + Profit

Or, Profit = Rs. 2,70,000 – Rs. 1,08,000 = Rs. 1,62,000.

Problem 22

The following costs and sales of a manufacturing company for the first half and second half of 1998-99 are given :

	First half	Second half
	Rs.	Rs.
Sales	24,00,000	30,00,000
Total costs	21,80,000	26,00,000

You are asked to determine :

(i) Contribution/sales ratio of the firm.
(ii) Annual fixed costs.
(iii) Break-even point.
(iv) Margin of safety as percentage of sales.

[Adapted—I.C.W.A. (Inter) June 1999]

Solution

	First half	*Second half*	*Change*
	Rs.	Rs.	Rs.
Sales	24,00,000	30,00,000	6,00,000
Total cost	21,80,000	26,00,000	4,20,000
Profit	2,20,000	4,00,000	1,80,000

(i) **Contribution/Sales Ratio**

Or, $\text{P/V Ratio} = \dfrac{\text{Change in Profit}}{\text{Change in Sales}} \times 100 = \dfrac{1{,}80{,}000}{6{,}00{,}000} \times 100 = 30\%$

(ii) **P/V Ratio = 30%**

So, Variable Cost/Sales Ratio = 100% – 30% = 70%

$\text{Variable Cost} = 70\% \text{ of total Sales} = \dfrac{70}{100} \times 54{,}00{,}000 = \text{Rs. } 37{,}80{,}000$

Hence, Fixed Cost = Total Cost – Variable Cost = Rs. 47,80,000 – Rs. 37,80,000 = Rs. 10,00,000

(iii) **Break-even point** $= \dfrac{\text{Fixed Cost}}{\text{P / V Ratio}} = \dfrac{\text{Rs. } 10{,}00{,}000}{30\%} = \text{Rs. } 33{,}33{,}333.$

(iv) **Margin of Safety as a percentage of sales**

Margin of Safety = Sales – BEP Sales

= Rs. 54,00,000 – Rs. 33,33,333 = Rs. 20,66,667

Margine of safety as percentage of sales =

$\dfrac{\text{Margin of Safety}}{\text{Sales}} \times 100 = \dfrac{\text{Rs. } 20{,}66{,}667}{\text{Rs. } 54{,}00{,}000} \times 100 = 38.3\%.$

Problem 23

The ratio of variable cost to sales is 70%. The break-even point occurs at 60% of the capacity sales when fixed costs are Rs. 90,000. Also compute profit at 75% of the capacity sales.

[Adapted—C.A. (Inter)]

Solution

Variable costs to sales = 70%

P/V Ratio = 100% – 70% = 30%

We know that Break-even Sales × P/V ratio = Fixed costs

$\therefore \text{BES} \times \dfrac{30}{100} = 90{,}000 \text{ or BES} = 90{,}000 \times \dfrac{100}{30} = \text{Rs. } 3{,}00{,}000$

It is given in the problem that break-even occurs at 60% capacity.

$\therefore$ Capacity Sales = 60% = Rs. 3,00,000

$= \dfrac{3{,}00{,}000}{60} \times 100 = \text{Rs. } 5{,}00{,}000$

Calculation of profit at 75% capacity

	75% capacity sales = $\frac{75}{100} \times 5,00,000$ =	Rs. 3,75,000
Less :	Variable cost $\frac{70}{100} \times$ Rs. 3,75,000 =	Rs. 2,62,500
		Rs. 1,12,500
Less :	Fixed costs	Rs. 90,000
	Profit	Rs. 22,500

Problem 24

X Ltd. made sales during a certain period for Rs. 1,00,000. The net profit for the same period was Rs. 10,000 and the fixed overheads were Rs. 15,000. Find out : (i) P/V Ratio; (ii) Break-even point of sales; (iii) Value of sales to earn a profit of Rs. 15,000 and (iv) Net profit from the sales of Rs. 1,50,000.

[C.U. B.Com. (Hons.) 1995]

Solution

Contribution = Fixed Overheads + Net Profit = Rs. 15,000 + Rs. 10,000 = Rs. 25,000

(i) **P/V Ratio** = $\frac{\text{Contribution}}{\text{Sales}} \times 100 = \frac{\text{Rs. } 25,000}{\text{Rs. } 1,00,000} \times 100 = 25\%$

(ii) **Break-even Point of Sales** $= \frac{\text{Fixed Expenses}}{\text{P / V Ratio}} = \frac{\text{Rs. } 15,000}{25\%}$

$= \frac{\text{Rs. } 15,000}{25} \times 100 = \text{Rs. } 60,000$

(iii) **Value of sales to earn a profit of Rs. 15,000**

$= \frac{\text{Fixed overheads + Desired profit}}{\text{P / V Ratio}} = \frac{\text{Rs. } 15,000 + \text{Rs. } 15,000}{25\%}$

$= \frac{\text{Rs. } 30,000}{25} \times 100 = \text{Rs. } 1,20,000$

(iv) **Profit when the sales is Rs. 1,50,000** $= \frac{15,000 + \text{Profit}}{\text{P / V Ratio}} = \text{Rs. } 1,50,000$

$15,000 + \text{Profit} = 1,50,000 \times \frac{25}{100}$

Or, Rs. 15,000 + Profit = Rs. 37,500

Or, Profit = Rs. 37,500 – Rs. 15,000 = Rs. 22,500

FINDING OUT THE SELLING PRICE

Problem 25

From the following particulars, find out the selling price per unit, if BEP is to be brought down to 9,000 units.

Variable cost per unit	Rs. 75
Selling price per unit	Rs. 100
Fixed expenses	Rs. 2,70,000

Solution

$$\text{Contribution per unit} = \frac{\text{Fixed Expenses}}{\text{BEP in units}} = \frac{\text{Rs. } 2,70,000}{9,000} = \text{Rs. } 30.00$$

Sale Price = Variable Cost + Contribution per unit

Sale Price = Rs. 75 + Rs. 30 = Rs. 105.

Problem 26

Following data have been extracted from the cost record of Suman Ltd. :

Total capacity 1,00,000 units

Capacity at BEP 40%

Variable Cost per unit Rs. 16

Fixed Costs Rs. 2,00,000

Find out selling price per unit for the BEP.

Solution

Capacity at BEP = 40%

$$\text{Capacity BEP} = \frac{\text{BEP in units}}{1,00,000} \times 100$$

$$40 = \frac{\text{BEP in units}}{1,00,000} \times 100 = \text{BEP in units} \times 100 = 1,00,000 \times 40$$

$$\text{BEP in units} = \frac{1,00,000 \times 40}{100} = 40,000 \text{ units.}$$

$$\text{Contribution per unit} = \frac{\text{FE}}{\text{BEP in units}} = \frac{\text{Rs. } 2,00,000}{40,000} = \text{Rs. } 5.00$$

Selling Price = Variable Cost + Contribution

S = Rs. 16.00 + Rs. 5 = Rs. 21.00.

FINDING OUT BEP IN RUPEES

Problem 27

The following data have been obtained from the cost records of Sail Ltd. :

	First year	Second year
	Rs.	Rs.
Sales	40,000	45,000
Profit	5,000	7,000

Calculate the BEP in Rupees.

Solution

$$\text{P/V Ratio} = \frac{\text{Change in Profit}}{\text{Change in sales}} \times 100 = \frac{\text{Rs. } 2,000}{\text{Rs. } 5,000} \times 100 = 40\%$$

$$\text{BEP} = \frac{\text{FE}}{\text{P/V Ratio}} = \text{Fixed Expenses} = (\text{S} \times \text{P/V Ratio}) - \text{Profit}$$

$$= \left(\text{Rs. } 40,000 \times \frac{40}{100}\right) - \text{Rs. } 5,000 = \text{Rs. } 16,000 - \text{Rs. } 5,000 = \text{Rs. } 11,000.$$

$$\therefore \text{BEP} = \frac{\text{Rs. } 11,000}{40\%} = \frac{11,000}{40} \times 100 = \text{Rs. } 27,500.$$

Problem 28

From the following data find out BEP in units :

Variable cost per unit	Rs. 10.00
Fixed overheads	Rs. 72,000
Selling price per unit	Rs. 16

Solution

$$\text{BEP in units} = \frac{S}{S - V} = \frac{\text{Rs. } 72{,}000}{16 - 10} = \frac{72{,}000}{6} = 12{,}000 \text{ units}$$

Problem 29

S Limited furnishes the following information relating to the half-year ended 30th June 1990 :

	Rs.
Fixed Expenses	50,000
Sales Value	2,00,000
Profit	50,000

During the second half of the same year the company has projected a loss of Rs. 10,000.

(i) Calculate the P/V ratio, break-even point and margin of safety for six months ending 30.6.1990.

(ii) Expected sales volume for second half of the year assuming that selling price and fixed expenses remain unchanged in the second half-year also.

(iii) The break-even point and margin of safety for the whole year 1990.

[Adapted—I.C.W.A. (Inter)]

Solution

		Rs.
(i)	Fixed Expenses	50,000
	Profit	50,000
	Contribution	1,00,000
	Sales	2,00,000

P/V Ratio $= \dfrac{\text{Contribution}}{\text{Sales}} \times 100 = \dfrac{\text{Rs. } 1{,}00{,}000}{\text{Rs. } 2{,}00{,}000} \times 100 = 50\%$

Break-even Point $= \dfrac{\text{Fixed Expenses}}{\text{P / V Ratio}} = \dfrac{\text{Rs. } 50{,}000}{50\%} = \text{Rs. } 1{,}00{,}000$

Margin of Safety = Rs. 2,00,000 – Rs. 1,00,000 = Rs. 1,00,000

(ii) **Contribution** = Fixed Expenses – Loss = Rs. 50,000 – Rs. 10,000 = Rs. 40,000

P/V Ratio = 50%.

$\therefore$ **Sales** $= \dfrac{\text{Contribution}}{\text{P / V Ratio}} = \dfrac{\text{Rs. } 40{,}000}{50\%} = \text{Rs. } 80{,}000$

(iii) **Fixed Expenses** = Rs. 1,00,000

P/V Ratio = 50%.

Break-even Point $= \dfrac{\text{Fixed Expenses}}{\text{P / V ratio}} = \dfrac{\text{Rs. } 1{,}00{,}000}{50\%} = \text{Rs. } 2{,}00{,}000$

Margin of Safety = Sales – BES = Rs. 2,80,000 – Rs. 2,00,000 = Rs. 80,000

Point to note

P/V ratio does not change with changes in level or volume, provided selling price remains the same.

Problem 30

Calculate number of units to be sold to earn a profit of Rs. 60,000 a year :

	Rs.	
Sale price	20	per unit
Variable manufacturing cost	11	" "
Variable selling cost	3	" "
Fixed factory overhead	Rs. 5,40,000	p.a.
Fixed selling cost	Rs. 2,52,000	p.a.

[Adapted—B.Com. Madras]

Solution

Contribution = SP – Variable Expenses

		Rs.	
	Sale price per unit	20	
Less :	Variable expenses (Rs. 11.00 + Rs. 3.00)	14	per unit
	Contribution	6	per unit

$$\text{Sales} = \frac{\text{Fixed Expenses} + \text{Profit}}{\text{Contribution per unit}}$$

$$= \frac{\text{Rs. } 5,40,000 + \text{Rs. } 2,52,000 + \text{Rs. } 60,000}{6}$$

$$= \frac{8,52,000}{6} = 1,42,000 \text{ units}$$

Problem 31

A company producing a single product sells it at Rs. 50 per unit. Unit variable cost is Rs. 35 and fixed costs amount to Rs. 12 lakh per annum. With this data you are required to calculate the following :

(a) P/V ratio and Break-even sales

(b) New Break-even sales if variable cost increases by Rs. 3 per unit, without increase in selling price.

(c) Increase in sales required if profits are to be increased by Rs. 2.4 lakhs.

(d) Percentage increase or decrease in sales valume units off-set.

(i) an increase of Rs. 3 in variable cost per unit.

(ii) a 10% increase in selling price without affecting existing profits quantum.

[Adapted—I.C.W.A. (Inter)]

Solution

(a) $$\text{P/V Ratio} = \frac{\text{Contribution per unit}}{\text{Sales}} \times 100 = \frac{50 - 35}{50} \times 100 = 30\%$$

$$\text{Break-even Sales} = \frac{\text{Fixed Expenses}}{\text{P/V Ratio}} = \frac{12 \text{ lakhs}}{30\%} = \text{Rs. } 40 \text{ lakhs}$$

(b) New Break-even Sales

$$\text{New P/V Ratio} = \frac{\text{Contribution} - \text{increase in VC}}{\text{Sales}} \times 100$$

$$= \frac{15 - 3}{50} \times 100 = 24\%.$$

$$\text{Revised BE Sales} = \frac{\text{Fixed Expenses}}{\text{P / V Ratio}} = \frac{\text{Rs. 12 lakhs}}{24\%} = \text{Rs. 50,00,000.}$$

(c) **Increase in Sales for increased profit**

$$\frac{\text{Fixed Cost + Desired Profit}}{\text{P / V Ratio}} = \frac{\text{Rs. 12,00,000 + 2,40,000}}{30\%}$$

= Total Sales Rs. 48,00,000.

Increase in Sales = Actual Sales – BE Sales = Rs. 48,00,000 – 40,00,000 = Rs. 8,00,000.

(d) (i) **Percentage increase in sales volume in units**

$$\frac{\text{Reduction in contribution}}{\text{New contribution}} \times 100 = \frac{3}{12} \times 100 = \frac{300}{12} = 25\%$$

(ii) % Decrease in sales volume

$$\frac{\text{Increase in contribution per unit}}{\text{New contribution per unit}} \times 100 = \frac{5}{20} \times 100 = 25\%.$$

Note : (a) New Sale Price – V.C. = New contribution = Rs. 55 – 35 = Rs. 20

(b) Increase in contribution = Rs. 20 – Rs. 15 = Rs. 5.

Problem 32

Raj corporation Ltd. has prepared the following budget estimates for the year 2002-2003.

Units sold	15,000
Fixed expenses	Rs. 34,000
Sales value	Rs. 1,50,000
Variable costs	6 per unit

You are required to :

(i) Find the P/V ratio, break-even point and margin of safety in each of the following cases.

(a) Decrease of 10% in selling price.

(b) Increase of 10% variable costs.

(c) Increase of sales volume by 2,000 units.

(d) Increase of Rs. 6,000 in fixed costs.

[Adapted—C.A. (Inter)]

Solution

	P/V Ratio	*Break-even Point*	*Margin of Safety*
i.	$\frac{\text{Contribution}}{\text{Sales}} \times 100$	$\frac{\text{Fixed Costs}}{\text{Contribution per unit}}$	Sales – BE Sales
(i)	$\frac{10 - 6}{10} \times 100 = 40\%$	$\frac{34,000}{4} = 8,500$	15,000 – 8,500 = 6,500 units

(ii) **In case of 10% decrease in seling price**

$\frac{\text{Rs. 9 – Rs. 6}}{\text{Rs. 9}} \times 100$	$\frac{\text{Rs. 34,000}}{3}$	15,000 – 11,333
= 33.33%	= 11,333 units	= 3,667 units

(iii) Increase of 10% in variable costs

$$\frac{10 - 6.6}{10} \times 100 \qquad \frac{34,000}{3.4} \qquad 15,000 - 10,000$$

$$= 34\% \qquad = 10,000 \text{ units} \qquad = 5,000 \text{ units}$$

(a) Increase of sales by 2000 units

$$\frac{10 - 6}{10} \times 100 \qquad \frac{34,000}{4} \qquad 17,000 - 8,500$$

$$= 40\% \qquad = 8,500 \text{ units} \qquad = 8,500 \text{ units}$$

(b) Increase of Rs. 6,000 in fixed costs

$$\frac{10 - 6}{10} \times 100 \qquad \frac{40,000\ (34,000 + 6,000)}{4} \qquad 15,000 - 10,000$$

$$= 40\% \qquad = 10,000 \text{ units} \qquad = 5,000 \text{ units}$$

Problem 33

Break-down of cost per unit at an activity level of 10,000 units of Zenith Razors is as follows :

		Rs.
	Raw materials	10
	Direct wages	8
	Chargeable expenses	2
	Variable overheads	4
	Fixed overheads	6
	Total cost per unit	30
Less :	Selling price per unit	32
	Profit per unit	2

How many units must be sold to break-even?

[Adapted—I.C.W.A. (Inter)]

Solution

		Rs.	Rs.
	Selling price per unit		32
Less :	***Variable costs***		
	Raw materials	10	
	Direct wages	8	
	Chargeable expenses	2	
	Variable overheads	4	24
	Contribution		8

Total Fixed Cost = 10,000 × Rs 6 = Rs. 60,000

$$\therefore \text{BEP} = \frac{\text{Fixed Cost}}{\text{Contribution per unit}} = \frac{\text{Rs. } 60,000}{\text{Rs. } 8} = 7,500 \text{ units}$$

Problem 34

From the following data calculate :

(i) P/V Ratio; (ii) Break-even Point; (iii) Margin of Safety

	Rs.
Total Sales	3,60,000
Selling price per unit	100
Variable cost per unit	50
Fixed costs	1,00,000

(iv) If the **selling price** is reduced to Rs. 90, by how much is the margin of safety **reduced?**

[Adapted—I.C.W.A. (Inter)]

Solution

(i) **P/V Ratio** $= \dfrac{\text{Contribution}}{\text{Sales}} \times 100$

Contribution = Selling Price – Variable Cost

= Rs. 100 – Rs. 50 = Rs. 50 per unit

P/V Ratio $= \dfrac{\text{Rs. }50}{\text{Rs. }100} \times 100 = 50\%$

(ii) **Break-even Point**

$$\text{BEP} = \frac{\text{Fixed Expenses}}{\text{P / V Ratio}} = \frac{\text{Rs. } 1,00,000}{50\%} = \frac{\text{Rs. } 1,00,000}{50} \times 100 = \text{Rs. } 2,00,000.$$

(iii) Margin of Safety = Present sales – Break-even sales

= Rs. 3,60,000 – Rs. 2,00,000 = Rs. 1,60,000

Alternatively : $\dfrac{\text{Profit}}{\text{P / V Ratio}}$

Profit = Contribution – Fixed Expenses.

Units produced = Sales ÷ Selling price per unit

= Rs. 3,60,000 ÷ 100 = 3,600 units

∴ Contribution = 3,600 × Rs. 50 = 1,80,000

Profit = Rs. 1,80,000 (C) – Rs. 1,00,000 (FC) = Rs. 80,000

∴ Margin of Safety $= \dfrac{\text{Profit}}{\text{P / V Ratio}} = \dfrac{\text{Rs. } 80,000}{50\%} = \dfrac{\text{Rs. } 80,000}{50} \times 100$

= Rs. 1,60,000

(iv) **New Sale Price** = 3,600 × Rs. 90 = Rs. 3,24,000

Contribution = Rs. 3,24,000 – Rs. 1,80,000 (VC) = Rs. 1,44,000

P/V Ratio $= \dfrac{\text{Contribution}}{\text{Sales}} \times 100 = \dfrac{\text{Rs. } 1,44,000}{3,24,000} \times 100 = 44.5\%$

New BEP $= \dfrac{\text{Fixed Expenses}}{\text{P / V Ratio}} = \dfrac{\text{Rs. } 1,00,000}{44.5\%}$ = Rs. 2,24,719 or Rs. 2,24,720

Reduced Margin of Safety = Rs. 2,24,720 – Rs. 2,00,000

(New BEP – Old BEP) = Rs. 24,720.

BREAK-EVEN VOLUME DUE TO INCREASED CAPACITY

Problem 35

From the following figures find the break-even volume :

Selling price per tonne	Rs. 69.50
Variable cost per tonne	Rs. 35.50
Fixed Expenses	Rs. 18.02 lakhs

If this volume represents 40% capacity, what is the additional profit for an added production of 40% capacity, the selling price of which is 10% lower for 20% capacity production and 15% lower than the existing price for the other 20% capacity?

[Adapted—I.C.W.A. (Inter)]

Solution

Break-even Sales × P/V Ratio = Fixed Cost

$$\text{BES} \times \frac{(\text{Rs. } 69{\cdot}50 - 35{\cdot}50)}{69{\cdot}50} \times 100$$

$$\text{BES} \times \frac{34}{69{\cdot}50} \times 100 = 48.92\%$$

∴ BES × 48.92% = Rs. 18·02 lakhs

$$\text{Or,} \quad \text{BES} = \frac{\text{Rs. } 18.02 \text{ lakhs}}{48.92\%} = \text{Rs. } 36{,}83{,}565$$

Contribution per tonne = Rs. 69·50 – Rs. 35.50 = Rs. 34.

$$\text{BES in units} = \frac{\text{Fixed Expenses}}{\text{Contribution per unit}} = \frac{18{\cdot}02 \text{ lakhs}}{\text{Rs. } 34} = 53{,}000 \text{ tonnes.}$$

40% Capacity = 53,000 tonnes

So, 80% Capacity = 1,06,000 tonnes

(i) **Profit for 20% capacity for which selling price falls by 10%.**

Revised selling price Rs. 69·50 – Rs. 6·95	= Rs. 62·55
Less : Variable cost	= Rs. 35·50
Contribution per tonne	Rs. 27·05

20% Capacity = 53,000 ÷ 2 = 26,500

So, Profit = 26,500 × Rs. 27·05 (since any contribution beyond B.E.S. is profit) = **Rs. 7,16,825.**

(ii) Profit for another 20% capacity for which selling price falls by 15%.

Revised sale price Rs. 69·500 – Rs. 10·425	= Rs. 59·075
Less : Variable cost	= Rs. 35·500
Contribution per tonne	Rs. 23·575

Profit = 26,500 units × Contribution per tonne

= 26,500 × Rs. 23.575 = **Rs. 6,24,738.**

Therefore, additional profit for 40% increased production = Profit in (i) + (ii)

= (i) Rs. 7,16,825 + (ii) Rs. 6,24,738 = Rs. 13,41,563.

Problem 36

From the following information calculate the break-even point and the turnover required to earn a profit of Rs. 30,000 :

Fixed overheads	Rs. 21,000
Variable costs	Rs. 2 per unit
Selling price	Rs. 5 per unit

If the company is earning a profit of Rs. 30,000, express the "Margin of Safety" available to it.

[Adapted—I.C.W.A. (Inter)]

Solution

(i) **Break-even Point**

Contribution per unit	Rs.
Sale price	5·00
Less : Variable cost	2·00
Contribution	3·00

Break-even Point = Fixed Expenses ÷ Contribution per unit

= Rs. 21,000 ÷ Rs. 3 = 7,000

Additional output required to earn a profit of Rs. 30,000.

$= \dfrac{\text{Rs. } 30{,}000}{\text{Rs. } 3} =$ 10,000

Total turnover in units to earn a profit of Rs. 30,000 17,000

(ii) So, **Turnover in amount** = 17,000 @ Rs. 5 per unit = Rs. 85,000

(iii) **Margin of Safety** :

Sale price 17,000 × Rs. 5 = Rs. 85,000

Less : Sale at Break-even point = 7,000 × Rs. 5 Rs. 35,000

17,000 – 7,000 = 10,000 × 5 = Rs. 50,000

Problem 37

The following figures are available from the records of Venus Enterprises as at 31st December :

	1994 Rs. (in lakhs)	1995 Rs. (in lakhs)
Sales	150	200
Profit	30	50

Calculate :

(a) the P/V ratio and total fixed expenses.

(b) the break-even level of sales.

(c) sales required to earn a profit at Rs. 90 lakhs.

(d) profit or loss that would arise if the sales were Rs 280 lakhs.

[Adapted—C.A. (Inter)]

Solution

(a) **P/V Ratio** $= \dfrac{\text{Change in Profit}}{\text{Change in Sales}} \times 100 = \dfrac{\text{Rs. 50 lakhs} - \text{Rs. 30 lakhs}}{\text{Rs. 200 lakhs} - \text{Rs. 150 lakhs}}$

$= \dfrac{\text{Rs. 20 lakhs}}{\text{Rs. 50 lakhs}} \times 100 = 40\%$

Fixed Expenses = Contribution – Profit

= (P/V Ratio × Sales) – Profit

Fixed Expenses for 1994 $= \left(\dfrac{40}{100} \times \text{150 lakhs}\right) - \text{30 lakhs}$

= Rs. 60 lakhs – 30 lakhs = Rs. 30 lakhs

Fixed Expenses for 1995 $= \left(\dfrac{40}{100} \times \text{Rs. 200 lakhs}\right) - \text{50 lakhs}$

= Rs. 80 lakhs – 50 lakhs = Rs. 30 lakhs

(b) **Break-even Point** $= \dfrac{\text{Fixed Expenses}}{\text{P / V Ratio}}$

$= \dfrac{\text{Rs. 30 lakhs}}{40\%} = \dfrac{\text{Rs. 30 lakhs}}{40} \times 100 = \text{Rs. 75 lakhs}$

(c) Sales required to earn a profit of Rs. 90 lakhs :

$\dfrac{\text{Fixed Cost + Required Profit}}{\text{P / V Ratio}} = \dfrac{\text{Rs. 30 lakhs + Rs. 90 Lakhs}}{40\%}$

$= \dfrac{\text{Rs. 120 lakhs}}{40} \times 100 = \text{Rs. 300 lakhs}$

(d) **Computation of profit or loss that would arise of the sales were Rs. 280 lakhs.**

Profit = Contribution – Fixed Expenses

= (P/V Ratio × Sales) – Fixed Expenses

$= (40\% \text{ of } 280 \text{ lakhs}) - \text{Rs. 30 lakhs.} = \left(280 \text{ lakhs} \times \dfrac{40}{100}\right) - \text{Rs. 30 lakhs}$

= Rs. 112 lakhs – Rs. 30 lakhs = Rs. 82 lakhs

Problem 38

From the data given below you are required to determine the Break-even Point and Margin of Safety :

	Rs.
Sales	6,00,000
Marginal Cost	3,50,000
Fixed Cost	1,50,000

[Adapted—I.C.W.A.]

Solution

		Rs.
	Sales	6,00,000
Less :	Marginal Cost	3,50,000
	Contribution	2,50,000
Less :	Fixed Cost	1,50,000
	Profit	1,00,000

Contribution to Sales Ratio $= \dfrac{2,50,000}{6,00,000} \times 100 = 41.667\%$

Break-even Point $= \dfrac{\text{Fixed Cost}}{\text{C / S Ratio}} \times 100$

$= \dfrac{\text{Rs. 1,50,000}}{41.667} \times 100 = \text{Rs. 3,60,000}$

Margin of Safety (Sale – BES) = Rs. 6,00,000 – Rs. 3,60,000 = Rs. 2,40,000

Problem 39

Present production and sales 8,000 units

Selling price – Rs. 20 per unit

Variable Cost per unit :

Direct Materials	Rs. 5·00
Direct Labour	Rs. 2·50
Variable Overhead	100% of Direct labour
Fixed Cost	Rs. 40,000

Find out :

(a) P/V Ratio; (b) Sales required to break-even; (c) Margin of Safety.

[Adapted—Bombay M.Com.]

Solution

Step I : Find out contribution per unit

Contribution = Sale – Variable expenses

		Rs.	Rs.
	Sales price per unit =		20·00
Less :	Variable expenses		
	Direct materials	5·00	
	Direct labour	2·50	
	Variable overhead = 100% of Direct wages	2·50	10·00
	Contribution		10·00 per unit

Step II : (a) $\textbf{P/V Ratio} = \frac{S - V}{S} \times 100 = \frac{20 - 10}{20} \times 100 = 50\%$

(b) $\textbf{Break-even Point} = \frac{\text{Fixed Expenses}}{\text{P / V Ratio}}$

$\textbf{BEP} = \frac{\text{Rs. } 40{,}000}{50\%} = \frac{40{,}000}{50} \times 100 = \text{Rs. } 80{,}000$

(c) **Margin of Safety** = Total Sales – BEP Sales

= (8,000 × Rs. 20) – Rs. 80,000 = Rs. 1,60,000 – Rs. 80,000 = Rs. 80,000

Problem 40

The following figures relating to the performance of a company of the years I and II are available. Assuming that (i) the ratio of variable cost to sales, and (ii) the fixed cost are the same for both the years, ascertain :

(a) the profit-volume ratio, (b) the amount of fixed costs, (c) the break-even point, and (d) the budgeted profit for the year III, if the budgeted sales for the year are Rs. 1 crore.

	Total Sales (Rs. in '000)	***Total Costs*** (Rs. in '000)
Year I	7,000	5,800
Year II	9,000	6,600

[Adapted—I.C.W.A. (Inter) 1991]

Solution

	Sales (Rs. in '000)	***Total Costs*** (Rs. in '000)	***Profit*** (Rs. in '000)
Year I	7,000	5,800	1,200
Year II	9,000	6,600	2,400
	2,000	800	1,200

(a) $\textbf{P/V Ratio} = \frac{\text{Chante in Profit}}{\text{Change in Sales}} \times 100 = \frac{\text{Rs. } 12{,}00{,}000}{\text{Rs. } 20{,}00{,}000} \times 100 = 60\%$

(b) **Fixed Expenses** = (P/V Ratio × Sales) – Profit = (60% of 70,00,000) – Rs. 12,00,000

= Rs. 42,00,000 – Rs. 12,00,000 = Rs. 30,00,000

(c) $BEP = \frac{\text{Fixed Expenses}}{\text{P / V Ratio}} = \frac{\text{Rs. } 30,00,000}{60\%} = \text{Rs. } 50,00,000$

(d) **Budgeted sales for 3rd Year** = Rs. 1,00,00,000

Therefore, Contribution = Sales × P/V Ratio = Rs. 1,00,00,000 × $\frac{60}{100}$ = Rs. 60,00,000

Less :	Fixed Expenses	= Rs. 30,00,000
	Budgeted Profit for the IIIrd year	= Rs. 30,00,000

Problem 41

The Asian Industries specialises in the manufacture of small capacity motors. The cost structure of a motor is as under :

Material	Rs. 50
Labour	Rs. 80
Variable Cost	75% of labour cost

Fixed overheads of the company amount to Rs. 2·40 lakhs per annum. The sale price of the motor is Rs. 230 each.

(a) Determine the number of motors that have to be manufactured and sold in a year in order to break-even.

(b) How many motors have to be made to make a profit of Rs. 1 lakh per year?

(c) If the sale price is reduced by Rs. 15 each how many motors have to be sold to break-even?

[Adapted—I.C.W.A. (Inter)]

Solution

(a) Find out contribution

		Rs.	Rs.
	Sale price per motor		230
Less :	Variable cost per motor		
	Material per unit	50	
	Labour	80	
	Variable overheads 75% of Rs. 80	60	190
	Contribution per unit		40
	Fixed Overheads per year	2,40,000	

$BEP = \frac{\text{Fixed cost}}{\text{Contribution per unit}} = \frac{\text{Rs. } 2,40,000}{40} = 6,000 \text{ units}$

(b) **Find out contribution in Rupees**

Contribution = F.C. + Profit = Rs. 2,40,000 + Rs. 1,00,000 = Rs. 3,40,000

The number of motors to be sold = $\frac{\text{Contribution in rupees}}{\text{Contribution per unit}} = \frac{\text{Rs. } 3,40,000}{40} = 8,500 \text{ units}$

(c) **Find out the new contribution**

New Sale Price = Rs. 230 – Rs. 15 = Rs. 215

New Contribution = Sale Price – Variable Expenses = Rs. 215 – Rs. 190 = Rs. 25

$BEP = \frac{\text{Fixed Costs}}{\text{Contribution}} = \frac{\text{Rs. } 2,40,000}{\text{Rs. } 25} = 9,600 \text{ motors}$

Problem 42

A Ltd. manufactures and sales four types of products under the board names P, Q, R, and S. The sales mix in value comprises $33\,^1/_3\%$, $41\,^2/_3\%$, $16\,^2/_3\%$ and $8\,^1/_3\%$ of P, Q, R and S, respectively. The total budgeted sales (100%) are Rs. 60,000 per month.

Operating costs are :

Variable Costs

Product	P	60% of selling price
"	Q	68% " " "
"	R	80% " " "
"	S	40% " " "

Fixed Cost Rs. 14,700.

Calculate the break-even point for the products on an overall basis.

[C.S. Final—Adapted]

Solution

		P	Q	R	S	Total
		Products				
		$33\frac{1}{3}\%$	$41\frac{2}{3}\%$	$16\frac{2}{3}\%$	$8\frac{1}{3}\%$	
		Rs.	Rs.	Rs.	Rs.	Rs.
	Sales value	20,000	25,000	10,000	5,000	60,000
Less :	Variable cost (based on given %)	12,000	17,000	8,000	2,000	39,000
	Contribution	8,000	8,000	2,000	3,000	21,000
Less :	Fixed cost					14,700
						6,300

$$\text{P/V Ratio} = \frac{\text{Contribution}}{\text{Sales}} \times 100$$

$$= \frac{\text{Rs. } 21{,}000}{60{,}000} \times 100 = 35\%$$

$$\text{Break-Even Point} = \frac{\text{Fixed Expenses}}{\text{P / V Ratio}} = \frac{\text{Rs. } 14{,}700}{35\%}$$

$$= \frac{\text{Rs. } 14{,}700}{35} \times 100 = 42{,}000 \text{ units.}$$

Problem 43

A single product company sells its products at Rs. 60 per unit. In 1996 the company operated on a margin of safety of 40%. The fixed costs amounted to Rs. 3,60,000 and variable cost ratio to sales was 80%.

In 1997, it is estimated that the variable cost will go up by 10% and the fixed cost will increase by 5%.

Find out the selling price required to be fixed in 1997 to earn the same P/V ratio as in 1996.

Assuming the same selling price of Rs. 60 per unit in 1997, find the number of units required to be produced and sold to earn the same profit as in 1996.

[C.A. (Inter) May 1998]

Solution

(a) **P/V ratio in 1996**

Contribution = S.P. – Variable Cost

= Rs. 60 – Rs. 48 (80% of Rs. 60) = Rs. 12.

P/V Ratio = $\frac{\text{Contribution}}{\text{Sales}} \times 100 = \frac{12}{60} \times 100 = 20\%$

(b) **Number of units sold in 1996**

Break-even Point = Fixed cost ÷ Contribution per unit

= Rs. 3,60,000 ÷ 12 = 30,000 units.

Break-even point will be 60% of units sold since margin of safety is 40%.

No. of units sold = Break-even points in units ÷ 60%.

= 30,000 ÷ 60% = $\frac{30,000}{60} \times 100$ = 50,000 units

(c) **Profit earned in 1996**

Total contribution = No. of units sold × Contribution per unit

= 50,000 × 12 = Rs. 6,00,000

Less : Fixed cost Rs. 3,60,000

Profit Rs. 2,40,000

(d) **Selling Price to be fixed in 1997**

Revised Variable Cost = Rs. 48 + $\left(\frac{10}{100} \times 48\right)$ = Rs. 48 + Rs. 4·80 = Rs. 52·80

Revised Fixed Cost = Rs. 3,60,000 × $\left(\frac{5}{100} \times 3,60,000\right)$ = Rs. 3,78,000

P/V Ratio for 1996 = 20%

Variable Cost ratio to selling price = 80%

Therefore, revised selling price per unit = Rs. 52·80 ÷ 80% = Rs. 66

(e) **No. of Units to be produced and sold in 1997** to earn the same profit

Profit in 1996 = Rs. 2,40,000

Fixed cost in 1997 = Rs. 3,78,000

Desired contribution = Rs. 6,18,000

Contribution per unit = Selling price per unit – Variable cost per unit

= Rs. 60 – Rs. 52·80 = Rs. 7·20

No. of Units to be produced in 1997

Desired contribution ÷ contribution per unit = Rs. 6,18,000 ÷ Rs. 7·20 = 85,834 units.

DROPING PRODUCTION OF ONE PRODUCT

Problem 44

The costs per unit of three products X, Y, and Z are given below :

Products	X	Y	Z
Direct materials (Rs.)	20	16	18
Direct labour (Rs.)	12	14	12
Variable overheads (Rs.)	8	10	6
Fixed Expenses (Rs.)	6	6	4
Cost per unit	46	46	40
Add : Profit	18	14	12
Sale price per unit	64	60	52
Number of units produced	10,000	5,000	8,000

Production arrangements are such that if one product is given-up the production of the others can be raised by 50%. The directors propose that product Z should be given up because the contribution from the product is the lowest. Present suitable analysis of the data indicating whether the proposal should be accepted.

[Delhi University B.Com. (Hons.) 1998]

Solution

Calculation of Contribution

	X	Y	Z
	Rs.	Rs.	Rs.
Variable Costs			
Material	20	16	18
Labour	12	14	12
Variable overhead	8	10	6
	40	40	36

Contribution = Sales – Variable Cost

	X	Y	Z
	Rs.	Rs.	Rs.
Sales	64	60	52
Less : Variable Cost	40	40	36
Contribution	24	20	16

Profit = Contribution – Fixed Cost

Total Contribution

Units sold × contribution per unit

	X	Y	Z
	Rs.	Rs.	Rs.
(i)	(10,000 × 24) = 2,40,000	(5,000 × 20) = 1,00,000	8,000 × 16 = 1,28,000
Less : Fixed cost	(10,000 × 6) = 60,000	(6 × 5,000) = 30,000	8,000 × 4 = 32,000
Profit	1,80,000	70,000	96,000

Total Profit = Rs. 1,80,000 + Rs. 70,000 + Rs. 96,000 = Rs. 3,46,000

(A) When product X is given up

	Y	Z
Sales units	7,500	12,000
	[5,000 + (50% of 5,000)]	[8,000 + (50% of 8,000)]
Contribution (Rs.)	7,500 × Rs. 20	12,000 × 16
	= Rs. 1,50,000	= Rs. 1,92,000

Profit = Contribution – Fixed expenses

Rs. 3,42,000 (Rs. 1,50,000 + Rs. 1,92,000) – Rs. 1,22,000 (60,000 + Rs. 30,000 + Rs. 32,000) – Fixed Costs remain the same = Rs. 3,42,000 – Rs. 1,22,000 = Rs. 2,20,000

(B) When product Y is given up

	X	Z
Sales (units)	15,000	12,000
Contribution (Rs)	(15,000 × 24) = Rs. 3,60,000	(12,000 × 16) = Rs. 1,92,000

Profit = Total Contribution – Total Fixed Expenses
= (Rs. 3,60,000 + Rs. 1,92,000) – Rs. 1,22,000 = Rs. 4,30,000

(C) When product Z is given up

	X	Y
Sales (units)	15,000	7,500
Contribution (Rs.)	(15,000 × 24) 3,60,000	(7,500 × 20) 1,50,000

Profit = (Rs. 3,60,000 + Rs. 1,50,000) – Rs. 1,22,000 = **Rs. 3,88,000.**

Conclusion = Product Y should be given up because the profit is maximum in that situation i.e. Rs. 4,30,000.

Problem 45

During the current year AB Ltd. showed a profit of Rs. 1,80,000 on a sale of Rs: 30,00,000. The variable expenses were Rs. 21,00,000.

You are required to work out :

(a) the break-even sales at present.

(b) the break-even sale, if variable cost prices increase by 5%.

(c) the break-even sale to maintain the profit as at present, if the selling price is reduced by 5%.

[Adapted—Madras M.Com.]

Solution

We have to find out the Fixed Cost.

Fixed Cost + Variable Cost + Profit = Sale price

= F.C. + Rs. 21,00,000 + Rs. 1,80,000 = Rs. 30,00,000

Or, F.C. = Rs. 30,00,000 – Rs. 21,00,000 – Rs. 1,80,000

Or, F.C. = Rs. 7,20,000

$$\textbf{P/V Ratio} = \frac{\text{Contribution}}{\text{Sales}} \times 100 \text{ (C = F.C. + Profit)}$$

$$= \text{P/V Ratio} = \frac{\text{Rs. 9,00,000}}{\text{Rs. 30,00,000}} \times 100 = 30\%$$

(a) **Break-even Point** $= \dfrac{\text{Fixed Cost}}{\text{P / V Ratio}} = \dfrac{\text{Rs. } 7{,}20{,}000}{30\%} = \text{Rs. } 24{,}00{,}000$

P/V Ratio $= \dfrac{C}{\text{Sales}} \times 100 = \dfrac{\text{Rs. } 7{,}95{,}000}{\text{Rs. } 30{,}00{,}000} \times 100 = 26.5\%$

(b) **Revised BEP** $= \dfrac{\text{Rs. } 7{,}20{,}000}{26.5\%} = \text{Rs. } 27{,}16{,}981$

Contribution = Sales – Variable Cost

= Rs. 30,00,000 – (Rs. 21,00,000 + 5% of Rs. 21,00,000)

= Rs. 30,00,000 – Rs. 22,05,000 = Rs. 7,95,000

(c) **New P/V Ratio**

	Sales	Rs. 30,00,000
Less :	Reduction @ 5%	Rs. 1,50,000
		Rs. 28,50,000
Less :	Variable Cost	Rs. 21,00,000
	Contribution	7,50,000

P/V Ratio $= \dfrac{C}{\text{Sale}} \times 100 = \dfrac{\text{Rs. } 7{,}50{,}000}{\text{Rs. } 28{,}50{,}000} \times 100 = 26{\cdot}3\%.$

So, Desired Sales Volume :

$$= \frac{\text{Fixed Cost + Desired Profit}}{\text{P / V Ratio}} = \frac{\text{Rs. } 7{,}20{,}000 + \text{Rs. } 1{,}80{,}000}{26 \cdot 3\%}$$

$$= \frac{\text{Rs. } 9{,}00{,}000}{26 \cdot 3\%} = \text{Rs. } 34{,}20{,}011$$

REVISED SELLING PRICE AT CURRENT P/V RATIO

Problem 46

Reprographics Ltd. manufactures a document-reproducing machine which has a variable cost structure as follows :

	Rs.
Materials	40
Labour	10
Overhead	4
Selling price	90

Sales during the current year are expected to be Rs. 13,50,000 and fixed overhead Rs. 1,40,000.

Under wage agreement an increase of 10% is payable to all direct workers from the beginning of the forthcoming year, while material costs are expected to increase by 7.5%; variable overhead costs by 5% and fixed overhead costs by 3%.

You are required to calculate :

(a) the new selling price if the current P/V ratio is to be maintained; and

(b) the quantity to be sold during the forthcoming year to yield the same amount of profit as the current year assuming the selling price to remain at Rs. 90.

[Adapted—C.A. (Inter)]

Solution

(a) **New selling price if the current P/V ratio is to be maintained**

	Existing Variable Cost Rs.	% increase	Revised Variable Cost Rs.
Material	40·00	7·5%	43·00
Labour	10·00	10·0%	11·00
Variable Overhead	4·00	5·0%	4·20
	54·00		58·20
Fixed Cost			1,40,000

Revised fixed cost with 3% increase (Rs. 1,400,000 + Rs. 4,200) = 1,44,200

$$\text{Current P/V Ratio} = \frac{S - V}{S} \times 100 = \frac{\text{Rs. } 90 - \text{Rs. } 54}{\text{Rs. } 90} \times 100 = \frac{36}{90} \times 100 = 40\%$$

Or, Current year's marginal cost = 100% – 40% = 60%

Now, if marginal cost is Rs. 60, then sales = Rs. 100

If marginal cost is Rs. 58·20 then sales = $\frac{100 \times 58 \cdot 20}{60}$ = Rs. 97

∴ New selling price is Rs. 97.

(b) **Quantity to be sold to yield same amount of profit**

		Rs.
	Current year's sales	13,50,000
	Contribution i.e. 40% of sales = $\frac{40}{100}$ × Rs. 13,50,000 =	5,40,000
Less :	Fixed Cost	1,40,000
	Profit	4,00,000
	Contribution of the forthcoming year	
	Revised fixed cost	1,44,200
Add :	Profit	4,00,000
	Total Contribution	5,44,200

Contribution per unit = Rs. 90 – Rs. 58·20 = Rs. 31·80

$$\text{Sales Quantity required} = \frac{\text{Total Contribution}}{\text{Contribution per unit}}$$

$$= \frac{\text{Rs. } 5,44,200}{\text{Rs. } 31 \cdot 80} = 17,114 \text{ units of machine.}$$

Problem 47

There are two similar plants under the same management. The Management desires to merge these two plants. The following particulars are available :

	Factory I	Factory II
Capacity	100%	60%
Sales	Rs. 300 lakhs	Rs. 120 lakhs
Variable Costs	Rs. 220 "	Rs. 90 "
Fixed costs	Rs. 40 "	Rs. 20 "

You are required to calculate :

(a) What the break-even capacity of the merged plant would be; and

(b) What the profitability on working at 75% of the merged capacity would be?

[D.U. M.Com.]

Solution

(a)

		Factory I (at 100% capacity)	Factory II (at 100% capacity)	Combined (at 100% capacity)
		Rs.	Rs.	Rs.
	Sales	300 lakhs	200 lakhs	500 lakhs
Less :	Variable Cost	200 "	150 "	370 "
	Contribution	100 "	50 "	130 "

$$\text{Break-even Volume in rupees} = \frac{\text{Fixed Cost}}{\text{Combined P / V Ratio}}$$

$$\text{P/V Ratio} = \frac{C}{S} \times 100 = \frac{130}{500} \times 100 = 26\%.$$

$$\text{Break-even Point} = \frac{\text{Fixed Costs}}{\text{P / V Ratio}} = \frac{\text{Rs. 60 lakhs}}{26\%} = \text{Rs. 230.8 lakhs}$$

(Total Fixed Cost = Rs. 40 lakhs + Rs. 20 lakhs = Rs. 60 lakhs)

$$\text{Break-even point (100\% capacity)} \quad \frac{\text{Break – even Sales}}{\text{Total capacity}} \times 100$$

$$= \frac{\text{Rs. 230·8 lakhs}}{\text{Rs. 500 lakhs}} \times 100 = 46{\cdot}15\%$$

The break-even capacity of the merged plant would be 46·15%.

(b) **Income Statement at 75% merged capacity**

		Rs.
	Sales 75% of Rs. 500 lakhs	375 lakhs
Less :	Variable Cost 75% of Rs. 370 lakhs	277.50 "
	Contribution	97.50 "
Less :	Fixed Cost	60.00
	Net Profit	37.50

Alternatively,

(Actual sales – BE sales) × P/V Ratio = (Rs. 375 lakhs – Rs. 230.769 lakhs) × 26%

= Rs. 37·50 lakhs

MAKE OR BUY DECISION

Problem 48

The Gamma Company is considering the feasibility of purchasing from a nearby jobber a component of necessary quantities at a unit price of Rs. 4·50. Transportation and storage costs for the component would be negligible and, therefore, can be ignored.

Gamma produces the component from a single raw material. The firm at present orders materials in Economic Order Quantity of 1,000 units at a unit cost of Re. 1·00, average annual usage is 10,000 units of the component. The yearly storage cost (including rent, taxes, return on inventory investment etc.) at present is computed at 50 paise per unit. The minimum inventory is set at 200 units.

Direct labour costs for the components are Rs. 3 per unit. Fixed manufacturing overhead is absorbed at Rs. 2 per unit based on a normal capacity of 10,000 units. In addition to the above costs the machines on which the components are produced is leased at Rs. 100 per month.

Should Gamma make or buy the component? Would you like to qualify your answer in any way?

[Adapted—D.U. B.Com. (Hons.) 1994]

Solution

The fixed cost element will not in any way affect the decision of **make or buy. It is the marginal costs that do influence the decision.**

Now, let us calculate the marginal costs (variable) in case the components are manufactured.

Materials cost of 10,000 units @ Rs. 1·00 per units =	Rs. 10,000
Direct wages of 10,000 units @ Rs. 3·00 =	Rs. 30,000
	Rs. 40,000

$$\text{Therefore, unit cost} = \frac{\text{Rs. } 40{,}000}{10{,}000} = \text{Rs. } 4$$

Since fixed costs like storage cost @ Re. 0·50 p.a. and lease cost of machine @ Rs. 2 remain the same it is profitable to manufacture the component.

DETERMINATION OF MINIMUM SALE PRICE

Problem 49

An umbrella manufacturer makes an average profit of Rs. 2·50 per unit on a selling price of Rs. 14·30 by producing and selling 60,000 units at 60% of potential capacity.

His cost of sales per unit is as follows :

Direct Materials	Rs. 3·50	
Direct Wages	Rs. 1·25	
Factory Overhead	Rs. 6·25	(50% fixed)
Sales Overhead	Re. 0·80	(25% variable)

During the current year he intends to produce the same number but estimates that his fixed costs would go up by 10% while the rates of direct materials and direct wages will increase by 8% and 6%, respectively. However, the selling price cannot be changed.

Under this situation, he obtains an offer to ensure the manufacturer an over-all profit of Rs. 1,67,300.

Solution **[Delhi University B.Com. (Hons.)]**

Statement of Marginal Cost for the current year.

			Rs.
Direct Materials	Rs. 3.50 + 0.21(6% increase)	=	3.710
Direct Wages	Rs. 1.25 + 0.10 (8% increase)	=	1.350
Factory Overhead	50% of Rs. 6·25	=	3.125
Sales Overhead	25% variable	=	0.200
Total Marginal Cost			8.385
Contribution (F.C. + Profit)			5.915
Selling Price per unit			14.300

(a) Statement of profit on sale of 60,000 units

			Rs.	Rs.
	Sales	(60,000 × Rs. 14·30) =		8,58,000
Less :	Variable cost	(60,000 × 8·385) =		5,03,100
	Contribution =			3,54,900
Less :	Fixed Cost (60,000 × 3·125)		1,87,500	
	Increase @ 10% in F.O.		18,750	
			2,06,250	
Add :	Sales overhead 60,000 × 0.66 (0·60 + 0·06)		39,600	2,45,850
	Profit			1,09,050

(**Note :** *Profit per unit will change due to rise in prices of raw materials, direct wages and fixed overhead.*)

Now, profit to be earned on 20,000 units (20%, or potential capacity of 1,00,000 units)

	Profit required	Rs. 1,67,300
Less :	Profit earned on 60,000 units	Rs. 1,09,050
	Additional profit to be earned	Rs. 58,250

(b) Statement of minimum sale price per unit

		Rs.
	Variable cost for 20,000 units @ Rs. 8·385 per unit = 20,000 × 8·385	1,67,700
Add :	Desired profit	58,250
		2,25,950

$$\text{So, selling price per unit} = \frac{\text{Rs. } 2,25,950}{20,000 \text{ units}} = \text{Rs. } 11{\cdot}30. \text{ (Approx.)}$$

Problem 50

The Reliable Battery Company furnishes you the following income information for the current year divided into two sub-parts :

	First half (Rs.)	*Second half* (Rs.)
Sales	8,10,000	10,26,000
Profit earned	21,600	64,800

From the above, you are required to compute the following assuming that the fixed cost remains the same in both periods :

(i) Profit/Volume Ratio

(ii) Fixed cost

(iii) Amount of profit or loss when sales are Rs. 6,48,000

(iv) Amount of sales required to earn profit of Rs. 1,08,000.

[Adapted—C.A. (Inter)]

Solution

1. $$\textbf{P/V Ratio} = \frac{\text{Change in Profit}}{\text{Change in Sales}} \times 100$$

$$\text{P/V Ratio} = \frac{\text{Rs. } 43,200}{\text{Rs. } 2,16,000} \times 100 = 20\%$$

2. **Variable Cost/Volume Ratio** = 80% (100% – 20%)

Total Sales Revenue = Fixed Cost + Variable Cost + Profit

Or, Rs. 18,36,000 = F.C. + (80% Rs. 18,36,000) + Rs. 86,400

Or, Rs. 18,36,000 – Rs. 15,55,200 = Fixed Cost

Or, Rs. 2,80,800 = **Fixed Cost** or, Fixed Cost = Rs. 2,80,800

3. **Income Statement when sales are Rs. 6,48,000**

		Rs.
	Sales Revenue	6,48,000
Less :	Variable Cost 80%	5,18,400
	Contribution	1,29,600
Less :	Fixed Cost	2,80,800
	Loss	(1,51,200)

4. **Required Sales Volume to earn profit**

$$= \frac{\text{Fixed Cost + Desired Profit}}{\text{P / V Ratio}} = \frac{\text{Rs. } 2,80,800 + 1,08,000}{20\%}$$

$$= \frac{\text{Rs. } 3,88,800}{20\%} = \text{Rs. } 19,44,000.$$

Problem 51

A company's report of operations for the two years shows the following results :

	1994	1995
	Rs.	Rs.
Sales	6,25,000	7,50,000
Profit/Loss	15,000 (loss)	20,000

(i) At what level of sales does the company break-even, assuming no change in its cost-volume-profit relationship?

(ii) Consider the following changes for the next year :

Decrease of 10% in selling price,

Decrease of 25% in variable cost,

Increase of Rs. 65,000 in fixed cost.

What sales volume would be needed to generate a profit equal to 10% of sales ?

[Adapted—C.U. M.Com. 1992]

Solution

(i) P/V Ratio

$$= \frac{\text{Change in profit}}{\text{Change in sales}} \times 100 = \frac{\text{Rs. } 35,000 \text{ (Rs. } 20,000 + \text{Rs. } 15,000)}{\text{Rs. } 1,25,000 \text{ (Rs. } 7,50,000 - \text{Rs. } 6,25,000}$$

$$= \frac{\text{Rs. } 35,000}{\text{Rs. } 1,25,000} \times 100 = 28\%.$$

Contribution at Rs. 7,50,000 sales $= \frac{28}{100} \times$ Rs. 7,50,000 = **Rs. 2,10,000**

Fixed cost = Contribution – Profit = Rs. 2,10,000 – Rs 20,000 = Rs. 1,90,000.

$$\textbf{BEP Sales} = \frac{\text{Fixed cost}}{\text{P / V Ratio}} = \frac{\text{Rs. } 1,90,000}{28\%} = \text{Rs. } 6,78,571.$$

(ii) **Under changed situation**

(a) Present selling price = Rs. 100 – (10% of Rs. 100) = Rs. 90.

(b) Present Variable Cost

Previous Variable Cost 100% – 28%		= Rs. 72
Less : 25% decrease	$\frac{25}{100} \times 72$	= Rs. 18
		Rs. 54

$$\text{P/V Ratio} = \frac{S - V}{S} \times 100 = \frac{\text{Rs. } 90 - \text{Rs. } 54}{\text{Rs. } 90} \times 100 = \frac{\text{Rs. } 36}{\text{Rs. } 90} \times 100 = 40\%$$

Previous Cost Price	Rs. 1,90,000
Add : Increase	Rs. 65,000
Fixed Cost	Rs. 2,55,000

$$\text{Required Sales} = \frac{\text{Fixed Cost + Desired Profit}}{\text{P/V Ratio}}$$

Hence, desired profit = 10% of sales

Let us assume that required sales is X

$$\text{Then, } X = \frac{\text{Rs. } 2{,}55{,}000 + \frac{10}{100}X}{40\%}$$

$$\text{Or, } X = \left(\frac{\text{Rs. } 2{,}55{,}000 + \frac{1}{10}X}{40}\right) \times 100$$

Or, 40X = 2,55,00,000 + 10X or 40X – 10X = 2,55,00,000

Or, 30X = 2,55,00,000

$$\text{Or, } X = \frac{2{,}55{,}00{,}000}{30} = \text{Rs. } 8{,}50{,}000$$

Problem 52

S. Ltd. furnishes the following particulars relating to the half-year ending 30th June 1996 :

	Rs.
Fixed Expenses	60,000
Sales Value	2,40,000
Profit	60,000

During the second half of the same year the company has a projected loss of Rs. 15,000.

Find out : (i) the P/V Ratio, BEP and margin of safety; (ii) Expected sales value of second half of the year assuming that selling price and fixed expenses remain unchanged in the second half of the year also. (iii) The BEP and Margin of safety for the whole year 1996.

[Adapted—I.C.W.A. (Inter)]

Solution

(i) (a) **P/V Ratio** $= \frac{S - V}{S}$ or $\frac{\text{Contribution}}{\text{Sales}} \times 100$

Contribution = **Fixed cost + Profit** = Rs. 60,000 + 60,000 = Rs. 1,20,000.

So, P/V Ratio $= \frac{\text{Rs. } 1{,}20{,}000}{\text{Rs. } 2{,}40{,}000} \times 100 = 50\%$.

(b) **Break-even Point**

$$\text{BEP} = \frac{\text{Fixed Expenses}}{\text{P / V Ratio}} = \frac{\text{Rs. } 60,000}{50\%} = \text{Rs. } 1,20,000.$$

(c) **Margin of safety**

Margin of safety = Sales – BEP Sales = Rs. 2,40,000 – Rs. 1,20,000 = Rs. 1,20,000.

(ii) **Expected Sales** (for the second half)

$$= \frac{\text{Expected Contribution}}{\text{P / V Ratio}} = \frac{\text{Fixed Cost} - \text{Loss}}{\text{P / V Ratio}}$$

$$= \frac{\text{Rs. } 60,000 - \text{Rs. } 15,000}{50\%} = \frac{\text{Rs. } 45,000}{50\%} = \text{Rs. } 90,000$$

(iii) **For the year 1996**

Total Sales = Rs. 2,40,000 + Rs. 90,000 = Rs. 3,30,000.

Fixed Expenses = Rs. 60,000 + Rs. 60,000 = Rs. 1,20,000.

P/V Ratio = 50%

Profit = Rs. 60,000 – Rs. 15,000 = Rs. 45,000

$$\text{BEP sales} = \frac{\text{Fixed Cost}}{\text{P / V Ratio}} = \frac{\text{Rs. } 1,20,000}{50\%} = \text{Rs. } 2,40,000$$

Margin of safety = Sales – BEP Sales

= Rs. 3,30,000 – Rs. 2,40,000 = Rs 90,000

$$\textbf{Alternatively} = \frac{\text{Profit}}{\text{P / V Ratio}} = \frac{\text{Rs. } 45,000}{50\%} = \text{Rs. } 90,000.$$

Problem 53

The following figures are available from the records of Venus Enterprises as at 31st March :

	1995 Rs. (in lakhs)	1996 Rs. (in lakhs)
Sales	150	200
Profit	30	50

Calculate :

(a) the P/V ratio and total fixed expenses,

(b) the break-even level of sales,

(c) Sales required to earn a profit of Rs. 90 lakhs,

(d) profit or loss that would arise if the sales were Rs. 280 lakhs.

[Adapted—C.A. (Inter)]

Solution

	1994-1995 Rs. (in lakhs)	1995-1996 Rs. (in lakhs)
Sales	150	200
Profit	30	50

(a) **P/V Ratio**

$$= \frac{\text{Change in contribution}}{\text{Change in sales}} \times 100$$

$$= \frac{\text{Rs. 20 lakhs } (50 - 30)}{\text{Rs. 50 lakhs } (200 - 150)} \times 100 = 40\%.$$

(b) **BEP Sales**

Contribution for the year 1994-95 = 40% of Rs. 150 lakhs	= Rs. 60 lakhs
Profit for the period	Rs. 30 lakhs
Fixed cost	Rs. 30 lakhs

$$\therefore \quad \text{BEP Sales} = \frac{\text{Fixed Cost}}{\text{P / V Ratio}} = \frac{\text{Rs. 30 lakhs}}{40\%} = \text{Rs. 75 lakhs.}$$

(c) **Sales required to earn a profit of Rs. 90 lakhs.**

$$= \frac{\text{Fixed cost + Profit}}{\text{P / V Ratio}} = \frac{\text{Rs. 30 lakhs + Rs. 90 lakhs}}{40\%}$$

$$= \frac{\text{Rs. 120 lakhs}}{40\%} = \text{Rs. 300 lakhs.}$$

(d) **Profit or loss when sales are Rs. 280 lakhs.**

Contribution from sales = 40% of Rs. 280 lakhs =	Rs. 112 lakhs
Less : Fixed costs	Rs. 30 lakhs
Profit	Rs. 82 lakhs

Since, Contribution = Fixed Costs + Profit.

PROFIT PLANNING

Marginal Costing helps the management to make effective profit planning so that the concern maximises the profits or can maintain a specified level of profit.

The following illustration will make the matter clear.

Problem 54

Two businesses, Y Ltd. and Z Ltd., sell same type of product in the same type of market. Their budgeted profit and loss accounts for the coming year are as follows :

		Y Ltd.		Z Ltd.	
		Rs.	Rs.	Rs.	Rs.
	Sales		1,50,000		1,50,000
Less :	Variable Cost	1,20,000		1,00,000	
	Fixed Cost	15,000	1,35,000	35,000	1,35,000
	Budgeted Net Profit		15,000		15,000

You are required to :

(a) Calculate the break-even point of each business;

(b) Calculate the sales volume at which each business will earn Rs. 5,000 profit;

(c) State which business is likely to earn greater in condition of :

(i) heavy demand for the product;

(ii) low demand for the product and briefly give your reasons.

[Madurai U. B.Com.]

Solution

(a) **Calculate P/V Ratio of both the companies.**

$$\text{P/V Ratio} = \frac{S - V}{S} \times 100$$

Y Ltd. | Z Ltd.

$$\frac{\text{Rs. } 30,000}{\text{Rs. } 1,50,000} \times 100 = 20\% \qquad \frac{\text{Rs. } 50,000}{\text{Rs. } 1,50,000} \times 100 = 33\frac{1}{3}\%$$

$$\text{BEP (Break-even point)} = \frac{\text{Fixed Expenses}}{\text{P/V Ratio}}$$

$$\text{BEP of Y Ltd.} = \frac{\text{Rs. } 15,000}{20\%} = \frac{\text{Rs. } 15,000 \times 100}{20} = \text{Rs. } 75,000$$

$$\text{BEP of Z Ltd.} = \frac{\text{Rs. } 35,000}{33\frac{1}{3}\%} = 35,000 \times \frac{300}{100} = \text{Rs. } 1,05,000.$$

(b) **The sales volume at the desired profit to be earned to be calculated as follows :**

$$\frac{\text{Fixed Expenses + Desired Profit}}{\text{P/V Ratio}}$$

$$\text{Y Ltd.} = \frac{\text{Rs. } 15,000 + \text{Rs. } 5,000}{20\%} = \frac{\text{Rs. } 20,000}{20} \times 100 = \text{Rs } 1,00,000$$

$$\text{Z Ltd.} = \frac{\text{Rs. } 35,000 + \text{Rs. } 5,000}{33\frac{1}{3}\%} = \frac{\text{Rs. } 40,000}{100} \times 300 = \text{Rs. } 1,20,000$$

Comments

(c) (i) In condition of heavy demand, a business with larger P/V Ratio can earn greater profit because of greater contribution. In that sense, Z Ltd. is expected to earn greater profit than that of Y Ltd.

(ii) In condition of low demand, a concern with lower break-even point is expected to earn more profit as it earns profit at a lower level of sales. From the above point of view Y Ltd., will start to earn profit when its sales reach the level of Rs. 75,000 but Z Ltd. will start earning profit at the sales level of Rs. 1,05,000.

Problem 55

Gamini Steel Ltd. manufactures a single product for which market demand exists for additional quantity, present sales of Rs. 60,000 per month, utilises only 60% capacity of the plant. Marketing Manager assures that with the reduction of 10% in the price he would be in a position to increase the sale by about 25% to 30%.

The following data are available :

(i)	Selling price	Rs. 10 per unit
(ii)	Variable cost	Rs. 3 per unit
(iii)	Semi-variable cost	**Rs. 6,000 fixed + 0·50 paise per unit**
(iv)	Fixed cost	**Rs. 20,000 at present level, estimated to be Rs. 24,000 at 80% output**

You are required to prepare the following statements :

(i) The operating profits at 60%, 70% and 80% level at current selling price and

(ii) The operating profits at proposed selling price at the above levels.

[D.U. B.Com. (Hons.)]

Solution

Statement of Profit

at current price and reduced price

	60% Capacity *6,000 units*	*70% Capacity* *7,000 units*	*80% Capacity* *8,000 units*
	Rs.	Rs.	Rs.
Fixed Costs	20,000	20,000	24,000
Semi-variable (fixed)	6,000	6,000	6,000
Variable costs @ Rs. 3 per unit	18,000	21,000	24,000
Semi-variable 0·50 paise per unit	3,000	3,500	4,000
Total Cost (A)	47,000	50,500	58,000
Sales at current price @ Rs. 10 per unit (B)	60,000	70,000	80,000
Profit at current price (B – A)	13,000	19,500	22,000
Sales price at reduced rate (C) @ Rs. 9 per unit	54,000	63,000	72,000
Profit at reduced price at present levels (C – A)	7,000	12,500	14,000

Problem 56

The following data relate to a manufacturing company :

Plant capacity	4,00,000	units p.a.
Present utilisation	40%	
Actuals for the year 1995 :		
Selling price	Rs. 50	per unit
Materials cost	Rs. 20	per unit
Variable Manufacturing Cost	Rs. 15	per unit
Fixed costs	Rs. 27,00,000	

In order to improve capacity utilisation the following proposals are considered :

Reduce selling price by 10%.

Spend additional Rs. 3,00,000 on sales promotion.

How many units should be made and sold in order to earn a profit of Rs. 5,00,000 per year?

Solution

Revised Sale price = Rs. 50 – $\left(\frac{10}{100} \times 100\right)$ = Rs. 50 – Rs. 5 = Rs. 45.

Contribution = Sales – Variable Cost

= Rs. 45 – Rs. 35 (Material Cost Rs. 20 + Manufacturing Cost Rs. 15) = Rs. 10 per unit

Fixed Cost = Rs. 27,00,000 + Rs. 3,00,000 (for sales promotion) = Rs. 30,00,000

$$\therefore \text{Sales in Units} = \frac{\text{Fixed cost + Desired profit}}{\text{Contribution per unit}}$$

$$= \frac{\text{Rs. } 30,00,000 + \text{Rs. } 5,00,000}{\text{Rs. } 10}$$ = 3,50,000 units are to be produced and sold.

The capacity utilisation will be :

Units produced	Capacity utilisation
4,00,000	100%
3,50,000	$\frac{100 \times 3,50,000}{4,00,000} = 87{\cdot}5\%$

Problem 57

Find out the profit from the following data :

	Rs.
Sales	80,000
Marginal cost	60,000
Break-even point	60,000 (Sales)

Solution

$$\text{P/V Ratio} = \frac{S - V}{S} \times 100 = \frac{\text{Rs. } 80,000 - \text{Rs. } 60,000}{80,000} \times 100$$

$$= \frac{\text{Rs. } 20,000}{80,000} \times 100 = 25\%.$$

$$\text{Break-even point} = \frac{\text{Fixed Cost}}{\text{P / V Ratio}}$$

$$\text{Or, Fixed cost} = \text{BEP} \times \text{P/V Ratio} = \text{Rs. } 60,000 \times \frac{25}{100} = \text{Rs. } 15,000.$$

Profit = Contribution – Fixed Cost

= S – V = Contribution – Fixed Cost

= Rs. 80,000 – Rs. 60,000 = Rs. 20,000 contribution

So, Profit = Rs. 20,000 – Rs. 15,000 = Rs. 5,000.

Problem 58

Modern Sports Ltd. has for the past several years produced boxing gloves which are sold at Rs. 28 per pair. Higher costs at recent years have made management to consider about the adequacy of this selling price.

The labour rate was increased from Rs. 1·75 per hour to Rs. 2·25 per hour and the cost of leather has gone up from Rs. 1·10 to Rs. 2·15 per square foot during the last 5 years. Fixed expenses have increased 25% from the level of Rs. 18,000 five years ago. Over the same period variable overhead has increased 30% or Rs. 3 per pair of gloves. Each glove requires 1·5 sq. ft. of leather and one hour of direct labour.

Calculate the selling price that the company has to charge under the new cost structure to break-even at the same number of units as five years ago.

[Adapted—B.Com. (Hons.) Delhi]

Solution

One pair of gloves need :

Raw material (leather) = 1·50 sq. ft. × 2 = 3 sq. ft.

Direct labour hours = 1 × 2 = 2 direct labour hours

Marginal Cost Statement (old)

	Per pair Rs.
Materials (leather) Rs. 1,10 × 3	3·30
Labour Rs. 1·75 × 2	3·50
*Variable overhead	10·00
Marginal cost	16·80
Contribution (Balancing figure)	11·20
Selling price (given)	28·00

Variable Overhead = 30% of Rs. 10 = Rs. 3

Now, Variable overhead = Rs. 10 + Rs. 3 = Rs. 13

$$\text{BEP} = \frac{\text{Fixed Expenses}}{\text{Contribution}} = \frac{\text{Rs. } 18{,}000}{\text{Rs. } 11 \cdot 20} = 1{,}607 \text{ units}$$

New Marginal Cost Statement

		Rs.
Materials	3 sq. fit. × Rs. 2·15	6.45
Direct labour (Wages)	2 × Rs. 2·25	4.50
Variable overhead Rs. 10 + Rs. 3		13.00
Marginal cost		23.95
* Fixed Expenses (25% increase over Rs. 18,000)		14.00
		37.95

New contribution = Rs. 18,000 + (25% of Rs. 18,000) = Rs. 22,500 ÷ 1,607 (BEP) = Rs. 14·00.

Problem 59

Kalyan University conducts a special course on Computer Application for a month during summer. For this purpose it invites application from graduates. An Entrance Test is given to the candidates and, based on the same, a final selection of a hundred candidates is made. The Entrance Test consists of four objective type of examinations and is spread over four days, one examination per day. Each candidate is charged a fee of Rs. 50 for taking up the Entrance Test. The following data was gathered for the past two years :

Kalyan University

Statement of Net Revenue from the Entrance Test for the course on "Computer Application".

	1994 Rs.	1995 Rs.
Gross Revenue (Fees collected) (A)	1,00,000	1,50,000
Evaluation valuation Cost	40,000	60,000
Question Booklet	20,000	30,000
Hall Rent at Rs. 2,000 per day	8,000	8,000
Honorarium to Chief Administrator	6,000	6,000
Supervision charges (One Supervisor for every 100 candidates @ Rs. 50 per day)	4,000	6,000
General Administration Expenses	6,000	6,000
Total Cost (B)	84,000	1,16,000
Net Revenue (A – B)	16,000	34,000

You are required to compute :

(a) The budgeted net revenue if 4,000 candidates take up the Entrance Test in 1996.

(b) The Break-even number of candidates.

(c) The number of candidates to be enrolled if the net income desired is Rs. 20,000.

[Adapted—C.A. (Inter)]

Solution

(i) **Statement showing the Budgeted Net Revenue for Entrance Test for 1996**

No. of candidates : 4,000

(A)	Fees to be collected		Rs.
	@ Rs. 50 per student	4,000 × Rs. 50	2,00,000
	Costs (variable)		
	Valuation (variable) @ Rs. 20 per student	4,000 × Rs. 20	80,000
	Question Booklets @ Rs. 10	4,000 × Rs. 10	40,000
Add :	**Fixed Costs**		
	Hall Rent	Rs. 8,000	
	Honorarium to Chief Administrator	Rs. 6,000	
	General Administration Expenses	Rs. 6,000	20,000
Add :	Semi-variable Cost		
	Supervision Expenses (4,000 ÷ 100) × (Rs. 50 × 4) = 40 × 200		8,000
(B)	**Total Cost**		1,48,000
(C)	**Net Revenue** = A – B = Rs. 2,00,000 – Rs. 1,48,000		= Rs. 52,000

(ii) **Break-even Point**

Since the invigilating cost varies on the basis of 100 students, contribution is calculated on the basis of 100 students :

	Rs.	Rs.
Fees for 100 students (100 × Rs. 50)		5,000
Less : Variable cost (100 × Rs. 30)	3,000	
Less : Invigilation cost (Rs. 50 × 4)	200	3,200
Contribution per 100 students		1,800

Fixed Cost = Rs. 20,000

$$\text{BEP} = \frac{\text{Fixed cost}}{\text{Contribution}} = \frac{\text{Rs. } 20{,}000}{1{,}800} \times 100 = 1{,}111{\cdot}11 \text{ candidates}$$

$$\text{Invigilation cost per student} = \frac{\text{Rs. } 50 \times 4}{100} = \text{Rs. } 2.$$

If BEP is taken as 1,111·11 candidates, there would be under-recovery of invigilation cost of Rs. 200 – (11·11 × Rs. 2) 22·22 = Rs. 177·78.

To recover the amount of Rs. 177·78, BEP will be increased by 8·88 $\left(\frac{\text{Rs. } 177{\cdot}78}{18}\right)$ units.

This will push the break-even point at the level of 1,120 candidates i.e. (1,111.11 + 8.88).

(iii) **The number of candidate for desired profit of Rs. 20,000**

$$= \frac{\text{Fixed Cost + Desired Profit}}{\text{Contributions per 100 students}} = \frac{20{,}000 + 20{,}000}{1{,}800} = 22.222$$

= 22.222 × 100 = 2,222.22 students or 2,223 students to be enrolled.

SELLING IN HOME MARKET / EXPORT

Problem 60

A factory produces 24,000 units, the cost sheet gives the following informaiton :

	Rs.
Direct materials	1,20,000
Direct wages	84,000
Variable Overheads	48,000
Semi-variable overheads	28,000
Fixed Overheads	80,000
Total Cost	3,60,000

The product is sold at Rs. 20 per unit.

The management proposes to increase the productions by 3,000 units for sale in the foreign market. It is estimated that the semi-variable overheads will increase by Rs. 1,000. But the product will be sold at Rs. 14 per unit in the foreign market. However, no capital expenditure will be incurred. The management seeks your advice as a Cost Accountant. What will you advise them? **[D.U. B.Com. (Hons.)]**

Solution

Total variable cost for 24,000 units

	Rs.
Materials	1,20,000
Wages (Direct)	84,000
Variable overheads	48,000
	2,52,000

$$\text{Variable cost per unit} = \frac{\text{Rs. } 2,52,000}{24,000} = \text{Rs. } 10.50$$

Profitability Statement for 3,000 units

	Rs.
Sale Price @ Rs. 14 per unit = 3,000 × 14 =	42,000
Less : Variable costs @ Rs. 10.50 = 3,000 × 10.50 =	31,500
	10,500
Less : Aditional semi-variable cost	1,000
Profit	9,500

Comment

If export order is accepted, there will be an additional profit of Rs. 9,500. Therefore, it is advised to accept export order.

Problem 61

From the following data, you are required to calculate the BEP and net sales at this point :

Direct Materials Cost (per unit)	Rs. 8
Direct Labour	Rs. 5
Fixed Overhead	Rs. 40,000
Variable Overhead @ 60% on direct labour	
Selling Price (per unit)	Rs. 25
Trade Discount	4%

If sales are 15% and 20% above the break-even volume, determine the net profit. **[Adapted—C.A.]**

Solution

			Rs.
	Selling price		25
Less :	Trade Discount @ 4%		1
			24
Less :	Variable Costs		
	Direct Material	8	
	Direct Labour	5	
	Variable Overhead $\left(5 \times \frac{60}{100}\right)$	3	16
	Contribution		8

$$\text{P/V Ratio} = \frac{C}{S} = \frac{\text{Rs. } 8}{\text{Rs. } 24} = \frac{1}{3} \text{ or } 33\frac{1}{3}\%$$

$$\text{BEP} = \frac{\text{Fixed Cost}}{\text{P / V Ratio}} = \frac{\text{Rs. } 24{,}000}{33\frac{1}{3}\%} = \text{Rs. } 72{,}000.$$

(i) Profit at BEP + 15% = Rs. 72,000 + $\frac{15}{100}$ × Rs. 72,000 = Rs. 82,800

Profit = (Actual Sales – BEP Sales) × P/V Ratio

= (Rs. 82,800 – Rs. 72,000) × $\frac{1}{3}$ = Rs. 10,800 × $\frac{1}{3}$ = Rs. 3,600

(ii) Profit BEP + 20% = Rs. 72,000 + 20% of Rs. 72,000 = Rs. 86,400.

Profit = (Rs. 86,400 – Rs. 72,000) × $\frac{1}{3}$ = Rs. 14,400 × $\frac{1}{3}$ = Rs. 4,800.

Problem 62

During 1994 AB Ltd. showed a profit of Rs. 1,80,000 on a sale of Rs. 30,00,000. The variable expenses were Rs. 21,00,000. You are required to work out :

(a) BE Sales at present;

(b) BE Sales if variable cost price increases by 5%.

(c) BE Sales to maintain the profit as at present if the selling price is reduced by 5%.

[Adapted—Madras M.Com.]

Solution

Sale Price = Fixed Cost + Variable Cost + Profit

∴ Fixed Cost = Sale Price – Profit – VC.

Or, F.C. = Rs. 30,00,000 – Rs. 21,00,000 – Rs. 1,80,000 = Rs. 7,20,000.

Contribution = F.C. + Profit = Rs. 7,20,000 + Rs. 1,80,000 = 9,00,000.

(a) **P/V Ratio** $= \frac{C}{S} \times 100 = \frac{\text{Rs. } 9{,}00{,}000}{\text{Rs. } 30{,}00{,}000} \times 100 = 30\%$

BEP $= \frac{\text{Fixed Cost}}{\text{P / V Ratio}} = \frac{\text{Rs. } 7{,}20{,}000}{30\%} = \text{Rs. } 24{,}00{,}000.$

(b) **P/V Ratio** $= \dfrac{\text{Rs. } 7{,}95{,}000 (\text{Rs. } 30{,}00{,}000 - \text{Rs. } 22{,}05{,}000)^*}{\text{Rs. } 30{,}00{,}000} \times 100$

$= 26{\cdot}5\%.$

> * Variable cost increases by 5% i.e. $21{,}00{,}000 + \left(\dfrac{5}{100} \times 21{,}00{,}000\right)$
>
> $=$ Rs. 21,00,000 + Re. 1,05,000
>
> $=$ Rs. 22,05,000

BEP $= \dfrac{\text{Fixed Cost}}{\text{P/V Ratio}} = \dfrac{\text{Rs. } 7{,}20{,}000}{26{\cdot}5\%}$ = Rs. 27,16,981.

(c) **Sales** = Rs. 30,00,000 – Rs. 1,50,000 = Rs. 28,50,000

Less : Variable Cost Rs. 21,00,000

Contribution Rs. 7,50,000

P/V Ratio $= \dfrac{C}{S} \times 100 = \dfrac{\text{Rs. } 7{,}50{,}000}{\text{Rs. } 28{,}50{,}000} \times 100 = 26\%$

Desired amount of sales $= \dfrac{\text{F.C. + Profit}}{\text{P/V Ratio}}$

$= \dfrac{\text{Rs. } 9{,}00{,}000 \; (\text{Rs. } 7{,}20{,}000 + 1{,}80{,}000)}{26\%}$

$=$ Rs. 34,61,539 (approx.).

Problem 63

Three basic product lines are manufactured and sold by Eastern Products Company under the following conditions :

Product Lines	*Selling Price (Rs.) (P/V Ratio)*	*Contribution to Volume Ratio*
A	200	10%
B	150	20%
C	100	40%

Over the past few years, half of the total sales volume was made up of sales of product A and four times as many units of product B were sold as of product C. The total fixed costs are approximately Rs. 1,30,000 per year.

The chief executive of the company hopes to improve the overall profit by selling a greater proportion of the more profitable lines. Next year, he anticipates the following sales mix :

Product A 30%, B 50%, C 20%.

You are required to (a) prepare a break-even chart for the existing sales-mix. Show the combined units of sale in 1,000 unit intervals ranging from 1,000 to 8,000 units. (b) Prepare a profit-volume graph for the existing-sales mix following the same scale and range as used for the break-even chart. (c) Draw another profit-volume graph for the sales-mix as envisaged by the chief executive.

[M.Com. Delhi]

Solution

Proposed Sale-mix

Products	*Units*	*Selling Price (Rs.)*	*Sales Revenue (Rs.)*	*VC (Rs.)*	*Contribution (Rs.)*	*P/V Ratio (Rs.)*
A	2,400	200	4,80,000	4,32,000	48,000	10
B	4,000	150	6,00,000	4,80,000	1,20,000	20
C	1,600	100	1,60,000	96,000	64,000	40
	8,000		12,40,000	10,08,000	2,32,000	18·71

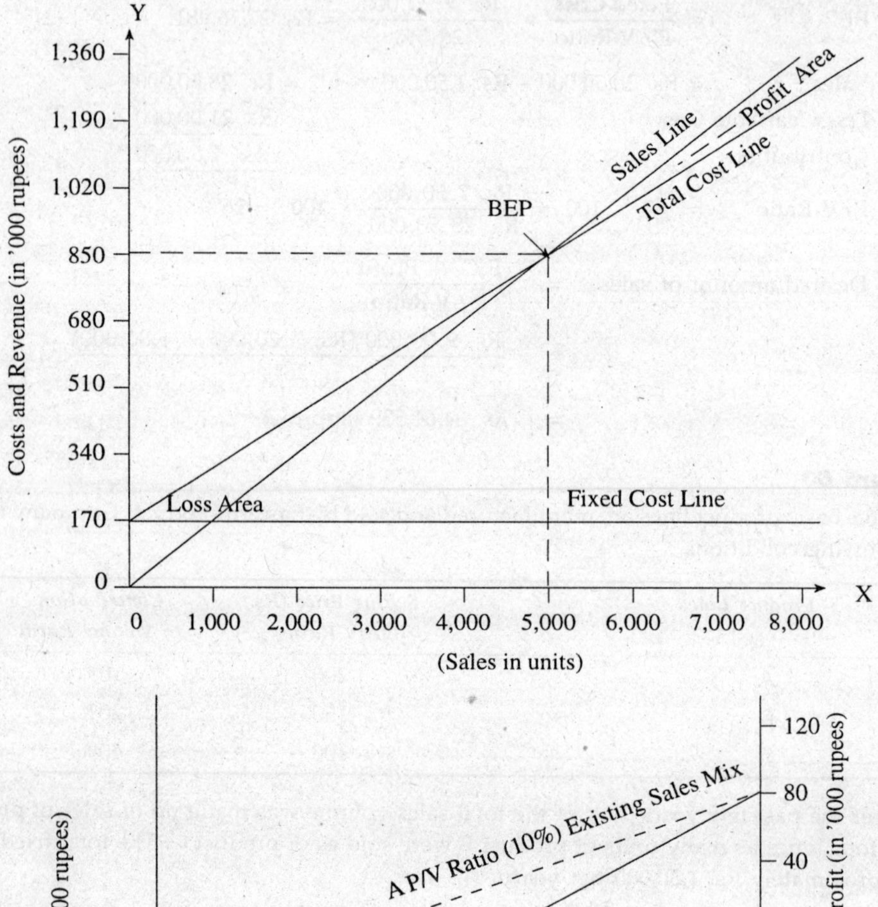

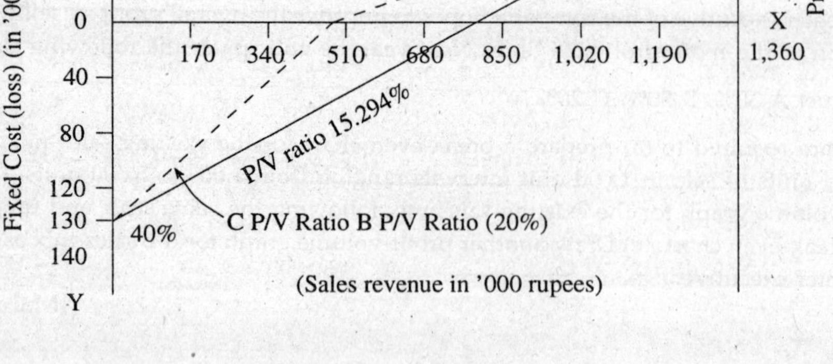

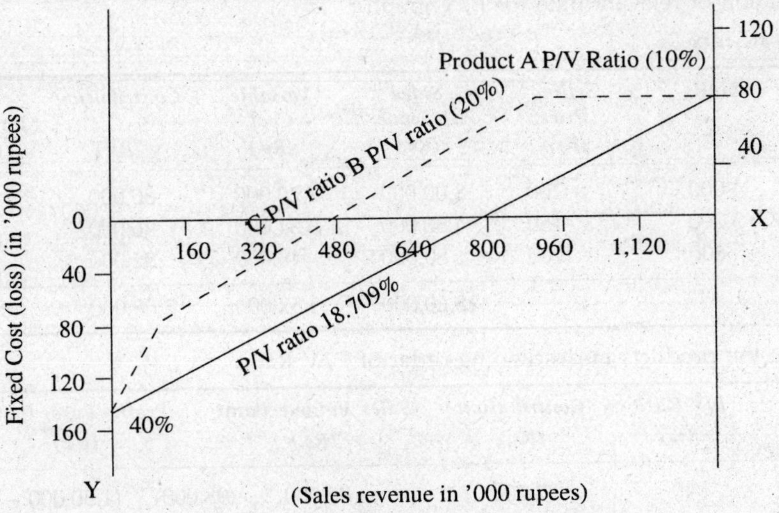

Arranging the products in descending order of P/V ratio :

	P/V Ratio (%)	Contribution (Rs.)	Sales Volume Point (Rs.)	Profit (Loss) Point (Rs.)
C	40	64,000	1,60,000	66,000 (1,30,000 – 64,000)
B	20	1,20,000	7,60,000	54,000 (1,20,000 – 66,000)
A	10	48,000	12,40,000	1,02,000 (54,000 + 48;000)

Product Lines	Selling Price Rs.	Sales Mix (units)	Sales Mix (SR) Adjusted Rs.	P/V Ratio (%)	V/V Ratio (%)	Total VC (Rs.)	Total Contribution (Rs.)
A	200	5	1,000	10	90	900	100
B	150	4	600	20	80	480	120
C	100	1	100	40	60	60	40

Combined P/V Ratio = $\frac{26}{100}$, P/V Ratio = $\frac{144}{170}$.

Determination of two points (for BE chart)

Products Mix of A, B and C	Sales Revenue (Rs.)	VC (Rs.)	FC (Rs.)	TC (Rs.)
1,000 units	1,70,000	1,44,000	1,30,000	2,74,000
8,000 units	13,60,000	11,52,000	1,30,000	12,82,000

Verification : BEP = $\frac{\text{Rs. } 21,30,000}{2,67,170}$ = Rs. 8,50,000

Determination of relevant date for P/V graph :

Existing sale-mix.

Product	*Units*	*Selling Price (Rs.)*	*Sales Revenue (Rs.)*	*Variable Cost (Rs.)*	*Contribution (Rs.)*	*P/V Ratio (%) (Rs.)*
A	4,000	200	8,00,000	7,20,000	80,000	10
B	3,200	150	4,80,000	3,84,000	96,000	20
C	800	100	80,000	48,000	32,000	40
			13,60,000	11,52,000	2,08,000	15·29

Arranging the products in descending order of P/V Ratio :

	P/V Ratio (%)	*Contribution (Rs.)*	*Sales Volume Point (Rs.)*	*Profit (Loss) Point (Rs.)*	
C	40	32,000	80,000	(98,000)	(1,30,000 – 32,000)
B	20	96,000	5,60,000	(2,000)	(98,000 – 96,000)
A	10	80,000	13,60,000	78,000	(2,000 less – 80,000)

Problem 64

A firm has two products, X and Y. Some data relating to them are given below :

Product	*Variable Cost Rs.*	*Selling Price Rs.*
X	80 per unit	100 per unit
Y	60 per unit	100 per unit

Fixed expenses of the firm are Rs. 5,000.

The sale of units of product X is three times that of units of product Y.

You are required to prepare a chart (graph) showing the break-even point and state the procedure that you adopt for this.

[M.Com. Delhi]

Solution

Product	*Selling Price Rs.*	*Sales Mix*	*Total Selling Price Rs.*	*Total Variable Cost Rs.*	*Total Contribution Rs.*	*P/V Ratio (%)*
X	100	3	300	240	60	20
Y	100	1	100	60	40	40
			400	300	100	

$$\text{Weighted P/V Ratio} = \frac{\text{Rs. } 100}{\text{Rs. } 400} = 25\%$$

$$\text{Weighted P/V Ratio} = \frac{\text{Rs. } 300}{\text{Rs. } 400} = 75\%$$

The P/V graph is preferred to the BE chart, because the P/V graph can portray the profit path of individual products also. Since sales revenue is not given in the question, let us assume that the total sales revenue of the firm is Rs. 30,000.

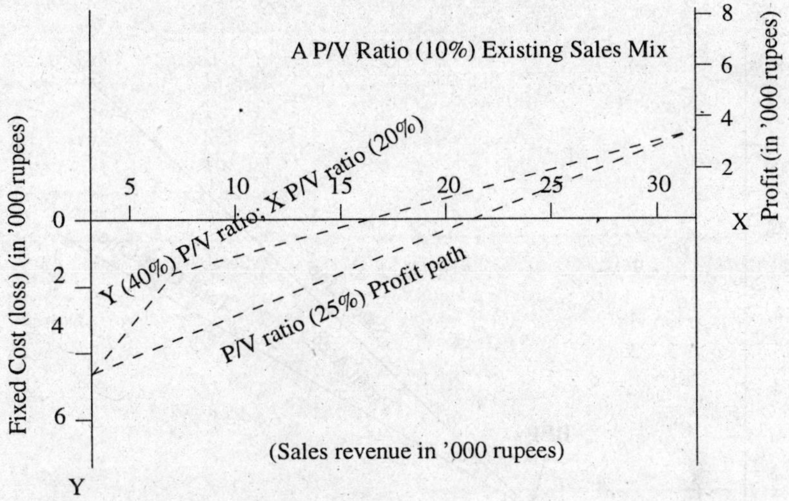

Product	*Selling Revenue* Rs.	*Variable Cost* Rs.	*Contribution* Rs.
X	22,500	18,000	4,500
Y	7,500	4,500	3,000
	30,000	22,500	7,500
Less : Fixed Costs			5,000
Net profit			2,500

Steps : Arranging the products in descending order of P/V Ratio.

	P/V Ratio	*Contribution* Rs.	*Sales Volume Point* Rs.	*Profit (Loss) Point* Rs.
X	40%	3,000	7,500	2,000 (5,000 – 3,000)
Y	20%	4,500	30,000	2,500 (2,000 loss – 4,500 contribution)

Problem 65

After a study of cost-volume relationships, the Kaling Tubes Company concluded that its costs for any given volume of sales could be expressed as Rs. 1,00,000 for fixed costs plus variable costs equal to 60% of sales. The company's range of volume was from zero to Rs. 8,00,000 of sales.

Prepare a graph which will illustrate this cost-volume relationship. Also draw a proper sales line to the graph to form break-even chart. Determine the break-even point.

A competitor operating a plant of the same size as Kaling also has fixed cost of approximately Rs. 1,00,000 per year, but his break-even point is Rs. 3,00,000 of sales.

What may be the probable causes of the difference between the break-even points of the Kaling Company and its competitors?

[M.Com. Delhi]

Solution

Since selling price per unit is not given, it is necessary to draw the cost-volume graph on the same scale so that a 45° line can be the proxy of the sales line.

Determination of two points for drawing the total cost line :

Sales Revenue	*FC*	*VC*	*TC*
Rs.	Rs.	Rs.	Rs.
1,00,000	1,00,000	60,000	1,60,000
8,00,000	1,00,000	4,80,000	5,80,000

The point of intersection of the TC line and sale line is BEP i.e., Rs. 2,50,000.

Verification : $\frac{\text{FC}}{\text{P / V Ratio}} = \frac{\text{Rs. } 1,00,000}{40\%} = \text{Rs. } 2,50,000.$

Possible cause for the differences in BEP :

1. The competitors are having a higher variable cost to volume ratio than the Kaling Tubes Ltd. It is $66\frac{2}{3}\%$ for the competitors assuming the selling price per unit for both the firms is the same.

$$\text{BEP} = \frac{\text{FC}}{\text{P / V ratio}} = \text{Rs. } 3,00,000 = \frac{\text{Rs. } 1,00,000}{\text{P / V ratio}}$$

$$\text{P/V ratio} = \frac{\text{Rs. } 1,00,000}{\text{Rs. } 3,00,000} = \frac{1}{3} \text{ or, } 33\frac{1}{3}\%$$

2. The competitors are having lower sales price per unit. Their prices per unit are $6\frac{2}{3}\%$ lower than those of the Kaling Tubes Ltd. as shown below :

$$\text{BEP} = \frac{\text{Rs. } 1,00,000}{(93\frac{1}{3}\% - 60\%)} = \frac{\text{Rs. } 1,00,000}{33\frac{1}{3}\%} = 3,00,000.$$

3. Partly due to higher variable cost to volume ratio or partly due to lower selling price, the sum of the difference is $6\frac{2}{3}\%$.

ASSIGNMENT

Theoretical Questions

1. Define 'Marginal Cost' and 'Marginal Costing'. How are variable costs and fixed costs treated in marginal costing?
2. What do you mean by marginal costing? Enumerate some of the advantages of the system.
3. Clearly explain the meaning of 'Contribution'. How is it related to profits?
4. State what you consider to be the advantages and disadvantages of marginal cost method.
5. What do you mean by P/V ratio?
6. Write short notes on :
   (i) P/V Ratio; (ii) Margin of Safety; (iii) Contribution; (iv) Angle of Incidence.
7. Define 'Marginal Costing'. What are its characteristics?
8. Find out the points of difference between Marginal Costing and Absorption Costing.
9. Draw a Break-even-chart with a few imaginary figures.
10. What do you mean by 'Absorption Costing'? How does it differ from Marginal Costing?
11. What do you mean by Break-even chart? What are the different methods of drawing Break-even-chart?
12. What are the assumptions underlying Break-even chart? What are its advantages?
13. What information do you get from profit Volume Graph? **[C.U. B.Com. (Hons.)]**
14. What information does margin of safety and Angle of Incidence express.
    [C.U. B.Com. (Hons.)]

Practical Problems

1. Present production and sales are 8,000 units. Selling price per unit is Rs. 20. Variable cost per unit :

Direct Materials	Rs. 5·00
Direct Labour	Rs. 2·50
Variable Overheads	100% of direct labour cost
Fixed Costs	Rs. 40,000

Find out : (i) P/V Ratio; (ii) Sales required to break-even; (iii) Margin of Safety.
[B.Com. Madras]

Ans. : (i) 50%, (ii) Rs. 80,000, (iii) Rs. 80,000.

2. Modern Machines Co. Ltd. places before you the following figures :

	Sales Rs.	Profit Rs.
1994	2,00,000	10,000
1995	1,80,000	2,000

You are required to :

(i) Determine the P/V Ratio; (ii) Sales at Break-even; (iii) Predict the expected profit or loss with sales of Rs. 1,50,000 and Rs. 3,00,000.

[Rajasthan M.Com.]

Ans. : (i) 40%; (ii) Rs. 1,75,000; (iii) Profit Rs. 50,000.

3. You are given the following data for the year 1995 of X Company :

	Rs.	%
Variable costs	6,00,000	60
Fixed costs	3,00,000	30
Net profit	1,00,000	10
	10,00,000	100

Find out (a) Break-even; (b) P/V Ratio; (c) Margin of safety.

[Karnataka B.Com.]

Ans. : (a) Rs. 7,50,000; (b) 40%; (c) Rs. 2,50,000.

4. Merry Manufacturer Limited has supplied you the following information in respect of one of its products :

	Rs.
Total fixed costs	18,000
Total variable costs	30,000
Total sales	60,000
Units sold	20,000 (units)

Find out (a) Contribution per unit; (b) Break-even point; (c) Margin of safety; (d) Profit and (e) Volume of sales to earn a profit of Rs. 24,000.

[Adapted—ACS (Final)]

Ans. : (a) Rs. 1·50 per unit; (b) 12,000; (c) 8,000 units; (d) Rs. 12,000; (e) 28,000; units.

5. The Cost Accountant of X Co. Ltd. furnished you the following information :

	Rs.
Fixed cost for the year	40,000
Net profit for the year	50,000
P/V Ratio	30%

(a) What is the amount of sales made during the year? (b) What will be the selling price per unit when variable cost per unit is Rs. 8·40 and P/V ratio is 40%?

[D.U. B.Com. (Pass) 1990]

Ans. : (a) Rs. 3,00,000; (b) R. 14.

Hints : V.C. Ratio = 100 – 40 = 60 when 60% = Rs. 8·40; 100% = Rs. 14.

6. Given the following information :

	Rs.
Fixed Costs	75,000
Sales	3,00,000
Direct Materials	1,00,000
Direct Labour	60,000
Direct Expenses	40,000

Calculate Break-even point.

[Kerala B.Com.]

Ans. : Rs. 2,25,000.

7. The following information relating to a company is given to you :

	Rs.
Sales	4,00,000
Fixed Cost	1,80,000
Variable Cost	2,50,000

Ascertain how much the value of sales must be increased for the company to break-even.

[Calicut B.Com.]

Ans. : Rs. 80,000.

8. From the following particulars, calculate the sales required to earn a profit of Rs. 1,20,000 :

	Rs.
Sales	6,00,000
Variable Costs	3,75,000
Fixed Cost	1,80,000

[Calicut B.Com.]

Ans. : Rs. 13,20,000.

9. From the following data compute Break-even sales and margin of safety :

	Rs.
Sales	10,00,000
Fixed Costs	3,00,000
Profit	3,00,000

[D.U. B.Com. (Pass) 1987]

Ans. : BES = Rs. 6,00,000; Margin of safety = Rs. 4,00,000.

10. From the following data calculate :

(i) Contribution per unit; (ii) Margin of safety; (iii) Volume of sales to earn a profit of Rs. 24,000.

	Rs.
Total Fixed Costs	18,000
Total Variable Costs	30,000
Total Sales	50,000
Units Sold	20,000

[D.U. B.Com. (Pass) 1994]

Ans. : (i) Re. 1·00; (ii) Rs. 45,000; (iii) 42,000 unit.

11. From the following information calculate the break-even point, the turnover required to earn a profit of Rs. 36,000 and the margin of safety at Rs. 36,000 profit :

Fixed overheads	Rs. 1,80,000
Variable cost per unit	Rs. 2·20
Selling price	Rs. 20·00

[Mysore B.Com. Part II 1990]

Ans. : BEP = Rs. 202,247, Rs. 2,42,297.

12. The Asian Industries specialises in the manufacture of small capacity motors. The cost structure of a motor is as under :

Material	Rs. 50
Labour	Rs. 80

Variable overheads 75% of labour cost.

Fixed overheads of the company amount to Rs. 2·40 lacs p.a. The sale price of the motor is Rs. 230 each.

(a) Determine the number of motors that have to be manufactured and sold in a year to break-even.

(b) How many motors have to be made and sold to make a profit of Rs. 1,00,000 per year?

(c) If the sales price is reduced by Rs. 15·00 each, how many motors have to be sold to break-even?

[I.C.W.A. (Inter) June 1980]

Ans. : (a) 6,000 units; (b) 8,500 units; (c) 9,600 units.

13. The following figures are extracted from the books of a manufacturing concern for the year 1995-96 :

	Rs.
Direct materials	2,05,000
Direct labour	75,000
Fixed overheads	60,000
Variable overheads	1,00,000
Sales	5,00,000

Calculate the Break-even point. What will be the effect on BEP of an increase of 10% in : (i) Fixed Expenses and (ii) Variable Expenses?

[C.S. (Inter) June 1992]

Ans. : (a) Rs. 2,50,000; (b) (i) Rs. 2,75,000; (ii) Rs. 3,65,854.

14. From the following data calculate :

(i) Break-even point expressed in amount of sales in rupees.

(ii) Number of units that must be sold to earn a profit of Rs. 60,000 per year.

(iii) How many units are to be sold to earn a net income of 10% of sales?

	Rs.	
Sale price	20	per unit
Variable manufacturing cost	11	per unit
Variable selling costs	3	per unit
Fixed factory overheads	5,40,000	per unit
Fixed selling costs	2,52,000	per unit

[D.U. B.Com. (Hons.) 1987]

Ans. : (i) Rs. 26,40,000; (ii) 1,42,000 units; (iii) 1,98,000 units.

15. A company budgets a production of 10,000 units. The variable cost is estimated at Rs. 12 per unit. The fixed costs are estimated Rs. 40,000. The selling price is fixed to earn a profit of 25% on cost. You are required to :

(i) compute break-even point in terms of units and sales; and (ii) compute how many units must be produced and sold to earn a profit of Rs. 60,000.

[D.U. B.Com. (Hons.)]

Ans. : (i) Rs. 1,00,000/5,000 units; (ii) 12,500 units.

16. From the particulars given below, calculate :

(i) Break-even sales, (ii) Margin of safety, and (ii) Sales to earn a profit of Rs. 4,000.

	Rs.
Selling price	20,000
Total cost	16,000
Variable cost	12,000

[D.U. B.Com. (Pass) 1992]

Ans. : (i) Rs. 10,000; (ii) Rs. 10,000; (iii) Rs. 20,000.

17. (i) What is Break-even Point? (ii) Find out Break-even point from the following information :

	Rs.
Total costs	60,000
Fixed costs	30,000
Sales	1,00,000

(iii) Also calculate the margin of safety.

Ans. : (i) Rs. 42,857 (approx.); (ii) R. 57,143.

18. Following information are given for the manufacturing of a product :

	Rs.	
Fixed expenses	4,00,000	
Material	10	per unit
Labour	5	per unit
Direct Expenses		
Fuel	3	per unit
Carriage inwards	2	per unit
Selling price	40	per unit

Calculate Break-even point in terms of units. Also find out new BEP if selling price reduced by 10% per unit.

Ans. : (i) 20,000 units, (ii) 25,000 units.

19. In a purely competitive market 10,000 pocket transistors can be manufactured and sold and a certain profit is generated. It is estimated that 2,000 pocket transistors need be manufactured and sold in a monopoly to earn the same profit.

Profit under both the conditions is targeted at Rs. 2,00,000. The variable cost per transistor is Rs. 100 and the total fixed cost is Rs. 37,000.

You are required to find out the unit selling price both under monopoly and competitive conditions.

[Adapted—I.C.W.A. Dec. 1985]

Ans. : Under monopoly = Rs. 218·50 p.u.; under competitive conditions sale price = Rs. 123·70 p.u.

20. Polestar Electronic decides to effect a 10% reduction in the price of its product because it is felt that such a step may lead to a greater volume of sales.

It is estimated that there are no prospects of a change in total fixed costs and variable costs per unit. The Directors wish to maintain net profit at the present level.

The following information has been obtained from its books :

Sales 10,000 units	Rs. 2,00,000
Variable costs	Rs. 15 per unit
Fixed costs	Rs. 40,000

How would the management proceed to implement this decision?

Ans. : Units to be sold = 16,667; Sales to be increased by 6,667 units.

21. From the following data calculate :

(i) Break-even point expressed in amount of sale in rupees.

(ii) Number of units that must be sold to earn a profit of Rs. 60,000.

	Rs.
Selling price	20 per unit
Variable manufacturing cost	11 per unit
Variable selling cost	3 per unit
Fixed factory overhead	5,40,000 p.a.
Fixed selling costs	2,52,000 p.a.

Ans. : Rs. 26,40,000; 1,42,000 units.

22. From the following data calculate the break-even point :

	Rs.
Selling price per unit	20
Direct material cost per unit	8
Direct labour cost per unit	2
Direct expenses per unit	2
Variable overheads per unit	3
Fixed overheads	20,000

If sales are 20% above the break-even point, determine the net profit.

[M.Com. C.U.]

Ans. : 4,000 units or Rs. 80,000, Rs. 4,00.

23. The Ancient Machine Company Ltd. places before you the following figures :

	Sales	Profit
	Rs.	Rs.
1994	1,00,000	5,000
1995	90,000	1,000

You are required to :

(i) Estimate the expected profit or loss with sales of : (a) Rs. 75,000; (b) Rs. 1,50,000.

(ii) Determine the P/V ratio; (iii) Determine sales at break-even point.

Ans. : (i) (a) Loss of Rs. 5,000; (b) Profit of Rs. 25,000; (ii) 40%; (iii) Rs. 1,75,000.

24. You are given the following data for costing year for a factory :

Budget output	1,00,000 units
Fixed expenses	Rs. 5,00,000
Variable expenses per unit	Rs. 10
Selling price per unit	Rs. 20

Draw a break-even chart showing the break-even point. If the selling price is reduced to Rs. 18 per unit, what will be the new break-even point?

[Jabalpur M.Com.]

25. A company budgets for a production of 1,50,000 units. The variable cost per unit is Rs. 14 fixed cost is Rs. 2 per unit. The company fixes its selling prices to fetch a profit of 15% or cost.
    (a) What is the break-even point?
    (b) What is the profit-volume ratio?
    (c) If it reduces its selling price by 5%, how does the revised selling price affect the break-even point and the P/V ratio?
    (d) If a profit increase of 10% is desired more than the budget, what should be the sales at the reduced price?

[D.U. B.Com. (Hons.) 1985]

Ans. : (a) 68,182 units; (b) 23·91%; (c) 19·90%; (d) Rs. 34,96,000.

26. From the following data find out the break-even point :

	Rs.
Selling price per unit	10·00
Trade discount 5%	
Direct materials cost per unit	3·00
Direct labour cost per unit	2·00
Fixed overheads	10,000
Variable overheads 100% on Wages.	

If sales are 10% and 15% above the break-even point determine the net profits.

Ans. : Profits Rs. 10,000 and Rs. 1,500.

27. You are given the following data for a costing year for a factory :

Budgeted output	1,00,000 units
Fixed expenses	Rs. 5,00,000
Variable expenses per unit	Rs. 10
Selling price per unit	Rs. 20

Determine the break-even point.

If the selling price is reduced to Rs. 18 per unit what will be the new break-even point?

[M.Com. Jodhpur]

Ans. : (i) 50,000 units; (ii) 62,506 units.

28. From the following information calculate (i) the break-even point and (ii) the turnover required to earn a profit of Rs. 30,000 :

	Rs.
Fixed overheads	21,000
Variable costs	2 per unit
Selling price	5 per unit

Ans. : (i) 60%; (ii) Rs. 85,000.

29.

	Sales	Profit
	Rs.	Rs.
Period I	10,000	2,000
Period II	15,000	4,000

You are required to calculate : (i) P/V Ratio; (ii) Fixed Cost; (iii) Break-even sales volume; (iv) Sales to earn a profit of Rs. 3,000; and (v) Profit when sales are Rs. 8,000.

[C.S. Inter]

Ans. : (i) 40%; (ii) Fixed cost Rs. 2,000; (iii) Rs. 5,000; (iv) Rs. 12,500; (v) Rs. 1,200 profit.

30. Rainbow Ltd. sold goods for Rs. 30,00,000 in a year. In that year the variable costs were Rs. 6,00,000 and fixed costs were Rs. 8,00,000. Find out : (i) P/V Ratio; (ii) Break-even sales; (iii) Break-even sales if selling price was reduced by 10% and fixed costs were increased by Rs. 1,00,000.

[C.U. B.Com. (Hons.) 2000]

Ans. : (i) 80%; (ii) Rs. 10,00,000; (iii) Rs. 11,57,110.

31. X. Ltd. sells 8000 units of its products at a loss of Rs. 16,000. Variable cost per unit is Rs. 12 and total fixed costs are Rs. 48,000. Calculate (i) Profit Volume Ratio; (ii) The number of units to be sold to earn a profit of Rs. 10,000; (iii) The amount of profit from a sale of 20,000 units.

[C.U. B.Com. (Hons.) 1999]

Ans. : (i) 25%; (ii) 14,500 units; (iii) 32,000 units.

32. A toy manufacturer earns an average net profit of Rs. 3 per piece in a selling price of Rs. 15 by producing and selling 60,000 pieces at 60% of the potential capacity. Composition of his cost of sales is :

	Rs.	
Direct materials	4·00	
Direct wages	1·00	
Works overhead	6·00	(50% fixed)
Sales overhead	1·00	(25% variable)

During the current year he intends to produce the same number but anticipates that :

(i) His fixed charges will go up by 10%.

(ii) Rates of direct labour will increase by 20%.

(iii) Rates of direct materials will increase by 5%.

(iv) Selling price cannot be increased.

Under these circumstances he obtains an order for a further 20% of his capacity.

What minimum price will you recommend for accepting the order to ensure the manufacturer an overall profit of Rs. 1,80,500?

[Adapted—Rajasthan M.Com.]

Ans. : Recommended selling price Rs 11·00.

33. Ambitious Enterprises is currently working at 50% capacity and produces 10,000 units at 60% working, raw materials cost increases by 2% and selling price falls by 2%. At 80% working raw material cost increases by 5% and selling price falls by 5%.

At 50% capacity working, the product costs Rs. 180 per unit and is sold at Rs. 200 per unit.

The unit cost of Rs. 180 is made up as follows :

	Rs.	
Materials	100	
Wages	30	
Factory overheads	30	(40% fixed)
Administrative overheads	20	(50% fixed)

Prepare a Marginal cost statement showing the estimated profit of the business when it is operated at 60% and 80% capacity.

[Adapted—Delhi B.Com. (Hons.)]

34. Sports Material Manufacturing Company's director gives the following information :

	Rs.
Sales (10,000 units)	1,00,000
Variable Cost	40,000
Fixed Cost	50,000

Find out the P/V ratio, break-even point and margin of safety.

Evaluate the effect of :

(a) 10% decrease in fixed cost

(b) 5% decrease in variable cost

(c) Rs. 5,000 variable cost of decrease accompanied by Rs. 15,000 fixed cost increase

(d) 10% decrease in selling price.

[Mysore University B.Com. 1991]

35. The following figures relating to the performance of a company for the years I and II are available. Assuming that (i) the ratio of variable costs to sales, and (ii) the fixed costs are the same for both the years, ascertain :

(a) the profit-volume ratio,

(b) the amount of fixed costs,

(c) the break-even point, and

(d) the budgeted profit for the year III, if the budgeted sales for that year are Rs. one crore.

	Total sales (Rs. in '000)	Total costs (Rs. in '000)
Year I	7,000	5,800
Year II	9,000	6,600

36. The following figures are available from the records of Venus Enterprises as at 31st March :

	1994 Rs. (in lakhs)	1995 Rs. (in lakhs)
Sales	150	200
Profit	30	50

Calculate :

(a) the P/V ratio and total fixed expenses

(b) the break-even level of sales

(c) sales required to earn a profit of Rs. 90 lakhs

(d) profit or loss that would arise if the sales were Rs. 280 lakhs.

[Adapted—C.A. (Inter) 1989]

Ans. : (a) P/V ratio 40%, Rs. 30 lakhs; (b) 75 lakhs; (c) Rs. 300 lakhs; (d) Rs. 82 lakhs.

37. A company earned a profit of Rs. 30,000 during the year 1994-95. If the marginal cost and selling price of a product are Rs. 8 and Rs. 10 per unit, respectively, find out the amount of margin of safety.

[Adapted—C.S. (Inter) May 1995]

Ans. : Rs. 1,50,000.

Hints : Margin of safety = $\dfrac{\text{Profit}}{\text{P / V Ratio}}$.

38. A company budgets for a production of 1,50,000 units. The variable cost per unit is Rs. 14 and fixed cost is Rs. 2 per unit. The company fixes its selling price to fetch a profit of 15% on cost.
   (a) What is the break-even point?
   (b) What is the P/V ratio?
   (c) If it reduces its selling price by 5%, how the revised selling price affects the break-even point and the profit-volume ratio?
   (d) If a profit increase of 10% is desired more than the budget, what should be the sales at the reduced prices?

Ans. (a) Break-even Point Rs. 12,49,549;
(b) P/V Ratio Rs. 23·91%;
(c) New Break-even point 86,207 units; New P/V ratio 19·90%;
(d) Sales in units for desired profit Rs. 34,96,000.

39.

	Sales Rs.	Profit Rs.
Period I	10,000	2,000
Period II	15,000	4,000

You are required to calculate :

(a) P/V ratio; (b) Fixed Cost; (c) Break-even sales volume; (d) Sales to earn a profit of Rs. 3,000 and (e) Profit when sales are 8,000.

[C.S. (Inter) 1995]

Ans. : (a) 40%; (b) Rs. 2,000; (c) Rs. 5,000; (d) Rs. 12,500 sales; (e) Rs. 1,200.

40. ABC Pvt. Ltd. manufactures and sells a standard product at fixed selling price.

The budgeted figures for 1994-95 are as under :

Production and sales	2	lakhs units
Variable cost	Rs. 56	per unit
Fixed cost	Rs. 48	lakhs
Profit margin	33.33%	

You are required to determine sales at break-even, both in terms of quantity and value, for the year 1994-95 at the above selling price.

[ACS Final 1986]

Ans. : Break-even point 7,000 unit; turnover Rs. 85,000 and 17,000 units;
Margin of Safety Rs. 50,000.

41. The cost per unit of three products X, Y and Z are given below :

Products	X	Y	Z
Direct Materials (Rs.)	20	16	18
Direct Labour (Rs.)	12	14	12
Variable Overheads (Rs.)	8	10	6
Fixed Expenses (Rs.)	6	6	4
	46	46	40
Profit (Rs.)	18	14	12
Sale Price (Rs.)	64	60	52
No. of units produced	10,000	5,000	8,0000

Production arrangements are such that if one product is given-up the production of the others can be raised by 50%. The directors propose that product Z should be given-up because the contribution from the product is the lowest.

Present suitable analysis of the data indicating whether the proposed should be acepted.

[D.U. B.Com. (Hons.) 1998]

Ans. : Product X should be dropped because in that case profit is minimum.

42. The following data is given :

	Rs.
Fixed expenses	10,00,000
Variable expenses	10 per unit
Selling price	15 per unit

Indicate the number of units to be manufactured and sold to break-even point and to earn a profit of Rs. 10,000.

What additional units would be necessary to increase the above profit by Rs. 5,000?

[Adapted—C.U. M.Com.]

Ans. : 20,000 units, 22,000 units, 1,000 units.

43. From the following data determine the break-even point and the Margin of Safety :

	Rs.
Sales	6,00,000
Marginal cost	3,50,000
Fixed cost	1,50,000

[I.C.W.A. (Inter) June 1990]

Ans. : Break-even point Rs. 3,60,000; Margin of safety Rs. 2,40,000.

44. S. Ltd. furnishes you the following information relating to the half-year ending 30.6.1993 :

	Rs.
Fixed Expenses	50,000
Sales Value	2,00,000
Profit	50,000

During the second half of the same year the company has projected a loss of Rs. 10,000.

Calculate :

(i) The P/V ratio, break-even point and margin of safety for six months ending 30.6.1993.

(ii) Expected sales volume for second half of the year assuming that selling price and fixed expenses remain unchanged in the second half-year also.

(iii) The break-even point and margin of safety for the whole year 1993.

[I.C.W.A (Inter) 1986]

Ans. : (i) P/V Ratio 50%; BEP Rs. 1,00,000; Margin of safety Rs. 1,00,000; (ii) Rs. 80,000; (iii) BEP Rs. 2,00,000; Margin of safety Rs. 80,000.

45. Two competing companies Hero Ltd. and Zero Ltd. sell the same type of product in the same market.

Their forecasted profit and loss accounts for the year ended December 1990 are as follows :

		Hero Ltd.		Zero Ltd.	
		Rs.	Rs.	Rs.	Rs.
	Sales		5,00,000		5,00,000
Less :	Variable cost of sales	4,00,000		3,00,000	
	Fixed Costs	50,000	4,50,000	1,50,000	4,50,000
			50,000		50,000

You are required to state which company is likely to earn greater profit in conditions of (a) low demand; and (b) high demand. **[I.C.W.A. Dec. 1990]**

Ans. : Hero Ltd.—Low Demand; Zero Ltd.—High Demand.

STANDARD COSTING 11

Learning Objectives

1. *Introduction*
2. *Definition*
3. *Advantages and Limitations*
4. *Standard Cost and Standard Costing*
5. *Standard Cost and Estimated Cost*
6. *Standard Costs and Budgetary Control*
7. *Types of Standard*
8. *Introduction of Standard Costing*
9. *Variances Analysis :*

   (i) Material Variances

   (ii) Labour Variances

   (iii) Overhead Variances

STANDARD COSTING 11

Introduction

The concept of 'Control'— a third and final link of managerial process—means the process of ensuring accomplishment of plan. This involves not only action to implement the plan but also the measurement of performance in comparison with the specified plan or some other standards, the communication of results to the appropriate authorities for taking corrective measures in time. Standard costs are predetermined costs and are used as a measure with which the actual cost as ascertained are compared. Standard costing seeks to measure the efficiency of performance and identify weakness in performance, if any, at an early stage so that appropriate managerial measures can be taken to remove the weakness for effective cost control. In standard costing, cost of a product or service is known in advance and deviations from actual are used for effective cost control purpose.

Definition of Standard Costing

Standard costing is a technique which established predetermined estimates of the costs of products and services and then compares these predetermined costs with actual costs. The predetermined costs are known as **standard costs** and the difference between the standard costs and actual costs is known as **variance**.

J. R. Brown and L. R. Howard define standard costing *"as a technique of cost accounting which compares the 'standard cost' of each product or service with the actual cost, to determine the efficiency of the operation, so that any remedial action may be taken"*.

I.C.M.A., London, has defined the term 'Standard Costing' as *"the preparation of standard costs of products and services"*.

In the words of **W. W. Bigg**—*"Standard costing is a logical extension of budgetary control in which the principles of comparing 'actual with plan' are applied to the costs of products and services as well as to functions and responsibility centres."*

Thus, standard costing involves :

(i) The setting of standards,

(ii) Ascertainment of actual results,

(iii) Comparing standards with actual costs to determine the variance,

(iv) Investigating the variances and taking appropriate action.

Standard Cost

Standard cost may simply be defined as 'predetermined cost'. More formally, a standard cost may be defined as a predetermined calculation of how much costs should be under specified working conditions.

The **I.C.M.A.** summaries the concept and purpose of standard cost as :

"A predetermined calculation of how much costs should be under specified working condition."

It is built up from an assessment of the value of cost elements and correlates technical specifications and the quantification of materials, labour and other costs to the prices and/ or wage rates expected to apply during the period in which the standard cost is expected to be used.

Its main purposes are to provide bases for control through variance accounting, for the valuation of stocks and work in progress, and, in some cases, for fixing selling prices.

The price and quantity are the two constituents of cost elements for which standards are specified. The production engineer specifies the quantity of materials to be required and the purchasing manager sets a standard price for the materials on the basis of current prices. Time department will set the labour times and wage rates will be set according to the type of labour required and anticipated average rates. Direct expenses will be assessed and overhead absorption rates will be calculated as appropriate. Standards are set before the commencement of a period and should cover all aspects of production.

Advantages of Standard Costing

The introduction of a system of standard costing may offer the following advantages :

(i) The setting of standards leads to economics by determining best materials and methods.

(ii) Actual performance may easily be compared with the predetermined standards. Showing separately the favourable or unfavourable variance.

(iii) A detailed analysis of variance enables the management to investigate the causes of inefficiencies of labour, of the use of materials and of the operation of plant and machineries.

(iv) A target of efficiency can be set for the employees to reach and the sense of cost consciousness is thereby stimulated.

(v) Since variances can be calculated, the operation of the principle 'management by exception' becomes possible.

(vi) Gains and losses arising out of market fluctuations in prices of raw materials, as distinct from variations due to manufacturing conversion are revealed.

(vii) Standard costs provide a valuable aid to the management in fixing up prices and formulating policies.

(viii) The effects of variations in the price and use of materials, the ratio of labour wages to other expenses and the volume of production are demonstrated at short intervals.

(ix) It is a management tool for having effective cost control.

(x) Costing procedures can be made simple.

(xi) It facilitates the evaluation of stock and optimises the use of plant facilities, current assets and working capital.

(xii) Since attention is focused on the variances, weak areas can be identified, as a result, management can take corrective and prompt actions on right spots.

(xiii) Better allocations and utilization of resources are possible due to critical study of all the operations, methods in respect of production, sales and administration.

(xiv) A properly developed standards costing system with full participation and involvement creates a positive and cost effective attitude through all levels of management.

(xv) Standard costing facilitates the integration of accounts so that reconciliation between cost accounts and financial accounts may be avoided.

Limitations

The standard costing suffers from the following limitations :

(i) It does not become effective without Budgetary Control.

(ii) Cost of its installation is very high.

(iii) Its effectiveness depends upon the efficiency of historical costing. It becomes effective only when historical costing periodically supplements it.

(iv) In volatile conditions with rapidly changing methods, rates and prices, standards become quickly out of date and, thus, lose their control and motivational effects. This may cause resentment and loss of goodwill.

(v) It may not be appropriate to the business to which it is applied.

(vi) A badly conceived standards costs may yield inaccurate and misleading results and, therefore, may not enjoy the confidence of the users of this system.

Applicability

Standard costing in practice is a detailed process and requires considerable development work before it becomes a useful management tool for taking managerial and economic decisions. It can gainfully be used in a variety of costing situations like batch and mass production, process manufacture, transport. However, the greatest benefit can be gained when the manufacturing method involves a substantial degree of repetition. Its major application in practice is in organisation involved in mass production and/or repetitive assembly work.

STANDARD COST AND STANDARD COSTING

Standard Cost

Standard cost is predetermined cost based on a technical estimate for materials labour and overhead for a selected period of time and for a prescribed set of working condition. The Institute of the Cost and Management Accountants of London defines standard cost as a predetermined calculation of how much costs should be under specified working conditions. It is built up from the assessment of the value of cost elements and correlates technical specifications and the quantification of materials labour and other costs to the prices and/or wages rates expected to apply during the period in which the standard cost is intended to be used. Its main purposes are to provide bases for control through variance accounting for the valuation of stock and work-in-progress and, in some costs, for fixing selling prices.

Standard Costing

Standard costing is a technique for the preparation of standard costs and variances and for analysing the causes of variances with a view to maintain maximum efficiency in production through better utilization of resources available to the business unit.

According to **W. W. Bigg** : *"Standard costing discloses the cost of deviations from standard and classifies these as to their causes, so that management is immediately informed of the sphere of operations in which remedial action is necessary."*

So, the above definition explains that the aims of standard costing are :

(i) Ascertainment of standard costs;

(ii) Measurement of actual costs;

(iii) Comparison of the actual costs with the standard costs to determine the variances;

(iv) Analysis of variances for the purpose of finding out the causes for variances;

(v) Taking the appropriate and quick actions to remove the weakness, if any, so that maximum efficiency in production may be achieved.

Difference between Standard Cost and Historical Cost

The meaning of 'Standard Cost' will be more illuminating to us if a line of distinction is drawn between 'Standard Cost' and 'Historical Cost'.

The following are the points of distinction :

(i) Recording

Standard Cost is determined and recorded before actual performance while Historical Cost is related to the past transactions i.e. the financial transactions are recorded after the actual performance.

(ii) High Degree of Efficiency

Standard Cost is an ideal cost which can be attained under normal conditions. But Historical Cost is actual and real cost i.e. it is related to past. On the other hand, Standard Cost is a predetermined cost related to future.

(iii) Evaluation of Efficiency

Standard cost serves as a measure of evaluation of efficiency since it helps the management to compare the budgeted cost with that of actual cost. Historical fails to provide any such technique.

(iv) Cost Control

Standard cost is very important for cost control but Historical Cost fails to provide any technique for cost control. Since it fails to make any comparison and fails to provide any yardstick for pointing out the possible causes for rises in cost. Standard cost can be used as an yardstick for pointing out the centre of responsibility through the analysis of variations.

(v) Planning and Control

Historical cost has its own value and carries historical significance. The actual financial position of the concern is made known through it. But it has no practical significance. It is not helpful to the management for planning for variance purposes and control. But standard cost is considered to be an effective managerial tool of cost control, future planning.

Standard Cost and Estimated Costs

The following are the points of difference between standard costs and estimated costs :

(i) Objective

Estimated costs are intended to ascertain what the costs will be while standard costs aim at what costs should be.

(ii) Calculation

Estimated costs are calculated on the basis of past performance being adjusted in the light of anticipated changes in the future. Standard costs, on the other hand, are ascertained on a scientific basis keeping in view certain conditions of efficiency.

(iii) Aid to Management

Estimated costs are not helpful to management in accomplishing management functions as they are not scientifically predetermined costs. But standard costs involves operational analysis and evaluation and a comprehensive review of internal and external factors. They become reliable yardsticks for product costing, product pricing, planning, co-ordination and price control purposes.

(iv) Emphasis

Estimated costs put emphasis on cost with which it is compared at the end of the accounting period. If the estimated costs are found higher or lower than actual costs, they are revised for the use in the next accounting year. In standard costing the emphasis is put on standard costs, i.e., what costs of material labour and overhead should be incurred if the factory is to be operated as a highly efficient unit. Under standard costing, actual costs are ascertained only to facilitate their comparison with standard costs.

(v) Use

The estimated costs are used only as a statistical data, whereas standard costs are used as a regular system from which variances are ascertained and the reasons for such variances are analysed and corrected measures are taken promptly.

(vi) Revision

Estimated cost is adjusted to the actual cost and expected changes in the coming period. While Standard Cost is not generally revised unless it has been set incorrectly or it has become irrelevant to the changed situations. Thus, Standard Cost is free from frequent changes or modifications.

(vii) Barometer of Efficiency

Estimated Cost—being only an expression of likely cost in the future—cannot be used to measure the efficiency or otherwise. But standard cost is used as a barometer of efficiency since it is compared with actual cost.

Standard Costs and Budgetary Control

Both Standard Costs and Budgetary Control are important tools in the hands of the management for planning operation and financial control of a business enterprise. In both of them, there are predetermined standards and actual are compared with predetermined standards to measure managerial efficiency in dealing with different resources—mainly financial resources. In both the cases, variances are identified and reasons for such variances are ascertained and remedial measures are adopted to remove the loopholes. So, both are valuable aids to management in controlling costs.

But in spite of their similarities in approach and objects, they do differ in many respects. **The points of difference are discussed below :**

1. Standard Costing can operate independently without the help of Budget while budgets, in absence of standard costs, cannot provide a reasonable base against which the actual results can be compared. But to get maximum efficiency out of budgetary control and standard, costing, both are to be linked up.
2. Standards are based on technical assessments whereas budgets are based on past actual that are adjusted to future trends.
3. The objectives of budgeting are different from standard costing. A budget is a planning for profit which reflects anticipated financial inflows and outflows. Though it is comprehensive in nature, it covers several business activities like production, purchase, selling and distribution, research and development; while standard costs are developed only for the production and related manufacturing cost. It also reflects planned costs.
4. Budgetary control deals with the operation of a department of a business as a whole while standard costing is applied to manufacturing of a production process or processes. So, Budgetary control is extensive whereas standard costing is intensive in its application.

5. In Budgetary control, variances are revealed in total. But in standard costing, variances are analysed in detail. It reveals variance through different accounts.
6. Budgets set up maximum limit of expenses above which actual expenses are not expected to be incurred. While standards set up targets which are to be attained by actual performance.
7. Budgets are equally important for planning organisation, coordination and control functions of management. Standard costs contribute relatively more to the control function rather than other managerial functions.
8. Budgets project financial accounts while standard costs project cost accounts. Budgetary control adopts a more general approach of giving service to management.
9. Budgets are anticipated costs meant to be used for, forecasting requirements of material labour, cash etc. On the contrary, standard costs do not forecast what the cost are expected to be. So, they cannot be used for the purpose of forecasting.
10. Review and revision of budgets is more frequently based on the changing circumstances than those of standard costs. They are more static and subject to less change.
11. Budgets are generally applied in such business which are of jobbing nature since jobs are better controlled through predetermined budget and cost for different jobs are ascertained historically. Standard costing can suitably be applied to those business where manufacturing is done under conditions of continuous processing or under mass production methods.

Conclusion

In spite of the above differences both have the same objectives of managerial control and are, therefore, interrelated and cannot function independently. Both are complimentary to each other.

Matz and Usry have observed that *"Standards are almost indispensable to the work of establishing and operating a budget"*.

A Study made by the **National Association of Accountants (U.S.A.)** concludes that *"Standard costs are specially valuable in developing the cost side of the budget because they provide a reliable and convenient source of data for converting the budgeted production schedule into requirements for raw materials, labour and services"*.

Types of Standard

There are different types of standard which are discussed below :

1. **Ideal Standard**

   This is the standard which can be attained under the most favourable conditions possible. In other words, ideal standards are based on perfect performance. It is assumed that there is no wastage, no idle time, no inefficiencies or other imperfections in the manufacturing process. But it is very difficult to attain such standards in practice.

2. **Expected Standard**

   This is the standard which may be anticipated to be attained during a future specified budget period. Expected standards are based on expected performance. In setting these standards, a reasonable allowance is made for wastage's and other inevitable lapses. It is more realistic than ideal standard. This type of standard is best suited from cost control point of view.

3. **Basic Standard**

   This is a standard which is established for use unaltered over a long period of time. Basic standards are set up for some base year and is not changed as material prices and labour rates change. It is suited for those items of expenses which are fixed in nature. But basic standard is of no practical importance from cost control point of view.

4. **Normal Standard**

   This standard is based on average performances of the past. They are attainable under normal conditions. If there is stability in the past performances, such standards may be useful from cost ascertainment point of view. But, for cost control, it is not so much effective.

Introduction of Standard Costing System in a Factory

Standard costing is a system of cost accounting which makes use of predetermined standard costs relating to each element of cost—material, labour and overhead. It is basically a technique of accounting which compares the standard cost of each product or service with the actual cost to determine the efficiency of the operations. So, that any remedial measure may be taken quickly. It is the most effective method for controlling performance and cost.

While introducing a standard costing system in a factory, the following preliminary steps are required :

1. **Review of Existing System of Costing**

   Before introduction of standard costing system, it is important to review the existing system of costing with special reference to existing forms and records.

2. **Study of Technical Aspect**

   It is essential to study the technical aspects because standard costing must be based on actual conditions in the factory. Technical aspects involve methods of production, different processes or stages of production, normal and abnormal losses and gains and input-output relations etc.

3. **Organisation Chart**

   Lines of authority and responsibility should clearly be defined so that responsibility may be assigned as and when required.

4. **Allocation and Apportionment of Overhead**

   The existing methods and policies in respect of allocation and apportionment should be reviewed in the background of standard costing principles.

5. **Staff Training**

   The staff concerned with the working of standard costing system should be properly trained up.

6. **Existing Controls**

   The existing control techniques like internal control, budgetary control should also be reviewed to avoid overlapping.

7. **Type of Standard**

   Setting up Standard costs for material, labour and overheads is a complicated task. So, an in-depth study should be made to determine the type of standard to be established.

8. **Standard Cost Manual**

   Standard cost manual should be prepared that should clearly define various terms and procedures to be used. This may provide a good guide to the staff.

1. VARIANCE ANALYSIS

1. MATERIAL VARIANCES

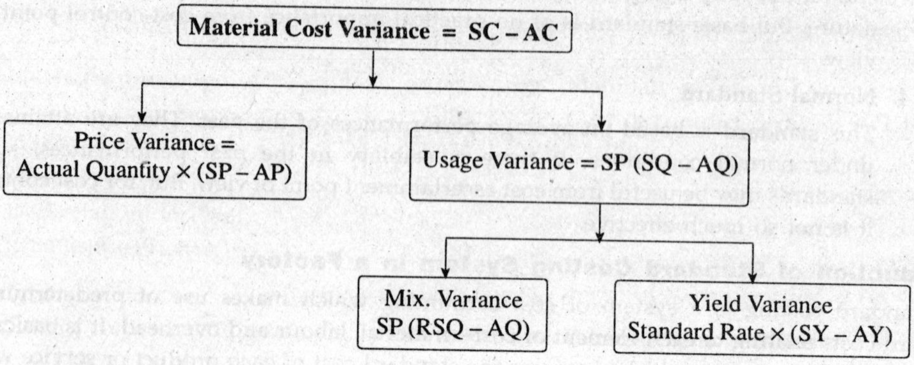

Some Definitions

1. Direct Materials Usage Variance

"The difference between the *standard quantity* specified for actual production and the *actual quantity* used at standard purchase price."

2. Direct Materials Price Variance

"The difference between the *standard price* and *actual price* for the *actual quantity* of materials."

$$\textbf{Standard Rate} = \frac{\text{Standard Cost for Standard Mix}}{\text{Standard Output}}$$

3. Direct Materials Total Variance

"The difference between the standard direct material cost of the actual production volume and the actual cost of direct material."

How to find out?

Formulae

(i) Actual quantity used for production × Standard price

Minus

(ii) Standard quantity for production × Standard price

} Usage Variance

Actual quantity purchased × Actual price

Minus

Actual quantity purchased × Standard price

} Price Variance

} Total Direct Material Variance

Note :

The actual usage is to be calculated as follows :

Opening stock + Purchase – Closing stock = USAGE

Causes of Material Variances

(i) Price Variances

(a) Buying lower or higher quality of materials than planned.

(b) Losing or gaining quantity discounts by purchasing in smaller or larger quantity of materials than planned.

(c) Paying higher or lower price than planned.

(d) Close substitute materials are bought due to unavailability of planned material.

(ii) **Usage variance**

(a) Buying of substitute materials because of unavailability of standard materials.

(b) Greater or lower yield from materials than expected or planned.

(c) Greater or lower rate of scrap than anticipated.

ALTERNATIVE APPROACH

Material Cost Variance

1. Actual Quantity × Actual Rate
2. Actual Quantity × Standard Rate
3. Standard Mix of Actual Quantity × Standard Price
4. Standard Quantity for Actual Output × Standard Rate.

Price Variance	=	2 – 1
Mix. Variance	=	3 – 2
Usage Variance	=	4 – 2
Yield Variance	=	4 – 3
Total Variance	=	4 – 1

Problem 1

Sanrare Perfumary Ltd. provides the following information from their records :

The standard material requirements for 10 kg. of a product are :

Materials	*Qnt.* (kg.)	*Rate per kg.* (Rs.)
A	8	10
B	6	6

During March, 1999, 100 kgs. of the product were produced. The actual consumptions of materials were as under :

Materials	*Qnt.* (kg.)	*Rate per kg.* (Rs.)
A	75	9
B	65	7

Calculate :

(i) Material Cost Variance

(ii) Matrial Price Variance

(iii) Material Usage Variance

[V.U. B.Com. (Hons.)]

Solution

Material	*Standard for 100 kgs.*			*Actual*		
	Qnt. kg.	*Rate* Rs.	*Amt.* Rs.	*Qnt.* kg.	*Rate* Rs.	*Amt.* Rs.
A	80	10	800	75	9	675
B	60	6	360	65	7	455
	140		1160	140		1130

1. **Material Cost Variance** Standard Cost – Actual Cost

1. **Material Cost Variance**	Standard Cost – Actual Cost			
	Rs. 1,160 – Rs. 1,130	=	Rs. 30	(F)
2. **Material Price Variance**	AQ (SP – AP)			
	A = 75 × (10 – 9)	=	Rs. 75	(F)
	B = 65 × (6 – 7)	=	Rs. 65	(A)
			Rs. 10	(F)
3. **Material Usage Variance**	SP × (SQ – AQ)			
	A = 10 × (80 – 75)	=	Rs. 50	(F)
	B = 6 × (60 – 65)	=	Rs. 30	(A)
Total Price Variance			Rs. 20	(F)

Problem 2

The Standard Material cost to produce a tonne of chemical is :

300 kgs. of material A @ Rs. 10 per kg.

400 kgs. of material B @ Rs. 5 per kg.

500 kgs. of material C @ Rs. 6 per kg.

During a period, 100 tonnes of mixture X were produced from the usage of :

35 tonnes of material A at a cost of Rs. 9,000 per tonne

42 tonnes of material B at a cost of Rs. 6,000 per tonne

53 tonnes of material C at a cost of Rs. 7,000 per tonne

Calculate material price, usuage and mix variances.

[Delhi U. B.Com. (Hons.)]

Solution

Statement

Material	*Standard*			*Actual*		
	Qnt. kg.	*Rate* Rs.	*Amount* Rs.	*Qnt.* kg.	*Rate* Rs.	*Amount* Rs.
A	30,000	10.00	3,00,000	35,000	9.00	3,15,000
B	40,000	5.00	2,00,000	42,000	6.00	2,52,000
C	50,000	6.00	3,00,000	53,000	7.00	3,71,000
Total	1,20,000		8,00,000	1,30,000		9,38,000

1. **Material Cost Variance**

Standard Cost for Actual Quantity – Actual Cost

= Rs. 8,00,000 – Rs. 9,38,000 = Rs. 1,38,000 (A)

2. **Material Price Variance** = AQ (SP – AP)

			Rs.	
A =	(Rs. 10 – Rs. 9) × 35,000	=	35,000	(F)
B =	(Rs. 5 – Rs. 6) × 42,000	=	42,000	(A)
C =	(Rs. 6 – Rs. 7) × 53,000	=	53,000	(A)
Total Price Variance		=	60,000	(A)

3. **Material Usage Variance** = SP (SQ – AB)

			Rs.
A =	(30,000 – 35,000) × 10	=	Rs. 50,000 (A)
B =	(40,000 – 42,000) × 5	=	Rs. 10,000 (A)
C =	(50,000 – 53,000) × 6	=	Rs. 18,000 (A)

4. **Material Mix Variance** = (Revised SQ – AQ) × Standard price

A = (32,500 – 35,000) × 10 = Rs. 25,000 (A)

B = $\left(\frac{1,30,000}{3} - 42,000\right) \times 5$ = Rs. 6,667 (F)

C = $\left(\frac{1,62,500}{3} - 53,000\right) \times 6$ = Rs. 7,000 (F)

Rs. 11,333 (A)

Working :

1. **Calculation of Standard Quantity**

$$\text{Revised Quantity} = \frac{\text{Total Actual Qnt.}}{\text{Total Standard Qnt.}} \times \text{Standard Qnt.}$$

$$A = \frac{1,30,000}{1,20,000} \times 30,000 = 32,500 \text{ kgs.}$$

$$B = \frac{1,30,000}{1,20,000} \times 40,000 = \frac{1,30,000}{3} \text{ or } 43,333 \text{ kgs.}$$

$$C = \frac{1,30,000}{1,20,000} \times 50,000 = \frac{1,62,500}{3} \text{ or } 54,167 \text{ kgs.}$$

Problem 3

From the following data compute :

(i) Material Cost Variance

(ii) Material Price Variance

(iii) Material Usage Variance

Srtandard quantity required 500 kgs.

Standard price @ Rs. 10 per kg.

Actual quantity used 600 kgs.

The above quantity was bought at Rs. 5,400.

Solution

Actual price per kg. = Rs. 5,400 ÷ 600 = Rs. 9.00.

1. **Material Price Variance** = Actual Quantity × (SP – AP)
   = 600 × (10 – 9) = Rs. 600 (F)

2. **Material Usage Variance** = Standard price × (SQ – AQ)
   = 10 × (500 – 600) = Rs. 1,000 (A)

3. **Material Cost Variance** = Standard Cost for actual quantity – Actual Cost
   = (500 × 10) – (600 × 9) = Rs. 400 (A)

Problem 4

From the following particulars compute :

(i) Material Cost Variance

(ii) Material Price Variance

(iii) Material Usage Variance

Quantity of material purchased :	5,000 units
Value of materials purchased :	Rs. 50,000
Standard Quantity of materials required for the product	5,500 units
Standard rate of material per unit	Rs. 10.50

Solution

1. **Material Price Variance** = AQ × (SP – AP)
   = 5,000 (10.50 – 10) = Rs. 2,500 (F)

2. **Material Usage Variance** = SP × (SQ – AQ)
   = 10.50 × (5,500 – 5,000) = Rs. 5,250 (F)

3. **Material Cost Variance** = Standard Cost for Actual Quantity – Actual Cost
   = Rs. 57,750 – Rs. 50,000 = Rs. 7,750 (F)

2. LABOUR VARIANCES

Labour variance analyses the variance of actual labour cost from standard labour cost due to the following factors :

(a) Rate of pay; (b) Labour efficiency; (c) Labour mix; (d) Idle time etc.

Labour Variance may be classified as follows :

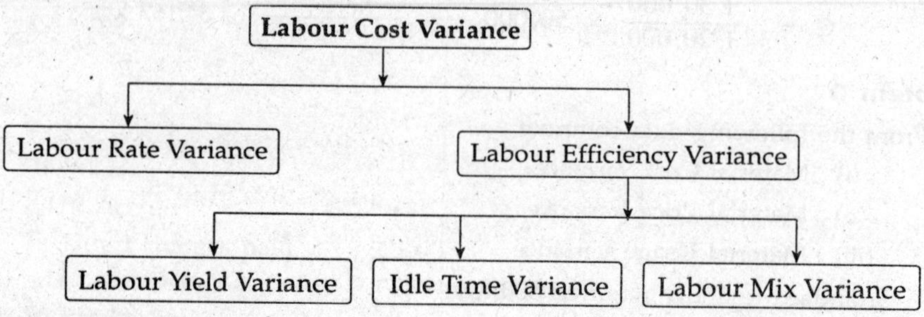

Labour Variances

Some definitions

(i) Direct Labour Rate Variance

Definition

"The difference between the standard and actual direct labour hour rate per hour for the total hours worked"—Terminology.

(ii) Direct Labour Efficiency Variance

"The difference between the standard hours for the actual production and the hours actually worked valued at the standard labour rate"—Terminology.

(iii) Direct Labour Total Variance

"The difference between the standard direct labour cost and the actual direct labour cost incurred for the production achieved"—Terminology.

(i) Labour Cost Variance

Formulae

(i) (Actual Labour Hours × Actual Rate)
Minus (Actual Labour Hours × Standard Rate)

Causes

Labour cost may arise due to changes in the following factors :

(i) Actual Wage Rate may be more or less than Standard Wage Rate.

(ii) Actual Labour Hours may be more or less than Standard Labour Hours.

(iii) There may be some idle hours due to abnormal situation like strike, lockout, shortage of power which were not considered at the time of fixing the standard labour cost.

(iv) There may be shortage of workers having standard level of efficiency.

(v) Actual Output may be more or less than Standard Output or yield.

(ii) Labour Rate Variance

According to **I.C.M.A., London**, Labour Rate Variance *"is that portion of labour (wages) variance which is due to the difference between the Standard Rate of pay specified and Actual Rate paid."*

Labour Rate Variance = (SR × AH) – (AR × AH)
= (SR – AR) × AH

Causes

Labour Rate variance may be caused by the following factors :

(i) Employment of more skilled and efficient workers who demand higher wages.

(ii) Scarce supply of labour might have raised the wage rates.

(iii) On the contrary, excess supply of labour might have lowered down the wage rate.

(iv) Overtime allowances, bonus and extra shift allowances might have been paid.

(v) Change in method of wage payment.

(vi) Due to government policy general wage rate might have gone up.

(vii) Due to an agreement with the trade unions there may be modification of terms and conditions of wage payment and as a result the rate of wages may go up.

(viii) Faulty recruitment and placement of workers.

(ix) New workmen now paid though not included in the standards.

(iii) Labour Time (efficiency) Variance

This is like Materials Quantity Variance. According to **I.C.M.A., London** *"it is that portion of labour (wages) variance which is due to the difference between standard labour hours specified for the output achieved and actual hours expended"*.

This variance reflects the efficiency or inefficiency of the workers.

Labour Efficiency Variance = (SH × SR) – (AH × SR) = SR × (SH – AH)

It is to be noted carefully that actual labour hours used in the formula should be labour hours actually taken for production.

Causes

Labour Efficiency Variance may be caused by :

(i) Go-slow tactics adopted by the trade unions.

(ii) Absence of maintenance up to standard level.

(iii) Poor quality of raw materials.

(iv) Loss in waiting time.

(v) Lack of proper and efficient supervision.

(iv) Idle-Time Variance

Sometimes workers may remain idle in the factory due to strike, power failures, machine break-down, etc. The hours for which workers are not provided with work facilities are known as idle hours. They get wages for these idle hours. Obvious idle hours do affect the labour cost variance. This kind of variance is undesirable and that is why reasons for these variances are to be identified and measures should be taken to control them.

Idle Time Variance = Idle Hours × S.R.

(v) Labour Yield Variance

This variance arises on account of the difference between Standard Yield and Actual Yield :

Labour Yield Variance = (AY – SY) × SLC per unit

(vi) Labour Mix. Variance

Labour Mix. Variance = (Revised Hours – Actual Hours) × S.R.

Revised Hours will be calculated :

RH = Actual Hours × Standard Mix Ratio.

Alternative Approach

Labour Cost Variances

1. Actual Hours × Actual Rate
2. Actual Hours × Standard Rate
3. Standard Hours for Actual Output × Standard Rate
   Or, Earned Standard Hours
4. Standard Hours is Standard Mix. for Actual Output × Standard Rate :

1.	Rate of Pay Variance	= 2 – 1
2.	Efficiency Variance	= 3 – 2
3.	Labour Mix. Variance	= 4 – 2
4.	Total Variance	= 3 – 1

Problem 5

The following information is obtained from a Standard Cost Card.

Labour Rate Rs. 2·00 per hour

Hours — 3 hours per unit

Actual production data are :

Units produced are 250

Labour rate Rs. 2·25 per hour

Hours worked—800

Calculate Labour Cost Variance and analyse it.

Solution

Standard Hours	=	250 × 3 = 750
Standard Labour Cost	=	750 × Rs. 2 = Rs. 1,500.
Actual Labour Cost	=	800 × 2.25 = Rs. 1,800

Analysis of Labour Cost Variance

	Labour Cost Variance (SLC – ALC) = Rs. 1,500 – Rs. 1,800 This is explained by		(–) 300 (A)
(i)	**Labour Rate Variance** = (SR – AR) × AH = (Rs. 2.00 – Rs. 2.25) × 800	200 (A)	
	Plus		
(ii)	**Labour Efficiency Variance** (SH – AH) × SR = (750 – 800) × Rs. 2	100 (A)	

Problem 6

Given for a factory :

Normal number of workers	100
Number of hours paid for in a week	80
Standard Rate of wages per hour	Rs. 1.60
Standard Output of the department per hour taking into account normal idle time	40 units

In the first week of January 2003 it was ascertained that 2,000 units were produced despite 20% idle time due to power failure and actual rate of wages was Rs. 1.80 per hour.

Calculate Labour Variances.

Solution

Standard hours for actual output $= \dfrac{2{,}000 \text{ units} \times 100}{40 \text{ units}} = 5{,}000$ hours

Standard Labour Cost	=	5,000 hours × Rs. 1.60 = Rs. 8,000
Actual Hours	=	100 × 80 = 8,000
Actual Labour Cost	=	8,000 × 1.80 = Rs. 14,400
Idle Hours	=	$8{,}000 \text{ hrs.} \times \dfrac{20}{100} = 1{,}600.$
Actual Hours for Efficiency Variance	=	8,000 – 1,600 = 6,400 hrs.

Analysis of Labour Cost Variance

			Rs.
	Labour Cost Variance	= (SLC – ALC) = Rs. 8,000 – Rs. 14,400	6,400 (A)
	Explained by :		
(i)	Labour Rate Variance (SR – AR) × AH.	= (Rs. 1.60 – Rs. 1.80) 8,000 = (–0·20) × 8,000)	1,600 (A)
(ii)	Labour Efficiency Variance	= (SH – AH) × SR = (5,000 – 6,400) × Rs. 1.60	2,240 (A)
(iii)	Idle Time Variance = Idle Hours × SR = 1,600 × Rs. 1.60		2,560 (A)

Problem 7

From the following data prepare a unit cost statement showing the prime cost of product A and B together with analysis of variances :

		Product A	*Product B*
Material :	Standard	600 kgs. @ Rs. 5.00	90 kgs. @ Rs. 3.00
	Actual	580 kgs. @ Rs. 5.50	100 kgs. @ Rs. 2.50
Labour :	Labour	80 hours @ Rs. 2.00	16 hours @ Rs. 2.80
	Actual	92 hours @ Rs. 1.75	14 hours @ Rs. 2.60

[Adapted—I.C.W.A. (Inter), June 1998]

Solution

Variance

	Product A	*Product B*
(1) **Material Price Variance**	= AQ × (SP – AQ) = 580 × (Rs. 5 – Rs. 5.50) = 580 × 0.50 = Rs. 290 (A)	AQ × (SP – AP) = 100 × (3 – 2.80) = 100 × 0.20 = Rs. 20 (F)
(2) **Material Usage Variance**	= (SQ – AQ) × SP (600 kgs. – 580 kgs.) × 5 = (20) × 5 = 100 (F)	(SQ – AQ) × SP (90 – 100) × Rs. 3 = Rs. 30 (A)
(3) **Material Cost Variance**	(Price Variance – Usage Varaince) Rs. 290 (A) – Rs. 100 (F) = Rs. 190 (A)	(Price Variance – Usage Varaince) Rs. 20 (F) – 30 (A) = Rs. 10 (A)
(4) **Labour Rate Variance**	(SR – AR) × AH (Rs. 2 – Rs. 1.75) × 92 = Rs. 23.00 (F)	(SR – AR) × AH (Rs. 2.80 – Rs. 2.60) × 14 = 0.20 × 14 hours = Rs. 2.80 (F)
(5) **Labour Efficiency Variance**	(SH – AH) × SR (80 hrs. – 92 hrs. × Rs. 2 = Rs. 24 (A)	(SH – AH) × SR (16 – 14) × 2.8 = Rs. 5.60 (F)
(6) **Labour Cost Variance**	Labour Rate Variance – Labour Efficiency Variance Rs. 23 (F) – Rs. 24 (A) = Re. 1.00 (A)	Labour Rate Variance + Labour Efficiency Variance Rs. 2.80 (F) + Rs. 5.60 (F) = Rs. 8.40 (F)

Cost Statement

Product A			*Product B*	
		Rs.		Rs.
Material :	600 kgs. × Rs. 5.00 =	3,000.00	90 kgs. × Rs. 3.00 =	270.00
Labour :	80 hrs. × Rs. 2.00 =	160.00	16 hours × Rs. 2.80 =	44.80
(A) **Standard Prime Cost**		3160.00		314.80
Material :	580 kgs. × Rs. 5.50 =	3,190	100 kgs. × Rs. 2.80 =	280.00
Labour :	92 hours × Rs. 1.75 =	161	14 hours × Rs. 2.60 =	36.40
(B) **Actual Prime Cost**		3,351		316.40
Total Cost Variance = Rs. 3,160 – Rs. 3,351= Rs. 191.00 (A)			Rs. 314.80 – Rs. 316.40 =Rs. 1.60 (A)	

Problem 8

A gang of workers normally consists of 30 men, 15 women and 10 boys. They are paid at standard hourly rates as under :

	Re.
Men	0.80
Women	0.60
Boys	0.40

In a normal working week of 40 hours, the gang is expected to produce 2,000 units of output. During the week ending 31st December, 2002, the gang consisted of 40 men, 10 women and 5 boys. The actual wages paid were @ Re 0.70, Re 0.65 and Re 0.30 respectively. 4 hours were lost due to abnormal idle time and 1,600 units were produced.

Calculate : (i) Wage Variance; (ii) Wage Rate Variance; (iii) Labour Efficiency Variance; (iv) Labour Mix Variance and (v) Labour Idle Time Variance.

[B.Com. (Hons.) Delhi University]

Solution

Workers	*Standard*			*Actual*		
	Hours	*Rate* (Rs.)	*Amount* (Rs.)	*Hours*	*Rate* (Rs.)	*Amount* (Rs.)
Men	1,200	0.80	960	1,600	0.70	1,120
Women	600	0.60	360	400	0.65	260
Boys	400	0.40	160	200	0.30	60
	2,200		1,480	2,200		1,440

1. **Labour Cost Variance** = (Actual Labour Cost – St. Labour Cost for Actual Output)

$$= \text{Rs. } 1{,}440 - \left(\frac{1{,}480}{2{,}000} \times 1{,}600\right) = \text{Rs. } 256 \text{ (A)}$$

2. **Wage Rate Variance** = Actual Hours paid × (Standard Rate – Actual Rate)

		Rs.
Men	= 1,600 × (0.80 – 0.70) =	160 (F)
Women	= 400 × (0.60 – 0.65) =	20 (A)
Boys	= 200 × (0.30 – 0.40) =	20 (A)

3. **Labour Efficiency Variance** = St. Rate × (St. Hours – Actual Hours)

Men $= 0.80 \times \left[\left(1{,}600 \times \frac{1{,}200}{2{,}000}\right) - 1{,}600\right]$

$= 0.80 \times (960 - 1{,}600) = \text{Rs. } 512 \text{ (A)}$

Women $= 0.60 \times \left[\left(\frac{600}{2{,}000} \times 1{,}600\right) - 400\right]$

$= 0.60 \times (480 - 400) = 48 \text{ (F)}$

Boys $= 0.40 \times \left(\frac{400}{2{,}000} \times 1{,}600\right) - 200$

$= 0.40 \times (320 - 200) = \text{Rs. } 48 \text{ (F)}$

4. **Labour Mix Variance** = St. Rate × (Actual time worked – Revised St. time)

Men $= \text{Re. } 0.80 \times \left(1{,}440 - \frac{1{,}980 \times 1{,}200}{2{,}220}\right)$

$= 0.80 \times (1{,}440 - 1{,}080) = \text{Rs. } 288 \text{ (A)}$

Problem 9

Calculate labour variances from the following data :

Gross direct wages	Rs. 36,000
Standard hours produced	2,000
Standard rate per hour	Rs. 15

Actual hours paid – 1,800 hours out of which hours not worked (abnormal idle time) are 50 hours.

Solution

(i) **Labour Cost Variance** = Standard cost of labour – Actual cost of labour
= (2,000 × Rs. 15) – (1,800 × 20)
= Rs. 30,000 – Rs. 36,000 = Rs. 6,000 (A)

(ii) **Labour Rate Variance** = Actual Time × (St. Rate – Actual Rate)
= 1,800 × (15 – 20) = Rs. 9,000 (A)

(iii) **Labour Efficiency Variance** = Standard Rate × (ST – AT)
= Rs. 15 × (2,000 – 1,750) = Rs. 3,750 (F)

(iv) **Idle Time Variance** = Abnormal Time × St. Rate
= 50 × Rs. 15 = 750 (A)

3. VARIABLE OVERHEAD VARIANCES

Classification :

(i) **Variance Overhead Cost Variance** = (SC – AC)

(ii) **Variable Overhead Expenditure Variance** = Actual hours worked × (SR – AR)

(iii) **Variable Overhead Efficiency Variance** = (SR × SH) – AH Worked

(i) **Variable Overhead Variance**

The difference between the actual overheads incurred and the variable overheads absorbed. This variance is simply the under-absorption of overheads.

(ii) **Variable Overhead Expenditure Variance**

Definition

The difference between the actual overheads incurred and the allowed variable overheads based on the actual hours worked is known as Variable Overhead Expenditure Variance (VOEV).

(iii) **Variable Overhead Efficiency Variance**

Definition

The difference between the variable overheads and the absorbed variable overheads is known as Variable Overhead Efficiency Variance.

Formulae

(i)	Actual Variance Overheads *Minus* Actual Labour hour × VOAR[1]	Variable Overhead Expenditure Variance	Total Variable Overhead Variance
(ii)	Actual Labour Hours × VOAR *Minus* SHP[2] × VOAR	Variable Overhead Efficiency Variance	

[1] VOAR = Variance Overhead Absorption Rate.

[2] SHP = Standard Hours of Production.

Problem 10

Budget for January 2003—Department A

	Rs.
Fixed Overhead	11,480
Variable Overhead	13,120
Labour Hours	3,280 hrs.
Standard Hours for Production	3,280 hrs.

Actual for January 2003—Department A

	Rs.
Fixed Overheads	12,100
Variable Overheads	13,930
Actual Labour Hours	3,150 hrs.
Standard Hours Produced	3,230 hrs.

Solution

FOAR[1] $= \dfrac{\text{Budgeted fixed overheads}}{\text{Budgeted Activity level}} = \dfrac{\text{Rs. } 11{,}480}{3{,}280 \text{ hrs.}} = \text{Rs. } 3.5 \text{ per hour.}$

VOAR[2] $= \dfrac{\text{Budgeted variable overheads}}{\text{Budgeted Activity level}} = \dfrac{\text{Rs. } 13{,}120}{3{,}280 \text{ std. hrs.}} = \text{Rs. } 4 \text{ per hour.}$

[1] FOAR = Fixed Overhead Absorption Rate.

[2] VOAR = Variable Overhead Absorption Rate.

(i) **Variable Overhead Expenditure Variance**

(A)	Actual Variable Overhead		= Rs. 13,930
	Minus Actual Labour Hours × VOAR		= Rs. 12,600
			Rs. 1,330 (A)

(ii) **Variable Overhead Efficiency Variance**

(B)	Actual Labour Hours × VOAR		= Rs. 12,600
	Minus SHP × VOAR	(3,230 × Rs. 4)	= Rs. 12,920
			Rs. 320 (F)

Total Variable Overhead Efficiency Variance

A – B = Rs. 1,330 (A) – Rs. 320 (FAV) = Rs. 1010 (A)

Problem 11

Calculate variable overhead expenditure variance from the following particulars :

Standard production	5,000 units
Actual production	4,000 units
Standard variable overhead	Rs. 15,000
Actual variable overhead	Rs. 11,200

Solution

Standard Variable Overhead Rate $= \frac{\text{Rs. } 15{,}000}{5{,}000} = \text{Rs. } 3$

Standard variable overhead cost = 4,000 × Rs. 3 = Rs. 12,000

Actual variable overhead cost = Rs. 11,200

∴ Variable overhead expenditure variable = SC – AC

= Rs. 12,000 – Rs. 11,200 = Rs. 800 (F)

Problem 12

From the following particulars calculate variable overhead expenditure variance :

Actual variable overhead expense	Rs. 14,250
Budgeted variable overhead expense	Rs. 17,000
Actual level of production	8,000 Standard hours
Normal capacity	10,000 Standard hours

[Adapted—I.C.W.A. (Inter)]

Solution

Variable Overhead Expenditure Variance = SC – AC

Standard Variable Overhead Expense = Standard rate × Actual output

Standard rate $= \frac{\text{Rs. } 17{,}000}{10{,}000} = \text{Rs. } 1.70.$

So, Standard Variable Overhead Cost = 8,000 × Rs. 1·70 = Rs. 13,600

∴ Variable Overhead Cost Variance = SC – AC = Rs. 13,600 – Rs. 14,250

= 650 (Adverse)

Problem 13

The standard cost card of a manufacturing concern includes the following particulars :

Variable overhead per unit – 2 hours @ 0·30 p. per hour = 0·60 p.

Actual operating hours 8,000 hours

Actual variable overhead expenses Rs. 2,600

Actual units produced 4,850

Calculate necessary cost variances.

[Adapted—C.A. Final]

Solution

We shall have to find out standard quantity and actual rate

$$\textbf{Standard Quantity} = \frac{\text{Actual operating hours}}{\text{Standard hours per unit}} = \frac{8{,}000}{2} = 4{,}000 \text{ units}$$

$$\textbf{Actual Rate} = \frac{\text{Actual overhead cost}}{\text{Standard hrs. worked}} = \frac{\text{Rs. } 2{,}600}{4{,}000} = 0{\cdot}65 \text{ p.}$$

(i) **Variable overhead cost variance** = SC – AC

Standard Cost = Actual Qnt. × S.R. = 4,850 × 0·60 p = Rs. 2,910

Variable overhead cost variance = Rs. 2,910 – Rs. 2,600 = 310 (F)

(ii) **Variable overhead expenses variance** = Standard unit × (SR – AR)

= 4,000 × (0·60 – 0·65) = Rs. 200 (A)

(iii) **Variable overhead efficiency variance** = SR × (AQ – SQ)

= 0·60 p × (4,850 – 4,000) = Rs. 510 (F)

4. SALES VARIANCES

A number of standard costing systems have been designed to present Material, Labour and Overhead cost variances as discused earlier. No doubt, these variables are invaluable, but many accountants do think that a system will remain incomplete if sales variances are not included in the presentation of information to the management.

There are two methods of calculating sales variances namely :

(i) **The Turnover Method** : This method shows the effect of a change in sales on turnover.

(ii) **The Margin Method** : This method shows the effect of a change in sales on profit margin.

Both the methods are very useful and should be understood by management accountants for taking managerial decisions.

Causes of Sales Variance

Sales variances are basically caused by two changes which may occur when comparing budgeted sales with actual sales.

(i) Those due to price and (ii) those due to volume.

The change in volume may be caused by (i) changes due to a change in quantity and (ii) changes due to a change in *'mix'* of sales.

An example will clarify the matter.

Change in price *Product*	*Budgeted*		*Actual*	
P	100 at Rs. 10	Rs. 1,000	100 at Rs. 11	1,100
Q	100 at Rs. 20	Rs. 2,000	100 at Rs. 15	1,500
	200	Rs. 3,000	200	Rs. 2,600

In the above case, the volume of sales is as budgeted, but the selling prices have changed in both the products.

Change in volume

P	100 at Rs. 10	Rs. 1,000	150 at Rs. 10	1,500
Q	100 at Rs. 20	Rs. 2,000	120 at Rs. 20	2,400
	200	Rs. 3,000	270	3,900

Here the price is as budgeted, but the volume has changed.

Change in quantity

P	100 at Rs. 10	Rs. 1,000	200 at Rs. 10	2,000
Q	100 at Rs. 20	Rs. 2,000	200 at Rs. 20	4,000
	200	Rs. 3,000	400	6,000

In the above situation, the price is as budgeted but the volume has changed.

Change in mix.

P	100 at Rs. 10	Rs. 1,000	120 at Rs. 10	Rs. 1,200
Q	100 at Rs. 20	Rs. 2,000	80 at Rs. 20	Rs. 1,600
	200	Rs. 3,000	200	Rs. 2,800

Here, the price and quantity are as budgeted but the 'mix' of products has changed from A 50% and B 50% to A 60% and B 40%.

(a) Sales Variance based on Turnover

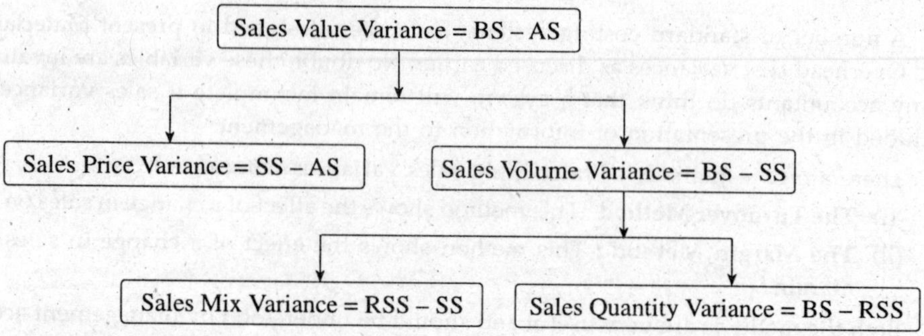

(i) ***Sales Value Variance :*** (Actual Value of Sales – Budgeted Vale of Sales)

Actual Sales = Actual Quantity sold × Actual selling price.

Budgeted Sales = Standard Quantity × Standard selling price.

If actual sales are more than the budgeted sales, there is favourable variance and if actual sales < budgeted sales the variance will be unfavourable.

(ii) ***Sales Price Variance :*** (Actual selling price – Budgeted selling price) × Actual Quantity

If actual sales price < budgeted sales, the variance is favourable and vice versa.

(iii) ***Sales Volume Variance*** : (Actual Quantity – Budgeted Quantity) × Budgeted selling price

If the actual quantity sold exceeds the budgeted sales quantity then the variance is favourable and if the actual quantity sold is *less than* budgeted sales quantity, the variance is taken as unfavourable.

(iv) ***Sales Mix Variance :*** (Actual mix quantity sold – Actual quantity in standard proportion) × standard selling price.

(Budgeted price per unit of actual mix – Budgeted price per unit of budgeted mix) × Total actual quantity.

(v) ***Sales Quantity Variance :*** (Total actual quantity – Total budgeted quantity) × Budgeted price per unit of budgeted mix.

Problem 14

The budgeted and actual sales of a concern manufacturing and marketing a single product are funished below :

Budgeted sales	10,000 units at Rs. 4 per unit.
Acutal sales	5,000 units at Rs. 3.50 per unit
	8,000 units at Rs. 4 per unit

Calculate : (a) Sales Price Variance

(b) Sales Volume Variance

Solution

(a)	**Sales Price Variance**	=	Actual Sales – Standard Sales
	Standard Sales	=	Standard Price × Actual Quantity
		=	13,000 × Rs. 4 = Rs. 52,000
	Actual Sales	=	Actual price × Actual quantity
		=	(5,000 × Rs. 3.50) + (8,000 × Rs. 4)
		=	Rs. 17,500 + Rs. 32,000 = Rs. 49,500
	Sales Price Variance	=	Rs. 52,000 – Rs. 49,500 = Rs. 2,500 (Adv.)
(b)	**Sales Volume Variance**	=	Standard Sales – Budgeted Sales
		=	Rs. 52,000 – 40,000 = Rs. 12,000 (Fav.)
(c)	**Sales Value Variance**	=	Actual Sales – Budgeted Sales
		=	Rs. 49,500 – Rs. 40,000 = Rs. 9,500 (Fav.)

(b) Variance based on Margin

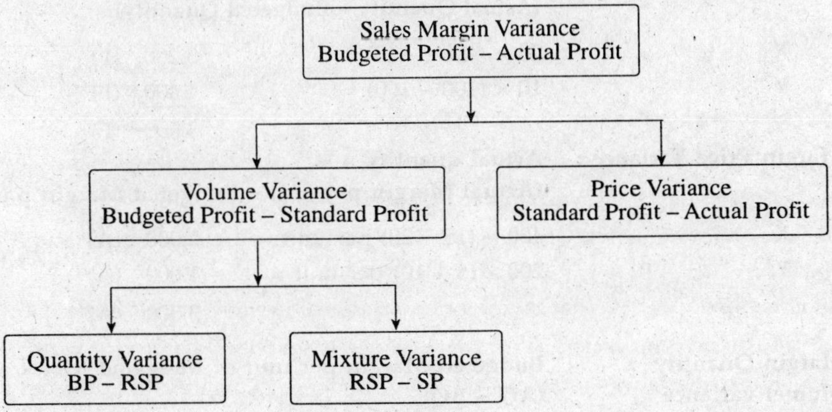

Sales Margin Variance = Quantity Variance + Mixture Variance + Price Variance

Or

BP – AP = (BP – RSP) + (RSP – SP) + (SP – AP)

The revised terminology of cost accounting published in 1966 by the Institute of Cost and Management Accountants favours this method of calculating sales variances.

Problem 15

Compute the following variances from the data given below :

(i) Total sales margin variance, (ii) Sales volume variance,

(iii) Sales margin price variance, (iv) Sales margin quantity variance.

Product	*Budgeted Qnt. Units*	*Actual Qnt. Units*	*Budgeted sale price per unit*	*Actual sale price per unit*	*Standard cost per unit*
			Rs.	Rs.	Rs.
X	240	400	50	45	30
Y	160	200	25	20	15

[C.A. Inter, May 1992]

Solution

Product	*Budgeted Sales price per unit*	*Budgeted cost per unit*	*Standard sales margin*	*Budgeted qnt.*	*Budgeted profit*	*Actual sales price*	*Actual sales margin*	*Actual sales qnt.*	*Actual profit*
	Rs.	Rs.	Rs.		Rs.	Rs.	Rs.		Rs.
X	50	30	20	240	4,800	45	15	400	6,000
Y	25	15	10	160	1,600	20	5	200	1,000
					6,400				7,000

1. **Total Sales Margin Variance : Actual Profit – Budgeted Profit**

   Rs. 7,000 – Rs. 6,400 = Rs. 600 (Fav.)

2. **Sales Margin Volume Variance : Budgeted Margin per unit × (Actual Quantity – Budgeted Quantity)**

X	20 × (400 – 240) =	3,200	(F)
Y	10 × (200 – 160) =	400	(F)
		3,600	(F)

3. **Sales Margin Price Variance : Actual quantity × (Actual Margin per unit – Budgeted Margin p.u.)**

X	400 × (15 – 20) per unit =	2,000	(A)
Y	200 × (5 – 10) per unit =	1,000	(A)
		3,000	(A)

4. **Sales Margin Quantity (sub-volume) variance : Budgeted Margin per unit of Budgeted Mix × (AQ – BQ)**

$$\frac{6,400}{400} \times (600 - 400) = 16 \times 200 = 3,200 \text{ (F)}$$

Problem 16

From the following particulars compute :

(a)	Material cost variance	
(b)	Material price variance	
(c)	Material usage variance	
	Quantity of materials purchased	3,000 units
	Value of materials purchased	Rs. 9,000
	Standard quantity of materials	
	Required per ton of output	30 units
	Standard rate of material	Rs. 2·50 per unit
	Opening stock of materials	Nil
	Closing stock of materials	500 units
	Output during the year	80 tons

[Delhi U. B.Com. (Hons.)]

Solution

(a) Quantity of materials consumed : 3,000 units – 500 units = 2,500 units

(b) Actual cost of materials per unit $= \frac{\text{Rs. } 9{,}000}{3{,}000} = \text{Rs. } 3$

(c) Standard material required per ton 30 units

(d) Standard material cost = 30 × 80 × Rs. 2·50 = 2,400 × 2·50 = Rs. 6,000

Actual cost = 2,500 × Rs. 3 = Rs. 7,500.

(i) Material Cost Variance = SC – AC

= Rs. 6,000 – Rs. 7,500 = Rs. 1,500 (A)

(ii) Material Price Variance = AQ × (SR – AR)

= 2,500 × (2·50 – 3·00) = Rs. 1,250 (A)

(iii) Material Usage Variance = SR × (SQ – AQ)

= Rs. 2·50 × (2,400 – 2,500)

= Rs. 2·50 × (–100) = 250 (A)

Reconciliation

MCV = MPV + MUV = 1,500 (A) = 1,250 (A) + 250 (A)

Problem 17

From the following data calculate the variances related to fixed expenses :

Particulars	*Standard*	*Actual*
Output of the month (units)	10,000	10,090
No. of days worked in the month	25	26
Efficiency of labour (%)	100	95
Fixed expenses for the month	15,000	15,150

Solution

	Units		Rs.
BQ (Budgeted Qnt.)	10,000	B.F.O.	15,000
AQ (Actual Qnt.)	10,090	A.F.O.	15,150

Revised Budgeted Quantity $= \frac{\text{Actual working days}}{\text{Standard working days}} \times \text{St. Output}$

$= \frac{26}{25} \times 10{,}000 = 10{,}400$ Standard Fixed Overhead

S.Q. = 10,400.

Standard Rate = $\frac{15,000}{10,000}$ = Rs. 1·50 per unit. S.F.O. = 10,090 units × 1.50 = Rs. 15,135

Fixed Overhead Variance = SFO – AFO = Rs. 15,135 – Rs. 15,150 = Rs. 15 (A)

Expenditure Variance = BFO – AFO = Rs. 15,000 – Rs. 15,150 = Rs. 150 (A)

Volume Variance = SR × (BQ – AQ) = Rs. 1·50 × (10,000 – 10,090) = Rs. 135 (F)

Reconciliation

FOHV = Exp. V + Vol V. = A

15 (A) = 150 (A) + 135 (F)

Capacity Variance = SR × (BQ – SQ)

= 1.50 (10,000 – 10,400)

= Rs. 600 (F)

Efficiency Variance = SR × (SQ – AQ)

= 1.50 × (10,400 – 10,090)

= Rs. 465 (A)

Reconciliation

Volume Variance = CAPV + Eff.V

135 (F) = 600 (F) + 465 (A)

Problem 18

From the following data for May 2002 of a factory calculate (a) Material cost variance, (b) Material price variance, (c) Material usage variance, (d) Material mix variance.

Name of Material	*Standard*		*Actual*	
	kg.	*Rate* Rs.	*kg.*	*Rate* Rs.
X	8,000	1·05	7,500	1·20
Y	3,000	2·15	3,300	2·30
Z	2,000	3·30	2,400	3·50

[Adapted—I.C.W.A. (Inter)]

Solution

(a) Material Cost Variance : Standard Cost – Actual Cost

	Standard			*Actual*		
	kg.	*Rate* Rs.	*Amount* Rs.	*kg.*	*Rate* Rs.	*Amount* Rs.
X	8,000	1·05	8,400	7,500	1·20	9,000
Y	3,000	2·15	6,450	3,300	2·30	7,590
Z	2,000	3·30	6,600	2,400	3·50	8,400
	13,000		21,450	13,200		24,990

∴ **Material Cost Variance** = Rs. 21,450 – Rs. 24,990 = Rs. 3,540 (Adverse).

(b) Material Price Variance : Actual Quantity (SP – AP)

X = 7,500 (Rs. 1·05 – Rs. 1·20) = Rs. 1,125 (A)

Y = 3,300 (Rs. 2·15 – Rs. 2·30) = Rs. 495 (A)

Z = 2,400 (Rs. 3·30 – Rs. 3·50) = Rs. 480 (A)

(c) Material Usage Variance : Standard Price (SQ – AQ)

X	=	Rs. 1·05 (8,000 – 7,500)	=	Rs. 525	(F)
Y	=	Rs. 2·15 (3,000 – 3,300)	=	Rs. 645	(A)
Z	=	Rs. 3·30 (2,000 – 2,400)	=	Rs. 1,320	(A)

(d) Material Mix. Variance : Standard price (Revised Standard Quantity – Actual Quantity)

$$\text{Revised Standard Quantity} = \frac{\text{Total of actual mix}}{\text{Total of standard mix}} \times \text{Standard quantity of each material.}$$

$$\therefore \textbf{ Revised standard quantity} = X = \frac{13,200}{13,000} \times 8,000 = 8,123$$

$$Y = \frac{13,200}{13,000} \times 3,000 = 3,046$$

$$Z = \frac{13,200}{13,000} \times 2,000 = 2,031$$

X	=	Rs. 1·05 (8,123 – 7,500)	= Rs.	654·15	(F)
Y	=	Rs. 2·15 (3,046 – 3,300)	= Rs.	546·10	(A)
Z	=	Rs. 3·30 (2,031 – 2,400)	= Rs.	1,217·70	(A)
Total			Rs.	1,109·65	(A)

Problem 19

The standard material and the standard cost per kg. of material required for the production of one unit of product X is as follows :

Material 10 kgs.

Standard price Rs. 15 per kg.

The actual production and related material data are as follows :

400 units of product x

Material used 4,200 kgs.

Price for material Rs. 14·90 per kg.

Calculate : (i) Material cost variance

(ii) Material price variance

(iii) Material usage variance.

Solution

(i) **Material Cost Variance :** Standard cost – Actual cost

Standard Cost = Standard Quantity × Standard Price

= (4,000 × 10) – (4,000 × 15)

= 40,000 – 60,000 = Rs. 10,000 (A)

(ii) **Material Price Variance :** (Standard price – Actual price) × Actual quantity

= (15 – 14·90) × 4,200 = (·10) × 4,200 = Rs. 420 (F)

(iii) **Material Usage Variance :**

= (SQ – AQ) × SP = (4,000 – 4,200) × 10

= – 200 × 10 = 2,000 (Adverse)

Problem 20

A manufacturing concern which has adopted standard costing furnished the following information :

Standard

Material for 70 kgs. of finished goods is 100 kgs.

Price of material Re. 1.00 per kgs.

Actual

Output	2,10,000 kgs.
Materials used	2,80,000
Cost of materials	Rs. 2,52,000

***Calculate* :**

(a) Material usage variance

(b) Material price variance

(c) Material cost variance

[C.A. (Inter)]

(a) **Material usage variance** = SP × (AQ – SQ)
= 1 × (2,80,000 – 3,00,000)
= Rs. 20,000 (Adverse)

(b) **Material price variance** = AQ (AP – SP)
= 2,80,000 × (0·9 – 1·00)
= 2,80,000 × 0·10 = Rs. 28,000 (Favourable)

(c) **Material cost variance** = Actual cost – Standard cost
= (AQ × AP) – (SQ × SP)
= (2,80,000 × 0·90) – (3,00,000 × 1)
= Rs. 48,000 (Favourable)

Working Notes :

1. **Standard quantity** :

Materials for 70 kgs. of finished Product = 100 kgs.

For 2,10,000 kgs. = $\frac{100 \times 2,10,000}{70}$ = 3,00,000 kgs.

2. **Actual price per kg.** = $\frac{2,52,000}{2,80,000}$ = Re. 0·90.

Problem 21

Modern Tiles Ltd. makes plastics tiles of standard size of 6" × 6" × 1/8". From the following information, you are required to calculate direct materials :

(i) The cost variance in total.

(ii) The cost variance sub-divided into (a) price and (b) usage.

(iii) The usage variance analysed as (a) mix, (b) yield.

A standard mix of the compound required to produce an output of 20,000 square feet of tiles 1/8" thick is as follows :

Direct Materials	*Quantity* (kgs.)	*Price per kg.* (Rs.)
A	600	0·90
B	400	0·65
C	500	0·40

During December 1995, 8 mixes were processed and actual materials consumed were :

Direct Material	Quantity (kgs.)	Price per kg.
A	5,000	0·85
B	2,900	0·60
C	4,400	0·45

Actual production for December 1995 was 6,20,000.

[Adapted—C.S. (Inter) Dec. 1996]

Solution

One mix of 20,000 sq. ft. of tiles produce 80,000 tiles (20,000 × 144" ÷ 36")

Standard Quantity for Actual Output :

$$A = 600 \times \frac{6,20,000}{80,000} = 4,650 \text{ kgs.}$$

$$B = 400 \times \frac{6,20,000}{80,000} = 3,100 \text{ kgs.}$$

$$C = 500 \times \frac{6,20,000}{80,000} = 3,875 \text{ kgs.}$$

Standard Cost = Standard Quantity × Standard Price

				Rs.
A	=	4,650 × Re. 0·90	=	4,185
B	=	3,100 × Re. 0·65	=	2,015
C	=	3,875 × Re. 0·40	=	1,550
				7,750

Actual cost = Actual Quantity × Actual Price

				Rs.
A	=	5,000 × 0·85	=	4,250
B	=	2,900 × 0·60	=	1,740
C	=	4,400 × 0·45	=	1,980
			=	7,970

Material Cost Variance = Standard Cost – Actual Cost

= Rs. 7,750 – Rs. 7,970 = Rs. 220 (A)

Material Price Variance = Actual Quantity (Standard Price – Actual Price)

				Rs.
A	=	5,000 × (Re 0·90 – Re 0·85)	=	250 (F)
B	=	2,900 × (Re 0·65 – Re 0·60)	=	145 (F)
C	=	4,400 × (Re 0·40 – Re 0·45)	=	220 (A)
				175 (F)

Material Usage Variance = Standard Price × (SQ – AQ)

A	=	Re 0·90 (4,650 – 5,000)	=	315 (A)
B	=	Re 0·65 (3,100 – 2,900)	=	130 (F)
C	=	Re 0·40 (3,875 – 4,400)	=	210 (A)
				395 (A)

Revised Standard Quantity

= (Total Actual Mix ÷ Total Standard Mix) × Standard Quantity

A	=	(12,300 ÷ 11,625) × 4,650	=	4,920
B	=	(12,300 ÷ 11,625) × 3,100	=	3,280
C	=	(12,300 ÷ 11,625) × 3,875	=	4,100

Material Mix Variance = Standard Price (Revised Standard Quantity – Actual Quantity)

A	=	Re. 0·90 (4,920 – 5,000)	=	72 (A)
B	=	Re. 0·65 (3,280 – 2,900)	=	247 (F)
C	=	Re. 0·40 (4,100 – 4,400)	=	120 (A)
				55 (F)

$$\textbf{Material Yield Variance} = \frac{\text{Standard cost}}{\text{Unit cost}} (\text{Standard yield} - \text{Actual yield})$$

(a) **Standard cost per unit** $= \dfrac{7{,}750}{6{,}20{,}000}$ = Re 0·0125

(b) **Standard yield for actual input** $= \dfrac{80{,}000}{1{,}500} \times 12{,}300$ = 6,56,000 tiles.

∴ **Material Yield Variance** = Re 0·0125 × (6,56,000 – 6,20,000) = Rs. 450 (A)

Note : A = Adverse, F = Favourable.

Problem 22

Gemini Chemical Industries provide the following information from their records. For making 10 kgs. of GEM Co., the standard material requirement is :

Material	Quantity (kgs.)	Rate per kg. (Rs.)
A	8	6·00
B	4	4·00

During April 1999, 1,000 kgs. of GEM Co. were produced. The actual consumption of materials is as under :

Material	Quantity (kgs.)	Rate per kg. (Rs.)
A	750	7·00
B	500	5·00

Calculate : (A) Material cost variance; (b) Material price variance; (c) Material usage variance.

Solution

M_1 = Actual cost of material used :

				Rs.
A	=	750 × Rs. 7,00	=	5,250
B	=	500 × Rs. 5·00	=	2,500
		1,250 kgs.		7,750

M_2 = Standard cost for materials used :

				Rs.
A	=	750 × Rs. 6	=	4,500
B	=	500 × Rs. 4	=	2,000
		1,250 kgs.		6,500

M_3 = Standard cost of material for standard production :

				Rs.
A	=	$\frac{1,000}{10} \times 8 \times$ Rs. 6	=	4,800
B	=	$\frac{1,000}{10} \times 4 \times$ Rs. 4	=	1,600
				6,400

M_4 = Standard Material cost.

A	=	8 kgs. × 6	=	Rs. 48
B	=	4 kgs. × 4	=	Rs. 16
				64

Therefore = (Rs. 64 ÷ 10) × 1,000 = Rs. 6,400.

(1) **Material cost variance** = $M_1 - M_2$ = Rs. 7,750 – Rs. 6,500 = Rs. 1,250 (A)

(2) **Material mix variance** = $M_2 - M_3$ = Rs. 6,500 – Rs. 6,400 = Rs. 100 (A)

(3) **Material usage variance** = $M_2 - M_4$ = Rs. 6,500 – Rs. 6,400 = Rs. 100 (A)

Problem 23

XYZ Company manufactures a product ABC by mixing three raw materials. For every 100 kgs. of ABC, 125 kgs. of raw materials used. In April 1990, there was an output of 5,600 kgs. of ABC. The standard and actual particulars of April 1990 are as follows :

	Standard		Actual	
	Mix	Price per kg.	Mix	Price per kg
	%	Rs.	%	Rs.
Raw material I	50	40	60	42
Raw material II	30	20	20	16
Raw material III	20	10	20	12

Calculate all variances.

[Adapted—I.C.W.A. (Inter)]

Solution

M_1 = **Actual cost of material used :**

Raw Material	*Mix %*	*Actual material used* Rs.	*Rate (Actual)* Rs.	*Amount* Rs.
I	60	4,200 (60% of 7,000)	42	1,76,400
II	20	1,400 (20% of 7,000)	16	22,400
III	20	1,400 (20% of 7,000)	12	16,800
		7,000*		2,15,600

* Input for 5,600 kgs. = $\frac{125 \times 5.600}{100}$ = 7,000 kgs.

M_2 = **Standard cost of actual production :**

Raw Material	*Mix %*	*Material used* kg.	*Rate (Standard)* Rs.	*Amount* Rs.
I	60	4,200	40	1,68,000
II	20	1,400	20	28,000
III	20	1,400	10	14,000
		7,000		2,10,000

M_3 = **Standard cost of material used if it had been used in standard proportion :**

Raw Material	*Mix %*	*Material used (in standard proportion) kg.*	*Rate (standard)* Rs.	*Amount* Rs.
I	50	3,500	40	1,40,000
II	30	2,100	20	42,000
III	20	1,400	10	14,000
		7,000		1,96,000

M_4 = **Standard material cost of output :**

Standard cost of 100 kg of ABC

Raw Material			*Kgs.*		
I	50% of 125	=	62·50 × Rs. 40	=	Rs. 2,500
II	30% of 125	=	37·50 × Rs. 20	=	Rs. 750
III	20% of 125	=	25·00 × Rs. 10	=	Rs. 250
			125		3,500
	Less loss		25		
			100		

Therefore, the standard cost of 5,600 kgs. $= \frac{5,600}{100} \times 3,500$ = Rs. 1,96,000

Calculation of Variances

(i) Material Price Variance $= M_1 - M_2$ = Rs. 2,15,600 – Rs. 2,10,000 = Rs. 5,600 (A)

(ii) Material Mix Variance $= M_2 - M_3$ = Rs. 2,10,000 – Rs. 1,96,000 = Rs. 14,000 (A)

(iii) Material Yield Variance $= M_3 - M_4$ = Rs. 1,96,000 – Rs. 1,96,000 = Nil

(iv) Material Usage Variance $= M_2 - M_4$ = Rs. 2,10,000 – Rs. 1,96,000 = Rs. 14,000 (A)

(v) Material Cost Variance $= M_1 - M_4$ = Rs. 2,15,600 – Rs. 1,96,000 = Rs. 19,600 (A)

Problem 24

Pragati Company manufactures a product 'P' by mixing three raw materials. For every 100 kgs. of output, 125 kgs. of raw material input are used. In April 1999, there was an output of 5,600 kgs. of 'P'. The standard and actual particulars of April 1999 are as follows :

Raw Material	*Standard*		*Actual*	
	Mix	*Price per kg.*	*Mix*	*Price per kg.*
I	50%	Rs. 40	60%	Rs. 42
II	30%	Rs. 20	20%	Rs. 16
III	20%	Rs. 10	20%	Rs. 12

Calculate all material variances. The actual quantity of material used was 7,000 kgs.

[Delhi University B.Com. (Hons.) 1997]

Solution

(a) **Calculation of Standard Cost**

Material	*Quantity* kgs.	*Rate* Rs.	*Amount* Rs.
I	3,500 (50%)	40	1,40,000
II	2,100 (30%)	20	42,000
III	1,400 (20%)	10	14,000
	7,000		1,96,000

(b) **Calculation of Actual Cost**

I	4,200 (60%)	42	1,76,400
II	1,400 (20%)	16	22,400
III	1,400 (20%)	12	16,800
	7,000		2,15,600

Material Cost Variance = Standard Cost – Actual Cost

I	Rs. 1,40,000 – Rs. 1,76,400	=	Rs. 36,400 (A)
II	Rs. 42,000 – Rs. 22,400	=	Rs. 19,600 (F)
III	Rs. 14,000 – Rs. 16,800	=	Rs. 2,800 (A)
			Rs. 19,600 (A)

Material Quantity Variance = (SQ – AQ) × SP.

I	(3,500 – 4,200) × 40	=	Rs. 28,000 (A)
II	(2,100 – 1,400) × 20	=	Rs. 14,000 (F)
III	(1,400 – 1,400) × 10	=	Nil
			Rs. 14,000 (A)

Material Price Variance = (SP – AP) × AQ

I	(40 – 42) × 4,200	=	Rs. 8,400 (A)
II	(20 – 16) × 1,400	=	Rs. 5,600 (F)
III	(10 – 12) × 1,400	=	Rs. 2,800 (A)
			Rs. 5,600 (A)

Material Mix Variance (Revised) = (SQ – AQ) × SP

I	(3,500 – 4,200) × 40	=	Rs. 28,000 (A)
II	(2,100 – 1,400) × 20	=	Rs. 14,000 (F)
III	(1,400 – 1,400) × 10	=	Nil
			Rs. 14,000 (A)

Problem 25

AB Ltd. has established the following standard mix producing 9 gallons of product A :

	Rs.
5 gallons of material X at Rs. 7 per gallon	35
3 gallons of material Y at Rs. 5 per gallon	15
2 gallons of material Z at Rs. 2 per gallon	4
	54

A standard loss of 10% of input is expected to occur. Actual input was as under :

53,000 gallons of material X at Rs. 7 per gallon

28,000 gallons of material Y at Rs. 5·30 per gallon

19,000 gallons of material Z at Rs. 2·20 per gallon.

Actual output for a period was 92,700 gallons of product 'A'.

Compute :

(a) **Material mix variance**

(b) **Material yield variance.**

[Delhi University B.Com. (Hons.) 1999]

Solution

(i) **Calculation of Actual Cost**

				Rs.
X	53,000	gallons @ Rs. 7·00	=	3,71,000
Y	28,000	gallons @ Rs. 5·30	=	1,48,400
Z	19,000	gallons @ Rs. 2·20	=	41,800
Total	1,00,000			5,61,200
Less : loss	7,300			
	92,700	gallons		

(ii) **Calculation of standard cost of 90,000 gallons**

				Rs.
X	50,000	gallons @ Rs. 7·00	=	3,50,000
Y	30,000	gallons @ Rs. 5·00	=	1,50,000
Z	20,000	gallons @ Rs. 2·00	=	40,000
Total	1,00,000			5,40,000
Less : loss	10,000			
	90,000	gallons		

(iii) **Materials Mix Variance**

(Revised Standard Quantity – Actual Quantity)

Standard price

X	(50,000 – 53,000) × Rs. 7	=	Rs. 21,000 (A)
Y	(30,000 – 28,000) × Rs. 5	=	Rs. 10,000 (F)
Z	(20,000 – 19,000) × Rs. 2	=	Rs. 2,000 (F)
			Rs. 9,000 (A)

Therefore, Material Mix Variance is Rs. 9,000 (A)

(iv) **Material Yield Variance**

(Actual Yield – Standard Yield) × Standard Cost per unit of output.

$$= (92{,}700 - 90{,}000) \times \frac{\text{Rs. } 5{,}40{,}000}{90{,}000} = \text{Rs. } 16{,}200 \text{ (F)}$$

Problem 26

Compute price, usage and mix variance from the data below :

		Standard			*Actual*		
		Qnt.	*Unit price*		*Qnt.*	*Unit price*	
			Rs.	Rs.		Rs.	Rs.
Material	A	6	1·50	9·00	5	2·40	12·00
Material	B	2	3·50	7·00	1	6·00	6·00
		8		16·00	6		18·00

[Adapted—Delhi B.Com. (Hons.)]

Solution

Material Price Variance : MPV = AQ × (SP – AP)

1.	Material A	= 5 × (1·50 – 2·40)	=	Rs. 4·50 (Adverse)
	Material B	= 1 × (Rs. 3·50 – Rs. 6·00)	=	Rs. 2·50 (Adverse)
				Rs. 7·00 (Adverse)
2.	**Usage Variance :** SP (SQ – AQ)			
	Material A	= Rs. 1·50 (6 – 5)	=	Rs. 1·50 (Fav.)
	Material B	= Rs. 3·50 (2 – 1)	=	Rs. 3·50 (Fav.)
				Rs. 5·00 (Fav.)

3. **Mix Variance :** (Revised Standard Quantity – Actual Quantity) × SP

Revised Standard Quantity $= \frac{\text{Total weight of actual mix}}{\text{Total weight of standard mix}} \times \text{Standard price}$

Material A $= \frac{6}{8} \times 6 = 4{\cdot}5$ kgs.

Material B $= \frac{6}{8} \times 2 = 1{\cdot}5$ kgs.

4. **Material Mix Variance :**

Material A	= 1·50 × (Rs. 4·50 – Rs. 5)	= Re. 0·75	(Adverse)
Material B	= 3·50 × (Rs. 1·50 – Re. 1.00)	= Rs. 1·75	(Fav.)
		Re. 1·00	(Fav.)

Problem 27

Mixers Ltd. is engaged in producing a standard mix using 60 kgs. of chemical X and 40 kgs. of chemical Y. The standard loss of production is 30%. The standard price of X is Rs. 5 per kg. and Y of Rs. 10 per kg.

The actual mix and yield were as follows :

X 80 kgs. @ Rs. 4·50 per kg.

Y 70 kgs. @ Rs. 8·00 per kg.

Actual yield 115 kgs.

Calculate : Direct Material Cost, Price, Wages, Mix and Yield Variance.

[D.U. B.Com. (Hons.) 1989]

Solution

	Standard			*Actual*		
	Qnt. kg.	Rate Rs.	Amount Rs.	Qnt. kg.	Rate Rs.	Amount Rs.
X	90[1]	5·00	450·00	80	4·50	360
Y	60[1]	10·00	600·00	70	8·00	560
	150		1,050.00	150		920

Working Notes :

(1) **Standard Mix for actual input of 150 kgs.**

X $= \frac{60}{100} \times 150$ = 90 kgs.

Y $= \frac{40}{100} \times 150$ = 60 kgs.

(2) **Standard output for Actual Mix.**

100 kgs. – loss 30% of 100 kgs. = 70 kgs.

150 kgs. 70% $= 70 \times \frac{150}{100} = 105$ kgs.

Actual mix Qnt. (given) = 115 kgs.

Standard cost per kg. $= \frac{\text{Rs. } 1{,}050}{105} = \text{Rs. } 10.$

Actual cost per kg. $= \frac{\text{Rs. } 920}{115} = \text{Rs. } 8.$

Calculation of variances

(i) **Direct Material Cost Variance = DMCV**

DMCV = Standard Cost of Actual output – Actual Cost

= Rs. 1,150 – Rs. 920 = Rs. 230 (F)

$\left(\text{Standard cost of actual output} = \frac{1{,}050}{105} \times 115\right) = \text{Rs. } 1{,}150.$

(ii) **Direct Material Price Variance** = DMPV = Actual Qnt. (SP – AP)

Material X	=	80 (Rs. 5·00 – Rs. 4·50)	= Rs. 40 (F)
Material Y	=	70 (Rs. 10·00 – Rs. 8·00)	= Rs. 140 (F)
			Rs. 180 (F)

(iii) **Direct Material Usage Variance** = DMUV = Standard Price for actual output (SQA – AQ)

$$X = 5 \times \left(\frac{90 \times 115}{105} - 80\right) = 93 \text{ (F)}$$

$$Y = 10 \times \left(\frac{60 - 115}{105} - 70\right) = 43 \text{ (A)}$$

(iv) **Direct Material Mix Variance** = Standard Rate (Std. Qnt. – Actual Qnt.)

X	=	Rs. 4 (90 – 80)	= 50 (F)
Y	=	Rs. 10 × (60 – 70)	= 100 (A)
			50 (A)

(v) **Direct Material Yield Variance** =

= Standard Cost per unit × (Actual Output – Std. Output)

= 10 × (115 – 105) = 100 (F)

Problem 28

Show Well Ltd. produces an article by blending two basic materials. It operates a standard costing system and the following standards have been set for raw materials :

Material	Standard Mix	Standard Price per Kg.
		Rs.
X	40%	4
Y	60%	5

The standard loss in processing is 15%. During March 1994, the company produced 1,700 kgs. of finished output.

The position of stock and purchases for the month of March 1994 is as under :

Material	Stock on 1.3.1994	Stock on 31.3.1994	Purchases during March 1994	
	kg.	kg.	kg.	Cost (Rs.)
X	35	5	800	3,400
Y	40	50	1,200	3,000

Calculate :

(i) Material price variance; (ii) Material usage variance; (iii) Material mix variance; (iv) Material yield variance and (v) Total material cost variance.

[D.U. B.Com. (Hons.) 1994]

Solution

	Standard				Actual		
Material	Qnt.	Rate	Amount		Qnt.	Rate	Amount
X	800 kgs.	Rs. 4	3,200	X	35	Rs. 4·00	Rs. 140·00
Y	1,200 kgs.	Rs. 3	3,600		795	Rs. 4·25	3,378·75
	2,000 kgs.		Rs. 6,800	Y	40	Rs. 3·00	120·00
					1,150	Rs. 2·50	2,875·00
					2,020		6,513·75

Note : Standard loss is 15%. Thus, to produce 1,700 kgs. of article, standard quantity of material required is $= \frac{100}{85} \times 1{,}700 = 2{,}000$ kg. $\therefore$ X = 800 kgs Y = 1,200 kgs. = 2,000 kgs

(1) **Material Price Variance = AQ × (SR – AR)**

X = For 795 kg. only = $795 \times (4 - 4{\cdot}25)$ = Rs. 198·75 (A)

Y = For 1,150 kg. only = $1{,}150 \times (3 - 2{\cdot}50)$ = Rs. 575·00 (F)

Total = Rs. 376·25 (F)

(2) **Material Usage Variance** = SR × (SQ for actual output – Act. Qty.)

X = $4 \times (800 - 830)$ = Rs. 120 (A)

Y = $3 \times (1{,}200 - 1{,}190)$ = 30 (F)

Total = Rs. 90 (A)

(3) **Material Yield Variance**

= Standard cost per unit of output × (Standard output for actual mix – Actual output)

$$= \frac{6{,}800}{1{,}700} \times \left[\left(\frac{1{,}700}{2{,}000} \times 2{,}020\right) - 1{,}700\right] = \text{Rs. } 4 \times (1{,}717 - 1{,}700) = \text{Rs. } 68 \text{ (A)}$$

(4) **Material Mix Variance** = SR × (RSQ – AQ)

Revised Standard Quantity = X = $\frac{2{,}020}{2{,}000} \times 800 = 808$ kgs.

Y = $\frac{2{,}020}{2{,}000} \times 1{,}200 = 1{,}212$ kgs.

MMV X = $4 \times (808 - 830)$ = Rs. 88 (A)

Y = $3 \times (1{,}212 - 1{,}190)$ = 66 (F)

Total = 22 (A)

(5) **Material Cost Variance** = **Standard Cost for Actual output – Actual cost**

MCV = 6,800 + 6,513·75 = Rs. 286·25 (F)

MCV = MPV + MUV = 376·25 (F) + 90 (A) = 286·25 (F)

MUV = MMV + MYV = 22 (A) + 68 (A) = Rs. 90 (A).

Problem 29

Bello Chemical Industries provide the following information from their records :

For making 10 kgs. of OMO, the standard material requirement is :

Material	*Quantity* (kgs.)	*Rate per kg.* (Rs.)
X	8	6·00
Y	4	4·00

During December 1990, 100 kgs. of OMO were produced. The actual consumption of materials is as under :

Material	Quantity (kgs.)	Rate per kg. (Rs.)
X	75	7·00
Y	50	5·00

Calculate :

(i) Material cost variance

(ii) Material price variance

(iii) Material usage variance

[D.U. B.Com. (Hons.) 1991]

Solution

For 100 kgs. of OMO

	Standard Quantity kgs.	Rate Rs.	Actual Quantity kgs.	Rate Rs.
X	80	6·00	75	7·00
Y	40	4·00	50	5·00

(i) **Material Cost Variance**

Actual Cost – Standard Cost

Actual Cost = (75 × 7) + (50 × 5) = Rs. 525 + 250 = Rs. 775

Less : Standard cost (80 × 6) + (40 × 4)= Rs. 480 + 160 = Rs. 640

Rs. 135 (A)

(ii) **Material Price Variance (MPV)**

Actual Quantity (Actual Price – Standard Price)

X = 75 (Rs. 7 – Rs. 6) = 75 × 1 = Rs. 75 (A)

Y = 50 (Rs. 5 – Rs. 4) = 50 × 1 = Rs. 50 (A)

= Rs. 75 + Rs. 50 = Rs. 125 (Adverse)

(iii) **Material Usage Variance (MUV)**

Standard Price (Actual Quantity – Standard Quantity)

X = 6(75 – 80) = Rs. 6 × 5 = Rs. 30 (F)

Y = 4 (50 – 40) = Rs. 4 × 10 = Rs. 40 (A)

= Rs. 30 (F) – Rs. 40 (A) = Rs. 10 (A)

Check : MCV = MPV + MUV = 135 (A) = 125 (A) + 10 (A).

Problem 30

The standard cost card a product shows : Material cost 2 kgs. @ Rs. 2·50 each = Rs. 5 per unit, wages 2 hours @ 0·50 p. each = Re. 1 per unit

The actual which have emerged from business operations are as follows :

Production	8,000 units
Material consumed 16,500 kgs. @ Rs. 2·40 each	Rs. 39,600
Wages paid for 18,000 hours @ Re. 0·40 each	Rs. 7,200

Calculate appropriate material and labour variances.

[Adapted—Delhi B.Com. (Hons.)]

Solution

(i) **Material Cost Variance** = SC – AC.
= 16,000 × 2·50 – 16,500 × Rs. 2·40
= Rs. 40,000 – Rs. 39,600 = 400 (F)

(ii) **Material Price Variance** = AQ × (SP – AP)
= 16,500 × (Rs. 2·50 – Rs. 2·40)
= Rs. 1,650 (F)

(iii) **Material Usage variance** = SR × (SQ – AQ)
= Rs. 2·50 × (16,000 – 16,500)
= Rs. 1,250 (Adverse)

(iv) **Labour Cost Variance** = SC – AC
= Rs. 8,000 – Rs. 7,200 = Rs. 800 (F)

(v) **Labour Rate Variance** = Actual hours × (SR – AR)
= 18,000 × (0·50 – 0·40)
= 1,800 (Favourable)

(vi) **Labour Efficiency Variance** = SR (Standard hours for actual production – Actual hours)
= Re 0·50 × (16,000 – 18,000) Rs. 1,000 (A)

Problem 31

A company manufacturing 'distemper' operates a costing system. The standard cost of one of the products of the company shows the following material standards :

Materials	*Qnt.*	*Standard* price per kg. (Rs.)	*Total*
A	40 kgs.	75	3,000
B	10 kgs.	50	500
C	50 kgs.	20	1,000
Material cost per unit (total)			4,500

The standard input mix is 100 kgs. and the standard output of the finished product is 90 kgs.

The actual results for a period are :

A	=	2,40,000	kgs. at Rs. 80 per kg.
B	=	40,000	kgs. at Rs. 52 per kg.
C	=	2,20,000	kgs. at Rs. 21 per kg.

Actual output of the finished goods = 4,20,000 kgs.
You are required to calculate the material price, mix and yield variance.

[I.C.W.A. (Inter)]

Solution

Working Notes :

Actual cost

Material	kg.	Rate Rs.	Amount (Rs. in lakhs)
A	2,40,000	80	192.00
B	40,000	52	20.80
C	2,20,000	21	46.20
Actual input	5,00,000		259.00
Less : Loss	80,000		—
	4,20,000		259.00

Note : Standard input mix is 100 kgs. and standard output is 90 kgs. i.e. 10% standard loss.

Standard Cost

Material		kgs.	*Rate* Rs.	*Amount* (Rs. in lakh)
A	$\frac{5,00,000}{100} \times 40$ =	2,00,000	75·00	150·00
B	$\frac{5,00,000}{100} \times 10$ =	50,000	50·00	25·00
C	$\frac{5,00,000}{100} \times 50$ =	2,50,000	20·00	50·00
Standard input		5,00,000		225·00
Less : loss @ 10%		50,000		—
		4,50,000		225·00

Standard Yield Rate (SYR) = $\frac{\text{Rs. 225 lakhs}}{\text{4,50,000 kgs.}}$ = Rs. 50 per kg.

Standard Cost for Actual Production (SCAP) = 4,20,000 kgs. @ Rs. 50 = Rs. 210 lakhs.

Standard Cost of Standard Mix (SCSM) = Rs. 225 lakhs.

Standard Cost of Actual Mix (SCAM)

Material	*SC* Rs.	*AM (kgs.)*	*Amount* (Rs. in lakhs)
A	75	2,40,000	180·00
B	50	40,000	20·00
C	20	2,20,000	44·00
		5,00,000	244·00

(i) **Material Price Variance** = AQ (SR – AR)

				(Rs. in lakhs)
A	=	2,40,000 (Rs. 75 – Rs. 80)	=	12·00 (A)
B	=	40,000 (Rs. 50 – Rs. 52)	=	0·80 (A)
C	=	2,20,000 (Rs. 20 – Rs. 21)	=	2·20 (A)
				15·00 (A)

(ii) **Material Yield Variance = SYR (AY – SY)** = Rs. 50 (4,20,000 – 4,50,000)

= Rs. 15 lakhs (A)

(iii) **Material Mix Variance = SCSM – SCAM** = Rs. 225 lakhs – 244 lakhs

= Rs. 19 lakhs (A)

Problem 32

Data relating to a job are as follows :

Standard rate of wages per hour	Rs. 10
Standard hours	300
Actual rate of wages per hour	Rs. 12
Actual hours	200

You are required to calculate

(i) Labour Cost Variance; (ii) Labour Rate Variance; (iii) Labour Efficiency Variance.

[D.U. B.Com. (Hons.)]

Solution

(i) **Labour Cost Variance = (SC – AC)**

(Standard Hours × Standard Rate) – (Actual Hours × Actual Rate)

= (300 × 10) – (200 × 12) = (3,000 – 2,400) = Rs. 600 (F)

(ii) **Labour Rate Variance**

Actual hours (SR – AR) = 200(10 –12) = Rs. 400 (A)

(iii) **Labour Efficiency Variance**

Standard Rate (Standard hours – Actual hours)

Rs. 10(300 hours – 200 hours) = Rs. 10(100) = Rs 1,000 (F)

Problem 33

From the following information of Orient Manufacturing Co. Ltd., determine (i) the Labour Cost Variance, (ii) Labour Rate Variance and (iii) Labour Efficiency Variance :

(i) Standard Labour Cost per unit of production is Rs. 15.

(ii) Time allotted per unit is 30 hours.

(iii) During the month of March 1996, 3,000 units are produced in 75,000 hours.

(iv) Actual payment of wages for the month is Rs. 45,000.

[C.U. B.Com. (Hons.) 1996]

Solution

Working Notes :

Standard hours = 3,000 units × 30 hours per unit = 90,000 hours.

$$\text{Standard rate of wages per hour} = \frac{\text{Rs. } 45{,}000(3{,}000 \times \text{Rs. } 15)}{90{,}000 \text{ units}} = 0{\cdot}50 \text{ paise}$$

$$\text{Actual rate of wages per hour} = \frac{\text{Rs. } 45{,}000}{75{,}000} = 0{\cdot}60 \text{ paise}$$

Labour Cost Variance :

Standard cost	=	90,000 × 0·50	=	Rs. 45,000
Less : Actual Cost			=	Rs. 45,000
				Nil

Labour Price Variance : Actual hours (SR – AR)

75,000(0·50 – 0·60) = Rs. 7,500 (A).

Labour Efficiency Variance : Standard Rate (Standard Hours – Actual Hours)

0·50(90,000 – 75,000) = 0·50(15,000) = 7,500 (F)

Reconciliation : Nil = 7,500 (A) – 7,500 (F)

Problem 34

The standard labour compliment and the actual labour compliment engaged in a week for a job are as under :

		Workers		
		Skilled	Semi-skilled	Unskilled
(A)	Standard number of workers in the gang	32	12	6
(B)	Standard wage rate per hour (Rs.)	3	2	1
(C)	Actual number of workers employed in the gang during the week	28	18	4
(D)	Actual wage rate per hour (Rs.)	4	3	2

During the 40-hour working week the gang produced 1,800 standard labour hours of work. Calculate :

(i) Labour efficiency variance
(ii) Rate of wages variance
(iii) Labour mix variance
(iv) Total labour cost variance.

[Adapted—C.A. (Inter)]

Solution

(a) **Standard wage rate of standard gang**

Category	*No. of Men*	*Hours/ Week*	*Total Hours*	*Standard Rate* (Rs.)	*Standard Wages* (Rs.)
Skilled	32	40	1,280	3	3,840
Semi-skilled	12	40	480	2	960
Unskilled	6	40	240	1	240
			2,000		5,040

∴ Standard rate per hour for standard gang = Rs. 5,040 ÷ 2,000 hrs. = Rs. 2·52.

(b) **Standard labour rate of actual gang**

Category	*No. of Men*	*Hours* (Rs.)	*Total Hours*	*Standard Rate* (Rs.)	*Standard Wages* (Rs.)
Skilled	28	40	1,120	3	3,360
Semi-skilled	18	40	720	2	1,440
Unskilled	4	40	160	1	160
			2,000		4,960

Standard rate per hour for actual gang = Rs. 4,960 ÷ 2,000 = Rs. 2·48.

(c) **Actual labour hour rate of actual gang**

Category	*No. of Men*	*Hours/ Week*	*Total Hours*	*Actual Rate* (Rs.)	*Actual Wages* (Rs.)
Skilled	28	40	1,120	4	4,480
Semi-skilled	18	40	720	3	2,160
Unskilled	4	40	160	2	320
			2,000		6,960

Actual rate per hour = Rs. 6,960 ÷ 2,000 = Rs. 3·48.

(A) Standard Cost of output = 1,800 st. hrs. @ Rs. 2·52 = Rs. 4,536.

(B) Actual hours at standard rate of standard gang = 2,000 @ Rs. 2·52 = Rs. 5,040.

(C) Actual hours at standard rate of actual gang = 2,000 × Rs. 2·48 = Rs. 4,960.

(D) Actual wage paid to actual gang = Rs. 6,960.

Variances :

(i)	**Efficiency variance** (A – B)	=	Rs. 504 (A)
(ii)	**Rate of wage variance** (C – D)	=	Rs. 2,000 (A)
(iii)	**Labour mix variance** (B – C)	=	Rs. 80 (F)
(iv)	**Total labour cost variance** (A – D)	=	Rs. 2,424 (A)

Problem 35

The standard cost of a product is :

Time 10 hours per unit

Cost Rs. 5 per hour

The actual performance was :

Production	1,000 units
Hours taken :	
Production	10,400 hours
Idle time	400 hours
	10,800 hours

Payments made Rs. 56,100 @ Rs. 5·20 per hour

Calculate :

(a) Labour rate variance

(b) Labour efficiency variance

(c) Idle time variance

(d) Labour cost variance.

Solution

We shall have to find out the Standard Cost of Actual Production (SCAP).

Actual production 1,000 × standard time 10 × Rs. 5 = Rs. 50,000

Actual cost = Time taken × Actual Cost per hour = 10,800 × Rs. 5·20 = Rs. 56,160

(a) **Labour Rate variance** = Actual hour (SR – AR)

= 10,800 (Rs. 5·00 – Rs. 5·20) = 10,800 × 0·20 = 2,160 (A)

(b) **Labour Efficiency variance**

SR(SH – AH) = Rs. 5(10,000 – 10,400) = Rs. 2,000 (A)

(c) **Idle Time variance**

SR(AHP – AHW) = Rs. 5(10,800 – 10,400) = Rs. 2,000 (A)

or Standard rate × Idle time = Rs. 5 × 400 = Rs. 2,000 (A)

(d) **Labour Cost Variance**

Standard cost – Actual cost

(Rs. 5 × 10,000) – (5·20 × 10,800) = Rs. 50,000 – Rs. 56,160 = Rs. 6,160 (A)

Problem 36

A gang of workers normally consists of 30 men, 15 women and 10 boys. They are paid at standard rates as under :

Men	Re. 0·80
Women	Re. 0·60
Boys	Re. 0·40

In a normal working week of 40 hours the gang is expected to produce 2,000 units of output.

During the week ended 31st March 1993, the gang consisted of 40 men, 10 women and 5 boys. The actual wages paid were @ Re. 0·70, Re. 0·65 and Re. 0·30, respectively. 4 hours were lost due to abnormal idle time and 1,600 units were produced.

Calculate :

(i) Labour cost variance,

(ii) Labour rate variance,

(iii) Labour efficiency variance,

(iv) Labour idle time variance.

[Delhi U. B.Com. (Hons.)]

Solution

Labour Cost Variance

Standard Cost

					Rs.
Men	30 × 40	=	1,200 hours @ Re. 0·80	=	960
Women	15 × 40	=	600 hours @ Re. 0·60	=	360
Boys	10 × 40	=	400 hours @ Re. 0·40	=	160
					1,480

$$\text{Standard Cost of Actual output} = \frac{1{,}480 \times 1{,}600}{2{,}000} = \text{Rs. } 1{,}184.$$

Actual Cost

					Rs.
Men	40 × 40	=	1,600 hours @ Re. 0·70	=	1,120
Women	10 × 40	=	400 hours @ Re. 0·65	=	260
Boys	5 × 40	=	200 hours @ Re. 0·30	=	60
					1,440

(i) Therefore, **Labour Cost Variance (LCV)**

= **Standard Cost – Actual Cost**

= Rs. 1,184 – Rs. 1,440 = Rs. 256 (Adverse)

(ii) **Labour Rate Variance (LRV)**

= (Standard Wage Rate – Actual Wage Rate) × Actual Total Hours

				Rs.	
Men	=	(0·80 – 0·70) × 1,600 hours	=	Rs. 160	(F)
Women	=	(0·60 – 0·65) × 400 hours	=	Rs. 20	(A)
Boys	=	(0·40 – 0·30) × 200 hours	=	Rs. 20	(F)
				Rs. 160	(F)

(iii) **Labour Efficiency Variance**

(Standard Hours for actual output – Actual hours for actual output) × Standard rates.

Men	=	(960 – 1,600) × 0·80	=	Rs. 512 (A)
Women	=	(480 – 400) × 0·60	=	Rs. 48 (F)
Boys	=	(320 – 200) × 0·40	=	Rs. 48 (F)
				Rs. 416 (A)

Standard Hours for Actual Output

Men = $1{,}200 \times \dfrac{1{,}600}{2{,}000}$ = Rs. 960

Women = $600 \times \dfrac{1{,}600}{2{,}000}$ = Rs. 480

Boys = $400 \times \dfrac{1{,}600}{2{,}000}$ = Rs. 320

(iv) **Labour Mix Variance (LMV)**

(Revised standard hours – Actual hours) × Standard wage rate

Effective standard hours = Total hours – Idle hours

Men	=	(40 × 40) – (40 × 4)	=	1,600 – 160	=	1,440
Women	=	(10 × 40) – (10 × 4)	=	400 – 40	=	360
Boys	=	(5 × 40) – (5 × 4)	=	200 – 20	=	180
Total effective hours =						1,980

Working Notes :

Revised Standard Hours Worked

Standard hours × $\dfrac{\text{Effective hours}}{\text{Stnd. total hours}}$

Men = $(30 \times 40) \times \dfrac{1{,}980}{2{,}200}$ = Rs. 1,080

Women = $(15 \times 40) \times \dfrac{1{,}980}{2{,}200}$ = Rs. 540

Boys = $(10 \times 40) \times \dfrac{1{,}980}{2{,}200}$ = Rs. 360

Hence, LMV are

Men	=	(1,080 – 1,440) × 0·80	=	Rs. 288 (A)
Women	=	(540 – 360) × 0·60	=	Rs. 108 (F)
Boys	=	(360 – 180) × 0·40	=	Rs. 72 (F)
				Rs. 108 (A)

Labour Idle Time Variance

Idle time × Std. wage rate

Men	=	(40 × 4) × 0·80	=	Rs. 128 (A)
Women	=	(10 × 4) × 0·60	=	Rs. 24 (A)
Boys	=	(5 × 4) × 0·40	=	Rs. 08 (A)
				160 (A)

Problem 37

Calculate the variances from the following information according to originating causes :

Standard Direct cost per unit

Material cost : 5 kgs. Rs. 50

Labour cost : 20 hours Rs. 10

For production of 500 units materials consumption amounted to Rs. 25,650 against 2·7 M.T. (2,700 kgs.). Wages payment was Rs. 6,050 for 11,000 hours including 20 hours idle time due to machine breakdown.

[Adapted—C.U. M.Com.]

Solution

Working Notes :

Standard rate of raw material = Rs. 50 ÷ 5	=	Rs. 10
Actual rate of material = Rs. 25,650 ÷ 2,700 kgs.	=	Rs. 9·50
Standard quantity for actual output = 500 units × 5 kgs.	=	2,500 kgs.
Actual quantity	=	2,700 kgs. (given)
Standard rate of direct labour = Rs. 10 ÷ 20	=	Re. 0·50
Actual rate of direct labour Rs. 6,050 + 11,000 hours	=	Re. 0·55 per hour.
Actual time excluding idle time = 11,000 – 20 hours	=	10,980 hours.

Calculation of Variance

(a)	**Material Cost Variance**	=	SC – AC
		=	Rs. 25,000 – Rs. 25,650
		=	Rs. 650 (Adverse)
(b)	**Material Price Variance**	=	AQ (SR – AR)
		=	2,700 (Rs. 10 – Rs. 9.50)
		=	Rs. 1,350 (F)
(c)	**Material Usage Variance**	=	SP per unit (SQ – AQ)
		=	Rs. 10 (2,500 – 2,700)
		=	Rs. 2,000 (Adverse)

Reconciliation

Material cost variance	=	Price variance + Usage variance
Rs. 650 (Adv.)	=	Rs. 1,350 (F) + Rs. 2,000 (A)
	=	650 (A)

Labour Variance

(a)	**Direct Labour Cost Variance**	=	SC – AC
		=	Rs. 5,000 – Rs. 6,050
		=	Rs. 1,050 (Adv.)
(b)	**Direct Labour Rate Variance**	=	Actual hours worked × (SR – AR)
		=	11,000 × (Re 0·50 – Re. 0·55)
		=	Rs. 550 (Adverse)
(c)	**Direct Labour Efficiency Variance**	=	Standard hourly rate (SH – AH)
		=	Re. 0·50 × (10,000 – 10,980)
		=	Rs. 490 (Adverse)
(d)	**Idle Time Variance**	=	Idle time × Standard rate per hour
		=	20 hrs. × Re. 0·50
		=	Rs. 10 (Adverse)

Reconciliation

Direct labour cost variance = Rate variance + Efficiency variance + Idle time variance

Rs. 1,050 (Adverse) = Rs. 550 (Adv.) + Rs. 490 (Adv.) + Rs. 10 (Adv.).

Problem 38

The following details relating to the product 'X' during the month of March 1989 are available.

You are required to compute the material and labour cost variances and also to reconcile the standard and the actual cost with the help of such variances.

Standard cost per unit

Materials 50 kgs. @ Rs. 40 per kg.

Labour 400 hours @ Re. 1·00 per hour

Actual cost per month

Materials 4,900 kgs. @ Rs 42 per kg.

Labour 39,600 hours @ Rs. 1·10 per hour

Actual production – 100 units

[Adapted—I.C.W.A. (Inter)]

Solution

Standard requirements of actual production :

Materials 50 kgs. × 100 = 500 kgs.

Labour 400 hours × 100 = 40,000 hours

1. Material Variances

(a) **Material Price Variance**

(Standard Price – Actual Price) × Actual Quantity

= (Rs. 40 – Rs. 42) × 4,900 kgs. = Rs. 2 × 4,900 kgs. = Rs. 9,800 (Adverse)

(b) **Material Usage Variance**

(Standard Quantity – Actual Qnt.) × Standard Price

= (5,000 – 4,900) × Rs. 40 = Rs. 4,000 (Favourable)

(c) **Material Cost Variance**

Rs. 9,800 A + 4,000 (F) = Rs. 5,800 (A)

2. Labour Variances

(a) Labour Rate Variance

(Standard Rate – Actual Rate) × Actual Hours

= (Re 1·00 – Rs. 1.10) × 39,600 = Rs. 3,960 (A)

(b) Labour Efficiency Variance

(Standard Hours – Actual Hours) × Standard Rate

= (40,000 – 39,600) × Re. 1,00 = Rs. 400 (F)

(c) Labour Cost Variance

Rs. 3,960 (A) + Rs. 400 (F) = Rs. 3,560 (A)

Reconciliation

		Rs.	
Actual Cost			
Material = 4,900 kgs. × Rs. 42 per kg.	=	2,05,800	
Labour = 39,600 hours × Rs. 1·10 per hour	=	43,560	
Total		2,49,360	
Standard Cost			
Materials = 5,000 kgs. @ Rs. 40 per kg.	=	2,00,000	
Labour = 40,000 hours @ Re. 1·00 per hour	=	40,000	
		2,40,000	
Variance			
Material cost (2,05,800 – 2,00,000)	=	5,800	(A)
Labour cost (43,560 – 40,000)	=	3,560	(A)
		Rs. 9,360	(A)

Problem 39

Direct labour strength of a section of a factory is 100 workers, paid at the rate of Rs. 6·00 per day of 8 hours each. The normal production level is 1,000 pieces per week of 48 hours. During a particular week an order for 1,500 pieces was completed working in all 7,650 hours, out of which 6,300 hours at normal wages and the balance 1,350 hours at overtime wages at double the normal rate. Total wages come to Rs. 6,300.

Calculate average labour cost per piece during the week and also analyse the various labour cost variances for the week.

[Adapted—I.C.W.A. (Inter)]

Solution

Average labour cost per piece = $\frac{\text{Rs. } 6{,}300}{1{,}500}$ Rs. 6,300 = Rs. 4·20 (Actual)

Labour cost per hour = Rs. 6 ÷ 8 = Rs. 0·75 per hour

Standard cost = 100 × 48 × $\frac{1{,}500}{1{,}000}$ = 7,200 hours @ Re. 0·75 = Rs. 5,400.

Actual Cost = Actual normal wages = $\frac{6{,}300}{9{,}000}$ = Re. 0·79 per hour

6,300 × Re. 0·70	=	Rs. 4,410
1,350 × Re. 0·70	=	Rs. 945
Overtime premium 7,650 hours	=	Rs. 945
		Rs. 6,300

(i) Labour Rate Variance	=	AHP (SR – AR)		Rs.	
	=	7,650 (Re. 0·75 – Re. 0·70)	=	382·50	(F)
(ii) Labour Efficiency Variance	=	SR (SH – AHP)			
	=	Re 0·75(7,200 – 7,650)	=	337·50	(A)

(iii) Overtime Variance	= 1,350 × Re. 0·70	=	945·00 (A)
(iv) Labour Cost Variance	= SC – AC		
	= Rs 5,400 – Rs. 6,300	=	900 (A)

Problem 40

From the following data of A Co. Ltd. relating to budgeted and actual performance for the month of March 1996, compute the direct material and direct labour cost variances :

Budgeted data for March 1996 :	
Units to be manufactured	1,50,000
Units of direct material required based on standard rates	4,95,000
Planned purchase of raw materials (units)	5,40,000
Average unit cost of direct material	Rs. 8
Direct labour hours per unit of finished goods	$^3/_4$th
Direct labour cost (total)	29,92,500
Actual data at the end of March 1996 :	Rs.
Units actually manufactured	1,60,000
Direct material cost (purchase cost based on units actually issued)	43,41,900
Direct material cost (purchase cost based on units actually purchased)	45,10,000
Average unit cost of Direct Material	Rs. 8·20
Total direct labour hours for March	1,25,000
Total direct labour cost for March	33,75,000

[Adapted—I.C.W.A. (Inter)]

Solution

Working Notes :

(i) **Actual units issued** (Direct Material) $= \dfrac{\text{Rs. } 43,41,900}{\text{Rs. } 8\cdot20}$ = 5,29,500

(ii) **Standard Quantity** $= \dfrac{4,95,000}{1,50,000}$ = 3·3 units of direct material for one unit of manufacturing.

(iii) Direct Labour Hour (DLH) $= 1,50,000 \times \dfrac{3}{4}$ = 1,12,500

(iv) Standard Rate $= \dfrac{\text{Rs. } 29,92,500}{1,12,500}$ = Rs. 26·60

(v) Actual Rate $= \dfrac{\text{Rs. } 33,75,000}{1,25,000}$ = Rs. 27

(vi) Standard cost for actual production = 1,60,000 × 3·3 = 5,28,000 units

Standard Cost = 5,28,000 × Rs. 8 = Rs. 42,24,000

Actual Cost = 5,29,500 × Rs. 8·20 = Rs. 43,41,900

1. Material Variances

(i)	**Material Price Variance**	=	**AQ (SR – AR)**
		=	5,29,500 (Rs. 8 – Rs. 8·20)
		=	Rs. 1,05,900 (A)
(ii)	**Material Usage Variance**	=	**SR (SQ – AQ)**
		=	Rs. 8 (5,28,000 – 5,29,500)
		=	Rs. 12,000 (A)
(iii)	**Material Cost Variance**	=	**SC – AC**
		=	Rs 42,24,000 – Rs. 43,41,900
		=	Rs. 1,17,900 (A)

2. Direct Labour Cost Variance

Standard cost for actual production (SC – AP)

$$1{,}60{,}000 \times \frac{3}{4} = 1{,}20{,}000 \text{ hours @ Rs. 26 per hour}$$

= **AHP × (SR – AR)**

= Rs. 31,92,000

Actual Cost = Rs. 33,75,000 i.e., 1,25,000 hours at Rs. 27.

(iv)	**Labour Rate Variance**	=	**AHP (SR – AR)**
		=	1,25,000 (Rs. 26·60 – Rs. 27)
		=	Rs. 50,000 (A)
(v)	**Labour Efficiency Variance**	=	**SR (SH – AHP)**
		=	Rs. 26·60 (1,20,000 – 1,25,000)
		=	Rs. 1,33,000 (A)
(vi)	**Labour Cost Variance**	=	**SC – AC**
		=	Rs. 31,92,000 – Rs. 33,75,000
		=	Rs. 1,83,000 (A)

Reconciliation

[Rs. 50,000 (A) + Rs. 1,33,000 (A)] = Rs. 1,83,000 (A)

Problem 41

From the following records of Apollo Bolt Nut Manufacturing Company, you are required to compute material and labour variances :

An input of 100 kgs. of material yields to a standard output of 10,000 units.
Standard price per kg. of material is Rs. 20.
Actual quantity of material issued and used by production department 10,000 kg.
Actual price per kg. of materials is Rs. 21 per kg.
Actual output is 9,00,000 units.
Number of employees is 200.
Standard wage rate per employee per day is Rs. 40.
Standard daily output per employee is 100 units.
Total number of days worked is 50 days.

Idle time paid for and included in the above—half day for each employee.
Actual wage rate per day is Rs. 45.

[Delhi University B.Com. (Hons.) 1998]

Solution

Material Variance

(i) **Material Cost Variance** = SC – AC

= Rs. [(9,000 × 20) – (10,000 × 21)]

= Rs. 30,000 (A)

(ii) **Material Price Variance** = (Standard Price – Actual Price) × Actual Quantity

= (Rs. 20 – Rs. 21) × 10,000

= Rs. 10,000 (A)

(iii) **Material Quantity Variance** = (Standard Quantity – Actual Quantity) × SP

= Rs. (9,000 – 10,000) × 20 = Rs. 20,000 (A)

Labour Variances

Workings :

(1) Mandays required for actual output. = $\frac{9,00,000}{100}$ = 9,000.

(2) Idle time = $\frac{1}{2}$ × 200 = 100 days.

∴ Actual Mandays = 200 × 50 = 10,000 days.

(1) **Labour Cost Variance** = Standard Cost – Actual Cost

= (9,000 × 40) – (10,000 × 45)

= Rs. 90,000 (A)

(2) **Labour Rate Variance** (Standard Rate – Actual Rate) × Actual days.

= (40 – 45) × 10,000 = Rs. 50,000 (A)

(3) **Labour Efficiency Variance** (Standard days – Actual days) × Standard Rate

= (9,000 – 10,000) × 40 = Rs. 40,000 (A)

(4) **Idle Time Variance** Idle time × Standard Rate

= 100 days × Rs. 40 = Rs. 4,000 (A)

Note : It is assumed that idle time variance is a sub-variance of labour efficiency variance.

Problem 42

The following figures are extracted from the books of a company :

	Budget	Actual
Output (in units)	6,000	6,500
Hours	3,000	3,300
Overheads		
Fixed	Rs. 1,200	Rs. 1,250
Variable	Rs. 6,000	Rs. 6,650
	Rs. 7,200	Rs. 7,900
Number of days	25	27

Compute and analyse the overhead variances.

Solution

(i) **Overhead Cost Variance** = (SO – RO)

= [(6,500 × Rs. 1·20) – Rs. 7,900]

= (Rs. 7,800 – Rs. 7,900) = Rs. 100 (A)

(ii) **Variable Overhead Cost Variance** = Budgeted Overhead – Actual Overhead

= (6,500 × Re. 1) – Rs. 6,650

= Rs. 6,500 – Rs. 6,650 = Rs. 150 (Adv.)

(iii) **Fixed Overhead Cost Variance** = Budgeted Overhead – Actual Overheads

= (6,500 × Re. 0·20) – Rs. 1,250

= Rs. 1,300 – Rs. 1,250 = Rs. 50 (F)

(iv) **Expenditure Variance** = Budgeted Overhead – Actual Overhead

= Rs. 1,200 – Rs. 1,250 = Rs. 50 (Adv.)

(v) **Fixed Overhead Volume Variance** = Recovered Overhead – Budgeted Overhead

= Rs. 1,300 – Rs. 1,200 = Rs. 100 (F)

(vi) **Efficiency Variance**

Recovered Overhead × Standard Overheads

= **(Standard rate per unit × Actual output) – (Standard rate per unit × Standard output for actual time)**

= (Re 0·20 × 6,000) – (Re 0·20 × 6,480)

= Rs. 1,300 – Rs. 1,296 = Rs. 4 (F)

(vii) **Capacity Variance**

Standard Overhead – Budgeted Overhead

= Rs. 1,296 – Rs. 1,200 = Rs. 96 (F)

(viii) **Calendar Variance**

Possible Overhead – Budgeted Overhead

= Rs. 1,296* – Rs. 1,200 Rs. 96 (F)

*Possible days × Standard rate per day = 27 × Rs. 48 = Rs. 1,296

(ix) **Revised Capacity Variance**

Standard Overhead – Possible Overhead

= Rs. 1,296 – Rs. 1,296 = 0.

Problem 43

The Cost Accountant of a Company was given the following information regarding the overheads for February 2003 :

(a) Overhead cost variance Rs. 1,400 adverse.

(b) Overheads volume variance Rs. 1,000 adverse.

(c) Budgeted hours for February 1996, 1,200 hours.

(d) Budgeted overheads for February 1996, Rs. 6,000.

(e) Actual rate of recovery of overheads Rs. 8 per hour.

You are required to assist him in computing the following for February 1996 :

(i) Overheads expenditure variance.

(ii) Actual overheads incurred.

(iii) Actual hours for actual production.

(iv) Overheads capacity variance.

(v) Overheads efficiency variances.

(vi) Actual hours for actual production.

[Adapted—C.A. (Inter)]

Solution

Computation of Variances

1. **Overhead Expenditure Variances**

= **Overhead cost variance – Overhead volume variance**

= Rs. 1,400 Adverse – Rs. 1,000 Adverse = Rs. 400 Adverse.

2. **Actual Overheads Incurred**

= **Budgeted Overhead – Overhead expenditure variance**

= Rs. 6,000 – Rs. 400 (Adverse)

= Rs. 6,000 – (–Rs. 400) = Rs. 6,400.

3. **Actual Hours for Actual Production**

$$= \frac{\text{Actual overheads}}{\text{Actual rate of recovery of overheads per hour}}$$

$$= \frac{\text{Rs. } 6,400}{\text{Rs. } 8} = 800 \text{ hours.}$$

4. **Overheads Capacity Variance**

Standard rate of recovery (Actual hours for actual production – Budgeted hours)

= Rs. 5*(800 hours – 1,200 hours) = Rs. 5 × (–Rs. 400 hours)

= Rs. 2,000 (Adverse)

5. **Overhead Efficiency Variance**

= **Overhead volume variance – Overhead capacity variance**

= Rs. 1,000 (A) – Rs. 2,000 (A) – Rs. 1,000 – (–Rs. 2,000)

= –Rs. 1,000 + Rs. 2,000 = Rs. 1,000 (Favourable)

6. **Standard Hours for Actual Production Volume Variance**

= Standard rate of overheads recovery
(Standard hours for actual production (SH) – Budgeted hours)

or, Rs. 1,000 (A) = 5 (SH – 1,200 hours)

$$\text{or, SH} - 1,200 \text{ hours} = \frac{-\text{Rs. } 1,000}{\text{Rs. } 5}$$

or, SH – 1,200 hours = –200 hours

or, SH = 1,200 hours – 200 hours

or, Standard hours for actual production = 1,000 hours

$$\text{*Note : Standard rate of recovery} = \frac{\text{Budgeted overheads}}{\text{Budgeted hours}} = \frac{\text{Rs. } 6,000}{1,200 \text{ hours}} = \text{Rs. 5 per hour}$$

Problem 44

Modern Tiles Ltd. makes plastic tiles of standard size of 6" × 6" × $\frac{1"}{8}$.

From the following information you are required to calculate the direct materials :

(i) the cost variance in total;

(ii) the cost variance subdivided into (a) price, (b) usage, and

(iii) the usage variance analysed to show (a) mixture, (b) yield.

A standard mix of the compound required to produce an output of 20,000 square feet of tiles of $^1/_8$" thickness is as follows :

Direct Materials	Qty. (kg.)	Price (Rs. per kg.)
A	600	0·90
B	400	0·65
C	500	0·40

During December 1995, eight mixes were processed and actual materials consumed were :

Direct Material	Qnt. (kg.)	Price (Rs. per kg.)
A	5,000	0·85
B	2,900	0·60
C	4,400	0·45

Actual production for December was 6,20,000 tiles.

[Adapted—C.S. (Inter) Dec. 1992]

Solution

Working Notes :

(i) One mix of 20,000 sq. fit. of tiles would produce $\frac{20,000}{6 \times 6}$ = 80,000 tiles

(ii) Standard quantity for actual output :

$$A = \frac{600 \times 6,20,000}{80,000} = 4,650 \text{ kgs.}$$

$$B = \frac{400 \times 6,20,000}{80,000} = 3,100 \text{ kgs.}$$

$$C = \frac{500 \times 6,20,000}{80,000} = 3,875 \text{ kgs.}$$

(iii) Standard Cost = Standard Quantity × Standard Price

A	=	4,650 kgs. × Rs. 0·90	=	Rs. 4,185
B	=	3,100 kgs. × Re. 0·65	=	Rs. 2,015
C	=	3,875 kgs. × Re. 0·40	=	Rs. 1,550
		Total		Rs. 7,750

(iv) Actual Cost = Actual Quantity × Actual Price

A	=	5,000 kgs. × Re. 0·85	=	Rs. 4,250
B	=	2,900 kgs. × Re. 0·60	=	Rs. 1,740
C	=	4,400 kgs. × Re. 0·45	=	Rs. 1,980
				Rs. 7,970

1. **Direct Material Cost Variance : Standard Cost – Actual Cost**

= Rs. 7,750 – Rs. 7,970 = Rs. 220 (Adverse)

2. **Direct Material Price Variance :**

Actual Quantity × (Standard Price – Actual Price)

A	=	5,000 kgs. × (0·90 – 0·85)	=	Rs. 250 (F)
B	=	2,900 kgs. × (0·65 – 0·60)	=	Rs. 145 (F)
C	=	4,400 kgs. × (0·40 – 0·45)	=	Rs. 220 (A)
				Rs. 175 (F)

3. **Direct Material Usage Variance :**

Standard Price – (Standard Quantity – Actual Quantity)

A	=	Re. 0·90 × (4,650 – 5,000)	=	Rs. 315 (A)
B	=	Re. 0·65 × (3,100 – 2,900)	=	Rs. 130 (F)
C	=	Re. 0·40 × (3,875 – 4,400)	=	Rs. 210 (A)
				Rs. 395 (A)

4. **Direct Material Mix Variance :**

Standard Price × (Revised Standard Quantity – Actual Quantity)

$$\text{Revised Standard Quantity} = \frac{\text{Total Weight of Actual Mix}}{\text{Total Weight of Standard Mix}} \times \text{Standard Quantity.}$$

$$A = \frac{12,300}{11,625} \times 4,650 = 4,920 \text{ kgs.}$$

$$B = \frac{12,300}{11,625} \times 3,100 = 3,280 \text{ kgs.}$$

$$C = \frac{12,300}{11,625} \times 3,875 = 4,100 \text{ kgs.}$$

5. **Direct Material Mix Variance :**

A	=	Re. 0·90 × (4,920 – 5,000)	=	Rs. 72 (A)
B	=	Re. 0·65 × (3,280 – 2,900)	=	Rs. 247 (F)
C	=	Re. 0·40 × (4,100 – 4,400)	=	Rs. 120 (A)
				Rs. 55 (F)

6. **Material Yield Variance :** Standard cost per unit × (Standard Yield – Actual Yield)

$$\text{Standard cost per unit} = \frac{\text{Rs. } 7,750}{6,20,000} = \text{Re. } 0{\cdot}0125$$

$$\text{Standard Yield for Actual Input} = \frac{80,000}{1,500} \times 12,300$$

= 6,56,000 tiles

Therefore, Yield Variance

= Re. 0·0125 × (6,56,000 – 6,20,000) = Rs. 450 (Adverse)

OVERHEAD VARIANCES

Problem 45

The following data has been collected from the cost records of a unit for computing the various fixed overhead variances for a period :

Number of budgeted working days	25
Budgeted man-hours per day	6,000
Output (budgeted) per man-hour (in units)	1
Fixed overhead cost as budgeted	Rs. 1,50,000
Actual number of working days	27
Actual man-hours per day	6,300
Actual output per man-hour (in units)	0.9
Actual fixed overhead incurred	Rs. 1,56,000

Calculate fixed overhead variances :

(a) Expenditure Varaince

(b) Calendar Variance

(c) Capacity Variance

(d) Efficiency Variance

(e) Volume Variance

(f) Fixed Cost Variance

[Adapted—I.C.W.A. (Inter)]

Solution

	Rs.	Rs.
(a) **Expenditure Variance**		
Actual Fixed overhead =	Rs. 1,56,000	
Less : Fixed overhead as per budget =	Rs. 1,50,000	
		6,000 (A)
(b) **Calendar Variance**		
Fixed overhead as per budget	1,50,000	
Less : Calendar days' budget for the period $\dfrac{\text{Actual no. of working days} \times \text{budgeted overhead}}{\text{Budgeted no. of working days}}$		
$\dfrac{27 \times 1,50,000}{25}$	1,62,000	
		12,000 (F)
(c) **Capacity Overhead**		
Calendar days' budget for the period	1,62,000	
Less : Actual hours worked × Actual no. of woking days × output per man-hour = (6,300 × 27 × 1)	1,70,100	
		8,100 (F)
(d) **Efficiency Variance**		
Actual hours worked × Actual no. of working days × output per man-hour	1,70,000	
Less : Standard Fixed overhead for actual production = (6,300 × 27 × 0.9 × Re. 1.00)	1,53,090	
		16,910 (A)

(e) **Volume Variance**

Calendar + Capacity + Efficiency

= Rs. 12,000 (F) + Rs. 8,100 (F) + Rs. 17,010 (A) = 3,190 (F)

(f) **Total Fixed Cost Variance**

Expenditure Variance + Volume Variance

= Rs. 6,000 (A) + Rs. 3,090 (F) = 2,910 (A)

Standard Fixed Overhead Rate

= [Rs. 1,50,00 ÷ (6,000 × 25)] = Re. 1.00.

ASSIGNMENT

Theoretical Questions

1. What is 'Standard Costing'? Bring out clearly the relationship between standard costing and budgetary control. **[Delhi U. B.Com. (Hons.) 1983]**
2. What do you mean by standard costing? How does it differ from budgetary control? **[C.U. B.Com. (Hons.) 1994]**
3. Define standard costing. What are its objects? **[C.U. B.Com. (Hons.) 1995]**
4. Define 'Variance Analysis'. List out types of variances. **[B.Com. Kerala]**
5. How does standard cost differ from estimated costs?
6. Enumerate the preliminary tasks required for introducing a standard costing system in a factory. **[C.A. (Inter), B.Com. Andhra]**
7. What are the several types of standards and what are the assumptions as to the factors on which these standards are based?

Practical Problems

1. The standard cost card for one unit of a product shows the following costs for material and labour :

   Material 4 pieces @ Rs. 5·00

   Labour 10 hours @ Rs. 1·25

   5,700 units of the product were manufactured during the month of March 1996 with following material and labour costs

   Material – 23,000 pieces @ Rs. 4·95

   Labour – 56,800 hours @ Rs. 1·52

   Calculate appropriate material and labour variances.

Ans. : MCV = Rs. 150 (F), MPV = Rs. 1,150 (F); MUV = Rs. 1,000 (A), LCV = Rs. 836 (A); LRV = Rs. 1,136 (A), LTV = Rs. 300 (F).

2. 80 kgs.of material A at a standard price of Rs. 2 per kg. and 40 kgs. of material B at a standard price of Rs 5 per kg. were to be used to manufacture 100 kgs. of a chemical.

   During a month 70 kgs. of material A priced at Rs. 2·10 per kg. and 50 kgs. of material B priced at Rs 4·50 per kg. were actually used and the output of the chemical was 102 kgs.

3. The standard cost of a certain chemical mixture is :

   35% material A at Rs. 25 per kg.

   65% material B at Rs. 36 per kg.

   A standard loss of 5% is expected in production.

During a period there is used :

125 kgs. of material A at Rs. 27 per kg. and

275 kgs. of material B at Rs. 35 per kg.

The actual output was 365 kgs.

Calculate :

(a) Material cost variance

(b) Material price variance

(c) Material mix variance

(d) Material yield variance.

[D.U. B.Com. (Hons.) 1985]

Ans. : (a) A = Rs. 13·25 (A); B = Rs. 359·72 (A), (b) A = Rs. 250 (A); B = Rs. 550 (F), (c) A = Rs. 375 (F); B = Rs. 540 (A), (d) Rs. 507·60 (A).

Hints : Material Yield Variance

= (Standard loss − Actual loss) × Standard output price

= (30 − 35) × 33·84 = Rs. 507·60 (A)

4. The following details relating to product 'X' during the month of March 1989 are available. You are required to compute the material and labour cost variances and also to reconcile the standard and the actual with the help of such variances.

Standard cost per unit :

Materials 50 kgs. @ Rs. 40 per kg.

Labour 400 hours @ Re. 1·00 per hour.

Actual cost for the month :

Material 4,900 kgs. @ 42 per kg.

Labour 39,600 hours @ Rs. 1·10 per hour.

Actual production 100 units.

[Adapted—I.C.W.A. (Inter) June 1989]

Ans. : Material price variance Rs. 200 (A); Material usage variance Rs. 100 (F).

5. The following information relates to a manufacturing process of a company :

Number of employees	200
Weekly hours worked	40
Standard wage rate	50 paise per hour
Standard output	250 units per hour

During first week of March 1996 four employees were paid at 45 paise per hour and two employees at 55 paise per hour, the rest employees were paid at standard rates. Idle time is one hour per employee. Actual output was 10,250 units. Calculate labour variances.

Hints	=	AH = 200 × 40	=	8,000 hours
ALC	=	4 × 40 × 0·45	=	Rs. 72
		2 × 40 × 0·55	=	Rs. 44
		196 × 40 × 0·50	=	Rs. 3,880
				Rs. 3,996

6. A manufacturing concern which has adopted standard costing furnished the following information :

Standard :

Material for 70 kgs. finished product 100 kgs.	
Price of materials	Re. 1 per kg.

Actual :

Output	2,10,000 kgs.
Materials used	2,80,000 kgs.
Cost of materials	Rs. 2,52,000

Calculate :

(a) Materials usage variance
(b) Materials price variance
(c) Materials cost variance

Ans. : (a) Rs. 20,000 (F); (b) 28,000 (F); (c) Rs. 48,000 (F).

7. The standard cost for a product is :

Time 10 hours per unit
Cost Rs. 5 per hour

The actual performance was :

Production	1,000 units
Hours taken	
Production	10,400 hours
Idle time	400 hours
Total time	10,800 hours

Payments made Rs. 56,160 @ Rs. 5·20 per hour.

Calculate :

(a) Labour rate variance; (b) Labour efficiency variance; (c) Idle time variance; (d) Labour cost variance. **[Meerut B.Com.]**

Ans. : @ Rs. 21,160 (A); (b) Rs. 2,000 (A); (c) Rs. 2,000 (A); (d) Rs. 6,160 (A).

8. S.V. Ltd. manufactures a simple product, the standard mix of which is :

Material A	60% at Rs. 20 per kg.
Material B	40% at Rs. 10 per kg.

Normal loss in production is 20% of input. Due to shortage of material A, the standard mix was changed. Actual results for March 1996 were :

Material A		105 kgs. at Rs. 20 per kg.
Material B		95 kgs. at Rs. 9 per kg.
Input	200 kgs.	
Loss	35 kgs.	
Output	165 kgs.	

Calculate :

(a) Material price variance; (b) Material usage variance; (c) Material mix variance; (d) Material yield variance. **[D.U. B.Com. (Hons.) 1990]**

Ans. : (a) Rs. 95 (F); (b) A = Rs. 375 (F); Material B = Rs. 125 (A);
(c) A = Rs. 300 (F), B = Rs. 150 (A); (d) Rs. 100 (A).

9. The standard cost card for one unit of a product shows the following costs for material and labour :

   Material 4 pieces @ Rs. 5.00

   Labour 10 hours @ Rs. 1·25

   5,700 units of the product were manufactured during the month of March 1996 with the following material and labour costs :

   Material—23,000 pieces @ Rs. 4.95

   Labour—56,800 hours @ Rs. 1·52

   Calculate appropriate material and labour variances.

   Ans. : (i) MCV = Rs. 150 (F); (ii) MPV = Rs. 1,150 (F); (iii) MUV = Rs. 1,000 (A); (iv) LCV = Rs. 836 (A); (v) LRV = Rs. 1,136 (A); (vi) LEV = Rs. 300 (F).

10. Trishul Industries turns out only one article, the prime cost standards for which have been established as follows :

	for completed piece
Materials = 5 lbs @ Rs. 4·20	Rs. 21
Labour = 3 hours @ Rs. 3	Rs. 9

The production schedule for the month of April 1996 required completion of 5,000 pieces. However, 5,120 pieces were actually completed.

Purchases for the month of April 1996 amounted to 30,000 lbs of material at the total invoice price or Rs. 1,35,000.

Production records for the month of April 1996 showed the following actual results :

Materials requisitioned and used	25,700 lbs
Direct labour = 15,150 hours	Rs. 48,480.

Calculate appropriate material and labour variances. **[D.U. B.Com. (Hons.)]**

Ans. : (i) MCV = Rs. 2,400 (A); (ii) MPV = Rs. 7,710 (A); (iii) MUV = Rs. 420 (A); (iv) LPV = Rs. 3,030 (A); (v) LEV = Rs. 630 (F); (vi) LCV = Rs. 2,400 (A).

11. The standard output per week in a factory is 2,000 units but the actual output for the week was 2,400 units. The total overhead expenses for the period were as follows :

	Actual (Rs.)	Standard (Rs.)
Fixed	900	800
Variable	500	500
Semivariable	1,050	900

The overtime work done during the week was equal to one day's work. Semivariable expenses are one-third fixed and two-third variable. Find out the different variances.

[M.Com. Rajasthan]

12. The stanndard materials inputs required for 1000 kgs. of a finished product are given below :

Material	Quantity kg.	Standard rate per kg. Rs.
P	450	20
Q	400	40
R	250	60
	1,100	
Less : Normal loss	100	
	1,000	

Actual production in a period was 20,000 kgs. of the finished product for which the actual quantity of material used and the prices paid thereof as under :

Material	*Quantity* kg.	*Standard rate per kg.* (in Rs.)
P	450	20
Q	400	40
R	250	60

***Calculate* :**

(i) Material Cost Variance;
(ii) Material Price Variance;
(iii) Material Usage Variance;
(iv) Material Mix Variance;
(v) Material Yield Variance.

[I.C.W.A. (Inter)]

Ans. : (i) Material Cost Variance = Rs. 39,500 (A);
(ii) Material Price Variance = Rs. 29,500 (A);
(iii) Material Usage Variance = Rs. 10000 (A);
(iv) Material Mix Variance = Rs. 26,363 (F);
(v) Material Yield Variance = Rs. 36,363 (A).

13. From the particulars given below, compute :

(i) Material Price Variance;
(ii) Material Usage Variance
(iii) Labour Rate Variance;
(iv) Idle Time Variance;
(v) labour Efficiency Variance.

1 tonne of material input yields a standard output of 1,00,000 units. The standard price of material is Rs. 20 per kg.

Number of employees engaged is 200. The standard wage rate per employee per day is Rs. 6. The standard daily output per employee is 100 units. The actual quantity of material used is 10 tonnes and the actual price paid is Rs. 21 per kg. Actual output obtained is 9,00,000 units. Actual number of days worked is 50 and actual rate of wages paid is Rs. 6.50 per day. Idle time paid for and included in above time is $^1/_2$ day.

[Adapted—C.A. (Inter)]

14. Standard labour hours and rate for production of one unit of Article A is given below :

	Per unit (hour)	*Rate per hour* (Rs.)	*Total* (Rs.)
Skilled worker	5	1.50	7.50
Unskilled worker	8	0.50	4.00
Semi-skilled worker	4	0.75	3.00
			14.50

Actual Data

		Rate per hour	Total
Articles produced 1,000 units		Rs.	Rs.
Skilled worker	4,500 hours	2.00	9,000
Unskilled worker	10,000 hours	0.45	4,500
Semi-skilled worker	4,200 hours	0.75	3,150
			16,650

Calculate :

(i) Labour Cost Variance
(ii) Labour Rate Variance
(iii) Labour Efficiency Variance
(iv) Labour Mix Variance.

Ans. : (i) Total Labour Cost Variance Rs. 2,150 (A)
(ii) Labour Rate Variance Rs. 1,750 (A)
(iii) Labour Efficiency Variance 400 (A)
(iv) Labour Mix Variance Rs. 1,050 (F)

15. From the particulars given below compute :
   (i) Material Price Variance
   (ii) Material Usage Variance
   (iii) Labour Rate Variance
   (iv) Idle Time Variance
   (v) Labour Efficiency Variance

1 tonne of material input yields a standard output of 1,00,000 unity. The standard price of material is Rs. 20 per kg. Number of employees engaged is 100 units. The standard wage rate per employee per day is Rs. 6.

The standard daily output per employee is 100 units. The actual quantity of materials used is 10 tonnes and the actual price is Rs. 21 per kg. Actual output is obtained is 9,00,000.

16. The standard output of the gang for the product was four units per hour.

During the month in question however, the actual composition of the gang and hourly rates paid were as follows :

Nature of Workers	*No. of Workers*	*Wage rate paid per worker per hour engaged*
Skilled	2	
Semi-skilled	3	
Unskilled	5	

The gang was engaged for 200 hours during the month, which included 12 hours where no production was possible due to machine break-down, 810 units of the product were recorded as output of the gang during the month.

You are required :
   (i) to compute the standard unit labour cost of the product;
   (ii) to compute the total variance in labour cost during the month; and
   (iii) analyse the variance in (ii) above and sub-variance and reconcile.

[I.C.W.A. (Inter)]

17. The standard labour complement and the actual labour complement engaged in a week for a job as under :

	Skilled workers	*Semi-skilled workers*	*Unskilled workers*
(a) Standard number of workers in the gang	32	12	6
(b) Standard wage rate per hour (Rs.)	3	2	1
(c) Actual number of workers employed in the gang during the work	28	18	4
(d) Actual wage rate per hour (Rs.)	4	3	2

During the 40 hour working week the gang product 1,800 standard labour hours of work.

Calculate :

(i) Labour efficiency variance;

(ii) Labour mix variance;

(iii) Rate of wage Variance;

(iv) Total Labour cost variance.

[C.A. (Inter)]

Ans. : (i) Rs. 504 (A); (ii) Rs. 80 (F); (iii) Rs. 2,000 (A); (iv) Rs. 2,424 (A).

18. Following are the standard and actual cost figures of a factory for a period. Compute the variances :

	Standard	Actual
Production units	20,000	22,000
Material 20,000 kg. at Re. 1.00	20,000	21,500 @ Re. 0.98 per kg.
Labour at Re 1.00 per hour	30,000	30,800 @ Rs. 1.10 per kg.
Fixed Overheads	25,000	27,000
	75,000	79,360

Ans. : (i) Material Cost Variance = Rs. 440 (F)

(ii) Material Price Variance = Rs. 440 (F)

(iii) Material Usage Variance = Nil

(iv) labour Cost Variance = Rs. 2,200 (F)

(v) Labour Rate Variance = Rs. 2,800 (A)

(vi) Labour Efficiency Variance = Rs. 5,000 (F)

19. AB Ltd. has established the following standard mix of producing 9 gallons of product A :

		Rs.
5 gallons of material X at Rs. 7 per gallon	=	35
3 gallons of material Y at Rs. 5 per gallon	=	15
2 gallons of material Z at Rs. 2 per gallon	=	4
		54

A standard loss of 10% of input is expected to occur.

Actual output was as under

53,000 gallons of material X at Rs. 7 per gallon.

28,000 gallons of material Y at Rs. 5.30 per gallon.

19,000 gallons of material Z at Rs. 2.20 per gallon.

Actual output for a period was Rs. 92,700 gallons of product A.

Compute :

(i) Material Mix Variance, (ii) Material Yield Variance.

[Adapted—Delhi University B.Com. (Hons.) 1999]

Ans. : (i) Material Mix Variance—Rs. 9,000 (Adv.)
(ii) Material Yield Variance—Rs. 16,200 (F)

20. The following was the composition of a gang of workers in a factory during a particular month in one of the production departments. The standard composition of worker and wage rate per hour were as below :

Skilled	:	The workers at a standard rate of Rs. 20 per hour each.
Semi-skilled	:	Four workers at a standard rate of Rs. 12 per hour each.
Unskilled	:	Four workers at a standard rate of Rs. 8 per hour each.

The standard output of the gang was four units per hour of the product.

During the month in question, however, the actual composition of the gang and hourly rate paid were as under :

Nature of Workers	*No. of Workers*	*Wage rate paid worker per hour engaged*
Skilled	2	Rs. 20
Semi-skilled	3	Rs. 14
Unskilled	5	Rs. 10

The gang was engaged for 200 hours during the month, which included 12 hours when no production was possible, due to machine break-down, 810 units of the product were recorded as output of the gang during the month.

You are required :

(a) to compute the standard unit labour cost of the product.

(b) to compute the total variance in labour cost during the month.

(c) to analyse the variance in (b) above in sub-variance and reconcile.

[I.C.W.A. (Inter)]

Ans. : (a) Rs. 30; (b) Rs. 2,100 (A);
(c) (i) Labour rate variance Rs 3,200 (A);
(ii) Labour Efficiency Variance Rs. 1,100 (F)

21. The standard material and labour cost for two products X and Y are :

Materials (same for both)

X		Y	
	Rs.		Rs.
5 kgs.	50	3 kgs.	30
10 hours	5	8 hours	4
	55		34

500 units of X and 200 units of Y were manufactured in a period against total material cost and labour cost as under :

Material :	Product X	:	2,700 kgs. material
	Product Y	:	700 kgs. material
Labour :	Product X	:	6,000 hours
	Product Y	:	2,000 hours

Reconcile the standard prime cost and actual prime cost for the production of 500 units of X and 200 units of Y.

[Adapted—I.C.W.A. (Inter)]

Ans. : (i) Material Price Variance Rs. 3,400 (A)

(ii) Material Usage Variance Rs. 3,000 (A)

(iii) Labour Rate Variance Rs. 400 (F)

(iv) Efficiency Variance Rs. 700 (A)

BUDGET AND BUDGETARY CONTROL 12

Learning Objectives :

1. *Definition of Budget*
2. *Purposes of Budget*
3. *Elements of Budget*
4. *Budgetary Control :*

   Definition, Principles, Characterisitcs
5. *Essentials of an Effective Budgeting*
6. *Merits and Demerits of Budgetary Control*
7. *Objectives of Budgetary Control*
8. *Requisites of Budgetary Control*
9. *Steps in Budgeting*
10. *Classification of Budget :*

    (a) On the basis of time

    (b) On the basis of functions

    (c) On the basis of flexibility

    (d) On the basis of nature of business
11. *Capital Budgeting—(a) Definition, (b) Importance and (c) Advantages*
12. *Zero Base Budgeting—(a) Definition, (b) Stages, (c) Advantages, (d) Limitations*
13. *Performance Budget*
14. *Responsibility Accounting—(a) Definition, (b) Pre-requisites, (c) Steps, (d) Responsibility Centres, (e) Limitations*
15. *Sales Budget—(a) Definition, (b) Factors to be considered for its preparation*
16. *Production Budget*
17. *Cash Budget—(a) Definition, (b) Objectives, (c) Methods of Preparing Cash Budget*
18. *Flexible Budget—(a) Definition, (b) Signification, (c) Operational Areas, (d) Difference between Fixed and Flexible Budget*

BUDGET AND BUDGETARY CONTROL 12

Definition of Budget

A Budget is a plan expressed in quantitative usually monetary terms, covering a specified period of time, usually one year. Many companies refer to their annual budget as a profit plan since it shows the planned activities that the company expects to undertake in its responsibility centers in order to obtain its profit goals.

In the words of *Charles T. Horngren, "A budget is a formal quantitative expression of management plans"*.

The Chartered Institute of Management Accountant of London (CIMA) defines a Budget in the following words. ***"A Budget is a plan quantified in monetary terms, prepared and approved prior to a defined period of time, usually*** showing planned income to be generated and/or expenditure to be incurred during that period and the capital to be employed to attain a given objective."

"A budget is a pre-determined statement of management policy during a given period which provides a standard for comparison with the result actually achieved."—J.R. Brown and L.R. Howard. Therefore, preplanning is a cardinal feature of budgetary control.

Purposes of Budget

The budget of an enterprise serves the following purposes :

(i) Budget is an aid in making and coordinating short-range plans.

(ii) It is a device for communicating these plans to the responsibility center managers.

(iii) Budget is a way of motivating managers to achieve their responsibility centers' goals.

(iv) It is a bench mark for controlling ongoing activities.

(v) Budget is a basis for evaluating the performance of responsibility centres and their managers.

(vi) It is a means of educating the managers in an organisation.

(vii) Under suitable condition, standard costing and budgetary control may go hand in hand and can harmonise and make the planning and control more effective.

Elements of Budget

A budget is defined as a "comprehensive and coordinated plan, expressed in financial terms, for the operations and resources, of an enterprise for some specified period in the future".—*J.M. Fremgen*. According to the above definition, the essential elements of a budget that average are :

(i) Plan;

(ii) Operations and resources;

(iii) Financial terms;

(iv) Specified future period;

(v) Comprehensiveness;

(vi) Coordination.

Plan

The term 'plan' with reference to budgeting has a *specific connotation*. Budgetary plan includes two aspects which have a bearing on the operations of an enterprise.

One set of factors that determine a firm's future operations are wholly external and beyond firm's control like general business conditions, government policy and size and composition of population.

The second set of factors that affect future activities are within the firm's control and discretion, i.e., they are internal like promotional programmes, manufacturing processes etc. Thus, budgeting not only suggests what will happen but should also make things happen. A budget is an expression partly of what the management expects to happen and partly of what the management intends to happen.

Operations and Resources

A budget is a mechanism to plan for the firm's operations and resources. A budget should qualify the revenues to be realised from products/services and the expenses to be incurred on goods or services used in generating revenues.

It also covers the resources of the firm. The budget makes plan for various assets to be used in its operations and the sources of funds to finance the assets both fixed and current assets.

Financial Terms

Budgets are always prepared in financial terms i.e., in terms of monetary value such as rupee, dollar, sterling etc.

Specified Future Period

Budget is prepared for a specified period of time, usually for a year. Sales budget, production budget, cash budget are all prepared for a financial period of one year.

Comprehensiveness

A budget is comprehensive i.e., all the activities and operations of an organisation are included in the budget. Budgets are prepared for each segment, facet, activity, division of an organisation. These activities, segments are integrated into an overall budget for the entire organisation. This overall budget is known as ***master budget***.

Coordination

The budget coordinates the various operational activities of an enterprise so as to take care of the situations and problems of each component. The budgets for each of the components are prepared in harmony with each other to make budgets more effective and meaningful.

BUDGETARY CONTROL

Definition

*"**Budgetary control** is a system of controlling costs which includes the preparation of **budget, coordinating** the departments and establishing responsibilities, comparing actual performance with that budgeted and acting upon results to achieve maximum profitability."*—**Brown and Howard**

CIMA defines budgeting control as *"The establishment of departmental budgets relating to responsibilities of executives to the requirements of a policy and the continuous comparison of actual* *with budgeted results, either to secure by individual action the objectives of that policy or to provide a firm basis for its revision".*

Budgetary control is therefore, means laying down in monetary and quantitative terms what exactly has to be done and how exactly it has to be done over the coming period and then to ensure that actual results do not deviate from the planned course.

Budgetary control is a tool of great potency for infusing forward looking dynamism and for harnessing the energies of people at all levels.

Principles of Budgetary Control

The following are the fundamental principles of budgetary control :

1. Establish a plan or target of performance which coordinates all the activities of the business.
2. Record the actual performance.
3. Compare the actual performance with that planned.
4. Calculate the differences or variances, and analyse the reasons for them.
5. Proper action is to be taken immediately to remedy the situation.

Characteristics of Budgetary Control

The salient features of Budgetary Control may be enumerated as follows :

(i) Budgetary Control determines the objectives to be achieved over the budget period. It also frames policies that are expected to be adopted for the achievement of these ends.

(ii) It addresses variety of activities that should be undertaken for the achievement of the objectives.

(iii) An effective budgetary control draws up a plan or a scheme of operation in respect of each class of activity, in physical as well as monetary terms, for the entire budget period and its parts.

(iv) It lays out a system of comparison of actual performance by each person, section or department with the relevant budget and determine the causes for the discripancies, if any.

(v) It ensures that corrective action will be taken, where the objective is not achieved and, that be not possible, for the revision of the plan.

In brief, it is a technique to assist the management in the **allocation of responsibility** and authority, to provide it with aid for making estimating and planning for the future and to facilitate the **analysis of the variations between estimated and actual performance**. By doing so, weak areas of performance are identified and corrective measures are taken so that objectives can be achieved.

Essentials of an Effective Budgeting

An effective budgeting system should have some essentials to ensure best results. The following are requisites :

(i) *Sound Forecasting*

Business forecasts are the foundation of budgets. The forecasts are discussed by the executives and when most profitable combinations of forecasts are selected, they become budgets. The more sound are the forecasts better results would come out of the budgeting.

(ii) *An adequate, planned and reliable Accounting System*

There should be a proper flow of accurate and timely information in the business which is 'must' for the preparation of budgets. The finance department should continuously supply financial data on the basis of which budget estimates and forecasts are to be made. If the data are wrong all the estimates will be wrong and the very objectives of budget will be misguiding.

(iii) *Efficient Organisation*

Preparation of Budget and its operation requires efficient, adequate and best organisation. Therefore, a budgeting system should always be supported by a sound organisational structure demarcating clearly the lines of authority and responsibility. Moreover, there should be true delegation of authority from top to lower levels of management so that executives at all levels may get the opportunity to make best decisions and get themselves involved in budget making exercise.

(iv) *Formation of Budget Committee*

It is the Budget Committee that receives the forecasts and targets of each department as well as periodic reports and finalises the final acceptable targets in form of **Mater Budget**. The Budget Committee also approves the departmental budgets. It is imperative that opportunities must be provided to the executives of all the departments for their participation in the process of budget making.

(v) *Cleanly defined Business Policies*

Budgets for each department should be prepared taking into account the policies set for particular department. Policies should be precise and clearly defined as well as free from any ambiguity.

(vi) *Availability of Standard Information*

It is very essential that sufficient and accurate relevant data should be made available to each department. Take for example, sales forecasts, production targets, price data may not flow from normal accounting system alone and these data should be collected and processed by using advanced statistical techniques and methods.

(vii) *Support of Top Management*

In order to make budgets effective, each member of top management should cooperate and should involve themselves enthusiastically in the process of budget making. The whole system of budget making should enjoy the active and spontaneous support of the top management.

(viii) *Good Reporting System*

An effective budgeting system also requires the presence of a proper feed back system. As work proceeds in the budget period, actual performance should not only be recorded but it should also be repaired with the budgeted performance. The variations should be reported promptly and clearly to the appropriate levels of management. The reporting system should be designed in such a way that along with variations, the causes of such variations and persons responsible for such variations are also reported so that management may decide about suitable remedial or corrective actions.

(ix) *Motivation*

All the employees or staff other than executives should be strongly and properly motivated towards budgeting system. There is need to make each member of the staff feel too much involved in the budget making system.

Merits of Budgetary Control

The following advantages can be drawn from budgetary control :

(i) Budgetary control ensures maximum utilisation of available resources with a view to achieving maximum profitability.

(ii) It leads to better coordination between different departments and hence better understanding between different functions.

(iii) It creates a sense of awareness at all levels of management in the process of achieving the planned targets.

(iv) It is a process of self-examination and self-criticisms which is essential for the success of any business enterprise.

(v) Budgeting gets the support and active participation of top management without which a budgeting programme cannot succeed.

(vi) Budgetary control directs capital expenditure in the most profitable time.

(vii) It helps in increasing productivity of men, materials and machine.

(viii) It acts as a yard-stick for measuring actual performance against targeted performance.

(ix) By comparing the actual with the targeted performance, budgetary control can identify the variances and helps to take remedial measures for correcting the variances.

Demerits of Budgetary Control

(i) Forecasting, planning or budgeting is not an exact science and a certain amount of judgement is present in any budgeting plan.

(ii) Lacking of support from the top management may lead to the collapse of plans.

(iii) Budgetary control is expensive.

(iv) It will be ineffective in a situation like strikes, lockout and economic revision.

(v) Budgetary control loses its importance when policies, programmes, techniques are to be changed to keep peace with socio-economic and political environment.

(vi) To be effective budgeting should be followed up by effective control system. Many organisations lack this effective control system which defeats the very purpose of budgeting.

(vii) Factors that cannot be controlled by the management cannot be incorporated in implementing the policies of budgetary control system.

Objectives of Budgetary Control

Objectives of Budgetary Control are outlined below :

1. To combine the ideas of all levels of management.
2. To coordinate the activities of the business.
3. To centralise control.
4. To decentralise responsibility on to each manager involved.
5. To plan and control income and expenditure in such a fashion so as to achieve maximum profitability.
6. To direct capital expenditure in profitable direction.
7. Budgetary control has to act as a guide to the management for taking management decisions when budgets are affected by unforeseeable conditions.
8. Budgetary control has to ensure the availability of sufficient working capital for efficient operations of the business.
9. It is to provide a yard stick against which actual performance can be compared with the targeted to identify the deviations, if any.
10. To show management when action is needed to remedy a deviation.

Requisites for Operation of a Budgetary Control

It is essential that there should be an efficient organisation of budgetary control which is to be operated effectively. It is not only an accounting exercise, but a management tool at all levels.

A number of preliminaries will be essential to make the budgetary control system efficient.

The ***preliminaries*** are discussed below :

1. *Well planned organisation*

There should be a well planned organisation set up with authority and responsibility clearly defined.

2. *Separate Departments to be established*

Centres or departments should be established for each of which budget will be set with the help of the head of department concerned.

3. *Accounting Records*

Adequate accounting records are to be introduced. It is essential that the accounting system should be able to record and analyst the information required for the preparation of budgets.

4. *General Instruction*

General instruction in technique of all concerned department should be given in operating the system. Each person must know the budget of his department, its objectives and how he fits into the plan. The person must feel that he is capable of carrying out the budgeted programmes efficiently and effectively.

5. *Preparation of an organisation chart*

An organisation chart is to be prepared organisation chart defines the functional responsibilities of each member of management and ensures that he knows his position in the organisation and his relationship to other members. It should be noted that in the preparation of each of the budget the accountant will play a big role, especially those involving costs.

6. *Budget Committee*

A budget committee should be established to formulate a general programme for preparing budgets and exercising overall control. The functions of budget committee will be :

(i) To provide the historical information to help managers in forecasting.

(ii) To issue instructions regarding budget requirements, dates for the receipt of budgets.

(iii) To define the general policies of the management in relation to budgets.

(iv) To advise the managers involved in preparation of budgets.

(v) To suggest revisions and amendments to budgets as and when required.

(vi) To see that budgets are prepared and submitted in due time.

(vii) To coordinate the budget programme.

(viii) To approve the Master Budgets after the functional budgets have been approved.

(ix) To identify the weak areas after making comparison of budgeted and actual results.

(x) To recommend corrective actions where necessary.

(xi) The finalisation of the functional budgets and their compilation into the Master Budget.

7. *Budget Manual*

Budget manual is to be prepared *"Budget manual is a document that sets out, the responsibilities of the persons engaged in, the routine of and the forms and records required for budgetary control".* ***—ICMA***

The main idea, behind the budget manual is to inform line executives before hand about procedures to be followed.

8. *Budget periods should be ascertained*

Budget periods vary between short-term and long-term. If the business experiences seasonal fluctuation the budget period may extend over one seasonal cycle. In that situation long-term budgets should be prepared.

In determining the length of the budget period, the following factors should be reasoned :

(i) The budget period should be long enough to complete production of various products.

(ii) The budget period should coincide with the financial accounting period to reconcile actual results with the budgeted estimates.

(iii) For a business of seasonal nature the budget period should cover at least one entire seasonal cycle.

(iv) In the case of capital expenditure budgets forecasts for a much longer periods than a year may be used.

9. *The Key Factor*

This is the factor the extent of whose influence must first be assessed in order to ensure that functional budgets are reasonable capable of fulfilment. The key factor is also known as 'limiting' or 'governing' or 'principal budget' factor. It is of vital importance. The key factor determines priorities in functional budgets.

The key factors that may affect budgeting are the following :

(a) **Materials**

(i) Availability of supply;

(ii) Restrictions imposed by licences, quotas etc.

(b) **Labour**

(i) General shortage;

(ii) Shortage in certain key process.

(c) **Plant**

(i) Insufficient capacity due to lack of capital;

(ii) or lack of space;

(iii) or lack of markets;

(iv) Bottlenecks in certain key process.

(d) **Sales**

(i) Low market demand;

(ii) Shortage of experienced salesmen;

(iii) Insufficient advertisement due to lack of money.

Probably, the sales demand is the most important key factor in industry. The success or otherwise of budgetary control rests on the forecast of sales during the budget period. Most of the budgets will be affected if sales figure proves to be inaccurate.

10. *Level of Activity*

It will be necessary to establish the normal level of activity, i.e. the level the company can reasonably be expected to achieve. This level is important in forecasting, for example, material and labour requirements and particularly production overhead budgets.

Steps in Budgeting

The following exhibit illustrates how the various resources and activities of an enterprise are coordinated through budgetary planning.

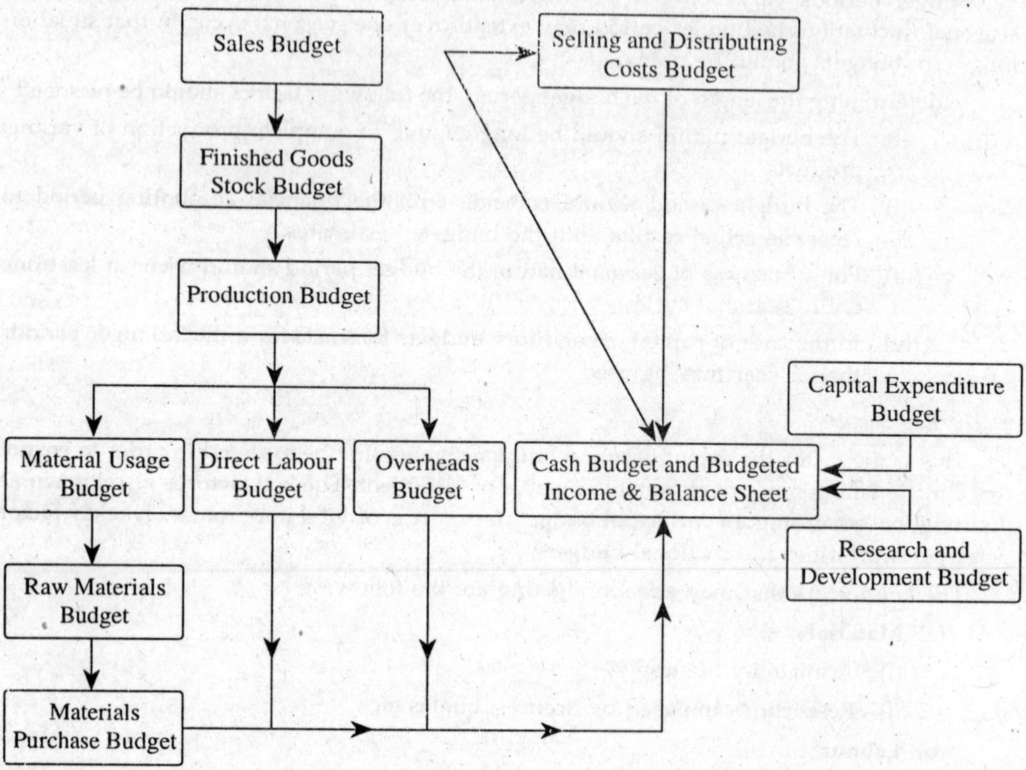

The above exhibit indicates that the first stage of budgeting exercise is the determination of the ***'key' factors*** or constants which impose overall limits to the budget plan. Among these factors are the productive capacity of the plant, the finance available to the firm, and, of course, the market conditions that impose a total limit on the output the firm is able to sell. Normally from the management point of view, the critical question is *'what is the firm able to sell in the budget period?'*, and this question summarises all the limits to the budget plan.

It is for this reason that the sales budget is at once the starting point and the fulcrum of the budgeting process.

The arrows in the above exhibit indicate the flow of relevant information. Once the level of sales is established, selling and distribution cost may be ascertained. The production budget itself is determined by the sales forecast, the desired level stock of finished goods and plant capacity. From the production budget may be estimated the production costs and cost schedules for materials, labour, and overheads.

In addition, the budgeting process for capital expenditure reflects decision taken in developing the long-range plan. The capital expenditure budget is concerned with expenditure during the budget period on the maintenance and improvement of the existing productive capacity. Moreover, Research and Development costs for improving methods of production and product improvement are associated with this budget.

From a financing point of view, the cash surplus or deficit arising out of the overall budget are revealed by the cash budget which incorporates all cash revenues and cash expenditures. This enables the firm to arrange its financial needs accordingly.

Finally, the projected results in terms of the overall net profits, and the changes in the structure of the firm's assets and liabilities are expressed in the budgeted profit and loss account and the budgeted balance sheet at the end of the budget period.

Budget coordinates the various activities of the firm in a simplified manner. So, budgetary planning is an activity which is of critical importance to the firm, and the problems involved are often complex and difficult ones to resolve. For example, a firm's sales policy cannot be considered in isolation from its pricing policy and its cost structure. The firm's production costs in relation to the required output may be too high to reach the profit target.

The role of the budget committee is, therefore, a very important and crucial one. It has not only to harmonize all the divisional budgets into an overall planning framework, but it has to deal with the numerous adjustments which may have to be made if the overall budget fails to meet some of the firm's stated objectives. Hence, the role of the budget committee is not only important in a practical sense, it embraces important and sensitive areas of policy making and management.

Classification of Budget

Budget may be classified as follows :

1. On the basis of time,
2. On the basis of function,
3. On the basis of flexibility,
4. On the basis of nature of business activity.

1. On the basis of time

According to time, budgets may be classified as : (i) Long-term Budget and (ii) Short-term Budget.

(i) Long-term Budgets :

Long-term budgets are prepared on the basis of long-term forecasts. It portrays a long range planning which extend from five to ten years. This is the reason that these budgets are prepared in terms of physical quantities rather than in rupee values.

(ii) Short-term Budgets :

Short-term budgets are those, which are prepared on the basis of short-term forecasts i.e. for a period of one to five years. These budgets are prepared in monetary units and are more precise than long-term budgets.

(iii) Current Budgets :

These budgets are prepared for a period that extends from one month to twelve months.

2. On the basis of function

Budgets for a period may also be classified according to the functions carried on in a business concern. The various functions of a business concern are interrelated. The various forecast of individual function are coordinated and then consolidated to show the total effect of all the functions. Therefore, budget for individual function is prepared and then a master budget is prepared consolidating all functional budgets. Thus budgets on the basis of functions may be :

(i) Master Budget or Summary Budget;

(ii) Functional Budgets or Subsidiary Budgets.

(i) Master Budget or Summary Budget :

The Master Budget is one that projects the activities of the business during the budget period. It commonly takes the form of budgeted Profit and Loss Account and Balance Sheet. It is prepared by the Budget Officer, and incorporates the details shown in the subsidiary budgets.

Master Budget that consolidates an organisation's overall plans for a shorter span of time is usually prepared on an annual basis.

The Master Budget is an integrative tool that cuts across divisional boundaries to coordinate the firm's diverse activities. A Master budget takes the macro view of the business enterprise and coordinates sales with production, raw materials, manpower, machinery and other resources.

The following exhibit shows the Master Budget of a non-manufacturing concern :

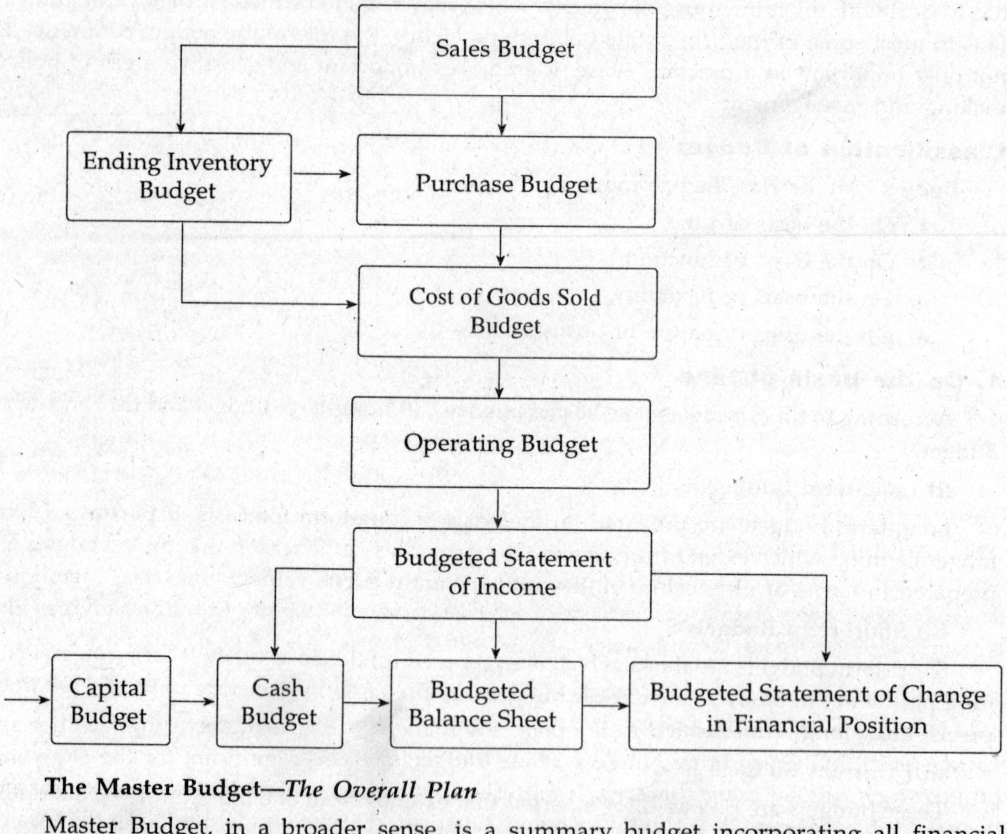

The Master Budget—*The Overall Plan*

Master Budget, in a broader sense, is a summary budget incorporating all financial budgets in a capsule form. From this view point, master budget depicts the picture of total plans of the budget period, and it covers information relating to sales, production, costs, profit and profit planning etc.

(ii) **Functional Budgets or Subsidiary Budgets**

Functional budgets are those that are prepared on the basis of approved forecasts for individual department. These functional budgets may vary in number from business to business. Normally, the following types of functional budgets are in vogue.

(a) Sales Budget, (b) Production Budget, (c) Raw Material Budget, (d) Labour Budget, (e) Plant Budget, (f) Research and Development Budget, (g) Overheads Budget, (h) Financial Budgets—Cash Budget, Capital Budget and Expenditure Budget.

3. On the basis of flexibility

(i) Fixed Budget and (ii) Flexible Budget.

(i) **Fixed Budget :** Fixed Budget are prepared for a fixed or standard volume of activity. They do not change with the change in the volume of activity. These budgets are prepared well in advance. They are not helpful for making comparison.

According to **I.C.M.A.** ***"a fixed budget is a budget designed to remain unchanged irrespective of the level of activity actually attained".***

Fixed budget is normally prepared when activities can fairly be forecast with reasonable certainty.

(i) Flexible Budget : The I.C.M.A. defines flexible budget as, ***"a budget which is designed to change in accordance with the level of activity attained".***

Basically, the idea of a flexible budget is that there shall be some standard of expenditure for varying levels of output. Flexible budgetary control has been developed with the objective of changing the budget figures progressively to correspond to the actual output. The preparation of budgets necessitates the analysis of all overheads into fixed, variable and semi-variable costs.

The I.C.M.A. defines the above costs as follows :

Fixed cost : a cost which tends to be unaffected by variation in volume of output.

Variable cost : a cost that tends to vary directly with the volume of output.

Semi-variable : a cost which partly fixed and partly variable.

4. On the basis of nature of business activity

On the above view point, budgets may be classified as :

(i) Operating Budgets or Revenue Budgets

(ii) Capital Expenditure Budgets

(i) ***Operating Budgets :***

Operating budgets are those that deal with the plans for routine activities, i.e., operations. These budgets are prepared on the basis of forecasts made in respect of routine activities like sales, production, costs, revenues etc.

(ii) ***Capital Expenditure Budgets :***

All budgets that are related to the plans aiming at creating manufacturing facilities are known as capital expenditure budgets. These budgets are very significant for the large and progressive manufacturing concerns. It represents estimated expenditure on all fixed assets during the budget period. It should be noted, however, that the budget period in the case of capital expenditure budget might differ from that of other budgets. This budget is subject to strict management control, because it may involve large amount of expenditure that needs top management's approval.

5. Plant Utilisation Budget

Plant utilisation budget is prepared in terms of working hours, weight or other convenient units of plant facilities required to carry out the programme laid down in the production budget. The objectives of Plant Utilisation Budget are :

(i) to determine the load on each process, cost or groups of machines for the budget period;

(ii) to indicate the process or cost centers which are overloaded so that corrective action can be taken;

(iii) to dovetail the sales, production budgets where it is not possible to increase the capacity of any of the overloaded processes;

(iv) to make effort to boost sales to utilise the surplus capacity.

6. Production Cost Budget

A product Cost Budget is the summary of material budget, labour budget, factory overhead budget. A Production Cost Budget is also known as Manufacturing Budget that consists of three budgets namely (i) material budget, (ii) labour budget and (iii) factory overhead budget.

7. Direct Material Budget

Direct Material Budget indicates the cost of direct material purchased.

The direct material budget is useful for the following reasons :

1. It helps the purchase department to prepare a schedule to ensure supply of material to the production departments as and when materials are required for production.
2. It helps the store department in fixing maximum and minimum levels of inventories.
3. It also helps the finance manager to ascertain the financial requirements to finance production targets.

Direct Material Budget consists of :

1. Material Usage Budget, 2. Purchase Budget.

The following example will clarify the matter.

Finolex Ltd.
Direct Materials Budget
for the year ended March 31, 2002

1. Materials Usage Budget

	Products		
	X	***Y***	***Total***
Budgeted production in units	1,00,000	1,25,000	2,25,000
Direct material requirements :			
Product X 10 kg. per unit	10,00,000		
Product Y 8 kg. per unit		10,00,000	
Cost per kg. (in Rupees)	2.00	2.50	
Cost of direct material used	Rs. 20,00,000	Rs. 25,00,000	45,00,000

8. Capital Budgeting

Definition

In the words of **R.M. Lynch**, *"Capital budgeting consists in planning for development of available capital for the purpose of maximizing the long-term profitability of the firm"*.

Charles T. Horngren defines Capital Budgeting as *"A long-term planning for making and financing proposed capital outlays"*.

Gitman L.J. has put, *"Capital Budgeting refers to the total process of generating, evaluating, selecting and following up of capital expenditure alternatives"*.

The capital budgeting decision, therefore, involves a current outlay or series of outlays of cash resources in return for anticipated flow of future benefits.

Importance

Capital budgetiing decision are of paramount importance in financial decision making.

Firstly, capital budgeting decisions affect the profitability of the firm. They also have a bearing on the competitive position of a firm.

Capital budgeting decisions determine the future destiny of a company. An opportune investment decision can result in a spectacular returns while an irrational investment decision can endanger the very survival of the firm.

Secondly, a capital expenditure decision has its effect over a long time span and inevitably affects the company's future cost structure.

Thirdly, capital expenditure decisions once made and implemented are not easily reversible without much financial loss.

Finally, It involves costs. Since most of the firms have scarce capital resources there is need for wise, thoughtful and correct investment decisions.

Advantages of Capital Expenditure Budget

Capital Expenditure Budget offer the following advantages :

(i) It highlights the capital development programmes and estimated capital expenditure during the budget period.

(ii) It provides a tool for controlling capital expenditure.

(iii) It enables the company to establish system of priorities in expenditure.

(iv) It provides some of the fixed-asset figures that will be required for the forecast Balance Sheet.

9. Zero Base Budgeting

Definition

Zero Base Budgeting is an operating planning and budgeting process which requires each manager to justify his entire budget requests in detail from scratch. Each manager has to justify why he should spend any money at all. This approach requires that all activities be identified as decision on packages which would be evaluated by a systematic analysis and ranked in order of importance.

Leonard Merewit has defined ZBB as a *"technique which complements and links the existing planning, budgeting and review process. It identifies alternatives and efficient methods of utgilizing limited resources in effective attainment of selected benefits. It is a flexible management approach which provides a credible rationale for re-allocating resources by focussing on a systematic review and justification of the funding and performance levels of current programmes or activities"*.

Devid Heminger has also explained ZBB as *"a management tool which provides a systematic method for evaluating all operations and programme, current or new, allows for budget reductions and expansions in a rational manner and allows re-allocation of resources from low to high priority programmes"*.

The above definition of ZBB suggests to examine a programme or function or responsibility from 'scratch'. The evaluator proceeds on the assumption that nothing is to be allowed simply since it was being done previously. The manager proposing the activity has to justify that the activity is essential and the outlay proposed is reasonable and rational in the present circumstance.

The ZBB technique suggests that an organization should not only make decisions about the proposed new programmes but it should also, from time to time, review the 'utility' and appropriateness of the existing programmes.

Stages of Zero Base Budgeting

1. Corporate objectives should be established and laid down in detail.
2. Each separate activity of the organization is identified and called decision package. A decision package is a document that identifies each activity and describes it in such a fashion so that management can (i) evaluate it and rank it against other activities competing for limited and scarce resources, and (ii) decide to approve or disapprove it.
3. Budget staff will compile operating expenses for packages approved by the departmental head.

Advantages of Zero Base Budgeting

Zero Base Budgeting has some distinct advantages, some of them are outlined below :

(i) The proposals for funds are strictly considered on merit basis and funds are allocated on the basis of priority.

(ii) This technique motivates managers to evolve cost effective ways of performing jobs. New ideas also emerge.

(iii) Obsolete operations and wastages are identified and eliminated.

(iv) Decision packages improve coordination within the firm and strengthen communication between different departments.

(v) Managers become aware of the value of inputs helping them to identify priorities.

(vi) Zero Base Budgeting is particularly useful in areas like service departments where it is often difficult to identify and quantity output.

(vii) ZBB aims at motivating the staff to take greater interest in the job because it involves staff in decision taking process.

(viii) ZBB is useful especially for service departments where it may be difficult to identify output.

Disadvantages of Zero Base Budgeting

(i) It is very expensive because the costs involved in preparing a vast number of decision packages in a large firm are very high.

(ii) Since more managers are involved in this process administration and communication of ZBB process may turn complicated.

(iii) Managers develop fear and feel threatened by ZBB and, therefore, may oppose new ideas and changes.

(iv) It involves a large amount of paper work and is very time consuming.

(v) The ranking of decision packages and allocation of resources is subjective to a certain degree that may lead to departmental conflict.

10. Performance Budget

Traditional budgeting does not provide a link between inputs in financial terms and output in physical terms. The term 'Performance Budget' was originally used in U.S.A. by the first Hoover Commission in 1949 when it recommended the adoption of a budget based on functions, programmes and activities.

Definition

A performance budget is a work plan which expresses for achievement in respect of various responsibility levels based on accepted norms and standards.

The National Institute of Bank Management, Mumbai has defined the performance budgeting technique as ***'the process of analysing identifying, simplifying and crystallising specific performance objectives of a job to be achieved over a period, within the frame work of organisational objectives, the purposes and objectives of the job. The technique is characterised by its specific direction towards the business objectives of the organisation".***

The above definition lays stress on the achievement of specific goals over a period of time.

The technique of performance budgeting calls for preparation of periodic performance reports which compare budget and actual performance to locate existing variances. Their preparation is greatly facilitated if the authority and responsibility for the incurrence of each cost element is clearly defined within the firm's organisational structure.

11. Responsibility Accounting

Responsibility Accounting is also known as Activity Accounting or Profitability Accounting. Responsibility Accounting is the root of zero base Budgeting and performance budgeting. Responsibility centres have their root in what is called responsibility accounting.

According to ***Charles T Horngren***, *"responsibility accounting is a system of accounting that recognises various responsibility centres throughout the organization and that reflects the plan of action of each of these centres by allocating particular revenue and costs to the one having the pertinent responsibility".*

It is widely considered as a part of Management Accounting and it can be explained as a system of collecting and reporting accounting information in terms of responsibility centres.

Pre-requisites of Responsibility Accounting

The following are the pre-requisites of Responsibility Accounting.

(i) The organisation should be divided into suitable responsibility centres.

(ii) Area of responsibility and authority of each centre should be well defined.

(iii) Each manager should know as what is expected of him. He should know the objectives and goals, he has to achieve.

(iv) The performance report of a centre should contain only the revenues, expenses, profits and investments controllable by the manager of that centre.

(v) Performance report of each centre should highlight the variances and items that require management's attention.

Steps in Responsibility Accounting

To make responsibility accounting effective and efficient, the following steps are suggested :

(i) Targets are set and should be communicated to each manager or executive.

(ii) A continuous appraisal of actual performance is to be made and actual results are to be conveyed to each manager of concerned responsibility centre.

(iii) The variances are to be reported to the higher management together with the names of managers of responsibility centres.

(iv) The corrective measures are to be suggested or taken and communicated to the concerned manager of each responsibility centre.

Responsibility Centres

Responsibility Accounting is a system of control that focuses attention on the responsibility centres. There are four types of responsibility centres that can be established in an organisation.

They are :

(i) Expenses centre.

(ii) Revenue centre.

(iii) Profit centre.

(iv) Investment centre.

Limitations of Responsibility Accounting

Like other management tools, responsibility accounting suffers from some limitations. Some of the limitations are stated below :

(i) It is practically difficult to design an organisation chart which might delineates lines of responsibility and grant authority required for responsibility assigned.

(ii) There is likely to be a conflict between individual interest and organisation interest leading to serious problems for implementation of policies.

(iii) A lot of passive resistance may be faced as a result of which basic objectives of the organisation may be lost.

(iv) This system ignores the personal reactions of the personnel involved in the process of implementation.

(v) There must exist a good reporting system without which the tool becomes useless and meaningless.

12. Sales Budget

Sales Budget is one of the functional budgets. Since sales forecast is the starting point of budgeting, sales budget assumes primary importance. The sales budget represents the total sales in physical quantities and values for a future budget period. Here the quantity that can be sold is the key factor for many business undertakings.

The purpose of sales budget is not to estimate or guess what the actual sales will be, but rather to develop a plan with clearly defined objectives towards which operational efforts are directed.

Factors to be considered for preparing the Sales Budget

The following factors are to be reckoned for preparing the sales budget.

(a) Reports of the salesmen who have the first hand information about the present market conditions for the product.

(b) General economic and political conditions are to seriously studied.

(c) Relative product profitability.

(d) Pricing policies.

(e) Market Research studies providing information like changes in fashion, tastes, consumers' preference, purchasing power of the consumers, and competitions' activities etc.

(f) Seasonal and cyclical variations.

(g) Advertising and sales promotion and their impact on the product market.

(h) Production capacity of the plant etc.

The Format of a Sales Budget

	Last Year		Budget Year		Northern Region		Southern Region		Central Region	
	Qnt.	*Value*	*Qnt.*	*Value*	*Qnt.*	*Value*	*Qnt.*	*Value*	*Qnt.*	*Value*
Product X										
1st Quarter										
2nd Quarter										
3rd Quarter										
4th Quarter										
Product Y										
Total										
General Total										

Example of Sales Budget

ABC Company

Sales Budget for the year ending March 2002

	Units	*Selling price per unit*	*Total*
		Rs.	Rs.
Product X	1,00,000	200	2,00,00,000
Product Y	50,000	250	1,25,00,000
			3,25,00,000

The Sales Budget may be prepared under the following classification or combination of classifications :

(a) Products or groups of products, (b) Areas, Towns, Salesmen, and Agents, (c) Types of customers like government, Export, Home Sales, Retail depots, (d) Period : months weeks etc.

Production Budget

A production budget incorporates the estimates of the total volume of production with the scheduling of operations by days, weeks and months. The production manager is responsible for the preparation of production budget. It is normally prepared in quantitative terms as units of output, tones of production. It is to be noted that sales budget should be used as basis for production estimates and forecasts.

Problem 1

The sales director of a manufacturing company reports that next year he expects to sole 50,000 units of a certain product.

The production manager consults the storekeeper and costs his figures as follows :

Two inside of raw materials A and B are required for manufacturing the product. Each unit of the product requires two units of A and three units of B.

The estimated opening balances at the commencement of the next year are :

Finished product 10,000 units : A 12,000 units; B 15,000 units. The desirable closing balances at the end of the year are :

Finished Product	14,000 units
A	13,000 units
B	16,000 "

Draw up a quantitative chart showing the Material Purchase Budget for the next year.

[C.U. M.Com.]

Solution

Production Budget

for the year ....

	Units	*Total*
Expected Sales	50,000	
Add : Closing Stock	14,000	
	64,000	
Less : Opening Stock	10,000	
Purchase Budget for the year		54,000

	Material A	*Material B*
	Units	*Units*
Consumption during the year	1,08,000	1,62,000
	(54,000 × 2)	(54,000 × 3)
Add : Desired stock at the end	13,000	16,000
	1,21,000	1,78,000
Less : Opening stock (Quantity to be purchased :	12,000	15,000
Quantity to be purchased	1,09,000	1,63,000

Problem 2

From the following particulars, prepare a production budget for the year 2001 assuming sales as limiting facts.

Product Group X	*Opening Stock*	*Budgeted Sales*
A	60,000	2,40,000
B	80,000	3,30,000
C	1,20,000	6,00,000
Product Group Y		
D	20,000	2,00,000
E	40,000	90,000

Stock of B and C is to be maintained at 20% above the existing level to sustain the budgeted sales. Stock level of A may be reduced by 10%. Stock of E is proposed to be raised by 40,000 units for export market not considered in sales budget given above.

Solution

Production Budget

(By product in units)

for the year ended 31st December 2001

	Product Group X			*Product Group Y*	
	A	B	C	D	E
Units required to meet sales budget	2,40,000	3,30,000	6,00,000	2,00,000	90,000
Add : Closing stock of finished goods	54,000	96,000	1,44,000	20,000	80,000
Total	2,94,000	4,26,000	7,44,000	2,20,000	1,70,000
Less : Opening Inventory of finished goods	60,000	80,000	1,20,000	20,000	40,000
Planned production Units	2,34,000	3,46,000	6,24,000	2,00,000	1,30,000

Problem 3

The following are the estimated sales of a company for eight months ending 30.11.1998 :

Months	Estimated Sales (units)
April, 1998	12,000
May, 1998	13,000
June, 1998	9,000
July, 1998	8,000
August, 1998	10,000
September, 1998	12,000
October, 1998	14,000
November, 1998	12,000

As a matter of policy, the company maintains the closing balance of finished goods and raw materials as follows :

Stock item	*Closing balance of a month*
Finished goods	50% of the estimated sales for the next month
Raw materials	5 estimated consumption for the next month

Every unit of production requires 2 kg. of raw materials costing Rs. 5 per kg.

Prepare Production Budget (in units) and Raw material purchase Budget (in units and cost) of the company for the half year ending 30th September 1998.

[Adapted—I.C.W.A. (Inter)]

Solution

Production Budget (in units)
for the half year ending 30th September 1998

Months	*Sale (in units) 50% of estimated for the next month sales*	*Closing Balance*	*Opening Balance*	*Production*
April 98	12,000	6,500	6,000	12,500
May, 98	13,000	5,400	6,500	11,000
June, 98	9,000	4,000	4,500	8,500
July, 1998	8,000	5,000	4,000	9,000
August 1998	10,000	6,000	5,00	11,000
September, 1998	12,000	7,000	6,000	13,000
				65,000

Purchase Budget (in cost and units)
for the year ended 30th Sept. 1998

	Consumption 2 kg. per unit	*Closing Balance*	*Opening Balance*	*Purchase in kg.*	*Rate (Rs.)*	*Amount (Rs.)*
April '98	25,000	22,000	25,000	22,000	5	1,10,000
May, '98	22,000	17,000	22,000	17,000	5	85,000
June '98	17,000	18,000	17,000	18,000	5	90,000
July '98	18,000	22,000	18,000	22,000	5	1,10,000
August '98	22,000	26,000	22,000	26,000	5	1,30,000
	26,000	26,000	26,000	26,000	5	1,30,000
	1,30,000					6,55,000

13. Cash Budget

The Cash Budget is one of the most important budgets to be prepared. It represents the cash requirements of the business during the budget period. It contains detailed estimates of cash receipts (cash inflows) and disbursements (cash outflows) either for the budget period or some other specific period. It is a useful tool in cash management of organisations as it reveals potential cash shortages as well as potential excess cash.

Objectives of Cash Budget

Cash budget is prepared with the following objectives :

(i) It indicates the cash availability for taking advantage of cash discount.

(ii) It indicates the cash requirement needed for capital expenditure for business expansion.

(iii) It determines the amount of loan to be taken from banks to manage working capital for a short period.

(iv) It shows the availability of excess funds for short-term investments to increase income of the organisation.

(v) Cash Budget helps the management in planning the financial requirements of bond redemption, payments to pension and retirement funds.

(vi) Efficient cash management is possible if cash budget is prepared.

Cash budgets help management to avoid having unnecessary idle cash on the one hand, and unnecessary 'nerve-racking' cash deficiencies, on the other.

Methods of Preparing Cash Budget

There are three recognised ways of preparing a cash budget.

1. The receipts and payments method.
2. The adjusted profit and loss method.
3. The Balance Sheet Method.

1. The Receipt and Payments Method

Under this method all anticipated cash receipts are carefully forecasted from a particular period. Cash receipts from the following sources are estimated :

(i) Cash sales; (ii) cash receipts from Debtors; (iii) dividends; (iv) interest on investments, (v) proceeds from sale of assets; (vi) royalties etc.

Cash disbursements required for the period are considered.

Cash disbursements consist :

(i) Cash purchases of raw materials;

(ii) Cash payments to creditors. This depends on credit terms extended by suppliers;

(iii) Payments for wages, salaries to staff, commission.

(iv) Payments for other factory office and administrative and selling and distribution overheads.

(v) Other disbursements including payments for fixed assets, short-term and long-term investments. Incase, there is an excess cash after meeting all obligations loans may be repaid.

Problem 4

From the following information, prepare a cash Budget for the months of January, 2003 to April 2003.

2003	*Expected Sales* Rs.	*Expected Purchase* Rs.
January	1,20,000	96,000
February	1,40,000	1,30,000
March	1,00,000	1,20,000
April	1,80,000	1,80,000

Wages to be paid to workers Rs. 10,000 each month. Balance at Bank on 1.1.2003 was Rs. 2,000.

It has been decided by the management that :

1. In the case of cash deficit within the limit of Rs. 10,000, arrangement can be made with bank.
2. Deficit of fund exceeding Rs. 10,000 but not exceeding Rs. 50,000 can be met by issuing 12% debentures.
3. In the case of deficit of fund exceeding Rs. 50,000, issue of shares is preferred (it is within the limit of Authorised Capital).

Solution

Cash Budget for the months of Jan. to March 2003

	Particulars	January Rs.	February Rs.	March Rs.	April Rs.
A.	Balance	20,000	24,000	14,000	Nil
B.	**Receipts**				
	Sales	1,20,000	1,40,000	1,00,000	1,80,000
	Issue of 12% Deb.			26,000	20,000
		1,40,000	1,64,000	1,40,000	2,00,000
C.	**Disbursements**				
	Purchase	96,000	1,30,000	1,20,000	1,80,000
	Wages	20,000	20,000	20,000	20,000
	Total	1,16,000	1,50,000	1,40,000	2,00,000
D.	Balance	24,000	14,000		
		1,40,000	1,64,000	Nil	Nil

2. Adjusted Profit and Loss Method

This method is termed as the **Cash Flow Statement** because it converts the profit and loss account into a cash forecast. This method is particularly useful for long-term forecasting, say, for a period of four or five years.

Preparation of cash budget under this method needs the following information :

(a) Expected cash balance at the beginning of the period.

(b) Net profit forecast for the period.

(c) Changes in working capital.

(d) Capital expenditure and sales of plant and machinery.

(e) Capital receipts

(f) Dividends.

In preparing the cash forecast one has to proceed with the budgeted profit for the period, then to adjust the figures for non-cash items already debited to Profit and Loss Account, changes in working capital, capital receipts and payments of dividends and tax.

A format of cash statement under this method is given below for clear understanding.

Cash Forecast for the Four Years 200X – 200X.

	Year 1 Rs.	Year 2 Rs.	Year 3 Rs.	Year 4 Rs.
Balance b/d				
(Opening cash and bank balance)				
Additions to cash				
(i) Budgeted Net Profit				
(ii) Depreciation written-off				
(iii) Intangible assets written-off.				
(iv) Provisions				
(v) Loss on sales of fixed assets				
(vi) Accrued expenses				
(vii) Reduction in current assets :				
(a) Stock				
(b) Sundry Debtors				
(c) Bills Receivables				
(viii) Increase in Current Liabilities				
(ix) Issue of Equity Shares				
(x) Long-term Loans				
(xi) Issue of Debentures				
A. Total Cash Inflow or Total Cash available				
Deductions				
Cash outflow :				
(i) Payment of dividend				
(ii) Increase in current assets :				
(a) Stock				
(b) Debtors				
(c) Inventories				
(d) Bills Receivable				
(iii) Decrease in current liabilities				
(a) Bills Payable				
(b) Sundry creditors				
(c) Outstanding Expenses				
B. Total Deductions				
Loan/Bank overdraft	XXX	XXX	XXX	XXX
Balance c/d	XXX	XXX	XXX	XXX

Preparation of cash budget under this method will relatively be easy if a budgeted profit and loss account and budgeted balance sheet are available for each budget period. Most of the items shown can be ascertained by comparing balances shown in the Balance Sheet of one year with those of the succeeding years.

Problem 5

Forecast Balance Sheet
as at 31st March 200X

	Rs.		Current Period Rs.	Rs.
Equity shares capital	35,00,000	Land and Buildings	17,50,000	
Reserves	3,50,000	*Less* : Depreciation	1,75,000	
Profit and Loss Account	5,60,000			15,75,000
10% Debentures	3,50,000	Plant and Machinery	28,00,000	
Creditors	2,10,000	*Less* : Depreciation	5,60,000	
Dividend Proposed	1,40,000			22,40,000
Accrued Expenses	30,000	Motor Vehicles	5,60,000	
		Less : Depreciation	1,40,000	
				4,20,000
		Stock :		
		Raw materials	1,75,000	
		Work-in-progress	1,05,000	
		Finished goods	70,000	
				3,50,000
		Debtors		3,15,000
		Bank		2,40,000
	51,40,000			51,40,000

Forecast Profit and Loss Account
for the year ended 31st March 200X

	Rs.	Rs.		Current Period Rs.
To Administrative Overheads			By Gross profit b/d	10,50,000
Salaries	1,70,000		" Interest received	26,200
Misc. Expenses	53,000		" Discount received	50,800
Rent and Rates	19,000	2,42,000		
To Selling Overheads :				
Salaries	90,000			
Expenses	40,000			
Delivery van	50,000			
Advertising	1,38,000			
Carriage	32,000			
		3,50,000		
		5,92,000		11,27,000

Contd.

B.F.		5,92,000		11,27,000
To Financial Expenses				
Interest on Debentures	35,500			
Audit fees	15,000			
Discount Allowed	32,300			
		82,800		
To Net profit c/d		4,52,200		
		11,27,000		11,27,000
To Dividend		2,80,000	By Balance b/d	5,60,000
" Balance c/d		7,32,200	" Net profit b/d	4,52,200
		10,12,200		10,12,200

Forecast Balance Sheet
as at 31st March 200X

			Current Period	
	Rs.		Rs.	Rs.
Issue shares capital	38,50,000	Land and Buildings	17,50,000	
Reserves	3,50,000	*Less* : Depreciation	2,10,000	
Profit kand Loss appropriation	7,32,200			15,40,000
10% Debentures	5,25,000	Plant and Machinery	35,00,000	
Creditors	2,45,000	*Less* : Depreciation	8,40,000	
Accrued Expenses	31,500			26,60,000
		Motor Vehicles	7,00,000	
		Less : Depreciation	2,80,000	
				4,20,000
		Stocks :		
		Raw Material	1,54,000	
		Work-in-progress	1,26,000	
		Finished goods	98,000	
				3,78,000
		Debtors		2,80,000
		Bank		4,55,700
	57,33,700			57,33,700

Solution

Cash Budget (Cash Flow Method)

			Period ....
	Rs.	Rs.	Rs.
Cash Balance			2,40,000
Additions to Cash			
Net Profit as per			
Profit and Loss Account		4,52,200	

Contd.

B. F.		4,52,200	2,40,000
Add : Depreciation :			
Land & Buildings	35,000		
Plant & Machinery	2,80,000		
Plant Vehicles	1,40,000		
		4,55,000	
Accrued Expenses		1,500	
Decrease in Current Assets			
Raw Materials		21,000	
Sundry Debtors		35,000	
Issue of Equity Shares (38,50,000 – 35,00,000)		3,50,000	
Issue of 10% Debentures		1,75,000	
Increase in Current Liabilities			
Creditors (2,45,000 – 2,10,000)		35,000	
			15,24,700
Cash Available			17,64,700
Cash Outflow :			
Dividend paid for last year (assumed)		1,40,000	
Dividend paid (current)		2,80,000	
Purchases :			
Plant and Machinery		7,00,000	
Motor vehicles		1,40,000	
Increase in Current Assets			
Work-in-progress		21,000	
Finished goods		28,000	13,09,000
			4,55,700

3. Balance Sheet Method

Under this method a budgeted Balance Sheet is prepared for the next period showing all items except cash and bank balance. The two sides of the Balance Sheet are then balanced, and the balancing figure is considered as cash.

If the assets side is larger than the liabilities side, this would reveal a bank overdraft; if the liabilities side is larger this will signify a balance at the bank.

Example

If we follow the Balance Sheet of the previous problem, the total of the liabilities side is Rs. 57,33,700.

	Rs.	Rs.
Therefore, Total of liabilities side		57,33,700
Less : Fixed Assets		
(i) Land and Building	15,40,000	
(ii) Plant and Machinery	26,60,000	
(iii) Motor vehicles	4,20,000	46,20,000
		11,13,700
Less : Current Assets (excluding cash)		
(i) Stock	3,78,000	
(ii) Debtors	2,80,000	6,58,000
Bank balance (balancing figure)		4,55,700

14. Flexible Budget

Before discussing flexible budget it seems to be appropriate to highlight upon fixed budget. According to **ICMA, London,** *"a fixed budget is a budget designed to remain unchanged irrespective of level of activity actually attained"*. Thus, a budget prepared for fixed level of activity is known as fixed budget.

In fixed budgetary control, the budgets prepared are based on one level of output, a level which has been carefully planned. In fact, fixed budget presents expected sales revenue, costs and profits or losses for a definite level of activity, a level which has carefully been planned to equate sales and production at the most profitable rate. Significantly, targets of fixed budget do not change with the changes of level of activity.

It is true, in some companies it becomes extremely difficult to forecast sales with even a reasonable chance of success. This situation may arise in case of following companies :

(i) companies that are greatly affected by weather condition, e.g., the soft drink industry;
(ii) which frequently introduce new products, e.g. the food camping industry;
(iii) companies in which production is carried out only when order is received, e.g. shipbuilding industry;
(iv) companies that are affected by changes in fashion;
(v) where large output is intended for export, e.g. production of consumers' goods.

Definition of Flexible Budget

The I.C.M.A. defines flexible budget as, *"budget which is designed to change in accordance with the level of activity actually attained"*.

The flexible budget (also called variable budget) is based on knowledge of cost behaviour pattern. It is prepared for a range, rather than a single level of activity. It is essentially a set of budgets that can be tailored to any level of activity. Ideally, the flexible budget is compiled after obtaining a detailed analysis of how each cost is affected by changes in activity.

In fixed budgetary control, the budget is prepared on the basis of one level of output, a level which has been carefully planned to equate sales and production at the most profitable rate. But if the level of output actually achieved differs considerably from that budgeted, large variances will arise. In some companies it seems extremely difficult to forecast sales with even a reasonable chance of success.

This situation may arise in case of the following companies :

(i) companies greatly affected by weather conditions, e.g. there is a great demand of cold drinks while demand falls during winter;
(ii) companies that introduce frequently new products, e.g. food canning industry;
(iii) in which production is carried on only after receiving order;
(iv) companies affected by change of fashion, e.g. millinery trade;
(v) where a large part of the output is intended for export, e.g. air conditioning equipment.

Flexible budgetary control has been developed with the objectives of changing the budget figures progressively to correspond with the actual output achieved. Some companies operate flexible budgets in conjunction with a fixed budget.

The preparation of flexible budgets necessitates the analysis of all overheads into *fixed, variable and semi-variable costs.* This analysis is very much significant in preparing flexible budget because varying levels of output need to be considered and they will have a different effect on each class of overhead.

Significance of Flexible Budgeting

The following advantages can be derived from flexible budgeting :

(i) it presents a detailed picture of output, costs, sales and profit for varying levels of business operations which makes the marginal analysis more practicable and feasible;

(ii) flexible budget is an indispensable tool for achieving *cost reduction* and *cost control;*

(iii) flexible budget is useful to forecast for varying level of operations;

(iv) it makes possible the comparison of actual performance and budgeted one for actual level of operation in a very easy and understandable way.

Operational Areas of Flexible Budget

Preparation of flexible budget is needed in the following cases :

(i) Where the business is subject to the vagaries of nature like agro-based industries, soft drinks, woolen industries etc.

(ii) Where the demand for the product depends upon customers' tastes and fashion like cotton textile and garment industries.

(iii) Where production is carried out only after receiving the customer's orders.

(iv) Where business depends heavily on export markets.

(v) Where sales are impredictable due to typical nature of business and influence of external factors e.g. luxury goods.

(vi) Where customer's reaction towards a new product is almost impossible to foresee and predict.

Problem 6

The following are the data of ABC Company for the month of June 2003. The Company is working at the capacity of 80%. It produces 8,000 units. The details are as follows :

	Rs.
Sales	1,92,000
Variable Cost	
Direct material	24,000
Direct labour	64,000
Idle time	3,200
Other indirect labour	800
Semi-variable Costs	
Plant maintenance (25% fixed)	31,000
Sales men's salaries (20% fixed)	18,800
Fixed Costs	45,000

You are required to calculate profit at 70% and 90% capacities.

Solution

ABC Company
Flexible Budget
for the month ended June 30, 2003

		Level of Activity		
		70%	80%	90%
		Rs.	Rs.	Rs.
Units		7,000	8,000	9,000
Sales		1,68,000	1,92,000	2,16,000
Variable Costs :				
Direct material	@ Rs. 3 per unit	21,000	24,000	27,000
Direct Labour	@ Rs. 8 per unit	56,000	64,000	72,000
Idle time	@ Re. 0.40	2,800	3,200	3,600
Other indirect labour	@ Re. 0.10	700	800	900
Variable Manufacturing Costs		80,500	92,000	1,03,500
Semi-variable Expenses :				
Plant Maintenance (25% fixed)		7,000	7,000	7,000
Variable	@ Rs. 3 per unit	21,000	24,000	27,000
Salesmen's Salaries (20% fixed)		2,800	2,800	2,800
(80% variable) @ Rs. 2 per unit		14,000	16,000	18,000
		1,25,300	1,41,800	1,58,300
Fixed Costs		45,000	45,000	45,000
Total Cost		1,70,300	1,86,800	2,03,300
Profit or Loss		(2,300)	5,200	12,700
		1,68,000	1,92,000	2,16,000

Difference between Fixed Budget and Flexible Budget

Fixed Budget	*Flexible Budget*
1. Fixed budget does not change with actual volume of activity achieved.	It can be recasted on the basis of activity level to be achieved. Therefore, it is not rigid but flexible in nature.
2. It operates on one level of activity and under one set of conditions. It assumes that there will be no change in the prevailing conditions. Such assumptions are obviously unrealistic.	It consists of various budgets for different levels of activity.
3. In this type of budget since all costs like fixed, variable and semi-variable are related to one level of activity, variance analysis fails to communicate useful information as a result of which decision making becomes difficult.	In flexible budget variance analysis provides useful information as each cost is analysed according to its behaviour.

Contd.

Fixed Budget	*Flexible Budget*
4. If the budgeted and actual activity levels differ significantly, then cost asscertainment and price fixation becomes difficult and fails to paint a clear picture.	Flexible budgeting at different levels of activity facilitates the ascertainment of cost, fixation of selling price and tendering of quotations.
5. When there is a difference between the two levels of activities comparison of actual performance with budgeted target becomes meaningless.	Flexible budget provides a meaningful basis of comparison of the actual performance with the budgeted targets as budgets for different level of activities are prepared taking into consideration of fixed, variable and semi-variable costs.

WORKED OUT PROBLEMS

Problem 7

Prepare a flexible budget for production at 80% and 100% activity on the basis of the following information :

Production at 50% capacity 10,000 units

Raw materials Rs. 100 per unit

Direct labour Rs. 50 per unit

Expenses Rs. 20 per unit

Factory expenses Rs. 1,00,000 (60% fixed)

Administration expenses 60,000 (50% variable)

Solution

Flexible Budget for Production

at 80% and 100% activity

	50% 10,000 units		80% 16,000 units		100% 20,000 units	
	Per unit	*Amount*	*Per unit*	*Amount*	*Per unit*	*Amount*
	Rs.	Rs.	Rs.	Rs.	Rs.	Rs.
1. Raw materials	100	10,00,000	100	16,00,000	100	20,00,000
2. Direct Labour	50	5,00,000	50	8,00,000	50	10,00,000
3. Expenses	20	2,00,000	20	3,20,000	20	4,00,000
Prime Cost	170	17,00,000	170.00	27,20,000	170	34,00,000
4. *Add* : Factory Expenses Fixed	6.00	60,000	3.75	60,000	3	60,000
Variable $\frac{40,000}{10,000}$ = Rs. 4.00	4.00	40,000	4.00	64,000	4	80,000
Works Cost	180.00	18,00,000	177.75	28,44,000	177.00	35,40,000
Add : Administration expenses (fixed)	3.00	30,000	1.875	30,000	1.50	30,000
	3.00	30,000	3.000	48,000	3.00	60,000
	186.00	18,60,000	182.625	29,22,000	181.5	36,30,000

Problem 8

Black and White Ltd. manufactures two products A and B. An estimate of the number of units expected to be sold in the first six months of 2003 is given below :

2003	Product A	Product B
January	2,000	4,000
February	2,400	3,800
March	2,500	3,600
April	3,000	3,200
May	3,200	3,000
June	3,600	2,800
July	3,600	2,400

It is anticipated that :

(i) there will be no work-in-progress at the end of any month;

(ii) finished units equal to 20% of the anticipated sales for the next month will be in stock at the end of each month including December 2002.

The budgeted production and production cost for the year ending 31.12.2003 are as follows :

	Product A	Product B
Production (in units)	40,000	45,000
(i) Direct material per unit (Rs.)	15	20
(ii) Direct wages	6	8
(iii) Works overhead cost apportionable in each type of production (in Rs.)	80,000	1,80,000

75% of overhead cost relates to production

You are required to prepare :

(a) a production budget showing the number of units to be manufactured each month.

(b) a summarised production cost budget for the 6 months period from January 2003 to June 2003.

Solution

Production Budget
for six months ending 30.6.2003

	Jan.	Feb.	March	April	May	June
Production A						
Sales	2,000	2,400	2,500	3,000	3,200	3,600
Add : Closing stock						
20% of next months sales	480	500	600	640	720	720
	2,480	2,900	3,100	3,640	3,920	4,320
Less : Opening stock	400	480	500	600	640	720
Total Production = 17,020 units	2,080	2,420	2,600	3,040	3,280	3,600
Product B						
Sales	4,000	3,800	3,600	3,200	3,000	2,800
Add : Closing stock						
20% of next months sales	760	720	640	600	560	480
	4,760	4,520	4,240	3,800	3,560	3,280
Less : Opening stock						
20% of same months sale	800	760	720	640	600	560
Total Production : 20,080 units	3,960	3,760	3,520	3,160	2,960	2,720

Production Cost Budget

for the six months ended 30.6.2003

		Product A		Product B	
Production : A 17,020 B 20,080		Cost per unit	Total	Cost per unit	Total
		Rs.	Rs.	Rs.	Rs.
1.	Direct Materials	15	2,55,300	20	4,01,600
2.	Direct wages	6	1,02,120	8	1,60,640
3.	Works Overhead				
	(80,000 ÷ 40,000)	2	34,040		
	(1,80,000 ÷ 45,000)			4	80,320
		23	3,91,460	32	6,42,560

Problem 9

A Single product company estimated its sales for the next quarterwise as under :

Quarters	Sales units
I	30,000
II	37,500
III	41,250
IV	45,000

The opening stock of finished goods is 10,000 units and the company expects to maintain the closing stock of finished goods of 16,250 units at the end of the year. The production pattern in each quarter is based on 80% of the sales of the current quarter and 20% of the sales of the next quarter.

The opening stock of raw materials in the beginning of the year is 10,000 kgs. and the closing stock at the end of the year is required to be maintained at 5,000 kgs. Each unit of finished output requires 2 kgs. of raw materials.

The company proposes to purchase the entire annual requirement of raw materials in the first three quarters in the proportion and at the prices given below :

Quarters	*Purchase of raw materials as a % to total annual requirement in quantity*	*Price per kg.*
		Rs.
I	30%	2
II	50%	3
III	20%	4

The value of the opening stock of raw materials in the beginning of the year is Rs. 20,000.

You are required to present the following for the next year quarterwise.

(i) Production budget in units,

(ii) Raw material consumption budget in quantity.

(iii) Raw material purchase budget in quantity and value.

(iv) Price store Ledger card of raw materials using FIFO method.

[Adapted—C.A. (Inter)]

Solution

Total Annual Production (in units)

Sales in 4 quarters

	I	30,000	
	II	37,500	
	III	41,250	
	IV	45,000	
			1,53,750
Add :	Closing balance		16,250
			1,70,000
Less :	Opening balance		10,000
			1,60,000

(i) **Production Budget** (in units)

	Quarters	I	II	III	IV	Total
		Units	Units	Units	Units	
	Sales	30,000	37,500	41,250	45,000	1,53,750
	Production in current quarter (30% of sales of current quarter)	24,000	30,000	33,000	36,000	
Add :	Production (20% of sales of next quarter)	7,500	8,250	9,000	12,250*	
		31,500	38,250	42,000	48,250**	1,60,000

* 1,60,000 – (31,500 + 38,250 + 42,000) = 48,250

** 48,250 – 36,000 = 12,250

(ii) **Raw Materials Consumption Budget in Quantity**

		Quarters				*Total*
		I	II	III	IV	
(a)	Units to be produced in each quarter	31,500	38,250	42,000	48,250	1,60,000
(b)	Raw materials consumption per unit (in kg)	2	2	2	2	
(c)	Total quantity of consumption of raw materials in kg (a × b)	63,000	76,500	84,000	96,500	3,20,000

(iii) **Raw Materials Purchase Budget in quantity**

	Raw materials required for production (in kg.)	3,20,000
Add :	Closing stock (kg.)	5,000
		3,25,000
Less :	Opening stock (kg.)	10,000
		3,15,000

Raw Materials Purchase Budget (in value)

Quarters		*Qnt. to be purchased* (kg.)	*Rate per kg.* Rs.	*Amount* Rs.
I	(30% of 3,15,000)	94,500	2	1,89,000
II	(50% of 3,15,000)	1,57,500	3	4,72,500
III	(20% of 3,15,000)	63,000	4	2,52,000
		3,15,000		9,13,500

(iv) **Store Ledger Card** **FIFO**

Date	*Receipts*			*Issues*			*Balance*		
	Qnt. kg.	*Rate* Rs.	*Amount* Rs.	*Qnt.* kg.	*Rate* Rs.	*Amount* Rs.	*Qnt.* kg.	*Rate* Rs.	*Amount* Rs.
Quarters							10,000	2	20,000
I	94,500	2	1,89,000	63,000	2	1,26,000	41,500	2	83,000
II	1,57,500	3	4,72,500	41,500	2	83,000			
				35,000	3	1,05,000	1,22,500	3	3,67,500
III	63,000	4	2,52,000	84,000	3	2,52,000	38,500	3	1,15,500
							63,000	4	2,52,000
IV				38,500	3	1,15,500			
				58,000	4	2,32,000	5,000	4	20,000

CASH BUDGET

Problem 10

From the following information available from a company, prepare Cash Budget (monthly) for April, May and June, 2003 :

(i)

Months (2003)	Sales Rs.	Purchases Rs.	Wages Rs.	Expenses Rs.
January (Actuals)	90,000	50,000	30,000	5,000
February (")	80,000	50,000	24,000	4,000
March (")	80,000	45,000	22,000	6,000
April (Budgeted)	85,000	48,000	25,000	7,000
May (")	75,000	42,000	20,000	6,000
June (")	78,000	44,000	23,000	5,000

(ii) 10% of the purchases and 20% of the sales are for cash.

(iii) Credit allowed to Debtors 1/2 month and credit received from creditors 1 month.

(iv) Wages are paid weekly.

(v) Opening cash balance is Rs. 15,000.

[Adapted—V.U., C.U. B.Com. (Hons.) 1998]

Solution

Cash Budget

for April, May and June 2003

Particulars		April Rs.	May Rs.	June Rs.
A.	**Receipts**			
	Cash in hand	15,000	21,450	25,800
	Cash sales (20%)	17,000	15,000	15,600
	Collection from Debtors	66,000	64,000	61,200
		98,000	1,00,450	1,02,600
B.	**Payments**			
	(a) Cash purchase (10%)	4,800	4,200	4,400
	(b) Payment to creditors for the last month	40,500	43,200	37,800
	(c) Wages $^1/_4$ of last month and $^3/_4$th of current month	24,250	21,250	22,250
	(d) Expenses (paid for the current month)	7,000	6,000	5,000
	(e) Cash in hand/overdraft	21,450	25,800	33,150
		98,000	1,00,450	1,02,600

Working Notes :

1. **Collecting from Debtors**

	March	April	May	June
Sales	80,000	85,000	75,000	78,000
Less : Cash sales 20%	16,000	17,000	15,000	15,600
Credit sales (80%)	64,000	68,000	60,000	62,400
50% for the previous month		32,000	34,000	30,000
50% for the current month		34,000	30,000	31,200
		66,000	64,000	61,200

Problem 11

From the following information prepare a cash budget for the quarter ending 30.6.2000 :

Months	Sales Rs.	Purchases Rs.	Wages Rs.	Misc. Expenses Rs.
February	1,20,000	84,000	10,000	7,000
March	1,30,000	1,00,000	12,000	8,000
April	80,000	1,04,000	8,000	6,000
May	1,16,000	1,06,000	10,000	12,000
June	88,000	80,000	8,000	6,000

Additional Information

(i) Cash on hand on 1.4.2000 Rs. 5,000.

(ii) Sales 20% realised in the month of sale discount allowed 2% balance realised after two months.

(iii) Purchases are paid one month after.

(iv) Wages—25% in arrears in the following month.

(v) Other expenses are paid at a lag of one month.

(vi) Income Tax Rs. 25,000 due on or before 30.6.2000.

[Adapted—C.U. B.Com. (Hons.) 2000]

Solution

Cash Budget for the quarter

ending 30th June, 2000

	April	May	June
	Rs.	Rs.	Rs.
Opening Balance	5,000	(320)	6,916
Add : Collection from Debtors	1,11,680	1,26,736	85,560
	1,16,680	1,26,416	92,476
Less : Payment to creditors	1,00,000	1,04,000	1,06,000
Wages	9,000	9,500	8,500
Other Expenses	8,000	6,000	12,000
Income Tax			25,000
Bank Overdraft/Cash in hand	(320)	6,916	(59,024)
	1,16,680	1,26,416	92,476

Working Notes :

1. Collection from Debtors

	April	May	June
	Rs.	Rs.	Rs.
20% of sales realised in the month of sales	16,000	23,200	22,000
Less : Discount	320	464	440
	15,680	22,736	21,560
Add : (i) 80% of sales 80% of Rs 1,20,000 (Feb.)	96,000		
(ii) 80% of Rs. 1,30,000 (March)		1,04,000	
(iii) 80% of Rs. 80,000			64,000
	1,11,680	1,26,736	85,560

Problem 12

From the following information of Moon Ltd. prepare a Cash Budget for the three months commencing on 1st June, 1990, when the bank balance was Rs. 10,000.

Months	Sales	Purchases	Wages	Selling Expenses	Overhead
	Rs.	Rs.	Rs.	Rs.	Rs.
April	1,00,000	70,000	85,000	3,500	4,000
May	1,20,000	80,000	9,500	3,500	4,500
June	1,40,000	90,000	9,500	3,500	6,000
July	1,60,000	1,00,000	12,000	3,500	6,500
August	1,80,000	1,10,000	14,000	3,500	7,000

A sale commission of 5% on sales 2 months after sales is payable in addition to the above selling expenses. Credit terms of sales are—payment by the end of the month following the month of supply.

On an average half of sales is paid on the due date, while the other half is paid during the next month.

Creditors are paid during the month following the month of supply. Plant purchased in June for Rs. 78,000 is payable on delivery Rs. 48,000 and the balance in two equal monthly instalments, in July and in August.

A dividend of Rs. 30,000 will be paid in September. Wages are paid 3/4th on due date while the other half is paid during the next month. Lag in payment of selling expenses and overheads is one month.

[C.U. B.Com. (Hons.)·1991]

Solution

Cash Budget of Moon Ltd.

for three months ending August 1990

	Particulars	June	July	August
		Rs.	Rs.	Rs.
	Receipts			
	Opening Balance	10,000	(27,500)	(25,775)
	Collection from Debtors	1,10,000	1,30,000	1,50,000
(A)	**Total Receipts**	1,20,000	1,02,500	1,24,225
(B)	**Payments**			
	Creditors (for last month)	80,000	90,000	1,00,000
	Plant purchased	48,000	15,000	15,000
	Wages :			
	$^3/_4$ of current month	7,125	9,000	10,500
	$^1/_4$ of previous month	2,375	2,375	3,000
	Selling expenses (last month)	3,500	3,500	3,500
	Overheads (for last month)	4,500	6,000	6,500
	Selling commission @ 20%			
	(on sales made two months back)	2,000	2,400	2,800
	Cash in hand/overdraft	(27,500)*	(25,775)	(17,075)
		1,20,000	1,02,500	1,24,225

* Overdraft amount has been put in bracket.

Problem 13

From the following particulars prepare a monthly Cash Budget for the quarter ended 31st March, 1998.

Months	Sales	Purchases	Wages	Expenses
	Rs.	Rs.	Rs.	Rs.
November	50,000	10,000	20,000	4,000
December	60,000	20,000	20,000	4,000
January	40,000	30,000	22,000	5,000
February	50,000	20,000	22,000	5,000
March	60,000	10,000	24,000	5,000

Additional Information

(a) 10% of sales and purchases are on cash, balance on credit.

(b) Credit to Debtors : One month, on an overage 50% of Debtors will make payment on due date while the rest will make payment one month thereafter.

(c) Credit from Creditors : 2 months 10% cash discount will be received if payment is made within one month and it is estimated that for 50% of purchases advantage of cash discount will be taken.

(d) Wages : To be paid twice in a month on the 1st and 16th respectively.

(e) Expenses are generally paid within the month.

(f) Plant costing Rs. 10,000 will be installed in February on payment of 25% of the cost in addition installation cost is Rs. 500. Balance amount is to be paid in three equal monthly instalments from the following month.

(g) Opening cash balance is Rs. 20,000.

[Adapted—C.U. M.Com.]

Solution

Cash Budget for the quarter
ended 31st March, 1998

	January Rs.	February Rs.	March Rs.
Receipts			
Cash Balance on 1.1.1998	20,000	31,900	28,750
Cash collected from Debtors Cash sales (10%)	4,000	5,000	6,000
Collection from Debtors (Note below)	49,500	45,000	40,500
	73,500	81,900	75,250
Payments			
Payment to creditors	12,600	21,150	21,600
Cash Purchase	3,000	2,000	1,000
Wages	21,000	22,000	23,000
Expenses	5,000	5,000	5,000
Plant		3,000	2,500
Cash in hand	31,900	28,750	22,150
	73,500	81,900	75,250

Working Notes :

		Nov.	Dec.	Jan.	Feb.	March
1.	Sales	50,000	60,000	40,000	50,000	60,000
Less :	Cash sales 10%	5,000	6,000	4,000	5,000	6,000
	Credit sales	45,000	54,000	36,000	45,000	54,000
	Collection from Debtors					
	50% for last month			22,500	27,000	18,000
	50% for month before last month			27,000	18,000	22,500
				49,500	45,000	40,500
	Purchases	10,000	20,000	30,000	20,000	10,000
Less :	Cash purchases (10%)	1,000	2,000	3,000	2,000	1,000
	Credit purchase	9,000	18,000	27,000	18,000	9,000

	January	February	March
	Rs.	Rs.	Rs.
Payment to creditors			
50% of previous month			
Less : Discount @ 10%	8,100	12,150	8,100
50% for two months back	4,500	9,000	13,500
	12,600	21,150	21,600

Problem 14

From the following particulars prepare monthly Cash Budget of the Sunclear Ltd. for October, November and December of 1996 :

Months	Purchases	Sales	Wages	Expenses
	Rs.	Rs.	Rs.	Rs.
July '96	40,000	60,000	8,000	10,000
August '96	60,000	80,000	10,500	12,000
September '96	50,000	70,000	17,500	12,500
October '96	70,000	90,000	17,100	11,600
November '96	80,000	1,00,000	12,000	11,800
December '96	60,000	1,20,000	12,000	12,300

(i) It is expected that 50% of sales will be in cash and 25% of the purchases can be made on credit.

(ii) Debtors are allowed 2 months credit but will receive 5% cash discount if they will pay off their dues within the month next to the month of sale. 80% of the Debtors normally clear their dues at the end of that period to avail the cash discount. Rest 20% of the debtors pay on the due date.

(iii) $^4/_5$ th of the credit purchases is paid after one month of that purchase and next to that month the balance $^1/_5$th is paid.

(iv) Wages are paid within 5th of the following month.

(v) Expenses include selling and distribution expenses which are 10% of the sales.

(vi) Any deficiency in cash at the end of a month will be met by taking short-term loan for two months from bank.

(vii) At the end of September, 1996 Sunclear Ltd. had Rs. 40,000 cash in hand.

[Adapted—C.U. B.Com. (Hons.) 1997]

Solution

Cash Budget

for the period from October to December 1996

	October 96	*November 96*	*December 96*
	Rs.	Rs.	Rs.
Receipts:			
Cash in hand	40,000	25,000	10,800
Cash sales 50% of sales	45,000	50,000	60,000
Collection from Debtors (as per note I)	34,600	41,200	47,000
	1,19,600	1,16,200	1,17,800

Payments :			
Cash purchases	52,500	60,000	45,000
Payment to creditors (Note 2)	13,000	16,500	19,500
Wages	17,500	17,100	12,000
Expenses	2,600	1,800	300
Selling and Distribution expenses	9,000	10,000	12,000
Cash in hand	25,000	10,800	29,000
	1,19,600	1,16,200	1,17,800

Working Notes :

	October	November	December
1. Collection from Debtors			
80% of Rs. 35,000	28,000	80% of Rs. 45,000 36,000	80% of Rs. 50,000 = 40,000
Less : Cash discount @ 5%	1,400	1,800	2,000
	26,600	34,200	38,000
Add : 20% of 50% of Rs. 80,000	8,000	(20% of 35,000) Rs. 7,000	(20% of Rs. 45,000) = 9,000
	34,600	41,200	47,000
2. Payment to creditors			
$^4/_5$ × Rs. 12,500	10,000	$^4/_5$ × Rs. 17,500 = 14,000	$^4/_5$ × 20,000 16,000
$^1/_5$ × Rs. 15,000	3,000	$^1/_5$ × 12,500 = 2,500	$^1/_5$ × 17,500 = 3,500
	13,000	16,500	19,500

Problem 15

A Ltd. has just established a small manufacturing unit to manufacture a new product which is expected to have a high margin. The company has made the following estimates of production, sales and costs :

(a) **Production and sales (in units)**

Months	*Production*	*Sales*
April 2000	2,000	—
May	3,000	—
June	4,000	1,000
July	5,000	2,000
August	5,000	4,000
September	5,000	5,000

Note : Both production and sales will stabilize at 5,000 units from September onwards.

(b) *Selling price and cost*

	Selling price per unit		Rs. 50
Less :	*Variable costs* :	Rs.	
	Materials	12	
	Labour	5	
	Overheads	5	22
	Contribution per unit		28

Note : Fixed costs are expected to be Rs. 10,000 per month.

The following additional information is also given :

(i) An initial stock of materials to meet three months requirements will be purchased during April, 2000. Further purchases will be made at the beginning of each month to have sufficient stock of materials for 3 months.

(ii) Suppliers of materials have agreed to give one month's credit.

(iii) Labour is to be paid half a month in arrears.

(iv) Variable overheads will be paid during the month following the month in which it is incurred.

(v) Fixed overheads will be incurred in advance at the beginning of every quarter.

(vi) Sales will be 50% cash and the balance will be on two months credit.

(vii) There will be an opening cash balance of Rs. 3,00,000 (in hand and bank).

Prepare a cash budget for A Ltd. for the six months ending 30th September 2000. Figures should be given monthly and the months, if any, during which additional funds are required should be clearly indicated.

[I.C.W.A. (Inter) December 2000]

Solution

Cash Budget

for the half-year ending 30th September 2000

Months	*April* Rs.	*May* Rs.	*June* Rs.	*July* Rs.	*August* Rs.	*September* Rs.
Opening Balance	3,00,000	2,65,000	1,34,500	67,000	(–)15,500	(–) 500
Receipts						
Cash Sales	—	—	25,000	50,000	1,00,000	1,25,000
Collection from Debtors	—	—	—	—	25,000	50,000
(A) Total Receipts	3,00,000	2,65,000	1,59,500	1,17,000	1,09,500	1,74,500
Payments						
Payments for purchases	—	1,08,000	60,000	60,000	60,000	60,000
Wages	5,000	12,500	17,500	22,500	25,000	25,000
Variable overhead	—	10,000	15,000	20,000	25,000	25,000
Fixed overhead	30,000	—	—	30,000	—	—
Total Payment	35,000	1,30,500	92,500	1,32,500	1,10,000	1,10,000
Balance in hand (A – B)	2,65,000	1,34,500	67,000	(–) 15,500	(–) 500	64,500
	3,00,000	2,65,000	1,59,500	1,17,000	1,09,500	1,74,500

Working Notes :

1. ***Calculation of purchases (in units and rupees) and payments.***

Months	*Opening balance units*	*Purchase units*	*Production units*	*Closing balance units*	*Purchase (in rupees)*	*Payments to creditors*
April 2000	—	9,000	2,000	7,000	1,08,000	—
May 2000	7,000	5,000	3,000	9,000	60,000	1,08,000
June 2000	9,000	5,000	4,000	10,000	60,000	60,000
July 2000	10,000	5,000	5,000	10,000	60,000	60,000
August	10,000	5,000	5,000	10,000	60,000	60,000
September	10,000	5,000	5,000	10,000	60,000	60,000

2. ***Collection from Debtors***

	Units sold	*Cash sales* Rs.	*Collection from Debtors* Rs.
April	—	—	—
May	—	—	—
June	1,000	25,000 (50% of 50,000)	—
July	2,000	50,000 (50% of Rs. 1,00,000	—
August	4,000	1,00,000 (50% of Rs. 2,00,000)	25,000
Sept.	5,000	1,25,000 (50% of Rs. 2,50,000)	50,000

3. ***Labour and Overhead***

	Wages due	*Wages paid*	*Variable overhead*	*Variable Overhead paid*
April	10,000	5,000	10,000	—
May	15,000	12,500	15,000	10,000
June	20,000	17,500	20,000	15,000
July	25,000	22,500	25,000	20,000
August	25,000	25,000	25,000	25,000
September	25,000	25,000	25,000	25,000

Problem 16

Prepare cash budget for Jan.-June from the following information :

(i) *The estimated sales and expenses are as follows :*

	Nov. Rs.	Dec. Rs.	Jan. Rs.	Feb. Rs.	Mar. Rs.	Apr. Rs.	May Rs.	June Rs.
Sales	2,00,000	2,20,000	1,20,000	1,00,000	1,50,000	2,40,000	2,00,000	2,00,000
Wages & Salaries	30,000	30,000	24,000	24,000	24,000	30,000	27,000	27,000
Misc. Exp.	27,000	27,000	21,000	30,000	24,000	27,000	27,000	27,000

(ii) 20% of the sales are on cash and the balance on credit.

(iii) The firm has a gross margin of 25% on sales.

(iv) 50% of credit sales are collected in the month following the sales, 30% in the second month and 20% in the third month.

(v) Material for the sale of each month is purchased one month in advance on a credit for two months.

(vi) The time lag in the payment of wages and salaries is one-third of a month and of miscellaneous expenses one month.

(vii) Debentures worth Rs. 40,000 were sold in January.

(viii) The firm maintains a minimum cash balance of Rs. 40,000. Funds can be borrowed @ 12% p.a. in the multiples of Rs. 1,000 the interest being payable on monthly basis.

(ix) Cash balance at the end of December is Rs. 60,000.

[Adapted—C.A. (Final)]

Solution

Working Notes :

1. *Collection from debtors*

(Rs. '000)

	Nov.	Dec.	Jan.	Feb.	Mar.	Apr.	May	June
Sales	200	220	120	100	150	240	200	200
Cash sales (20%)	40	44	24	20	30	48	40	40
Credit Sales (80%)	160	176	96	80	120	192	160	·160
Collection 50% in the month following		80	88	48	40	60	96	80
30% in 2nd month			48	52.8	28.8	24	36	57.6
20% in 3rd month			*	32.0	35.2	19.2	16	24.0
			136	132.8	104.0	103.2	148	161.6

* In the absence of information about sales of October nil collection for that month is assumed.

2. *Cost of Goods Sold*

	Nov.	Dec.	Jan.	Feb.	Mar.	Apr.	May	June
75% of sales	150	165	90	75	112.5	180	150	150
Purchases one month in advance	165	90	75	112.5	180	150	150	150*
Payment to supplier on 2 month credit			165	90	75	112.5	180	150

*Purchases for the month of June is assumed as in May in the absence of sales figure for July.

3. ***Payment of Wages & Salaries due for the month***

	Dec.	Jan.	Feb.	Mar.	Apr.	May	June
Time lag 1/3rd of a month	30	24	24	24	30	27	27
1/3 of last month		10	8	8	8	10	9
2/3 of current month		16	16	16	20	18	18
Total Payment		26	24	24	28	28	27

Cash Budget

for the period from January to June

	Jan. Rs.	Feb. Rs.	Mar. Rs.	Apr. Rs.	May Rs.	June Rs.
Cash in hand	60,000	42,000	59,800	64,800	51,500	40,500
Cash sales	24,000	20,000	30,000	48,000	40,000	40,000
Collection from debtors (W.No.1)	1,36,000	1,32,800	1,04,000	1,03,200	1,48,000	1,61,600
Sales of debentures	40,000	—	—	—	—	—
Total Cash available before current financing (A)	2,60,000	1,94,800	1,93,800	2,16,000	2,39,500	2,42,100
Payments :						
Creditors for supplies (Note 2)	1,65,000	90,000	75,000	1,12,500	1,80,000	1,50,000
Wages and salaries (Note 3)	26,000	24,000	24,000	28,000	28,000	27,000
Misc. Expenses (Time lag 1 month)	27,000	21,000	30,000	24,000	27,000	27,000
Minimum cash balance	40,000	40,000	40,000	40,000	40,000	40,000
Total Cash needed	2,58,000	1,75,000	1,69,000	2,04,500	2,75,000	2,44,000
Surplus/(deficinecy)	2,000	19,800	24,800	11,500	(35,500)	(1,900)
Financing :						
Borrowing	—	—	—	—	36,000	3,000
Repayment Interest @ 12% p.a.	—	—	—	—	—	(360)*
Total effect of financing/repayment (C)	—	—	—	—	36,000	2,640
Closing cash balance (A+C–B)	42,000	59,800	64,800	51,500	40,500	40,740

$$* \text{ Rs. } 36{,}000 \times \frac{12}{100} \times \frac{1}{12} = \text{Rs. } 360.$$

Problem 17

Draw up a Flexible Budget for overhead expenses on the basis of the following data and determine the overhead rates of 70%, 80% and 90% plant capacity.

Expenses	At 80% capacity Rs.
Indirect Labour	12,000
Stores including spares	4,000
Power (30% fixed)	20,000
Repairs and Maintenance (60% fixed)	2,000
Depreciation	11,000
Insurance	3,000
Salary	10,000
Total Overhead	62,000
Estimated direct labour hours	1,24,000 hours

[C.U. B.Com. (General) Part-II 2003]

Solution

Flexible Budget for Overhead Expenses

	Capacity		
	70%	80%	90%
	Rs.	Rs.	Rs.
Indirect Labour	10,500	12,000	13,500
Stores including spares	3,500	4,000	4,500
Power (fixed)	6,000	6,000	6,000
(variable)	12,250	14,000	15,750
Repairs and Maintenance (60% fixed)	1,200	1,200	1,200
Repairs variable	700	800	900
Depreciation	9,625	11,000	12,375
Insurance	3,000	3,000	3,000
Salaries	10,000	10,000	10,000
Total overhead	56,775	62,000	67,225
Labour hour rate (Overheads ÷ Labour hours)	1,24,000	1,24,000	1,24,000
	= Rs. 0.458	= Rs. 0.5	= Re. 0.542

Problem 18

A department of a company X attains sale of Rs. 6,00,000 at 80% of its normal capacity and its expenses are given below :

1.	***Administration Costs***	
	Office salaries	Rs. 90,000
	General Expenses	2% of sales
	Depreciation	Rs. 7,500
	Rates and taxes	Rs. 8,750
2.	***Selling Costs***	
	Salaries	8% of sales
	Travelling expenses	2% of sales
	Sales office	1% of sales
	General expenses	1% of sales
3.	***Distribution Costs***	
	Wages	Rs. 15,000
	Rent	1% of sales
	Other expenses	.4% of sales

Draw up flexible administration, selling and distribution costs budgets, operating at 90%, 100% and 110% of normal capacity.

[B.U. B.Com. (Hons.)]

Solution

X Ltd.
Flexible Budget for the period ......

Level of Activity

Particulars	Basis	80% Rs.	90% Rs.	100% Rs.	110% Rs.
Sales		6,00,000	6,75,000	7,50,000	8,25,000
1. **Administration Costs**					
Office Salaries	Fixed	90,000	90,000	90,000	90,000
General expenses	2% of sales	12,000	13,500	15,000	16,500
Depreciation	Fixed	7,500	7,500	7,500	7,500
Rates and Taxes	Fixed	8,750	8,750	8,750	8,750
A. Total		1,18,250	1,19,750	1,21,250	1,22,750
2. **Selling Costs**					
Salaries	8% of sales	48,000	54,000	60,000	66,000
Traveling expenses	2% of sales	12,000	13,500	15,000	16,500
Sales office expenses	1% of sales	6,000	6,750	7,500	8,250
General expenses	1% of sales	6,000	6,750	7,500	8,250
B. Total		72,000	81,000	90,000	99,000
3. **Distribution Costs**					
Wages	Fixed	15,000	15,000	15,000	15,000
Rent	1% of sales	6,000	6,750	7,500	8,250
Other expenses	4% of sales	24,000	27,000	30,000	33,000
C. Total Cost		45,000	48,750	52,500	56,250
Total Costs (A + B + C)		2,35,250	2,49,500	2,63,750	2,78,000

Problem 19

A factory is currently running at 50% capacity and produces 5,000 units at a cost of Rs. 90 per unit as per details below :

	Rs.
Materials	50
Labour	15
Factory Overhead	15 (Rs. 6 fixed)
Administrative overheads	10 (Rs. 5 fixed)

The current selling price is Rs. 100 per unit. At 60% working, material cost per unit increases by 2% and selling price per unit falls by 2%.

Estimate profit of the factory at 60% working.

[C.U. B.Com. (Hons.) 1995]

Solution

Flexible Budget

Showing the profit at 60% capacity

		50% capacity 5,000 units		*60% capacity 6,000 units*	
		per unit Cost Rs.	*Total Cost* Rs.	*Cost per unit* Rs.	*Total cost* Rs.
1.	Sales	100.00	5,00,000	98.00[1]	15,88,000
2.	*Less : Variable Costs :*				
	(a) Materials	50.00	2,50,000	51.00[2]	3,06,000
	(b) Wages	15.00	75,000	15.00	90,000
	(c) *Variable Overheads :*				
	(i) Factory Overhead	9.00	45,000	9.00	54,000
	(ii) Administration overheads	5.00	25,000	5.00	30,000
		79.00	3,95,000	80.00	4,80,000
	Contribution (1–2)	21.00	1,05,000	18.00	1,08,000
	Less : Fixed Costs				
	(a) Factory Overhead	(6.00)	(30,000)	(5.00)[3]	(30,000)
	(b) Administration overhead	(5.00)	(25,000)	(4.17)[4]	(25,000)
	Next Profit	10.00	50,000	8.33	53,000

Working Notes :

1. Selling price per unit at 60% level = Rs. 100 – (2% of 100)
   = Rs. 100 – Rs. 2 = **Rs. 98 per unit**

2. Material cost increased by 2% at 60% level.
   Therefore material cost Rs. 50 + (2% of Rs. 50)
   = Rs. 50 + Re. 1 = **Rs. 51**

3. Factory overheads Rs. 6 per unit i.e., 5,000 × 6 = Rs. 30,000

   At 60% level per unit fixed cost $= \frac{\text{Rs. } 30{,}000}{6{,}000} =$ **Rs. 5.00**

4. Administration overhead : Rs. 5 per unit, so for 5,000 units
   = 5,000 × 5 = Rs. 25,000

   At 60% level i.e. for 6,000 units fixed overhead $= \frac{\text{Rs. } 25{,}000}{6{,}000} =$ **Rs. 4.17 per unit**

Problem 20

The following data are available for a manufacturing company for a yearly period :

		Rs. (in lakhs)
1.	**Fixed Expenses :**	
	Wages and salaries	9.5
	Rent, Rates and Taxes	6.6
	Depreciation	7.4
	Sundry Administrative expenses	6.5

Contd.

2.	**Semi-variable Expenses :**	
	Maintenance and Repair	3.5
	Indirect labour	7.9
	Sales departments' salaries	3.8
	Sundry administrative expenses	2.8
3.	**Variable Expenses (at 50% of capacity) :**	
	Materials	21.7
	Labour	20.4
	Other expenses	7.9
		98.00

Assume that the fixed expenses remain constant at all levels of production; semi-variable expenses remain constant between 45% and 65% of capacity increasing by 10% between 65% and 80% of capacity and by 20% between 80% and 100% capacity.

Sales at various levels are :

	Rs. (in lakhs.)
50% capacity	100
60% capacity	120
75% capacity	150
90% capacity	200

Prepare a flexible budget for the year at 60% and 90% capacity and estimate the profit at these levels of output.

[Adpated—C.S. (Inter)]

Solution

FLEXIBLE BUDGET

(Rs. in lakhs.)

Capacity		*60%*		*90%*
1. **Fixed Expenses**				
Wages and salaries	9.50		9.50	
Rent, Rates and Taxes	6.60		6.60	
Depreciation	7.40		7.40	
Sundry Administrative Exp.	6.50		6.50	
		30.00		30.00
2. **Semi-variable Expenses**				
Maintenance and Repairs	3.50		4.20 (20% increase)	
Indirect Labour	7.90		9.48 (20% increase)	
Sales departments' salaries	3.80		4.56 (20% increase)	
Sundry Administrative Exp.	2.80		3.36 (20% increase)	
Total		18.00		21.60

3. **Variable Expenses**				
Materials	$\left(21.7 \times \frac{60\%}{50\%}\right)$	26,04	$\left(21.7 \times \frac{90\%}{50\%}\right)$	39.06
Labour	$\left(20.4 \times \frac{60\%}{50\%}\right)$	24.48	$\left(20.4 \times \frac{90\%}{50\%}\right)$	36.72
Other Expenses	$\left(7.9 \times \frac{60\%}{50\%}\right)$	9.48	$\left(7.9 \times \frac{90\%}{50\%}\right)$	14.22
Total Cost (1 + 2 + 3)		108.00		141.60
Sales		120.00		180.00
Profit		12.00		38.40

Problem 21

A factory engaged in manufacturing plastic buckets is working at 40% capacity and produces 10,000 buckets per month. The present cost break-up for one bucket is as under :

	Rs.
Materials	20
labour	6
Overheads	10 (60% fixed)

The selling price is Rs. 40 per bucket. If it is decided to work the factory at 50% capacity, selling price falls by 3%. At 90% capacity, the selling price falls by 5% accompanied by a similar fall in the price of materials.

You are required to prepare a statement showing the profits at 50% and 90% capacities and also determine the break-even points at each of the production levels

[I.C.W.A. (Inter)]

Solution

Flexible Budget

Particulars	*Capacity*		
	40%	50%	90%
Production and sales in units	10,000	12,500	22,500
Selling price per unit (Rs.)	40	38.80	38
(a) **Sales value**	4,00,000	4,85,000	8,55,000
Less : **Total variable costs :**			
Material	2,00,000	2,50,000	4,27,500
Labour	60,000	75,000	1,35,000
Variable Overheads	40,000	50,000	90,000
(b) **Total variable cost**	3,00,000	3,75,000	6,52,000
(c) **Contribution (a – b)**	1,00,000	1,10,000	2,02,500
Less : **Fixed Overheads**	60,000	60,000	60,000
Profits	40,000	50,000	1,42,500
Contribution per unit	10.00	8.80	9,00
Break-even point in units	6,000	6,181	6,667
$\frac{\text{Total fixed overheads}}{\text{Contribution per unit}}$	$\frac{60,000}{10.00}$	$\frac{60,000}{8.80}$	$\frac{1,42,500}{9.00}$

Working Notes :

		Rs.	Rs.
1.	Contribution per unit :		
	Selling price		40
	Less : Variable cost :		
	Material	20	
	Labour	6	
	Variable overheads		
	40% of Rs. 10	4	
			30
	Contribution per unit		10
2.	Fixed Overheads for one bucket		6 (60% of Rs. 10)

Total fixed overheads per month = 10,000 × 6 = 60,000

Problem 22

Draw up a flexible budget for overhead expenses on the basis of the following data and determine the overhead rates at 70%, 80% and 90% plant capacity :

	At 70% Capacity Rs.	At 80% Capacity Rs.	At 90% Capacity Rs.
Variable Overheads :			
Indirect labour	—	12,000	
Stores including spares	—	4,000	
Semi-variable Overheads :			
Power (30% fixed and 70% variable)	—	20,000	—
Repairs and maintenance (60% fixed and 40% variable)	—	2,000	—
Fixed Overheads :			
Depreciation		11,000	
Insurance		3,000	
Salaries		10,000	
Total overheads		62,000	
Estimated direct Labour hours		1,24,000 hours	

Solution

Flexible Budget

for the period ......

		At 70% Capacity Rs.	At 80% Capacity Rs.	At 90% Capacity Rs.
1.	**Variable Overheads :**			
	(a) Indirect labour	10,500 $\left(\frac{12,000}{8} \times 7\right)$	12,000	13,500 $\left(\frac{12,000}{8} \times 9\right)$

	(b) Stores including spares	3,500	4,000	4,500
		$\left(\frac{4,000}{8} \times 7\right)$		$\left(\frac{4,000}{8} \times 9\right)$
2.	**Semi-variable Overheads :**			
	(a) Power (30% fixed)	6,000	6,000	6,000
	(70% Variable)	12,250	14,000	15,750
		$\left(\frac{14,000}{8} \times 7\right)$		
	(b) Repairs and Maintenance			
	Fixed (60% of 2,000)	1,200	1,200	1,200
	Variable (40% of 2,000)	700	800	900
3.	**Fixed Overheads :**			
	(a) Depreciation	11,000	11,000	11,000
	(b) Insurance	3,000	3,000	3,000
	(c) Salaries	10,000	10,000	10,000
	Total Overheads	58,150	62,000	65,850
	$\frac{\text{Overhead}}{\text{Direct Labour hours}}$	$\frac{58,150}{124.000}$	$\frac{62,000}{124.000}$	$\frac{65,850}{124.000}$
	Direct Labour Hour Rate	0.536	0.500	0.472

Problem 23

Galaxy Pvt. Ltd. is engaged in production of certain TV parts, 100% capacity being 10,000 units. Given are the information for January and February 1999 :

Month	*January*	*February*
Parts produced (in units)	6,000	9,000
Elements of overhead costs	Rs.	Rs.
Salaries	3,000	3,000
Power	3,000	3,900
Consumable stores	3,000	4,500
Repairs	4,000	4,600
Shop labour	1,500	2,250
Depreciation	2,500	2,500
Inspection	1,000	1,300

Rate of production per hour is 10 units. Direct material costs are Rs. 2 per unit and direct labour costs per hour Rs. 8.

You are required to compute :

(a) Cost of production at 50%, 80% and 100% capacity respectively showing separately the fixed, semi-variable and variable expenses in the flexible budget, and

(b) Show the overhead absorption rate per unit at 100% capacity.

[I.C.W.A. ((Inter) June, 2000]

Solution

Flexible Budget

	Capacity		
	50%	80%	100%
T.V. parts produced (in units)	5,000	8,000	10,000
Production hours	500	800	1,000
	Rs.	Rs.	Rs.
Direct material @ Rs. 2.00 per unit	10,000	16,000	20,000
Wages @ Rs. 8 per hour	4,000	6,400	8,000
(A) Prime Cost	14,000	22,400	28,000
Add : **Factory overheads**			
1. **Variable**			
(i) Consumable Stores @ 0.50 per unit (3,000 ÷ 6,000)	2,500	4,000	5,000
(ii) Shop labour @ Re. 0.25 per unit (Rs. 1,500 ÷ 6,000)	1,250	2,000	2,500
2. **Fixed Expenses**			
(i) Salaries	3,000	3,000	3,000
(ii) Depreciation	2,500	2,500	2,500
3. **Semi-variable**			
Repairs (note 1)	3,800	4,400	4,800
Power (note 2)	2,700	3,600	4,200
Inspection (note 3)	900	1,200	1,400
(B) Factory Overhead	16,650	20,700	23,400
(a) **Total cost of production A + B**	30,650	43,100	51,400

(b) Overhead absorption rate at 100% capacity = $\frac{23,400}{10,000}$ = Rs. 2.34 per unit

Problem 24

A department of Tek India Company attains sale of Rs. 6,00,000 at 80% of its normal capacity and its expenses are given below :

1.	**Administration Costs :**	
	Office salaries	Rs. 90,000
	General expenses	2% of sales
	Depreciation	Rs. 7,500
	Rent and Taxes	Rs. 8,750
2.	**Distribution Costs :**	
	Wages	Rs. 15,000
	Rent	1% of sales
	Other expenses	4% of sales
3.	**Selling Costs :**	
	Salaries	8% of sales
	Travelling expenses	2% of sales
	Sales office expenses	1% of sales
	General expenses	1% of sales

Draw up flexible administration, selling and distribution costs budget operating at 90%, 100% and 110% of normal capacity.

[Delhi University B.Com. (Hons.)]

Solution

(i) At 80% capacity sale is Rs. 6,00,000

At 90% $= \text{Rs. } 6{,}00{,}000 \times \frac{90}{80} = \text{Rs. } 6{,}75{,}000$

100% $= \frac{\text{Rs. } 6{,}00{,}000}{80} \times 100 = \text{Rs. } 7{,}50{,}000$

110% $= \frac{\text{Rs. } 6{,}00{,}000}{80} \times 110 = \text{Rs. } 8{,}25{,}000$

Flexible Budget for Administration, Distribution and Selling costs

	Particulars	90% Rs.	100% Rs.	110% Rs.
	Sales (as per note)	6,75,000	7,50,000	8,25,000
1.	**Administration Costs**			
	Office salaries	90,000	90,000	90,000
	General Expenses (2% of sales)	13,500	15,000	16,500
	Depreciation	7,500	7,500	7,500
	Rent and taxes	8,750	8,750	8,750
2.	**Distribution Costs**			
	Wages	15,000	15,000	15,000
	Rent (1% of sales)	6,750	7,500	8,250
	Other Expenses (4% on sales)	27,000	30,000	33,000
3.	**Selling Costs**			
	Salaries (8% of sales)	54,000	60,000	66,000
	Travelling expenses (2% of sales)	13,500	15,000	16,500
	Sales office expenses (1% of sales)	6,750	7,500	8,250
	General expenses (1% of sales)	6,750	7,500	8,250
	Total	2,49,500	2,63,750	2,78,000

Problem 25

From the following data prepare a flexible budget for production of 40,000 units and 75,000 units, distinctly showing variable cost and fixed cost as well as total cost. Also indicate element-wise cost per unit. Budgeted output is 1,00,000 units and budgeted cost per unit is as follows :

	Rs.
Direct Material	95
Direct Labour	50
Production Overhead (variable)	40
Production overhead (fixed)	5
Administration overhead (fixed	5
Selling overhead (10% fixed)	10
Distribution overhead (20% fixed)	15

[D.U. B.Com. (Hons.) 2000]

Solution

Flexible Budget

Production		75,000 units		40,000 units	
		Cost per unit	*Total Cost*	*Cost per unit*	*Total cost*
		Rs.	Rs.	Rs.	Rs.
1.	**Fixed Costs**				
	Production Overhead	6.67	5,00,000	12.50	5,00,000
	Administration Overhead	6.67	5,00,000	12.50	5,00,000
	Selling overhead	1.33	1,00,000	2.50	1,00,000
	Distribution Overhead	4.00	3,00,000	7.50	3,00,000
	Total	18.67	14,00,000	35.00	14,00,000
2.	**Variable Costs**				
	Materials	95.00	71,25,000	95.00	38,00,000
	Labour	50.00	37,50,000	50.00	20,00,000
	Production Overhead	40.00	30,00,000	40.00	16,00,000
	Selling Overhead	9.00	6,75,000	9.00	3,60,000
	Distribution Overhead	12.00	9,00,000	12.00	4,80,000
	Total	206.00	1,54,50,000	206.00	82,40,000
	Total Cost (1 + 2)	224.67	1,68,50,000	241.00	96,40,000

Performance Budget

Problem 26

Z. Ltd. had a profit plan approved for selling 5,000 units per month at an average selling price of Rs. 10 per unit. The budgeted variable cost of production was Rs. 4 per unit and the fixed costs were budgeted at Rs. 20,000, the planned income being Rs. 10,000 p.m.

Due to shortage of raw materials only, 4,000 units could be produced and the cost of production was increased by 0.50 paise per unit. The selling price was raised by Re. 1.00 per unit. In order to improve the production process, an expenditure of Rs. 1,000 was incurred for research and development activities.

You are required to prepare a performance budget and a summary profit.

[Adapted—I.C.W.A.I. (Inter)]

Solution

Performance Budget

	Original plan	*Adjusted plan*	*Actual position*
	Rs.	Rs.	Rs.
Sales	50,000 5,000 × 10	40,000 (4,000 × 10)	44,000 (4,000 × 11)
Less : Variable Costs	20,000 (5,000 × 4)	16,000 (4,000 × 4)	18,000 (4,000 × 4.50)
Contribution	30,000	24,000	26,000
Less : Fixed cost	20,000	20,000	21,000*
Net Profit	10,000	4,000	5,000

* Rs. 20,000 + Rs. 1,000 for research and development.

Summary Report in Profit Plan

	Rs.	
Planned Income	10,000	
(a) Selling price variance [4,000 × (11 – 10)]	4,000	(F)
(b) Variance Cost variance [4,000 × (4 – 4.50)]	2,000	(F)
(c) Fixed cost variance (Rs. 21,000 – Rs. 20,000)	1,000	(F)
(d) Profit volume variance (1,000 × 6)	6,000	(A)
(e) Total variance (7,000 – 6,000)	1,000	
Actual Income	5,000	

Problem 27

The cost sheet of a company based on a budgeted volume of sales of 3,00,000 units per quarter as under :

	Rs. (per unit)
Direct materials	5.00
Direct wages	2.00
Factory overheads (50% fixed)	6.00
Selling and Administration Overhead (1/3rd variable)	3.00
Selling price	18.00

When the budget was discussed it was felt that the company would be able to achieve only a volume of 2,50,000 units of production and sales per quarter. The company, therefore, decided that an aggressive sales promotion campaign should be launched to achieve the following improved operations :

Proposal I

(a) Sell 4,00,000 units per quarter by spending Rs. 2,00,000 on special advertising.

(b) The factory fixed costs will increase by Rs. 4,00,000 per quarter.

Proposal II

Sell 5,00,000 units per quarter subject to the following conditions :

(a) An overall price reduction of Rs. 2 per unit is allowed on all sales.

(b) Variable selling and administration cost will increase by 5%.

(c) Direct Material costs will be reduced by 1% due to purchase price discount.

(d) The fixed factory cost will increase by Rs. 2,00,000 more.

You are required to prepare a Flexible Budget at 2,50,000, 4,00,000 and 5,00,000 units of output per quarter and calculate the profit at each of the above levels of output.

[C.A. (Inter) May 2002]

Solution

Flexible Budget

Units (to be sold)	2,50,000	4,00,000	5,00,000
	Rs.	Rs.	Rs.
Sales (2,50,000 × 18)	45,00,000		
(4,00,000 × 18)		72,00,000	
(5,00,000 × 16)			80,00,000
(A) **Variable Cost**	45,00,000	72,00,000	80,00,000
(a) Direct Materials			
(2,50,000 × 5)	12,50,000		
(4,00,000 × 5)		20,00,000	
(5,00,000 × 4.95)			24,75,000
(b) Direct labour @ Rs. 2 per unit	5,00,000	8,00,000	10,00,000
(c) Factory Overheads @ Rs. 3 per unit	7,50,000	12,00,000	15,00,000
(d) Selling and Administration overheads			
(2,50,000 × Re. 1.00)	2,50,000		
(4,00,000 × Re. 1.00)		4,00,000	
(5,00,000 × Rs. 1.05)			5,25,000
(B) **Total Variable Costs**	27,50,000	44,00,000	55,00,000
(C) **Contribution (A – B)**	17,50,000	28,00,000	25,00,000
Less : **Fixed Costs**			
Factory Overheads	9,00,000	9,00,000	9,00,000
Selling and Administration Overhead	6,00,000	6,00,000	6,00,000
Insurance in fixed costs		4,00,000	6,00,000
Advertisement costs		2,00,000	
Profit	2,50,000	7,00,000	4,00,000

Problem 28

Based on the following information, prepare a Cash Budget for ABC Ltd.

Particular	*1st quarter*	*2nd quarter*	*3rd quarter*	*4th quarter*
Receipts :	Rs.	Rs.	Rs.	Rs.
Opening Cash Balance	10,000			
Collection from Debtors	1,25,000	1,50,000	1,60,000	2,21,000
Payments :				
Purchase of materials	20,000	35,000	35,000	54,200
Other Expenses	25,000	20,000	20,000	17,000
Salaries and wages	90,000	95,000	95,000	1,09,200
Income Tax	5,000	—	—	—
Purchase of machinery	—	—	—	20,000

The company desires to maintain a cash balance of Rs. 15,000 at the end of each quarter. Cash can be borrowed or repaid in multiples of Rs. 500 at an interest of 10% per annum.

Management does not want to borrow more than what is necessary and wants to repay as early as possible.

In any event loans cannot be extented beyond 4 quarters. Interest is computed and paid when the principal is repaid.

Assume that borrowings take place at the beginning and repayments are made at the end of the quarters. **[Adapted—I.C.W.A. (Inter)]**

Solution

Cash Budget of ABC Ltd.

	1st quarter Rs.	2nd quarter Rs.	3rd quarter Rs.	4th quarter Rs.
Opening Cash Balance	10,000	15,000	15,000	15,325
Collection from Debtors	1,25,000	1,50,000	1,60,000	2,21,000
A. Total Receipts	1,35,000	1,65,000	1,75,000	2,36,325
Payments				
Purchase of materials	20,000	35,000	35,000	54,200
Other expenses	25,000	20,000	20,000	17,000
Salary and wages	90,000	95,000	95,000	1,09,200
Income Tax	5,000	—	—	—
Purchase of Machinery	—	—	—	20,000
Cash Balance	15,000	15,000	15,325	23,825
Borrowings/Repayment including interest	(20,000)	—	9,675[1]	12,100[2]
	1,35,000	1,65,000	1,75,000	2,36,325

Working Notes :

1. Interest on borrowings

Interest is to be calculated on the amount of loan repaid.

Therefore, interest on Rs. 9,000 @ 10% p.a. for 9 months

$= 9{,}000 \times \frac{10}{100} \times \frac{9}{12} =$ Rs. 675.

Total repayment is Rs. 9,000 + Rs. 625 (Principal + Interest) = Rs. 9,625

2. Interest on Rs. 11,000 (20,000 – 9,000) @ 10% for 12 months since loan is repaid at the end of 4th quarter = Rs. $11{,}000 \times \frac{10}{100} =$ Rs. 1,100.

Repayment = Principal + Interest = Rs. 11,000 + Rs. 1,100 = Rs. 12,100

Problem 29

Unique Cements Ltd. has a cement plant with an annual capacity of 10 lakh tonnes. The estimates of costs are as under :

Budget Year (1994-1995)	*Rupees per tonne*
(a) Manufacturing variable costs	280
(b) packing (bags) costs	100
(c) Variable marketing costs	30

The estimates of fixed cost for the budget year (1994-1995) are as under :

Capacity utilisation level	80%	90%	100%
		(Rupees in lakhs)	
Manufacturing fixed costs	300	330	350
Depreciation	400	400	400
Marketing fixed costs	250	270	300

The net sales price realisation per tonne of cement likely to be achieved for various capacity utilisation levels are as under :

Capacity-utilisation level (%)	*Price realisation per tonne of cement*
80	630
90	620
100	610

(a) Prepare a statement showing the expected results at various levels of capacity utilisation given above.

(b) What would be the profits at different capacity-utilisation levels given above, if there is a price rise of 10% in packing (bags) costs.

Solution

(a) **Statement of Profit at various capacity levels**

Capacity utilisation levels	80%	90%	100%
Tonnes	8 lakhs	9 lakhs	10 lakhs
Price per tonne (Rs.)	630	620	610
		(Rupees in lakhs)	
Sales value	5,040	5,580	6,100
Less : Variable cost at Rs. 410 per tonne	3,280	3,690	4,100
Contribution	1,760	1,890	2,000
Less : Fixed costs	950	1,000	1,050
Profit	810	890	950
(b) Sale value	5,040	5,580	6,100
Less : Variable cost at Rs. 420* per tonne	3,360	3,780	4,200
Contribution	1,680	1,800	1,900
Less : Fixed costs	950	1,000	1,050
Profit	730	800	850

* Packing cost increases by 10%, then variable cost will be Rs. 410 + Rs. 10 = Rs. 420.

Problem 30

The monthly budgets for manufacturing overheads of a concern for two levels of activity were as follows :

Capacity	60%	100%
Budgeted production units	600	1,000
	Rs.	Rs.
Wages	1,200	2,000
Consumable stores	900	1,500
Maintenance	1,100	1,500
Power and Fuel	1,600	2,000
Depreciation	4,000	4,000
Insurance	1,000	1,000

You are required to :

(i) Indicate which of the items are fixed, variable and semi-variable.

(ii) Prepare a budget for 80% capacity; and

(iii) Find the total cost, both fixed and variable, per unit of output at 60%, 80% and 100% of capacity.

[Adapted—C.S. (Inter)]

Solution

(i) Calculation of Fixed, Variable and Semi-variable Costs

Fixed cost

(a) **The following items have fixed costs :**

(a) Depreciation as it remains the same at 60% and 100% levels of production.

(b) Insurance—for the above stated reason.

(b) **Variable cost**

(a) Wages at 60% level—Rs. 1,200 ÷ 600 = Rs. 2

100% level—Rs. 2,000 ÷ 1,000 = Rs. 2

Consumable stores

60% level—Rs. 900 ÷ 600 = Rs. 1.50

100% level Rs. 1,500 ÷ 1,000 = Rs. 1.50

(c) **Semi-variable costs**

(a) *Maintenance* :

	1,000 units	Rs. 1,500
	600 units	Rs. 1,100
Difference	400 units	Rs. 400

$$\text{Variable Cost} = \frac{\text{Rs. } 400}{400 \text{ units}} = \text{Re } 1.00 \text{ per unit}$$

Fixed : Total Cost – Variable Cost

Rs. 1,500 – Rs. 1,000 (1,000 × 1) = Rs. 500

(b) *Power and Fuel*

	1,000 units	Rs. 2,00
	600 units	Rs. 1,600
Difference	400	Rs. 400

$$\text{Variable} = \frac{\text{Rs. } 400}{400 \text{ units}} = \text{Re } 1.00 \text{ per unit}$$

Fixed = Total cost – Variable cost = Rs. 2,000 – 1,000 (1,000 × 1) = Rs. 1,000

$$\text{Budget for 80\% capacity} = 800 \left(\frac{1,000}{100} \times 80\right) \text{ units}$$

(ii)

Flexible Budget
Showing total cost

	60%	80%	100%
Capacity	60%	80%	100%
Units	600	800	1,000
A. **Fixed Costs**			
Depreciation	4,000	4,000	4,000
Insurance	1,000	1,000	1,000
Maintenance	500	500	500
Power and Fuel	1,000	1,000	1,000
Total Fixed Costs	6,500	6,500	6,500

B. Variable Costs			
Wages @ Rs. 2.00 per unit	1,200	1,600	2,000
Consumable stores @ Rs. 105 per unit	900	1,200	1,500
Maintenance @ Re. 1.00 per unit	600	800	1,000
Power and Fuel @ Re. 1.00 per unit	600	800	1,000
	3,300	4,400	5,500
Total Cost (A + B)	9,800	10,900	12,000
Fixed Cost per unit	6,500 ÷ 600	6,500 ÷ 800	6,500 ÷ 1,000
Fixed Cost ÷ units	10.833	8.125	6.50
Variable cost per unit	3,300 ÷ 600	4,400 ÷ 800	5,500 ÷ 1,000
	Rs. 5.50	Rs. 5.50	Rs. 5.50
Total Cost per unit	9,800 ÷ 600	10,900 ÷ 800	12,000 ÷ 1,000
	= 16.333	= 13.625	Rs. 12.00

ASSIGNMENT

Theoretical Questions

1. What is meant by Budget? What are its objectives? To what extent is the preparation of the budget influenced by the existence of a key or limiting factor?
[C.U. B.Com. (Hons.)]
2. What is a budget? What is meant by Budgetary Control? How do you distinguish between the two? What is the importance of Budgetary Control?
[C.U. B.Com. (Hons.)]
3. What is cash budget? What are its advantages? State two methods of preparing cash budget.
4. What is the importance of cash budget?
5. What is Master Budget?
6. What are the steps in budgeting?
7. What is flexible budget? What is its importance?
8. What do you mean by Performance Budget?
9. What is Zero-Base Budgeting? What are its advantages and limitations?
10. What do you mean Responsibility Accounting? What are its pre-requisites?

Practical Problem

1. Dasgupta & Co. wishes to arrange overdraft facilities with its Bankers during the period April to June, 2003 when it will be manufacturing mostly for stock. Prepare a Cash Budget for the above period from the following data, indicating the extent of. bank facilities the company will require at the end of each month :

	Sales	Purchases	Wages
(a)	Rs.	Rs.	Rs.
February 2003	1,80,000	1,24,800	12,000
March	1,92,000	1,44,000	14,000
April	1,08,000	2,43,000	11,000
May	1,74,000	2,46,000	10,000
June	1,26,000	2,68,000	15,000

(b) 50% of credit sales are realised in the month following the sales and the remaining 50% in the second month following. Creditors are paid in the month following the month of purchase.

(c) Cash at Bank on 1.4.2003 (estimated) Rs. 25,000.

Ans. : (i) April—Bank Balance Rs. 53,000;
(ii) May—Bank Overdraft Rs. 51,000;
(iii) June—Bank Overdraft Rs. 1,66,000.

2. From the following information prepare cash budget for the months of January to April :

Expected Sales	Rs.	*Expected Purchases*	Rs.
January	60,000	January	48,000
February	40,000	February	80,000
March	45,000	March	81,000
April	40,000	April	90,000

Wages to be paid to workers Rs. 5,000 each month. Balance at Bank on 1st January Rs. 8,000. It has been decided by the management that :

(i) In the case of deficit of fund within the limit of Rs. 10,000 arrangement can be made with the Bank.

(ii) In the case of deficit of fund exceeding Rs. 10,000 but within the limit of Rs. 42,000, issue of debentures is to be favoured.

(iii) In the case of deficit of fund exceeding Rs. 42,000, issue of shares is preferred (considering the fact that it is within the limit of authorised capital).

[Adapted—M.Com. Madras]

Ans. : (a) January—Cash balance Rs. 15,000.
(b) February—Issue of debentures Rs. 30,000.
(c) March—Issue of debentures Rs. 41,000.
(d) April—Issue of shares Rs. 55,000.

3. Prepare a Cash Budget for the three months ending 30th June, 1986 from the information given below :

(a)

Months	*Sales* Rs.	*Purchases* Rs.	*Wages* Rs.	*Overheads* Rs.
February	14,000	9,600	3,000	1,700
March	15,000	9,000	3,000	1,900
April	16,000	9,200	3,200	2,000
May	17,000	10,000	3,600	2,200
June	18,000	10,400	4,000	2,300

(b) ***Credit terms are*** :

Sales/Debtors 10% sales are on cash, 50% of the credit sales are collected next month and the balance in the following month.

Creditors :	Materials	2 months
	Wages	$\frac{1}{4}$th month
	Overheads	$\frac{1}{2}$ month

(c) Cash and Bank balance on 1st April, 1986 is expected to be Rs. 6,000.

(d) ***Other relevant information*** :

(i) Plant and Machinery will be installed in February, 1986 at a cost of Rs. 90,000. The monthly instalment of Rs. 2,000 is payable from April onwards.

(ii) Dividend @ 5% on preference share capital of Rs. 2,00,000 will be paid on 1st June.

(iii) Advance to be received for sale of vehicles Rs. 9,000 in June.

(iv) Dividend from investments amounted to Rs. 1,000 expected to be received in June.

(v) Income-tax (advance) to be paid in June, is Rs. 2,000.

[I.C.W.A. Inter—Adapted]

Ans. : Cash balance : (a) April Rs. 3,950; (b) May Rs. 3,000; (c) June Rs. 300

4. From the following information available from a company, prepare cash budget (monthly) for April, May and June 1998 :

(i)

Months	Sale Rs.	Purchase Rs.	Wages Rs.	Expenses Rs.
1998				
January (Actual)	90,000	50,000	30,000	5,000
February (")	80,000	50,000	24,000	4,000
March (")	80,000	45,000	22,000	6,000
April (Budgeted)	85,000	48,000	25,000	7,000
May (")	75,000	42,000	20,000	6,000
June (Budgeted)	78,000	44,000	23,000	5,000

(ii) 10% of the purchases and 20% of sales are for cash.

(iii) Credit allowed to debtors 1/2 month and credit received from the creditors for one month.

(iv) Wages are paid weekly.

(v) Opening cash balance was Rs. 15,000.

[Vidyasagar University B.Com. (Hons.) 1998]

5. From the following information prepare a cash budget for Bengal Drugs Ltd. for the first 4 months of 2003 :

(i) Sales are 75% for credit and rest for cash.

(ii) Terms of credit sales 50% are collected in the month after the sale 30% in the next month and 20% in the third month.

(iii) The company has a gross margin of 25% on sales and payment is made for previous month's sale.

(iv) Wages and salaries are paid in the following month.

(v) Payment of overheads is made in the same month.

(vi) Half-yearly debenture interest is paid in March and September 12% 1,000 Debentures were issued in the year 2000.

(vii) Depreciation is charged @ 20% on Rs. 5,00,000.

(viii) A plant was bought at Rs. 1,00,000 on 1.1.2003 and monthly instalment of Rs. 10,000 is paid every month starting from February 2003.

(ix) Advance Income-tax is due in March amounted to Rs. 25,000.

(x) Opening cash balance on 1.1.2003 was Rs. 1,10,000.

Additional Information

Months	Sales Rs.	Wages Rs.	Overheads Rs.
October	4,00,000	25,000	5,000
November	6,00,000	30,000	6,000
December	7,00,000	30,000	6,000
January	8,60,000	35,000	7,500
February	8,80,000	35,000	7,500
March	10,00,000	40,000	8,000
April	10,40,000	40,000	8,000

6. A newly started company wishes to prepare a cash budget from January. Prepare Cash Budget for the first six months from the following estimated revenues and expenses.

Months	*Total Sales* Rs.	*Materials* Rs.	*Wages* Rs.	*Production Overheads* Rs.	*Selling and Distribution Overheads* Rs.
January	20,000	20,000	4,000	3,200	800
February	22,000	14,000	4,400	3,300	900
March	24,000	14,000	4,600	3,300	800
April	26,000	12,000	4,600	3,400	900
May	28,000	12,000	4,800	3,500	900
June	30,000	16,000	4,800	3,600	1,000

Cash balance on 1st January was Rs. 10,000. A new machine is to be installed at Rs. 30,000 on credit to be repaid by two equal instalment in March and April.

Sales commission @ 5% on total sales is to be paid within the month following actual sales.

Rs. 10,000 being the amount of second call may be received in March. Security premium amounting to Rs. 2,000 is also receivable with 2nd call.

(i)	Period of credit allowed by suppliers	2 months.
(ii)	Period of credit allowed to customers	1 month

(iii) Delay in payment of Overhead 1 month

(iv) Delay in payment of wages 1/2 month

Assume cash sales to be 50% of total sales.

Ans. : Cash Balance : January Rs. 18,000; February Rs. 29,800; March Rs. 20,000; April Rs. 6,100; May Rs. 8,800; June Rs. 15,200

7. From the following information supplied by Bright Limited, prepare a Cash Budget for the period from 1st September, 1989 to 31st December 1989 :

Months	*Credit Purchases*	*Credit Sales*	*Wages*	*Selling Expenses*	*Overheads*
	Rs.	Rs.	Rs.	Rs.	Rs.
July	85,000	1,60,000	32,000	8,000	10,000
August	92,000	1,85,000	37,000	9,500	11,500
September	1,00,000	2,10,000	42,000	10,500	13,000
October	1,20,000	2,45,000	49,000	12,500	14,500
November	90,000	1,78,000	35,500	8,900	10,500
December	98,000	1,82,000	36,000	9,000	11,000

Additional Information :

(a) Expected cash balance on 1st September Rs. 10,500.

(b) Period of credit allowed to Debtors 2 months.

(c) Period of credit allowed by creditors 1 month.

(d) Lag in payment of wages, selling expenses and overheads—1 month.

(e) Selling commission @ 2% on sales is payable after sales.

(f) Expenditure on machinery worth Rs. 50,000 is payable in October.

(g) Expected cash sales per month Rs. 15,000.

(h) No commission is payable on cash sales.

[C.U. B.Com. (Hons.) 1989]

Ans. : Cash in hand : September Rs. 31,800; October Rs. 12,100; November Rs. 36,200; December Rs. 1,48,640.

8. From the following data prepare a Cash Budget for the quarter October to December :

		Rs.
(a) Sales for the month of	August	20,000
	September	25,000
	October	30,000
	November	30,000
	December	32,000

All the sales are on credit. Half of the dues are collected in the month of sale on which a cash discount of 20% is allowed and the other half are realised in the next month.

(b) Materials are purchased for cash on which a rebate of 5% is offered by the supplier. If the company buys on credit payment can be deferred by one month foregoing the rebate. The purchase budget for the next quarter is : October Rs. 12,500, November Rs. 15,000 and December Rs. 18,000.

(c) The direct labour budget is :

October Rs. 7,000, November Rs. 7,000 and December Rs. 7,000.

(d) The manufacturing overhead budget is :

	Department A	Department B	General Factory
	Rs.	Rs.	Rs.
October	2,400	1,550	800
November	2,400	1,550	800
December	2,500	1,650	900

The above estimates include the quarter's provision for depreciation amounting to Rs. 900 for department A and Rs. 750 for department B.

(e) The general overheads budget for the quarter is Rs. 3,500 (out of which Rs. 200 is for depreciation and Rs. 300 for bad debt reserve.).

(f) An old machine is to be replaced with an additional outlay of Rs. 17,000 in the month of December.

(g) The cash balance on 1st October may be taken as Rs. 15,000.

Ans. October Cash balance Rs. 15,425;
November " " Rs. 15,975;
December Bank overdraft Rs. 2,825.

9. From the following information prepare a cash budget for the months of January to April 2003 :

	Expected Sales	Expected Purchases
	Rs.	Rs.
January	60,000	48,000
February	40,000	80,000
March	45,000	81,000
April	40,000	90,000

Wages to be paid to workers Rs. 5,000 each month. Balance at Bank on 1st January 2003 was Rs. 8,000. It has been decided by the management that :

(a) In the case of deficit of fund within the limit of Rs. 10,000 arrangement can be made with the Bank.

(b) In the case of deficit of fund exceeding Rs. 10,000 but not exceeding Rs. 42,000 issue of Debenture is to be preferred.

(c) In the case of deficit of fund exceeding Rs. 42,000 issue of shares is preferred (it is within the limit of authorised capital).

10. A factory is currently running at 50% capacity and produces 5,000 units at a cost of Rs. 90 per unit as per details below :

	Rs.
Material	50
Labour	15
Factory overheads	15 (Rs. 6 fixed)
Administrative overheads	10 (Rs. 5 fixed)

The current selling price is Rs. 100 per unit. At 60% working material cost per unit increases by 2% and selling price per unit falls by 2%.

Estimate profit of the factory at 60% working.

[C.U. B.Com. (Hons.) 1995]

Ans. : Profit at 60% working is Rs. 53,000

11. Prepare a flexible budget on the basis of the following information for the year 2001 :

	Rs.	
Direct material	90,000	
Direct labour	60,000	
Direct expenses	30,000	
Machine expenses	15,000	
Power	15,000	
Factory overheads (80% fixed)	12,000	
Administrative overheads	18,000	(60% fixed)
Selling overheads (50% fixed)	6,000	
Sales at Rs. 3 per unit	3,00,000	

During the year the entire production was sold and the factory was working at 60% capacity. You are to assume the following :

(i) that price of direct material and wages will increase by 10% and 5% respectively.

(ii) that capacity will be 80%.

12. A Co. produces a standard product. The estimated costs per unit are as follows :

Raw materials Rs. 4, Direct labour Rs. 2, Variable overheads Rs. 5.

The semi-variable costs are indirect materials Rs. 235; indirect labour Rs. 156, Repairs Rs. 570. The variable costs per unit included in semi-variables are :

Indirect materials Re. 0.05; Indirect labour 0.08; Repairs Re. 0.10. The fixed costs are Factory Rs. 2,000, Selling and distribution 2,500.

The above costs are for 70% normal producing 700 units. The selling price is Rs. 30 per unit.

Prepare a Flexible Budget for 60%, 80% and 100% normal capacities with the help of the above data.

[Rajasthan University M.Com.]

13. Production costs of Jyoti Udyog Ltd. are as follows :

	Level of Capacity		
	60%	70%	80%
Output (in units)	1,200	1,400	1,600
Cost (in Rupees)			
Direct Materials	24,000	28,000	32,000
Direct Labour	7,200	8,400	9,600
Factory Overheads	12,800	13,600	14,400
Works Cost	44,000	50,000	56,000

A proposal to increase production to 90% level of activity is under consideration of the management. The proposal is not expected to involve any increase in fixed factory overheads.

Prepare a statement showing the prime cost, total marginal cost and total factory cost at 80% level of capacity.

[Adapted—B.Com. (Hons.) Delhi University]

Ans. : Total Factory Cost Rs. 62,000.

Hints : Overheads are to be classified into fixed and variable.

14. A factory engaged in manufacturing plastic toys is working at 40% capacity and produces 10,000 toys per month. The present cost break up for one toy is as under :

	Rs.
Material	10
Labour	3
Overhead	5 (60% fixed)

The selling price Rs. 20 per toy. It is decided to work the factory at 50% capacity, the selling price falls by 3%. At 90% capacity the selling price falls by 5% accompanied by a similar fall in the price of material. You are required to prepare a statement showing profit at 50% and 90% capacities.

[B.Com. (Hons.) Delhi]

Ans. : Profit Rs. 20,000 at 40% capacity; Profit Rs. 25,000 at 50%; Profit Rs. 71,250 at 90%.

15. Prepare a flexible budget for overheads on the basis of data given below. Ascertain the overhead rates at 50, 60 and 70% capacity.

	At 50% capacity	*At 60% capacity*	*At 70% capacity*
	Rs.	Rs.	Rs.
Variable Overheads :			
Indirect materials		6,000	
Indirect Labour		18,000	
Semi-variable overheads :			
Electricity (40% fixed)		30,000	
Repairs and maintenance (80% fixed)		3,000	
Fixed Overheads :			
Depreciation		16,500	
Insurance		4,500	
Salaries		15,000	
Total Overheads		93,000	

Estimated direct labour hours 1,86,000

Ans. : (a) At 50% capacity level Re. 0.55; (b) At 60% capacity level Re. 0.50.

16. Prepare a Flexible Budget for overheads on the basis of data given below. Ascertain the overheads rates at 50, 60 and 70% capacity.

	At 50% capacity	*At 60% capacity*	*At 70% capacity*
	Rs.	Rs.	Rs.
Variable Overheads :			
Indirect materials		6,000	
Indirect labour		18,000	
Semi-variable Overhead :			
Electricity (40% fixed)		30,000	
Repairs and maintenance (80% fixed)		3,000	

Fixed Overheads :	
Depreciation	16,500
Insurance	4,500
Salaries	15,000
	93,000

Estemated direct labour hours at 60% capacity 1,86,000

[B.U. B.Com. (Hons.)]

Ans. :	50% capacity,	60% capacity,	70% capacity.
	Rs.	Rs.	Rs.
Total overheads	85,900	93,000	1,00,100
Overhead rate per direct labour (Re)	0.55	0.50	0.46

17. From the following data, prepare a flexible budget for production of 40,000 units and 75,000 units distinctly showing variable and fixed cost as well as total cost. Also indicate elementwise cost per unit. Budgeted output is 1,00,000 units and budgeted cost per unit is as follows :

		Rs.
(i)	Direct material	95
(ii)	Direct labour	50
(iii)	Production overhead (variable)	40
(iv)	Production overhead (fixed)	5
(v)	Administration overhead (fixed)	5
(vi)	Selling overhead (10% fixed)	10
(vii)	Distribution overhead (20% fixed)	15

[Delhi University B.Com. (Hons.)]

Ans. : Total cost of 75,000 units = Rs. 1,68,50,000,
Total cost of 40,000 units = Rs. 96,40,000.

18. Draw up a flexible budget for overhead expenses on the basis of the following data and determine the overhead rates at 70%, 80% and 90% plant capacity.

	At 70% Capacity Rs.	At 80% Capacity Rs.	At 90% Capacity Rs.
Variable overhead :			
Indirect labour		12,000	
Stores including spares		4,000	
Semi-variable overheads :			
Power (30% fixed)		20,000	
Repairs and maintenance (60% fixed)			
Fixed Overheads :			
Depreciation		11,000	
Insurance		3,000	
Salaries		10,000	

Extimated direct labour hours 1,24,000 hours

[Adapted—B.Com. Madurai]

Ans. : (a) At 79% capacity Re. 0.536;
(b) At 80% capacity Re. 0.500; (c) At 90% capacity Re. 0.472.

19. A company incurs the following expenses to produce 1,000 units of an article :

	Rs.
Direct materials	30,000
Direct labour	15,000
Power (20% fixed)	10,000
Repairs and maintenance (15% fixed)	8,000
Depreciation (40% variable expenses)	6,000
Administrative expenses (100% fixed)	12,000

Prepare a Flexible Budget showing individual expenses of production levels at 1,500 units and 2,000 units.

[C.U. B.Com. (Hons.) 1998]

Ans. : 1,000, 1,500, 2,000;

Total cost Rs. 81,000; Rs. 1,12,100; Rs. 1,43,200.

20. For the production of 10,000 electrical automatic irons the following are the budgeted expenses :

	Per unit Rs.
Direct material	60
Direct labour	30
Variable Overheads	25
Fixed Overheads (Rs. 1,50,000)	15
Variable expenses (direct)	5
Selling expenses (10% fixed)	15
Administration expenses (Rs. 50,000 fixed for all levels of production)	5
Distribution expenses (20% fixed)	5
Total cost of sale per unit	160

Prepare a flexible budget for production of 6,000, 7,000 and 8,000 irons.

[Adapted—B.Com. Punjab]

Ans. : Total cost—Rs. 10,50,000 for 6,000 units;

Rs. 11,87,500 for 7,000 units; Rs. 13,25,000 for 8,000 units.

21. Deepak Electronics Ltd. had prepared its budget for the year ended 31.3.2002 based on the production of 1,00,000 units of their only product as under :

	Rs.
Raw materials	2,52,000
Direct labour	75,000
Direct expenses	10,000
Works overhead (60% fixed)	2,25,000
Administration Overheads	40,000
Selling Overheads (50% fixed)	20,000

For want of demand, the actual production for that period was only 60,000 units.

Calculate the budgeted cost per unit under both the original plan and under the actual performance.

[Adapted—M.Com. Bombay]

Ans. : Total Cost : (a) Original, (1,00,000 units)—Rs. 6,22,000,

(b) Actual (60,000)—Rs. 4,47,200.

22. Prepare a Flexible Budget for production at 80% and 100% activity on the basis of the following information :

Production at 50% capacity	5,000 units
Raw material Rs. 80 per unit	
Direct Labour Rs. 50 per unit	
Expenses Rs. 15 per unit	
Factory expenses Rs. 50,000 (50% fixed)	
Administration expenses Rs. 60,000 (60% variable)	

Ans. : Cost of production : 80% capacity Rs. 13,06,600,
100% capacity Rs. 16,21,000.

23. Prepare a Flexible Budget on the basis of the following information for the year ended 31.3.2002.

Particulars	Amount 2001-2002 Rs.
Direct materials	1,60,000
Direct labour	1,40,000
Chargeable expenses	50,000
Machine expenses	30,000
Motive power	10,000
Factory overheads (80% Fixed)	24,000
Office Overheads (60% Fixed)	36,000
Selling Overheads (50% Fixed)	12,000
Sales (selling price being Rs. 500 per unit)	5,00,000

During the year all the units produced were sold and the factory was working at the capacity of 60%. The flexible budget is to be prepared with the following assumptions :

(i) That capacity will be 75% and

(ii) That the price of direct material will increase by 20% and that wages will increase by 10%.

24. A factory is currently working at 50% capacity and produces 10,000 units. Estimate the profit of the company when it works at 60% and 80% capacity and offer your comment.

At 60% working, raw material cost increases by 2% and selling price by 2%. At 80% raw material cost increases by 5% and selling price falls by 5%.

At 50% capacity the product costs are Rs. 180 per unit and is sold at Rs. 200 per unit. The unit cost of Rs. 180 is made up as follows :

	Rs.
Material	100
Labour	30
Factory overhead	30 (40% fixed)
Administrative overhead	20 (50% fixed)

[Adapted—I.C.W.A. (Inter)]

Profit

Ans. : 50% capacity Rs. 2,00,000, Rs. 20 per unit.
60% capacity Rs. 2,12,000, Rs. 17.67 per unit.
80% capacity Rs. 2,12,000, Rs. 13.25 per unit.

25. A Limited Company is to be incorporated to take over a running business. It is proposed to raise Rs. 50 lakhs by issuing Equity Shares and balance of capital required in first six months is to be financed by a financial institution. The latter is to be given 8% Debentures to the extent of Rs. 1 lakh above the amount required, secured on Fixed Assets.

Initial investments consist of :

	Rs.
Freehold Premises	20 lakhs
Plant	8 lakhs
Stock	5 lakhs
Motor vans and other items	6 lakhs

Payments on account of the above items are to be made in the month of incorporation.

Estimates of transactions for the first six months commencing from July are given below :

Sales :	Rs. (in lakhs)
July	12.50
August	15.00
September	18.00
October	22.00
November	23.00

For each of the next three months Rs. 24 lakhs Gross profit on sales to be at the rate of 20%.

Debtors : To get two months credit.

Creditors : To be paid at the end of the month of purchase.

Expenses :

(a) Preliminary expenses Rs. 50,000 to be paid in August.

(b) General expenses Rs. 40,000 per month payable at the end of each month.

(c) Wages and salaries payable on the first day of the next month, Rs. 70,000 for each of first three months and Rs. 85,000 per month thereafter.

Assume that shares and debentures are issued on 1st July.

Draw up a Cash Budget and budgeted Final Account upto 31st December, and Balance Sheet as on that date.

[Adapted—C.A. Final]

Ans. : (i) Net Profit Rs. 20.46 lakhs

(ii) Balance Sheet : Total Rs. 90.70 lakhs.

26. The cost of an article at the capacity level of 5,000 units is given under 'A' below. For a variation of 25% in capacity above or below this level, the individual expenses vary as indicated under 'B' below :

	A	B
	Rs.	
Material Cost	25,000	100% varying
Labour Cost	15,000	100% varying
Power	1,250	80% varying
Repairs and Maintenance	2,000	75% varying
Stores	1,000	100% varying

Inspection	500	20% varying
Depreciation	10,000	100% varying
Administration		
Overheads	5,000	25% varying
Selling Overheads	3,000	50% varying
	62,750	
Cost per unit	12.55	

Prepare the Production Cost Budget at 4,000 and 6,000.

[Adapted—Bangalore U. M.Com.]

Ans. : Total Cost : For 4,000 units Rs. 53,480, For 6,000 units Rs. 72,020, Cost per unit : 4,000 — Rs. 13.37, 6,000—Rs. 12.00.

RATIO ANALYSIS 13

Learning Objectives :

1. *Introduction*
2. *Users of Financial Statements*
3. *Ratio Analysis—Nature*
4. *Uses of Accounting Ratios*
5. *Limitations of Ratio Analysis*
6. *Types of Ratios :*
   (a) Liquidity Ratios
   (b) Leverage Ratios
   (c) Activity Ratios
   (d) Profitability Ratios
7. *Solved Problems*
8. *Assignment for Practice*

RATIO ANALYSIS 13

FINANCIAL STATEMENT ANALYSIS

Introduction

Financial Statements refer to income statements and balance sheet of a firm. Financial Statements analysis is the groundwork for making plans. It is true that one has to understand the past for anticipating the future. Therefore, Financial Statements Analysis is *an important management tool to identify the financial strengths and weaknesses* of a firm and the management can plan accordingly to remove the weaknesses, if any, and can lead the firm to the path of success.

The basic limitation of the traditional financial statements comprising the balance sheet and the profit and loss account is that they do not give all the information regarding the financial operation of a firm. Undoubtedly, they provide some extremely useful information to the extent the balance sheet mirrors the financial position on a particular date in terms of the structures of assets, liabilities and owners equity, etc. and the profit and loss account shows the results obtained and the cost incurred during the year. The financial statements provide a summarised view of the financial position and operations of the firm.

Financial analysis is the process of identifying the financial strengths and weaknesses of the firm by properly establishing relationships between the items of the balance sheet and the income statements.

In the words of **Metcalf R. W.** and **P. L. Titard,** *"The analysis of financial statements is a process of evaluating relationships between component parts of financial statements to obtain a better understanding of the firm's position and performances".*

Users of Financial Statements

The users of financial analysis are :

(a) *Management* : to see the resources of the firm are used most *effectively* and *efficiently* and the financial position are sound.

(b) *Creditors* : they are interested in the firm's liquidity position so that the firm can meet its debts within a short period of time.

(c) *The suppliers of long term debt* : they are concerned with firm's long-term solvency and servival

(d) *Investors* : are interested in firm's profitability and solvency because they expect reasonable return on their investments and their investments are secured.

Ratio Analysis

Definition

Ratio Analysis is a powerful tool of financial analysis. A ratio is defined as *"the indicated quotient of two mathematical expressions and as the relationship between two or more things"*— ***Webster's New Collegiate Dictionary.***

Ratio Analysis may be defined as the systematic use of ratio to interpret the financial statements so that the strength and weaknesses of a firm as well as its historical performance and current financial condition can be determined.

The term 'ratio' refers to the numerical or quantitative relationship between two items or variables.

In financial analysis, a ratio is used as an index or yardstick for evaluating the financial position and performance of a firm. As a matter of fact, an accounting figure conveys meaning when it is related to some other relevant information. Therefore, ratios help to summaries the large quantities of financial data and to make qualitative judgement about firm's financial performance and financial position.

The accounting ratios serve many purpose, they can assist management in its basic functions like forecasting, planning, co-ordination, control, and communication. If they are used properly they can improve efficiency and therefore, profits.

Uses of Accounting Ratios

Some of the possible uses of accounting ratios are summarized below :

1. Accounting ratios may be very useful for forecasting likely events in the future since past ratios indicate trends in costs, sales, profit and other relevant facts.
2. Ideal ratios can be established and the relationships between primary ratios may be used to establish the desirable co-ordination or balance. Normally, this is linked with the Budgetary Control.
3. Control may be materially assisted by the use of ratios and can be made effective.
4. "Communication" is the process used to impart knowledge within the business or to outside shareholders or other interested parties. Accounting ratios can play vital role in informing what has happened from one period to another.
5. Accounting ratios may be used as measures of efficiency. In fact, accounting ratios aid uniformity and, therefore, can made comparisons much more valid.
6. Ratio analysis helps investment decisions. An investor is interested in both solvency and profitability of a firm. The investor can take his investment decision studying both solvency as well as profitability ratios.

There is no doubt that ratios can be an invaluable aid to management and others who are interested in analysing the operations and the state of affairs of a business. Absolute figures may be misleading unless compared one with another, ratios provide the means of showing the interrelationships which exist.

According to ***W.H. Beaver***, *"Ratio analysis is being as a device to diagnose the financial health of a business concern"*. It facilitates the work of gauging the profitability, solvency and activity of the concern. Undoubtedly, it is a powerful tool for both internal and external analysis and can be used as guidelines for managerial and other economic decisions.

Limitations of Ratio Analysis

"The ratio analysis is an aid to management in taking credit decisions, but as a mechanical substitute for thinking and judgement, it is worse than useless."—***Hunt, Williams & Donaldson***

Though ratios are precious tools in the hands of the analyst but its significance emanates from proper use of these ratios. Misuse and mishandling of the ratios may lead the management and other users to a wrong decisions.

There are some limiting factors for the use of ratios. These limiting factors are as follows :

(i) Ratios are not end in themselves but they are means to achieve a particular end.

(ii) The accuracy and correctness of ratios are totally dependent upon the reliability of the data contained in financial statements on the basis of which ratios are calculated.

(iii) The analyst or the user must have comprehensive but practical knowledge and experience about the concerns whose statements are used for calculating ratios.

(iv) In case of inter-firm comparison, there must be uniformity in the accounting plan used by both the firms.

(v) Ratios may make the comparative study complicated and misleading on account of changes in price level.

(vi) Inter-firm comparison through ratio analysis should not be undertaken in the case of concerns which are not associated or comparable.

Types of Ratios

In view of the requirements of the various users of ratios, we may classify them into the following four important categories.

1. Liquidity Ratios
2. Leverage or Capital Structure Ratios
3. Activity Ratios
4. Profitability Ratios.

The following is the summary of some of the most important financial ratios :

1. Liquidity Ratios (They are also know as Balance Sheet Ratios.)

The very object of liquidity ratio is to measure the firm's short-term solvency. The measure the firm's capability to pay off its current liabilities. A firm must have sufficient current assets so that it can liquidate current liabilities as and when required.

The following are the liquidity ratios which are determined from the figures of the Balance Sheet.

(a) **Current Ratio** : $\dfrac{\text{Current Assets}}{\text{Current Liabilities}}$

(b) **Quick or Acid Test Ratio** : $\dfrac{\text{Current Assets} - \text{Inventory}}{\text{Current Liabilities}}$

(c) **Cash Ratio** : $\dfrac{\text{Cash} + \text{Marketable Securities}}{\text{Current Liabilities}}$

(i) Current Assets consists of :

- Cash in hand;
- Cash at Bank;
- Sundry Debtors or Book Debts;
- Bills Receivable;
- Inventories;
  (a) Raw Materials
  (b) Work-in-progress
  (c) Finished goods
- Prepaid expenses.

(ii) Current Liabilities include the following :
- Sundry creditors
- Bills payable
- Outstanding liabilities
- Provision for taxation
- Proposed Dividend.

Current assets are those which are expected to be converted into cash or are realisable within the next financial year in the usual course of business activities.

Current liabilities are those financial obligations of the firm that are payable in the next financial year.

* Is Bank overdraft in a current liability or long-term liability? There is a controversy over the matter nevertheless consistency is expected to be followed.

2. Leverage Ratios (they are also known as Balance Sheet ratios)

The object of leverage ratios is to measure the long-term solvency of the firm.

(i) **Total Debt Ratio** $= \dfrac{\text{Total Debt}}{\text{Capital Employed}}$

(ii) **Debt-Equity Ratio** $= \dfrac{\text{Net Worth}}{\text{Total Debt}}$

(iii) **Capital Equity Ratio** $= \dfrac{\text{Capital Employed or Net Assets}}{\text{Net Worth}}$

(iv) **Capital Gearing Ratio** $= \dfrac{\text{Fixed Interest bearing Securities}}{\text{Equity Share Capital or Owners' Equity}}$

(v) **Interest Coverage** $= \dfrac{\text{*EBIT + Depreciation}}{\text{Interest}}$

(vi) **Proprietary Ratio** $= \dfrac{\text{Proprietory Fund}}{\text{Total Assets}}$

* EBIT = Earning before Interest and Income-tax.

3. Activity Ratios : These ratios indicate how the resources of the Firm have been used for earning profits

(i) **Inventory Turnover** $= \dfrac{\text{Cost of Goods Sold or Sales}}{\text{Average Inventory}}$

(ii) **Inventory Velocity** $= \dfrac{\text{360 days}}{\text{Inventory Turnover}}$

(iii) **Debtors Turnover** $= \dfrac{\text{Credit Sales or Sales}}{\text{Debtors}}$

(iv) **Collection Period** $= \dfrac{\text{360 days}}{\text{Debtors Turnover}}$

(v) **Assets Turnover** $= \dfrac{\text{Sales}}{\text{Net Assets or Capital Employed}}$

(vi) **Working Capital Turnover** $= \dfrac{\text{Sales}}{\text{** Net Working Capital}}$

(vii) Fixed Assets Turnover $= \dfrac{\text{Sales}}{\text{Fixed Assets}}$

** Net Working Capital = Current Assets – Current Liabilities

4. Profitability Ratios

(i) **Gross Profit Ratio or Gross Margin** $= \dfrac{\text{Gross Profit}}{\text{Sales}} \times 100$

(ii) (a) **Net Margin** $= \dfrac{\text{Profit after tax}}{\text{Sales}} \times 100$

(b) **Net Margin** $= \dfrac{\text{EBIT}}{\text{Sales}} \times 100$

(iii) **Return on Investment** $= \dfrac{\text{EBIT}}{\text{Net assets or Capital Employed}} \times 100$

(iv) **Return on Equity** $= \dfrac{\text{Profit after tax}}{\text{Net Worth}} \times 100$

Now, we propose to discuss the nature of each ratio their interpretation.

Liquid Ratios

1. **Current Ratio** $= \dfrac{\text{*Current Assets}}{\text{*Net Liabilities}}$

- Current Assets include cash, bank, and other assets that can be converted into cash within a year, such a marketable securities, debtors and inventories. Prepaid expenses are also treated as current assets as they have to be paid in the near future.
- Current liabilities include all financial obligations that have to be made within a year, such as trade creditors, bills payable, short-term loans, outstanding expenses, income-tax liability and long-term debts maturing in the current year.

Interpretation

Current ratio measures the firm's ability to meet short-term obligations. It indicates the availability of current assets in rupees to meet the current liabilities.

The higher the ratio, greater the margin of safety. In fact, the main weakness of this ratio is that it does not reckon the quality of assets but the quantity of assets, which is not rational. Therefore, too much of reliance on current ratio should not be placed in measuring firm's short-term solvency.

Conventionally, a current **ratio of 2 : 1 is ideal ratio** but in practice there is no logic to follow this ratio. Firm with less than 2 to 1 ratios may do well. The current ratio fails to measure the quality of assets. For example, if the firm's currents assets consist of slow paying debtors or slow moving stock or obsolete stock, then the firm's ability to pay its current obligations will be impaired. Nonetheless, the current ratio is a crude-and-quick measure of the firm's liquidity.

2. **Acid Test Ratio or Quick Ratio** $= \dfrac{\text{Current Assets – Inventories}}{\text{Current Liabilities}}$

In the opinion of some authors $= \dfrac{\text{C.A. – Inventories}}{\text{C.L. – B.O.}}$

Interpretation

Acid Text Ratio establishes a relationship between quick or liquid assets and current liabilities. Liquid assets refer to those assets, which can be converted into cash quickly and easily without a loss in value. In that sense, cash and bank balances are more liquid than the other assets. Other current assets that are reckoned relatively liquid are book debts, bills receivable and marketable securities. For this purpose inventories normally cannot be or may not be converted into cash immediately.

Normally, **one is to one** ratio is considered as an ideal quick ratio. It does mean liquid assets = current liabilities. It is a more penetrating test of liquidity than the current ratio but is to be used cautiously. Practically speaking, in some cases inventories may be more liquid than book debts in case of some firms.

Nevertheless, the quick ratio is an important index of measuring firm's liquidity.

3. **Cash Ratio** $= \dfrac{\text{Cash + Marketable Securities}}{\text{Current Liabilities}}$

Problem 1

The Balance Sheet of Y Ltd. shows the following current assets and liabilities as on 31.3.2003 :

	Rs.	
Cash at Bank	50,000	
Sundry debtors	10,00,000	
Inventories	5,00,000	
Marketable securities	2,00,000	
Prepaid expenses	10,000	
		17,60,000
Sundry creditors	4,00,000	
Income-tax payable	2,00,000	
Bills payable	1,00,000	
Outstanding liabilities	30,000	
		7,30,000

From the above data you are required to find out the liquid ratios.

Solution

1. **Current Ratio** $= \dfrac{\text{Current Assets}}{\text{Current Liabilities}} = \dfrac{17,60,000}{7,30,000} = 2.41$

2. **Liquid Ratio** $= \dfrac{\text{Current Assets - Inventories}}{\text{Current Liabilities}} = \dfrac{12,60,000}{7,30,000} = 1.726$

3. **Cash Ratio** $= \dfrac{\text{Cash at Bank + Cash in hand}}{\text{Current Liabilities}} = \dfrac{50,000}{7,30,000} = 0.0684$

Leverage Ratios

There are two types of leverage ratios. They are structural ratios and coverage ratios. Structural ratios are based on the proportions of debt and equity in the capital structure of the firm, whereas coverage ratios are derived from the relationship between debt servicing commitments and sources of funds for meeting theses obligation.

Structural Ratios

(i) **Total Debt Ratio** $= \dfrac{\text{Total Debt}}{\text{Capital Employed}}$

(ii) **Debt Equity Ratio** $= \dfrac{\text{Debt}}{\text{Equity}}$

(iii) **Proprietary Ratio** $= \dfrac{\text{Owner's Equity}}{\text{Total Assets}}$

(iv) **Capital Gearing Ratio** $= \dfrac{\text{Fixed Income} - \text{Learing Fund}}{\text{Total long - term Fund}}$

Interpretations

(i) Total Debt Ratio or Debt Equity Ratio :

The above ratio is an important tool of financial analysis to appraise the financial structure of a firm. It has important implications from the view point of creditors, owners and the firm itself.

The high Debt Equity Ratio indicates a danger signal for creditors because in case of failure of business, the creditors will lose heavily.

This ratio indicates the relationship or role of outsiders in financing the business of the firm.

In case of low debt-equity ratio, creditors claim a high stake and implies sufficient safety margin against shrinkage in assets.

On the other hand, the servicing of debt becomes less burden some for the company.

It is evident that both high and low debt-equity ratios are not desirable. It can be rationally said that other's money should be in reasonable proportion to the owner's capital and the owners should have sufficient stake in the fortunes of the firm.

Capital structure ratios establish the relationship between the Creditors' Fund and Owners' Capital. Therefore, to judge the long-term financial position of the firm, financial leverage or capital structure ratios are calculated.

Problem 2

Following is the Balance Sheet of X Ltd. as on 31.3.2003

	Rs.		Rs.
Share Capital	3,00,000	**Fixed Assets**	5,00,000
Reserves and Surplus	2,80,000	Other Non-current Assets	2,00,000
10% Long-term Debentures	1,00,000	**Current Assets**	
12% Other long-term Debt	2,00,000	*Inventories* :	
11% Short-term loan	3,00,000	Raw materials	2,00,000
Trade creditors	95,000	Stock-in-process	1,00,000
Provisions	2,05,000	Finished goods	2,00,000
		Debtors	2,00,000
		Cash at Bank	80,000
	14,80,000		14,80,000

You are required to calculate Liquidity and Capital Structure ratios.

Solution

1. Liquidity Ratios

1. **Current Ratio :** $\frac{CA}{CL} = \frac{7,80,000}{3,00,000} = 2.6 : 1$

2. **Quick Ratio :** $\frac{CA - \text{Inventories}}{CL} = \frac{2,80,000}{3,00,000} = 0.93 : 1$

2. Leverage Ratios

1. **Debt Ratio :** $\frac{\text{Total Debt}}{\text{Capital Employed}} = \frac{\text{Rs. } 6,00,000}{\text{Rs. } 11,80,000} = 0.508$

This means that the lenders have financed 50.8 per cent or half of the company's net assets. The owners have provided 49.2%.

2. **Debt Equity Ratio :** $\frac{\text{Total Debt}}{\text{Net Worth}} = \frac{\text{Rs. } 6,00,000}{\text{Rs. } 5,80,000} = 1.03 : 1$

3. **Capital Gearing Ratio :** $\frac{\text{Fixed interest bearing securities}}{\text{Equity share capital}} = \frac{\text{Rs. } 6,00,000}{\text{Rs. } 3,00,000} = 2 : 1$

4. **Proprietary Ratio :** $\frac{\text{Proprietors' Fund}}{\text{Total Assets}} = \frac{\text{Rs. } 3,00,000 + \text{Rs. } 2,80,000}{14,80,000}$

$= \frac{\text{Rs. } 5,80,000}{\text{Rs. } 14,80,000} = 0.39 : 1$

Proprietary Ratio calculated above shows that the owners have financed 39% of total assets of the firm.

5. **Capital Equity Ratio :** $\frac{\text{Capital Employed}}{\text{Net Worth}} = \frac{\text{Rs. } 11,80,000}{\text{Rs. } 5,80,000} = 2.03 : 1$

3. Activity Ratios

The activity ratios are applied to evaluate the **efficiency of management** in utilizing the assets to generate sales and profits. These ratios are also known as turnover ratios because they indicate the speed with which assets are being turned-over or converted into sales. In this sense, activity ratios involve a relationship between sales and assets. These ratios are derived from both income statements and Balance Sheet.

Problem 3.

Zinc India Ltd.

Trading and Profit and Loss Account

For the year ended 31.3.2003

Dr.		Rs.			*Cr.* Rs.
To	Opening Stock	2,00,000	By	Sales	14,00,000
"	Purchases (Net)	6,00,000			
"	Wages	2,00,000			
"	Carriage Inward	50,000			
"	Gross Profit	4,00,000	By	Closing Stock	50,000
		14,50,000			14,50,000
To	Operating Expenses	1,00,000	By	Gross Profit	4,00,000
"	Net Profit	3,00,000			
		4,00,000			4,00,000

Balance Sheet
as on 31.3.2003

Equity Share Capital	4,00,000	Fixed Assets	7,00,000
Reserves	2,50,000		
10% Debentures	2,00,000	Debtors	1,75,000
Trade Creditors	1,50,000		
Outstanding Expenses	25,000	Stock	50,000
		Cash at Bank	1,00,000
	10,25,000		10,25,000

You are required to show the activity ratios of X Ltd. and comment on them.

Solution

1. **Inventory Turnover** = $\dfrac{\text{Cost of goods sold}}{\text{Average inventory}} = \dfrac{\text{Rs. } 10,00,000}{\text{Rs. } 1,25,000} = 8 : 1$

(Cost of goods sold = Rs. 2,00,000 + Rs. 6,00,000 + Rs. 2,00,000 + 50,000 – 50,000)

Zinc India Ltd. is turning its inventory of finished goods into sales (at cost) 8 times in a year.

2. **Inventory Velocity** = $\dfrac{\text{360 days}}{8} = 45$ days.

In case, the cost of goods sold figure is not available to an outside analyst from published annual accounts, he may compute inventory turnover as :

$$\frac{\text{Sales}}{\text{Average Inventory}}$$

In this situation, the inventory turnover ratio will be :

$$\frac{\text{Sales}}{\text{Inventory}} = \frac{\text{Rs. } 14,00,000}{\text{Rs. } 50,000} = 28 : 1$$

Or, $\dfrac{\text{Sales}}{\text{Average Inventory}} = \dfrac{\text{Rs. } 14,00,000}{\text{Rs. } 1,25,000} = 8$

3. **Debtors Turnover** = $\dfrac{\text{Credit Sales}}{\text{Average Debtors}} = \dfrac{\text{Rs. } 14,00,000}{\text{Rs. } 1,75,000} = 8$

Collection Period = $\dfrac{\text{Debtors}}{\text{Sales}} \times 360 = \dfrac{\text{Rs. } 1,75,000}{14,00,000} \times 360 = 45$ days.

4. **Assets Turnover Ratio** : $\dfrac{\text{Sales}}{\text{Net Assets}} = \dfrac{\text{Rs. } 14,00,000}{\text{Rs. } 8,50,000} = 1.645 : 1$

(Net Assets = FA + CA – CL = Rs. 7,00,000 + Rs. 3,25,000 – Rs. 1,75,000 = Rs. 8,50,000)

5. **Fixed Assets Turnover Ratio** = $\dfrac{\text{Sales}}{\text{F.A.}} = \dfrac{\text{Rs. } 14,00,000}{\text{Rs. } 7,00,000} = 2 : 1.$

4. Profitability Ratios

A company should earn sufficient profits for its survival and growth. It is an established fact that *"sufficient profit must be earned by a business unit and sustain the operations of the business, to be able to obtain funds from investors for expansion and growth and to contribute towards the social overheads for the welfare of the society".—**Drucker P.F.***

The profitability ratios are calculated to measure the operating efficiency of the company. Moreover, management, creditors and owners are equally interested in the profitability of the firm.

Creditors like to receive interest and repayment of principal regularly. Shareholders want to get a reasonable return on their investments and management wants to satisfy all interested parties thereby to create goodwill for the organisation. All these are possible when the company earns substantial profits.

There are generally two types of profitability ratios :

1. ***Profitability in relation to sales.***
2. ***Profitability in relation to investment.***

1. **Profitability in relation to Sales :**

(a) **Gross Profit Margin :** $\dfrac{\text{Gross Profit}}{\text{Sales}} \times 100$

The gross profit margin reflects the efficiency with which the management produces each unit of product. It measures also the efficiency of both purchase and sales departments. The efficiency of these two departments reduces the cost of goods sold and thereby increases the efficiency of competitiveness in a competitive and global markets.

Obviously, a high gross profit margin is a sign of good management. A gross profit margin ratio may be higher due to any of the following factors :

(i) higher sale price, cost of goods sold remaining constant;

(ii) lower cost of goods sold, sales prices remaining constant;

(iii) a combination of variations in sales prices and costs; and

(iv) an increase in the proportionate volume of higher margin items.

(b) **Net Profit Margin =** $\dfrac{\text{Profit after tax}}{\text{Sales}} \times 100$

The net profit margin establishes relationship between net profit and sales and points out management's efficiency in manufacturing, administration and selling its products.

The high net profit margin enables a company to survive in a situation of adverse economic conditions. A firm with high net profit margin can make better use of favourable market and economic conditions such as rising sales prices, falling cost of production or increasing demand for the product. Such a firm has the ability to accelerate its profits at a faster rate.

Net profit margin for evaluating operating performance may be computed in the following manner :

Net Profit Margin = $\dfrac{\text{EBIT(I} - \text{T)}}{\text{Sales}} \times 100$

(c) **Operating Expense Ratio :** $\dfrac{\text{Operating Expenses}}{\text{Sales}} \times 100$

(i) Operating Expenses = Cost of goods sold + office and administrative expenses + selling expenses. Interest is not considered.

This ratio is a yardstick of operating efficiency. A higher operating expense ratio is unfavourable since it will leave a small amount of operating income to meet interest and dividends.

(d) **Administrative Expenses Ratio =** $\dfrac{\text{Administrative Expenses}}{\text{Net Sales}} \times 100$

(e) **Selling Expense Ratio =** $\dfrac{\text{Selling Expenses}}{\text{Net sales}} \times 100$

Interpretation

The operating expense ratio is used for measuring the operating efficiency. It is advisable to use this ratio very cautiously since it is affected by a number of factors, such as external uncontrollable factors, internal factors.

Taxes are not controllable by a firm, and also one may not know the marginal corporate tax rate while analysing the published data, it is more appropriate to use the following measures of ROI for comparing the operating efficiency of firm.

2. **Profitability in relation to investment :**

(i) **Return on Investment**

Return on Investment

POTA (Return on Total Asset)	RONA (Return on Net Asset)
$= \dfrac{EBIT(I - T)}{\text{Total Assets}}$	$\dfrac{EBIT(I - T)}{\text{Net Assets}}$

Since taxes are not controllable by management and since opportunities for availing tax incentives differ from firm to firm, it is more prudent to use before tax measure of Return on Investment. The term investment may refer to total assets or net assets. Net assets mean capital employed.

The before tax ratios are :

(i) $ROI = ROTA = \dfrac{EBIT}{TA}$

(ii) $ROI = RONA = \dfrac{EBIT}{NA^*}$

Net Assets = Capital employed.

(ii) ***Return on Equity*** $= \dfrac{PAT^*\text{(Profit After Tax)}}{\text{Net Worth}^*}$

*Net worth = Equity + Reserves and surplus.

*Profit is to be calculated after deducting dividend from PAT.

(iii) ***Earning per Share (EPS)***

The earning per share is calculated by dividing the profit after taxes by the total number of Equity shares. Therefore, EPS is equal to

$$EPS = \frac{\text{Profit After Tax (PAT)}}{\text{No. of Equity Shares}}$$

EPS calculations made over the years indicate the trend of profitability of the firm. This trend can easily guide the investors in taking investment decisions. But, it fails to reflect how much is paid as dividend and how much is retained in the business.

(iv) ***Dividend per Share (DPS)***

The net profits after taxes belong to shareholders. But the income which they actually receive is the amount of earnings distributed as cash dividend (including interim dividend, if any).

$$DPS = \frac{\text{Earning paid to Equity Shareholders}}{\text{No. of Ordinary Shares}}$$

(v) ***Dividend Payout Ratio***

$$\text{Pay out Ratio} = \frac{\text{Dividend Per Share (DPS)}}{\text{Earning Per Share (EPS)}}$$

(vi) ***Price Earning Ratio***

$$\text{Price Earning Ratio} = \frac{\text{Market Value Per Share}}{\text{Earnings Per Share}} \text{ or } \frac{MV}{EPS}$$

This ratio indicates investor's judgement or expectations about the firm's performance. Management is also interested in this market appraisal of the firm's performance and will like to identity the causes of weak performance if the P/E ratio declines.

WORKED-OUT PROBLEMS

Problem 4

Ramdhari Ltd. has following earnings during the year 1999 :

Profit before tax	Rs. 24,46,000	
Tax at	60%	
Proposed Dividend	20%	
Capital of the company is :		
9% Preference Shares		Rs. 10,00,000
Equity Shares		Rs. 30,00,000
		(30,000 Shares of Rs. 100 each)

Reserves as at the beginning of the year Rs. 22,00,000.

From the above compute (for equity shares)

(i) Earnings per share
(ii) Book value per share
(iii) Earnings Yield ratio
(iv) Price/Earnings ratio
(v) Dividend Payment ratio

The current market price of the equity shares is Rs. 200.

[I.C.W.A.—Adapted]

Solution

$$\textbf{(i) Earning Per Share} = \frac{\text{Net Profit} - \text{Pref. Div.} - \text{Tax}}{\text{Equity Shares}}$$

$$= \frac{\text{Rs. } 24{,}46{,}000 - \text{Rs. } 90{,}000 - \text{Rs. } 14{,}67{,}600}{30{,}000}$$

$$= \textbf{Rs. 29.61 per share}$$

(ii) Book Value Per Share

			Rs.	Rs.
	Net profit		24,46,000	
Less :	Pref. Dividend	90,000		
	Pref. Dividend	6,00,000		
	Tax	14,67,600		
			21,57,600	2,88,400
	Share capital (30,000 × 100)			30,00,000
	Reserves			22,00,000
				54,88,400

Fund transfer for Equity shareholders

Value per share $= \dfrac{\text{Rs. } 54,88,400}{30,000} = \text{Rs. } 182.95$

(iii) **Earning Yield Ratio** $= \dfrac{\text{Net Profit} - \text{Pref. Div.} - \text{Tax}}{\text{Shareholders' Fund}} \times 100$

$= \dfrac{\text{Rs. } 24,46,000 - \text{Rs. } 90,000 - \text{Rs. } 14,67,400}{\text{Rs. } 54,88,400} \times 100$

$= \mathbf{16.2\%}$

(iv) **Price Earning Ratio** $= \dfrac{\text{Earning Per share}}{\text{Market Value}} = \dfrac{\text{Rs. } 29.61}{200} = \text{Rs. } 14.85$

(v) **Dividend Payment Ratio** $= \dfrac{\text{Proposed Div.}}{\text{Net Profit}} \times 100$

$= \dfrac{\text{Rs. } 6,00,000}{\text{Rs. } 8,88,400} \times 100 = 67.6\%$

Problem 5

From the following information prepare a summarised Balance Sheet in the books of X Ltd. as at 31st December, 2003 assuming the capital is composed of Equity Shares of Rs. 10 each :

Liquid Ratio	1.5
Current Ratio	2.5
Asset (Fixed) Proprietorship Fund Ratio	0.75
Working Capital	Rs. 1,20,000
Reserves and Surplus	Rs. 60,000
Bank Overdraft	Rs. 20,000

[C.U. B.Com. (Hons.)]

Solution

Workings :

(i) **Working Capital** = Current Assets (CA) – Current Liabilities (CL)

or, Rs. 1,20,000 = CA – CL

CA = Rs. 1,20,000 + CL

Current Ratio $= \dfrac{CA}{CL}$

or, $2.5 = \dfrac{\text{Rs. } 1,20,000 + CL}{CL} = \text{Rs. } 90,000.$

or, 2.5 CL = Rs. 1,20,000 + CL

or, 1.5 CL = Rs. 1,20,000

$CL = \dfrac{\text{Rs. } 1,20,000}{1.5} = \text{Rs. } 80,000$

CA = Rs. 1,20,000 + Rs. 80,000 = Rs. 2,00,000

(ii) **Quick Ratio** $= \dfrac{\text{Quick Assets}}{\text{Quick Liabilities}}$

$1.5 = \dfrac{CA - \text{Stock}}{CL - \text{Bank O/D}}$

$$1.5 = \frac{\text{Rs. } 2{,}00{,}000 - \text{Stock}}{\text{Rs. } 80{,}000 - \text{Rs. } 20{,}000}$$

1.5 × Rs. 60,000 = Rs. 2,00,000 – Stock

Stock = Rs. 2,00,000 – Rs. 90,000 = Rs. 1,10,000

Other Current Assets = Rs. 2,00,000 – Rs. 1,10,000 = Rs. 90,000

(iii) **Fixed Asset Proprietorship Ratio** $= \frac{\text{Fixed Asset}}{\text{Proprietory Fund}} = .75$

In the absence of any information assuming that there is no long-term loan, no investment and no fictitious assets.

Proprietary Fund = Fixed Asset + Working Capital

= Fixed Asset + Rs. 1,20,000

$$\therefore \frac{\text{Fixed Assets}}{\text{Fixed Asset} + \text{Rs. } 1{,}20{,}000} = .75$$

Fixed Asset = .75 Fixed Asset + Rs. 90,000

.25 Fixed Asset = Rs. 90,000

$$\therefore \text{Fixed Asset} = \frac{\text{Rs. } 90{,}000}{.25} = \text{Rs. } 3{,}60{,}000$$

$$\text{Proprietary Fund} = \frac{\text{Fixed Asset}}{.75} = \frac{\text{Rs. } 3{,}60{,}000}{.75} = \text{Rs. } 4{,}80{,}000.$$

Again, Proprietary Fund = Share Capital + Reserve & Surplus.

∴ Share Capital = Proprietary Fund – Reserve & Surplus

= Rs. 4,80,000 – Rs. 60,000

= Rs. 4,20,000

(iv) **Creditor** = Current Liabilities – Bank O/D

= Rs. 80,000 – Rs. 20,000 = Rs. 60,000

X Ltd.

Balance Sheet as at 31.12.98

Liabilities	Rs.	Assets	Rs.
Share Capital :		Fixed Assets	3,60,000
42,000 Equity Shares or Rs. 10 each	4,20,000	Current Assets :	
Reserve and Surplus	60,000	Stock	1,10,000
Current Liabilities :		Others	90,000
Sundry Creditors	60,000		
Bank Overdraft	20,000		
	5,60,000		5,60,000

Problem 6

From the following date relating to a firm, prepare balance sheet of the firm as at 31.12.98 :

Annual Sales	Rs. 36,00,000
Sales to Net Worth	4 times
Current liabilities to net worth	50%
Total Debt to net worth	80%
Current ratio	3

Sales to Inventory	6 times
Average Collection period	73 days
Fixed Assets to net worth	30%

[B.U. B.Com. (Hons) 1998]

Solution

Balance Sheet
as at 31.12.98

Liabilities	Rs.	Assets	Rs.
Net worth	9,00,000	Fixed Assets	2,70,000
Long-term debt	2,70,000	Stock	6,00,000
Current liabilities	4,50,000	Debtors	7,20,000
		Cash & Bank	30,000
	16,20,000		16,20,000

Workings :

(i) **Net Worth**

Sales to Net worth = 4 times

or $4 = \dfrac{\text{Sales}}{\text{Net worth}}$ or $4 = \dfrac{\text{Rs. } 36{,}00{,}000}{\text{Net worth}}$

or, Net worth $\dfrac{\text{Rs. } 36{,}00{,}000}{4}$ = Rs. 9,00,000

(ii) **Current Liabilities**

Current liabilities to Net worth = 50%

or, $\dfrac{50}{100} = \dfrac{\text{Current Liabilities}}{\text{Net Worth}}$

or, $.50 = \dfrac{\text{Current Liabilities}}{\text{Rs. } 9{,}00{,}000}$

or, Current Liabilities = .50 × Rs. 9,00,000 = Rs. 4,50,000

(iii) **Long-Term Debt**

Total Debt to Net worth = 80%

or, $\dfrac{80}{100} = \dfrac{\text{Total Debt}}{\text{Net worth}}$

or, $.80 = \dfrac{\text{Total Debt}}{\text{Rs. } 9{,}00{,}000}$

or Total debt = .80 × Rs. 9,00,000 = Rs. 7,20,000

Long-term debt = Total Debt – Current liabilities

= Rs. 7,20,000 – Rs. 4,50,000

= Rs. 2,70,000

(iv) **Current Assets**

Current Ratio = 3

Current Ratio = $\dfrac{\text{Current Assets}}{\text{Current Liabilities}}$

$$\text{or, } 3 = \frac{\text{Current Assets}}{\text{Rs. } 4{,}50{,}000}$$

or, Current Assets = 3 × Rs. 4,50,000 = Rs. 13,50,000

(v) **Inventory**

Sales to Inventory = 6 times

$$\text{or, } 6 \; \frac{\text{Sales}}{\text{Inventory}}$$

$$\text{or, } 6 = \frac{\text{Rs. } 36{,}00{,}000}{\text{Inventory}}$$

$$\text{or, Inventory} = \frac{\text{Rs. } 36{,}00{,}000}{6} = \text{Rs. } 6{,}00{,}000$$

(vi) **Debtors**

Average Collection Period = 73 days

$$\text{or, Average Collection Period} = \frac{365}{\text{Credit Sales}} \times \text{Debtors}$$

$$\text{or, } 73 = \frac{365}{36{,}00{,}000} \times \text{Debtors}$$

$$\text{or, Debtors} = \frac{73 \times 36{,}00{,}000}{365} = \text{Rs. } 7{,}20{,}000$$

(vii) **Cash and Bank**

Current Assets = Stock + Debtors + Cash & Bank

or, Rs. 13,50,000 = Rs. 6,00,000 + Rs. 7,20,000 + Cash & Bank

or, Cash & Bank = Rs. 13,50,000 – Rs. 13,20,000 = Rs. 30,000

(viii) **Fixed Assets**

Fixed Assets to Net Worth = 30%

$$\text{or, } .30 = \frac{\text{Fixed Assets}}{\text{Net Worth}}$$

$$\text{or, } .30 = \frac{\text{Fixed Assets}}{9{,}00{,}000}$$

or, Fixed Asset = Rs. 9,00,000 × .30 = Rs. 2,70,000.

Problem 7

From the following particulars prepare the balance sheet of Shri Mohan Ram & Co. Ltd.

Current ratio	2
Working Capital	Rs. 4,00,000
Capital block to current assets	3 : 2
Fixed assets to turnover	1 : 3
Sales cash/credit	1: 2
Debentures/shares capital	1 : 2
Stock Velocity	2 months
Creditors Velocity	2 months
Debtors Velocity	3 months
Gross Profit ratio	25% (to sales)

Capital block :	
Net profit	10% of turnover
Reserve	$2^1/_2$ of turnover

Workings :

Since current Ratio is 2 current assets must be twice of current liabilities. In case of current liabilities are X. Current Assets will be 2X.

$\therefore$ 2X – X = 4,00,000

X = 4,00,000

Thus : Current Liabilities	Rs. 4,00,000
Current Assets	Rs. 8,00,000
Capital Block	Rs. 12,00,000

Since the total liabilities are Rs. 16,00,000 (i.e. Rs. 12,00,000 + Rs. 4,00,000), the total assets will also be Rs. 16,00,000.

Fixed Assets (Rs. 16,00,00 – Rs. 8,00,000)	Rs.	8,00,000
Turnover (Rs. 8,00,000 × 3)	Rs.	24,00,000
Credit Sales	Rs.	16,00,000
Cash Sales	Rs.	8,00,000
Debtors Velocity		3 months
Debtors are therefore (Rs. 16,00,000 × $^3/_{12}$)	Rs.	4,00,000
Gross profit (Rs. 24,00,000 × 25/10)	Rs.	6,00,000
Cost of Sales	Rs.	18,00,000
Stock turnover		2 months
Stock is therefore (Rs. 18,00,000 × 2/12)	Rs.	3,00,000
Creditors Velocity		2 months
Creditors are therefore (Rs. 18,00,000 × 2/12)	Rs.	3,00,000
Cash Balance (Rs. 8,00,000 – Rs. 7,00,000)	Rs.	1,00,000
Reserves (Rs. 24,00,000 × 2.5/100)	Rs.	60,000
Profit (Rs. 24,00,000 × 10/100)	Rs.	2,40,000
Block or Fixed Capital	Rs.	12,00,000
Reserves and Profit	Rs.	3,00,000
Debentures and Share Capital	Rs.	9,00,000
Share Capital	Rs.	6,00,000
Debentures	Rs.	3,00,000

Shri Mohan Ram & Co. Ltd.

Balance Sheet as on ....

Liabilities	Rs.	Assets	Rs.
Shares Capital	6,00,000	Fixed Assets	8,00,000
Reserves	60,000	Current Assets :	
Profit & Loss Account	2,40,000	Debtors	4,00,000
Debentures	3,00,000	Stock	3,00,000
Sundry Creditors	3,00,000	Cash	1,00,000
Other Current Liabilities	1,00,000		
	16,00,000		16,00,00

Problem 8

The Balance Sheets of Pilcom Ltd. for the last 3 years read as below :

	1994	1995	1996
Sources		(Rupees in lakhs)	
Share Capital (shares of Rs. 10)	2,000	2,000	3,000
Share Premium	1,500	1,500	500
Reserves (after 10% dividend)	1,500	1,700	1,800
Long-Term loan	1,000	800	800
	6,000	6,000	6,100
Represented by			
Fixed Assets	2,000	2,500	3,000
Less : Depreciation	700	950	1,250
	1,300	1,550	1,750
Capital Work-in-progress	800	900	700
Investments	200	200	200
	2,300	2,650	2,650
Net Current Assets :			
Current Assets :			
Debtors	1,700	1,800	1,850
Stocks	1,800	1,900	2,400
Cash and Bank	500	500	500
Others	400	600	1,400
	4,400	4,800	6,150
Current Liabilities	700	1,450	2,700
	3,700	3,350	3,450
Total Assets	6,000	6,000	6,100
Sales	3,900	4,000	5,000

Sales excludes excise duty and sales tax at 20%

Calculate for the years 1995 and 1996 :

(i) Fixed Assets Turnover Ratio

(ii) Stock Turnover Ratio

(iii) Debtors Turnover Ratio in terms of number of days' sales

(iv) Earnings per share.

Solution

Calculation of Ratios

	1995		1996	
	Rs. in lakhs	Ratio	Rs. in lakhs	Ratio
(i) Fixed Assets Turnover Ratio				
Sales / Average Fixed Assets				
Sales (Excluding excise duty and sales tax)	4,000		5,000	
Average Fixed Assets (Net)	1,425		1,650	
Ratio (times)		2.80		3.03

(ii)	**Stock Turnover Ratio**			
	Sales	4,000		5,000
	Average Inventory			
	Sales (Net) ÷			
	Average Inventory	1,850		2,150
	Ratio (times)		2.16	2.33
(iii)	**Debtors Turnover Ratio in terms of number of days' sales**			
	$\frac{\text{Average Receivables}}{\text{Credit Sales}} \times$ No. of days in a year			
	Average Receivables			
	$= \frac{\text{Opening Debtors + Closing Debtors}}{2}$	1,750		1,825
	Credit Sales	4,800		6,000
	(Inclusive of excise duty and sales tax)			
	Ratio (days)		133	111
(iv)	**Earnings Per Share**			
	$\frac{\text{Earnings attributable to equity shareholders}}{\text{Number of Equity Shares}}$			
	Increase in Reserves during the year	200		100
	Add : Dividends	200		300
	Total Earning for the year (after tax)	400		400
	Ratio (Rs.)		0.2	1.33

Problem 9

From the information given below prepare a comparative statement of suitable management ratios for your company to indicate **profitability** and **liquidity** trend over a period of two years.

Comment on the significance of the ratios shown in the statement and indicate how individual ratios are inter-related.

Balances Sheet
as at 31st, December

		1985 Rs. (000)	1986 Rs. (000)
Fixed Assets :			
	Land and Buildings at cost	2,727	3,343
	Plant : At cost	868	1,062
Less :	Depreciation	(395)	(475)
	(a)	3,200	3,930
Add :	*Current Assets* :		
	Stock and Work-in-progress	2,862	3,436
	Debtors	2,643	2,574
	Balance at Bank	360	123
	(b) Total Assets	9,065	10,063
Less :	Current Liabilities	3,107	2,338
	(c) Capital employed	5,958	7,725

Profit and Loss Account

for the year ended 31st December

		1985 Rs. (000)		1986 Rs. (000)
Sales		9,371		12,282
Production costs	6,091		6,755	
Selling and Distribution costs	1,171		1,696	
Administrative costs	1,028		1,228	
		8,290		9,679
Profit before tax		1,081		2,603

[Adapted—C.A. (Final)]

Solution

Comparatively Statement indicating Profitability and Liquidity Ratios for 1985 and 1986 :

Profitability Ratios :		1985 (Rs. in '000)	1986
1. **Gross Profit Ratio**	$\frac{\text{Gross Profit}}{\text{Sales}} \times 100$	$\frac{3,280}{9,371} \times 100 = 35\%$	$\frac{5,527}{12,282} \times 100 = 45\%$
2. **Net Profit Ratio**	$\frac{\text{Net Profit}}{\text{Sales}} \times 100$	$\frac{1,081}{9,371} \times 100 = 11.5\%$	$\frac{2,603}{12,282} \times 100 = 21.2\%$
3. **Return on Investment (ROI)**	$\frac{\text{Net Profit}}{\text{Capital Employed}} \times 100$	$\frac{1,081}{5,958} \times 100 = 18.1\%$	$\frac{2,603}{7,725} \times 100 = 33.7\%$
4. **Capital Turnover Ratio**	$\frac{\text{Sales}}{\text{Capital Employed}}$	$\frac{9,371}{5,958} = 1.57$ times	$\frac{12,282}{7,725} = 1.59$ times

*This ratio may be further analysed as under :

		1985	1986
(i) **Production Cost to Sales Ratio**	$\frac{\text{Production Cost}}{\text{Sales}} \times 100$	$\frac{6,091}{9,371} \times 100 = 65\%$	$\frac{6,755}{12,282} \times 100 = 55\%$
(ii) **Selling & Distribution Costs to Sales Ratio**	$\frac{\text{Selling \& Distribution Cost}}{\text{Sales}} \times 100$	$\frac{1,771}{9,371} \times 100 = 12.5\%$	$\frac{1,696}{12,282} \times 100 = 13.8\%$
(iii) **Administrative Cost to Sales Ratio**	$\frac{\text{Administrative Cost}}{\text{Sales}} \times 100$	$\frac{1,028}{9,371} \times 100 = 11\%$	$\frac{1,228}{12,282} \times 100 = 10\%$

Liquidity Ratios :

1. Current Ratio $= \dfrac{\text{Current Assets}}{\text{Current Liabilities}}$ $\dfrac{5,865}{3,107} = 1.89 : 1$ $\dfrac{6,133}{2,338} = 2.62 : 1$

2. Quick Ratio $= \dfrac{\text{Quick Assets}}{\text{Current Liabilities}}$ $\dfrac{3,003}{3,107} = .97 : 1$ $\dfrac{2,697}{2,338} = 1.15 : 1$

Comment on the Significance of the Ratios :

The above ratios show marked improvement in profitability and liquidity of the company in 1986 over 1985. This has been possible mainly by controlling cost of production is as depicted by production costs to sales ratio.

Problem 10

From the following ratios relating to the activities of Ray & Co. find out :

(a) Sales; (b) Sundry Debtors; (c) Closing Stock, (d) Sundry Debtors :

Debtors Velocity	3 months
Stock Velocity	8 months
Creditors Velocity	4 months
Gross Profit Ratio	25%

Gross profit for the current year ended 31.3.2003 amounts to Rs. 5,00,000. Closing stock of the year is 20,000 above the opening stock. Bills receivable amount to Rs. 30,000 and bills payable to Rs. 15,000.

Solution

(a) ***Sales*** = 25% of Sales = Rs. 5,00,000

$$\text{Sales} = \text{Rs. } 5{,}00{,}000 \times \frac{100}{25} = \text{Rs. } 20{,}00{,}000.$$

(b) ***Sundry Debtors*** $= \dfrac{\text{Credit sales}}{\text{Debtors Velocity}} = \text{Rs. } 20{,}00{,}000 \times \dfrac{3}{12}$

$$= \frac{20{,}00{,}000}{4} = \text{Rs. } 5{,}00{,}000$$

Closing Debtors = Rs. 5,00,000 – Bills Receivable

= Rs. 5,00,000 – Rs. 20,000 = Rs. 4,80,000.

(c) ***Closing Stock*** $= \dfrac{\text{Cost of goods sold}}{\text{Stock turnover}} = \dfrac{\text{Sales} - \text{Gross Profit}}{8 \text{ months}}$

$$= \frac{\text{Rs. } 20{,}00{,}000 - \text{Rs. } 5{,}00{,}000}{12} \times 8$$

Average Stock = Rs. 10,00,000

Closing stock is Rs. 20,000 above opening stock

$$\text{Opening stock} = \frac{(\text{Rs. } 10{,}00{,}000 + \text{Rs. } 10{,}00{,}000) - \text{Rs. } 20{,}000}{2}$$

= Rs. 9,80,000 ÷ 2 = Rs. 4,90,000

∴ Closing stock = Rs. 4,90,000 + Rs. 20,000 = 5,10,000

(d) ***Sundry Creditors*** :

Credit Purchase = Cost of goods sold + Closing stock – Opening stock

= Rs. 15,00,000 + Rs. 5,10,000 – Rs. 4,90,000 = Rs. 15,20,000

$$\text{Creditors} = \frac{\text{Credit Purchase}}{\text{Creditors volecity 4 months}} = \frac{\text{Rs. } 15{,}20{,}000}{12} \times 4$$

$$= \text{Rs. } 5{,}06{,}667$$

Here, Sundry creditors or payable include Bills Payable.

Therefore, Sundry creditors = Rs. 5,06,667 – Rs. 15,000 = **Rs. 4,91,667.**

INVENTORY TURNOVER RATIO

Problem 11

From the following information available from the Bin Cards of a concern for a period of one year :

(a) Calculate the inventory turnover of materials A, B and C.

(b) If the prices of A, B and C be respectively Rs. 10 per unit, Rs. 8 per kg. and Rs. 5 per litre, then what is the turnover of materials A, B and C.

(c) Find the period for which the average inventory in respect of each A, B and C is held :

	Material A	*Material B*	*Material C*
Opening stock	7000 units	2000 kg.	10,000 litres
Purchases	1,15,000 units	1,10,000 "	12,000 "
Closing stock	2,000 "	12,000 "	18,000 "

[Adapted—Bombay M.Com.]

Solution

Statement of Inventory Turnover Ratio

	Materials A	Materials B	Materials C	Total
	Rs.	Rs.	Rs.	Rs.
Price	10	8	5	
Opening stock	70,000	16,000	50,000	1,36,000
Add : Purchases	11,50,000	8,80,000	60,000	20,90,000
	12,20,000	8,96,000	1,10,000	22,26,000
Less : Closing stock	20,000	96,000	90,000	2,06,000
	12,00,000	8,00,000	20,000	20,20,000

$$\text{Average Inventory} = \frac{\text{Opening stock + Closing stock}}{2}$$

	A	B	C
	Rs.	Rs.	Rs.
	$\frac{70{,}000 + 20{,}000}{2}$	$\frac{96{,}000 + 16{,}000}{2}$	$\frac{1{,}36{,}000 + 2{,}06{,}000}{2}$
	45,000	56,000	1,71,000
Inventory Turnover $\frac{\text{Material Consumed}}{\text{Average Inventory}}$	$\frac{12{,}00{,}000}{45{,}000}$	$\frac{8{,}00{,}000}{56{,}000}$	$\frac{20{,}000}{70{,}000}$
	26.67	14.28	0.29
Period for which inventory was held	$\frac{365}{26.67}$	$\frac{365}{14.28}$	$\frac{365}{0.29}$
	= 14 days	= 26 days	= 1,259 days

Problem 12

From the information given below calculate :

(i) Working Capital

(ii) Capital Employed

(iii) Current Ratio

(iv) Acid Test Ratio

(v) Debt Equity Ratio and

(vi) Asset Proprietorship Ratio.

Balance Sheet of X Company Ltd.

As on 31st Dec. 1995

Liabilities	Rs.	Rs.	Assets	Rs.	Rs.
Shareholders Fund			**Fixed Assets :**		1,80,000
Equity Share cap.	1,50,000		Current Assets :		
12% Pref. Sh. Cap.	30,000		Stores	12,000	
Reserve & Surplus	24,000	2,04,000	Stock-in-Trade	32,000	
15% Debentures		48,000	Sundry Debtors	10,000	
Current Liabilities :			Cash-in-hand	2,000	
Bank Loan	12,000		Cash at Bank	4,000	60,000
Sundry Creditors	16,000		Preliminary Expenses		48,000
Proposed Dividend	2,000		Discount on issue		
Provision for Taxation	10,000	40,000	of Debentures		4,000
		2,92,000			2,92,000

[C.U. B.Com. (Hons.) 1996]

Solution

(i) Statement Showing Computation of Working Capital of X Co. Ltd. as on 31st December 1995 :

	Rs.	Rs.
Current Assets		
Stores	12,000	
Stock-in-Trade	32,000	
Sundry Debtors	10,000	
Cash in hand	2,000	
Cash at Bank	4,000	
Gross Working Capital		60,000
Less : Current Liabilities :		
Bank Loan	12,000	
Sundry Creditors	16,000	
Proposed Dividend	2,000	
Provision for Taxation	10,000	40,000
Net Working Capital		20,000

(ii) Statement showing Computation of Capital Employed of X Co. Ltd. as on 31st Dec. 1995 :

	Rs.	Rs.
Fixed Assets		1,80,000
Current Assets :		
Stores	12,000	
Stock-in-Trade	32,000	
Sundry Debtors	10,000	
Cash in hand	2,000	
Cash at Bank	4,000	60,000
Gross Capital Employed		2,40,000
Less : Current Liabilities		
Bank Loan	12,000	
Sundry Creditors	16,000	
Proposed Dividend	2,000	
Provision for Taxation	10,000	
		40,000
Net Capital Employed		2,00,000
Less : Long Term Liabilities :		
15% Debentures		48,000
Proprietors' Capital Employed		1,52,000

(iii) **Current Ratio** $= \dfrac{\text{Total Current Assets}}{\text{Total Current Liabilities}} = \dfrac{\text{Rs. } 60,000}{\text{Rs. } 40,000} = \dfrac{3}{2} = 1.5 : 1$

(iv) **Acid Test Ratio or Quick Ratio** $= \dfrac{\text{Total Quick Assets}}{\text{Total Quick Liabilities}}$

$$\frac{\text{Quick Assets (CA − Inventories)}}{\text{Total Current Liabilities − Bank Overdraft}}$$

$$\frac{\text{Rs. } 60,000 - \text{Rs. } (12,000 + 32,000)}{\text{Rs. } 40,000 - \text{Rs. } 12,000} = \frac{\text{Rs. } 16,000}{\text{Rs. } 28,000} = 0.57 : 1$$

(v) **Debt Equity Ratio** $= \dfrac{\text{Total Debt}}{\text{Total Equity}} = \dfrac{\text{Current Liabilities + Debentures}}{\text{Share Capital + Reserves and Surplus}}$

$$\frac{\text{Rs. } 40,000 + \text{Rs. } 48,000}{\text{Rs. } (1,50,000 + 30,000) + \text{Rs. } 24,0000} = \frac{\text{Rs. } 88,000}{\text{Rs. } 2,04,000} = 0.43 : 1$$

(vi) **Asset Proprietorship Ratio** $= \dfrac{\text{Total Proprietors' Fund or Equity}}{\text{Total Assets}}$

$$= \frac{\text{Rs. } 2,04,000}{\text{Rs. } (1,80,000 + 60,000)} = \frac{\text{Rs. } 2,04,000}{\text{Rs. } 2,40,000} = 0.85 : 1.$$

Problem 13

From the following particulars prepare the Balance Sheet of Light Ltd. for the year ended 31.3.1989 :

Fixed Assets to Net Worth	5 : 8
Current Ratio	2 : 1
Acid Test Ratio	1 : 1
Reserves to Proprietors' Fund	1 : 5
Current Liabilities	Rs. 3,60,000
Cash in hand	Rs. 15,000
Fixed Assets	Rs. 6,00,000

[C.U. B.Com. (Hons.) 1990]

Solution

Workings :

1. **Fixed Assets to Net Worth** $= \frac{5}{8}$ or, $\frac{6,00,000}{\text{Net Worth}} = \frac{5}{8}$

$\therefore$ Net Worth $= 6,00,000 \times \frac{8}{5}$ = Rs. 9,60,000

2. **Reserve to Proprietors' Fund** = 1 : 5

or, $\frac{\text{Reserves}}{\text{Proprietors's Fund}} = \frac{1}{5+1} = \frac{1}{6}$

or, $\frac{\text{Reserves}}{9,60,000} = \frac{1}{6}$

$\therefore$ Reserves $= 9,60,000 \times \frac{1}{6}$ = Rs. 1,60,000.

3. **Capital** = Proprietors' Fund or Net Worth – Reserves
= Rs. 9,60,000 – 1,60,000 = Rs. 8,00,000.

4. **Current Ratio** = 2 : 1

$\therefore \frac{CA}{CL} = \frac{2}{1}$ or $\frac{CA}{3,60,000} = \frac{2}{1}$

$\therefore$ Current Assets = 3,60,000 × 2 = Rs. 7,20,000

5. **Acid Test Ratio** = 1 : 1

$\therefore \frac{CA - \text{Stock}}{CL} = 1$ or, $\frac{7,20,000 - \text{Stock}}{3,60,000} = 1$

$\therefore$ 7,20,000 – Stock = 3,60,000

or, Stock = Rs. 3,60,000

6. **Debtors** = Current Assets – Stock – Cash in hand
= 7,20,000 – 3,60,000 – 15,000
= Rs. 3,45,000.

Balance Sheet of Light Ltd.
as at 31.03.89

Liabilities	Amount Rs.	Assets	Amount Rs.
Equity Share Capital	8,00,000	Fixed Assets	6,00,000
Reserve and Surplus	1,60,000	Stock	3,60,000
Current Liabilities	3,60,000	Sundry Debtors	3,45,000
		Cash in hand	15,000
	13,20,000		13,20,000

Problem 14

Balance Sheet of XYZ Co.
as at 31.12.2001

	Rs.		Rs.
Equity share Capital	2,00,000	Goodwill	1,20,000
Profit	60,000	Fixed Assets	2,80,000
Capital Reserve	40,000	Stock	60,000
Loan (Mortgage)	1,60,000	Debtors	60,000
Creditors	80,000	Investment	20,000
Provision for Taxation	60,000	Cash at Bank	60,000
	6,00,000		6,00,000

You are required to find out the long-term solvency ratios.

Solution

Long-term Solvency Ratios

1. **Debt-Equity Ratio** $= \dfrac{\text{Outsiders' Funds}}{\text{Shareholders' Funds}} = \dfrac{\text{Rs. } 1,60,000}{3,00,000} = 8 : 15 = 1 : 1.875$

2. **Proprietary Ratio** $= \dfrac{\text{Shareholders' Funds}}{\text{Total Assets}} \times 100 = \dfrac{\text{Rs. } 3,00,000}{6,00,000} \times 100 = 50\%$

Problem 15

The Profit and Loss Account and Balance Sheet of Happy Ltd. is given below :

Profit and Loss Account
for the year ended 31st Marc, 2003

		Rs.		Rs.
To	Opening Stock	90,000	By Sales	9,00,000
"	Purchases	5,60,000	" Closing Stock	90,000
"	Wages	2,14,000		
"	Gross Profit	1,26,000		
		9,90,000		9,90,000

To	Salaries	16,000	By	Gross Profit	1,26,000
"	Electricity	10,000			
"	Miscellaneous Expenses	10,000			
"	Depreciation	30,000			
"	Net Profit	60,000			
		1,26,000			1,26,000

Balance Sheet

as at 31.3.2003

	Rs.		Rs.	Rs.
Share Capital		Fixed Assets	5,40,000	
Equity Shares	1,80,000	*Less* : Depreciation	1,50,000	
Reserves and Surplus	1,20,000			3,90,000
Secured Loans	2,10,000	*Current Assets* :		
Current Liabilities :		Stock		90,000
Sundry Creditors	90,000	Sundry Debtors		1,05,000
		Cash at Bank		15,000
	6,00,000			6,00,000

Calculate :

(i) Liquidity and Solvency test ratios;

(ii) Profitability test ratios; and

(iii) Overall measures ratios.

[Adapted—C.S. (Inter)]

Solution

1. **Liquidity Ratios**

(a) **Current Ratio** $= \frac{\text{Current Assets}}{\text{Current Liabilities}} = \frac{\text{Rs. } 2,10,000}{\text{Rs. } 90,000} = 2.33$

The ideal Ratio is 2.

(b) **Liquid Ratio** $= \frac{\text{Liquid Assets}}{\text{Current Liabilities}} = \frac{\text{Rs. } 1,20,000}{\text{Rs. } 90,000} = 1.33$

The ideal ratio is 1.

2. **Solvency Ratios**

(i) **Debt-equity ratio** : (a) $\frac{\text{Total Debts}}{\text{Shareholders' Fund}} = \frac{\text{Rs. } 2,10,000}{\text{Rs. } 3,00,000} = 0.7$

(b) $\frac{\text{Debts}}{\text{Long-term fund*}} = \frac{\text{Rs. } 2,10,000}{\text{Rs. } 5,10,000} = 0.41$

*Long-term funds include secured loan.

(c) $\frac{\text{External Equities}}{\text{Internal Equities}} = \frac{\text{Rs. } 3,00,000}{\text{Rs. } 3,00,000} = 1$

(ii) **Fixed Assets Ratio** : $\frac{\text{Fixed Assets}}{\text{Long-term Funds}} = \frac{\text{Rs. } 3,90,000}{\text{Rs. } 5,10,000} = 0.76$

3. **Profitability Ratios**

(i) Gross Profit Ratio : $\frac{\text{Gross Profit}}{\text{Net Sales}} \times 100 = \frac{\text{Rs. } 1,26,000}{9,00,000} \times 100 = 14\%.$

(ii) Net Profit Ratio : $\frac{\text{Net Profit}}{\text{Net Sales}} \times 100 = \frac{\text{Rs. } 60,000}{9,00,000} \times 100 = 6.7\%.$

4. **Overall Ratios**

(i) Return on Shareholders Investment : $\frac{\text{Net Profit}}{\text{Shareholders' Fund}} \times 100$

$$= \frac{\text{Rs. } 60,000}{\text{Rs. } 3,00,000} \times 100 = 20\%$$

(ii) Return on Capital Employed : $\frac{\text{Net Profit}}{\text{Capital Employed*}} \times 100$

$$= \frac{\text{Rs. } 6,00,000}{5,10,000} \times 100 = 11.7\%$$

*Capital employed = Fixed Assets + Current Assets – Current Liabilities
i.e. Rs. 3,90,000 + Rs. 2,10,000 – Rs. 90,000 = Rs. 6,00,000 – 90,000 = Rs. 5,10,000.

Problem 16

The following extracts of financial information relate to Curious Ltd.

Balance Sheet
as at 31st December

(Rupees in lakhs)

	1995	1994
Share Capital	10	10
Reserves and Surplus	30	10
Loan Funds	60	70
	100	90
(a) Fixed Assets (Net)	30	20
Current Assets :		
Stocks	30	20
Debtors	30	30
Cash and Bank Balances	10	20
Other Current Assets	30	10
	100	80
Less : **Current Liabilities**	30	20
(b) Net	70	60
Total Assets (a + b)	100	90
Sales (Rs. lakhs)	270	300

(i) Calculate for the two years Debt Equity Ratio; Quick Ratio and Working Capital Turnover Ratio and;

(ii) Find out the sales volume that should have been generated in 1995 if the company were to have maintained its working capital turnover ratio.

[C.A. (Inter)]

Solution

(i) ***Debt – Equity Ratio :*** $\dfrac{\text{Debt}}{\text{Equity}} = \dfrac{\text{Loan Fund}}{\text{Share Capital + Reserves}}$

1994	1995
$\dfrac{70}{20} = 3.5$	$\dfrac{60}{40} = 1.5$

(ii) ***Quick Ratio :*** $\dfrac{\text{Quick Assets}}{\text{Quick Liabilities}} = \dfrac{\text{Debtors + Cash}}{\text{Quick Liabilities}}$

1994	1995
$\dfrac{30 + 20}{20} = 2.5 : 1$	$\dfrac{30 + 10}{30} = 1.33 : 1$

(iii) ***Working Capital Turnover :***

Ratio $\dfrac{\text{Sales}}{\text{Working Capital}}$

1994	1995
$\dfrac{300}{60} = 5$	$\dfrac{270}{70} = 3.86$

(iv) ***Sales volume to be maintained :***

Working capital turnover ratio in 1994 = 5 times

Therefore, sales volume to be maintained in 1995

$5 = \dfrac{\text{Required Sales}}{70}$ or required sales = 70 × 5 = Rs. 350 lakhs.

Problem 17

From the following ratios and information relating to the activities of Bengal Traders Ltd. find out :

(a) Sales for the year 1993
(b) Sundry Debtors on 31.12.1993
(c) Closing Stock on 31.12.93 and
(d) Sundry Creditors on 31.12.93

Debtors velocity	3 months
Stock velocity	6 months
Creditors velocity	2 months
Gross Profit Ratio 20%	

Gross profit for the year ended 31st Dec. 1993 was Rs. 5,00,000. Stock as on 31st December 1993 was Rs. 20,000 higher than that of the opening stock. Bills Receivable and Bills Payable were Rs. 60,000 and Rs. 36,667 respectively at the end of the year. **[C.U. B.Com. 1994]**

Solution

(a) Gross Profit Ratio $= \dfrac{\text{Gross Profit}}{\text{Net Sales}} \times 100\% = 20\%$

or, $\dfrac{\text{Rs. 5,00,000}}{\text{Net Sales}}$ 100% = 20%

or, Net Sales = Rs. 5,00,000 × $\dfrac{100}{20}$ = Rs. 25,00,000

(b) Debtors velocity (period) is 3 months

$$\text{So, Debtors velocity} = \frac{\text{12 months (i.e. one year)}}{\text{2 months}} = 4 \text{ times}$$

$$\text{Again, No. of Debtors velocity} = \frac{\text{Credit Sales}}{\text{Closing Receivables}}$$

$$= \frac{\text{Credit Sales}}{\text{Sundry Debtors + Bills Receivables}}$$

$$\text{or, } = \frac{25,00,000}{\text{Sundry Debtors} + 60,000} = 4$$

$$\text{or, Sundry Debtors} + 60,000 = \frac{25,00,000}{4} = 6,25,000$$

or, Sundry Debtors = 6,25,000 – 60,000 = Rs. 5,65,000.

(c) Stock Velocity (Period) is 6 months.

$$\text{So, Stock Velocity/Turnover} = \frac{\text{12 months (i.e. one year)}}{\text{6 months}} = 2 \text{ times}$$

$$\text{Now, No. of Stock Velocity} = \frac{\text{(Direct) Cost of Goods Sold}}{\text{Average Stock}} = 2 \text{ times}$$

Here, (Direct) Cost of Goods sold = Sales – G.P.
= Rs. 25,00,000 – Rs. 5,00,000 = Rs. 20,00,000

2 Average stock = Rs. 20,00,000

Average stock = Rs. 20,00,000 ÷ 2 = Rs. 10,00,000

Therefore, total stock = Rs. 10,00,000 + Rs. 10,00,000 = Rs. 20,00,000

$$\text{Opening stock} = \frac{\text{Rs. } 20,00,000 - \text{Rs. } 20,000}{2} = \text{Rs. } 19,80,000 \div 2 = \text{Rs. } 9,90,000$$

Closing stock = Rs. 9,90,000 + 20,000 = Rs. 10,10,000.

(d) Here Creditors' Velocity (Period) is 2 months

$$\text{So No. of Creditors' Velocity} = \frac{\text{12 months (i.e. one year)}}{\text{2 months}} = 6 \text{ times.}$$

Cost of Goods Sold = Opening Stock + Purchase – Closing Stock

or, 20,00,000 = 9,90,000 + Purchase – 10,10,000

or, Purchase = Rs. (20,00,000 + 10,10,000 – 9,90,000) = Rs. 20,20,000.

Creditors' Velocity = 2 months

$$\text{Total Payables} = \text{Credit Purchases} \times \frac{2}{12}$$

= Rs. 20,20,000 ÷ 6 = Rs. 3,36,667

Sundry Creditors = Rs. 3,36,667 – Bill Payable
= Rs. 3,36,667 – Rs. 36,667 = Rs. 3,00,000

Problem 18

From the following information relating to Moon Light Ltd. prepare a Balance Sheet as on 31.12.97 :

(i)	Current Ratio	2.5
(ii)	Liquid Ratio	1.5
(iii)	Net Working Capital	Rs. 3,00,000
(iv)	Cost of Sales/Closing Stock	8 times
(v)	G.P. Ratio	25%
(vi)	Average Debt Collecting Period	1.5 months
(vii)	Fixed Assets/Shareholders' Net worth	0.75
(viii)	Reserves & surplus/Share Capital	0.50

[C.U. B.Com. (Hons.) 1998]

Solution

Working Notes :

(i) ***Current Assets and Current Liabilities :***

Current Ratio = 2.5

Working Capital = 2.5 – 1.0 = 1.5 (CA – CL)

or 1.5 = Rs. 3,00,000

$$2.5 = \text{Rs. } 3,00,000 \times \frac{2.5}{1.5} = \text{Rs. } 5,00,000$$

Current Liability = C.A. – Working Capital

= Rs. 5,00,000 – Rs. 3,00,000 = Rs. 2,00,000

(ii) ***Stock***

$$\text{Liquid Ratio} = \frac{\text{CA} - \text{Stock}}{\text{CL}}$$

$$1.5 = \frac{\text{Rs. } 5,00,000 - \text{Stock}}{\text{Rs. } 2,00,000 - \text{Nil}}$$

Rs. 3,00,000 = Rs. 5,00,000 – Stock

∴ Stock = Rs. 2,00,000

(iii) ***Cost of Sales / Closing stock*** = 8 times

∴ Cost of sale = Closing Stock × 8 times = Rs. 2,00,000 × 8

= Rs. 16,00,000

(iv) ***Sales***

G.P. Ratio is 25% of sales. Therefore Cost of Sales is 75% of Sales.

$$\therefore \text{Sales} = \frac{\text{Rs. } 16,00,000}{75} \times 100 = \text{Rs. } 21,33,333.$$

(v) ***Debtors***

Average Collection Period = 1.5 months.

$$\therefore \text{Average Debtors} = \frac{1.5 \times 21,33,333}{12} = \text{Rs. } 2,66,667$$

(vi) **Cash & Bank**

Current Assets = Debtors + Cash & Bank

Rs. 5,00,000 = Rs. 2,66,667 + 2,00,000 + Cash & Bank

∴ Cash & Bank = Rs. 5,00,000 – 4,66,667 = Rs. 33,333.

(vii) **Net Worth**

Fixed Assets/Shareholders' Net Worth = .75.

Shareholders net worth = Fixed Assets + Net working capital.

Net working capital = Net worth – Fixed Assets.

Net working capital = 1.00 – 0.75 = 0.25

0.25 = Rs. 3,00,000

$$1 = 3{,}00{,}000 \times \frac{1}{.25}$$

Net worth = Rs. 12,00,000.

Fixed Assets = Rs. 12,00,000 – Rs. 3,00,000 = Rs. 9,00,000.

In the absence of any information it is assumed that there is a no long-term loan, no investment and no fictitious assets.

(viii) **Share Capital and Reserves and Surplus** = Reserves & Surplus/Share Capital

$$\frac{\text{Reserves and Surplus (R \& S)}}{\text{Share Capital}} = 0.50.$$

Net worth = Reserves & Surplus + Share Capital

or 0.5 + 1.0 = Rs. 12,00,000

or 1.5 = Rs. 12,00,000

$$\text{or } 1 = \frac{12{,}00{,}000}{1.5} \times 1 = \text{Rs. } 8{,}00{,}000$$

Equity Share Capital = Rs. 8,00,000

Reserve Surplus = 12,00,000 – Rs. 8,00,000 = Rs. 4,00,000

Balance Sheet of Moon Light Ltd.

as on 31.12.97

Liabilities	Rs.	Assets	Rs.
Share Capital	8,00,000	Fixed Assets	9,00,000
Reserves & Surplus	4,00,000	Stock	2,00,000
Current Liabilities	2,00,000	Debtors	2,66,667
		Cash & Bank	33,333
	14,00,000		14,00,000

Notes : 1. It is assumed that entire sales were made on credit.

2. It is further assumed that opening and closing balances are same. So closing debtors is equal to average debtors.

∴ Debtors = Rs. 2,66,667.

Problem 19

Using the following data complete the Balance Sheet of X Limited as at 31.12.2000 :

(i) Gross profit 25% of sales

(ii) Gross profit Rs. 1,20,000

(iii) Shareholders' equity Rs. 20,000

(iv) Credit sales to total sales 80%

(v) Total turnover to total assets 4 times

(vi) Cost of sales to inventory 10 times

(vii) Average collection period = 5 days, assume 365 days in a year

(viii) Long-term debt ?

(ix) Current ratio 1.5

(x) Sundry creditors Rs. 60,000

Balance Sheet of X Limited

as at 31.3.2000

Liabilities	Rs.	Assets	Rs.
Sundry creditors	—	Cash	—
Long-term Debt	—	Sundry Debtors	—
Share Capital	—	Inventory	—
	—	Fixed Assets	—

[C.A. (Inter) November 2000]

Solution

Balance Sheet of X Limited

as at 31.12.2000

Liabilities	Rs.	Rs.	Assets	Rs.	Rs.
Sundry Creditors		60,000	Cash		48,740
Long-term Debt		40,000	Sundry Debtors		5,260
(Balancing figure)			Inventory		36,000
Share Capital		20,000	Fixed Assets		30,000
		1,20,000			1,20,000

Working Notes :

1. ***Sales***

Gross Profit = 25% on Sales = Rs. 1,20,000

Sales = $1{,}20{,}000 \times \frac{100}{25}$ = Rs. 4,80,000

Credit sales = 80% of total sales

= $\frac{80}{100} \times 4{,}80{,}000$ = Rs. 3,84,000

2. ***Cost of goods sold*** = Sales – Gross Profit

= Rs. 4,80,000 – Rs. 1,20,000 = Rs. 3,60,000

3. ***Closing inventory*** = $\frac{\text{Cost of goods sold}}{\text{Inventory}}$ = 10 times

or, Inventory = $\frac{\text{Rs. } 3{,}60{,}000}{10}$ = Rs. 36,000

4. ***Total Assets*** = $\frac{\text{Total Turnover}}{\text{Total Assets}}$ = 4 times

Total Assets = $\frac{\text{Total Turnover}}{4} = \frac{\text{Rs. } 4{,}80{,}000}{4}$ = Rs. 1,20,000

5. ***Current Assets*** = Current Ratio = 1.5 : 1

$$\frac{CA}{CL} = 1.5 \text{ or } \frac{CA}{\text{Rs. } 60,000} = 1.5 \text{ or CA = Rs. } 90,000.$$

(i) Sundry Debtors : $\frac{\text{Debtors}}{\text{Credit Sales}} = \frac{5 \text{ days}}{365}$

$$365 \text{ Debtors} = \frac{\text{Rs. } 3,84,000}{365} \times 5 = \text{Rs. } 5,260$$

(ii) Cash Balance : Current Assets = Rs. 90,000

Cash = Rs. 90,000 – Rs. 5,260 – Rs. 36,000 = Rs. 48,740.

Determination of Working Capital

Problem 20

Important ratios of a firm for the year 1999 are given below :

1.	Stock velocity	4
2.	Debt collection period	2 months
3.	Creditors payment period	73 days
4.	Gross profit	Rs. 2,00,000
5.	Gross profit margin	20%
6.	Cash and Bank balance	5% of sales
7.	Credit purchases	25%

The firm expects an increase of 50% in sales in the ensuing year.

Estimate the working capital requirement of the firm for the ensuing year.

[Adapted—C.A. (Inter) May 2000]

Solution

1\. (a) ***Sales for 1999***

Gross profit margin 20% of sales = Rs. 2,00,000

$$\therefore \text{Sales} = \text{Rs. } 2,00,000 \times \frac{100}{20} = \text{Rs. } 10,00,000$$

(b) ***Sales for 2000***

(i) Estimated sales = 150% of Rs. 10,00,000 = Rs. 15,00,000

(ii) Gross profit @ 20% of sales i.e. $\frac{20}{100} \times 15,00,000 = \text{Rs. } 3,00,000.$

2\. ***Stock***

Cost of goods sold = Sales – Gross profit

= Rs. 15,00,000 – Rs. 3,00,000 = Rs. 12,00,000

$$\text{Stock} = \frac{\text{Cost of goods sold}}{\text{Stock velocity}}$$

$$= \frac{\text{Rs. } 12,00,000}{12} \times 4 = \text{Rs. } 4,00,000$$

3\. ***Debtors***

$$= \frac{\text{Credit Sales} \times \text{Debt collection period}}{12} = \text{Rs. } 15,00,000 \times \frac{2}{12} = \text{Rs. } 2,50,000$$

4\. ***Creditors***

Cost of goods sold has been considered as credit purchase assuming opening and closing stock are same.

Creditors payment period = 73 days.

$\therefore$ Credit Purchase = 25% of total purchase $= \frac{25}{100} \times 12{,}00{,}000 =$ Rs. 3,00,000

Creditors = Credit Purchase $\times \frac{73}{365}$ = Rs. 3,00,000 $\frac{1}{5}$ = Rs. 60,000

5. ***Cash and Bank balance***

5% of sales = Rs. 15,00,000 $\times \frac{5}{100}$ = Rs. 75,000

Estimation of Working Capital Requirement for 2000

	Rs.
Current Assets	
Stock (2)	3,00,000
Debtors (3)	2,50,000
Cash and Bank balance (5)	75,000
	6,25,000
Less : Current Liabilities :	
Creditors (4)	60,000
	5,65,000

Problem 21

The Directors of Bharucha Enterprises Ltd. ask you to ascertain :

(a) Proprietary Funds (b) Fixed Assets

(c) Closing Debtors (d) Closing Creditors

(e) Closing Stock (f) Share Capital

(g) Cash and Bank balances.

From the following information :

(i) Inventory turnover ratio is 6 times.
Year end debtors are outstanding for 2 months
Year end creditors are outstanding for 73 days.

(ii) Ratios of cost of goods sold to :
(a) Proprietors funds is 2 : 1
(b) Fixed assets 4 : 1

(iii) Ratio of gross profit to sales is 20%.

(iv) Closing stock is greater than the opening stock by Rs. 10,000.

(v) The gross profit for the year ended 31st March, 1998 is Rs. 1,20,000.

(vi) Reserves and Surplus appearing in the Balance Sheet as at 31st March, 1998 total to Rs. 40,000.

[Adapted—C.A. (Inter)]

Solution

(a) ***Proprietors' Fund*** $= \frac{\text{Cost of goods sold}}{\text{Proprietors Fund}} = \frac{2}{1}$

Proprietors' Fund $= \frac{\text{Rs. } 4{,}80{,}000}{2}$ = Rs. 2,40,000

(b) ***Fixed Assets*** $= \dfrac{\text{Cost of goods sold}}{\text{Fixed Assets}} = \dfrac{4}{1}$

Fixed Assets $= \dfrac{\text{Cost of goods sold}}{4} = \dfrac{\text{Rs. } 4,80,000}{4} = \text{Rs. } 1,20,000$

(c) ***Closing Debtors***

Year end debtors are outstanding for 2 months

Sales $= \dfrac{\text{Gross profit}}{20\%} \times 100\% = \text{Rs. } 1,20,000 \times 5 = \text{Rs. } 6,00,000$

Therefore, closing debtors $\dfrac{2}{12} \times \text{Rs. } 6,00,000 = \text{Rs. } 1,00,000$

(d) ***Closing Creditors***

Purchase $\times \dfrac{73 \text{ days}}{365 \text{ days}} = \text{Rs. } 4,90,000 \times \dfrac{73}{365} = \text{Rs. } 98,000.$

(Purchase = Cost of goods sold + Closing stock – Opening stock

= Rs. 4,80,000 + 85,000 – 75,000 = Rs. 4,90,000)

(e) ***Closing Stock***

Inventory turnover ratio is 6 times

$= \dfrac{\text{Cost of goods sold}}{\text{Inventory turnover ratio}} = \text{Average Inventory}$

$= \dfrac{\text{Rs. } 4,80,000}{6} = \text{Rs. } 80,000.$

Let the opening stock x

Closing stock = x + 10,000

Average inventory $= \dfrac{\text{Opening stock + Closing stock}}{2}$

$\text{Rs. } 80,000 = \dfrac{2x + \text{Rs. } 10,000}{2}$

= Rs. 1,60,000 = Rs. 2x + Rs. 10,000

or (–) 2x = (–) Rs. 1,60,000 + Rs. 10,000

or $2x = \text{Rs. } 1,50,000 \text{ or } x = \dfrac{1,50,000}{2} = \text{Rs. } 75,000$

So, opening stock = Rs. 75,000

Closing stock = Rs. 75,000 + Rs. 10,000 = Rs. 85,000

(f) ***Share Capital***

Proprietors' Fund = Share capital + Reserves and Surplus.

Rs. 2,40,000 = x + 40,000

or x = 2,40,000 – 40,000 = Rs. 2,00,000.

(g) ***Cash in hand and Bank Balance***

Proprietors' Fund + Creditors

= Fixed Assets + Debtors + Inventory + Cash and Bank balance.

= Rs. 2,40,000 + Rs. 98,000

= Rs. 1,20,000 + Rs. 1,00,000 + 85,000 + Cash and Bank balance.

or, Rs. 3,38,000 – Rs. 3,05,000 = Rs. 33,000

ASSIGNMENT

Theoretical Questions

1. What do you mean by financial statements?
2. What do you mean by ratio analysis?
3. What are the advantages of ratio analysis?
4. Who are the users of financial statements?
5. What is the importance of ratio analysis? What are its limitations?
6. What do you mean by Ratio Analysis? Discuss its uses and limitations.
7. Discuss the role of the following ratios in the interpretation of financial statements :
   (i) Debt Turnover Ratio.
   (ii) Acid Test Ratio.
   (iii) Capital Gearing Ratio.

[C.U. B.Com. (Hons.) 1982]

8. Explain the following ratios :
   (i) Gearing Ratio
   (ii) Gross Profit Ratio
   (iii) Acid Test Ratio
   (iv) Return on Investment (ROI)

[C.U. B.Com. (General) 2001]

9. What do you mean by Ratio Analysis? Explain the following ratios :
   (a) Capital Gearing Ratio
   (b) Gross Profit Ratio
   (c) Return on Investment (ROI)
   (d) Operating Ratio

[C.U. B.Com. (Hons.) 1995]

Practical Problems

1. You have been furnished with the financial information of Strong Ltd. for the year 1.4.2002-31.3.2003 :

(a) **Balance Sheet**
as on 31.3.2003

Liabilities	Rs.	Assets	Rs.
Equity Share Capital		Plant	6,00,000
(Rs. 10 each)	10,00,000	Land & Buildings	1,20,000
Retained Earning	3,68,000	Sundry Debtors	3,20,000
Sundry Creditors	1,00,000	Stock	4,80,000
Bills Payable	1,90,000	Prepaid Insurance	12,000
Outstanding Liabilities	34,000	Cash	1,60,000
	16,92,000		16,92,000

(b)

Statement of Profit

for the year ended 31st March 2003

		Rs.
	Sales	40,00,000
Less :	Cost of goods sold	30,80,000
		9,20,000
Less :	Operating Expenses	6,80,000
	Net Profit	2,40,000
Less :	Tax @ 35%	84,000
	Net profit after taxes	1,56,000

Sundry Debtors and stock at the beginning of the year were Rs. 3,00,000 and Rs. 4,00,000 respectively.

Determine the following ratios :

(a) Current ratio; (b) Acid Test ratio; (c) Stock Turnover; (d) Debtors Turnover; (e) Gross Profit ratio; (f) Net Profit ratio, (g) Operating ratio.

Ans. : (a) 3 : 1; (b) 1.48 : 1; (c) 7 times; (d) 12 : 12 times, (e) 23%; (f) 3.9%; (g) 17%.

2. From the following information prepare a summarsed Balance Sheet in the books of X Ltd. as at 31st December, 1983 assuming the capital is composed of Equity Shares of Rs. 10 each.

   Liquid Ratio 1.5

   Current Ratio 2.5

   Assets (Fixed) Proprietorship Fund Ratio 0.75

   Working capital Rs. 1,20,000

   Reserves and Surplus Rs. 60,000

   Bank Overdraft Rs. 20,000

[C.U. B.Com. (Hons.)]

3. From the following ratios and information relating to the activities of Bengal Traders Ltd. find out :

   (a) Sales for the year 1993

   (b) Sundry Debtors on 31.12.1993

   (c) Sundry Creditors on 31.12.1993; and

   (d) Closing Stock :

Debtors velocity	3 months
Stock velocity	6 months
Creditors velocity	2 months
Gross profit ratio	20%.

Gross profit for the year ended 31.12.1993 was Rs. 5,00,000. Stock as on 31st December 1993 was Rs. 20,000 higher than that of the opening stock. Bills Receivable and Bills Payable were Rs. 60,000 and Rs. 36,667, respectively at the end of the year.

[C.U. B.Com. (Hons.) 1994]

4. With the help of information given below prepare a Trading Account, Profit and Loss Account and Balance Sheet of Sunshine Ltd.

(a) Gross Profit Ratio 25%; (b) Net Profit/Sales 20%; (c) Sales Inventory Ratio 10; (d) Fixed Assets/Total Current Assets 5/8; (e) Current Ratio = 1; (f) Fixed Assets/share capital = 5/4; (g) Fixed Assets Rs. 8,00,000; (h) Closing stock Rs. 80,000.

[C.U. B.Com. (Hons.)]

5. The following financial statement is summarised from the books of Armstrong Ltd. as at 31st March, 1983.

Capital and Liabilities	Rs.	**Property and Assets**	Rs.
Paid up Capital	15,00,000	Fixed Assets	16,50,000
Reserves and surplus	6,00,000	Stock-in-trade	9,10,000
Debentures (long-term)	5,00,000	Book Debts	12,40,000
Bank Overdraft	2,00,000	Investment—short-term	1,60,000
Sundry Creditors	12,00,000	Cash	40,000
	40,00,000		40,00,000

Annual Sales – Rs. 74,40,000; Gross Profit Rs. 7,44,000.

You are required to calculate the following ratios for the year and comment on the financial position as revealed by these ratios :

(i) Debt Equity Ratio; (ii) Current Ratio; (iii) Proprietory Ratio; (iv) G.P. Ratio; (v) Debtors Turnover Ratio; (vi) Stock Turnover Ratio.

[Adapted—C.U. B.Com. (Hons.) 1983]

Ans. : (i) 0.904; (ii) 1.67 : 1; (iii) 0.525; (iv) 10%; (v) 6 times; (vi) 7.358 times.

6. From the following information prepare a Balance Sheet as detail as possible :

(i)	Gross Profit	Rs. 80,000
(ii)	Gross Profit to cost of goods sold	1/3
(iii)	Stock velocity	6 times
(iv)	Opening stock	Rs. 36,000
(v)	Current Assets	Rs. 1,50,000
(vi)	Fixed Assets turnover ratio	8 times
(vii)	Accounts Receivable velocity (Year of 360 days)	72 days
(viii)	Accounts payable velocity	90 days
(ix)	Bills Receivable	Rs. 20,000
(x)	Bills Payable	Rs. 5,000

[V.U. B.Com. (Hons.) 1999]

Ans. : B/S Total Rs. 27,10,000

7. With the following information given below prepare Trading Account, Profit and Loss Account and Balance Sheet of Sunshine Ltd.

(a)	Gross Profit Ratio	25%
(b)	Net Profit/sales	20%
(c)	Sales Inventory Ratio	10
(d)	Fixed Assets/Total Current Assets	5/8

(e)	Current Ratio	1
(f)	Fixed Assets/Share Capital	$\frac{5}{4}$
(g)	Fixed Assets	Rs. 8,00,000
(h)	Closing Stock	Rs. 80,000

[Adapted—C.U. B.Com. (Hons.)]

Ans. : Gross Profit Rs. 2,00,000

Balance Sheet Total Rs.

8. The Trading and Profit and Loss Account for the year ended 31.3.2002 and the Balance Sheet as on that date of Bharat Electricals Ltd. are given below :

Trading and Profit and Loss Account

Dr. *Cr.*

		Rs.			Rs.
To	Opening Stock	75,000	By	Sales (Net)	4,00,000
"	Purchases (Net)	2,25,000	"	Closing Stock	80,000
"	Wages	50,000			
"	Gross Profit	1,30,000			
		4,80,000			4,80,000
To	Administration Expenses	65,000	By	Gross Profit	1,30,000
"	Sales Overheads	15,000			
"	Net Profit	50,000			
		1,30,000			1,30,000

Balance Sheet

as on 31.3.2002

Capital + Liabilities		Rs.	Assets		Rs.
Proprietors Fund			*Fixed Assets*		2,50,000
Equity Share capital		1,00,000	*Currents :*		
10% Preference			Stock	60,000	
share capital		1,50,000	Debtors	90,000	
Reserves and Surplus		50,000	Cash	50,000	
					2,00,000
15% Debentures		75,000			
Current Liabilities	25,000				
Sundry Creditors	50,000	75,000			
		4,50,000			4,50,000

You are required to work out the following ratios with brief remarks :

(i) Current Ratio; (ii) Liquid Ratio; (iii) Debt Equity Ratio; (iv) Proprietory Ratio; (v) Gross Profit Ratio; (vi) Stock Turnover Ratio; (vii) Return on Investment Ratio; (viii) Net Profit to Proprietors' Equity Ratio.

[V.U. B.Com. (Hons.) 1993—Adapted]

9. M/s Raj and Sons Ltd. present you the following :

Balance Sheet
as on 31.12.2002

		Rs.		Rs.
Equity Share Capital		50,000	Fixed Assets	87,500
8% Preference Share Capital		10,000	Investments	25,000
Reserve Fund		40,000	Stock	30,000
6% Debentures		20,000	Sundry Debtors	13,500
Profit and Loss Account			Bank Balance	7,000
2001	1,000		Preliminary Expenses	8,000
2002	20,000	21,000		
Sundry Creditors		30,000		
		1,71,000		1,71,000

The directors intend to transfer a sum of Rs. 5,000 out of current year's profits to provision for tax.

You are required to calculate the following ratios :

(a) Return on capital employed

(b) Current Ratio

(c) Fixed Assets to Net worth

(d) Debt to equity

[Adapted—M.Com. Nagpur]

Ans. : (a) 12.7%; (b) 2.14; (c) 0.81; (d) 0.4 74 : 1.

10. X Co. Ltd.

Balance Sheet
as on 31.3.1993

Liabilities	Rs.	Assets	Rs.
Equity share Capital	1,00,000	Fixed Assets	2,00,000
Pref. Share Capital	50,000	Stock	75,000
General Reserve	25,000	Debtors	25,000
Debentures	50,000	Bank	20,000
Bank Loan (short-term)	50,000	Cash	5,000
Loan (Long-term)	50,000	Preliminary Expenses	15,000
Sundry Creditors	15,000	Discount of Shares	10,000
Provision for taxation	10,000		
	3,50,000		3,50,000

From the above Balance Sheet of X Co. Ltd. calculate the following :

(a) Current Ratio; (b) Acid Test Ratio; (c) Proprietory Ratio; (d) Debt Equity Ratio.

[B.U. B.Com. (Hons.)]

11. From the following Balance Sheet of Calcutta Trading Company Ltd. you are required to calculate :

(i) Current Ratio; (ii) Acid Test Ratio; (iii) Debt-Equity Ratio; (iv) Proprietary Ratio; (v) Capital Gearing Ratio—and to comment on the financial condition of the company :

Balance Sheet

as at 31st December, 1994

Liabilities	Rs.	Assets	Rs.
8% Preference share Capital	2,00,000	Goodwill	25,000
Equity Share Capital	3,00,000	Land & Building	3,00,000
General Reserve	50,000	Machinery	1,95,000
Profit & Loss Account	10,000	Furniture	50,000
7% Mortgage Debentures	1,50,000	Stock-in-trade	1,00,000
Sundry Creditors	30,000	Sundry Debtors	40,000
Bills Payable	10,000	Bills Receivable	6,000
		Cash at Bank	30,000
		Underwriting Commission	4,000
	7,50,000		7,50,000

[Adapted—B.U. B.Com. (Hons.)]

12. From the following information make out a statement of proprietor's funds with details :

(i) Current Ratio 2.5.
(ii) Liquid Ratio 1.5.
(iii) Proprietary Ratio (fixed assets / proprietary fund) 0.75.
(iv) Working capital Rs. 60,000.
(v) Reserves and surplus Rs. 40,000.
(vi) Bank overdraft Rs. 10,000 and
(vii) There is no long-term loan or fictitious assets.

[Adapted—C.S. (Inter)]

Ans. : Proprietors Funds Rs. 2,40,000.

13. From the following details, make out the Balance Sheet with as many details as possible :

(i)	Stock velocity	6
(ii)	Gross Profit Ratio	20%
(iii)	Debtors velocity	2 months
(iv)	Creditors velocity	73 days
(v)	Capital Turnover Ratio	2
(vi)	Fixed Assets Turnover	4

Gross profit was Rs. 60,000. Reserves and Surplus amount to Rs. 20,000. Closing stock was Rs. 5,000 in excess of opening stock.

Ans. : Total of Balance Sheet Rs. 1,69,000 :
(a) Fixed Assets—Rs.60,000; (b) Creditors—Rs. 49,000;
(c) Debtors—Rs. 50,000; (d) Purchase—Rs. 2,45,000;
(e) Capital—Rs. 1,20,000.

14. With the help of the information given below, prepare a Trading Account, Profit and Loss Account and Balance Sheet of X Ltd.

(a) Gross profit Ratio = 25%
(b) Net Profit/sales Ratio = 20%
(c) Sales/Inventory Ratio = 10
(d) Fixed Assets/Total Current Assets = 5/7
(e) Current Ratio = 1
(f) Fixed Assets/Share Capital = 5/4
(g) Fixed Assets = Rs. 10,00,000
(h) Closing Stock = Rs. 1,00,000.

[C.U. B.Com. (Hons.)]

15. Following are the ratios relating to the trading activities of an organisation :

(i)	Debtors velocity	3 months
(ii)	Stock velocity	4 months
(iii)	Creditors velocity	2 months
(iv)	Gross profit ratio	25%
(v)	Capital Turnover Ratio	3
(vi)	Fixed Assets Turnover Ratio	4

The gross Profit for the year ended 31st March, 1991 was Rs. 7,50,000. Stock as on 31st March 1991 was Rs. 30,000 more than it was on 1st April, 1990.

At the end of the year, Bills Payable and Bills Receivable were Rs. 45,000 and Rs. 50,000, respectively and Bank Overdraft was Rs. 1,10,000.

Make necessary assumptions that you think fit.

Prepare the Statement of Proprietory Fund for the year ended 31.3.1991.

[Adapted—C.U. B.Com. (Hons.)]

16. From the information given below calculate : (a) Working capital, (b) Current Ratio, and (c) Acid-test Ratio.

Also comment on the funancial condition of the Company (from the given Balance Sheet).

Balance Sheet of A Ltd.
as on 31.12.1988

Liabilities	Rs.	Assets	Rs.
Equity Share Capital	1,50,000	Fixed Assets	1,90,000
Preference Share Capital	40,000	Stock	52,000
General Reserve	24,000	Debtors	30,000
Debentures	40,000	Bank	5,000
Bank loan (short-term)	12,000	Cash	2,000
Sundry Creditors	16,000	Preliminary expenses	10,000
Provision for taxation	10,000	Discount on shares	3,000
	2,92,000		2,92,000

[B.U. B.Com. (Hons.)]

Ans. : (a) Rs. 51,000; (b) 2.34 : 1; (c) 0.97 : 1.

17. What do you mean by Proprietary Ratio and Debt-Equity Ratio?

From the following Balance Sheet calculate the above two ratios and bring out their significance :

Liabilities	Rs.	Assets	Rs.
Equity share Capital	8,00,000	Fixed Assets	6,00,000
8% Pref. Share Capital	2,00,000	Investment	2,00,000
Reserve	2,00,000	Current Assets	12,00,000
6% Debenture	4,00,000		
Current Liabilities	4,00,000		
	20,00,000		20,00,000

18. With the help of the following ratios regarding Subhas Ghai films, draw the Balance Sheet of the company for the year 2001 :

Current Ratio	2.5
Liquidity Ratio	1.5
Net working Capital	Rs. 3,00,000
Stock turnover ratio (Cost of sales/closing stock)	6 times
Gross Profit Ratio	20%
Fixed Assets Turnover Ratio (on cost of sales)	2 times
Debt collection period	2 months
Fixed Assets to Shareholders Net worth	0.80
Reserve and Surplus to capital	0.50

[Madras University B.Com. 2002]

19. From the folowing information, relating to a limited company, prepare a statement of proprietors fund :

(i) Current Ratio	2
(ii) Liquid Ratio	1.5
(iii) Fixed Assets/Proprietory Fund	3/4
(iv) Working Capital	Rs. 75,000
(v) Reserves and Surplus	Rs. 50,000
(vi) Bank Overdraft	Rs. 10,000

There were no long-term loans or fictitious assets.

[C.A. (Inter)]

Ans. : Proprietary Fund Rs. 3,00,000.

20. From the following figures make out a statement of proprietors' Fund :

Current Ratio	2.5
Liquid Ratio	1.75
Proprietary Ratio (Fixed Assets to Proprietary Fund)	0.80
Capital Gearing Ratio (Equity share capital to preference share capital)	6
Working capital	Rs. 75,000
Reserves and Surplus	Rs. 25,000
Bank Overdraft	Rs. 20,000

There is no long-term loan, investment or fictitious assets.

C.A.—Rs. 1,25,000; C.L.—30,000; F.A.—3,00,000; Profit 3,75,000.

UNIVERSITY OF CALCUTTA

B. Com. (Honours)—Part-I

2000

Costing (New Syllabus)

1. P. Ltd. has supplied the following information in respect of incompleted contract as on 31.3.99 :

	Contract A	Contract B
	Rs.	Rs.
Contract price	2,40,000	1,50,000
Works certified	2,16,000	1,00,000
Estimated cost of completion of contract	2,10,000	1,20,000
Cash received	1,60,000	80,000
Uncertified work	10,000	7,000
Cost of contract (expenditure incurred upto 31.3.99)	180,000	95,000

Calculate the profit to be carried to Profit and Loss Account for the year ended 31.3.99.

Ans. : Contract A—Rs. 20,000; B—Rs. 6,400

2. A worker produced 180 units in a week. The guranteed weekly wage payment for 44 hrs. is Rs. 77. The expected time to produce one unit is 16 minutes which is further raised by 25% under the incentive scheme. What will be the earning per hour of the worker under the Halsey and Rowan Schemes.

Ans. : Halsey Rs. 2·06; Rowan Rs. 2·27

3. About 200 units are required per quarter Rs. 100 per order is incurred for placing an order. The inventory carrying cost per unit is Rs. 4. The re-order level is 350 units. The minimum usage is 25 units per week and the re-order periods is 4-6 weeks.

Compute—(a) Economic order quantity; (b) Maximum level.

Ans. : (a) 200 units; (b) 450 units

4. Explain 'abnormal loss' and state how it should be dealt with in Process Costing.

5. From the following information, compute the raw material purchased :

	Rs.
Opening stock of raw materials	20,000
Closing stock of raw materials	30,000
Direct Wages	2,10,000
Factory overland	60% of direct wages
General overhead	10% of works cost
Cost of production	6,88,600

Ans. : Rs. 3,00,000

6. Write short notes **(any two)** :

(a) Escalation clause : (b) Cost centre; (c) Wastage.

7. P. Ltd. a manufacturer of fans, manufactured and sold 2,000 fans during the year ended 31.3.99. Following is the Profit and Loss Account of the company during the year.

Profit and Loss Account

for the year ended 31.3.99

		Rs.			Rs.
To	Opening stock of raw materials	20,000	By	Sales	6,00,000
"	Purchases of raw materials	1,30,000	"	Closing stock of raw materials	30,000
"	Wages	1,80,000			
"	Manufacturing expenses	75,000			
"	Gross Profit c/d	2,25,000			
		6,30,000			6,30,000

Contd.

		Rs.			Rs.
To	Rent, rates and taxes	20,000	By	Gross profit b/d	2,25,000
"	Administration expenses	1,00,000	"	Dividend received	3,000
"	Selling and distribution expenses	45,000			
"	Preliminary expenses written off	8,000			
"	Donation	5,000			
"	Net Profit c/d	50,000			
		2,28,000			2,28,000

The estimates made by the company for the year ended 31.3.2000 are as under :

(a) The production and sales of fans will increase by 50%.

(b) The price of material per fan would increase by 20%.

(c) The labour cost per fan would go up by 10%.

(d) Of the manufacturing expenses Rs. 15,000 are fixed and the balance are variable. The variable portion will be in the same proportion of material consumed and wages as in the previous year.

(e) Administration expenses are to be charged at the same respective percentage as in the previous year.

(f) Selling and distribution expenses per fan would remain unchanged.

(g) Selling price per fan will decrease by 10%.

You are required to prepare two separate cost sheets for the years 1998-99 and 1999-2000 showing cost, profit and selling price per fan and the total cost, total profit and total sales.

Ans. : 1998-1999—Rs. 6,60,000; Rs. 30 per fan;
1999-2000—Rs. 8,10,000; Rs. 72,832 (loss); Rs. 24·28 per fan

8. (a) What do you mean by 'Composite Unit'?

(b) Raju the owner of a taxi supplies the following information :

Cost of taxi—Rs. 1,50,000 with total of life of 2,50,000 kms., Driver's salary—Rs. 700 p.m., Cleaner's salary—Rs. 300 p.m., Repairs—Rs. 3,600 p.a., Garage rent—Rs. 2,400 p.a., Tax—Rs. 1,200 p.a., Diesel consumption 8 kms. per litre, Diesel cost Rs. 8 per litre, Oil and other sundries Rs. 20 per 125 kms.

The taxi runs 100 kms per day for an average of 25 days in a month. 20% of the distance has been run without any passenger.

Calculate the cost of running the taxi per km.

9. A. Ltd. has three production departments P_1, P_2, and P_3 and two service departments S_1 and S_2. The following data are extracted from the records of the company for a particular given period :

	Rs.		Rs.
Rent and rates	25,000	Power	7,500
General lighting	3,000	Depreciation on machinery	50,000
Indirect wages	7,500	Sundries	50,000

Other information :

	P_1	P_2	P_3	S_1	S_2
Direct wages (Rs.)	15,000	10,000	15,000	7,500	2,500
H.P. of machines used	60	30	50	10	—
Cost of machinery (Rs.)	3,00,000	4,00,000	5,00,000	25,000	25,000
Floor space (Sq. ft.)	2,000	2,500	3,000	2,000	500
No. of light points	10	15	20	10	5
Production hours worked	6,226	4,028	4,066	—	—

Expenses of the service departments S_1 and S_2 are apportioned as below :

	P_1	P_2	P_3	S_1	S_2
S_1	20%	30%	40%	—	10%
S_2	40%	20%	30%	10%	—

You are required to :

(a) Compute overhead rate per production hour of each production department.

(b) Determine the total cost of Product x which is processed for manufacture in department P_1, P_2 and P_3 for 4 hours, 5 hours, and 3 hours respectively, given that its direct material cost is Rs. 250 and direct labour cost is Rs. 150.

Ans. : (a) P_1 Rs. 7·50 per hour

P_2 Rs. 11·25 per hour

P_3 Rs. 15·00

(b) Rs. 531·25

UNIVERSITY OF CALCUTTA

B. Com. (Honours)—Part-I

2001

Costing (New Syllabus)

1. A manufacturing company provides you with a summary of its production costs at three production levels :

Cost Item	1,000 Units	2,000 Units	3,000 Units
	Rs.	Rs.	Rs.
A	5,000	5,000	5,000
B	1,400	1,800	2,200
C	3,000	6,000	9,000

(i) Indicate the cost behaviour for the cost items.

(ii) What would be total costs if the company produces 2,500 units?

Ans. : Fixed cost : A— Rs. 5,000, B— Rs. 1,000, C—Nil, (Total) = Rs. 6,000.

Variable cost : A— Nil, B— Rs. 1,000, C— Rs. (2,500 × 3) = Rs. 7,500, (Total) = Rs. 8,500.

∴ Total— Rs. 14,500

2. Modern Manufacturing Company, Kolkata, purchased a material of 20 tonnes from a mining company. The following data is available for the lot of material purchased :

(i) Invoice Price of Material @ Rs. 2,000 per tonne;

(ii) Trade discount @ 20% on Invoice Price;

(iii) Excise Duty @ 10% on Invoice Price;

(iv) Sales Tax @ 10%;

(v) Freight and Insurance @ 2%;

(vi) Other charges for delivery @ Rs. 100 per tonne;

(vii) Cost of containers @ Rs. 20 per box of 1 quintal;

(viii) Cost of loading and unloading @ 1% of total cost.

Compute total material purchase cost and cost per tonne to Modern Manufacturing Company.

Ans. : Total Cost Rs. 46,860·60; Unit Cost Rs. 2,343·03

3. A truck starts with a load of 10 tonnes of goods from station D. It unloads 3 tonnes at station E and rest of goods at station F. It reaches back directly to station D after getting reloaded with 8 tonnes of goods at station F. The distance from D to E, E to F and then from F to D are 80 kms, 120 kms, and 160 kms, respectively. Compute tonne-kms for the truck service.

Ans. : DE— 800 Tonne-km, EF—840 Tonne-km, FD— 1,280 Tonne-km; Total — 2,920 Tonne-km

4. Mohit Ltd. furnished the following information in relation to the production of 2,000 units of Product 'N' for the year 2000 :

	Rs.
(i) Direct material	2,00,000
(ii) Direct labour	1,50,000
(iii) Indirect wages (50% fixed)	40,000

(iv) Consumable stores (70% variable)	30,000
(v) Office rent (100% fixed)	60,000
(vi) Selling expenses (40% variable)	80,000

In the year 2001, it is estimated that the production will be increased by 50%. The price of material and labour will go up by 10% and 20% respectively. You are required to compute selling price per unit of product 'N' for the year 2001 if the company wishes to maintain profit @ 10% on cost.

Ans. : Sale price per unit Rs. 310·39

5. State the implications of cost-plus contracts from the view points of (a) contractor and (b) contractee. What is the relevance of escalation clause provided in the contract?

6. Write short notes on (any **two**) :
   (a) Over-recovery of Overhead; (b) Stores Ledger; (c) Cost Unit.

7. (a) In a factory a job can be executed either through workman Pradip or Arindam. Pradip takes 32 hours to complete the job while Arindam finishes it in 30 hours. The standard time to finish the job is 40 hours.

The raw material input cost and hourly wage rate are same for both the workers. Pradip is entitled to receive bonus according to Halsey plan while Arindam is paid bonus as per Rowan plan. Works overheads are recovered on the job at Rs. 15 per labour hour worked. The factory cost of the job comes to Rs. 5,200 irrespective of the workmen engaged.

Find out hourly wage rate and cost of raw materials input.

Ans. : Wage Rate per hour Rs. 20; Material Cost for the job Rs. 4,000

(b) During the same period, the factory received a job order the details of which are given below :

Raw Material Cost	Rs. 5,000
Standard Labour Time	200 hours
Actual Time (Job done by Arindam)	150 hours
Administration Overhead	15% of works cost
Selling and Distribution Overhead	10% of total cost
Profit Margin	20% on sales

What price do you recommend for the job?

Ans. : Total Cost for the job Rs. 14,056; Price for the job Rs. 17,570

8. (a) What is a Composite Machine-Hour Rate?

(b) Three machines P, Q and R which are of different nature are used in a department of a factory. From the following information, compute machine-hour rate of machine R :

(i) Total Cost of machine P, Q and R is Rs. 50,000, out of which cost of machine R is Rs. 10,000. Its estimated scrap value and working life are Rs. 1,000 and 18,000 hours respectively.

(ii) Rent (Total area 1,000 sq. ft. and machine R occupies 250 sq. ft)	Rs. 780 p.a.
(iii) Lighting (Total light points 12, out of which 2 points used for machine R)	Rs. 288 p.a.

(iv) Insurance for all machines	Rs. 45 per quarter
(v) Consumable stores for machine R	Rs. 60 p.m.
(vi) Salary of supervisor (supervisor devotes $\frac{1}{4}$th of his time for machine R)	Rs. 6,000 p.a.
(vii) Repairs and maintenance for the entire life of machine R	Rs. 1,800 p.a.

(viii) Machine R consumes 5 units of power per hour at a cost of Rs. 16 per 100 units.

(ix) Machine R will work 2,000 hours p.a., out of which normal idle time estimated at 8% of total working hours and time for routine maintenance estimated at 40 hours p.a.

Ans. : Machine Houre Rate Rs. 2·79; Effective Working Hours 1,800

9. Z Ltd. produced product X through three processes—P_1, P_2 and P_3. On January 1, raw materials 1,000 units were introduced in process P_1 at Rs. 50 per unit. The details of expenses incurred on the three process during the year 2000 were as under :

	P_1	P_2	P_3
Sundry other materials	Rs. 1,600	Rs. 3,315	Rs. 3,220
Labour	Rs. 2,600	Rs. 8,000	Rs. 6,392
Normal loss (% of input)	5%	10%	5%
Scrap value per unit	Re. 1	Rs. 3	Rs. 6
Actual output (units)	940	846	410
Sales price of output per unit	Rs. 70	Rs. 100	Rs. 200

Entire output of P_1 was passed to the next process while $\frac{1}{2}$ of the output of P_2 was passed to the next process and the balance was sold. The entire output of P_3 was sold. Management expenses and selling expenses were Rs. 6,000 and Rs. 9,000 respectively. These are not allocable to the processes.

You are required to prepare—(a) Process A/cs and (b) Statement of Profit.

Ans. : (a) P_1—Abnormal Loss 10 units; P_2—Normal Loss 94 units, Finished Goods 846 units, Transfer to P_3 423 units at Rs. 32,306; P_3—Abnormal Gain 8 units, Finished Goods 410 units at Rs. 42,624; (b) Net Profit Rs. 34,539 including Abnormal Gain of Rs. 224

CALCUTTA UNIVERSITY

B.Com. (Honours)—Part-I

2002

Costing

First Group

1. The following data are available in respect of a material 'MMI' used in the production of a goods of M/s Bright Ltd. for the year 2001 :

   Cost of the Materials per unit—Rs. 50; Weekly consumption—300 units; Ordering cost per order—Rs. 650; Stock holding cost—2% per month (on cost).

   Compute (a) Economic Ordering Quantity, (b) Optimum No. of Orders per year and (c) Time lag between two consecutive orders.

2. The following transactions took place in respect of a Material "MP–6" in the store of a manufacturing company in the month of November, 2001 :

   Opening Stock—400 units @ Rs. 15 per unit; Purchased on 11.11.2001—8,000 units @ Rs. 10 per unit; Issued on 19.11.2001—7,800 units.

   The company follows "Simple Average Method" for pricing of material issues. What is the value of closing stock of materials as on 19.11.2001?

3. A product is produced after passing it through three processes—A, B and C. From the following particulars prepare Process B Account for the year 2001 :

   Output of Process A transferred 3,000 units @ Rs. 5 each; Process Materials added—Rs. 1,000; Direct Wages—Rs. 10,000; Direct Expenses—Rs. 4,000; Production Overhead—20% of Wages; Output of Process B—2,750 units; Normal loss—10%; Scrap value of lost units—Rs. 2 per unit.

4. In a factory, 20 workers are employed in the production of goods. From the following particulars compute the Wage Bill for the workers for the month of January, 2002 :

   Basic Wage @ Rs. 1,000 p.m. per worker; Dearness Allowance @ 900 p.m. per worker; Bonus for the month @ 20% of Basic Wages plus D.A.; Other Allowances @ Rs. 200 p.m.; Own and Employer's contribution to P.F. @ 10% of Basic Wages; Own and Employer's contribution to ESI @ 2% of Basic Wages; Professional Tax deducted from Salary—Rs. 20 p.m.

5. Distinguish between Halsey Scheme and Rowan Scheme for providing incentive bonus to workers.

6. (a) What is a composite unit? (b) A truck carried 45 tons during a six-day week and travelled a total distance of 135 miles as given below :

Day	*Distance travelled (miles)*	*Tons carried*
Monday	10	5
Tuesday	20	10
Wednesday	30	5
Thursday	40	10
Friday	25	10
Saturday	10	5
	135	45

Calculate ton-miles for the week.

Second Group

7. From the following particulars regarding the single output of Anirban & Co. for the quarter ended on 31st December, 2001, prepare (a) a statement of Cost of Production and (b) a statement of Profit or Loss, assuming weighted of finished goods.

Average Method is followed by the company for valuation of closing stock :

		1.10.2001	31.12.2001
Stock		Rs.	Rs.
Raw Materials		40,000	50,000
Work-in-progress		50,000	70,000
Finished Goods		72,000 (4,000 units)	? (5,000 units)
Purchase of Raw Materials	:	Rs. 1,60,000;	
Direct Labour	:	Rs. 1,10,000;	
Chargeable Expenses	:	Rs. 40,000;	
Machine Hour Rate	:	16 per hour;	
Machine Hour worked	:	5,000 hours;	
Office & Administration overhead	:	@ Rs. 4.80 per unit;	
Selling & Distribution overhead	:	@ Rs. 3.00 per unit;	
Sale of 24,000 units	:	Rs. 26 per unit.	

What would be the difference in stock value if the company follows FIFO method for valuation of closing stock of finished goods?

8. In Moon Light Manufacturing Company, the output is produced through three machine departments A, B and C. The company follows pre-determined factory overhead adsorption rates for the machine departments. Hourly rates fixed up for the year 2001 are Rs. 16.00 per hour for Dept. A, Rs. 18.80 per hour for Dept. B and Rs. 17.50 per hour for Dept. C.

The actual expenses of these machine departments for the year 2001 are as follows :

	Rs.		Rs.
Depreciation on Machinery	20,000	Repairs to Machinery	12,000
Rent of Factory Shed	18,000	Lighting	4,000
Indirect Materials	10,000	Canteen Expenses	15,000
Indirect Wages	12,000	Insurance of Machines	8,000
Power	16,000	Sundry Expenses	18,000

The particulars relating to the machine departments are given below :

Departments	*Machine A*	*Machine B*	*Machine C*
Area Occupied (Sq. ft.)	800	600	400
Value of Machinery (Rs.)	80,000	60,000	60,000
Direct Wages (Rs.)	50,000	40,000	30,000
Direct Materials (Rs.)	60,000	80,000	60,000
No. of Light Points	9	5	6

Power of Machines (H.P.)	20	40	20
No. of Workers	12	8	10
Actual Working Hours	3,000	2,500	2,000

You are required to (a) calculate overhead absorption rate per working hour for the departments, (b) compute the price to be charged for a Job which requires materials of Rs. 1,500 and wages of Rs. 1,000 assuming the office & administration overhead is charged @ 20% on works cost, selling & distribution overhead @ 20% on cost of production and profit @ 25% on sale (The job requires 15, 12 and 10 hours of time in machines A, B and C respectively) and (c) determine over or under absorption of factory overhead

9. A firm of Building Contractors undertook a contract for Rs. 3,00,000. The following particulars are furnished for the year ended 31st March, 2001 :

Materials	Rs.
Direct Purchase	50,000
Issued from stores	10,000
Wages for labour	40,000
General Plant in use :	
Written down value	90,000
Depreciation thereon	10,000
Direct expenses	2,500
Sub-contract charges	6,000
Share of general overhead	2,000
Materials in hand on 31.3.2001	2,000
Materials lost by fire	500
Salvage value thereof	150
Wages accrued on 31.3.2001	6,000
Direct expenses accrued on 31.3.2001	1,000
Cash received (90% of works certified)	1,62,000
Cost of uncertified work	5,000

Prepare Contract Account, value the work-in-progress and show how the various items would appear in the Balance Sheet.

2003

Costing (General)

Second Paper

Group A

1. Answer any *five* questions :

(a) What is cost plus contract? (b) What is Profit on incomplete Contract? (c) Give two Advantages of Job Costing. (d) Distinguish between Fixed overhead and Variable overhead. (e) What Chargeable Expenses? Give example. (f) What is an idle facility? (g) What is labour Turnover? (h) Mention any two advantages of the FIFO method.

2. Answer any *three* questions :

(a) What is E.O.Q.? Represent Graphically. Calculate E.O.Q. from the following :

(i) Quantity 600 units; (ii) Ordering cost Rs. 12 per order; (iii) Carrying cost 20%; (iv) Price per unit Rs. 20.

(b) Out of LIFO and FIFO which method would you recommend when for pricing of stores and why?

(c) Describe the four expenses and four Income which are excluded from Cost Accounts.

(d) Using the following data calculate the wages payable to workman under the (i) Halsey Premium Bonus Plan and (ii) Rowan Bonus Plan.

Time Allowed	48 hours
Time Taken	40 hours
Rate per hour	Re. 1

(e) From the following particulars compute—(i) Maximum stock level; (ii) Minimum stock level and (iii) Recorder level.

Normal consumption per month	1,000 litres
Maximum " " "	8,000 "
Minimum consumption " "	4,000 "
Lead time " " "	2 to 4 months
Re-order quantity " "	10,000 units

3. From the following information prepare a Statement of Cost for the year 2002.

	Rs.
Opening Stock of :	
Raw Materials	18,000
Finished Goods	5,000
Closing Stock of :	
Raw Materials	10,000
Finished Goods	6,000
Purchase of Raw Materials	90,000
Indirect Wages (Factory)	3,000
Factory Supervision	2,000
Direct Wages	18,000
Power & Fuel	5,000

Depreciation on Plant and Machinery	7,000
Carriage Outward	3,000
Office Salaries	8,000
Office Rent	6,000
Sundry Office Expenses	9,000
Salesmen's Salaries	3,000

Or

Mirik Construction Ltd. entered into a contract for constructing a building. The contract value is Rs. 6,50,000 to be realised in instalments on the basis of the value of work certified by the architect subject to a retention of 10%. The work commenced on 1.4.2001 but it remained incomplete in 31.12.2001 when the final accounts are to be prepared. The detailed information are :

	Rs.
Plant charged to contract at the commencement	32,000
Materials charged to contract	1,80,000
Wages paid	87,000
Expenses incurred on the contract	38,750

Total establishment expenses amounted to Rs. 41,000 out of which 25% is attributable to this contract. Out of the materials issued to the contract, material costing Rs. 4,000 were sold for Rs. 5,000. A part of the plant (cost Rs. 2,000) was damaged on 1.10.2001 and the scrap realised Rs. 300 only. Plant costing Rs. 3,000 was transferred to another contract site on 31.12.2001. Plant is to be depreciated @ 10% p.a.; Materials in hand on 31.12.2001 Rs. 17,500; Cash received from the contractee Rs. 3,06,000; Cost of work yet to be certified is Rs. 30,000.

Prepare a Contract Account.

VIDYASAGAR UNIVERSITY

2003

Costing

Elective General

1. Answer any **ten** questions, taking **six** from **Section I** and **four** from **Section II.**

Section I

(a) Name the methods of Costing most appropriate to the following industries :

(i) Ready-made Garments; (ii) Brick works; (iii) Colliery; (iv) Paper Mills.

(b) Give two examples of selling overheads.

(c) Give a blank specimen form of Purchase Requisition.

(d) Mention two advantages of FIFO method.

(e) When does overtime work become necessary?

(f) Give two examples of Semi-variable overhead.

(g) State two limitations of Job-costing.

(h) Maximum stock level = Re-order level + ? —(Minimum Consumption × ?).

(i) Find out the price to be quoted for the following job whose costs are : Material Rs. 200; Labour Rs. 300, Overhead 50% of Labour Cost, Profit 25% on Cost Price.

Section II

(j) What is 'Farm Accounting'?

(k) Give two examples of 'Farm Inputs'.

(l) What is 'Multiple Cropping'?

(m) State two important 'Books of Accounts' to be kept for recording farm transactions.

(n) Give two examples of 'Farm Joint Products'.

(o) Give examples of important 'Farm Operations'.

Costing

[Answer any **three** questions]

2. (a) What do you mean by 'Cost Accounting'? What are its advantages?

(b) State the relation between Cost Accounting and Management Accounting.

3. (a) Distinguish between a Stores Ledger and a Bin Card.

(b) From the following information you are required to prepare a cost sheet :

	Rs.	Rs.
Finished Stock on 1.1.99 (800 units)		64,000
Raw Materials used :		
M_1 100 tons @ Rs. 800 per ton	80,000	
M_2 700 tons @ Rs. 200 per ton	1,40,000	2,20,000
Direct wages		1,00,000
Factory overhead		80% of Direct wages
Administrative overhead		25% of works cost
Selling overhead		Re. 1 per unit sold

4. Write short notes on any **four** of the following :

(a) Economic Order Quantity, (b) Perpetual Inventory System, (c) Incentive Wage Plans, (d) Costing Method, (e) Costing Techniques, (f) Absorption of Overheads.

5. (a) What do you mean by the terms :

(i) Minimum Level, (ii) Maximum Level and (iii) Ordering Level of Stock?

(b) Two components X and Y are consumed as follows :

(i) Normal usage—200 units per week each.

(ii) Minimum usage—100 units per week each.

(iii) Maximum usage—300 units per week each.

Re-order quantity of the components are as follows : (i) Component X—800 units; (ii) Component Y—1,200 units.

Re-order period in respect of the components are as follows :

Component X—6 to 8 weeks; Component Y—3 to 5 weeks.

On the basis of the above particulars you are required to calculate for each component—(i) Minimum Level, (ii) Maximum Level and (iii) Average Level of Stock.

6. (a) Calculate the total monthly remuneration of three workers—A, B and C from the following data :

(i) Standard production per month per workers 4,500 units.

(ii) Actual production for the month : A—3,500 units; B—3,800 units; C—2,600 units.

(iii) Price Work Wage Rate is Re. 1 per unit.

(iv) Additional production Bonus is paid @ Rs. 10 for each percentage of actual production over 60% of Standard Production stated above.

(v) Dearness Allowance is fixed at Rs. 500 per month for each worker.

(b) Distinguish between Halsey System and Rowan System of Incentive Wage Plans.

7. From the following particulars prepare Contract Account, Contractee Account and Work-in-Progress Account as on 31.03.02

	Rs.
Materials issued to site	5,60,000
Labour engaged on site	2,20,000
Overhead charges allocated	50,000
Plant issued to site	2,00,000
Uncertified work	30,000
Certified work	10,00,000
Contract price	12,50,000
Cash received	8,00,000
Material sold (Cost Rs. 5,000)	7,000
Material at site on 31.03.02	25,000
Plant at site on 31.03.02	1,60,000

Estimated further expenses to complete the work : Materials Rs. 80,000; Labour Rs. 75,000 and Overhead Rs. 50,000. The estimated value of plant on Completion Rs. 60,000.